ENGLAND RUGBY CHRONICLE SINCE 1969 - VOLUME THREE: 2000-2010

Second edition with corrections and additions

Andrew Shurmer

First published 2010 by Anoeth Limited.
Second revised edition published 2015 by Anoeth Limited.

ISBN 978-0-9575865-1-2

A catalogue record for this book is available from the British Library.

Printed and bound in Great Britain by CreateSpace.

This is not an official publication of the Rugby Football Union (RFU) or any other official rugby governing body. We welcome comments, corrections and additions to this book. Please send them to the author at:

andrew.shurmer@englandrugbychronicle.com

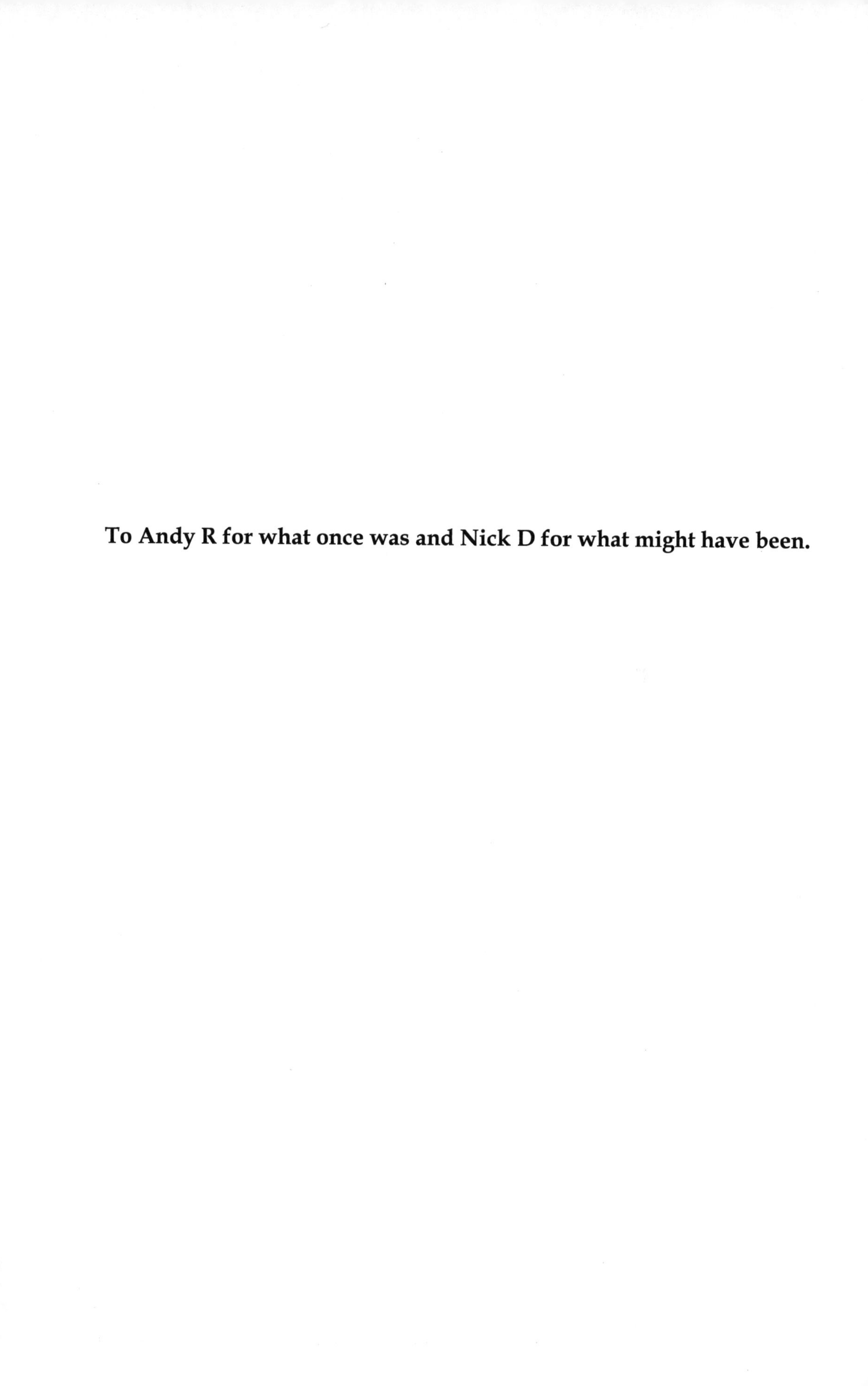

To Andy R for what once was and Nick D for what might have been.

CONTENTS

PREFACE

Welcome to Volume Three of the England Rugby Chronicle! This is the third volume in an intended series of three books which are designed to provide a detailed history of the representative career of every man who played for an adult England Rugby Union team between 1st January 1969 and 31st July 2010 respectively. Volume One covered the period between 1st January 1969 and 4th August 1990. Volume Two involved the period between 5th August 1990 and 31st July 2000, while the third and final Volume duly deals with the period between 1st August 2000 and 31st July 2010. All the information contained therein has been collated together from many hundreds of different written and visual sources to form a reference guide that is intended to be both informative and entertaining. Each Volume can be used as either a stand-alone source or in conjunction with its two sister books.

It is intriguing to see how the 7-a-side variation of Rugby Union has changed between the first and the last IRB World Sevens tournaments listed in this Volume of the England Rugby Chronicle, which were played in Durban on 18th-19th November 2000 and in Edinburgh 29th-30th May 2010 respectively. For the former competition the game of sevens was just starting to shake off an unwanted reputation as a frivolous end of season antidote to the serious business of 15-a-side World Cups, 6 Nations and Tri-Nations tournaments. By contrast in the latter competition sevens was a truly global sport where the result was gloriously unpredictable in that Kenya could beat New Zealand and England could lose to the Cook Islands! The IRB World Sevens series was now been taken very seriously indeed with a number of participants centrally contracting their players to exclusively play the 7-a-side variation. A further shift in emphasis was demonstrated on 9th October 2009 when the IOC decided to include sevens in the 2016 Olympic Games instead of the hitherto dominant 15-a-side game. The ten years between 2000 and 2010 also saw significantly fewer sevens sides being raised by the traditional invitational teams such as the Barbarians, the Penguins and the Public School Wanderers, with newer invitational sides like the Samurai duly stepping in to fill the breach.

While the face of sevens did indeed change between 2000 and 2010, the game of Rugby Union as a whole still remained unstinting in its ability to deliver brilliant, disastrous, contentious and bizarre incidents! Volume Three of the England Rugby Chronicle describes a number of such incidents in the two Match Notes sections that accompany the formal match statistics. Examples include:

a) *brilliant* - tries scored by Jason Robinson against France in 2002, Ugo Monye against Wales in 2003, Paul Sackey against Argentina in 2006 and Ben Youngs against Australia in 2010 respectively.
b) *disastrous* - tries conceded to Joe Roff at Melbourne in 2001, Waisale Serevi at Hong Kong in 2005, Florian Fritz at Stade de France in 2006 and Kurt Baker at Twickenham in 2010 respectively.
c) *contentious* - Ben Cohen's disallowed try against Ireland in 2004 and Mark Cueto's disallowed try against South Africa in the World Cup Final in 2007 respectively.
d) *bizarre* - Isoa Damu's failure to touch the ball down for a try at Twickenham in 2007 and Matthew Clarkin's acrobatic roll in Brussels in 2009 respectively!

On a personal note this book is the product of an ongoing eight year battle with a variety of sources that sadly do not always agree about their subject matter. In spite of this I have always looked to present the correct information. This book is dedicated to Andy and Nick, who have passed over but will never be forgotten. I would also like to thank the multitude who deserve it and offer up the hope that those who don't deserve it get the requisite period in the sin-bin for their efforts!

Andrew Shurmer *30th November 2010*

PREFACE TO THE SECOND EDITION

Welcome to a revised edition of Volume Three of the England Rugby Chronicle! This second edition has been produced following further research which brought relevant new information to light after the first edition went to press. An extra 4 pages worth of fresh material has therefore now been added.

On a personal note this book is the product of what is now an eleven year battle with those recalcitrant sources! Hopefully you will get as much pleasure from reading it as I did when I was putting it together. This book is still dedicated to the inspirational Andy and Nick. The usual bouquets and brickbats are extended to the helpers and hinderers!

Andrew Shurmer *7th October 2015*

ENGLAND RUGBY CHRONICLE - CRITERIA

OVERVIEW

Since 1st January 1969 English players have taken part in over 1000 representative rugby union matches. This England Rugby Chronicle (or ERC) is unique in that will records every single one of these matches from an English perspective, going in date order from this starting point of 1st January 1969 right up to 31st July 2010. As such it is possible to follow the representative career of every English player who was involved at some point in these matches.

The aim of the ERC is to provide the following comprehensive details about each individual game from the viewpoint of the team containing an English player:

- The reason for the game
- The venue where the game was played
- The management and or coaching staff for the team
- The final score
- The team that took the field
- The replacements bench
- The scorers
- Details of other players included in the squad
- Any notable rule or scoring value changes
- Reasons for cancelled games
- Kick-off times (1)
- Any players unavailable due to injury, illness, family, work or other rugby commitments
- Any initially selected players who later withdrew due to injury, illness, family, work or other rugby commitments
- Notable appearances by players in preliminary England Trial Matches
- Any nationality changes for English players
- Footnote details of England Schools 19 Group, England Schools 18 Group, England Colts, England U19 and England U18 matches (2)
- Footnote details of other invitational matches that do not merit a mention in the main body of the text
- Footnote details of other English or foreign invitational teams
- Any extreme weather conditions

- Any notable scores, incidents, injuries or contentious moments
- Periodic score updates, including half-time, midway through the first half and midway through the second half, with special emphasis on the first and last five minutes of a 15-a-side match and the first and last three minutes of a 7-a-side match (3)
- Tournament results for the 5 Nations and 6 Nations Championships (including 'A', U20 and Students level) will be given in full from 1st January 1969 to 31st July 2010
- Annual standings for the IRB World Sevens Series will be given in full
- Other tournaments and competitions will give the finishing position of the team containing an English player

This veritable mine of information will be split into five separate sections in the ERC. In this way the reader has a choice in that he or she can peruse as little or as much data as personally required. These five sections are as follows:

1) England player **match Results, teams and scorers** since 1969
2) England player **tour match Results, teams and scorers** since 1969
3) England player **Match Notes** since 1969
4) England player tour **Match Notes** since 1969
5) England team and player **Records** since 1969

The first two sections are therefore concerned with what actually happened, whereas the third and fourth sections detail how and indeed why these results occurred. Each Volume will contain the first four sections mentioned above for the period in question. In addition, the third and final Volume will contain the fifth section which will tie the first four sections together by providing a statistical analysis of literally who did what during the entire period from 1st January 1969-31st July 2010. The rationale behind these separate sections is explained in more detail below:

MATCH RESULTS, TEAMS AND SCORERS

These two sections list the time, date and final outcome of the match in question, together with a list of the coaching staff, touring squad members, players, bench replacements and scorers. If the author considered that the relevant team could or should have done better, then that team is marked with an asterisk and a fantasy rugby position assigned beneath the actual result. While rugby is indeed not a matter of life and death (it is more serious that that) this fantasy section is designed to provide a little light relief and not a list of grievances for the powers that be to investigate! The ERC is strictly concerned with the following **core teams**:

- English full cap international teams
- English representative teams, i.e. below the full cap international level
- Combined representative teams containing at least one English player or squad member
- Combined teams assembled for individual matches, tournaments or tours who contained at least one player who appeared for an English full cap international or representative team
- Major (4) or ongoing (5) English, Irish, Welsh, Scottish, French or Italian invitational teams containing at least one English player, where that team was either **a)** playing an overseas touring team, **b)** going on a tour whose purpose was conceived after 31st December 1968 (6), **c)** playing Celebration or Anniversary matches against English, Irish, Welsh, Scottish, French or Italian club, county or regional opponents, **d)** playing a Commemorative/Fund-raising/Charity/Stadium or Stand Opening match against English, Irish, Welsh, Scottish, French or Italian club, county or regional opponents where the reason for that game was conceived after 31st December 1968 (7), **e)** playing other English, Irish, Welsh, Scottish, French or Italian invitational opponents, **f)** playing the Combined Services team that is based on the British Army, Royal Navy and Royal Air Force or **g)** playing in Sevens tournaments where social invitational teams (8) did not form the majority of the field
- Cornish full cap or uncapped XV teams (9) containing at least one English player (10), where that team was **a)** playing in the County Championship Semi-Final or Final, **b)** playing a foreign touring team (11), **c)** going on a tour whose purpose was conceived after 31st December 1968, **d)** playing English, Irish, Welsh, Scottish, French or Italian invitational opponents or **e)** playing Celebration or Anniversary matches against English, Irish, Welsh, Scottish, French or Italian club, county or regional opponents

All teams containing an English player are listed in full where possible. English players, managers and coaches and players are denoted by normal black type throughout. Non-English players, managers and coaches are also rendered in normal black type, but additionally have their surnames followed by brackets which contain a 2 or 3 letter abbreviation of their country of allegiance. These abbreviations can be found in the **Key**. Full international, representative or invitational teams containing English players are listed in bold capital type throughout. Other full international, representative or combined teams are denoted by normal capital type, with other invitational teams being rendered in underlined lower case type. English county and club teams are listed in lower case type throughout. Provincial, county and club teams from outside England are also denoted by lower case type, but their names are additionally followed by brackets which contain a 2 or 3 letter abbreviation of their country of origin. Uniformed and forces teams are distinguished from provincial, county and club teams by being rendered in lower case type followed by brackets which contain a 3 letter abbreviation of the word 'services'.

The English representative teams are defined in the ERC as follows, with bold type depicting the next level down and normal type denoting the date order of the teams fielded in that particular level:

- **England XV**
- The Rest (12)
- D.L. Sanders' XV
- R.F.U. International XV
- RFU President's XV
- England Invitation XV
- **England B**
- England A
- England Saxons
- **England Emerging Players/Emerging England Players/Emerging England**
- **England U25**
- England U23
- The Rest of England U23 XV
- England U21
- England U21 A
- England U21 South XV / England U21 North XV
- England U20
- **English Students**
- England Students
- Combined England Students
- England Students Rest XV
- England Students U21
- England Students R.F.U. U21 XV
- England Students R.F.U.
- **England [7s]**
- English Bulldogs (13)
- Dick Best's Selection
- England Select VII
- RFU President's VII
- Young England
- England VII

- Dig Deep England
- **Rest of England**
- England Rugby Partnership XV
- English National Divisions XV
- England Counties

Combined international representative teams are defined in the ERC as follows:
- British Lions
- British Isles XV
- British & Irish Lions
- England & Wales XV
- Devon & Cornwall XV / Cornwall & Devon XV
- Oxford & Cambridge / Oxbridge XV (14)

Combined teams assembled for individual matches, tournaments or tours are defined in the ERC as follows:
- Oxford Past and Present
- President's RFU XV
- Carwyn James XV
- Cambridge Past and Present
- I.R.F.U. President's XV
- Sandy Sanders VII
- World XV [1977]
- XV du Président
- Rugby Union Writers Club Invitation XV
- British Selection XV
- Rest of the World XV [1980]
- W.R.U. President's XV [1981]
- Barbarian World XV
- Bill Beaumont's International XV
- Five Nations XV [1982]
- Western Province President's Centenary XV
- W.R.U. President's World XV/W.R.U. President's XV [1984]
- M.R. Steele-Bodger's International XV
- World Invitation XV
- Five Nations XV [1986]
- J.R.F.U. President XV
- World XV [1988]
- World Select XV
- British Isles Student Select
- FNB International XV

- Four Home Unions XV
- World XV [1992a]
- World XV [1992b]
- Hong Kong R.F.U. President's VII
- International Select XV [1995]
- World XV [1996/1998]
- Sella World XV
- British Lions Invitation XV
- Fran Cotton's Home Nations XV
- Dean Richards XV
- UK Students [7s]
- Will Carling's World XV
- Rest of the World XV
- Premiership All Stars
- AJ Hignell's XV
- Great Britain [7s]
- British Students
- Jason Leonard XV
- North
- Martin Johnson XV
- Britain and Ireland XV
- Great Britain Students
- World XV [2006]
- Coronation World XV
- Help for Heroes XV
- International Select XV [2008]
- Help for Heroes VII
- XV Europe

Major ongoing English, Irish, Welsh, Scottish, French or Italian invitational teams are defined as follows:

- Barbarians
- Penguins
- Public School Wanderers
- Anti-Assassins
- Wigan (15)
- Samurai (16)
- Irish Wolfhounds
- Crawshay's Welsh
- Co-Optimists
- Welsh Academicals

- Saltires
- French Barbarians
- Zebre
- South African Barbarians
- Australian Barbarians

Three other ongoing English invitational teams are considered to be of minor historic importance and will only be mentioned in footnotes unless they play a match against any of the chronicle's core teams (17). These teams are Major R.V. Stanley's XV, M.R. Steele-Bodger's XV and R.F. Oakes' Memorial XV. A further three English invitational teams are now considered to be extinct (18) and as such will be confined to the footnotes. These teams were the Tankards, Bos'uns and the Luddites.

The following teams will only be listed when they play matches against any of the chronicle's core teams or contain notable English players:

- Other international, representative and regional teams
- Club teams affiliated to their national governing body
- English, Irish, Welsh, Scottish, French and Italian social invitational teams such as the White Hart Marauders, Jedi and Skyrunners
- Major invitational teams from outside England, Ireland, Wales, Scotland, France or Italy
- Social invitational teams from outside England, Ireland, Wales, Scotland, France or Italy
- Teams from the individual British services (19)

MATCH NOTES

These two sections give relevant pre and post-game information and additionally contain **match reports** from over 1000 representative rugby union matches involving English players since 1st January 1969. The author has compiled these match reports by actually watching the matches wherever possible and also sourcing books and newspapers printed at the time. Please refer to the Bibliography for the complete list of the sources used. As such the reports are designed to be both accurate and informative! Hopefully a few long-standing myths will have been deconstructed along the way. Match timings where given are accurate to a margin of one minute.

RECORDS

This section will contain four distinct rolls of honour. The first roll is entitled Achievements. This is subdivided into two separate categories as follows: The first category contains a table which summarises the annual results of the **6 Nations Championship** played between England, Scotland, Ireland, Wales, France and Italy. However instead of merely incorporating the championship results since 1969, this table also includes all the final standings from every season going back to 1883, when this competition was initially devised as the International Championship. This is done for the sake of completeness in that it paints the most accurate picture of the historical strength of each of the six competing nations.

The second category lists the **competition results** successfully attained by the England international and representative teams between 1st January 1969 and 31st July 2010. These accomplishments will be defined as follows:

- Winners
- Finalists
- Semi-Finalists
- 3rd Place
- 4th Place
- Quarter-Finalists
- 5th Place
- 6th Place
- 7th Place
- 8th Place
- Plate Winners
- Plate Finalists
- Plate Semi-Finalists
- Bowl Winners
- Bowl Finalists
- Bowl Semi-Finalists
- Bowl Quarter-Finalists

The winners section will begin with the 5 and 6 Nations Championship and those awards or trophies associated with it, namely the Grand Slam, Triple Crown, Calcutta Cup and Millennium Trophy. Following this victories will be given in descending date order based on the first year that the championship, tournament or trophy was won. The finalists, semi-finalists, 3rd-8th place positions and quarter-finalists sections will follow the same descending date order format.

The second roll of honour is called **Caps** and will list the English players who have appeared in full cap and non-cap international matches at either 15-a-side or 7-a-side level between 1st January 1969 and 31st July 2010. This roll will contain separate sections on:

- England international cap holders from 1969
- England unused bench replacements (cap matches) from 1969 (20)
- England non-cap match appearances from 1969
- England unused bench replacements (non-cap matches) from 1969 (21)
- England tour match appearances from 1969
- England tour squad appearances from 1969
- England sevens competition appearances from 1973 (22)
- England IRB World Sevens competition appearances from 2000

The third roll of honour is entitled **Points** and will list the English players who have scored points in full cap and non-cap international matches at either 15-a-side or 7-a-side level between 1st January 1969 and 31st July 2010. This roll will contain separate sections on:

- England cap match points scorers from 1969
- England non-cap match points scorers from 1969
- England tour match points scorers from 1969
- England sevens competition points scorers from 1973 (23)
- England Rugby World Cup Sevens competition point scorers from 1993
- England Commonwealth Sevens competition points scorers from 1998 (24)
- England IRB World Sevens competition points scorers from 2000 (25)

The fourth roll of honour is called **Captaincy** and will list the English players who have led the team in full cap and non-cap international matches at either 15-a-side or 7-a-side level between 1st January 1969 and 31st July 2010. This roll will contain separate sections on:

- England cap match captains from 1969
- England non-cap match captains from 1969
- England tour match captains from 1969
- England sevens competition captains from 1973 (26)
- England IRB World Sevens competition captains from 2000 (27)

Notes

(1) All kick-offs are given in local time
(2) These 4 teams were not considered for the main body of the text due to the low percentage of English schoolboy internationals attaining full cap honours since 1st January 1969
(3) Periodic is defined by the ERC as every 10 minutes
(4) Major is defined by the ERC as fulfilling at least 2 of points a) to g)
(5) Ongoing is defined here as having more than 20 years of history behind the club
(6) This excludes the Barbarians Easter tour of South Wales, which ran from 1901 until 1996
(7) This excludes the Mobbs Memorial Match between the Barbarians and an East Midlands XV, which has been played annually since 1921
(8) Social invitation teams are defined here as outfits who have no affiliation to their national governing body, or are formed with a view to playing in one particular tournament, or were initially formed with a view to playing non-competitive rugby
(9) This excludes the Cornwall A, B and U23 teams
(10) The Cornish have historic reasons for viewing themselves as a separate nation outside England but their team - while seen as independent in all but name - continues to be affiliated to the RFU, so in view of this ongoing anomaly the ERC will treat Cornwall as another international country containing English players (which also allows the Cornwall & Devon XV to be included as a core team because Cornwall is being treated as this separate international country, but by contrast the South & South East of England cannot be defined as a core team because Cornwall is not mentioned in this team's title)
(11) Foreign is defined here as a team from outside England, Wales and Scotland
(12) The Rest played an England XV in numerous Final England Trial Matches until 1987
(13) The English Bulldogs played in the WDA/British Airways International Sevens Tournament in 1986 as part of Sport Aid, where national teams competed under assumed nicknames
(14) Oxford & Cambridge/Oxbridge XV went on a number of international tours where they played international or representative opposition
(15) Wigan are a professional rugby league side who have been invited to play rugby union on 2 separate occasions, and as such the ERC will treat them as an invitational rugby union side
(16) The ERC excludes Samurai St George, who are used as a development side for the England Sevens team
(17) The ERC considers them to be of minor importance because they were all formed with the specific intention of playing 1 annual match
(18) Extinct is defined here as having not played a match in the last 20 years up to 31st July 2010
(19) The ERC considers the individual service teams, such as the successful Army sevens team, to be the equivalent of a civilian English club team
(20) This section is restricted to uncapped players only
(21) This section is restricted to uncapped players only
(22) Excluding the IRB World Sevens competition, which is listed separately
(23) Excluding the Rugby World Cup Sevens, Commonwealth Sevens and IRB World Sevens competitions; The author has provided as full a list as possible from available sources
(24) The author has provided as full a list as possible from available sources
(25) The author has provided as full a list as possible from available sources
(26) Excluding the IRB World Sevens competition, which is listed separately; The author has provided a full a list as possible from available sources
(27) The author has provided as full a list as possible from available sources

KEY

1. *Abbreviations:*
In the ERC foreign players and/or provincial, county and club teams are followed by brackets which contain a 2 or 3 letter abbreviation denoting their country. These abbreviations are as follows in alphabetical order:

- ARA = Arabian Gulf
- AR = Argentina
- AU = Australia
- BAH = Bahrain
- BAR = Barbados
- BEL = Belgium
- BER = Bermuda
- BOT = Botswana
- BRA = Brazil
- CAN = Canada
- CAY = Cayman Islands
- CHI = Chile
- CHN = China
- COO = Cook Islands
- CO = Cornwall
- CRO = Croatia
- CZE = Czechoslovakia/Czech Republic
- DEN = Denmark
- FIJ = Fiji
- FR = France
- GEO = Georgia
- GER = West Germany/Germany
- HOL = Netherlands
- HON = Hong Kong
- HUN = Hungary
- IND = Indonesia
- IR = Ireland
- IT = Italy
- IVO = Ivory Coast
- JAP = Japan
- KEN = Kenya
- KOR = South Korea/Korea
- LAT = Latvia
- MAL = Malaysia
- MAU = Mauritius

- MEX = Mexico
- MOR = Morocco
- NAM = Namibia
- NIU = Niue
- NOR = Norway
- NZ = New Zealand
- PAP = Papua New Guinea
- PAR = Paraguay
- POL = Poland
- POR = Portugal
- ROM = Romania
- RUS = USSR/CIS/Russia
- SA = South Africa
- SAM = Western Samoa/Samoa
- SC = Scotland
- SER = Services teams
- SIN = Singapore
- SLO = Slovenia
- SOL = Solomon Islands
- SP = Spain
- SRI = Ceylon/Sri Lanka
- SWA = Swaziland
- SWE = Sweden
- SWI = Switzerland
- TAH = Tahiti
- TAI = Taiwan/Kwang-Hua Taipei/Chinese Taipei
- TAN = Tanzania
- THA = Thailand
- TON = Tonga
- TRI = Trinidad & Tobago
- TUN = Tunisia
- UGU = Uganda
- UKR = Ukraine
- URU = Uruguay
- US = USA
- WA = Wales
- ZAM = Zambia
- ZI = Rhodesia/Zimbabwe

2. *ERC Notation:*

Team notation for the 15-a-side game

The starting line-ups are listed in the modern shirt numbering order of 1 to 15, unless there are any obvious positional anomalies which are duly referred to in the pre-match notes e.g. a player wearing the right wing's number 14 shirt but actually playing on the left wing. The bench replacements are listed in alphabetical order. Touring and tournament squad members are also listed in alphabetical order.

Team notation for the 7-a-side game

The starting line-ups are listed in their positional order from loose-head prop to wing. The bench replacements are listed in alphabetical order. Tournament squad members are listed in shirt number order where available. Failing that, these squad members are listed in or either positional or alphabetical order.

Player notation

Each individual player is denoted in a unique manner throughout the ERC. A player's first chronological appearance in each Volume is indicated by the appearance of both his forename and surname in the team notation. A player's forename can be his official **Christian** name, a **preferred playing name** based on any of his other given names, a **nickname** or a **derivative name** based on his Christian or any of his other given names. Preferred playing names are denoted in italics (or bold type in the case of New Zealand) after the official Christian name, whereas nicknames and derivative names are listed in inverted commas after the official Christian name and/or other given names. Brackets denote where a player either used a shortened version of his official surname or changed his surname in the course of his career.

After this first chronological appearance the player is listed solely by his surname in the team notation, with the following exceptions:

a) Where 2 or more players have the same surnames. In this case the player is denoted by both the initial of his forename and his surname e.g. Brian Moore is referred to as B. Moore.

b) Where 2 or more players have both the same surname and a forename beginning with the same letter. In this case the player is denoted by both his forename and his surname e.g. Jonny Wilkinson is referred to as Jonny Wilkinson.

c) Where 2 or more players have both the same surname and forename. In this case the player is denoted by both his forename and his surname, with his surname then being followed by a number depicting his chronological position in the ERC. The only exception to this rule is when such a player appears among the scorers, in which case his chronological number is both omitted in the scoring notation and retained in the team notation for the corresponding match. In addition where possible the player's other given name will be listed on his first chronological appearance, with his forename consequently being denoted in italics. For example, Richard Hill the England scrum half [1984-91] is listed as *Richard* John Hill (1) in his first chronological appearance in the ERC and Richard Hill (1) thereafter unless he appears amongst the scorers, where he is merely listed as Richard Hill. By contrast Richard Hill the England flanker [1997-2004] is listed as *Richard* Anthony Hill (2) on his first chronological appearance and Richard Hill (2) thereafter unless he appears among the scorers, where he is merely listed as Richard Hill.

A player's first chronological 15-a-side appearance in either a touring squad, tournament squad or amongst the bench replacements is denoted by his team position being listed in brackets after his name e.g. (scrum half). Thereafter his team position is only referred to in a touring squad, tournament squad or amongst the bench replacements if it has clearly changed from the one originally listed e.g. Austin Healey was variously selected as a scrum half, fly half, wing and full back during his career! A player's first chronological 7-a-side appearance in a tournament squad is denoted by his team position being listed in brackets after his name e.g. (forward). Once again his team position is only referred to thereafter in a tournament squad when it has obviously changed. A player's team position will only be listed amongst the tour match bench replacements if it represents a clear change from his normal position.

A player's team position may occasionally be listed where team notations are unable to be given in full. This is done independently of any subsequent listing of that player's position in a touring squad, tournament squad or amongst the bench replacements.

Touring and tournament squad annotation for the 15-a-side game

The ERC lists those members of the touring or tournament squad who did not actually play in a major match, plus the overall squad size where available, further to the right on the line in the **England player match Results, teams and scorers** section which describes the nature of the trip or competition. Brackets are used to denote where a player either withdrew after originally being selected, played in a tour match, left the squad early, joined the squad later or was unavailable for selection by the end of proceedings. Notes relating to both the tour or tournament and those aforementioned members of the touring or tournament squad are indicated in the line immediately below.

Tournament squad annotation for the 7-a-side game

The full tournament squad, plus the overall squad size where available, are listed further to the right on the line in the **England player match Results, teams and scorers** section which describes the nature of the competition. Brackets are used to denote whether a player either withdrew after originally being selected or was unavailable for selection by the end of the competition. Notes relating to both the tournament and this aforementioned tournament squad are indicated in the line immediately below.

Captaincy notation

Captains for individual matches in England, Wales or Scotland are indicated where available in italics in the line above the game in question. For tours overseas the captain is denoted in italics in the line above the first cap international, non-cap international or major match. Thereafter the captaincy is not mentioned unless a new player takes over, in which case he is listed in italics above the respective cap international, non-cap international or major match on the tour. For tour matches the captain is denoted in italics in the line above the first game. Thereafter the captaincy is not mentioned unless a new player takes over, in which case he is listed in italics above the respective tour match. For 15-a-side and 7-a-side tournaments the captain is denoted in italics above the first match in the competition. Thereafter the captaincy is not mentioned unless a new player takes over, in which case he is listed in italics above the respective tournament match.

Management and coaching notation

Each manager and/or coach is denoted in a unique manner throughout the ERC. The manager and/or coach is listed by both his forename and surname. When there are 2 or more players, managers or coaches with both the same surname and forename, then the manager and or/coach's surname is followed by a number depicting his chronological position in the ERC. If a person both i) makes his first chronological appearance in the ERC as a manager and/or coach (rather than a player) and ii) is known by another given name, nickname or derivative name instead of his official Christian name, then either: a) his preferred other given name will be denoted in italics (or bold type in the case of New Zealand) after the official Christian name or b) his nickname or derivative name will be listed in inverted commas after the official Christian name and/or any other given names.

Members of the management and/or coaching team for individual matches in England, Wales or Scotland are indicated where available in italics above the game in question. Notes concerning members of this management and/or coaching team are where available usually indicated to the immediate right of the person's name. For tours overseas the management and/or coaching team are denoted in italics on the line in the **England player match Results, teams and scorers** section which describes the nature of the trip. Notes relating to this management and/or coaching team are given below the touring squad's details. Thereafter the management and/or coaching team are not mentioned again unless a new person takes over, in which case he is listed in italics (alongside his colleagues if he has any) above the respective cap international, non-cap international or major match on the tour. For minor tour matches the management and/or coaching team are denoted in italics on the line in the **England player tour match Results, teams and scorers** section which describes the nature of the trip. Thereafter the management and/or coaching team are not mentioned again unless a new person takes over, in which case he is listed in italics (alongside his colleagues if he has any) above the respective tour match. For 15-a-side and 7-a-side tournaments the management and/or coaching team is denoted in italics above the first match in the competition. Notes concerning members of this management and/or coaching team are where available usually indicated to the immediate right of the person's name. Thereafter the management and/or coaching team are not mentioned again unless a new person takes over, in which case he is listed in italics (alongside his colleagues if he has any) above the respective tournament match.

Scoring notation

The scorers for both the 15 and 7-a-side games are sub-divided into the following methods:

a) try
b) penalty goal
c) drop goal
d) conversion
e) goal from a mark (until August 1977)

Within these sub-divisions the players are listed in order of scoring, except where the same player scored more than once using the same method. In this case the player is listed in the scoring sequence at the point when he achieved his first example of that particular method, with the total number of this kind of score being given in brackets after his name.

Match notation

Matches are given in date order in the ERC except where an overseas tour or tournament is taking place. On these occasions the following rules apply:
i) For an overseas tour the cap internationals, non-cap internationals or major matches are given in the **England player match Results, teams and scorers** section, while the minor matches are given in the separate **England player tour match Results, teams and scorers** section. The final major tour match may be followed by the relevant team's final series result in the case of contested tours like the British Lions. Any unrelated match whose date falls between the first and last major game of the tour will be duly listed out of date order below either the last tour match or the overall tour result if listed. The date of the first tour match, whether it be a major or minor game, determines at which point the major tour matches are listed in the **England player match Results, teams and scorers** section because this initial date clearly indicates when the tour actually started. Thus when two tours occur simultaneously, or when a tour takes place at the same time as a tournament, it does not always follow that the major matches will be listed in strict consecutive date order in the ERC. For example in June-July 2005 the British & Irish Lions tour of New Zealand is listed before the England Counties tour of Argentina and Uruguay in the **England player match Results, teams and scorers** section, despite the first major match of the former tour (against New Zealand at Christchurch on 25th June 2005) being played after the corresponding initial major game on the latter tour (against an Argentina XV at Sante Fe on 12th June 2005). The British Lions tour is listed first because the initial match was played against Bay of Plenty at Rotorua on 4th June 2005, which predates the kick-off of the first match on the England Counties tour (namely the Atlético del Rosario Invitación XV game) by 11 days.
ii) All the England or relevant competing team's matches for a tournament are listed consecutively in date order after the first game. The final tournament match is followed by England's (or indeed the relevant competing team) overall tournament result, with the 5 Nations Championship, 5 Nations Student Championship, U21 5 Nations Championship, 'A' International Championship, 6 Nations Championship, U21 6 Nations Championship, U20 6 Nations Championship and IRB World Sevens Series rankings all being listed in full throughout. Any unrelated non-tournament match whose date falls between the first and last game of a stand-alone competition will be duly listed out of date order below the overall tournament result. The corresponding students, age group and second team tournaments (or series of friendly matches) are listed in order below the overall 5 or 6 Nations Championship result because they are deemed to have taken place simultaneously with the main competition. Once again only the relevant

England team's matches are listed, with the first game being followed in date order by the subsequent ones. Any match whose date falls between the first and last game of the main 5 or 6 Nations Championship, but is not related to this aforementioned group of tournaments (or series of games), is listed out of date order below the second team tournament (or series of games).

When a cap, non-cap or combined international team went on an overseas tour which involved matches being played against both i) a cap or non-cap international team and ii) a second or lower representative team from the same country, then the game(s) against the higher ranking team are defined as major matches and thus listed in the **England player match Results, teams and scorers** section, with the game(s) against the lower ranking team being duly listed as minor matches in the **England player tour match Results, teams and scorers** section. For example, when the England team toured Argentina in June 2002 they played both the full Argentine side and Argentina A. The ERC duly defines the game against Argentina as a major match, whereas the game against Argentina A is considered to be a minor match.

When an age group international or invitational team went on an overseas tour which involved matches being played against two or more different levels of representative team from the same country, then the game(s) against the highest ranking team are defined as major matches, with the game(s) against the lower ranking team being accordingly listed as minor matches. For example when the Penguins team toured Mexico in June-July 2004 they played a Mexico XV and a Mexico Select XV in succession. The ERC duly defines the Mexico XV game as a major match, whereas the Mexico Select XV game is considered to be a minor match.

A number of overseas countries have created their own named Barbarians sides in emulation of the foundation of the original Barbarian Football Club in England in 1890. Some of these sides like the French Barbarians have subsequently selected English players and are thus are already to be found within the ERC. In addition other overseas countries have created invitational sides in obvious emulation of the original Barbarians. Some of these sides like the Australian Barbarians have duly gone on to select England players and are therefore already included in the ERC. Other overseas Barbarians and/or invitational sides such as the New Zealand Barbarians and the Lupi have yet to include any English players. They are thus only to be found in the ERC when they play against other teams who do fulfil the criteria for inclusion. The ERC defines these games as a) major matches when the foreign Barbarian and/or invitational team has historically contained players from more than one country and b) minor matches when the foreign Barbarians and/or invitational team has to date only contained players from one country.

When a cap international team went on an overseas tour where both a test series was played against one particular country and another major match was played against either a second country or an invitational team, then all these major games are listed in date order, with a broken line being used to signify which match was not actually part of the main test series. A broken line is also used to signify those major matches on an incoming or overseas tour which had either individual sponsorship arrangements or trophies to be contested. For example on 26th June 2004 England contested the Cook Cup against Australia in Brisbane as part of an overall tour of New Zealand and Australia which had already contained two cap international matches against New Zealand.

General notes about tours or tournaments are listed in the line below the tour or tournament squad listing in the **England player match Results, teams and scorers** section. However both the **England player Match Notes** and **England player tour Match Notes** sections contain detailed observations about the specific individual games already mentioned in the corresponding parts of the **England player match Results, teams and scorers** and **England player tour match Results, teams and scorers** sections. These comments are divided into two parts:

i) Pre and Post Match notes – these concern events both during the build up to the game and afterwards.
ii) Match reports – these relate to moments that occurred during the game itself.

<u>Venue notation</u>
Playing venues are listed with the street, town, city and/or province in which they are situated, with the exception of obviously historical venues such as Twickenham and Murrayfield, which are deemed not to require any further identification other than a brief introductory comment in the **England player match notes** section!

Records notation

The following rules apply in the ERC **Records** section:

i) Players are indicated in italics when they are still currently playing Rugby Union.

ii) Uncapped players are listed in bold type.

iii) While the RFU have been awarding England caps since 1871, the aim of the ERC is to document the period between 1st January 1969 and 31st July 2010. Players not winning caps after 1st January 1969 are thus excluded from the scope of this Records section.

iv) Players who won caps both before and after 1st January 1969 are listed with their full amount of caps for the sake of completeness, with the amount of caps being won before 1st January 1969 being referred to in the notes column.

v) Players are listed with their team positions in bold type when they have the most match appearances in that particular position.

vi) Players with equal numbers of appearances are listed in the date order when they played their first 15-a-side match or 7-a-side competition in that particular section. If 15-a-side players also played this initial match at the same time, then precedence is given to those who started the game rather than came on later as a replacement. If these players either started the game at the same time or came on as a replacement during the match, then they are listed in the following position order: Prop, Hooker, Lock, Flanker, Number 8, Scrum half, Fly half, Centre, Wing and Full back. Failing that attempt to separate them they are finally listed in alphabetical order! If 7-a-side players also played in this initial competition at the same time, then they are listed in this order of position: Forward, Prop, Hooker, Forward/Back, Back/Forward, Back, Scrum half, Fly half, Centre and Wing. If these players still cannot be separated because played in the same position, they are then listed in alphabetical order!

vii) Players with equal numbers of points are listed in the date order when they played their first 15-a-side match or 7-a-side competition in that particular section. If they played in this initial match or competition at the same time, then they are listed in their positional order as outlined above. Once again any failure to separate them at that point will see them listed in alphabetical order!

viii) If players were honoured with the starting captaincy in equal numbers of either 15-a-side matches or 7-a-side competitions, then the number of times they were made acting captain is taken into consideration, with these temporary captaincy appearances being listed in brackets after the initial total for matches or competitions started as captain. If there are no appearances as acting captain to consider, then these players are listed in the date order when they started their first match or competition as captain.

GLOSSARY

Abbreviations in order of appearance:-

[ ] = this match was not an England cap international game
* = the denoted team could or should have drawn or won the respective match
CC = Calcutta Cup
TC = Triple Crown
tm = tour match
?? = unknown match captain
GS = Grand Slam
C = match cancelled
?# = unknown competition finishing position
?@ = unknown match venue
L = match lost
W = match won
ab = match abandoned
? = unknown Coach or Manager
SC = team scratched from the competition
WO = match walk-over
aet = after extra time
MT = Millennium Trophy
BP = Bonus point

PART 1
ENGLAND PLAYER MATCH RESULTS, TEAMS & SCORERS
2000-2010

2000

OTHER MATCHES

STUDENT RUGBY WORLD CUP

Italy

[*Other squad members:* Simon Danielli (*wing*), Benjamin 'Ben' Gollings (*fly half/full back*), James Ogilvie-Bull (*centre*)]

(squad of 26)

[This tournament was originally scheduled with a First Round consisting of 1 Pool of four and 2 Pools of three teams, but this structure was changed on 27th July 2000 to 3 Pools of three teams after Georgia withdrew from the competition; Simon Brading and Phil Christophers travelled later as replacements; Simon Danielli was capped for England Schools 18 Group in March 1998]

[**MANAGER:** *Anthony 'Tony' Lanaway*] [**COACH:** *Peter Drewett*] [**ASSISTANT COACH:** *Peter Cook (1)*]

CAPTAIN: *??*

First Round - Pool 'C'

[5th Aug WALES STUDENTS 0 **ENGLAND STUDENTS** 22]

Campo Tevere, CUS Roma, Stadio degli Eucalipti, Rome

[*Team:* Haydn Jeffreys, Edward 'Ed' Mallett, James Lofthouse, Philip 'Phil' Graham]

[*Bench:* Simon Amor (*scrum half/fly half*), ?, ?, ?, ?, ?, ?]

[*Scorers:* **try** by E. Mallett, **penalty goals** by Lofthouse (5), **conversion** by Lofthouse]

[8th Aug JAPAN STUDENTS 14 **ENGLAND STUDENTS** 35]

Campo delle Bandiere, CUS Roma, Stadio degli Eucalipti, Rome

[*Team:* Simon Miall, James Cockle, Christopher 'Chris' Simpson-Daniel, Amor, Philip 'Phil' Christophers, Ayoola Erinle, Alistair 'Ali' Newmarch]

[*Bench:* Lofthouse (*fly half*) (rep), Bryan Shelbourne (*scrum half*), ?, ?, ?, ?, ?]

[*Scorers:* **tries** by Christophers, Erinle, Chris Simpson-Daniel and Newmarch, **penalty goals** by Amor (2) and Lofthouse, **conversions** by Amor (2) and Lofthouse]

CAPTAIN: *Andy Beattie*

Quarter-Final

[13th Aug ITALY STUDENTS 11 **ENGLAND STUDENTS** 30]

Stadio Comunale, Rieti

[*Team:* Jeffreys, Richard Protherough, Timothy 'Tim' Payne, Miall, James Winterbottom, Ben Cole, Anthony 'Tony' Roques, Andrew 'Andy' Beattie, Shelbourne, Lofthouse, Christophers, Simon Brading, Simon Brocklehurst, Newmarch, Phil Graham]

[*Bench:* Amor (rep), Adam Bidwell (*centre*) (rep), Cockle (*flanker*) (rep), Simon Daws (*flanker*) (rep), Josh Hooker (*prop*) (rep), Tom Robinson (*hooker*) (rep), Chris Simpson-Daniel (*scrum half*) (rep)]

[*Scorers:* **tries** by Christophers, Newmarch and Phil Graham, **penalty goals** by Lofthouse (2) and Amor, **conversions** by Lofthouse (3)]

CAPTAIN: *Ben Cole*
Semi-Final
[16th Aug FRANCE STUDENTS 34 **ENGLAND STUDENTS** 15]
Stadio Comunale Tommaso Fattori, L'Aquila
[*Team:* Craig Mitcherson, Protherough, T. Payne, Miall, E. Mallett, B. Cole, Roques, Cockle, Shelbourne, Amor, Christophers, Brading, Brocklehurst, Newmarch, Jon Fabian]
[*Bench:* A. Beattie (*number 8*) (rep), Daws (rep), Phil Graham (*wing/full back*) (rep), Jeffreys (*prop*) (rep), Lofthouse (rep), T. Robinson (rep), Chris Simpson-Daniel (rep)]
[*Scorers:* **penalty goals** by Amor (5)]
Third Place Play-Off
[19th Aug SCOTLAND STUDENTS 25 **ENGLAND STUDENTS** 18]
Stadio Comunale Tommaso Fattori, L'Aquila
[*Team:* Mitcherson, T. Robinson, T. Payne, J. Winterbottom, E. Mallett, Cockle, Daws, A. Beattie, Chris Simpson-Daniel, Lofthouse, Christophers, Bidwell, Brocklehurst, Newmarch, Phil Graham]
[*Bench:* Amor, Fabian (*full back*) (rep), Miall (*lock*) (rep), Protherough (*hooker*) (rep), Shelbourne (rep), ?, ?]
[*Scorers:* **tries** by Phil Graham and A. Beattie, **penalty goals** by Lofthouse (2), **conversion** by Lofthouse]
POSITION: 4TH PLACE
[England were scheduled to hold the Student Rugby World Cup in 2004 but this idea was eventually abandoned; On 12th May 2006 it was announced that the Student Rugby World Cup was scheduled to be held at Stellenbosch in South Africa on either 1st-21st July 2007 or 7th-20th October 2007, but this idea was eventually abandoned too]

CWMTAWE SEVENS

Pontardawe RFC, Parc Ynysderw, Ynysderw Road, Pontardawe, Swansea
[*Tournament squad:* Russell 'Russ' Earnshaw (*forward*), Nigel Simpson (*back/forward*), David 'Dave' Scully (*scrum half*), Nick Drake (*wing*) (never travelled as withdrew), Martin Dawson (*wing*) (never travelled as withdrew), Michael 'Mike' Umaga (SAM) (*fly half/centre*), Mike Schmid (CAN) (*forward*) (never travelled as withdrew), Andy Northey (*centre*) (never travelled as withdrew), Isaac Feaunati (SAM) (*forward*) (never travelled as withdrew), Leon Greef (ZI) (*forward*) (never travelled as withdrew), Stuart Dixon (*centre*), Neil Spence (*forward*), Paul Manley (*forward*), Michael Wood (*wing*), Howard Parr (*forward*), Kevin Pike (*back*)]
(squad of 10)
[Samurai International RFC founded 1996 by Terry Sands; Paul Manley, Howard Parr, Neil Spence, Kevin Pike, Stuart Dixon and Michael Wood were not part of the original squad of 10 that was announced on 4th August 2000; Paul Manley was capped for England Colts in March 1987; Martin Dawson was capped for England Schools 18 Group in April 1990; Michael Wood was capped for England Schools 18 Group in March 1994]
[NO COACH NOMINATED]
CAPTAIN: *Dave Scully*
First Round - Pool 'C'
[5th Aug Pontardawe (*WA*) 0 **SAMURAI** 59]
[*Team:*]
[*Bench:*]
[*Scorers:*]

[5th Aug Cwmgors (*WA*) 0 **SAMURAI** 48]
[*Team:*]
[*Bench:*]
[*Scorers:*]
[5th Aug Llandovery (*WA*) 0 **SAMURAI** 47]
[*Team:*]
[*Bench:*]
[*Scorers:*]
Quarter-Final
[5th Aug Saracens 0 **SAMURAI** 43]
[*Team:*]
[*Bench:*]
[*Scorers:*]
Semi-Final
[5th Aug Bridgend (*WA*) 0 **SAMURAI** 29]
[*Team:*]
[*Bench:*]
[*Scorers:*]
Final
[5th Aug Swansea (*WA*) 33 **SAMURAI** 24]
[*Team:* N. Spence, Earnshaw, P. Manley, Scully, M. Umaga (SAM), Stuart Dixon, N. Simpson]
[*Bench:* H. Parr, Pike, Michael Wood]
[*Scorers:* **tries** by Stuart Dixon (2), M. Umaga (SAM) and Earnshaw, **conversions** by Scully (2)]
POSITION: LOSING FINALISTS

EUROBET MIDDLESEX CHARITY SEVENS
RUSSELL-CARGILL MEMORIAL CUP
Twickenham
[*Tournament squad:* Andrew Williams (3) (WA) (*scrum half*), Apolosi Satala (FIJ) (*forward*), Gerrie Engelbrecht (SA) (*forward*) Paul Williams (1) (WA) (*fly half*), Mathew 'Matty' Isaac (AU) (*scrum half*), Archer Dames (SA) (*wing*), Manueli Nawalu (FIJ) (*wing*), Adrian Durston (WA) (*centre*), N. Drake, Ben Harvey (*scrum half/fly half*)]
(squad of 10)
[This venue in London was officially called Twickenham Stadium, but it was usually just referred to as Twickenham; Ben Harvey was the nephew of the actress Jan Harvey]
[**COACH:** *Colin Hillman* (WA)]
CAPTAIN: *??*
First Round
[12th Aug London Wasps 12 **SAMURAI** 14]
[*Team:*]
[*Bench:*]
[*Scorers:*]
Quarter-Final
[12th Aug Penguins 26 **SAMURAI** 12]
[*Team:*]
[*Bench:*]

[*Scorers:*]
POSITION: LOSING QUARTER-FINALISTS

GERMAN RUGBY UNION CENTENARY MATCH

[NO COACH NOMINATED]
CAPTAIN: *Scott Hastings* (SC)
[12th Aug GERMANY 19 **BARBARIANS** 47]
Eilenriede-Stadion, Hannover
[*Team:* Jeffrey 'Jeff' Probyn, Frank 'Frankie' Sheahan (IR), Samuel *Trevor* Revan, Derwyn Jones (WA), John Langford (AU), Earnshaw, Daniel 'Danny' Collins, Scott Hutton (SC), Peter Stringer (IR), Shaun Connor (WA), Shaun Longstaff (SC), Trevor Walsh (AU), Duncan Roke, Pete Davies, Stephen 'Steve' Swindells]
[*Bench:* Julian Brammer (*hooker*) (rep), Warwick Bullock (*prop*) (rep), Richard Elliott (*scrum half*) (rep), Alun Harries (WA) (*wing*) (rep), Scott Hastings (SC) (*centre*) (rep), Julian Horrobin (*lock/flanker/number 8*) (rep), Matthew 'Matt' Jones (*fly half*) (rep)]
[*Scorers:* **tries** by Roke (2), Trevor Walsh (AU), Derwyn Jones (WA), J. Langford (AU), Earnshaw and Horrobin, **conversions** by Swindells (2), S. Connor (WA) (3) and Matt Jones]
[Match to commemorate the 100th Anniversary of the foundation of the Deutscher Rugby-Verband (German Rugby Union) in 1900]

REMEMBRANCE MATCH

[NO COACH NOMINATED]
CAPTAIN: *No captain appointed*
[7th Nov COMBINED SERVICES (*SER*) C **BARBARIANS** C]
Kingsholm, Gloucester
[*Team:* Revan, Andy Cuthbert, Gary Powell (WA), Paul Clapham, Stephen 'Steve' Moore (WA), Lee Crofts, Mark Ellis, S. Hutton (SC), R. Elliott, S. Connor (WA), Longstaff (SC), Alex Lawson (WA), Trevor Walsh (AU), A. Harries (WA), Cerith Rees (WA)]
[*Bench:* Bullock, Derwyn Jones (WA) (*lock*), Matt Jones, Rhodri Jones (WA) (*scrum half*), John Lawn (*hooker*), Ma'ama Molitika (TON) (*flanker/number 8*)]
[*No scorers*]
[Match to commemorate the members of the British uniformed services who lost their lives during armed conflict]

EMIRATES AIRLINE SOUTH AFRICA SEVENS
IRB WORLD SEVENS SERIES 2000-2001 ROUND 1

ABSA Stadium, Durban
[*Tournament squad:* A. Beattie (*forward*) (never travelled as withdrew), Steven 'Steve' Booth (*wing*) (never travelled as withdrew), Darren Carr (*wing*) (never travelled as withdrew), D. Collins (*forward*) (never travelled as withdrew), Michael 'Mike' Friday (*scrum half*) (never travelled as withdrew), Andrew 'Andy' Gomarsall (*scrum half*) (never travelled as withdrew), Richard Haughton (*wing*) (never travelled as withdrew), Charles 'Charlie' Hodgson (*fly half*) (never travelled as withdrew), N. Simpson (never travelled as withdrew), Stuart Williams (*forward*) (never travelled as withdrew), James Brown (*fly half*), Jonathan 'Jon' Pritchard (*fly half/centre*), Benjamin 'Ben' Breeze (*wing*), Fabian (*back/forward*), Henry Cripps (*centre*), Phil Graham (*back/forward*), William 'Will' Harrison (*forward*), Erinle (*centre*), Mark Sowerby (*forward*), Jamie Greenlees (*wing*), Robert 'Rob' Stewart (2) (*scrum half*), Simon Stacey (*forward*)]
(*squad of 12*)

[The ABSA Stadium was previously called King's Park Stadium, Durban; Andy Beattie, Steve Booth, Darren Carr, Danny Collins, Mike Friday, Andy Gomarsall, Richard Haughton, Charlie Hodgson, Nigel Simpson and Stuart Williams all initially selected but were then withdrawn by their clubs on 7th November 2000 due to an ongoing row about promotion and relegation between the RFU and EFDR; Adrian Thompson then had to pick Second Division players from outside the Zurich Premiership clubs on 10th November 2000; Mark Sowerby played in the Penguins team that won the COBRA Tens at Kuala Lumpur on 22nd-23rd January 1994; Andy Gomarsall captained England Schools 18 Group to a Grand Slam in April 1992; James Brown and Jon Pritchard were capped for England Schools 18 Group in March 1996; Charlie Hodgson was capped for England Schools 18 Group in January 1999; Steve Booth became a Rugby Union player in August 2000 when he joined Leicester]

[Adrian Thompson was appointed as a full-time Coach on 16th October 2000; Adrian Thompson sat on the bench for England against Australia in November 1988 and against Scotland in February 1989]

[**MANAGER:** *John Elliott*] [**COACH:** *Adrian Thompson*]

CAPTAIN: *Mark Sowerby*

First Round - Pool 'C'

18th Nov AUSTRALIA 43 **ENGLAND** 0

[*Team:*]

[*Bench:*]

[*No scorers*]

18th Nov ARGENTINA 24 **ENGLAND** 7

[*Team:*]

[*Bench:*]

[*Scorers:* **try** by Greenlees, **conversion** by Rob Stewart]

18th Nov ZIMBABWE 15 **ENGLAND** 5

[*Team:*]

[*Bench:*]

[*Scorers:* **try** by Pritchard]

[Bowl Quarter-Final:]

[19th Nov GEORGIA 10 **ENGLAND** 7 **]**

[*Team:*]

[*Bench:*]

[*Scorers:* **try** by Greenlees, **conversion** by James Brown]

POSITION: FIRST ROUND LOSERS [*BOWL QUARTER-FINALISTS*]

[England did not score any competition points in this Round of the 2000-2001 IRB World Sevens Series]

AUSTRALIAN TOUR TO FRANCE, SCOTLAND AND ENGLAND 2000
THE INVESTEC INTERNATIONAL
COOK CUP MATCH

[**TEAM MANAGER:** *Clive Woodward*] [**HEAD COACH:** Richard *Andrew 'Andy' Robinson*] [**ASSISTANT COACHES:** William *Brian Ashton* & *Phil Larder*]

CAPTAIN: *Martin Johnson*

18th Nov **ENGLAND** 22 AUSTRALIA 19

Twickenham

[*Team:* Jason Leonard, Philip 'Phil' Greening, Philip 'Phil' Vickery, Martin Johnson, Daniel 'Danny' Grewcock, *Richard* Anthony Hill (2), Neil Back, Lawrence Dallaglio, Kyran Bracken, Jonathan 'Jonny' Wilkinson, Daniel 'Dan' Luger, Michael 'Mike' Catt, Michael 'Mike' Tindall, Austin Healey, Matthew 'Matt' Perry]

[*Bench:* Iain Balshaw (*wing/full back*) (rep), Stephen 'Steve' Borthwick (*lock*), Martin Corry (*lock/flanker/number 8*), Matthew 'Matt' Dawson (*scrum half*) (rep), David Flatman (*prop*) (rep), William 'Will' Greenwood (*centre*), Mark Regan (*hooker*) (rep)]

[*Scorers:* **try** by Luger, **penalty goals** by Jonny Wilkinson (4), **drop goal** by Jonny Wilkinson, **conversion** by Jonny Wilkinson]

[Clive Woodward was appointed on 16th September 1997; Clive Woodward won 21 caps for England between 1980-84 and was capped for the British Lions in June 1980; Phil Larder was appointed on 17th November 1997; Phil Larder was appointed Coach of the England Rugby League team on 17th July 1995, guided them to the Rugby League World Cup Final at Wembley on 28th October 1995 and was the Coach when the Great Britain Rugby League Team toured Papua New Guinea, Fiji and New Zealand in September-November 1996; Brian Ashton was appointed on 23rd May 1998; Brian Ashton toured Australia with England in May 1975; Andy Robinson was appointed on 7th June 2000; Andy Robinson was capped for England in June 1988 and played for a British Lions XV against France at Parc des Princes on 4th October 1989]

EMIRATES AIRLINE DUBAI RUGBY SEVENS
IRB WORLD SEVENS SERIES 2000-2001 ROUND 2
EMIRATES INTERNATIONAL TROPHY

Dubai Exiles Stadium, Dubai

[*Tournament squad:* Breeze, James Brown, Cripps, Erinle, Fabian, Phil Graham, Greenlees, W. Harrison, Pritchard, Sowerby, Stacey, Rob Stewart (2)]

(squad of 12)

[Adrian Thompson had to pick Second Division players once again; Rob Stewart (2) not mentioned in the tournament programme; Jon Pritchard won 20 England U21 caps and pledged his allegiance to England in January 2000, but later switched this allegiance to Wales, playing for Wales 7s in June 2001 and for Wales A in November 2001]

[**MANAGER:** *John Elliott*] [**COACH:** *Adrian Thompson*]

CAPTAIN: *Mark Sowerby*

First Round - League W

23rd Nov ARABIAN GULF 0 **ENGLAND** 27

[*Team:*]

[*Bench:*]

[*Scorers:* **tries** by Erinle, Phil Graham, Rob Stewart (2) and James Brown, **conversion** by James Brown]

23rd Nov GEORGIA 12 **ENGLAND** 33
[*Team:*]
[*Bench:*]
[*Scorers:* **tries** by Fabian (2), Erinle (2) and Sowerby, **conversions** by Fabian (4)]

23rd Nov NEW ZEALAND 40 **ENGLAND** 7
[*Team:* Sowerby, Fabian]
[*Bench:*]
[*Scorers:* **try** by Sowerby, **conversion** by Fabian]

Quarter-Final

24th Nov FIJI 43 **ENGLAND** 0
[*Team:*]
[*Bench:*]
[*No scorers*]

[Plate Semi-Final:]

[24th Nov SOUTH AFRICA 45 **ENGLAND** 0]
[*Team:*]
[*Bench:*]
[*No scorers*]

POSITION: LOSING QUARTER-FINALISTS [*PLATE SEMI-FINALISTS*]

[England scored 4 competition points in this Round of the 2000-2001 IRB World Sevens Series]

ARGENTINE TOUR TO ENGLAND 2000
THE INVESTEC INTERNATIONAL

[**TEAM MANAGER:** *Clive Woodward*] [**HEAD COACH:** *Andy Robinson*] [**ASSISTANT COACHES:** *Brian Ashton & Phil Larder*]

CAPTAIN: *Martin Johnson*

25th Nov **ENGLAND** 19 ARGENTINA 0
Twickenham

[*Team:* J. Leonard, M. Regan, Julian White, Martin Johnson, Grewcock, Richard Hill (2), Back, Dallaglio, Matt Dawson, Jonny Wilkinson, Luger, M. Catt, Tindall, Ben Cohen, Balshaw]

[*Bench:* K. Bracken (*scrum half*), Corry (rep), Flatman (rep), W. Greenwood (rep), Matt Perry (*centre/full back*), Vickery (*prop*) (rep), Dorian West (*hooker*) (rep)]

[*Scorers:* **try** by B. Cohen, **penalty goals** by Jonny Wilkinson (3), **drop goal** by Jonny Wilkinson, **conversion** by Jonny Wilkinson]

SOUTH AFRICAN TOUR TO IRELAND, WALES AND ENGLAND 2000

[**MANAGER:** *Tony Macarthur* (AU)] [**COACHES:** *Philip Thomas 'Phil' Davies (2)* (WA) & *Adrian Davies* (WA)]

CAPTAIN: *Mike Shelley*

[28th Nov **ENGLISH NATIONAL DIVISIONS XV** 35 SOUTH AFRICA XV 30]
Worcester RFC, Sixways Stadium, Pershore Lane, Hindip, Worcester

[*Team:* Michael 'Mike' Shelley, Andrew Lamerton (WA), Christopher 'Chris' Budgen, Julian

Hyde, Thomas Philip 'Tom' Palmer (2), Steve Barnes, Cameron Mather (SC), Ian Patten, Scott Benton, Richard Le Bas, Spencer Bromley, Stephen 'Steve' Ravenscroft, Roke, Daniel 'Dan' Scarbrough, Benjamin 'Ben' Hinshelwood (SC)]
[*Bench:* Hesekaia 'Hese' Fakatou (TON) (*flanker/number 8*) (rep), Chris Hall (*wing*) (rep), B. Harvey (*scrum half/fly half*) (rep), Matt Holt (AU) (*hooker*) (rep), Liam Mooney (IR) (*prop*) (rep), Stephen 'Steve' Pope (*prop*) (rep), Benjamin 'Ben' Whetstone (*centre/wing*) (rep)]
[*Scorers:* **tries** by Scarbrough and L. Mooney (IR), **penalty goals** by Le Bas (6) and B. Harvey, **conversions** by Le Bas (2)]
[The English National Divisions XV was composed of players from outside the Zurich Premiership who played in the National Leagues]
[Tony Macarthur was appointed on 4th October 2000; Phil Davies (2) and Adrian Davies were both appointed on 7th November 2000; Tony Macarthur once managed Shirley Bassey!; Phil Davies (2) won 46 caps for Wales between 1985-95; Adrian Davies was capped for Wales in October 1990]

THE INVESTEC INTERNATIONAL

[**TEAM MANAGER:** *Clive Woodward*] [**HEAD COACH:** *Andy Robinson*] [**ASSISTANT COACHES:** *Brian Ashton* & *Phil Larder*]
CAPTAIN: *Martin Johnson*

2nd Dec **ENGLAND** 25 SOUTH AFRICA 17
Twickenham
[*Team:* J. Leonard, Greening, Julian White, Martin Johnson, Grewcock, Richard Hill (2), Back, Dallaglio, Matt Dawson, Jonny Wilkinson, Luger, W. Greenwood, Tindall, B. Cohen, Matt Perry]
[*Bench:* Balshaw (rep), K. Bracken, Corry (rep), Flatman, Healey (*wing*) (rep), M. Regan (rep), Vickery (rep)]
[*Scorers:* **try** by W. Greenwood, **penalty goals** by Jonny Wilkinson (6), **conversion** by Jonny Wilkinson]

THE SCOTTISH AMICABLE CHALLENGE

[**COACHES:** *Robert 'Bob' Dwyer* (AU) & *John Hart (1)* (NZ)]
CAPTAIN: *Lawrence Dallaglio*

[10th Dec **BARBARIANS*** 31 SOUTH AFRICA XV 41]
Millennium Stadium, Cardiff
[*Team:* Richard Harry (AU), Allen 'Naka' Drotske (SA), Mauricio Reggiardo (AR), Norm Maxwell (NZ), David Giffin (AU), Jim Williams (AU), Dallaglio, Ronald 'Ron' Cribb (NZ), Agustin Pichot (AR), Carlos Spencer (NZ), Chris Latham (AU), Daniel Herbert (AU), Brian O'Driscoll (IR), Matthew 'Matt' Burke (AU), Christian Cullen (NZ)]
[*Bench:* Balshaw (rep), Peter Clohessy (IR) (*prop*) (rep), Mark Hammett (NZ) (*hooker*) (rep), Neil Jenkins (WA) (*fly half*) (rep), Byron Kelleher (NZ) (*scrum half*) (rep), Malcolm O'Kelly (IR) (*lock*) (rep), Andrew 'Andy' Ward (IR) (*flanker*) (rep)]
[*Scorers:* **tries** by Brian O'Driscoll (IR), Pichot (AR), Latham (AU) and C. Cullen (NZ), **penalty goal** by Matt Burke (AU), **conversions** by Matt Burke (AU) (4)]
[Bob Dwyer was appointed on 25th August 2000; Bob Dwyer was the Coach when Australia won the World Cup at Twickenham on 2nd November 1991; John Hart (1) was appointed on 9th November 2000]

ENGLAND U21 MATCH

[**MANAGER:** *Nigel Melville*] [**COACH:** *Dean Ryan*]

CAPTAIN: *Mark Tucker*

[20th Dec **ENGLAND U21 A XV** 27 WALES U21 A XV 26]
Bridgwater & Albion RFC, College Way, Bath Road, Bridgwater

[*Team:* Adam Webb, Andrew 'Andy' Titterrell, James Isaacson, Karl Rudzki, Phillip 'Phil' Murphy (1), Robert 'Rob' Devonshire, Declan Danaher, Ian Clarke, Alex Page, C. Hodgson, James Tapster, Mark Tucker, Sam Cox, Anthony Elliott, Sean Marsden]

[*Bench:* Benjamin 'Ben' Hampson (*scrum half*), Matthew 'Matt' Leek (*fly half/centre*), Rhys Oakley (*flanker*), Jonathan 'Johnny' Roddam (*hooker*), Ollie Smith (1) (*prop*), Ross Winney (*fly half/centre*), ?]

[*Scorers:* **tries** by Sam Cox (2) and A. Elliott (2), **penalty goal** by C. Hodgson, **conversions** by C. Hodgson (2)]

[Nigel Melville was appointed on 7th September 2000; Nigel Melville won 13 caps for England between 1984-88; Dean Ryan was appointed on 9th November 2000; Dean Ryan was capped for England in July 1990]

2001
RUGBY WORLD CUP SEVENS
MELROSE CUP

Estadio José Maria Minella, Mar del Plata

[*Tournament squad:* Joseph 'Joe' Worsley (*forward*), Kristian 'Kris' Chesney (*forward*), Grant Seely (*forward*), Ben Johnston (*forward*), Friday, Paul Sampson (*scrum half/fly half/wing*), Owen Joshua 'Josh' Lewsey (*back/forward*), N. Simpson, Robert 'Rob' Thirlby (*back/forward*), Paul Sackey (*wing*)]

(squad of 10)

[Richard Hill (2), Neil Back, Lawrence Dallaglio, Kyran Bracken, Mike Catt, Iain Balshaw and Dan Luger all unavailable for this tournament due to their 6 Nations Championship commitments; Jason Robinson, Andy Gomarsall, Tom Beim, Michael Stephenson, Adam Vander and Ben Gollings were all members of a provisional squad of 16 in January 2001; The final 10 man tournament squad was announced on 17th January 2001; Mike Friday was the tournament captain; The England squad departed for Argentina on 21st January 2001; England only had four days to prepare for this tournament; England played a practice match against Georgia on 24th January 2001; Ben Johnston was capped for England Colts in March 1998; Joe Worsley was capped for both England Schools 18 Group in March 1995 and England Colts in March 1996; Paul Sampson was capped for England Schools 18 Group in January 1995 and came on as a replacement for M.R. Steele-Bodger's XV against Cambridge University at Grange Road on 29th November 2000; Josh Lewsey was capped as a fly half for England Colts in March 1996 and was originally selected to play for the Combined Services against an Argentine XV at Portsmouth on 21st November 2000 but then withdrew; Rob Thirlby toured Canada with England Colts in August-September 1995]

[**MANAGER:** *John Elliott*] [**COACH:** *Adrian Thompson*]

CAPTAIN: *Joe Worsley*

First Round - Pool 'C'

26th Jan CHILE 7 **ENGLAND** 21

[*Team:* Chesney, Ben Johnston, J. Worsley, Sampson, J. Lewsey, R. Thirlby, Sackey]

[*Bench:* Friday, N. Simpson (rep), Seely]

[*Scorers:* **tries** by Sampson, R. Thirlby and J. Lewsey, **conversions** by Sampson (3)]

CAPTAIN: *Mike Friday*

26th Jan ZIMBABWE 7 **ENGLAND** 28

[*Team:* Ben Johnston, Seely, J. Worsley, Friday, Sampson, J. Lewsey, Sackey]

[*Bench:* Chesney, N. Simpson (rep), R. Thirlby (rep)]

[*Scorers:* **tries** by Sampson, Sackey, Ben Johnston and R. Thirlby, **conversions** by Sampson (4)]

26th Jan SPAIN 14 **ENGLAND*** 12

[*Team:* Chesney, Seely, J. Worsley, Friday, Sampson, J. Lewsey, Sackey]

[*Bench:* Ben Johnston, N. Simpson (rep), R. Thirlby (rep)]

[*Scorers:* **tries** by Chesney and Sackey, **conversion** by Sampson]

CAPTAIN: *Joe Worsley*

27th Jan JAPAN 7 **ENGLAND** 24

[*Team:* Ben Johnston, Seely, J. Worsley, Sampson, J. Lewsey, R. Thirlby, Sackey]

[*Bench:* Chesney, Friday (rep), N. Simpson (rep)]

[*Scorers:* **tries** by R. Thirlby, J. Lewsey, Ben Johnston and Sampson, **conversions** by Sampson (2)]

CAPTAIN: *Mike Friday*

27th Jan NEW ZEALAND 17 **ENGLAND** 7

[*Team:* Ben Johnston, Seely, J. Worsley, Friday, R. Thirlby, J. Lewsey, Sampson]
[*Bench:* Chesney, Sackey, N. Simpson]
[*Scorers:* **try** by R. Thirlby, **conversion** by Sampson]

Quarter-Final

28th Jan AUSTRALIA 33 **ENGLAND** 5

[*Team:* Ben Johnston, Seely, J. Worsley, Friday, R. Thirlby, J. Lewsey, Sampson]
[*Bench:* Chesney (rep), Sackey (rep), N. Simpson (rep)]
[*Scorers:* **try** by Sampson]

POSITION: LOSING QUARTER-FINALISTS

6 NATIONS CHAMPIONSHIP

[**TEAM MANAGER:** *Clive Woodward*] [**HEAD COACH:** *Andy Robinson*] [**ASSISTANT COACHES:** *Brian Ashton & Phil Larder*]

CAPTAIN: *Martin Johnson*

3rd Feb WALES 15 **ENGLAND** 44

Millennium Stadium, Cardiff

[*Team:* J. Leonard, D. West, Vickery, Martin Johnson, Grewcock, Richard Hill (2), Back, Dallaglio, Matt Dawson, Jonny Wilkinson, Luger, M. Catt, W. Greenwood, B. Cohen, Balshaw]
[*Bench:* Corry (rep), Healey (*scrum half*) (rep), Matt Perry (rep), M. Regan, Tindall (*centre*) (rep), Julian White (*prop*), Trevor Woodman (*prop*) (rep)]
[*Scorers:* **tries** by W. Greenwood (3), Matt Dawson (2) and B. Cohen, **penalty goals** by Jonny Wilkinson (2), **conversions** by Jonny Wilkinson (4)]

17th Feb **ENGLAND** 80 ITALY 23

Twickenham

[*Team:* J. Leonard, D. West, Vickery, Martin Johnson, Grewcock, Richard Hill (2), Back, Dallaglio, Matt Dawson, Jonny Wilkinson, B. Cohen, M. Catt, W. Greenwood, Healey, Balshaw]
[*Bench:* K. Bracken (rep), Corry (rep), M. Regan (rep), Jason Robinson (*wing/full back*) (rep), Tindall, Trevor Woodman (rep), J. Worsley (*flanker/number 8*) (rep)]
[*Scorers:* **tries** by Healey (2), Balshaw (2), B. Cohen, M. Regan, J. Worsley, W. Greenwood, Jonny Wilkinson and Dallaglio, **penalty goals** by Jonny Wilkinson (4), **conversions** by Jonny Wilkinson (9)]

3rd March **ENGLAND** 43 SCOTLAND 3

Twickenham

[*Team:* J. Leonard, D. West, Vickery, Martin Johnson, Grewcock, Richard Hill (2), Back, Dallaglio, Matt Dawson, Jonny Wilkinson, B. Cohen, M. Catt, W. Greenwood, Healey, Balshaw]
[*Bench:* K. Bracken (rep), Corry, Matt Perry, M. Regan (rep), Jason Robinson (rep), Trevor Woodman, J. Worsley (rep)]
[*Scorers:* **tries** by Dallaglio (2), Richard Hill, Balshaw (2) and W. Greenwood, **penalty goal** by Jonny Wilkinson, **conversions** by Jonny Wilkinson (5)]

CAPTAIN: *No captain appointed*

24th Mar IRELAND P **ENGLAND** P

Lansdowne Road

[*Team not selected*]
[*Bench not selected*]

[*No scorers*]
CAPTAIN: *Martin Johnson*
7th April **ENGLAND** 48 FRANCE 19
Twickenham
[*Team:* J. Leonard, Greening, Julian White, Martin Johnson, S. Borthwick, Richard Hill (2), Back, Dallaglio, Matt Dawson, Jonny Wilkinson, B. Cohen, M. Catt, W. Greenwood, Healey, Balshaw]
[*Bench:* K. Bracken (rep), Corry (rep), Flatman (rep), Matt Perry (rep), Jason Robinson (rep), D. West (rep), J. Worsley (rep)]
[*Scorers:* **tries** by W. Greenwood, Richard Hill, Balshaw, Greening, M. Catt and Matt Perry, **penalty goals** by Jonny Wilkinson (2), **conversions** by Jonny Wilkinson (6)]
CAPTAIN: *No captain appointed*
5th May IRELAND P **ENGLAND** P
Lansdowne Road
[*Team not selected*]
[*Bench not selected*]
[*No scorers*]
CAPTAIN: *Matt Dawson* [*Neil Back took over when Matt Dawson was injured in the 1st half*]
20th Oct IRELAND 20 **ENGLAND*** 14
Lansdowne Road
[*Team:* J. Leonard, Greening, Julian White, Simon Shaw, Grewcock, Corry, Back, Richard Hill (2), Matt Dawson, Jonny Wilkinson, Jason Robinson, M. Catt, W. Greenwood, Luger, Balshaw]
[*Bench:* S. Borthwick, K. Bracken (rep), Healey (*wing*) (rep), Lewis Moody (*flanker*) (rep), Matt Perry, Christopher *Graham* Rowntree (*prop*) (rep), D. West (rep)]
[*Scorers:* **try** by Healey, **penalty goals** by Jonny Wilkinson (3)]
POSITION: **1ST 8 +149 CC** [Ireland 8 +40 MT, Scotland 5 -24, Wales 5 -41, France 4 -23, Italy 0 -101]
FANTASY: ***1ST 10 GS TC CC MT***

OTHER MATCHES

ENGLAND STUDENTS MATCHES

[**MANAGER:** *Tony Lanaway*] [**COACH:** *Richard* John *Hill (1)*] [**ASSISTANT COACH:** *Ian* Robert *Smith (2)*]
CAPTAIN: *Ed Mallett*
[2nd Feb WALES STUDENTS 29 **ENGLAND STUDENTS** 29]
Brewery Field, Bridgend
[*Team:* Jeffreys, Matt Cairns, T. Payne, E. Mallett, Peter Short, Cockle, Ben Lewitt, A. Beattie, Scott Bemand, Amor, Simon Hunt, Brading, Euan Kenworthy, Adam Billig, Newmarch]
[*Bench:* James Brooks (*fly half*) (rep), Chris Collins (*hooker*), Lofthouse (rep), P. Richards (*prop*), Lee Starling (*flanker*), Dan Taberner (*scrum half*), John Welch (*centre*) (rep)]
[*Scorers:* **tries** by Brading, B. Lewitt and Billig, **penalty goals** by Amor (4), **conversion** by Amor]
CAPTAIN: *Scott Bemand*
[2nd Mar **ENGLAND STUDENTS** 33 SCOTLAND STUDENTS 10]
Sedgley Park RFC, Park Lane, Whitefield, Manchester
[*Team:* Bemand, Amor, Brading]

[*Bench:* ?, ?, ?, ?, ?, ?, ?]
[*Scorers:* **tries** by ?, ?, ? and ?, **penalty goals** by Amor (3), **conversions** by Amor (2)]
[23rd Mar IRELAND STUDENTS C **ENGLAND STUDENTS** C]
Trinity College, Dublin
[*Team not selected*]
[*Bench not selected*]
[*No scorers*]
[6th April **ENGLAND STUDENTS** 25 FRANCE STUDENTS 14]
Worcester RFC, Sixways Stadium, Pershore Lane, Hindip, Worcester
[*Team:* John Brooks, M. Cairns, T. Payne, Kieran Roche, P. Short, Howard Quigley, B. Lewitt, Adam Balding, Bemand, Amor, Simon Hunt, Alex Cadwallader, Kenworthy, Billig, Newmarch]
[*Bench:* Cockle (rep), ?, ?, ?, ?, ?, ?]
[*Scorers:* **tries** by B. Lewitt, Cockle and Balding, **penalty goals** by Amor (2), **conversions** by Amor (2)]
[Richard Hill (1) and Ian Smith (2) were both appointed on 13th January 2001; Peter Drewett was appointed Manager of England U19 on 1st November 2001; Richard Hill (1) won 29 caps for England between 1984-91]

U21 6 NATIONS CHAMPIONSHIP

[**MANAGER:** *Nigel Melville*] [**COACH:** *Dean Ryan*]
CAPTAIN: *Mark Tucker*
[2nd Feb WALES U21 27 **ENGLAND U21** 12]
Sardis Road, Pwllgwaun, Pontypridd
[*Team:* Luke Harbut, Titterrell, Jonathan 'Jon' Dawson, Phil Murphy (1), Rudzki, Jonathan 'Jon' Dunbar, D. Danaher, I. Clarke, A. Page, C. Hodgson, Christophers, M. Tucker, Sam Cox, Thomas 'Tom' Voyce, Marsden]
[*Bench:* Devonshire (*flanker*) (rep), A. Elliott (*wing*), James Grindal (*scrum half*) (rep), Isaacson (*prop*) (rep), M. Leek (rep), Martin Purdy (*lock*) (rep), Matthew 'Matt' Williams (1) (*hooker*)]
[*Scorers:* **penalty goals** by C. Hodgson (4)]
[17th Feb **ENGLAND U21** 47 ITALY U21 18]
Stoop Memorial Ground, Langhorn Drive, Twickenham
[*Team:* Harbut, Titterrell, Isaacson, Louis Deacon, M. Purdy, Devonshire, D. Danaher, Alexander 'Alex' Alesbrook, Grindal, C. Hodgson, Michael Stephenson, M. Tucker, Sam Cox, Voyce, Marsden]
[*Bench:* Alexander 'Alex' Clarke (*prop*) (rep), A. Elliott (rep), Alex Hadley (*lock*), M. Leek, A. Page (*scrum half*) (rep), Matt Williams (1) (rep), ?]
[*Scorers:* **tries** by M. Tucker, C. Hodgson, M. Stephenson, Voyce (2) and Alex Clarke, **penalty goals** by C. Hodgson (3), **conversions** by C. Hodgson (4)]
[2nd Mar **ENGLAND U21** 62 SCOTLAND U21 29]
Webb Ellis Road, Rugby
[*Team:* Harbut, Matt Williams (1), Isaacson, L. Deacon, Rudzki, I. Clarke, D. Danaher, Alesbrook, Grindal, Andrew 'Andy' Goode, M. Stephenson, M. Tucker, Sam Cox, Voyce, Marsden]
[*Bench:* Christophers (*wing*) (rep), J. Dawson (*prop*), C. Hodgson (*fly half*) (rep), A. Page (rep), M. Purdy, Titterrell (*hooker*), ?]
[*Scorers:* **tries** by Andy Goode, Marsden (3), M. Stephenson, M. Tucker, Voyce (2) and Christophers, **penalty goal** by Andy Goode, **conversions** by Andy Goode (5) and C.

Hodgson (2)]

[23rd Mar IRELAND U21 C **ENGLAND U21** C]

Donnybrook, Dublin

[*Team not selected*]

[*Bench not selected*]

[*No scorers*]

[6th April **ENGLAND U21** 10 FRANCE U21 8]

Newbury RFC, Monks Lane, Newbury

[*Team:* Harbut, James Parkes, Isaacson, L. Deacon, Rudzki, I. Clarke, D. Danaher, Alesbrook, Grindal, Andy Goode, M. Stephenson, M. Tucker, Sam Cox, Voyce, Marsden]

[*Bench:* Christophers (rep), J. Dawson (rep), J. Dunbar (*flanker*) (rep), M. Leek, A. Page, M. Purdy, Titterrell]

[*Scorers:* **try** by Voyce, **penalty goal** by Andy Goode, **conversion** by Andy Goode]

POSITION: 2ND 6 +49 [*INCOMPLETE:*
France Played 5: 8pts +85, Wales Played 4: 6pts +23,
Ireland Played 2: 2pts +31, Scotland Played 4: 2pts -45,
Italy Played 5: 0pts -143]

'A' INTERNATIONAL CHAMPIONSHIP

[**MANAGER:** *Gerald 'Ged' Glynn*] [**COACH:** *John Wells*] [**ASSISTANT COACH:** *Ellery Hanley*]

CAPTAIN: *Steve Borthwick*

[2nd Feb WALES A 19 **ENGLAND A*** 19]

The Racecourse Ground, Wrexham

[*Team:* Flatman, Richard Kirke, John Mallett, Benedict 'Ben' Kay, S. Borthwick, Steve White-Cooper, Moody, J. Worsley, Martyn Wood, Andy Goode, Jason Robinson, James 'Jamie' Noon, Leon Lloyd, David Rees (2), Sampson]

[*Bench:* Christopher 'Chris' Fortey (*hooker*) (rep), Gomarsall (*scrum half*), Robin 'Rob' Hardwick (*prop*) (rep), Andrew 'Andy' Hazell (*flanker*), Alastair 'Ali' Hepher (*fly half*) (rep), Tom May (*fly half/centre/wing/full back*) (rep), Seely (*number 8*)]

[*Scorers:* **try** by Sampson, **penalty goals** by Andy Goode (3), **drop goal** by Andy Goode, **conversion** by Andy Goode]

[16th Feb **ENGLAND A** 44 ITALY A 3]

Goldington Road, Goldington, Bedford

[*Team:* Flatman, Andrew 'Andy' Long, Julian White, S. Borthwick, Kay, Seely, Moody, William 'Will' Johnson, Martyn Wood, Andy Goode, Nnamdi Ezulike, J. Lewsey, L. Lloyd, Liam Botham, Sampson]

[*Bench:* Robert 'Rob' Fidler (*lock*) (rep), Gomarsall (rep), Hardwick, Kirke (*hooker*), T. May, Paul Volley (*flanker*) (rep), David 'Dave' Walder (*fly half/full back*) (rep)]

[*Scorers:* **tries** by Ezulike, J. Lewsey, Sampson, S. Borthwick, W. Johnson and Walder, **penalty goals** by Andy Goode (2), **conversions** by Andy Goode and Walder (3)]

[2nd Mar **ENGLAND A** 60 SCOTLAND A 20]

Headingley Stadium, Leeds

[*Team:* Flatman, A. Long, Hardwick, S. Borthwick, Kay, White-Cooper, Volley, Will Johnson, Martyn Wood, Walder, David Rees (2), T. May, L. Lloyd, Sampson, J. Lewsey]

[*Bench:* Benton (*scrum half*) (rep), Rob Fidler (rep), Greening (*hooker*) (rep), Hazell (rep), Alexander 'Alex' King (*fly half*) (rep), J. Mallett (*prop*) (rep), Noon (*centre*) (rep)]

[*Scorers:* **tries** by Sampson (2), White-Cooper, Hardwick, David Rees, S. Borthwick, Martyn Wood and Greening, **penalty goals** by Walder (2), **conversions** by Walder (5) and A. King

(2)]

CAPTAIN: *No captain appointed*

[23rd Mar IRELAND A C **ENGLAND A** C]

Thomond Park, Limerick

[*Team not selected*]

[*Bench not selected*]

[*No scorers*]

CAPTAIN: *Ben Kay*

[6th April **ENGLAND A** 23 FRANCE A 22]

Recreation Ground, Redruth

[*Team:* Michael 'Mike' Worsley, A. Long, Ricky Nebbett, Rob Fidler, Kay, Patrick 'Pat' Sanderson, Volley, W. Johnson, Nicholas 'Nick' Walshe, C. Hodgson, Sampson, T. May, L. Lloyd, David Rees (2), J. Lewsey]

[*Bench:* Mark Cornwell (*lock*) (rep), A. King (rep), Kirke (rep), Noon (rep), Adrian Olver (*prop*) (rep), Richard 'Ricky' Pellow (*scrum half*), Alexander 'Alex' Sanderson (*flanker/number 8*) (rep)]

[*Scorers:* **tries** by Sampson and P. Sanderson, **penalty goals** by C. Hodgson (3), **conversions** by C. Hodgson (2)]

POSITION: **2ND 7 +82** [*INCOMPLETE:*
France Played 5: 8pts +64, Scotland Played 4: 4pts -5,
Wales Played 4: 3pts -18, Ireland Played 2: 2pts +20,
Italy Played 5: 0pts -143]

FANTASY: ***1ST 10 GS TC***

[Ged Glynn, John Wells and Ellery Hanley were all appointed on 9th November 2000; John Wells played for an England XV against an Italy XV at Rovigo on 1st May 1990; Ellery Hanley was capped 36 times for Great Britain at Rugby League between 1984-93, was appointed Great Britain Rugby League Coach in August 1994 and was the Coach when the England Rugby League team played in the European Championship in February 1995; Ellery Hanley resigned on 25th September 2001 due to a contractual dispute with the RFU]

TELECOM 2GO NEW ZEALAND INTERNATIONAL SEVENS
IRB WORLD SEVENS SERIES 2000-2001 ROUND 3

WestpacTrust Stadium, Wellington

[*Tournament squad:* Sowerby, Earnshaw, A. Elliott (*wing*), Friday, Dean Dewdney (*scrum half/wing*), S. Booth, R. Haughton, Darren Carr, N. Simpson, James 'Jim' Brownrigg (*forward*), James Brooks (*scrum half/fly half*), Stuart Bellinger (*forward*)]

(squad of 12)

[Mark Sowerby played in the White Hart Marauders team that won the Henley International Sevens on 13th May 2001, played in the Bradford Bulls team that won the Middlesex Sevens at Twickenham on 17th August 2002 and played in the White Hart Marauders team that reached the Final of the Cwmtawe Sevens at Pontardawe on 2nd August 2003; Dean Dewdney was capped for Zimbabwe in May 1996 and played for Major R.V. Stanley's XV against Oxford University at Iffley Road on 18th November 1998]

[**MANAGER:** *John Elliott*] [**COACH:** *Adrian Thompson*]

CAPTAIN: *Mark Sowerby*

First Round - Pool 'B'

9th Feb CHINA 14 **ENGLAND** 33
[*Team:*]
[*Bench:*]
[*Scorers:* **tries** by Earnshaw, S. Booth, R. Haughton (2) and A. Elliott, **conversions** by James Brooks (4)]

9th Feb USA 17 **ENGLAND*** 12
[*Team:*]
[*Bench:*]
[*Scorers:* **tries** by A. Elliott and R. Haughton, **conversion** by S. Booth]

9th Feb FIJI 41 **ENGLAND** 5
[*Team:*]
[*Bench:*]
[*Scorers:* **try** by N. Simpson]

[Bowl Quarter-Final:]

[10th Feb NIUE 7 **ENGLAND** 22]
[*Team:*]
[*Bench:*]
[*Scorers:* **tries** by James Brooks and N. Simpson (3), **conversion** by S. Booth]

[Bowl Semi-Final:]

[10th Feb SOUTH AFRICA 31 **ENGLAND** 12]
[*Team:*]
[*Bench:*]
[*Scorers:* **tries** by Brownrigg (2), **conversion** by S. Booth]

POSITION: FIRST ROUND LOSERS [*BOWL SEMI-FINALISTS*]

[England did not score any competition points in this Round of the 2000-2001 IRB World Sevens Series]

BRISBANE SEVENS
IRB WORLD SEVENS SERIES 2000-2001 ROUND 4

Suncorp Stadium, Lang Park, Brisbane
[*Tournament squad not selected*]
[**MANAGER:** *John Elliott*] [**COACH:** *Adrian Thompson*]
CAPTAIN: *No captain appointed*

16th Feb *No opponents named* C **ENGLAND** C
[*Team not selected*]
[*Bench not selected*]
[*No scorers*]

ALASTAIR HIGNELL BENEFIT MATCH

[CAMBRIDGE PAST AND PRESENT: [NO COACH NOMINATED]]
[AJ HIGNELL XV: [NO COACH NOMINATED]]
CAPTAIN: *Michael Count* [Cambridge Past and Present]
CAPTAIN: *Phil de Glanville* [AJ Hignell XV]

[7th Mar **CAMBRIDGE PAST AND PRESENT** 55 **AJ HIGNELL XV** 46]

University Football Ground, Grange Road, Cambridge

[CAMBRIDGE PAST & PRESENT: [*Team:* Mike Tweedie (IR), Stefan Rodgers, James Meredith (WA), E. Mallett, Angus Innes (AU), M. Purdy, Michael 'Mike' Haslett (IR), Michael

Count, Mark Chapman-Smith (NZ), Amor, Matthew 'Matt' Singer (WA), Christopher 'Chris' Davis, David Quinlan (IR), Paul Surridge (NZ), John *Stuart* Moffat (SC)]
[*Bench:* Anthony 'Tony' Dalwood (*centre/full back*) (rep), Christiaan 'Chris' Derksen (SA) (*hooker*) (rep), Peter Dunn (*fly half*) (rep), Mark Edwards (IR) (*scrum half*), Nicholas 'Nick' Hill (AU) (*centre*), Neil Lomax (*wing/full back*) (rep), Marco Rivaro (IT) (*wing*) (rep), Ronan Workman (IR) (*prop*) (rep)]
[*Scorers:* **tries** by P. Surridge (NZ) (2), Chris Davis, Haslett (IR), P. Dunn, Count, D. Quinlan (IR) (2) and Dalwood, **conversions** by Amor (2), P. Surridge (NZ), Count and Lomax]**]**
[AJ HIGNELL XV: [*Team:* Andrew 'Andy' Le Chevalier, Saul Nelson (WA), Tim Marston, Charlie Simpson (IR), Jim Evans, Steve Cheeseborough, Richard Nias, B. Cole, James Bramhall, Ken Iwabuchi (JAP), N. Drake, Philip 'Phil' de Glanville, Paul Reeves (SA), Jonathan 'Jon' Sleightholme, Robert 'Rob' Ashforth]
[*Bench:* Andrew 'Andy' Craig (NZ) (*lock*) (rep), M. Leek (rep), Lee Mears (*prop/hooker*), John O'Reilly (*scrum half*) (rep), Richard Siveter (*prop*) (rep), Gareth Williams (3) (*centre/wing*) (rep), ?]
[*Scorers:* **tries** by de Glanville, Ashforth, Iwabuchi (JAP), N. Drake, P. Reeves (SA), J. Sleightholme (2) and C. Simpson (IR), **conversions** by Iwabuchi (JAP) and Ashforth (2)]**]**
[Match organised by Cambridge University to raise money for Alastair Hignell's multiple sclerosis treatment]

CREDIT SUISSE FIRST BOSTON HONG KONG SEVENS
IRB WORLD SEVENS SERIES 2000-2001 ROUND 5

Hong Kong Stadium, Eastern Hospital Road, So Kon Po, Hong Kong
[*Tournament squad:* J. Sleightholme (*wing*), Nicholas 'Nick' Marsh (*wing*), Mark Cueto (*wing*), N. Simpson, Mark Meenan (*fly half*), Sebastian 'Seb' FitzGerald (*fly half*), Rob Stewart (2), James 'Jamie' Hamilton (*scrum half*), Miall (*forward*), Earnshaw, Luke Sherriff (*prop*), Chris Davis (*forward*)]
(squad of 12)
[Several sevens specialists were unavailable due to their Zurich Premiership and 6 Nations Championship commitments; Mark Meenan played for Ireland in the U19 World Championship in Wales in March-April 1999, but had switched his allegiance to England by January 2000]
[MANAGER: *John Elliott*] **[COACH:** *Adrian Thompson*]
CAPTAIN: *Jon Sleightholme*
First Round - Pool 'D'

30th Mar JAPAN 14 **ENGLAND** 28
[*Team:* Earnshaw, Meenan, J. Sleightholme]
[*Bench:* S. FitzGerald (rep)]
[*Scorers:* **tries** by Meenan, Earnshaw (2) and J. Sleightholme, **conversions** by Meenan (4)]
31st Mar SINGAPORE 5 **ENGLAND** 66
[*Team:* ?, ?, ?, Jamie Hamilton, Meenan, N. Simpson, J. Sleightholme]
[*Bench:* Cueto (rep), S. FitzGerald (rep), N. Marsh, ?, ?]
[*Scorers:* **tries** by N. Simpson (3), Jamie Hamilton (2), J. Sleightholme (2), Meenan, Chris Davis and Cueto, **conversions** by Meenan (4) and S. FitzGerald (4)]
31st Mar SAMOA 28 **ENGLAND** 0
[*Team:* S. FitzGerald]
[*Bench:*]
[*No scorers*]

Quarter-Final

1st April FIJI 22 **ENGLAND** 7

[*Team:* Sherriff, Chris Davis, Miall, Jamie Hamilton, Meenan, N. Simpson, J. Sleightholme]
[*Bench:* Cueto (rep), Earnshaw, S. FitzGerald (rep), N. Marsh, Rob Stewart (2) (rep)]
[*Scorers:* **try** by N. Simpson, **conversion** by Meenan]

POSITION: LOSING QUARTER-FINALISTS

[England scored 8 competition points in this Round of the 2000-2001 IRB World Sevens Series]

SHANGHAI SEVENS
IRB WORLD SEVENS SERIES 2000-2001 ROUND 6

Yuanshen Stadium, Pudong, Shanghai

[*Tournament squad:* Chesney, Chris Davis, N. Simpson, Timothy 'Tim' Stimpson (*back/forward*), Gomarsall, R. Thirlby, Meenan, A. Elliott, S. FitzGerald, Gollings (*fly half/centre*), R. Haughton, Brownrigg]

(squad of 12)

[Tim Stimpson was capped for England Schools 18 Group in January 1991]

[**MANAGER:** *John Elliott*] [**COACH:** *Adrian Thompson*]

CAPTAIN: *Andy Gomarsall*

First Round - Pool 'B'

7th April CHINA 14 **ENGLAND** 22

[*Team:*]
[*Bench:*]
[*Scorers:* **tries** by R. Thirlby (2) and N. Simpson (2), **conversion** by Gomarsall]

7th April WALES 0 **ENGLAND** 29

[*Team:*]
[*Bench:*]
[*Scorers:* **tries** by R. Thirlby (2), Gomarsall and N. Simpson (2), **conversions** by Gomarsall (2)]

7th April AUSTRALIA 43 **ENGLAND** 0

[*Team:*]
[*Bench:*]
[*No scorers*]

Quarter-Final

8th April SOUTH AFRICA 24 **ENGLAND** 7

[*Team:*]
[*Bench:*]
[*Scorers:* **try** by R. Thirlby, **conversion** by Gomarsall]

[Plate Semi-Final:]

[8th April ARGENTINA 17 **ENGLAND** 19]

[*Team:*]
[*Bench:*]
[*Scorers:* **tries** by Meenan, Gomarsall and N. Simpson, **conversions** by Meenan and Gomarsall]

CAPTAIN: *??*

[Plate Final:]

[8th April FIJI 45 **ENGLAND** 14]

[*Team:* Chesney, Chris Davis, R. Thirlby, S. FitzGerald, Meenan, N. Simpson, A. Elliott]

[*Bench:* Brownrigg, Gollings, Gomarsall (rep), R. Haughton, Stimpson]
[*Scorers:* **tries** by Meenan and R. Thirlby, **conversions** by Meenan and R. Thirlby]
POSITION: LOSING QUARTER-FINALISTS [*PLATE FINALISTS*]
[*England scored 6 competition points in this Round of the 2000-2001 IRB World Sevens Series*]

TILNEY MELROSE SEVENS
LADIES CENTENARY CUP

The Greenyards, Melrose
[*Tournament squad:* Sherriff, Alain Studer (SWI) (*forward*), Miall, Friday (never travelled as withdrew, replaced by Alex Page), Conan Sharman (SC) (*centre/wing*), J. Sleightholme (captain; never travelled due to bereavement, replaced by David Irving), Simon Webster (SC) (*centre/wing*), Darren Burns (SC) (*forward*), Longstaff (SC) (*wing*), Owain Williams (WA) (*forward*), A. Page (*scrum half*), David Irving (SC) (*scrum half*)]
(squad of 10)
[Jon Sleightholme withdrew the day before the tournament due to a family bereavement and was initially due to be replaced by Chris Paterson, who then proved to be unavailable due to his BBC commentating commitments, which meant that it was David Irving who actually played in the competition, where he duly won a much-coveted Melrose winner's medal!; Jon Sleightholme played in the White Hart Marauders team that won the Henley International Sevens on 13th May 2001]
[The first round was a qualifying round]
[NO COACH NOMINATED]
CAPTAIN: *Shaun Longstaff* (SC)
Second Round
[14th April West of Scotland (*SC*) 14 **BARBARIANS** 33]
[*Team:*]
[*Bench:*]
[*Scorers:* **tries** by Studer (SWI), Longstaff (SC), A. Page, Sharman (SC) and Sherriff, **conversions** by Sharman (SC) (4)]
Quarter-Final
[14th April Kirkcaldy (*SC*) 14 **BARBARIANS** 26]
[*Team:*]
[*Bench:*]
[*Scorers:* **tries** by Sharman (SC) (2), Longstaff (SC) and D. Irving (SC), **conversions** by Sharman (SC) (2) and D. Irving (SC)]
Semi-Final
[14th April Glasgow Hawks (*SC*) 12 **BARBARIANS** 24]
[*Team:*]
[*Bench:*]
[*Scorers:* **tries** by Sharman (SC), D. Burns (SC) (2) and Sherriff, **conversions** by Sharman (SC) (2) and D. Irving (SC) (2)]
Final
[14th April Nawaka (*FIJ*) 19 **BARBARIANS** 38]
[*Team:* D. Burns (SC), Sherriff, O. Williams (WA), A. Page, S. Webster (SC), Sharman (SC), Longstaff (SC)]
[*Bench:* D. Irving (SC) (rep), Miall, Studer (SWI)]
[*Scorers:* **tries** by Sharman (SC) (2), S. Webster (SC) (3) and Longstaff (SC), **conversions**

by Sharman (SC) (2) and D. Irving (SC) (2)]
POSITION: WINNERS

BANK OF SCOTLAND BORDER LEAGUE CENTENARY MATCH

[NO COACH NOMINATED]
CAPTAIN: *Graham Shiel* (SC)
[16th April Border League Select XV (*SC*) 31 **BARBARIANS*** 24]
The Greenyards, Melrose
[*Team:* Jocky Bryce (SC), Lawn, Bruce Douglas (SC), Robbie Brown (SC), Miall, C. Mather (SC), Studer (SWI), Vuniani Derenalagi (FIJ), R. Elliott, Andrew *Graham* Shiel (SC), Phil Graham, Lalai Driu (FIJ), Neil Boobyer (WA), Temesia Kaumaia (FIJ), Matt Cardey (WA)]
[*Bench:* Michael 'Mike' Armstrong (*hooker*) (rep), Bullock (rep), Chapman-Smith (NZ) (*scrum half*) (rep), Norman Ligairi (FIJ) (*wing/full back*) (rep), Sailosi Nawavu (FIJ) (*flanker*) (rep), Apisai Naro (FIJ) (*number 8*) (rep)]
[*Scorers:* **tries** by Cardey (WA), Phil Graham, J. Bryce (SC) and Studer (SWI), **conversions** by G. Shiel (SC) (2)]
[Match to commemorate the 100th Anniversary of the foundation of the Border League in the South of Scotland in 1901]

MALAYSIA SEVENS
IRB WORLD SEVENS SERIES 2000-2001 ROUND 7

MPPJ Stadium, Petaling Jaya, Kelana Jaya
[*Tournament squad:* Brownrigg, Chris Davis, Miall, A. Elliott, N. Simpson, Rob Stewart (2), Meenan (never travelled as withdrew), Paul Dunkley (*fly half*), James Tapster (*wing*), Simon Hunt (*back/forward*), Sackey (never travelled as withdrew), N. Drake, Amor (*scrum half/fly half*), Toby Bainbridge-Kay (*scrum half*)]
(squad of 12)
[Simon Amor and Toby Bainbridge-Kay not in original squad; A revised squad of 13 was announced on 19th April 2001]
[**MANAGER:** *John Elliott*] [**COACH:** *Adrian Thompson*]
CAPTAIN: *Chris Davis*
First Round - Pool 'A'
21st April MALAYSIA 10 **ENGLAND** 31
[*Team:*]
[*Bench:*]
[*Scorers:* **tries** by Simon Hunt (3), Tapster and Brownrigg, **conversions** by Amor (2) and Dunkley]
21st April WALES 24 **ENGLAND** 14
[*Team:*]
[*Bench:*]
[*Scorers:* **tries** by Simon Hunt and Amor, **conversions** by Amor (2)]
21st April NEW ZEALAND 33 **ENGLAND** 5
[*Team:*]
[*Bench:*]
[*Scorers:* **try** by Chris Davis]
[Bowl Quarter-Final:]
[22nd Apr TAIWAN 0 **ENGLAND** 38]
[*Team:*]
[*Bench:*]

[*Scorers:* **tries** by Tapster, Simon Hunt (3), N. Drake and N. Simpson, **conversions** by Amor (4)]
[Bowl Semi-Final:]
[22nd Apr JAPAN 7 **ENGLAND** 34]
[*Team:*]
[*Bench:*]
[*Scorers:* **tries** by Brownrigg, Simon Hunt (3), Rob Stewart and N. Simpson, **conversions** by Amor (2)]
[Bowl Final:]
[22nd Apr KOREA 24 **ENGLAND** 12]
[*Team:*]
[*Bench:*]
[*Scorers:* **tries** by N. Drake and Rob Stewart, **conversion** by Amor]
POSITION: FIRST ROUND LOSERS [*BOWL FINALISTS*]
[England did not score any competition points in this Round of the 2000-2001 IRB World Sevens Series]

VOLKSWAGEN JAPAN SEVENS
IRB WORLD SEVENS SERIES 2000-2001 ROUND 8

Chichibunomiya Rugby Stadium, Tokyo
[*Tournament squad:* Brownrigg, Chris Davis, Miall, A. Elliott, N. Simpson, Rob Stewart (2), Meenan, Dunkley (never travelled as withdrew), Tapster, Simon Hunt, Sackey (never travelled as withdrew), N. Drake, Amor, A. Sanderson (*forward*)]
(squad of 12)
[Simon Amor and Alex Sanderson not in original squad]
[MANAGER: *John Elliott*] **[COACH:** *Adrian Thompson*]
CAPTAIN: *Chris Davis*
First Round - Pool 'B'
29th April MALAYSIA 5 **ENGLAND** 31
[*Team:*]
[*Bench:*]
[*Scorers:* **tries** by Tapster (2), Amor, Simon Hunt and N. Simpson, **conversions** by Amor (3)]
29th April JAPAN 7 **ENGLAND** 24
[*Team:*]
[*Bench:*]
[*Scorers:* **tries** by Amor, Tapster, Rob Stewart and Simon Hunt, **conversions** by Amor (2)]
29th April AUSTRALIA 26 **ENGLAND** 0
[*Team:* Brownrigg, Chris Davis, N. Simpson, Rob Stewart (2), Amor, Simon Hunt, N. Drake]
[*Bench:* A. Elliott, Meenan, Miall (rep), A. Sanderson (rep), Tapster (rep)]
[*No scorers*]
Quarter-Final
30th April NEW ZEALAND 26 **ENGLAND** 7
[*Team:*]
[*Bench:*]
[*Scorers:* **try** by Simon Hunt, **conversion** by Amor]
[Plate Semi-Final:]
[30th Apr CANADA 5 **ENGLAND** 29]
[*Team:*]
[*Bench:*]

[*Scorers:* **tries** by Amor and Simon Hunt (4), **conversions** by Amor (2)]
[Plate Final:]
[30th Apr SOUTH AFRICA 38 **ENGLAND** 15]
[*Team:*]
[*Bench:*]
[*Scorers:* **tries** by Simon Hunt (2) and N. Simpson]
POSITION: LOSING QUARTER-FINALISTS [*PLATE FINALISTS*]
[England scored 6 competition points in this Round of the 2000-2001 IRB World Sevens Series]

ENGLAND STUDENTS MATCH

[**COACH:** *?*]
CAPTAIN: *??*
[5th May **ENGLAND STUDENTS U21** 32 COMBINED SERVICES U21 (*SER*) 21]
Twickenham
[*Team:* Alex Clarke, John Williams (3), Josh Hooker, Andy Monighan, Min Aung, Sherriff, Simon Dawes, Anthony 'Tony' Jackson, Simon Dyson, Peter Murphy, Michael Lennon, Christopher 'Chris' Brain, Cadwallader, Simon Hunt, Jonathan 'Jonny' Hylton]
[*Bench:* J. Dunbar, Terry Ellis (*hooker*), Erinle (*centre*), Will Green (2) (*scrum half*), C. Hodgson, T. Payne (*prop*), Rudzki (*lock*)]
[*Scorers:* **tries** by Hylton (2), Lennon and John Williams, **penalty goals** by Peter Murphy (4)]

FIRST SCOTTISH AMICABLE TOUR MATCH

[**COACH:** *Bob Dwyer* (AU)]
CAPTAIN: *Gary Teichmann* (SA)
[20th May WALES XV 38 **BARBARIANS** 40]
Millennium Stadium, Cardiff
[*Team:* Garry Pagel (SA), Trevor Leota (SAM), Craig Dowd (NZ), Tom Bowman (AU), *Ian* Donald Jones (2) (NZ), Benjamin 'Ben' Clarke, Josh Kronfeld (NZ), Gary Teichmann (SA), Joost van der Westhuizen (SA), Johannes Jacobus 'Braam' van Straaten (SA), Joeli Vidiri (NZ), Kevin Maggs (IR), Jason Little (AU), Luger, Percival 'Percy' Montgomery (SA)]
[*Bench:* Robin Brooke (NZ) (*lock*) (rep), Drotske (SA) (*hooker*) (rep), Adrian Garvey (SA) (*prop*) (rep), Gomarsall (rep), Timothy 'Tim' Horan (AU) (*centre*) (rep), Patrick 'Pat' Lam (SAM) (*flanker/number 8*) (rep), Friedrich Lombard (SA) (*wing*) (rep)]
[*Scorers:* **tries** by Luger, Vidiri (NZ), F. Lombard (SA) (2), Drotske (SA) and P. Montgomery (SA), **conversions** by van Straaten (SA) (5)]
[Bob Dwyer was appointed on 17th May 2001]

SECOND SCOTTISH AMICABLE TOUR MATCH

[**COACH:** *Bob Dwyer* (AU)]
CAPTAIN: *Tim Horan* (AU)
[24th May SCOTLAND XV 31 **BARBARIANS** 74]
Murrayfield
[*Team:* Kevin Yates, Richard Cockerill, A. Garvey (SA), R. Brooke (NZ), John Langford (AU), Ben Clarke, Angus Gardiner, Lam (SAM), van der Westhuizen (SA), P. Montgomery (SA), F. Lombard (SA), Horan (AU), Maggs (IR), Jonah Lomu (NZ), Geordan Murphy (IR)]
[*Bench:* Bowman (AU) (*lock*) (rep), Philippe Carbonneau (FR) (*scrum half*) (rep), C. Dowd (NZ) (*prop*) (rep), Drotske (SA) (rep), Patrick 'Pat' Howard (AU) (*fly half/centre*) (rep), Kronfeld (NZ) (*flanker*) (rep), van Straaten (SA) (*fly half*) (rep)]

[*Scorers:* **tries** by Lomu (NZ) (4), F. Lombard (SA) (2), Cockerill, van der Westhuizen (SA), Maggs (IR), Bowman (AU), Ben Clarke and Lam (SAM), **conversions** by P. Montgomery (SA) (6) and van Straaten (SA)]

TETLEY'S COUNTY CHALLENGE

COUNTY CHALLENGE CUP

[**COACH:** *Barry Trevaskis* (CO)]

CAPTAIN: *Ian Sanders*

[26th May **CORNWALL** 19 Yorkshire 47]
Twickenham

[*Team:* Neil Douch (CO), Neil Clark, Nicholas 'Nick' Croker (CO), Lee Soper, Simon O'Sullivan (CO), Alastair Durant (CO), Ian Boase (CO), Laka Laka Waganivere (FIJ), Ian Sanders, James Hendy (CO), Adryan Winnan, Shane Kirman (NZ), Andrew 'Andy' Hymans (SA), Stephen 'Steve' Larkins (CO), James Hawken (CO)]

[*Bench:* Liam Chapple (CO) (*scrum half*) (rep), Jonathan Clifton-Griffith (CO) (*hooker*) (rep), Jason Hobson (*prop*) (rep), Andrew 'Andy' Joint (CO) (*lock*) (rep), David Moyle (CO) (*prop*) (rep), John Navin (CO) (*flanker*) (rep), Christopher 'Chris' Trace (CO) (*wing/full back*) (rep)]

[*Scorers:* **try** by J. Hendy (CO), **penalty goals** by Larkins (CO) (4), **conversion** by Larkins (CO)]

[On 5th April 2001 the RFU announced that this match would replace the County Championship, which they had cancelled on 30th March 2001 due to a fixture backlog created by floods during the autumn and an outbreak of foot and mouth disease in England]

[Barry Trevaskis was appointed on 4th October 2000; Barry Trevaskis won 50 caps for Cornwall between 1976-89; Alan Mitchell resigned from his post of Chairman of Selectors on 19th March 2001 and the Cornish Rugby Football Union (CRFU) subsequently decided to leave the position vacant until 29th June 2001; Barry Trevaskis was sacked on 3rd October 2001]

THIRD SCOTTISH AMICABLE TOUR MATCH

[ENGLAND XV: [*Other squad members:* Oliver 'Olly' Barkley (*fly half/centre*), Benton, Alex Brown (*lock*), Joseph 'Joe' Ewens (*centre*), Flatman, C. Fortey, Darren Garforth (*prop*), W. Johnson (*flanker/number 8*), A. Long (*hooker*), Moody, Noon, Tom Palmer (2) (*lock*), Richard Pool-Jones (*flanker*) (withdrew, replaced by Pat Sanderson), David Rees (2) (*wing*), Sackey (*wing*), P. Sanderson (*flanker*), Stephen 'Steve' Thompson (2) (*hooker*), Voyce (*wing/full back*), Fraser Waters (*centre*), White-Cooper (*lock/flanker*), ?]**]**

(squad of 43)

[Jason Leonard, Phil Greening, Phil Vickery, Martin Johnson, Danny Grewcock, Richard Hill (2), Neil Back, Lawrence Dallaglio, Matt Dawson, Jonny Wilkinson, Dan Luger, Ben Cohen, Jason Robinson, Mike Catt, Will Greenwood, Austin Healey, Iain Balshaw and Matt Perry all unavailable due to their British & Irish Lions commitments; Richard Pool-Jones withdrew on 21st May 2001 due to club commitments; Steve Thompson (2) was known as Steve Walter until August 2000; Steven J. 'Steve' Thompson (1) was capped as a centre for England Schools 18 Group in March 1990, captained England Colts for 5 matches in March-April 1991 and played as a fly half for England Students before May 1999; Richard Pool-Jones was capped for England Schools 18 Group in April 1986; Olly Barkley was capped for England Schools 18 Group in March 1999; Fraser Waters was capped for England Schools 18 Group in March 1994]

[BARBARIANS: [*English squad members:* Ben Clarke (*flanker/number 8*), Luger (*wing*), Kevin Yates (*prop*)]]
[Ben Clarke retired due to injury in April 2002]
[ENGLAND XV: [TEAM MANAGER: *Clive Woodward*] **[HEAD COACH:** *Andy Robinson*] **[ASSISTANT COACHES:** *Brian Ashton* & *Phil Larder*]]
[BARBARIANS: [COACH: *Bob Dwyer* (AU)]]
CAPTAIN: *Kyran Bracken* [*Josh Lewsey took over when Kyran Bracken temporarily went off injured in the 1st half*] [England XV]
CAPTAIN: *Gary Teichmann* (SA) [Barbarians]
27th May **ENGLAND XV*** 29 **BARBARIANS** 43
Twickenham
[ENGLAND XV: [*Team:* Trevor Woodman, M. Regan, Julian White, S. Shaw, S. Borthwick, A. Sanderson, Hazell, J. Worsley, K. Bracken, Walder, M. Stephenson, J. Lewsey, L. Lloyd, Sampson, Stimpson]
[*Bench:* Corry (rep), Ben Johnston (*centre*) (rep), Kay (*lock/flanker/number 8*) (rep), A. King (rep), Rowntree (rep), D. West (rep), Martyn Wood (*scrum half*) (rep)]
[*Scorers:* **tries** by Sampson (2), M. Stephenson and Ben Johnston, **penalty goal** by Walder, **conversions** by Walder (3)]]
[BARBARIANS: [*Team:* C. Dowd (NZ), Drotske (SA), Pagel (SA), R. Brooke (NZ), Ian Jones (2) (NZ), Lam (SAM), Kronfeld (NZ), Teichmann (SA), Gomarsall, van Straaten (SA), Lomu (NZ), P. Howard (AU), J. Little (AU), Vidiri (NZ), G. Murphy (IR)]
[*Bench:* Bowman (AU) (rep), Carbonneau (FR) (rep), Cockerill (*hooker*) (rep), A. Gardiner (*flanker*) (rep), A. Garvey (SA) (rep), Jeremy Guscott (*centre*) (rep), F. Lombard (SA) (rep)]
[*Scorers:* **tries** by P. Howard (AU), Vidiri (NZ), Guscott, Lomu (NZ), Lam (SAM), Teichmann (SA) and A. Garvey (SA), **conversions** by van Straaten (SA) (4)]]

EMIRATES AIRLINE LONDON SEVENS
IRB WORLD SEVENS SERIES 2000-2001 ROUND 9

London
[*Tournament squad:* K. Roche (*forward*), Roques (*forward*), Paul Gustard (*forward*), Seely, John Rudd (*wing*), N. Simpson, Amor, Simon Hunt, Meenan, R. Thirlby, Bramhall (*scrum half*), Bainbridge-Kay (withdrew, replaced by Richard Haughton), R. Haughton]
(squad of 12)
[Paul Gustard toured Canada with England Colts in August-September 1995; John Rudd played for England in the U19 World Championship in France in April 2000]
[MANAGER: *John Elliott*] **[COACH:** *Adrian Thompson*]
CAPTAIN: *Nigel Simpson*
First Round - Pool 'D'
27th May **ENGLAND** 36 WEST INDIES 5
Stoop Memorial Ground, Langhorn Drive, Twickenham
[*Team:* K. Roche, Seely, Simon Hunt, Bramhall, Meenan, N. Simpson, R. Thirlby]
[*Bench:* P. Gustard (rep), Roques (rep), J. Rudd (rep), ?, ?]
[*Scorers:* **tries** by N. Simpson, Simon Hunt, K. Roche, R. Thirlby, Seely and J. Rudd, **conversions** by Bramhall and Meenan (2)]
27th May **ENGLAND** 19 WALES 0
Stoop Memorial Ground, Langhorn Drive, Twickenham
[*Team:* P. Gustard, Seely, Simon Hunt, Amor, Meenan, N. Simpson, R. Thirlby]
[*Bench:* R. Haughton (rep), K. Roche (rep), J. Rudd (rep), ?, ?]
[*Scorers:* **tries** by Simon Hunt, J. Rudd and Amor, **conversions** by Amor and R. Haughton]

27th May **ENGLAND** 22 SAMOA 19
Stoop Memorial Ground, Langhorn Drive, Twickenham
[*Team:* P. Gustard, Seely, Simon Hunt, Amor, R. Thirlby, N. Simpson, R. Haughton]
[*Bench:* Bramhall (rep), Roques (rep), J. Rudd (rep), ?, ?]
[*Scorers:* **tries** by Simon Hunt (3) and R. Haughton, **conversion** by Amor]
Quarter-Final
28th May **ENGLAND*** 12 FIJI 14
Twickenham
[*Team:* P. Gustard, Seely, Simon Hunt, Amor, R. Thirlby, N. Simpson, R. Haughton]
[*Bench:* Bramhall (rep), Roques (rep), J. Rudd (rep), ?, ?]
[*Scorers:* **tries** by N. Simpson and J. Rudd, **conversion** by Amor]
[Plate Semi-Final:]
[28th May **ENGLAND** 33 ARGENTINA 14]
Twickenham
[*Team:* P. Gustard, Seely, Roques, Bramhall, Meenan, Simon Hunt, J. Rudd]
[*Bench:* Amor (rep), K. Roche (rep), N. Simpson (rep), ?, ?]
[*Scorers:* **tries** by Gustard, Simon Hunt, N. Simpson, Roques and J. Rudd, **conversions** by Bramhall (2) and Meenan (2)]
[Plate Final:]
[28th May **ENGLAND** 7 SOUTH AFRICA 31]
Twickenham
[*Team:* P. Gustard, K. Roche, Roques, Amor, Simon Hunt, N. Simpson, J. Rudd]
[*Bench:* Bramhall (rep), Meenan (rep), Seely (rep), ?, ?]
[*Scorers:* **try** by Roques, **conversion** by Amor]
POSITION: LOSING QUARTER-FINALISTS [*PLATE FINALISTS*]
FANTASY: *SEMI-FINALISTS*
[England scored 6 competition points in this Round of the 2000-2001 IRB World Sevens Series]

EMIRATES AIRLINE WALES SEVENS
IRB WORLD SEVENS SERIES 2000-2001 ROUND 10

Wales
[*Tournament squad:* K. Roche, Roques, P. Gustard, Seely, J. Rudd, N. Simpson, Amor (never travelled as withdrew), Simon Hunt, Meenan (never travelled as withdrew), R. Thirlby (never travelled as withdrew), Bramhall (never travelled as withdrew), Bainbridge-Kay (never travelled as withdrew), Gerald Arasa (*centre/wing*), James Brooks, Matthew 'Matt' Carrington (*fly half*), R. Haughton, John 'Johnny' Howard (*scrum half*)]
(squad of 12)
[Gerald Arasa, James Brooks, John Howard and Matt Carrington were added to a revised squad of 12 on 1st June 2001; Matt Carrington played for New Zealand U21 and was the son of Ken Carrington, who was capped for New Zealand in June 1971; Gerald Arasa was capped for England Schools 18 Group in January 1999]
[**MANAGER:** *John Elliott*] [**COACH:** *Adrian Thompson*]
CAPTAIN: *Nigel Simpson*
First Round - Pool 'C'
2nd June SPAIN 19 **ENGLAND** 19
Rodney Parade, Newport
[*Team:* K. Roche, Seely, Simon Hunt, Johnny Howard, James Brooks, N. Simpson, J. Rudd]
[*Bench:* Arasa (rep), Carrington (rep), Roques (rep), ?, ?]

[*Scorers:* **tries** by James Brooks, K. Roche and Roques, **conversions** by James Brooks (2)]

2nd June GEORGIA 17 **ENGLAND** 12

Rodney Parade, Newport

[*Team:* P. Gustard, K. Roche, Roques, Johnny Howard, Carrington, N. Simpson, R. Haughton]

[*Bench:* Arasa (rep), J. Rudd (rep), Seely (rep), ?, ?]

[*Scorers:* **tries** by Roques and R. Haughton, **conversion** by P. Gustard]

2nd June FIJI 19 **ENGLAND*** 15

Rodney Parade, Newport

[*Team:* P. Gustard, Seely, Roques, Johnny Howard, James Brooks, Arasa, R. Haughton]

[*Bench:* Carrington (rep), J. Rudd (rep), N. Simpson (rep), ?, ?]

[*Scorers:* **tries** by Seely (2) and R. Haughton]

[Bowl Quarter-Final:]

[3rd June FRANCE 12 **ENGLAND** 17]

Millennium Stadium, Cardiff

[*Team:* P. Gustard, Seely, Roques, Johnny Howard, James Brooks, Arasa, R. Haughton]

[*Bench:* Carrington (rep), J. Rudd (rep), N. Simpson (rep), ?, ?]

[*Scorers:* **tries** by Roques (2) and James Brooks, **conversion** by James Brooks]

[Bowl Semi-Final:]

[3rd June CANADA 14 **ENGLAND** 29]

Millennium Stadium, Cardiff

[*Team:* P. Gustard, Seely, Roques, James Brooks, Carrington, N. Simpson, J. Rudd]

[*Bench:* Arasa (rep), Johnny Howard, R. Haughton (rep), K. Roche (rep), ?]

[*Scorers:* **tries** by Roques, J. Rudd, N. Simpson, James Brooks and R. Haughton, **conversions** by Carrington (2)]

[Bowl Final:]

[3rd June PORTUGAL 26 **ENGLAND** 35]

Millennium Stadium, Cardiff

[*Team:* P. Gustard, Seely, Roques, James Brooks, Carrington, N. Simpson, J. Rudd]

[*Bench:* Arasa (rep), Johnny Howard, R. Haughton (rep), K. Roche (rep), ?]

[*Scorers:* **tries** by J. Rudd, N. Simpson, James Brooks, R. Haughton and Roques, **conversions** by Carrington (5)]

POSITION: FIRST ROUND LOSERS [*BOWL WINNERS*]

[England scored 2 competition points in this Round of the 2000-2001 IRB World Sevens Series]

RANKING: 7TH 32 [*New Zealand 162*, Australia 150, Fiji 124, Samoa 92, South Africa 82, Argentina 50, Canada 26, Wales 19, USA 16, Korea 14, France 12, Cook Islands 12, Portugal 4, Zimbabwe 4, Georgia 4, Ireland 2, Hong Kong 1]

PENGUINS TOUR TO GERMANY AND ARGENTINA 2001

[**MANAGER:** *Alan Wright*] [**COACH:** *Craig Brown* (NZ)]

[*Other squad members:* Breeze (*wing*), David 'Dave' Clare (IR) (*prop*), Luis Criscuolo (AR) (*fly half/centre/full back*), Alan Dignan (IR) (*back*), Filippo Fratti (IT) (*scrum half*) (tm), Gary French (*hooker*), Mark Giacheri (IT) (*lock*), Charles 'Charlie' Harrison (*scrum half*), Bernard Jackman (IR) (*hooker*), Kevin James (WA) (*wing*), Feki Latuselu (TON) (*number 8*), Nicholas 'Nick' Marval (*centre*), David 'Dave' Moore (IR) (*flanker/number 8*), Nawavu (FIJ), Matthew 'Matt' Oliver (*centre*), Warren O'Kelly (IR) (*prop*), Darragh O'Mahony (IR) (*wing*), Riccardo

Piovan (IT) (*number 8*), Taniela Qauqau (FIJ) (*centre/wing*), Graham Quinn (IR) (*lock*), Saula Rabaka (FIJ) (*fly half*), Iain Sinclair (SC) (*flanker*), Michael 'Mike' Tamati (NZ) (*centre*)]
(squad of 26)
[Penguin International RFC founded 1959; Nick Marval played for Major R.V. Stanley's XV against Oxford University at Iffley Road on 15th November 2000]
CAPTAIN: *Andre Fox* (SA)
[2nd June GERMANY 8 **PENGUINS** 101]
Fritz-Grunebaum-Sportpark, Heidelberg-Kirchheim
[*Team:* Andre Fox (SA) (*lock*), J. Winterbottom, James Brown]
[*Bench:*]
[*Scorers:*]

ENGLAND TOUR TO CANADA AND AMERICA 2001

[**TEAM MANAGER:** *Clive Woodward*] [**HEAD COACH:** *Brian Ashton*] [**ASSISTANT COACHES:** *John Wells*, *Ellery Hanley*, *Paul Grayson* & *Dave Reddin*]
[*Other squad members:* Benton (left the tour injured, replaced by Nick Walshe) (tm), Alex Brown (injured during the tour) (tm), Ewens (injured during the tour) (tm), Rob Fidler (travelled later as a replacement) (tm), C. Fortey (tm), Garforth (never travelled as withdrew, replaced by Ricky Nebbett), Paul Grayson (*fly half*) (originally travelled as kicking Coach), Hazell (tm), Ellery Hanley (*flanker/number 8/fly half*) (originally travelled as defensive Coach, injured on the tour), Ben Johnston (never travelled as injured), Nebbett (*prop*) (tm), Pool-Jones (never travelled as withdrew, replaced by Pat Sanderson), David Rees (2) (tm), Sackey (tm), A. Sanderson (tm), Steve Thompson (2) (tm), Walshe (*scrum half*) (travelled later as a replacement) (tm), Trevor Woodman (tm)]
(squad of 41)
[Mike Tindall, Kevin Sorrell and Tom Beim were unavailable for this tour due to injury; Jason Leonard, Phil Greening, Phil Vickery, Martin Johnson, Danny Grewcock, Richard Hill (2), Martin Corry, Neil Back, Lawrence Dallaglio, Matt Dawson, Jonny Wilkinson, Dan Luger, Ben Cohen, Jason Robinson, Mike Catt, Will Greenwood, Austin Healey, Iain Balshaw and Matt Perry all unavailable as they were in the squad for the simultaneous British & Irish Lions tour of Australia; Darren Garforth chose to rest his body for the forthcoming England domestic season and thus was no longer available to tour; Richard Pool-Jones chose to honour a promise to his club Stade Français to complete their remaining domestic fixtures and thus was also no longer available to tour; Ben Johnston withdrew due to injury on the day of the squad's departure and was not replaced; The England squad departed for Canada on 28th May 2001; Nick Walshe travelled later as a replacement on 7th June 2001; Joe Ewens, Alex Brown and Paul Sampson remained with the tour party after being injured; Rob Fidler was added to the original squad of 40 on 10th June 2001 to provide injury cover for Ben Kay; Paul Grayson won 32 caps for England between 1995-2004]
CAPTAIN: *Kyran Bracken*
2nd June CANADA 10 **ENGLAND** 22
Fletcher's Fields, Markham, Toronto
[*Team:* Rowntree, D. West, Julian White, S. Borthwick, Kay, Corry, Moody, J. Worsley, K. Bracken, Walder, M. Stephenson, Noon, L. Lloyd, Sampson, J. Lewsey]
[*Bench:* Flatman, A. King, A. Long, P. Sanderson (rep), S. Shaw (*lock*) (rep), Stimpson (*full back*) (rep), Martyn Wood]
[*Scorers:* **tries** by K. Bracken, D. West and J. Lewsey (2), **conversion** by Walder]

CAPTAIN: *Kyran Bracken [Ben Kay took over when Kyran Bracken was injured in the 1st half; Dorian West took over when Ben Kay was injured in the 2nd half]*

9th June CANADA 20 **ENGLAND** 59

Swangard Stadium, Burnaby, Toronto

[*Team:* Rowntree, D. West, Julian White, S. Shaw, Kay, White-Cooper, Moody, J. Worsley, K. Bracken, Walder, M. Stephenson, Noon, L. Lloyd, Sampson, J. Lewsey]

[*Bench:* S. Borthwick (rep), Flatman (rep), A. King (rep), M. Regan (rep), P. Sanderson (rep), Stimpson (rep), Martyn Wood (rep)]

[*Scorers:* **tries** by S. Shaw (2), penalty try, J. Worsley, Walder (2), Noon and Martyn Wood, **penalty goals** by Walder (3), **conversions** by Walder (5)]

CAPTAIN: *Kyran Bracken*

16th June USA 19 **ENGLAND** 48

Matthew J. Boxer Stadium, Balboa Park, San Francisco

[*Team:* Rowntree, D. West, Julian White, S. Shaw, S. Borthwick, White-Cooper, Moody, J. Worsley, K. Bracken, Walder, M. Stephenson, Noon, F. Waters, L. Lloyd, J. Lewsey]

[*Bench:* Barkley (rep), Flatman (rep), A. Long (rep), Tom Palmer (2) (rep), P. Sanderson (rep), Voyce (rep), Martyn Wood (rep)]

[*Scorers:* **tries** by D. West, P. Sanderson, J. Lewsey (2), J. Worsley, L. Lloyd (2) and Moody, **conversions** by Walder (4)]

GRAND PRIX OF EUROPE INTERNATIONAL SEVENS TOURNAMENT

Fritz-Grunebaum-Sportpark, Heidelberg-Kirchheim

[*Tournament squad:* Friday, Nawavu (FIJ) (*forward*), Hamish Innes (AU) (*forward*), Rabaka (FIJ) (*fly half*), Qauqau (FIJ) (*centre/wing*), Breeze, Rory Jenkins (*forward*), Daren O'Leary (*wing*), M. Oliver (*centre*), Darragh O'Mahony (IR) (*wing*)]

(squad of 10)

[Hamish Innes was the brother of Angus Innes; Rory Jenkins was capped for England Colts in March 1989 and played for M.R. Steele-Bodger's XV against Cambridge University at Grange Road on 28th November 2001; Ben Breeze played in a Welsh Trial Match at St. Helen's on 29th January 2000, played for Wales A in November 2001 and played for Wales 7s in May 2002; Richard Kinsey played for the Barbarians against the Lupi at the Stadio Flaminio on 11th June 1997]

[**MANAGER:** *William 'Bill' Calcraft* (AU)] [**COACH:** *Richard Kinsey*]

CAPTAIN: *Mike Friday*

First Round - Pool 'A'

[3rd June Comite Alpes Maritimes (*FR*) 0 **PENGUINS** 35]

[*Team:*]

[*Bench:*]

[*Scorers:*]

[3rd June POLAND 14 **PENGUINS** 33]

[*Team:*]

[*Bench:*]

[*Scorers:*]

Semi-Final

[3rd June NETHERLANDS 0 **PENGUINS** 36]

[*Team:*]

[*Bench:*]

[*Scorers:*]

Final

[3rd June GERMANY 7 **PENGUINS** 57]

[*Team:*]

[*Bench:*]

[*Scorers:*]

POSITION: WINNERS

BRITISH & IRISH LIONS TOUR TO AUSTRALIA 2001

[**MANAGER:** *Donal Lenihan* (IR)] [**COACH:** *Graham Henry* (NZ)] [**ASSISTANT COACHES:** *Andy Robinson* & *Phil Larder*]

[*Other squad members:* M. Catt (*fly half/centre/full back*) (returned home as injured, replaced by Scott Gibbs) (tm), B. Cohen (*wing*) (tm), Dallaglio (*flanker/number 8*) (returned home as injured, replaced by David Wallace) (tm), Jeremy Davidson (IR) (*lock*) (tm), Ian *Scott* Gibbs (WA) (*centre*) (travelled later as a replacement) (tm), Greening (returned home as injured, replaced by Gordon Bulloch), W. Greenwood (tm), Tyrone Howe (IR) (*wing*) (travelled later as a replacement) (tm), Luger (returned home as injured, replaced by Tyrone Howe) (tm), Robin McBryde (WA) (*hooker*) (returned home as injured, replaced by Dorian West) (tm), Scott Murray (SC) (*lock*) (tm), M. O'Kelly (IR) (tm), Mark Taylor (WA) (*centre*) (tm), Simon Taylor (2) (SC) (*number 8*) (returned home as injured, replaced by Martin Corry) (tm), David Wallace (IR) (*flanker*) (travelled later as a replacement) (tm), David 'Dai' Young (WA) (*prop*) (tm)]

(squad of 37)

[From 15th September 2000 onwards the British Isles squad was referred to as the British & Irish Lions to reflect the political reality that the Republic of Ireland had not been part of the United Kingdom since 1922!; Donal Lenihan was appointed on 11th February 2000; Graham Henry was appointed as Coach on 23rd June 2000 after Ian McGeechan had turned the post down on no less than four separate occasions between 28th April 2000 and 14th June 2000!; Andy Robinson was appointed on 4th July 2000; Phil Larder was appointed on 21st October 2000; Donal Lenihan won 52 caps for Ireland between 1981-92; Mark Regan, Julian White and Peter Stringer were included in a provisional list of 67 players that was announced by Graham Henry on 21st February 2001; The Lions squad departed for Australia on 1st June 2001; Gordon Bulloch travelled later as a supplementary replacement for Phil Greening; Martin Corry travelled later as a replacement for Simon Taylor (2); Gordon Bulloch became a permanent squad member on 17th June 2001 after Phil Greening left the tour injured; Dorian West travelled later as a supplementary replacement for Robin McBryde and then became a permanent squad member on 29th June 2001 after McBryde returned home injured; Andy Nicol travelled to Australia as a supporters' tour guide and was promptly drafted into the squad on the morning of the third test as a supplementary replacement for Austin Healey!; David Wallace was the brother of Richard and Paul Wallace; Jonny Wilkinson's goal-kicking fell below its normal standard in the test match series after he had trouble finding the 'sweet spot' on the Australian-made balls; Iain Balshaw lost form on this tour after he was unaccountably ordered to keep to a game-plan that involved running down the middle of the pitch to actively seek contact with the opposition players, instead of his usual game of exploiting space on the wings]

[Tom 'Rusty' Richards won an Olympic Gold medal for Australia at Rugby Union at the White City Stadium, London on 26th October 1908 before being capped for Australia in December 1908, was capped for the British Lions in August 1910 while he was living in South Africa and then won another cap for Australia in November 1912!]

BUNDABERG RUM TEST SERIES

TOM RICHARDS TROPHY

CAPTAIN: *Martin Johnson*

[30th Jun AUSTRALIA 13 **BRITISH & IRISH LIONS** 29]

Wooloongabba Stadium, Brisbane

[*Team:* Tom Smith (2) (SC), Keith Wood (IR), Vickery, Martin Johnson, Grewcock, Corry, Richard Hill (2), Leon *Scott* Quinnell (WA), Robert 'Rob' Howley (WA), Jonny Wilkinson, Jason Robinson, Robert 'Rob' Henderson (IR), Brian O'Driscoll (IR), Dafydd James (WA), Matt Perry]

[*Bench:* Balshaw (rep), Gordon Bulloch (SC) (*hooker*) (rep), Colin Charvis (WA) (*flanker/number 8*) (rep), Matt Dawson, Healey (*wing*), J. Leonard (*prop*) (rep), Martyn Williams (WA) (*flanker*)]

[*Scorers:* **tries** by Jason Robinson, Dafydd James (WA), Brian O'Driscoll (IR) and Scott Quinnell (WA), **penalty goal** by Jonny Wilkinson, **conversions** by Jonny Wilkinson (3)]

[7th July AUSTRALIA 35 **BRITISH & IRISH LIONS** 14]

Colonial Stadium, Melbourne

[*Team:* Tom Smith (2) (SC), K. Wood (IR), Vickery, Martin Johnson, Grewcock, Richard Hill (2), Back, Scott Quinnell (WA), Howley (WA), Jonny Wilkinson, Jason Robinson, R. Henderson (IR), Brian O'Driscoll (IR), Dafydd James (WA), Matt Perry]

[*Bench:* Balshaw (rep), Corry (rep), Matt Dawson (rep), N. Jenkins (WA) (rep), J. Leonard (rep), D. West, Martyn Williams (WA)]

[*Scorers:* **try** by Back, **penalty goals** by Jonny Wilkinson (3)]

[14th July AUSTRALIA 29 **BRITISH & IRISH LIONS*** 23]

Stadium Australia, Sydney Olympic Park, Homebush Bay, Sydney

[*Team:* Tom Smith (2) (SC), K. Wood (IR), Vickery, Martin Johnson, Grewcock, Corry, Back, Scott Quinnell (WA), Matt Dawson, Jonny Wilkinson, Jason Robinson, R. Henderson (IR), Brian O'Driscoll (IR), Dafydd James (WA), Matt Perry]

[*Bench:* Balshaw (rep), Charvis (WA) (rep), Darren Morris (WA) (*prop*) (rep), Andrew 'Andy' Nicol (SC) (*scrum half*), Ronan O'Gara (IR) (*fly half*), D. West, Martyn Williams (WA)]

[*Scorers:* **tries** by Jason Robinson and Jonny Wilkinson, **penalty goals** by Jonny Wilkinson (3), **conversions** by Jonny Wilkinson (2)]

POSITION: SERIES LOSERS

FANTASY: *SERIES WINNERS*

RICOH SOUTHERN HEMISPHERE UNDER 21 RUGBY CHAMPIONSHIP

Sydney Showground, Sydney Olympic Park, Homebush Bay, Sydney

[*Other squad members:* Arasa, Tom Barlow (1) (*flanker/number 8*), Simon Hunt (*wing/full back*), Alan Low (*prop*), Phil Murphy (1) (*lock*), Chris Simpson-Daniel (never travelled as injured)]

(squad of 28)

[Andy Goode was unavailable for this tournament due to injury; The England U21 squad arrived in Australia on 17th June 2001; Alan Low played for England in the U19 World Championship in France in April 2000; Tom Barlow (1) was capped for England Schools 18 Group in January 1999; Chris Simpson-Daniel retired due to injury in 2002]

(<u>During the First Round a bonus point was awarded for scoring 4 or more tries in a match and for losing by seven points or less</u>)

[**MANAGER:** *Nigel Melville*] [**COACH:** *Dean Ryan*]

CAPTAIN: *Mark Tucker*
First Round - Pool 'A'
[20th Jun IRELAND U21 10 **ENGLAND U21** 15]
[*Team:* Alex Clarke, J. Parkes, Isaacson, Jim Evans, Rudzki, D. Danaher, Alesbrook, I. Clarke, Grindal, C. Hodgson, Christophers, M. Tucker, Sam Cox, A. Elliott, Marsden]
[*Bench:* Nicholas 'Nick' Cox (*prop*), Devonshire, B. Hampson, Andrew 'Andy' Higgins (2) (*centre*), M. Leek (rep), M. Purdy, Titterrell]
[*Scorers:* **tries** by Marsden and Christophers, **drop goal** by M. Leek, **conversion** by M. Leek]
[23rd Jun NEW ZEALAND U21 63 **ENGLAND U21** 3]
[*Team:* Alex Clarke, J. Parkes, Isaacson, Jim Evans, Rudzki, Devonshire, D. Danaher, I. Clarke, Grindal, C. Hodgson, A. Elliott, M. Tucker, Christophers, R. Haughton, Marsden]
[*Bench:* Alesbrook (*flanker/number 8*), N. Cox, B. Hampson, Andy Higgins (2) (rep), M. Leek, M. Purdy, Titterrell]
[*Scorers:* **penalty goal** by C. Hodgson]
[27th Jun ARGENTINA U21 26 **ENGLAND U21** 42 **BP**]
[*Team:* Jim Evans, Rudzki, R. Haughton, M. Leek, Sam Cox]
[*Bench:* C. Hodgson, ?, ?, ?, ?, ?, ?]
[*Scorers:* **tries** by Jim Evans (2), R. Haughton (2) and Sam Cox, **penalty goals** by M. Leek (3), **conversions** by M. Leek (4)]
Third Place Play-Off
[30th Jun FRANCE U21 36 **ENGLAND U21** 6]
[*Team:* M. Leek]
[*Bench:* C. Hodgson, ?, ?, ?, ?, ?, ?]
[*Scorers:* **penalty goals** by M. Leek (2)]
POSITION: 4TH PLACE

TUSKER SAFARI SEVENS

TUSKER TROPHY

RFU of East Africa Ground, Ngong Road, Nairobi
[*Tournament squad:* Amor, Bemand (*scrum half*), Daws (*forward*), Kenworthy (*back*), B. Lewitt (*forward*), Peter Murphy (*scrum half/fly half*), Newmarch (*wing*), Peter Nicholas (*hooker*), Nnamdi Obi (*wing*), Quigley (*forward*), J. Rudd, Sherriff]
(squad of 12)
[*This tournament was played at high altitude*]
[COACH: *?*]
CAPTAIN: *??*
First Round - Pool 'B'
[23rd Jun ZAMBIA L **ENGLAND STUDENTS U21** W]
[*Team:*]
[*Bench:*]
[*Scorers:*]
[23rd Jun TANZANIA L **ENGLAND STUDENTS U21** W]
[*Team:*]
[*Bench:*]
[*Scorers:*]

[23rd Jun KENYA 10 **ENGLAND STUDENTS U21** 15]
[*Team:*]
[*Bench:*]
[*Scorers:*]
Quarter-Final
[24th Jun UGANDA 12 **ENGLAND STUDENTS U21** 35]
[*Team:*]
[*Bench:*]
[*Scorers:*]
Semi-Final
[24th Jun Bristol University Select 31 **ENGLAND STUDENTS U21** 7]
[*Team:*]
[*Bench:*]
[*Scorers:*]
POSITION: LOSING SEMI-FINALISTS

CWMTAWE SEVENS

Pontardawe RFC, Parc Ynysderw, Ynysderw Road, Pontardawe, Swansea
[*Tournament squad:* Bainivalu 'Bul' Bulumakau (FIJ) (*forward*), Andy Dawling (*hooker*), A. Satala (FIJ), Howard Graham (*scrum half*), Emosi Naisaramaki (FIJ) (*fly half*), Filipe Tawayaga (FIJ) (*centre*), Saula Roko (FIJ) (*wing*), Epeli Qolikibua (FIJ) (*fly half*), Mathew Raikosa (FIJ) (*forward/back*), Ken Kainoco (FIJ) (*forward/back*)]
(squad of 10)
[Andy Dawling played for Major R.V. Stanley's XV against Oxford University at Iffley Road on 18th November 1998 and captained the British Army to victory at the Middlesex Sevens at Twickenham on 18th August 2001; Howard Graham came on as a replacement for Major R.V. Stanley's XV against Oxford University at Iffley Road on 18th November 1998, played for the White Hart Marauders at the Tusker Safari Sevens in Nairobi on 23rd-24th June 2000 and played in the British Army team that won the Middlesex Sevens at Twickenham on 18th August 2001]
[NO COACH NOMINATED]
CAPTAIN: *Howard Graham*
First Round - Pool 'D'
[4th Aug Brynamman (*WA*) 0 **SAMURAI** 47]
[*Team:*]
[*Bench:*]
[*Scorers:*]
[4th Aug Abercrave (*WA*) 0 **SAMURAI** 45]
[*Team:*]
[*Bench:*]
[*Scorers:*]
[4th Aug Llandovery (*WA*) 0 **SAMURAI** 40]
[*Team:*]
[*Bench:*]
[*Scorers:*]
Quarter-Final
[4th Aug Neath (*WA*) 10 **SAMURAI** 45]
[*Team:*]
[*Bench:*]

[*Scorers:*]

Semi-Final

[4th Aug   Swansea (*WA*)   12   **SAMURAI**   33]
[*Team:*]
[*Bench:*]
[*Scorers:*]

Final

[4th Aug   Samurai-Ecosse   15   **SAMURAI**   28]
[*Team:* Bulumakau (FIJ), Dawling, A. Satala (FIJ), Graham, Naisaramaki (FIJ), Tawayaga (FIJ), S. Roko (FIJ)]
[*Bench:* Qolikibua (FIJ) (rep), Raikosa (FIJ) (rep), Kainoco (FIJ) (rep)]
[*Scorers:* **tries** by Naisaramaki (FIJ) (2), Bulumakau (FIJ) and Qolikibua (FIJ), **conversions** by H. Graham (2) and Qolikibua (FIJ) (2)]

POSITION: WINNERS

WORLD GAMES SEVENS

Yabase Stadium, Akita City, Japan

[*Tournament squad:* Chris McCarey (IR) (*prop*), *Gareth* John Williams (5) (WA) (*hooker*), Sherriff, Rob Stewart (2), Justin Thomas (WA) (*fly half*), Emyr Lewis (2) (WA) (*fly half*), Andrew 'Andy' Maxwell (2) (IR) (*wing*), Simon Hunt (never travelled, replaced by Nigel Simpson), Mark Lee (SC) (*hooker/scrum half*), J. Rudd, N. Simpson]

(squad of 10)

[This was the 6th World Games; The World Games was an event run every 4 years by the International World Games Association (IWGA), an organisation that was founded as the World Games Council in 1980 and recognised by the International Olympic Committee (IOC) on 27th October 2000; The International Rugby Board (IRB) received an invitation to play in this tournament in November 1997; The Great Britain team consisted of players from England, Wales, Scotland and Northern Ireland; Colin Hillman was the Coach when Wales played in the Commonwealth Sevens at Manchester on 2nd-4th August 2002]

[**MANAGER:** *John Ryan (2)* (WA)] [**COACH:** *Colin Hillman* (WA)]

CAPTAIN: *Mark Lee* (SC)

Preliminary League - Pool 'B'

[25th Aug   AUSTRALIA   31   **GREAT BRITAIN**   0]
[*Team:*]
[*Bench:*]
[*No scorers*]

[25th Aug   SOUTH AFRICA   43   **GREAT BRITAIN**   5]
[*Team:*]
[*Bench:*]
[*Scorers:* **try** by ?]

[25th Aug   JAPAN   38   **GREAT BRITAIN**   7]
[*Team:*]
[*Bench:*]
[*Scorers:* **try** by ?, **conversion** by ?]

First Round

[26th Aug   FIJI   35   **GREAT BRITAIN**   0]
[*Team:*]
[*Bench:*]

[*No scorers*]
Consolation Match
[26th Aug SOUTH AFRICA 22 **GREAT BRITAIN*** 19]
[*Team:*]
[*Bench:*]
[*Scorers:* **tries** by ?, ? and ?, **conversions** by ? (2)]
[The winner of this match went through to the 4th/5th Place Play-Off]
7th/8th Place Play-Off
[26th Aug JAPAN 19 **GREAT BRITAIN** 21]
[*Team:*]
[*Bench:*]
[*Scorers:* **tries** by ?, ? and ?, **conversions** by ? (3)]
POSITION: 7TH PLACE [FIRST ROUND LOSERS]

AUSTRALIAN TOUR TO ENGLAND, SPAIN, FRANCE AND WALES 2001

[**MANAGER & COACH:** *Tony MacArthur* (AU)] [**ASSISTANT COACHES:** *Adrian Davies* (WA), *Ian Bremner* & *Richard Cockerill*]
CAPTAIN: *Dave Sims*
[28th Oct **ENGLISH NATIONAL DIVISIONS XV** 22 AUSTRALIA XV 34]
Welford Road, Leicester
[*Team:* S. Pope, Chris Ritchie, Phil Sluman, David 'Dave' Sims, Robert 'Rob' Baxter, Earnshaw, N. Spence, Richard Baxter, Alex Birkby, Simon Binns, Harvey Thorneycroft, James Shanahan, Roke, George Truelove, Peter Massey]
[*Bench:* Ben Ayres (*scrum half*) (rep), Sam Blythe (*hooker*) (rep), Phil Greaves (*centre*) (rep), Leigh Hinton (*full back*) (rep), J. Hyde (*lock*) (rep), Nick Lloyd (*prop*) (rep), Gary Willis (*flanker*) (rep)]
[*Scorers:* **try** by P. Greaves, **penalty goals** by Binns (4), **drop goal** by Binns, **conversion** by Binns]
[Tony MacArthur was appointed on 4th October 2001; Richard Cockerill won 27 caps for England between 1997-99]

REMEMBRANCE MATCH

[**NO COACH NOMINATED**]
CAPTAIN: *Andy Gomarsall*
[6th Nov COMBINED SERVICES (*SER*) 14 **BARBARIANS** 50]
United Services Recreation Ground, Burnaby Road, Portsmouth
[*Team:* John Davies (WA), Marcus Thomas (WA), Ceri Jones (2) (WA), Andrew 'Andy' Reed (SC), Rob Baxter, Peter Buxton, Horrobin, Richard Baxter, Gomarsall, Jason Strange (WA), Brendon Daniel, Roke, Brocklehurst, Charlie Keenan (SC), Ian Calder (NZ)]
[*Bench:* Bullock (rep), Dale Burn (WA) (*scrum half*) (rep), Criscuolo (AR) (rep), Andy Cuthbert (*hooker*) (rep), J. Hyde (rep), Shanahan (*fly half/centre*) (rep), Michael 'Mike' 'Buster' White (*flanker*) (rep)]
[*Scorers:* **tries** by Keenan (SC) (2), John Davies (WA), I. Calder (NZ), Richard Baxter, B. Daniel, Criscuolo (AR) and Dale Burn (WA), **conversions** by J. Strange (WA) (5)]
[Match to commemorate the members of the British uniformed services who lost their lives during armed conflict]

EMIRATES AIRLINE DUBAI RUGBY SEVENS
IRB WORLD SEVENS SERIES 2001-2002 ROUND 1

Dubai Exiles Stadium, Dubai

[*Tournament squad not selected*]

[*Joe Lydon was appointed England Sevens Coach on 3rd October 2001; Joe Lydon won 30 caps for Great Britain at Rugby League between 1983-92 and played for an Ireland XIII at Rugby League in March 1995*]

[**MANAGER:** *John Elliott*] [**COACH:** *Joseph 'Joe' Lydon*]

CAPTAIN: *No captain appointed*

8th Nov *No opponents named* C **ENGLAND** C

[*Team not selected*]

[*Bench not selected*]

[*No scorers*]

ROMANIAN TOUR TO ENGLAND 2001

[**MANAGER:** *Tony Lanaway*] [**COACH:** *Richard Hill (1)*] [**ASSISTANT COACH:** *Ian Smith (2)*]

CAPTAIN: *Howard Quigley*

[8th Nov **ENGLAND STUDENTS*** 11 ROMANIA XV 21]

University Football Ground, Grange Road, Cambridge

[*Team:* Danny Porte, Roddam, T. Payne, Rudzki, Adam Harris, Jonathan Pettemerides, B. Lewitt, Quigley, Graham Barr, Jake Niarchos, Simon Hunt, Phillip 'Phil' Greenaway, Cadwallader, Josh Frapp, Christopher 'Chris' Borrett]

[*Bench:* Jonathan 'Jonny' Barrett (*hooker*), Ed Binham (*centre*) (rep), Nathan Bland (*flanker*), Dominic Castle (*scrum half*), Robert 'Rob' Hunt (*wing*) (rep), Edward 'Ed' Norris (*lock*), A. Webb (*prop*)]

[*Scorers:* **try** by Frapp, **penalty goals** by Niarchos (2)]

[*Richard Hill (1) and Ian Smith (2) were both appointed on 1st November 2001*]

[*Blood substitution time limit introduced*]

AUSTRALIAN TOUR TO ENGLAND, SPAIN, FRANCE AND WALES 2001
FIRST INVESTEC CHALLENGE MATCH
COOK CUP MATCH

[**TEAM MANAGER:** *Clive Woodward*] [**HEAD COACH:** *Andy Robinson*] [**ASSISTANT COACHES:** *Brian Ashton & Phil Larder*]

CAPTAIN: *Neil Back*

10th Nov **ENGLAND** 21 AUSTRALIA 15

Twickenham

[*Team:* Rowntree, D. West, Vickery, Kay, Grewcock, Richard Hill (2), Back, J. Worsley, K. Bracken, Jonny Wilkinson, Luger, M. Catt, W. Greenwood, Healey, Jason Robinson]

[*Bench:* S. Borthwick, B. Cohen, C. Hodgson, J. Leonard, Moody, Matt Perry, M. Regan]

[*Scorers:* **penalty goals** by Jonny Wilkinson (5), **drop goals** by Jonny Wilkinson (2)]

[*On 8th November 2001 the IRB announced that blood substitutions would now be subject to a 15 minute time limit*]

EMIRATES AIRLINE SOUTH AFRICA SEVENS
IRB WORLD SEVENS SERIES 2001-2002 ROUND 2

ABSA Stadium, Durban

[*Tournament squad:* Amor, Geoff Appleford (*back/forward*), Nicholas 'Nick' Duncombe (*scrum half*), A. Elliott, James Forrester (*forward*), Friday, P. Sanderson (*forward*), N. Simpson, James Simpson-Daniel (*centre/wing*), M. Stephenson (*centre/wing*), R. Thirlby, Ian Vass (*scrum half*)]

(*squad of 12*)

[Nick Duncombe was capped for England Schools 18 Group in January 1999 and played for England in the U19 World Championship in Chile in April 2001; Ian Vass was capped for England Schools 18 Group in January 1999 and played for England in the U19 World Championship in France in April 2000; James Simpson-Daniel played for England in the U19 World Championship in Chile in April 2001; James Simpson-Daniel was the brother of Chris Simpson-Daniel]

[Mike Friday captained England in the Rugby World Cup Sevens at Mar del Plata on 26th-28th January 2001]

[**MANAGER:** *John Elliott*] [**COACH:** *Joe Lydon*] [**PLAYER-COACH:** *Mike Friday*]

CAPTAIN: *Pat Sanderson*

First Round - Pool 'A'

17th Nov ARABIAN GULF 14 **ENGLAND** 38

[*Team:* Appleford, P. Sanderson, R. Thirlby, Friday, Vass, J. Simpson-Daniel, M. Stephenson]

[*Bench:* Amor (rep), Duncombe (rep), N. Simpson (rep), ?, ?]

[*Scorers:* **tries** by P. Sanderson, Vass, R. Thirlby (2), Appleford and Duncombe, **conversions** by R. Thirlby (4)]

17th Nov GEORGIA 0 **ENGLAND** 34

[*Team:*]

[*Bench:*]

[*Scorers:* **tries** by A. Elliott, Forrester (2), P. Sanderson, J. Simpson-Daniel and R. Thirlby, **conversions** by J. Simpson-Daniel (2)]

17th Nov NEW ZEALAND 28 **ENGLAND** 0

[*Team:*]

[*Bench:*]

[*No scorers*]

Quarter-Final

18th Nov AUSTRALIA 7 **ENGLAND** 27

[*Team:*]

[*Bench:*]

[*Scorers:* **tries** by P. Sanderson, R. Thirlby (2), and M. Stephenson (2), **conversion** by R. Thirlby]

Semi-Final

18th Nov SAMOA 24 **ENGLAND** 7

[*Team:*]

[*Bench:*]

[*Scorers:* **try** by N. Simpson, **conversion** by R. Thirlby]

POSITION: LOSING SEMI-FINALISTS

[England scored 12 competition points in this Round of the 2001-2002 IRB World Sevens Series]

ROMANIAN TOUR TO ENGLAND 2001
SECOND INVESTEC CHALLENGE MATCH

[**TEAM MANAGER:** *Clive Woodward*] [**HEAD COACH:** *Andy Robinson*] [**ASSISTANT COACHES:** *Brian Ashton & Phil Larder*]

CAPTAIN: *Neil Back* [*Kyran Bracken took over when Neil Back was substituted at half-time*]

17th Nov **ENGLAND** 134 ROMANIA 0
Twickenham

[*Team:* Rowntree, M. Regan, J. Leonard, Kay, S. Borthwick, Moody, Back, J. Worsley, Healey, C. Hodgson, Luger, Tindall, W. Greenwood, B. Cohen, Jason Robinson]

[*Bench:* K. Bracken (rep), M. Catt (rep), Grewcock (*lock*) (rep), A. Sanderson (rep), D. West, Julian White (rep), Jonny Wilkinson (*fly half/centre*)]

[*Scorers:* **tries** by B. Cohen (3), C. Hodgson (2), Moody (2), Healey, Jason Robinson (4), Tindall (2), A. Sanderson, Luger (3), M. Regan and J. Worsley, **penalty goals** by C. Hodgson (2), **conversions** by C. Hodgson (14)]

FIJIAN TOUR TO ITALY AND FRANCE 2001

[NO COACH NOMINATED]

CAPTAIN: *Olivier Roumat* (FR)

[17th Nov **FRENCH BARBARIANS*** 15 FIJI XV 17]
Stade Félix Mayol, Toulon

[*Team:* Patrice Collazo (FR), Noël Curnier (FR), Franck Tournaire (FR), Olivier Roumat (FR), Mike James (CAN), Christophe Milhères (FR), Pool-Jones, Phil Murphy (2) (CAN), Jérôme Fillol (FR), David Skréla (FR), Raphael Poulain (FR), John 'Jack' Isaac (FR), Franck Comba (FR), Philippe Bernat-Salles (FR), Nicolas Brusque (FR)]

[*Bench:* Yann Delaigue (FR) (*fly half*) (rep), Delmotte (FR) (*centre*) (rep), Stéphane Franchini (FR) (*lock*) (rep), Aubin Hueber (FR) (*scrum half*) (rep), Michel Konieck (FR) (*hooker*) (rep), Sylvain Marconnet (FR) (*prop*) (rep), Sergueev (RUS) (*lock*) (rep)]

[*Scorers:* **tries** by Milhères (FR) and Marconnet (FR), **penalty goal** by D. Skréla (FR), **conversion** by D. Skréla (FR)]

SOUTH AFRICA 'A' TOUR TO ENGLAND 2001

[**MANAGER & COACH:** *Tony MacArthur* (AU)] [**ASSISTANT COACHES:** *Adrian Davies* (WA), *Ian Bremner & Richard Cockerill*]

CAPTAIN: *Dave Sims*

[21st Nov **ENGLISH NATIONAL DIVISIONS XV** 9 SOUTH AFRICA A 33]
Worcester RFC, Sixways Stadium, Pershore Lane, Hindip, Worcester

[*Team:* S. Pope, Ritchie, Sluman, Sims, Rob Baxter, Nathan Carter, Thomas 'Tom' Jordan, Richard Baxter, Birkby, Binns, Greenlees, Shanahan, Ed Jennings, Truelove, Phil Graham]

[*Bench:* Blythe (rep), Andrew 'Andy' Brown (*scrum half*) (rep), Matthew 'Matt' Cornish (*flanker*) (rep), P. Greaves (rep), J. Hyde (rep), N. Lloyd (rep), Steven 'Steve' Vile (*fly half*) (rep)]

[*Scorers:* **penalty goals** by Binns (3)]

SOUTH AFRICAN TOUR TO FRANCE, ITALY AND ENGLAND 2001
THIRD INVESTEC CHALLENGE MATCH

[**TEAM MANAGER:** *Clive Woodward*] [**HEAD COACH:** *Andy Robinson*] [**ASSISTANT COACHES:** *Brian Ashton & Phil Larder*]

CAPTAIN: *Martin Johnson*

24th Nov **ENGLAND** 29 SOUTH AFRICA 9

Twickenham

[*Team:* Rowntree, D. West, Vickery, Martin Johnson, Grewcock, Richard Hill (2), Back, J. Worsley, K. Bracken, Jonny Wilkinson, Luger, M. Catt, W. Greenwood, Healey, Jason Robinson]

[*Bench:* B. Cohen, C. Hodgson, Kay (rep), J. Leonard, Moody (rep), M. Regan, Tindall (rep)]

[*Scorers:* **try** by Luger, **penalty goals** by Jonny Wilkinson (7), **drop goal** by M. Catt]

AUSTRALIAN TOUR TO ENGLAND, SPAIN, FRANCE AND WALES 2001
SCOTTISH AMICABLE CHALLENGE

[**COACH:** *Bob Dwyer* (AU)] [**ASSISTANT COACH:** *Philippe Sella* (FR)]

CAPTAIN: *Rob Howley* (WA)

[28th Nov **BARBARIANS*** 35 AUSTRALIA XV 49]

Millennium Stadium, Cardiff

[*Team:* Darren Morris (WA), Raphäel Ibañez (FR), D. Young (WA), Ian Jones (2) (NZ), Mark Andrews (SA), Cornelius 'Corné' Krige (SA), Olivier Magne (FR), Paul Miller (NZ), Howley (WA), van Straaten (SA), Stefan Terblanche (SA), P. Howard (AU), Stéphane Glas (FR), Breyton Paulse (SA), P. Montgomery (SA)]

[*Bench:* Cockerill (rep), C. Dowd (NZ) (rep), Lam (SAM) (rep), Simon Maling (NZ) (*lock*) (rep), Mat Rogers (AU) (*wing*) (rep), C. Spencer (NZ) (*fly half/full back*) (rep), Werner Swanepoel (SA) (*scrum half*) (rep)]

[*Scorers:* **tries** by Paulse (SA) (3), Glas (FR) and Lam (SAM), **conversions** by van Straaten (SA) (5)]

[Philippe Sella won 111 caps for France between 1982-95]

ENGLAND U21 MATCH

[**MANAGER:** *Ged Glynn*] [**COACH:** *Paul Westgate*]

CAPTAIN: *Alex Page*

[19th Dec WALES U21 A XV 21 **ENGLAND U21 A XV*** 21]

Sardis Road, Pwllgwaun, Pontypridd

[*Team:* N. Cox, James Buckland, Mark Irish, Richard Hunt, Andrew 'Andy' Springgay, Chris Morgan, Simon Cross, Matthew 'Matt' Styles, A. Page, Matthew 'Matt' Honeyben, Edward 'Ed' Thrower, Will Wigram, Cadwallader, J. Rudd, Hylton]

[*Bench:* Alex Crockett (*centre*) (rep), Darren Fox (*flanker*), Michael Holford (*prop*), Matthew 'Matt' Parr (*prop*), Roddam, Vass (*scrum half*), Nick Wainwright (*fly half*)]

[*Scorers:* **tries** by Irish and Thrower, **penalty goals** by Thrower (3), **conversion** by Thrower]

[A Combined Midlands & North U21 XV lost 17-15 to France South East U21 and a Combined London & South West U21 XV lost 27-23 to France South West U21 respectively at Broadstreet RFC on 14th November 2001]

2002
OTHER MATCHES
CERVEZA CRISTAL SANTIAGO SEVENS
IRB WORLD SEVENS SERIES 2001-2002 ROUND 3

Estadio San Carlos de Apoquindo, Santiago

[*Tournament squad:* Cueto, Forrester (never travelled as withdrew, replaced by Simon Amor), Hazell (*forward*) (never travelled as withdrew, replaced by Adam Balding), J. Simpson-Daniel, Duncombe (never travelled as withdrew, replaced by Ian Vass), Gollings, R. Thirlby (never travelled as injured, replaced by Nigel Simpson), J. Lewsey, Friday (injured during the tournament), Appleford, Earnshaw, R. Haughton (injured during the tournament), Vass, Amor, Balding (*forward*), N. Simpson]

(squad of 12)

[This round of the IRB World Sevens Series was originally scheduled to take place in Punta del Este but the IRB changed its location to Santiago on 6th December 2001 due to the deteriorating economic situation in Uruguay; Pat Sanderson selected as captain in the original training squad of 15 but withdrew due to injury; Declan Danaher, Nigel Simpson, Simon Amor and Ben Johnston all in original training squad of 15; James Forrester, Andy Hazell and Nick Duncombe initially selected but withdrew on the day of the squad's departure due to club commitments; The England squad departed for Chile on 31st December 2001; Mike Friday was the tournament captain]

[Damian McGrath was appointed on 4th December 2001; Damian McGrath was the Assistant Coach when the England Rugby League team played in the Rugby League World Cup in October-November 2000]

[**MANAGER:** *John Elliott*] [**COACH:** *Joe Lydon*] [**ASSISTANT COACH:** *Damian McGrath*] [**PLAYER-COACH:** *Mike Friday*]

CAPTAIN: *Mike Friday*

First Round - Pool 'C'

4th Jan URUGUAY 0 **ENGLAND** 54

[*Team:* Balding]

[*Bench:*]

[*Scorers:* **tries** by R. Haughton (3), Appleford (2), Balding, Gollings and J. Lewsey, **conversions** by Gollings (7)]

4th Jan FRANCE 17 **ENGLAND** 15

[*Team:* Balding]

[*Bench:*]

[*Scorers:* **tries** by R. Haughton (2) and Gollings]

4th Jan SOUTH AFRICA 7 **ENGLAND** 12

[*Team:* Balding, Gollings]

[*Bench:*]

[*Scorers:* **tries** by Amor and Gollings, **conversion** by Gollings]

CAPTAIN: *??*

Quarter-Final

5th Jan FIJI 36 **ENGLAND** 7

[*Team:* Balding]

[*Bench:*]

[*Scorers:* **try** by Gollings, **conversion** by Gollings]

[Plate Semi-Final:]
[5th Jan AUSTRALIA 7 **ENGLAND** 15 **]**
[*Team:* Balding]
[*Bench:*]
[*Scorers:* **tries** by J. Simpson-Daniel, Amor and Cueto]
[Plate Final:]
[5th Jan SAMOA 21 **ENGLAND** 12 **]**
[*Team:* Balding, Gollings, Cueto]
[*Bench:*]
[*Scorers:* **tries** by Cueto and J. Lewsey, **conversion** by Gollings]
POSITION: LOSING QUARTER-FINALISTS [*PLATE FINALISTS*]
[England scored 6 competition points in this Round of the 2001-2002 IRB World Sevens Series]

MAR DEL PLATA SEVENS
IRB WORLD SEVENS SERIES 2001-2002 ROUND 4

Estadio José Maria Minella, Mar del Plata
[*Tournament squad:* Cueto, Forrester (never travelled as withdrew, replaced by Simon Amor), Hazell (never travelled as withdrew, replaced by Adam Balding), J. Simpson-Daniel, Duncombe (never travelled as withdrew, replaced by Ian Vass), Gollings, R. Thirlby (never travelled as withdrew, replaced by Nigel Simpson), J. Lewsey, Friday, Appleford, Earnshaw, R. Haughton, Amor, Balding, Vass, N. Simpson]
(squad of 12)
[Pat Sanderson unavailable due to injury; Andy Hazell and Nick Duncombe unavailable due to club commitments; Rob Thirlby initially selected but then withdrew due to club commitments]
[**MANAGER:** *John Elliott*] [**COACH:** *Joe Lydon*] [**ASSISTANT COACH:** *Damian McGrath*] [**PLAYER-COACH:** *Mike Friday*]
CAPTAIN: *Mike Friday*
First Round - Pool 'B'
11th Jan PARAGUAY 0 **ENGLAND** 45
[*Team:*]
[*Bench:*]
[*Scorers:* **tries** by R. Haughton (2), J. Simpson-Daniel (2), Cueto (2) and Gollings, **conversions** by J. Simpson-Daniel (3) and Gollings (2)]
11th Jan CHILE 0 **ENGLAND** 43
[*Team:* Gollings, J. Simpson-Daniel, Cueto]
[*Bench:* R. Haughton (rep)]
[*Scorers:* **tries** by Gollings (4), Cueto, J. Simpson-Daniel and Balding, **conversions** by Gollings (4)]
11th Jan AUSTRALIA 12 **ENGLAND*** 7
[*Team:*]
[*Bench:*]
[*Scorers:* **try** by Gollings, **conversion** by Amor]
Quarter-Final
12th Jan NEW ZEALAND 26 **ENGLAND** 5
[*Team:*]
[*Bench:*]
[*Scorers:* **try** by J. Simpson-Daniel]

[Plate Semi-Final:]

[12th Jan SAMOA 12 **ENGLAND** 19 **]**

[*Team:*]

[*Bench:*]

[*Scorers:* **tries** by Cueto, Gollings and Amor, **conversions** by Gollings (2)]

[Plate Final:]

[12th Jan AUSTRALIA 15 **ENGLAND*** 12 aet**]**

[*Team:* Appleford, Gollings]

[*Bench:*]

[*Scorers:* **tries** by Gollings and Appleford, **conversion** by Gollings]

POSITION: LOSING QUARTER-FINALISTS [*PLATE FINALISTS*]

FANTASY: *LOSING QUARTER-FINALISTS* [*PLATE WINNERS*]

[England scored 6 competition points in this Round of the 2001-2002 IRB World Sevens Series]

6 NATIONS CHAMPIONSHIP

[**TEAM MANAGER:** *Clive Woodward*] [**HEAD COACH:** *Andy Robinson*] [**ASSISTANT COACHES:** *Brian Ashton & Phil Larder*]

CAPTAIN: *Martin Johnson*

2nd Feb SCOTLAND 3 **ENGLAND** 29

Murrayfield

[*Team:* Rowntree, Steve Thompson (2), Julian White, Martin Johnson, Kay, Richard Hill (2), Back, J. Worsley, K. Bracken, Jonny Wilkinson, B. Cohen, Tindall, W. Greenwood, Healey, Jason Robinson]

[*Bench:* Balshaw (rep), Corry, Duncombe (*scrum half*) (rep), Grewcock (rep), C. Hodgson (rep), J. Leonard (rep), M. Regan]

[*Scorers:* **tries** by Jason Robinson (2), Tindall and B. Cohen, **penalty goal** by Jonny Wilkinson, **conversions** by Jonny Wilkinson (2) and C. Hodgson]

16th Feb **ENGLAND** 45 IRELAND 11

Twickenham

[*Team:* Rowntree, Steve Thompson (2), Vickery, Martin Johnson, Kay, Richard Hill (2), Back, J. Worsley, K. Bracken, Jonny Wilkinson, B. Cohen, Tindall, W. Greenwood, Healey, Jason Robinson]

[*Bench:* Balshaw (rep), Duncombe (rep), Grewcock (rep), C. Hodgson (rep), J. Leonard (rep), Moody (rep), D. West]

[*Scorers:* **tries** by Jonny Wilkinson, B. Cohen, W. Greenwood (2), J. Worsley and Kay, **penalty goal** by Jonny Wilkinson, **conversions** by Jonny Wilkinson (6)]

2nd Mar FRANCE 20 **ENGLAND*** 15

Stade de France, Paris

[*Team:* Rowntree, Steve Thompson (2), Vickery, Martin Johnson, Kay, Richard Hill (2), Back, J. Worsley, K. Bracken, Jonny Wilkinson, B. Cohen, Tindall, W. Greenwood, Healey, Jason Robinson]

[*Bench:* Corry (rep), Duncombe, Grewcock (rep), J. Leonard (rep), Luger (rep), Henry Paul (*fly half/centre*) (rep), D. West (rep)]

[*Scorers:* **tries** by Jason Robinson and B. Cohen, **penalty goal** by Jonny Wilkinson, **conversion** by Jonny Wilkinson]

[**TEAM MANAGER:** *Clive Woodward*] [**HEAD COACH:** *Andy Robinson*] [**ASSISTANT COACH:** *Phil Larder*]

CAPTAIN: *Neil Back*

23rd Mar **ENGLAND** 50 WALES 10

Twickenham

[*Team:* Rowntree, Steve Thompson (2), Julian White, Grewcock, Kay, Moody, Back, Richard Hill (2), K. Bracken, Jonny Wilkinson, B. Cohen, Tindall, W. Greenwood, Luger, Healey]

[*Bench:* Balshaw, Corry (rep), Matt Dawson (rep), J. Leonard, Stimpson (rep), D. West (rep), J. Worsley (rep)]

[*Scorers:* **tries** by W. Greenwood, Jonny Wilkinson, Luger (2) and Stimpson, **penalty goals** by Jonny Wilkinson (4), **drop goal** by Jonny Wilkinson, **conversions** by Jonny Wilkinson (5)]

CAPTAIN: *Neil Back* [*Martin Johnson took over when Neil Back was substituted in the 2nd half*]

7th April ITALY 9 **ENGLAND** 45

Stadio Flaminio, Rome

[*Team:* Rowntree, Steve Thompson (2), Julian White, Grewcock, Kay, Moody, Back, Richard Hill (2), K. Bracken, Jonny Wilkinson, B. Cohen, Tindall, W. Greenwood, Luger, Jason Robinson]

[*Bench:* Dallaglio (rep), Matt Dawson (rep), Healey (*wing*) (rep), C. Hodgson (rep), J. Leonard (rep), Martin Johnson (*lock*) (rep), D. West (rep)]

[*Scorers:* **tries** by W. Greenwood (2), B. Cohen, Jason Robinson, Dallaglio and Healey, **penalty goal** by Jonny Wilkinson, **conversions** by Jonny Wilkinson (5) and Matt Dawson]

POSITION: 2ND 8 +131 TC CC MT [*France 10 +81 GS*, Ireland 6 +7, Scotland 4 -37, Wales 2 -69, Italy 0 -113]

FANTASY: ***1ST 10 GS TC CC MT***

[Brian Ashton took a temporary leave of absence from his post of Assistant Coach for personal reasons on 20th March 2002 and was then appointed Manager of the RFU National Academy on 24th April 2002]

OTHER MATCHES

ENGLAND STUDENTS MATCHES

[**MANAGER:** *Tony Lanaway*] [**COACH:** *Richard Hill (1)*] [**ASSISTANT COACH:** *Ian Smith (2)*]

CAPTAIN: *Scott Bemand*

[1st Feb SCOTLAND STUDENTS 14 **ENGLAND STUDENTS** 19]

Stewart's Melville FP RFC, Inverleith, Ferry Road, Edinburgh

[*Team:* Porte, M. Cairns, John Brooks, P. Short, K. Roche, Quigley, B. Lewitt, Thomas 'Tom' Hayman, Bemand, James Brown, Karelle Dixon, Ben Thompson, Cadwallader, Simon Hunt, Hylton]

[*Bench:* J. Barrett, Kevin Barrett (*scrum half*), A. Harris (*lock*), R. Hunt, Niarchos (*fly half*), T. Payne, L. Starling]

[*Scorers:* **tries** by Simon Hunt, B. Lewitt and K. Roche, **conversions** by James Brown (2)]

[15th Feb **ENGLAND STUDENTS** 17 IRELAND STUDENTS 18]

Bournemouth RFC, Chapel Gate, Parley Lane, Hurn, Christchurch

[*Team:* John Brooks, J. Barrett, Porte, P. Short, K. Roche, Quigley, L. Starling, T. Hayman, Bemand, Niarchos, K. Dixon, Robert 'Rob' Hoadley, Cadwallader, Simon Hunt, B. Thompson]

[*Bench:* K. Barrett (rep), James Brown (*fly half*) (rep), M. Cairns (*hooker*) (rep), A. Harris (rep), R. Hunt, B. Lewitt (*flanker*) (rep), T. Payne (rep)]

[*Scorers:* **tries** by Simon Hunt (2) and B. Lewitt, **conversion** by James Brown]

CAPTAIN: *Matt Cairns*

[1st Mar FRANCE STUDENTS 22 **ENGLAND STUDENTS** 15]
Stade Léon Sausset, Tournon

[*Team:* John Brooks, M. Cairns, Henry Nwume, A. Harris, P. Short, K. Roche, B. Lewitt, Quigley, K. Barrett, James Brown, K. Dixon, R. Hunt, Cadwallader, Simon Hunt, B. Thompson]

[*Bench:* J. Barrett, Bemand (*scrum half*), Hoadley (*centre/wing*) (rep), T. Hayman (*number 8*), Ryan Hopkins (*prop*), L. Starling, Sam Walton (*prop/hooker*)]

[*Scorers:* **tries** by Simon Hunt and K. Dixon, **penalty goal** by James Brown, **conversion** by Hoadley]

CAPTAIN: *Scott Bemand*

[22nd Mar **ENGLAND STUDENTS** 35 WALES STUDENTS 6]
Ashton Gate, Bristol

[*Team:* S. Walton, M. Cairns, Porte, P. Short, K. Roche, Quigley, B. Lewitt, T. Hayman, Bemand, James Brown, Simon Hunt, B. Thompson, Cadwallader, K. Dixon, N. Marsh]

[*Bench:* J. Barrett, K. Barrett, Neil Hallett (*fly half/full back*), A. Harris, R. Hopkins, R. Hunt, Andrew 'Andy' Walters (*flanker*)]

[*Scorers:* **tries** by Cadwallader, B. Lewitt (2) and T. Hayman, **penalty goals** by James Brown (3), **conversions** by James Brown (3)]

[Ian Smith (2) was appointed Assistant Coach of England U19 on 12th November 2002]

U21 6 NATIONS CHAMPIONSHIP

[**COACH:** *Nigel Melville*]

CAPTAIN: *Mark Soden*

[1st Feb SCOTLAND U21 16 **ENGLAND U21** 31]
Dunbar RFC, Hallhill Healthy Living Centre, Kellie Road, Dunbar

[*Team:* N. Cox, Roddam, Irish, Stuart Hooper, M. Purdy, Mark Soden, James 'Jim' Scaysbrook, Phillip 'Phil' Davies (3), A. Page, Barkley, Voyce, Andy Higgins (2), Oliver James 'Ollie' Smith (2), A. Elliott, A. Winnan]

[*Bench:* Billig (*centre/wing/full back*), Buckland (*hooker*) (rep), Devonshire (rep), Jonathan 'Jon' Goodridge (*full back*), Stephen 'Steve' Green (*lock*) (rep), J. Simpson-Daniel (*centre/wing*) (rep), Vass (rep)]

[*Scorers:* **tries** by Voyce, Barkley (2) and J. Simpson-Daniel, **penalty goal** by Barkley, **conversions** by Barkley (3) and A. Winnan]

[15th Feb **ENGLAND U21** 28 IRELAND U21 23]
Coundon Road, Coventry

[*Team:* N. Cox, Roddam, Irish, S. Hooper, M. Purdy, Forrester, Scaysbrook, Soden, Harry Ellis, Barkley, Voyce, Crockett, Billig, J. Simpson-Daniel, A. Winnan]

[*Bench:* Buckland (rep), I. Clarke (*flanker/number 8*) (rep), Goodridge (rep), S. Green, Alistair 'Ali' McKenzie (*prop*) (rep), A. Page, Thrower (*full back*) (rep)]

[*Scorers:* **tries** by Crockett (2) and J. Simpson-Daniel, **penalty goals** by Barkley (3), **conversions** by Barkley (2)]

[1st Mar FRANCE U21 21 **ENGLAND U21*** 19]
Stade de la Vallée du Cher, Tours

[*Team:* N. Cox, Roddam, Irish, S. Hooper, M. Purdy, Soden, Scaysbrook, Forrester, Harry Ellis, Barkley, Voyce, Crockett, Ollie Smith (2), J. Simpson-Daniel, Thrower]

[*Bench:* Billig, Devonshire (rep), A. Elliott (rep), S. Green, M. Holford (rep), Titterrell (rep), Vass]

[*Scorers:* **tries** by Barkley and Forrester, **penalty goals** by Barkley (3)]

[22nd Mar **ENGLAND U21*** 35 WALES U21 36]
Newbury RFC, Monks Lane, Newbury
[*Team:* M. Holford, Roddam, Irish, S. Hooper, M. Purdy, Chris Morgan, Scaysbrook, Soden, Vass, Barkley, Voyce, Crockett, Billig, A. Elliott, Goodridge]
[*Bench:* Buckland, I. Clarke, N. Cox (rep), James Hamilton (*lock*), Andy Higgins (2) (rep), A. McKenzie, A. Page]
[*Scorers:* **tries** by Chris Morgan, Voyce, Vass and Barkley, **penalty goals** by Barkley (3), **conversions** by Barkley (3)]
[6th April ITALY U21 15 **ENGLAND U21** 50]
Stadio Santa Colomba, Benevento
[*Team:* M. Holford, Buckland, Irish, S. Hooper, M. Purdy, Forrester, Chris Morgan, Soden, Vass, Barkley, Voyce, Crockett, J. Simpson-Daniel, A. Elliott, Billig]
[*Bench:* I. Clarke, N. Cox, James Hamilton, Andy Higgins (2), A. McKenzie, A. Page, Matthew 'Matt' Thompson (*hooker*) (rep)]
[*Scorers:* **tries** by A. Elliott (2), Andy Higgins (2), Crockett, Barkley, Chris Morgan and M. Holford, **conversions** by Barkley (5)]
POSITION: 3RD 6 +52 [*France 10 +98 GS*, Wales 8 +92 TC, Ireland 4 +45, Italy 2 -190, Scotland 0 -97]
FANTASY: *1ST 10 GS TC*
[Nigel Melville was appointed on 5th December 2001 and on 6th March 2002 announced that he would be leaving his post of Coach after the Italy U21 match at Benevento on 6th April 2002]

'A' INTERNATIONAL CHAMPIONSHIP

[**COACH:** *Ged Glynn*] [**ASSISTANT COACHES:** *John Wells & Damian McGrath*]
CAPTAIN: *Steve Borthwick*
[1st Feb SCOTLAND A 6 **ENGLAND A*** 6]
Stirling County RFC, Bridgehaugh Park, Stirling
[*Team:* Flatman, A. Long, Nebbett, Tom Palmer (2), S. Borthwick, P. Buxton, A. Sanderson, Hazell, Walshe, Andy Goode, Stephen 'Steve' Hanley, F. Waters, H. Paul, Cueto, J. Lewsey]
[*Bench:* Alex Brown (rep), Hall Charlton (*scrum half*), D. Danaher (*flanker/number 8*) (rep), Ben Johnston, T. May (rep), Titterrell, M. Worsley (*prop*) (rep)]
[*Scorers:* **penalty goals** by Andy Goode (2)]
CAPTAIN: *Nick Walshe*
[15th Feb **ENGLAND A*** 18 IRELAND A 25]
Franklin's Gardens, Northampton
[*Team:* M. Worsley, Titterrell, Nebbett, Alex Brown, Tom Palmer (2), P. Buxton, D. Danaher, A. Sanderson, Walshe, Andy Goode, J. Lewsey, F. Waters, H. Paul, Sackey, Matt Perry]
[*Bench:* Charlton, Christophers, Flatman (rep), C. Fortey (rep), T. May, Andrew 'Andy' Sheridan (*lock*) (rep), White-Cooper (rep)]
[*Scorers:* **penalty goals** by Andy Goode (6)]
CAPTAIN: *Steve Borthwick*
[1st Mar FRANCE A 19 **ENGLAND A*** 13]
Parc Municipal des Sports de Beaublanc, Limoges
[*Team:* Flatman, M. Regan, Julian White, S. Borthwick, Tom Palmer (2), D. Danaher, P. Sanderson, A. Sanderson, Matt Dawson, Andy Goode, Sackey, J. Lewsey, F. Waters, Cueto, Balshaw]
[*Bench:* P. Buxton (*flanker/number 8*) (rep), Christophers (rep), C. Fortey (rep), Phil Jones (*fly half*) (rep), Sheridan (rep), Trevor Woodman (rep), Walshe]

[*Scorers:* **try** by penalty try, **penalty goals** by Andy Goode and Phil Jones, **conversion** by Andy Goode]

[22nd Mar **ENGLAND A*** 21 WALES A 29]
Ashton Gate, Bristol

[*Team:* Trevor Woodman, M. Regan, Nebbett, Tom Palmer (2), S. Borthwick, W. Johnson, Forrester, Balding, Duncombe, Phil Jones, Scarbrough, Ben Johnston, F. Waters, Cueto, Sampson]

[*Bench:* S. Booth (*wing/full back*) (rep), Christophers (rep), Mark Cornwell (rep), Andy Goode (*fly half*), P. Gustard (*flanker/number 8*) (rep), Shelley (*prop*) (rep), Walshe]

[*Scorers:* **tries** by M. Regan (2), **penalty goals** by Phil Jones (3), **conversion** by Phil Jones]

[6th April ITALY A 22 **ENGLAND A*** 21]
Stadio CUS Napoli, Naples

[*Team:* M. Worsley, M. Regan, Hardwick, Mark Cornwell, S. Borthwick, Ben Sturnham, Volley, J. Worsley, Duncombe, H. Paul, Christophers, Ben Johnston, T. May, S. Booth, Scarbrough]

[*Bench:* James Brooks (rep), C. Fortey, Gollings (rep), P. Gustard (rep), Noon (rep), Roques (*flanker*), Shelley (rep)]

[*Scorers:* **tries** by S. Booth and Mark Cornwell, **penalty goals** by H. Paul (3), **conversion** by H. Paul]

POSITION: **6TH 1 -22** [*Ireland 8 +141 TC*, France 8 +26, Wales 8 +20, Scotland 3 -69, Italy 2 -96]

FANTASY: ***1ST 10 GS TC***

[Damian McGrath was appointed on 4th December 2001; Ged Glynn was appointed Coach of Spain in February 2004]

BRISBANE WORLD RUGBY SEVENS
IRB WORLD SEVENS SERIES 2001-2002 ROUND 5

Ballymore Stadium, Brisbane

[*Tournament squad:* Forrester, Christopher 'Chris' Jones (*forward*), Appleford, L. Lloyd (*centre/wing*) (injured during the tournament), Jonathan 'Joe' Shaw (*back*), R. Thirlby, Noon (*back/forward*), Amor, Harry Ellis (*scrum half*), Gollings, M. Stephenson, R. Haughton]
(squad of 12)

[This tournament was originally scheduled to take place on 15th-16th February 2002; Phil Christophers, Olu Ikeowu, Mike Friday, Ben Johnston and Andy Titterrell all in original 13 man training squad on 21st January 2002; Mike Friday in travelling squad of 13 but did not actually play in the tournament; Joe Shaw was capped for England Schools 18 Group in March 1998]

[**MANAGER:** *John Elliott*] [**COACH:** *Joe Lydon*] [**ASSISTANT COACHES:** *Damian McGrath & Mike Friday*]

CAPTAIN: *Rob Thirlby*

First Round - Pool 'D'

2nd Feb TONGA 0 **ENGLAND** 33

[*Team:* Appleford, ?, ?, Amor, R. Thirlby, Noon, R. Haughton]

[*Bench:* ?, ?, ?, ?, ?]

[*Scorers:* **tries** by Appleford, Noon, R. Haughton, J. Shaw and L. Lloyd, **conversions** by Amor (4)]

2nd Feb CANADA 0 **ENGLAND** 29

[*Team:* Appleford, ?, Chris Jones, Amor, R. Thirlby, ?, R. Haughton]

[*Bench:* ?, ?, ?, ?, ?]

[*Scorers:* **tries** by R. Haughton, Appleford, Chris Jones, M. Stephenson and Amor, **conversions** by Amor (2)]

2nd Feb SOUTH AFRICA 17 **ENGLAND** 5

[*Team:* Amor]

[*Bench:*]

[*Scorers:* **try** by Amor]

Quarter-Final

3rd Feb AUSTRALIA 29 **ENGLAND*** 12

[*Team:*]

[*Bench:*]

[*Scorers:* **tries** by Harry Ellis and Forrester, **conversion** by Gollings]

[Plate Semi-Final:]

[3rd Feb FIJI 17 **ENGLAND*** 12 aet**]**

[*Team:* Gollings]

[*Bench:*]

[*Scorers:* **tries** by Noon and M. Stephenson, **conversion** by Gollings]

POSITION: LOSING QUARTER-FINALISTS [*PLATE SEMI-FINALISTS*]

[England scored 4 competition points in this Round of the 2001-2002 IRB World Sevens Series]

TELECOM MORE MOBILE NEW ZEALAND INTERNATIONAL SEVENS

IRB WORLD SEVENS SERIES 2001-2002 ROUND 6

WestpacTrust Stadium, Wellington

[*Tournament squad:* Forrester (never travelled as withdrew, replaced by Andy Dawling), Chris Jones, Appleford, L. Lloyd (never travelled as injured, replaced by Simon Hunt), J. Shaw, R. Thirlby, Noon (never travelled as withdrew, replaced by Mike Friday), Amor, Harry Ellis, Gollings, M. Stephenson, R. Haughton, Dawling (*forward*), Simon Hunt, Friday]

(squad of 12)

[James Forrester and Jamie Noon selected but withdrew due to club commitments; Chris Jones, Simon Amor, Richard Haughton, Simon Hunt, Andy Dawling and Mike Friday all not mentioned in the tournament programme; Ben Johnston, Andy Titterrell, Declan Danaher, Phil Christophers and Olu Ikeowu all in original 13 man training squad on 21st January 2002]

[**MANAGER:** *John Elliott*] [**COACH:** *Joe Lydon*] [**ASSISTANT COACH:** *Damian McGrath*] [**PLAYER-COACH:** *Mike Friday*]

CAPTAIN: *Mike Friday*

First Round - Pool 'A'

8th Feb PAPUA NEW GUINEA 0 **ENGLAND** 36

[*Team:* Chris Jones, Gollings, R. Haughton]

[*Bench:*]

[*Scorers:* **tries** by R. Haughton (3), Chris Jones, Amor and M. Stephenson, **conversions** by Gollings (2) and Amor]

8th Feb USA 21 **ENGLAND** 26

[*Team:* Appleford, Gollings]

[*Bench:*]

[*Scorers:* **tries** by Appleford, Gollings (2) and R. Haughton, **conversions** by Gollings (3)]

8th Feb NEW ZEALAND 50 **ENGLAND** 7
[*Team:*]
[*Bench:*]
[*Scorers:* **try** by Gollings, **conversion** by Gollings]
CAPTAIN: *??*
Quarter-Final
9th Feb FIJI 14 **ENGLAND** 19
[*Team:* Dawling, Appleford, Simon Hunt, Harry Ellis, Amor, Gollings, M. Stephenson]
[*Bench:* Friday (rep), R. Haughton (rep), Chris Jones, J. Shaw (rep), R. Thirlby]
[*Scorers:* **tries** by Dawling, Gollings and M. Stephenson, **conversions** by Gollings (2)]
CAPTAIN: *Mike Friday*
Semi-Final
9th Feb SAMOA 36 **ENGLAND** 5
[*Team:* M. Stephenson]
[*Bench:*]
[*Scorers:* **try** by M. Stephenson]
POSITION: LOSING SEMI-FINALISTS
[England scored 12 competition points in this Round of the 2001-2002 IRB World Sevens Series]

BEIJING SEVENS
IRB WORLD SEVENS SERIES 2001-2002 ROUND 7

National Olympic Sports Centre, Beijing
[*Tournament squad:* A. Sanderson (never travelled as injured, replaced by Joe Shaw), Greening (*hooker*), Appleford, J. Lewsey, Friday, H. Paul (never travelled as withdrew), Noon, Amor, Harry Ellis (never travelled as injured, replaced by Nnamdi Ezulike), Gollings (never travelled as withdrew), Balshaw (*wing*) (never travelled as withdrew), R. Haughton, J. Shaw, Ezulike (*wing*), J. Simpson-Daniel]
(squad of 10)
[This tournament was originally scheduled to take place on 27th-28th April 2002; Pat Sanderson was unavailable for this tournament due to injury; Iain Balshaw and Henry Paul in original squad of 12 but were withdrawn by their clubs Bath and Gloucester respectively on the day of the squad's departure; Ben Gollings was withdrawn by his club Harlequins six hours before the squad departed on 11th March 2002!; James Simpson-Daniel was added to the squad on the day of its departure; Mike Friday was the tournament captain]
[**MANAGER:** *John Elliott*] [**COACH:** *Joe Lydon*] [**ASSISTANT COACH:** *Damian McGrath*] [**PLAYER-COACH:** *Mike Friday*]
CAPTAIN: *Mike Friday*
First Round - Pool 'C'
16th Mar HONG KONG 0 **ENGLAND** 43
[*Team:* J. Lewsey, Greening, J. Shaw, Amor, J. Simpson-Daniel, Appleford, R. Haughton]
[*Bench:* Ezulike (rep), Friday (rep), Noon (rep), ?, ?]
[*Scorers:* **tries** by J. Lewsey (2), Greening, Amor, R. Haughton, Appleford and Ezulike, **conversions** by J. Lewsey (2), Greening and J. Simpson-Daniel]
16th Mar CANADA 10 **ENGLAND** 7
[*Team:* J. Lewsey, Greening, J. Shaw, Friday, J. Simpson-Daniel, Appleford, R. Haughton]
[*Bench:* Amor (rep), Ezulike (rep), Noon (rep), ?, ?]
[*Scorers:* **try** by Appleford, **conversion** by Amor]

16th Mar SAMOA 5 **ENGLAND** 7
[*Team:* J. Lewsey, Greening, Noon, Amor, J. Simpson-Daniel, Appleford, R. Haughton]
[*Bench:* Ezulike (rep), Friday (rep), J. Shaw (rep), ?, ?]
[*Scorers:* **try** by Noon, **conversion** by Amor]
Quarter-Final
17th Mar FIJI 28 **ENGLAND** 14
[*Team:* J. Lewsey, Greening, Noon, Amor, J. Simpson-Daniel, Appleford, R. Haughton]
[*Bench:* Ezulike (rep), Friday (rep), J. Shaw (rep), ?, ?]
[*Scorers:* **tries** by R. Haughton and J. Simpson-Daniel, **conversions** by Amor and J. Simpson-Daniel]
[Plate Semi-Final:]
[17th Mar USA 12 **ENGLAND** 21 **]**
[*Team:* J. Lewsey, Noon, J. Shaw, Amor, J. Simpson-Daniel, Appleford, R. Haughton]
[*Bench:* Ezulike (rep), Friday (rep), Greening (rep), ?, ?]
[*Scorers:* **tries** by R. Haughton, Appleford and Amor, **conversions** by Amor (3)]
[Plate Final:]
[17th Mar SAMOA 14 **ENGLAND** 33 **]**
[*Team:* J. Lewsey, Noon, J. Shaw, Amor, J. Simpson-Daniel, Appleford, R. Haughton]
[*Bench:* Ezulike (rep), Friday (rep), Greening (rep), ?, ?]
[*Scorers:* **tries** by Amor, Appleford, R. Haughton and J. Simpson-Daniel (2), **conversions** by Amor (4)]
POSITION: LOSING QUARTER-FINALISTS [*PLATE WINNERS*]
[England scored 8 competition points in this Round of the 2001-2002 IRB World Sevens Series]

CREDIT SUISSE FIRST BOSTON HONG KONG SEVENS
IRB WORLD SEVENS SERIES 2001-2002 ROUND 8

Hong Kong Stadium, Eastern Hospital Road, So Kon Po, Hong Kong
[*Tournament squad:* A. Sanderson (never travelled as injured), Greening, Appleford, J. Lewsey, Friday (never played as withdrew), H. Paul (*back/forward*), Noon, Amor, Harry Ellis (never travelled as injured), Gollings, Balshaw (never travelled as withdrew), R. Haughton, J. Shaw, J. Simpson-Daniel, M. Stephenson, P. Sanderson (never travelled as injured, replaced by Tony Roques), Roques]
(squad of 12)
[Iain Balshaw selected but withdrew as he was now required to join the full England international squad for the match against Wales; Mike Friday in original playing squad of 12 but eventually travelled as Assistant Coach; Declan Danaher was included in a revised training squad; Phil Greening was the tournament captain]
[**MANAGER:** *John Elliott*] [**COACH:** *Joe Lydon*] [**ASSISTANT COACHES:** *Damian McGrath & Mike Friday*]
CAPTAIN: *Phil Greening*
First Round - Pool 'F'
22nd Mar JAPAN 0 **ENGLAND** 47
[*Team:* Noon, Greening, J. Lewsey, Amor, Gollings, H. Paul, R. Haughton]
[*Bench:* Roques (rep), J. Simpson-Daniel (rep), M. Stephenson (rep), ?, ?]
[*Scorers:* **tries** by R. Haughton, Amor (2), Gollings, J. Simpson-Daniel (2) and Roques, **conversions** by Amor (6)]
23rd Mar THAILAND 5 **ENGLAND** 33
[*Team:* Noon, J. Lewsey, Roques, Gollings, H. Paul, J. Simpson-Daniel, M. Stephenson]

[*Bench:* Appleford (rep), R. Haughton (rep), J. Shaw (rep), ?, ?]
[*Scorers:* **tries** by J. Lewsey (2), Gollings, Appleford and H. Paul, **conversions** by Gollings (3) and H. Paul]

23rd Mar ARGENTINA 5 **ENGLAND** 19
[*Team:* Roques, Greening, J. Lewsey, Amor, Gollings, H. Paul, R. Haughton]
[*Bench:* J. Simpson-Daniel (rep), Noon (rep), M. Stephenson (rep), ?, ?]
[*Scorers:* **tries** by H. Paul, R. Haughton and Gollings, **conversions** by Amor (2)]

Quarter-Final

24th Mar SAMOA 5 **ENGLAND** 19
[*Team:* Roques, Greening, J. Lewsey, Amor, Gollings, H. Paul, R. Haughton]
[*Bench:* Appleford (rep), Noon (rep), J. Simpson-Daniel (rep), ?, ?]
[*Scorers:* **tries** by H. Paul and R. Haughton (2), **conversions** by Amor (2)]

Semi-Final

24th Mar WALES 12 **ENGLAND** 19
[*Team:* Roques, Greening, J. Lewsey, Amor, Gollings, H. Paul, R. Haughton]
[*Bench:* Appleford (rep), Noon (rep), J. Shaw, J. Simpson-Daniel, M. Stephenson (rep)]
[*Scorers:* **tries** by Gollings, Amor and J. Lewsey, **conversions** by Amor (2)]

CAPTAIN: *Simon Amor*

Final

24th Mar FIJI 20 **ENGLAND** 33
[*Team:* Noon, J. Lewsey, Roques, Amor, Gollings, H. Paul, M. Stephenson]
[*Bench:* Appleford (rep), J. Shaw (rep), J. Simpson-Daniel (rep), ?]
[*Scorers:* **tries** by Amor, J. Simpson-Daniel (3) and Gollings, **conversions** by Amor (4)]

POSITION: WINNERS

[England scored 30 competition points in this Round of the 2001-2002 IRB World Sevens Series]

TILNEY MELROSE SEVENS

LADIES CENTENARY CUP

The Greenyards, Melrose

[*Tournament squad:* Dawling, François Mounier (FR) (*forward*), Miall, Brett Robinson (AU) (*forward*), D. Burns (SC), A. Page, Arwel Thomas (WA) (*fly half*), Cerith Rees (WA) (*fly half*), James Strong (WA) (*wing*), Keenan (SC) (*wing*)]

(squad of 10)

[The first round was a qualifying round]

[NO COACH NOMINATED]

CAPTAIN: *??*

Second Round

[13th April Selkirk (*SC*) 19 **BARBARIANS** 40]
[*Team:*]
[*Bench:*]
[*Scorers:* **tries** by A. Page (2), Strong (WA), Keenan (SC) (2) and Brett Robinson (AU), **conversions** by Arwel Thomas (WA) (5)]

Quarter-Final

[13th April Melrose (*SC*) 21 **BARBARIANS** 26 aet]
[*Team:* A. Page, Arwel Thomas (WA), Keenan (SC)]
[*Bench:*]
[*Scorers:* **tries** by Keenan (SC), Strong (WA), D. Burns (SC) and A. Page, **conversions** by

Arwel Thomas (WA) (3)]

Semi-Final

[13th April Boroughmuir (*SC*) 19 **BARBARIANS** 12]

[*Team:* D. Burns (SC)]

[*Bench:*]

[*Scorers:* **tries** by D. Burns (SC) and Keenan (SC), **conversion** by Arwel Thomas (WA)]

POSITION: LOSING SEMI-FINALISTS

SINGAPORE SEVENS

IRB WORLD SEVENS SERIES 2001-2002 ROUND 9

National Stadium, Kallang

[*Tournament squad:* Luger (*wing*) (injured during the tournament), Gollings, Duncombe, Noon, M. Stephenson, R. Thirlby, Greening (captain; never travelled as injured, replaced by Ben Lewitt), Sampson, F. Waters (*centre*) (injured during the tournament), Phil Jones (*fly half/centre*), N. Simpson, R. Haughton, B. Lewitt (injured during the tournament)]

(squad of 12)

[This tournament was originally scheduled to take place on 20th-21st April 2002; Pat Sanderson was unavailable for this tournament due to injury]

[**MANAGER:** *John Elliott*] [**COACH:** *Joe Lydon*] [**ASSISTANT COACHES:** *Damian McGrath & Mike Friday*]

CAPTAIN: *Jamie Noon*

First Round - Pool 'D'

20th April CANADA 0 **ENGLAND** 31

[*Team:* Noon, B. Lewitt, N. Simpson, Duncombe, Gollings, F. Waters, R. Haughton]

[*Bench:* Luger (rep), Sampson (rep), R. Thirlby (rep), ?, ?]

[*Scorers:* **tries** by Gollings (4) and R. Haughton, **conversions** by Gollings (3)]

20th April TAIWAN 7 **ENGLAND** 28

[*Team:* Gollings, Phil Jones, Sampson]

[*Bench:*]

[*Scorers:* **tries** by Phil Jones (2) and Sampson (2), **conversions** by Gollings (2), Phil Jones and Sampson]

20th April ARGENTINA 19 **ENGLAND*** 14

[*Team:* Gollings, F. Waters, Sampson]

[*Bench:*]

[*Scorers:* **tries** by Sampson and F. Waters, **conversions** by Gollings (2)]

Quarter-Final

21st April SOUTH AFRICA 7 **ENGLAND** 15

[*Team:* Luger]

[*Bench:*]

[*Scorers:* **tries** by Sampson (2) and F. Waters]

Semi-Final

21st April NEW ZEALAND 19 **ENGLAND*** 10

[*Team:* Gollings]

[*Bench:*]

[*Scorers:* **tries** by Gollings and Noon]

POSITION: LOSING SEMI-FINALISTS

[England scored 12 competition points in this Round of the 2001-2002 IRB World Sevens Series]

MALAYSIA SEVENS

IRB WORLD SEVENS SERIES 2001-2002 ROUND 10

MPPJ Stadium, Petaling Jaya, Kelana Jaya

[*Tournament squad:* David Rees (2) (*wing*), Jamie Williams (*back*) (never travelled as withdrew, replaced by Howard Graham), R. Haughton, J. Shaw, Scarbrough (*back/forward*), K. Barrett (*scrum half*), B. Lewitt, Dawling, Phil Jones, Earnshaw, N. Simpson, Howard Graham (*back/forward*)]

(squad of 11)

[Pat Sanderson and Phil Greening were unavailable for this tournament due to injury; Andy Dawling played in the British Army team that won the Cwmtawe Sevens at Pontardawe on 3rd August 2002 and played for the Penguins in the COBRA Tens at Petaling Jaya on 30th-31st August 2003; Howard Graham captained the British Army to victory at the Cwmtawe Sevens at Pontardawe on 3rd August 2002 and 4th August 2007, captained the British Army to victory at the Middlesex Sevens at Twickenham on 14th August 2004, captained the Penguins in the COBRA Tens at Petaling Jaya on 11th-12th September 2004 and 10th-11th September 2005 and captained the White Hart Marauders team that reached the Final of the Amsterdam Heineken Sevens on 19th-20th May 2007]

[**MANAGER:** *John Elliott*] [**COACH:** *Joe Lydon*] [**ASSISTANT COACHES:** *Damian McGrath & Mike Friday*]

CAPTAIN: *Howard Graham*

First Round - Pool 'D'

27th April JAPAN 0 **ENGLAND** 31

[*Team:* N. Simpson, H. Graham, B. Lewitt, K. Barrett, Phil Jones, J. Shaw, R. Haughton]

[*Bench:* Dawling, Earnshaw (rep), David Rees (2) (rep), Scarbrough (rep)]

[*Scorers:* **tries** by Phil Jones, R. Haughton, Scarbrough (2) and David Rees, **conversions** by H. Graham (3)]

27th April THAILAND 0 **ENGLAND** 34

[*Team:* Earnshaw, H. Graham, B. Lewitt, K. Barrett, Phil Jones, Scarbrough, David Rees (2)]

[*Bench:* Dawling (rep), R. Haughton (rep), J. Shaw, N. Simpson (rep)]

[*Scorers:* **tries** by Earnshaw, Phil Jones (3), David Rees and Scarbrough, **conversions** by H. Graham (2)]

27th April AUSTRALIA 14 **ENGLAND** 7

[*Team:* Earnshaw, H. Graham, B. Lewitt, K. Barrett, Phil Jones, Scarbrough, David Rees (2)]

[*Bench:* Dawling, R. Haughton (rep), J. Shaw, N. Simpson (rep)]

[*Scorers:* **try** by R. Haughton, **conversion** by H. Graham]

Quarter-Final

28th April SOUTH AFRICA 19 **ENGLAND** 0

[*Team:* Earnshaw, H. Graham, B. Lewitt, K. Barrett, Phil Jones, J. Shaw, David Rees (2)]

[*Bench:* Dawling, R. Haughton (rep), Scarbrough (rep), N. Simpson (rep)]

[*No scorers*]

[Plate Semi-Final:]

[28th Apr WALES 5 **ENGLAND** 22 **]**

[*Team:* ?, H. Graham, ?, ?, ?, Scarbrough, R. Haughton]

[*Bench:* David Rees (2), J. Shaw (rep), ?, ?]

[*Scorers:* **tries** by R. Haughton, Scarbrough and J. Shaw (2), **conversion** by H. Graham]

[Plate Final:]
[28th Apr ARGENTINA 7 **ENGLAND** 43]
[*Team:* Dawling, H. Graham, B. Lewitt, K. Barrett, Phil Jones, Scarbrough, David Rees (2)]
[*Bench:* Earnshaw (rep), R. Haughton (rep), J. Shaw, N. Simpson (rep)]
[*Scorers:* **tries** by Phil Jones (3), Scarbrough, David Rees and K. Barrett (2), **conversions** by H. Graham (3) and Phil Jones]
POSITION: LOSING QUARTER-FINALISTS [*PLATE WINNERS*]
[England scored 8 competition points in this Round of the 2001-2002 IRB World Sevens Series]

ENGLAND STUDENTS MATCH

[**MANAGER:** *Ian Robson*] [**COACHES:** *Steve Hill* & *Mark Tainton*]
CAPTAIN: *??*
[4th May **ENGLAND STUDENTS U21** 23 COMBINED SERVICES U21 (*SER*) 19]

Twickenham
[*Team:* Simon Legg, Ben Gotting, Dan Chesham, Ben Gulliver, James Hudson, Benjamin 'Ben' Woods, Tom Miklausic, Benjamin 'Ben' Durham, Timothy 'Tim' Sinnett, N. Wainwright, William 'Will' Kershaw-Naylor, Paul Murphy, Duncan Murray, Richard Briggs, Hylton]
[*Bench:* N. Clark (*hooker*), James Gaunt (*scrum half*), G. Hill, M. Honeyben (*fly half*) (rep), Ben Hughes (*lock/number 8*), Peter Knight (2) (*flanker*), M. Lamb]
[*Scorers:* **tries** by N. Wainwright and Hylton, **penalty goals** by Paul Murphy (3), **conversions** by Paul Murphy (2)]

TETLEY'S COUNTY CHAMPIONSHIP SEMI-FINAL

[**CHAIRMAN OF SELECTORS:** *Terry Carter* (CO)] [**COACH:** *Nick Brokenshire* (CO)] [**ASSISTANT COACHES:** *Darren Chapman* (CO) & *Anthony 'Tony' Cook* (CO)]
CAPTAIN: *Steve Larkins* (CO)
[18th May **CORNWALL** 10 Gloucestershire 22 aet]

Recreation Ground, Redruth
[*Team:* Peter Risdon (CO), Barry Lucas (CO), Steve Rush (CO), Julian Wilce (CO), Soper, Richard Carroll (CO), Kevin Penrose (CO), James Lancaster (NZ), Ricky Pellow, James 'Jimmy' Tucker (CO), J. Hawken (CO), Kirman (NZ), Craig Bonds (CO), Marc Richards (CO), Larkins (CO)]
[*Bench:* John Arnold (CO) (*flanker/number 8*) (rep), Chris Hammond (CO) (*flanker*) (rep), Hymans (SA) (*centre/wing*) (rep), D. Moyle (CO) (rep), Mark Richards (CO) (*scrum half/centre*), Dave Risdon (CO) (*hooker*) (rep), Tom Sincock (CO) (*fly half/wing/full back*)]
[*Scorers:* **try** by Kirman (NZ), **penalty goal** by Larkins (CO), **conversion** by Larkins (CO)]
POSITION: LOSING SEMI-FINALISTS
[Terry Carter was appointed on 29th June 2001; Nick Brokenshire was appointed on 3rd October 2001; Darren Chapman and Tony Cook were both appointed in February 2002; Darren Chapman won 38 caps for Cornwall between 1987-94; Tony Cook won a record 102 caps for Cornwall between 1982-98]

EMIRATES AIRLINE LONDON SEVENS
IRB WORLD SEVENS SERIES 2001-2002 ROUND 11

Twickenham
[*Tournament squad:* White-Cooper (*forward*), Roques, Greening, T. May (*back/forward*), H.

Paul, J. Lewsey, Sampson, M. Stephenson, K. Barrett, Gollings, R. Haughton, Duncombe] ***(squad of 12)***
[Pat Sanderson was unavailable for this tournament due to injury; Simon Amor, Ben Johnston and Rob Thirlby in original training squad of 13; Tom May and Richard Haughton were not part of the original training squad; Kevin Barrett played for the White Hart Marauders in the Hong Kong Tens at Hong Kong Football Club on 16th-17th March 2005 and played in the Samurai team that won the Amsterdam Heineken Sevens on 21st-22nd May 2005]
[**MANAGER:** *John Elliott*] [**COACH:** *Joe Lydon*] [**ASSISTANT COACHES:** *Damian McGrath & Mike Friday*]
CAPTAIN: *Phil Greening*
First Round - Pool 'B'

24th May **ENGLAND** 40 CANADA 0
[*Team:* Greening, J. Lewsey, Roques, Duncombe, Gollings, H. Paul, Sampson]
[*Bench:* K. Barrett (rep), R. Haughton (rep), T. May (rep), M. Stephenson, White-Cooper]
[*Scorers:* **tries** by Gollings, Roques, J. Lewsey and R. Haughton (3), **conversions** by Gollings (5)]

24th May **ENGLAND** 34 SPAIN 14
[*Team:* Greening, T. May, White-Cooper, K. Barrett, H. Paul, M. Stephenson, Sampson]
[*Bench:* Duncombe (rep), Gollings (rep), R. Haughton, J. Lewsey (rep), Roques]
[*Scorers:* **tries** by Sampson (2), M. Stephenson, T. May, White-Cooper and K. Barrett, **conversions** by H. Paul (2)]

24th May **ENGLAND** 27 SAMOA 0
[*Team:* Greening, J. Lewsey, Roques, Duncombe, Gollings, H. Paul, R. Haughton]
[*Bench:* K. Barrett (rep), T. May (rep), Sampson (rep), M. Stephenson, White-Cooper]
[*Scorers:* **tries** by R. Haughton (2), J. Lewsey (2) and Gollings, **conversion** by Gollings]

Quarter-Final

25th May **ENGLAND** 26 AUSTRALIA 14
[*Team:* Greening, J. Lewsey, Roques, Duncombe, Gollings, H. Paul, R. Haughton]
[*Bench:* K. Barrett (rep), T. May (rep), Sampson (rep), M. Stephenson, White-Cooper]
[*Scorers:* **tries** by Roques, Greening, Sampson and J. Lewsey, **conversions** by Gollings (3)]

Semi-Final

25th May **ENGLAND*** 12 SOUTH AFRICA 26
[*Team:* Greening, J. Lewsey, Roques, Duncombe, Gollings, H. Paul, R. Haughton]
[*Bench:* K. Barrett, T. May (rep), Sampson (rep), M. Stephenson (rep), White-Cooper]
[*Scorers:* **tries** by J. Lewsey and Gollings, **conversion** by Gollings]

POSITION: LOSING SEMI-FINALISTS
[England scored 12 competition points in this Round of the 2001-2002 IRB World Sevens Series]

FIRST PRUDENTIAL TOUR MATCH

[ENGLAND XV: [*Other squad members:* Balshaw (withdrew due to injury), K. Bracken (withdrew due to injury, replaced by Andy Gomarsall), B. Cohen (withdrew), Mark Cornwell (withdrew due to injury), Dallaglio (captain; withdrew due to injury), D. Danaher (withdrew due to injury), Matt Dawson (withdrew due to injury, replaced by Nick Walshe), Duncombe (withdrew), W. Greenwood (withdrew due to illness, being replaced by Ben Johnston), J. Lewsey (withdrew), Robert 'Robbie' Morris (*prop*), Scarbrough (*wing/full back*) (withdrew due to injury, being replaced by Kevin Sorrell), S. Shaw (withdrew due to injury, replaced by Ed Pearce), Sheridan (withdrew due to injury, replaced by Alex Codling), M. Stephenson

(withdrew), Tindall (withdrew due to injury), Jonny Wilkinson (withdrew), M. Worsley (withdrew due to injury, replaced by Robbie Morris)]]
(squad of 27)
[Steve Borthwick, Alex Brown, Danny Grewcock, Richard Hill (2) and Dan Luger were all unavailable for this match due to injury; Julian White was initially unavailable due to injury and then on 14th May 2002 a RFU hearing found him guilty of fighting an opponent in a Zurich Premiership match on 5th May 2002 and thus banned him for 3 weeks; Martin Johnson, Lewis Moody, Neil Back, Charlie Hodgson, Austin Healey and Jason Robinson were all unavailable due to club commitments; Lawrence Dallaglio was made England captain on 30th April 2002 but withdrew from this match due to injury; Nick Duncombe, Josh Lewsey, Ben Johnston and Michael Stephenson all selected but then withdrew on 14th May 2002 as they were now required to play for the England Sevens team; Ben Cohen selected but then withdrew on 14th May 2002 as he had reached the maximum number of games permitted by an agreement between the RFU and the English Zurich Premiership clubs; Jonny Wilkinson selected but then withdrew on 14th May 2002 after Clive Woodward decided to rest him for this match; Kyran Bracken, Will Greenwood and Dan Scarbrough withdrew on 20th May 2002; Ben Johnston was added to the squad again on 20th May 2002!; Matt Dawson withdrew on 22nd May 2002; Robbie Morris, Alex Codling, Grant Seely, Hugh Vyvyan, Nick Walshe, Phil Christophers, Geoff Appleford, Kevin Sorrell, James Simpson-Daniel, Dan Scarbrough and Michael Horak were all not part of the original squad]
[BARBARIANS: [*English squad members:* J. Leonard, Matt Perry (withdrew due to injury)]]
[Rod Macqueen and Philippe Sella were both appointed on 25th March 2002; Rod Macqueen was the Coach when Australia both won the World Cup at the Millennium Stadium on 6th November 1999 and beat the British & Irish Lions 2-1 in a series held in June-July 2001]
[ENGLAND XV: [HEAD COACH: *Clive Woodward*] **[COACH:** *Andy Robinson*] **[ASSISTANT COACH:** *Phil Larder*]]
[BARBARIANS: [COACH: *Rod Macqueen* (AU)] **[ASSISTANT COACH:** *Philippe Sella* (FR)]]
CAPTAIN: *Phil Vickery* [England XV]
CAPTAIN: *Todd Blackadder* (NZ) [Barbarians]
26th May **ENGLAND XV** 53 **BARBARIANS** 29
Twickenham
[ENGLAND XV: [*Team:* Trevor Woodman, Steve Thompson (2), Vickery, Alex Codling, Hugh Vyvyan, P. Gustard, Forrester, J. Worsley, Gomarsall, Walder, Christophers, Ben Johnston, Appleford, J. Simpson-Daniel, Michael Horak]
[*Bench:* Flatman (rep), Phil Jones (rep), Edward 'Ed' Pearce (*lock/flanker/number 8*) (rep), M. Regan (rep), Seely (rep), Kevin Sorrell (*centre*) (rep), Walshe (rep)]
[*Scorers:* **tries** by Forrester, Steve Thompson, J. Simpson-Daniel, Horak, Christophers (2) and Walder, **penalty goals** by Walder (2), **conversions** by Walder (5) and Gomarsall]]
[BARBARIANS: [*Team:* Christian Califano (FR), Drotske (SA), A. Garvey (SA), K. Roche, Ian Jones (2) (NZ), Todd Blackadder (NZ), Kupu Vanisi (NZ), Simon Taylor (2) (SC), Pichot (AR), van Straaten (SA), Lomu (NZ), Pita Alatini (NZ), Glas (FR), Pieter Rossouw (SA), C. Cullen (NZ)]
[*Bench:* Thomas Castaignède (FR) (*fly half/centre*) (rep), C. Dowd (NZ) (rep), Lam (SAM) (rep), Kronfeld (NZ) (rep), Mauro Ledesma (AR) (*hooker*) (rep), P. Montgomery (SA) (*fly half/full back*) (rep), Mark Robinson (2) (NZ) (*scrum half*) (rep)]

[*Scorers:* **tries** by Ian Jones (NZ), P. Montgomery (SA), Simon Taylor (SC) (2) and Lam (SAM), **conversions** by van Straaten (SA) (2)]]

SECOND PRUDENTIAL TOUR MATCH

[**COACH:** *Rod Macqueen* (AU)] [**ASSISTANT COACH:** *Philippe Sella* (FR)]
CAPTAIN: *Pat Lam* (SAM)

[29th May WALES XV 25 **BARBARIANS** 40]
Millennium Stadium, Cardiff

[*Team:* C. Dowd (NZ), Ibañez (FR), Reggiardo (AR), George Wilson 'Doddie' Weir (SC), K. Roche, Patrick 'Pat' Lam (SAM), Kronfeld (NZ), Jim Williams (AU), Mark Robinson (2) (NZ), van Straaten (SA), Noon, Alatini (NZ), Ollie Smith (2), Gerhardus Marthinus 'Thinus' Delport (SA), P. Montgomery (SA)]

[*Bench:* Botham (*centre/wing/full back*) (rep), Chesney (*lock/flanker*) (rep), A. Garvey (SA) (rep), Ledesma (AR) (rep), Pieter Muller (SA) (*centre*) (rep), Ryan Strudwick (SA) (*lock/number 8*) (rep), Ofisa 'Junior' Tonu'u (NZ) (*scrum half/fly half*) (rep)]

[*Scorers:* **tries** by Ollie Smith, Delport (SA) (2), A. Garvey (SA) (2) and Lam (SAM), **conversions** by van Straaten (SA) (5)]

EMIRATES AIRLINE CARDIFF SEVENS
IRB WORLD SEVENS SERIES 2001-2002 ROUND 12

Millennium Stadium, Cardiff

[*Tournament squad:* P. Sanderson, Roques, Greening, Appleford (never travelled as injured, replaced by Phil Jones), Noon, T. May, Sampson, M. Stephenson, R. Thirlby, Gollings, R. Haughton, Duncombe, Phil Jones]

(squad of 12)

[James Forrester, James Simpson-Daniel and Henry Paul were unavailable for this tournament due to club commitments; Phil Jones returned to Rugby League in August 2004 and then came back to Rugby Union in August 2005 when he joined Sedgley Park]

[**MANAGER:** *John Elliott*] [**COACH:** *Joe Lydon*] [**ASSISTANT COACHES:** *Damian McGrath & Mike Friday*]

CAPTAIN: *Phil Greening*

First Round - Pool 'B'

31st May FRANCE 7 **ENGLAND** 10
[*Team:* T. May, Greening, P. Sanderson, Duncombe, Gollings, R. Thirlby, R. Haughton]
[*Bench:* Phil Jones, Noon, Roques (rep), Sampson (rep), M. Stephenson (rep)]
[*Scorers:* **tries** by R. Haughton and M. Stephenson]

31st May RUSSIA 10 **ENGLAND** 28
[*Team:* Roques, Greening, Noon, Duncombe, Gollings, Phil Jones, Sampson]
[*Bench:* R. Haughton, T. May (rep), P. Sanderson (rep), R. Thirlby (rep)]
[*Scorers:* **tries** by Sampson (2), Gollings and R. Thirlby, **conversions** by Gollings (4)]

31st May WALES 14 **ENGLAND** 28
[*Team:* Roques, Greening, P. Sanderson, Duncombe, Noon, Phil Jones, R. Haughton]
[*Bench:* Gollings (rep), T. May (rep), Sampson, R. Thirlby (rep)]
[*Scorers:* **tries** by P. Sanderson, R. Haughton, Phil Jones and Roques, **conversions** by Phil Jones (3) and Gollings]

Quarter-Final

1st June SCOTLAND 0 **ENGLAND** 17
[*Team:* Roques, Greening, P. Sanderson, Duncombe, Gollings, R. Thirlby, R. Haughton]

[*Bench:* T. May (rep), Noon (rep), Sampson (rep)]
[*Scorers:* **tries** by Gollings (2) and R. Thirlby, **conversion** by Gollings]
Semi-Final
1st June FIJI 0 **ENGLAND** 24
[*Team:* Roques, Greening, P. Sanderson, Duncombe, Gollings, R. Thirlby, Sampson]
[*Bench:* R. Haughton (rep), T. May (rep), Noon (rep)]
[*Scorers:* **tries** by Sampson (2), R. Haughton and Gollings, **conversions** by Gollings (2)]
Final
1st June NEW ZEALAND 24 **ENGLAND*** 12
[*Team:* Roques, Greening, P. Sanderson, Duncombe, Gollings, R. Thirlby, Sampson]
[*Bench:* R. Haughton (rep), T. May (rep), Noon (rep)]
[*Scorers:* **tries** by R. Thirlby and Gollings, **conversion** by Gollings]
POSITION: LOSING FINALISTS
FANTASY: *WINNERS*
[England scored 16 competition points in this Round of the 2001-2002 IRB World Sevens Series]
RANKING: 3RD 126 [*New Zealand 198*, South Africa 136, Fiji 122, Australia 108, Samoa 90, Argentina 86, Wales 50, France 20, Scotland 13, USA 12, Canada 8, Namibia 2, Cook Islands 2, Morocco 1]

THIRD PRUDENTIAL TOUR MATCH

[**COACH:** *Rod Macqueen* (AU)] [**ASSISTANT COACH:** *Philippe Sella* (FR)]
CAPTAIN: *Ian Jones (2)* (NZ)
[1st June SCOTLAND XV 27 **BARBARIANS** 47]
Murrayfield
[*Team:* C. Dowd (NZ), Ledesma (AR), Reggiardo (AR), Ian Jones (2) (NZ), Strudwick (SA), Chesney, Kronfeld (NZ), Jim Williams (AU), Mark Robinson (2) (NZ), van Straaten (SA), P. Rossouw (SA), Alatini (NZ), P. Muller (SA), Delport (SA), P. Montgomery (SA)]
[*Bench:* Botham (rep), Barry Everitt (IR) (*fly half*) (rep), A. Garvey (SA) (rep), P. Gustard (rep), Ibañez (FR) (*hooker*) (rep), K. Roche (*lock/flanker/number 8*) (rep), Tonu'u (NZ) (rep)]
[*Scorers:* **tries** by Chesney, Jim Williams (AU), Alatini (NZ), Kronfeld (NZ), Mark Robinson (NZ), Ian Jones (NZ) and P. Muller (SA), **conversions** by van Straaten (SA) (5) and Everitt (IR)]

LISBON SEVENS

Lisbon
[PENGUINS: [*Tournament squad:* David 'Dave' McCallum (AU) (*centre*), P. Sanderson, Peter Miller (AU) (*wing*), Gregor Lawson (SC) (*fly half*), Faimafili *Caine* Elisara (HOL) (*forward*), Meenan, Timothy 'Tim' O'Brien (2) (AU) (*forward*), Waisale Serevi (FIJ) (*fly half*), Sharman (SC), Shane Thompson (CAN) (*scrum half/centre*)]**]**
(squad of 10)
[Gregor Lawson was the son of Alan Lawson]
[SAMURAI: [*Tournament squad:* Engelbrecht (SA), Earnshaw, B. Lewitt, Ryan Davis (*back*), Shaun Welch (SC) (*scrum half*), Friday, R. Thirlby, Oriol Ripol (SP) (*wing*), N. Drake, William 'Will' Oldham (SC) (*forward*), Bromley (*back*)]**]**
(squad of 10)
[Mike Friday originally travelled as Coach; Ben Lewitt played for the Samurai in the Hong Kong Tens at Hong Kong Football Club on 24th-25th March 2004]
[PENGUINS: [**MANAGER:** *Craig Brown* (NZ)] [**ASSISTANT MANAGER:** *John Kerr* (SC)] [**COACH:** *Bill Calcraft* (AU)]**]**

[SAMURAI: [COACH: *Colin Hillman* (WA)] **[PLAYER-COACH:** *Mike Friday*]]
CAPTAIN: *Waisale Serevi* (FIJ) [Penguins]
CAPTAIN: *Gerrie Engelbrecht* (SA) [Samurai]

First Round - Group ?

[8th June Lousã (*POR*) 0 **PENGUINS** 68]
[*Team:*]
[*Bench:*]
[*Scorers:*]
[8th June Belenenses (*POR*) 7 **PENGUINS** 38]
[*Team:*]
[*Bench:*]
[*Scorers:*]
[8th June White Hart Marauders 12 **PENGUINS** 35]
[*Team:*]
[*Bench:*]
[*Scorers:*]

First Round - Group ?

[8th June Samurai Sharks L **SAMURAI** W]
[*Team:*]
[*Bench:*]
[*Scorers:*]
[8th June GDS Cascais (*POR*) L **SAMURAI** W]
[*Team:*]
[*Bench:*]
[*Scorers:*]
[8th June Técnico (*POR*) L **SAMURAI** W]
[*Team:*]
[*Bench:*]
[*Scorers:*]

Quarter Final - Group ?

[9th June GDS Cascais (*POR*) 0 **PENGUINS** 49]
[*Team:*]
[*Bench:*]
[*Scorers:*]
[9th June Euskarians (*FR*) 7 **PENGUINS** 35]
[*Team:*]
[*Bench:*]
[*Scorers:*]

Quarter Final - Group ?

[9th June Direito (*POR*) L **SAMURAI** W]
[*Team:*]
[*Bench:*]
[*Scorers:*]
[9th June White Hart Marauders L **SAMURAI** W]
[*Team:*]
[*Bench:*]
[*Scorers:*]

Semi-Final
[9th June White Hart Marauders 0 **PENGUINS** 47]
[*Team:*]
[*Bench:*]
[*Scorers:* **try** by W. Serevi (FIJ)]
[9th June Euskarians (*FR*) 5 **SAMURAI** 15]
[*Team:*]
[*Bench:*]
[*Scorers:*]
Final
[9th June **PENGUINS** 24 **SAMURAI** 38]
[PENGUINS: [*Team:*]
[*Bench:*]
[*Scorers:* **try** by W. Serevi (FIJ)]]
[SAMURAI: [*Team:* Friday]
[*Bench:*]
[*Scorers:* **tries** by Ripol (SP) (2), B. Lewitt, R. Davies, Bromley and Engelbrecht (SA), **conversions** by ? (4)]]
POSITION: LOSING FINALISTS [Penguins]
POSITION: WINNERS [Samurai]

IRB U21 WORLD CHAMPIONSHIP

South Africa
[*Other squad members:* A. Elliott, Goodridge (returned home as injured, replaced by Jonny Hylton), Andy Higgins (2), A. McKenzie, Chris Morgan (*flanker*) (never travelled as injured, replaced by Magnus Lund)]
(squad of 26)
[On 12th November 2001 the IRB announced that they would be holding an U21 World Championship in South Africa in June 2002; Brian Ashton was appointed on 24th April 2002; James Forrester, Olly Barkley and Alex Crockett were unavailable for this tournament due to injury; England U21 were ranked in Pool D and played their matches against the 3 teams in Pool A; The England U21 squad departed for South Africa on 8th June 2002; Jonny Hylton joined the squad before the New Zealand U21 match as a replacement for the injured Jon Goodridge; David Tibbott, Alex Alesbrook, Brett Sturgess and Andrew Kyriacou travelled later as replacements for Alex Cadwallader, Ian Clarke, Adam Halsey and Ben Gotting respectively; The England U21 squad was stricken by food poisoning shortly before the Ireland U21 match; Nigel Redman won 20 caps for England between 1984-97, was appointed joint Coach of England U19 on 27th October 2000 and was then appointed Assistant Coach of England U19 on 1st November 2001]
(During the First Round a bonus point was awarded for scoring 4 or more tries in a match and for losing by seven points or less)
[MANAGER: *Peter Drewett*] **[COACH:** *Brian Ashton*] **[ASSISTANT COACHES:** *Nigel Redman & Paul Grayson*]
CAPTAIN: *Mark Soden*
First Round - Pool 'D'
[14th Jun NEW ZEALAND U21 67 **ENGLAND U21** 23]
Ellis Park Stadium, Johannesburg
[*Team:* M. Holford, Buckland, Irish, S. Hooper, M. Purdy, I. Clarke, Scaysbrook, Soden, Paul

Hodgson, M. Honeyben, J. Rudd, Cadwallader, Billig, Simon Hunt, Voyce]
[*Bench:* N. Cox, Phil Davies (3) (*flanker/number 8*), Gotting (*hooker*), B. Hampson, Mike McCarthy (*lock*), Thrower, Sam Vesty (*fly half/centre/full back*)]
[*Scorers:* **tries** by M. Holford (2) and Billig, **penalty goals** by M. Honeyben (2), **conversion** by Simon Hunt]

CAPTAIN: *Martin Purdy*

[18th Jun ITALY U21 12 **ENGLAND U21** 41 **BP**]
Rand Afrikaans University Stadium, Johannesburg
[*Team:* N. Cox, Gotting, Adam Halsey, M. McCarthy, M. Purdy, I. Clarke, Magnus Lund, Phil Davies (3), B. Hampson, Vesty, J. Rudd, Spencer Davey, Voyce, Hylton, Billig]
[*Bench:* Buckland (rep), P. Hodgson (*flanker/scrum half*) (rep), M. Holford, M. Honeyben, S. Hooper (*lock*) (rep), Soden (*flanker/number 8*) (rep), Thrower (rep)]
[*Scorers:* **tries** by Hylton, M. Purdy, Billig, I. Clarke and Voyce, **penalty goals** by Vesty (2), **conversions** by Vesty (5)]

CAPTAIN: *Mark Soden* [*Martin Purdy took over when Mark Soden was sent off in the 1st half*]

[21st Jun ARGENTINA U21 17 **ENGLAND U21** 20]
Witts University Stadium, Johannesburg
[*Team:* M. Holford, Buckland, Irish, S. Hooper, M. Purdy, Phil Davies (3), Lund, Soden, P. Hodgson, B. Hampson, Simon Hunt, David Tibbott, Billig, Voyce, Hylton]
[*Bench:* N. Cox (rep), Gotting, P. Hodgson, M. McCarthy (rep), J. Rudd (*wing*) (rep), Vesty (rep), ?]
[*Scorers:* **tries** by Voyce and Hylton, **penalty goals** by Voyce (2), **conversions** by Simon Hunt and Vesty]
[England U21 failed to score enough bonus points to get into the top 4 teams and thus did not have a chance of playing for a place in the final]

CAPTAIN: *Martin Purdy*

5th/6th/7th/8th Place Semi-Final

[25th Jun IRELAND U21 28 **ENGLAND U21*** 15]
Rand Afrikaans University Stadium, Johannesburg
[*Team:* N. Cox, Buckland, Irish, S. Hooper, M. Purdy, Alesbrook, Scaysbrook, Phil Davies (3), B. Hampson, M. Honeyben, Voyce, Tibbott, Simon Hunt, J. Rudd, Hylton]
[*Bench:* P. Hodgson (rep), M. Holford (rep), Andrew Kyriacou (*hooker*) (rep), Lund (*flanker*) (rep), M. McCarthy (rep), Brett Sturgess (*prop*) (rep), Vesty (rep)]
[*Scorers:* **tries** by Phil Davies and S. Hooper (2)]

CAPTAIN: *Mark Soden*

7th/8th Place Play-Off

[28th Jun ARGENTINA U21 14 **ENGLAND U21** 74]
Ellis Park Stadium, Johannesburg
[*Team:* M. Holford, Buckland, Sturgess, S. Hooper, M. McCarthy, Scaysbrook, Lund, Soden, P. Hodgson, Vesty, Simon Hunt, Tibbott, Billig, J. Rudd, Hylton]
[*Bench:* Ed Burrill (*full back*) (rep), S. Davey (*centre*) (rep), Phil Davies (3) (rep), B. Hampson (rep), Kyriacou (rep), ?, ?]
[*Scorers:* **tries** by Hylton, M. McCarthy, Simon Hunt (3), Billig, J. Rudd (3), P. Hodgson and Scaysbrook, **penalty goal** by Simon Hunt, **conversions** by Simon Hunt (8)]

POSITION: 7TH PLACE

FANTASY: ***5TH PLACE***

PENGUINS TOUR TO AMERICA AND CANADA 2002

[**MANAGERS:** *Bill Calcraft* (AU) & *Alan Wright*] [**PLAYER-COACH:** *Craig Brown* (NZ)]
[*Other squad members:* Chris Allen (2) (IR) (*hooker*), Paul Beal (*prop*), Craig Brown (NZ) (*flanker*), Collazo (FR) (*prop*), Earnshaw (*flanker/number 8*), C. Elisara (HOL) (*lock/number 8*), C. Harrison, Graeme Inglis (IR) (*centre/wing*), Eion Keane (IR) (*lock*), D. McCallum (AU) (*centre/wing*), Meenan (*fly half/full back*), Rory Jenkins (*flanker*), G. Lawson (SC) (*fly half/full back*), Tim O'Brien (2) (AU) (*flanker*), J. O'Reilly, Eric Peters (SC) (*flanker/number 8*) (withdrew), Martin Ridley (AU) (*centre*), Peter Robertson (SC) (*hooker*), Paul Rollerson (*lock*), Shane Thompson (CAN) (*centre*), Tamati (NZ), Matthew 'Matt' Volland (*prop*)]
(squad of 23)
[This tour replaced the scheduled trip to China, which was cancelled at short notice; Bill Calcraft and Alan Wright were Manager for the New York and Toronto legs respectively!; Eric Peters left the tour on 16th June 2002 as he was now required to join the simultaneous Scotland tour of Canada and America]
CAPTAIN: *Mark Denney*
[18th Jun Toronto Renegades (*CAN*) 7 **PENGUINS** 32]
Oakville Crusaders RC, Crusaders Park, Oakville, Ontario
[*Team:* Mark Denney]
[*Bench:*]
[*Scorers:*]

ENGLAND TOUR TO ARGENTINA 2002

[**HEAD COACH:** *Clive Woodward*] [**COACH:** *Andy Robinson*] [**ASSISTANT COACH:** *Phil Larder*]
[*Other squad members:* Peter 'Pete' Anglesea (*flanker/number 8*) (tm), Thomas 'Tom' Beim (*wing/full back*) (tm), Cueto (*wing*) (tm), D. Danaher (tm), Rob Fidler (tm), J. Lewsey (*fly half/centre/wing/full back*) (never travelled as injured, replaced by Tom May), L. Lloyd (*centre/wing*) (never travelled as injured, replaced by Tom Beim), May (tm), Robbie Morris (tm), E. Pearce (never travelled as injured, replaced by Rob Fidler), David Rees (2) (tm), S. Shaw (never travelled as injured, replaced by Ed Pearce), J. Simpson-Daniel (never travelled as injured, replaced by David Rees (2))]
(squad of 30)
[This tour replaced the scheduled trip to Fiji, Samoa and Tonga in June-July 2002 which was cancelled by the RFU on 26th March 2002 due to a dispute over the playing itinerary; Lawrence Dallaglio was made England captain on 30th April 2002 but was unavailable for this tour due to injury; Julian White, Tom Palmer (2), Mark Cornwell, Steve Borthwick, Kyran Bracken, Dan Luger, Mike Catt, Mike Tindall, Steve Booth, Iain Balshaw, Dan Scarbrough and Matt Perry all unavailable due to injury; Martin Johnson, Danny Grewcock, Richard Hill (2), Neil Back, Matt Dawson, Jonny Wilkinson, Austin Healey, Will Greenwood and Jason Robinson were all rested for this tour by Clive Woodward; Simon Shaw initially selected but withdrew due to injury, being replaced by Ed Pearce who then himself withdrew due to injury and was replaced by Rob Fidler; The England squad departed for Argentina on 10th June 2002; Tom Beim was capped for England Schools 18 Group in April 1993; David Rees (2) retired in May 2010]

SHELL CUP MATCH

CAPTAIN: *Phil Vickery*

22nd Jun ARGENTINA 18 **ENGLAND** 26

CA Vélez Sársfield, Estadio José Amalfitani, Buenos Aires

[*Team:* Flatman, Steve Thompson (2), Vickery, Codling, Kay, A. Sanderson, Moody, J. Worsley, Gomarsall, C. Hodgson, Christophers, Ben Johnston, Appleford, Stimpson, Horak]

[*Bench:* Balding (*number 8*), M. Regan, K. Sorrell, H. Vyvyan (*lock/number 8*), Walder, Walshe, Trevor Woodman]

[*Scorers:* **tries** by Kay and Christophers, **penalty goals** by C. Hodgson (3) and Stimpson, **conversions** by C. Hodgson (2)]

ENGLAND COUNTIES TOUR TO CHILE 2002

[**MANAGER:** *Rob Udwin*] [**ASSISTANT MANAGER:** *Danny Hodgson*] [**COACH:** *Bob Hood*] [**ASSISTANT COACH:** *Tommy Borthwick*]

[*Other squad members:* Jan Bonney (*fly half/centre*) (tm), Shaun Brady (*flanker/number 8*) (tm), Andy Brown (tm), Lee Fortey (*prop*) (tm), Luke Jones (*flanker*) (tm), Ian Kennedy (*fly half/full back*) (tm), Neil Kerfoot (*wing*) (tm), Andrew 'Andy' Lee (*fly half*) (never travelled as withdrew, replaced by Craig Raymond), Simon Martin (*centre*) (tm), Dave Muckalt (*lock/flanker/number 8*) (tm), Ricky Pellow (tm), Wayne Reed (*prop*) (never travelled as withdrew, replaced by Terry Sigley), Dean Schofield (*lock*) (tm), John Sewell (2) (*number 8*) (tm), Terry Sigley (*prop*) (tm), Glen Wilson (*flanker/number 8*) (tm), J. Winterbottom (*lock*) (tm)]

(squad of 26)

[On 21st September 2001 the RFU approved the formation of an England Counties team, which would consist of players from outside the Zurich Premiership who had played in the County Championship; Lee Soper was unavailable for this tour due to military commitments; Wayne Reed and Andy Lee withdrew due to work commitments; The England Counties squad departed for Chile on 18th June 2002; Luke Jones played for England Students; Jan Bonney was capped as a wing for England Colts in March 1990]

CAPTAIN: *Tony Windo*

[29th Jun CHILE 21 **ENGLAND COUNTIES** 33]

Centro de Alto Rendimiento de Rugby, La Reina, Santiago

[*Team:* Anthony 'Tony' Windo, Gregg Botterman, Richard Moore (*prop*), ?, Jason Oakes (*lock*), ?, ?, ?, ?, Craig Raymond (*fly half*), Mark Kirkby (*wing*), Mike Davies, ?, David 'Dave' Strettle (*wing*), Andrew 'Andy' Hodgson]

[*Bench:* Lawn (rep), Michael 'Mike' Scott (1) (*fly half*) (rep), ?, ?, ?, ?, ?]

[*Scorers:* **tries** by Craig Raymond, Strettle, Kirkby (2) and Lawn, **conversions** by Craig Raymond (4)]

COMMONWEALTH SEVENS

City of Manchester Stadium

[*Tournament squad:* Roques, P. Sanderson, H. Paul, Amor, Duncombe, Gollings, Sampson, Appleford, J. Lewsey, Greening, Marcus St. Hilaire (*wing*), R. Thirlby]

(squad of 12)

[This tournament was played on a pitch which was only 92 metres long and 6 metres narrower than normal; Leon Lloyd was unavailable for this tournament due to injury; Jason Robinson was unavailable due to family commitments; Lawrence Dallaglio, Declan Danaher, James Forrester, Andy Hazell, Lewis Moody, Mike Friday, Ian Vass,

***Austin Healey, Nigel Simpson, Mark Cueto, Dan Luger and Jason Robinson were all included in a preliminary squad of 25 selected on 13th December 2001; Neil Baxter, Harry Ellis, Russ Earnshaw, Richard Haughton, Ben Johnston, Jamie Noon, James Simpson-Daniel, Michael Stephenson and Fraser Waters were all included in an original 20 man training squad on 25th June 2002; Michael Horak and Marcus St. Hilaire were included in a revised 20 man training squad on 2nd July 2002 after Fraser Waters and Ben Johnston withdrew due to injury; England played practice matches against Wales, Scotland and the Samurai at Coventry on 7th July 2002; Richard Haughton and James Simpson-Daniel were included in a provisional 14 man training squad on 11th July 2002; The final 12 man tournament squad was announced on 24th July 2002 with James Simpson-Daniel not being selected due to injury; Marcus St. Hilaire was capped for England at Rugby League in October 1999, played in this tournament after Leeds Rhinos released him from his Rugby League contract, returned to Rugby League on 23rd August 2002 when he joined Huddersfield and played Rugby League for England in the Rugby League World Sevens in February 2003*]**

[**MANAGER:** *John Elliott*] [**COACH:** *Joe Lydon*] [**ASSISTANT COACHES:** *Damian McGrath & Mike Friday*]

CAPTAIN: *Phil Greening*

First Round - Pool 'C'

2nd Aug **ENGLAND** 24 COOK ISLANDS 12
[*Team:* P. Sanderson, Greening, J. Lewsey, Duncombe, Gollings, H. Paul, R. Thirlby]
[*Bench:* Amor, Appleford (rep), Roques (rep), Sampson (rep), St. Hilaire]
[*Scorers:* **tries** by R. Thirlby, Gollings and J. Lewsey (2), **conversions** by Gollings (2)]

2nd Aug **ENGLAND** 33 KENYA 12
[*Team:* Roques, Greening, H. Paul, Amor, Gollings, Appleford, St. Hilaire]
[*Bench:* Duncombe, J. Lewsey, Sampson (rep), P. Sanderson (rep), R. Thirlby (rep)]
[*Scorers:* **tries** by Gollings, H. Paul (2), Greening and Sampson, **conversions** by Amor (4)]

3rd Aug **ENGLAND** 19 SAMOA 7
[*Team:* P. Sanderson, Greening, J. Lewsey, Amor, Gollings, H. Paul, R. Thirlby]
[*Bench:* Appleford (rep), Duncombe (rep), Roques (rep), Sampson, St. Hilaire]
[*Scorers:* **tries** by Greening and Amor (2), **conversions** by Amor (2)]

Quarter-Final

3rd Aug **ENGLAND*** 5 FIJI 7
[*Team:* Roques, Greening, J. Lewsey, Amor, Gollings, H. Paul, Sampson]
[*Bench:* Appleford, Duncombe (rep), P. Sanderson (rep), St. Hilaire, R. Thirlby (rep)]
[*Scorers:* **try** by Sampson]

[Plate Semi-Final:]

[4th Aug **ENGLAND** 29 CANADA 0 **]**
[*Team:* Roques, Greening, P. Sanderson, Duncombe, H. Paul, Appleford, J. Lewsey]
[*Bench:* Amor, Gollings (rep), Sampson (rep), St. Hilaire (rep), R. Thirlby]
[*Scorers:* **tries** by J. Lewsey, P. Sanderson, Greening and Sampson (2), **conversions** by H. Paul (2)]

[Plate Final:]

[4th Aug **ENGLAND** 36 AUSTRALIA 12 **]**
[*Team:* Roques, Greening, P. Sanderson, Duncombe, Gollings, H. Paul, J. Lewsey]
[*Bench:* Amor (rep), Appleford (rep), Sampson (rep), St. Hilaire]
[*Scorers:* **tries** by Gollings, Greening, Roques, J. Lewsey, Duncombe and H. Paul,

conversions by Gollings (3)]
POSITION: LOSING QUARTER-FINALISTS [*PLATE WINNERS*]

DEREK MORGAN MATCH

[BRITISH STUDENTS: [MANAGER: *Ron Tennick*]]
[PENGUINS: [PLAYER-COACH: *Craig Brown* (NZ)]]
CAPTAIN: *??* [British Students]
CAPTAIN: *Tim O'Brien (2)* (AU) [Penguins]
[2nd Oct **BRITISH STUDENTS** 17 **PENGUINS** 50]
Iffley Road, Oxford
[BRITISH STUDENTS: [*Team:* Tom Snellgrove (WA), N. Clark, R. Hopkins, A. Harris, Dylan Alexander, Daniel 'Dan' Teague (SC), Joe El Abd, T. Hayman, Gaunt, M. Honeyben, K. Dixon, R. Hunt, Gareth Chapman (WA), William 'Will' Ellerby, Murray Strang (SC)]
[*Bench:* James Boyle, B. Durham (*flanker/number 8*), Gotting, Will Green (2) (rep), Simon Legg (*prop*), Andy Spence (SC) (*fly half*), Strettle (*wing*)]
[*Scorers:* **tries** by K. Dixon and W. Green, **penalty goal** by M. Honeyben, **conversions** by M. Honeyben (2)]]
[PENGUINS: [*Team:* P. Beal, Conrad Burke (SA), Kevin Tkachuk (CAN), Steven 'Steve' Martin (WA), J. Winterbottom, White-Cooper, Tim O'Brien (2) (AU), Stewart Eru (NZ), Paul Newton, Eddie McLaughlin (NZ), ?, D. McCallum (AU), John Allen (2) (AU), William 'Will' Rubie, H. Graham]
[*Bench:* C. Brown (NZ) (*flanker*), John Dick (*wing*), Friday (*scrum half*), Mark Lloyd (*flanker*), Ryan O'Neill (*full back*), Sam Reay (*centre*), John Simmons (2) (NZ)]
[*Scorers:* **tries** by Rubie (3), D. McCallum (AU), John Allen (AU), McLaughlin (NZ), P. Newton and H. Graham, **conversions** by H. Graham (5)]]
[Match to celebrate Derek Morgan's appointment as President of the RFU]
[Ron Tennick played for an England XV against the Rest in a Final England Trial Match at Twickenham on 18th January 1969]

NEW ZEALAND TOUR TO ENGLAND, FRANCE AND WALES 2002

FIRST INVESTEC CHALLENGE MATCH

[**HEAD COACH:** *Clive Woodward*] [**COACH:** *Andy Robinson*] [**ASSISTANT COACH:** *Phil Larder*]
CAPTAIN: *Martin Johnson*
9th Nov **ENGLAND** 31 NEW ZEALAND 28
Twickenham
[*Team:* Trevor Woodman, Steve Thompson (2), Vickery, Martin Johnson, Grewcock, Moody, Richard Hill (2), Dallaglio, Matt Dawson, Jonny Wilkinson, B. Cohen, Tindall, W. Greenwood, J. Simpson-Daniel, Jason Robinson]
[*Bench:* Back (*flanker*) (rep), Healey (rep), Ben Johnston (rep), Kay (rep), J. Leonard, M. Regan, Stimpson]
[*Scorers:* **tries** by Moody, Jonny Wilkinson and B. Cohen, **penalty goals** by Jonny Wilkinson (3), **drop goal** by Jonny Wilkinson, **conversions** by Jonny Wilkinson (2)]

REMEMBRANCE MATCH

[NO COACH NOMINATED]

CAPTAIN: *Doddie Weir* (SC)

[12th Nov COMBINED SERVICES (*SER*) 27 **BARBARIANS*** 26]

Devonport Services RFC, Rectory Stadium, Second Avenue, Devonport, Plymouth

[*Team:* Mark Dorrington, Ben Phillips (WA), Christopher 'Chris' Horsman, Andrew 'Andy' Hawken (CO), D. Weir (SC), G. Willis, Hedley Verity, Ultan O'Callaghan (IR), Ian Fairley (SC), Killian Keane (IR), Matthew Watkins (WA), Kanogo Njuru (SWE), Murdoch (AU), Matthew 'Matt' Mostyn (IR), Wayne Proctor (WA)]

[*Bench:* Richard Baxter (*flanker/number 8*) (rep), Ross Blake (SC) (*scrum half/fly half*), Ian Brown (*lock*) (rep), Richard *Graham* Dawe (*hooker*) (rep), Ngalu Taufo'ou (TON) (*prop*) (rep), Piran Trethewey (NZ) (*wing*) (rep), Winney (rep)]

[*Scorers:* **tries** by Verity, D. Weir (SC), Horsman and W. Proctor (WA), **conversions** by K. Keane (IR) (3)]

[Match to commemorate the members of the British uniformed services who lost their lives during armed conflict]

ENGLAND U21 TRIAL MATCHES

[*Other England U21 South XV squad members:* Tom Allen (*centre*), James Bailey (*wing*), Matthew Bourne (*flanker*), Ian Critchley (*prop*), Daniel 'Danny' Gray (*fly half*), Duncan Hayward (*centre*), P. Hodgson, Ross Laidlaw (*fly half*), Ian Martin (*scrum half*), Daniel 'Dan' Miller (*prop*), Ugo Monye (*centre/wing*), Jonathan 'Jon' Pendlebury (*lock*), Tom Pierce (*flanker*), Mark Rimmer (lock), Christopher 'Chris' Rowland (*prop/hooker*), M. Styles (*flanker/number 8*), S. Walton]

(squad of 23)

[Ian Critchley toured Canada, New Zealand and Australia with England Schools 18 Group in July-August 2001; Chris Rowland, Jon Pendlebury and James Bailey played for England in the U19 World Championship in Italy in March 2002; Peter Drewett was appointed in September 2002; Jon Callard, Nigel Redman and Paul Grayson were all appointed on 24th October 2002; Jon Callard was capped for England in November 1993]

[**MANAGER:** *Peter Drewett*] [**COACH:** *Jonathan 'Jon' Callard*] [**ASSISTANT COACHES:** *Nigel Redman & Paul Grayson*]

CAPTAIN: *??*

[13th Nov FRANCE U21 WEST XV 22 **ENGLAND U21 SOUTH XV** 18]

Centre National de Rugby, Domaine de Bellejame, Marcoussis

[*Team:* Matthew 'Matt' Stevens, Joshua 'Josh' Lord (*flanker*), Richard Martin-Redman, Pat Sykes (*wing*), Andrew 'Andy' Frost]

[*Bench:* Thomas 'Tom' Lambert (*hooker*) (rep), ?, ?, ?, ?, ?, ?]

[*Scorers:* **tries** by A. Frost and T. Lambert, **penalty goals** by A. Frost (2), **conversion** by A. Frost]

[*Other England U21 North XV squad members:* Adam Caves (*hooker*) (never travelled as withdrew, replaced by Richard Oxley), Peter Cook (2) (*prop*), Christian 'Chris' Day (*lock*), Brett Deacon (*flanker/number 8*), Alex Gluth (*prop*), Danny 'Dan' Hipkiss (*centre*), Christopher 'Chris' Hyndman (*centre*), Stephen James 'Steve' Jones (2) (*fly half/full back*), Kyriacou, Lund, Neil Mason (*flanker*), Chris Mayor (*centre/wing/full back*), Lee Morley (*lock*), Geoffrey 'Geoff' Parling (*lock*), M. Parr, Shaun Richardson (*scrum half*), Benjamin J. 'Ben' Russell (1) (*fly half*), Warren Spragg (*fly half/centre/full back*), Richard Wigglesworth (*scrum half*), B. Woods (*flanker*)]

(squad of 23)
[Chris Day, Geoff Parling and Richard Wigglesworth toured Canada, New Zealand and Australia with England Schools 18 Group in July-August 2001 and played for England in the U19 World Championship in Italy in March 2002; Warren Spragg toured Canada, New Zealand and Australia with England Schools 18 Group in July-August 2001; Ben Russell (1) played for England in the U19 World Championship in Italy in March 2002; Alex Gluth, Adam Caves, Lee Morley and Brett Deacon played for England in the U19 World Championship in Chile in April 2001; Brett Deacon was the brother of Louis Deacon; Steve Jones (2) played for Scotland U21 in February 2004]
[**MANAGER:** *Peter Drewett*] [**COACH:** *Jon Callard*] [**ASSISTANT COACHES:** *Nigel Redman* & *Paul Grayson*]
CAPTAIN: *??*
[13th Nov FRANCE U21 EAST XV 31 **ENGLAND U21 NORTH XV** 20]
Centre National de Rugby, Domaine de Bellejame, Marcoussis
[*Team:* Strettle, Stuart Brown (*full back*)]
[*Bench:* M. Holford (rep), Richard Oxley (*hooker*) (rep), ?, ?, ?, ?, ?]
[*Scorers:* **tries** by Stuart Brown, Strettle and Oxley, **penalty goal** by Stuart Brown, **conversion** by Stuart Brown]

AUSTRALIAN TOUR TO IRELAND, ENGLAND AND ITALY 2002
SECOND INVESTEC CHALLENGE MATCH
COOK CUP MATCH
[**HEAD COACH:** *Clive Woodward*] [**COACH:** *Andy Robinson*] [**ASSISTANT COACH:** *Phil Larder*]
CAPTAIN: *Martin Johnson*
16th Nov **ENGLAND** 32 AUSTRALIA 31
Twickenham
[*Team:* J. Leonard, Steve Thompson (2), Vickery, Martin Johnson, Kay, Moody, Back, Richard Hill (2), Matt Dawson, Jonny Wilkinson, B. Cohen, Tindall, W. Greenwood, J. Simpson-Daniel, Jason Robinson]
[*Bench:* Dallaglio (rep), Gomarsall, Grewcock, Healey (*wing*) (rep), Robbie Morris, M. Regan, Stimpson]
[*Scorers:* **tries** by B. Cohen (2), **penalty goals** by Jonny Wilkinson (6), **conversions** by Jonny Wilkinson (2)]

SOUTH AFRICAN TOUR TO FRANCE, SCOTLAND AND ENGLAND 2002
THIRD INVESTEC CHALLENGE MATCH
[**HEAD COACH:** *Clive Woodward*] [**COACH:** *Andy Robinson*] [**ASSISTANT COACH:** *Phil Larder*]
CAPTAIN: *Martin Johnson*
23rd Nov **ENGLAND** 53 SOUTH AFRICA 3
Twickenham
[*Team:* J. Leonard, Steve Thompson (2), Vickery, Martin Johnson, Kay, Moody, Back, Richard Hill (2), Matt Dawson, Jonny Wilkinson, Christophers, Tindall, W. Greenwood, B. Cohen, Jason Robinson]

[*Bench:* Dallaglio (rep), Gomarsall (rep), Grewcock (rep), Healey (rep), Robbie Morris, M. Regan, Stimpson (rep)]
[*Scorers:* **tries** by B. Cohen, W. Greenwood (2), penalty try, Back, Richard Hill and Dallaglio, **penalty goals** by Jonny Wilkinson (2), **conversions** by Jonny Wilkinson, Matt Dawson, Gomarsall (2) and Stimpson (2)]
[A North v South Challenge was scheduled to be played at Twickenham on 30th November 2002 to raise money for developing rugby nations, but the IRB cancelled this match on 4th October 2002 when it became clear that they would be unable to raise sufficiently competitive teams from both the northern and southern hemispheres because many potential players had extensive club and international commitments in the period in question]

EMIRATES AIRLINE DUBAI RUGBY SEVENS
IRB WORLD SEVENS SERIES 2002-2003 ROUND 1

Dubai Exiles Stadium, Dubai
[*Tournament squad:* Amor, Matthew 'Matt' Cannon (*fly half/centre*), Gollings, R. Haughton, Hylton (*forward/back*), Rob Laird (*back/forward*), Lund (*forward*), Mayor (*back*), Ryan Peacey (*forward*), Benjamin T. 'Ben' Russell (2) (*forward*), Sampson (injured during the tournament), R. Thirlby]
(squad of 12)
[England played a training match against the Army at Aldershot on 25th November 2002; Ben Russell (2) captained England in the U19 World Championship in Italy in March 2002]
[**MANAGER:** *John Elliott*] [**COACH:** *Joe Lydon*] [**ASSISTANT COACH:** *Mike Friday*]
CAPTAIN: *Simon Amor*
First Round - Pool 'B'
6th Dec CANADA 5 **ENGLAND** 26
[*Team:* Ben Russell (2), Amor, Gollings]
[*Bench:*]
[*Scorers:* **tries** by Amor, Ben Russell, R. Thirlby and Lund, **conversions** by Gollings (3)]
6th Dec ARABIAN GULF 5 **ENGLAND** 49
[*Team:* Amor, Gollings]
[*Bench:*]
[*Scorers:* **tries** by R. Haughton (2), Gollings (2), Sampson, Laird and Peacey, **conversions** by Gollings (5) and Amor (2)]
6th Dec WALES 0 **ENGLAND** 33
[*Team:* Amor]
[*Bench:*]
[*Scorers:* **tries** by R. Haughton, Amor, R. Thirlby, Ben Russell and Gollings, **conversions** by Amor and Gollings (3)]
Quarter-Final
7th Dec NEW ZEALAND 19 **ENGLAND*** 7
[*Team:* Amor, Gollings]
[*Bench:*]
[*Scorers:* **try** by Ben Russell, **conversion** by Gollings]
[Plate Semi-Final:]
[7th Dec ARGENTINA 12 **ENGLAND** 19]
[*Team:* Amor, R. Haughton]
[*Bench:*]

[*Scorers:* **tries** by R. Haughton (2) and Amor, **conversions** by Gollings (2)]
[Plate Final:]
[7th Dec FIJI 29 **ENGLAND** 5]
[*Team:* Amor]
[*Bench:*]
[*Scorers:* **try** by Amor]
POSITION: LOSING QUARTER-FINALISTS [*PLATE FINALISTS*]
FANTASY: *WINNERS*
[England scored 6 competition points in this Round of the 2002-2003 IRB World Sevens Series]

EMIRATES AIRLINE SOUTH AFRICA SEVENS
IRB WORLD SEVENS SERIES 2002-2003 ROUND 2

Outeniqua Park Stadium, George
[*Tournament squad:* Amor, M. Cannon, Gollings, R. Haughton, Hylton, Laird, Lund, Mayor, Peacey, Ben Russell (2), Sampson (never travelled as injured, replaced by Ben Russell (1)), R. Thirlby, Ben Russell (1) (*fly half*)]
(squad of 12)
[MANAGER: *John Elliott*] **[COACH:** *Joe Lydon*] **[ASSISTANT COACH:** *Mike Friday*]
CAPTAIN: *Simon Amor*
First Round - Pool 'B'
13th Dec FRANCE 10 **ENGLAND** 19
[*Team:* Ben Russell (2), M. Cannon, Lund, Amor, Gollings, R. Thirlby, R. Haughton]
[*Bench:* Hylton, Laird (rep), Mayor (rep), Peacey (rep), Ben Russell (1)]
[*Scorers:* **tries** by Gollings, R. Thirlby and Peacey, **conversions** by Gollings (2)]
13th Dec NAMIBIA 7 **ENGLAND** 19
[*Team:* Ben Russell (2), Laird, Peacey, Amor, Gollings, Mayor, R. Thirlby]
[*Bench:* M. Cannon, R. Haughton (rep), Hylton (rep), Lund, Ben Russell (1) (rep)]
[*Scorers:* **tries** by R. Thirlby, Mayor and R. Haughton, **conversions** by Gollings (2)]
13th Dec AUSTRALIA 19 **ENGLAND*** 14
[*Team:* Ben Russell (2), M. Cannon, Lund, Amor, Gollings, R. Thirlby, R. Haughton]
[*Bench:* Hylton (rep), Laird, Mayor, Peacey (rep), Ben Russell (1) (rep)]
[*Scorers:* **tries** by Gollings and Lund, **conversions** by Amor and Gollings]
Quarter-Final
14th Dec NEW ZEALAND 19 **ENGLAND*** 7
[*Team:* Ben Russell (2), M. Cannon, Lund, Amor, Ben Russell (1), Gollings, R. Thirlby]
[*Bench:* R. Haughton (rep), Hylton (rep), Laird (rep), Mayor, Peacey]
[*Scorers:* **try** by R. Thirlby, **conversion** by Gollings]
[Plate Semi-Final:]
[14th Dec SAMOA 19 **ENGLAND*** 12]
[*Team:* Ben Russell (2), Laird, Lund, Amor, Gollings, Hylton, R. Haughton]
[*Bench:* M. Cannon (rep), Mayor, Peacey (rep), Ben Russell (1) (rep)]
[*Scorers:* **tries** by Gollings (2), **conversion** by Gollings]
POSITION: LOSING QUARTER-FINALISTS [*PLATE SEMI-FINALISTS*]
[England scored 4 competition points in this Round of the 2002-2003 IRB World Sevens Series]

ENGLAND U21 MATCH

[**MANAGER:** *Peter Drewett*] [**COACH:** *Jon Callard*] [**ASSISTANT COACHES:** *Nigel Redman & Paul Grayson*]

CAPTAIN: *Michael Holford*

[18th Dec **ENGLAND U21 A XV** 28 WALES U21 A XV 5]

Newbury RFC, Monks Lane, Newbury

[*Team:* Peter Cook (2), Kyriacou, M. Holford, Pendlebury, James Hamilton, N. Mason, B. Woods, Luke Abraham, Wigglesworth, Spragg, John Holtby, Hipkiss, T. Allen, J. Bailey, A. Frost]

[*Bench:* Day (rep), Gluth (rep), P. Hodgson (rep), Monye (rep), Parling (rep), C. Rowland (rep), Timothy 'Tim' Taylor (*fly half/full back*) (rep)]

[*Scorers:* **tries** by B. Woods, Hipkiss and T. Allen, **penalty goals** by A. Frost (3), **conversions** by A. Frost (2)]

2003
OTHER MATCHES
BRISBANE SEVENS
IRB WORLD SEVENS SERIES 2002-2003 ROUND 3

Ballymore Stadium, Brisbane

[*Tournament squad:* Lund, R. Thirlby, Gollings, Amor, R. Haughton, Philip 'Phil' Dowson (*forward*), Johnny Howard, Nathan McAvoy (*centre/wing*), Monye (*back/forward*), H. Paul, Roques, William 'Will' Skinner (*forward*)]

(squad of 12)

[Paul Sampson unavailable due to injury; Nathan McAvoy was capped for England at Rugby League in June 1996, toured Papua New Guinea, Fiji and New Zealand with the Great Britain Rugby League team in September-November 1996, played in the Bradford Bulls team that won the Middlesex Sevens at Twickenham on 17th August 2002 and became a Rugby Union player on 29th January 2003 when he joined Saracens; Will Skinner played for England in the U19 World Championship in France in April 2003]

[**MANAGER:** *John Elliott*] [**COACH:** *Joe Lydon*] [**ASSISTANT COACH:** *Mike Friday*]

CAPTAIN: *Simon Amor*

First Round - Pool 'D'

1st Feb COOK ISLANDS 0 **ENGLAND** 21

[*Team:* Amor, Gollings, R. Haughton]

[*Bench:*]

[*Scorers:* **tries** by R. Haughton (2) and R. Thirlby, **conversions** by Gollings (3)]

1st Feb JAPAN 19 **ENGLAND** 22

[*Team:* Amor, N. McAvoy]

[*Bench:* Gollings (rep)]

[*Scorers:* **tries** by N. McAvoy (2), Johnny Howard and Gollings, **conversion** by Gollings]

1st Feb FIJI 14 **ENGLAND** 19

[*Team:* Dowson, Amor, Gollings]

[*Bench:*]

[*Scorers:* **tries** by Dowson and Gollings (2), **conversions** by Gollings (2)]

Quarter-Final

2nd Feb SAMOA 5 **ENGLAND** 27

[*Team:* Amor, Monye]

[*Bench:* R. Haughton (rep)]

[*Scorers:* **tries** by Monye (2), R. Haughton (2) and H. Paul, **conversion** by Gollings]

Semi-Final

2nd Feb NEW ZEALAND 14 **ENGLAND** 19

[*Team:* Roques, H. Paul, Lund, Amor, Gollings, ?, Monye]

[*Bench:* Dowson, R. Haughton, W. Skinner, ?, ?]

[*Scorers:* **tries** by Amor, Monye and Gollings, **conversions** by Gollings (2)]

Final

2nd Feb FIJI 14 **ENGLAND** 28

[*Team:* Roques, H. Paul, Lund, Amor, Gollings, N. McAvoy, Monye]

[*Bench:* R. Haughton, Johnny Howard, W. Skinner, R. Thirlby]

[*Scorers:* **tries** by Roques, Monye (2) and Gollings, **conversions** by Gollings (4)]

POSITION: WINNERS

[*England scored 20 competition points in this Round of the 2002-2003 IRB World Sevens Series*]

TELECOM NEW ZEALAND INTERNATIONAL SEVENS
IRB WORLD SEVENS SERIES 2002-2003 ROUND 4

WestpacTrust Stadium, Wellington
[*Tournament squad:* Amor, Dowson, Gollings, R. Haughton, Johnny Howard, Lund, N. McAvoy, Monye, H. Paul, Roques, W. Skinner, R. Thirlby]
(*squad of 12*)
[*Paul Sampson unavailable due to injury; Simon Amor was the tournament captain*]
[**MANAGER:** *John Elliott*] [**COACH:** *Joe Lydon*] [**ASSISTANT COACH:** *Mike Friday*]

CAPTAIN: *Tony Roques*
First Round - Pool 'A'

7th Feb PAPUA NEW GUINEA 0 **ENGLAND** 49
[*Team:* Roques, ?, ?, Jonny Howard, Gollings, ?, R. Haughton]
[*Bench:* Amor, H. Paul, R. Thirlby (rep), ?, ?]
[*Scorers:* **tries** by R. Haughton (3), Gollings (2), Roques and R. Thirlby, **conversions** by Gollings (7)]

CAPTAIN: *Simon Amor*

7th Feb TONGA 17 **ENGLAND** 28
[*Team:* Amor, Gollings]
[*Bench:*]
[*Scorers:* **tries** by Gollings, Monye (2) and N. McAvoy, **conversions** by Gollings (4)]

7th Feb NEW ZEALAND 24 **ENGLAND** 0
[*Team:* Monye]
[*Bench:* R. Thirlby (rep)]
[*No scorers*]

Quarter-Final

8th Feb SOUTH AFRICA 7 **ENGLAND** 17
[*Team:* Roques, Dowson, H. Paul]
[*Bench:*]
[*Scorers:* **tries** by Roques, Dowson and Monye, **conversion** by Gollings]

Semi-Final

8th Feb AUSTRALIA 15 **ENGLAND** 21
[*Team:* Lund, Gollings]
[*Bench:*]
[*Scorers:* **tries** by Lund, Gollings and R. Haughton, **conversions** by Gollings (3)]

Final

8th Feb NEW ZEALAND 38 **ENGLAND** 26
[*Team:* ?, ?, ?, Amor, Gollings, H. Paul, N. McAvoy]
[*Bench:*]
[*Scorers:* **tries** by H. Paul, Monye, Gollings and Dowson, **conversions** by Gollings (3)]

POSITION: LOSING FINALISTS

[*England scored 16 competition points in this Round of the 2002-2003 IRB World Sevens Series*]

6 NATIONS CHAMPIONSHIP

[**HEAD COACH:** *Clive Woodward*] [**COACH:** *Andy Robinson*] [**ASSISTANT COACH:** *Phil Larder*]

CAPTAIN: *Martin Johnson*

15th Feb **ENGLAND** 25 FRANCE 17

Twickenham

[*Team:* J. Leonard, Steve Thompson (2), Julian White, Martin Johnson, Kay, Moody, Back, Richard Hill (2), Gomarsall, Jonny Wilkinson, B. Cohen, C. Hodgson, W. Greenwood, Luger, Jason Robinson]

[*Bench:* Christophers, Dallaglio (rep), Grewcock (rep), M. Regan (rep), Rowntree (rep), J. Simpson-Daniel, Walshe]

[*Scorers:* **try** by Jason Robinson, **penalty goals** by Jonny Wilkinson (5), **drop goal** by Jonny Wilkinson, **conversion** by Jonny Wilkinson]

22nd Feb WALES 9 **ENGLAND** 26

Millennium Stadium, Cardiff

[*Team:* Rowntree, Steve Thompson (2), Robbie Morris, Martin Johnson, Kay, Richard Hill (2), Back, Dallaglio, K. Bracken, Jonny Wilkinson, B. Cohen, C. Hodgson, W. Greenwood, Luger, Jason Robinson]

[*Bench:* Christophers (rep), Gomarsall (rep), Grewcock (rep), M. Regan, J. Simpson-Daniel (rep), M. Worsley, J. Worsley (rep)]

[*Scorers:* **tries** by W. Greenwood and J. Worsley, **penalty goals** by Jonny Wilkinson (2), **drop goals** by Jonny Wilkinson (2), **conversions** by Jonny Wilkinson (2)]

CAPTAIN: *Jonny Wilkinson* [*Lawrence Dallaglio took over when Jonny Wilkinson was injured in the 2nd half*]

9th March **ENGLAND** 40 ITALY 5

Twickenham

[*Team:* Rowntree, Steve Thompson (2), Robbie Morris, Grewcock, Kay, J. Worsley, Richard Hill (2), Dallaglio, Matt Dawson, Jonny Wilkinson, Luger, Tindall, W. Greenwood, J. Simpson-Daniel, J. Lewsey]

[*Bench:* K. Bracken (rep), C. Hodgson (rep), M. Regan (rep), A. Sanderson (rep), S. Shaw (rep), Ollie Smith (2) (*centre/wing*) (rep), M. Worsley (rep)]

[*Scorers:* **tries** by J. Lewsey (2), Steve Thompson, J. Simpson-Daniel, Tindall and Luger, **conversions** by Jonny Wilkinson (4) and Matt Dawson]

CAPTAIN: *Martin Johnson*

22nd Mar **ENGLAND** 40 SCOTLAND 9

Twickenham

[*Team:* Rowntree, Steve Thompson (2), J. Leonard, Martin Johnson, Kay, Richard Hill (2), Back, Dallaglio, Matt Dawson, Jonny Wilkinson, B. Cohen, Tindall, W. Greenwood, Jason Robinson, J. Lewsey]

[*Bench:* Grayson (rep), Gomarsall, Grewcock (rep), Luger (rep), M. Regan, Trevor Woodman (rep), J. Worsley (rep)]

[*Scorers:* **tries** by J. Lewsey, B. Cohen and Jason Robinson (2), **penalty goals** by Jonny Wilkinson (4), **conversions** by Jonny Wilkinson (3) and Grayson]

30th Mar IRELAND 6 **ENGLAND** 42

Lansdowne Road

[*Team:* Rowntree, Steve Thompson (2), J. Leonard, Martin Johnson, Kay, Richard Hill (2), Back, Dallaglio, Matt Dawson, Jonny Wilkinson, B. Cohen, Tindall, W. Greenwood, Jason Robinson, J. Lewsey]

[*Bench:* K. Bracken (rep), Grayson (rep), Grewcock (rep), Luger (rep), D. West, Trevor

Woodman (rep), J. Worsley (rep)]
[*Scorers:* **tries** by Dallaglio, Tindall, W. Greenwood (2) and Luger, **penalty goal** by Jonny Wilkinson, **drop goals** by Jonny Wilkinson (2), **conversions** by Jonny Wilkinson (3) and Grayson]
POSITION: 1ST 10 +127 GS TC CC MT [Ireland 8 +22, France 6 +78, Scotland 4 -80, Italy 2 -85, Wales 0 -62]

OTHER MATCHES

ENGLAND STUDENTS MATCHES

[**MANAGER:** *Tony Lanaway*] [**COACH:** *Richard Hill (1)*] [**ASSISTANT COACH:** *Steve Hill*]
CAPTAIN: *Ben Gerry*
[14th Feb **ENGLAND STUDENTS*** 28 FRANCE STUDENTS 30]
Sedgley Park RFC, Park Lane, Whitefield, Manchester
[*Team:* Adam Hopcroft, N. Clark, Porte, James Hudson, P. Short, Ben Gerry, El Abd, T. Hayman, K. Barrett, M. Honeyben, Obi, Andrew 'Andy' Vilk, Billig, Rubie, B. Thompson]
[*Bench:* C. Collins, Charlie Edwards (*lock*), Matthew 'Matt' Evans (1) (*flanker*), Mark Foster (*wing*), Gaunt, Joe Horn-Smith (*prop*), Winney (rep)]
[*Scorers:* **tries** by T. Hayman (2), El Abd and Billig, **conversions** by Winney (4)]
[21st Feb WALES STUDENTS 17 **ENGLAND STUDENTS** 23]
St. Helen's, Swansea
[*Team:* Hopcroft, N. Clark, Porte, James Hudson, P. Short, B. Gerry, El Abd, T. Hayman, K. Barrett, Winney, Obi, Vilk, Billig, Rubie, B. Thompson]
[*Bench:* C. Collins, Matt Evans (1), M. Foster (rep), Gaunt (rep), L. Hinton, Horn-Smith, Nick Rouse (*lock*) (rep)]
[*Scorers:* **tries** by B. Gerry (2), T. Hayman and Vilk, **penalty goal** by Winney]
CAPTAIN: *No captain appointed*
[7th Mar **ENGLAND STUDENTS** C ITALY STUDENTS C]
Rectory Field, Charlton Road, Blackheath
[*Team:* Hopcroft, N. Clark, Horn-Smith, James Hudson, P. Short, Matt Evans (1), El Abd, T. Hayman, Barr, Winney, Obi, Vilk, Billig, K. Dixon, L. Hinton]
[*Bench:* C. Collins, M. Foster, Gaunt, B. Gerry (*flanker*), Oliver 'Ollie' Phillips (*wing*), Porte (*prop*), Rouse]
[*No scorers*]
[21st Mar **ENGLAND STUDENTS** C SCOTLAND STUDENTS C]
?@
[*Team not selected*]
[*Bench not selected*]
[*No scorers*]
[Steve Hill was appointed on 12th November 2002]

U21 6 NATIONS CHAMPIONSHIP

[**MANAGER:** *Peter Drewett*] [**COACH:** *Jon Callard*] [**ASSISTANT COACHES:** *Nigel Redman & Paul Grayson*]
CAPTAIN: *Chris Day*
[14th Feb **ENGLAND U21** 26 FRANCE U21 25]
Newbury RFC, Monks Lane, Newbury
[*Team:* Peter Cook (2), Kyriacou, M. Stevens, James Hamilton, Day, B. Woods, Scaysbrook, Ben Russell (2), Clive Stuart-Smith, Spragg, Holtby, Hipkiss, Hyndman, Monye, A. Frost]
[*Bench:* S. Davey, P. Hodgson, M. Holford (rep), Ryan Peacey (*flanker*) (rep), Pendlebury

(rep), C. Rowland, T. Taylor (rep)]
[*Scorers:* **tries** by Monye (2) and M. Stevens, **penalty goals** by A. Frost and Spragg (2), **conversion** by Spragg]
[21st Feb WALES U21 35 **ENGLAND U21** 9]
The Gnoll, Neath
[*Team:* Peter Cook (2), Kyriacou, M. Stevens, Pendlebury, Day, B. Woods, Scaysbrook, Ben Russell (2), Stuart-Smith, Spragg, Holtby, Hipkiss, S. Davey, Marcel Garvey, Mayor]
[*Bench:* P. Hodgson (rep), M. Holford (rep), Lund (rep), Monye (rep), Parling (rep), C. Rowland (rep), T. Taylor (rep)]
[*Scorers:* **penalty goals** by Spragg (3)]
[7th Mar **ENGLAND U21** 34 ITALY U21 3]
Newbury RFC, Monks Lane, Newbury
[*Team:* Peter Cook (2), Kyriacou, M. Holford, James Hamilton, Day, B. Woods, Scaysbrook, Lund, P. Hodgson, Spragg, Mayor, Hipkiss, Christian 'Chris' Bell, J. Bailey, Thrower]
[*Bench:* Hyndman, Pendlebury, Ben Russell (2) (*flanker/number 8*), M. Stevens (*prop*), Stuart-Smith (*scrum half*), T. Taylor, M. Thompson (rep)]
[*Scorers:* **tries** by Mayor, Hipkiss, Lund, B. Woods and J. Bailey, **penalty goal** by Thrower, **conversions** by Thrower (3)]
[21st Mar **ENGLAND U21** 15 SCOTLAND U21 12]
Newbury RFC, Monks Lane, Newbury
[*Team:* Peter Cook (2), Kyriacou, M. Holford, Parling, Day, B. Woods, Scaysbrook, Lund, P. Hodgson, Spragg, Monye, Hipkiss, C. Bell, M. Garvey, Thrower]
[*Bench:* J. Bailey (rep), Pendlebury (rep), Ben Russell (2) (rep), M. Stevens (rep), Stuart-Smith, T. Taylor, M. Thompson]
[*Scorers:* **tries** by Lund (2) and Thrower]
[28th Mar IRELAND U21 21 **ENGLAND U21*** 20]
Ravenhill Park, Belfast
[*Team:* Peter Cook (2), Kyriacou, M. Holford, Parling, Day, B. Woods, Scaysbrook, Lund, P. Hodgson, Spragg, Mayor, S. Davey, Henry 'Harry' Barratt, J. Bailey, Thrower]
[*Bench:* Pendlebury (rep), Ben Russell (2) (rep), M. Stevens (rep), Stuart-Smith (rep), T. Taylor (rep), M. Thompson (rep), Thomas 'Tom' Williams (*wing/full back*) (rep)]
[*Scorers:* **tries** by J. Bailey and S. Davey, **penalty goals** by Thrower (2), **conversions** by Thrower (2)]
POSITION: **3RD 6 +8** [*Wales 10 +58 GS TC*, Ireland 8 +20, France 4 +49, Scotland 2 -19, Italy 0 -116]
FANTASY: ***2ND 8***

'A' INTERNATIONAL CHAMPIONSHIP

[**COACH:** *Joe Lydon*] [**ASSISTANT COACHES:** *Simon Hardy* & *Phil Keith-Roach*]
CAPTAIN: *Dorian West*
[14th Feb **ENGLAND A** 30 FRANCE A 13]
Franklin's Gardens, Northampton
[*Team:* M. Worsley, D. West, Robbie Morris, S. Borthwick, Tom Palmer (2), A. Sanderson, Hazell, J. Worsley, Martyn Wood, Grayson, M. Garvey, Ben Johnston, Ollie Smith (2), Scarbrough, J. Lewsey]
[*Bench:* Benton, Corry, Chris Jones (*lock/flanker/number 8*) (rep), A. King (rep), Noon (rep), Shelley, Titterrell]
[*Scorers:* **tries** by J. Worsley and Scarbrough, **penalty goals** by Grayson (6), **conversion** by Grayson]

CAPTAIN: *No captain appointed*
[21st Feb WALES A C **ENGLAND A** C]
The Racecourse Ground, Wrexham
[*Team not selected*]
[*Bench not selected*]
[*No scorers*]
CAPTAIN: *Dorian West*
[7th Mar **ENGLAND A** 43 ITALY A 11]
Franklin's Gardens, Northampton
[*Team:* Shelley, D. West, Maurice Fitzgerald, S. Borthwick, Tom Palmer (2), Corry, Hazell, Forrester, Gomarsall, A. King, Christophers, Ben Johnston, Noon, M. Garvey, Scarbrough]
[*Bench:* Chris Jones (rep), Neal Hatley (*prop*) (rep), Titterrell (rep), Adam Vander (*flanker*) (rep), Walshe (rep), F. Waters (rep), Martyn Wood (rep)]
[*Scorers:* **tries** by D. West, Ben Johnston, Hazell (2), F. Waters, M. Garvey and Vander, **conversions** by A. King (2), Gomarsall and Martyn Wood]
CAPTAIN: *Kyran Bracken*
[21st Mar **ENGLAND A** 78 SCOTLAND A 6]
Franklin's Gardens, Northampton
[*Team:* M. Worsley, Titterrell, Robbie Morris, S. Borthwick, Chris Jones, A. Sanderson, Vander, Forrester, K. Bracken, A. King, Cueto, H. Paul, J. Simpson-Daniel, Christophers, Scarbrough]
[*Bench:* Corry (rep), M. Fitzgerald (*prop*), Ben Johnston (rep), H. Vyvyan (rep), Walshe (rep), F. Waters (rep), D. West]
[*Scorers:* **tries** by Scarbrough (2), Christophers (2), Cueto (3), Forrester (2), K. Bracken and F. Waters, **penalty goal** by A. King, **conversions** by A. King (10)]
CAPTAIN: *Martin Corry*
[28th Mar IRELAND A 24 **ENGLAND A*** 21]
Donnybrook, Dublin
[*Team:* M. Worsley, M. Regan, Robbie Morris, S. Shaw, Chris Jones, Corry, Vander, Forrester, Walshe, A. King, Cueto, Ben Johnston, F. Waters, Christophers, Scarbrough]
[*Bench:* Barkley (rep), M. Fitzgerald (rep), Tom Palmer (2) (rep), M. Stephenson (rep), Titterrell (rep), H. Vyvyan (rep), Martyn Wood]
[*Scorers:* **tries** by Scarbrough (2), **penalty goals** by Barkley and A. King, **drop goal** by A. King, **conversion** by A. King]
POSITION: **1ST 6 +118** [France 6 +60, Ireland 5 +10, Italy 2 -97, Scotland 1 -91]
FANTASY: ***1ST 8***
[Joe Lydon, Simon Hardy and Phil Keith-Roach were all appointed on 29th January 2003; Simon Hardy played for England U23 against Italy in May 1979]
[On 28th April 2003 the SRU announced that the Scotland A team would not be playing in 2004 for financial reasons; The 'A' International Championship was abolished by the Six Nations Committee on 5th August 2003]

JARROD CUNNINGHAM SALSA FOUNDATION BENEFIT MATCH

[**COACH:** *Wayne Smith* (NZ)]
CAPTAIN: *Rob Howley* (WA)
[6th Mar London Irish All-Stars 33 **BARBARIANS** 66]
Stoop Memorial Ground, Langhorn Drive, Twickenham
[*Team:* Kelvin Todd, Matt Sexton (NZ), A. Garvey (SA), Michael 'Mick' Galwey (IR), Glenn Delaney (NZ), David Hunter (SA), Darren Fox, Royston 'Roy' Winters, Howley (WA), W.

Serevi (FIJ), Ripol (SP), Daryl Gibson (NZ), Viliame Satala (FIJ), J. Sleightholme, P. Montgomery (SA)]
[*Bench:* Kevin Brennan (*scrum half*) (rep), Critchley (rep), Denney (*centre*) (rep), Simon Hepher (*lock/flanker/number 8*) (rep), Leota (SAM) (*hooker*) (rep), L. Starling (rep), Tonu'u (NZ) (rep)]
[*Scorers:* **tries** by Ripol (SP), V. Satala (FIJ), Darren Fox, G. Delaney (NZ), P. Montgomery (SA), W. Serevi (FIJ) (3), Brennan and Denney, **conversions** by W. Serevi (FIJ) (8)]
[Match arranged to raise money for the Jarrod Cunningham SALSA Foundation, which was a charity set up by Jarrod Cunningham after he had been diagnosed with a form of Motor Neurone Disease]
[Wayne Smith won 17 caps for New Zealand between 1980-85 and toured South Africa with the New Zealand Cavaliers team in April-May 1986]

NIG CHALLENGE
NEIL BACK TESTIMONIAL MATCH

[**COACH:** *Zinzan Brooke* (NZ)]
CAPTAIN: *Richard Cockerill*

[7th Mar	Leicester XV	21	**BARBARIANS**	12]

Welford Road, Leicester
[*Team:* C. Dowd (NZ), Cockerill, Darren Morris (WA), Brent Cockbain (WA), Troy Jaques (AU), Alexandre 'Alex' Audebert (SC), Warren Brosnihan (SA), Jim Williams (AU), Morgan Williams (CAN), Nicky Little (FIJ), Pierre Bondouy (FR), Norman 'Norm' Berryman (NZ), Sebastien Bonetti (FR), Diego Albanese (AR), Delport (SA)]
[*Bench:* Denney (rep), A. Garvey (SA), Leota (SAM) (rep), Miall, V. Satala (FIJ) (*centre*) (rep), W. Serevi (FIJ) (*fly half/full back*) (rep), Ben Wheeler (*flanker*) (rep)]
[*Scorers:* **tries** by N. Berryman (NZ) and Albanese (AR), **conversion** by N. Little (FIJ)]
[Match organised as a testimonial game for Neil Back; Zinzan Brooke won 58 caps for New Zealand between 1987-97]

VIÑA DEL MAR SEVENS
IRB WORLD SEVENS SERIES 2002-2003 ROUND 5

Estadio Sausalito, Viña del Mar
[*Tournament squad not selected*]
[This tournament was originally scheduled to take place on 10th-11th January 2003 but was then postponed by the IRB on 27th December 2002 due to transport problems, with the IRB then rescheduling it on 29th January 2003]
[**MANAGER:** *John Elliott*] [**COACH:** *Joe Lydon*] [**ASSISTANT COACH:** *Mike Friday*]
CAPTAIN: *No captain appointed*

7th March	*No opponents named*	C	**ENGLAND**	C

[*Team not selected*]
[*Bench not selected*]
[*No scorers*]

CREDIT SUISSE FIRST BOSTON HONG KONG SEVENS
IRB WORLD SEVENS SERIES 2002-2003 ROUND 6

Hong Kong Stadium, Eastern Hospital Road, So Kon Po, Hong Kong
[*Tournament squad:* Amor, Appleford, Dowson, Greening, R. Haughton, Johnny Howard, Monye, Noon, H. Paul, Gareth Raynor (*wing*) (never travelled as withdrew, replaced by Matt Cannon), Roques, R. Thirlby, M. Cannon]

(squad of 12)
[The order of the First Round draw was changed on 25th March 2003 because Italy, France and Argentina had all withdrawn from the competition due to fears about the spread of the Severe Acute Respiratory Syndrome (SARS) virus; Ben Gollings was unavailable for this tournament due to family commitments; Simon Amor was the tournament captain; The England squad arrived in Hong Kong on 25th March 2003; Gareth Raynor became a Rugby Union player in June 2002 when he signed for Leicester and then returned to Rugby League in June 2003, where he was capped for Great Britain in November 2005]
[**MANAGER:** *John Elliott*] [**COACH:** *Joe Lydon*] [**ASSISTANT COACH:** *Mike Friday*]
CAPTAIN: *Phil Greening*
First Round - Pool 'B'
28th Mar SINGAPORE 0 **ENGLAND** 52
[*Team:* R. Thirlby, Greening, Noon, Johnny Howard, H. Paul, Appleford, R. Haughton]
[*Bench:* Amor (rep), M. Cannon (rep), Dowson (rep), Monye, ?]
[*Scorers:* **tries** by Noon (2), R. Thirlby (2), Appleford (2), R. Haughton and M. Cannon, **conversions** by H. Paul (2), R. Thirlby, Noon, R. Haughton and Amor]
CAPTAIN: *Simon Amor*
29th Mar CHINESE TAIPEI 5 **ENGLAND** 43
[*Team:* Roques, Greening, Dowson, Amor, H. Paul, Appleford, Monye]
[*Bench:* M. Cannon (rep), R. Haughton, Johnny Howard (rep), R. Thirlby (rep), ?]
[*Scorers:* **tries** by Monye (4), Johnny Howard, R. Thirlby and Roques, **conversions** by Amor (3) and Johnny Howard]
29th Mar TONGA 7 **ENGLAND** 42
[*Team:* Roques, Greening, Dowson, Amor, H. Paul, Noon, Monye]
[*Bench:* Appleford (rep), R. Haughton (rep), R. Thirlby (rep), ?, ?]
[*Scorers:* **tries** by R. Haughton (2), Monye (2), Dowson and Greening, **conversions** by Amor (5) and H. Paul]
Quarter-Final
30th Mar AUSTRALIA 14 **ENGLAND** 19
[*Team:* Roques, Greening, Noon, Amor, H. Paul, Appleford, Monye]
[*Bench:* Dowson (rep), R. Haughton (rep), R. Thirlby (rep), ?, ?]
[*Scorers:* **tries** by Amor, Monye and Noon, **conversions** by Amor (2)]
Semi-Final
30th Mar FIJI 19 **ENGLAND** 24
[*Team:* Roques, Greening, Dowson, Amor, H. Paul, R. Thirlby, Monye]
[*Bench:* Appleford (rep), R. Haughton (rep), Noon (rep), ?, ?]
[*Scorers:* **tries** by R. Thirlby, H. Paul, Greening and Roques, **conversions** by H. Paul and Amor]
Final
30th Mar NEW ZEALAND 17 **ENGLAND** 22
[*Team:* Roques, Greening, Dowson, Amor, H. Paul, R. Thirlby, Monye]
[*Bench:* Appleford (rep), R. Haughton (rep), Noon (rep), ?, ?]
[*Scorers:* **tries** by Monye, H. Paul and R. Haughton (2), **conversion** by Amor]
POSITION: WINNERS
[England scored 30 competition points in this Round of the 2002-2003 IRB World Sevens Series]

BEIJING SEVENS
IRB WORLD SEVENS SERIES 2002-2003 ROUND 7

National Olympic Sports Centre, Beijing

[*Tournament squad:* Amor, Appleford, M. Cannon, Dowson, R. Haughton, P. Hodgson (*scrum half*), Lund, Monye, Raynor, Roques, R. Thirlby, ?]

(squad of 12)

[Phil Greening, Johnny Howard, Jamie Noon and Henry Paul were all unavailable for this tournament due to club commitments; One other player was due to be added to the squad to bring it up to the required strength of 12 but the tournament was cancelled before this could be done]

[**MANAGER:** *John Elliott*] [**COACH:** *Joe Lydon*] [**ASSISTANT COACH:** *Mike Friday*]

CAPTAIN: *No captain appointed*

5th April *No opponents named* C **ENGLAND** C

[*Team not selected*]

[*Bench not selected*]

[*No scorers*]

SINGAPORE SEVENS
IRB WORLD SEVENS SERIES 2002-2003 ROUND 8

National Stadium, Kallang

[*Tournament squad not selected*]

[**MANAGER:** *John Elliott*] [**COACH:** *Joe Lydon*] [**ASSISTANT COACH:** *Mike Friday*]

CAPTAIN: *No captain appointed*

26th April *No opponents named* C **ENGLAND** C

[*Team not selected*]

[*Bench not selected*]

[*No scorers*]

MALAYSIA SEVENS
IRB WORLD SEVENS SERIES 2002-2003 ROUND 9

MPPJ Stadium, Petaling Jaya, Kelana Jaya

[**MANAGER:** *John Elliott*] [**COACH:** *Joe Lydon*] [**ASSISTANT COACH:** *Mike Friday*]

CAPTAIN: *No captain appointed*

3rd May *No opponents named* C **ENGLAND** C

[*Team not selected*]

[*Bench not selected*]

[*No scorers*]

TETLEY'S COUNTY CHAMPIONSHIP SEMI-FINAL

[**CHAIRMAN OF SELECTORS:** *Terry Carter* (CO)] [**COACH:** *Nick Brokenshire* (CO)] [**ASSISTANT COACH:** *Darren Chapman* (CO)]

CAPTAIN: *Steve Evans* (CO)

[17th May **CORNWALL*** 13 Lancashire 23]

Recreation Ground, Redruth

[*Team:* Martin Rice (CO), Viliami Ma'asi (TON), Jonathan Wright (CO), Wilce (CO), R. Carroll (CO), J. Lancaster (NZ), Penrose (CO), Soper, Ricky Pellow, Steve Evans (CO), Richard 'Rocky' Newton (CO), Bede Brown (NZ), Paul Gadsdon (CO), Bonds (CO), Larkins (CO)]

[*Bench:* Neil Corin (CO) (*lock/flanker*), Mark Harper (CO) (*hooker*), J. Hawken (CO) (*centre/wing/full back*) (rep), Sam Heard (*prop*), Navin (CO) (rep), Alan Paver (CO) (*prop*) (rep), Mark Richards (CO)]
[*Scorers:* **tries** by R. Newton (CO) and J. Hawken (CO), **penalty goal** by Larkins (CO)]
POSITION: LOSING SEMI-FINALISTS

TETLEY'S NATIONAL COUNTIES SEVEN-A-SIDE TOURNAMENT

Twickenham
[*Tournament squad:* J. Lancaster (NZ) (*forward*), Alan *Paul* Thirlby (CO) (*scrum half/fly half*), N. Corin (CO) (*forward*), Sebastian 'Seb' Berti (CHI) (*fly half*), Nick Brown (CO) (*back/forward*), R. Thirlby, Ian Hambly (CO) (*centre*), Bede Brown (NZ) (*fly half/centre*), Lewis Vinnicombe (*wing*), Sam Hocking (CO) (*forward*), Sam Harrison (1) (CO) (*hooker*)]
(squad of 11)
[Sam Harrison (1) not mentioned in the tournament programme; Graham Still won 11 caps for Cornwall between 1975-84]
[The first 2 rounds were qualifying rounds]
[**MANAGER:** *Graham Still* (CO)]
CAPTAIN: *Rob Thirlby*
Semi-Final
[24th May Eastern Counties 0 **CORNWALL** 47]
[*Team:* J. Lancaster (NZ), Sam Harrison (1) (CO), N. Corin (CO), P. Thirlby (CO), Berti (CHI), R. Thirlby, Vinnicombe]
[*Bench:* Bede Brown (NZ), N. Brown (CO), I. Hambly (CO) (rep), S. Hocking (CO)]
[*Scorers:* **tries** by N. Corin (CO) (2), R. Thirlby, Berti (CHI), I. Hambly (CO), Vinnicombe and P. Thirlby (CO), **conversions** by P. Thirlby (CO) (6)]
Final
[24th May Yorkshire 31 **CORNWALL** 33]
[*Team:* J. Lancaster (NZ), Sam Harrison (1) (CO), N. Corin (CO), P. Thirlby (CO), Berti (CHI), R. Thirlby, Vinnicombe]
[*Bench:* Bede Brown (NZ), N. Brown (CO), I. Hambly (CO) (rep), S. Hocking (CO)]
[*Scorers:* **tries** by Vinnicombe, R. Thirlby (2), N. Corin (CO) and I. Hambly (CO), **conversions** by P. Thirlby (CO) (4)]
POSITION: WINNERS

FIRST LLOYDS TSB TOUR MATCH

[**ENGLAND XV:** [*Other squad members:* Balding, M. Cairns, Daniel 'Dan' Hyde (*flanker/number 8*) (withdrew due to injury), Luger (withdrew due to injury), Sheridan (*prop*) (withdrew due to injury), M. Stephenson (withdrew due to injury)]]
(squad of 28)
[Austin Healey, Charlie Hodgson and James Simpson-Daniel unavailable due to injury; Steve Thompson (2), Steve Borthwick, Simon Shaw, Danny Grewcock, Joe Worsley, Paul Volley, Lawrence Dallaglio, Matt Dawson, Paul Grayson, Alex King, Olly Barkley, Ben Cohen, Mike Tindall, Mike Catt, Stuart Abbott, Josh Lewsey and Iain Balshaw were all unavailable due to club commitments; Jason Leonard, Martin Johnson, Richard Hill (2), Neil Back, Jonny Wilkinson and Will Greenwood were rested for this match; Andy Sheridan was converted from a lock to a prop by his club Bristol in October 2002]
[**BARBARIANS:** [*English squad members:* Balshaw, Matt Perry]]
[Alan Solomons was appointed on 22nd January 2003; Philippe Sella was appointed on 7th April 2003]

[ENGLAND XV: [HEAD COACH: *Clive Woodward*] **[COACH:** *Andy Robinson*] **[ASSISTANT COACH:** *Phil Larder*]]
[BARBARIANS: [HEAD COACH: *Alan Solomons* (SA)] **[ASSISTANT COACH:** *Philippe Sella* (FR)]]
CAPTAIN: *Phil Vickery* [England XV]
CAPTAIN: *Taine Randell* (NZ) [Barbarians]

25th May **ENGLAND XV*** 36 **BARBARIANS** 49
Twickenham

[ENGLAND XV: [*Team:* M. Worsley, M. Regan, Vickery, Codling, Alex Brown, Corry, Michael Lipman, Chris Jones, K. Bracken, Walder, Christophers, Ben Johnston, Noon, Cueto, Scarbrough]
[*Bench:* Amor (rep), Anglesea (rep), Flatman (rep), K. Sorrell (rep), Titterrell (rep), H. Vyvyan (rep), Walshe (rep)]
[*Scorers:* **tries** by Lipman, Noon (2), Walder and Walshe, **drop goal** by Walder, **conversions** by Walder (4)]]
[BARBARIANS: [*Team:* Califano (FR), Matt Sexton (NZ), Carl Hayman (NZ), Albertus Johannes 'A.J.' Venter (SA), Mark Connors (AU), Jerry Collins (NZ), Samuel 'Sam' Harding (NZ), Taine Randell (NZ), Mark Robinson (2) (NZ), David Humphreys (IR), Trevor *Bruce* Reihana (NZ), Jonathan Bell (IR), T. Castaignède (FR), Aisea Tuilevu (FIJ), P. Montgomery (SA)]
[*Bench:* Felipe Contepomi (AR) (*fly half*) (rep), Darren Edwards (WA) (*scrum half*) (rep), D. Gibson (NZ) (*centre*) (rep), Ibañez (FR) (rep), Francois 'Hottie' Louw (SA) (*lock*) (rep), Strudwick (SA), Tournaire (FR) (*prop*) (rep)]
[*Scorers:* **tries** by T. Castaignède (FR), Califano (FR), Mark Robinson (NZ), Jonathan Bell (IR), Ibañez (FR), Reihana (NZ) and Tournaire (FR), **conversions** by D. Humphreys (IR) (7)]]

SECOND LLOYDS TSB TOUR MATCH

[HEAD COACH: *Alan Solomons* (SA)] **[ASSISTANT COACH:** *Philippe Sella* (FR)]
CAPTAIN: *Mick Galwey* (IR)

[28th May SCOTLAND XV 15 **BARBARIANS** 24]
Murrayfield

[*Team:* André-Henri 'Ollie' le Roux (SA), Ibañez (FR), A. Garvey (SA), Galwey (IR), H. Louw (SA), Troy Flavell (NZ), Santiago Phelan (AR), A.J. Venter (SA), Darren Edwards (WA), Contepomi (AR), Aurélien Rougerie (FR), D. Gibson (NZ), De Wet Barry (SA), Scott Staniforth (AU), Conrad Jantjes (SA)]
[*Bench:* Magne (FR) (*flanker*) (rep), Matt Perry (rep), Pichot (AR) (rep), Matt Sexton (NZ) (*hooker*) (rep), Cristian Stoica (IT) (*centre*), Strudwick (SA) (rep), Tournaire (FR) (rep)]
[*Scorers:* **tries** by S. Staniforth (AU), Darren Edwards (WA), O. le Roux (SA) and Rougerie (FR), **conversions** by Contepomi (AR) (2)]

EMIRATES AIRLINE CARDIFF SEVENS
IRB WORLD SEVENS SERIES 2002-2003 ROUND 10

Cardiff Arms Park
[*Tournament squad:* M. Cannon, Lund, R. Thirlby, Gollings, Amor, Cueto, Dowson, Monye, P. Hodgson, P. Sanderson, James Brooks, Roke (*centre*)]
(squad of 12)
[Tony Roques, Phil Greening, Henry Paul and Richard Haughton were all unavailable for this tournament due to club commitments; Simon Amor was the tournament

***captain*]**
[MANAGER: *John Elliott*] **[COACH:** *Joe Lydon*] **[ASSISTANT COACH:** *Mike Friday*]
CAPTAIN: *Pat Sanderson*
First Round - Pool 'B'
31st May WALES 26 **ENGLAND*** 14
[*Team:* Dowson, P. Hodgson, P. Sanderson, James Brooks, Gollings, R. Thirlby, Monye]
[*Bench:* M. Cannon (rep), Cueto (rep), Lund (rep), Roke]
[*Scorers:* **tries** by Monye and Cueto, **conversions** by Gollings (2)]
31st May RUSSIA 0 **ENGLAND** 31
[*Team:* Dowson, Lund, P. Sanderson, James Brooks, Gollings, R. Thirlby, Monye]
[*Bench:* M. Cannon (rep), Cueto (rep), P. Hodgson, Roke (rep)]
[*Scorers:* **tries** by Dowson, James Brooks, Monye, P. Sanderson and R. Thirlby, **conversions** by Gollings (3)]
31st May FRANCE 12 **ENGLAND** 19
[*Team:* Dowson, Lund, P. Sanderson, James Brooks, Gollings, R. Thirlby, Cueto]
[*Bench:* M. Cannon (rep), P. Hodgson (rep), Monye (rep), Roke]
[*Scorers:* **tries** by R. Thirlby, Cueto and Gollings, **conversions** by Gollings (2)]
CAPTAIN: *Simon Amor*
Quarter-Final
1st June NEW ZEALAND 10 **ENGLAND** 14
[*Team:* Dowson, Lund, P. Sanderson, Amor, Gollings, R. Thirlby, Monye]
[*Bench:* James Brooks (rep), M. Cannon (rep), Cueto (rep), P. Hodgson, Roke]
[*Scorers:* **tries** by R. Thirlby and Lund, **conversions** by Gollings and Amor]
Semi-Final
1st June SOUTH AFRICA 22 **ENGLAND*** 10
[*Team:* Dowson, Lund, P. Sanderson, Amor, R. Thirlby, James Brooks, Monye]
[*Bench:* M. Cannon (rep), Cueto (rep), P. Hodgson (rep), Roke]
[*Scorers:* **tries** by Monye (2)]
POSITION: LOSING SEMI-FINALISTS
[England scored 12 competition points in this Round of the 2002-2003 IRB World Sevens Series]

THIRD LLOYDS TSB TOUR MATCH

[HEAD COACH: *Alan Solomons* (SA)] **[ASSISTANT COACH:** *Philippe Sella* (FR)]
CAPTAIN: *Mark Connors* (AU)
[31st May WALES XV 35 **BARBARIANS** 48]
Millennium Stadium, Cardiff
[*Team:* O. le Roux (SA), Matt Sexton (NZ), Tournaire (FR), Strudwick (SA), Connors (AU), Sam Harding (NZ), Magne (FR), A.J. Venter (SA), Mark Robinson (2) (NZ), Contepomi (AR), Reihana (NZ), D. Gibson (NZ), Stoica (IT), Tuilevu (FIJ), P. Montgomery (SA)]
[*Bench:* Darren Edwards (WA), Galwey (IR) (*lock/flanker/number 8*) (rep), A. Garvey (SA) (rep), Ibañez (FR) (rep), Matt Perry (rep), Phelan (AR) (*flanker*), S. Staniforth (AU) (*centre/wing/full back*) (rep)]
[*Scorers:* **tries** by Reihana (NZ), Magne (FR), Sam Harding (NZ), Tuilevu (FIJ), Galwey (IR), A. Garvey (SA) and Mark Robinson (NZ), **conversions** by Contepomi (AR) (4)]

EMIRATES AIRLINE LONDON SEVENS
IRB WORLD SEVENS SERIES 2002-2003 ROUND 11

Twickenham

[*Tournament squad:* R. Thirlby, Gollings, Amor, R. Haughton, Dowson, N. McAvoy, Monye, H. Paul, Roques, Greening (injured during the tournament), P. Sanderson, James Brooks]
(squad of 12)

[Matt Cannon in original training squad of 13; Phil Greening was the tournament captain]

[**MANAGER:** *John Elliott*] [**COACH:** *Joe Lydon*] [**ASSISTANT COACH:** *Mike Friday*]
CAPTAIN: *Phil Greening*

First Round - Pool 'B'

6th June **ENGLAND** 29 SCOTLAND 5
[*Team:* Dowson, Greening, Roques, Amor, R. Thirlby, H. Paul, R. Haughton]
[*Bench:* James Brooks (rep), N. McAvoy, Monye (rep), P. Sanderson (rep)]
[*Scorers:* **tries** by R. Haughton (2), R. Thirlby, Monye and James Brooks, **conversions** by Amor (2)]

6th June **ENGLAND** 19 GEORGIA 7
[*Team:* Dowson, Roques, P. Sanderson, Amor, H. Paul, N. McAvoy, Monye]
[*Bench:* James Brooks (rep), Greening (rep), R. Haughton (rep), R. Thirlby]
[*Scorers:* **tries** by Monye, Amor and P. Sanderson, **conversions** by Amor (2)]
CAPTAIN: *Simon Amor [Pat Sanderson took over when Simon Amor was substituted at half-time]*

6th June **ENGLAND** 35 ARGENTINA 5
[*Team:* Dowson, Roques, P. Sanderson, Amor, Gollings, H. Paul, R. Haughton]
[*Bench:* James Brooks (rep), N. McAvoy, Monye (rep), R. Thirlby (rep)]
[*Scorers:* **tries** by R. Haughton, H. Paul, Dowson, R. Thirlby and Gollings, **conversions** by Gollings (5)]
CAPTAIN: *Simon Amor [Pat Sanderson took over when Simon Amor was substituted in the 2nd half]*

Quarter-Final

7th June **ENGLAND** 50 ITALY 0
[*Team:* Dowson, Roques, P. Sanderson, Amor, Gollings, R. Thirlby, Monye]
[*Bench:* James Brooks (rep), R. Haughton (rep), N. McAvoy (rep), H. Paul]
[*Scorers:* **tries** by R. Thirlby (3), Dowson, Roques, P. Sanderson, Gollings and James Brooks, **conversions** by Gollings (5)]
CAPTAIN: *Simon Amor [Pat Sanderson took over when Simon Amor was substituted in the 2nd half]*

Semi-Final

7th June **ENGLAND** 26 SOUTH AFRICA 5
[*Team:* Dowson, Roques, P. Sanderson, Amor, Gollings, H. Paul, R. Haughton]
[*Bench:* James Brooks (rep), N. McAvoy, Monye (rep), R. Thirlby (rep)]
[*Scorers:* **tries** by Amor, Roques (2) and Gollings, **conversions** by Gollings (3)]
CAPTAIN: *Simon Amor [Pat Sanderson took over when Simon Amor was substituted in the 2nd half]*

Final

7th June **ENGLAND** 31 FIJI 24
[*Team:* Dowson, Roques, P. Sanderson, Amor, Gollings, H. Paul, R. Haughton]
[*Bench:* James Brooks (rep), N. McAvoy, Monye (rep), R. Thirlby (rep)]

[*Scorers:* **tries** by Roques, H. Paul, Gollings, Amor and Monye, **conversions** by Gollings (3)]
POSITION: WINNERS
[England scored 20 competition points in this Round of the 2002-2003 IRB World Sevens Series]
RANKING: 2ND 108 [*New Zealand 112*, Fiji 94, South Africa 82, Australia 66, Samoa 58, Argentina 36, France 20, Wales 14, Kenya 12, Tonga 10, Canada 6, Scotland 5, Italy 4, Georgia 4, Namibia 2, Cook Islands 2, Korea 2, USA 1]
FANTASY: ***1ST 122***

ENGLAND TOUR TO NEW ZEALAND AND AUSTRALIA 2003

[**HEAD COACH:** *Clive Woodward*] [**COACH:** *Andy Robinson*] [**ASSISTANT COACH:** *Phil Larder*]
[*Other squad members:* Stuart Abbott (*centre*) (tm), Balshaw (flew to Canada after first tour match) (tm), Corry (tm), Grewcock (never travelled as suspended, replaced by Tom Palmer (2)), Hazell (flew to Canada after first tour match) (tm), Ben Johnston (flew to Canada after first tour match) (tm), Noon (tm), Tom Palmer (2) (flew to Canada after first tour match) (tm), S. Shaw (returned home as injured), J. Simpson-Daniel (flew to Canada after first tour match) (tm), Volley (flew to Canada after first tour match) (tm), M. Worsley (flew to Canada after first tour match) (tm)]
(squad of 37)
[Julian White, Lewis Moody, Austin Healey, Charlie Hodgson and Ollie Smith (2) were all unavailable for this tour due to injury; On 25th May 2003 Danny Grewcock was sent off for striking an opponent in the Parker Pen Shield Final and was thus duly banned for 2 weeks from 1st June 2003 onwards; Danny Grewcock was initially included in the squad announced on 27th May 2003 but he then withdrew after he decided not to appeal against his ban; The England squad departed for New Zealand on 2nd June 2003; Mike Worsley, Tom Palmer (2), Paul Volley, Andy Hazell, Ben Johnston, James Simpson-Daniel and Iain Balshaw all flew to Canada on 10th June 2003 as they were now required to join the England A squad for the simultaneous Churchill Cup tournament; Simon Shaw returned home injured on 16th June 2003 and was not replaced; Stuart Abbott played for South Africa U23 in June 2000]
CAPTAIN: *Martin Johnson*
14th June NEW ZEALAND 13 **ENGLAND** 15
WestpacTrust Stadium, Wellington
[*Team:* Rowntree, Steve Thompson (2), J. Leonard, Martin Johnson, Kay, Richard Hill (2), Back, Dallaglio, K. Bracken, Jonny Wilkinson, B. Cohen, Tindall, W. Greenwood, Jason Robinson, J. Lewsey]
[*Bench:* S. Borthwick, Gomarsall, Grayson, Luger (rep), Vickery (rep), D. West, J. Worsley (rep)]
[*Scorers:* **penalty goals** by Jonny Wilkinson (4), **drop goal** by Jonny Wilkinson]

COOK CUP MATCH

CAPTAIN: *Martin Johnson*
21st June AUSTRALIA 14 **ENGLAND** 25
Telstra Dome, Melbourne
[*Team:* Trevor Woodman, Steve Thompson (2), Vickery, Martin Johnson, Kay, Richard Hill (2), Back, Dallaglio, K. Bracken, Jonny Wilkinson, B. Cohen, Tindall, W. Greenwood, Jason Robinson, J. Lewsey]

[*Bench:* S. Borthwick (rep), Matt Dawson (rep), A. King, J. Leonard, Luger, M. Regan, J. Worsley (rep)]
[*Scorers:* **tries** by W. Greenwood, Tindall and B. Cohen, **penalty goals** by Jonny Wilkinson (2), **conversions** by Jonny Wilkinson (2)]

ENGLAND COUNTIES TOUR TO ROMANIA AND FRANCE 2003

[**MANAGER:** *Rob Udwin*] [**ASSISTANT MANAGER:** *Danny Hodgson*] [**COACH:** *Bob Hood*] [**ASSISTANT COACH:** *Tommy Borthwick*]
[*Other squad members:* Martin Giraud (*wing*) (tm), Ed Thorpe (*number 8*)]
(squad of 26)
[The England Counties squad travelled to Romania on 7th June 2003; The England Counties squad returned home after the Romania match and then travelled to France shortly before the France Amateurs match; Martin Giraud played for Wales U21 in 1996 but qualified for England due to residency]
CAPTAIN: *Tony Windo*
[14th Jun ROMANIA 45 **ENGLAND COUNTIES** 23]
Stadionul National "Lia Manoliu", Bucharest
[*Team:* Windo, M. Armstrong, Martin O'Keefe, J. Oakes, Soper, Florent Rossigneux, N. Bland, G. Wilson, Paul Knight (2), Peter Murphy, Kirkby, Bonney, Craig Cooper, James Moore, Robert 'Rob' Hitchmough]
[*Bench:* Paul Arnold (2) (*lock*) (rep), S. Brady (rep), Andy Brown (rep), Muckalt (rep), Paul Price (*prop/hooker*) (rep), Sigley (rep), John Swords (*centre/wing*) (rep)]
[*Scorers:* **tries** by Soper and penalty try, **penalty goals** by J. Moore (3), **conversions** by J. Moore (2)]
[24th Jun FRANCE AMATEURS 26 **ENGLAND COUNTIES*** 24]
Stade Ernest Argeles, Blagnac
[*Team:* Windo, M. Armstrong, O'Keefe, J. Oakes, Soper, Rossigneux, S. Brady, Muckalt, Andy Brown, Peter Murphy, Kirkby, Bonney, Sean Casey, J. Moore, Hitchmough]
[*Bench:* Paul Arnold (2) (rep), S. Brady (rep), C. Cooper (*centre/wing*) (rep), David 'Dave' Knight (*centre/wing/full back*) (rep), Paul Knight (2) (*scrum half*) (rep), P. Price (rep), Sigley (rep), G. Wilson (rep)]
[*Scorers:* **tries** by J. Moore, S. Brady and S. Casey, **penalty goal** by J. Moore, **conversions** by J. Moore (3)]

IRB U21 WORLD CHAMPIONSHIP

England
[*Other squad members:* Peter Cook (2) (never travelled, replaced by Aston Croall), Kyriacou (never travelled, replaced by Rob Hawkins), Robbie Morris (never travelled, replaced by Jason Hobson), Ben Russell (2) (never travelled, replaced by John Hart (2)), T. Taylor (returned home as injured, replaced by Andy Reay)]
(squad of 26)
[Harry Ellis and Dan Hipkiss initially selected but withdrew due to injury, being replaced by Clive Stuart-Smith and James Bailey respectively; England U21 were ranked in Pool C and played their matches against the 3 teams in Pool B; Andy Reay travelled later as a replacement for Tim Taylor; Richard Martin-Redman travelled later as a replacement for Ben Skirving; Dan Hipkiss, Tom Williams and Harry Ellis travelled later as replacements for Spencer Davey, Ugo Monye and Paul Hodgson respectively]
(During the First Round a bonus point was awarded for scoring 4 or more tries in a match and for losing by seven points or less)
[**MANAGER:** *Peter Drewett*] [**COACH:** *Jon Callard*] [**ASSISTANT COACHES:** *Nigel Redman*

& *Paul Grayson*]

CAPTAIN: *Chris Day*

First Round - Pool 'C'

[13th Jun **ENGLAND U21*** 22 AUSTRALIA U21 52]

Iffley Road, Oxford

[*Team:* M. Holford, C. Rowland, M. Stevens, Pendlebury, Day, Lund, B. Woods, Benjamin 'Ben' Skirving, Stuart-Smith, Bradley 'Brad' Davies, M. Garvey, S. Davey, C. Bell, Monye, Thrower]

[*Bench:* H. Barratt (*centre/wing/full back*), Aston Croall (*prop*) (rep), John Hart (2) (*number 8*) (rep), Rob Hawkins (*hooker*) (rep), P. Hodgson, Peacey (rep), A. Winnan (*fly half/wing/full back*)]

[*Scorers:* **tries** by C. Rowland, M. Holford and penalty try, **penalty goal** by Thrower, **conversions** by Thrower (2)]

CAPTAIN: *Paul Hodgson*

[17th Jun **ENGLAND U21** 69 JAPAN U21 3 **BP**]

Newbury RFC, Monks Lane, Newbury

[*Team:* Croall, R. Hawkins, J. Hobson, Pendlebury, Parling, John Hart (2), Peacey, Skirving, P. Hodgson, A. Winnan, H. Barratt, Andrew 'Andy' Reay, C. Bell, J. Bailey, Thrower]

[*Bench:* Brad Davies (*fly half*), Day, M. Holford, Monye (rep), C. Rowland (rep), Stuart-Smith, B. Woods]

[*Scorers:* **tries** by A. Reay, J. Bailey (3), Thrower, C. Bell, J. Hobson, Monye (2) and H. Barratt (2), **conversions** by Thrower (7)]

CAPTAIN: *Chris Day*

[21st Jun **ENGLAND U21*** 16 FRANCE U21 21 **BP**]

Henley RFC, Dry Leas, Marlow Road, Henley-on-Thames

[*Team:* Croall, C. Rowland, M. Stevens, Pendlebury, Day, B. Woods, Peacey, John Hart (2), Stuart-Smith, A. Winnan, M. Garvey, S. Davey, H. Barratt, J. Bailey, Thrower]

[*Bench:* Brad Davies, R. Hawkins (rep), J. Hobson (rep), P. Hodgson, Lund (rep), Parling, A. Reay (*centre*) (rep)]

[*Scorers:* **try** by J. Bailey, **penalty goals** by Thrower (3), **conversion** by Thrower]

[England U21 failed to score enough bonus points to get into the top 4 teams and thus did not have a chance of playing for a place in the final]

5th/6th/7th/8th Place Semi-Final

[25th Jun **ENGLAND U21** 27 WALES U21 44]

Henley RFC, Dry Leas, Marlow Road, Henley-on-Thames

[*Team:* M. Holford, R. Hawkins, M. Stevens, Parling, Day, B. Woods, Peacey, John Hart (2), P. Hodgson, A. Winnan, H. Barratt, A. Reay, C. Bell, J. Bailey, Thrower]

[*Bench:* Brad Davies (rep), M. Garvey (*wing*) (rep), J. Hobson (rep), Lund (rep), Martin-Redman (*flanker/number 8*) (rep), C. Rowland (rep), Stuart-Smith (rep)]

[*Scorers:* **tries** by C. Bell (2) and A. Reay, **penalty goals** by Thrower (2), **conversions** by Thrower and A. Winnan (2)]

7th/8th Place Play-Off

[29th Jun **ENGLAND U21*** 22 SCOTLAND U21 33]

Newbury RFC, Monks Lane, Newbury

[*Team:* M. Holford, C. Rowland, M. Stevens, Pendlebury, Day, B. Woods, Lund, John Hart (2), Stuart-Smith, Brad Davies, H. Barratt, Hipkiss, C. Bell, T. Williams, A. Winnan]

[*Bench:* Croall (rep), Harry Ellis (*scrum half*) (rep), R. Hawkins, Martin-Redman (rep), Parling

(rep), A. Reay (rep), Thrower (rep)]
[*Scorers:* **tries** by C. Bell, T. Williams and M. Holford, **penalty goal** by A. Winnan, **conversions** by A. Winnan (2)]

POSITION: 8TH PLACE

FANTASY: *7TH PLACE*

[On 29th June 2003 France beat Wales 24-20 in the 5th/6th Place Play-Off match but on 8th July 2003 the IRB retrospectively changed this result, awarding the match to Wales after they complained that France had broken the competition rules by failing to provide a second front row replacement during the match]

CHURCHILL CUP

Canada
[*No other squad members*]
(squad of 30)
[On 7th November 2002 the RFU announced that they had signed a memorandum of understanding with both the Canadian Rugby Union (Rugby Canada) and the United States of America Rugby Football Union (USA Rugby), for a Strategic Alliance which featured the holding of a Churchill Cup tournament at Vancouver in June 2003; The IRB approved this competition on 14th November 2002; Jim Mallinder and Steve Diamond were both appointed on 31st March 2003; Jim Mallinder was capped for England in May 1997; Steve Diamond sat on the bench for England against Argentina in June 1997; Julian White, Maurice Fitzgerald, Alex Sanderson, Lewis Moody, Adam Vander, James Forrester, Austin Healey, Charlie Hodgson, Ollie Smith (2) and Tom May were all unavailable for this tournament due to injury; Mike Catt was rested for this tournament; Tom Palmer (2) initially selected but withdrew as he was now required to join the simultaneous England tour of New Zealand and Australia, being replaced by Alex Codling; The England A squad departed for Canada on 7th June 2003; Henry Paul and Phil Greening were in the original squad but travelled later due to their England 7s commitments; The original squad of 23 was later augmented to 30 on 10th June 2003 when Mike Worsley, Tom Palmer (2), Paul Volley, Andy Hazell, Ben Johnston, James Simpson-Daniel and Iain Balshaw flew in from New Zealand; Tom Palmer (2) returned home injured after the First Round USA match without being replaced]
[**COACH:** David *James 'Jim' Mallinder*] [**ASSISTANT COACH:** *Steve Diamond*]

CAPTAIN: *Hugh Vyvyan*

First Round

[14th Jun CANADA 7 **ENGLAND A** 43]
Thunderbird Stadium, Vancouver
[*Team:* Sheridan, Titterrell, William Robert 'Will' Green (1), Alex Brown, Codling, Anglesea, D. Hyde, H. Vyvyan, Martyn Wood, Walder, Christophers, H. Paul, F. Waters, Cueto, Scarbrough]
[*Bench:* Barkley (rep), M. Cairns (rep), Flatman (rep), N. Hatley (rep), Horak (*full back*) (rep), Chris Jones (rep), Walshe (rep)]
[*Scorers:* **tries** by Scarbrough, Titterrell, Martyn Wood, F. Waters, Cueto and M. Cairns, **penalty goals** by Walder (3), **conversions** by Walder and Flatman]
[21st Jun USA 10 **ENGLAND A** 36]
Thunderbird Stadium, Vancouver
[*Team:* M. Worsley, Greening, Flatman, Tom Palmer (2), Chris Jones, Volley, Hazell, H. Vyvyan, Walshe, Barkley, J. Simpson-Daniel, Ben Johnston, F. Waters, Balshaw, Horak]

[*Bench:* Anglesea (rep), M. Cairns (rep), Will Green (1) (*prop*) (rep), N. Hatley (rep), H. Paul (rep), Scarbrough (rep), Martyn Wood (rep)]
[*Scorers:* **tries** by Horak (4), Balshaw and Anglesea, **conversions** by Barkley (3)]
Final
[28th Jun USA 6 **ENGLAND A** 43]
Thunderbird Stadium, Vancouver
[*Team:* Sheridan, Titterrell, Will Green (1), Alex Brown, Codling, Anglesea, D. Hyde, H. Vyvyan, Martyn Wood, Walder, J. Simpson-Daniel, H. Paul, Ben Johnston, Cueto, Balshaw]
[*Bench:* Barkley (rep), Christophers (rep), Flatman (rep), Greening (rep), Chris Jones (rep), Volley (rep), M. Worsley (rep)]
[*Scorers:* **tries** by Ben Johnston, H. Vyvyan, Anglesea, H. Paul, Greening and Balshaw, **penalty goal** by Walder, **conversions** by Walder (4) and Barkley]
POSITION: WINNERS

ENGLAND 'A' TOUR TO JAPAN 2003

[**COACH:** *Jim Mallinder*] [**ASSISTANT COACH:** *Steve Diamond*]
[*Other squad members:* Alex Brown (tm), M. Cairns (tm), Christophers (tm), Flatman (tm), Horak (tm), Walshe (tm), F. Waters (tm)]
(squad of 29)
[Julian White, Maurice Fitzgerald, Tom Palmer (2), Alex Sanderson, Lewis Moody, Adam Vander, James Forrester, Austin Healey, Charlie Hodgson, Ollie Smith (2), Tom May and Adam Vander were all unavailable for this tour due to injury; Mike Catt was rested for this tour; The England A squad departed for Japan from Canada on 29th June 2003 and arrived on 1st July 2003]
CAPTAIN: *Hugh Vyvyan*
[6th July JAPAN 20 **ENGLAND A** 55]
National Olympic Stadium, Tokyo
[*Team:* M. Worsley, Greening, Will Green (1), Codling, Chris Jones, Anglesea, Hazell, H. Vyvyan, Martyn Wood, Walder, J. Simpson-Daniel, H. Paul, Ben Johnston, Cueto, Balshaw]
[*Bench:* Barkley (rep), N. Hatley (rep), D. Hyde (rep), Scarbrough (rep), Sheridan (rep), Titterrell (rep), Volley (rep)]
[*Scorers:* **tries** by M. Worsley, Martyn Wood (2), Balshaw (2), J. Simpson-Daniel, Will Green, N. Hatley and Ben Johnston, **conversions** by Walder (5)]

GREENE KING HENLEY INTERNATIONAL SEVENS

Henley RFC, Dry Leas, Marlow Road, Henley-on-Thames
[*Tournament squad:* James Haskell (*prop*), R. Thirlby, Will Matthews (*forward*), Martin Freeman (*wing*)]
[The Young England Sevens team was formed as a development side for the full England Sevens team; Young England prepared for this tournament by participating in the Cayman International Sevens at George Town on 20th-21st June 2003; Joe Lydon was appointed on 23rd July 2003; James Haskell played for England in the U19 World Championship in France in April 2003]
[**COACH:** *Joe Lydon*]
CAPTAIN: *Rob Thirlby*
First Round
[10th Aug **YOUNG ENGLAND** 40 Apache 0]
[*Team:*]
[*Bench:*]
[*Scorers:*]

Quarter-Final
[10th Aug **YOUNG ENGLAND** 5 British Army (*SER*) 17]
[*Team:*]
[*Bench:*]
[*Scorers:*]
[Shield Qualifying Round:]
[10th Aug **YOUNG ENGLAND** 17 UGANDA CRANES 26]
[*Team:*]
[*Bench:*]
[*Scorers:*]
POSITION: LOSING QUARTER-FINALISTS

LONDON PRIDE MIDDLESEX SEVENS
RUSSELL-CARGILL MEMORIAL CUP
Twickenham
[*Tournament squad:* Akinola 'Aki' Abiola (*wing*), J. Bailey (*wing*), Rodd Penney (*centre*), R. Thirlby, Burrill (*back*), Matt Rhodes (*scrum half*), P. Hodgson, Haskell, Tom Rees (*forward*), B. Woods (*forward*), W. Matthews]
(squad of 11)
[Young England wore navy blue shirts for this tournament; Ed Burrill played for the Samurai in the Hong Kong Tens at Hong Kong Football Club on 24th-25th March 2004; Tom Rees and Aki Abiola played for England in the U19 World Championships in France in April 2003 and Italy in March 2002 respectively]
[**COACH:** *Joe Lydon*]
CAPTAIN: *Rob Thirlby*
First Round
[16th Aug **YOUNG ENGLAND** 26 London Irish 10]
[*Team:*]
[*Bench:*]
[*Scorers:* **try** by Haskell]
Quarter-Final
[16th Aug **YOUNG ENGLAND** 0 Newcastle Falcons 42]
[*Team:*]
[*Bench:*]
[*No scorers*]
POSITION: LOSING QUARTER-FINALISTS

FIRST INVESTEC CHALLENGE MATCH
[*Other squad members:* Back, Balshaw, K. Bracken, B. Cohen, Dallaglio, Matt Dawson, W. Greenwood, Grayson, Hazell, Richard Hill (2) (*flanker/number 8*), Martin Johnson, Kay, J. Lewsey, Jason Robinson, Rowntree, Steve Thompson (2), Tindall, Titterrell, Vickery, Jonny Wilkinson, Trevor Woodman]
(squad of 43)
[First warm-up match for the 2003 World Cup; Charlie Hodgson unavailable due to injury; A 43 man World Cup training squad was announced on 9th July 2003]
[**HEAD COACH:** *Clive Woodward*] [**COACH:** *Andy Robinson*] [**ASSISTANT COACH:** *Phil Larder*]

CAPTAIN: *Jason Leonard*

23rd Aug WALES 9 **ENGLAND** 43

Millennium Stadium, Cardiff

[*Team:* J. Leonard, M. Regan, Julian White, Grewcock, S. Shaw, Corry, Moody, J. Worsley, Gomarsall, A. King, Luger, S. Abbott, Noon, J. Simpson-Daniel, Scarbrough]

[*Bench:* S. Borthwick (rep), Will Green (1) (rep), Healey, A. Sanderson (rep), Ollie Smith (2) (rep), Walder (rep), D. West (rep)]

[*Scorers:* **tries** by Moody, Luger, J. Worsley, S. Abbott and D. West, **penalty goals** by A. King (3), **drop goal** by A. King, **conversions** by A. King (2) and Walder]

SECOND WORLD CUP WARM-UP MATCH

[*Other squad members:* S. Abbott, Back, K. Bracken, Dallaglio, Matt Dawson, Will Green (1) (never travelled as withdrew), W. Greenwood, Richard Hill (2), Martin Johnson, Kay, A. King, Luger, M. Regan, Jason Robinson, Scarbrough, J. Simpson-Daniel, Titterrell, Vickery, Jonny Wilkinson, Trevor Woodman, J. Worsley]

(squad of 43)

[Second warm-up match for the 2003 World Cup; Charlie Hodgson unavailable due to injury; Will Green (1) chose not to travel to Marseille due to family reasons]

[**HEAD COACH:** *Clive Woodward*] [**COACH:** *Andy Robinson*] [**ASSISTANT COACH:** *Phil Larder*]

CAPTAIN: *Dorian West [Paul Grayson took over when Dorian West was substituted in the 2nd half]*

30th Aug FRANCE 17 **ENGLAND*** 16

Stade Vélodrome, Marseille

[*Team:* Rowntree, D. West, Julian White, S. Borthwick, Grewcock, Corry, Moody, A. Sanderson, Healey, Grayson, B. Cohen, Tindall, Ollie Smith (2), J. Lewsey, Balshaw]

[*Bench:* Gomarsall (rep), Hazell, J. Leonard (rep), Noon (rep), S. Shaw (rep), Steve Thompson (2) (rep), Walder]

[*Scorers:* **try** by Tindall, **penalty goals** by Grayson (3), **conversion** by Grayson]

SECOND INVESTEC CHALLENGE MATCH

[*Other squad members:* Dallaglio, Gomarsall, Grewcock, Healey, A. King (withdrew due to injury, replaced by Mike Catt), Luger, M. Regan, Rowntree, J. Simpson-Daniel, Ollie Smith (2), Tindall, Vickery, J. Worsley]

(squad of 35)

[Third warm-up match for the 2003 World Cup; Charlie Hodgson unavailable due to injury; Clive Woodward reduced his World Cup training squad from 43 to 35 on 1st September 2003; Alex King withdrew from the World Cup training squad on 4th September 2003 due to injury; Mark Regan, Phil Vickery, Joe Worsley, Lawrence Dallaglio, Mike Tindall and James Simpson-Daniel were all unavailable for this match due to injury]

[**HEAD COACH:** *Clive Woodward*] [**COACH:** *Andy Robinson*] [**ASSISTANT COACH:** *Phil Larder*]

CAPTAIN: *Martin Johnson [Neil Back took over when Martin Johnson was substituted in the 2nd half]*

6th Sept **ENGLAND** 45 FRANCE 14

Twickenham

[*Team:* Trevor Woodman, Steve Thompson (2), Julian White, Martin Johnson, Kay, Richard Hill (2), Back, Corry, K. Bracken, Jonny Wilkinson, B. Cohen, S. Abbott, W. Greenwood, Balshaw, Jason Robinson]

[*Bench:* Matt Dawson (rep), Grayson (rep), J. Leonard (rep), J. Lewsey (rep), Moody (rep), S. Shaw (rep), D. West (rep)]
[*Scorers:* **tries** by B. Cohen (2), Jason Robinson, Balshaw and J. Lewsey, **penalty goals** by Jonny Wilkinson (4), **conversions** by Jonny Wilkinson (3) and Grayson]

WORLD CUP

WEBB ELLIS CUP

Australia
[*No other squad members*]
(squad of 30)
[Charlie Hodgson and Alex King were unavailable for this tournament due to injury; The World Cup squad of 30 was announced on 7th September 2003; The England squad departed for Australia on 1st October 2003; Austin Healey was initially invited to travel to Australia to provide potential scrum half injury cover for Kyran Bracken, Matt Dawson and Andy Gomarsall, but Healey then himself proved to be unavailable due to a calf injury, which meant that it was Martyn Wood who actually travelled to Australia on 12th October 2003!; Martyn Wood was not officially added to the squad and returned home on 16th October 2003 after the scrum half injury crisis abated; Will Greenwood temporarily travelled home on 19th October 2003 due to a family illness and then returned to Australia on 27th October 2003; Martin Corry briefly returned home on 26th October 2003 for family reasons and then arrived back in Australia on 31st October 2003; Simon Shaw travelled to Australia on 2nd November 2003 as a replacement for Danny Grewcock; Austin Healey travelled to Australia on 9th November 2003 as a potential replacement for Iain Balshaw and Josh Lewsey, but was not officially added to the squad and duly returned home on 12th November 2003 after both Balshaw and Josh Lewsey passed a fitness test]
(During the First Round a bonus point was awarded for scoring 4 or more tries in a match and for losing by seven points or less)
[**HEAD COACH:** *Clive Woodward*] [**COACH:** *Andy Robinson*] [**ASSISTANT COACH:** *Phil Larder*]
CAPTAIN: *Martin Johnson*
First Round - Pool 'C'
12th Oct GEORGIA 6 **ENGLAND** 84 **BP**
Subiaco Oval, Perth
[*Team:* Trevor Woodman, Steve Thompson (2), Vickery, Martin Johnson, Kay, Richard Hill (2), Back, Dallaglio, Matt Dawson, Jonny Wilkinson, B. Cohen, Tindall, W. Greenwood, Jason Robinson, J. Lewsey]
[*Bench:* Grayson (rep), Gomarsall (rep), Grewcock, J. Leonard (rep), Luger (rep), Moody (rep), M. Regan (rep)]
[*Scorers:* **tries** by Tindall, Matt Dawson, Steve Thompson, Back, Dallaglio, W. Greenwood (2), M. Regan, B. Cohen (2), Jason Robinson and Luger, **penalty goals** by Jonny Wilkinson (2), **conversions** by Jonny Wilkinson (5) and Grayson (4)]
18th Oct SOUTH AFRICA 6 **ENGLAND** 25
Subiaco Oval, Perth
[*Team:* Trevor Woodman, Steve Thompson (2), Vickery, Martin Johnson, Kay, Moody, Back, Dallaglio, K. Bracken, Jonny Wilkinson, B. Cohen, Tindall, W. Greenwood, J. Lewsey, Jason Robinson]
[*Bench:* Corry, Gomarsall, Grayson, J. Leonard (rep), Luger (rep), D. West, J. Worsley (rep)]

[*Scorers:* **try** by W. Greenwood, **penalty goals** by Jonny Wilkinson (4), **drop goals** by Jonny Wilkinson (2), **conversion** by Jonny Wilkinson]

26th Oct SAMOA 22 **ENGLAND** 35 **BP**

Telstra Dome, Melbourne

[*Team:* J. Leonard, M. Regan, Julian White, Martin Johnson, Kay, J. Worsley, Back, Dallaglio, Matt Dawson, Jonny Wilkinson, B. Cohen, Tindall, S. Abbott, Balshaw, Jason Robinson]

[*Bench:* M. Catt (rep), Corry, Gomarsall, Luger, Moody (rep), Steve Thompson (2) (rep), Vickery (rep)]

[*Scorers:* **tries** by Back, penalty try, Balshaw and Vickery, **penalty goals** by Jonny Wilkinson (2), **drop goal** by Jonny Wilkinson, **conversions** by Jonny Wilkinson (3)]

CAPTAIN: *Phil Vickery [Martin Johnson took over when Phil Vickery was substituted in the 2nd half]*

2nd Nov URUGUAY 13 **ENGLAND** 111 **BP**

Suncorp Stadium, Lang Park, Brisbane

[*Team:* J. Leonard, D. West, Vickery, Corry, Grewcock, J. Worsley, Moody, Dallaglio, Gomarsall, Grayson, Luger, M. Catt, S. Abbott, Balshaw, J. Lewsey]

[*Bench:* K. Bracken (rep), W. Greenwood (rep), Martin Johnson (rep), Kay, Jason Robinson (rep), Steve Thompson (2), Julian White (rep)]

[*Scorers:* **tries** by Moody, J. Lewsey (5), Balshaw (2), M. Catt (2), Gomarsall (2), Luger, S. Abbott, Jason Robinson (2) and W. Greenwood, **conversions** by Grayson (11) and M. Catt (2)]

CAPTAIN: *Martin Johnson*

Quarter-Final

9th Nov WALES 17 **ENGLAND** 28

Suncorp Stadium, Lang Park, Brisbane

[*Team:* J. Leonard, Steve Thompson (2), Vickery, Martin Johnson, Kay, Moody, Back, Dallaglio, Matt Dawson, Jonny Wilkinson, B. Cohen, Tindall, W. Greenwood, Luger, Jason Robinson]

[*Bench:* S. Abbott (rep), K. Bracken (rep), M. Catt (rep), S. Shaw, D. West, Trevor Woodman (rep), J. Worsley]

[*Scorers:* **try** by W. Greenwood, **penalty goals** by Jonny Wilkinson (6), **drop goal** by Jonny Wilkinson, **conversion** by Jonny Wilkinson]

Semi-Final

16th Nov FRANCE 7 **ENGLAND** 24

Telstra Stadium, Sydney Olympic Park, Homebush Bay, Sydney

[*Team:* Trevor Woodman, Steve Thompson (2), Vickery, Martin Johnson, Kay, Richard Hill (2), Back, Dallaglio, Matt Dawson, Jonny Wilkinson, B. Cohen, M. Catt, W. Greenwood, Jason Robinson, J. Lewsey]

[*Bench:* Balshaw, K. Bracken (rep), Corry, J. Leonard (rep), Moody (rep), Tindall (rep), D. West (rep)]

[*Scorers:* **penalty goals** by Jonny Wilkinson (5), **drop goals** by Jonny Wilkinson (3)]

Final

22nd Nov AUSTRALIA 17 **ENGLAND** 20 aet

Telstra Stadium, Sydney Olympic Park, Homebush Bay, Sydney

[*Team:* Trevor Woodman, Steve Thompson (2), Vickery, Martin Johnson, Kay, Richard Hill

(2), Back, Dallaglio, Matt Dawson, Jonny Wilkinson, B. Cohen, Tindall, W. Greenwood, Jason Robinson, J. Lewsey]
[*Bench:* Balshaw (rep), K. Bracken, M. Catt (rep), Corry, J. Leonard (rep), Moody (rep), D. West]
[*Scorers:* **try** by Jason Robinson, **penalty goals** by Jonny Wilkinson (4), **drop goal** by Jonny Wilkinson]
POSITION: WINNERS

OTHER MATCHES

ESS REMEMBRANCE MATCH

[NO COACH NOMINATED]
CAPTAIN: *Dan Baugh* (CAN)
[11th Nov COMBINED SERVICES (*SER*) 8 **BARBARIANS** 26]
Army Rugby Stadium, Queen's Avenue, Aldershot
[*Team:* Adam Black, Paul Young (WA), Joaquim Ferreira (POR), Scott MacLeod (SC), Peter 'Pete' Taylor, Ian Boobyer (WA), Jason Forster (WA), Dan Baugh (CAN), Luis Pissarra (POR), Craig Warlow (WA), Andrew Turnbull (SC), Jamie Robinson (WA), Whetstone, Cameron 'Cammie' Murray (SC), Gonçalo Malheiro (POR)]
[*Bench:* Richard Baxter (rep), N. Boobyer (WA) (*centre*) (rep), Andy Cuthbert (rep), Paul Evans (*lock*) (rep), Paul John (WA) (*scrum half*) (rep), Porte (rep), Tony Yapp (*fly half*) (rep)]
[*Scorers:* **tries** by Baugh (CAN), Whetstone, Jason Forster (WA) and Malheiro (POR), **conversions** by Malheiro (POR) (3)]
[*Match to commemorate the members of the British uniformed services who lost their lives during armed conflict*]

ENGLAND SEVENS TRAINING MATCH

[ENGLAND VII: [MANAGER: *John Elliott*] **[COACH:** *Joe Lydon*] **[ASSISTANT COACH:** *Mike Friday*]]
[SAMURAI: [MANAGER: *Terrence 'Terry' Sands*] **[COACHES:** *Jim Fitzsimons* (NZ) & *Colin Hillman* (WA)] **[PLAYER-COACH:** *Mike Friday*]]
CAPTAIN: *Simon Amor* [England VII]
CAPTAIN: *??* [Samurai]
2nd Dec **ENGLAND VII** 35 **SAMURAI** 30
Rashid School, Dubai
[ENGLAND VII: [*Team:*]
[*Bench:*]
[*Scorers:*]]
[SAMURAI: [*Team:*]
[*Bench:* Friday (rep)]
[*Scorers:*]]
[*Practice match played prior to the Emirates Airline Dubai Rugby Sevens*]
[*Colin Hillman died of cancer in July 2009*]

ENGLAND U21 TRIAL MATCH

[ENGLAND U21 NORTH XV: [MANAGER: *Peter Drewett*] **[COACH:** *Jon Callard*] **[ASSISTANT COACH:** *Nigel Redman*]]
[ENGLAND U21 SOUTH XV: [MANAGER: *Peter Drewett*] **[COACH:** *Jon Callard*] **[ASSISTANT COACH:** *Nigel Redman*]]

CAPTAIN: *Geoff Parling* [England U21 North XV]
CAPTAIN: *Nils Mordt* [England U21 South XV]

[2nd Dec **ENGLAND U21 NORTH XV** 26 **ENGLAND U21 SOUTH XV** 26]

Broadstreet RFC, Ivor Preece Field, Binley Woods, Coventry

[ENGLAND U21 NORTH XV: [*Team:* Tom French (2), Stuart Friswell, Matthew 'Matt' Hampson, James Percival, Parling, L. Abraham, Ed Williamson, Mark Hopley, Rhodri McAtee, Ben Russell (1), H. Barratt, Chris Briers, T. Allen, Yomi Akinyemi, Jon Clarke]

[*Bench:* Iyran Clunis (*hooker*) (rep), Nathan Jones (*scrum half*) (rep), Thomas 'Tom' Ryder (*lock/number 8*) (rep), Thomas 'Tom' Warren (*flanker*) (rep), James Wellwood (*centre/wing*) (rep)]

[*Scorers:* **tries** by M. Hampson, T. Warren, Friswell and T. Allen, **conversions** by Ben Russell (3)**]]**

[ENGLAND U21 SOUTH XV: [*Team:* James Graham, James Greenwood, Michael 'Mike' Guess, Tom Parker (1), William 'Will' Bowley, Richard Thorpe, Christopher 'Chris' Cracknell, Tom Guest, Joseph 'Joe' Bedford, Adrian Jarvis, Delon Armitage, Nils Mordt, A. Frost, M. Foster, T. Williams]

[*Bench:* Andrew 'Andy' Buist (*lock*) (rep), Cameron Dott (*hooker*) (rep), Mark Hanson (2) (*prop*) (rep), Ross Laidlaw (rep), Luke Narraway (*flanker*) (rep), Gregory 'Greg' Nicholls (*scrum half*) (rep), Simon Whatling (*fly half/centre*) (rep)]

[*Scorers:* **tries** by J. Greenwood, D. Armitage, T. Williams and Cracknell, **conversions** by A. Jarvis (2) and Ross Laidlaw**]]**

EMIRATES AIRLINE DUBAI RUGBY SEVENS
IRB WORLD SEVENS SERIES 2003-2004 ROUND 1

Dubai Exiles Stadium, Dubai

[*Tournament squad:* Amor, Appleford, James Brooks, Dowson, Gollings, R. Haughton, Hipkiss (*back/forward*), Monye, P. Sanderson, Tom Rees, Roques, R. Thirlby]

(squad of 12)

[Neil Baxter and Phil Greening in original training squad of 10 but withdrew due to injury; Simon Amor was the tournament captain; Tom Rees played for M.R. Steele-Bodger's XV against Cambridge University at Grange Road on 26th November 2003]

[**MANAGER:** *John Elliott*] [**COACH:** *Joe Lydon*] [**ASSISTANT COACH:** *Mike Friday*]

CAPTAIN: *Ben Gollings*

First Round - Pool 'A'

4th Dec MOROCCO 0 **ENGLAND** 45

[*Team:* Appleford, Dowson, P. Sanderson, James Brooks, Gollings, Hipkiss, Monye]

[*Bench:* Amor (rep), R. Haughton, Roques, Tom Rees (rep), R. Thirlby (rep)]

[*Scorers:* **tries** by Monye (2), Gollings (3), Hipkiss and R. Thirlby, **conversions** by Gollings (5)]

CAPTAIN: *Simon Amor*

4th Dec SRI LANKA 0 **ENGLAND** 75

[*Team:* Appleford, Roques, Tom Rees, James Brooks, Amor, R. Thirlby, R. Haughton]

[*Bench:* Dowson, Gollings (rep), Hipkiss (rep), Monye, P. Sanderson (rep)]

[*Scorers:* **tries** by Amor (2), R. Haughton (2), Appleford, Tom Rees, R. Thirlby, Gollings (2), P. Sanderson and James Brooks, **conversions** by Amor (5), R. Haughton and Gollings (4)]

4th Dec FRANCE 0 **ENGLAND** 40

[*Team:* Roques, ?, ?, Amor, Gollings, Appleford, Monye]

[*Bench:* R. Haughton, Hipkiss, R. Thirlby (rep), ?, ?]

[*Scorers:* **tries** by Monye, Roques, Amor (2), R. Thirlby and Appleford, **conversions** by Gollings (4) and Amor]

Quarter-Final

5th Dec ARGENTINA 5 **ENGLAND** 14

[*Team:* Roques, Appleford, Dowson, Amor, Gollings, R. Thirlby, Monye]

[*Bench:* James Brooks (rep), R. Haughton, Hipkiss (rep), Tom Rees, P. Sanderson (rep)]

[*Scorers:* **tries** by Monye and R. Thirlby, **conversions** by Gollings (2)]

CAPTAIN: *Ben Gollings*

Semi-Final

5th Dec SOUTH AFRICA 13 **ENGLAND*** 12

[*Team:* Roques, Dowson, P. Sanderson, James Brooks, Gollings, Appleford, R. Haughton]

[*Bench:* Hipkiss (rep), Monye (rep), Tom Rees, R. Thirlby (rep)]

[*Scorers:* **tries** by R. Haughton and R. Thirlby, **conversion** by Gollings]

POSITION: LOSING SEMI-FINALISTS

FANTASY: *WINNERS*

[*England scored 12 competition points in this Round of the 2003-2004 IRB World Sevens Series*]

EMIRATES AIRLINE SOUTH AFRICA SEVENS
IRB WORLD SEVENS SERIES 2003-2004 ROUND 2

Outeniqua Park Stadium, George

[*Tournament squad:* Appleford, Roques, Tom Rees, James Brooks, Hipkiss, P. Sanderson, Monye, Dowson, R. Thirlby, Gollings, Amor (captain; never travelled as injured, replaced by Matt Rhodes), R. Haughton, Rhodes]

(*squad of 12*)

[*Tony Roques was the tournament captain*]

[**MANAGER:** *John Elliott*] [**COACH:** *Joe Lydon*] [**ASSISTANT COACH:** *Mike Friday*]

CAPTAIN: *Tony Roques*

First Round - Pool 'A'

12th Dec CANADA 0 **ENGLAND** 38

[*Team:* Appleford, Roques, P. Sanderson, James Brooks, Gollings, Hipkiss, Monye]

[*Bench:* Dowson, R. Haughton, Tom Rees, Rhodes, R. Thirlby]

[*Scorers:* **tries** by Monye (2), James Brooks (2), Gollings and P. Sanderson, **conversions** by Gollings (4)]

12th Dec ZAMBIA 0 **ENGLAND** 33

[*Team:* Dowson, Roques, Tom Rees, James Brooks, R. Thirlby, Appleford, R. Haughton]

[*Bench:* Gollings, Hipkiss (rep), Monye (rep), Rhodes, P. Sanderson]

[*Scorers:* **tries** by Dowson, James Brooks, Tom Rees (2) and R. Thirlby, **conversions** by James Brooks (3) and R. Thirlby]

12th Dec ARGENTINA 5 **ENGLAND** 26

[*Team:* Appleford, Roques, P. Sanderson, James Brooks, Gollings, Hipkiss, R. Thirlby]

[*Bench:* Dowson (rep), R. Haughton (rep), Monye, Tom Rees, Rhodes]

[*Scorers:* **tries** by James Brooks, Gollings (2) and R. Haughton, **conversions** by Gollings (2) and R. Thirlby]

CAPTAIN: *Geoff Appleford*

Quarter-Final

13th Dec FRANCE 0 **ENGLAND** 50

[*Team:* Appleford, Dowson, Tom Rees, James Brooks, Gollings, Thirlby, R. Haughton]

[*Bench:* Hipkiss (rep), Monye (rep), Rhodes, Roques, P. Sanderson (rep)]
[*Scorers:* **tries** by R. Thirlby (2), James Brooks (2), R. Haughton, Gollings, Appleford and Dowson, **conversions** by Gollings (3) and James Brooks (2)]
CAPTAIN: *Tony Roques*
Semi-Final
13th Dec SOUTH AFRICA 7 **ENGLAND** 19
[*Team:* Appleford, Roques, P. Sanderson, James Brooks, Gollings, R. Thirlby, R. Haughton]
[*Bench:* Dowson, Monye (rep), Tom Rees (rep), Rhodes]
[*Scorers:* **tries** by Gollings (2) and R. Thirlby, **conversions** by Gollings (2)]
CAPTAIN: *Geoff Appleford*
Final
13th Dec NEW ZEALAND 14 **ENGLAND** 38
[*Team:* Appleford, Dowson, P. Sanderson, James Brooks, Gollings, R. Thirlby, R. Haughton]
[*Bench:* Hipkiss (rep), Monye (rep), Tom Rees (rep)]
[*Scorers:* **tries** by R. Thirlby (3), R. Haughton and Gollings (2), **conversions** by Gollings (4)]
POSITION: WINNERS
[England scored 20 competition points in this Round of the 2003-2004 IRB World Sevens Series]

ZURICH WORLD CHAMPIONS CHALLENGE

[*Other squad members:* Balshaw (withdrew due to injury, replaced by Ben Cohen), C. Hodgson (withdrew from bench due to injury), Moody (withdrew due to injury, replaced by Corry), M. Regan (withdrew from team due to injury), Steve Thompson (2) (withdrew from team due to injury), Vickery (captain; withdrew due to injury, replaced by Matt Stevens), M. Worsley (withdrew due to injury, replaced by Trevor Woodman)]
(squad of 22)
[Match to celebrate England winning the 2003 World Cup; Julian White and Jonny Wilkinson were unavailable for this match due to injury; Jason Leonard, Dorian West, Martin Johnson, Ben Kay, Lawrence Dallaglio, Neil Back, Matt Dawson, Mike Catt, Will Greenwood, Dan Luger and Josh Lewsey were all rested for this match; An agreement between the RFU and Premier Rugby limited selection to no more than 3 players from each Zurich Premiership club; Mike Worsley, Phil Vickery, Lewis Moody and Iain Balshaw all in original squad of 22 but then withdrew due to injury on 15th December 2003]
[**HEAD COACH:** *Clive Woodward*] [**COACH:** *Andy Robinson*] [**ASSISTANT COACH:** *Phil Larder*]
CAPTAIN: *Richard Hill (2) [Andy Gomarsall took over when Richard Hill (2) went off injured in both the 1st and 2nd half]*
20th Dec **ENGLAND XV** 42 New Zealand Barbarians 17
Twickenham
[*Team:* Trevor Woodman, Titterrell, M. Stevens, Grewcock, S. Shaw, Corry, Richard Hill (2), J. Worsley, Gomarsall, Grayson, B. Cohen, S. Abbott, Ollie Smith (2), J. Simpson-Daniel, Jason Robinson]
[*Bench:* K. Bracken (rep), Gollings (rep), A. Long, P. Sanderson (rep), Sheridan (rep), Tindall (rep), H. Vyvyan (rep)]
[*Scorers:* **tries** by B. Cohen (2), Grayson, M. Stevens, J. Simpson-Daniel and Tindall, **penalty goals** by Grayson (2), **conversions** by Grayson (3)]

JEAN-CLAUDE BAQUÉ SHIELD MATCH

[**MANAGER:** *Rob Udwin*] [**ASSISTANT MANAGER:** *Danny Hodgson*] [**COACH:** *Bob Hood*] [**ASSISTANT COACH:** *Tommy Borthwick*]

CAPTAIN: *Jamie Hamilton*

[28th Dec **ENGLAND COUNTIES*** 18 FRANCE AMATEURS 27]
Henley RFC, Dry Leas, Marlow Road, Henley-on-Thames

[*Team:* Robert 'Rob' Faulkner, Joe Duffy, Neil Collins, Clapham, Soper, Craig Hammond, Matt Evans (1), Muckalt, Jamie Hamilton, Lee Cholewa, Ben Murphy, Bonney, Freeman Payne, C. Cooper, J. Moore]

[*Bench:* S. Brady (rep), Jon Higgins (*fly half*) (rep), Hitchmough (*fly half/wing/full back*) (rep), P. Price, Gareth Roberts (2) (*prop*) (rep), Malcolm 'Mal' Roberts (*centre/wing/full back*) (rep), Richard Senior (*flanker*) (rep)]

[*Scorers:* **tries** by Soper and J. Moore, **penalty goals** by J. Moore (2), **conversion** by J. Moore]

[*Jean-Claude Baqué was the President of FIRA-AER; Nick Bartlett, Andrew Boyle, Mike Blakeburn, John Carter, Lee Crofts, Lee Morley, Ed Norris, Tim Stannard, Luke Walters, Ben Wheeler, Mike Worden, Jody Peacock, Neil Starling and James Tapster were all members of an interim training squad of 36 at Broadstreet RFC, Coventry on 20th December 2003*]

2004
OTHER MATCHES
AXA NEW ZEALAND INTERNATIONAL SEVENS
IRB WORLD SEVENS SERIES 2003-2004 ROUND 3

WestpacTrust Stadium, Wellington

[*Tournament squad:* Amor, James Brooks, Dowson, Gollings, R. Haughton (never travelled as withdrew, replaced by Nnamdi Obi), Hipkiss, Lund (never travelled as withdrew, replaced by Kai Horstmann), Monye (never travelled as injured, replaced by Rodd Penney), N. Mordt (*back/forward*), T. Rees, Roques, R. Thirlby, Kai Horstmann (*forward*), Obi, Penney]
(squad of 12)
[Richard Haughton withdrew due to club commitments]
[**MANAGER:** *John Elliott*] [**COACH:** *Joe Lydon*] [**ASSISTANT COACH:** *Mike Friday*]
CAPTAIN: *Simon Amor*
First Round - Pool 'A'

6th Feb	KENYA	17	**ENGLAND**	26

[*Team:* Dowson, Amor, Gollings]
[*Bench:*]
[*Scorers:* **tries** by Dowson, Hipkiss, Gollings and Amor, **conversions** by Gollings (3)]

6th Feb	PAPUA NEW GUINEA	0	**ENGLAND**	26

[*Team:* Dowson, Amor]
[*Bench:*]
[*Scorers:* **tries** by R. Thirlby (2), James Brooks and Tom Rees, **conversions** by Gollings (3)]

6th Feb	AUSTRALIA	17	**ENGLAND**	26

[*Team:* Roques, ?, ?, Amor, Gollings, ?, Obi]
[*Bench:* Hipkiss (rep)]
[*Scorers:* **tries** by Obi, Gollings (2) and Hipkiss, **conversions** by Gollings (3)]
Quarter-Final

7th Feb	SAMOA	7	**ENGLAND**	19

[*Team:* Amor, Gollings, R. Thirlby]
[*Bench:*]
[*Scorers:* **tries** by R. Thirlby (2) and Amor, **conversions** by Gollings (2)]
Semi-Final

7th Feb	FIJI	15	**ENGLAND***	10 aet

[*Team:* Amor, R. Thirlby, Obi]
[*Bench:*]
[*Scorers:* **tries** by R. Thirlby and Obi]
POSITION: LOSING SEMI-FINALISTS
[England scored 12 competition points in this Round of the 2003-2004 IRB World Sevens Series]

TEAM ROC USA SEVENS
IRB WORLD SEVENS SERIES 2003-2004 ROUND 4

Home Depot Center, Carson City, Los Angeles

[*Tournament squad:* Appleford, R. Haughton, P. Sanderson, Monye, Amor, Roques, Tom Rees, James Brooks, Hipkiss, Dowson, Gollings, R. Thirlby]
(squad of 12)

[**MANAGER:** *John Elliott*] [**COACH:** *Joe Lydon*] [**ASSISTANT COACH:** *Mike Friday*]
CAPTAIN: *Simon Amor*
First Round - Pool 'A'
14th Feb USA 0 **ENGLAND** 40
[*Team:* Dowson, Roques, P. Sanderson, Amor, Gollings, Appleford, Monye]
[*Bench:* James Brooks (rep), R. Haughton (rep), Hipkiss (rep), ?, ?]
[*Scorers:* **tries** by Gollings (2), Amor, Hipkiss and R. Haughton (2), **conversions** by Gollings (4) and James Brooks]
14th Feb TRINIDAD & TOBAGO 0 **ENGLAND** 50
[*Team:* Dowson, Tom Rees, R. Thirlby, James Brooks, Gollings, Hipkiss, Monye]
[*Bench:* Appleford (rep), R. Haughton (rep), P. Sanderson (rep), ?, ?]
[*Scorers:* **tries** by Tom Rees, Hipkiss (2), Monye (2), R. Thirlby, Appleford and P. Sanderson, **conversions** by Gollings (5)]
14th Feb SAMOA 19 **ENGLAND*** 17
[*Team:* Dowson, Roques, P. Sanderson, Amor, Gollings, Appleford, R. Haughton]
[*Bench:* Hipkiss (rep), Monye (rep), R. Thirlby (rep), ?, ?]
[*Scorers:* **tries** by Dowson, Gollings and Amor, **conversion** by Gollings]
Quarter-Final
15th Feb NEW ZEALAND 22 **ENGLAND** 0
[*Team:* P. Sanderson, Roques, R. Thirlby, Amor, Gollings, Appleford, Monye]
[*Bench:* Dowson (rep), R. Haughton (rep), Hipkiss (rep), ?, ?]
[*No scorers*]
[Plate Semi-Final:]
[15th Feb SOUTH AFRICA 7 **ENGLAND** 33 **]**
[*Team:* P. Sanderson, Roques, Tom Rees, Amor, Gollings, R. Thirlby, R. Haughton]
[*Bench:* Appleford (rep), Dowson (rep), Hipkiss (rep), ?, ?]
[*Scorers:* **tries** by P. Sanderson, R. Thirlby, Gollings and R. Haughton (2), **conversions** by Gollings (4)]
[Plate Final:]
[15th Feb CANADA 0 **ENGLAND** 55 **]**
[*Team:* Dowson, Tom Rees, P. Sanderson, Amor, Gollings, Appleford, R. Haughton]
[*Bench:* Hipkiss (rep), Monye (rep), Roques (rep), ?, ?]
[*Scorers:* **tries** by Tom Rees, P, Sanderson, Gollings, Amor, R. Haughton (2), Hipkiss and Monye (2), **conversions** by Gollings (4) and Amor]
POSITION: LOSING QUARTER-FINALISTS [*PLATE WINNERS*]
[England scored 8 competition points in this Round of the 2003-2004 IRB World Sevens Series]

6 NATIONS CHAMPIONSHIP

[**HEAD COACH:** *Clive Woodward*] [**COACH:** *Andy Robinson*] [**ASSISTANT COACH:** *Phil Larder*]
CAPTAIN: *Lawrence Dallaglio*
15th Feb ITALY 9 **ENGLAND** 50
Stadio Flaminio, Rome
[*Team:* Trevor Woodman, Steve Thompson (2), Vickery, Grewcock, Kay, J. Worsley, Richard Hill (2), Dallaglio, Gomarsall, Grayson, B. Cohen, W. Greenwood, Jason Robinson, J. Lewsey, Balshaw]
[*Bench:* Barkley (rep), Matt Dawson (rep), Chris Jones (rep), J. Leonard (rep), H. Paul (rep), M. Regan (rep), S. Shaw (rep)]

[*Scorers:* **tries** by Balshaw, Jason Robinson (3), J. Lewsey, Grayson and Chris Jones, **penalty goals** by Grayson (3), **conversions** by Grayson (3)]

21st Feb SCOTLAND 13 **ENGLAND** 35

Murrayfield

[*Team:* Trevor Woodman, Steve Thompson (2), Vickery, Grewcock, Kay, Chris Jones, Richard Hill (2), Dallaglio, Gomarsall, Grayson, B. Cohen, W. Greenwood, Jason Robinson, J. Lewsey, Balshaw]

[*Bench:* Barkley, Matt Dawson (rep), J. Leonard, H. Paul (rep), M. Regan, A. Sanderson, S. Shaw (rep)]

[*Scorers:* **tries** by B. Cohen, Balshaw, J. Lewsey and Grewcock, **penalty goals** by Grayson (3), **conversions** by Grayson (3)]

6th March **ENGLAND*** 13 IRELAND 19

Twickenham

[*Team:* Trevor Woodman, Steve Thompson (2), Vickery, S. Borthwick, Kay, J. Worsley, Richard Hill (2), Dallaglio, Matt Dawson, Grayson, B. Cohen, W. Greenwood, Jason Robinson, J. Lewsey, Balshaw]

[*Bench:* Back, Barkley (rep), Gomarsall, Chris Jones (rep), M. Regan (rep), J. Simpson-Daniel (rep), M. Stevens]

[*Scorers:* **try** by Matt Dawson, **penalty goals** by Grayson (2), **conversion** by Grayson]

20th Mar **ENGLAND** 31 WALES 21

Twickenham

[*Team:* Trevor Woodman, Steve Thompson (2), Vickery, Grewcock, Kay, Chris Jones, Richard Hill (2), Dallaglio, Matt Dawson, Barkley, B. Cohen, W. Greenwood, Tindall, J. Lewsey, Jason Robinson]

[*Bench:* S. Borthwick, M. Catt (rep), Gomarsall, M. Regan, J. Simpson-Daniel, Julian White (rep), J. Worsley (rep)]

[*Scorers:* **tries** by B. Cohen (2) and J. Worsley, **penalty goals** by Barkley (4), **conversions** by Barkley (2)]

27th Mar FRANCE 24 **ENGLAND*** 21

Stade de France, Paris

[*Team:* Trevor Woodman, Steve Thompson (2), Vickery, Grewcock, Kay, J. Worsley, Richard Hill (2), Dallaglio, Matt Dawson, Barkley, B. Cohen, W. Greenwood, Tindall, J. Lewsey, Jason Robinson]

[*Bench:* S. Borthwick (rep), M. Catt (rep), Corry, Gomarsall, M. Regan, J. Simpson-Daniel, Julian White (rep)]

[*Scorers:* **tries** by B. Cohen and J. Lewsey, **penalty goals** by Barkley (3), **conversion** by Barkley]

POSITION: **3RD 6 +64 CC** [*France 10 +84 GS*, Ireland 8 +46 TC MT, Wales 4 +9, Italy 2 -110, Scotland 0 -93]

FANTASY: ***1ST 10 GS TC CC MT***

OTHER MATCHES

ENGLAND STUDENTS MATCHES

[**MANAGER:** *Tony Lanaway*] [**COACH:** *Richard Hill (1)*] [**ASSISTANT COACH:** *Steve Hill*]

CAPTAIN: *Ross Winney*

[14th Feb ITALY U25 25 **ENGLAND STUDENTS*** 21]

Stadio Comunale di Telese Terme, Benevento

[*Team:* Chesham, Robin Scothern, Matthew 'Matt' Street, James Hudson, Jon Chance, B.

Woods, John Tenconi, T. Hayman, Haydn Thomas, Winney, Chris Wyles, James Whittingham, C. Cooper, Tom Tombleson, Luke Sayer]
[*Bench:* Justin Abrahams (*fly half/centre*), Andrew 'Andy' Dalgleish (*hooker*) (rep), Owen Evans (*fly half/centre*), Hopcroft (*prop*), Andrew 'Andy' Houston (*scrum half*), James Jones (*flanker*), Tom Skelding (*lock*)]
[*Scorers:* **tries** by Dalgleish and Whittingham, **penalty goals** by Whittingham (3), **conversion** by Whittingham]
[19th Mar **ENGLAND STUDENTS** 48 WALES STUDENTS 12]
Clifton RFC, Station Road, Cribbs Causeway, Henbury, Bristol
[*Team:* M. Street, Dalgleish, Hopcroft, Simon Gibbons, Skelding, B. Woods, Tenconi, T. Hayman, Haydn Thomas, Winney, C. Wyles, Whittingham, O. Evans, Tombleson, Sayer]
[*Bench:* Abrahams, M. Foster, Gaunt, James Jones, Ogilvie, Scothern, Wayne Thompson (*prop*)]
[*Scorers:* **tries** by Skelding, Haydn Thomas (2), C. Wyles (2), Winney and B. Woods, **penalty goal** by Whittingham, **conversions** by Whittingham (5)]
[26th Mar FRANCE STUDENTS 43 **ENGLAND STUDENTS** 8]
Stade Municipal Georges Vuillermet, Lyon
[*Team:* Simon Carter, Dalgleish, Hopcroft, Gibbons, Skelding, Christopher 'Chris' Lowrie, Tenconi, T. Hayman, Haydn Thomas, Winney, C. Wyles, Whittingham, O. Phillips, Tombleson, Sayer]
[*Bench:* Abrahams, M. Foster, Gaunt, James Jones (rep), Ogilvie, Scothern, W. Thompson]
[*Scorers:* **try** by James Jones, **penalty goal** by Whittingham]

U21 6 NATIONS CHAMPIONSHIP

[**MANAGER:** *Peter Drewett*] [**COACH:** *Jon Callard*] [**ASSISTANT COACH:** *Nigel Redman*]
CAPTAIN: *Clive Stuart-Smith*
[14th Feb ITALY U21 3 **ENGLAND U21** 57]
Stadio Leone, Pomigliano D'Arco, Naples
[*Team:* Nick Wood, R. Hawkins, David Wilson (2), Percival, Day, Lund, W. Skinner, Skirving, Stuart-Smith, A. Jarvis, M. Garvey, A. Reay, C. Bell, J. Bailey, Jon Clarke]
[*Bench:* H. Barratt, Croall, Friswell (*hooker*) (rep), N. Mordt (*centre*), Ben Russell (2), T. Warren, Wigglesworth]
[*Scorers:* **tries** by M. Garvey (2), A. Reay, Day, Lund (2), Jon Clarke, Friswell and Skirving, **conversions** by A. Jarvis (6)]
[20th Feb SCOTLAND U21 9 **ENGLAND U21** 27]
Stirling County RFC, Bridgehaugh Park, Stirling
[*Team:* N. Wood, R. Hawkins, David Wilson (2), Percival, Day, Lund, W. Skinner, Skirving, Stuart-Smith, A. Jarvis, M. Garvey, N. Mordt, C. Bell, J. Bailey, Jon Clarke]
[*Bench:* H. Barratt, Brad Davies (rep), Friswell, Tom Parker (1) (*lock*), Ben Russell (2) (rep), T. Warren (rep), Wigglesworth]
[*Scorers:* **tries** by Skirving (2), Stuart-Smith and Ben Russell, **penalty goal** by A. Jarvis, **conversions** by A. Jarvis (2)]
[5th Mar **ENGLAND U21** 27 IRELAND U21 19]
Kingsholm, Gloucester
[*Team:* N. Wood, R. Hawkins, David Wilson (2), Percival, Day, Ben Russell (2), W. Skinner, Skirving, Stuart-Smith, A. Jarvis, Monye, A. Reay, C. Bell, M. Garvey, Jon Clarke]
[*Bench:* J. Bailey, Brad Davies (rep), Friswell, M. Hopley (*number 8*), Tom Parker (1), T. Warren, Wigglesworth]
[*Scorers:* **tries** by A. Reay, Ben Russell and C. Bell (2), **penalty goal** by A. Jarvis,

conversions by A. Jarvis and Brad Davies]

[19th Mar **ENGLAND U21** 22 WALES U21 19]

Kingsholm, Gloucester

[*Team:* N. Wood, R. Hawkins, Guess, Percival, Day, Ben Russell (2), W. Skinner, Skirving, Stuart-Smith, A. Jarvis, Monye, A. Reay, C. Bell, M. Garvey, Jon Clarke]

[*Bench:* J. Bailey, Brad Davies (rep), Friswell, Narraway (rep), Tom Parker (1) (rep), T. Warren (rep), Wigglesworth]

[*Scorers:* **tries** by Skirving (2) and A. Reay, **penalty goal** by Brad Davies, **conversions** by A. Jarvis and Brad Davies]

[26th Mar FRANCE U21 18 **ENGLAND U21** 25]

Parc Municipal des Sports, Brive-la-Gaillarde

[*Team:* N. Wood, R. Hawkins, T. Warren, Percival, Day, Ben Russell (2), Tom Rees, Skirving, Stuart-Smith, Brad Davies, M. Garvey, A. Reay, C. Bell, J. Bailey, Jon Clarke]

[*Bench:* H. Barratt, Croall, Friswell (rep), Ross Laidlaw (rep), Narraway (rep), Parling (rep), Wigglesworth (rep)]

[*Scorers:* **tries** by R. Hawkins, C. Bell and Tom Rees, **penalty goals** by Ross Laidlaw (2), **conversions** by Brad Davies (2)]

POSITION: 1ST 10 +90 GS TC [France 7 +66, Ireland 7 +60, Wales 4 +24, Scotland 2 -94, Italy 0 -146]

[Matt Hampson, Andrew Kyriacou, Geoff Parling, James Haskell, Luke Myring, Spencer Davey, Andy Frost and Tom Williams were all members of an original training squad of 35 at Worcester RFC on 2nd February 2004]

'A' INTERNATIONAL MATCHES

[**COACH:** *Joe Lydon*] [**ASSISTANT COACH:** *Steve Diamond*]

CAPTAIN: *Mike Catt*

[6th Mar FRANCE A 26 **ENGLAND A*** 22]

Stade Aimé Giral, Perpignan

[*Team:* M. Worsley, Titterrell, Robbie Morris, Alex Brown, Tom Palmer (2), A. Beattie, Hazell, Forrester, Harry Ellis, M. Catt, R. Haughton, H. Paul, Tindall, Christophers, Scarbrough]

[*Bench:* M. Cairns (rep), Perry Freshwater (*prop/hooker*) (rep), P. Sanderson (rep), Ollie Smith (2) (rep), Stuart Turner (rep), H. Vyvyan (rep), Martyn Wood (rep)]

[*Scorers:* **try** by P. Sanderson, **penalty goals** by H. Paul (5), **conversion** by H. Paul]

CAPTAIN: *No captain appointed*

[19th Mar ITALY A C **ENGLAND A** C]

Stadio Comunale, Pomezia

[*Team not selected*]

[*Bench not selected*]

[*No scorers*]

[Joe Lydon and Steve Diamond were both appointed on 27th February 2004]

CATHAY PACIFIC/CREDIT SUISSE HONG KONG SEVENS
IRB WORLD SEVENS SERIES 2003-2004 ROUND 5

Hong Kong Stadium, Eastern Hospital Road, So Kon Po, Hong Kong

[*Tournament squad:* Amor, Appleford, Neil Baxter (*wing*), Dowson, Gollings, R. Haughton, Horstmann, H. Paul (never travelled as withdrew, replaced by Tom Williams), Peter Richards (*scrum half/hooker*), P. Sanderson, Scarbrough, R. Thirlby, T. Williams (*back*)]

(squad of 12)

[Tony Roques and Phil Greening were unavailable for this tournament due to injury;

Henry Paul was withdrawn by his club Gloucester, who refused to release him from his Zurich Premiership commitments; Peter Richards was capped for England Schools 18 Group in March 1996; Neil Baxter gained a temporary release from his Rugby League club Salford Reds to play Rugby Union for England in the U19 World Championship in Chile in April 2001 and then became a Rugby Union player in October 2003 when he joined Leicester]

[MANAGER: *John Elliott*] **[COACH:** *Joe Lydon*] **[ASSISTANT COACH:** *Mike Friday*]

CAPTAIN: *Simon Amor*

First Round - Pool 'B'

26th Mar CHINA 0 **ENGLAND** 49

[*Team:* Appleford, Dowson, Horstmann, Peter Richards, Gollings, Scarbrough, R. Thirlby]
[*Bench:* Amor (rep), Neil Baxter (rep), R. Haughton, P. Sanderson (rep), T. Williams]
[*Scorers:* **tries** by Gollings (2), Appleford (2), Neil Baxter, Peter Richards and P. Sanderson, **conversions** by Gollings (7)]

27th Mar SCOTLAND 12 **ENGLAND** 38

[*Team:* P. Sanderson, Peter Richards, Dowson, Amor, Gollings, Scarbrough, R. Haughton]
[*Bench:* Appleford (rep), Neil Baxter (rep), Horstmann, R. Thirlby, T. Williams (rep)]
[*Scorers:* **tries** by Scarbrough, Peter Richards, Gollings, R. Haughton, Appleford and Amor, **conversions** by Gollings (3) and Amor]

27th Mar GEORGIA 0 **ENGLAND** 42

[*Team:* Appleford, P. Sanderson, Horstmann, Amor, Gollings, R. Thirlby, R. Haughton]
[*Bench:* Neil Baxter, Dowson (rep), Peter Richards (rep), Scarbrough (rep), T. Williams]
[*Scorers:* **tries** by R. Haughton (3), P. Sanderson, Horstmann and Scarbrough, **conversions** by Gollings (6)]

Quarter-Final

28th Mar FIJI 12 **ENGLAND** 17

[*Team:* Appleford, Dowson, P. Sanderson, Amor, Gollings, R. Thirlby, R. Haughton]
[*Bench:* Neil Baxter (rep), Horstmann (rep), Peter Richards (rep), Scarbrough, T. Williams]
[*Scorers:* **tries** by P. Sanderson, R. Haughton and R. Thirlby, **conversion** by Gollings]

Semi-Final

28th Mar SOUTH AFRICA 7 **ENGLAND** 15

[*Team:* P. Sanderson, Peter Richards, Dowson, Amor, Gollings, Appleford, R. Haughton]
[*Bench:* Neil Baxter, Horstmann (rep), Scarbrough (rep), R. Thirlby (rep), T. Williams]
[*Scorers:* **tries** by R. Haughton (2) and Peter Richards]

Final

28th Mar ARGENTINA 12 **ENGLAND** 22

[*Team:* P. Sanderson, Peter Richards, Dowson, Amor, Gollings, Appleford, R. Haughton]
[*Bench:* Neil Baxter, Horstmann (rep), Scarbrough (rep), R. Thirlby (rep), T. Williams]
[*Scorers:* **tries** by Amor, Peter Richards, R. Haughton and R. Thirlby, **conversion** by Gollings]

POSITION: WINNERS

[England scored 30 competition points in this Round of the 2003-2004 IRB World Sevens Series]

STANDARD CHARTERED SEVENS, SINGAPORE
IRB WORLD SEVENS SERIES 2003-2004 ROUND 6

National Stadium, Kallang

[*Tournament squad:* Amor, Neil Baxter, Dowson, Gollings, R. Haughton, Horstmann, Tom Rees, Peter Richards, Sampson, Scarbrough, R. Thirlby, T. Williams]

(squad of 12)
[Neil Baxter became an American Football player in November 2004 and then returned to Rugby Union in November 2005 when he joined Wasps!; Paul Sampson played for M.R. Steele-Bodger's XV against Cambridge University at Grange Road on 26th November 2003]
[On 22nd April 2004 Joe Lydon announced that he would be leaving his post of England Sevens Coach on 24th May 2004]
[**MANAGER:** *John Elliott*] [**COACH:** *Joe Lydon*] [**ASSISTANT COACH:** *Mike Friday*]
CAPTAIN: *Simon Amor*
First Round - Pool 'B'
3rd April JAPAN 0 **ENGLAND** 28
[*Team:* Dowson, Peter Richards, Horstmann, Amor, Gollings, R. Thirlby, Neil Baxter]
[*Bench:* R. Haughton (rep), Tom Rees, Sampson, Scarbrough (rep), T. Williams (rep)]
[*Scorers:* **tries** by Amor, Dowson, R. Thirlby and Peter Richards, **conversions** by Gollings (3) and Amor]
3rd April HONG KONG 5 **ENGLAND** 26
[*Team:* Dowson, Peter Richards, Scarbrough, Sampson, Amor, R. Thirlby, T. Williams]
[*Bench:* Neil Baxter (rep), Gollings (rep), R. Haughton, Horstmann (rep), Tom Rees]
[*Scorers:* **tries** by Gollings, Sampson, Neil Baxter and R. Thirlby, **conversions** by Gollings (3)]
3rd April FRANCE 14 **ENGLAND** 14
[*Team:* Dowson, Peter Richards, Horstmann, Amor, Gollings, R. Thirlby, R. Haughton]
[*Bench:* Neil Baxter (rep), Tom Rees (rep), Sampson, Scarbrough (rep), T. Williams]
[*Scorers:* **tries** by R. Thirlby and Neil Baxter, **conversions** by Gollings and Amor]
Quarter-Final
4th April ARGENTINA 21 **ENGLAND** 0
[*Team:* Dowson, Tom Rees, Horstmann, Amor, Gollings, R. Thirlby, R. Haughton]
[*Bench:* Neil Baxter (rep), Peter Richards, Sampson, Scarbrough (rep), T. Williams (rep)]
[*No scorers*]
[Plate Semi-Final:]
[4th April FIJI 19 **ENGLAND** 5]
[*Team:* Dowson, Tom Rees, Horstmann, Amor, Gollings, Scarbrough, R. Thirlby]
[*Bench:* Neil Baxter (rep), R. Haughton (rep), Peter Richards, Sampson, T. Williams (rep)]
[*Scorers:* **try** by Gollings]
POSITION: LOSING QUARTER-FINALISTS [*PLATE SEMI-FINALISTS*]
[England scored 4 competition points in this Round of the 2003-2004 IRB World Sevens Series]

ROSSLYN PARK 125TH ANNIVERSARY MATCH

[**MANAGER:** *John Allen (2)* (AU)]
CAPTAIN: *Stewart Eru* (NZ)
[2nd May Rosslyn Park 48 **OXBRIDGE XV** 53]
Rosslyn Park FC, Priory Lane, Upper Richmond Road, Roehampton
[*Team:* Jakobus *Rudolf* Bosch (SA), Gareth Forde (AU), Nwume, David 'Dave' Lubans (AU), Gavin Webster, Matthew 'Mat' Hocken (NZ), Richie Woods (IR), Eru (NZ), Ben Dormer (NZ), Barr, Simon Frost (SA), Jason Wright (NZ), Adam Magro (AU), John Bradshaw (SA), Ryan O'Mahoney (SA)]
[*Bench:* Abiola (*wing*) (rep), B. Durham, Gaunt, Allan Fergus 'Fergie' Gladstone (SC) (*hooker*), T. Hayman, Dafydd Lewis (WA) (*fly half*), Anton van Zyl (SA) (*lock*)]

[*Scorers:* **tries** by Hocken (NZ), J. Bradshaw (SA) (3), Abiola, O'Mahoney (SA) (2), Lubans (AU), Barr and Eru (NZ), **penalty goal** by ?]
[Match to commemorate the 125th Anniversary of the foundation of Rosslyn Park FC in 1879]

FIRST STAFFWARE CHALLENGE TOUR MATCH

[*English squad members:* Back, J. Leonard]
[Bob Dwyer was appointed on 13th April 2004]
[**COACH:** *Bob Dwyer* (AU)]
CAPTAIN: *Taine Randell* (NZ)
[22nd May SCOTLAND XV 33 **BARBARIANS** 40]
Murrayfield
[*Team:* Greg Feek (NZ), Anton Oliver (NZ), Izak Jacobus 'Cobus' Visagie (SA), M. Andrews (SA), M. O'Kelly (IR), Aaron Persico (IT), Randell (NZ), Robert 'Bobby' Skinstad (SA), Mark Robinson (2) (NZ), D. Humphreys (IR), Vilimoni Delasau (FIJ), Brian O'Driscoll (IR), T. Castaignède (FR), Shane Horgan (IR), C. Cullen (NZ)]
[*Bench:* Matt Burke (AU) (*fly half/centre/full back*) (rep), Neil de Kock (SA) (*scrum half*) (rep), O. le Roux (SA) (*prop*) (rep), Brad Mika (NZ) (*lock*) (rep), Eric Miller (IR) (*flanker/number 8*) (rep), Matt Sexton (NZ) (rep), Terblanche (SA) (*wing*) (rep)]
[*Scorers:* **tries** by Delasau (FIJ), Mark Robinson (NZ), Horgan (IR) (2), C. Cullen (NZ) and Randell (NZ), **conversions** by D. Humphreys (IR) (5)]

SECOND STAFFWARE CHALLENGE TOUR MATCH
STAFFWARE CHALLENGE TROPHY

[*English squad members:* Back]
[**COACH:** *Bob Dwyer* (AU)]
CAPTAIN: *Matt Burke* (AU)
[26th May WALES XV 42 **BARBARIANS** 0]
Ashton Gate, Bristol
[*Team:* O. le Roux (SA), Matt Sexton (NZ), Richard Bands (SA), Mika (NZ), Connors (AU), Magne (FR), Andre Vos (SA), E. Miller (IR), N. de Kock (SA), Matt Burke (AU), Paulse (SA), Nathan Grey (AU), Damien Traille (FR), Dafydd James (WA), Reihana (NZ)]
[*Bench:* T. Castaignède (FR) (rep), Owen Finegan (AU) (*lock/flanker*) (rep), D. Humphreys (IR) (*fly half*) (rep), J. Leonard (rep), A. Oliver (NZ) (*hooker*) (rep), Persico (IT) (*flanker*) (rep), Mark Robinson (2) (NZ) (rep)]
[*No scorers*]

EMIRATES AIRLINE BORDEAUX SEVENS
IRB WORLD SEVENS SERIES 2003-2004 ROUND 7

Stade Jacques Chaban-Delmas, Bordeaux
[*Tournament squad:* Amor, Appleford, James Brooks, Dowson, Gollings, R. Haughton, Horstmann, Monye, H. Paul, Roques, P. Sanderson, R. Thirlby]
(squad of 12)
[The Stade Jacques Chaban-Delmas, Bordeaux was previously called Stade Municipal, Parc Lescure, Bordeaux; Jamie Noon, Peter Richards and Ben Russell (2) in original training squad of 15; Simon Amor was the tournament captain]
[On 22nd April 2004 Mike Friday was appointed to succeed Joe Lydon as Coach on 24th May 2004, but Joe Lydon was still involved with the selection of the team for the Bordeaux Sevens and London Sevens!]

[**MANAGER:** *John Elliott*] [**COACH:** *Mike Friday*] [**ASSISTANT COACH:** *Damian McGrath*]
CAPTAIN: *Simon Amor*
First Round - Pool 'B'
28th May KENYA 5 **ENGLAND** 31
[*Team:* Appleford, Roques, Dowson, Amor, Gollings, H. Paul, Monye]
[*Bench:* James Brooks, R. Haughton (rep), Horstmann, P. Sanderson (rep), R. Thirlby (rep)]
[*Scorers:* **tries** by Monye, Dowson, Amor, Gollings and R. Haughton, **conversions** by Gollings (3)]
CAPTAIN: *Ben Gollings*
28th May SPAIN 12 **ENGLAND** 36
[*Team:* P. Sanderson, Roques, Horstmann, James Brooks, Gollings, R. Thirlby, R. Haughton]
[*Bench:* Amor, Appleford, Dowson (rep), Monye (rep), H. Paul (rep)]
[*Scorers:* **tries** by P. Sanderson, Gollings, R. Thirlby (3) and Monye, **conversions** by Gollings (2) and H. Paul]
CAPTAIN: *Simon Amor*
28th May AUSTRALIA 12 **ENGLAND** 19
[*Team:* P. Sanderson, Roques, Dowson, Amor, Gollings, H. Paul, Monye]
[*Bench:* Appleford, James Brooks (rep), R. Haughton (rep), Horstmann (rep), R. Thirlby]
[*Scorers:* **tries** by Monye (2) and Amor, **conversions** by Gollings (2)]
Quarter-Final
29th May CANADA 0 **ENGLAND** 36
[*Team:* Appleford, Dowson, P. Sanderson, Amor, Gollings, H. Paul, R. Haughton]
[*Bench:* James Brooks, Horstmann, Monye (rep), Roques (rep), R. Thirlby (rep)]
[*Scorers:* **tries** by Gollings, R. Haughton, Dowson and Monye (3), **conversions** by Gollings (2) and Amor]
Semi-Final
29th May SOUTH AFRICA 14 **ENGLAND** 17
[*Team:* Appleford, Roques, Dowson, Amor, Gollings, H. Paul, Monye]
[*Bench:* James Brooks, R. Haughton (rep), Horstmann (rep), P. Sanderson, R. Thirlby (rep)]
[*Scorers:* **tries** by Amor and Monye, **penalty goal** by Amor, **conversions** by Gollings (2)]
Final
29th May NEW ZEALAND 28 **ENGLAND** 19
[*Team:* Appleford, Roques, Dowson, Amor, Gollings, H. Paul, Monye]
[*Bench:* James Brooks, R. Haughton (rep), Horstmann (rep), P. Sanderson, R. Thirlby (rep)]
[*Scorers:* **tries** by Amor, H. Paul and Horstmann, **conversions** by Amor and Gollings]
POSITION: LOSING FINALISTS
[England scored 16 competition points in this Round of the 2003-2004 IRB World Sevens Series]

THIRD STAFFWARE CHALLENGE TOUR MATCH

STAFFWARE CHALLENGE TROPHY

[ENGLAND XV: [*Other squad members:* Goodridge, N. Lloyd (withdrew due to injury), M. Stephenson, Stuart-Smith (withdrew due to injury, replaced by Hall Charlton)]**]**
(squad of 26)
[David Flatman and Jonny Wilkinson unavailable due to injury; Pat Sanderson, Richard Haughton and Henry Paul unavailable due to their England Sevens commitments; Perry Freshwater, David Barnes, Tim Payne, Dorian West, Andy Titterrell, George Chuter, Lee Mears, Julian White, Will Green (1), Matt Stevens, Stuart Turner, Simon Shaw, Steve Borthwick, Danny Grewcock, Ben Kay, Louis Deacon, Rob

***Fidler, Chris Jones, Joe Worsley, Andy Beattie, Will Johnson, Michael Lipman, Lawrence Dallaglio, Martin Corry, Martyn Wood, Peter Richards, Scott Benton, Harry Ellis, Charlie Hodgson, Alex King, Andy Goode, Olly Barkley, Austin Healey, Tom Voyce, Stuart Abbott, Mike Tindall, Ollie Smith (2), Fraser Waters, Leon Lloyd, Mark Cueto, Josh Lewsey, Jason Robinson and Matt Perry were all unavailable due to club commitments; Trevor Woodman, Steve Thompson (2), Richard Hill (2), Matt Dawson, Andy Gomarsall, Ben Cohen and James Simpson-Daniel were all rested for this match by Clive Woodward*]**

[BARBARIANS: [*English squad members:* Back]]

[ENGLAND XV: [TEAM MANAGER: *Clive Woodward*] **[HEAD COACH:** *Andy Robinson*] **[ASSISTANT COACH:** *Phil Larder*]]

[BARBARIANS: [COACH: *Bob Dwyer* (AU)]]

CAPTAIN: *Hugh Vyvyan* [England XV]

CAPTAIN: *Anton Oliver* (NZ) [*Mark Andrews* (SA) *took over when Anton Oliver was substituted in the 2nd half*] [Barbarians]

30th May **ENGLAND XV** 12 **BARBARIANS** 32

Twickenham

[ENGLAND XV: [*Team:* M. Worsley, M. Regan, Robbie Morris, Mark Cornwell, Alex Brown, D. Hyde, Hazell, H. Vyvyan, Walshe, Walder, M. Garvey, K. Sorrell, Noon, Sackey, Horak]

[*Bench:* P. Buxton (rep), Charlton, J. Dawson (rep), C. Fortey, Darren Fox, T. May, Scarbrough (rep)]

[*Scorers:* **penalty goals** by Walder (4)]]

[BARBARIANS: [*Team:* J. Leonard, A. Oliver (NZ), C. Visagie (SA), M. O'Kelly (IR), M. Andrews (SA), Finegan (AU), Vos (SA), Randell (NZ), Mark Robinson (2) (NZ), D. Humphreys (IR), Reihana (NZ), N. Grey (AU), Brian O'Driscoll (IR), Horgan (IR), T. Castaignède (FR)]

[*Bench:* Matt Burke (AU) (rep), N. De Kock (SA) (rep), Feek (NZ) (*prop*) (rep), Magne (FR) (rep), Matt Sexton (NZ) (rep), B. Skinstad (SA) (*flanker/number 8*) (rep), Traille (FR) (*centre*) (rep)]

[*Scorers:* **tries** by J. Leonard, Horgan (IR), Reihana (NZ), B. Skinstad (SA) and M. O'Kelly (IR), **penalty goal** by D. Humphreys (IR), **conversions** by D. Humphreys (IR) (2)]]

EMIRATES AIRLINE LONDON SEVENS
IRB WORLD SEVENS SERIES 2003-2004 ROUND 8

Twickenham

[*Tournament squad:* Appleford, Roques, H. Paul, James Brooks, Horstmann, P. Sanderson, Monye (injured during the tournament), Dowson, R. Thirlby, Gollings, Amor, Peter Richards]

(squad of 12)

***[Jamie Noon and Ben Russell (2) in original training squad of 15; Richard Haughton in original training squad of 15 but withdrew due to injury*]**

[MANAGER: *John Elliott*] **[COACH:** *Mike Friday*] **[ASSISTANT COACH:** *Damian McGrath*]

CAPTAIN: *Simon Amor*

First Round - Pool 'B'

5th June **ENGLAND** 12 SCOTLAND 7

[*Team:* Dowson, Roques, Appleford, James Brooks, Amor, Peter Richards, Monye]

[*Bench:* Gollings (rep), Horstmann (rep), H. Paul, P. Sanderson, R. Thirlby (rep)]

[*Scorers:* **tries** by Amor and Peter Richards, **conversion** by Amor]

5th June **ENGLAND** 40 ITALY 0

[*Team:* Horstmann, Peter Richards, P. Sanderson, Amor, Gollings, H. Paul, R. Thirlby]

[*Bench:* Appleford (rep), James Brooks (rep), Dowson, Roques (rep)]
[*Scorers:* **tries** by H. Paul, Amor, R. Thirlby (3) and Gollings, **conversions** by Gollings (5)]

5th June **ENGLAND** 40 FRANCE 7

[*Team:* Horstmann, Peter Richards, P. Sanderson, Amor, Gollings, H. Paul, R. Thirlby]
[*Bench:* Appleford, James Brooks (rep), Dowson (rep), Roques (rep)]
[*Scorers:* **tries** by Gollings (2), Amor, Peter Richards and R. Thirlby (2), **conversions** by Gollings (5)]

Quarter-Final

6th June **ENGLAND** 14 AUSTRALIA 5

[*Team:* Roques, Peter Richards, P. Sanderson, Amor, Gollings, H. Paul, R. Thirlby]
[*Bench:* Appleford (rep), James Brooks (rep), Dowson (rep), Horstmann]
[*Scorers:* **tries** by P. Sanderson and R. Thirlby, **conversions** by Gollings (2)]

Semi-Final

6th June **ENGLAND** 14 FIJI 12

[*Team:* Dowson, Peter Richards, P. Sanderson, Amor, Gollings, H. Paul, R. Thirlby]
[*Bench:* Appleford (rep), James Brooks (rep), Horstmann, Roques (rep)]
[*Scorers:* **tries** by Gollings and R. Thirlby, **conversions** by Gollings (2)]

Final

6th June **ENGLAND** 22 NEW ZEALAND 19

[*Team:* Dowson, Roques, P. Sanderson, Amor, Gollings, H. Paul, R. Thirlby]
[*Bench:* Appleford (rep), James Brooks (rep), Horstmann, Peter Richards (rep)]
[*Scorers:* **tries** by R. Thirlby, Gollings, H. Paul and Amor, **conversion** by Gollings]

POSITION: WINNERS

[England scored 20 competition points in this Round of the 2003-2004 IRB World Sevens Series]

RANKING: 2ND 122 [*New Zealand 128*, Argentina 98, Fiji 84, South Africa 74, Samoa 60, France 37, Australia 34, Canada 22, Scotland 12, Tonga 8, Kenya 8, Korea 2, Cook Islands 1]

FANTASY: *1ST 130*

[The IRB deducted 32 points from South Africa after finding them guilty of fielding an ineligible player in Dubai and George]

BATTLE OF THE CENTURIONS - TRIBUTE TO RUGBY LEGENDS MATCH

LEGENDS CUP

[**MANAGER:** *Mike Scott (2)*] [**COACH:** *Roger Uttley*]

CAPTAIN: *Jason Leonard*

[6th June NEIL JENKINS XV 80 **JASON LEONARD XV** 80]

Millennium Stadium, Cardiff

[*Team:* J. Leonard, D. West, Garforth, Steve Williams (2) (WA), William 'Bill' Davison, Phillip *Kingsley* Jones (WA), Back, Vos (SA), Grindal, Paul Burke (IR), J. Sleightholme, John Leslie (SC), Nicholas 'Nick' Greenstock, Nicholas 'Nick' Beal, Kenneth 'Kenny' Logan (SC)]
[*Bench Replacements:* Nigel Davies (WA) (*centre*) (rep*)*, A. Deacon (*prop*) (rep), Leota (SAM) (rep), Epi Taione (TON) (*flanker/number 8/centre/wing*) (rep)]
[*Scorers:* **tries** by J. Leslie (SC), Grindal, P. Burke (IR) (2), ?, ?, Back, ?, N. Beal, ?, N. Davies (WA) and ?, **conversions** by P. Burke (IR) (10)]

[Match organised by the WRU as a testimonial game for Neil Jenkins; Roger Uttley won 23 caps for England between 1973-80 and was capped for the British Lions in June 1974]

PORTUGUESE NATIONAL DAY MATCH

[*Other squad members:* Baugh (CAN) (*flanker*) (never travelled), Z. Brooke (NZ) (*number 8*) (originally selected as player-coach, actually travelled as coach), Leo Cullen (IR) (*lock*), Garan Evans (WA) (*full back*) (never travelled as withdrew), Dafydd James (WA) (*centre/wing*), K. Logan (SC) (*wing*) (never travelled as withdrew), Gary Longwell (IR) (*lock*) (never travelled as withdrew, replaced by Leo Cullen), S. Moffat (SC) (*wing/full back*) (never travelled as withdrew, replaced by Emyr Lewis (2)), Andy Moore (2) (WA) (*scrum half*) (never travelled as withdrew, replaced by Rhodri Jones), D. West (returned home as injured, replaced by Rhys Thomas)]

(squad of 22)

[Match to commemorate the 100th Anniversary of the first rugby match being played in Portugal in 1903; Zinzan Brooke was appointed on 4th June 2004; Garan Evans selected but withdrew as he was required to act as a standby replacement for the Wales tour of Argentina; Stuart Moffat selected but withdrew as he was now required to join the Scotland tour of Australia as a replacement; Cambridge University toured Portugal in September 1996, beating a Portuguese XV 35-20]

[**COACH:** *Zinzan Brooke* (NZ)]

CAPTAIN: *Rob Baxter*

[10th Jun PORTUGAL 34 **BARBARIANS** 66]

Estádio de Honra, Estádio Universitário, Lisbon

[*Team:* Nebbett, Leota (SAM), John Davies (WA), Rob Baxter, Alfred Vakacokavanua (FIJ), Junior Paramore (SAM), Volley, B. Skinstad (SA), Benton, Mark Mapletoft, D. O'Leary, Mike Mullins (IR), L. Lloyd, Nicholas 'Nick' Baxter, Emyr Lewis (2) (WA)]

[*Bench:* Matthew 'Matt' Allen (*centre*) (rep), P. Burke (IR) (*fly half*) (rep), Rhodri Jones (WA) (rep), Taione (TON) (rep), Robin Sowden-Taylor (WA) (*flanker*) (rep), Matthew 'Mattie' Stewart (SC) (*prop*) (rep), Thomas *Rhys* Thomas (WA) (*hooker*) (rep)]

[*Scorers:* **tries** by M. Mullins (IR) (3), Benton, Vakacokavanua (FIJ), Paramore (SAM), Volley, B. Skinstad (SA), M. Allen and penalty try, **conversions** by Mapletoft (8)]

PENGUINS TOUR TO HONG KONG 2004

[**MANAGER:** *Craig Brown* (NZ)] [**COACH:** *Bill Calcraft* (AU)]

[*Other squad members:* Arthur Brenton (*lock*) (tm), Ross Blake (SC), Breeze (WA) (tm), Carlo Di Ciacca (SC) (*hooker*), David 'Dave' Dillon (NZ) (*flanker*), Dowson (*flanker/number 8*) (tm), Giacheri (IT), Gulliver (*lock*), Andy Higgins (2), Christopher 'Chris' Johnson (1) (*hooker*), Sam Johnstone (*prop*), Peter Jorgensen (AU) (*centre/wing*), Joel Nasmith (NZ) (*scrum half*), Raymond Rodan (FIJ) (*wing/full back*), Rossigneux (*flanker/number 8*), W. Serevi (FIJ) (captain; never travelled as withdrew), Gareth Smith (AU) (*wing/full back*), Mark Sweeney (1) (AU) (*fly half/full back*) (tm), Tamati (NZ), Doug Tausili (SAM) (*centre*), Blair Urlich (NZ) (*flanker/number 8*)]

(squad of 23)

[Rescheduled tour to commemorate the 50th Anniversary of the foundation of the Hong Kong R.F.U. in 1952; This tour was originally scheduled for June 2003 but had to be postponed due to fears about the spread of the SARS virus; Waisale Serevi selected but withdrew due to club commitments; Chris Johnson (1) was capped for England Colts in March 1992]

CAPTAIN: *Craig de Goldi* (NZ)

[10th Jun HONG KONG 0 **PENGUINS** 86]

King's Park Sports Ground, Hong Kong

[*Team:* Stuart 'Stu' Wilson (2) (AU) (*prop*), Laurent Gomez (FR) (*prop*), Craig de Goldi (NZ)

(*flanker*)]
[*Bench:*]
[*Scorers:* **tries** by L. Gomez (FR), ?, ?, ?, ?, ?, ?, ?, ?, ?, ?, ? and ?]

IRB U21 WORLD CHAMPIONSHIP

Scotland
[*Other squad members:* Jon Clarke (*wing/full back*) (never travelled as injured, replaced by Delon Armitage), R. Hawkins (never travelled as injured, replaced by Cameron Dott), M. Hopley (never travelled as injured, replaced by Chris Cracknell), Lund (never travelled as injured, replaced by Richard Thorpe), Monye (returned home as injured, replaced by Luke Myring), Wigglesworth (never travelled as injured, replaced by Joe Bedford)]
(squad of 26)
[Rob Hawkins withdrew from the World Cup squad on 26th May 2004 due to injury; Ed Williamson and Luke Myring trained with the squad at Newbury RFC between May 31st and June 4th 2004 to provide injury cover; Mark Hopley, Magnus Lund, Jon Clarke and Richard Wigglesworth all withdrew from the World Cup squad on 4th June 2004 due to injury; Clive Stuart-Smith was the tournament captain; England U21 were ranked in Pool D and played their matches against the 3 teams in Pool A; Chris Goodman travelled later as a replacement for Ben Russell (2); Luke Myring travelled later as a replacement for Ugo Monye]
(During the First Round a bonus point was awarded for scoring 4 or more tries in a match and for losing by seven points or less)
[MANAGER: *Peter Drewett*] **[COACH:** *Jon Callard*] **[ASSISTANT COACH:** *Nigel Redman*]
CAPTAIN: *Clive Stuart-Smith*
First Round - Pool 'D'
[11th Jun NEW ZEALAND U21 42 **ENGLAND U21** 13]
Gala RFC, Netherdale, Nether Road, Galashiels
[*Team:* N. Wood, Friswell, T. Warren, Percival, Day, Narraway, Tom Rees, Ben Russell (2), Stuart-Smith, A. Jarvis, J. Bailey, A. Reay, C. Bell, M. Garvey, D. Armitage]
[*Bench:* H. Barratt, J. Bedford (*scrum half*), Cracknell (*flanker/number 8*) (rep), Brad Davies (rep), Dott (rep), Parling (rep), Tom French (2) (*prop*) (rep)]
[*Scorers:* **try** by A. Reay, **penalty goals** by A. Jarvis and Brad Davies, **conversion** by A. Jarvis]
[15th Jun SCOTLAND U21 14 **ENGLAND U21** 25]
Gala RFC, Netherdale, Nether Road, Galashiels
[*Team:* Croall, Friswell, Tom French (2), Parling, Day, R. Thorpe, Tom Rees, Ben Russell (2), Stuart-Smith, Brad Davies, J. Bailey, N. Mordt, C. Bell, M. Garvey, D. Armitage]
[*Bench:* H. Barratt, J. Bedford, Cracknell (rep), Dott (rep), A. Jarvis (*fly half*) (rep), Narraway (rep), T. Warren (rep)]
[*Scorers:* **tries** by D. Armitage, Tom Rees and R. Thorpe, **penalty goals** by Brad Davies and D. Armitage, **conversions** by D. Armitage (2)]
[19th Jun WALES U21 14 **ENGLAND U21** 23]
Raeburn Place, Stockbridge, Edinburgh
[*Team:* N. Wood, Friswell, T. Warren, Percival, Day, Parling, Tom Rees, Cracknell, Stuart-Smith, A. Jarvis, D. Armitage, A. Reay, C. Bell, M. Garvey, Luke Myring]
[*Bench:* H. Barratt (rep), J. Bedford, Brad Davies, Dott, Tom French (2) (rep), Narraway (rep), R. Thorpe (*flanker/number 8*) (rep)]
[*Scorers:* **tries** by N. Wood, H. Barratt and M. Garvey, **penalty goals** by Myring and A. Jarvis, **conversion** by A. Jarvis]

[England U21 failed to score any bonus points, which prevented them from getting into the top 4 teams and thus playing for a place in the final]

CAPTAIN: *Chris Bell*

5th/6th/7th/8th Place Semi-Final

[23rd Jun ARGENTINA U21 13 **ENGLAND U21** 39]

Gala RFC, Netherdale, Nether Road, Galashiels

[*Team:* N. Wood, Friswell, Tom French (2), Day, Parling, Narraway, Tom Rees, R. Thorpe, J. Bedford, A. Jarvis, H. Barratt, N. Mordt, C. Bell, J. Bailey, Myring]

[*Bench:* D. Armitage (*centre/wing/full back*), Croall (rep), Brad Davies (rep), Dott (rep), Chris Goodman (*number 8*) (rep), Stuart-Smith (rep), T. Warren (rep)]

[*Scorers:* **tries** by N. Wood, J. Bedford, C. Bell, H. Barratt, Narraway and J. Bailey, **penalty goal** by A. Jarvis, **conversions** by A. Jarvis (3)]

CAPTAIN: *Clive Stuart-Smith*

5th/6th Place Play-Off

[27th Jun WALES U21 19 **ENGLAND U21** 26]

Cartha Queens Park RFC, Dumbreck Road, Dumbreck, Glasgow

[*Team:* N. Wood, Friswell, T. Warren, Percival, Day, Narraway, Tom Rees, R. Thorpe, Stuart-Smith, A. Jarvis, M. Garvey, A. Reay, C. Bell, H. Barratt, Myring]

[*Bench:* J. Bailey (rep), J. Bedford, Croall (rep), Brad Davies, Tom French (2) (rep), Goodman (rep), Parling (rep)]

[*Scorers:* **tries** by Tom Rees, C. Bell and Parling, **penalty goals** by A. Jarvis (3), **conversion** by A. Jarvis]

POSITION: 5TH PLACE

ENGLAND TOUR TO NEW ZEALAND AND AUSTRALIA 2004

[**TEAM MANAGER:** *Clive Woodward*] [**HEAD COACH:** *Andy Robinson*] [**ASSISTANT COACHES:** *Phil Larder & Joe Lydon*]

[*Other squad members:* Christophers, Harry Ellis, Flatman, Will Green (1) (added to the revised squad after the Eden Park test match)]

(squad of 33)

[On 22nd April 2004 Joe Lydon was appointed to become England Assistant Coach on 24th May 2004; Neil Back was unavailable for this tour; Phil Vickery, Lewis Moody, Jonny Wilkinson and Iain Balshaw were all unavailable due to injury; Ben Kay, Will Greenwood and Jason Robinson were rested for this tour by Clive Woodward; Tim Payne was added to the original squad of 30 on 31st May 2004 to provide injury cover for David Flatman; The England squad departed for New Zealand on 3rd June 2004; Mike Worsley and Will Green (1) were added to the revised squad on 20th June 2004 to provide injury cover for Matt Stevens and Trevor Woodman respectively; Clive Woodward resigned on 1st September 2004, with the RFU accepting his resignation on 2nd September 2004]

PHILIPS SERIES

CAPTAIN: *Lawrence Dallaglio*

12th June NEW ZEALAND 36 **ENGLAND** 3

Carisbrook Stadium, Dunedin

[*Team:* Trevor Woodman, Steve Thompson (2), Julian White, S. Shaw, Grewcock, Chris Jones, Richard Hill (2), Dallaglio, Matt Dawson, C. Hodgson, B. Cohen, M. Catt, Tindall, J. Simpson-Daniel, J. Lewsey]

[*Bench:* S. Abbott (rep), Barkley, S. Borthwick (rep), Gomarsall (rep), M. Regan (rep), M. Stevens (rep), J. Worsley (rep)]

[*Scorers:* **penalty goal** by C. Hodgson]

19th June	NEW ZEALAND	36	**ENGLAND**	12

Eden Park, Auckland

[*Team:* Trevor Woodman, M. Regan, Julian White, S. Shaw, S. Borthwick, J. Worsley, Richard Hill (2), Dallaglio, Gomarsall, C. Hodgson, B. Cohen, S. Abbott, Tindall, Voyce, J. Lewsey]

[*Bench:* Barkley (rep), Matt Dawson (rep), Grewcock (rep), Lipman (*flanker*) (rep), M. Stevens (rep), Titterrell (rep), F. Waters (rep)]

[*Scorers:* **penalty goals** by C. Hodgson (4)]

FIRST COOK CUP MATCH

CAPTAIN: *Lawrence Dallaglio*

26th June	AUSTRALIA	51	**ENGLAND**	15

Suncorp Stadium, Lang Park, Brisbane

[*Team:* T. Payne, M. Regan, Julian White, S. Shaw, S. Borthwick, J. Worsley, Richard Hill (2), Dallaglio, Gomarsall, C. Hodgson, B. Cohen, Tindall, M. Catt, Voyce, J. Lewsey]

[*Bench:* Barkley (rep), Corry (rep), Matt Dawson (rep), Lipman (rep), Steve Thompson (2) (rep), F. Waters (rep), M. Worsley (rep)]

[*Scorers:* **tries** by Richard Hill and Dallaglio, **penalty goal** by C. Hodgson, **conversion** by C. Hodgson]

ENGLAND COUNTIES TOUR TO CANADA 2004

[**MANAGER:** *Rob Udwin*] [**ASSISTANT MANAGER:** *Danny Hodgson*] [**COACH:** *Mark Nelson*] [**ASSISTANT COACH:** *Paul Westgate*]

[*Other squad members:* James Aston (*wing*) (tm), R. Faulkner (*prop*) (tm), Benjamin 'Ben' Foden (*scrum half/wing/full back*) (tm), Ricky Hyslop (*centre*) (tm)]

(squad of 26)

[Mark Nelson and Paul Westgate were both appointed on 22nd January 2004; The RFU also announced on 22nd January 2004 that the England Counties team would participate against France Amateurs, Spain and Portugal in a tournament in June 2004, but this idea was eventually abandoned; The England Counties squad departed for Canada on 8th June 2004]

CAPTAIN: *Craig Hammond*

[18th Jun	RUGBY CANADA SUPER LEAGUE ALL-STARS	17	**ENGLAND COUNTIES**	38]

Ellerslie Rugby Park, Edmonton

[*Team:* Justin Wring, Mark Luffman, Kristyan 'Kris' Fullman, Paul Arnold (2), J. Oakes, Craig Hammond, David 'Dave' Wilks, E. Thorpe, Shaun Perry, Thomas William 'Tom' Barlow (2), Strettle, Paul Mooney, Mal Roberts, Matthew 'Matt' Jess, J. Moore]

[*Bench:* Craig Jones (*fly half*) (rep), Lowrie (*flanker/number 8*) (rep), O'Keefe (*prop*) (rep), P. Price (rep), Senior, Spragg, Paul Williams (3) (*lock/flanker*) (rep)]

[*Scorers:* **tries** by Fullman, P. Mooney (2), Jess, E. Thorpe and J. Moore, **conversions** by J. Moore (4)]

CHURCHILL CUP

Canada

[*Other squad members:* David Barnes (*prop*), A. Beattie (*lock/flanker/number 8*) (never travelled as injured, replaced by Will Johnson), Freshwater (never travelled as withdrew, replaced by David Barnes), D. Hyde, Mears, T. Payne (never travelled due to becoming

replacement on full England tour of New Zealand and Australia), Robbie Morris (never travelled as injured, replaced by Micky Ward), M. Stephenson]
(squad of 27)
[Jim Mallinder and Steve Diamond were both appointed on 15th April 2004; Andy Sheridan, Graham Rowntree, Tom Palmer (2), Pete Anglesea, Alex Sanderson, James Forrester, Ollie Smith (2) and Steve Hanley were all unavailable for this tournament due to injury; Perry Freshwater initially selected but then chose to honour a promise to his club Perpignan to complete their remaining fixtures and thus was no longer available to tour; Tim Payne was added to the original squad of 27 on 28th May 2004 as potential injury cover but then withdrew on 31st May 2004 as he was now required to join the simultaneous England tour of New Zealand and Australia; The England A squad departed for Canada on 3rd June 2004; Pat Sanderson, Peter Richards, Henry Paul and Jamie Noon were in the original squad but did not travel until 7th June 2004 due to their England 7s commitments; Michael Horak was in the original squad but did not travel until 7th June 2004 due to family commitments]
[The competition rules stated that, in the event of the scores being level at the end of the Final, two extra time halves of 10 minutes each would then be played]
[**COACH:** *Jim Mallinder*] [**ASSISTANT COACH:** *Steve Diamond*]
CAPTAIN: *Hugh Vyvyan*
First Round
[13th Jun CANADA 23 **ENGLAND A** 48]
Rugby Park, Calgary
[*Team:* M. Worsley, M. Cairns, Will Green (1), L. Deacon, Alex Brown, P. Sanderson, Hazell, H. Vyvyan, Martyn Wood, A. King, Scarbrough, H. Paul, Noon, Cueto, Horak]
[*Bench:* Richard Birkett (*lock*) (rep), George Chuter (*hooker*) (rep), W. Johnson (rep), Peter Richards (*scrum half*) (rep), K. Sorrell (rep), Walder (rep), Michael 'Micky' Ward (*prop*) (rep)]
[*Scorers:* **tries** by Horak, Cueto, Noon (2), H. Vyvyan, Hazell and Scarbrough (2), **conversions** by A. King (2) and Walder (2)]
Final
[19th Jun NEW ZEALAND MAORI 26 **ENGLAND A*** 19 aet]
Commonwealth Stadium, Edmonton
[*Team:* M. Worsley, Chuter, Will Green (1), Alex Brown, L. Deacon, W. Johnson, Hazell, H. Vyvyan, Martyn Wood, Walder, Sackey, H. Paul, Noon, Cueto, Scarbrough]
[*Bench:* R. Birkett (rep), M. Cairns (rep), Horak, Peter Richards (rep), P. Sanderson (rep), K. Sorrell (rep), Micky Ward (rep)]
[*Scorers:* **try** by Noon, **penalty goals** by Walder (4), **conversion** by Walder]
POSITION: **LOSING FINALISTS**
FANTASY: ***WINNERS***

PENGUINS TOUR TO MEXICO 2004

[**MANAGER:** *Craig Brown* (NZ)] [**COACH:** *Steve Hill*]
[*Other squad members:* James 'Jamie' Astbury (*flanker*), Barr (*scrum half*), Dave Bassett (*prop*), P. Beal, Karl Cleere (IR) (*prop*), Antonio da Cunha (POR) (*number 8*), K. Dixon (*wing*), Dormer (NZ) (*scrum half*), Henry Head (IR) (*lock*), G. Inglis (IR), James Jones, John Kilbride (IR) (*scrum half*), Dafydd Lewis (WA), Alan Maher (IR) (*lock*), Glen McLellan (SC) (*lock*), Neil Meikle (SC) (*hooker*), O'Mahoney (SA) (*full back*), George Oommen (SC) (*flanker*), Andrew 'Andy' Prior (CAN) (*lock*), Dylan Pugh (WA) (*fly half*), P. Robertson (SC), Ali

Rowe (SC) (*wing*), Sharman (SC) (*centre/wing*), Nopera Stewart (NZ) (*centre/wing/full back*), Swords, Neil Wardingley (*wing*), Winney, J. Winterbottom]
(squad of 29)
[James Winterbottom captained the Penguins to victory in the Mexican Tens at Dos Rios on 26th June 2004]
CAPTAIN: *Dave Gorrie* (NZ)
[27th Jun MEXICO XV 0 **PENGUINS** 92]
Las Caballerizas, Dos Rios
[*Team:* David 'Dave' Gorrie (NZ) (*number 8*)]
[*Bench:*]
[*Scorers:*]

HENLEY INTERNATIONAL SEVENS

Henley RFC, Dry Leas, Marlow Road, Henley-on-Thames
[*Tournament squad not selected*]
[Mike Friday was appointed on 26th May 2004]
[**COACH:** *Mike Friday*]
CAPTAIN: *No captain appointed*
[1st Aug **YOUNG ENGLAND** C *No opponents named* C]
[*Team not selected*]
[*Bench not selected*]
[*No scorers*]

COMPASS GROUP INTERNATIONAL SEVENS

Stoop Memorial Ground, Langhorn Drive, Twickenham
[*Tournament squad:* J. Bedford (*scrum half*), Cracknell (*forward*) (injured during the tournament), Goodman (*forward*), Oliver 'Olly' Morgan (*back*), Rob Vickerman (*forward/back*)]
[Rob Vickerman played for England in the U19 World Championship in South Africa in March-April 2004; Olly Morgan played for England in the U19 World Championships in France in April 2003 and South Africa in March-April 2004]
[**COACH:** *Mike Friday*]
CAPTAIN: *Joe Bedford*
First Round - Pool Four
[6th Aug **YOUNG ENGLAND** L Samurai W]
[*Team:*]
[*Bench:*]
[*Scorers:*]
[6th Aug **YOUNG ENGLAND** L Gloucester W]
[*Team:*]
[*Bench:*]
[*Scorers:*]
[6th Aug **YOUNG ENGLAND** W Pacific Coast Grizzlies (*US*) L]
[*Team:*]
[*Bench:*]
[*Scorers:*]
[Bowl Quarter-Final:]
[7th Aug **YOUNG ENGLAND** 12 Saracens 15]
[*Team:*]
[*Bench:*]

[*Scorers:*]
[Jug Semi-Final:]
[7th Aug **YOUNG ENGLAND** L Australian Legends (*AU*) W **]**
[*Team:*]
[*Bench:*]
[*Scorers:*]
POSITION: FIRST ROUND LOSERS [*BOWL QUARTER-FINALISTS*]

KBR REMEMBRANCE MATCH

[NO COACH NOMINATED]
CAPTAIN: *Ed Orgee*
[9th Nov COMBINED SERVICES (*SER*) 38 **BARBARIANS*** 36]
Army Rugby Stadium, Queen's Avenue, Aldershot
[*Team:* George Davis, Ritchie, J. Hobson, Matthew 'Matt' Veater (WA), Edward 'Ed' Orgee, A. Hawken (CO), Ioan Cunningham (WA), A. da Cunha (POR), Pissarra (POR), Ian Humphreys (IR), Nick Baxter, Kevin Utterson (SC), Andrew Trimble (IR), 'Aisea Havili (TON), Malheiro (POR)]
[*Bench:* David 'Dave' Addleton (*hooker*) (rep), Graeme Cowe (SC) (*scrum half*) (rep), P. Evans (rep), Richard Liddington (US) (*prop*) (rep), Chris Morgan (rep), A. Turnbull (*wing*) (rep), Stephen Ward (WA) (*fly half/centre*) (rep)]
[*Scorers:* **tries** by Nick Baxter (2), G. Davis, Trimble (IR) (2) and I. Humphreys (IR), **conversions** by I. Humphreys (IR) (3)]
[*Match to commemorate the members of the British uniformed services who lost their lives during armed conflict*]

CANADIAN TOUR TO ENGLAND 2004
FIRST INVESTEC CHALLENGE MATCH

[**HEAD COACH:** *Andy Robinson*] [**ASSISTANT COACHES:** *Phil Larder, Dave Alred* & *Joe Lydon*]
CAPTAIN: *Jason Robinson* [*Mike Tindall took over when Jason Robinson was substituted in the 2nd half*]
13th Nov **ENGLAND** 70 CANADA 0
Twickenham
[*Team:* Rowntree, Steve Thompson (2), Julian White, Grewcock, S. Borthwick, Moody, Hazell, Corry, Gomarsall, C. Hodgson, J. Lewsey, H. Paul, Tindall, Cueto, Jason Robinson]
[*Bench:* Charlton, B. Cohen (rep), W. Greenwood (rep), Kay (rep), Sheridan (rep), Titterrell (rep), H. Vyvyan (rep)]
[*Scorers:* **tries** by Jason Robinson (3), J. Lewsey (2), Tindall, Cueto (2), C. Hodgson, W. Greenwood, Moody and H. Vyvyan, **conversions** by C. Hodgson (2) and H. Paul (3)]
[*Andy Robinson became acting Head Coach on 2nd September 2004 and was then formally appointed as Head Coach on 15th October 2004*]

SOUTH AFRICAN TOUR TO WALES, IRELAND, ENGLAND AND SCOTLAND 2004
SECOND INVESTEC CHALLENGE MATCH

[**HEAD COACH:** *Andy Robinson*] [**ASSISTANT COACHES:** *Phil Larder, Dave Alred & Joe Lydon*]

CAPTAIN: *Jason Robinson*

20th Nov **ENGLAND** 32 SOUTH AFRICA 16
Twickenham

[*Team:* Rowntree, Steve Thompson (2), Julian White, Grewcock, S. Borthwick, J. Worsley, Moody, Corry, Gomarsall, C. Hodgson, J. Lewsey, H. Paul, Tindall, Cueto, Jason Robinson]

[*Bench:* B. Cohen, Harry Ellis (rep), W. Greenwood (rep), Hazell (rep), Kay (rep), Sheridan, Titterrell]

[*Scorers:* **tries** by C. Hodgson and Cueto, **penalty goals** by C. Hodgson (5), **drop goal** by C. Hodgson, **conversions** by C. Hodgson (2)]

ENGLAND U21 DEVELOPMENT MATCHES

[**MANAGER:** *Peter Drewett*] [**COACH:** *Jim Mallinder*] [**ASSISTANT COACH:** *Nigel Redman*]

CAPTAIN: *??*

[24th Nov FRANCE U21 WEST XV 17 **ENGLAND U21 SOUTH XV** 7]
Stade de l'Etang Neuf, Centre National de Rugby, Domaine de Bellejame, Marcoussis

[*Team:* Croall, David 'Dave' Ward, Laurence Ovens, Gary Johnson, Richard Blaze, Guest, Steffon Armitage, R. Thorpe, J. Bedford, Shane Geraghty, Jess, R. Davis, Wellwood, Topsy Ojo, Mike Brown]

[*Bench:* Dott, Duncan James (*scrum half*), Adam Newton (*flanker/number 8*), George Robson (*lock*), Ben Russell (1), James Thomas (*prop*), Joe Woodward (*wing/full back*)]

[*Scorers:* **try** by Croall, **conversion** by R. Davis]

[**MANAGER:** *Peter Drewett*] [**COACH:** *Jim Mallinder*] [**ASSISTANT COACH:** *Nigel Redman*]

CAPTAIN: *??*

[24th Nov FRANCE U21 EAST XV 22 **ENGLAND U21 NORTH XV** 25]
Stade de l'Etang Neuf, Centre National de Rugby, Domaine de Bellejame, Marcoussis

[*Team:* Michael Cusack, Stuart Mackie, Aaron Liffchak, T. Ryder, Sean Cox, Ben Lloyd, Cracknell, M. Hopley, Lee Dickson, Tobias 'Toby' Flood, Paul Diggin, Whatling, Adam Dehaty, Thom Evans, Kieron Lewitt]

[*Bench:* Clunis, Thomas 'Tom' Croft (*lock/flanker*), Foden, Chris Hallam (*flanker/number 8*), James Hoyle (*centre*), Tom Muggeridge (*prop*), Ben Patston (*fly half/full back*)]

[*Scorers:* **tries** by M. Hopley, Cracknell and Ben Lloyd, **penalty goals** by T. Flood (2), **conversions** by T. Flood (2)]

[*Jim Mallinder was appointed on 12th October 2004*]

AUSTRALIAN TOUR TO SCOTLAND, FRANCE AND ENGLAND 2004
THIRD INVESTEC CHALLENGE MATCH
SECOND COOK CUP MATCH

[**HEAD COACH:** *Andy Robinson*] [**ASSISTANT COACHES:** *Phil Larder, Dave Alred & Joe Lydon*]

CAPTAIN: *Jason Robinson*

27th Nov **ENGLAND*** 19 AUSTRALIA 21

Twickenham

[*Team:* Rowntree, Steve Thompson (2), Julian White, Grewcock, S. Borthwick, J. Worsley, Moody, Corry, Gomarsall, C. Hodgson, J. Lewsey, H. Paul, Tindall, Cueto, Jason Robinson]

[*Bench:* B. Cohen (rep), Harry Ellis (rep), W. Greenwood (rep), Hazell, Kay, Sheridan, Titterrell]

[*Scorers:* **tries** by Moody, J. Lewsey and Cueto, **conversions** by Tindall (2)]

EMIRATES AIRLINE DUBAI RUGBY SEVENS
IRB WORLD SEVENS SERIES 2004-2005 ROUND 1
EMIRATES INTERNATIONAL TROPHY

Dubai Exiles Stadium, Dubai

[*Tournament squad:* Amor, Appleford, J. Bailey (never travelled as withdrew, replaced by Ollie Phillips), Horstmann, Monye, Peter Richards, Roques, Sampson, P. Sanderson, Neil Starling (*fly half/centre*), Mathew 'Matt' Tait (*centre*), R. Thirlby, O. Phillips (*centre/wing*)]

(squad of 12)

[James Bailey was withdrawn by his club Gloucester in order to fulfil his Zurich Premiership commitments; Delon Armitage, James Brooks, Ben Russell (2), Ben Skirving and Andy Vilk all in original 18 man training squad on 22nd-23rd November 2004; Neil Starling was the son of Dave Starling; Matt Tait played for the Jedi invitational team in the Henley International Sevens at Henley on 10th August 2003, played for England in the U19 World Championship in South Africa in March-April 2004 and played for Loughborough University at the Middlesex Sevens at Twickenham on 14th August 2004]

[Juliette Reilly was appointed in September 2004]

[**MANAGER:** *Juliette Reilly*] [**COACH:** *Mike Friday*] [**ASSISTANT COACH:** *Damian McGrath*]

CAPTAIN: *Simon Amor*

First Round - Pool 'B'

2nd Dec SCOTLAND 19 **ENGLAND** 24

[*Team:* Roques, Horstmann, Appleford, Amor, N. Starling, M. Tait, Sampson]

[*Bench:* Monye (rep), O. Phillips, Peter Richards (rep), P. Sanderson, R. Thirlby (rep)]

[*Scorers:* **tries** by N. Starling, Amor, Monye and Peter Richards, **conversions** by Amor (2)]

2nd Dec UGANDA 7 **ENGLAND** 34

[*Team:* Monye, Peter Richards, P. Sanderson, Amor, N. Starling, R. Thirlby, O. Phillips]

[*Bench:* Appleford, Horstmann (rep), Roques, Sampson (rep), M. Tait (rep)]

[*Scorers:* **tries** by Monye (2), O. Phillips, Amor, P. Sanderson and Sampson, **conversions** by Amor (2)]

2nd Dec FRANCE 14 **ENGLAND** 26

[*Team:* Roques, Peter Richards, P. Sanderson, Amor, Appleford, M. Tait, Sampson]

[*Bench:* Horstmann (rep), Monye, O. Phillips (rep), N. Starling, R. Thirlby (rep]

[*Scorers:* **tries** by Peter Richards, Amor and R. Thirlby (2), **conversions** by Amor (3)]
Quarter-Final
3rd Dec AUSTRALIA 5 **ENGLAND** 24
[*Team:* Roques, Peter Richards, P. Sanderson, Amor, Appleford, M. Tait, Monye]
[*Bench:* Horstmann (rep), O. Phillips, Sampson, N. Starling, R. Thirlby (rep)]
[*Scorers:* **tries** by Peter Richards, Monye (2) and Amor, **conversions** by Amor (2)]
Semi-Final
3rd Dec SOUTH AFRICA 5 **ENGLAND** 14
[*Team:* Roques, Peter Richards, P. Sanderson, Amor, Appleford, M. Tait, Monye]
[*Bench:* Horstmann, Sampson, O. Phillips, N. Starling (rep), R. Thirlby (rep)]
[*Scorers:* **tries** by Roques and Peter Richards, **conversions** by Amor (2)]
Final
3rd Dec FIJI 21 **ENGLAND** 26
[*Team:* Roques, Peter Richards, P. Sanderson, Amor, Appleford, M. Tait, Sampson]
[*Bench:* Horstmann, Monye, O. Phillips, N. Starling (rep), R. Thirlby (rep)]
[*Scorers:* **tries** by P. Sanderson, N. Starling, M. Tait and R. Thirlby, **conversions** by Amor, Sampson and R. Thirlby]
POSITION: WINNERS
[England scored 20 competition points in this Round of the 2004-2005 IRB World Sevens Series]

NEW ZEALAND TOUR TO ITALY, WALES AND FRANCE 2004
GARTMORE CHALLENGE
GARTMORE CHALLENGE TROPHY
[*English squad members:* M. Catt (withdrew due to injury), Chris Jones (withdrew due to injury)]
[Bob Dwyer was appointed on 13th September 2004; Rob Howley was appointed on 18th November 2004; Rob Howley won 59 caps for Wales between 1996-2002 and was capped for the British & Irish Lions in June 2001]
[**HEAD COACH:** *Bob Dwyer* (AU)] [**ASSISTANT COACH:** *Rob Howley* (WA)]
CAPTAIN: *Justin Marshall* (NZ)
[4th Dec **BARBARIANS** 19 NEW ZEALAND XV 47]
Twickenham
[*Team:* Bill Young (AU), Brendan Cannon (AU), Faan Rautenbach (SA), Daniel Vickerman (AU), Albert van den Berg (SA), Schalk Burger (SA), Phil Waugh (AU), Xavier Rush (NZ), Justin Marshall (NZ), Matt Giteau (AU), Sireli Bobo (FIJ), Morgan Turinui (AU), Lote Tuqiri (1) (AU), Latham (AU), M. Rogers (AU)]
[*Bench:* Gcobani Bobo (SA) (*centre*) (rep), Gary Botha (SA) (*hooker/flanker*) (rep), Werner Greeff (SA) (*full back*) (rep), *Andrea Lo Cicero* Vaina (IT) (*prop*) (rep), Radike Samo (AU) (*lock/flanker*) (rep), Tuilevu (FIJ) (*wing*) (rep), A.J. Venter (SA) (*lock/flanker/number 8*) (rep)]
[*Scorers:* **tries** by X. Rush (NZ), Lo Cicero (IT) and van den Berg (SA), **conversions** by Giteau (AU) and M. Rogers (AU)]

EMIRATES AIRLINE SOUTH AFRICA SEVENS
IRB WORLD SEVENS SERIES 2004-2005 ROUND 2
Outeniqua Park Stadium, George
[*Tournament squad:* Appleford, Roques, Peter Richards, N. Starling, O. Phillips, Sampson, Horstmann, R. Thirlby, Gollings, R. Haughton, M. Tait]
(squad of 11)

[Simon Amor and Ugo Monye unavailable due to injury; Pat Sanderson unavailable after a RFU hearing on 7th December 2004 found him guilty of striking an opponent in a Zurich Premiership match on 26th November 2004 and thus banned him for 2 weeks; Tony Roques was the tournament captain]

[**MANAGER:** *Juliette Reilly*] [**COACH:** *Mike Friday*] [**ASSISTANT COACH:** *Damian McGrath*]

CAPTAIN: *Tony Roques*

First Round - Pool 'B'

10th Dec KENYA 0 **ENGLAND** 26

[*Team:* Appleford, Horstmann, Roques, Sampson, Gollings, N. Starling, O. Phillips]

[*Bench:* R. Haughton (rep), Peter Richards (rep), M. Tait, R. Thirlby (rep)]

[*Scorers:* **tries** by N. Starling (3) and Peter Richards, **conversions** by Gollings (3)]

CAPTAIN: *Ben Gollings*

10th Dec IRELAND 19 **ENGLAND** 31

[*Team:* Horstmann, Peter Richards, R. Thirlby, Sampson, Gollings, N. Starling, M. Tait]

[*Bench:* Appleford, R. Haughton (rep), O. Phillips (rep), Roques (rep)]

[*Scorers:* **tries** by Peter Richards (2), M. Tait (2) and Sampson, **conversions** by Gollings (3)]

CAPTAIN: *Tony Roques*

10th Dec AUSTRALIA 12 **ENGLAND** 24

[*Team:* Appleford, Horstmann, Roques, Peter Richards, Gollings, M. Tait, R. Haughton]

[*Bench:* O. Phillips, Sampson (rep), N. Starling (rep), R. Thirlby (rep)]

[*Scorers:* **tries** by R. Haughton, Appleford, Roques and Peter Richards, **conversions** by Gollings (2)]

Quarter-Final

11th Dec TUNISIA 0 **ENGLAND** 52

[*Team:* Horstmann, Peter Richards, Roques, Sampson, Gollings, N. Starling, O. Phillips]

[*Bench:* Appleford (rep), R. Haughton, M. Tait, R. Thirlby (rep)]

[*Scorers:* **tries** by Sampson, O. Phillips (3), Gollings (2), N. Starling and Peter Richards, **conversions** by Gollings (6)]

Semi-Final

11th Dec FIJI 19 **ENGLAND** 12

[*Team:* Appleford, Horstmann, Roques, Peter Richards, Gollings, M. Tait, R. Haughton]

[*Bench:* O. Phillips, Sampson, N. Starling (rep), R. Thirlby (rep)]

[*Scorers:* **tries** by M. Tait and N. Starling, **conversion** by Gollings]

POSITION: LOSING SEMI-FINALISTS

[England scored 12 competition points in this Round of the 2004-2005 IRB World Sevens Series]

2005
OTHER MATCHES
AXA NEW ZEALAND INTERNATIONAL SEVENS
IRB WORLD SEVENS SERIES 2004-2005 ROUND 3

WestpacTrust Stadium, Wellington

[*Tournament squad:* Amor, Appleford, J. Bailey, James Brooks, Gollings, O. Phillips, Peter Richards, Roques, Ben Russell (2), N. Starling (never travelled as injured, replaced by Dan Hipkiss), R. Thirlby, Vilk (*back/forward*), Hipkiss]

(squad of 12)

[Delon Armitage, Phil Dowson, Richard Haughton, Kai Horstmann, Will Matthews, Ugo Monye, Paul Sampson, Pat Sanderson, Ben Skirving, Matt Tait and Rob Vickerman all in original training squad of 24 on 17th-20th January 2005; Neil Starling withdrew on the day of the squad's departure; Simon Amor was the tournament captain]

[**MANAGER:** *Juliette Reilly*] [**COACH:** *Mike Friday*] [**ASSISTANT COACH:** *Damian McGrath*]

CAPTAIN: *Ben Gollings*

First Round - Pool 'A'

4th Feb CANADA 5 **ENGLAND** 31

[*Team:* Appleford, Vilk, Ben Russell (2), James Brooks, Gollings, J. Bailey, R. Thirlby]
[*Bench:* Amor, Hipkiss (rep), O. Phillips (rep), Peter Richards (rep), Roques]
[*Scorers:* **tries** by James Brooks, Gollings, Appleford, J. Bailey and O. Phillips, **conversions** by Gollings (3)]

CAPTAIN: *Simon Amor*

4th Feb NIUE 7 **ENGLAND** 41

[*Team:* Vilk, Peter Richards, Ben Russell (2), Amor, Gollings, Hipkiss, O. Phillips]
[*Bench:* Appleford, J. Bailey (rep), James Brooks (rep), Roques, R. Thirlby]
[*Scorers:* **tries** by O. Phillips (2), Gollings, Ben Russell, Amor, James Brooks and Vilk, **conversions** by Gollings (3)]

4th Feb SAMOA 10 **ENGLAND** 21

[*Team:* Appleford, Peter Richards, Ben Russell (2), Amor, Gollings, R. Thirlby, O. Phillips]
[*Bench:* J. Bailey (rep), James Brooks (rep), Hipkiss, Roques, Vilk (rep)]
[*Scorers:* **tries** by Gollings, Peter Richards and O. Phillips, **conversions** by Gollings (3)]

Quarter-Final

5th Feb FIJI 24 **ENGLAND** 19

[*Team:* Roques, Vilk, Ben Russell (2), Amor, Gollings, Appleford, R. Thirlby]
[*Bench:* J. Bailey (rep), James Brooks, Hipkiss, O. Phillips, Peter Richards]
[*Scorers:* **tries** by R. Thirlby, Appleford and J. Bailey, **conversions** by Gollings (2)]

CAPTAIN: *Ben Gollings*

[Plate Semi-Final:]

[5th Feb SCOTLAND 19 **ENGLAND*** 17 **]**

[*Team:* Appleford, Roques, Ben Russell (2), James Brooks, Gollings, Hipkiss, O. Phillips]
[*Bench:* Amor, J. Bailey (rep), Peter Richards, R. Thirlby, Vilk (rep)]
[*Scorers:* **tries** by Hipkiss and O. Phillips (2), **conversion** by Gollings]

POSITION: LOSING QUARTER-FINALISTS [*PLATE SEMI-FINALISTS*]

FANTASY: *LOSING QUARTER-FINALISTS* [*PLATE WINNERS*]

[England scored 4 competition points in this Round of the 2004-2005 IRB World Sevens Series]

6 NATIONS CHAMPIONSHIP

[**HEAD COACH:** *Andy Robinson*] [**ASSISTANT COACHES:** *Phil Larder, Dave Alred & Joe Lydon*]

CAPTAIN: *Jason Robinson*

5th Feb WALES 11 **ENGLAND*** 9

Millennium Stadium, Cardiff

[*Team:* Rowntree, Steve Thompson (2), Julian White, Grewcock, Kay, Chris Jones, Hazell, J. Worsley, Matt Dawson, C. Hodgson, J. Lewsey, Noon, M. Tait, Cueto, Jason Robinson]

[*Bench:* Barkley (rep), S. Borthwick (rep), B. Cohen, Harry Ellis (rep), Forrester (*flanker*) (rep), Titterrell, Vickery (rep)]

[*Scorers:* **penalty goals** by C. Hodgson (3)]

13th Feb **ENGLAND*** 17 FRANCE 18

Twickenham

[*Team:* Rowntree, Steve Thompson (2), Vickery, Grewcock, Kay, J. Worsley, Moody, Corry, Harry Ellis, C. Hodgson, J. Lewsey, Barkley, Noon, Cueto, Jason Robinson]

[*Bench:* S. Borthwick, B. Cohen (rep), Matt Dawson (rep), Hazell (rep), H. Paul, Sheridan, Titterrell]

[*Scorers:* **tries** by Barkley and J. Lewsey, **penalty goal** by C. Hodgson, **conversions** by C. Hodgson (2)]

27th Feb IRELAND 19 **ENGLAND*** 13

Lansdowne Road

[*Team:* Rowntree, Steve Thompson (2), M. Stevens, Grewcock, Kay, J. Worsley, Moody, Corry, Harry Ellis, C. Hodgson, J. Lewsey, Barkley, Noon, Cueto, Jason Robinson]

[*Bench:* Duncan Bell (*prop*), S. Borthwick, Matt Dawson (rep), Andy Goode, Hazell, Ollie Smith (2), Titterrell]

[*Scorers:* **try** by Corry, **penalty goal** by C. Hodgson, **drop goal** by C. Hodgson, **conversion** by C. Hodgson]

CAPTAIN: *Martin Corry*

12th Mar **ENGLAND** 39 ITALY 7

Twickenham

[*Team:* Rowntree, Steve Thompson (2), M. Stevens, Grewcock, Kay, J. Worsley, Moody, Corry, Harry Ellis, C. Hodgson, J. Lewsey, Barkley, Noon, Cueto, Balshaw]

[*Bench:* Duncan Bell (rep), S. Borthwick (rep), Matt Dawson (rep), Andy Goode (rep), Hazell (rep), Ollie Smith (2) (rep), Titterrell (rep)]

[*Scorers:* **tries** by Cueto (3), Steve Thompson, Balshaw and Hazell, **penalty goal** by C. Hodgson, **conversions** by C. Hodgson (2) and Andy Goode]

19th Mar **ENGLAND** 43 SCOTLAND 22

Twickenham

[*Team:* M. Stevens, Steve Thompson (2), Duncan Bell, Grewcock, Kay, J. Worsley, Moody, Corry, Harry Ellis, C. Hodgson, J. Lewsey, Barkley, Noon, Cueto, Balshaw]

[*Bench:* S. Borthwick (rep), Matt Dawson (rep), Andy Goode (rep), Hazell (rep), Ollie Smith (2) (rep), Titterrell (rep), M. Worsley (rep)]

[*Scorers:* **tries** by Noon (3), J. Worsley, J. Lewsey, Harry Ellis and Cueto, **conversions** by C. Hodgson (4)]

POSITION: **4TH 4 +44 CC** [*Wales 10 +74 GS TC*, France 8 +52, Ireland 6 +25 MT, Scotland 2 -71, Italy 0 -124]

FANTASY: ***1ST 10 GS TC CC MT***

OTHER MATCHES

U21 6 NATIONS CHAMPIONSHIP

[**MANAGER:** *Peter Drewett*] [**COACH:** *Jim Mallinder*] [**ASSISTANT COACH:** *Nigel Redman*]

CAPTAIN: *Tom Rees*

[4th Feb WALES U21 32 **ENGLAND U21** 21]

Rodney Parade, Newport

[*Team:* Croall, Dave Ward, Martin Halsall, Blaze, Sean Cox, Haskell, Tom Rees, Goodman, J. Bedford, Ross Broadfoot, Thomas 'Tom' Varndell, R. Davis, Matt Cornwell, Wellwood, O. Morgan]

[*Bench:* Neil Briggs (*hooker/flanker*) (rep), Cracknell (rep), M. Cusack (*prop*) (rep), Foden (rep), M. Hampson (*prop*) (rep), Dan Smith (*lock/flanker*) (rep), Whatling (rep)]

[*Scorers:* **tries** by Tom Rees, Haskell and Wellwood, **penalty goals** by Broadfoot (2)]

[11th Feb **ENGLAND U21*** 17 FRANCE U21 20]

Franklin's Gardens, Northampton

[*Team:* Croall, Dave Ward, M. Hampson, Blaze, Dan Smith, Tom Rees, David Seymour, Goodman, Foden, R. Davis, Varndell, Whatling, Matt Cornwell, Diggin, Broadfoot]

[*Bench:* Tom Biggs (*wing*) (rep), M. Cusack (rep), L. Dickson (*scrum half*), Haskell (*flanker/number 8*) (rep), S. Mackie (*hooker*), T. Ryder (rep), Wellwood (rep)]

[*Scorers:* **tries** by Matt Cornwell and Blaze, **penalty goal** by Broadfoot, **conversions** by Broadfoot (2)]

CAPTAIN: *Ryan Davis*

[25th Feb IRELAND U21 6 **ENGLAND U21** 28]

Donnybrook, Dublin

[*Team:* M. Cusack, N. Briggs, Croall, Blaze, T. Ryder, Haskell, David Seymour, M. Hopley, Foden, T. Flood, Varndell, R. Davis, Matt Cornwell, Biggs, O. Morgan]

[*Bench:* Sean Cox (*lock*) (rep), L. Dickson (rep), M. Hampson (rep), S. Mackie (rep), Ojo (*wing*) (rep), R. Thorpe (rep), Whatling (rep)]

[*Scorers:* **tries** by M. Cusack, Varndell (2) and O. Morgan (2), **penalty goal** by T. Flood]

[11th Mar **ENGLAND U21** 31 ITALY U21 14]

Franklin's Gardens, Northampton

[*Team:* M. Cusack, N. Briggs, M. Hampson, Blaze, T. Ryder, Haskell, David Seymour, M. Hopley, Foden, T. Flood, Varndell, R. Davis, Matt Cornwell, Biggs, O. Morgan]

[*Bench:* Sean Cox (rep), L. Dickson (rep), S. Mackie (rep), Ojo (rep), W. Thompson (rep), R. Thorpe (rep), Whatling (rep)]

[*Scorers:* **tries** by O. Morgan, Varndell and David Seymour, **penalty goals** by T. Flood (4), **conversions** by T. Flood (2)]

CAPTAIN: *Tom Rees*

[18th Mar **ENGLAND U21*** 17 SCOTLAND U21 19]

Franklin's Gardens, Northampton

[*Team:* M. Cusack, N. Briggs, W. Thompson, Blaze, Sean Cox, Tom Rees, David Seymour, Haskell, L. Dickson, T. Flood, Varndell, Whatling, Matt Cornwell, Biggs, O. Morgan]

[*Bench:* Broadfoot (*fly half*) (rep), R. Davis (*fly half/centre/full back*) (rep), Foden (rep), Halsall (*prop*) (rep), M. Hopley (rep), T. Ryder (rep), Dave Ward (*hooker*) (rep)]

[*Scorers:* **try** by Foden, **penalty goals** by T. Flood (4)]

POSITION: **4TH 4 +23** [*Wales 10 +100 GS TC*, France 8 +98, Scotland 6 +8, Ireland 2 -52, Italy 0 -143]

FANTASY: ***2ND 8***

[*Jim Mallinder was appointed on 12th October 2004*]

ENGLAND STUDENTS MATCHES

[**MANAGER:** *Tony Lanaway*] [**COACH:** *Richard Hill (1)*] [**ASSISTANT COACH:** *Steve Hill*]

CAPTAIN: *Tom Hayman*

[11th Feb **ENGLAND STUDENTS** 10 FRANCE STUDENTS 6]
Rectory Field, Charlton Road, Blackheath

[*Team:* Irish, Dalgleish, G. Davis, A. Harris, Skelding, B. Wheeler, Lowrie, T. Hayman, Haydn Thomas, Brad Davies, M. Foster, Abrahams, Whittingham, Jonan Boto, Sayer]

[*Bench:* Gibbons (*lock*), Sacha Harding (*flanker*) (rep), A. Houston, Alistair 'Ali' James (*centre/wing*) (rep), Scothern, W. Thompson (rep), C. Wyles (*centre/wing*) (rep)]

[*Scorers:* **try** by penalty try, **penalty goal** by Whittingham, **conversion** by Whittingham]

[25th Feb FRANCE STUDENTS 23 **ENGLAND STUDENTS** 6]
Stade Henri Desgranges, La Roche-sur-Yon

[*Team:* D. Bassett, Dalgleish, W. Thompson, A. Harris, Skelding, B. Wheeler, Lowrie, T. Hayman, Haydn Thomas, Adam Staniforth, M. Foster, Abrahams, Whittingham, O. Evans, Sayer]

[*Bench:* Gibbons, Sacha Harding, A. Houston, A. James, Robert 'Rob' Vickers (*hooker*), C. Wyles, ?]

[*Scorers:* **penalty goals** by Whittingham (2)]

CAPTAIN: *Andy Dalgleish*

[11th Mar **ENGLAND STUDENTS*** 27 ITALY U25 27]
Iffley Road, Oxford

[*Team:* Irish, Dalgleish, D. Bassett, Skelding, Gibbons, Lowrie, Tom Lawy, Toby Walker, A. Houston, Abrahams, Joseph Ajuwa, Whittingham, Robert 'Rob' Jewell, M. Foster, Rory Teague]

[*Bench:* Matt Corker (*lock/number 8*), Alex Hayman (*centre*), Simon Lovegrove (*prop*), W. Matthews (*flanker/number 8*), Neil Taylor (*centre*), Vickers, Chris Worsley (*scrum half*)]

[*Scorers:* **tries** by Ajuwa, M. Foster (2) and Lawy, **penalty goal** by Whittingham, **conversions** by Whittingham (2)]

[There was an England Students Final Trial at Castlecroft on 5th January 2005]

'A' INTERNATIONAL MATCH

[**HEAD COACH:** *Brian Ashton*] [**ASSISTANT COACHES:** *John Wells & Jon Callard*]

CAPTAIN: *Hugh Vyvyan*

[11th Feb **ENGLAND A** 30 FRANCE A 20]
Recreation Ground, Bath

[*Team:* Freshwater, Chuter, Duncan Bell, L. Deacon, Alex Brown, A. Beattie, Lund, H. Vyvyan, Gomarsall, Andy Goode, Christophers, C. Bell, Ollie Smith (2), Voyce, Balshaw]

[*Bench:* James Brown, M. Cairns, Ben Johnston, Robbie Morris (rep), Tom Palmer (2) (rep), Scaysbrook (*flanker/number 8*) (rep), Walshe (rep)]

[*Scorers:* **tries** by Duncan Bell, Ollie Smith, L. Deacon and Balshaw, **penalty goals** by Andy Goode (2), **conversions** by Andy Goode (2)]

[Brian Ashton, John Wells and Jon Callard were all appointed on 27th January 2005; On 29th September 2005 Brian Ashton was appointed Head Coach of England A for a second time, but then on 1st November 2005 he resigned and also announced that he would be leaving his post of Manager of the RFU National Academy on 17th December 2005]

JEAN-CLAUDE BAQUÉ SHIELD MATCH

[**CHAIRMAN OF SELECTORS:** *Peter Hartley*] [**MANAGER:** *Rob Udwin*] [**ASSISTANT MANAGER:** *Danny Hodgson*] [**COACH:** *Mark Nelson*] [**ASSISTANT COACH:** *Paul Westgate*]

CAPTAIN: *Craig Hammond*

[12th Feb **ENGLAND COUNTIES** 38 FRANCE AMATEURS 0]

Newbury RFC, Monks Lane, Newbury

[*Team:* R. Faulkner, Caves, N. Collins, Daniel 'Dan' Cook, Paul Arnold (2), Craig Hammond, Wilks, Earnshaw, S. Perry, Duncan Hughes, James Aston, Chris Malherbe, Isaac Richmond, J. Moore, Mal Roberts]

[*Bench:* Des Brett (*prop*) (rep), Joseph 'Joe' Clark (*hooker*) (rep), Oliver 'Ollie' Cook (*flanker/number 8*) (rep), Kirkby (*wing*) (rep), Andrew Smith (*lock*) (rep), Spragg (rep), Ollie Thomas (*fly half*) (rep)]

[*Scorers:* **tries** by J. Moore, James Aston, Craig Hammond, Mal Roberts, Wilks and Spragg, **conversions** by J. Moore (4)]

[Peter Hartley was appointed on 4th January 2005]

TEAM ROC USA SEVENS
IRB WORLD SEVENS SERIES 2004-2005 ROUND 4

Home Depot Center, Carson City, Los Angeles

[*Tournament squad:* Appleford, Roques, Ben Russell (2), James Brooks, Hipkiss, O. Phillips, J. Bailey, Vilk, R. Thirlby, Gollings, Peter Richards, Dowson]

(squad of 12)

[Simon Amor unavailable due to injury; Peter Richards was the tournament captain]

[**MANAGER:** *Juliette Reilly*] [**COACH:** *Mike Friday*] [**ASSISTANT COACH:** *Damian McGrath*]

CAPTAIN: *Peter Richards*

First Round - Pool 'A'

12th Feb TONGA 12 **ENGLAND** 19

[*Team:* Dowson, Roques, Ben Russell (2), James Brooks, Appleford, Peter Richards, O. Phillips]

[*Bench:* J. Bailey (rep), Gollings (rep), Hipkiss, R. Thirlby, Vilk (rep)]

[*Scorers:* **tries** by James Brooks, J. Bailey and Gollings, **conversions** by Gollings (2)]

CAPTAIN: *Ben Gollings*

12th Feb WEST INDIES 7 **ENGLAND** 52

[*Team:* Roques, Vilk, Ben Russell (2), James Brooks, Gollings, Hipkiss, R. Thirlby]

[*Bench:* Appleford, J. Bailey (rep), Dowson (rep), O. Phillips (rep), Peter Richards]

[*Scorers:* **tries** by R. Thirlby (2), J. Bailey (3), Hipkiss (2) and Roques, **conversions** by Gollings (4) and James Brooks (2)]

CAPTAIN: *Peter Richards*

12th Feb FIJI 10 **ENGLAND** 14

[*Team:* Dowson, Peter Richards, Ben Russell (2), James Brooks, Gollings, Appleford, R. Thirlby]

[*Bench:* J. Bailey (rep), Hipkiss, O. Phillips, Roques (rep), Vilk]

[*Scorers:* **tries** by R. Thirlby and Appleford, **conversions** by Gollings (2)]

Quarter-Final

13th Feb SAMOA 7 **ENGLAND** 28

[*Team:* Appleford, Roques, Dowson, James Brooks, Gollings, Peter Richards, R. Thirlby]

[*Bench:* J. Bailey (rep), Hipkiss (rep), O. Phillips, Ben Russell (2) (rep), Vilk]

[*Scorers:* **tries** by James Brooks, Appleford, Gollings and Dowson, **conversions** by Gollings (4)]

Semi-Final

13th Feb ARGENTINA 17 **ENGLAND** 0

[*Team:* Appleford, Roques, Dowson, James Brooks, Gollings, Peter Richards, R. Thirlby]

[*Bench:* J. Bailey (rep), Hipkiss, O. Phillips. Ben Russell (2) (rep), Vilk (rep)]

[*No scorers*]

POSITION: LOSING SEMI-FINALISTS

[England scored 12 competition points in this Round of the 2004-2005 IRB World Sevens Series]

IRB RUGBY AID MATCH

[**MANAGER:** *Serge Blanco* (FR)] [**COACH:** *Clive Woodward*] [**ASSISTANT COACHES:** *Brian Ashton* & *Gareth Jenkins* (WA)]

CAPTAIN: *Lawrence Dallaglio*

[5th Mar **NORTH** 19 SOUTH 54]

Twickenham

[*Team:* John Yapp (WA), Titterrell, Horsman, Marco Bortolami (IT), Donnchadh 'Donncha' O'Callaghan (IR), Dallaglio, P. Sanderson, Simon Taylor (2) (SC), Gareth Cooper (WA), D. Humphreys (IR), B. Cohen, Ceri Sweeney (WA), Ollie Smith (2), Mirco Bergamasco (IT), Christopher 'Chris' Paterson (SC)]

[*Bench:* Ibañez (FR) (rep), E. Miller (IR) (rep), William Michael 'Mike' Phillips (2) (WA) (*scrum half*) (rep), Cédric Soulette (FR) (*prop*) (rep), M. Tait (*centre*) (rep), M. Taylor (WA) (rep), Jonathan Thomas (WA) (*lock/number 8*) (rep)]

[*Scorers:* **tries** by Titterrell, P. Sanderson and Bergamasco (IT), **conversions** by D. Humphreys (IR) and C. Sweeney (WA)]

[Serge Blanco and Clive Woodward were both appointed on 2nd February 2005; Brian Ashton and Gareth Jenkins were both appointed on 16th February 2005; Gareth Jenkins played for a Wales XV against Japan in Tokyo on 24th September 1975 and toured America and Canada with the Barbarians in May-June 1976]

RUGBY WORLD CUP SEVENS

MELROSE CUP

Hong Kong Stadium, Eastern Hospital Road, So Kon Po, Hong Kong

[*Tournament squad:* Appleford, Roques, P. Sanderson, Peter Richards, H. Paul, N. Starling, Monye, Dowson, R. Thirlby, Gollings, Amor, R. Haughton]

(squad of 12)

[Ollie Phillips was unavailable for this tournament due to injury; Ben Russell (2) and Andy Vilk in original 15 man training squad announced on 1st March 2005; England had a pre-tournament training camp at Imperial College, Harlington on 7th-10th March 2005; Matt Tait in original 15 man training squad but withdrew on 11th March 2005 due to injury and illness, being replaced by James Brooks who was in turn not selected for the World Cup squad of 12; The England squad departed for Hong Kong on 13th March 2005; The final 12 man tournament squad was named on 14th March 2005]

[**MANAGER:** *Juliette Reilly*] [**COACH:** *Mike Friday*] [**ASSISTANT COACH:** *Damian McGrath*]

CAPTAIN: *Simon Amor*

First Round - Pool 'B'

18th Mar GEORGIA 0 **ENGLAND** 47

[*Team:* Dowson, Roques, N. Starling, Amor, Gollings, H. Paul, Monye]

[*Bench:* Appleford (rep), R. Haughton (rep), Peter Richards, P. Sanderson, R. Thirlby (rep)]
[*Scorers:* **tries** by Gollings, Monye (2), H. Paul, Roques, N. Starling and R. Haughton, **conversions** by Gollings (4) and Amor (2)]

CAPTAIN: *Ben Gollings*

18th Mar ITALY 0 **ENGLAND** 41

[*Team:* Appleford, Roques, P. Sanderson, Peter Richards, Gollings, R. Thirlby, R. Haughton]
[*Bench:* Amor (rep), Dowson, Monye (rep), H. Paul, N. Starling (rep)]
[*Scorers:* **tries** by Haughton (3), Gollings, Peter Richards, R. Thirlby and Monye, **conversions** by Gollings (3)]

CAPTAIN: *Simon Amor*

18th Mar FRANCE 28 **ENGLAND*** 17

[*Team:* Dowson, Peter Richards, P. Sanderson, Amor, Appleford, H. Paul, Monye]
[*Bench:* Gollings, R. Haughton (rep), Roques (rep), N. Starling (rep), R. Thirlby]
[*Scorers:* **tries** by Monye, Dowson and Appleford, **conversion** by Amor]

19th Mar CHINESE TAIPEI 0 **ENGLAND** 41

[*Team:* Appleford, Roques, P. Sanderson, Amor, Gollings, H. Paul, R. Haughton]
[*Bench:* Dowson, Monye (rep), Peter Richards, N. Starling (rep), R. Thirlby (rep)]
[*Scorers:* **tries** by R. Haughton (2), Gollings, H. Paul, R. Thirlby, Monye and N. Starling, **conversions** by Gollings (2) and Amor]

19th Mar SAMOA 7 **ENGLAND** 12

[*Team:* Dowson, Roques, P. Sanderson, Amor, Gollings, H. Paul, Monye]
[*Bench:* Appleford (rep), Peter Richards (rep), N. Starling, R. Thirlby (rep)]
[*Scorers:* **tries** by Monye and Amor, **conversion** by Gollings]

Quarter-Final

20th Mar SCOTLAND 0 **ENGLAND** 36

[*Team:* Dowson, Roques, P. Sanderson, Amor, Gollings, Peter Richards, R. Haughton]
[*Bench:* Appleford (rep), Monye, N. Starling (rep), R. Thirlby (rep)]
[*Scorers:* **tries** by R. Haughton, Peter Richards, Roques, Gollings, R. Thirlby and Appleford, **conversions** by Gollings (2) and Amor]

Semi-Final

20th Mar FIJI 24 **ENGLAND*** 19 aet

[*Team:* Dowson, Roques, P. Sanderson, Amor, Gollings, Peter Richards, R. Haughton]
[*Bench:* Appleford (rep), N. Starling (rep), R. Thirlby (rep)]
[*Scorers:* **tries** by Gollings, Roques and Amor, **conversions** by Gollings (2)]

POSITION: LOSING SEMI-FINALISTS
FANTASY: *WINNERS*

OTHER MATCHES
STANDARD CHARTERED SEVENS, SINGAPORE
IRB WORLD SEVENS SERIES 2004-2005 ROUND 5

National Stadium, Kallang

[*Tournament squad:* Amor, Appleford, D. Armitage (*centre/wing*), James Brooks, Gollings, R. Haughton, W. Matthews, Peter Richards, Roques, Skirving (*forward*), M. Tait (never travelled as injured, replaced by Dan Hipkiss), R. Thirlby, Hipkiss]
(squad of 12)
[*Henry Paul was unavailable for this tournament due to injury; Simon Amor was the tournament captain*]

[**MANAGER:** *Juliette Reilly*] [**COACH:** *Mike Friday*] [**ASSISTANT COACH:** *Damian McGrath*]
CAPTAIN: *Ben Gollings*
First Round - Pool 'B'
16th April KENYA 7 **ENGLAND** 24
[*Team:* Appleford, Roques, W. Matthews, James Brooks, Gollings, Peter Richards, R. Haughton]
[*Bench:* Amor, D. Armitage (rep), Hipkiss, Skirving, R. Thirlby]
[*Scorers:* **tries** by R. Haughton (2), Gollings and Appleford, **conversions** by Gollings (2)]
16th April HONG KONG 0 **ENGLAND** 38
[*Team:* Hipkiss, Roques, Skirving, Peter Richards, Gollings, D. Armitage, R. Thirlby]
[*Bench:* Amor, Appleford, James Brooks (rep), R. Haughton, W. Matthews]
[*Scorers:* **tries** by D. Armitage (2), James Brooks, R. Thirlby, Peter Richards and Skirving, **conversions** by James Brooks (2), D. Armitage and Gollings]
16th April SCOTLAND 5 **ENGLAND** 21
[*Team:* Roques, Peter Richards, W. Matthews, James Brooks, Gollings, Appleford, R. Thirlby]
[*Bench:* Amor, D. Armitage, R. Haughton (rep), Hipkiss, Skirving]
[*Scorers:* **tries** by Roques, Peter Richards and R. Haughton, **conversions** by Gollings (2) and James Brooks]
Quarter-Final
17th April AUSTRALIA 14 **ENGLAND** 17
[*Team:* Appleford, Roques, W. Matthews, James Brooks, Gollings, Peter Richards, R. Haughton]
[*Bench:* Amor, D. Armitage, Hipkiss, Skirving, R. Thirlby]
[*Scorers:* **tries** by W. Matthews, Appleford and R. Haughton, **conversion** by Gollings]
Semi-Final
17th April FIJI 12 **ENGLAND** 14
[*Team:* Appleford, Roques, W. Matthews, James Brooks, Gollings, Peter Richards, R. Haughton]
[*Bench:* Amor, D. Armitage, Hipkiss, Skirving, R. Thirlby]
[*Scorers:* **tries** by R. Haughton and Gollings, **conversions** by Gollings (2)]
Final
17th April NEW ZEALAND 26 **ENGLAND** 5
[*Team:* Appleford, Roques, W. Matthews, James Brooks, Gollings, Peter Richards, R. Haughton]
[*Bench:* Amor, D. Armitage, Hipkiss (rep), Skirving, R. Thirlby]
[*Scorers:* **try** by Hipkiss]
POSITION: LOSING FINALISTS
[England scored 16 competition points in this Round of the 2004-2005 IRB World Sevens Series]

NEW ZEALAND ARMY TOUR TO ENGLAND AND WALES 2005

[NO COACH NOMINATED]
CAPTAIN: *??*
[5th May **PUBLIC SCHOOL WANDERERS** 24 New Zealand Army (*NZ*) 48]
Iffley Road, Oxford
[*Team:* Dalgleish, S. FitzGerald, Adam Slade]

[*Bench:*]
[*Scorers:*]

ZURICH TEST

[*Other squad members:* Back, G. Bulloch (SC), Cueto, Matt Dawson, W. Greenwood, Gavin Henson (WA) (*fly half/centre/full back*), Richard Hill (2), C. Hodgson, Gethin Jenkins (WA) (*prop*), *Stephen* Michael Jones (2) (WA) (*fly half*), J. Lewsey, Paul O'Connell (IR) (*lock*), Brian O'Driscoll (IR) (*centre*), M. O'Kelly (IR), Dwayne Peel (WA) (*scrum half*), Jason Robinson, Tomos 'Tom' Shanklin (WA) (*centre/wing*), Sheridan, M. Stevens, Simon Taylor (2) (SC), Gareth Thomas (2) (WA) (*centre/wing/full back*), Titterrell, Martyn Williams (WA)]
(squad of 45)
[Warm-up match for the British & Irish Lions tour of New Zealand in June-July 2005; Clive Woodward was appointed on 6th February 2004; Ian McGeechan, Gareth Jenkins & Mike Ford were all appointed on 21st October 2004; Ian McGeechan won 32 caps for Scotland between 1972-79 and was capped for the British Lions in June 1974; Mike Ford won 10 caps for Great Britain at Rugby League between 1987-93, was capped for England at Rugby League in November 1992 and retired in July 2001; On 19th May 2005 a RFU hearing found Neil Back guilty of striking an opponent in the Zurich Premiership Final on 14th May 2005 and thus banned him for 4 weeks; On 5th March 2008 the IRB retrospectively ruled that this game was a cap international match]
[**HEAD COACH:** *Clive Woodward*] [**COACHES:** *Ian McGeechan* (SC), *Gareth Jenkins* (WA) & *Mike Ford*]
CAPTAIN: *Michael Owen* (WA)
[23rd May **BRITISH & IRISH LIONS*** 25 ARGENTINA 25]
Millennium Stadium, Cardiff
[*Team:* Rowntree, S. Byrne (IR), John Hayes (IR), D. O'Callaghan (IR), Grewcock, Corry, Moody, Michael Owen (WA), Gareth Cooper (WA), Jonny Wilkinson, Shane Williams (WA), Gordon D'Arcy (IR), Ollie Smith (2), Denis Hickie (IR), G. Murphy (IR)]
[*Bench:* Christopher 'Chris' Cusiter (SC) (*scrum half*) (rep), Dallaglio, Horgan (IR) (*centre/wing*) (rep), Kay (rep), O'Gara (IR), Steve Thompson (2) (rep), Julian White (rep)]
[*Scorers:* **try** by Ollie Smith, **penalty goals** by Jonny Wilkinson (6), **conversion** by Jonny Wilkinson]

BARBARIANS MATCH

[*English squad members:* M. Regan, S. Shaw, Ollie Smith (2)]
[Bob Dwyer and Pat Howard were both appointed on 10th May 2005; Pat Howard won 20 caps for Australia between 1993-97]
[**COACH:** *Bob Dwyer* (AU)] [**ASSISTANT COACH:** *Pat Howard* (AU)]
CAPTAIN: *David Humphreys* (IR)
[24th May SCOTLAND XV 38 **BARBARIANS** 7]
Pittodrie Stadium, Aberdeen
[*Team:* Lo Cicero (IT), Sheahan (IR), Darren Morris (WA), Longwell (IR), A.J. Venter (SA), Finegan (AU), Semo Sititi (SAM), E. Miller (IR), Bryan Redpath (SC), D. Humphreys (IR), S. Bobo (FIJ), Maggs (IR), Matt Burke (AU), Brian Lima (SAM), Girvan Dempsey (IR)]
[*Bench:* Christopher *Selborne* Boome (SA) (*lock*) (rep), T. Castaignède (FR) (rep), Ibañez (FR) (rep), K. Logan (SC) (rep), John 'Jonny' O'Connor (IR) (*flanker*) (rep), Mark Robinson (2) (NZ) (rep), C. Visagie (SA) (*prop*) (rep)]
[*Scorers:* **try** by Lo Cicero (IT), **conversion** by D. Humphreys (IR)]

TIBCO CHALLENGE

[ENGLAND XV: [*Other squad members:* Barkley (withdrew due to injury, replaced by Sam Vesty), C. Bell (*centre*) (withdrew due to injury), Cueto (withdrew), Freshwater (withdrew), Will Green (1) (withdrew, replaced by Micky Ward), Greening (withdrew due to injury, replaced by Lee Mears), Hazell (withdrew due to injury, replaced by Magnus Lund), Lund, Monye, Tindall (withdrew due to injury, replaced by Ayoola Erinle), Vickery (withdrew due to injury, replaced by Robbie Morris), Jonny Wilkinson (withdrew)]**]**

(squad of 29)

[Joe Lydon, Simon Hardy, Phil Keith-Roach and Damian McGrath were all appointed on 8th April 2005; Graham Rowntree, Andy Sheridan, Steve Thompson (2), Andy Titterrell, Julian White, Matt Stevens, Danny Grewcock, Ben Kay, Richard Hill (2), Neil Back, Lewis Moody, Lawrence Dallaglio, Martin Corry, Matt Dawson, Will Greenwood, Ollie Smith (2), Josh Lewsey and Jason Robinson all unavailable due to their British & Irish Lions commitments; Mark Cueto withdrew on 17th April 2005 as he was now required to go on the British & Lions tour of New Zealand; Will Green (1) withdrew on 3rd May 2005 after he announced that he no longer wished to be considered for selection to the England team; Jonny Wilkinson withdrew on 8th May 2005 as he was now required to go on the British & Lions tour of New Zealand; Perry Freshwater withdrew on 16th May 2005 due to club commitments; Phil Greening retired due to injury in October 2005]

[ENGLAND XV: [HEAD COACH: *Joe Lydon*] [**ASSISTANT COACHES:** *Simon Hardy, Phil Keith-Roach* & *Damian McGrath*]**]**

[BARBARIANS: [COACH: *Bob Dwyer* (AU)] [**ASSISTANT COACH:** *Pat Howard* (AU)]**]**

CAPTAIN: *Pat Sanderson* [England XV]

CAPTAIN: *Corné Krige* (SA) [Barbarians]

28th May **ENGLAND XV*** 39 **BARBARIANS** 52

Twickenham

[ENGLAND XV: [*Team:* M. Worsley, Chuter, Micky Ward, L. Deacon, Tom Palmer (2), Chris Jones, P. Sanderson, H. Vyvyan, Gomarsall, Andy Goode, J. Simpson-Daniel, Noon, Erinle, Sackey, Voyce]

[*Bench:* Forrester (rep), S. Hooper (rep), Mears (rep), Robbie Morris (rep), Peter Richards (rep), M. Tait (rep), Vesty (rep)]

[*Scorers:* **tries** by Sackey (2), Erinle, Forrester and P. Sanderson, **penalty goals** by Andy Goode (2), **conversions** by Andy Goode (2) and Vesty (2)]**]**

[BARBARIANS: [*Team:* Tom Smith (2) (SC), M. Regan, C. Visagie (SA), S. Shaw, Boome (SA), Krige (SA), Jonny O'Connor (IR), Sébastien Chabal (FR), Mark Robinson (2) (NZ), C. Spencer (NZ), Reihana (NZ), Trevor Halstead (SA), T. Castaignède (FR), Wendell Sailor (AU), Robert *Brent* Russell (SA)]

[*Bench:* Matt Burke (AU) (rep), D. Humphreys (IR) (rep), Ibañez (FR) (rep), Lo Cicero (IT) (rep), B. Redpath (SC) (*scrum half*) (rep), Sititi (SAM) (*flanker*) (rep), A.J. Venter (SA) (rep)]

[*Scorers:* **tries** by Reihana (NZ) (2), Sailor (AU) (2), C. Spencer (NZ), Halstead (SA) and Brent Russell (SA) (2), **conversions** by Reihana (NZ) (6)]**]**

EMIRATES AIRLINE LONDON SEVENS
IRB WORLD SEVENS SERIES 2004-2005 ROUND 6

Twickenham

[*Tournament squad:* Appleford, Roques, W. Matthews, Peter Richards, Hipkiss, M. Tait, J. Bailey, Dowson, R. Thirlby, Gollings, Amor, R. Haughton]

(squad of 12)

[Henry Paul and Ollie Phillips were unavailable for this tournament due to injury; Delon Armitage and Andy Vilk in original 14 man training squad announced on 14th May 2005]
[**MANAGER:** *Juliette Reilly*] [**COACH:** *Mike Friday*] [**ASSISTANT COACH:** *Damian McGrath*]
CAPTAIN: *Simon Amor*
First Round - Pool 'B'
4th June **ENGLAND** 29 FRANCE 0
[*Team:* Roques, Peter Richards, Dowson, Amor, Gollings, M. Tait, R. Haughton]
[*Bench:* Appleford, J. Bailey (rep), Hipkiss, W. Matthews, R. Thirlby]
[*Scorers:* **tries** by Dowson, Peter Richards, R. Haughton (2) and J. Bailey, **conversions** by Gollings (2)]
4th June **ENGLAND** 33 GEORGIA 5
[*Team:* Hipkiss, W. Matthews, Roques, Amor, R. Thirlby, Appleford, J. Bailey]
[*Bench:* Dowson, Gollings (rep), R. Haughton, Peter Richards, M. Tait (rep)]
[*Scorers:* **tries** by Hipkiss, Roques, W. Matthews, J. Bailey and M. Tait, **conversions** by Amor (3) and Gollings]
4th June **ENGLAND*** 15 SAMOA 19
[*Team:* W. Matthews, Peter Richards, Dowson, Amor, Gollings, M. Tait, R. Haughton]
[*Bench:* Appleford (rep), J. Bailey, Hipkiss, Roques (rep), R. Thirlby (rep)]
[*Scorers:* **tries** by Dowson, M. Tait and R. Thirlby]
Quarter-Final
5th June **ENGLAND** 40 SCOTLAND 7
[*Team:* Appleford, Roques, Dowson, Amor, Gollings, Peter Richards, R. Haughton]
[*Bench:* J. Bailey, Hipkiss, W. Matthews, M. Tait, R. Thirlby (rep)]
[*Scorers:* **tries** by R. Haughton (3), Gollings, R. Thirlby and Amor, **conversions** by Gollings (5)]
Semi-Final
5th June **ENGLAND** 33 ARGENTINA 7
[*Team:* Appleford, Roques, Dowson, Amor, Gollings, Peter Richards, R. Haughton]
[*Bench:* J. Bailey, Hipkiss, W. Matthews, M. Tait (rep), R. Thirlby (rep)]
[*Scorers:* **tries** by Dowson, Gollings (2), Amor and M. Tait, **conversions** by Gollings (4)]
Final
5th June **ENGLAND*** 12 SOUTH AFRICA 21
[*Team:* Appleford, Roques, Dowson, Amor, Gollings, Peter Richards, R. Haughton]
[*Bench:* J. Bailey, Hipkiss (rep), W. Matthews, M. Tait, R. Thirlby (rep)]
[*Scorers:* **tries** by R. Haughton and Gollings, **conversion** by Gollings]
POSITION: LOSING FINALISTS
FANTASY: *WINNERS*
[England scored 16 competition points in this Round of the 2004-2005 IRB World Sevens Series]

NOBOK CHALLENGE - JONNO V JONAH

NOBOK CHALLENGE TROPHY
[**MANAGER:** *Jason Leonard*] [**PLAYER-COACH:** *Pat Howard* (AU)]
CAPTAIN: *Martin Johnson*
[4th June **MARTIN JOHNSON XV** 33 JONAH LOMU XV 29]
Twickenham
[*Team:* Tom Smith (2) (SC), Ibañez (FR), Darren Morris (WA), Martin Johnson, Chris Jones, J. Worsley, Magne (FR), Chabal (FR), K. Bracken, Andy Goode, Healey, Noon, Tony Marsh

(FR), Erinle, Gregor Townsend (SC)]
[*Bench:* Victor Costello (IR) (*flanker/number 8*) (rep), Anthony Foley (IR) (*number 8*) (rep), Will Green (1) (rep), R. Henderson (IR) (*centre*) (rep), P. Howard (AU) (rep), Jonathan Humphreys (WA) (*hooker*) (rep), W. Johnson (rep), L. Lloyd (rep), Morgan Williams (CAN) (*scrum half*) (rep)]
[*Scorers:* **tries** by Healey (3), Erinle and L. Lloyd, **conversions** by Andy Goode (4)]
[Match organised as a testimonial game for Martin Johnson]
[Jason Leonard and Pat Howard were both appointed on 30th March 2005; Jason Leonard won 114 caps for England between 1990-2004 and was capped for the British Lions in June 1993; Pat Howard was originally only involved as the Coach for this match!]

BRITISH & IRISH LIONS TOUR TO NEW ZEALAND 2005

[**MANAGER:** *Bill Beaumont*] [**HEAD COACH:** *Clive Woodward*] [**ASSISTANT COACHES:** *Andy Robinson*, *Eddie O'Sullivan* (IR), *Phil Larder*, *Ian McGeechan* (SC), *Gareth Jenkins* (WA) & *Mike Ford*]
[*Other squad members:* Balshaw (never travelled as injured, replaced by Mark Cueto), Cockbain (WA) (*lock*) (travelled later as a replacement for Danny Grewcock) (tm), Gareth Cooper (WA) (*scrum half*) (tm), Cusiter (SC) (tm), Dallaglio (returned home as injured, replaced by Simon Easterby) (tm), G. D'Arcy (IR) (*centre/wing*) (tm), J. Hayes (IR) (*prop*) (tm), Hickie (IR) (*wing*) (tm), C. Hodgson (tm), M. O'Kelly (IR) (returned home as injured, replaced by Simon Shaw), Michael Owen (WA) (*lock/flanker/number 8*) (tm), Shanklin (WA) (returned home as injured) (tm), S. Shaw (travelled later as a replacement) (tm), Sheridan (tm), Ollie Smith (2) (tm), M. Stevens (tm), Simon Taylor (2) (SC) (returned home as injured, replaced by Ryan Jones), Titterrell (tm), Jason White (SC) (*flanker*) (travelled later as a replacement for Richard Hill (2))]
(squad of 45)
[Bill Beaumont and Clive Woodward were both appointed on 6th February 2004; Bill Beaumont won 34 caps for England between 1975-82 and captained the British Lions on their tour of South Africa in May-July 1980; Andy Robinson, Eddie O'Sullivan, Phil Larder, Ian McGeechan, Gareth Jenkins & Mike Ford were all appointed on 21st October 2004; Trevor Woodman, Phil Vickery and Mike Tindall were unavailable for this tour due to injury; Jonny Wilkinson was added to the original squad of 44 on 8th May 2005; Brian O'Driscoll was the tour captain; The Lions squad departed for New Zealand on 24th May 2005; Stephen Jones (2) was in the original squad but did not travel until 30th May 2005 due to club commitments; Gareth Thomas (2) missed the first match of the tour due to club commitments; Jason Robinson missed the first two matches of the tour due to family commitments; Tom Shanklin returned home injured after the first test and was not replaced]

DHL LIONS SERIES TROPHY

[**MANAGER:** *Bill Beaumont*] [**HEAD COACH:** *Clive Woodward*] [**ASSISTANT COACHES:** *Eddie O'Sullivan* (IR), *Andy Robinson* & *Phil Larder*]
CAPTAIN: *Brian O'Driscoll* (IR) [*Martin Corry took over when Brian O'Driscoll was injured in the 1st half*]
[25th Jun NEW ZEALAND 21 **BRITISH & IRISH LIONS** 3]
Jade Stadium, Christchurch
[*Team:* Gethin Jenkins (WA), S. Byrne (IR), Julian White, P. O'Connell (IR), Kay, Richard Hill (2), Back, Corry, D. Peel (WA), Stephen Jones (2) (WA), Gareth Thomas (2) (WA), Jonny Wilkinson, Brian O'Driscoll (IR), J. Lewsey, Jason Robinson]

[*Bench:* Matt Dawson (rep), W. Greenwood (rep), Grewcock (rep), Horgan (IR) (rep), Ryan Jones (WA) (*flanker/number 8*) (rep), Rowntree, Steve Thompson (2) (rep)]
[*Scorers:* **penalty goal** by Jonny Wilkinson]
CAPTAIN: *Gareth Thomas (2)* (WA)
[2nd July NEW ZEALAND 48 **BRITISH & IRISH LIONS** 18]
WestpacTrust Stadium, Wellington
[*Team:* Gethin Jenkins (WA), Steve Thompson (2), Julian White, D. O'Callaghan (IR), P. O'Connell (IR), Simon Easterby (IR), Moody, Ryan Jones (WA), D. Peel (WA), Jonny Wilkinson, Shane Williams (WA), Henson (WA), Gareth Thomas (2) (WA), Jason Robinson, J. Lewsey]
[*Bench:* S. Byrne (IR) (*hooker*) (rep), Corry (rep), Matt Dawson, Horgan (IR) (rep), Stephen Jones (2) (WA) (*fly half*) (rep), Rowntree (rep), Martyn Williams (WA)]
[*Scorers:* **tries** by Gareth Thomas (WA) and S. Easterby (IR), **penalty goals** by Jonny Wilkinson (2), **conversion** by Jonny Wilkinson]
CAPTAIN: *Gareth Thomas (2)* (WA) [*Paul O'Connell* (IR) *took over when Gareth Thomas (2) went off in the 2nd half due to illness*]
[9th July NEW ZEALAND 38 **BRITISH & IRISH LIONS*** 19]
Eden Park, Auckland
[*Team:* Gethin Jenkins (WA), S. Byrne (IR), Julian White, D. O'Callaghan (IR), P. O'Connell (IR), S. Easterby (IR), Moody, Ryan Jones (WA), D. Peel (WA), Stephen Jones (2) (WA), J. Lewsey, Gareth Thomas (2) (WA), W. Greenwood, Cueto, G. Murphy (IR)]
[*Bench:* G. Bulloch (SC) (rep), Corry (rep), Matt Dawson (rep), Horgan (IR) (rep), O'Gara (IR) (rep), Rowntree (rep), Martyn Williams (WA) (rep)]
[*Scorers:* **try** by Moody, **penalty goals** by Stephen Jones (WA) (4), **conversion** by Stephen Jones (WA)]
POSITION: SERIES LOSERS

TRIBUTE TO RUGBY'S LEGENDS

[**COACH:** *Derek Quinnell* (WA)]
CAPTAIN: *Scott Quinnell* (WA)
[5th June **BRITAIN AND IRELAND XV** 57 THE WORLD XV 67]
Millennium Stadium, Cardiff
[*Team:* J. Leonard, M. Regan, Darren Morris (WA), Jonathan *Craig* Quinnell (WA), D. Weir (SC), Anthony 'Tony' Diprose, Volley, Scott Quinnell (WA), K. Bracken, N. Jenkins (WA), K. Logan (SC), John Devereux (WA), Allan Bateman (WA), Dafydd James (WA), Mark Van Gisbergen (NZ)]
[*Bench (Forwards):* John Davies (WA) (*prop*) (rep), Galwey (IR) (rep), J. Humphreys (WA) (rep), Gareth Llewellyn (WA) (*lock*) (rep), Derek *Gavin* Quinnell (WA) (*lock/flanker/number 8*) (rep), Tom Smith (2) (SC) (*prop*) (rep), Gavin Thomas (WA) (*flanker*) (rep), Christopher 'Chris' Wyatt (WA) (*lock*) (rep)]
[*Bench (Backs):* Garan Evans (WA) (rep), Paul John (WA) (rep), A. King (rep), Alistair 'Ally' McCoist (SC) (*wing*) (rep), G. Townsend (SC) (*fly half/centre*) (rep)]
[*Scorers:* **tries** by Dafydd James (WA) (2), Garan Evans (WA) (2), Scott Quinnell (WA), Van Gisbergen (NZ), G. Quinnell (WA), McCoist (SC) and special replacement, **conversions** by K. Logan (SC), McCoist (SC) (4) and ball girl]
[Match organised by the WRU as a testimonial game for both Scott Quinnell and Rob Howley]
[Derek Quinnell was appointed on 8th April 2005; Derek Quinnell won 23 caps for Wales between 1972-80 and was capped for the British Lions in July 1971]

IRB U21 WORLD CHAMPIONSHIP

Argentina

[*Other squad members:* Broadfoot (never travelled as injured, replaced by Ben Russell (1)), R. Davis (never travelled as injured, replaced by Shane Geraghty), Tom Rees (*flanker*) (captain; never travelled as injured, replaced by Will Skinner), David Wilson (2) (*prop*) (never travelled as injured, replaced by Dylan Hartley)]

(squad of 26)

[England U21 were ranked in Pool B and played their matches against the 3 teams in Pool C; The England U21 squad departed for Argentina on 3rd June 2005; Nigel Redman was appointed Coach of England U19 on 29th September 2005]

(During the First Round a bonus point was awarded for scoring 4 or more tries in a match and for losing by seven points or less)

[MANAGER: *Peter Drewett*] **[COACH:** *Jim Mallinder*] **[ASSISTANT COACH:** *Nigel Redman*]

CAPTAIN: *Matt Cornwell*

First Round - Pool 'B'

[9th June SAMOA U21 22 **ENGLAND U21** 52 **BP**]

Maristas RC, Mendoza

[*Team:* Croall, N. Briggs, W. Thompson, Blaze, Sean Cox, Haskell, David Seymour, M. Hopley, Foden, T. Flood, Biggs, Whatling, Matt Cornwell, Varndell, O. Morgan]

[*Bench:* Bowley (*lock*) (rep), L. Dickson (rep), Geraghty (*fly half/centre*) (rep), Goodman (rep), Dylan Hartley (*prop/hooker*) (rep), Ben Russell (1) (rep), Dave Ward (rep)]

[*Scorers:* **tries** by O. Morgan, N. Briggs, Varndell (2), Biggs (2) and D. Hartley (2), **conversions** by T. Flood (5) and Ben Russell]

[13th Jun SOUTH AFRICA U21 34 **ENGLAND U21** 16]

Liceo RC, Mendoza

[*Team:* M. Cusack, N. Briggs, W. Thompson, Blaze, Sean Cox, Haskell, David Seymour, Goodman, L. Dickson, T. Flood, Diggin, Geraghty, Dehaty, Varndell, Matt Cornwell]

[*Bench:* Biggs (rep), Croall (rep), Foden (rep), D. Hartley (rep), M. Hopley (rep), Ben Russell (1) (rep), W. Skinner (*flanker/number 8*) (rep)]

[*Scorers:* **try** by M. Hopley, **penalty goals** by T. Flood (3), **conversion** by Ben Russell]

[17th Jun FRANCE U21 37 **ENGLAND U21** 27 **BP**]

Mendoza RC, Mendoza

[*Team:* M. Cusack, Dave Ward, W. Thompson, Blaze, Sean Cox, Haskell, David Seymour, M. Hopley, Foden, T. Flood, Varndell, Whatling, Matt Cornwell, Biggs, O. Morgan]

[*Bench:* Bowley (rep), N. Briggs (rep), Croall (rep), L. Dickson, Geraghty (rep), D. Hartley (rep), W. Skinner (rep)]

[*Scorers:* **tries** by O. Morgan, Foden, T. Flood and Haskell, **penalty goal** by T. Flood, **conversions** by T. Flood (2)]

CAPTAIN: *Simon Whatling*

5th/6th/7th/8th Place Semi-Final

[21st Jun ARGENTINA U21 20 **ENGLAND U21** 6]

Mendoza RC, Mendoza

[*Team:* D. Hartley, N. Briggs, Croall, Blaze, Bowley, W. Skinner, David Seymour, M. Hopley, L. Dickson, T. Flood, Varndell, Whatling, Dehaty, Biggs, O. Morgan]

[*Bench:* M. Cusack (rep), Foden (rep), Geraghty (rep), Haskell (rep), Ben Russell (1) (rep), W. Thompson (rep), Dave Ward (rep)]

[*Scorers:* **penalty goals** by T. Flood and Geraghty]

CAPTAIN: *Matt Cornwell*
7th/8th Place Play-Off
[25th Jun WALES U21 32 **ENGLAND U21** 57]
Liceo RC, Mendoza
[*Team:* D. Hartley, N. Briggs, W. Thompson, Blaze, Sean Cox, Haskell, W. Skinner, M. Hopley, Foden, T. Flood, Varndell, Whatling, Matt Cornwell, Diggin, O. Morgan]
[*Bench:* Croall (rep), L. Dickson (rep), Geraghty (rep), Goodman (rep), Ben Russell (1), David Seymour (*flanker*) (rep), Dave Ward (rep)]
[*Scorers:* **tries** by Varndell (3), Diggin, T. Flood, Foden, Haskell, L. Dickson and Geraghty, **conversions** by T. Flood (6)]
POSITION: 7TH PLACE

GMF PARIS SEVENS
IRB WORLD SEVENS SERIES 2004-2005 ROUND 7

Stade Jean Bouin, Paris
[*Tournament squad:* Appleford (injured during the tournament), Roques, W. Matthews, R. Vickerman, Hipkiss, D. Armitage, J. Bailey, Vilk, R. Thirlby, Gollings, Amor (injured during the tournament), R. Haughton]
(squad of 12)
[This tournament was originally scheduled to be held at the Stade Jacques Chaban-Delmas in Bordeaux on 27th-28th May 2005 but the IRB and FFR changed both the date and the venue on 11th February 2005; Henry Paul and Ollie Phillips were unavailable for this tournament due to injury; Simon Amor was the tournament captain; Rob Vickerman played in the Samurai team that won the Amsterdam Heineken Sevens on 21st-22nd May 2005; Geoff Appleford retired due to injury in January 2007]
[Damian McGrath was appointed Assistant Coach of England U19 on 29th September 2005]
[**MANAGER:** *Juliette Reilly*] [**COACH:** *Mike Friday*] [**ASSISTANT COACH:** *Damian McGrath*]
CAPTAIN: *Simon Amor*
First Round - Pool 'B'
10th June CANADA 5 **ENGLAND** 42
[*Team:* Roques, Vilk, W. Matthews, Amor, Gollings, D. Armitage, R. Haughton]
[*Bench:* Appleford (rep), J. Bailey (rep), Hipkiss, R. Thirlby, R. Vickerman (rep)]
[*Scorers:* **tries** by R. Haughton, Gollings (2), D. Armitage, Vilk and R. Vickerman, **conversions** by Gollings (6)]
CAPTAIN: *Ben Gollings*
10th June PORTUGAL 0 **ENGLAND** 29
[*Team:* Appleford, Roques, Hipkiss, Gollings, R. Thirlby, Vilk, J. Bailey]
[*Bench:* D. Armitage (rep), R. Haughton, W. Matthews (rep), R. Vickerman (rep)]
[*Scorers:* **tries** by Vilk, Appleford, Hipkiss, R. Vickerman and W. Matthews, **conversions** by Gollings (2)]
10th June SCOTLAND 5 **ENGLAND** 26
[*Team:* Appleford, Roques, W. Matthews, Gollings, R. Thirlby, Vilk, R. Haughton]
[*Bench:* D. Armitage, J. Bailey, Hipkiss, R. Vickerman]
[*Scorers:* **tries** by Gollings, R. Haughton, Vilk and Hipkiss, **conversions** by Gollings (3)]
Quarter-Final
11th June SAMOA 21 **ENGLAND*** 14
[*Team:* Roques, W. Matthews, Hipkiss, Gollings, R. Thirlby, Vilk, R. Haughton]
[*Bench:* Amor (rep), D. Armitage (rep), J. Bailey (rep), R. Vickerman]

[*Scorers:* **tries** by penalty try and J. Bailey, **conversions** by Gollings (2)]
CAPTAIN: *Simon Amor*
[Plate Semi-Final:]
[11th Jun AUSTRALIA 0 **ENGLAND** 24]
[*Team:* Roques, Vilk, R. Vickerman, Amor, Gollings, D. Armitage, J. Bailey]
[*Bench:* R. Haughton (rep), Hipkiss, W. Matthews (rep), R. Thirlby (rep)]
[*Scorers:* **tries** by Gollings (2), D. Armitage and R. Haughton, **conversions** by Gollings (2)]
CAPTAIN: *Ben Gollings*
[Plate Final:]
[11th Jun SOUTH AFRICA 26 **ENGLAND*** 19]
[*Team:* Roques, Vilk, R. Vickerman, Gollings, R. Thirlby, D. Armitage, J. Bailey]
[*Bench:* R. Haughton (rep), Hipkiss, W. Matthews]
[*Scorers:* **tries** by R. Thirlby (2) and R. Haughton, **conversions** by Gollings (2)]
POSITION: LOSING QUARTER-FINALISTS [*PLATE FINALISTS*]
FANTASY: LOSING QUARTER-FINALISTS [*PLATE WINNERS*]
[England scored 6 competition points in this Round of the 2004-2005 IRB World Sevens Series]
RANKING: 3RD 86 [*New Zealand 116*, Fiji 88, South Africa 76, Argentina 68, Samoa 46, Australia 42, France 30, Scotland 22, Kenya 6, Tunisia 4, Portugal 2, Canada 2]
FANTASY: *2ND 96*

ENGLAND COUNTIES TOUR TO ARGENTINA AND URUGUAY 2005

[**CHAIRMAN OF SELECTORS:** *Peter Hartley*] [**MANAGER:** *Jim Robinson*] [***ASSISTANT MANAGER:*** *Danny Hodgson*] [**COACH:** *Paul Westgate*] [**ASSISTANT COACH:** *Ben Ryan*]
[*Other squad members:* Andrew 'Andy' MacRae (*wing*) (tm), Johnathan 'Johnny' Williams (*prop*) (tm)]
(squad of 26)
[On 4th January 2005 Jim Robinson was appointed to succeed Rob Udwin as Manager after the France Amateurs match on 12th February 2005; Jim Robinson was the Manager when England played in the U19 World Championship in Wales in March-April 1999; Paul Westgate and Ben Ryan were both appointed on 17th May 2005; Ben Ryan sat on the bench for England U21 against Belgium in September 1991; The England Counties squad arrived in Argentina on 5th June 2005; The England Counties squad travelled to Uruguay on 16th June 2005]
CAPTAIN: *Craig Hammond*
[12th Jun ARGENTINA XV 36 **ENGLAND COUNTIES** 10]
Club de Rugby Ateneo Inmaculada, Santa Fe
[*Team:* R. Faulkner, Stewart Pearl, Dan Parkes, Chris Bentley, Rouse, Craig Hammond, Wilks, E. Thorpe, Andy Brown, Duncan Hughes, Jess, I. Richmond, Malherbe, C. Wyles, B. Thompson]
[*Bench:* Lee Blackett (*centre*) (rep), Glenn Cooper (*hooker*) (rep), Matthew 'Matt' Long (*prop*) (rep), David 'Dave' McCormack (*scrum half*) (rep), James Ponton (*flanker/number 8*), O. Thomas (rep), G. Wilson (rep)]
[*Scorers:* **try** by Jess, **penalty goal** by Duncan Hughes, **conversion** by Duncan Hughes]
[18th Jun URUGUAY 9 **ENGLAND COUNTIES** 29]
British School, Montevideo
[*Team:* R. Faulkner, Glenn Cooper, M. Long, Paul Arnold (2), Rouse, Craig Hammond, Wilks, E. Thorpe, Andy Brown, Duncan Hughes, C. Wyles, Blackett, Malherbe, Jess, B. Thompson]

[*Bench:* C. Bentley (*lock*) (rep), D. McCormack (rep), D. Parkes (*prop*) (rep), Pearl (*hooker*) (rep), Ponton (rep), P. Price
(rep), I. Richmond (*centre*) (rep), O. Thomas (rep)]
[*Scorers:* **tries** by Jess (2), Glenn Cooper, M. Long and Blackett, **conversions** by Duncan Hughes and O. Thomas]

PUBLIC SCHOOL WANDERERS TOUR TO SRI LANKA 2005

[**MANAGER:** *Rolph James* (WA)] [**ASSISTANT MANAGER:** *Gavin Holmes*]
[*Other squad members:* Nick Baxter (*wing*) (tm), Brennan, Andrew Clatworthy (WA) (*prop*), B. Harvey (tm), Steve Martin (WA) (*lock*), Lee May (WA) (*prop*), Duncan Murray (*centre*), M. Oliver, Neil Watkins (WA) (*lock*)]
(squad of 22)
[Steve White-Cooper was the tour captain; Ben Harvey was not part of the original squad; The Public School Wanderers squad arrived in Sri Lanka on 12th June 2005; Steve Martin was the son of Allan Martin; Duncan Murray captained Wales U18 in April 1999; Duncan Murray played for Arabian Gulf 7s in December 2009 and was capped for the United Arab Emirates in April 2011; Rolph James died of cancer in June 2010]
CAPTAIN: *Steve White-Cooper*

[16th Jun	SRI LANKAN RFU PRESIDENT'S XV	7	**PUBLIC SCHOOL WANDERERS**	63]

Colombo Hockey & Football Club Grounds, Maitland Crescent, Colombo
[*Team:* Daniel 'Dan' Leek, Christopher 'Chris' Small, James Campbell (WA), Kevin Burke (WA), ?, White-Cooper, Simon Granger, James 'Jim' Jenner, Richard Smith (WA), Rhys Edwards (WA), ?, Tombleson, Andrew Harrison, George Dixon, O'Neill]
[*Bench:* Chris Evans (*flanker*) (rep)]
[*Scorers:* **tries** by A. Harrison (2), George Dixon, Granger, Tombleson (2), J. Campbell (WA), K. Burke (WA), Small and D. Leek, **penalty goal** by Rhys Edwards (WA), **conversions** by Rhys Edwards (WA) (5)]

TUSKER SAFARI SEVENS

TUSKER TROPHY

RFU of East Africa Ground, Ngong Road, Nairobi
[*Tournament squad:* Kern Yates (*forward*), Mark Evans (*forward*), B. Harvey, Lucas Onyango (KEN) (*wing*)]
[This tournament was played at high altitude; Kern Yates was capped for England Schools 18 Group in April 1992; Ben Harvey played in the Samurai team that won the Amsterdam Heineken Sevens on 20th-21st May 2006]
[NO COACH NOMINATED]
CAPTAIN: *Ben Harvey*
First Round - Pool 'D'

[17th Jun	TANZANIA	5	**PUBLIC SCHOOL WANDERERS**	47]

[*Team:*]
[*Bench:*]
[*Scorers:*]

[17th Jun	Shujaa (*KEN*)	14	**PUBLIC SCHOOL WANDERERS**	10]

[*Team:*]
[*Bench:*]
[*Scorers:* **tries** by Mark Evans and Onyango (KEN)]

[18th Jun	SWAZILAND	0	**PUBLIC SCHOOL WANDERERS**	40]

[*Team:*]
[*Bench:*]
[*Scorers:*]

[18th Jun	NAMIBIA	7	**PUBLIC SCHOOL WANDERERS**	31]

[*Team:*]
[*Bench:*]
[*Scorers:*]

Quarter-Final

[19th Jun	Western Province (*SA*)	17	**PUBLIC SCHOOL WANDERERS***	14]

[*Team:* B. Harvey, Onyango (KEN)]
[*Bench:*]
[*Scorers:*]

[Plate Quarter-Final:]

[19th Jun	Bristol University Select	21	**PUBLIC SCHOOL WANDERERS**	19 **]**

[*Team:*]
[*Bench:*]
[*Scorers:*]

POSITION: LOSING QUARTER-FINALISTS [*PLATE QUARTER-FINALISTS*]

CHURCHILL CUP

Canada

[*Other squad members:* Barkley (never travelled as injured, replaced by Andy Higgins (2)), Will Green (1) (never travelled as withdrew, replaced by Micky Ward), Greening (never travelled as injured, replaced by Lee Mears), Hazell (never travelled as injured, replaced by Magnus Lund), Lund (never travelled as injured), Tindall (never travelled as injured, replaced by Ayoola Erinle), Vickery (never travelled as injured, replaced by Robbie Morris), H. Vyvyan (never travelled as injured, replaced by Phil Dowson), Micky Ward (never travelled as injured, replaced by Stuart Turner), Jonny Wilkinson (never travelled as withdrew), M. Worsley (never travelled as injured, replaced by Mike Shelley)]

(squad of 25)

[Joe Lydon, Simon Hardy and Damian McGrath were all appointed on 8th April 2005; Phil Keith-Roach was also appointed on 8th April 2005 but later withdrew due to illness; Duncan Bell, Andy Beattie, Alex King and Leon Lloyd were all unavailable for this tournament; David Flatman and Steve Borthwick were unavailable due to injury; Joe Worsley, Harry Ellis, Ben Cohen and Jamie Noon were all rested for this tournament; Will Green (1) in original squad of 26 but withdrew on 3rd May 2005 after he announced that he no longer wished to be considered for selection to the England team, being replaced by Micky Ward who then himself had to withdraw due to injury on 3rd June 2005; Jonny Wilkinson withdrew on 8th May 2005 as he was now required to go on the British & Irish Lions tour of New Zealand; Andy Hazell initially selected but withdrew on 12th May 2005 due to injury, being replaced by Magnus Lund; Magnus Lund withdrew on the day of the squad's departure on 9th June 2005 due to injury and was not replaced; Damian McGrath was appointed Assistant Coach of England U19 on 29th September 2005 and then sacked on 27th April 2006; Mike Worsley retired due to injury in May 2006; Will Green (1) retired in May 2007]

[**COACH:** *Joe Lydon*] [**ASSISTANT COACHES:** *Simon Hardy* & *Damian McGrath*]
CAPTAIN: *Pat Sanderson*
First Round
[19th Jun CANADA 5 **ENGLAND A** 29]
Commonwealth Stadium, Edmonton
[*Team:* Freshwater, Chuter, Stuart Turner, L. Deacon, Tom Palmer (2), Chris Jones, P. Sanderson, Dowson, Gomarsall, Andy Goode, Monye, C. Bell, J. Simpson-Daniel, Sackey, Vesty]
[*Bench:* Erinle (rep), Forrester (rep), S. Hooper (rep), Mears (rep), Robbie Morris (rep), Peter Richards (rep), Voyce (rep)]
[*Scorers:* **tries** by Sackey, Vesty, Voyce, J. Simpson-Daniel and P. Sanderson, **conversions** by Andy Goode (2)]
Final
[26th Jun ARGENTINA A 16 **ENGLAND A** 45]
Commonwealth Stadium, Edmonton
[*Team:* Freshwater, Mears, Stuart Turner, L. Deacon, Tom Palmer (2), Chris Jones, P. Sanderson, Dowson, Peter Richards, Andy Goode, M. Tait, C. Bell, J. Simpson-Daniel, Sackey, Voyce]
[*Bench:* Chuter (rep), Erinle (rep), Forrester (rep), Gomarsall (rep), Andy Higgins (2) (rep), S. Hooper (rep), Shelley (rep)]
[*Scorers:* **tries** by J. Simpson-Daniel, Voyce (2), Sackey and Gomarsall, **penalty goals** by Andy Goode (3) and Peter Richards, **conversions** by Andy Goode (3) and Gomarsall]
POSITION: WINNERS

WORLD GAMES SEVENS

MSV-Arena, Duisburg
[*Tournament squad:* Ross Rennie (SC) (*forward*), Gareth Williams (4) (WA) (*hooker*), Richard Vernon (SC) (*forward*), James Mathias (*forward*), Oliver 'Oli' Brown (SC) (*forward*), Rory Lawson (SC) (*scrum half*), A. Turnbull (SC) (*centre/wing*), Alistair 'Ali' Warnock (SC) (*fly half*), Cameron Johnston (SC) (*wing*), Jamie Blackwood (SC) (*scrum half*), Strettle (*wing*) (injured during the tournament)]
(squad of 11)
[Peter Gallagher and Rob Moffat were both appointed on 5th May 2005; Rob Moffat played for a Scotland XV against Japan in September 1977; The Great Britain squad travelled to Germany on 20th July 2005; Rory Lawson was the brother of Gregor Lawson and the son of Alan Lawson; Dave Strettle played in the Samurai team that won the Amsterdam Heineken Sevens on 21st-22nd May 2005]
[**MANAGER:** *Peter Gallagher* (SC)] [**COACH:** *Rob Moffat* (SC)]
CAPTAIN: *??*
First Round - Pool 'A'
[22nd Jul GERMANY 7 **GREAT BRITAIN** 24]
[*Team:* Rennie (SC), Gareth Williams (4) (WA), J. Mathias, R. Lawson (SC), Warnock (SC), A. Turnbull (SC), Cameron Johnston (SC)]
[*Bench:* Blackwood (SC), O. Brown (SC) (rep), Strettle (rep), Vernon (SC) (rep)]
[*Scorers:* **tries** by A. Turnbull (SC), Warnock (SC) and Strettle (2), **conversions** by Warnock (SC) (2)]
[22nd Jul JAPAN 7 **GREAT BRITAIN** 26]
[*Team:* Vernon (SC), Gareth Williams (4) (WA), O. Brown (SC), Blackwood (SC), Warnock (SC), A. Turnbull (SC), Strettle]

[*Bench:* Cameron Johnston (SC) (rep), R. Lawson (SC) (rep), J. Mathias (rep), Rennie (SC)]
[*Scorers:* **tries** by Warnock (SC) (2), O. Brown (SC) and A. Turnbull (SC), **conversions** by Warnock (SC) (2) and R. Lawson (SC)]
[22nd Jul FIJI 33 **GREAT BRITAIN** 17]
[*Team:* Vernon (SC), Gareth Williams (4) (WA), O. Brown (SC), Blackwood (SC), Warnock (SC), A. Turnbull (SC), Strettle]
[*Bench:* Cameron Johnston (SC) (rep), R. Lawson (SC) (rep), J. Mathias (rep), Rennie (SC)]
[*Scorers:* **tries** by Warnock (SC), Rennie (SC) and Cameron Johnston (SC), **conversion** by R. Lawson (SC)]
Semi-Final
[23rd July SOUTH AFRICA 52 **GREAT BRITAIN** 0]
[*Team:* Rennie (SC), Gareth Williams (4) (WA), J. Mathias, R. Lawson (SC), Warnock (SC), A. Turnbull (SC), Cameron Johnston (SC)]
[*Bench:* Blackwood (SC), O. Brown (SC), Vernon (SC)]
[*No scorers*]
Third Place Play-Off
[23rd July ARGENTINA 22 **GREAT BRITAIN** 10]
[*Team:* Vernon (SC), Gareth Williams (4) (WA), O. Brown (SC), Blackwood (SC), Warnock (SC), A. Turnbull (SC), Cameron Johnston (SC)]
[*Bench:* R. Lawson (SC), J. Mathias, Rennie (SC)]
[*Scorers:* **tries** by O. Brown (SC) and Warnock (SC)]
POSITION: 4TH PLACE
[On 3rd October 2009 it was announced that the Four Home Unions had agreed to enter a Great Britain team in the proposed Olympic Sevens tournament at the 2016 Olympic Games in Rio de Janeiro]

LLOYDS TSB CWMTAWE SEVENS

Pontardawe RFC, Parc Ynysderw, Ynysderw Road, Pontardawe, Swansea
[*Tournament squad:* Nicolas Alberts (SA) (*forward*), Earnshaw, Tristan Prosser-Shaw (*forward*), Chris MacDonald (WA) (*scrum half*), Craig Richards (WA) (*wing*), Strettle]
[Rob Appleyard was capped for Wales in July 1997; Russ Earnshaw captained the Samurai to victory at the Amsterdam Heineken Sevens on 20th-21st May 2006]
[**COACH:** *Rob Appleyard* (WA)]
CAPTAIN: *??*
First Round - Pool 'A'
[6th Aug Gorseinion (*WA*) 0 **SAMURAI** 38]
[*Team:*]
[*Bench:*]
[*Scorers:*]
[6th Aug Bath Bandits 7 **SAMURAI** 24]
[*Team:*]
[*Bench:*]
[*Scorers:*]
[6th Aug Llangennech (*WA*) 5 **SAMURAI** 41]
[*Team:*]
[*Bench:*]
[*Scorers:*]

Quarter-Final

[6th Aug Neath (*WA*) 10 **SAMURAI** 17]
[*Team:*]
[*Bench:*]
[*Scorers:*]

Semi-Final

[6th Aug Welsh Wizards 19 **SAMURAI*** 12]
[*Team:* Strettle]
[*Bench:*]
[*Scorers:* **tries** by Strettle and Prosser-Shaw, **conversion** by ?]

POSITION: LOSING SEMI-FINALISTS

AUSTRALIAN TOUR TO FRANCE, ENGLAND, IRELAND AND WALES 2005
FIRST INVESTEC CHALLENGE MATCH
COOK CUP MATCH

[**HEAD COACH:** *Andy Robinson*] [**ASSISTANT COACHES:** *Phil Larder, Dave Alred & Joe Lydon*]

CAPTAIN: *Martin Corry*

12th Nov **ENGLAND** 26 AUSTRALIA 16
Twickenham

[*Team:* Sheridan, Steve Thompson (2), Vickery, S. Borthwick, Grewcock, P. Sanderson, Moody, Corry, Matt Dawson, C. Hodgson, B. Cohen, Tindall, Noon, Cueto, J. Lewsey]
[*Bench:* Barkley (rep), L. Deacon (*lock*), Harry Ellis, Chris Jones, Mears, M. Stevens, Van Gisbergen (*full back*) (rep)]
[*Scorers:* **tries** by B. Cohen and Cueto, **penalty goals** by C. Hodgson (2) and Barkley, **drop goal** by C. Hodgson, **conversions** by C. Hodgson and Barkley]

ATKINS REMEMBRANCE RUGBY MATCH

[**COACH:** *Zinzan Brooke* (NZ)]

CAPTAIN: *Bobby Skinstad* (SA)

[15th Nov COMBINED SERVICES (*SER*) 6 **BARBARIANS** 45]
Newbury RFC, Monks Lane, Newbury

[*Team:* Paul James (WA), Gareth Williams (5) (WA), Benjamin 'Ben' Evans (WA), Lubans (AU), Craig Hammond, Jason Forster (WA), Jonathan Edwards (WA), B. Skinstad (SA), Pissarra (POR), Richard McCarter (IR), Nick Baxter, Taliesin 'Tal' Selley (WA), Malherbe, Kenny Bingham, Malheiro (POR)]
[*Bench:* Dormer (NZ) (rep), Chris Hart (*lock/flanker*) (rep), Dafydd Lewis (WA) (rep), S. Pope (rep), Ravenscroft (*centre*) (rep), Ritchie (*hooker*) (rep)]
[*Scorers:* **tries** by B. Skinstad (SA), Jonathan Edwards (WA), Malheiro (POR), Nick Baxter, Gareth Williams (WA), K. Bingham and Jason Forster (WA), **conversions** by Malheiro (POR) (3) and Dafydd Lewis (WA) (2)]

[Match to commemorate the members of the British uniformed services who lost their lives during armed conflict]

[Zinzan Brooke was appointed on 27th October 2005]

NEW ZEALAND TOUR TO WALES, IRELAND, ENGLAND AND SCOTLAND 2005

SECOND INVESTEC CHALLENGE MATCH

[**HEAD COACH:** *Andy Robinson*] [**ASSISTANT COACHES:** *Phil Larder, Dave Alred & Joe Lydon*]

CAPTAIN: *Martin Corry*

19th Nov **ENGLAND*** 19 NEW ZEALAND 23

Twickenham

[*Team:* Sheridan, Steve Thompson (2), Vickery, S. Borthwick, Grewcock, P. Sanderson, Moody, Corry, Matt Dawson, C. Hodgson, B. Cohen, Tindall, Noon, Cueto, J. Lewsey]

[*Bench:* Barkley, L. Deacon, Harry Ellis, Chris Jones, Mears, M. Stevens (rep), Van Gisbergen]

[*Scorers:* **try** by Corry, **penalty goals** by C. Hodgson (4), **conversion** by C. Hodgson]

SAMOAN TOUR TO SCOTLAND AND ENGLAND 2005

THIRD INVESTEC CHALLENGE MATCH

[**HEAD COACH:** *Andy Robinson*] [**ASSISTANT COACHES:** *Phil Larder, Dave Alred & Joe Lydon*]

CAPTAIN: *Martin Corry*

26th Nov **ENGLAND** 40 SAMOA 3

Twickenham

[*Team:* Sheridan, Steve Thompson (2), M. Stevens, S. Borthwick, L. Deacon, P. Sanderson, Moody, Corry, Harry Ellis, C. Hodgson, Voyce, Tindall, J. Simpson-Daniel, Cueto, J. Lewsey]

[*Bench:* Barkley (rep), Forrester (rep), Freshwater (rep), Mears (rep), Peter Richards, S. Shaw (rep), Varndell (*wing*) (rep)]

[*Scorers:* **tries** by Voyce (2), C. Hodgson, Harry Ellis and Varndell, **penalty goals** by C. Hodgson (3), **conversions** by C. Hodgson (3)]

EMIRATES AIRLINE DUBAI RUGBY SEVENS

IRB WORLD SEVENS SERIES 2005-2006 ROUND 1

EMIRATES INTERNATIONAL TROPHY

Dubai Exiles Stadium, Dubai

[*Tournament squad:* Amor, Foden (*scrum half/centre*), Gollings, Hylton, W. Matthews, N. Mordt, Narraway (*forward*), H. Paul, Ben Russell (2), M. Tait, Varndell (*wing*), Vilk]

(squad of 12)

[Phil Dowson and Tony Roques were unavailable for this tournament due to injury; Paul Sampson and Dan Luger in original training squad; Simon Amor was the tournament captain]

[Terry Sands was appointed on 29th September 2005; Phil Greening was appointed on 13th October 2005; Phil Greening won 24 caps for England between 1996-2001]

[**MANAGER:** *Terry Sands*] [**COACH:** *Mike Friday*] [**ASSISTANT COACH:** *Phil Greening*]

CAPTAIN: *Simon Amor*

First Round - Pool 'C'

1st Dec KENYA 7 **ENGLAND** 52

[*Team:* Narraway, Ben Russell (2), N. Mordt, Amor, Gollings, H. Paul, Varndell]

[*Bench:* Foden (rep), Hylton, W. Matthews, M. Tait (rep), Vilk (rep)]

[*Scorers:* **tries** by Varndell (2), Amor, H. Paul (2), N. Mordt, Foden and M. Tait, **conversions**

by Gollings (6)]
CAPTAIN: *Ben Gollings*
1st Dec UGANDA 0 **ENGLAND** 48
[*Team:* Narraway, W. Matthews, Hylton, Foden, Gollings, Vilk, M. Tait]
[*Bench:* Amor (rep), N. Mordt (rep), H. Paul, Ben Russell (2), Varndell (rep)]
[*Scorers:* **tries** by Hylton (2), Gollings, M. Tait (2), Vilk, Foden and Varndell, **conversions** by Gollings and Amor (3)]
CAPTAIN: *Simon Amor*
1st Dec AUSTRALIA 5 **ENGLAND** 33
[*Team:* Narraway, Ben Russell (2), N. Mordt, Amor, Gollings, H. Paul, Varndell]
[*Bench:* Foden (rep), Hylton, W. Matthews, M. Tait, Vilk]
[*Scorers:* **tries** by Varndell (2), Amor, Gollings and Foden, **conversions** by Gollings (3) and Amor]
Quarter-Final
2nd Dec ARGENTINA 12 **ENGLAND** 24
[*Team:* Narraway, Ben Russell (2), N. Mordt, Amor, Gollings, H. Paul, Varndell]
[*Bench:* Foden, Hylton (rep), W. Matthews (rep), M. Tait (rep), Vilk]
[*Scorers:* **tries** by Varndell (2) and M. Tait (2), **conversions** by Gollings (2)]
Semi-Final
2nd Dec SAMOA 5 **ENGLAND** 7
[*Team:* Narraway, Ben Russell (2), Vilk, Amor, Gollings, H. Paul, Varndell]
[*Bench:* Foden, Hylton, W. Matthews, N. Mordt, M. Tait (rep)]
[*Scorers:* **try** by Varndell, **conversion** by Amor]
Final
2nd Dec FIJI 26 **ENGLAND** 28
[*Team:* Narraway, Ben Russell (2), N. Mordt, Amor, Gollings, H. Paul, Varndell]
[*Bench:* Foden, Hylton, W. Matthews, M. Tait, Vilk]
[*Scorers:* **tries** by Varndell (2) and Gollings (2), **conversions** by Gollings (4)]
POSITION: WINNERS
[England scored 20 competition points in this Round of the 2005-2006 IRB World Sevens Series]

EMIRATES AIRLINE SOUTH AFRICA SEVENS
IRB WORLD SEVENS SERIES 2005-2006 ROUND 2

Outeniqua Park Stadium, George
[*Tournament squad:* Narraway, Luger, W. Matthews, N. Mordt, H. Paul, Foden, Hylton, Vilk, J. Bailey, Gollings, Amor, M. Tait]
(squad of 12)
[Phil Dowson and Tony Roques were unavailable for this tournament due to injury; Tom Varndell unavailable due to club commitments; Simon Amor was the tournament captain; Dan Luger played for Samurai St George in the Dubai International Invitation Rugby Sevens on 30th November-2nd December 2005]
[**MANAGER:** *Terry Sands*] [**COACH:** *Mike Friday*] [**ASSISTANT COACH:** *Phil Greening*]
CAPTAIN: *Ben Gollings*
First Round - Pool 'C'
9th Dec CANADA 0 **ENGLAND** 40
[*Team:* Narraway, Vilk, W. Matthews, Foden, Gollings, H. Paul, Hylton]
[*Bench:* Amor, J. Bailey (rep), Luger (rep), N. Mordt, M. Tait]

[*Scorers:* **tries** by Hylton, Vilk (2), Gollings (2) and Narraway, **conversions** by Gollings (5)]
CAPTAIN: *Simon Amor*

9th Dec	PORTUGAL	0	**ENGLAND**	36

[*Team:* Narraway, Vilk, N. Mordt, Amor, Gollings, H. Paul, M. Tait]
[*Bench:* J. Bailey (rep), Foden (rep), Hylton, Luger, W. Matthews (rep)]
[*Scorers:* **tries** by Gollings, Vilk, Narraway (2), M. Tait and Amor, **conversions** by Gollings (2) and Amor]

9th Dec	SAMOA	21	**ENGLAND**	22

[*Team:* Narraway, Vilk, N. Mordt, Amor, Gollings, H. Paul, M. Tait]
[*Bench:* J. Bailey (rep), Foden (rep), Hylton, Luger (rep), W. Matthews]
[*Scorers:* **tries** by N. Mordt, Vilk and Foden, **penalty goal** by Amor, **conversions** by Gollings and Amor]

Quarter-Final

10th Dec	FRANCE	5	**ENGLAND**	26

[*Team:* Narraway, Vilk, W. Matthews, Amor, H. Paul, M. Tait, Foden]
[*Bench:* J. Bailey, Gollings (rep), Hylton (rep), Luger (rep), N. Mordt]
[*Scorers:* **tries** by Vilk, Foden (2) and Gollings, **conversions** by Amor and Gollings (2)]

Semi-Final

10th Dec	FIJI	28	**ENGLAND**	22

[*Team:* Narraway, Vilk, N. Mordt, Amor, Gollings, H. Paul, M. Tait]
[*Bench:* J. Bailey (rep), Foden (rep), Hylton, Luger (rep), W. Matthews]
[*Scorers:* **tries** by Gollings, M. Tait, Vilk and Narraway, **conversion** by Amor]

POSITION: LOSING SEMI-FINALISTS

[England scored 12 competition points in this Round of the 2005-2006 IRB World Sevens Series]

2006
OTHER MATCHES
AXA NEW ZEALAND INTERNATIONAL SEVENS
IRB WORLD SEVENS SERIES 2005-2006 ROUND 3

WestpacTrust Stadium, Wellington

[*Tournament squad:* Narraway, Ben Russell (2), David Seymour (*forward*), N. Mordt, H. Paul, Danny Care (*scrum half*), Strettle, Vilk, O. Phillips, Gollings, Amor, M. Tait]

(squad of 12)

[Tony Roques and Richard Haughton were unavailable for this tournament due to injury; Simon Amor was the tournament captain; Danny Care played in the England team that reached the Final of the Commonwealth Youth Games Rugby Sevens at Bendigo, Victoria on 2nd-3rd December 2004 and played for England in the U19 World Championship in South Africa in April 2005; Dave Strettle played for Samurai St George in the Dubai International Invitation Rugby Sevens on 30th November-2nd December 2005]

[**MANAGER:** *Terry Sands*] [**COACH:** *Mike Friday*] [**ASSISTANT COACH:** *Phil Greening*]

CAPTAIN: *Simon Amor*

First Round - Pool 'A'

3rd Feb SCOTLAND 5 **ENGLAND** 12

[*Team:* Narraway, Ben Russell (2), Vilk, Amor, Gollings, H. Paul, O. Phillips]

[*Bench:* Care, N. Mordt, David Seymour, Strettle (rep), M. Tait (rep)]

[*Scorers:* **tries** by Amor and H. Paul, **conversion** by Gollings]

CAPTAIN: *Ben Gollings*

3rd Feb PAPUA NEW GUINEA 0 **ENGLAND** 64

[*Team:* Narraway, N. Mordt, David Seymour, Care, Gollings, M. Tait, Strettle]

[*Bench:* Amor, H. Paul (rep), O. Phillips (rep), Ben Russell (2) (rep), Vilk]

[*Scorers:* **tries** by Strettle (5), Care (2), M. Tait, O. Phillips and Ben Russell, **conversions** by Gollings (4) and Care (3)]

CAPTAIN: *Simon Amor*

3rd Feb AUSTRALIA 7 **ENGLAND** 19

[*Team:* Narraway, Vilk, David Seymour, N. Mordt, Amor, Gollings, H. Paul, M. Tait]

[*Bench:* Care (rep), N. Mordt, O. Phillips, Ben Russell (2) (rep), Strettle (rep)]

[*Scorers:* **tries** by M. Tait, H. Paul and Gollings, **conversions** by Gollings (2)]

Quarter-Final

4th Feb FRANCE 19 **ENGLAND*** 14

[*Team:* Narraway, Ben Russell (2), N. Mordt, Amor, Gollings, H. Paul, M. Tait]

[*Bench:* Care (rep), O. Phillips, David Seymour, Strettle (rep), Vilk]

[*Scorers:* **tries** by M. Tait and Strettle, **conversions** by Gollings and Amor]

[Plate Semi-Final:]

[4th Feb SAMOA 17 **ENGLAND** 21]

[*Team:* Narraway, Ben Russell (2), N. Mordt, Amor, Care, M. Tait, Strettle]

[*Bench:* Gollings (rep), H. Paul (rep), O. Phillips, David Seymour, Vilk (rep)]

[*Scorers:* **tries** by N. Mordt (2) and Narraway, **conversions** by Amor (3)]

[Plate Final:]

[4th Feb ARGENTINA 10 **ENGLAND** 14]

[*Team:* Narraway, Vilk, N. Mordt, Amor, Care, M. Tait, Strettle]

[*Bench:* Gollings (rep), H. Paul (rep), O. Phillips, Ben Russell (2), David Seymour]

[*Scorers:* **tries** by Vilk and M. Tait, **conversions** by Amor (2)]
POSITION: LOSING QUARTER-FINALISTS [*PLATE WINNERS*]
FANTASY: *WINNERS*
[England scored 8 competition points in this Round of the 2005-2006 IRB World Sevens Series]

6 NATIONS CHAMPIONSHIP

[HEAD COACH: *Andy Robinson*] **[ASSISTANT COACHES:** *Phil Larder, Dave Alred & Joe Lydon*]
CAPTAIN: *Martin Corry*

4th Feb **ENGLAND** 47 WALES 13
Twickenham
[*Team:* Sheridan, Steve Thompson (2), M. Stevens, S. Borthwick, Grewcock, J. Worsley, Moody, Corry, Harry Ellis, C. Hodgson, B. Cohen, Tindall, Noon, Cueto, J. Lewsey]
[*Bench:* Dallaglio (rep), Matt Dawson (rep), Andy Goode (rep), Mears (rep), S. Shaw (rep), Voyce (rep), Julian White (rep)]
[*Scorers:* **tries** by Cueto, Moody, Tindall, Dallaglio, Matt Dawson and Voyce, **penalty goals** by C. Hodgson (3), **conversions** by C. Hodgson (2) and Andy Goode (2)]

11th Feb ITALY 16 **ENGLAND** 31
Stadio Flaminio, Rome
[*Team:* Sheridan, Steve Thompson (2), M. Stevens, S. Borthwick, Grewcock, J. Worsley, Moody, Corry, Harry Ellis, C. Hodgson, B. Cohen, Tindall, Noon, Cueto, Voyce]
[*Bench:* Dallaglio (rep), Matt Dawson (rep), Andy Goode, Mears (rep), S. Shaw (rep), J. Simpson-Daniel (rep), Julian White (rep)]
[*Scorers:* **tries** by Tindall, C. Hodgson, Cueto and J. Simpson-Daniel, **penalty goal** by C. Hodgson, **conversions** by C. Hodgson (4)]
CAPTAIN: *Martin Corry [Mike Tindall took over when Martin Corry was substituted in the 2nd half]*

25th Feb SCOTLAND 18 **ENGLAND*** 12
Murrayfield
[*Team:* Sheridan, Steve Thompson (2), Julian White, S. Borthwick, Grewcock, J. Worsley, Moody, Corry, Harry Ellis, C. Hodgson, B. Cohen, Tindall, Noon, Cueto, J. Lewsey]
[*Bench:* Chuter, Dallaglio (rep), Matt Dawson (rep), Freshwater (rep), Andy Goode, S. Shaw (rep), Voyce]
[*Scorers:* **penalty goals** by C. Hodgson (4)]
CAPTAIN: *Martin Corry*

12th Mar FRANCE 31 **ENGLAND** 6
Stade de France, Paris
[*Team:* M. Stevens, Steve Thompson (2), Julian White, S. Borthwick, Grewcock, J. Worsley, Moody, Corry, Matt Dawson, C. Hodgson, B. Cohen, Tindall, Noon, Cueto, J. Lewsey]
[*Bench:* Dallaglio (rep), Harry Ellis (rep), Andy Goode (rep), Mears (rep), S. Shaw (rep), Sheridan (rep), Voyce (rep)]
[*Scorers:* **penalty goals** by C. Hodgson and Andy Goode]

18th Mar **ENGLAND*** 24 IRELAND 28
Twickenham
[*Team:* Sheridan, Mears, Julian White, S. Borthwick, S. Shaw, J. Worsley, Moody, Corry, Harry Ellis, Andy Goode, B. Cohen, S. Abbott, Noon, Cueto, Voyce]
[*Bench:* Dallaglio, Matt Dawson (rep), Freshwater (rep), Grewcock (rep), Steve Thompson (2) (rep), Tindall (rep), Walder]

[*Scorers:* **tries** by Noon and S. Borthwick, **penalty goals** by Andy Goode (4), **conversion** by Andy Goode]
POSITION: **4TH 4 +14** [*France 8 +63*, Ireland 8 +34 TC MT, Scotland 6 -3 CC, Wales 3 -55, Italy 1 -53]
FANTASY: ***2ND 8 TC CC MT***
[*On 25th January 2006 the Six Nations Committee unveiled a specially commissioned Triple Crown Trophy, which was thereafter awarded to either England, Ireland, Wales or Scotland if they beat the other three of these aforementioned four teams in a single 6 Nations Championship season*]
[*Phil Larder, Dave Alred and Joe Lydon were all sacked on 27th April 2006*]

OTHER MATCHES

U21 6 NATIONS CHAMPIONSHIP

[**MANAGER:** *Peter Drewett*] [**COACH:** *Jim Mallinder*] [**ASSISTANT COACH:** *Dorian West*]
CAPTAIN: *Matt Cornwell*
[3rd Feb **ENGLAND U21** 26 WALES U21 18]
Worcester RFC, Sixways Stadium, Pershore Lane, Hindip, Worcester
[*Team:* D. Hartley, Chris Brooker, David Wilson (2), Blaze, T. Croft, Christopher 'Chris' Robshaw, Michael Hills, Jordan Crane, Foden, Ryan Lamb, Mike Brown, Anthony Allen, Matt Cornwell, Hoyle, O. Morgan]
[*Bench:* N. Briggs, Geraghty (rep), Haskell (rep), Mark Lambert (*prop*) (rep), Ojo (rep), Nick Runciman (*scrum half*), T. Ryder]
[*Scorers:* **tries** by O. Morgan, Mike Brown and J. Crane, **penalty goals** by R. Lamb (3), **conversion** by R. Lamb]
[9th Feb ITALY U21 3 **ENGLAND U21** 48]
Stadio Alessandro Lamarmora, Biella
[*Team:* D. Hartley, Brooker, David Wilson (2), Blaze, T. Croft, Haskell, Hills, J. Crane, Foden, R. Lamb, Mike Brown, Anthony Allen, Matt Cornwell, Ojo, Geraghty]
[*Bench:* N. Briggs (rep), Thom Evans (*wing/full back*) (rep), Hoyle (rep), M. Lambert (rep), Robshaw (*flanker/number 8*) (rep), N. Runciman (rep), T. Ryder (rep)]
[*Scorers:* **tries** by Ojo (4), Foden, R. Lamb, Haskell and D. Hartley, **conversions** by Geraghty (3) and J. Crane]
[24th Feb SCOTLAND U21 22 **ENGLAND U21** 49]
Falkirk Stadium
[*Team:* D. Hartley, N. Briggs, David Wilson (2), Blaze, T. Croft, Haskell, Hills, J. Crane, Foden, R. Lamb, Thom Evans, Anthony Allen, Matt Cornwell, Ojo, Mike Brown]
[*Bench:* Nick Abendanon (*wing/full back*) (rep), M. Lambert (rep), Tajiv 'Tosh' Masson (*centre*) (rep), Robshaw (rep), Alex Rogers (*prop*) (rep) N. Runciman (rep), T. Ryder (rep)]
[*Scorers:* **tries** by Foden (2), Thom Evans (2) and Anthony Allen (2), **penalty goals** by R. Lamb (3), **conversions** by R. Lamb (5)]
[11th Mar FRANCE U21 17 **ENGLAND U21** 30]
Stade Municipal, Périgueux
[*Team:* A. Rogers, D. Hartley, David Wilson (2), Blaze, T. Croft, Haskell, Hills, J. Crane, Foden, T. Flood, Abendanon, Anthony Allen, Matt Cornwell, Thom Evans, Mike Brown]
[*Bench:* N. Briggs (rep), Sean Cox (rep), R. Lamb (*fly half*) (rep), M. Lambert (rep), Ojo, Alex Rae (*lock*), N. Runciman]
[*Scorers:* **tries** by T. Flood, Mike Brown and Hills, **penalty goals** by T. Flood (2) and Mike Brown, **conversions** by T. Flood (2) and R. Lamb]

[17th Mar **ENGLAND U21** 40 IRELAND U21 5]
Worcester RFC, Sixways Stadium, Pershore Lane, Hindip, Worcester
[*Team:* A. Rogers, D. Hartley, David Wilson (2), Blaze, T. Croft, Haskell, Hills, J. Crane, Foden, T. Flood, Abendanon, Anthony Allen, Matt Cornwell, Thom Evans, Mike Brown]
[*Bench:* N. Briggs (rep), Sean Cox (rep), R. Lamb (rep), M. Lambert (rep), Ojo (rep), Alex Rae (rep), N. Runciman (rep)]
[*Scorers:* **tries** by Haskell, David Wilson, Abendanon (2) and J. Crane, **penalty goals** by T. Flood (3), **conversions** by T. Flood (3)]
POSITION: 1ST 10 +128 GS TC [France 8 +98, Wales 6 +27, Scotland 4 -64, Ireland 2 -33, Italy 0 -156]
[In 2005 the Six Nations Committee specially commissioned an U21 Six Nations Championship Trophy, which was awarded annually to the winners of the U21 and U20 6 Nations Championship from 2006 onwards]
[Dorian West was appointed on 29th September 2005; Dorian West won 21 caps for England between 1998-2003 and was appointed Assistant Coach of England U19 on 12th October 2004; On 7th November 2005 Jim Mallinder was appointed to succeed Brian Ashton as Manager of the RFU National Academy on 17th December 2005]

'A' INTERNATIONAL MATCHES

[**HEAD COACH:** *John Wells*] [**ASSISTANT COACHES:** *Jon Callard & Anthony 'Tony' 'Tosh' Askew*]
CAPTAIN: *Perry Freshwater*
[3rd Feb ITALY A 13 **ENGLAND A** 57]
Stadio Maurizio Natali, Colleferro
[*Team:* Freshwater, Titterrell, Duncan Bell, L. Deacon, Tom Palmer (2), H. Vyvyan, Lund, Skirving, S. Perry, Shane Drahm, Varndell, S. Abbott, Ollie Smith (2), Sackey, Jon Clarke]
[*Bench:* M. Cairns (rep), Forrester (rep), Nick Kennedy (*lock*) (rep), Stuart Turner (rep), Vesty (rep), Walder, Wigglesworth (rep)]
[*Scorers:* **tries** by S. Abbott, Varndell (4), H. Vyvyan, Ollie Smith and Forrester, **penalty goal** by Drahm, **conversions** by Drahm (4), D. Walder (2) and Ollie Smith]
CAPTAIN: *Shaun Perry* [*Nick Walshe took over when he came on as a substitute in the 2nd half*]
[17th Mar **ENGLAND A** 18 IRELAND A 33]
Kingsholm, Gloucester
[*Team:* T. Payne, Titterrell, Stuart Turner, L. Deacon, Tom Palmer (2), A. Beattie, Lipman, Chris Jones, S. Perry, Drahm, C. Bell, Ollie Smith (2), Jon Clarke, Sackey, Van Gisbergen]
[*Bench:* D. Armitage (rep), M. Cairns (rep), Tom Rees, Vesty (rep), Walshe (rep), Dan Ward-Smith (*lock/flanker/number 8*) (rep), N. Wood (*prop*) (rep)]
[*Scorers:* **tries** by Sackey and Lipman, **penalty goals** by Drahm (2), **conversion** by Drahm]
[John Wells and Jon Callard were both appointed on 1st November 2005; Tosh Askew was appointed joint Coach of England U19 on 27th October 2000, was appointed Coach of England U19 on 1st November 2001 and was then appointed Assistant Coach of England A on 29th September 2005; Tosh Askew was sacked on 27th April 2006; John Wells was appointed England Assistant Coach on 23rd May 2006]

ENGLAND STUDENTS MATCHES

[**MANAGER:** *Tony Lanaway*] [**COACH:** *Steve Hill*] [**ASSISTANT COACH:** *Paul Hull*]

CAPTAIN: *Kevin Brennan*

[4th Feb **ENGLAND STUDENTS** 6 FRANCE STUDENTS 41]

Twickenham

[*Team:* Irish, Dalgleish, W. Thompson, Richard Graham, James Hanks, James Jones, Tom Yellowlees, Greg Irvin, Brennan, Richard Vasey, Tombleson, Thomas 'Tom' Gregory, A. James, George Dixon, James 'Jamie' Lennard]

[*Bench:* Robert Anderson (*lock*) (rep), R. Faulkner (rep), Daniel 'Dan' James (*hooker*) (rep), Lowrie (rep), Christopher 'Chris' Pilgrim (*scrum half*) (rep), Pritchard (rep), Whittingham (*fly half/centre/full back*) (rep)]

[*Scorers:* **penalty goals** by Lennard (2)]

[10th Feb ITALY U25 44 **ENGLAND STUDENTS** 31]

Stadio Comunale, Nuoro, Sardinia

[*Team:* R. Faulkner, Dalgleish, W. Thompson, R. Graham, Hanks, James Jones, Lowrie, Irvin, Brennan, Vasey, Tombleson, T. Gregory, Pritchard, A. James, Lennard]

[*Bench:* R. Anderson (rep), George Dixon (*centre/wing*) (rep), Irish (*prop*) (rep), Dan James (rep), C. Pilgrim (rep), Whittingham (rep), Yellowlees (*flanker*) (rep)]

[*Scorers:* **tries** by Tombleson, T. Gregory and Pritchard, **penalty goals** by Lennard (4), **conversions** by Lennard (2)]

CAPTAIN: *Andy Dalgleish*

[10th Mar FRANCE STUDENTS 17 **ENGLAND STUDENTS** 3]

Stade Marcel Tribut, Dunkirk

[*Team:* W. Thompson, Dalgleish, Irish, R. Anderson, R. Graham, Mark George, Lowrie, Irvin, C. Pilgrim, Whittingham, Tombleson, Pritchard, T. Gregory, George Dixon, Lennard]

[*Bench:* Greg Collett (*fly half/centre*) (rep), R. Faulkner (rep), Tobias 'Toby' Henry (*scrum half*) (rep), Dan James (rep), James Lumby (*flanker*) (rep), Stephen 'Steve' Pape (*lock*) (rep), Vasey (*fly half*) (rep)]

[*Scorers:* **penalty goal** by Lennard]

[There was an England Students Final Trial at Castlecroft on 4th January 2006]

[Steve Hill and Paul Hull were both appointed on 21st November 2005; Paul Hull was capped for England in June 1994]

USA SEVENS
IRB WORLD SEVENS SERIES 2005-2006 ROUND 4

Home Depot Center, Carson City, Los Angeles

[*Tournament squad:* Narraway, Ben Russell (2) (never travelled as withdrew, replaced by Will Matthews), David Seymour, N. Mordt, H. Paul, Care, Strettle, Vilk, O. Phillips, Gollings, Amor (never travelled as withdrew, replaced by Dan Luger), M. Tait, W. Matthews, Luger]

(squad of 12)

[Tony Roques and Richard Haughton were unavailable for this tournament due to injury]

[**MANAGER:** *Terry Sands*] [**COACH:** *Mike Friday*] [**ASSISTANT COACH:** *Phil Greening*]

CAPTAIN: *Henry Paul*

First Round - Pool 'A'

11th Feb KENYA 5 **ENGLAND** 26

[*Team:* Narraway, N. Mordt, David Seymour, Care, H. Paul, M. Tait, Strettle]

[*Bench:* Gollings, Luger (rep), W. Matthews (rep), O. Phillips (rep), Vilk]

[*Scorers:* **tries** by David Seymour, Narraway, M. Tait and Strettle, **conversions** by Care (3)]
11th Feb USA 0 **ENGLAND** 45
[*Team:* Narraway, Vilk, David Seymour, Care, Gollings, H. Paul, Strettle]
[*Bench:* Luger (rep), N. Mordt (rep), O. Phillips (rep), M. Tait]
[*Scorers:* **tries** by Vilk, Strettle (3), Gollings (2) and N. Mordt, **conversions** by Gollings (5)]
11th Feb FRANCE 19 **ENGLAND** 24
[*Team:* Narraway, Vilk, David Seymour, Gollings, H. Paul, M. Tait, Strettle]
[*Bench:* Care, Luger (rep), N. Mordt (rep), O. Phillips (rep)]
[*Scorers:* **tries** by Narraway, Strettle (2) and Gollings, **conversions** by Gollings (2)]
Quarter-Final
12th Feb ARGENTINA 15 **ENGLAND** 19
[*Team:* Narraway, Vilk, David Seymour, Gollings, H. Paul, M. Tait, Strettle]
[*Bench:* Care (rep), Luger, N. Mordt, O. Phillips]
[*Scorers:* **tries** by Strettle and M. Tait (2), **conversions** by Gollings (2)]
Semi-Final
12th Feb SOUTH AFRICA 0 **ENGLAND** 38
[*Team:* Narraway, Vilk, David Seymour, Gollings, H. Paul, M. Tait, Strettle]
[*Bench:* Care (rep), Luger, N. Mordt (rep), O. Phillips (rep)]
[*Scorers:* **tries** by Strettle, Vilk (3), M. Tait and Gollings, **conversions** by Gollings (4)]
Final
12th Feb FIJI 5 **ENGLAND** 38
[*Team:* Narraway, Vilk, David Seymour, Gollings, H. Paul, M. Tait, Strettle]
[*Bench:* Care (rep), Luger (rep), N. Mordt (rep), O. Phillips]
[*Scorers:* **tries** by Strettle, Vilk (2), M. Tait, N. Mordt and Gollings, **conversions** by Gollings (4)]

POSITION: WINNERS

[England scored 20 competition points in this Round of the 2005-2006 IRB World Sevens Series]

JEAN-CLAUDE BAQUÉ SHIELD MATCH

[**CHAIRMAN OF SELECTORS:** *Peter Hartley*] [**MANAGER:** *Jim Robinson*] [**ASSISTANT MANAGER:** *Danny Hodgson*] [**COACH:** *Paul Westgate*] [**ASSISTANT COACH:** *Alan Buzza*]
CAPTAIN: *James Winterbottom*
[11th Mar FRANCE AMATEURS 16 **ENGLAND COUNTIES** 29]
Stade Jean Guiral, Beaune
[*Team:* Duncan Cormack, Caves, W. Reed, J. Winterbottom, Richard Stott, Mark Evans, John Munro, James Rodwell, Toby Handley, O. Thomas, Hamish Smales, Malherbe, C. Briers, Phil Reed, Oliver Viney]
[*Bench:* D. Brett (rep), Brocklehurst (*centre*) (rep), Simon Elkinson (*hooker*) (rep), N. Hallett (rep), Richard Snowball (*lock*) (rep), Vinnicombe (*wing/full back*) (rep), Stean Williams (*flanker*) (rep)]
[*Scorers:* **tries** by W. Reed, Viney, Malherbe and H. Smales, **penalty goal** by O. Thomas, **conversions** by O. Thomas (3)]
[Ben Ryan was unavailable due to work commitments, with Alan Buzza consequently being made acting Assistant Coach on 6th March 2006; Alan Buzza sat on the bench for England against Ireland in January 1990]

COMMONWEALTH SEVENS

Telstra Dome, Melbourne

[*Tournament squad:* Lund, David Seymour, Ben Russell (2), N. Mordt, H. Paul, R. Haughton, Varndell, Vilk, Care, Gollings, Amor, M. Tait]

(squad of 12)

[Tony Roques and Will Matthews were unavailable for this tournament due to injury; Luke Narraway and Rob Thirlby both unavailable due to club commitments; Ben Lewitt, Dan Luger and Dave Strettle were all members of an initial 15 man training squad announced on 28th February 2006; The England squad departed for Australia on 5th March 2006; On 6th March 2006 the England squad arrived at the Sports Super Centre at Runaway Bay on the Gold Coast of Australia for a pre-tournament training camp; The final 12 man tournament squad was named on 14th March 2006; Simon Amor was the tournament captain; The Telstra Dome had its retractable roof closed for this tournament; Danny Care played for England in the U19 World Championship at Dubai in April 2006]

[**MANAGER:** *Terry Sands*] [**COACH:** *Mike Friday*] [**ASSISTANT COACH:** *Phil Greening*]

CAPTAIN: *Simon Amor*

Preliminary Round - Pool 'C'

16th Mar COOK ISLANDS 5 **ENGLAND** 35

[*Team:* David Seymour, Vilk, Lund, Amor, H. Paul, Gollings, Varndell]

[*Bench:* Care (rep), R. Haughton (rep), N. Mordt, Ben Russell (2) (rep), M. Tait]

[*Scorers:* **tries** by Varndell, H. Paul, David Seymour, Lund and Care, **conversions** by Gollings (5)]

CAPTAIN: *Ben Gollings*

16th Mar SRI LANKA 0 **ENGLAND** 61

[*Team:* David Seymour, N. Mordt, Ben Russell (2), Care, Gollings, M. Tait, R. Haughton]

[*Bench:* Amor, Lund (rep), H. Paul (rep), Varndell (rep), Vilk]

[*Scorers:* **tries** by David Seymour (2), M. Tait (3), R. Haughton, Varndell (2) and N. Mordt, **conversions** by Gollings (6), N. Mordt and Care]

CAPTAIN: *Simon Amor*

16th Mar AUSTRALIA 12 **ENGLAND** 14

[*Team:* David Seymour, Vilk, Lund, Amor, H. Paul, M. Tait, Varndell]

[*Bench:* Care, Gollings, R. Haughton (rep), N. Mordt (rep), Ben Russell (2) (rep)]

[*Scorers:* **tries** by Amor and Varndell, **conversions** by Amor (2)]

Quarter-Final

17th Mar SAMOA 14 **ENGLAND** 17

[*Team:* David Seymour, N. Mordt, Lund, Amor, H. Paul, M. Tait, Varndell]

[*Bench:* Care, Gollings, R. Haughton (rep), Ben Russell (2) (rep), Vilk]

[*Scorers:* **tries** by M. Tait (3), **conversion** by Amor]

Semi-Final

17th Mar FIJI 14 **ENGLAND** 21

[*Team:* David Seymour, Vilk, Lund, Amor, H. Paul, M. Tait, Varndell]

[*Bench:* Care, Gollings (rep), R. Haughton (rep), N. Mordt, Ben Russell (2)]

[*Scorers:* **tries** by Amor and M. Tait (2), **conversions** by Amor (3)]

Final

17th Mar NEW ZEALAND 29 **ENGLAND*** 21

[*Team:* Lund, David Seymour, Ben Russell (2), Amor, H. Paul, M. Tait, Varndell]

[*Bench:* Care, Gollings (rep), R. Haughton, N. Mordt, Vilk (rep)]

[*Scorers:* **tries** by M. Tait, Vilk and Gollings, **conversions** by Amor (2) and Gollings]
POSITION: LOSING FINALISTS [*SILVER MEDALISTS*]
FANTASY: *WINNERS*

CATHAY PACIFIC/CREDIT SUISSE HONG KONG SEVENS
IRB WORLD SEVENS SERIES 2005-2006 ROUND 5

Hong Kong Stadium, Eastern Hospital Road, So Kon Po, Hong Kong
[*Tournament squad:* Luger, Ben Russell (2), David Seymour, N. Mordt, H. Paul, Strettle, Varndell, Vilk, Foden, Gollings, Amor, M. Tait]
(squad of 12)
[Tony Roques was unavailable for this tournament due to injury; Luke Narraway and Rob Thirlby both unavailable due to club commitments; The England squad travelled to Bali after the Commonwealth Games for a pre-tournament training camp; Simon Amor was the tournament captain; The England squad arrived in Hong Kong on 26th March 2006]
[**MANAGER:** *Terry Sands*] [**COACH:** *Mike Friday*] [**ASSISTANT COACH:** *Phil Greening*]
CAPTAIN: *Ben Gollings*
First Round - Pool 'B'
31st Mar HONG KONG 0 **ENGLAND** 52
[*Team:* David Seymour, Luger, Ben Russell (2), Foden, Gollings, M. Tait, Strettle]
[*Bench:* Amor, N. Mordt (rep), H. Paul (rep), Varndell, Vilk (rep)]
[*Scorers:* **tries** by Gollings, Strettle (4), M. Tait, Luger and Ben Russell, **conversions** by Gollings (6)]
CAPTAIN: *Simon Amor*
1st April USA 5 **ENGLAND** 40
[*Team:* David Seymour, Vilk, Ben Russell (2), Amor, Gollings, H. Paul, Varndell]
[*Bench:* Foden (rep), Luger (rep), N. Mordt, Strettle, M. Tait (rep)]
[*Scorers:* **tries** by Gollings (2), Amor, Varndell, Vilk and M. Tait, **conversions** by Gollings (5)]
1st April CANADA 12 **ENGLAND** 36
[*Team:* David Seymour, Luger, Ben Russell (2), Amor, Gollings, M. Tait, Strettle]
[*Bench:* Foden (rep), N. Mordt, H. Paul (rep), Varndell (rep), Vilk]
[*Scorers:* **tries** by Strettle (2), Luger, David Seymour and Varndell (2), **conversions** by Gollings (2) and H. Paul]
Quarter-Final
2nd April SAMOA 10 **ENGLAND** 14
[*Team:* David Seymour, Vilk, Ben Russell (2), Amor, Gollings, M. Tait, Varndell]
[*Bench:* Foden, Luger, N. Mordt, H. Paul (rep), Strettle (rep)]
[*Scorers:* **tries** by Amor and Vilk, **conversions** by Gollings (2)]
Semi-Final
2nd April SOUTH AFRICA 0 **ENGLAND** 24
[*Team:* David Seymour, Vilk, Ben Russell (2), Amor, Gollings, M. Tait, Varndell]
[*Bench:* Foden (rep), Luger, N. Mordt (rep), H. Paul (rep), Strettle (rep)]
[*Scorers:* **tries** by M. Tait, Amor, Varndell and Strettle, **conversions** by Gollings (2)]
Final
2nd April FIJI 24 **ENGLAND** 26
[*Team:* David Seymour, Vilk, Ben Russell (2), Amor, Gollings, M. Tait, Varndell]
[*Bench:* Foden, Luger, N. Mordt, H. Paul (rep), Strettle (rep)]
[*Scorers:* **tries** by Varndell, Gollings (2) and M. Tait, **conversions** by Gollings (3)]

POSITION: WINNERS
[England scored 30 competition points in this Round of the 2005-2006 IRB World Sevens Series]

QINETIQ CHALLENGE MATCH

[NO COACH NOMINATED]
CAPTAIN: *Bobby Skinstad* (SA)

[4th April Royal Navy (*SER*) 10 **BARBARIANS** 31]
Plymouth Albion RFC, Brickfields Recreation Ground, Madden Road, Plymouth
[*Team:* W. Reed, Dalgleish, Peter Bucknall, Andrew Smith, C. Bentley, Danny Thomas, Cornish, B. Skinstad (SA), Greig Laidlaw (SC), Dafydd Lewis (WA), K. Bingham, Mark Fatialofa (SAM), Jonathan 'Jon' Bryant (WA), Nacanieli 'Nat' Saumi (FIJ), Jonathan 'Jon' Ufton]
[*Bench:* Nick Burnett (CO) (*flanker*) (rep), G. Davis (*prop*) (rep), I. Humphreys (IR) (*fly half*) (rep), Brett Luxton (*lock/number 8*) (rep), A. Page (rep), Ritchie (rep)]
[*Scorers:* **tries** by Dafydd Lewis (WA), Danny Thomas, Saumi (FIJ), B. Skinstad (SA) and I. Humphreys (IR), **conversions** by Ufton (3)]
[Match to commemorate the Centenary of the Royal Navy Rugby Union, which was founded in 1906]

STANDARD CHARTERED SEVENS, SINGAPORE
IRB WORLD SEVENS SERIES 2005-2006 ROUND 6

National Stadium, Kallang
[*Tournament squad:* Luger, Ben Russell (2), David Seymour, N. Mordt, H. Paul, Strettle, Varndell, Vilk, Foden, Gollings, Amor, M. Tait]
(squad of 12)
[Tony Roques unavailable due to injury; Luke Narraway was unavailable for this tournament due to club commitments; Simon Amor was the tournament captain; Henry Paul returned to Rugby League on 27th April 2006 and then came back for a final stint in Rugby Union in September 2008 when he joined Leeds Carnegie]
[**MANAGER:** *Terry Sands*] [**COACH:** *Mike Friday*] [**ASSISTANT COACH:** *Phil Greening*]
CAPTAIN: *Simon Amor*
First Round - Pool 'B'

8th April KENYA 12 **ENGLAND** 26
[*Team:* David Seymour, Luger, Ben Russell (2), Amor, Gollings, H. Paul, Strettle]
[*Bench:* Foden, N. Mordt, M. Tait, Varndell (rep), Vilk]
[*Scorers:* **tries** by H. Paul, Varndell (2) and David Seymour, **conversions** by Gollings (2) and Amor]
CAPTAIN: *Ben Gollings*

8th April KOREA 5 **ENGLAND** 47
[*Team:* N. Mordt, Vilk, Ben Russell (2), Foden, Gollings, H. Paul, Varndell]
[*Bench:* Amor, Luger, David Seymour, Strettle (rep), M. Tait]
[*Scorers:* **tries** by Varndell (2), H. Paul, Gollings, Foden (2) and Strettle, **conversions** by Gollings (6)]
CAPTAIN: *Simon Amor*

8th April SAMOA 14 **ENGLAND*** 12
[*Team:* David Seymour, N. Mordt, Ben Russell (2), Amor, Gollings, H. Paul, Strettle]
[*Bench:* Foden, Luger, M. Tait, Varndell (rep), Vilk]
[*Scorers:* **tries** by N. Mordt and Varndell, **conversion** by H. Paul]

Quarter-Final

9th April AUSTRALIA 14 **ENGLAND** 26

[*Team:* David Seymour, Vilk, Ben Russell (2), Amor, Gollings, H. Paul, Varndell]
[*Bench:* Foden, Luger, N. Mordt, Strettle, M. Tait]
[*Scorers:* **tries** by Varndell, Gollings and Amor (2), **conversions** by Gollings (3)]

Semi-Final

9th April SOUTH AFRICA 14 **ENGLAND** 33

[*Team:* David Seymour, Vilk, Ben Russell (2), Amor, Gollings, H. Paul, Varndell]
[*Bench:* Foden (rep), Luger, N. Mordt (rep), Strettle, M. Tait (rep)]
[*Scorers:* **tries** by Gollings (2), Vilk, Amor and M. Tait, **conversions** by H. Paul and Gollings (3)]

Final

9th April FIJI 40 **ENGLAND** 19

[*Team:* David Seymour, Vilk, Ben Russell (2), Amor, Gollings, M. Tait, Varndell]
[*Bench:* Foden (rep), Luger, N. Mordt, H. Paul (rep), Strettle (rep)]
[*Scorers:* **tries** by Varndell, M. Tait and Vilk, **conversions** by Gollings (2)]

POSITION: LOSING FINALISTS

[England scored 16 competition points in this Round of the 2005-2006 IRB World Sevens Series]

MATT HAMPSON CHALLENGE MATCH

[**MANAGER:** *Peter Drewett*] [**COACH:** *Jim Mallinder*] [**ASSISTANT COACH:** *Dorian West*]

CAPTAIN: *Jordan Crane*

[16th May Leicester Tigers Development XV 17 **ENGLAND U21 XV** 36]

Welford Road, Leicester

[*Team:* A. Rogers, Brooker, M. Lambert, T. Ryder, Blaze, Haskell, Hills, J. Crane, Foden, Sam Robinson, Diggin, R. Davis, Matt Riley, Abendanon, Mike Brown]
[*Bench:* Sean Cox, Iain Grieve (*flanker/number 8*) (rep), James Honeyben (*scrum half*) (rep), Lennard (*full back*) (rep), W. Matthews (rep), Tom Mercey (*prop*), Phil Nilson (*hooker*)]
[*Scorers:* **tries** by Hills (2), Diggin, Mike Brown and Haskell, **penalty goal** by Mike Brown, **conversions** by Mike Brown (2) and Lennard (2)]

[Match arranged to raise money for the Matt Hampson Trust Fund; Matt Hampson suffered a severe neck injury during an England U21 training session at Franklin's Gardens on 15th March 2005]

RICHARD HILL TESTIMONIAL SPECIAL

[**COACH:** *Bob Dwyer* (AU)] [**ASSISTANT COACHES:** *Mike Ruddock* (WA) & *Craig Dowd* (NZ)]

CAPTAIN: *Lawrence Dallaglio*

[21st May Saracens 14 **WORLD XV** 64]

Vicarage Road, Watford

[*Team:* David 'Dave' Hewett (NZ), M. Regan, Peter Bracken (IR), Daniel Leo (SAM), Tom Palmer (2), Finegan (AU), Sam Harding (NZ), Dallaglio, Mark Robinson (2) (NZ), C. Spencer (NZ), Balshaw, F. Waters, Joseph 'Joe' Roff (AU), Reihana (NZ), Matt Burke (AU)]
[*Bench:* Califano (FR) (*prop*) (rep), Cédric Desbrosse (FR) (*centre*) (rep), Ibañez (FR) (rep), Rodger Siaosi *Toutai* Kefu (AU) (*number 8*) (rep), J. Marshall (NZ) (*scrum half*) (rep), Isa Nacewa (FIJ) (*fly half/centre/wing/full back*) (rep), X. Rush (NZ) (*flanker/number 8*) (rep)]
[*Scorers:* **tries** by Balshaw, C. Spencer (NZ) (2), Matt Burke (AU) (2), Mark Robinson (NZ), Nacewa (FIJ) (2), M. Regan and Reihana (NZ), **conversions** by Matt Burke (AU) (6) and

referee]

[Match organised as a testimonial game for Richard Hill (2)]

[Bob Dwyer was appointed on 21st February 2006; Mike Ruddock and Craig Dowd were both appointed on 18th May 2006; Mike Ruddock played for Wales B in October 1982; Craig Dowd won 59 caps for New Zealand between 1993-2000]

GMF PARIS SEVENS
IRB WORLD SEVENS SERIES 2005-2006 ROUND 7

Stade Sébastien Charléty, Paris

[*Tournament squad:* W. Matthews, Ben Russell (2), David Seymour, O. Phillips, Hipkiss, Strettle, J. Bailey, Vilk, R. Thirlby, Gollings, Amor, R. Haughton]

(squad of 12)

[Tony Roques and Nils Mordt were unavailable for this tournament due to injury; Ben Foden, Jonny Hylton, Dan Luger and Luke Narraway all in original 16 man training squad]

[Phil Greening was the Coach when the Samurai won the Amsterdam Heineken Sevens on 20th-21st May 2006]

[**MANAGER:** *Terry Sands*] [**COACH:** *Mike Friday*] [**ASSISTANT COACH:** *Phil Greening*]

CAPTAIN: *Simon Amor*

First Round - Pool 'B'

27th May SCOTLAND 7 **ENGLAND** 24

[*Team:* David Seymour, Vilk, Ben Russell (2), Amor, Gollings, Hipkiss, Strettle]

[*Bench:* J. Bailey, R. Haughton (rep), W. Matthews, O. Phillips, R. Thirlby]

[*Scorers:* **tries** by Strettle, Gollings, Vilk and R. Haughton, **conversions** by Gollings and Amor]

27th May RUSSIA 7 **ENGLAND** 26

[*Team:* W. Matthews, David Seymour, R. Thirlby, Amor, Gollings, O. Phillips, J. Bailey]

[*Bench:* R. Haughton (rep), Hipkiss (rep), Ben Russell (2), Strettle, Vilk]

[*Scorers:* **tries** by R. Thirlby, J. Bailey, Hipkiss and R. Haughton, **conversions** by Gollings (2) and Amor]

27th May FRANCE 12 **ENGLAND** 19

[*Team:* David Seymour, Vilk, Ben Russell (2), Amor, Gollings, Hipkiss, Strettle]

[*Bench:* J. Bailey, R. Haughton (rep), W. Matthews (rep), O. Phillips, R. Thirlby (rep)]

[*Scorers:* **tries** by Strettle, Hipkiss and R. Haughton, **conversions** by Gollings (2)]

Quarter-Final

28th May AUSTRALIA 29 **ENGLAND*** 17

[*Team:* David Seymour, Vilk, Ben Russell (2), Amor, Gollings, R. Thirlby, R. Haughton]

[*Bench:* J. Bailey, Hipkiss (rep), W. Matthews (rep), O. Phillips, Strettle (rep)]

[*Scorers:* **tries** by Ben Russell, Vilk and R. Thirlby, **conversion** by Gollings]

[Plate Semi-Final:]

[28th May ARGENTINA 14 **ENGLAND*** 12]

[*Team:* W. Matthews, Vilk, Ben Russell (2), Amor, Gollings, Hipkiss, R. Haughton]

[*Bench:* J. Bailey, O. Phillips (rep), David Seymour, Strettle (rep), R. Thirlby]

[*Scorers:* **tries** by Vilk and Hipkiss, **conversion** by Gollings]

POSITION: LOSING QUARTER-FINALISTS [*PLATE SEMI-FINALISTS*]

FANTASY: *WINNERS*

[England scored 4 competition points in this Round of the 2005-2006 IRB World Sevens Series]

GARTMORE CHALLENGE

GARTMORE CHALLENGE TROPHY

[ENGLAND XV: [*Other squad members:* Noon, Sackey (withdrew due to injury, replaced by Delon Armitage), Voyce, Walshe, J. Worsley (withdrew due to injury, replaced by James Haskell)]]

(*squad of 24*)

[*John Wells and Mike Ford were both appointed on 23rd May 2006; Brian Ashton was appointed on 25th May 2006; Andy Sheridan, Matt Stevens, Phil Vickery, Steve Borthwick, Richard Hill (2), Lawrence Dallaglio, Shaun Perry, Jonny Wilkinson, Shane Drahm, Paul Sackey and Jon Clarke all unavailable due to injury; Graham Rowntree, George Chuter, Andy Titterrell, Julian White, Stuart Turner, Chris Jones, Ben Kay, Dean Schofield, Lewis Moody, Magnus Lund, Richard Wigglesworth, Andy Goode, Sam Vesty and Tom Varndell all unavailable due to club commitments; Steve Thompson (2), Danny Grewcock, Martin Corry, Harry Ellis, Charlie Hodgson, Ben Cohen, Mike Tindall, Mark Cueto and Josh Lewsey were all rested for this match by Andy Robinson*]

[*Bob Dwyer was appointed on 11th April 2006; Mike Ruddock was appointed on 18th May 2006*]

[ENGLAND XV: [HEAD COACH: *Andy Robinson*] **[ASSISTANT COACHES:** *Brian Ashton, John Wells* & *Mike Ford*]]

[BARBARIANS: [COACH: *Bob Dwyer* (AU)] **[ASSISTANT COACH:** *Mike Ruddock* (WA)]]

CAPTAIN: *Pat Sanderson* [England XV]

CAPTAIN: *Raphäel Ibañez* (FR) [Barbarians]

28th May **ENGLAND XV** 46 **BARBARIANS** 19
Twickenham

[ENGLAND XV: [*Team:* T. Payne, Mears, Duncan Bell, James Hudson, Alex Brown, Forrester, Lipman, P. Sanderson, Peter Richards, Barkley, Balshaw, M. Catt, M. Tait, J. Simpson-Daniel, Van Gisbergen]

[*Bench:* S. Abbott (rep), D. Armitage (rep), D. Barnes (rep), Bemand (rep), Haskell (rep), David Paice (*prop/hooker*) (rep), K. Roche (rep)]

[*Scorers:* **tries** by J. Simpson-Daniel (2), Barkley, Forrester, D. Barnes and D. Armitage, **penalty goals** by Barkley (2), **conversions** by Barkley (5)]]

[BARBARIANS: [*Team:* Lo Cicero (IT), Ibañez (FR), Califano (FR), Robert 'Bob' Casey (IR), Tom Palmer (2), X. Rush (NZ), Magne (FR), Kefu (AU), Mark Robinson (2) (NZ), C. Spencer (NZ), Roff (AU), Dominic Feau'nati (SAM), T. Castaignède (FR), Reihana (NZ), Matt Burke (AU)]

[*Bench:* P. Bracken (IR) (*prop*) (rep), Sam Harding (NZ) (*flanker*) (rep), Leo (SAM) (*lock/flanker/number 8*) (rep), J. Marshall (NZ) (rep), Nacewa (FIJ) (rep), M. Regan (rep), F. Waters (rep)]

[*Scorers:* **tries** by Magne (FR), Reihana (NZ) and Matt Burke (AU), **conversions** by Matt Burke (AU) (2)]]

BARBARIANS MATCH

[*Other squad members:* K. Bracken, Justin Fitzpatrick (IR) (*prop*), Brad Macleod-Henderson (SA) (*flanker/number 8*), Gethin *Rhys* Williams (2) (WA) (*full back*) (never travelled as withdrew, replaced by Ugo Monye)]

(*squad of 26*)

[*Pat Howard was appointed on 11th April 2006*]

[**COACH:** *Pat Howard* (AU)]

CAPTAIN: *Will Greenwood*

[31st May SCOTLAND XV 66 **BARBARIANS** 19]

Murrayfield

[*Team:* Tkachuk (CAN), Pieter Dixon (SA), John Davies (WA), James Hamilton, H. Louw (SA), Kieron Dawson (IR), Jason Forster (WA), Daniel 'Dan' Browne (NZ), Jason Spice (NZ), Christopher 'Chris' Malone (AU), Lee Robinson, Sonny Parker (WA), W. Greenwood, L. Lloyd, S. Hanley]

[*Bench:* Olivier Azam (FR) (*hooker*) (rep), Darren Crompton (*prop*) (rep), Maggs (IR) (*centre*) (rep), T. Marsh (FR) (*centre*) (rep), Miall (rep), Monye (rep), Jacob 'Jake' Rauluni (FIJ) (*scrum half*) (rep), B. Skinstad (SA) (rep)]

[*Scorers:* **tries** by K. Dawson (IR), S. Hanley and T. Marsh (FR), **conversions** by C. Malone (AU) (2)]

TUNISIAN TOUR TO ENGLAND 2006

[**CHAIRMAN OF SELECTORS:** *Peter Hartley*] [**MANAGER:** *Jim Robinson*] [**ASSISTANT MANAGER:** *Danny Hodgson*] [**COACH:** *Ben Ryan*] [**ASSISTANT COACH:** *Jim Thorp*]

CAPTAIN: *Duncan Cormack*

[3rd June **ENGLAND COUNTIES** 35 TUNISIA 7]

Broadstreet RFC, Ivor Preece Field, Binley Woods, Coventry

[*Team:* D. Cormack, Joe Duffey, W. Reed, B. Luxton, Paul Arnold (2), Mark Evans, N. Spence, Rodwell, Paul Knight (2), O. Thomas, Kerfoot, C. Briers, Malherbe, H. Smales, Viney]

[*Bench:* Ed Barnes (*fly half*) (rep), K. Bingham (*scrum half/wing*) (rep), David 'Dave' Campton (*lock*) (rep), Glenn Cooper (rep), R. Hopkins (rep), D. Knight (rep), J. Munro (*flanker*) (rep)]

[*Scorers:* **tries** by Rodwell (2), Paul Knight, D. Cormack and E. Barnes, **conversions** by O. Thomas (3) and E. Barnes (2)]

[Ben Ryan and Jim Thorp were both appointed on 15th May 2006; Jim Thorp was an England U21 squad member in May 1996]

WORLD XV TOUR TO SOUTH AFRICA 2006

[**COACH:** *Bob Dwyer* (AU)] [**ASSISTANT COACHES:** *Mike Ruddock* (WA) & *Craig Dowd* (NZ)]

[*Other squad members:* Desbrosse (FR) (tm), Drotske (SA) (tm), Finegan (AU) (tm), Kefu (AU) (tm), Lo Cicero (IT)]

(squad of 26)

[Bob Dwyer was appointed on 21st February 2006; Mike Ruddock and Craig Dowd were both appointed on 18th May 2006; The World XV squad arrived in South Africa on 30th May 2006; Thomas Castaignède joined the French touring squad after the South African XV match; Raphäel Ibañez joined the French touring squad after the South Africa XV match, being replaced by Naka Drotske]

CAPTAIN: *Justin Marshall* (NZ)

[3rd June SOUTH AFRICA XV 30 **WORLD XV*** 27]

Ellis Park Stadium, Johannesburg

[*Team:* Hewett (NZ), Ibañez (FR), C. Visagie (SA), Tom Palmer (2), Samo (AU), X. Rush (NZ), Magne (FR), Chabal (FR), J. Marshall (NZ), C. Spencer (NZ), Nacewa (FIJ), F. Waters, T. Castaignède (FR), Reihana (NZ), Matt Burke (AU)]

[*Bench:* Califano (FR) (rep), Sam Harding (NZ) (rep), Ludovic Mercier (FR) (*fly half*) (rep), Julien Pierre (FR) (*lock*) (rep), M. Regan (rep), Mark Robinson (2) (NZ) (rep), Roff (AU) (*wing/full back*) (rep)]

[*Scorers:* **tries** by J. Marshall (NZ) and Nacewa (FIJ), **penalty goals** by Matt Burke (AU) (5), **conversion** by Matt Burke (AU)]

EMIRATES AIRLINE LONDON SEVENS
IRB WORLD SEVENS SERIES 2005-2006 ROUND 8

Twickenham

[*Tournament squad:* W. Matthews, Ben Russell (2), Narraway, O. Phillips, Hylton, Strettle, J. Bailey, Vilk, Foden, Gollings, Amor, R. Haughton]

(squad of 12)

[Tony Roques and Nils Mordt were unavailable for this tournament due to injury; Simon Amor was the tournament captain; Jonny Hylton played in the Samurai team that won the Amsterdam Heineken Sevens on 20th-21st May 2006]

[MANAGER: *Terry Sands*] **[COACH:** *Mike Friday*] **[ASSISTANT COACH:** *Phil Greening*]

CAPTAIN: *Simon Amor*

First Round - Pool 'B'

3rd June **ENGLAND** 26 KENYA 0

[*Team:* Narraway, Vilk, Ben Russell (2), Amor, Gollings, Foden, R. Haughton]

[*Bench:* J. Bailey, Hylton, W. Matthews, O. Phillips, Strettle (rep)]

[*Scorers:* **tries** by Gollings, Foden, Vilk and Strettle, **conversions** by Gollings (3)]

CAPTAIN: *Ben Gollings*

3rd June **ENGLAND** 51 GERMANY 0

[*Team:* Narraway, W. Matthews, Hylton, J. Bailey, Gollings, O. Phillips, Strettle]

[*Bench:* Foden (rep), R. Haughton (rep), Ben Russell (2), Vilk]

[*Scorers:* **tries** by Strettle (2), J. Bailey, Gollings, R. Haughton, O. Phillips, Hylton, W. Matthews and Narraway, **conversions** by Gollings (2) and R. Haughton]

3rd June **ENGLAND*** 19 AUSTRALIA 24

[*Team:* W. Matthews, Vilk, Ben Russell (2), J. Bailey, Gollings, Hylton, Strettle]

[*Bench:* R. Haughton (rep), Narraway (rep), O. Phillips (rep)]

[*Scorers:* **tries** by Vilk (2) and Strettle, **conversions** by Gollings (2)]

Quarter-Final

4th June **ENGLAND** 14 FRANCE 7

[*Team:* Narraway, Vilk, Ben Russell (2), J. Bailey, Gollings, R. Haughton, Strettle]

[*Bench:* O. Phillips (rep)]

[*Scorers:* **tries** by R. Haughton and Ben Russell, **conversions** by Gollings (2)]

Semi-Final

4th June **ENGLAND** 7 SAMOA 15

[*Team:* Narraway, Vilk, Ben Russell (2), J. Bailey, Gollings, R. Haughton, Strettle]

[*Bench:* O. Phillips (rep)]

[*Scorers:* **try** by Strettle, **conversion** by Gollings]

POSITION: LOSING SEMI-FINALISTS

[England scored 12 competition points in this Round of the 2005-2006 IRB World Sevens Series]

RANKING: 2ND 122 [*Fiji 144*, South Africa 110, New Zealand 76, Samoa 72, Argentina 64, France 50, Australia 40, Kenya 13, Scotland 12, Wales 8, Canada 4, Portugal 2, China 1]

FANTASY: ***1ST 150***

BARCLAYS CHURCHILL CUP

Canada & USA

[*Other squad members:* Drahm (*fly half*) (never travelled as injured, replaced by Dave Walder), Forrester (never travelled as injured, replaced by Kai Horstmann), Andy Higgins (2) (injured during the tournament), Sackey (never travelled as injured, replaced by Andy Higgins (2))]

(squad of 28)

[The England A team was officially renamed as the England Saxons on 15th May 2006; Luke Narraway and Richard Haughton were in the original squad but travelled later due to their England 7s commitments; David Barnes was the tournament captain; The England Saxons squad departed for Canada on 29th May 2006; James Forrester retired due to injury in October 2008; Andy Higgins (2) failed to take drugs tests on both 13th May and 14th May 2009 and a subsequent RFU Disciplinary Panel on 3rd August 2009 found Andy Higgins (2) guilty of 'conduct prejudicial to the interests of the game' and thus banned him for 9 months, with the ban running from 1st June 2009 until 28th February 2010; Andy Higgins (2) consequently retired on 17th August 2009 but then changed his mind on 28th May 2010]

[Jon Callard and Simon Hardy were both appointed on 23rd May 2006]

(During the First Round a bonus point was awarded for scoring 4 or more tries in a match and for losing by seven points or less)

[**COACH:** *Jon Callard*] [**ASSISTANT COACH:** *Simon Hardy*]

CAPTAIN: *Paul Hodgson*

First Round - Pool 'B'

[3rd June SCOTLAND A 13 **ENGLAND SAXONS*** 7 **BP**]

York University Stadium, Toronto

[*Team:* D. Barnes, Buckland, Stuart Turner, James Hudson, Schofield, A. Beattie, David Seymour, Horstmann, P. Hodgson, Walder, C. Bell, Vesty, Ben Johnston, D. Armitage, Horak]

[*Bench:* A. Crockett (rep), N. Kennedy (rep), D. Paice (rep), K. Roche (rep), Micky Ward (rep), Wigglesworth, B. Woods (rep)]

[*Scorers:* **try** by penalty try, **conversion** by Walder]

CAPTAIN: *Ben Johnston* [*David Barnes took over when Ben Johnston was temporarily sin-binned in the 2nd half*]

[10th Jun CANADA 11 **ENGLAND SAXONS** 41 **BP**]

York University Stadium, Toronto

[*Team:* Micky Ward, D. Paice, Robbie Morris, N. Kennedy, K. Roche, Narraway, David Seymour, Horstmann, Wigglesworth, Walder, A. Crockett, C. Bell, Ben Johnston, R. Haughton, D. Armitage]

[*Bench:* D. Barnes (rep), Buckland (rep), Erinle (*wing*) (rep), James Hudson (*lock*) (rep), Stuart-Smith (rep), Vesty (rep), B. Woods (rep)]

[*Scorers:* **tries** by R. Haughton, D. Armitage (2), Horstmann, C. Bell and B. Woods, **penalty goal** by Walder, **conversions** by Walder (4)]

CAPTAIN: *Clive Stuart-Smith*

[Plate Final:]

[17th Jun IRELAND A 30 **ENGLAND SAXONS*** 27 **]**

Commonwealth Stadium, Edmonton

[*Team:* D. Barnes, Buckland, Stuart Turner, James Hudson, N. Kennedy, K. Roche, David

Seymour, Horstmann, Stuart-Smith, Walder, Erinle, Vesty, Ben Johnston, R. Haughton, D. Armitage]
[*Bench:* A. Beattie (rep), Horak, Narraway (rep), D. Paice (rep), Micky Ward (rep), Wigglesworth, B. Woods (rep)]
[*Scorers:* **tries** by Horstmann, Erinle, Vesty and Ben Johnston, **penalty goal** by Walder, **conversions** by Walder (2)]
POSITION: FIRST ROUND LOSERS [*PLATE FINALISTS*]

BARBARIANS TOUR TO GEORGIA 2006

[**MANAGER:** *Micky Steele-Bodger*] [**PLAYER-COACH:** *Pat Howard* (AU)]
[*Other squad members:* Hipkiss (never travelled as injured, replaced by Ugo Monye), Spice (NZ) (*scrum half*) (never travelled as injured, replaced by Ian Vass), Rhys Williams (2) (WA) (never travelled as injured, replaced by Neil Hallett)]
(squad of 25)
[Pat Howard was appointed on 11th April 2006; Micky Steele-Bodger was capped for England in January 1947 and was Manager on the England XV tour to Canada in September-October 1967; Pat Howard originally travelled as Coach]
CAPTAIN: *Bobby Skinstad* (SA)
[4th June GEORGIA 19 **BARBARIANS** 28]
FC Lokomotivi Tbilisi, Mikheil Meshki Stadium, Vake, Tbilisi
[*Team:* Justin Fitzpatrick (IR), Azam (FR), Darren Crompton, James Hamilton, Miall, Macleod-Henderson (SA), W. Skinner, B. Skinstad (SA), J. Rauluni (FIJ), C. Malone (AU), L. Robinson, Maggs (IR), T. Marsh (FR), Monye, N. Hallett]
[*Bench:* D. Browne (NZ) (*number 8*) (rep), John Davies (WA) (rep), Pieter Dixon (SA) (*hooker*) (rep), Jason Forster (WA) (*flanker*) (rep), S. Hanley (rep), P. Howard (AU) (rep), L. Lloyd (rep), H. Louw (SA) (rep), Tkachuk (CAN) (*prop*) (rep), Vass (rep)]
[*Scorers:* **tries** by Monye, S. Hanley (2) and N. Hallett, **conversions** by C. Malone (AU) (3) and N. Hallett]

IRB U21 WORLD CHAMPIONSHIP

France
[*Other squad members*: N. Briggs (never travelled as injured, replaced by Rob Webber)]
(squad of 26)
[On 7th March 2006 Peter Drewett announced that he would be leaving his post of Manager after the IRB U21 World Championship in France in June 2006; Dylan Hartley, Nick Abendanon and Olly Morgan were unavailable for this tournament due to injury; Matt Tait and Tom Varndell unavailable because they were required to go on the full England tour of Australia in June 2006; The England U21 squad travelled to France on 5th June 2006; Jim Mallinder was appointed England Saxons Coach on 24th November 2006; Dorian West was appointed England Saxons Assistant Coach on 2nd January 2007]
(During the First Round a bonus point was awarded for scoring 4 or more tries in a match and for losing by seven points or less)
[**MANAGER:** *Peter Drewett*] [**COACH:** *Jim Mallinder*] [**ASSISTANT COACH:** *Dorian West*]
CAPTAIN: *Matt Cornwell*
First Round - Pool 'B'
[9th June FIJI U21 8 **ENGLAND U21** 34 **BP**]
Stade Louis Darragon, Vichy
[*Team:* David Wilson (2), Robert 'Rob' Webber, Mercey, T. Ryder, T. Croft, Haskell,

Robshaw, J. Crane, Care, R. Lamb, Diggin, T. Flood, Matt Cornwell, Ojo, Mike Brown]
[*Bench:* Anthony Allen (*centre*) (rep), Blaze (*lock*) (rep), Brooker (*hooker*) (rep), R. Davis, Grieve, M. Lambert (rep), Uche Oduoza (*wing*)]
[*Scorers:* **tries** by T. Flood, Anthony Allen, Diggin and J. Crane, **penalty goals** by T. Flood (2), **conversions** by T. Flood (4)]
CAPTAIN: *Jordan Crane*
[13th Jun NEW ZEALAND U21 29 **ENGLAND U21** 14]
Stade Louis Darragon, Vichy
[*Team:* A. Rogers, Brooker, David Wilson (2), Blaze, T. Croft, Haskell, Hills, J. Crane, Care, R. Lamb, Diggin, T. Flood, Anthony Allen, Ojo, Mike Brown]
[*Bench:* Foden (rep), M. Lambert, Riley (*centre/wing*) (rep), Robshaw, T. Ryder (rep), Oduoza (rep), R. Webber (*hooker*) (rep)]
[*Scorers:* **tries** by Haskell and Ojo, **conversions** by T. Flood (2)]
CAPTAIN: *Matt Cornwell*
[17th Jun SCOTLAND U21 12 **ENGLAND U21** 31 **BP**]
Stade Emile Pons, Riom
[*Team:* A. Rogers, Brooker, M. Lambert, T. Ryder, Blaze, Robshaw, Hills, J. Crane, Foden, R. Lamb, Oduoza, Anthony Allen, Matt Cornwell, Ojo, Mike Brown]
[*Bench:* Care (*scrum half*), R. Davis, Grieve (rep), Haskell (rep), Riley, R. Webber, David Wilson (2) (rep)]
[*Scorers:* **tries** by Anthony Allen, J. Crane (2), A. Rogers and Haskell, **conversions** by R. Lamb (3)]
[England U21 failed to score enough bonus points to get into the top 4 teams and thus did not have a chance of playing for a place in the final]
5th/6th/7th/8th Place Semi-Final
[21st Jun WALES U21 11 **ENGLAND U21** 13]
Stade Louis Darragon, Vichy
[*Team:* A. Rogers, Brooker, David Wilson (2), Blaze, T. Croft, Grieve, Hills, Haskell, Foden, T. Flood, Riley, R. Davis, Matt Cornwell, Ojo, Mike Brown]
[*Bench:* Anthony Allen (rep), Care (rep), J. Crane (*number 8*) (rep), R. Lamb (rep), Mercey (rep), Robshaw (rep), R. Webber (rep)]
[*Scorers:* **try** by David Wilson, **penalty goals** by T. Flood (2), **conversion** by R. Lamb]
5th/6th Place Play-Off
[25th Jun IRELAND U21 8 **ENGLAND U21** 32]
Stade Maurice Couturier, Cournon d'Auvergne
[*Team:* A. Rogers, Brooker, David Wilson (2), Blaze, T. Croft, Haskell, Hills, J. Crane, Care, R. Lamb, Diggin, Anthony Allen, Matt Cornwell, Ojo, Mike Brown]
[*Bench:* T. Flood (*fly half/centre*) (rep), Foden (rep), M. Lambert (rep), Riley (rep), Robshaw (rep), T. Ryder (rep), R. Webber (rep)]
[*Scorers:* **tries** by Care, A. Rogers (2), Anthony Allen and Hills, **penalty goal** by R. Lamb, **conversions** by R. Lamb (2)]
POSITION: 5TH PLACE

ANDY MULLIGAN TROPHY MATCH

[*Other squad members:* Breeze (WA), Brenton, Marc Camburn (NZ) (*centre*), Gorrie (NZ) (*number 8*), Head (IR), R. Henderson (IR), Duncan Hodge (*fly half*) (SC), Jorgensen (AU), Rida Joauher (FR) (*wing*), Khrist Kopetzky (FR) (*fly half/full back*), Paul Laffin (IR) (*prop*), Steven 'Steve' Lawrie (SC) (*hooker*), Nasmith (NZ), Paul Neville (IR) (*flanker/number 8*), Mike

Prendergast (IR) (*scrum half*), Reece Robinson (NZ) (*lock/flanker*), Rossigneux, Nicolas le Roux (FR) (*full back*), Urlich (NZ), Ian Warbrick (SC) (*wing*)]
(squad of 24)
[Match to commemorate the 100th Anniversary of the foundation of Paris Université Club (PUC) in 1906; Andy Mulligan won 22 caps for Ireland between 1956-61, was capped for the British Lions in September 1959, played for PUC between 1962-65 and died in February 2001; John Rutherford won 42 caps for Scotland between 1979-87 and was capped for the British Lions in July 1983]
[MANAGER: *Craig Brown* (NZ)] **[COACH:** *John Rutherford* (SC)]
CAPTAIN: *Rod Moore* (AU)
[10th Jun Paris Université Club Past & Present (*FR*) 7 **PENGUINS** 40]
Stade Sébastien Charléty, Paris
[*Team:* Matt Dunning (AU) (*prop*), James McCormack (AU) (*hooker*), Rod Moore (AU) (*prop*), de Goldi (NZ)]
[*Bench:*]
[*Scorers:* **tries** by J. McCormack (AU), de Goldi (NZ), ?, ?, ? and ?, **conversions** by ? (5)]

ENGLAND TOUR TO AUSTRALIA 2006

[HEAD COACH: *Andy Robinson*] **[ASSISTANT COACHES:** *Brian Ashton, John Wells & Mike Ford*]
[*Other squad members:* Duncan Bell, Bemand, J. Simpson-Daniel (injured during the tour), Titterrell, Van Gisbergen]
(squad of 30)
[Andy Sheridan, Matt Stevens, Phil Vickery, Steve Borthwick, Richard Hill (2), Lawrence Dallaglio, Shaun Perry, Jonny Wilkinson and Jon Clarke were unavailable for this tour due to injury; Steve Thompson (2), Danny Grewcock, Martin Corry, Harry Ellis, Charlie Hodgson, Ben Cohen, Mike Tindall, Mark Cueto and Josh Lewsey were all rested for this tour by Andy Robinson; The England squad departed for Australia on 29th May 2006]

COOK CUP SERIES

CAPTAIN: *Pat Sanderson*
11th June AUSTRALIA 34 **ENGLAND** 3
Telstra Stadium, Sydney Olympic Park, Homebush Bay, Sydney
[*Team:* Rowntree, Mears, Julian White, L. Deacon, Alex Brown, Lund, Moody, P. Sanderson, Peter Richards, Barkley, Voyce, M. Catt, M. Tait, Varndell, Balshaw]
[*Bench:* Chuter (rep), Andy Goode (rep), Chris Jones (rep), Noon (rep), T. Payne (rep), Walshe (rep), J. Worsley (rep)]
[*Scorers:* **penalty goal** by Barkley]
17th June AUSTRALIA 43 **ENGLAND** 18
Telstra Dome, Melbourne
[*Team:* Rowntree, Chuter, Julian White, Chris Jones, Kay, J. Worsley, Lipman, P. Sanderson, Peter Richards, Andy Goode, M. Tait, M. Catt, Noon, Varndell, Balshaw]
[*Bench:* S. Abbott (rep), Barkley (rep), L. Deacon (rep), Lund (rep), Mears (rep), T. Payne (rep), Walshe (rep)]
[*Scorers:* **tries** by Chuter and Varndell, **penalty goal** by Andy Goode, **drop goal** by Andy Goode, **conversion** by Andy Goode]
POSITION: SERIES LOSERS

WORLD UNIVERSITY RUGBY SEVENS CHAMPIONSHIP

CUS Roma, Stadio degli Eucalipti, Rome

[*Tournament squad:* Patrick 'Pat' Benson (*hooker*), Patrick Dias (*centre*), Tom Dickens (WA) (*scrum half*), George Dixon (*centre/wing*), T. Gregory (*centre*), John Houston (SC) (*centre*), Simon Hunt, Thomas 'Tom' Jarvis (*centre/wing*), Liam Lonergan (*centre*), Peter McKee (SC) (*fly half*), Alastair Simmie (*fly half*), Graham Thomson (SC) (*scrum half*)]

(squad of 12)

[This tournament was the 2nd World University Rugby Sevens Championship; The World University Rugby Sevens Championship was an event run every 2 years by the Fédération Internationale du Sports Universitaire (FISU), an organisation that was founded in 1949; Great Britain were not involved in the first World University Rugby Sevens Championship, which was held at Beijing in China on 16th-17th September 2004; The Great Britain Students team was organised by the British Universities Sports Association (BUSA), an organisation that was founded in November 1994 when the UAU merged with the British Universities Sports Federation; Keith Green, Liam Middleton and Ian Minto were all appointed in May 2006; The Great Britain Students squad travelled to Italy on 2nd August 2006; Simon Hunt played for the Samurai in the Hong Kong Tens at Hong Kong Football Club on 24th-25th March 2004 and played in the Samurai team that won the Amsterdam Heineken Sevens on 20th-21st May 2006 and 19th-20th May 2007]

[**MANAGER:** *Keith Green*] [**COACHES:** *Liam Middleton* (ZI) & *Ian Minto*]

CAPTAIN: *John Houston* (SC)

First Round - Pool 'B'

[4th Aug Ukrainian Universities (*UKR*) 0 **GREAT BRITAIN STUDENTS** 38]

[*Team:*]

[*Bench:*]

[*Scorers:* **tries** by ?, ?, ?, ?, ? and ?, **conversions** by ? (4)]

[4th Aug Moroccan Universities (*MOR*) 0 **GREAT BRITAIN STUDENTS** 45]

[*Team:*]

[*Bench:*]

[*Scorers:* **tries** by ?, ?, ?, ?, ?, ? and ?, **conversions** by ? (5)]

Quarter-Final

[5th Aug ITALY STUDENTS 12 **GREAT BRITAIN STUDENTS** 24]

[*Team:*]

[*Bench:*]

[*Scorers:* **tries** by Simmie, Simon Hunt, T. Jarvis and G. Thomson (SC), **conversions** by Simmie (2)]

Semi-Final

[5th Aug Spanish Universities (*SP*) 19 **GREAT BRITAIN STUDENTS** 24]

[*Team:*]

[*Bench:*]

[*Scorers:* **tries** by Simmie, Simon Hunt, G. Thomson (SC) and Dickens (WA), **conversions** by Simmie (2)]

Final

[5th Aug FRANCE STUDENTS 33 **GREAT BRITAIN STUDENTS** 10]

[*Team:* Dickens (WA)]

[*Bench:*]

[*Scorers:* **tries** by Simmie and Lonergan]

POSITION: LOSING FINALISTS [*SILVER MEDALISTS*]

LAWRENCE HAMBLIN HENLEY INTERNATIONAL SEVENS

Henley RFC, Dry Leas, Marlow Road, Henley-on-Thames

[*Tournament squad:* James 'Jamie' Murray (SC) (*forward*), Angus Martyn (SC) (*forward*), O. Brown (SC) (never travelled as withdrew), M. Cannon (*hooker*), Llyr Lane (WA) (*scrum half*) (never travelled as withdrew, replaced by Ross Blake), Matt Vaughan (NZ) (*fly half*), Gert De Kock (SA) (*back*), Warnock (SC) (never travelled as withdrew, replaced by Carl McWilliam), Kirk King (*wing*), Malherbe (*centre*), Richard Carter (WA) (*wing*) (never travelled as withdrew, replaced by Rory Watson), Ross Blake (SC) (*scrum half/fly half*), Carl McWilliam (NZ) (*fly half*), Rory Watson (SC) (*wing*)]

(squad of 11)

[**MANAGER:** *Terry Sands*] [**COACH:** *Owen Scrimgeour* (NZ)]

CAPTAIN: *Jamie Murray* (SC)

First Round

[6th Aug Henley Hawks 0 **SAMURAI** 34]

[*Team:* J. Murray (SC), M. Cannon, Martyn (SC), Ross Blake (SC), M. Vaughan (NZ), De Kock (SA), R. Watson (SC)]

[*Bench:* Malherbe (rep), McWilliam (NZ)]

[*Scorers:* **tries** by De Kock (SA) (2), M. Vaughan (NZ) (2), Martyn (SC) and Malherbe, **conversions** by M. Vaughan (NZ) (2)]

Quarter-Final

[6th Aug British Army (*SER*) 12 **SAMURAI** 19]

[*Team:* J. Murray (SC), M. Cannon, Martyn (SC), Ross Blake (SC), ?, De Kock (SA), K. King]

[*Bench:* Malherbe, R. Watson (SC), ?]

[*Scorers:* **tries** by De Kock (SA) and Martyn (SC) (2), **conversions** by Ross Blake (SC) (2)]

Semi-Final

[6th Aug Hartpury College 12 **SAMURAI** 17]

[*Team:* J. Murray (SC), M. Cannon, Ross Blake (SC), M. Vaughan (NZ), ?, R. Watson (SC)]

[*Bench:* K. King (rep), McWilliam (NZ), ?]

[*Scorers:* **tries** by Ross Blake (SC) and M. Cannon (2), **conversion** by M. Vaughan (NZ)]

Final

[6th Aug Scorpions 24 **SAMURAI** 19]

[*Team:* J. Murray (SC), M. Cannon, Martyn (SC), Ross Blake (SC), M. Vaughan (NZ), ?, R. Watson (SC)]

[*Bench:* K. King (rep), McWilliam (NZ) (rep), ?]

[*Scorers:* **tries** by Ross Blake (SC), Martyn (SC) and J. Murray (SC), **conversions** by M. Vaughan (NZ) and McWilliam (NZ)]

POSITION: LOSING FINALISTS

NEW ZEALAND TOUR TO ENGLAND, FRANCE AND WALES 2006

FIRST INVESTEC CHALLENGE MATCH

[**HEAD COACH:** *Andy Robinson*] [**ASSISTANT COACHES:** *Brian Ashton*, *John Wells* & *Mike Ford*] [**SELECTOR:** Christopher *Robert 'Rob' Andrew*]

CAPTAIN: *Martin Corry*

5th Nov **ENGLAND*** 20 NEW ZEALAND 41

Twickenham

[*Team:* Sheridan, Chuter, Julian White, Grewcock, Kay, Corry, Moody, P. Sanderson, S. Perry, C. Hodgson, B. Cohen, Anthony Allen, Noon, Sackey, Balshaw]

[*Bench:* Andy Goode, Chris Jones, Lund (rep), Mears (rep), Peter Richards (rep), Stuart Turner, Van Gisbergen]
[*Scorers:* **tries** by Noon, B. Cohen and S. Perry, **penalty goal** by C. Hodgson, **conversion** by C. Hodgson]
[*Match to celebrate the official opening of the new South Stand at Twickenham*]
[*Rob Andrew was appointed Elite Director of Rugby on 18th August 2006 and his duties included sitting alongside the 4 England Coaches on a five man selection panel; Rob Andrew won 71 caps for England between 1985-97 and was capped for the British Lions in July 1989*]

ARGENTINE TOUR TO ENGLAND AND ITALY 2006
SECOND INVESTEC CHALLENGE MATCH

[**HEAD COACH:** *Andy Robinson*] [**ASSISTANT COACHES:** *Brian Ashton, John Wells & Mike Ford*] [**SELECTOR:** *Rob Andrew*]
CAPTAIN: *Martin Corry*
11th Nov **ENGLAND*** 18 ARGENTINA 25
Twickenham
[*Team:* Freshwater, Chuter, Julian White, Grewcock, Kay, Corry, Moody, P. Sanderson, S. Perry, C. Hodgson, B. Cohen, Anthony Allen, Noon, Sackey, Balshaw]
[*Bench:* T. Flood (rep), J. Lewsey (rep), Mears (rep), Lund (rep), Tom Palmer (2) (rep), Peter Richards (rep), Stuart Turner]
[*Scorers:* **tries** by Sackey and Balshaw, **penalty goals** by C. Hodgson and T. Flood, **conversion** by C. Hodgson]

ATKINS REMEMBRANCE RUGBY MATCH

[**NO COACH NOMINATED**]
CAPTAIN: *Andy Dalgleish*
[14th Nov COMBINED SERVICES (*SER*) 25 **BARBARIANS** 33]
Newbury RFC, Monks Lane, Newbury
[*Team:* Tom Davies (WA), Dalgleish, Cai Griffiths (WA), Mark Cornwell, Brenton, Iain Dick (WA), Jonathan Edwards (WA), Richard Morris (WA), G. Laidlaw (SC), Arwel Thomas (WA), K. Bingham, Jonathan Bell (IR), Albert Finney (IR), T. Howe (IR), N. Hallett]
[*Bench:* Dafydd Lewis (WA) (rep), B. Luxton (rep), Alan MacDonald (SC) (*flanker*), Malherbe (*centre*) (rep), S. Pope (rep), Ritchie (rep), Scully (*scrum half*) (rep)]
[*Scorers:* **tries** by Richard Morris (WA) (2), K. Bingham, Mark Cornwell and penalty try, **conversions** by N. Hallett (3) and Dafydd Lewis (WA)]
[*Match to commemorate the members of the British uniformed services who lost their lives during armed conflict*]

SOUTH AFRICAN TOUR TO IRELAND AND ENGLAND 2006
THIRD INVESTEC CHALLENGE MATCH

[**HEAD COACH:** *Andy Robinson*] [**ASSISTANT COACHES:** *Brian Ashton, John Wells & Mike Ford*] [**SELECTOR:** *Rob Andrew*]
CAPTAIN: *Martin Corry*
18th Nov **ENGLAND** 23 SOUTH AFRICA 21
Twickenham
[*Team:* Sheridan, Chuter, Julian White, Tom Palmer (2), Kay, J. Worsley, P. Sanderson, Corry, Peter Richards, C. Hodgson, B. Cohen, Noon, M. Tait, Cueto, J. Lewsey]
[*Bench:* Andy Goode (rep), T. Flood, Chris Jones (rep), Mears (rep), Moody (rep), S. Perry

(*scrum half*) (rep), Vickery (rep)]
[*Scorers:* **tries** by Cueto and Vickery, **penalty goals** by C. Hodgson (2) and Andy Goode, **conversions** by Andy Goode (2)]

FOURTH INVESTEC CHALLENGE MATCH

[**HEAD COACH:** *Andy Robinson*] [**ASSISTANT COACHES:** *Brian Ashton, John Wells & Mike Ford*] [**SELECTOR:** *Rob Andrew*]

CAPTAIN: *Martin Corry*

25th Nov **ENGLAND** 14 SOUTH AFRICA 25
Twickenham
[*Team:* Vickery, Mears, Julian White, Tom Palmer (2), Chris Jones, J. Worsley, P. Sanderson, Corry, Peter Richards, Andy Goode, B. Cohen, Noon, M. Tait, Cueto, J. Lewsey]
[*Bench:* Chuter (rep), T. Flood (rep), Kay (rep), Moody (rep), T. Payne, S. Perry (rep), Van Gisbergen]
[*Scorers:* **try** by Cueto, **penalty goals** by Andy Goode (3)]
[Andy Robinson announced his resignation on 29th November 2006]

AUSTRALIAN TOUR TO WALES, ITALY, IRELAND AND SCOTLAND 2006

[**COACH:** *Nicholas 'Nick' Mallett* (SA)]

CAPTAIN: *No captain appointed*

[29th Nov **BARBARIANS** C AUSTRALIA XV C]
Twickenham
[*Team not selected*]
[*Bench not selected*]
[*No scorers*]
[Nick Mallett was appointed on 23rd August 2006; Nick Mallett played for the Rest against an England XV in a Final England Trial Match at Twickenham on 5th January 1980, played for the S.A.R.B. President's XV against a Five Nations XV at Ellis Park Stadium, Johannesburg on 24th July 1982, was capped for South Africa in October 1984 and was appointed Coach of South Africa on 25th September 1997 before resigning on 27th September 2000]

EMIRATES AIRLINE DUBAI RUGBY SEVENS
IRB WORLD SEVENS SERIES 2006-2007 ROUND 1
EMIRATES INTERNATIONAL TROPHY

Dubai Exiles Stadium, Dubai
[*Tournament squad:* Haskell, T. Croft (*prop*), Hills (*prop*), Dominic 'Dom' Shabbo (*forward*), Abendanon (*centre/wing*), Strettle, Jack Adams (*fly half/centre*) (never travelled as withdrew, replaced by Marcel Garvey), Vilk, R. Thirlby, Gollings, Amor, David Doherty (*wing*), M. Garvey (*wing*)]
(squad of 12)
[The England squad departed for Dubai on 26th November 2006; Dom Shabbo played in the England team that reached the Final of the Commonwealth Youth Games Rugby Sevens at Bendigo, Victoria on 2nd-3rd December 2004 and played for England in the U19 World Championship in South Africa in April 2005; David Doherty played for England in the U19 World Championships in South Africa in April 2005 and Dubai in April 2006]
[**MANAGER:** *Terry Sands*] [**COACH:** *Mike Friday*] [**ASSISTANT COACH:** *Phil Greening*]

CAPTAIN: *Simon Amor*

First Round - Pool 'B'

1st Dec SCOTLAND 0 **ENGLAND** 38

[*Team:* Haskell, Shabbo, T. Croft, Amor, Gollings, Vilk, Strettle]

[*Bench:* Abendanon (rep), D. Doherty (rep), M. Garvey (rep), Hills, R. Thirlby]

[*Scorers:* **tries** by Vilk, Haskell, Strettle, Abendanon, M. Garvey and T. Croft, **conversions** by Gollings (4)]

1st Dec ZIMBABWE 0 **ENGLAND** 29

[*Team:* Hills, Vilk, T. Croft, Amor, R. Thirlby, Abendanon, D. Doherty]

[*Bench:* M. Garvey (rep), Gollings (rep), Haskell, Shabbo (rep), Strettle]

[*Scorers:* **tries** by Vilk (2), R. Thirlby, M. Garvey and D. Doherty, **conversions** by Amor and Gollings]

1st Dec FRANCE 10 **ENGLAND** 19

[*Team:* Haskell, Vilk, Hills, Amor, Gollings, Abendanon, Strettle]

[*Bench:* T. Croft, D. Doherty, M. Garvey (rep), Shabbo (rep), R. Thirlby (rep)]

[*Scorers:* **tries** by Gollings (2) and Abendanon, **conversions** by Gollings (2)]

Quarter-Final

2nd Dec AUSTRALIA 5 **ENGLAND** 21

[*Team:* Haskell, Vilk, T. Croft, Amor, Gollings, Abendanon, Strettle]

[*Bench:* D. Doherty (rep), M. Garvey, Hills (rep), Shabbo, R. Thirlby (rep)]

[*Scorers:* **tries** by Strettle (2) and Gollings, **conversions** by Gollings (3)]

Semi-Final

2nd Dec SOUTH AFRICA 19 **ENGLAND** 0

[*Team:* Haskell, Vilk, T. Croft, Amor, Gollings, Abendanon, Strettle]

[*Bench:* D. Doherty, M. Garvey, Hills (rep), Shabbo (rep), R. Thirlby (rep)]

[*No scorers*]

POSITION: LOSING SEMI-FINALISTS

[England scored 12 competition points in this Round of the 2006-2007 IRB World Sevens Series]

SOUTH AFRICAN TOUR TO IRELAND AND ENGLAND 2006

[**COACH:** *Bob Dwyer* (AU)] [**ASSISTANT COACH:** *Bryan Redpath* (SC)]

CAPTAIN: *Lawrence Dallaglio*

[3rd Dec **WORLD XV** 7 SOUTH AFRICA XV 32]

Walkers Stadium, Filbert Way, Leicester

[*Team:* Hewett (NZ), Fabio Ongaro (IT), C. Visagie (SA), S. Shaw, Alister 'Al' Campbell (AU), Michael Owen (WA), Jonny O'Connor (IR), Dallaglio, J. Marshall (NZ), T. Castaignède (FR), Andrew 'Drew' Mitchell (AU), Andrew 'Andy' Farrell, Ryan Cross (AU), Clinton Schiscofske (AU), Matt Perry]

[*Bench:* Alberto *Vernet* Basualdo (AR) (*hooker*) (rep), Gareth Cooper (WA) (rep), Pablo Gómez Cora (AR) (*centre*) (rep), David Croft (AU) (*flanker*) (rep), Delport (SA) (*full back*) (rep), Nicholas 'Nic' Henderson (AU) (*prop*) (rep), Takuro Miuchi (JAP) (*number 8*) (rep)]

[*Scorers:* **try** by D. Mitchell (AU), **conversion** by Schiscofske (AU)]

[Match arranged to commemorate the 100th Anniversary of the first South African tour to the British Isles in 1906]

[Bob Dwyer and Bryan Redpath were both appointed on 24th October 2006; Bryan Redpath won 60 caps for Scotland between 1993-2003]

EMIRATES AIRLINE SOUTH AFRICA SEVENS
IRB WORLD SEVENS SERIES 2006-2007 ROUND 2

Outeniqua Park Stadium, George

[*Tournament squad:* Haskell, T. Croft, Hills, Shabbo, Danny Gray (*fly half*), Charlie Amesbury (*wing*), M. Garvey (injured during the tournament), Vilk, R. Thirlby, Gollings, Amor, D. Doherty]

(squad of 12)

[Danny Gray and Charlie Amesbury played for Samurai St George in the Dubai International Invitation Rugby Sevens on 30th November-2nd December 2006; Marcel Garvey played in the Samurai team that won the Amsterdam Heineken Sevens on 19th-20th May 2007]

[On 29th November 2006 Mike Friday announced that he would be leaving his post of Coach after the South Africa Sevens at George on 8th-9th December 2006; Terry Sands resigned in December 2006; Mike Friday was appointed Assistant Coach of the England Women Sevens team on 21st November 2007]

[**MANAGER:** *Terry Sands*] [**COACH:** *Mike Friday*] [**ASSISTANT COACH:** *Phil Greening*]

CAPTAIN: *Simon Amor*

First Round - Pool 'B'

8th Dec WALES 14 **ENGLAND*** 14

[*Team:* Hills, Vilk, T. Croft, Amor, Gollings, R. Thirlby, D. Doherty]

[*Bench:* Amesbury, M. Garvey (rep), Danny Gray, Haskell (rep), Shabbo (rep)]

[*Scorers:* **tries** by R. Thirlby and D. Doherty, **conversions** by Gollings (2)]

8th Dec PORTUGAL 5 **ENGLAND** 58

[*Team:* Hills, Vilk, Haskell, Amor, Danny Gray, R. Thirlby, M. Garvey]

[*Bench:* Amesbury (rep), T. Croft, D. Doherty (rep), Gollings, Shabbo (rep)]

[*Scorers:* **tries** by Vilk, M. Garvey (3), R. Thirlby (2), Amor, Amesbury and D. Doherty (2), **conversions** by Danny Gray and Amor (3)]

8th Dec ARGENTINA 7 **ENGLAND** 26

[*Team:* Hills, Vilk, Haskell, Amor, Danny Gray, R. Thirlby, D. Doherty]

[*Bench:* Amesbury (rep), T. Croft (rep), M. Garvey, Gollings (rep), Shabbo]

[*Scorers:* **tries** by Hills, D. Doherty (2) and R. Thirlby, **conversions** by Amor (3)]

Quarter-Final

9th Dec SAMOA 0 **ENGLAND** 24

[*Team:* Hills, Vilk, Haskell, Amor, Danny Gray, R. Thirlby, Amesbury]

[*Bench:* T. Croft (rep), D. Doherty, Gollings (rep), Shabbo (rep)]

[*Scorers:* **tries** by Hills, Haskell (2) and Shabbo, **conversions** by Gollings (2)]

Semi-Final

9th Dec SOUTH AFRICA 10 **ENGLAND*** 7

[*Team:* Hills, Vilk, Haskell, Amor, Danny Gray, Gollings, Amesbury]

[*Bench:* T. Croft, D. Doherty, Shabbo]

[*Scorers:* **try** by Hills, **conversion** by Gollings]

POSITION: LOSING SEMI-FINALISTS

[England scored 12 competition points in this Round of the 2006-2007 IRB World Sevens Series]

2007
OTHER MATCHES
NEW ZEALAND INTERNATIONAL SEVENS
IRB WORLD SEVENS SERIES 2006-2007 ROUND 3

WestpacTrust Stadium, Wellington
[*Tournament squad:* Ben Russell (2), Roques, Hills, Narraway, Danny Gray, Amesbury, N. Mordt, Vilk, R. Thirlby, M. Foster (*centre/wing*), Amor, David Smith (2) (*wing*)]
(squad of 12)
[Ben Gollings was unavailable for this tournament due to club commitments; The England squad departed for New Zealand on 28th January 2007; Tony Roques captained Samurai St George in the Dubai International Invitation Rugby Sevens on 30th November-2nd December 2006]
[Ben Ryan was appointed on 13th December 2006; Craig Townsend was appointed in January 2007; Craig Townsend was the brother of Gregor Townsend]
[**MANAGER:** *Craig Townsend* (SC)] [**COACH:** *Ben Ryan*] [**ASSISTANT COACH:** *Phil Greening*]
CAPTAIN: *Simon Amor*
First Round - Pool 'C'
2nd Feb SCOTLAND 12 **ENGLAND** 33
[*Team:* Hills, Vilk, Narraway, Amor, Danny Gray, M. Foster, Amesbury]
[*Bench:* N. Mordt, Roques (rep), Ben Russell (2) (rep), David Smith (2), R. Thirlby (rep)]
[*Scorers:* **tries** by Hills (2), Amor, R. Thirlby and Vilk, **conversions** by Amor (4)]
2nd Feb PAPUA NEW GUINEA 7 **ENGLAND** 22
[*Team:* Ben Russell (2), Vilk, Roques, Amor, N. Mordt, R. Thirlby, David Smith (2)]
[*Bench:* Amesbury (rep), M. Foster, Danny Gray, Hills (rep), Narraway]
[*Scorers:* **tries** by David Smith, R. Thirlby, Vilk and Amesbury, **conversion** by Amor]
2nd Feb SAMOA 19 **ENGLAND*** 12
[*Team:* Hills, Vilk, Narraway, Amor, Danny Gray, R. Thirlby, Amesbury]
[*Bench:* M. Foster, N. Mordt (rep), Roques (rep), Ben Russell (2) (rep), David Smith (2)]
[*Scorers:* **tries** by Danny Gray and N. Mordt, **conversion** by Amor]
Quarter-Final
3rd Feb NEW ZEALAND 14 **ENGLAND*** 7
[*Team:* Roques, Vilk, Ben Russell (2), Amor, Danny Gray, N. Mordt, R. Thirlby]
[*Bench:* Amesbury (rep), M. Foster, Hills, Narraway, David Smith (2)]
[*Scorers:* **try** by Danny Gray, **conversion** by Amor]
[Plate Semi-Final:]
[3rd Feb CANADA 7 **ENGLAND** 29]
[*Team:* Ben Russell (2), Vilk, Roques, Amor, Danny Gray, N. Mordt, R. Thirlby]
[*Bench:* Amesbury (rep), M. Foster (rep), Hills, Narraway, David Smith (2) (rep)]
[*Scorers:* **tries** by Danny Gray (2), R. Thirlby (2) and Roques, **conversions** by Amor (2)]
[Plate Final:]
[3rd Feb FRANCE 12 **ENGLAND** 21]
[*Team:* Ben Russell (2), Vilk, Roques, Amor, Danny Gray, N. Mordt, R. Thirlby]
[*Bench:* Amesbury (rep), M. Foster (rep), Hills, Narraway, David Smith (2)]
[*Scorers:* **tries** by Amor, Roques and Danny Gray, **conversions** by Amor (3)]
POSITION: LOSING QUARTER-FINALISTS [*PLATE WINNERS*]

[England scored 8 competition points in this Round of the 2006-2007 IRB World Sevens Series]

6 NATIONS CHAMPIONSHIP

[**HEAD COACH:** *Brian Ashton*] [**ASSISTANT COACHES:** *John Wells & Mike Ford*]

CAPTAIN: *Phil Vickery*

3rd Feb **ENGLAND** 42 SCOTLAND 20
Twickenham
[*Team:* Freshwater, Chuter, Vickery, L. Deacon, Grewcock, J. Worsley, Lund, Corry, Harry Ellis, Jonny Wilkinson, Jason Robinson, A. Farrell, Tindall, J. Lewsey, O. Morgan]
[*Bench:* T. Flood (rep), Mears (rep), Tom Palmer (2), Tom Rees (rep), Peter Richards, M. Tait, Julian White (rep)]
[*Scorers:* **tries** by Jason Robinson (2), Jonny Wilkinson and Lund, **penalty goals** by Jonny Wilkinson (5), **drop goal** by Jonny Wilkinson, **conversions** by Jonny Wilkinson (2)]

10th Feb **ENGLAND** 20 ITALY 7
Twickenham
[*Team:* Freshwater, Chuter, Vickery, L. Deacon, Grewcock, Nick Easter, Lund, Corry, Harry Ellis, Jonny Wilkinson, Jason Robinson, A. Farrell, Tindall, J. Lewsey, Balshaw]
[*Bench:* T. Flood (rep), Mears (rep), Tom Palmer (2) (rep), S. Perry, Tom Rees (rep), M. Tait (rep), Julian White (rep)]
[*Scorers:* **try** by Jason Robinson, **penalty goals** by Jonny Wilkinson (5)]

24th Feb IRELAND 43 **ENGLAND** 13
Croke Park, Dublin
[*Team:* Freshwater, Chuter, Vickery, L. Deacon, Grewcock, J. Worsley, Lund, Corry, Harry Ellis, Jonny Wilkinson, Strettle, A. Farrell, Tindall, J. Lewsey, O. Morgan]
[*Bench:* T. Flood, Mears (rep), Tom Palmer (2) (rep), S. Perry (rep), Tom Rees (rep), M. Tait (rep), Julian White (rep)]
[*Scorers:* **try** by Strettle, **penalty goals** by Jonny Wilkinson (2), **conversion** by Jonny Wilkinson]

CAPTAIN: *Mike Catt*

11th Mar **ENGLAND** 26 FRANCE 18
Twickenham
[*Team:* T. Payne, Chuter, Julian White, Corry, Tom Palmer (2), J. Worsley, Tom Rees, Easter, Harry Ellis, T. Flood, Jason Robinson, M. Catt, Tindall, Strettle, J. Lewsey]
[*Bench:* L. Deacon (rep), Geraghty (rep), Lund (rep), Mears, S. Perry (rep), M. Tait (rep), Stuart Turner]
[*Scorers:* **tries** by T. Flood and Tindall, **penalty goals** by T. Flood (3) and Geraghty, **conversions** by T. Flood and Geraghty]

CAPTAIN: *Mike Catt* [*Jason Robinson took over when Mike Catt was injured in the 2nd half*]

17th Mar WALES 27 **ENGLAND*** 18
Millennium Stadium, Cardiff
[*Team:* T. Payne, Chuter, Julian White, Corry, Tom Palmer (2), Haskell, Tom Rees, J. Worsley, Harry Ellis, T. Flood, Jason Robinson, M. Catt, M. Tait, Strettle, Cueto]
[*Bench:* L. Deacon (rep), Geraghty (rep), Lund (rep), Mears (rep), Noon, S. Perry (rep), Stuart Turner (rep)]
[*Scorers:* **tries** by Harry Ellis and Jason Robinson, **penalty goal** by T. Flood, **drop goal** by T. Flood, **conversion** by T. Flood]

POSITION: **3RD 6 +4 CC** [*France 8 +69*, Ireland 8 +65 TC MT, Italy 4 -53, Wales 2 -27, Scotland 2 -58]

FANTASY: ***3RD 8 CC***

[Brian Ashton was appointed Head Coach on 20th December 2006]

OTHER MATCHES

U21 6 NATIONS CHAMPIONSHIP

[**MANAGER:** *John Elliott*] [**COACH:** *Nigel Redman*] [**ASSISTANT COACH:** *Mark Mapletoft*]

CAPTAIN: *Danny Care*

[2nd Feb **ENGLAND U20** 31 SCOTLAND U20 5]

Recreation Ground, Bath

[*Team:* Daniel 'Dan' Cole, Matthew 'Matt' Mullan, Jack Forster, David 'Dave' Attwood, Phil Hoy, Alex Shaw, Chevvy Pennycook, David Tait, Care, Sebastian 'Seb' Jewell, Selorm Kuadey, Adam Powell, Adam Thompstone, Oliver 'Ollie' Dodge, Frankie Neale]

[*Bench:* Charles 'Charlie' Beech (*prop*) (rep), Matthew 'Matt' Cox (*flanker/number 8*) (rep), Hugo Ellis (*number 8*) (rep), Charlie Gower (*centre*) (rep), Ross McMillan (*hooker*) (rep), Tom Parker (2) (*scrum half*) (rep), James Tirrell (*scrum half/full back*) (rep)]

[*Scorers:* **tries** by D. Tait (2), Tom Parker, M. Cox and Hugo Ellis, **conversions** by Neale (3)]

[9th Feb **ENGLAND U20** 30 ITALY U21 10]

Recreation Ground, Bath

[*Team:* C. Beech, Mullan, Mercey, Attwood, Hoy, A. Shaw, Pennycook, D. Tait, Care, S. Jewell, Kuadey, Adam Powell, Tom Youngs, O. Dodge, D. Doherty]

[*Bench:* M. Cox (rep), Jack Forster (*prop*) (rep), Hugo Ellis (rep), Neale (*fly half/full back*), Tom Parker (2), Tom Standfield (*hooker*) (rep), Tirrell (rep)]

[*Scorers:* **tries** by O. Dodge, Adam Powell, C. Beech and S. Jewell, **penalty goal** by D. Doherty, **drop goal** by Care, **conversions** by D. Doherty (2)]

[23rd Feb IRELAND U20 13 **ENGLAND U20** 6]

Dubarry Park, Athlone

[*Team:* C. Beech, Mullan, D. Cole, Attwood, Hoy, A. Shaw, Pennycook, D. Tait, Care, S. Jewell, Kuadey, Adam Powell, T. Youngs, O. Dodge, D. Doherty]

[*Bench:* Richard Bolt (*scrum half*), M. Cox (rep), Hugo Ellis (rep), Mercey, Neale (rep), Standfield (rep), Jordan Turner-Hall (*centre*) (rep)]

[*Scorers:* **penalty goals** by D. Doherty (2)]

[9th Mar **ENGLAND U20** 13 FRANCE U21 32]

Franklin's Gardens, Northampton

[*Team:* D. Cole, Mullan, Mercey, Attwood, Hoy, M. Cox, Andrew 'Andy' Saull, Hugo Ellis, Care, S. Jewell, Kuadey, Adam Powell, Dominic 'Dom' Waldouck, O. Dodge, D. Doherty]

[*Bench:* C. Beech (rep), Luke Cozens (*fly half*) (rep), R. McMillan (rep), Pennycook (*flanker*) (rep), Danny Pointon (*scrum half*), A. Shaw (*flanker/number 8*), T. Youngs (*centre*) (rep)]

[*Scorers:* **try** by penalty try, **penalty goals** by D. Doherty (2), **conversion** by D. Doherty]

[16th Mar WALES U20 21 **ENGLAND U20*** 21]

Rodney Parade, Newport

[*Team:* D. Cole, Mullan, Mercey, Attwood, Hoy, A. Shaw, Saull, Hugo Ellis, Care, Cozens, T. Youngs, Adam Powell, Waldouck, D. Doherty, David Smith (2)]

[*Bench:* C. Beech (rep), M. Cox, O. Dodge (*wing*) (rep), R. McMillan (rep), Pennycook (rep), Pointon (rep), Ben Thomas (*lock*)]

[*Scorers:* **tries** by D. Doherty and T. Youngs, **penalty goals** by Cozens (3), **conversion** by Cozens]

POSITION: **3RD 5 +20** [*Ireland 10 +46 GS TC*, France 8 +127, Italy 4 -52, Wales 3 +19, Scotland 0 -160]

FANTASY: ***3RD 6***

[On 26th May 2006 it was announced that the Four Home Unions had agreed to enter U20 teams in the 2007 U21 Six Nations Championship]

[Nigel Redman was appointed on 3rd December 2006; On 13th December 2006 Mark Mapletoft was appointed to become England U20 Assistant Coach on 1st January 2007; Mark Mapletoft was capped for England in June 1997]

ENGLAND SAXONS INTERNATIONAL MATCHES

[**COACH:** *Jim Mallinder*] [**ASSISTANT COACH:** *Dorian West*]

CAPTAIN: *Jamie Noon*

[2nd Feb **ENGLAND SAXONS** 34 ITALY A 5]

Sandy Park Stadium, Sandy Park Way, Exeter

[*Team:* N. Wood, Titterrell, Stuart Turner, Schofield, Alex Brown, Haskell, Scaysbrook, J. Crane, S. Perry, Geraghty, Abendanon, Barkley, Noon, Strettle, Mike Brown]

[*Bench:* Easter (*flanker/number 8*) (rep), D. Hartley (rep), Chris Jones (rep), Mercey (rep), Varndell (rep), Nouredienne Albert Colin 'Chev' Walker (*centre*) (rep), Wigglesworth (rep)]

[*Scorers:* **tries** by Abendanon, Mike Brown (2), Schofield and D. Hartley, **penalty goal** by Geraghty, **conversions** by Geraghty (3)]

CAPTAIN: *Mike Catt*

[9th Feb IRELAND A 5 **ENGLAND SAXONS** 32]

Ravenhill Park, Belfast

[*Team:* T. Payne, D. Hartley, Stuart Turner, Schofield, Alex Brown, Chris Jones, Scaysbrook, J. Crane, Peter Richards, Geraghty, Strettle, M. Catt, C. Walker, Cueto, Mike Brown]

[*Bench:* Abendanon, Barkley (rep), Haskell (rep), Titterrell (rep), Wigglesworth (rep), N. Wood (rep), B. Woods (rep)]

[*Scorers:* **tries** by D. Hartley, Haskell, Strettle and Wigglesworth, **penalty goal** by Geraghty, **drop goal** by M. Catt, **conversions** by Geraghty (3)]

[Jim Mallinder was appointed on 24th November 2006; Dorian West was appointed on 2nd January 2007]

ENGLAND STUDENTS MATCHES

[**MANAGER:** *Tony Lanaway*] [**COACH:** *Steve Hill*] [**ASSISTANT COACH:** *Patrick Jerram*]

CAPTAIN: *No captain appointed*

[10th Feb SPAIN A C **ENGLAND STUDENTS** C]

Campo Central de la Ciudad Universitaria, Madrid

[*Team not selected*]

[*Bench not selected*]

[*No scorers*]

CAPTAIN: *Greg Irvin*

[23rd Feb FRANCE STUDENTS 6 **ENGLAND STUDENTS** 8]

Stade Lucien Desprats, Cahors

[*Team:* Kevin Davis, Joe Clark, Liffchak, Ian Kench, Chance, Douglas Abbott, Thomas 'Tom' Malaney, Irvin, T. Henry, Simmie, Ryan Owen, T. Gregory, Tibbott, T. Jarvis, Alex *Jack* Smales]

[*Bench:* R. Anderson (rep), Rory Damant (*fly half/centre*) (rep), Tom George (*number 8*) (rep), Dan James (rep), Richard 'Ricky' Lutton (*prop*) (rep), C. Pilgrim (rep), Duncan Steele (*fly half/centre/full back*) (rep)]

[*Scorers:* **try** by Simmie, **penalty goal** by T. Henry]
[9th Mar **ENGLAND STUDENTS** 19 FRANCE STUDENTS 10]
Iffley Road, Oxford
[*Team:* K. Davis, Joe Clark, Liffchak, Kench, Chance, D. Abbott, Malaney, Irvin, T. Henry, Simmie, R. Owen, T. Gregory, Tibbott, T. Jarvis, J. Smales]
[*Bench:* R. Anderson (rep), Damant (rep), T. George (rep), Dan James (rep), Lutton (rep), C. Pilgrim (rep), D. Steele (rep)]
[*Scorers:* **try** by R. Owen, **penalty goals** by Simmie (4), **conversion** by Simmie]
[*There was an England Students Final Trial at Loughborough University on 10th January 2007*]
[*This was Tony Lanaway's 12th and final season as Manager of England Students since he was appointed in 1996!; Patrick Jerram was appointed on 9th January 2007*]

STEINLAGER USA SEVENS
IRB WORLD SEVENS SERIES 2006-2007 ROUND 4

PETCO Park, San Diego
[*Tournament squad:* John Brake (*back/forward*), Roques, Hills, Shabbo, Danny Gray, Amesbury, N. Mordt, Vilk, R. Thirlby, M. Foster, Amor, David Smith (2)]
(*squad of 12*)
[*Will Matthews and Ben Russell (2) were unavailable for this tournament due to injury; Ben Gollings was unavailable due to club commitments; John Brake played for Samurai St George in the Dubai International Invitation Rugby Sevens on 30th November-2nd December 2006*]
[*Phil Greening resigned after this tournament*]
[**MANAGER:** *Craig Townsend* (SC)] [**COACH:** *Ben Ryan*] [**ASSISTANT COACH:** *Phil Greening*]
CAPTAIN: *Simon Amor*
First Round - Pool 'C'
10th Feb KENYA 14 **ENGLAND** 26
[*Team:* Hills, Vilk, Roques, Amor, Danny Gray, N. Mordt, R. Thirlby]
[*Bench:* Amesbury, Brake, M. Foster (rep), Shabbo (rep), David Smith (2) (rep)]
[*Scorers:* **tries** by R. Thirlby (2), Vilk and Shabbo, **conversions** by Amor (3)]
10th Feb USA 10 **ENGLAND** 26
[*Team:* Hills, Vilk, Brake, Amor, Danny Gray, Amesbury, R. Thirlby]
[*Bench:* M. Foster (rep), N. Mordt, Roques, Shabbo, David Smith (2)]
[*Scorers:* **tries** by Amor (2) and Amesbury (2), **conversions** by Amor (3)]
10th Feb AUSTRALIA 19 **ENGLAND** 14
[*Team:* Hills, Vilk, Shabbo, Amor, Danny Gray, R. Thirlby, M. Foster]
[*Bench:* Amesbury (rep), Brake (rep), N. Mordt (rep), Roques, David Smith (2)]
[*Scorers:* **tries** by R. Thirlby (2), **conversions** by Amor (2)]
Quarter-Final
11th Feb NEW ZEALAND 19 **ENGLAND*** 7
[*Team:* Hills, Vilk, Roques, Amor, Danny Gray, N. Mordt, R. Thirlby]
[*Bench:* Amesbury (rep), Brake, M. Foster, Shabbo (rep), David Smith (2)]
[*Scorers:* **try** by Amesbury, **conversion** by Amor]
[Plate Semi-Final:]
[11th Feb SOUTH AFRICA 21 **ENGLAND*** 14 **]**
[*Team:* Shabbo, Vilk, Roques, Amor, Danny Gray, N. Mordt, Amesbury]
[*Bench:* Brake, M. Foster, Hills, David Smith (2)]

[*Scorers:* **tries** by Shabbo (2), **conversions** by Amor (2)]
POSITION: LOSING QUARTER-FINALISTS [*PLATE SEMI-FINALISTS*]
[England scored 4 competition points in this Round of the 2006-2007 IRB World Sevens Series]

AIB CLUB INTERNATIONAL MATCH

[**CHAIRMAN OF SELECTORS:** *Peter Hartley*] [**MANAGER:** *Jim Robinson*] [**ASSISTANT MANAGER:** *Danny Hodgson*] [**COACH:** *Ben Ryan*] [**ASSISTANT COACH:** *David 'Dave' Baldwin*]

CAPTAIN: *Duncan Cormack*

[23rd Feb IRELAND CLUB XV 20 **ENGLAND COUNTIES*** 17]
Donnybrook, Dublin

[*Team:* D. Cormack, Liam Wordley, W. Reed, Snowball, J. Winterbottom, Mike Blakeburn, N. Spence, T. Hayman, Barr, M. Leek, Mark Sweeney (2), Mark Bedworth, Malherbe, Alastair Bressington, N. Hallett]

[*Bench:* Craig Aikman (*scrum half*) (rep), David 'Dave' Allen (*flanker*) (rep), Bevon Armitage (*centre/wing*) (rep), Tom Doran (*hooker*) (rep), Matthew 'Matt' Owen (*lock*) (rep), Tristan Roberts (*fly half*) (rep), James Tideswell (*prop*) (rep)]

[*Scorers:* **tries** by Malherbe and Bedworth, **penalty goal** by N. Hallett, **conversions** by N. Hallett (2)]

[Dave Baldwin was appointed on 12th September 2006; Dave Baldwin toured Argentina with England in May-June 1997]

JEAN-CLAUDE BAQUÉ SHIELD MATCH

[**CHAIRMAN OF SELECTORS:** *Peter Hartley*] [**MANAGER:** *Jim Robinson*] [**ASSISTANT MANAGER:** *Danny Hodgson*] [**COACH:** *Ben Ryan*] [**ASSISTANT COACH:** *Dave Baldwin*]

CAPTAIN: *Duncan Cormack*

[10th Mar **ENGLAND COUNTIES** 41 FRANCE AMATEURS 10]
Rectory Field, Charlton Road, Blackheath

[*Team:* D. Cormack, L. Wordley, W. Reed, Snowball, J. Winterbottom, Blakeburn, N. Spence, T. Hayman, Barr, M. Leek, Mark Sweeney (2), Bedworth, Malherbe, Bressington, N. Hallett]

[*Bench:* Aikman (rep), D. Allen (rep), B. Armitage (rep), Doran (rep), Matt Owen (rep), T. Roberts (rep), Tideswell (rep)]

[*Scorers:* **tries** by N. Hallett (2), Bedworth, Bressington, W. Reed and D. Allen, **penalty goal** by N. Hallett, **conversions** by N. Hallett (4)]

[Ben Ryan resigned on 27th March 2007 so that he could concentrate on his coaching roles with the RFU National Academy and the England Sevens team]

FIRST ARMY CENTENARY MATCH

[NO COACH NOMINATED]

CAPTAIN: *John Blaikie* (NZ)

[21st Mar Army (*SER*) 48 **OXBRIDGE XV** 24]
Army Rugby Stadium, Queen's Avenue, Aldershot

[*Team:* Oliver 'Ollie' Tomaszczyk (*prop*), Richard Schwikkard (SA) (*prop*), John Blaikie (NZ) (*lock*), Chance, Craig McMahon (AU) (*fly half*), Tombleson, Tim Catling (*centre*)]

[*Bench:*]

[*Scorers:* **tries** by Tombleson (2) and Chance, **penalty goal** by McMahon (AU), **conversions** by McMahon (AU) (2) and T. Catling]

[First match to commemorate the 100th Anniversary of the foundation of the Army Rugby Union in 1906]

CATHAY PACIFIC/CREDIT SUISSE HONG KONG SEVENS
IRB WORLD SEVENS SERIES 2006-2007 ROUND 5

Hong Kong Stadium, Eastern Hospital Road, So Kon Po, Hong Kong
[*Tournament squad:* T. Williams, Roques, David Seymour, N. Mordt, Ben Russell (2), Amesbury, James Brooks, Vilk, Care, J. Adams, Amor, D. Doherty]
(squad of 12)
[Ben Gollings was unavailable for this tournament due to club commitments; Isoa Damu in original training squad of 13 but withdrew due to injury; The England squad arrived in Hong Kong on 26th March 2007]
[**MANAGER:** *Craig Townsend* (SC)] [**COACH:** *Ben Ryan*]
CAPTAIN: *Simon Amor*
First Round - Pool 'E'
30th Mar HONG KONG 7 **ENGLAND** 38
[*Team:* Ben Russell (2), Vilk, David Seymour, Amor, Care, D. Doherty, T. Williams]
[*Bench:* J. Adams (rep), Amesbury, James Brooks, N. Mordt, Roques (rep)]
[*Scorers:* **tries** by T. Williams, Amor, Vilk, Care (2) and D. Doherty, **conversions** by Amor (4)]
31st Mar KOREA 14 **ENGLAND** 38
[*Team:* David Seymour, N. Mordt, Roques, Amor, James Brooks, J. Adams, Amesbury]
[*Bench:* Care (rep), D. Doherty, Ben Russell (2) (rep), Vilk, T. Williams (rep)]
[*Scorers:* **tries** by Amesbury (4), N. Mordt and J. Adams, **conversions** by Amor (4)]
31st Mar ARGENTINA 14 **ENGLAND** 19
[*Team:* Ben Russell (2), Vilk, David Seymour, Amor, James Brooks, J. Adams, D. Doherty]
[*Bench:* Amesbury, Care (rep), N. Mordt (rep), Roques, T. Williams (rep)]
[*Scorers:* **tries** by Amor and James Brooks (2), **conversions** by Amor (2)]
Quarter-Final
1st April NEW ZEALAND 26 **ENGLAND** 0
[*Team:* Ben Russell (2), Vilk, David Seymour, Amor, James Brooks, J. Adams, Amesbury]
[*Bench:* Care (rep), D. Doherty (rep), N. Mordt, Roques, T. Williams (rep)]
[*No scorers*]
POSITION: LOSING QUARTER-FINALISTS
[England scored 8 competition points in this Round of the 2006-2007 IRB World Sevens Series]

SECOND ARMY CENTENARY MATCH

[**COACH:** *Zinzan Brooke* (NZ)]
CAPTAIN: *Joe Roff* (AU)
[4th April Army (*SER*) 0 **BARBARIANS** 14]
Stoop Memorial Ground, Langhorn Drive, Twickenham
[*Team:* Justin Fitzpatrick (IR), Steve Scott (SC), David 'Dai' Maddocks (WA), G. Robson, Oliver 'Ollie' Hodge, Craig Hammond, Tom Johnson, Sherriff, Stuart-Smith, Gonzalo Quesada (AR), Roff (AU), Matt Cornwell, Maggs (IR), Thompstone, N. Hallett]
[*Bench:* Brennan (rep), Paul Clark (*lock*) (rep), Dalgleish (rep), Finney (IR) (*centre*) (rep), S. Jewell (*fly half/centre*) (rep), W. Reed (rep), Mark Waugh (IR) (*flanker*) (rep)]
[*Scorers:* **tries** by Thompstone and G. Robson, **conversions** by Quesada (AR) (2)]
[Second match to commemorate the 100th Anniversary of the foundation of the Army Rugby Union]
[Zinzan Brooke was appointed on 23rd March 2007]

ADELAIDE SEVENS
IRB WORLD SEVENS SERIES 2006-2007 ROUND 6

Adelaide Oval, Adelaide
[*Tournament squad: Isoa Damu*(damu) (*forward*), Roques, Hills, Brake, Ben Russell (2), Amesbury, James Brooks, Vilk, Care, J. Adams, Amor, D. Doherty]
(squad of 12)
[Ben Gollings was unavailable for this tournament due to club commitments; Isoa Damu was born in Fiji but qualified for England after completing a residency period of 3 years as part of the British Army!; Simon Amor was the tournament captain; The England squad arrived in Australia on 3rd April 2007; Isoa Damu played in the British Army team that won the Middlesex Sevens at Twickenham on 14th August 2004, played for the Combined Services against the Barbarians at Aldershot on 9th November 2004 and played for Samurai St George in the Dubai International Invitation Rugby Sevens on 30th November-2nd December 2006]
[MANAGER: *Craig Townsend* (SC)] **[COACH:** *Ben Ryan*]
CAPTAIN: *Simon Amor*
First Round - Pool 'A'
7th April TONGA 12 **ENGLAND** 5
[*Team:* Damu, Vilk, Ben Russell (2), Amor, James Brooks, J. Adams, Amesbury]
[*Bench:* Brake (rep), Care (rep), D. Doherty, Hills (rep), Roques]
[*Scorers:* **try** by Amor]
CAPTAIN: *Tony Roques*
7th April CANADA 12 **ENGLAND** 31
[*Team:* Damu, Hills, Roques, Care, James Brooks, Brake, D. Doherty]
[*Bench:* J. Adams, Amesbury (rep), Amor, Ben Russell (2) (rep), Vilk (rep)]
[*Scorers:* **tries** by Damu (2), James Brooks, Amesbury and Care, **conversions** by Care (3)]
CAPTAIN: *Simon Amor*
7th April FIJI 12 **ENGLAND** 20
[*Team:* Damu, Vilk, Ben Russell (2), Amor, Care, Brake, Amesbury]
[*Bench:* J. Adams, James Brooks (rep), D. Doherty, Hills, Roques]
[*Scorers:* **tries** by Care, Amesbury and Brake, **penalty goal** by Amor, **conversion** by Amor]
Quarter-Final
8th April KENYA 17 **ENGLAND*** 12
[*Team:* Damu, Vilk, Ben Russell (2), Amor, Care, Brake, Amesbury]
[*Bench:* J. Adams, James Brooks (rep), D. Doherty, Hills, Roques]
[*Scorers:* **tries** by Damu (2), **conversion** by Amor]
[Plate Semi-Final:]
[8th April AUSTRALIA 26 **ENGLAND** 21]
[*Team:* Damu, Hills, Roques, Amor, Care, J. Adams, Amesbury]
[*Bench:* Brake (rep), James Brooks, D. Doherty (rep), Ben Russell (2) (rep), Vilk]
[*Scorers:* **tries** by Care (2) and Damu, **conversions** by Amor (3)]
POSITION: LOSING QUARTER-FINALISTS [*PLATE SEMI-FINALISTS*]
[England scored 4 competition points in this Round of the 2006-2007 IRB World Sevens Series]

BARCLAYS CHURCHILL CUP

England

[*Other squad members:* Balshaw (withdrew), Brooker, Diggin (*wing*) (released after first match), A. Jarvis, Lipman (released after first match), K. Roche (released after first match), David Seymour (released after first match), Skirving (*number 8*) (withdrew)]

(squad of 36)

[Iain Balshaw and Ben Skirving initially selected for the original squad of 38, but both then withdrew without being replaced on 8th May and 15th May 2007 respectively as they were now required to join the simultaneous England tour of South Africa; Neal Hatley was the tournament captain]

[Jim Mallinder and Dorian West both resigned on 8th June 2007]

(During the First Round a bonus point was awarded for scoring 4 or more tries in a match and for losing by seven points or less)

[**COACH:** *Jim Mallinder*] [**ASSISTANT COACH:** *Dorian West*]

CAPTAIN: *Neal Hatley* [*Phil Dowson took over when Neal Hatley was substituted in the 1st half*]

First Round - Pool 'A'

[18th May **ENGLAND SAXONS** 51 USA 3 **BP**]

Edgeley Park, Hardcastle Road, Edgeley, Stockport

[*Team:* N. Hatley, D. Paice, John Brooks, Blaze, Jim Evans, Dowson, W. Skinner, J. Crane, Wigglesworth, R. Lamb, Ojo, Geraghty, K. Sorrell, Scarbrough, D. Armitage]

[*Bench:* L. Dickson (rep), Jack Forster (rep), N. Kennedy (rep), Mercey (rep), N. Mordt (rep), M. Thompson (rep), B. Woods (rep)]

[*Scorers:* **tries** by Ojo, J. Crane (2), D. Armitage (2), Jim Evans, Jack Forster, Dowson and L. Dickson, **conversions** by R. Lamb (3)]

CAPTAIN: *Neal Hatley* [*Phil Dowson took over when Neal Hatley was substituted in the 2nd half*]

[28th May **ENGLAND SAXONS** 18 SCOTLAND A 3]

Twickenham

[*Team:* N. Hatley, D. Paice, John Brooks, Blaze, Jim Evans, Haskell, W. Skinner, Dowson, Wigglesworth, Daniel 'Danny' Cipriani, Voyce, Barkley, K. Sorrell, Sackey, Abendanon]

[*Bench:* J. Crane (rep), T. Croft (*lock/flanker/number 8*) (rep), L. Dickson (rep), Jack Forster (rep), Mercey (rep), N. Mordt (rep), M. Thompson (rep)]

[*Scorers:* **tries** by D. Paice and Abendanon, **penalty goals** by Barkley and N. Mordt, **conversion** by Barkley]

CAPTAIN: *Neal Hatley* [*Phil Dowson took over when Neal Hatley was injured in the 1st half*]

Final

[2nd June **ENGLAND SAXONS** 17 NEW ZEALAND MAORI 13]

Twickenham

[*Team:* N. Hatley, D. Paice, John Brooks, Blaze, Jim Evans, Haskell, W. Skinner, Dowson, Wigglesworth, Barkley, Voyce, N. Mordt, K. Sorrell, Sackey, Cipriani]

[*Bench:* J. Crane (rep), T. Croft (rep), L. Dickson (rep), Erinle (rep), Jack Forster (rep), Mercey (rep), M. Thompson (rep)]

[*Scorers:* **tries** by Sackey, Voyce and T. Croft, **conversion** by Barkley]

POSITION: WINNERS

BARBARIANS TOUR TO TUNISIA AND SPAIN 2007

[**MANAGER:** *Micky Steele-Bodger*] [**COACH:** *Zinzan Brooke* (NZ)]

[*Other squad members:* Azam (FR) (never travelled as injured, replaced by Andy Dalgleish), Richard Parks (WA) (*flanker*) (never travelled as withdrew, replaced by Jon Mills)]

(squad of 25)

[Zinzan Brooke was appointed on 9th May 2007; The Barbarians squad arrived in Tunisia on 17th May 2007]

CAPTAIN: *Hugh Vyvyan*

[19th May TUNISIA 10 **BARBARIANS** 33]

El Menzah Olympic Stadium, Tunis

[*Team:* Dorian Williams (WA), Dalgleish, John Davies (WA), Miall, H. Louw (SA), Craig Hammond, Jason Forster (WA), H. Vyvyan, Stuart-Smith, Nicholas 'Nick' Macleod (WA), T. Howe (IR), Garry Law (SC), Matt Cornwell, Rhys Williams (WA), S. Moffat (SC)]

[*Bench:* Guy Easterby (IR) (*scrum half*) (rep), C. Griffiths (WA) (*prop*) (rep), J. Hayter (rep), O. Hodge (*lock*) (rep), Jonathan 'Jon' Mills (WA) (*flanker/number 8*) (rep), L. Robinson (*wing*) (rep), Nicholas 'Nicky' Robinson (WA) (*fly half*) (rep)]

[*Scorers:* **tries** by Rhys Williams (WA), T. Howe (IR) (2), John Davies (WA) and O. Hodge, **conversions** by N. Macleod (WA) (4)]

[23rd May SPAIN 26 **BARBARIANS** 52]

Estadio Manuel Martinez Valero, Elche

[*Team:* Justin Fitzpatrick (IR), J. Hayter, C. Griffiths (WA), O. Hodge, H. Louw (SA), J. Mills (WA), T. Johnson, H. Vyvyan, G. Easterby (IR), Nicky Robinson (WA), L. Robinson, Maggs (IR), Matt Cornwell, Rhys Williams (WA), S. Moffat (SC)]

[*Bench:* Dalgleish (rep), Craig Hammond (*lock/flanker*) (rep), Law (SC) (*centre*) (rep), N. Macleod (WA) (*fly half/centre/full back*) (rep), Miall (rep), Stuart-Smith (rep), Dorian Williams (WA) (*prop*) (rep)]

[*Scorers:* **tries** by L. Robinson (3), Matt Cornwell, S. Moffat (SC) (2) and Rhys Williams (WA) (2), **conversions** by Nicky Robinson (WA) (6)]

ENGLAND TOUR TO SOUTH AFRICA 2007

[**HEAD COACH:** *Brian Ashton*] [**ASSISTANT COACHES:** *John Wells* & *Mike Ford*]

[*Other squad members:* P. Buxton (never travelled as injured, replaced by Ben Skirving), B. Cohen (never travelled as withdrew, replaced by Iain Balshaw), A. Farrell (*centre/flanker*) (taken ill during the tour), Ojo (travelled later as a replacement), Peter Richards (taken ill during the tour), Strettle (returned home due to illness, replaced by Nick Abendanon), N. Wood (returned home as injured, replaced by Matt Stevens)]

(squad of 31)

[Andy Sheridan, Tim Payne, James Forrester, Dan Ward-Smith, Charlie Hodgson, Mike Catt, Mike Tindall, Mark Cueto and Olly Morgan were all unavailable for this tour due to injury; Harry Ellis initially unavailable due to club commitments and later because he ruptured the anterior cruciate ligament in his knee in the Guinness Premiership Semi-Final match on 5th May 2007; Perry Freshwater unavailable at first due to club commitments and then because he seriously injured his elbow in a Perpignan club match on 13th May 2007; Phil Vickery, David Barnes, George Chuter, Lee Mears, Julian White, Duncan Bell, Steve Borthwick, Danny Grewcock, Ben Kay, Tom Palmer (2), Simon Shaw, James Haskell, Joe Worsley, Andy Beattie, Lewis Moody, Tom Rees, Michael Lipman, Martin Corry, Lawrence Dallaglio, Jordan Crane, Nick Walshe, Olly Barkley, Andy Goode, Dave Walder, Nick Abendanon, Tom Voyce, Fraser Waters, Ayoola Erinle, Ollie Smith (2), Chev Walker, Tom Varndell, Paul Sackey, Josh Lewsey

and Mark Van Gisbergen were all unavailable due to club commitments; Dylan Hartley unavailable due to suspension; Ben Cohen initially selected but then withdrew due to family commitments; Peter Buxton selected but withdrew on the day of the squad's departure, being replaced by Ben Skirving; The England squad departed for South Africa on 15th May 2007; Matt Stevens initially unavailable due to club commitments but then travelled later as a replacement for Nick Wood; Dan Scarbrough initially travelled on 25th May 2007 to replace the hospitalised Dave Strettle (who later rejoined the tour) and then became a replacement for the injured Iain Balshaw; Nick Abendanon travelled later as a replacement for Dave Strettle; Topsy Ojo was added to the squad on 31st May 2007 to provide illness cover for James Simpson-Daniel and Mike Brown]

VODACOM INCOMING TOUR

CAPTAIN: *Jason Robinson*

26th May SOUTH AFRICA 58 **ENGLAND** 10

Vodacom Park Stadium, Bloemfontein

[*Team:* Kevin Yates, M. Regan, Stuart Turner, Schofield, Alex Brown, Chris Jones, Hazell, Easter, Gomarsall, Jonny Wilkinson, Jason Robinson, T. Flood, M. Tait, Balshaw, Mike Brown]

[*Bench:* Anthony Allen, M. Cairns (rep), Darren Crompton (rep), S. Perry (rep), P. Sanderson (rep), J. Simpson-Daniel (rep), Winters (*lock/flanker/number 8*) (rep)]

[*Scorers:* **try** by J. Simpson-Daniel, **penalty goal** by Jonny Wilkinson, **conversion** by Jonny Wilkinson]

CAPTAIN: *Jonny Wilkinson*

2nd June SOUTH AFRICA 55 **ENGLAND*** 22

Loftus Versfeld Stadium, Pretoria

[*Team:* Kevin Yates, M. Regan, M. Stevens, Winters, Alex Brown, Easter, Lund, Skirving, Gomarsall, Jonny Wilkinson, Scarbrough, T. Flood, M. Tait, Noon, Mike Brown]

[*Bench:* Abendanon (rep), Anthony Allen, Chris Jones (rep), S. Perry (rep), Schofield (rep), Titterrell (rep), Stuart Turner (rep)]

[*Scorers:* **try** by Scarbrough, **penalty goals** by Jonny Wilkinson (5), **conversion** by Jonny Wilkinson]

EMIRATES AIRLINE LONDON SEVENS
IRB WORLD SEVENS SERIES 2006-2007 ROUND 7

Twickenham

[*Tournament squad:* Damu, Roques, Hills, Foden (*centre*), Ben Russell (2), Amesbury, T. Williams, Vilk, Care, R. Thirlby, Amor, D. Doherty (withdrew as injured, replaced by Noah Cato), Noah Cato (*wing*)]

(squad of 12)

[Richard Haughton was unavailable for this tournament due to injury; Ben Gollings unavailable due to club commitments; David Doherty played for Major R.V. Stanley's XV against Oxford University at Iffley Road on 14th November 2007; Noah Cato played in the White Hart Marauders team that reached the Final of the Amsterdam Heineken Sevens on 19th-20th May 2007]

[Russ Earnshaw was appointed before this tournament; Russ Earnshaw played for England at the Commonwealth Sevens at Petaling Jaya on 12th-14th September 1998, played for the Barbarians against Germany at Hannover on 12th August 2000, played for England at the Hong Kong Sevens on 30th March-1st April 2001, played for the English National Divisions XV against an Australian XV at Welford Road on 28th

October 2001, toured America and Canada with the Penguins in June 2002 and played for England Counties against France Amateurs at Newbury on 12th February 2005]
[**MANAGER:** *Craig Townsend* (SC)] [**COACH:** *Ben Ryan*] [**ASSISTANT COACH:** *Russ Earnshaw*]
CAPTAIN: *Simon Amor*
First Round - Pool 'D'

26th May	**ENGLAND**	19	PORTUGAL	14

[*Team:* Roques, Vilk, Ben Russell (2), Amor, Care, Foden, R. Thirlby]
[*Bench:* Amesbury, Cato (rep), Damu, Hills (rep), T. Williams (rep)]
[*Scorers:* **tries** by Foden and R. Thirlby (2), **conversions** by Amor (2)]

26th May	**ENGLAND**	0	WALES	22

[*Team:* Hills, Vilk, Damu, Amor, Care, Foden, Amesbury]
[*Bench:* Cato, Roques, Ben Russell (2) (rep), R. Thirlby (rep), T. Williams (rep)]
[*No scorers*]

26th May	**ENGLAND**	17	SOUTH AFRICA	14

[*Team:* Roques, Vilk, Damu, Amor, Care, Foden, R. Thirlby]
[*Bench:* Amesbury (rep), Cato, Hills, Ben Russell (2) (rep), T. Williams]
[*Scorers:* **tries** by Care (3), **conversion** by Amor]
[Bowl Quarter-Final:]

[27th May	**ENGLAND**	19	KENYA	0]

[*Team:* Roques, Vilk, Damu, Amor, Care, Foden, R. Thirlby]
[*Bench:* Amesbury, Cato (rep), Hills, Ben Russell (2) (rep), T. Williams (rep)]
[*Scorers:* **tries** by Foden (2) and T. Williams, **conversions** by Amor (2)]
[Bowl Semi-Final:]

[27th May	**ENGLAND**	17	FRANCE	7]

[*Team:* Roques, Vilk, Damu, Amor, Care, Foden, R. Thirlby]
[*Bench:* Amesbury (rep), Cato, Hills (rep), Ben Russell (2) (rep), T. Williams]
[*Scorers:* **tries** by Damu (2) and Foden, **conversion** by Amor]
[Bowl Final:]

[27th May	**ENGLAND**	10	PORTUGAL	0]

[*Team:* Roques, Vilk, Damu, Amor, Care, Foden, R. Thirlby]
[*Bench:* Amesbury (rep), Cato, Hills (rep), Ben Russell (2), T. Williams]
[*Scorers:* **tries** by Damu and Hills]
POSITION: FIRST ROUND LOSERS [*BOWL WINNERS*]
[England scored 2 competition points in this Round of the 2006-2007 IRB World Sevens Series]

EMIRATES AIRLINE EDINBURGH SEVENS
IRB WORLD SEVENS SERIES 2006-2007 ROUND 8
NED HAIG CUP

Murrayfield
[*Tournament squad:* Damu, Roques, Hills, Foden, Ben Russell (2) (never travelled as withdrew, replaced by David Seymour), Amesbury, T. Williams, Vilk, Care, R. Thirlby, Amor (captain; never travelled as withdrew, replaced by Danny Gray), Cato, David Seymour, Danny Gray]
(*squad of 12*)
[Richard Haughton was unavailable for this tournament due to injury; Ben Gollings unavailable due to club commitments; Ben Russell (2) and Simon Amor were initially

selected but then withdrew due to family commitments; Simon Amor was appointed Head Coach of the England Women Sevens team on 21st November 2007; Michael Hills played in the Samurai team that won the Amsterdam Heineken Sevens on 16th-17th May 2009]

[**MANAGER:** *Craig Townsend* (SC)] [**COACH:** *Ben Ryan*] [**ASSISTANT COACH:** *Russ Earnshaw*]

CAPTAIN: *Tony Roques*

First Round - Pool 'D'

2nd June GEORGIA 0 **ENGLAND** 24

[*Team:* David Seymour, Roques, Damu, Care, Danny Gray, Foden, Amesbury]
[*Bench:* Cato (rep), Hills (rep), R. Thirlby, Vilk, T. Williams (rep)]
[*Scorers:* **tries** by Damu, Amesbury, Care and Roques, **conversions** by Care (2)]

2nd June ARGENTINA 19 **ENGLAND*** 14

[*Team:* David Seymour, Vilk, Roques, Care, Danny Gray, Foden, R. Thirlby]
[*Bench:* Amesbury (rep), Cato, Damu (rep), Hills (rep), T. Williams]
[*Scorers:* **tries** by R. Thirlby and Care, **conversions** by Care (2)]

2nd June NEW ZEALAND 38 **ENGLAND** 0

[*Team:* David Seymour, Roques, Damu, Care, R. Thirlby, Foden, Amesbury]
[*Bench:* Cato, Danny Gray, Hills (rep), Vilk (rep), T. Williams (rep)]
[*No scorers*]

[Bowl Quarter-Final:]

[3rd June CANADA 7 **ENGLAND** 29 **]**

[*Team:* Hills, Vilk, Roques, Care, R. Thirlby, Foden, Cato]
[*Bench:* Amesbury, Danny Gray (rep), David Seymour (rep), T. Williams (rep)]
[*Scorers:* **tries** by Foden, Cato (2) and R. Thirlby (2), **conversions** by Care (2)]

[Bowl Semi-Final:]

[3rd June AUSTRALIA 19 **ENGLAND** 24 aet**]**

[*Team:* David Seymour, Vilk, Roques, Foden, Care, T. Williams, Amesbury]
[*Bench:* Cato (rep), Danny Gray, Hills (rep)]
[*Scorers:* **tries** by Vilk, Care (2) and Hills, **conversions** by Care (2)]

[Bowl Final:]

[3rd June PORTUGAL 0 **ENGLAND** 31 **]**

[*Team:* David Seymour, Vilk, Roques, Foden, Care, T. Williams, Amesbury]
[*Bench:* Cato (rep), Danny Gray (rep), Hills (rep)]
[*Scorers:* **tries** by T. Williams (2), Hills and Cato (2), **conversions** by Care (3)]

POSITION: FIRST ROUND LOSERS [*BOWL WINNERS*]

[England scored 2 competition points in this Round of the 2006-2007 IRB World Sevens Series]

RANKING: 5TH 52 [*New Zealand 130*, Fiji 128, Samoa 122, South Africa 92, Wales 38, Australia 32, France 28, Scotland 26, Argentina 23, Kenya 22, Tonga 10, Canada 8, Tunisia 6, Portugal 2, USA 2, Russia 1]

ENGLAND COUNTIES TOUR TO RUSSIA 2007

[**CHAIRMAN OF SELECTORS:** *Peter Hartley*] [**MANAGER:** *Jim Robinson*] [**ASSISTANT MANAGER:** *Danny Hodgson*] [**COACH:** *Harvey Biljon* (SA)] [**ASSISTANT COACH:** *Dave Baldwin*]

[*Other squad members:* Timothy 'Tim' Mathias (*prop*), Neale (injured during the tour), Chris Rainbow (*flanker*) (injured during the tour), H. Smales (*centre/wing*), Viney (*wing/full back*)]

(*squad of 26*)

[Harvey Biljon was appointed on 25th April 2007; England Counties became the first English adult representative rugby side to play in Russia; The England Counties squad departed for Russia on 3rd June 2007; The England Counties squad arrived in Siberia on 4th June 2007; The England Counties squad travelled to Moscow on 8th June 2007]

CAPTAIN: *Duncan Cormack*

[16th Jun RUSSIA 21 **ENGLAND COUNTIES** 23]

Slava Stadium, Moscow

[*Team:* D. Cormack, L. Wordley, Tideswell, Alex Davidson, Campton, Blakeburn, Chris Morgan, Gregor Hayter, Paul Knight (2), Mark Woodrow, Arran Cruickshanks, Bedworth, Malherbe, T. Jarvis, M. Leek]

[*Bench:* Glenn Cooper, C. Pilgrim, Scott Rawlings (*centre*), Carl Rimmer (*prop*) (rep), N. Spence (*flanker*) (rep), J. Winterbottom (rep)]

[*Scorers:* **tries** by Malherbe (2), **penalty goals** by M. Woodrow (3), **conversions** by M. Woodrow (2)]

FALKLANDS 25 TASK FORCE TROPHY MATCH

[MANAGER: *Ian Bullerwell*] **[COACHES:** *Steve Hill* & *Joe Roff* (AU)]

CAPTAIN: *Howard Graham*

[16th Jun Falklands Task Force XV (*SER*) 33 **PENGUINS*** 33]

Stoop Memorial Ground, Langhorn Drive, Twickenham

[*Team:* Rod Moore (AU), Chris Johnson (1), S. Carter, Jon-Lee Phillips, Brenton, James Bucknall, O. Brown (SC), Ken Aseme (US), Nicky Griffiths (WA), Kieran Hallett (IR), Felise Ah-Ling (SAM), Bryan Milne (NZ), H. Graham, Andrew 'Andy' Wright, J. Smales]

[*Bench:* Barr (rep), James 'Jamie' Fleming (*flanker/number 8*) (rep), Gaunt (rep), Rory Greenslade-Jones (WA) (*centre/wing*) (rep), Head (IR) (rep), Le Chevalier (rep), Matt Miles (WA) (*hooker*) (rep), Matt Price (*hooker*) (rep), Strong (WA) (*wing*) (rep)]

[*Scorers:* **tries** by O. Brown (SC), Gaunt, J-L Phillips, Nicky Griffiths (WA) and Greenslade-Jones (WA), **conversions** by K. Hallett (IR) (3) and Nicky Griffiths (WA)]

[Match to commemorate the 25th Anniversary of the liberation of the Falkland Islands on 14th June 1982]

[Ian Bullerwell was an international referee between 1988-90; Joe Roff won 86 caps for Australia between 1995-2004]

CWMTAWE SEVENS

Pontardawe RFC, Parc Ynysderw, Ynysderw Road, Pontardawe, Swansea

[*Tournament squad:* Earnshaw, Gareth Williams (4) (WA), M. Cannon, Simon Hunt, R. Thirlby, Thomas 'Tom' Hockedy (*wing*), Aaron Bramwell (WA) (*wing*), Nick Wakley (WA) (*wing*)]

[Tom Hockedy played for Samurai St George in the Dubai International Invitation Rugby Sevens on 30th November-2nd December 2006]

[NO COACH NOMINATED]

CAPTAIN: *??*

First Round - Pool 'H'

[4th Aug Glamorgan Young Farmers (*WA*) 7 **SAMURAI** 28]

[*Team:*]

[*Bench:*]

[*Scorers:*]

[4th Aug Brammers International (*FR*) 0 **SAMURAI** 33]
[*Team:*]
[*Bench:*]
[*Scorers:*]
Quarter-Final
[4th Aug Llanelli Scarlets (*WA*) 24 **SAMURAI*** 19]
[*Team:*]
[*Bench:*]
[*Scorers:* **try** by Simon Hunt]
POSITION: LOSING QUARTER-FINALISTS

FIRST INVESTEC CHALLENGE MATCH

[*Other squad members:* Abendanon, Barkley, M. Catt, Cipriani (*fly half/full back*), Cueto (*full back*) (withdrew from team due to injury), Freshwater, Haskell, C. Hodgson, Kay, J. Lewsey, Mears, Noon, Tom Palmer (2), Tom Rees, Peter Richards (withdrew from bench due to injury), Sackey, Tindall, Ward-Smith, Kevin Yates]
(squad of 40)
[First warm-up match for the 2007 World Cup; Ben Cohen unavailable due to family commitments; Danny Grewcock unavailable after a European Rugby Cup (ERC) hearing on 11th June 2007 found him guilty of punching an opponent in the European Challenge Cup Final on 19th May 2007 and thus banned him for 6 weeks from 4th August 2007 onwards; Louis Deacon, Andy Hazell, Magnus Lund, Shane Geraghty, Fraser Waters and Olly Morgan were all members of the 47 man World Cup training squad announced on 15th June 2007; Julian White was a member of the 47 man World Cup training squad but withdrew on 12th July 2007 due to family and work commitments and was not replaced; Brian Ashton reduced his World Cup training squad from 46 to 40 on 13th July 2007; Tom Rees, Dan Ward-Smith and Mike Tindall were unavailable for this match due to injury]
[**HEAD COACH:** *Brian Ashton*] [**ASSISTANT COACHES:** *John Wells* & *Mike Ford*]
CAPTAIN: *Phil Vickery* [*Martin Corry took over when Phil Vickery went off injured at half-time; Jonny Wilkinson took over when Martin Corry was substituted in the 2nd half*]
4th Aug **ENGLAND** 62 WALES 5
Twickenham
[*Team:* Sheridan, M. Regan, Vickery, S. Shaw, S. Borthwick, Corry, J. Worsley, Easter, S. Perry, Jonny Wilkinson, Jason Robinson, A. Farrell, Hipkiss, Strettle, M. Tait]
[*Bench:* Chuter (rep), Dallaglio (rep), T. Flood (rep), Gomarsall, Moody (rep), M. Stevens (rep)]
[*Scorers:* **tries** by Easter (4), S. Borthwick, Dallaglio, S. Perry, Jason Robinson and M. Tait, **penalty goal** by Jonny Wilkinson, **conversions** by Jonny Wilkinson (7)]

SECOND INVESTEC CHALLENGE MATCH

[*Other squad members:* Chuter, Cueto, Easter, A. Farrell, T. Flood, Freshwater, Hipkiss, C. Hodgson, Moody (withdrew from team due to injury), Tom Palmer (2), Tom Rees, Peter Richards, Jason Robinson, Strettle, M. Tait, Tindall, Ward-Smith, Kevin Yates, Wigglesworth]
(squad of 41)
[Second warm-up match for the 2007 World Cup; Ben Cohen unavailable due to family commitments; Julian White unavailable due to family and work commitments; Danny Grewcock unavailable due to suspension; Richard Wigglesworth was added to the World Cup training squad on 6th August 2007 to provide injury cover for Peter Richards; Dan Ward-Smith was released from the World Cup training squad on 7th

August 2007 as he was not match fit; Dave Strettle withdrew from the World Cup training squad on 9th August 2007 due to injury; Tom Rees, Peter Richards, Mike Tindall and Mark Cueto were unavailable for this match due to injury]
[**HEAD COACH:** *Brian Ashton*] [**ASSISTANT COACHES:** *John Wells & Mike Ford*]
CAPTAIN: *Mike Catt*

11th Aug	**ENGLAND***	15	FRANCE	21

Twickenham
[*Team:* Sheridan, M. Regan, M. Stevens, S. Shaw, Kay, Haskell, J. Worsley, Dallaglio, S. Perry, Barkley, J. Lewsey, M. Catt, Noon, Sackey, Abendanon]
[*Bench:* S. Borthwick, Cipriani, Corry (rep), Gomarsall (rep), Mears (rep), Vickery (rep), Jonny Wilkinson (rep)]
[*Scorers:* **penalty goals** by Barkley (4), **drop goal** by Gomarsall]

THIRD INVESTEC CHALLENGE MATCH

[*Other squad members:* M. Catt, Chuter (withdrew from team due to injury), Kay, Moody, Noon, Peter Richards, M. Tait, Sheridan]
(squad of 30)
[Third warm-up match for the 2007 World Cup; Ben Cohen unavailable due to family commitments; Julian White unavailable due to family and work commitments; Danny Grewcock unavailable due to suspension; Richard Wigglesworth was left out of the World Cup squad of 30 on 13th August 2007 but continued to train alongside them in order to provide injury cover for Peter Richards; Lewis Moody and Peter Richards were unavailable for this match due to injury; Andy Sheridan was unavailable for this match due to illness]
[**HEAD COACH:** *Brian Ashton*] [**ASSISTANT COACHES:** *John Wells & Mike Ford*]
CAPTAIN: *Phil Vickery [Martin Corry took over when Phil Vickery went off injured at half-time]*

18th Aug	FRANCE	22	**ENGLAND**	9

Stade Vélodrome, Marseille
[*Team:* Freshwater, M. Regan, Vickery, S. Shaw, S. Borthwick, Corry, Tom Rees, Easter, S. Perry, Jonny Wilkinson, Jason Robinson, A. Farrell, Hipkiss, J. Lewsey, Cueto]
[*Bench:* Barkley (rep), Dallaglio (rep), Gomarsall (rep), Mears (rep), Sackey (rep), M. Stevens (rep), J. Worsley (rep)]
[*Scorers:* **penalty goals** by Jonny Wilkinson (3)]

FIRA-AER EUROPEAM' FESTIVAL

France
[*Other squad members:* D. Hyde (never travelled as injured, replaced by James Kellard), L. Wordley (*hooker*) (never travelled as injured, replaced by Dean Bick)]
(squad of 26)
[This EuropeAm' Festival was organised by FIRA-AER as a friendly competition involving France Amateurs, Belgium, England Counties, Russia, Spain and the French Armed Forces; While there was no official competition winner, England Counties did finish the Festival with a better points difference than France Amateurs, who had also scored two wins and a draw in their 3 matches!; This Festival was not organised on a round-robin basis, so England Counties did not play either Belgium or the French Armed Forces during the competition; The England Counties squad travelled to France on 5th September 2007]
[**CHAIRMAN OF SELECTORS:** *Peter Hartley*] [**MANAGER:** *Jim Robinson*] [**ASSISTANT MANAGER:** *Danny Hodgson*] [**COACH:** *Harvey Biljon* (SA)] [**ASSISTANT COACH:** *Dave*

Baldwin]
CAPTAIN: *Jim Jenner*
[6th Sept RUSSIA 10 **ENGLAND COUNTIES** 76]
Stade Municipal Marius-Lacoste, Fleurance
[*Team:* Darren Jacques, Glenn Cooper, Tideswell, Matt Owen, Snowball, Matthew 'Matt' Payne, D. Allen, Jenner, Aikman, T. Roberts, Nicholas 'Nick' Royle, P. Mooney, Malherbe, T. Jarvis, Neale]
[*Bench:* Dean Bick (*hooker*) (rep), Dan Cooper (*flanker*) (rep), Kyle Dench (*centre*) (rep), James Doherty (*scrum half*) (rep), James Kellard (*flanker/number 8*) (rep), C. Rowland (rep), Simmie (*fly half*) (rep)]
[*Scorers:* **tries** by Royle, Aikman (3), Jenner, Malherbe, Neale, M. Payne, D. Bick (2), Dench and J. Doherty, **conversions** by T. Roberts (8)]
CAPTAIN: *Tom Bason*
[10th Sep SPAIN XV 15 **ENGLAND COUNTIES** 21]
Stade des Cordeliers, Morlaàs
[*Team:* C. Rowland, D. Bick, Peter Joyce, Matt Owen, Thomas 'Tom' Bason, Kellard, D. Cooper, David Archer, J. Doherty, T. Roberts, T. Jarvis, P. Mooney, Dench, Royle, J. Smales]
[*Bench:* Aikman (rep), D. Allen (rep), Glenn Cooper (rep), Jacques (*prop*) (rep), Malherbe (rep), Neale (rep), Snowball (rep)]
[*Scorers:* **tries** by Glenn Cooper and Royle, **penalty goals** by T. Roberts (3), **conversion** by Neale]
CAPTAIN: *Jim Jenner*
[13th Sep FRANCE AMATEURS 21 **ENGLAND COUNTIES*** 21]
Stade Municipal, Saint-Paul-lès-Dax
[*Team:* Jacques, Glenn Cooper, Tideswell, Bason, Snowball, M. Payne, Kellard, Jenner, Aikman, T. Roberts, Royle, Dench, Malherbe, T. Jarvis, Neale]
[*Bench:* D. Archer (*number 8*) (rep), D. Cooper (rep), J. Doherty (rep), P. Joyce (*prop*) (rep), P. Mooney (*centre*) (rep), C. Rowland (rep), J. Smales (*fly half/wing/full back*) (rep)]
[*Scorers:* **tries** by Jenner and Royle, **penalty goals** by T. Roberts (3), **conversion** by T. Roberts]

WORLD CUP
WEBB ELLIS CUP

France
[*Other squad members:* Abendanon]
(squad of 30)
[The World Cup squad of 30 was announced on 13th August 2007; Tim Payne, James Forrester and Harry Ellis were unavailable for this tournament due to injury; Ben Cohen unavailable due to family commitments; Julian White unavailable due to family and work commitments; Danny Grewcock unavailable due to suspension; Phil Vickery was the tournament captain; Stuart Turner was initially invited to travel to France to provide potential front row injury cover, but then himself proved to be unavailable due to injury, which meant that it was Darren Crompton who actually travelled to France on 13th September 2007!; Darren Crompton was not officially added to the squad and returned home on 15th September 2007; Toby Flood travelled to France on 17th September 2007 as a replacement for Jamie Noon; Stuart Turner travelled to France on the same day as potential front row injury cover, but was not officially added to the

squad; Nick Abendanon travelled to France on 15th October 2007 to replace Josh Lewsey]

(<u>During the First Round a bonus point was awarded for scoring 4 or more tries in a match and for losing by seven points or less</u>)

[HEAD COACH: *Brian Ashton*] **[ASSISTANT COACHES:** *John Wells & Mike Ford*]

CAPTAIN: *Phil Vickery* [*Martin Corry took over when Phil Vickery was substituted in the 2nd half*]

First Round - Pool 'A'

8th Sept USA 10 **ENGLAND** 28

Stade Félix Bollaert, Lens

[*Team:* Sheridan, M. Regan, Vickery, S. Shaw, Kay, J. Worsley, Tom Rees, Dallaglio, S. Perry, Barkley, Jason Robinson, M. Catt, Noon, J. Lewsey, Cueto]

[*Bench:* Chuter (rep), Corry (rep), A. Farrell (rep), Moody (rep), Peter Richards (rep), M. Stevens (rep), M. Tait (rep)]

[*Scorers:* **tries** by Jason Robinson, Barkley and Tom Rees, **penalty goals** by Barkley (3), **conversions** by Barkley (2)]

CAPTAIN: *Martin Corry*

14th Sept SOUTH AFRICA 36 **ENGLAND** 0

Stade de France, Paris

[*Team:* Sheridan, M. Regan, M. Stevens, S. Shaw, Kay, Corry, Tom Rees, Easter, S. Perry, M. Catt, Sackey, A. Farrell, Noon, J. Lewsey, Jason Robinson]

[*Bench:* S. Borthwick (rep), Chuter (rep), Freshwater (rep), Gomarsall (rep), Moody (rep), Peter Richards (*centre*) (rep), M. Tait (rep)]

[*No scorers*]

22nd Sep SAMOA 22 **ENGLAND** 44 **BP**

Stade de la Beaujoire, Nantes

[*Team:* Sheridan, Chuter, M. Stevens, S. Shaw, Kay, Corry, J. Worsley, Easter, Gomarsall, Jonny Wilkinson, Cueto, Barkley, M. Tait, Sackey, J. Lewsey]

[*Bench:* S. Borthwick (rep), A. Farrell, Freshwater (rep), Hipkiss (rep), Moody (rep), M. Regan, Peter Richards (*scrum half*)]

[*Scorers:* **tries** by Corry (2) and Sackey (2), **penalty goals** by Jonny Wilkinson (4), **drop goals** by Jonny Wilkinson (2), **conversions** by Jonny Wilkinson (3)]

CAPTAIN: *Martin Corry* [*Phil Vickery took over when he came on as a substitute in the 2nd half*]

28th Sept TONGA 20 **ENGLAND** 36 **BP**

Parc des Princes

[*Team:* Sheridan, Chuter, M. Stevens, S. Borthwick, Kay, Corry, Moody, Easter, Gomarsall, Jonny Wilkinson, Cueto, Barkley, M. Tait, Sackey, J. Lewsey]

[*Bench:* Dallaglio (rep), A. Farrell (rep), Hipkiss (rep), Mears (rep), Peter Richards (rep), Vickery (rep), J. Worsley]

[*Scorers:* **tries** by Sackey (2), M. Tait and A. Farrell, **penalty goals** by Jonny Wilkinson (2), **drop goals** by Jonny Wilkinson (2), **conversions** by Jonny Wilkinson (2)]

CAPTAIN: *Phil Vickery [Martin Corry took over when Phil Vickery was substituted in the 2nd half]*

Quarter-Final

6th Oct AUSTRALIA 10 **ENGLAND** 12

Stade Vélodrome, Marseille

[*Team:* Sheridan, M. Regan, Vickery, S. Shaw, Kay, Corry, Moody, Easter, Gomarsall, Jonny Wilkinson, J. Lewsey, M. Catt, M. Tait, Sackey, Jason Robinson]

[*Bench:* Chuter (rep), Dallaglio (rep), T. Flood (rep), Hipkiss, Peter Richards (rep), M. Stevens (rep), J. Worsley (rep)]

[*Scorers:* **penalty goals** by Jonny Wilkinson (4)]

CAPTAIN: *Phil Vickery [Martin Corry took over when Phil Vickery was substituted in the 2nd half]*

Semi-Final

13th Oct FRANCE 9 **ENGLAND** 14

Stade de France, Paris

[*Team:* Sheridan, M. Regan, Vickery, S. Shaw, Kay, Corry, Moody, Easter, Gomarsall, Jonny Wilkinson, J. Lewsey, M. Catt, M. Tait, Sackey, Jason Robinson]

[*Bench:* Chuter (rep), Dallaglio (rep), T. Flood (rep), Hipkiss (rep), Peter Richards (rep), M. Stevens (rep), J. Worsley (rep)]

[*Scorers:* **try** by J. Lewsey, **penalty goals** by Jonny Wilkinson (2), **drop goal** by Jonny Wilkinson]

CAPTAIN: *Phil Vickery [Martin Corry took over when Phil Vickery was substituted at half-time]*

Final

20th Oct SOUTH AFRICA 15 **ENGLAND*** 6

Stade de France, Paris

[*Team:* Sheridan, M. Regan, Vickery, S. Shaw, Kay, Corry, Moody, Easter, Gomarsall, Jonny Wilkinson, Cueto, M. Catt, M. Tait, Sackey, Jason Robinson]

[*Bench:* Chuter (rep), Dallaglio (rep), T. Flood (rep), Hipkiss (rep), Peter Richards (rep), M. Stevens (rep), J. Worsley (rep)]

[*Scorers:* **penalty goals** by Jonny Wilkinson (2)]

POSITION: LOSING FINALISTS

FANTASY: ***WINNERS***

OTHER MATCHES

ATKINS REMEMBRANCE RUGBY MATCH

[**COACH:** *Graham Dawe*]

CAPTAIN: *Jannie Bornman* (SA)

[14th Nov COMBINED SERVICES (*SER*) 27 **BARBARIANS*** 24]

Plymouth Albion RFC, Brickfields Recreation Ground, Madden Road, Plymouth

[*Team:* Dorian Williams (WA), Diego Zarzosa (SP), Nigel Hall (NZ), Rob McCusker (WA), O. Hodge, Jannie Bornman (SA), Roques, Matt Evans (1), Gareth Williams (6) (WA), Quesada (AR), Nicolas 'Nic' Sestaret (FR), Tristan Davies (WA), Liam Roberts (WA), Matt Moore, Andrew 'Andy' Birkett (CO)]

[*Bench:* D. Allen (rep), Brad Davies (rep), Duffey (*hooker*) (rep), Andrew 'Andy' Kennedy (IR) (*lock/number 8*) (rep), McAtee (WA) (*scrum half/centre/wing*) (rep), Wihan Neethling (SA) (*full back*) (rep), D. Parkes (rep)]

[*Scorers:* **tries** by M. Moore, Zarzosa (SP) and Sestaret (FR) (2), **conversions** by Brad Davies (2)]

[Match to commemorate the members of the British uniformed services who lost their lives during armed conflict]
[Graham Dawe was appointed on 8th November 2007; Graham Dawe was capped for England in February 1987]

EMIRATES AIRLINE DUBAI RUGBY SEVENS
IRB WORLD SEVENS SERIES 2007-2008 ROUND 1
EMIRATES INTERNATIONAL TROPHY

Dubai Exiles Stadium, Dubai
[*Tournament squad:* Damu, Guest (*forward*), Matthew 'Matt' Banahan (*forward/centre/wing*), Brake, Foden, T. Youngs (*forward/back*), A. Elliott, Vilk, Joseph 'Joe' Simpson (*scrum half*), J. Adams, Liam Gibson (*wing*), Simon Hunt]
(*squad of 12*)
[Joe Simpson played for England in the U19 World Championships at Dubai in April 2006 and Ireland in April 2007]
[**MANAGER:** *Craig Townsend* (SC)] [**COACH:** *Ben Ryan*] [**ASSISTANT COACH:** *Russ Earnshaw*]
CAPTAIN: *Andy Vilk*
First Round - Pool 'D'

30th Nov TUNISIA 12 **ENGLAND** 27
[*Team:* Banahan, Vilk, Damu, Foden, J. Adams, Simon Hunt, A. Elliott]
[*Bench:* Brake (rep), L. Gibson (rep), Guest (rep), J. Simpson, T. Youngs]
[*Scorers:* **tries** by Damu (2), A. Elliott (2) and Simon Hunt, **conversion** by Foden]

30th Nov CANADA 24 **ENGLAND*** 24
[*Team:* Guest, Vilk, Damu, Foden, J. Adams, Brake, L. Gibson]
[*Bench:* Banahan (rep), A. Elliott, Simon Hunt, J. Simpson (rep), T. Youngs (rep)]
[*Scorers:* **tries** by Brake, J. Adams (2) and Damu, **conversions** by Foden (2)]

30th Nov SOUTH AFRICA 22 **ENGLAND** 10
[*Team:* Guest, Vilk, Damu, Foden, J. Adams, Simon Hunt, A. Elliott]
[*Bench:* Banahan (rep), Brake (rep), L. Gibson, J. Simpson (rep), T. Youngs (rep)]
[*Scorers:* **tries** by A. Elliott and Banahan]

Quarter-Final

1st Dec SAMOA 19 **ENGLAND** 26
[*Team:* Guest, Vilk, Damu, Foden, J. Adams, Simon Hunt, A. Elliott]
[*Bench:* Banahan (rep), Brake (rep), L. Gibson, J. Simpson, T. Youngs]
[*Scorers:* **tries** by A. Elliott (2), Guest and Simon Hunt, **conversions** by Foden (3)]

Semi-Final

1st Dec FIJI 22 **ENGLAND*** 21
[*Team:* Guest, Vilk, Damu, Foden, J. Adams, Simon Hunt, A. Elliott]
[*Bench:* Banahan (rep), Brake (rep), L. Gibson, J. Simpson, T. Youngs (rep)]
[*Scorers:* **tries** by penalty try, Foden and Guest, **conversions** by Foden (3)]

POSITION: LOSING SEMI-FINALISTS
[England scored 12 competition points in this Round of the 2007-2008 IRB World Sevens Series]

GARTMORE CHALLENGE
GARTMORE CHALLENGE TROPHY
[*Other squad members:* Luke Charteris (WA) (*lock*) (withdrew, replaced by Michael Owen), Sheridan (withdrew, replaced by J.D. Moller)]
(squad of 22)
[Eddie O'Sullivan was appointed on 29th August 2007]
[**COACH:** *Eddie O'Sullivan* (IR)]
CAPTAIN: *Mark Regan* [*Justin Marshall* (NZ) *took over when Mark Regan was substituted in the 2nd half*]
[1st Dec **BARBARIANS** 22 SOUTH AFRICA XV 5]
Twickenham
[*Team:* Federico Pucciariello (IT), M. Regan, Salesi Ma'afu (AU), Cockbain (WA), Justin Harrison (AU), Jerry Collins (NZ), Martyn Williams (WA), Rocky Elsom (AU), J. Marshall (NZ), Giteau (AU), Isoa Neivua (FIJ), Ma'a Nonu (NZ), Conrad Smith (NZ), Josevata 'Joe' Rokocoko (NZ), Jason Robinson]
[*Bench:* Schalk Brits (SA) (*hooker*) (rep), B. Cohen (rep), Flavell (NZ) (*lock/flanker*) (rep), Peter Grant (SA) (*fly half*) (rep), Jan Daniel 'J.D.' Moller (SA) (*prop*) (rep), Michael Owen (WA) (rep), Shanklin (WA) (rep)]
[*Scorers:* **tries** by Giteau (AU), Martyn Williams (WA) and Elsom (AU), **penalty goal** by Giteau (AU), **conversions** by Giteau (AU) (2)]

EMIRATES AIRLINE SOUTH AFRICA SEVENS
IRB WORLD SEVENS SERIES 2007-2008 ROUND 2
Outeniqua Park Stadium, George
[*Tournament squad:* Damu, Guest, Banahan, Brake, Foden, T. Youngs, A. Elliott, Vilk, J. Simpson, J. Adams, L. Gibson, Simon Hunt]
(squad of 12)
[**MANAGER:** *Craig Townsend* (SC)] [**COACH:** *Ben Ryan*] [**ASSISTANT COACH:** *Russ Earnshaw*]
CAPTAIN: *Andy Vilk*
First Round - Pool 'A'
7th Dec ZIMBABWE 7 **ENGLAND** 24
[*Team:* Guest, Vilk, Brake, J. Simpson, T. Youngs, Foden, L. Gibson]
[*Bench:* J. Adams (rep), Banahan (rep), Damu, A. Elliott, Simon Hunt (rep)]
[*Scorers:* **tries** by J. Simpson, Vilk, T. Youngs and J. Adams, **conversions** by J. Simpson and Foden]
7th Dec KENYA 17 **ENGLAND** 7
[*Team:* Simon Hunt, Vilk, Damu, Foden, J. Adams, T. Youngs, A. Elliott]
[*Bench:* Banahan (rep), Brake, L. Gibson, Guest (rep), J. Simpson (rep)]
[*Scorers:* **try** by T. Youngs, **conversion** by Foden]
7th Dec NEW ZEALAND 26 **ENGLAND*** 24
[*Team:* Guest, Vilk, Damu, Foden, J. Adams, Simon Hunt, A. Elliott]
[*Bench:* Banahan (rep), Brake (rep), L. Gibson, J. Simpson, T. Youngs]
[*Scorers:* **tries** by Simon Hunt, Foden, Guest and Damu, **conversions** by Foden (2)]
[Bowl Quarter-Final:]
[8th Dec CANADA 5 **ENGLAND** 35]
[*Team:* Banahan, Vilk, Damu, J. Simpson, J. Adams, Foden, L. Gibson]
[*Bench:* Brake, A. Elliott, Guest, Simon Hunt (rep), T. Youngs (rep)]

[*Scorers:* **tries** by J. Simpson (2), Banahan and Foden (2), **conversions** by J. Simpson (2) and Foden (3)]

[Bowl Semi-Final:]

[8th Dec AUSTRALIA 14 **ENGLAND** 29]

[*Team:* Guest, Vilk, Damu, J. Simpson, J. Adams, Foden, A. Elliott]

[*Bench:* Banahan (rep), Brake, L. Gibson, Simon Hunt (rep), T. Youngs]

[*Scorers:* **tries** by A. Elliott, J. Adams, Guest, Foden and Simon Hunt, **conversions** by Foden (2)]

[Bowl Final:]

[8th Dec WALES 21 **ENGLAND*** 19]

[*Team:* Guest, Vilk, Damu, J. Simpson, J. Adams, Simon Hunt, A. Elliott]

[*Bench:* Banahan (rep), Brake (rep), L. Gibson, T. Youngs]

[*Scorers:* **tries** by A. Elliott (2) and J. Simpson, **conversions** by J. Simpson (2)]

POSITION: FIRST ROUND LOSERS [*BOWL FINALISTS*]

FANTASY: *FIRST ROUND LOSERS* [*BOWL WINNERS*]

[England did not score any competition points in this Round of the 2007-2008 IRB World Sevens Series]

2008
OTHER MATCHES
NEW ZEALAND INTERNATIONAL SEVENS
IRB WORLD SEVENS SERIES 2007-2008 ROUND 3

Westpac Stadium, Wellington

[*Tournament squad:* Damu, James Collins (*forward*), Banahan, Brake (*scrum half*), Shabbo, T. Youngs (never travelled as injured, replaced by Uche Oduoza), A. Elliott, Vilk, Care, Gollings, Erinle, Simon Hunt, Oduoza (*forward/wing*)]

(squad of 12)

[Westpac Stadium was previously called WestpacTrust Stadium]

[**MANAGER:** *Craig Townsend* (SC)] [**COACH:** *Ben Ryan*] [**ASSISTANT COACH:** *Russ Earnshaw*]

CAPTAIN: *Andy Vilk*

First Round - Pool 'B'

1st Feb COOK ISLANDS 21 **ENGLAND*** 17

[*Team:* Shabbo, James Collins, Damu, Care, Gollings, Vilk, A. Elliott]

[*Bench:* Banahan (rep), Brake, Erinle (rep), Simon Hunt (rep), Oduoza (rep)]

[*Scorers:* **tries** by Damu, Gollings and Care, **conversion** by Gollings]

1st Feb WALES 15 **ENGLAND** 5

[*Team:* Simon Hunt, Vilk, Damu, Care, Gollings, Erinle, A. Elliott]

[*Bench:* Banahan (rep), Brake, James Collins, Oduoza (rep), Shabbo (rep)]

[*Scorers:* **try** by Gollings]

1st Feb FIJI 17 **ENGLAND** 7

[*Team:* Shabbo, Vilk, Damu, Brake, Gollings, Erinle, Oduoza]

[*Bench:* Banahan (rep), Care, James Collins (rep), A. Elliott (rep), Simon Hunt]

[*Scorers:* **try** by Gollings, **conversion** by Gollings]

[Bowl Quarter-Final:]

[2nd Feb CANADA 17 **ENGLAND** 33]

[*Team:* Shabbo, Vilk, Damu, Brake, Gollings, Erinle, A. Elliott]

[*Bench:* Banahan (rep), Care, James Collins (rep), Simon Hunt (rep), Oduoza]

[*Scorers:* **tries** by Shabbo, Brake, A. Elliott, Gollings and Banahan, **conversions** by Gollings (4)]

[Bowl Semi-Final:]

[2nd Feb FRANCE 5 **ENGLAND** 14]

[*Team:* Shabbo, Vilk, Damu, Care, Gollings, Erinle, Oduoza]

[*Bench:* Banahan (rep), Brake, James Collins (rep), A. Elliott, Simon Hunt (rep)]

[*Scorers:* **tries** by Erinle and Shabbo, **conversions** by Gollings (2)]

[Bowl Final:]

[2nd Feb ARGENTINA 7 **ENGLAND** 12]

[*Team:* Shabbo, Vilk, Damu, Care, Gollings, Erinle, A. Elliott]

[*Bench:* Banahan (rep), Brake (rep), James Collins, Simon Hunt (rep), Oduoza]

[*Scorers:* **tries** by A. Elliott and Banahan, **conversion** by Gollings]

POSITION: FIRST ROUND LOSERS [*BOWL WINNERS*]

[England scored 2 competition points in this Round of the 2007-2008 IRB World Sevens Series]

6 NATIONS CHAMPIONSHIP

[**HEAD COACH:** *Brian Ashton*] [**ASSISTANT COACHES:** *John Wells & Mike Ford*]

CAPTAIN: *Phil Vickery [Jonny Wilkinson took over when Phil Vickery was substituted in the 2nd half]*

2nd Feb **ENGLAND*** 19 WALES 26
Twickenham

[*Team:* Sheridan, M. Regan, Vickery, S. Shaw, S. Borthwick, Haskell, Moody, Narraway, Gomarsall, Jonny Wilkinson, Strettle, T. Flood, Tindall, Sackey, Balshaw]

[*Bench:* Cipriani (rep), Kay (rep), Mears (rep), Tom Rees (rep), M. Stevens (rep), Lesley Vainikolo (*wing*) (rep), Wigglesworth]

[*Scorers:* **try** by T. Flood, **penalty goals** by Jonny Wilkinson (3), **drop goal** by Jonny Wilkinson, **conversion** by Jonny Wilkinson]

CAPTAIN: *Steve Borthwick*

10th Feb ITALY 19 **ENGLAND** 23
Stadio Flaminio, Rome

[*Team:* T. Payne, M. Regan, M. Stevens, S. Shaw, S. Borthwick, Haskell, Lipman, Easter, Gomarsall, Jonny Wilkinson, Vainikolo, T. Flood, Noon, Sackey, Balshaw]

[*Bench:* Cipriani (rep), J. Hobson, Kay (rep), Mears (rep), Narraway (rep), M. Tait (rep), Wigglesworth (rep)]

[*Scorers:* **tries** by Sackey and T. Flood, **penalty goals** by Jonny Wilkinson (3), **conversions** by Jonny Wilkinson (2)]

CAPTAIN: *Phil Vickery*

23rd Feb FRANCE 13 **ENGLAND** 24
Stade de France, Paris

[*Team:* Sheridan, M. Regan, Vickery, S. Shaw, S. Borthwick, Haskell, Lipman, Easter, Wigglesworth, Jonny Wilkinson, Vainikolo, T. Flood, Noon, Sackey, Balshaw]

[*Bench:* Cipriani, T. Croft (rep), P. Hodgson, Kay (rep), Mears (rep), M. Stevens (rep), M. Tait (rep)]

[*Scorers:* **tries** by Sackey and Wigglesworth, **penalty goals** by Jonny Wilkinson (3), **drop goal** by Jonny Wilkinson, **conversion** by Jonny Wilkinson]

CAPTAIN: *Phil Vickery [Steve Borthwick took over when Phil Vickery was substituted in the 2nd half]*

8th March SCOTLAND 15 **ENGLAND** 9
Murrayfield

[*Team:* Sheridan, Mears, Vickery, S. Shaw, S. Borthwick, T. Croft, Lipman, Easter, Wigglesworth, Jonny Wilkinson, Vainikolo, T. Flood, Noon, Sackey, Balshaw]

[*Bench:* Chuter (rep), C. Hodgson (rep), P. Hodgson, Kay (rep), Narraway (rep), M. Stevens (rep), M. Tait (rep)]

[*Scorers:* **penalty goals** by Jonny Wilkinson (3)]

CAPTAIN: *Phil Vickery [Steve Borthwick took over when Phil Vickery was substituted in the 2nd half]*

15th Mar **ENGLAND** 33 IRELAND 10
Twickenham

[*Team:* Sheridan, Mears, Vickery, S. Shaw, S. Borthwick, T. Croft, Lipman, Easter, Wigglesworth, Cipriani, Vainikolo, T. Flood, Noon, Sackey, Balshaw]

[*Bench:* Chuter (rep), Haskell (rep), P. Hodgson (rep), Kay (rep), M. Stevens (rep), M. Tait (rep), Jonny Wilkinson (rep)]

[*Scorers:* **tries** by Sackey, M. Tait and Noon, **penalty goals** by Cipriani (4), **conversions** by Cipriani (3)]

POSITION: **2ND 6 +25 MT** [*Wales 10 +74 GS TC*, France 6 +10, Ireland 4 -6, Scotland 2 -54 CC, Italy 2 -57]

FANTASY: ***2ND 8 MT***

[Brian Ashton was sacked on 16th April 2008]

OTHER MATCHES

U20 6 NATIONS CHAMPIONSHIP

[**MANAGER:** *John Elliott*] [**COACH:** *Nigel Redman*] [**ASSISTANT COACH:** *Mark Mapletoft*]

CAPTAIN: *Hugo Ellis*

[1st Feb **ENGLAND U20** 28 WALES U20 15]

Kingsholm, Gloucester

[*Team:* Nathanael 'Nathan' Catt, Joe Gray, Alex Corbisiero, Gregor Gillanders, Scott Hobson, Jonathan 'Jon' Fisher, M. Cox, Hugo Ellis, Ben Youngs, Alex Goode, Miles Benjamin, Turner-Hall, Luke Eves, Cato, Greig Tonks]

[*Bench:* Jonny Arr (*scrum half*), Scott Freer (*prop/hooker*), Billy Moss (*prop*) (rep), Daniel 'Dan' Norton (*centre/wing/full back*) (rep), Tom Sargeant (*flanker/number 8*) (rep), Sebastian 'Seb' Stegmann (*wing*) (rep), B. Thomas]

[*Scorers:* **tries** by Cato, M. Benjamin and L. Eves, **penalty goals** by Alex Goode (3), **conversions** by Alex Goode (2)]

[9th Feb ITALY U20 13 **ENGLAND U20** 22]

Stadio Sciorba, Genoa

[*Team:* N. Catt, Joe Gray, Corbisiero, B. Thomas, S. Hobson, Jon Fisher, M. Cox, Hugo Ellis, B. Youngs, Alex Goode, Cato, Turner-Hall, L. Eves, Stegmann, Tonks]

[*Bench:* Arr (rep), Freer (rep), Robert 'Rob' Miller (*fly half*) (rep), B. Moss (rep), D. Norton (rep), Sargeant, Saull (*flanker*) (rep)]

[*Scorers:* **tries** by Corbisiero, Cato and Saull, **penalty goal** by Alex Goode, **conversions** by Alex Goode (2)]

[22nd Feb FRANCE U20 6 **ENGLAND U20** 24]

Stade des Alpes, Grenoble

[*Team:* N. Catt, Joe Gray, Corbisiero, B. Thomas, S. Hobson, Jon Fisher, M. Cox, Hugo Ellis, B. Youngs, Alex Goode, Cato, Turner-Hall, L. Eves, Stegmann, D. Norton]

[*Bench:* Freer (rep), R. Miller (rep), B. Moss (rep), Sargeant (rep), Saull (rep), Charlie Sharples (*wing*) (rep), J. Simpson (*scrum half*) (rep)]

[*Scorers:* **tries** by Cato and Corbisiero, **penalty goals** by Alex Goode (3) and R. Miller, **conversion** by Alex Goode]

[7th Mar SCOTLAND U20 15 **ENGLAND U20** 41]

Falkirk Stadium

[*Team:* N. Catt, Joe Gray, Corbisiero, B. Thomas, S. Hobson, Jon Fisher, M. Cox, Hugo Ellis, J. Simpson, R. Miller, Mark Odejobi, Alex Goode, L. Eves, Stegmann, Cato]

[*Bench:* Brake (*scrum half/centre/wing*) (rep), Freer (rep), Greg King (*centre*) (rep), Graham Kitchener (*lock*) (rep), B. Moss (rep), Sargeant (rep), B. Youngs (*scrum half/fly half*) (rep)]

[*Scorers:* **tries** by Stegmann, Cato (2), Hugo Ellis, J. Simpson and M. Cox, **penalty goal** by Alex Goode, **conversions** by Alex Goode (2) and R. Miller (2)]

CAPTAIN: *Hugo Ellis [Nathan Catt took over when Hugo Ellis went off injured at half-time]*

[14th Mar **ENGLAND U20** 43 IRELAND U20 14]

Kingsholm, Gloucester

[*Team:* N. Catt, Joe Gray, Corbisiero, Kitchener, S. Hobson, Jon Fisher, M. Cox, Hugo Ellis, J. Simpson, Adam Greendale, Odejobi, Alex Goode, L. Eves, Stegmann, Cato]

[*Bench:* James Cannon (*lock*) (rep), Freer (rep), G. King (rep), B. Moss (rep), D. Norton (rep), Saull (rep), B. Youngs (rep)]
[*Scorers:* **tries** by Stegmann, Hugo Ellis, L. Eves, M. Cox, Cato, N. Catt and Odejobi, **conversions** by Alex Goode (4)]
POSITION: 1ST 10 +95 GS TC [Wales 8 +33, France 6 +7, Ireland 4 -34, Italy 2 -46, Scotland 0 -55]

ENGLAND SAXONS INTERNATIONAL MATCHES

[**COACH:** *Stephen 'Steve' Bates*] [**ASSISTANT COACHES:** *Simon Hardy & Graham Rowntree*]
CAPTAIN: *Jordan Crane*
[1st Feb **ENGLAND SAXONS** 31 IRELAND A 13]
Welford Road, Leicester
[*Team:* N. Wood, D. Paice, J. Hobson, Tom Palmer (2), N. Kennedy, Dowson, B. Woods, J. Crane, L. Dickson, R. Lamb, D. Armitage, Geraghty, Ollie Smith (2), Varndell, Abendanon]
[*Bench:* Anthony Allen, Mike Brown (*wing/full back*) (rep), Grindal (rep), D. Hartley (rep), W. Skinner (rep), George Skivington (*lock*) (rep), David Wilson (2) (rep)]
[*Scorers:* **tries** by D. Paice, Varndell (2) and D. Armitage, **penalty goals** by R. Lamb and D. Armitage (2), **conversion** by D. Armitage]
CAPTAIN: *Phil Dowson*
[9th Feb ITALY A 15 **ENGLAND SAXONS** 38]
Stadio Aldo Campo, Ragusa, Sicily
[*Team:* Alex Clarke, D. Paice, Jon Golding, P. Short, N. Kennedy, Dowson, B. Woods, Guest, L. Dickson, A. Jarvis, J. Rudd, A. Crockett, D. Armitage, Biggs, Abendanon]
[*Bench:* John Brooks (*prop*) (rep), Mike Brown (rep), Care (rep), A. Long (rep), Ojo (rep), W. Skinner (rep), Springgay (*lock*) (rep)]
[*Scorers:* **tries** by Guest, D. Armitage, Biggs, N. Kennedy and A. Crockett, **penalty goal** by A. Jarvis, **conversions** by A. Jarvis (5)]
[Steve Bates, Simon Hardy and Graham Rowntree were all appointed on 8th January 2008; Graham Rowntree won 54 caps for England between 1995-2006 and was capped for the British & Irish Lions in May 2005]

USA SEVENS
IRB WORLD SEVENS SERIES 2007-2008 ROUND 4

PETCO Park, San Diego
[*Tournament squad:* Damu, James Collins, Banahan, Brake, Shabbo, Oduoza, A. Elliott, Vilk, K. Barrett, Gollings, Tombleson (*wing*), Simon Hunt]
(squad of 12)
[**MANAGER:** *Craig Townsend* (SC)] [**COACH:** *Ben Ryan*] [**ASSISTANT COACH:** *Russ Earnshaw*]
CAPTAIN: *Andy Vilk*
First Round - Pool 'D'
9th Feb MEXICO 0 **ENGLAND** 48
[*Team:* Damu, James Collins, Shabbo, K. Barrett, Gollings, Vilk, Oduoza]
[*Bench:* Banahan (rep), Brake, A. Elliott, Simon Hunt, Tombleson]
[*Scorers:* **tries** by Damu, Oduoza (3), K. Barrett, Gollings and Banahan (2), **conversions** by Gollings (4)]
9th Feb USA 21 **ENGLAND** 28
[*Team:* Brake, James Collins, Damu, K. Barrett, Gollings, Vilk, A. Elliott]

[*Bench:* Banahan, Simon Hunt, Oduoza (rep), Shabbo, Tombleson]
[*Scorers:* **tries** by Brake (2), A. Elliott and Gollings, **conversions** by Gollings (4)]
9th Feb SOUTH AFRICA 10 **ENGLAND** 14
[*Team:* Damu, Vilk, Banahan, K. Barrett, Gollings, Brake, A. Elliott]
[*Bench:* James Collins, Simon Hunt (rep), Oduoza (rep), Shabbo, Tombleson]
[*Scorers:* **tries** by Gollings (2), **conversions** by Gollings (2)]
Quarter-Final
10th Feb KENYA 17 **ENGLAND*** 7
[*Team:* Banahan, James Collins, Brake, K. Barrett, Gollings, Vilk, A. Elliott]
[*Bench:* Simon Hunt, Oduoza, Shabbo, Tombleson]
[*Scorers:* **try** by Gollings, **conversion** by Gollings]
[Plate Semi-Final:]
[10th Feb FIJI 21 **ENGLAND*** 14]
[*Team:* Simon Hunt, James Collins, Shabbo, Brake, Gollings, Vilk, Oduoza]
[*Bench:* Banahan, K. Barrett, A. Elliott, Tombleson]
[*Scorers:* **tries** by Oduoza and Shabbo, **conversions** by Gollings (2)]
POSITION: LOSING QUARTER-FINALISTS [*PLATE SEMI-FINALISTS*]
[England scored 4 competition points in this Round of the 2007-2008 IRB World Sevens Series]

ENGLAND STUDENTS MATCH

[**MANAGER:** *Keith Green*] [**COACH:** *Steve Hill*] [**ASSISTANT COACHES:** *Patrick Jerram, Paul Westgate* & *Philip 'Phil' Harvey*]
CAPTAIN: *Ian Kench*
[23rd Feb FRANCE STUDENTS 45 **ENGLAND STUDENTS** 9]
Stade Léon Sausset, Tournon
[*Team:* K. Davis, Jonathan Moyce, Liffchak, Kench, Simon Pitfield, Andries Pretorius, Malaney, Lumby, T. Henry, Vasey, Scott Armstrong, T. Gregory, Giles Pryor, T. Jarvis, Peter Wackett]
[*Bench:* Peter Browne (*lock/number 8*) (rep), Joe Clark (rep), Michael 'Mike' Denbee (*flanker/number 8*) (rep), Phillip 'Phil' Ellis (*centre*) (rep), Horn-Smith (rep), T. Roberts (rep), Dominic 'Dom' Shaw (*scrum half*) (rep)]
[*Scorers:* **penalty goals** by Vasey (3)]
[England Students amalgamated with the English Universities team on 2nd November 2007; There was an England Students Final Trial at Loughborough University on 9th January 2008]
[Keith Green, Paul Westgate and Phil Harvey were all appointed on 2nd November 2007; Keith Green was the Manager when the English Universities played their final game at Twickenham on 5th May 2007; Phil Harvey played for England U21 in December 1995]

FOUR NATIONS COLLEGES STUDENT RUGBY TOURNAMENT

[**MANAGER:** *Keith Green*] [**COACH:** *Steve Hill*] [**ASSISTANT COACHES:** *Patrick Jerram, Paul Westgate* & *Phil Harvey*]
CAPTAIN: *Michael Rickner*
[7th Mar Scottish Universities (*SC*) 0 **ENGLAND STUDENTS** 42]
Lasswade RFC, Hawthornden, Polton, Bonnyrigg
[*Team:* Richard 'Ricky' Whitehall, Matthew 'Matt' Cross, Lutton, Adrian Griffiths, P. Browne, Michael Rickner, Denbee, Thomas 'Tommy' Booth, D. Shaw, T. Roberts, Hockedy, P. Ellis, T.

Gregory, A. Wright, Christopher 'Chris' Ashwin]
[*Bench:* R. Anderson (rep), Peter Clarke (1) (*flanker*) (rep), Thomas 'Tom' Fidler (*prop*) (rep), T. Henry (rep), Drew Locke (*fly half/centre/wing*) (rep), Moyce (*hooker*) (rep), Timothy 'Tim' Stevenson (*fly half*) (rep)]
[*Scorers:* **tries** by A. Wright (2), Rickner (2), Peter Clarke and T. Henry, **conversions** by T. Roberts (6)]

CAPTAIN: *Ian Kench*

[14th Mar **ENGLAND STUDENTS** 30 Irish Colleges (*IR*) 14]
Henley RFC, Dry Leas, Marlow Road, Henley-on-Thames
[*Team:* Liffchak, Moyce, Horn-Smith, Kench, A. Griffiths, Peter Clarke (1), Denbee, Andries Pretorius, D. Shaw, T. Stevenson, Hockedy, P. Ellis, T. Gregory, A. Wright, T. Jarvis]
[*Bench:* S. Armstrong (*wing*) (rep), Ashwin (*fly half/full back*) (rep), Cross (*hooker*) (rep), K. Davis (*prop*) (rep), T. Henry (rep), Lumby (rep), Pitfield (*lock/flanker*) (rep)]
[*Scorers:* **tries** by A. Griffiths, A. Wright, Hockedy (2) and T. Stevenson, **penalty goal** by T. Stevenson, **conversion** by T. Stevenson]

CAPTAIN: *Phil Ellis*

[3rd May **ENGLAND STUDENTS** 38 COMBINED SERVICES U23 (*SER*) 26]
Twickenham
[*Team:* T. Fidler, Cross, Lutton, Pitfield, A. Griffiths, Rickner, Peter Clarke (1), P. Browne, Jamie Hood, Ashwin, Hockedy, P. Ellis, D. Locke, Mike Coady, Wackett]
[*Bench:* Denbee (rep), Dias (*centre*) (rep), Moyce (rep), Edward 'Ed' Pickles (*prop*) (rep), Andries Pretorius (*flanker*) (rep), Christopher 'Chris' Rowley (*scrum half*) (rep), T. Stevenson (rep)]
[*Scorers:* **tries** by J. Hood, P. Ellis, Denbee, Hockedy and P. Browne, **penalty goals** by Ashwin (3), **conversions** by Ashwin (2)]

POSITION: WINNERS

[This competition was also billed as a Colleges Four Nations Tournament; This tournament was not officially approved by the RFU]

CATHAY PACIFIC/CREDIT SUISSE HONG KONG SEVENS
IRB WORLD SEVENS SERIES 2007-2008 ROUND 5

Hong Kong Stadium, Eastern Hospital Road, So Kon Po, Hong Kong
[*Tournament squad:* Mayor, James Collins, Jon Fisher (*forward*), Brake, Cato, M. Cox (*forward*), A. Elliott, Vilk, K. Barrett, Gollings, B. Youngs (*scrum half/fly half*), Simon Hunt] ***(squad of 12)***

[Isoa Damu and Dom Shabbo were unavailable for this tournament due to injury; Matt Banahan and Danny Care unavailable due to club commitments; The England squad arrived in Hong Kong on 23rd March 2008]

[**MANAGER:** *Craig Townsend* (SC)] [**COACH:** *Ben Ryan*] [**ASSISTANT COACH:** *Russ Earnshaw*]

CAPTAIN: *Andy Vilk*

First Round - Pool 'B'

28th Mar CANADA 12 **ENGLAND** 24
[*Team:* Simon Hunt, Vilk, Brake, K. Barrett, Gollings, Mayor, A. Elliott]
[*Bench:* Cato, James Collins, M. Cox (rep), Jon Fisher, B. Youngs]
[*Scorers:* **tries** by Brake, Mayor, Gollings and M. Cox, **conversions** by Gollings (2)]

29th Mar SRI LANKA 7 **ENGLAND** 47
[*Team:* Simon Hunt, James Collins, Brake, B. Youngs, Gollings, Vilk, Cato]

[*Bench:* K. Barrett, M. Cox, A. Elliott (rep), Jon Fisher (rep), Mayor (rep)]
[*Scorers:* **tries** by Gollings (2), Brake, Simon Hunt, Cato, Mayor and A. Elliott, **conversions** by Gollings (6)]

29th Mar SAMOA 5 **ENGLAND** 7
[*Team:* Simon Hunt, Vilk, Brake, K. Barrett, Gollings, Mayor, A. Elliott]
[*Bench:* Cato (rep), James Collins, M. Cox (rep), Jon Fisher, B. Youngs (rep)]
[*Scorers:* **try** by Simon Hunt, **conversion** by Gollings]

Quarter-Final

30th Mar SAMOA 17 **ENGLAND*** 12
[*Team:* Simon Hunt, Vilk, M. Cox, K. Barrett, Gollings, Brake, A. Elliott]
[*Bench:* Cato (rep), James Collins (rep), Jon Fisher, Mayor, B. Youngs (rep)]
[*Scorers:* **tries** by A. Elliott and Vilk, **conversion** by Gollings]

POSITION: LOSING QUARTER-FINALISTS

[England scored 8 competition points in this Round of the 2007-2008 IRB World Sevens Series]

ADELAIDE SEVENS
IRB WORLD SEVENS SERIES 2007-2008 ROUND 6

Adelaide Oval, Adelaide

[*Tournament squad:* Mayor, James Collins (injured during pre-tournament training), Jon Fisher (never travelled as withdrew, replaced by Tom Tombleson), Brake, Cato, M. Cox, A. Elliott, Vilk, K. Barrett, Gollings, B. Youngs, Simon Hunt, Tombleson]

(squad of 12)

[Isoa Damu and Dom Shabbo were unavailable for this tournament due to injury; Jon Fisher initially selected but then withdrew due to Heineken Cup commitments; James Collins pulled a hamstring in a training session the day before the tournament began; Simon Hunt's off the field behaviour at this tournament was deemed to be unacceptable and as a consequence he was not considered for further selection to the England Sevens team until September 2010; John Brake played in the Samurai team that won the Amsterdam Heineken Sevens on 16th-17th May 2009 and played in the Samurai St George team that won the ULR Anglican Premier International Sevens at Bury St. Edmunds on 9th May 2010]

[**MANAGER:** *Craig Townsend* (SC)] [**COACH:** *Ben Ryan*] [**ASSISTANT COACH:** *Russ Earnshaw*]

CAPTAIN: *Andy Vilk*

First Round - Pool 'D'

5th April FIJI 31 **ENGLAND*** 12
[*Team:* Simon Hunt, Vilk, M. Cox, K. Barrett, Gollings, Brake, Cato]
[*Bench:* A. Elliott, Mayor, Tombleson, B. Youngs]
[*Scorers:* **tries** by Simon Hunt and K. Barrett, **conversion** by Gollings]

5th April KENYA 17 **ENGLAND** 10
[*Team:* Simon Hunt, Vilk, M. Cox, K. Barrett, B. Youngs, Brake, Cato]
[*Bench:* A. Elliott, Mayor, Tombleson]
[*Scorers:* **tries** by Simon Hunt and Vilk]

5th April FRANCE 19 **ENGLAND*** 12
[*Team:* Tombleson, Vilk, M. Cox, B. Youngs, K. Barrett, Mayor, A. Elliott]
[*Bench:* Brake (rep), Cato (rep), Simon Hunt (rep)]
[*Scorers:* **tries** by B. Youngs and A. Elliott, **conversion** by B. Youngs]

[Bowl Quarter-Final:]

[6th April USA 26 **ENGLAND*** 19 aet]

[*Team:* Tombleson, Vilk, M. Cox, K. Barrett, Mayor, Brake, Cato]
[*Bench:* A. Elliott, Simon Hunt (rep), B. Youngs (rep)]
[*Scorers:* **tries** by Tombleson, Brake and Simon Hunt, **conversions** by K. Barrett and B. Youngs]

[Shield Semi-Final:]

[6th April WALES 19 **ENGLAND*** 14]

[*Team:* Simon Hunt, Vilk, Brake, B. Youngs, K. Barrett, Mayor, Cato]
[*Bench:* M. Cox, A. Elliott, Tombleson]
[*Scorers:* **tries** by Mayor and Brake, **conversions** by B. Youngs (2)]

POSITION: FIRST ROUND LOSERS [*SHIELD SEMI-FINALISTS*]

[England did not score any competition points in this Round of the 2007-2008 IRB World Sevens Series]

EDINBURGH ACADEMICALS 150TH ANNIVERSARY MATCH

[**COACH:** *John Jeffrey* (SC)]

CAPTAIN: *Gordon Bulloch* (SC)

[9th April Edinburgh Academicals (*SC*) 0 **BARBARIANS** 43]

Raeburn Place, Stockbridge, Edinburgh

[*Team:* Dorian Williams (WA), G. Bulloch (SC), Taufo'ou (TON), J-L. Phillips, Peter Sidoli (WA), Tammas McVie (SC), Genaro Fessia (AR), G. Quinnell (WA), N. Runciman, R. Miller, Craig Morgan (WA), N. Macleod (WA), M. Allen, Lee Best, S. Moffat (SC)]
[*Bench:* Ross Blake (rep), Ben Evans (WA) (*prop*) (rep), Craig Hammond (rep), T. Howe (IR) (rep), Ledua Jope (FIJ) (*flanker/number 8*) (rep), Andrea Moretti (IT) (*hooker*) (rep), Ross Samson (SC) (*scrum half*) (rep)]
[*Scorers:* **tries** by N. Macleod (WA), Fessia (AR) (2), S. Moffat (SC), Craig Hammond, Samson (SC) and L. Best, **conversions** by R. Miller (2) and N. Macleod (WA) (2)]

[Edinburgh Academical FC founded 1857]

[John Jeffrey was appointed on 20th February 2008; John Jeffrey won 40 caps for Scotland between 1984-91]

EMIRATES AIRLINE LONDON SEVENS
IRB WORLD SEVENS SERIES 2007-2008 ROUND 7

Twickenham

[*Tournament squad:* Biggs (*wing*), R. Webber (*forward*), Cracknell, L. Dickson (*scrum half*), Foden, T. Youngs, J. Adams, Vilk, K. Barrett, Gollings, Oduoza, O. Phillips]

(squad of 12)

[Isoa Damu was unavailable for this tournament due to injury; Andy Vilk was the tournament captain]

[**MANAGER:** *Craig Townsend* (SC)] [**COACH:** *Ben Ryan*] [**ASSISTANT COACH:** *Russ Earnshaw*]

CAPTAIN: *Ben Gollings*

First Round - Pool 'B'

24th May **ENGLAND** 29 SPAIN 7

[*Team:* T. Youngs, R. Webber, Cracknell, L. Dickson, Gollings, J. Adams, Biggs]
[*Bench:* K. Barrett, Foden (rep), Oduoza (rep), O. Phillips (rep), Vilk]
[*Scorers:* **tries** by Biggs (3), L. Dickson and J. Adams, **conversions** by Gollings (2)]

CAPTAIN: *Andy Vilk*

24th May **ENGLAND** 33 FRANCE 5

[*Team:* R. Webber, Vilk, O. Phillips, K. Barrett, Gollings, Foden, Oduoza]

[*Bench:* J. Adams, Biggs (rep), Cracknell (rep), L. Dickson, T. Youngs (rep)]

[*Scorers:* **tries** by Gollings, Foden (2), K. Barrett and Oduoza, **conversions** by Gollings (4)]

24th May **ENGLAND** 7 SOUTH AFRICA 22

[*Team:* Oduoza, Vilk, R. Webber, L. Dickson, Gollings, Foden, O. Phillips]

[*Bench:* J. Adams, K. Barrett (rep), Biggs (rep), Cracknell, T. Youngs (rep)]

[*Scorers:* **try** by O. Phillips, **conversion** by Gollings]

Quarter-Final

25th May **ENGLAND** 17 NEW ZEALAND 12

[*Team:* R. Webber, Vilk, Cracknell, K. Barrett, Gollings, Foden, Oduoza]

[*Bench:* J. Adams, Biggs (rep), L. Dickson, O. Phillips, T. Youngs]

[*Scorers:* **tries** by Foden, K. Barrett and Biggs, **conversion** by Gollings]

Semi-Final

25th May **ENGLAND*** 12 SAMOA 14

[*Team:* R. Webber, Vilk, Cracknell, K. Barrett, Gollings, Foden, Oduoza]

[*Bench:* J. Adams, Biggs (rep), L. Dickson (rep), O. Phillips (rep), T. Youngs]

[*Scorers:* **tries** by Biggs and Foden, **conversion** by Foden]

POSITION: LOSING SEMI-FINALISTS

[England scored 12 competition points in this Round of the 2007-2008 IRB World Sevens Series]

BARBARIANS TOUR TO BELGIUM 2008

[**COACH:** *Dai Young* (WA)]

[*Other squad members:* Michael Claassens (SA) (*scrum half*), Delport (SA), Grewcock (never travelled as withdrew, replaced by Santiago Dellapè), Peter Hewat (AU) (*wing/full back*), Seilala Mapusua (SAM) (*centre*), Craig Newby (NZ) (*flanker/number 8*), Ryan Powell (WA) (*scrum half*) (never travelled as withdrew, replaced by Mark Robinson (2)), Jaco Pretorius (SA) (*centre*), Pucciariello (IT) (*prop*), C. Visagie (SA)]

(squad of 30)

[Dai Young was appointed on 12th February 2008; Dai Young won 54 caps for Wales between 1987-2001 and was capped for the British Lions in July 1989; Danny Grewcock and Ryan Powell in original squad but withdrew due to club commitments; The Barbarians squad travelled to Belgium on 22nd May 2008; Danny Grewcock retired in May 2011 but then came out of retirement to play for a H4H Northern Hemisphere XV against a Southern Hemisphere XV at Twickenham on 3rd December 2011]

CAPTAIN: *Mark Regan*

[24th May BELGIUM XV 10 **BARBARIANS** 84]

Stade Roi Baudouin, Brussels

[*Team:* Collazo (FR), M. Regan, Darren Crompton, Chesney, Justin Harrison (AU), Molitika (TON), D. Croft (AU), Mitchell 'Mitch' Chapman (AU), Gomarsall, Glen Jackson (NZ), Vainikolo, Tyrone Smith (AU), Turinui (AU), Gareth Thomas (2) (WA), Balshaw]

[*Bench:* Sébastien Bruno (FR) (*hooker*) (rep), Santiago Dellapè (IT) (*lock*) (rep), Stephen Larkham (AU) (*fly half/full back*) (rep), Mark Robinson (2) (NZ) (rep), O. le Roux (SA) (rep), Ross Skeate (SA) (*lock*) (rep), Pedrie Wannenburg (SA) (*flanker/number 8*) (rep)]

[*Scorers:* **tries** by Chesney, M. Chapman (AU), Balshaw (3), Turinui (AU) (2), Gareth Thomas (WA) (4), Wannenburg (SA), Molitika (TON) and Vainikolo, **conversions** by G. Jackson (NZ) (4), Larkham (AU) (2) and Balshaw]

FIRST GARTMORE CHALLENGE MATCH

[**COACH:** *Dai Young* (WA)]

CAPTAIN: *Morgan Turinui* (AU)

[27th May **BARBARIANS** 14 IRELAND XV 39]

Kingsholm, Gloucester

[*Team:* O. le Roux (SA), Bruno (FR), C. Visagie (SA), Chesney, Skeate (SA), Newby (NZ), D. Croft (AU), Wannenburg (SA), M. Claassens (SA), Larkham (AU), Vainikolo, J. Pretorius (SA), Turinui (AU), Sosene Anesi (NZ), Hewat (AU)]

[*Bench:* M. Chapman (AU) (*lock/flanker/number 8*) (rep), Collazo (FR) (rep), Dellapè (IT) (rep), Gomarsall (rep), G. Jackson (NZ) (*fly half*) (rep), M. Regan (rep), Tyrone Smith (AU) (*centre*) (rep)]

[*Scorers:* **tries** by Newby (NZ) and Wannenburg (SA), **conversions** by Hewat (AU) (2)]

[*Dai Young was appointed on 12th February 2008*]

EMIRATES AIRLINE EDINBURGH SEVENS
IRB WORLD SEVENS SERIES 2007-2008 ROUND 8
NED HAIG CUP

Murrayfield

[*Tournament squad:* Biggs, O. Cook (*forward*), Cracknell, Michael 'Micky' Young (*scrum half*), Rodwell (*forward*), T. Youngs, J. Adams, Vilk, K. Barrett, Gollings, Oduoza, O. Phillips]

(squad of 12)

[*Isoa Damu was unavailable for this tournament due to injury*]

[**MANAGER:** *Craig Townsend* (SC)] [**COACH:** *Ben Ryan*] [**ASSISTANT COACH:** *Russ Earnshaw*]

CAPTAIN: *Andy Vilk*

First Round - Pool 'A'

31st May PORTUGAL 0 **ENGLAND** 22

[*Team:* Cracknell, Vilk, T. Youngs, K. Barrett, Gollings, J. Adams, Oduoza]

[*Bench:* Biggs (rep), O. Cook (rep), O. Phillips (rep), Rodwell, Micky Young]

[*Scorers:* **tries** by Oduoza (2), O. Phillips and Biggs, **conversion** by Gollings]

31st May RUSSIA 17 **ENGLAND*** 17

[*Team:* O. Cook, Vilk, T. Youngs, Micky Young, Gollings, O. Phillips, Biggs]

[*Bench:* J. Adams (rep), K. Barrett (rep), Cracknell, Oduoza (rep), Rodwell]

[*Scorers:* **tries** by O. Phillips, Micky Young and Oduoza, **conversion** by Gollings]

31st May NEW ZEALAND 21 **ENGLAND*** 12

[*Team:* Cracknell, Vilk, T. Youngs, K. Barrett, Gollings, J. Adams, Oduoza]

[*Bench:* Biggs (rep), O. Cook, O. Phillips (rep), Rodwell, Micky Young]

[*Scorers:* **tries** by Gollings and J. Adams, **conversion** by Gollings]

Quarter-Final

1st June SOUTH AFRICA 0 **ENGLAND** 10

[*Team:* Cracknell, Vilk, T. Youngs, K. Barrett, Gollings, J. Adams, Oduoza]

[*Bench:* Biggs, O. Cook, O. Phillips (rep), Rodwell, Micky Young]

[*Scorers:* **tries** by J. Adams and K. Barrett]

Semi-Final

1st June WALES 0 **ENGLAND** 7

[*Team:* Cracknell, Vilk, T. Youngs, K. Barrett, Gollings, J. Adams, Oduoza]

[*Bench:* Biggs (rep), O. Cook, O. Phillips (rep), Rodwell, Micky Young]

[*Scorers:* **try** by Gollings, **conversion** by Gollings]

Final

1st June NEW ZEALAND 24 **ENGLAND*** 14

[*Team:* Cracknell, Vilk, T. Youngs, K. Barrett, Gollings, J. Adams, Oduoza]

[*Bench:* Biggs (rep), O. Cook (rep), O. Phillips (rep), Rodwell, Micky Young]

[*Scorers:* **tries** by Oduoza and O. Phillips, **conversions** by Gollings (2)]

POSITION: LOSING FINALISTS

FANTASY: *WINNERS*

[England scored 16 competition points in this Round of the 2007-2008 IRB World Sevens Series]

RANKING: 5TH 54 [*New Zealand 154*, South Africa 106, Samoa 100, Fiji 94, Argentina 43, Kenya 38, Australia 30, Wales 30, Scotland 26, Tonga 22, France 8, USA 6, Cook Islands 4, Portugal 4, Canada 2, Russia 1]

SECOND GARTMORE CHALLENGE MATCH

GARTMORE CHALLENGE TROPHY

[ENGLAND XV: [*Other squad members:* Anthony Allen, Alex Clarke, Noon, Robshaw, Tindall]**]**

(squad of 27)

[Rob Andrew, Graham Rowntree and Jon Callard were all appointed on 16th April 2008; Martin Johnson was involved in the selection process for this match but did not officially become England Team Manager until 1st July 2008 due to family commitments; Louis Deacon, Alex Brown, Lewis Moody, Jonny Wilkinson, Danny Cipriani, Shane Geraghty, Andy Farrell and James Simpson-Daniel all unavailable due to injury; Tim Payne, Lee Mears, Phil Vickery, Matt Stevens, Simon Shaw, Richard Blaze, Steve Borthwick, Ben Kay, Tom Palmer (2), Tom Croft, James Haskell, Joe Worsley, Michael Lipman, Tom Rees, Jordan Crane, Harry Ellis, Matt Banahan, Olly Barkley, Dom Waldouck, Dan Hipkiss, Paul Sackey, Tom Varndell, Josh Lewsey and Nick Abendanon all unavailable due to club commitments]

[ENGLAND XV: [TEAM MANAGER: *Rob Andrew*] **[COACHES:** *John Wells*, *Mike Ford*, *Graham Rowntree* & *Jon Callard*]**]**

[BARBARIANS: [COACH: *Dai Young* (WA)]**]**

CAPTAIN: *Nick Easter* [England XV]

CAPTAIN: *Mark Regan* [*Andy Gomarsall took over when Mark Regan was substituted in the 2nd half*] [Barbarians]

1st June **ENGLAND XV** 17 **BARBARIANS** 14

Twickenham

[ENGLAND XV: [*Team:* N. Lloyd, D. Paice, J. Hobson, Chris Jones, N. Kennedy, Narraway, W. Skinner, Easter, Wigglesworth, C. Hodgson, Strettle, T. Flood, M. Tait, Ojo, Mike Brown]

[*Bench:* Care (rep), Guest (*flanker/number 8*) (rep), D. Hartley (rep), S. Hooper (rep), Monye (rep), Peter Richards (rep), David Wilson (2) (rep)]

[*Scorers:* **tries** by Easter and M. Tait, **penalty goal** by T. Flood, **conversions** by T. Flood and Mike Brown]**]**

[BARBARIANS: [*Team:* Pucciariello (IT), M. Regan, C. Visagie (SA), Chesney, Justin Harrison (AU), Jerry Collins (NZ), Molitika (TON), Wannenburg (SA), Gomarsall, Larkham (AU), Balshaw, Mapusua (SAM), Turinui (AU), Gareth Thomas (2) (WA), Delport (SA)]

[*Bench:* Bruno (FR) (rep), M. Claassens (SA) (rep), Collazo (FR) (rep), D. Croft (AU) (rep), Dellapè (IT) (rep), G. Jackson (NZ) (rep), J. Pretorius (SA) (rep)]

[*Scorers:* **tries** by Mapusua (SAM) and Gareth Thomas (WA), **conversions** by Gomarsall and G. Jackson (NZ)]**]**

IRB JUNIOR WORLD CHAMPIONSHIP

Wales

[*No other squad members*]

(squad of 26)

[On 8th May 2007 the IRB announced that they would be holding a Junior World Championship in 2008; This IRB Junior World Championship amalgamated the previous IRB U21 World Championship and IRB U19 World Championship competitions; On 14th March 2008 the IRB unveiled a specially commissioned IRB Junior World Championship Trophy, which was thereafter awarded to the winners of the IRB Junior World Championship; Carl Fearns was unavailable for this tournament due to injury; Hugo Ellis was the tournament captain; On 18th May 2008 Nigel Redman announced that he would be leaving his post of Coach on 1st July 2008]

(During the First Round a bonus point was awarded for scoring 4 or more tries in a match and for losing by seven points or less)

[**MANAGER:** *John Elliott*] [**COACH:** *Nigel Redman*] [**ASSISTANT COACH:** *Mark Mapletoft*]

CAPTAIN: *Hugo Ellis*

First Round - Pool 'C'

[6th June FIJI U20 17 **ENGLAND U20** 41 **BP**]

Rodney Parade, Newport

[*Team:* N. Catt, Freer, Corbisiero, S. Hobson, B. Thomas, Jon Fisher, Calum Clark, Hugo Ellis, J. Simpson, Alex Goode, M. Benjamin, Turner-Hall, Odejobi, Stegmann, Cato]

[*Bench:* M. Cox (rep), Gillanders (*lock*), Joe Gray (*hooker*) (rep), R. Miller (rep), B. Moss (rep), Alex Tait (*centre/full back*) (rep), B. Youngs (rep)]

[*Scorers:* **tries** by M. Benjamin (2), Cato, Alex Goode, Stegmann and Turner-Hall, **penalty goal** by Alex Goode, **conversions** by Alex Goode (4)]

[10th Jun CANADA U20 18 **ENGLAND U20** 60 **BP**]

Rodney Parade, Newport

[*Team:* B. Moss, Joe Gray, Freer, Courtney Lawes, Gillanders, Jon Fisher, M. Cox, Hugo Ellis, B. Youngs, R. Miller, C. Sharples, Alex Tait, L. Eves, Odejobi, Cato]

[*Bench:* M. Benjamin (*wing*) (rep), James Clark (*hooker*) (rep), Corbisiero (*prop*) (rep), Alex Goode (*fly half/centre/full back*), S. Hobson (*lock/flanker*) (rep), J. Simpson (rep), B. Thomas (rep)]

[*Scorers:* **tries** by Jon Fisher, M. Cox, Odejobi, R. Miller, B. Youngs (2), L. Eves, Hugo Ellis and Cato, **penalty goal** by R. Miller, **conversions** by R. Miller (6)]

[14th Jun AUSTRALIA U20 13 **ENGLAND U20** 18]

Rodney Parade, Newport

[*Team:* N. Catt, Joe Gray, Corbisiero, S. Hobson, Gillanders, Jon Fisher, Calum Clark, Hugo Ellis, J. Simpson, Alex Goode, M. Benjamin, Turner-Hall, L. Eves, Stegmann, Cato]

[*Bench:* M. Cox, Freer, R. Miller, B. Moss, Alex Tait (rep), B. Thomas, B. Youngs (rep)]

[*Scorers:* **tries** by M. Benjamin (2), **penalty goals** by Alex Goode (2), **conversion** by Alex Goode]

Semi-Final

[18th Jun SOUTH AFRICA U20 18 **ENGLAND U20** 26]

Cardiff Arms Park

[*Team:* N. Catt, Joe Gray, Corbisiero, B. Thomas, Gillanders, M. Cox, Calum Clark, Hugo Ellis, J. Simpson, Alex Goode, M. Benjamin, Turner-Hall, L. Eves, Cato, Alex Tait]

[*Bench:* Jon Fisher (*flanker*) (rep), Freer, S. Hobson, R. Miller, B. Moss, Odejobi (*wing*) (rep), B. Youngs]
[*Scorers:* **tries** by J. Simpson, Cato and Corbisiero, **penalty goals** by Alex Goode (3), **conversion** by Alex Goode]
CAPTAIN: *Hugo Ellis* [*Nathan Catt took over when Hugo Ellis was substituted in the 2nd half*]
Final
[22nd Jun NEW ZEALAND U20 38 **ENGLAND U20** 3]
Liberty Stadium, Swansea
[*Team:* N. Catt, Joe Gray, Corbisiero, B. Thomas, Gillanders, Jon Fisher, Calum Clark, Hugo Ellis, J. Simpson, Alex Goode, M. Benjamin, Turner-Hall, L. Eves, Odejobi, Cato]
[*Bench:* M. Cox (rep), Freer (rep), S. Hobson (rep), R. Miller (rep), B. Moss (rep), Stegmann (rep), B. Youngs (rep)]
[*Scorers:* **penalty goal** by Alex Goode]
POSITION: LOSING FINALISTS

ENGLAND COUNTIES TOUR TO AMERICA AND CANADA 2008

[**CHAIRMAN OF SELECTORS:** *Peter Hartley*] [**MANAGER:** *Danny Hodgson*] [**ASSISTANT MANAGER:** *Martyn 'Sid' Cole*] [**COACH:** *Harvey Biljon* (SA)] [**ASSISTANT COACH:** *Dave Baldwin*]
[*Other squad members:* A. Davidson (*lock*) (never travelled as injured, replaced by Steve Pape), Jess (*wing*) (never travelled as withdrew, replaced by Andrew Fenby)]
(squad of 26)
[Danny Hodgson and Sid Cole were both appointed on 25th February 2008; Chris Rainbow was unavailable for this tour due to injury; Matt Jess initially selected but then withdrew due to club commitments; Liam Wordley was the tour captain; The England Counties squad departed for America on 3rd June 2008]
CAPTAIN: *Liam Wordley*
[6th June USA SELECT XV 3 **ENGLAND COUNTIES** 27]
Baker Field Athletics Complex, Columbia University, New York
[*Team:* T. Mathias, L. Wordley, Philip 'Phil' Boulton, Matt Owen, Pape, Kellard, Denbee, Mark Evans, N. Jones, Gavin Beasley, Andrew Fenby, Oliver 'Ollie' Winter, Rawlings, Oliver 'Ollie' Brennand, Benjamin 'Ben' Coulbeck]
[*Bench:* Daniel 'Dan' Collier (*lock*) (rep), J. Doherty (rep), Sebastian 'Seb' Moss (*flanker/number 8*) (rep), Petrus du Plessis (*prop*) (rep), Richard Wainwright (*fly half*) (rep), Christopher 'Chris' Whitehead (*hooker*) (rep), Andre Wilson (*fly half/centre*) (rep)]
[*Scorers:* **tries** by O. Brennand, Fenby (2), Rawlings and Coulbeck, **conversion** by Beasley]
CAPTAIN: *Dan Hyde*
[9th June USA SELECT XV 16 **ENGLAND COUNTIES** 31]
Baker Field Athletics Complex, Columbia University, New York
[*Team:* Johnny Williams, Whitehead, P. du Plessis, Pape, D. Collier, D. Hyde, Denbee, S. Moss, J. Doherty, Richard Wainwright, O. Brennand, Jason Duffy, A. Wilson, T. Jarvis, Coulbeck]
[*Bench:* Beasley (*fly half*) (rep), Boulton (*prop*) (rep), N. Jones (rep), Kellard (rep), Matt Owen (rep), Winter (*centre*) (rep), L. Wordley (rep)]
[*Scorers:* **tries** by J. Doherty, Pape, Richard Wainwright and L. Wordley, **penalty goal** by Richard Wainwright, **conversions** by Richard Wainwright (4)]

——— ——— ———

TEKSAVVY KENT CUP

CAPTAIN: *Liam Wordley*

[13th Jun CANADA SELECT XV 6 **ENGLAND COUNTIES** 31]

Chatham-Kent Community Athletic Complex, Chatham, South Ontario

[*Team:* T. Mathias, L. Wordley, Boulton, Pape, Matt Owen, D. Hyde, Kellard, Mark Evans, N. Jones, Richard Wainwright, Fenby, Rawlings, Winter, T. Jarvis, Coulbeck]

[*Bench:* Beasley (rep), Denbee (rep), J. Doherty (rep), S. Moss (rep), P. du Plessis (rep), Whitehead (rep), A. Wilson (rep)]

[*Scorers:* **tries** by Mark Evans, Winter, Coulbeck and T. Jarvis (2), **conversions** by Beasley (3)]

BARCLAYS CHURCHILL CUP

USA & Canada

[*Other squad members:* Alex Brown (never travelled as injured, replaced by Stuart Hooper), Mercey (travelled later as a replacement for David Wilson (2)), Adam Powell (*centre*), Varndell (never travelled as withdrew, replaced by Tom Biggs), Waldouck (*centre*) (never travelled as withdrew, replaced by Adam Powell), R. Webber]

(squad of 28)

[Lesley Vainikolo was rested for this tournament; Dom Waldouck and Tom Varndell initially selected but withdrew as they were now required to join the simultaneous England tour of New Zealand; Will Skinner was the tournament captain; The England Saxons squad departed for Canada on 2nd June 2008; Tom French (2) travelled later as a replacement for Nick Lloyd; David Wilson (2) flew to New Zealand after the Ireland A match, being replaced by Tom Mercey]

[On 13th March 2008 Toby Booth was appointed to become the England Saxons Assistant Coach for the 2008 Churchill Cup]

(<u>During the First Round a bonus point was awarded for scoring 4 or more tries in a match and for losing by seven points or less</u>)

[**COACH:** *Steve Bates*] [**ASSISTANT COACHES:** *Simon Hardy & Toby Booth*]

CAPTAIN: *Will Skinner [Jordan Crane took over when Will Skinner was substituted in the 2nd half]*

First Round - Pool 'B'

[7th June USA 10 **ENGLAND SAXONS** 64 **BP**]

Twin Elm Rugby Park, Nepean, Ottawa

[*Team:* N. Lloyd, Chuter, David Wilson (2), Blaze, Skivington, Chris Jones, W. Skinner, J. Crane, P. Hodgson, R. Lamb, Banahan, Anthony Allen, Ollie Smith (2), Biggs, Foden]

[*Bench:* Abendanon (rep), S. Armitage (*flanker*) (rep), Jack Forster (rep), Guest (rep), Monye (rep), Robshaw (rep), Titterrell (rep)]

[*Scorers:* **tries** by Banahan (3), Skivington, Anthony Allen, Foden, <u>penalty try</u>, Biggs and Monye, **penalty goal** by R. Lamb, **conversions** by R. Lamb (8)]

CAPTAIN: *George Chuter [Jordan Crane took over when George Chuter was substituted in the 2nd half]*

[14th Jun IRELAND A 12 **ENGLAND SAXONS** 34 **BP**]

Fletcher's Fields, Markham, Toronto

[*Team:* Alex Clarke, Chuter, David Wilson (2), Skivington, Chris Jones, J. Crane, S. Armitage, Guest, P. Hodgson, R. Lamb, Banahan, Anthony Allen, Ollie Smith (2), Monye, Abendanon]

[*Bench:* Blaze (rep), L. Dickson (rep), Foden (rep), Jack Forster (rep), A. Jarvis (rep), Robshaw (rep), Titterrell (rep)]
[*Scorers:* **tries** by Banahan (2), S. Armitage, Monye, Anthony Allen and Abendanon, **conversions** by R. Lamb and A. Jarvis]
CAPTAIN: *Will Skinner*
Final
[21st Jun SCOTLAND A 19 **ENGLAND SAXONS** 36]
Toyota Park, Bridgeview, Chicago
[*Team:* Alex Clarke, Chuter, Jack Forster, Chris Jones, Skivington, Robshaw, W. Skinner, J. Crane, P. Hodgson, R. Lamb, Banahan, Anthony Allen, Ollie Smith (2), Monye, Abendanon]
[*Bench:* S. Armitage (rep), L. Dickson (rep), Foden (rep), Tom French (2) (rep), S. Hooper (rep), A. Jarvis (rep), Titterrell (rep)]
[*Scorers:* **tries** by Banahan, Abendanon, J. Crane and Monye, **penalty goals** by R. Lamb (4), **conversions** by R. Lamb (2)]
POSITION: WINNERS

ENGLAND TOUR TO NEW ZEALAND 2008

[**TEAM MANAGER:** *Rob Andrew*] [**COACHES:** *John Wells, Mike Ford, Graham Rowntree & Jon Callard*]
[*Other squad members:* Cipriani (never travelled as injured, replaced by Dan Hipkiss), Easter (returned home as injured), D. Hartley, Hipkiss (never travelled as injured, replaced by Dom Waldouck), N. Kennedy, Lipman, Sackey (never travelled as injured, replaced by Tom Varndell), Waldouck, David Wilson (2) (travelled later as a replacement for Andy Sheridan)]
(squad of 32)
[Rob Andrew, Graham Rowntree and Jon Callard were all appointed on 16th April 2008; Martin Johnson provided input into the selection process for this tour even though he did not officially take up his post of Team Manager until 1st July 2008; Phil Vickery, Simon Shaw, Louis Deacon, Lewis Moody, Harry Ellis, Jonny Wilkinson, Shane Geraghty, Andy Farrell, James Simpson-Daniel and Josh Lewsey were all unavailable for this tour due to injury; The England squad departed for New Zealand on 2nd June 2008; Nick Easter returned home injured on 8th June 2008 and was not replaced; David Wilson (2) joined the tour on 16th June 2008]

IVECO SERIES

CAPTAIN: *Steve Borthwick*
14th June NEW ZEALAND 37 **ENGLAND*** 20
Eden Park, Auckland
[*Team:* Sheridan, Mears, M. Stevens, Tom Palmer (2), S. Borthwick, Haskell, Tom Rees, Narraway, Wigglesworth, C. Hodgson, Strettle, Barkley, Tindall, Ojo, Mike Brown]
[*Bench:* Care (rep), Kay (rep), Noon (rep), D. Paice (rep), T. Payne (rep), M. Tait, J. Worsley (rep)]
[*Scorers:* **tries** by Ojo (2), **penalty goals** by Barkley (2), **conversions** by Barkley (2)]
21st June NEW ZEALAND 44 **ENGLAND** 12
AMI Stadium, Christchurch
[*Team:* T. Payne, Mears, M. Stevens, Tom Palmer (2), S. Borthwick, Haskell, Tom Rees, Narraway, Care, T. Flood, Varndell, Noon, Tindall, Ojo, M. Tait]
[*Bench:* Barkley (rep), T. Croft (rep), J. Hobson (rep), Kay (rep), D. Paice (rep), Peter Richards (rep), J. Worsley (rep)]
[*Scorers:* **tries** by Care and Varndell, **conversion** by Barkley]

BACK TO BALLYMORE MATCH

[**MANAGER:** *Daniel Herbert* (AU)] [**COACH:** *Alan Jones* (AU)] [**ASSISTANT COACH:** Robert *Alexander 'Alec' Evans* (AU)]

CAPTAIN: *Ben Gollings*

[13th July Queensland XV (*AU*) 61 **AUSTRALIAN BARBARIANS** 17]
Ballymore Stadium, Brisbane

[*Team:* Pek Cowan (AU), Jeremy Paul (AU), Ma'afu (AU), Sitaleki Timani (TON), M. Chapman (AU), Scott Robertson (NZ), Beau Robinson (AU), Kefu (AU), Sam Cordingley (AU), Gollings, Luger, Taione (TON), Zane Mitchell (AU), Ratu Nasiganiyavi (AU), Mark Gerrard (AU)]

[*Bench:* Jason Harrington (AU) (*lock/flanker*) (rep), Daniel 'Dan' Palmer (AU) (*prop*) (rep), Quesada (AR) (*fly half*) (rep), Moses Rauluni (FIJ) (*scrum half*) (rep), Andrew Shaw (AU) (*flanker/number 8*) (rep), John Ulugia (AU) (*hooker*) (rep), Andrew Walker (AU) (*wing*) (rep)]

[*Scorers:* **tries** by J. Paul (AU) (2) and Cordingley (AU), **conversion** by Gollings]

[Match organised by the Queensland Rugby Union to raise money for both the Queensland Reds development tour of Ireland in August-September 2008 and the Souths rugby club in Brisbane, who incurred massive legal costs when they were taken to court over their plans to create a second pitch]

[Alan Jones and Alec Evans were both appointed on 17th June 2008; Daniel Herbert won 67 caps for Australia between 1994-2002; Alan Jones and Alec Evans were the Coach and Assistant Coach respectively when Australia won an unofficial Grand Slam by beating England, Ireland, Wales and Scotland in November-December 1984]

WORLD UNIVERSITY RUGBY SEVENS CHAMPIONSHIP

Estadio Universitario Monte Cronos, Campus de Rabanales, Córdoba

[*Tournament squad:* Dias, Peter Clarke (1) (*forward*), Pitfield (*forward*), Simon Lilley (*wing*), J. Hood (*forward*), Sam Smee (*centre/wing*), H. Smales (*centre/wing*), C. Rowley (*scrum half*), G. Thomson (SC), Harry Whittington (*fly half*), Gareth 'Gaz' Williams (forward), Idrusu Labri (*wing*)]

(squad of 12)

[Dave Morris was appointed on 9th July 2008; The Great Britain Students team was organised by the British Universities & Colleges Sport (BUCS), an organisation that was founded in June 2008 when University College Sport merged with the BUSA; The Great Britain Students squad arrived in Spain on 14th July 2008; Simon Pitfield played for Major R.V. Stanley's XV against Oxford University at Iffley Road on 19th November 2008]

[**MANAGER:** *Tim Stevens*] [**COACH:** *Dave Morris* (WA)] [**ASSISTANT COACH:** *Paul March*]

CAPTAIN: *??*

First Round - Pool 'B'

[17th July ROMANIA STUDENTS 12 **GREAT BRITAIN STUDENTS** 19]
[*Team:*]
[*Bench:*]
[*Scorers:*]

[17th July Portuguese Universities (*POR*) 0 **GREAT BRITAIN STUDENTS** 17]
[*Team:*]
[*Bench:*]
[*Scorers:*]

[17th July CHINESE TAIPEI STUDENTS 0 **GREAT BRITAIN STUDENTS** 36]
[*Team:*]

[*Bench:*]
[*Scorers:*]
[18th July Spanish Universities (*SP*) 12 **GREAT BRITAIN STUDENTS** 5]
[*Team:*]
[*Bench:*]
[*Scorers:*]
[18th July Canadian Universities (*CAN*) 0 **GREAT BRITAIN STUDENTS** 5]
[*Team:*]
[*Bench:*]
[*Scorers:*]
Quarter-Final
[19th July RUSSIA STUDENTS 12 **GREAT BRITAIN STUDENTS** 0]
[*Team:*]
[*Bench:*]
[*No scorers*]
[Plate Semi-Final:]
[19th July CHINESE TAIPEI STUDENTS 14 **GREAT BRITAIN STUDENTS** 21 **]**
[*Team:*]
[*Bench:*]
[*Scorers:*]
[Plate Final:]
[19th July ROMANIA STUDENTS 10 **GREAT BRITAIN STUDENTS** 14 **]**
[*Team:*]
[*Bench:*]
[*Scorers:*]
POSITION: LOSING QUARTER-FINALISTS [*PLATE WINNERS*]

TONGA CORONATION MATCH

[*Other squad members:* Matt Burke (AU), Chresten Davis (NZ) (*lock/flanker*), Finegan (AU), M. Gerrard (AU) (*centre/wing/full back*), D. Giffin (AU) (*lock*), Stuart Grimes (SC) (*lock*), Craig Joiner (SC), Kefu (AU), Brendan Laney (SC) (*fly half/centre/full back*), David Lemi (SAM) (*wing*), Lima (SAM) (*centre/wing*), Mark Mayerhofler (NZ) (*centre*), Persico (IT), Saula Radidi (FIJ) (*centre*), Roff (AU), V. Satala (FIJ), Sititi (SAM), George Stowers (SAM) (*flanker/number 8*), Fereti 'Freddie' Tuilagi (SAM) (*centre/wing*), H. Vyvyan (never travelled as withdrew)]
(squad of 26)
[Match to celebrate the forthcoming coronation of King George V Tupou of Tonga; Ilivasi Tabua won 10 caps for Australia between 1993-95 and also won 17 caps for Fiji between 1995-99!]
[**MANAGER:** *Darren Towart*] [**COACH:** *Daniel Herbert* (AU)] [**ASSISTANT COACH:** *Ilivasi Tabua* (FIJ)]
CAPTAIN: *Colin Charvis* (WA)
[31st July TONGA XV 60 **CORONATION WORLD XV** 26]
Teufaiva Stadium, Nuku'alofa
[*Team:* David Hilton (SC), J. Paul (AU), Jone Railomo (FIJ) (*prop*), Charvis (WA), Kronfeld (NZ), Gollings, M. Taylor (WA)]
[*Bench:* Nasiganiyavi (AU) (*wing*) (rep), Isireli 'Sireli' Temo (FIJ) (*prop*) (rep)]
[*Scorers:* **try** by Nasiganiyavi (AU)]

[*Experimental Law Variations introduced*]

CWMTAWE SEVENS

Pontardawe RFC, Parc Ynysderw, Ynysderw Road, Pontardawe, Swansea

[*Tournament squad:* R. Thirlby, Jonathan Hooper (WA) (*scrum half*), Gerard Viguurs (HOL) (*wing*), Ryan Tomlinson (CAN) (*fly half/centre*), Gareth Bowen (WA) (*fly half*), Jon Paine (IR) (*forward*), Dan Connolly (WA) (*centre/wing*), Malherbe, Nio Aiono (SAM) (*forward*), Greg Summers (*wing*), B. Gerry (*forward*), Sam Brown (*scrum half*), Justin Wilson (NZ) (*wing*) (never travelled as withdrew)]

(squad of 12)

[**MANAGERS:** *Terry Sands* & *John Pennycuick*] [**COACH:** *Eugene Martin* (NZ)]

CAPTAIN: *Rob Thirlby*

First Round - Pool 'E'

[2nd Aug	CSG Old Boys (*WA*)	0	**SAMURAI**	28	]

[*Team:*]
[*Bench:*]
[*Scorers:*]

[2nd Aug	Old Breconians (*WA*)	12	**SAMURAI**	35	]

[*Team:*]
[*Bench:*]
[*Scorers:*]

Quarter-Final

[2nd Aug	Covenant Brothers (*FIJ*)	5	**SAMURAI**	24	]

[*Team:*]
[*Bench:*]
[*Scorers:*]

Semi-Final

[2nd Aug	KooGa Wailers	28	**SAMURAI**	7	]

[*Team:*]
[*Bench:*]
[*Scorers:*]

POSITION: LOSING SEMI-FINALISTS

[On 1st May 2008 the IRB announced 13 Experimental Law Variations (ELVs) including: 1) a rolling maul could now be collapsed legally, 2) a quick lineout throw could now be taken at any angle towards the tryline of the team throwing in the ball, 3) each team had to put a minimum of two players into a lineout, but after that the non-throwing team now did not have to match the number of any further players put into the lineout by the team throwing in the ball, 4) an offside line now existed 5 metres behind the rearmost foot of the players either forming or feeding a scrum, 5) the corner flag was no longer considered to be touch in-goal unless the ball was grounded against it; These ELVs were introduced on a 12 month trial basis and officially came into effect on 1st August 2008 for both the southern hemisphere and northern hemisphere respectively]

[The 2009 Cwmtawe Sevens was cancelled on 30th July 2009 due to heavy rain]

HELP FOR HEROES RUGBY CHALLENGE MATCH

[**HELP FOR HEROES XV:** [**TEAM MANAGER:** *Phil de Glanville*] [**COACH:** *Nigel Redman*] [**ASSISTANT COACH:** *Jon Callard*]]

[**INTERNATIONAL SELECT XV:** [**TEAM MANAGER:** *Ieuan Evans* (WA)] [**COACH:** *Eddie O'Sullivan* (IR)] [**ASSISTANT COACH:** *Phil Davies (2)* (WA)]]

CAPTAIN: *Lawrence Dallaglio* [Help for Heroes XV]
CAPTAIN: *Scott Gibbs* (WA) [*Gareth Llewellyn* (WA) *took over when Scott Gibbs was substituted in the 1st half*] [International Select XV]

[20th Sep **HELP FOR HEROES XV** 29 **INTERNATIONAL SELECT XV** 10]
Twickenham

[HELP FOR HEROES XV: [*Team:* N. Catt, M. Regan, Mercey, Rob Sugden, S. Hobson, Cornish, Richard Hill (2), Dallaglio, J. Simpson, Alex Goode, Luger, W. Greenwood, Jason Robinson, Odejobi, Mal Roberts]
[*Bench:* H. Barratt (rep), Martin Johnson (rep), Gareth Leonard (SC) (*prop*) (rep), Richard 'Jack' Matthews (*hooker*) (rep), Martin Offiah (*wing*) (rep), Tom O'Keeffe (*lock*) (rep), Dave Pascoe (*scrum half*) (rep), Shabbo (*wing/full back*) (rep), Volley (rep)]
[*Scorers:* **tries** by Richard Hill, N. Catt, W. Greenwood and J. Simpson, **penalty goal** by Alex Goode, **conversions** by Alex Goode (2) and Dallaglio]**]**
[INTERNATIONAL SELECT XV: [*Team:* Hilton (SC), G. Bulloch (SC), Darren Morris (WA), Gareth Llewellyn (WA), H. Parr, Dafydd Jones (WA), Charvis (WA), Joe Kava (FIJ), G. Easterby (IR), Rhys Priestland (WA), K. Logan (SC), Gibbs (WA), Angelo Flammia, Kristian Phillips (WA), Justin Bishop (IR)]
[*Bench:* S. Byrne (IR) (rep), Marshall 'Marsh' Cormack (SC) (*lock*) (rep), Zak Feaunati (SAM) (*number 8*) (rep), Dafydd Hewitt (WA) (*centre*) (rep), M. Lee (SC) (*flanker*) (rep), Rhodes (*scrum half/fly half*) (rep), Shaun Ruwers (SA) (*prop*) (rep), M. Stephenson (rep), Micky Young (*scrum half*) (rep)]
[*Scorers:* **tries** by K. Phillips (WA) and K. Logan (SC)]**]**
[Match to raise money for the Joint Services Rehabilitation Centre at Headley Court in Surrey]
[Phil de Glanville was appointed on 3rd June 2008; Phil de Glanville won 38 caps for England between 1992-99; Nigel Redman and Jon Callard were both appointed on 15th July 2008]
[Ieuan Evans was appointed on 3rd June 2008; Ieuan Evans won 72 caps for Wales between 1987-98 and was capped for the British Lions in July 1989; Eddie O'Sullivan and Phil Davies (2) were both appointed on 15th July 2008]

ATKINS REMEMBRANCE RUGBY MATCH

[**COACH:** *Rob Baxter*]
CAPTAIN: *Danny Thomas*

[4th Nov COMBINED SERVICES (*SER*) 14 **BARBARIANS** 33]
Plymouth Albion RFC, Brickfields Recreation Ground, Madden Road, Plymouth
[*Team:* Windo, Joäo Correia (POR), R. Hopkins, Hocken (BEL), Chris Gittins (WA), Vasco Uva (POR), Danny Thomas, Kyle Marriott, William 'Will' Runciman, Rhys Jones (WA), Christopher 'Chris' Czekaj (WA), Diogo Mateus (POR), Selley (WA), McAtee (WA), Douglas 'Dougie' Flockhart (SC)]
[*Bench:* Bolt (rep), Brenton (rep), Mark Davies (*fly half*) (rep), Jamie Miller (*flanker*) (rep), Neethling (SA) (rep), Ritchie (rep), Sturgess (rep)]
[*Scorers:* **tries** by V. Uva (POR), McAtee (WA), D. Flockhart (SC) (2) and Czekaj (WA), **conversions** by Rhys Jones (WA) (2) and Mark Davies (2)]
[Match to commemorate the members of the British uniformed services who lost their lives during armed conflict]
[Rob Baxter was appointed on 27th October 2008; Rob Baxter played for the English National Divisions XV against both an Australian XV at Welford Road on 28th October 2001 and South Africa A at Worcester on 21st November 2001]

PACIFIC ISLANDERS TOUR TO ENGLAND, FRANCE AND ITALY 2008

FIRST INVESTEC CHALLENGE MATCH

[**TEAM MANAGER:** *Martin Johnson*] [**COACH:** *Brian Smith* (IR)] [**ASSISTANT COACHES:** *John Wells, Mike Ford & Graham Rowntree*]

CAPTAIN: *Steve Borthwick*

8th Nov **ENGLAND** 39 PACIFIC ISLANDERS 13

Twickenham

[*Team:* Sheridan, Mears, M. Stevens, S. Borthwick, N. Kennedy, T. Croft, Tom Rees, Easter, Care, Cipriani, Monye, Riki Flutey, Noon, Sackey, D. Armitage]

[*Bench:* Harry Ellis (rep), T. Flood (rep), D. Hartley (rep), Haskell (rep), Lipman (rep), Tom Palmer (2) (rep), Vickery (rep)]

[*Scorers:* **tries** by Sackey (2), Cipriani, N. Kennedy and Mears, **penalty goals** by Cipriani (2), **conversions** by Cipriani (4)]

[*On 16th April 2008 Martin Johnson was appointed to become England Team Manager on 1st July 2008; Martin Johnson won 84 caps for England between 1993-2003 and captained both the British Lions on their tour of South Africa in May-July 1997 and the British & Irish Lions on their tour of Australia in June-July 2001; Brian Smith was appointed on 14th July 2008; Brian Smith was capped for Australia in May 1987 and was then capped for Ireland in November 1989; Graham Rowntree was appointed on 7th August 2008*]

AUSTRALIAN TOUR TO ITALY, ENGLAND, FRANCE AND WALES 2008

SECOND INVESTEC CHALLENGE MATCH

COOK CUP MATCH

[**TEAM MANAGER:** *Martin Johnson*] [**COACH:** *Brian Smith* (IR)] [**ASSISTANT COACHES:** *John Wells, Mike Ford & Graham Rowntree*]

CAPTAIN: *Steve Borthwick*

15th Nov **ENGLAND*** 14 AUSTRALIA 28

Twickenham

[*Team:* Sheridan, Mears, Vickery, S. Borthwick, Tom Palmer (2), T. Croft, Tom Rees, Easter, Care, Cipriani, Monye, Flutey, Noon, Sackey, D. Armitage]

[*Bench:* Harry Ellis (rep), T. Flood (rep), D. Hartley (rep), Haskell (rep), Lipman (rep), S. Shaw (rep), M. Stevens (rep)]

[*Scorers:* **try** by Easter, **penalty goals** by Cipriani (2), **drop goal** by D. Armitage]

SOUTH AFRICAN TOUR TO WALES, SCOTLAND AND ENGLAND 2008

THIRD INVESTEC CHALLENGE MATCH

[**TEAM MANAGER:** *Martin Johnson*] [**COACH:** *Brian Smith* (IR)] [**ASSISTANT COACHES:** *John Wells, Mike Ford & Graham Rowntree*]

CAPTAIN: *Steve Borthwick*

22nd Nov **ENGLAND** 6 SOUTH AFRICA 42

Twickenham

[*Team:* T. Payne, Mears, Vickery, S. Borthwick, Tom Palmer (2), Haskell, Tom Rees, Easter,

Care, Cipriani, Monye, Flutey, Noon, Sackey, D. Armitage]
[*Bench:* T. Croft (rep), J. Crane (rep), Harry Ellis (rep), D. Hartley (rep), T. Flood (rep), S. Shaw (rep), M. Stevens (rep)]
[*Scorers:* **penalty goals** by Cipriani (2)]

EMIRATES AIRLINE DUBAI RUGBY SEVENS
IRB WORLD SEVENS SERIES 2008-2009 ROUND 1
EMIRATES INTERNATIONAL TROPHY

The Sevens, Dubai
[*Tournament squad:* Damu, Greg Barden (*forward/centre*), R. Vickerman, Micky Young, Rodwell, Oduoza, O. Phillips, Josua 'Josh' Drauniniu (*centre/wing*), K. Barrett, Gollings (injured during pre-tournament training), Biggs, Cracknell]
(squad of 12)
[Andy Vilk was unavailable for this tournament due to club commitments; The England squad arrived in Dubai on 22nd November 2008; Ben Gollings injured his calf in a training session before the tournament began; England played a practice match against the British Heart Foundation on 25th November 2008]
[Sean Bettinson was appointed on 10th November 2008]
[**MANAGER:** *Sean Bettinson*] [**COACH:** *Ben Ryan*] [**ASSISTANT COACH:** *Russ Earnshaw*]
CAPTAIN: *Ollie Phillips*
First Round - Pool 'D'
28th Nov PORTUGAL 7 **ENGLAND** 31
[*Team:* Damu, R. Vickerman, Cracknell, K. Barrett, O. Phillips, Drauniniu, Oduoza]
[*Bench:* Barden (rep), Biggs (rep), Rodwell, Micky Young (rep)]
[*Scorers:* **tries** by Drauniniu, Damu, Cracknell, Oduoza and Barden, **conversions** by O. Phillips (3)]
28th Nov USA 10 **ENGLAND** 24
[*Team:* Damu, R. Vickerman, Cracknell, K. Barrett, O. Phillips, Drauniniu, Oduoza]
[*Bench:* Barden, Biggs (rep), Rodwell (rep), Micky Young (rep)]
[*Scorers:* **tries** by O. Phillips (2), R. Vickerman and Damu, **conversions** by O. Phillips (2)]
28th Nov FIJI 5 **ENGLAND** 28
[*Team:* Damu, R. Vickerman, Cracknell, K. Barrett, O. Phillips, Drauniniu, Oduoza]
[*Bench:* Barden (rep), Biggs (rep), Rodwell, Micky Young (rep)]
[*Scorers:* **tries** by Damu (2), Oduoza and Micky Young, **conversions** by O. Phillips (4)]
Quarter-Final
29th Nov ARGENTINA 5 **ENGLAND** 15
[*Team:* Damu, R. Vickerman, Cracknell, K. Barrett, O. Phillips, Drauniniu, Biggs]
[*Bench:* Barden (rep), Oduoza, Rodwell (rep), Micky Young (rep)]
[*Scorers:* **tries** by Drauniniu, Damu and Biggs]
Semi-Final
29th Nov NEW ZEALAND 19 **ENGLAND** 21
[*Team:* Damu, R. Vickerman, Cracknell, K. Barrett, O. Phillips, Drauniniu, Oduoza]
[*Bench:* Barden, Biggs (rep), Rodwell, Micky Young]
[*Scorers:* **tries** by R. Vickerman, O. Phillips and Drauniniu, **conversions** by O. Phillips (3)]
Final
29th Nov SOUTH AFRICA 19 **ENGLAND*** 12
[*Team:* Damu, R. Vickerman, Cracknell, K. Barrett, O. Phillips, Drauniniu, Oduoza]
[*Bench:* Barden, Biggs (rep), Rodwell, Micky Young (rep)]

[*Scorers:* **tries** by Biggs and Micky Young, **conversion** by Micky Young]

POSITION: LOSING FINALISTS

FANTASY: ***WINNERS***

[*England scored 16 competition points in this Round of the 2008-2009 IRB World Sevens Series*]

NEW ZEALAND TOUR TO SCOTLAND, IRELAND WALES AND ENGLAND 2008

FOURTH INVESTEC CHALLENGE MATCH

SIR EDMUND HILLARY SHIELD

[**TEAM MANAGER:** *Martin Johnson*] [**COACH:** *Brian Smith* (IR)] [**ASSISTANT COACHES:** *John Wells, Mike Ford & Graham Rowntree*]

CAPTAIN: *Steve Borthwick*

29th Nov **ENGLAND** 6 NEW ZEALAND 32
Twickenham

[*Team:* T. Payne, Mears, Vickery, S. Borthwick, N. Kennedy, Haskell, Lipman, Easter, Care, T. Flood, Monye, Flutey, Noon, Sackey, D. Armitage]

[*Bench:* Cipriani (rep), T. Croft (rep), Harry Ellis (rep), D. Hartley (rep), Hipkiss (rep), Tom Rees (rep), M. Stevens (rep)]

[*Scorers:* **penalty goals** by T. Flood and D. Armitage]

[*On 27th November 2008 the RFU unveiled the specially commissioned Sir Edmund Hillary Shield, which was thereafter awarded to the winners of non-World Cup matches played between England and New Zealand; Sir Edmund Hillary reached the summit of Mount Everest on 29th May 1953 and died in January 2008*]

AUSTRALIAN TOUR TO ITALY, ENGLAND, FRANCE AND WALES 2008

OLYMPIC GAMES CENTENARY MATCH

CORNWALL CUP

[**COACH:** *Jake White* (SA)] [**ASSISTANT COACH:** *Eddie Jones* (AU)]

CAPTAIN: *John Smit* (SA)

[3rd Dec **BARBARIANS*** 11 AUSTRALIA XV 18]
Wembley Stadium

[*Team:* Pucciariello (IT), John Smit (SA), Cencus Johnston (SAM), John Philip 'Bakkies' Botha (SA), Johann Muller (SA), Jerry Collins (NZ), Richard 'Richie' McCaw (NZ), S. Burger (SA), Fourie du Preez (SA), Francois Steyn (SA), Bryan Habana (SA), Jean de Villiers (SA), Rico Gear (NZ), Rokocoko (NZ), P. Montgomery (SA)]

[*Bench:* Rodney Blake (AU) (*prop*) (rep), George Gregan (AU) (*scrum half*) (rep), Chris Jack (NZ) (*lock/flanker*) (rep), Nick Koster (SA) (*number 8*) (rep), M. Regan (rep), Ollie Smith (2) (rep), Shane Williams (WA) (*scrum half/wing*) (rep)]

[*Scorers:* **try** by Jerry Collins (NZ), **penalty goals** by P. Montgomery (SA) (2)]

[*Match organised by the British Olympic Association (BOA) to celebrate the centenary of the Rugby Union competition at the 1908 Olympic Games in London; This aforementioned tournament was won by an Australian XV, who beat a Great Britain XV 32-3 in the Final at the White City Stadium, London on 26th October 1908*]

[*The RFU chose Cornwall to represent Great Britain in the Rugby Union competition at the 1908 Olympic Games in London*]

[Jake White was appointed on 17th September 2008; Eddie Jones was appointed on 7th October 2008; Jake White and Eddie Jones were the Coach and Assistant Coach respectively when South Africa won the World Cup at Stade de France on 20th October 2007]

EMIRATES AIRLINE SOUTH AFRICA SEVENS
IRB WORLD SEVENS SERIES 2008-2009 ROUND 2

Outeniqua Park Stadium, George

[*Tournament squad:* Damu, Barden, R. Vickerman, Micky Young, Rodwell, Oduoza (never travelled as injured, replaced by Charlie Simpson-Daniel)), O. Phillips (captain; never travelled as injured, replaced by Rhys Crane), Drauniniu (never travelled as injured, replaced by Mat Turner)), K. Barrett, Gollings, Biggs, Cracknell, Charles 'Charlie' Simpson-Daniel (*scrum half*), Rhys Crane (*wing*), Mathew 'Mat' Turner (*centre/wing*)]

(squad of 12)

[Andy Vilk was unavailable for this tournament due to club commitments; Mat Turner played for South Africa U20 in February 2008; Charlie Simpson-Daniel was the brother of Chris and James Simpson-Daniel]

[**MANAGER:** *Sean Bettinson*] [**COACH:** *Ben Ryan*] [**ASSISTANT COACH:** *Russ Earnshaw*]

CAPTAIN: *Ben Gollings*

First Round - Pool 'A'

5th Dec TUNISIA 7 **ENGLAND** 42

[*Team:* Damu, R. Vickerman, Cracknell, K. Barrett, Micky Young, Gollings, Biggs]

[*Bench:* Barden (rep), R. Crane, Rodwell, Charlie Simpson-Daniel (rep), M. Turner (rep)]

[*Scorers:* **tries** by Gollings, Micky Young (3), R. Vickerman and Barden, **conversions** by Gollings (6)]

5th Dec FRANCE 7 **ENGLAND** 21

[*Team:* Damu, R. Vickerman, Cracknell, K. Barrett, Micky Young, Gollings, Biggs]

[*Bench:* Barden (rep), R. Crane (rep), Rodwell (rep), Charlie Simpson-Daniel, M. Turner]

[*Scorers:* **tries** by Cracknell, Gollings and Micky Young, **conversions** by Gollings (3)]

5th Dec NEW ZEALAND 19 **ENGLAND*** 7

[*Team:* Damu, R. Vickerman, Cracknell, K. Barrett, Micky Young, Gollings, Biggs]

[*Bench:* Barden (rep), R. Crane, Rodwell, Charlie Simpson-Daniel (rep), M. Turner (rep)]

[*Scorers:* **try** by R. Vickerman, **conversion** by Gollings]

Quarter-Final

6th Dec SOUTH AFRICA 17 **ENGLAND** 12

[*Team:* Damu, R. Vickerman, Cracknell, K. Barrett, Micky Young, Gollings, Biggs]

[*Bench:* Barden (rep), R. Crane, Rodwell (rep), Charlie Simpson-Daniel, M. Turner]

[*Scorers:* **tries** by Micky Young and Damu, **conversion** by Gollings]

[Plate Semi-Final:]

[6th Dec SAMOA 19 **ENGLAND** 20]

[*Team:* Damu, R. Vickerman, Cracknell, K. Barrett, Micky Young, Gollings, Biggs]

[*Bench:* Barden (rep), R. Crane (rep), Rodwell, Charlie Simpson-Daniel, M. Turner (rep)]

[*Scorers:* **tries** by Micky Young, Gollings and M. Turner (2)]

[Plate Final:]

[6th Dec PORTUGAL 7 **ENGLAND** 24]

[*Team:* Damu, R. Vickerman, Cracknell, K. Barrett, Micky Young, Gollings, Biggs]

[*Bench:* Barden (rep), R. Crane, Rodwell, Charlie Simpson-Daniel (rep), M. Turner (rep)]

[*Scorers:* **tries** by Damu, Micky Young, M. Turner and K. Barrett, **conversions** by Gollings (2)]

POSITION: LOSING QUARTER-FINALISTS [*PLATE WINNERS*]
[*England scored 8 competition points in this Round of the 2008-2009 IRB World Sevens Series*]

2009

OTHER MATCHES

ENGLAND SAXONS INTERNATIONAL MATCH

[**COACH:** *Stuart Lancaster*] [**ASSISTANT COACH:** *Paul Hull*]

CAPTAIN: *Phil Dowson*

[30th Jan **ENGLAND SAXONS** 66 PORTUGAL 0]

Edgeley Park, Hardcastle Road, Edgeley, Stockport

[*Team:* D. Cole, R. Webber, David Wilson (2), J. Crane, Skivington, Kearnan Myall, Saull, Dowson, Harry Ellis, E. Barnes, Cato, Adam Powell, Waldouck, Varndell, Abendanon]

[*Bench:* N. Catt (*prop*) (rep), Jon Fisher (rep), Alex Goode (rep), Mercey (rep), J. Simpson (rep), Matt Smith (1) (*fly half/centre/full back*) (rep), Joe Ward (*hooker*) (rep)]

[*Scorers:* **tries** by Harry Ellis (2), Adam Powell (2), Varndell (2), Cato, Waldouck, Matt Smith and J. Crane, **conversions** by E. Barnes (4) and Alex Goode (4)]

[Stuart Lancaster was appointed on 6th August 2008; Stuart Lancaster was capped for Scotland U21 in April 1991 but later switched his allegiance to England; On 6th May 2008 Stuart Lancaster was appointed to become Head of Elite Player Development on 1st June 2008; Paul Hull was appointed on 13th January 2009]

PARC Y SCARLETS OPENING CELBRATION MATCH

CARWYN JAMES MEMORIAL TROPHY

[**COACH:** *Eddie O'Sullivan* (IR)]

CAPTAIN: *Anton Oliver* (NZ) [*Mark Regan took over when Anton Oliver was substituted in the 2nd half*]

[31st Jan Llanelli Scarlets (*WA*) 40 **BARBARIANS*** 24]

Parc y Scarlets, Llanelli

[*Team:* Pucciariello (IT), A. Oliver (NZ), J. Dawson, Deiniol Jones (WA), D. Vickerman (AU), Persico (IT), Steve Tandy (WA), Molitika (TON), Michael 'Mike' Petri (US), Gordon Ross (SC), Voyce, Marius Goosen (SA), Jamie Robinson (WA), Brian Carney (IR), Ben Blair (NZ)]

[*Bench:* Charvis (WA) (rep), B. Evans (WA) (rep), G. Quinnell (WA) (rep), M. Regan (rep), Mark Robinson (2) (NZ) (rep), Jeremy Staunton (IR) (*fly half/centre*) (rep), Tomás de Vedia (AR) (*wing/full back*) (rep)]

[*Scorers:* **tries** by Carney (IR), B. Blair (NZ), Staunton (IR) and de Vedia (AR), **conversions** by B. Blair (NZ) (2)]

[Match to celebrate the official opening of the Parc y Scarlets]

[On 27th January 2009 Llanelli Scarlets unveiled a specially commissioned Carwyn James Memorial Trophy]

[Kingsley Jones was appointed Coach on 24th September 2008 but then withdrew on 13th January 2009 due to work commitments; Eddie O'Sullivan was appointed on 13th January 2009]

NEW ZEALAND INTERNATIONAL SEVENS

IRB WORLD SEVENS SERIES 2008-2009 ROUND 3

Westpac Stadium, Wellington

[*Tournament squad:* Damu, Ben Jones (*scrum half*), R. Vickerman, D. Norton (*centre/wing*), Barden (never travelled as injured, replaced by James Rodwell), Charlie Simpson-Daniel (injured during pre-tournament training), O. Phillips, Vilk, K. Barrett, Gollings, Biggs, Cracknell, Rodwell]

(squad of 12)

[The England squad arrived in New Zealand on 4th February 2009; Russ Earnshaw was listed on the bench in the tournament teamsheets but never actually changed into a playing kit!]
[**MANAGER:** *Sean Bettinson*] [**COACH:** *Ben Ryan*] [**ASSISTANT COACH:** *Russ Earnshaw*]
CAPTAIN: *Ollie Phillips*
First Round - Pool 'C'
6th Feb FRANCE 10 **ENGLAND** 26
[*Team:* Damu, R. Vickerman, Cracknell, K. Barrett, Gollings, O. Phillips, Biggs]
[*Bench:* B. Jones, D. Norton (rep), Rodwell (rep), Vilk (rep)]
[*Scorers:* **tries** by K. Barrett, O. Phillips, Damu and Vilk, **conversions** by Gollings (3)]
6th Feb CANADA 7 **ENGLAND** 34
[*Team:* Damu, R. Vickerman, Cracknell, K. Barrett, Gollings, O. Phillips, Biggs]
[*Bench:* B. Jones (rep), D. Norton (rep), Rodwell, Vilk (rep)]
[*Scorers:* **tries** by O. Phillips, Biggs, Damu, R. Vickerman, Gollings and D. Norton, **conversions** by Gollings (2)]
6th Feb ARGENTINA 13 **ENGLAND** 5
[*Team:* Damu, R. Vickerman, Cracknell, K. Barrett, Gollings, O. Phillips, Biggs]
[*Bench:* B. Jones, D. Norton (rep), Rodwell, Vilk (rep)]
[*Scorers:* **try** by K. Barrett]
Quarter-Final
7th Feb FIJI 10 **ENGLAND** 31
[*Team:* Damu, R. Vickerman, Cracknell, K. Barrett, Gollings, O. Phillips, Biggs]
[*Bench:* B. Jones (rep), D. Norton, Rodwell (rep), Vilk (rep)]
[*Scorers:* **tries** by Biggs, R. Vickerman, O. Phillips, Cracknell and Gollings, **conversions** by Gollings (3)]
Semi-Final
7th Feb KENYA 0 **ENGLAND** 24
[*Team:* Damu, R. Vickerman, Cracknell, K. Barrett, Gollings, O. Phillips, Biggs]
[*Bench:* B. Jones, D. Norton (rep), Rodwell (rep), Vilk (rep)]
[*Scorers:* **tries** by O. Phillips (3) and Cracknell, **conversions** by Gollings (2)]
Final
7th Feb NEW ZEALAND 17 **ENGLAND** 19
[*Team:* Damu, R. Vickerman, Cracknell, K. Barrett, Gollings, O. Phillips, Biggs]
[*Bench:* B. Jones, D. Norton, Rodwell, Vilk (rep)]
[*Scorers:* **tries** by O. Phillips, R. Vickerman and Damu, **conversions** by Gollings (2)]
POSITION: WINNERS
[England scored 20 competition points in this Round of the 2008-2009 IRB World Sevens Series]

6 NATIONS CHAMPIONSHIP

[**TEAM MANAGER:** *Martin Johnson*] [**COACH:** *Brian Smith* (IR)] [**ASSISTANT COACHES:** *John Wells*, *Mike Ford* & *Graham Rowntree*]
CAPTAIN: *Steve Borthwick*
7th Feb **ENGLAND** 36 ITALY 11
Twickenham
[*Team:* Sheridan, Mears, Vickery, S. Borthwick, N. Kennedy, Haskell, S. Armitage, Easter, Harry Ellis, Andy Goode, Cueto, Flutey, Noon, Sackey, D. Armitage]
[*Bench:* T. Croft (rep), Foden (rep), Geraghty (rep), D. Hartley (rep), M. Tait (rep), Julian White (rep), J. Worsley (rep)]

[*Scorers:* **tries** by Andy Goode, Harry Ellis (2), Flutey and Cueto, **penalty goal** by Andy Goode, **conversions** by Andy Goode (4)]

14th Feb WALES 23 **ENGLAND*** 15

Millennium Stadium, Cardiff

[*Team:* Sheridan, Mears, Vickery, S. Borthwick, N. Kennedy, Haskell, J. Worsley, Easter, Harry Ellis, Andy Goode, Cueto, Flutey, Tindall, Sackey, D. Armitage]

[*Bench:* T. Croft (rep), T. Flood (rep), D. Hartley (rep), P. Hodgson, Narraway (rep), M. Tait (rep), Julian White (rep)]

[*Scorers:* **tries** by Sackey and D. Armitage, **drop goal** by Andy Goode, **conversion** by T. Flood]

28th Feb IRELAND 14 **ENGLAND*** 13

Croke Park, Dublin

[*Team:* Sheridan, Mears, Vickery, S. Borthwick, N. Kennedy, Haskell, J. Worsley, Easter, Harry Ellis, T. Flood, Cueto, Flutey, Tindall, Sackey, D. Armitage]

[*Bench:* Care (rep), T. Croft (rep), Andy Goode (rep), D. Hartley (rep), Narraway (rep), M. Tait (rep), Julian White (rep)]

[*Scorers:* **try** by D. Armitage, **penalty goals** by T. Flood and D. Armitage, **conversion** by Andy Goode]

15th Mar **ENGLAND** 34 FRANCE 10

Twickenham

[*Team:* Sheridan, Mears, Vickery, S. Borthwick, S. Shaw, T. Croft, J. Worsley, Easter, Harry Ellis, T. Flood, Monye, Flutey, Tindall, Cueto, D. Armitage]

[*Bench:* Care (rep), Andy Goode (rep), D. Hartley (rep), Haskell (rep), N. Kennedy (rep), M. Tait (rep), Julian White (rep)]

[*Scorers:* **tries** by Cueto, Flutey (2), D. Armitage and J. Worsley, **penalty goal** by T. Flood, **conversions** by T. Flood (3)]

21st Mar **ENGLAND** 26 SCOTLAND 12

Twickenham

[*Team:* Sheridan, Mears, Vickery, S. Borthwick, S. Shaw, T. Croft, J. Worsley, Easter, Harry Ellis, T. Flood, Monye, Flutey, Tindall, Cueto, D. Armitage]

[*Bench:* Care (rep), Andy Goode (rep), D. Hartley (rep), Haskell (rep), N. Kennedy (rep), M. Tait (rep), Julian White (rep)]

[*Scorers:* **tries** by Monye, Flutey and M. Tait, **penalty goals** by T. Flood (2), **drop goal** by Care, **conversion** by T. Flood]

POSITION: **2ND 6 +54 CC** [*Ireland 10 +48 GS TC MT*, France 6 +23, Wales 6 +19, Scotland 2 -23, Italy 0 -121]

FANTASY: ***1ST 10 GS TC CC MT***

OTHER MATCHES

U20 6 NATIONS CHAMPIONSHIP

[**MANAGER:** *Stuart Lancaster*] [**COACH:** *Mark Mapletoft*] [**ASSISTANT COACH:** Stephen *Martin Haag*]

CAPTAIN: *Calum Clark*

[6th Feb **ENGLAND U20** 17 ITALY U20 0]

Worcester RFC, Sixways Stadium, Pershore Lane, Hindip, Worcester

[*Team:* Ben Moon, Jamie George, Bob Baker, James Gaskell, Kitchener, Lawes, Calum Clark, Christopher 'Chris' York, B. Youngs, Rory Clegg, Will Hurrell, L. Eves, Henry Trinder, Stegmann, C. Sharples]

[*Bench:* James Clark (rep), Shaun Knight (*prop*) (rep), R. Miller (rep), Joshua 'Josh' Ovens

(*flanker*) (rep), Tonks (*centre/full back*) (rep), Daniel 'Dan' White (*scrum half*) (rep), Daniel 'Dan' Williams (*lock/number 8*) (rep)]
[*Scorers:* **tries** by H. Trinder, L. Eves and Stegmann, **conversion** by Rory Clegg]

[13th Feb WALES U20 16 **ENGLAND U20** 28]
Brewery Field, Bridgend
[*Team:* Ben Moon, J. George, B. Baker, Gaskell, Kitchener, J. Ovens, Calum Clark, York, Dan White, R. Miller, Hurrell, Tonks, H. Trinder, Stegmann, Thomas 'Tom' Homer]
[*Bench:* Freddie Burns (*centre/full back*) (rep), James Clark (rep), Peter Elder (*lock*) (rep), Sam Harrison (2) (*scrum half*), Shaun Knight (rep), Sargeant (rep), Mike Stanley (*centre*)]
[*Scorers:* **tries** by York, H. Trinder, Calum Clark and R. Miller, **conversions** by R. Miller (4)]

[27th Feb IRELAND U20 19 **ENGLAND U20*** 18]
Dubarry Park, Athlone
[*Team:* Ben Moon, J. George, Shaun Knight, Gaskell, Elder, J. Ovens, Calum Clark, York, Dan White, Rory Clegg, Hurrell, Tom Casson, George Lowe, Stegmann, Tonks]
[*Bench:* B. Baker (*prop*) (rep), F. Burns, Arthur Ellis (*hooker*), Carl Fearns (*flanker/number 8*) (rep), Sam Harrison (2) (rep), Sargeant, James Short (*wing*) (rep)]
[*Scorers:* **tries** by J. Ovens, Hurrell and Lowe, **penalty goal** by Rory Clegg]

CAPTAIN: *Luke Eves*

[13th Mar **ENGLAND U20*** 11 FRANCE U20 31]
Worcester RFC, Sixways Stadium, Pershore Lane, Hindip, Worcester
[*Team:* Ben Moon, J. George, B. Baker, Gaskell, Dan Williams, Jamie Gibson, Jacob Rowan, York, Dan White, Rory Clegg, Stegmann, Casson, L. Eves, Lowe, Tonks]
[*Bench:* F. Burns (rep), Elder (rep), A. Ellis (rep), Sam Harrison (2) (rep), Hurrell (*wing/full back*) (rep), Joseph 'Joe' Marler (*prop*) (rep), Sargeant (rep)]
[*Scorers:* **try** by Lowe, **penalty goals** by Rory Clegg (2)]

[20th Mar **ENGLAND U20** 20 SCOTLAND U20 6]
Worcester RFC, Sixways Stadium, Pershore Lane, Hindip, Worcester
[*Team:* Marler, James Clark, Ben Moon, Dan Williams, Elder, J. Gibson, J. Rowan, York, Jordi Pasqualin, R. Miller, J. Short, L. Eves, H. Trinder, Lowe, Tonks]
[*Bench:* Rory Clegg (*fly half*) (rep), J. George (*hooker*) (rep), Hurrell (rep), Shaun Knight (rep), Sargeant (rep), Dan White (rep), Daniel 'Danny' Wright (*lock*) (rep)]
[*Scorers:* **tries** by H. Trinder, J. Gibson and Lowe, **penalty goal** by R. Miller, **conversion** by R. Miller]

POSITION: **3RD 6 +22** [*France 8 +97*, Ireland 8 -2, Scotland 6 -21, Wales 2 -16, Italy 0 -80]

FANTASY: ***1ST 10 GS TC***

[*On 6th May 2008 Stuart Lancaster was appointed to become England U20 Manager after the IRB Junior World Championship in Wales in June 2008; On 18th May 2008 Mark Mapletoft and Martin Haag were appointed to become England U20 Coach and England U20 Assistant Coach respectively on 1st July 2008; Martin Haag was capped for England in May 1997 and was the Assistant Coach when England U18 toured Australia in August 2007; Stuart Lancaster was unable to actually attend the Italy U20 match due to his England Saxons commitments*]

ENGLAND SAXONS INTERNATIONAL MATCH

[**COACH:** *Stuart Lancaster*] [**ASSISTANT COACH:** *Paul Hull*]

CAPTAIN: *George Skivington*

[6th Feb IRELAND A C **ENGLAND SAXONS** C]
Donnybrook, Dublin
[*Team:* Mullan, D. Paice, David Wilson (2), J. Crane, Skivington, Robshaw, W. Skinner,

Guest, P. Hodgson, Cipriani, Banahan, Turner-Hall, Waldouck, Ojo, Abendanon]
[*Bench:* D. Cole (*prop*), Dowson, S. Hooper, Stephen Myler (*fly half/full back*), J. Simpson, Strettle, R. Webber]
[*No scorers*]

USA SEVENS
IRB WORLD SEVENS SERIES 2008-2009 ROUND 4

PETCO Park, San Diego
[*Tournament squad:* Damu, B. Jones, R. Vickerman, D. Norton, Barden (never travelled as injured, replaced by James Rodwell), Charlie Simpson-Daniel (never travelled as injured, replaced by Mat Turner), O. Phillips, Vilk, K. Barrett, Gollings, Biggs, Cracknell, Rodwell, M. Turner]
(*squad of 12*)
[**MANAGER:** *Sean Bettinson*] [**COACH:** *Ben Ryan*] [**ASSISTANT COACH:** *Russ Earnshaw*]
CAPTAIN: *Ollie Phillips*
First Round - Pool 'C'
14th Feb SCOTLAND 12 **ENGLAND** 22
[*Team:* Damu, R. Vickerman, Cracknell, K. Barrett, Gollings, O. Phillips, Biggs]
[*Bench:* B. Jones, D. Norton (rep), Rodwell, M. Turner, Vilk (rep)]
[*Scorers:* **tries** by K. Barrett, Damu, Biggs and D. Norton, **conversion** by Gollings]
14th Feb JAPAN 12 **ENGLAND** 35
[*Team:* Damu, Vilk, Cracknell, K. Barrett, Gollings, O. Phillips, Biggs]
[*Bench:* B. Jones (rep), D. Norton, Rodwell (rep), M. Turner (rep), R. Vickerman]
[*Scorers:* **tries** by Biggs (2), O. Phillips, Cracknell and B. Jones, **conversions** by Gollings (5)]
14th Feb SAMOA 15 **ENGLAND*** 12
[*Team:* Rodwell, Vilk, Cracknell, K. Barrett, Gollings, O. Phillips, Biggs]
[*Bench:* B. Jones, D. Norton, M. Turner, R. Vickerman]
[*Scorers:* **tries** by K. Barrett (2), **conversion** by Gollings]
Quarter-Final
15th Feb FIJI 10 **ENGLAND** 12
[*Team:* Rodwell, R. Vickerman, Cracknell, K. Barrett, Gollings, O. Phillips, Biggs]
[*Bench:* B. Jones, D. Norton, M. Turner, Vilk]
[*Scorers:* **tries** by penalty try and R. Vickerman, **conversion** by Gollings]
Semi-Final
15th Feb SOUTH AFRICA 19 **ENGLAND** 22
[*Team:* Rodwell, R. Vickerman, Cracknell, K. Barrett, Gollings, O. Phillips, Biggs]
[*Bench:* B. Jones, D. Norton, M. Turner, Vilk (rep)]
[*Scorers:* **tries** by Gollings, O. Phillips (2) and Biggs, **conversion** by Gollings]
Final
15th Feb ARGENTINA 19 **ENGLAND*** 14
[*Team:* Rodwell, R. Vickerman, Cracknell, K. Barrett, Gollings, O. Phillips, Biggs]
[*Bench:* B. Jones, D. Norton, M. Turner, Vilk (rep)]
[*Scorers:* **tries** by Biggs and Gollings, **conversions** by Gollings (2)]
POSITION: LOSING FINALISTS
FANTASY: *WINNERS*
[England scored 16 competition points in this Round of the 2008-2009 IRB World Sevens Series]

AIB CLUB INTERNATIONAL MATCH

[**CHAIRMAN OF SELECTORS:** *Peter Hartley*] [**MANAGER:** *Danny Hodgson*] [**ASSISTANT MANAGER:** *Michael 'Mike' Old*] [**COACH:** *Harvey Biljon* (SA)] [**ASSISTANT COACH:** *Dave Baldwin*]

CAPTAIN: *Liam Wordley*

[27th Feb IRELAND CLUB XV 13 **ENGLAND COUNTIES*** 13]
Donnybrook, Dublin

[*Team:* Jacques, L. Wordley, Rupert Harden, Luke Collins, Bason, J. Lord, Kellard, Robert 'Rob' Baldwin, J. Doherty, Beasley, Samuel 'Sam' Smith, Bedworth, Billig, Mark Billings, Robert 'Rob' Cook]

[*Bench:* B. Gerry (*hooker*) (rep), Jack Harrison (*centre*) (rep), Christopher 'Chris' Johnson (2) (*fly half*) (rep), Paul Knight (2) (rep), Simon Legg (rep), J. Rule (rep), Jason Smithson (*flanker/number 8*) (rep)]

[*Scorers:* **try** by J. Doherty, **penalty goals** by Bedworth (2), **conversion** by Bedworth]

[Mike Old was appointed in October 2008; Mike Old was the son of Alan Old; Peter Hartley died on 3rd March 2009]

ENGLAND STUDENTS MATCHES

[**MANAGER:** *Keith Green*] [**COACH:** *Paul Westgate*] [**ASSISTANT COACH:** *James Farndon*]

CAPTAIN: *Phil Ellis*

[27th Feb Irish Colleges (*IR*) 10 **ENGLAND STUDENTS** 13]
City of Derry RFC, Judge's Road, Strathfoyle, Derry

[*Team:* B. Moss, Moyce, James Hall, A. Griffiths, Kench, Pitfield, Andrew 'Andy' Bridgeman, Ben Maidment, Rob Springall, William 'Will' Nelson, D. Locke, P. Ellis, David Butler, Sean Morris, Grant Pointer]

[*Bench:* Alan Awcock (*wing/full back*) (rep), Adam Bellamy (*hooker*), T. Fidler, T. Henry (rep), Malaney (*flanker*) (rep), Paul Trendell (*fly half*), Rob Wood (*lock/flanker*) (rep)]

[*Scorers:* **tries** by D. Locke and Pointer, **penalty goal** by Pointer]

[13th Mar **ENGLAND STUDENTS** 15 French Universities (*FR*) 13]
Clifton RFC, Station Road, Cribbs Causeway, Henbury, Bristol

[*Team:* B. Moss, Moyce, T. Fidler, Kench, R. Wood, Pitfield, Malaney, Maidment, T. Henry, W. Nelson, D. Locke, P. Ellis, D. Butler, Awcock, Pointer]

[*Bench:* Bellamy (rep), Bridgeman (*flanker*), Phil Burgess (*flanker/number 8*) (rep), James Hall (*prop*) (rep), Sean Morris (*wing*), Springall (*scrum half*), Trendell (rep)]

[*Scorers:* **tries** by Pointer (2), **penalty goal** by Pointer, **conversion** by Pointer]

[There was an England Students Final Trial at Loughborough University on 7th January 2009]

[James Farndon was appointed in September 2008]

RUGBY WORLD CUP SEVENS

MELROSE CUP

The Sevens, Dubai

[*Tournament squad:* Damu, Charlie Simpson-Daniel, R. Vickerman, Drauniniu, Rodwell, Varndell, O. Phillips, Vilk, K. Barrett, Gollings, Biggs, Cracknell]

(squad of 12)

[The final 12 man tournament squad was named on 19th February 2009; On 24th February 2009 the England squad arrived at Jabel Ali in Dubai for a pre-tournament training camp]

[**MANAGER:** *Sean Bettinson*] [**COACH:** *Ben Ryan*] [**ASSISTANT COACH:** *Russ Earnshaw*]

CAPTAIN: *Ollie Phillips*
First Round - Pool 'E'
5th March HONG KONG 5 **ENGLAND** 42
[*Team:* Damu, R. Vickerman, Cracknell, K. Barrett, Gollings, O. Phillips, Biggs]
[*Bench:* Drauniniu (rep), Rodwell, Charlie Simpson-Daniel, Varndell (rep), Vilk (rep)]
[*Scorers:* **tries** by Biggs, Varndell (2), Gollings (2) and Drauniniu, **conversions** by Gollings (6)]
6th March TUNISIA 24 **ENGLAND** 26
[*Team:* Damu, R. Vickerman, Cracknell, K. Barrett, Gollings, O. Phillips, Varndell]
[*Bench:* Biggs (rep), Drauniniu, Rodwell (rep), Charlie Simpson-Daniel (rep), Vilk]
[*Scorers:* **tries** by Varndell (2), Cracknell and Gollings, **conversions** by Gollings (3)]
6th March KENYA 7 **ENGLAND** 26
[*Team:* Damu, R. Vickerman, Cracknell, K. Barrett, Gollings, O. Phillips, Varndell]
[*Bench:* Biggs, Drauniniu (rep), Rodwell, Charlie Simpson-Daniel, Vilk (rep)]
[*Scorers:* **tries** by K. Barrett, Varndell and Damu (2), **conversions** by Gollings (3)]
Quarter-Final
7th March SAMOA 31 **ENGLAND*** 26 aet
[*Team:* Damu, R. Vickerman, Cracknell, K. Barrett, Gollings, O. Phillips, Varndell]
[*Bench:* Biggs, Drauniniu (rep), Rodwell, Charlie Simpson-Daniel, Vilk (rep)]
[*Scorers:* **tries** by Varndell (2), O. Phillips and Drauniniu, **conversions** by Gollings (3)]
POSITION: LOSING QUARTER-FINALISTS
FANTASY: ***WINNERS***
[*On 26th May 2009 the IRB announced that the Rugby World Cup Sevens would be replaced by the proposed Olympic Sevens competition at the 2016 Olympic Games in Rio de Janeiro; On 9th October 2009 the IOC duly voted to include Rugby Sevens in both the 2016 and the 2020 Olympic Games; On 17th December 2009 the IRB confirmed that there would be another Rugby World Cup Sevens tournament in 2013 before the Olympic Sevens took over as the pinnacle of the seven-a-side variation of the game*]

JEAN-CLAUDE BAQUÉ SHIELD MATCH

[**MANAGER:** *Danny Hodgson*] [**ASSISTANT MANAGER:** *Mike Old*] [**COACH:** *Harvey Biljon* (SA)] [**ASSISTANT COACH:** *Dave Baldwin*]
CAPTAIN: *Liam Wordley*
[15th Mar **ENGLAND COUNTIES*** 19 FRANCE AMATEURS 27]
Twickenham
[*Team:* Jacques, L. Wordley, Harden, L. Collins, J. Lord, Bason, Kellard, Smithson, J. Doherty, Chris Johnson (2), Sam Smith, Bedworth, Billig, Jack Harrison, R. Cook]
[*Bench:* R. Baldwin (*number 8*) (rep), Beasley (rep), Billings (rep), B. Gerry (rep), Paul Knight (2), Simon Legg, J. Rule (rep)]
[*Scorers:* **tries** by Billig, L. Collins and R. Baldwin, **conversions** by Bedworth (2)]
[*Harvey Biljon resigned on 23rd April 2009*]

BLACKHEATH 150TH ANNIVERSARY MATCH

[**COACH:** *Mike Rayer* (WA)]

CAPTAIN: *Paul Volley* [*Gordon Bulloch* (SC) *took over when Paul Volley was substituted at half-time*]

[18th Mar Blackheath 45 **BARBARIANS** 57]

Rectory Field, Charlton Road, Blackheath

[*Team:* Nigel Hall (NZ), G. Bulloch (SC), Patrick Palmer (WA), J. Cannon, Heino Senekal (NAM), John Dalziel (SC), M. Lee (SC), Volley, Walshe, McCarter (IR), Donavan Van Vuuren (SA), David Bishop (2) (WA), S. Jewell, Simon Hunt, Kevin Morgan (WA)]

[*Bench:* J. Dawson (rep), O. Dodge (rep), Head (IR) (rep), Lumby (rep), Ritchie (rep), Owen Ruttley (WA) (*scrum half*) (rep), Shanahan (rep)]

[*Scorers:* **tries** by Dalziel (SC), Simon Hunt (2), David Bishop (WA), S. Jewell, M. Lee (SC) (2), G. Bulloch (SC) and K. Morgan (WA), **conversions** by McCarter (IR) (3) and Walshe (3)]

[Blackheath FC founded 1858]

[Mike Rayer was appointed on 10th March 2009; Mike Rayer won 21 caps for Wales between 1991-94]

OXBRIDGE TOUR TO JAPAN 2009

[**MANAGERS:** *Stewart Eru* (NZ) & *Tim Stevens*] [**COACHES:** *Steve Hill* & *Ian Minto*]

[*Other squad members:* Andrew 'Andy' Daniel (*prop*) (tm)]

(squad of 26)

[Peter Clarke (1) was made tour captain because he was the winning skipper from the Varsity Match at Twickenham on 11th December 2008; The Oxbridge squad departed for Japan on 19th March 2009]

YOKOHAMA PORT & KEIO UNIVERSITY 150TH ANNIVERSARY MATCH

CAPTAIN: *Peter Clarke (1)*

[28th Mar All Keio University (*JAP*) 25 **OXBRIDGE XV*** 19]

Mitsuzawa Stadium, Yokohama

[*Team:* K. Davis, Daniel 'Dan' Rosen, Lutton, Conor O'Keeffe (IR), Robert 'Bert' Payne, Peter Clarke (1), Malaney, Chris Davies, Brendan McKerchar (SC), T. Henry, William 'Will' Browne, Willem Klopper (SA), Jonathan 'Jon' Burnett (AU), Sean Morris, Chris Mahony (NZ)]

[*Bench:* Fred Burdon (*centre*) (rep), T. Catling (*fly half/centre/wing/full back*) (rep), Alex Cheeseman (*flanker/centre*) (rep), Niall Conlon (IR) (*prop*) (rep), Matt Crockett (WA) (*hooker*) (rep), T. Gregory (*centre*) (rep), Kench (*lock*) (rep), Rhidian McGuire (WA) (*scrum half*) (rep), Joseph 'Joe' Wheeler (*flanker*) (rep), Peter Wright (2) (*number 8*) (rep)]

[*Scorers:* **tries** by Mahony (NZ) (2) and Sean Morris, **conversions** by T. Gregory (2)]

[Match to commemorate the 150th Anniversaries of the foundation of Keio University in 1858 and the opening of the Port of Yokohama in 1859 respectively]

CATHAY PACIFIC/CREDIT SUISSE HONG KONG SEVENS

IRB WORLD SEVENS SERIES 2008-2009 ROUND 5

Hong Kong Stadium, Eastern Hospital Road, So Kon Po, Hong Kong

[*Tournament squad:* Damu, B. Jones, R. Vickerman, Drauniniu, Rodwell, Varndell, O. Phillips, Charlie Simpson-Daniel (never travelled as injured, replaced by Dan Caprice), K. Barrett, Gollings, Biggs, Cracknell, Dan Caprice (*centre/wing*)]

(squad of 12)

[Andy Vilk was unavailable for this tournament due to club commitments; Ollie Phillips was the tournament captain]

[**MANAGER:** *Sean Bettinson*] [**COACH:** *Ben Ryan*] [**ASSISTANT COACH:** *Russ Earnshaw*]

CAPTAIN: *Ben Gollings*
First Round - Pool 'B'
27th Mar CHINA 0 **ENGLAND** 54
[*Team:* Damu, R. Vickerman, Cracknell, K. Barrett, Gollings, Drauniniu, Varndell]
[*Bench:* Biggs (rep), Caprice (rep), B. Jones, O. Phillips, Rodwell (rep)]
[*Scorers:* **tries** by Drauniniu (2), Damu, K. Barrett (2) and Caprice (3), **conversions** by Gollings (7)]
CAPTAIN: *Ollie Phillips*
28th Mar JAPAN 0 **ENGLAND** 50
[*Team:* Damu, R. Vickerman, Rodwell, K. Barrett, O. Phillips, Drauniniu, Varndell]
[*Bench:* Biggs (rep), Caprice (rep), Cracknell, Gollings, B. Jones (rep)]
[*Scorers:* **tries** by Damu (2), R. Vickerman (3), Varndell (2) and B. Jones, **conversions** by O. Phillips (5)]
28th Mar WALES 19 **ENGLAND** 26
[*Team:* Damu, R. Vickerman, Cracknell, K. Barrett, O. Phillips, Drauniniu, Varndell]
[*Bench:* Biggs (rep), Caprice (rep), Gollings, B. Jones, Rodwell (rep)]
[*Scorers:* **tries** by Damu, K. Barrett, O. Phillips and Cracknell, **conversions** by O. Phillips (3)]
CAPTAIN: *Ben Gollings*
Quarter-Final
29th Mar FIJI 10 **ENGLAND*** 7
[*Team:* Damu, R. Vickerman, Cracknell, K. Barrett, Gollings, Drauniniu, Varndell]
[*Bench:* Biggs (rep), Caprice, B. Jones, O. Phillips (rep), Rodwell (rep)]
[*Scorers:* **try** by R. Vickerman, **conversion** by Gollings]
POSITION: LOSING QUARTER-FINALISTS
FANTASY: *WINNERS*
[England scored 8 competition points in this Round of the 2008-2009 IRB World Sevens Series]

ADELAIDE SEVENS
IRB WORLD SEVENS SERIES 2008-2009 ROUND 6

Adelaide Oval, Adelaide
[*Tournament squad:* Damu (never travelled as injured, replaced by Neil Starling), B. Jones, R. Vickerman (never travelled as withdrew), Drauniniu, Rodwell, Varndell, O. Phillips, Charlie Simpson-Daniel (never travelled as injured, replaced by Dan Caprice), K. Barrett, Gollings, Biggs (never travelled as withdrew), Cracknell, Caprice, Starling]
(*squad of 10*)
[Andy Vilk was unavailable for this tournament due to club commitments; Rob Vickerman and Tom Biggs selected but withdrew due to club commitments and were not replaced]
[**MANAGER:** *Sean Bettinson*] [**COACH:** *Ben Ryan*] [**ASSISTANT COACH:** *Russ Earnshaw*]
CAPTAIN: *Ollie Phillips*
First Round - Pool 'A'
3rd April AUSTRALIA 21 **ENGLAND*** 17
[*Team:* Rodwell, B. Jones, Cracknell, K. Barrett, Gollings, O. Phillips, Varndell]
[*Bench:* Caprice (rep), Drauniniu (rep), Starling]
[*Scorers:* **tries** by Varndell and O. Phillips (2), **conversion** by Gollings]
4th April PORTUGAL 0 **ENGLAND** 29
[*Team:* Rodwell, Starling, Cracknell, Gollings, O. Phillips, Drauniniu, Varndell]

[*Bench:* Caprice, B. Jones (rep), Mika Taufaao (TON) (*fly half*) (rep)]
[*Scorers:* **tries** by Varndell (2), Drauniniu (2) and Rodwell, **conversions** by Gollings (2)]
4th April SAMOA 24 **ENGLAND*** 24
[*Team:* Rodwell, Starling, Cracknell, Gollings, O. Phillips, Drauniniu, Varndell]
[*Bench:* Caprice (rep), B. Jones (rep), Taufaao (TON)]
[*Scorers:* **tries** by Varndell (2), O. Phillips and Gollings, **conversions** by Gollings (2)]
Quarter-Final
5th April FIJI 40 **ENGLAND** 0
[*Team:* Rodwell, Starling, Cracknell, B. Jones, Gollings, O. Phillips, Drauniniu]
[*Bench:* Caprice (rep), Taufaao (TON)]
[*No scorers*]
[Plate Semi-Final:]
[5th April NEW ZEALAND 14 **ENGLAND** 21 **]**
[*Team:* Rodwell, Starling, Cracknell, Gollings, O. Phillips, Caprice, Varndell]
[*Bench:* Drauniniu (rep), B. Jones, Taufaao (TON)]
[*Scorers:* **tries** by Rodwell, Cracknell and Caprice, **conversions** by Gollings (3)]
[Plate Final:]
[5th April AUSTRALIA 19 **ENGLAND** 24 aet**]**
[*Team:* Rodwell, Starling, Cracknell, Gollings, O. Phillips, Caprice, Varndell]
[*Bench:* Drauniniu (rep), B. Jones, Taufaao (TON)]
[*Scorers:* **tries** by Varndell, O. Phillips, Rodwell and Gollings, **conversions** by Gollings (2)]
POSITION: LOSING QUARTER-FINALISTS [*PLATE WINNERS*]
[England scored 8 competition points in this Round of the 2008-2009 IRB World Sevens Series]

ENGLAND STUDENTS MATCHES

[MANAGER: *Keith Green*] **[COACH:** *Paul Westgate*] **[ASSISTANT COACH:** *James Farndon*]
CAPTAIN: *Phil Ellis*
[11th April NETHERLANDS 7 **ENGLAND STUDENTS** 68]
Nationaal Rugby Centrum, Sportpark "De Eendracht", Bok de Korverweg, Amsterdam
[*Team:* B. Moss, Moyce, James Hall, Kench, Pitfield, P. Burgess, Malaney, Maidment, T. Henry, Trendell, Awcock, P. Ellis, D. Locke, Sean Morris, Pointer]
[*Bench:* Bellamy (rep), Bridgeman (rep), D. Butler (*centre*) (rep), Lutton (rep), W. Nelson (*fly half/full back*) (rep), Springall (rep), R. Wood (rep)]
[*Scorers:* **tries** by D. Locke, Pitfield (2), Maidment, James Hall, Kench, P. Burgess, P. Ellis (2) and Awcock, **penalty goals** by Pointer (2), **conversions** by Pointer (2), Trendell (2) and W. Nelson (2)]
[2nd May **ENGLAND STUDENTS** 65 COMBINED SERVICES U23 (*SER*) 8]
Twickenham
[*Team:* Lutton, Bellamy, James Hall, Pitfield, R. Wood, P. Burgess, Bridgeman, Maidment, T. Henry, Trendell, Awcock, P. Ellis, D. Locke, D. Butler, Pointer]
[*Bench:* Will Chudleigh (*scrum half*) (rep), Kench (rep), Malaney (rep), Moyce (rep), W. Nelson (rep), Barney Purbrook (*prop*) (rep), Gareth Wynne (*wing*) (rep)]
[*Scorers:* **tries** by P. Burgess (2), R. Wood (2), Awcock, D. Locke, Kench, P. Ellis, Purbrook and Maidment, **penalty goal** by Pointer, **conversions** by Pointer (6)]

LONDON FLOODLIT SEVENS

Rosslyn Park FC, Priory Lane, Upper Richmond Road, Roehampton

[*Tournament squad:* Barden, K. Barrett, Drauniniu, D. Norton, Oduoza (withdrew), O. Phillips, Tom Powell (*forward*), Rodwell, Starling, Micky Young]

(squad of 9)

[The Help for Heroes VII was added to this tournament at short notice after Blackheath withdrew; The Help for Heroes VII wore sleeveless shirts in this tournament!]

[**COACH:** *Ben Ryan*]

CAPTAIN: *Ollie Phillips*

First Round - Pool 'D'

[6th May Loughborough University 14 **HELP FOR HEROES VII** 31]

[*Team:*]

[*Bench:*]

[*Scorers:*]

[6th May British Army (*SER*) 7 **HELP FOR HEROES VII** 31]

[*Team:*]

[*Bench:*]

[*Scorers:*]

Semi-Final

[6th May Saracens 7 **HELP FOR HEROES VII** 26]

[*Team:*]

[*Bench:*]

[*Scorers:* **tries** by Rodwell, O. Phillips, K. Barrett and D. Norton, **conversions** by ? (3)]

Final

[6th May Harlequins 10 **HELP FOR HEROES VII** 31]

[*Team:* Rodwell, Barden, ?, K. Barrett, O. Phillips, D. Norton, Drauniniu]

[*Bench:* Gus Qasevakatini (FIJ) (*wing*) (rep), Micky Young]

[*Scorers:* **tries** by O. Phillips, D. Norton, Barden (2) and Qasevakatini (FIJ), **conversions** by O. Phillips (3)]

POSITION: WINNERS

DAN JAMES MEMORIAL MATCH

[**MANAGER:** *John Elliott*] [**COACH:** *Mark Mapletoft*] [**ASSISTANT COACH:** *Martin Haag*]

CAPTAIN: *Calum Clark*

[13th May Loughborough University 23 **ENGLAND U20 XV*** 20]

Loughborough Students RFC, Loughborough University, Loughborough

[*Team:* Marler, James Clark, B. Baker, Gaskell, Dan Williams, York, Calum Clark, Fearns, David 'Dave' Lewis, R. Miller, Jack Cobden, Tonks, Lowe, C. Sharples, Rory Clegg]

[*Bench:* L. Eves (*centre*) (rep), J. George (rep), Hurrell (rep), Kitchener (rep), Shaun Knight (rep), Ben Moon (*prop*) (rep), Pasqualin (*scrum half*) (rep), J. Rowan (*flanker*) (rep), H. Trinder (*centre/wing*) (rep)]

[*Scorers:* **tries** by Calum Clark and L. Eves, **penalty goals** by R. Miller and Rory Clegg, **conversions** by R. Miller (2)]

[Match arranged to raise money for the Dan James Trust for spinal research; Dan James played for England Students in February 2006 and died on 12th September 2008; England U20 prepared for the 2009 Junior World Championship by having a pre-tournament training camp at Loughborough University on 13th-18th May 2009; This training camp commenced with the match against Loughborough University]

[*Majority of ELVs ratified*]

EMIRATES AIRLINE LONDON SEVENS

IRB WORLD SEVENS SERIES 2008-2009 ROUND 7

Twickenham

[*Tournament squad:* Biggs, Barden, R. Vickerman, Micky Young, Rodwell, Oduoza, O. Phillips, Starling, K. Barrett, Gollings, D. Norton, Cracknell]

(squad of 12)

[Isoa Damu was unavailable for this tournament due to injury; Andy Vilk unavailable due to club commitments; Ross Batty, Dan Caprice and Josh Drauniniu in original 16 man training squad; Tom Varndell in revised training squad of 14 but withdrew due to club commitments; Tom Powell in revised training squad of 14; Ollie Phillips was the tournament captain]

[**MANAGER:** *Sean Bettinson*] [**COACH:** *Ben Ryan*] [**ASSISTANT COACH:** *Russ Earnshaw*]

CAPTAIN: *Ollie Phillips*

First Round - Pool 'B'

23rd May **ENGLAND** 20 FRANCE 14

[*Team:* Cracknell, R. Vickerman, Rodwell, K. Barrett, Micky Young, O. Phillips, Biggs]

[*Bench:* Barden (rep), Gollings (rep), D. Norton, Oduoza (rep), Starling]

[*Scorers:* **tries** by K. Barrett, O. Phillips, Cracknell and Gollings]

CAPTAIN: *Ben Gollings*

23rd May **ENGLAND** 61 GEORGIA 0

[*Team:* Rodwell, R. Vickerman, Starling, Micky Young, Gollings, D. Norton, Biggs]

[*Bench:* Barden (rep), K. Barrett (rep), Cracknell, Oduoza (rep), O. Phillips]

[*Scorers:* **tries** by Gollings, Biggs (2), Micky Young (2), Rodwell, R. Vickerman and Oduoza (2), **conversions** by Gollings (8)]

CAPTAIN: *Ollie Phillips*

23rd May **ENGLAND** 31 SAMOA 14

[*Team:* Cracknell, R. Vickerman, Rodwell, K. Barrett, Gollings, O. Phillips, Biggs]

[*Bench:* Barden, D. Norton, Oduoza (rep), Starling (rep), Micky Young (rep)]

[*Scorers:* **tries** by K. Barrett, Gollings, Cracknell, Micky Young and R. Vickerman, **conversions** by Gollings (3)]

Quarter-Final

24th May **ENGLAND** 26 AUSTRALIA 12

[*Team:* Cracknell, R. Vickerman, Rodwell, K. Barrett, Gollings, O. Phillips, Biggs]

[*Bench:* Barden, D. Norton, Oduoza (rep), Starling (rep), Micky Young (rep)]

[*Scorers:* **tries** by Rodwell, Biggs, Gollings and R. Vickerman, **conversions** by Gollings (3)]

Semi-Final

24th May **ENGLAND** 26 SCOTLAND 12

[*Team:* Cracknell, R. Vickerman, Rodwell, K. Barrett, Gollings, O. Phillips, Biggs]

[*Bench:* Barden (rep), D. Norton, Oduoza (rep), Starling, Micky Young (rep)]

[*Scorers:* **tries** by O. Phillips, Biggs, Barden and Gollings, **conversions** by Gollings (3)]

CAPTAIN: *Ollie Phillips* [*Ben Gollings took over when Ollie Phillips was substituted in the 2nd half*]

Final

24th May **ENGLAND** 31 NEW ZEALAND 26 aet

[*Team:* Cracknell, R. Vickerman, Rodwell, K. Barrett, Gollings, O. Phillips, Biggs]

[*Bench:* Barden, D. Norton (rep), Oduoza (rep), Starling, Micky Young (rep)]

[*Scorers:* **tries** by Oduoza, Micky Young (2), Rodwell and D. Norton, **conversions** by Gollings (3)]
POSITION: WINNERS
[England scored 20 competition points in this Round of the 2008-2009 IRB World Sevens Series]
[On 13th May 2009 the IRB announced the completion of the 12 month ELV trial period basis and stated that 10 of the ELVs would be fully incorporated into the Laws of Rugby Union, whereas the remaining 3 ELVs were being abandoned; As a consequence it was decreed that a quick lineout throw could legally be taken backwards at any angle, the 5 metre offside line would exist at the base of a scrum and players could lawfully hit the corner flag in the act of scoring, but it was once again illegal to collapse a rolling maul and each team did actually have to match the number of players put into the lineout by the team throwing in the ball; These rule changes officially came into effect on 23rd May 2009 for both the southern hemisphere and northern hemisphere respectively]

EMIRATES AIRLINE EDINBURGH SEVENS
IRB WORLD SEVENS SERIES 2008-2009 ROUND 8
NED HAIG CUP

Murrayfield
[*Tournament squad:* Biggs, Barden, R. Vickerman, Micky Young, Rodwell, Oduoza, O. Phillips, Starling, K. Barrett, Gollings, D. Norton, Cracknell]
(squad of 12)
[Isoa Damu was unavailable for this tournament due to injury; Andy Vilk unavailable due to club commitments; Ollie Phillips was the tournament captain]
[**MANAGER:** *Sean Bettinson*] [**COACH:** *Ben Ryan*] [**ASSISTANT COACH:** *Russ Earnshaw*]
CAPTAIN: *Ollie Phillips*
First Round - Pool 'C'
30th May SCOTLAND 33 **ENGLAND*** 17
[*Team:* Cracknell, R. Vickerman, Rodwell, K. Barrett, Gollings, O. Phillips, Biggs]
[*Bench:* Barden (rep), D. Norton (rep), Oduoza (rep), Starling, Micky Young (rep)]
[*Scorers:* **tries** by Rodwell, Oduoza and Gollings, **conversion** by Gollings]
30th May CANADA 12 **ENGLAND** 26
[*Team:* Rodwell, R. Vickerman, Starling, K. Barrett, Gollings, O. Phillips, Oduoza]
[*Bench:* Barden (rep), Biggs, Cracknell, D. Norton (rep), Micky Young]
[*Scorers:* **tries** by Gollings (2), Starling and O. Phillips, **conversions** by Gollings (3)]
30th May KENYA 21 **ENGLAND*** 14
[*Team:* Rodwell, Barden, Starling, Micky Young, Gollings, O. Phillips, Oduoza]
[*Bench:* K. Barrett, Biggs (rep), Cracknell, D. Norton (rep)]
[*Scorers:* **tries** by Barden and O. Phillips, **conversions** by Gollings (2)]
CAPTAIN: *Ben Gollings [Ollie Phillips took over when Ben Gollings was substituted in the 2nd half]*
[Bowl Quarter-Final:]
[31st May GEORGIA 7 **ENGLAND** 31 **]**
[*Team:* Rodwell, Barden, Starling, K. Barrett, Gollings, D. Norton, Biggs]
[*Bench:* Oduoza (rep), O. Phillips (rep), Micky Young (rep)]
[*Scorers:* **tries** by D. Norton, Rodwell, Oduoza (2) and Micky Young, **conversions** by Gollings (3)]

CAPTAIN: *Ollie Phillips*
[Bowl Semi-Final:]
[31st May PORTUGAL 7 **ENGLAND** 31]
[*Team:* Rodwell, Barden, Starling, K. Barrett, Gollings, O. Phillips, Oduoza]
[*Bench:* Biggs (rep), D. Norton (rep), Micky Young (rep)]
[*Scorers:* **tries** by Oduoza (2), Rodwell, Gollings and Biggs, **conversions** by Gollings (2) and Micky Young]
[Bowl Final:]
[31st May FRANCE 15 **ENGLAND** 26]
[*Team:* Rodwell, Barden, Starling, K. Barrett, Micky Young, O. Phillips, Oduoza]
[*Bench:* Biggs (rep), Gollings, D. Norton]
[*Scorers:* **tries** by Oduoza (2), Rodwell and O. Phillips, **conversions** by O. Phillips (3)]
POSITION: FIRST ROUND LOSERS [*BOWL WINNERS*]
FANTASY: *LOSING SEMI-FINALISTS*
[England scored 2 competition points in this Round of the 2008-2009 IRB World Sevens Series]
RANKING: 3RD 98 [*South Africa 132*, Fiji 102, New Zealand 88, Argentina 68, Kenya 64, Samoa 40, Australia 30, Scotland 24, Wales 24, USA 20, Portugal 15, France 8, Tonga 4, Canada 3, Cook Islands 2]
FANTASY: *1ST 138*

BRITISH & IRISH LIONS TOUR TO SOUTH AFRICA 2009

[**MANAGER:** *Gerald Davies* (WA)] [**HEAD COACH:** *Ian McGeechan* (SC)] [**ASSISTANT COACHES:** *Warren Gatland* (NZ), *Rob Howley* (WA), *Shaun Edwards*, *Graham Rowntree* & *Neil Jenkins* (WA)]
[*Other squad members:* Michael 'Mike' Blair (SC) (*scrum half*) (tm), Keith Earls (IR) (*centre/full back*) (tm), Stephen Ferris (IR) (*flanker/number 8*) (left the tour injured, replaced by Ryan Jones) (tm), Jeremiah 'Jerry' Flannery (IR) (*hooker*) (never travelled as injured, replaced by Ross Ford), Stephen *Leigh* Halfpenny (WA) (*wing/full back*) (left the tour as injured) (tm), Nathan Hines (SC) (*lock*) (tm), Ryan Jones (WA) (travelled later as a replacement for Stephen Ferris, returned home injured), Euan Murray (SC) (*prop*) (left the tour injured, replaced by John Hayes) (tm), Tomás O'Leary (IR) (*scrum half*) (never travelled as injured, replaced by Mike Blair), Andrew 'Andy' Powell (WA) (*number 8*) (tm), Alan Quinlan (IR) (*lock/flanker/number 8*) (never travelled as suspended, replaced by Tom Croft), Shanklin (WA) (never travelled as injured)]
(squad of 38)
[Gerald Davies was appointed on 20th November 2007; Gerald Davies won 46 caps for Wales between 1966-78, was capped for the British Lions in July 1968 and captained the Barbarians against a British Lions XV at Twickenham on 10th September 1977; Ian McGeechan was appointed on 14th May 2008; Warren Gatland, Rob Howley and Shaun Edwards were all appointed on 22nd October 2008; Warren Gatland toured Australia, Wales & Ireland, France and Argentina with New Zealand in June-July 1988, October-November 1989, October-November 1990 and June-July 1991 respectively and also captained a New Zealand XV against England B in June 1992; Shaun Edwards was capped 36 times for Great Britain at Rugby League between 1985-94, played in the Wigan team that won the Middlesex Sevens at Twickenham on 11th May 1996 and played for Ireland at Rugby League in November 1998; Graham Rowntree was appointed on 11th December 2008; Neil Jenkins was appointed on 8th June and arrived in South Africa on 11th June 2009; Neil Jenkins won 87 caps for Wales

***between 1991-2002 and was capped for the British Lions in June 1997; Alan Quinlan was banned for 12 weeks on 13th May 2009 after being found guilty of gouging the eyes of an opponent in a Heineken Cup match on 1st May 2009 and he subsequently withdrew from the squad on 20th May 2009 after his appeal was turned down by the ERC; James Hook was added to the squad the day before its departure to provide injury cover for Leigh Halfpenny; The Lions squad departed for South Africa on 24th May 2009; Leigh Halfpenny was in the original squad but did not arrive until 2nd June 2009 due to injury; Gordon D'Arcy travelled later as a supplementary replacement for Riki Flutey and Keith Earls; Gordon D'Arcy became a permanent squad member on 11th June 2009 after Leigh Halfpenny left the tour injured; Ryan Jones arrived in South Africa on 11th June and then left the tour on 12th June 2009 because he had been concussed on the simultaneous Wales tour of Canada and America!; Tim Payne was added to the original squad of 37 on 21st June 2009 to provide injury cover for Andy Sheridan; Lee Byrne left the tour injured on 25th June 2009 and was not replaced; Gethin Jenkins, Adam Jones (2) and Brian O'Driscoll all returned home injured on 1st July 2009 and were not replaced*]**

CASTLE SOUTH AFRICA 2009 LIONS SERIES TROPHY

CAPTAIN: *Paul O'Connell* (IR)

[20th Jun SOUTH AFRICA 26 **BRITISH & IRISH LIONS*** 21]

ABSA Stadium, Durban

[*Team:* Gethin Jenkins (WA), Mears, Vickery, Alun-Wyn Jones (WA), P. O'Connell (IR), T. Croft, D. Wallace (IR), James 'Jamie' Heaslip (IR), Mike Phillips (2) (WA), Stephen Jones (2) (WA), Monye, James 'Jamie' Roberts (WA), Brian O'Driscoll (IR), Thomas 'Tommy' Bowe (IR), Lee Byrne (WA)]

[*Bench:* Harry Ellis, *Adam* Rhys Jones (2) (WA) (*prop*) (rep), Robert 'Rob' Kearney (IR) (*wing/full back*) (rep), D. O'Callaghan (IR) (*lock*) (rep), O'Gara (IR), Matthew Rees (WA) (*hooker*) (rep), Martyn Williams (WA) (rep)]

[*Scorers:* **tries** by T. Croft (2) and Mike Phillips (WA), **conversions** by Stephen Jones (WA) (3)]

[27th Jun SOUTH AFRICA 28 **BRITISH & IRISH LIONS*** 25]

Loftus Versfeld Stadium, Pretoria

[*Team:* Gethin Jenkins (WA), M. Rees (WA), Adam Jones (2) (WA), S. Shaw, P. O'Connell (IR), T. Croft, D. Wallace (IR), Heaslip (IR), Mike Phillips (2) (WA), Stephen Jones (2) (WA), Luke Fitzgerald (IR), J. Roberts (WA), Brian O'Driscoll (IR), Bowe (IR), R. Kearney (IR)]

[*Bench:* Harry Ellis, Ross Ford (SC) (*hooker*), Alun-Wyn Jones (WA) (*lock/flanker*) (rep), O'Gara (IR) (rep), Sheridan (rep), Martyn Williams (WA) (rep), Shane Williams (WA) (rep)]

[*Scorers:* **try** by R. Kearney (IR), **penalty goals** by Stephen Jones (WA) (5), **drop goal** by Stephen Jones (WA), **conversion** by Stephen Jones (WA)]

[4th July SOUTH AFRICA 9 **BRITISH & IRISH LIONS** 28]

Coca-Cola Park, Johannesburg

[*Team:* Sheridan, M. Rees (WA), Vickery, S. Shaw, P. O'Connell (IR), J. Worsley, Martyn Williams (WA), Heaslip (IR), Mike Phillips (2) (WA), Stephen Jones (2) (WA), Shane Williams (WA), Flutey, Bowe (IR), Monye, R. Kearney (IR)]

[*Bench:* T. Croft (rep), Harry Ellis (rep), R. Ford (SC) (rep), J. Hayes (IR) (rep), James Hook (WA) (*fly half/centre*), Alun-Wyn Jones (WA) (rep), D. Wallace (IR) (rep)]

[*Scorers:* **tries** by Shane Williams (WA) (2) and Monye, **penalty goals** by Stephen Jones (WA) (3), **conversions** by Stephen Jones (WA) (2)]

POSITION: SERIES LOSERS

FANTASY: ***SERIES WINNERS***

BARBARIANS MATCH

[ENGLAND XV: [*Other squad members:* Chuter, J. Crane, T. Croft (withdrew, replaced by Chris Jones), Cueto, Hipkiss, Kay, O. Morgan (*full back*), N. Kennedy, Tom Rees, Strettle (withdrew as injured, replaced by Matt Banahan), M. Tait, Vesty, Julian White, Wigglesworth]**]**

(squad of 34)

[Tom Palmer (2), Toby Flood, Mike Tindall and Paul Sackey all unavailable due to injury; Olly Barkley unavailable for personal reasons; Jonny Wilkinson was rested for this match; Tom Croft withdrew on 20th May 2009 as he was now required to go on the British & Lions tour of South Africa]

[Dai Young was appointed on 19th January 2009; Eddie O'Sullivan was appointed on 31st January 2009 but then withdrew on 16th March 2009 due to work commitments; Mike Catt was appointed on 16th March 2009; Mike Catt won 75 caps for England between 1994-2007 and was capped for the British Lions in July 1997]

[ENGLAND XV: [TEAM MANAGER: *Martin Johnson*] **[COACH:** *Brian Smith* (IR)] [**ASSISTANT COACHES:** *John Wells* & *Mike Ford*]**]**

[BARBARIANS: [COACH: *Dai Young* (WA)] **[PLAYER-ASSISTANT COACH:** *Mike Catt*]**]**

CAPTAIN: *Steve Borthwick* [England XV]

CAPTAIN: *Martin Corry* [Barbarians]

30th May **ENGLAND XV*** 26 **BARBARIANS** 33

Twickenham

[ENGLAND XV: [*Team:* T. Payne, D. Hartley, David Wilson (2), S. Borthwick, L. Deacon, Robshaw, Moody, Easter, Care, Andy Goode, Banahan, Turner-Hall, Noon, Foden, D. Armitage]

[*Bench:* S. Armitage (rep), Haskell (rep), P. Hodgson (rep), Chris Jones, T. May (rep), Steve Thompson (2) (rep), N. Wood (rep)]

[*Scorers:* **tries** by Foden, Turner-Hall, T. May and Banahan, **conversions** by Andy Goode (3)]**]**

[BARBARIANS: [*Team:* Clarke Dermody (NZ), Brits (SA), Greg Somerville (NZ), Corry, C. Jack (NZ), Jerry Collins (NZ), Serge Betsen (FR), Elsom (AU), J. Marshall (NZ), G. Jackson (NZ), Balshaw, G. D'Arcy (IR), J. Lewsey, Douglas 'Doug' Howlett (NZ), B. Blair (NZ)]

[*Bench:* Brendon James 'B. J.' Botha (SA) (*prop*) (rep), Bruno (FR) (rep), M. Catt (rep), Nasiganiyavi (AU) (rep), Paul Tito (NZ) (*lock*) (rep), P. Waugh (AU) (*flanker*) (rep), Chris Whitaker (AU) (*scrum half*) (rep)]

[*Scorers:* **tries** by Balshaw (2), C. Jack (NZ), Elsom (AU) and G. D'Arcy (IR), **conversions** by B. Blair (NZ) (4)]**]**

IRB TOSHIBA JUNIOR WORLD CHAMPIONSHIP

Japan

[*Other squad members:* Casson (*centre*) (never travelled as injured, replaced by Jack Cobden), Stegmann (never travelled as injured, replaced by Will Hurrell)]

(squad of 26)

[Seb Stegmann initially selected for this tournament but then ruptured the anterior cruciate ligament in his knee; The England U20 squad departed for Japan on 27th May 2009; Calum Clark was the tournament captain; Martin Haag resigned on 23rd June 2009]

(During the First Round a bonus point was awarded for scoring 4 or more tries in a match and for losing by seven points or less)

[**MANAGER:** *John Elliott*] [**COACH:** *Mark Mapletoft*] [**ASSISTANT COACH:** *Martin Haag*]

CAPTAIN: *Luke Eves* [*Carl Fearns took over when Luke Eves was substituted at half-time*]
First Round - Pool 'B'
[5th June JAPAN U20 0 **ENGLAND U20** 43 **BP**]
Chichibunomiya Rugby Stadium, Tokyo
[*Team:* Marler, J. George, B. Baker, Dan Williams, Gaskell, York, J. Ovens, Fearns, B. Youngs, Rory Clegg, Cobden, Tonks, L. Eves, Lowe, Homer]
[*Bench:* James Clark (rep), Kitchener (rep), Lawes (*lock/flanker*) (rep), Dave Lewis (*scrum half*) (rep), R. Miller (rep), B. Moon (rep), H. Trinder (rep)]
[*Scorers:* **tries** by J. Ovens, York, L. Eves, Lowe, Fearns and Lawes, **penalty goal** by Homer, **conversions** by Homer (5)]
CAPTAIN: *Luke Eves*
[9th June SCOTLAND U20 7 **ENGLAND U20** 30 **BP**]
Chichibunomiya Rugby Stadium, Tokyo
[*Team:* B. Moon, J. George, Shaun Knight, Gaskell, Kitchener, Lawes, J. Ovens, York, Dave Lewis, R. Miller, Hurrell, L. Eves, H. Trinder, C. Sharples, Homer]
[*Bench:* B. Baker (rep), James Clark (rep), Rory Clegg (rep), Cobden (*centre/wing*) (rep), Fearns (rep), Dan Williams (*lock/flanker/number 8*) (rep), B. Youngs (rep)]
[*Scorers:* **tries** by C. Sharples, H. Trinder, L. Eves and Fearns, **penalty goals** by Homer (2), **conversions** by Homer (2)]
CAPTAIN: *Calum Clark* [*Luke Eves took over when Calum Clark was substituted in the 2nd half*]
[13th Jun SAMOA U20 7 **ENGLAND U20** 52 **BP**]
Chichibunomiya Rugby Stadium, Tokyo
[*Team:* B. Moon, James Clark, B. Baker, Dan Williams, Kitchener, Lawes, Calum Clark, Fearns, B. Youngs, Rory Clegg, Lowe, L. Eves, H. Trinder, C. Sharples, Homer]
[*Bench:* Gaskell (*lock*) (rep), J. George (rep), Shaun Knight, Dave Lewis (rep), R. Miller (rep), J. Ovens (rep), Tonks (rep)]
[*Scorers:* **tries** by H. Trinder (2), Lowe, Fearns (2), B. Youngs and C. Sharples, **penalty goals** by Homer (2) and Rory Clegg, **conversions** by Homer (4)]
CAPTAIN: *Calum Clark*
Semi-Final
[17th Jun SOUTH AFRICA U20 21 **ENGLAND U20** 40]
Chichibunomiya Rugby Stadium, Tokyo
[*Team:* B. Moon, James Clark, B. Baker, Kitchener, Gaskell, Lawes, Calum Clark, Fearns, B. Youngs, Rory Clegg, C. Sharples, L. Eves, H. Trinder, Lowe, Homer]
[*Bench:* Cobden (rep), J. George (rep), Shaun Knight (rep), Dave Lewis, R. Miller, J. Ovens, Dan Williams]
[*Scorers:* **tries** by B. Youngs, Gaskell, Lawes and H. Trinder, **penalty goals** by Homer (4), **conversions** by Homer (4)]
Final
[21st Jun NEW ZEALAND U20 44 **ENGLAND U20*** 28]
Chichibunomiya Rugby Stadium, Tokyo
[*Team:* B. Moon, J. George, B. Baker, Kitchener, Gaskell, Lawes, Calum Clark, Fearns, B. Youngs, Rory Clegg, C. Sharples, L. Eves, H. Trinder, Lowe, Homer]
[*Bench:* James Clark (rep), Cobden (rep), Shaun Knight (rep), Dave Lewis (rep), R. Miller (rep), J. Ovens (rep), Dan Williams (rep)]

[*Scorers:* **tries** by Gaskell, Fearns and Dave Lewis, **penalty goals** by Homer (3), **conversions** by Homer and R. Miller]

POSITION: LOSING FINALISTS

FANTASY: *WINNERS*

ENGLAND COUNTIES TOUR TO KOREA AND JAPAN 2009

[**MANAGER:** *Danny Hodgson*] [**ASSISTANT MANAGER:** *Mike Old*] [**COACH:** *Dave Baldwin*] [**ASSISTANT COACH:** *Tommy Borthwick*]

[*Other squad members:* James Aston (tm), Gareth Collins (*wing*) (tm), P. Joyce (tm), Paul Ralph (*lock*) (tm)]

(squad of 26)

[Tommy Borthwick was appointed on 27th April 2009; The England Counties squad departed for Korea on 31st May 2009]

CAPTAIN: *Matt Long*

[5th Jun KOREA RUGBY UNION PRESIDENT'S XV 10 **ENGLAND COUNTIES** 108]

Seongnam Stadium, Seoul

[*Team:* C. Rowland, Joe Graham, M. Long, Mike Howard, Matt Owen, Eniola 'Eni' Gesinde, Rainbow, S. Moss, Tom Richardson, M. Woodrow, Stephen 'Steve' Parsons, Patrick Leach, Jack Harrison, Royle, Chris Bishay]

[*Bench:* Dench (rep), Tom Eaton (*fly half*) (rep), Owen Hambly (*hooker*) (rep), Robert 'Rob' O'Donnell (*prop*) (rep), Smithson (rep), Wayne Sprangle (*flanker*) (rep), Huw Thomas (2) (*scrum half*) (rep)]

[*Scorers:* **tries** by S. Parsons (4), Royle (2), Bishay (2), P. Leach, M. Howard, Joe Graham, Dench, Sprangle, Matt Owen, Jack Harrison and M. Woodrow, **conversions** by M. Woodrow (12) and Eaton (2)]

CHURCHILL CUP

USA

[*Other squad members:* Banahan (*centre/wing*) (never travelled as withdrew, replaced by Matt Smith (1)), Corbisiero (never travelled as injured, replaced by Mark Lambert), Alex Goode (never travelled as injured)]

(squad of 27)

[Matt Mullan, David Paice, Richard Blaze, George Skivington, Michael Lipman, Will Skinner, James Simpson-Daniel, Topsy Ojo and Mike Brown were all unavailable for this tournament due to injury; Matt Banahan initially selected but withdrew as he was now required to join the simultaneous England tour of Argentina; Neil Briggs was added to the original squad of 26 on the day of its departure to provide injury cover for Joe Ward; Nick Kennedy was added to the original squad of 26 on the day of its departure; The England Saxons squad departed for America on 1st June 2009]

(During the First Round a bonus point was awarded for scoring 4 or more tries in a match and for losing by seven points or less)

[**COACH:** *Stuart Lancaster*] [**ASSISTANT COACH:** *Paul Hull*]

CAPTAIN: *Stuart Hooper*

First Round - Pool 'B'

[6th June ARGENTINA JAGUARS 20 **ENGLAND SAXONS** 28]

Infinity Park, Glendale

[*Team:* Flatman, R. Webber, D. Cole, P. Short, S. Hooper, Chris Jones, B. Woods, Narraway, J. Simpson, Cipriani, Varndell, Geraghty, Waldouck, Matt Smith (1), Abendanon]

[*Bench:* N. Briggs (rep), Dowson (rep), Guest (rep), M. Lambert (rep), Mercey (rep), Myler

(rep), Micky Young (rep)]
[*Scorers:* **tries** by Matt Smith, J. Simpson and Varndell, **penalty goals** by Cipriani (2), **drop goal** by Myler, **conversions** by Cipriani (2)]
CAPTAIN: *Phil Dowson*
[14th Jun USA 17 **ENGLAND SAXONS** 56 **BP**]
Infinity Park, Glendale
[*Team:* Flatman, R. Webber, D. Cole, P. Short, N. Kennedy, Dowson, B. Woods, Guest, Micky Young, Myler, Cato, Bradley 'Brad' Barritt, Waldouck, Varndell, Abendanon]
[*Bench:* N. Briggs (rep), Cipriani (rep), Chris Jones (rep), M. Lambert (rep), Narraway (rep), J. Simpson (rep), Matt Smith (1) (rep)]
[*Scorers:* **tries** by N. Kennedy, Micky Young, R. Webber, Guest, Varndell, Barritt and Cato, **penalty goals** by Myler (3), **conversions** by Myler (6)]
Final
[21st Jun IRELAND A 49 **ENGLAND SAXONS*** 22]
Dick's Sporting Goods Park, Commerce City
[*Team:* Flatman, R. Webber, D. Cole, S. Hooper, N. Kennedy, Dowson, B. Woods, Narraway, Micky Young, Myler, Varndell, Barritt, Waldouck, Cato, Abendanon]
[*Bench:* Cipriani (rep), Geraghty (rep), Guest (rep), Mercey (rep), Schofield (rep), J. Simpson (rep), Joe Ward (rep)]
[*Scorers:* **tries** by B. Woods and Varndell, **penalty goals** by Myler (4)]
POSITION: LOSING FINALISTS
FANTASY: ***WINNERS***

ENGLAND TOUR TO ARGENTINA 2009

[**TEAM MANAGER:** *Martin Johnson*] [**COACH:** *Brian Smith* (IR)] [**ASSISTANT COACHES:** *John Wells* & *Mike Ford*]
[*Other squad members:* T. Croft (never travelled as withdrew), Foden (never travelled), N. Kennedy (never travelled as withdrew), Moody, O. Morgan, Noon, Tom Rees (never travelled), Strettle (never travelled as injured, replaced by Matt Banahan), Turner-Hall (never travelled), Wigglesworth, N. Wood]
(squad of 34)
[Tom Palmer (2), Toby Flood, Mike Tindall and Paul Sackey were all unavailable for this tour due to injury; Olly Barkley unavailable for personal reasons; Jonny Wilkinson was rested for this tour; Tom Croft withdrew on 20th May 2009 as he was now required to go on the simultaneous British & Lions tour of South Africa; Nick Kennedy withdrew on 1st June 2009 as he was now required to join the England Saxons squad for the simultaneous Churchill Cup tournament; Tom Rees, Ben Foden and Jordan Turner-Hall were released from the tour on the day of the squad's departure; The England squad departed for Argentina on 7th June 2009]

STANDARD BANK CUP

CAPTAIN: *Steve Borthwick*
6th June ARGENTINA 15 **ENGLAND** 37
Old Trafford
[*Team:* T. Payne, D. Hartley, David Wilson (2), S. Borthwick, L. Deacon, Haskell, S. Armitage, Easter, Care, Andy Goode, Banahan, T. May, Hipkiss, Cueto, D. Armitage]
[*Bench:* J. Crane (rep), P. Hodgson (rep), Kay (rep), M. Tait (rep), Steve Thompson (2) (rep), Vesty (rep), Julian White (rep)]
[*Scorers:* **tries** by Banahan and D. Armitage (2), **penalty goals** by Andy Goode (4), **drop**

goals by Andy Goode (2), **conversions** by Andy Goode (2)]

QUILMES MATCH

CAPTAIN: *Steve Borthwick*

13th June ARGENTINA 24 **ENGLAND*** 22

Estadio Padre Ernesto Martearena, Salta

[*Team:* T. Payne, D. Hartley, Julian White, S. Borthwick, L. Deacon, Robshaw, S. Armitage, Easter, Care, Andy Goode, Banahan, T. May, Hipkiss, Cueto, D. Armitage]

[*Bench:* Chuter (rep), Haskell (rep), P. Hodgson (rep), Kay (rep), M. Tait (rep), Vesty (rep), David Wilson (2) (rep)]

[*Scorers:* **try** by Banahan, **penalty goals** by Andy Goode (5), **conversion** by Andy Goode]

BARBARIANS TOUR TO AUSTRALIA 2009

[**COACH:** *Dai Young* (WA)] [**ASSISTANT COACH:** *Mike Catt*]

[*Other squad members:* G. D'Arcy (IR) (never travelled as withdrew), Elsom (AU) (*flanker/number 8*) (left the tour injured, replaced by David Lyons), Peter Grant (SA) (never travelled as withdrew, replaced by Ratu Nasiganiyavi), Justin Harrison (AU) (*lock*) (never travelled as withdrew, replaced by Phil Waugh), Howlett (NZ) (*wing/full back*) (never travelled as withdrew), Nasiganiyavi (AU), Iestyn Thomas (2) (WA) (*prop*) (never travelled as injured, replaced by Clarke Dermody), Dimitri Yachvili (FR) (*scrum half*) (never travelled as withdrew, replaced by Chris Whitaker)]

(squad of 25)

[Dai Young was appointed on 19th January 2009; Eddie O'Sullivan was appointed on 31st January 2009 but then withdrew on 16th March 2009 due to work commitments; Mike Catt was appointed on 16th March 2009; Justin Harrison initially selected but withdrew after he announced his retirement on 21st May 2009; Dimitri Yachvili initially selected but withdrew as he was now required to join the French tour of New Zealand and Australia; Peter Grant initially selected but withdrew as he was now required to join the South African training squad for the simultaneous British & Irish Lions tour; Glen Jackson was added to the original squad of 24 on 22nd May 2009; Gordon D'Arcy and Doug Howlett both withdrew on the day of the squad's departure for personal reasons; The Barbarians squad departed for Australia on 30th May 2009]

[Nick Shehadie won 30 caps for Australia between 1947-58 and played for the Barbarians against an Australian XV at Cardiff Arms Park on 22nd February 1958]

NICK SHEHADIE CUP

CAPTAIN: *Phil Waugh* (AU)

[6th June AUSTRALIA XV 55 **BARBARIANS** 7]

Sydney Football Stadium, Sydney

[*Team:* Dermody (NZ), Bruno (FR), B.J. Botha (SA), C. Jack (NZ), Tito (NZ), Jerry Collins (NZ), P. Waugh (AU), David Lyons (AU), Whitaker (AU), Luke McAlister (NZ), J. Lewsey, Mapusua (SAM), Sonny Bill Williams (NZ), Balshaw, G. Murphy (IR)]

[*Bench:* Betsen (FR) (*flanker*) (rep), B. Blair (NZ) (*full back*) (rep), Brits (SA) (*hooker*) (rep), Corry (rep), G. Jackson (NZ) (rep), J. Marshall (NZ) (rep), Somerville (NZ) (*prop*) (rep)]

[*Scorers:* **try** by Balshaw, **conversion** by McAlister (NZ)]

TUSKER SAFARI SEVENS

TUSKER TROPHY

RFU of East Africa Ground, Ngong Road, Nairobi

[*Tournament squad:* O. Cook, Lewis Evans (WA) (*forward*), Martyn (SC), Matthew Pewtner (WA) (*forward/centre*), Thomas 'Tom' Edwards (WA) (*scrum half*), Neil Chivers (*fly half*),

Gareth Davies (2) (WA) (*fly half*), Simon Hunt, Jacob Abbott (*forward*), Ifan Evans (WA) (*hooker/wing*), Tirrell (*scrum half/wing*), David Evans (WA) (*wing*)]
(squad of 12)
[This tournament was played at high altitude]
[**MANAGER:** *William 'Will' Thomas* (WA)] [**COACH:** *Mark Hewitt*]
CAPTAIN: *Angus Martyn* (SC)
First Round - Pool 'C'

[20th Jun	Shujaa (*KEN*)	5	**SAMURAI**	22	]

[*Team:*]
[*Bench:*]
[*Scorers:*]

[20th Jun	MOROCCO	0	**SAMURAI**	29	]

[*Team:*]
[*Bench:*]
[*Scorers:*]

[20th Jun	EMERGING BOKS	26	**SAMURAI**	24	]

[*Team:*]
[*Bench:*]
[*Scorers:*]
Quarter-Final

[21st Jun	ZIMBABWE	0	**SAMURAI**	17	]

[*Team:*]
[*Bench:*]
[*Scorers:*]
Semi-Final

[21st Jun	KENYA	24	**SAMURAI**	0	]

[*Team:*]
[*Bench:*]
[*No scorers*]
POSITION: LOSING SEMI-FINALISTS

MIDDLESEX CHARITY SEVENS
RUSSELL-CARGILL MEMORIAL CUP
Twickenham
[SAMURAI: [*Tournament squad:* Roques, Chase Minnaar (SA) (*forward*), Marius Schoeman (SA) (*forward/wing*), Humphrey Kayange (KEN) (*forward/fly half*), Michael Fedo (SC) (*forward*), Julien Palmer (NZ) (*forward*), Amor, Collins Injera (KEN) (*wing*), Ryno Benjamin (*centre/wing*) (SA) (never travelled as withdrew, replaced by Nick Wakley), Peceli Nacamavuto (FIJ) (*centre*), Willie Bishop (AU) (*fly half/centre*), Tim Walsh (AU) (*scrum half/fly half/centre*), Gollings (withdrew due to injury), Wakley (WA)]]
(squad of 12)
[Mike Friday was appointed on 3rd August 2009; Joe Lydon was appointed on 5th August 2009; Simon Amor was the tournament captain; Mike Friday did not actually attend the tournament; Humphrey Kayange and Collins Injera were brothers]
[HELP FOR HEROES VII: [*Tournament squad:* Peter Jericevich (SC) (*scrum half*), M. Woodrow (*fly half*), M. Turner, Barden, Simon Hunt, Selley (WA) (*centre/wing*), Rory Hutton (SC) (*fly half*), Titterrell (*hooker*), David Akinluyi (*wing*), T. Powell, Oduoza, Chris Brightwell (*forward*)]]
(squad of 12)

[Ben Ryan was appointed on 3rd August 2009; Dai Jenkins and Stephen Gemmell were both appointed on 5th August 2009; Dai Jenkins was the Manager when Wales won the Plate competition at the 2006 Commonwealth Sevens in Melbourne on 16th-17th March 2006; Stephen Gemmell was the Coach when Scotland played in the Rugby World Cup Sevens in Dubai on 5th-7th March 2009; Paul John was appointed joint Coach on 5th August 2009 but withdrew due to family commitments; Mat Turner played in the Samurai team that won the Amsterdam Heineken Sevens on 16th-17th May 2009]
[SAMURAI: [MANAGER: *Terry Sands*] **[COACHES:** *Joe Lydon* & *Mike Friday*]**]**
[HELP FOR HEROES VII: [MANAGER: *David 'Dai' Jenkins* (WA)] **[COACHES:** *Ben Ryan* & *Stephen Gemmell* (SC)]**]**

CAPTAIN: *Simon Amor* [Samurai]

CAPTAIN: *Greg Barden* [Help for Heroes VII]

First Round

CAPTAIN: *Humphrey Kayange* (KEN) [*Simon Amor took over when he came on as a substitute in the 2nd half*]

[15th Aug Northampton Saints 12 **SAMURAI** 17]
[*Team:* Minnaar (SA), Schoeman (SA), Julien Palmer (NZ), T. Walsh (AU), Kayange (KEN), W. Bishop (AU), Injera (KEN)]
[*Bench:* Amor (rep), Fedo (SC), Nacamavuto (FIJ), Roques (rep), Wakley (WA) (rep)]
[*Scorers:* **tries** by Schoeman (SA), Kayange (KEN) and W. Bishop (AU), **conversion** by W. Bishop (AU)]

CAPTAIN: *Greg Barden*

[15th Aug Sale Sharks 21 **HELP FOR HEROES VII** 29]
[*Team:* T. Powell, Barden, Brightwell, Jericevich (SC), Rory Hutton (SC), Selley (WA), Oduoza]
[*Bench:* Akinluyi, Simon Hunt (rep), Titterrell, M. Turner (rep), M. Woodrow (rep)]
[*Scorers:* **tries** by Barden, Jericevich (SC) (2), Rory Hutton (SC) and M. Turner, **conversions** by Jericevich (SC) and M. Turner]

Quarter-Final

CAPTAIN: *Simon Amor* [*Humphrey Kayange* (KEN) *took over when Simon Amor was substituted in the 2nd half*]

[15th Aug Leeds Carnegie 17 **SAMURAI** 33]
[*Team:* Minnaar (SA), Schoeman (SA), Roques, Amor, T. Walsh (AU), Kayange (KEN), Injera (KEN)]
[*Bench:* W. Bishop (AU) (rep), Fedo (SC), Nacamavuto (FIJ) (rep), Julien Palmer (NZ) (rep), Wakley (WA)]
[*Scorers:* **tries** by Kayange (KEN), Injera (KEN) (2), Roques and Minnaar (SA), **conversions** by T. Walsh (AU) (4)]

CAPTAIN: *Greg Barden*

[15th Aug Newcastle Falcons 34 **HELP FOR HEROES VII** 5]
[*Team:* Barden, Titterrell, Brightwell, Jericevich (SC), Rory Hutton (SC), Selley (WA), Oduoza]
[*Bench:* Akinluyi (rep), Simon Hunt, T. Powell, M. Turner (rep), M. Woodrow (rep)]
[*Scorers:* **try** by M. Turner]

CAPTAIN: *Simon Amor*

Semi-Final

[15th Aug Newcastle Falcons 17 **SAMURAI** 28]
[*Team:* Minnaar (SA), Schoeman (SA), Roques, Amor, T. Walsh (AU), Kayange (KEN), Injera (KEN)]

[*Bench:* W. Bishop (AU) (rep), Fedo (SC), Nacamavuto (FIJ), Julien Palmer (NZ) (rep), Wakley (WA)]
[*Scorers:* **tries** by Injera (KEN) (2), Julien Palmer (NZ) and W. Bishop (AU), **conversions** by T. Walsh (AU) (3) and Amor]
Final
[15th Aug London Irish 26 **SAMURAI*** 19]
[*Team:* Julien Palmer (NZ), Roques, Minnaar (SA), Amor, T. Walsh (AU), Kayange (KEN), Injera (KEN)]
[*Bench:* W. Bishop (AU) (rep), Fedo (SC) (rep), Nacamavuto (FIJ) (rep), Schoeman (SA), Wakley (WA)]
[*Scorers:* **tries** by Injera (KEN), W. Bishop (AU) and Nacamavuto (FIJ), **conversions** by Amor (2)]
POSITION: LOSING FINALISTS [Samurai]
FANTASY: *WINNERS* [Samurai]
POSITION: LOSING QUARTER-FINALISTS [Help for Heroes VII]

AUSTRALIAN TOUR TO ENGLAND, IRELAND, SCOTLAND AND WALES 2009
FIRST INVESTEC CHALLENGE MATCH
COOK CUP MATCH

[**TEAM MANAGER:** *Martin Johnson*] [**COACH:** *Brian Smith* (IR)] [**ASSISTANT COACHES:** *John Wells, Mike Ford & Graham Rowntree*]
CAPTAIN: *Steve Borthwick*
7th Nov **ENGLAND*** 9 AUSTRALIA 18
Twickenham
[*Team:* T. Payne, Steve Thompson (2), David Wilson (2), L. Deacon, S. Borthwick, T. Croft, Moody, J. Crane, Care, Jonny Wilkinson, Banahan, Geraghty, Hipkiss, Cueto, Monye]
[*Bench:* Duncan Bell (rep), Erinle (rep), Andy Goode, D. Hartley (rep), Haskell (rep), P. Hodgson (rep), Lawes (rep)]
[*Scorers:* **penalty goals** by Jonny Wilkinson (2), **drop goal** by Jonny Wilkinson]

ATKINS REMEMBRANCE RUGBY MATCH

[**COACH:** *Glenn Delaney* (NZ)]
CAPTAIN: *Craig Hammond*
[11th Nov COMBINED SERVICES (*SER*) 22 **BARBARIANS*** 19]
Army Rugby Stadium, Queen's Avenue, Aldershot
[*Team:* Ryan Grant (SC), T. Youngs, Rob Dugard, Jean-Pierre 'Tim' Schumacher (HOL), Steven Turnbull (SC), Dalziel (SC), Rhys Shellard (WA), Craig Hammond, Robert 'Rob' Lewis (WA), David Blair (SC), David Slemen, Selley (WA), James Lewis (WA), S. Webster (SC), Craig Morgan (WA)]
[*Bench:* Head (IR) (rep), McCarter (IR) (*fly half*) (rep), Neale (rep), C. Pilgrim (rep), Porte (rep), Ritchie (rep), Sean-Michael Stephen (CAN) (*flanker/number 8*) (rep)]
[*Scorers:* **tries** by Shellard (WA), Head (IR) and Neale, **conversions** by D. Blair (SC) and McCarter (IR)]
[Match to commemorate the members of the British uniformed services who lost their lives during armed conflict]
[Glenn Delaney was appointed on 30th October 2009]

ARGENTINE TOUR TO ENGLAND, WALES AND SCOTLAND 2009

SECOND INVESTEC CHALLENGE MATCH

[**TEAM MANAGER:** *Martin Johnson*] [**COACH:** *Brian Smith* (IR)] [**ASSISTANT COACHES:** *John Wells, Mike Ford & Graham Rowntree*]

CAPTAIN: *Steve Borthwick*

14th Nov **ENGLAND** 16 ARGENTINA 9

Twickenham

[*Team:* T. Payne, D. Hartley, Duncan Bell, L. Deacon, S. Borthwick, T. Croft, Moody, Haskell, P. Hodgson, Jonny Wilkinson, Banahan, Geraghty, Hipkiss, Cueto, Monye]

[*Bench:* Care (rep), Paul Doran-Jones (*prop*) (rep), Erinle, Andy Goode (rep), Lawes, Steve Thompson (2) (rep), J. Worsley (rep)]

[*Scorers:* **try** by Banahan, **penalty goals** by Jonny Wilkinson (2), **drop goal** by Jonny Wilkinson, **conversion** by Jonny Wilkinson]

FIRA-AER 75TH ANNIVERSARY MATCH

[**MANAGER:** *Michel Arpaillange* (FR)] [**COACHES:** *Tomaz Morais* (POR) & *Tomasz Putra* (POL)]

CAPTAIN: *Matthew Clarkin*

[14th Nov French Barbarians 39 **XV EUROPE*** 26]

Stade Roi Baudouin, Brussels

[*Team:* Olivier Tissot (FR), Joan Caudullo (FR), Vincent Débaty (BEL), Sorin Socol (ROM), Gonçalo Uva (POR), Lund, Matthew Clarkin, Robert Mohr (GER), Pablo Feijoo (SP), Nicolas Laharrague (FR), Sepp Visser (HOL), Christophers, Miguel Portela (POR), Samuele Pace (IT), David Chartier (POL)]

[*Bench:* Rémy Bonfils (FR) (*hooker*) (rep), Ionut *Tiberius* Dimofte (ROM) (*fly half/centre*) (rep), Pierre Hendrickx (BEL) (*lock*) (rep), Juan Murre (POR) (*prop*) (rep), Pissarra (POR) (*scrum half*) (rep), César Sempere (SP) (*full back*) (rep), Bastien Sipielski (POL) (*prop*) (rep), Mathieu Verschelden (BEL) (*lock*) (rep)]

[*Scorers:* **tries** by Laharrague (FR), Bonfils (FR), Dimofte (ROM) and Visser (HOL), **conversions** by Laharrague (FR) (2) and Chartier (POL)]

[Match to commemorate the 75th Anniversary of the foundation of FIRA in 1934]

[Tomaz Morais was appointed on 27th August 2009; Tomaz Morais won 20 caps for Portugal between 1991-95; Michel Arpaillange and Tomasz Putra were both appointed on 20th October 2009; Tomasz Putra won 10 caps for Poland]

NEW ZEALAND TOUR TO WALES, ITALY, ENGLAND AND FRANCE 2009

THIRD INVESTEC CHALLENGE MATCH

SIR EDMUND HILLARY SHIELD

[**TEAM MANAGER:** *Martin Johnson*] [**COACH:** *Brian Smith* (IR)] [**ASSISTANT COACHES:** *John Wells, Mike Ford & Graham Rowntree*]

CAPTAIN: *Steve Borthwick*

21st Nov **ENGLAND*** 6 NEW ZEALAND 19

Twickenham

[*Team:* T. Payne, D. Hartley, Duncan Bell, S. Shaw, S. Borthwick, J. Worsley, Moody, Haskell, P. Hodgson, Jonny Wilkinson, Monye, Erinle, Hipkiss, Banahan, Cueto]

[*Bench:* Care (rep), T. Croft (rep), L. Deacon (rep), Geraghty (rep), M. Tait (rep), Steve Thompson (2) (rep), David Wilson (2) (rep)]
[*Scorers:* **penalty goals** by Jonny Wilkinson (2)]

FIJIAN TOUR TO SCOTLAND, IRELAND AND ENGLAND 2009
THIRD INVESTEC CHALLENGE MATCH

[**TEAM MANAGER:** *Martin Johnson*] [**COACH:** *Brian Smith* (IR)] [**ASSISTANT COACHES:** *John Wells, Mike Ford & Graham Rowntree*]
CAPTAIN: *No captain appointed*

28th Nov **ENGLAND** C FIJI C
Twickenham
[*Team not selected*]
[*Bench not selected*]
[*No scorers*]

EMIRATES AIRLINE DUBAI RUGBY SEVENS
IRB WORLD SEVENS SERIES 2009-2010 ROUND 1
EMIRATES INTERNATIONAL TROPHY

The Sevens, Dubai
[*Tournament squad:* Damu, Brightwell, Christian Wade (*wing*), D. Norton, Rodwell, Jake Abbott (*hooker*), Royle (*wing*), Caprice, K. Barrett, Gollings, M. Turner, Cracknell]
(squad of 12)
[On 5th November 2009 the IRB announced that the 2009-2010 World Sevens Series would use a revised points system where the Winners, Runners-Up, Semi-Finalists, Plate Winners, Plate Runners-Up, Plate Semi-Finalists and Bowl Winners in a Round with 24 teams were awarded 30, 25, 20, 16, 10, 8 and 5 points respectively, whereas the Winners, Runners-Up, Semi-Finalists, Plate Winners, Plate Runners-Up, Plate Semi-Finalists and Bowl Winners in a Round containing 16 teams were awarded 24, 20, 16, 12, 8, 6 and 4 points respectively; Ollie Phillips unavailable due to club commitments; Christian Wade toured Argentina and South Africa with England U18 in July-August 2008 and July-August 2009 respectively; The England squad arrived in Dubai on 26th November 2009]
[**MANAGER:** *Will Beeley*] [**COACH:** *Ben Ryan*] [**ASSISTANT COACH:** *Russ Earnshaw*]
CAPTAIN: *Kevin Barrett*

First Round - Pool 'C'

4th Dec USA 12 **ENGLAND** 40
[*Team:* Damu, Jake Abbott, Cracknell, K. Barrett, Gollings, D. Norton, Royle]
[*Bench:* Brightwell (rep), Caprice, Rodwell, M. Turner (rep), Wade (rep)]
[*Scorers:* **tries** by D. Norton (3), K. Barrett, Gollings and M. Turner, **conversions** by Gollings (5)]

4th Dec RUSSIA 0 **ENGLAND** 28
[*Team:* Damu, Jake Abbott, Cracknell, K. Barrett, Gollings, D. Norton, M. Turner]
[*Bench:* Brightwell, Caprice (rep), Rodwell (rep), Royle, Wade]
[*Scorers:* **tries** by Gollings, Damu and Caprice (2), **conversions** by Gollings (4)]

4th Dec KENYA 10 **ENGLAND** 27
[*Team:* Damu, Jake Abbott, Cracknell, K. Barrett, Gollings, D. Norton, Royle]
[*Bench:* Brightwell (rep), Caprice, Rodwell, M. Turner (rep), Wade (rep)]
[*Scorers:* **tries** by Royle (2), Jake Abbott, Gollings and M. Turner, **conversion** by Gollings]

Quarter-Final

5th Dec ARGENTINA 12 **ENGLAND** 17 aet

[*Team:* Damu, Jake Abbott, Cracknell, K. Barrett, Gollings, D. Norton, Royle]
[*Bench:* Brightwell (rep), Caprice, Rodwell, M. Turner (rep), Wade]
[*Scorers:* **tries** by Royle, D. Norton and Gollings, **conversion** by Gollings]

Semi-Final

5th Dec SAMOA 28 **ENGLAND*** 19

[*Team:* Damu, Jake Abbott, Cracknell, K. Barrett, Gollings, D. Norton, Royle]
[*Bench:* Brightwell, Caprice (rep), Rodwell, M. Turner, Wade]
[*Scorers:* **tries** by Royle and Cracknell (2), **conversions** by Gollings (2)]

POSITION: LOSING SEMI-FINALISTS

FANTASY: ***LOSING FINALISTS***

[England scored 16 competition points in this Round of the 2009-2010 IRB World Sevens Series]

EMIRATES AIRLINE SOUTH AFRICA SEVENS
IRB WORLD SEVENS SERIES 2009-2010 ROUND 2

Outeniqua Park Stadium, George

[*Tournament squad:* Damu, Brightwell, Wade, D. Norton, Rodwell, Jake Abbott, Royle, Caprice, K. Barrett, Gollings, M. Turner (never travelled due to illness), Cracknell]

(squad of 11)

[Ollie Phillips unavailable due to club commitments; Mat Turner selected but withdrew due to illness and was not replaced; Kevin Barrett was the tournament captain]

[**MANAGER:** *Will Beeley*] [**COACH:** *Ben Ryan*] [**ASSISTANT COACH:** *Russ Earnshaw*]

CAPTAIN: *Kevin Barrett [Ben Gollings took over when Kevin Barrett was substituted in the 2nd half]*

First Round - Pool 'D'

11th Dec TUNISIA 0 **ENGLAND** 45

[*Team:* Damu, Jake Abbott, Rodwell, K. Barrett, Gollings, D. Norton, Wade]
[*Bench:* Brightwell (rep), Caprice (rep), Cracknell, Royle (rep)]
[*Scorers:* **tries** by Jake Abbott (2), Wade (2), D. Norton, Gollings and Royle, **conversions** by Gollings (5)]

CAPTAIN: *Kevin Barrett*

11th Dec ARGENTINA 7 **ENGLAND** 17

[*Team:* Damu, Jake Abbott, Cracknell, K. Barrett, Gollings, D. Norton, Royle]
[*Bench:* Brightwell, Caprice (rep), Rodwell (rep), Wade (rep)]
[*Scorers:* **tries** by Wade (2) and Damu, **conversion** by Gollings]

CAPTAIN: *Ben Gollings*

11th Dec SCOTLAND 19 **ENGLAND** 29

[*Team:* Damu, Brightwell, Rodwell, Caprice, Gollings, D. Norton, Wade]
[*Bench:* Jake Abbott (rep), K. Barrett, Cracknell]
[*Scorers:* **tries** by D. Norton (2), Caprice, Brightwell and Gollings, **conversions** by Gollings (2)]

CAPTAIN: *Kevin Barrett*

Quarter-Final

12th Dec NEW ZEALAND 22 **ENGLAND*** 19

[*Team:* Damu, Jake Abbott, Cracknell, K. Barrett, Gollings, D. Norton, Wade]

[*Bench:* Brightwell, Caprice (rep), Rodwell]
[*Scorers:* **tries** by Gollings (2) and K. Barrett, **conversions** by Gollings (2)]
[Plate Semi-Final:]
[12th Dec AUSTRALIA 5 **ENGLAND** 24 **]**
[*Team:* Damu, Brightwell, Rodwell, K. Barrett, Gollings, Caprice, Wade]
[*Bench:* Jake Abbott (rep), Cracknell, D. Norton (rep)]
[*Scorers:* **tries** by Wade (2), Caprice and Gollings, **conversions** by Gollings (2)]
CAPTAIN: *Kevin Barrett* [*Ben Gollings took over when Kevin Barrett was substituted in the 2nd half*]
[Plate Final:]
[12th Dec SOUTH AFRICA 7 **ENGLAND** 21 **]**
[*Team:* Damu, Jake Abbott, Cracknell, K. Barrett, Gollings, D. Norton, Wade]
[*Bench:* Brightwell (rep), Caprice (rep), Rodwell (rep)]
[*Scorers:* **tries** by D. Norton, Wade and Damu, **conversions** by Gollings (3)]
POSITION: LOSING QUARTER-FINALISTS [*PLATE WINNERS*]
FANTASY: *LOSING FINALISTS*
[England scored 12 competition points in this Round of the 2009-2010 IRB World Sevens Series]

2010

OTHER MATCHES

ENGLAND U20 TRAINING MATCH

[**MANAGER:** *Stuart Lancaster*] [**COACH:** *Mark Mapletoft*] [**ASSISTANT COACH:** *Rob Hunter* (SC)]

CAPTAIN: *Jacob Rowan*

[21st Jan Cambridge University 7 **ENGLAND U20 XV** 61]

University Football Ground, Grange Road, Cambridge

[*Team:* Marler, J. George, Shaun Knight, Calum Green, D. Wright, Will Welch, J. Rowan, Alex Gray, Sam Harrison (2), Jake Sharp, Sam Smith, Tom Catterick, Jonny May, Hurrell, Jonathan Joseph]

[*Bench:* A. Ellis (rep), Kieran Brookes (*prop*) (rep), Elder (rep), Owen Farrell (*fly half/centre*) (rep), Lee Imiolek (*prop*) (rep), Charlie Matthews (*lock*) (rep), Sam Stuart (*scrum half/centre*) (rep), Mako Vunipola (*prop*) (rep), Wade (*wing*) (rep), Jackson Wray (*lock/number 8*) (rep)]

[*Scorers:* **tries** by Sam Smith (3), Jonny May (2), Catterick (2), C. Matthews and A. Ellis, **conversions** by J. Sharp (8)]

[England U20 prepared for the 2010 U20 6 Nations Championship by having a pre-tournament training camp at Cambridge University on 18th-24th January 2010]

[On 9th October 2009 Rob Hunter was appointed to become England U20 Assistant Coach on 1st December 2009]

ENGLAND STUDENTS MATCH

[**MANAGER:** *Keith Green*] [**COACH:** *Paul Westgate*] [**ASSISTANT COACH:** *James Farndon*]

CAPTAIN: *Phil Burgess*

[30th Jan PORTUGAL XV 21 **ENGLAND STUDENTS*** 18]

Estádio Universitário, Lisbon

[*Team:* Matt Berry, Bellamy, Oliver 'Ollie' Mines, Jon Aston, Andrew Archibald, Mark Wilson, P. Burgess, Maidment, W. Chudleigh, Paul Roberts, Hockedy, Matt Humphries, Tom Mitchell (2), Sean Morris, John Bordiss]

[*Bench:* Tim Brockett (*prop*) (rep), Royce Cadman (*lock*) (rep), Patrick Crossley (*hooker*) (rep), James Crozier (*wing/full back*) (rep), G. Nicholls (rep), Alex Waddingham (*flanker*) (rep), Mike Ward (*fly half*) (rep)]

[*Scorers:* **tries** by M. Humphries and P. Burgess, **penalty goals** by P. Roberts (2), **conversion** by P. Roberts]

[England Students had a training camp at Birmingham University on 5th-6th January 2010]

ENGLAND SAXONS INTERNATIONAL MATCH

[**COACH:** *Stuart Lancaster*] [**ASSISTANT COACHES:** *Simon Hardy & Andy Farrell*]

CAPTAIN: *George Skivington*

[31st Jan **ENGLAND SAXONS** 17 IRELAND A 13]

Recreation Ground, Bath

[*Team:* N. Wood, D. Paice, Doran-Jones, Attwood, Skivington, Tom Wood, Saull, Dowson, B. Youngs, Geraghty, Cato, Barritt, Waldouck, Strettle, Alex Goode]

[*Bench:* M. Benjamin (rep), Jon Clarke, Mercey (rep), Narraway (rep), Parling (rep), R. Webber (rep), Micky Young (rep)]

[*Scorers:* **tries** by Strettle and Geraghty, **penalty goal** by Geraghty, **conversions** by Geraghty (2)]

[Simon Hardy and Andy Farrell were both appointed on 4th January 2010; Andy Farrell was capped 34 times for Great Britain at Rugby League between 1993-2004, played for England in the Rugby League World Cup Final at Wembley on 28th October 1995 and was capped for England at Rugby Union in January 2007]

NEW ZEALAND INTERNATIONAL SEVENS
IRB WORLD SEVENS SERIES 2009-2010 ROUND 3

Westpac Stadium, Wellington
[*Tournament squad:* Damu (never travelled as injured, replaced by Tom Powell), Brightwell, Wade, D. Norton, Rodwell, Jake Abbott, Royle, Caprice, K. Barrett, Gollings, M. Turner, Donald 'Don' Barrell (*forward*), T. Powell]
(squad of 12)
[Chris Cracknell and Ollie Phillips unavailable due to club commitments; Kevin Barrett was the tournament captain; Don Barrell played for England in the U19 World Championship in South Africa in April 2005]
[**MANAGER:** *Will Beeley*] [**COACH:** *Ben Ryan*] [**ASSISTANT COACH:** *Russ Earnshaw*]
CAPTAIN: *Kevin Barrett*
First Round - Pool 'C'
5th Feb USA 7 **ENGLAND** 31
[*Team:* Rodwell, Jake Abbott, Brightwell, K. Barrett, Gollings, M. Turner, Wade]
[*Bench:* Barrell (rep), Caprice, D. Norton (rep), T. Powell, Royle (rep)]
[*Scorers:* **tries** by Gollings, M. Turner (2), Jake Abbott and K. Barrett, **conversions** by Gollings (3)]
CAPTAIN: *Kevin Barrett* [*Ben Gollings took over when Kevin Barrett was injured in the 2nd half*]
5th Feb TONGA 19 **ENGLAND** 24
[*Team:* Rodwell, Jake Abbott, Brightwell, K. Barrett, Gollings, D. Norton, Wade]
[*Bench:* Barrell, Caprice (rep), T. Powell, Royle (rep), M. Turner]
[*Scorers:* **tries** by Wade, D. Norton, Brightwell and Caprice, **conversions** by Gollings (2)]
CAPTAIN: *Ben Gollings*
5th Feb KENYA 10 **ENGLAND** 24
[*Team:* Rodwell, Jake Abbott, Brightwell, Caprice, Gollings, M. Turner, Wade]
[*Bench:* Barrell (rep), D. Norton, T. Powell (rep), Royle (rep)]
[*Scorers:* **tries** by Caprice (2), M. Turner and Brightwell, **conversions** by Gollings (2)]
Quarter-Final
6th Feb CANADA 0 **ENGLAND** 31
[*Team:* Rodwell, Jake Abbott, Brightwell, Caprice, Gollings, M. Turner, D. Norton]
[*Bench:* Barrell (rep), T. Powell (rep), Royle, Wade (rep)]
[*Scorers:* **tries** by Caprice, Gollings (2) and M. Turner (2), **conversions** by Gollings (3)]
Semi-Final
6th Feb FIJI 28 **ENGLAND*** 19
[*Team:* Rodwell, Brightwell, Barrell, Caprice, Gollings, M. Turner, Wade]
[*Bench:* Jake Abbott, D. Norton (rep), T. Powell (rep), Royle]
[*Scorers:* **tries** by Wade, M. Turner and Gollings, **conversions** by Gollings (2)]
POSITION: LOSING SEMI-FINALISTS
FANTASY: ***LOSING FINALISTS***
[England scored 16 competition points in this Round of the 2009-2010 IRB World Sevens Series]

6 NATIONS CHAMPIONSHIP

[**TEAM MANAGER:** *Martin Johnson*] [**COACH:** *Brian Smith* (IR)] [**ASSISTANT COACHES:** *John Wells, Mike Ford & Graham Rowntree*]

CAPTAIN: *Steve Borthwick*

6th Feb **ENGLAND** 30 WALES 17

Twickenham

[*Team:* T. Payne, D. Hartley, David Wilson (2), S. Shaw, S. Borthwick, Haskell, Moody, Easter, Care, Jonny Wilkinson, Monye, T. Flood, M. Tait, Cueto, D. Armitage]

[*Bench:* S. Armitage (rep), D. Cole (rep), L. Deacon (rep), Foden, Hipkiss (rep), P. Hodgson (rep), Steve Thompson (2) (rep)]

[*Scorers:* **tries** by Haskell (2) and Care, **penalty goals** by Jonny Wilkinson (3), **conversions** by Jonny Wilkinson (3)]

14th Feb ITALY 12 **ENGLAND** 17

Stadio Flaminio, Rome

[*Team:* T. Payne, D. Hartley, D. Cole, S. Shaw, S. Borthwick, Haskell, Moody, Easter, Care, Jonny Wilkinson, Monye, Flutey, M. Tait, Cueto, D. Armitage]

[*Bench:* S. Armitage (rep), L. Deacon (rep), T. Flood, P. Hodgson (rep), Mullan (*prop/hooker*) (rep), Steve Thompson (2) (rep), David Wilson (2) (rep)]

[*Scorers:* **try** by M. Tait, **penalty goals** by Jonny Wilkinson (3), **drop goal** by Jonny Wilkinson]

27th Feb **ENGLAND*** 16 IRELAND 20

Twickenham

[*Team:* T. Payne, D. Hartley, D. Cole, S. Shaw, S. Borthwick, Haskell, Moody, Easter, Care, Jonny Wilkinson, Monye, Flutey, M. Tait, Cueto, D. Armitage]

[*Bench:* L. Deacon (rep), T. Flood, Foden (rep), P. Hodgson (rep), Mears (rep), David Wilson (2) (rep), J. Worsley (rep)]

[*Scorers:* **try** by D. Cole, **penalty goals** by Jonny Wilkinson (2), **drop goal** by Johnny Wilkinson, **conversion** by Jonny Wilkinson]

13th Mar SCOTLAND 15 **ENGLAND*** 15

Murrayfield

[*Team:* T. Payne, D. Hartley, D. Cole, L. Deacon, S. Borthwick, Haskell, J. Worsley, Easter, Care, Jonny Wilkinson, Monye, Flutey, M. Tait, Cueto, D. Armitage]

[*Bench:* T. Flood (rep), Foden (rep), Lawes (rep), Moody (rep), Steve Thompson (2) (rep), David Wilson (2) (rep), B. Youngs (rep)]

[*Scorers:* **penalty goals** by Jonny Wilkinson (3) and T. Flood (2)]

CAPTAIN: *Lewis Moody*

20th Mar FRANCE 12 **ENGLAND*** 10

Stade de France, Paris

[*Team:* T. Payne, D. Hartley, D. Cole, S. Shaw, L. Deacon, J. Worsley, Moody, Easter, Care, T. Flood, Christopher 'Chris' Ashton, Flutey, Tindall, Cueto, Foden]

[*Bench:* Haskell (rep), Tom Palmer (2) (rep), M. Tait (rep), Steve Thompson (2) (rep), Jonny Wilkinson (rep), David Wilson (2) (rep), B. Youngs]

[*Scorers:* **try** by Foden, **penalty goal** by Jonny Wilkinson, **conversion** by T. Flood]

POSITION: **3RD 5 +12 CC** [*France 10 +66 GS*, Ireland 6 +11 MT, Wales 4 -4, Scotland 3 -17, Italy 2 -68]

FANTASY: ***1ST 10 GS TC CC MT***

[*England went to the Algarve for warm-weather training from 25th January to 29th January 2010*]

OTHER MATCHES

U20 6 NATIONS CHAMPIONSHIP

[**MANAGER:** *Stuart Lancaster*] [**COACH:** *Mark Mapletoft*] [**ASSISTANT COACH:** *Rob Hunter (SC)*]

CAPTAIN: *Jacob Rowan*

[5th Feb **ENGLAND U20** 41 WALES U20 14]

Kingsholm, Gloucester

[*Team:* Marler, J. George, Shaun Knight, Calum Green, Gaskell, W. Welch, J. Rowan, A. Gray, Sam Harrison (2), F. Burns, Sam Smith, Rory Clegg, Homer, Hurrell, Catterick]

[*Bench:* Rob Buchanan (*prop/hooker*) (rep), Imiolek (rep), Jonathan Joseph (*centre/full back*) (rep), C. Matthews (rep), Jonny May (*centre/wing*) (rep), Stuart (rep), Jackson Wray (rep)]

[*Scorers:* **tries** by Marler (2), J. George, J. Rowan and Jonny May, **penalty goals** by F. Burns (2), **conversions** by F. Burns (2) and Homer (3)]

[12th Feb ITALY U20 10 **ENGLAND U20** 16]

Stadio Mario e Romolo Pacifici, San Donà di Piave

[*Team:* Marler, J. George, Shaun Knight, D. Wright, C. Matthews, W. Welch, J. Rowan, Jackson Wray, Sam Harrison (2), F. Burns, Jonny May, Casson, Jonathan Joseph, Hurrell, Catterick]

[*Bench:* Sam Edgerley (*wing*) (rep), Elder (rep), A. Ellis (rep), Imiolek (rep), George Kruis (*lock/flanker*) (rep), J. Sharp (*fly half*) (rep), Stuart (rep)]

[*Scorers:* **try** by Jonny May, **penalty goals** by F. Burns (3), **conversion** by F. Burns]

[26th Feb **ENGLAND U20*** 10 IRELAND U20 25]

Kingsholm, Gloucester

[*Team:* Imiolek, J. George, Shaun Knight, D. Wright, C. Matthews, Jackson Wray, J. Rowan, A. Gray, Sam Harrison (2), F. Burns, Jonny May, Casson, Jonathan Joseph, Hurrell, Jack Wallace]

[*Bench:* Brookes (rep), A. Ellis (rep), Kruis (rep), Marler (rep), Pasqualin (rep), J. Sharp (rep), Wade (rep)]

[*Scorers:* **try** by penalty try, **penalty goal** by F. Burns, **conversion** by F. Burns]

[12th Mar SCOTLAND U20 6 **ENGLAND U20** 27]

Firhill, Glasgow

[*Team:* Imiolek, J. George, Marler, Calum Green, C. Matthews, J. Gibson, J. Rowan, Jackson Wray, Sam Harrison (2), Rory Clegg, Sam Smith, Casson, Andrew 'Andy' Forsyth, Marcus Watson, Catterick]

[*Bench:* Mark Atkinson (*fly half/centre*) (rep), A. Ellis (rep), Jonathan Joseph (rep), Pasqualin (rep), Vunipola (rep), W. Welch (*flanker*) (rep), D. Wright (rep)]

[*Scorers:* **tries** by Forsyth, M. Watson and C. Matthews, **penalty goals** by Rory Clegg (2), **conversions** by Rory Clegg (3)]

[21st Mar FRANCE U20 33 **ENGLAND U20** 47]

Stade du Préhembert, St Nazaire

[*Team:* Marler, J. George, Shaun Knight, Calum Green, C. Matthews, W. Welch, J. Rowan, J. Gibson, Sam Harrison (2), Rory Clegg, Sam Smith, Casson, Forsyth, M. Watson, Homer]

[*Bench:* M. Atkinson (rep), Catterick (*fly half/full back*) (rep), Charlie Davies (*scrum half*) (rep), A. Ellis (rep), Imiolek (rep), Jackson Wray (rep), D. Wright (rep)]

[*Scorers:* **tries** by J. Gibson (2), M. Watson, Casson and Sam Smith, **penalty goals** by Homer (4), **conversions** by Homer (5)]

POSITION: **2ND 8 +53** [*Ireland 8 +85 TC*, Wales 6 +17, France 5 -25, Scotland 3 -56, Italy 0 -74]
FANTASY: ***1ST 10 GS TC***

ENGLAND SAXONS INTERNATIONAL MATCH

[**COACH:** *Stuart Lancaster*] [**ASSISTANT COACHES:** *Simon Hardy* & *Andy Farrell*]
CAPTAIN: *George Skivington*
[7th Feb ITALY A 5 **ENGLAND SAXONS** 31]
Stadio Comunale, Mogliano Veneto
[*Team:* Flatman, R. Webber, Doran-Jones, Parling, Skivington, Robshaw, Hendre Fourie, Dowson, Micky Young, Geraghty, M. Benjamin, Barritt, Jon Clarke, Strettle, Cipriani]
[*Bench:* Attwood (*lock*) (rep), Alex Goode (rep), Mercey (rep), Vickers (rep), Waldouck, Wigglesworth (rep), T. Wood (*flanker/number 8*) (rep)]
[*Scorers:* **tries** by M. Benjamin, penalty try, Alex Goode and Strettle, **penalty goal** by Geraghty, **conversions** by Geraghty and Alex Goode (3)]

USA SEVENS
IRB WORLD SEVENS SERIES 2009-2010 ROUND 4

Sam Boyd Stadium, Las Vegas
[*Tournament squad:* Damu (never travelled as injured, replaced by Tom Powell), Brightwell, Wade, D. Norton, Rodwell, Jake Abbott, Royle, Caprice, K. Barrett (captain; never travelled as injured, replaced by Ollie Lindsay-Hague), Gollings, M. Turner, Barrell, T. Powell, Oliver 'Ollie' Lindsay-Hague (*back*)]
(squad of 12)
[Chris Cracknell and Ollie Phillips unavailable due to club commitments; This tournament was played on a pitch which was narrower than normal]
[**MANAGER:** *Will Beeley*] [**COACH:** *Ben Ryan*] [**ASSISTANT COACH:** *Russ Earnshaw*]
CAPTAIN: *Ben Gollings*
First Round - Pool 'D'
13th Feb WALES 10 **ENGLAND** 26
[*Team:* Rodwell, Brightwell, Barrell, Caprice, Gollings, M. Turner, Wade]
[*Bench:* Jake Abbott, Lindsay-Hague, D. Norton (rep), T. Powell (rep), Royle (rep)]
[*Scorers:* **tries** by Gollings (2), D. Norton and Rodwell, **conversions** by Gollings (3)]
13th Feb JAPAN 5 **ENGLAND** 24
[*Team:* Rodwell, Jake Abbott, Brightwell, Caprice, Gollings, D. Norton, Wade]
[*Bench:* Barrell (rep), Lindsay-Hague (rep), T. Powell, Royle (rep), M. Turner]
[*Scorers:* **tries** by Jake Abbott, Wade (2) and Caprice, **conversions** by Gollings (2)]
13th Feb ARGENTINA 12 **ENGLAND*** 12
[*Team:* T. Powell, Jake Abbott, Barrell, Lindsay-Hague, Gollings, M. Turner, Royle]
[*Bench:* Brightwell, Caprice (rep), D. Norton, Rodwell (rep), Wade]
[*Scorers:* **tries** by Royle (2), **conversion** by Gollings]
Quarter-Final
14th Feb KENYA 26 **ENGLAND*** 21 aet
[*Team:* Rodwell, Jake Abbott, Brightwell, Caprice, Gollings, D. Norton, Wade]
[*Bench:* Barrell (rep), Lindsay-Hague, T. Powell (rep), Royle, M. Turner (rep)]
[*Scorers:* **tries** by Wade, Gollings and D. Norton, **conversions** by Gollings (3)]

[Plate Semi-Final:]
[14th Feb SOUTH AFRICA 27 **ENGLAND*** 14]
[*Team:* Rodwell, Jake Abbott, Barrell, Caprice, Gollings, M. Turner, Wade]
[*Bench:* Brightwell, Lindsay-Hague, D. Norton (rep), T. Powell (rep), Royle (rep)]
[*Scorers:* **tries** by Gollings and D. Norton, **conversions** by Gollings (2)]
POSITION: LOSING QUARTER-FINALISTS [*PLATE SEMI-FINALISTS*]
FANTASY: *LOSING SEMI-FINALISTS*
[England scored 6 competition points in this Round of the 2009-2010 IRB World Sevens Series]

ENGLAND COUNTIES MATCH

[**MANAGER:** *Danny Hodgson*] [**ASSISTANT MANAGER:** *Mike Old*] [**COACH:** *Dave Baldwin*] [**ASSISTANT COACH:** *Jan Bonney*]
CAPTAIN: *Tom Bason*
[26th Feb **ENGLAND COUNTIES** 29 IRELAND CLUB XV 25]
Stourbridge RFC, Stourton Park, Bridgnorth Road, Stourbridge
[*Team:* Johnny Williams, Joe Graham, Heard, Matt Owen, Bason, Daniel 'Dan' Legge, Darren Fox, T. Powell, Luke Baldwin, James Brown, David Howells, S. Jewell, Jack Harrison, Sam Ulph, Neale]
[*Bench:* Matthew 'Matt' Hall (*hooker*) (rep), Ben Harris (*lock*), Alex Nash (*flanker/number 8*), S. Parsons (*wing*) (rep), T. Richardson (*scrum half*), Riley (rep), T. Warren (rep)]
[*Scorers:* **tries** by Neal (3) and L. Baldwin, **penalty goal** by Ulph, **conversions** by Ulph (3)]
[Jan Bonney was appointed on 6th January 2010; Jan Bonney toured Chile and Romania & France with England Counties in June 2002 and June 2003 respectively]

ENGLAND STUDENTS MATCHES

[**MANAGER:** *Keith Green*] [**COACH:** *Paul Westgate*] [**ASSISTANT COACH:** *James Farndon*]
CAPTAIN: *Phil Burgess*
[26th Feb **ENGLAND STUDENTS** 42 Irish Colleges (*IR*) 9]
Gosforth RFC, Druid Park, Ponteland Road, Woolsington
[*Team:* Berry, Bellamy, Mines, Cadman, Archibald, M. Wilson, Evan Stewart, P. Burgess, G. Nicholls, Mike Ward, Crozier, M. Humphries, Tom Mitchell (2), Sean Morris, Louis Messer]
[*Bench:* Brockett (rep), W. Chudleigh (rep), Crossley (rep), Hockedy (*wing*) (rep), Maidment (*number 8*) (rep), P. Roberts (*fly half*) (rep), Will Warden (*lock*) (rep)]
[*Scorers:* **tries** by P. Burgess (2), E. Stewart, M. Wilson, M. Humphries and Sean Morris, **penalty goals** by Crozier (2), **conversions** by Crozier (3)]
[19th Mar French Universities (*FR*) 35 **ENGLAND STUDENTS*** 22]
Stade Émile Pons, Riom
[*Team:* Berry, Bellamy, Mines, Warden, Archibald, M. Wilson, E. Stewart, P. Burgess, Josh Leach, P. Roberts, Hockedy, M. Humphries, Tom Mitchell (2), Sean Morris, Messer]
[*Bench:* Brockett (rep), Cadman (rep), Crossley (rep), Crozier (rep), Maidment (rep), Harry Peck (*scrum half*) (rep), Mike Ward (rep)]
[*Scorers:* **tries** by Sean Morris, Messer and Hockedy, **penalty goal** by P. Roberts, **conversions** by P. Roberts and Crozier]
[Keith Green resigned after the French Universities match]

JEAN-CLAUDE BAQUÉ SHIELD MATCH

[**MANAGER:** *Danny Hodgson*] [**ASSISTANT MANAGER:** *Mike Old*] [**COACH:** *Dave Baldwin*] [**ASSISTANT COACH:** *Jan Bonney*]

CAPTAIN: *Tom Bason*

[19th Mar FRANCE AMATEURS 29 **ENGLAND COUNTIES** 11]

Stade Vélodrome, Roubaix

[*Team:* Johnny Williams, Joe Graham, Andrew Fahey, Bason, R. Anderson, Dan Legge, Darren Fox, R. Baldwin, T. Richardson, James Brown, Hylton, Bedworth, Damant, H. Smales, Neale]

[*Bench:* Daniel 'Dan' Baines (*flanker*) (rep), Barr (rep), G. Collins (*wing/full back*) (rep), James Fitzpatrick (*centre*) (rep), Nick Flynn (*prop*) (rep), Matt Hall (rep), Matt Owen (rep)]

[*Scorers:* **try** by Darren Fox, **penalty goals** by Neale (2)]

ADELAIDE SEVENS
IRB WORLD SEVENS SERIES 2009-2010 ROUND 5

Adelaide Oval, Adelaide

[*Tournament squad:* T. Powell, Brightwell, Wade, Drauniniu, Rodwell, Jake Abbott, Royle, Caprice, O. Phillips (never travelled as injured, replaced by Ollie Lindsay-Hague), Gollings, M. Turner, Barrell, Lindsay-Hague]

(squad of 12)

[Isoa Damu and Kevin Barrett unavailable due to injury; Chris Cracknell unavailable due to club commitments]

[**MANAGER:** *Will Beeley*] [**COACH:** *Ben Ryan*] [**ASSISTANT COACH:** *Russ Earnshaw*]

CAPTAIN: *Ben Gollings*

First Round - Pool 'D'

19th Mar USA 24 **ENGLAND*** 21

[*Team:* T. Powell, Jake Abbott, Brightwell, Caprice, Gollings, M. Turner, Wade]

[*Bench:* Barrell, Drauniniu (rep), Lindsay-Hague, Rodwell (rep), Royle (rep)]

[*Scorers:* **tries** by M. Turner, Gollings and Royle, **conversions** by Gollings (3)]

20th Mar NIUE 0 **ENGLAND** 38

[*Team:* Rodwell, T. Powell, Barrell, Caprice, Gollings, M. Turner, Royle]

[*Bench:* Jake Abbott (rep), Brightwell, Drauniniu (rep), Lindsay-Hague (rep), Wade]

[*Scorers:* **tries** by T. Powell, Gollings, Royle, Barrell, Jake Abbott and Lindsay-Hague, **conversions** by Gollings (4)]

20th Mar AUSTRALIA 17 **ENGLAND*** 12

[*Team:* Rodwell, Brightwell, T. Powell, Caprice, Gollings, M. Turner, Wade]

[*Bench:* Jake Abbott (rep), Barrell, Drauniniu (rep), Lindsay-Hague, Royle]

[*Scorers:* **tries** by M. Turner and T. Powell, **conversion** by Gollings]

[Bowl Quarter-Final:]

[21st Mar PAPUA NEW GUINEA 0 **ENGLAND** 47]

[*Team:* Rodwell, Jake Abbott, Barrell, Lindsay-Hague, Gollings, Drauniniu, Royle]

[*Bench:* Brightwell (rep), T. Powell (rep), M. Turner, Wade]

[*Scorers:* **tries** by Gollings (2), Rodwell (2), Lindsay-Hague, Royle and Brightwell, **conversions** by Gollings (6)]

[Bowl Semi-Final:]

[21st Mar FRANCE 0 **ENGLAND** 19]

[*Team:* Rodwell, Brightwell, T. Powell, Lindsay-Hague, Gollings, M. Turner, Wade]

[*Bench:* Jake Abbott (rep), Barrell (rep), Drauniniu (rep), Royle]

[*Scorers:* **tries** by Wade, Brightwell and Lindsay-Hague, **conversions** by Gollings (2)]
[Bowl Final:]
[21st Mar KENYA 12 **ENGLAND** 33]
[*Team:* Rodwell, Brightwell, T. Powell, Lindsay-Hague, Gollings, M. Turner, Wade]
[*Bench:* Jake Abbott, Barrell, Drauniniu (rep), Royle]
[*Scorers:* **tries** by Wade (2), T. Powell, penalty try and Jake Abbott, **conversions** by Gollings (4)]
POSITION: FIRST ROUND LOSERS [*BOWL WINNERS*]
FANTASY: *LOSING FINALISTS*
[England scored 4 competition points in this Round of the 2009-2010 IRB World Sevens Series]

CATHAY PACIFIC/CREDIT SUISSE HONG KONG SEVENS
IRB WORLD SEVENS SERIES 2009-2010 ROUND 6

Hong Kong Stadium, Eastern Hospital Road, So Kon Po, Hong Kong
[*Tournament squad:* T. Powell, Brightwell, Wade, Drauniniu, Rodwell, Jake Abbott, Royle, Caprice (never played as injured), O. Phillips (never travelled as injured, replaced by Ollie Lindsay-Hague), Gollings, M. Turner, Barrell, Lindsay-Hague]
(squad of 12)
[Isoa Damu and Kevin Barrett unavailable due to injury; Chris Cracknell unavailable due to club commitments; Dan Caprice was injured during the preceding Adelaide Sevens tournament]
[**MANAGER:** *Will Beeley*] [**COACH:** *Ben Ryan*] [**ASSISTANT COACH:** *Russ Earnshaw*]
CAPTAIN: *Ben Gollings* [*Mat Turner took over when Ben Gollings was substituted at half-time*]
First Round - Pool 'E'
26th Mar HONG KONG 0 **ENGLAND** 45
[*Team:* Rodwell, Brightwell, T. Powell, Lindsay-Hague, Gollings, M. Turner, Wade]
[*Bench:* Jake Abbott (rep), Barrell, Drauniniu (rep), Royle (rep)]
[*Scorers:* **tries** by Lindsay-Hague (2), Wade, Rodwell, Royle (2) and T. Powell, **conversions** by Gollings (3) and M. Turner (2)]
CAPTAIN: *Ben Gollings* [*Mat Turner took over when Ben Gollings was substituted at half-time*]
27th Mar JAPAN 0 **ENGLAND** 45
[*Team:* Rodwell, Jake Abbott, T. Powell, Lindsay-Hague, Gollings, M. Turner, Royle]
[*Bench:* Barrell (rep), Brightwell, Drauniniu (rep), Wade (rep)]
[*Scorers:* **tries** by Gollings, Royle (2), Jake Abbott, Drauniniu, Rodwell and Lindsay-Hague, **conversions** by Gollings (3) and Drauniniu (2)]
CAPTAIN: *Ben Gollings*
27th Mar WALES 5 **ENGLAND** 26
[*Team:* Rodwell, Brightwell, T. Powell, Lindsay-Hague, Gollings, M. Turner, Wade]
[*Bench:* Jake Abbott (rep), Barrell, Drauniniu (rep), Royle (rep)]
[*Scorers:* **tries** by Rodwell, Wade, Lindsay-Hague and Royle, **conversions** by Gollings (3)]
Quarter-Final
28th Mar AUSTRALIA 19 **ENGLAND** 26
[*Team:* Rodwell, Brightwell, T. Powell, Lindsay-Hague, Gollings, M. Turner, Wade]
[*Bench:* Jake Abbott (rep), Barrell, Drauniniu, Royle]
[*Scorers:* **tries** by Wade (2), Rodwell and T. Powell, **conversions** by Gollings (3)]

Semi-Final

28th Mar	SAMOA	28	**ENGLAND***	24

[*Team:* Rodwell, Brightwell, T. Powell, Lindsay-Hague, Gollings, M. Turner, Royle]
[*Bench:* Jake Abbott (rep), Barrell, Drauniniu, Wade (rep)]
[*Scorers:* **tries** by Brightwell, Lindsay-Hague, M. Turner and Rodwell, **conversions** by Gollings (2)]

POSITION: LOSING SEMI-FINALISTS

FANTASY: *LOSING FINALISTS*

[England scored 20 competition points in this Round of the 2009-2010 IRB World Sevens Series]

LONDON FLOODLIT SEVENS

Rosslyn Park FC, Priory Lane, Upper Richmond Road, Roehampton

[*Tournament squad:* Jake Abbott, Brake, Brightwell, A. Cheeseman (*forward/centre*), Simon Hunt, T. Powell, Rodwell, Manu Tuilagi (*centre*), M. Turner]

(squad of 9)

[The Dig Deep England team was not officially approved by the RFU; Manu Tuilagi was the brother of Alesana and Freddie Tuilagi]

[**COACH:** *Ben Ryan*]

CAPTAIN: *Mat Turner*

First Round - Pool 'C'

[6th May	**DIG DEEP ENGLAND**	38	Esher	7	]

[*Team:*]
[*Bench:*]
[*Scorers:*]

[6th May	**DIG DEEP ENGLAND**	40	Loughborough University	7	]

[*Team:*]
[*Bench:*]
[*Scorers:*]

Semi-Final

[6th May	**DIG DEEP ENGLAND**	24	Wasps	10	]

[*Team:*]
[*Bench:*]
[*Scorers:* **tries** by M. Tuilagi (2) and Simon Hunt (2), **conversions** by ? (2)]

Final

[6th May	**DIG DEEP ENGLAND**	17	Saracens	5	]

[*Team:* Rodwell, Brightwell, T. Powell, Brake, M. Turner, M. Tuilagi, Simon Hunt]
[*Bench:* Jake Abbott, A. Cheeseman]
[*Scorers:* **tries** by Brake, Simon Hunt and T. Powell, **conversion** by ?]

POSITION: WINNERS

DAN JAMES MEMORIAL MATCH

[**MANAGER:** *Charlotte Gibbons*] [**COACH:** *Mark Mapletoft*] [**ASSISTANT COACH:** *Rob Hunter* (SC)]

CAPTAIN: *Jacob Rowan*

[19th May	Loughborough University	11	**ENGLAND U20 XV**	29 ab]

Loughborough Students RFC, Loughborough University, Loughborough

[*Team:* Marler, A. Ellis, Shaun Knight, Kruis, C. Matthews, W. Welch, J. Rowan, Jackson

Wray, Charlie Davies, F. Burns, M. Watson, Forsyth, Jonny May, Wade, Catterick]
[*Bench:* Casson (rep), Rory Clegg (rep), J. George (rep), A. Gray (*flanker/number 8*) (rep), Calum Green (*lock*) (rep), Sam Harrison (2) (rep), Homer (*centre/wing/full back*) (rep), Sam Smith (*wing/full back*) (rep), Alex Waller (*prop*) (rep)]
[*Scorers:* **tries** by Wade, M. Watson, Marler and Jonny May, **penalty goal** by F. Burns, **conversions** by F. Burns (3)]
[*This was the second Dan James Memorial Match*]
[*Charlotte Gibbons was appointed on 20th April 2010*]

EMIRATES AIRLINE LONDON SEVENS
IRB WORLD SEVENS SERIES 2009-2010 ROUND 7

Twickenham
[*Tournament squad:* T. Powell, Brightwell, Wade, Micky Young, Rodwell, Varndell, O. Phillips (withdrew, replaced by Ollie Lindsay-Hague), R. Vickerman, K. Barrett, Gollings, M. Turner, Barden, Lindsay-Hague]
(squad of 12)
[Isoa Damu unavailable due to injury; Chris Cracknell unavailable due to suspension; Ollie Lindsay-Hague, John Brake and Simon Hunt in original training squad of 15; Ollie Phillips was withdrawn by his club Stade Français the day before the tournament, being replaced by Ollie Lindsay-Hague; Ben Gollings was the tournament captain]
[**MANAGER:** *Will Beeley*] [**COACH:** *Ben Ryan*] [**ASSISTANT COACH:** *Russ Earnshaw*]
CAPTAIN: *Ben Gollings* [*Kevin Barrett took over when Ben Gollings was injured in the 2nd half*]
First Round - Pool 'D'
22nd May **ENGLAND** 29 RUSSIA 5
[*Team:* Rodwell, R. Vickerman, T. Powell, K. Barrett, Gollings, M. Turner, Varndell]
[*Bench:* Barden, Brightwell (rep), Lindsay-Hague, Wade (rep), Micky Young (rep)]
[*Scorers:* **tries** by T. Powell, Gollings, Rodwell, Wade and M. Turner, **conversions** by Gollings (2)]
CAPTAIN: *Ben Gollings* [*Kevin Barrett took over when Ben Gollings was substituted in the 2nd half*]
22nd May **ENGLAND** 36 SCOTLAND 10
[*Team:* Rodwell, R. Vickerman, T. Powell, K. Barrett, Gollings, M. Turner, Wade]
[*Bench:* Barden, Brightwell (rep), Lindsay-Hague, Varndell (rep), Micky Young (rep)]
[*Scorers:* **tries** by Wade, Gollings, Rodwell, M. Turner and Varndell (2), **conversions** by Gollings (2) and Micky Young]
CAPTAIN: *Kevin Barrett*
22nd May **ENGLAND** 5 AUSTRALIA 38
[*Team:* Rodwell, Brightwell, T. Powell, K. Barrett, Micky Young, M. Turner, Varndell]
[*Bench:* Barden (rep), Gollings, Lindsay-Hague (rep), R. Vickerman, Wade (rep)]
[*Scorers:* **try** by Micky Young]
CAPTAIN: *Ben Gollings* [*Kevin Barrett took over when Ben Gollings was sin-binned in the 1st half*]
Quarter-Final
23rd May **ENGLAND*** 12 SOUTH AFRICA 17
[*Team:* Rodwell, R. Vickerman, T. Powell, K. Barrett, Gollings, M. Turner, Varndell]
[*Bench:* Barden, Brightwell, Lindsay-Hague, Wade (rep), Micky Young (rep)]
[*Scorers:* **tries** by Varndell and T. Powell, **conversion** by Gollings]

CAPTAIN: *Ben Gollings*
[Plate Semi-Final:]
[23rd May **ENGLAND*** 19 NEW ZEALAND 22]
[*Team:* Rodwell, R. Vickerman, T. Powell, Micky Young, Gollings, M. Turner, Wade]
[*Bench:* Barden, K. Barrett, Brightwell, Lindsay-Hague, Varndell]
[*Scorers:* **tries** by T. Powell, Gollings and Wade, **conversions** by Gollings (2)]
POSITION: LOSING QUARTER-FINALISTS [*PLATE SEMI-FINALISTS*]
FANTASY: *LOSING SEMI-FINALISTS*
[England scored 6 competition points in this Round of the 2009-2010 IRB World Sevens Series]

PENGUINS TOUR TO PORTUGAL 2010

[**MANAGER:** *Ben Dormer* (NZ)] [**ASSISTANT MANAGER:** *Craig Brown* (NZ)] [**COACHES:** *Steve Hill*, *John McKittrick* (NZ) & *Riccardo Franconi* (IT)]
[*Other squad members:* Alessandro Boscolo (IT) (*lock*), Martin Dufficy (IR) (*fly half*), T. George (*flanker*), T. Gregory, Hugh Hogan (IR) (*flanker/number 8*), Neilus Keogh (IR) (*lock*), James Knight (SC) (*centre*) (never travelled as withdrew, replaced by Henry Strethfield), Sam MacDonald (IR) (*lock/number 8*), Joris Matheron (FR) (*flanker*), Martin Nutt (*centre/wing/full back*), Ben Penga (SC) (*number 8*), Anthony 'Tony' Penn (NZ) (*prop*), M. Price, Edward 'Ed' Rosa (*hooker*), Edoardo Rotella (IT) (*scrum half/wing*), Kenny Sewell (*scrum half/fly half*), Mark Sexton (IR) (*centre*), Chad Shepherd (NZ) (*scrum half*), Andrew 'Andy' Skinstad (SA) (*centre*), Jeff Stewart (*fly half/full back*), Henry Strethfield, Tama Tuirirangi (NZ) (*prop*), J. Wallace (*full back*) (never travelled as withdrew, replaced by Martin Dufficy), John 'Jon' West (*number 8*)]
(squad of 24)
[AEIS Agronomia founded 1935; John McKittrick was the Coach when the USA played in the Rugby World Cup Sevens at Mar del Plata on 26th-28th January 2001 and was the Coach when the Cook Islands played in the Commonwealth Sevens at Manchester on 2nd-4th August 2002; The Penguins squad travelled to Portugal on 23rd May 2010; Tom George played for Major R.V. Stanley's XV against Oxford University at Iffley Road on 17th November 2009; Andy Skinstad was the brother of Bobby Skinstad]

AEIS AGRONOMIA 75TH ANNIVERSARY MATCH

CAPTAIN: *Marcus Di Rollo* (SC)
[29th May AEIS Agronomia (*POR*) 17 **PENGUINS** 30]
Campo A, Complexo Desportivo da Tapada
[*Team:* Steven 'Steve' Ketchin (SC) (*flanker*), Marcus Di Rollo (SC)]
[*Bench:*]
[*Scorers:*]

EMIRATES AIRLINE EDINBURGH SEVENS
IRB WORLD SEVENS SERIES 2009-2010 ROUND 8
NED HAIG CUP

Murrayfield
[*Tournament squad:* T. Powell, Brightwell, Royle, Micky Young, Rodwell, Varndell (never travelled as withdrew, replaced by Uche Oduoza), O. Phillips (never travelled as withdrew, replaced by Ollie Lindsay-Hague), R. Vickerman, K. Barrett, Gollings, M. Turner, Barden, Lindsay-Hague, Oduoza]
(squad of 12)
[Isoa Damu unavailable due to injury; Christian Wade unavailable due to his IRB

***Junior World Championship commitments; Chris Cracknell unavailable due to suspension; Ollie Phillips in original squad but was withdrawn by his club Stade Français, being replaced by Ollie Lindsay-Hague; Tom Varndell in original squad but withdrew due to his Churchill Cup commitments; Uche Oduoza played in the Samurai St George team that won the ULR Anglican Premier International Sevens at Bury St. Edmunds on 9th May 2010*]**
[**MANAGER:** *Will Beeley*] [**COACH:** *Ben Ryan*] [**ASSISTANT COACH:** *Russ Earnshaw*]
CAPTAIN: *Ben Gollings*
First Round - Pool 'C'
29th May PORTUGAL 5 **ENGLAND** 17
[*Team:* Rodwell, R. Vickerman, T. Powell, Micky Young, Gollings, M. Turner, Oduoza]
[*Bench:* Barden (rep), K. Barrett, Brightwell, Lindsay-Hague (rep), Royle (rep)]
[*Scorers:* **tries** by M. Turner, Royle and Lindsay-Hague, **conversion** by Gollings]
29th May CANADA 26 **ENGLAND*** 19
[*Team:* Rodwell, R. Vickerman, Brightwell, K. Barrett, Gollings, M. Turner, Oduoza]
[*Bench:* Barden, Lindsay-Hague, T. Powell (rep), Royle (rep), Micky Young (rep)]
[*Scorers:* **tries** by Oduoza, Royle and Rodwell, **conversions** by Gollings (2)]
29th May AUSTRALIA 21 **ENGLAND*** 21
[*Team:* Rodwell, R. Vickerman, T. Powell, Micky Young, Gollings, M. Turner, Oduoza]
[*Bench:* Barden (rep), K. Barrett, Brightwell, Lindsay-Hague (rep), Royle (rep)]
[*Scorers:* **tries** by Gollings, Oduoza and M. Turner, **conversions** by Gollings (3)]
Quarter-Final
30th May SCOTLAND 7 **ENGLAND** 19
[*Team:* Rodwell, R. Vickerman, T. Powell, Micky Young, Gollings, M. Turner, Oduoza]
[*Bench:* Barden (rep), K. Barrett, Brightwell, Lindsay-Hague, Royle (rep)]
[*Scorers:* **tries** by M. Turner and Royle (2), **conversions** by Gollings (2)]
Semi-Final
30th May SAMOA 15 **ENGLAND*** 12
aet
[*Team:* Rodwell, Barden, T. Powell, Micky Young, Gollings, M. Turner, Oduoza]
[*Bench:* K. Barrett (rep), Brightwell, Lindsay-Hague (rep), Royle (rep)]
[*Scorers:* **tries** by T. Powell and Barden, **conversion** by Gollings]
POSITION: LOSING SEMI-FINALISTS
FANTASY: *WINNERS*
[*England scored 16 competition points in this Round of the 2009-2010 IRB World Sevens Series*]
RANKING: 5TH 96 [*Samoa 164*, New Zealand 149, Australia 122, Fiji 108, South Africa 80, Argentina 62, Kenya 52, Wales 34, USA 32, Canada 15, Scotland 12]
FANTASY: *1ST 161*

FIRST MASTERCARD TROPHY MATCH

[ENGLAND XV: [*Other squad members:* D. Armitage, C. Ashton (*wing*), Banahan, Chuter, D. Cole, T. Croft, Flatman, T. Flood, Geraghty, H. Fourie (*flanker*), D. Hartley (withdrew as injured, replaced by George Chuter), Lawes, Moody, Monye, Parling, Robshaw, S. Shaw, Waldouck, R. Webber, Wigglesworth, Jonny Wilkinson, David Wilson (2), B. Youngs]**]**
(*squad of 44*)
[*Andy Sheridan, Steve Borthwick and Riki Flutey unavailable due to injury; Phil Vickery and Louis Deacon were rested for this match*]
[*Philippe Saint-André and Kingsley Jones were both appointed on 13th April 2010;*

Philippe Saint-André won 69 caps for France between 1990-97; Kingsley Jones won 10 caps for Wales between 1996-98]

[**ENGLAND XV:** [**TEAM MANAGER:** *Martin Johnson*] [**COACH:** *Brian Smith* (IR)] [**ASSISTANT COACHES:** *John Wells, Mike Ford & Graham Rowntree*]]

[**BARBARIANS:** [**COACH:** *Philippe Saint-André* (FR)] [**ASSISTANT COACH:** *Kingsley Jones* (WA)]]

CAPTAIN: *Nick Easter* [England XV]

CAPTAIN: *Xavier Rush* (NZ) [Barbarians]

30th May **ENGLAND XV** 35 **BARBARIANS*** 26

Twickenham

[**ENGLAND XV:** [*Team:* J. Golding, Steve Thompson (2), Doran-Jones, Attwood, Tom Palmer (2), Haskell, S. Armitage, Easter, Care, C. Hodgson, Strettle, Shontayne Hape, Tindall, Cueto, Foden]

[*Bench:* Barkley (rep), Mears (rep), T. Payne (rep), M. Tait (rep), Ward-Smith (rep), J. Simpson (rep), J. Worsley (rep)]

[*Scorers:* **tries** by Haskell, Hape, Foden and Tindall, **penalty goals** by C. Hodgson (2) and Barkley, **conversions** by C. Hodgson (2) and Barkley]]

[**BARBARIANS:** [*Team:* Rodrigo Roncero (AR), Benoît August (FR), Julian White, Skeate (SA), Kay, Rodney So'oialo (NZ), Martyn Williams (WA), X. Rush (NZ), Kelleher (NZ), Jean-Baptiste Élissalde (FR), Cédric Heymans (FR), Florian Fritz (FR), Casey Laulala (NZ), Sackey, Paul Warwick (AU)]

[*Bench:* Fabrice Estebanez (FR) (*fly half/centre*) (rep), Cencus Johnston (SAM) (*prop*) (rep), Pierre Mignoni (FR) (*scrum half*) (rep), Ken Owens (WA) (*hooker*) (rep), David Smith (3) (SAM) (*wing*) (rep), George Smith (AU) (*flanker*) (rep), Jérôme Thion (FR) (*lock*) (rep)]

[*Scorers:* **tries** by Sackey (2), David Smith (SAM) and Cencus Johnston (SAM), **conversions** by J-B. Élissalde (FR) (3)]]

SECOND MASTERCARD TROPHY MATCH

[**COACH:** *Philippe Saint-André* (FR)] [**ASSISTANT COACH:** *Kingsley Jones* (WA)]

CAPTAIN: *Xavier Rush* (NZ) [*George Smith* (AU) *took over when Xavier Rush was substituted in the 2nd half*]

[4th June IRELAND XV 23 **BARBARIANS** 29]

Thomond Park, Limerick

[*Team:* D. Barnes, Brits (SA), Cencus Johnston (SAM), Thion (FR), M. O'Kelly (IR), A. Quinlan (IR), George Smith (AU), X. Rush (NZ), Mignoni (FR), Brock James (AU), David Smith (3) (SAM), Ratu *Seru* Rabeni (FIJ), Laulala (NZ), Heymans (FR), Warwick (AU)]

[*Bench:* August (FR) (*hooker*) (rep), J-B. Élissalde (FR) (*scrum half/fly half*) (rep), Estebanez (FR) (rep), Kelleher (NZ) (rep), So'oialo (NZ) (*flanker/number 8*) (rep), Julian White (rep), Martyn Williams (WA) (rep)]

[*Scorers:* **tries** by X. Rush (NZ), George Smith (AU) and Heymans (FR), **penalty goals** by Brock James (AU) (3) and J-B. Élissalde (FR), **conversion** by Brock James (AU)]

[Philippe Saint-André and Kingsley Jones were both appointed on 13th April 2010]

ENGLAND COUNTIES TOUR TO CANADA 2010

[**MANAGER:** *Danny Hodgson*] [**ASSISTANT MANAGER:** *Mike Old*] [**COACH:** *Dave Baldwin*] [**ASSISTANT COACH:** *Jan Bonney*]

[*Other squad members:* William 'Will' Fraser (*flanker*) (left the tour as injured) (tm) Charlie Ingall (*wing*) (tm), Tom Kessell (*scrum half*) (tm), Cameron Mitchell (*centre*) (never travelled as withdrew, replaced by Kyle Dench)]

(squad of 26)

[Matt Rhodes was unavailable for this tour due to injury; Peter Joyce was unavailable due to family commitments; Owen Hambly was unavailable due to work commitments; Cameron Mitchell initially selected but withdrew for personal reasons; Matt Long was the tour captain; The England Counties squad departed for Canada on 31st May 2010; Will Fraser left the tour injured after the Ontario Blues match and was not replaced; Charlie Ingall played for Ireland U18 in April 2007; On 8th June 2010 Danny Hodgson announced that he would be leaving his post of England Counties Manager after this tour; On 8th June 2010 Mike Old was appointed to succeed Danny Hodgson as Manager after this England Counties tour]

CAPTAIN: *Matt Long*

[12th Jun British Columbia Bears (*CAN*) 7 **ENGLAND COUNTIES XV** 46]

Capilano RFC, Klahanie Park, West Vancouver

[*Team:* M. Long, Roddam, Craig Voisey, Louis McGowan, Harry Spencer, M. Wilson, Baines, Mark Evans, Will Cliff, Paul Humphries, T. Jarvis, Steve Hamilton, Henry Staff, James Tincknell, G. Collins]

[*Bench:* L. Collins (*lock*) (rep), Dench (rep), Phil Eggleshaw (*flanker/number 8*) (rep), N. Flynn (rep), Matt Hall (rep), Fergus Mulchrone (*wing*) (rep), Winney (rep), Gavin Woods (*prop*) (rep)]

[*Scorers:* **tries** by Staff (2), Tincknell (2), T. Jarvis, L. McGowan and Eggleshaw, **penalty goal** by Winney, **conversions** by P. Humphries (2) and Winney (2)]

IRB JUNIOR WORLD CHAMPIONSHIP

Argentina

[*Other squad members:* Catterick (never travelled as injured, replaced by Rob Buchanan), Hurrell (never travelled as injured, replaced by Marcus Watson)]

(squad of 26)

[On 1st April 2010 Mark Mapletoft announced that he would be leaving his post of England U20 Coach on 1st July 2010; Charlotte Gibbons was appointed on 20th April 2010; England U20 prepared for this 2010 Junior World Championship by having a pre-tournament training camp at North Bristol RFC on 10th-14th May 2010; James Gaskell was unavailable for this tournament due to injury; Jacob Rowan was the tournament captain; On 28th May 2010 Diccon Edwards was appointed to succeed Rob Hunter as Assistant Coach on 1st July 2010; The England U20 squad arrived in Argentina on 30th May 2010; On 7th June 2010 Rob Hunter was appointed to become England U20 Coach on 1st July 2010]

(<u>During the First Round a bonus point was awarded for scoring 4 or more tries in a match and for losing by seven points or less</u>)

[**MANAGER:** *Charlotte Gibbons*] [**COACH:** *Mark Mapletoft*] [**ASSISTANT COACH:** *Rob Hunter* (SC)]

CAPTAIN: *Jacob Rowan*

First Round - Pool 'B'

[5th June ARGENTINA U20 22 **ENGLAND U20** 48 **BP**]

Estadio El Coloso del Parque, Rosario

[*Team:* Marler, A. Ellis, Shaun Knight, Calum Green, C. Matthews, W. Welch, J. Rowan, Jackson Wray, Sam Harrison (2), F. Burns, M. Watson, Casson, Jonny May, Wade, Homer]

[*Bench:* Rory Clegg (rep), Charlie Davies (rep), Forsyth (*centre/full back*) (rep), J. George (rep), A. Gray (rep), Imiolek (rep), Kruis (rep)]

[*Scorers:* **tries** by Jonny May (3), J. Rowan and Wade, **penalty goals** by Homer (5), **conversions** by Homer (4)]

[9th June IRELAND U20 21 **ENGLAND U20** 36]

Estadio El Coloso del Parque, Rosario

[*Team:* Imiolek, J. George, Vunipola, Kruis, C. Matthews, J. Gibson, J. Rowan, A. Gray, Charlie Davies, Rory Clegg, Sam Smith, Casson, Forsyth, Wade, Homer]

[*Bench:* R. Buchanan (rep), F. Burns (rep), Calum Green (rep), Sam Harrison (2) (rep), Marler (rep), Jonny May (rep), Jackson Wray (rep)]

[*Scorers:* **tries** by J. Gibson and F. Burns (2), **penalty goals** by Homer (5), **conversions** by Homer (3)]

CAPTAIN: *Jamie George*

[13th Jun FRANCE U20 9 **ENGLAND U20** 17]

Estadio El Coloso del Parque, Rosario

[*Team:* Marler, J. George, Shaun Knight, Calum Green, Kruis, J. Gibson, W. Welch, A. Gray, Sam Harrison (2), Rory Clegg, Sam Smith, Casson, Forsyth, M. Watson, F. Burns]

[*Bench:* Charlie Davies, A. Ellis, Homer (rep), Imiolek (rep), C. Matthews (rep), Jonny May (rep), Jackson Wray (rep)]

[*Scorers:* **try** by J. Gibson, **penalty goals** by F. Burns (3), **drop goal** by F. Burns]

CAPTAIN: *Jacob Rowan*

Semi-Final

[17th Jun AUSTRALIA U20 28 **ENGLAND U20*** 16]

Estadio El Coloso del Parque, Rosario

[*Team:* Marler, J. George, Shaun Knight, Calum Green, C. Matthews, J. Gibson, J. Rowan, Jackson Wray, Charlie Davies, Rory Clegg, Sam Smith, Casson, Forsyth, Wade, Homer]

[*Bench:* F. Burns (rep), A. Ellis (rep), Sam Harrison (2) (rep), Imiolek (rep), Kruis (rep), Jonny May (rep), W. Welch (rep)]

[*Scorers:* **tries** by Sam Smith and Jonny May, **penalty goals** by Homer (2)]

Third Place Play-Off

[21st Jun SOUTH AFRICA U20 27 **ENGLAND U20*** 22]

Estadio El Coloso del Parque, Rosario

[*Team:* Marler, J. George, Vunipola, Calum Green, Kruis, W. Welch, J. Rowan, J. Gibson, Sam Harrison (2), F. Burns, M. Watson, Casson, Jonny May, Wade, Homer]

[*Bench:* R. Buchanan (rep), Rory Clegg (rep), Charlie Davies (rep), A. Gray (rep), C. Matthews (rep), Shaun Knight (rep), Sam Smith (rep)]

[*Scorers:* **tries** by M. Watson, F. Burns and Marler, **penalty goal** by Rory Clegg, **conversions** by F. Burns (2)]

POSITION: 4TH PLACE

FANTASY: ***LOSING FINALISTS***

ENGLAND TOUR TO AUSTRALIA AND NEW ZEALAND 2010

[**TEAM MANAGER:** *Martin Johnson*] [**COACH:** *Brian Smith* (IR)] [**ASSISTANT COACHES:** *John Wells*, *Mike Ford* & *Graham Rowntree*]

[*Other squad members:* S. Armitage (tm), Attwood (tm), Banahan (tm), Barkley (tm), Barritt (*fly half/centre*) (tm), Doran-Jones (tm), Dowson (tm), Flatman (tm), H. Fourie (left the tour injured, replaced by Phil Dowson) (tm), Geraghty (tm), J. Golding (*prop*) (tm), D. Hartley (never travelled as injured, replaced by George Chuter), C. Hodgson (tm), P. Hodgson (tm), Mears (tm), Monye (tm), Parling (tm), Robshaw (tm), J. Simpson (never travelled as injured, replaced by Paul Hodgson), Strettle (tm), Waldouck (tm), Ward-Smith (tm), R. Webber (tm), Wigglesworth (tm), J. Worsley (tm)]

(squad of 45)
[Andy Sheridan, Steve Borthwick and Riki Flutey were unavailable for this tour due to injury; Phil Vickery and Louis Deacon were rested for this tour; Joe Simpson selected but withdrew on the day of the squad's departure due to injury, being replaced by Paul Hodgson; The England squad departed for Australia on 31st May 2010; Phil Dowson flew in from Canada on 11th June 2010; Brad Barritt was added to the original squad of 44 on 17th June 2010 to provide injury cover for Dom Waldouck; Jon Golding, Steve Thompson (2), Simon Shaw, David Wilson (2), Tom Palmer (2), Tom Croft, Joe Worsley, Lewis Moody, Nick Easter, Paul Hodgson, Toby Flood, Jonny Wilkinson, Ugo Monye, Matt Banahan, Shontayne Hape, Mike Tindall, Mark Cueto all returned home on 20th June 2010, having been released from the tour by Martin Johnson; The remaining 28 players in the squad flew to New Zealand on the same day; Dan Ward-Smith retired due to injury in August 2011; Joe Worsley retired due to injury in November 2011]

BUNDABERG RUM TEST SERIES

COOK CUP

CAPTAIN: *Lewis Moody* [*Nick Easter took over when Lewis Moody was substituted in the 2nd half*]

12th June AUSTRALIA 27 **ENGLAND*** 17

Subiaco Oval, Perth

[*Team:* T. Payne, Steve Thompson (2), D. Cole, S. Shaw, Tom Palmer (2), T. Croft, Moody, Easter, Care, T. Flood, C. Ashton, Hape, Tindall, Cueto, Foden]

[*Bench:* Chuter (rep), Haskell (rep), Lawes (rep), M. Tait (rep), Jonny Wilkinson (rep), David Wilson (2) (rep), B. Youngs (rep)]

[*Scorers:* **tries** by penalty try (2), **penalty goal** by T. Flood, **conversions** by T. Flood (2)]

CAPTAIN: *Lewis Moody*

19th June AUSTRALIA 20 **ENGLAND** 21

ANZ Stadium, Sydney Olympic Park, Homebush Bay, Sydney

[*Team:* T. Payne, Steve Thompson (2), D. Cole, Lawes, Tom Palmer (2), T. Croft, Moody, Easter, B. Youngs, T. Flood, C. Ashton, Hape, Tindall, Cueto, Foden]

[*Bench:* D. Armitage (rep), Care (rep), Chuter (rep), Haskell, S. Shaw (rep), Jonny Wilkinson (rep), David Wilson (2) (rep)]

[*Scorers:* **tries** by B. Youngs and C. Ashton, **penalty goals** by T. Flood (2) and Jonny Wilkinson, **conversion** by T. Flood]

POSITION: SERIES SHARED

FANTASY: *SERIES WINNERS*

CHURCHILL CUP

USA

[*Other squad members:* Dowson (flew to Australia after the first match), P. Hodgson (never travelled as withdrew, replaced by Lee Dickson), S. Hooper (never travelled as injured, replaced by James Hudson), D. Paice (never travelled as injured, replaced by Andy Titterrell), Tom Rees (never travelled as injured, replaced by Kearnan Myall)]

(squad of 26)
[Danny Cipriani was unavailable for this tour due to injury; Paul Hodgson initially selected but withdrew as he was now required to go on the simultaneous England tour of Australia and New Zealand; George Skivington was the tournament captain; The England Saxons squad departed for America on 1st June 2010; Phil Dowson flew to Australia after the first match and was not replaced; Brad Barritt flew to Australia after the second match and was not replaced; On 18th June 2011 the RFU announced that

the agreement with Rugby Canada and USA Rugby to hold the Churchill Cup tournament would not be renewed beyond the 2011 competition because Canada and America were now included on the IRB's tournaments and tour schedule for 2012 onwards]
(<u>During the First Round a bonus point was awarded for scoring 4 or more tries in a match and for losing by seven points or less</u>)
[COACH: *Stuart Lancaster*] **[ASSISTANT COACHES:** *Simon Hardy & Andy Farrell*]
CAPTAIN: *George Skivington*
First Round - Pool 'B'
[9th June RUSSIA 17 **ENGLAND SAXONS** 49 **BP**]
Infinity Park, Glendale
[*Team:* N. Wood, Vickers, Duncan Bell, Kitchener, Skivington, T. Wood, Saull, Narraway, Micky Young, Myler, Varndell, Anthony Allen, Jon Clarke, J. Simpson-Daniel, Abendanon]
[*Bench:* Barritt (rep), N. Catt (rep), Corbisiero (rep), L. Dickson (rep), Alex Goode (rep), Myall (*lock/flanker*) (rep), Titterrell (rep)]
[*Scorers:* **tries** by Saul, Abendanon, Narraway, Varndell (2), Micky Young and Myler, **conversions** by Myler (7)]
[13th Jun USA 9 **ENGLAND SAXONS** 32 **BP**]
Infinity Park, Glendale
[*Team:* N. Wood, Titterrell, Corbisiero, James Hudson, Skivington, Myall, Saull, Narraway, L. Dickson, Alex Goode, Varndell, Barritt, Anthony Allen, Ollie Smith (2), Abendanon]
[*Bench:* Duncan Bell (rep), Jon Clarke (rep), Kitchener (rep), Tom Lindsay (*hooker*) (rep), Myler (rep), T. Wood (rep), Micky Young (rep)]
[*Scorers:* **tries** by Varndell (2), Anthony Allen and Narraway, **penalty goals** by Alex Goode (2), **conversions** by Alex Goode (2) and Myler]
Final
[19th Jun CANADA 18 **ENGLAND SAXONS** 38]
Red Bull Arena, Harrison, New Jersey
[*Team:* N. Wood, Titterrell, Corbisiero, James Hudson, Skivington, T. Wood, Saull, Narraway, L. Dickson, Myler, Abendanon, Anthony Allen, Jon Clarke, J. Simpson-Daniel, Alex Goode]
[*Bench:* Duncan Bell (rep), Kitchener (rep), Myall (rep), Ollie Smith (2) (rep), Varndell (rep), Vickers (rep), Micky Young (rep)]
[*Scorers:* **tries** by Abendanon, Alex Goode, Jon Clarke and Narraway, **penalty goals** by Myler (4), **conversions** by Myler (3)]
POSITION: WINNERS

<u>RUGBYROCKS LONDON SEVENS</u>
<u>*NATIONAL SEVENS SERIES 2010 ROUND 1*</u>
Athletic Ground, Kew Foot Road, Richmond
[*Tournament squad:* Rhys Jones (WA) (*fly half*), Mark Bright (NZ) (*forward*), Geoff Griffiths (*forward*), Gavin Dacey (WA) (*centre*), Simon Hunt, Zane Winslade (NZ) (*forward*), Greig Ryan (SC) (*forward*), Carl Murray (NZ) (*forward/back*), Graham Spiers (SC) (*wing*), Mike Davis (2) (NZ) (*fly half*), Tom Wiley (NZ) (*wing*), Ripol (SP) (*scrum half*)]
(squad of 12)
[The RFU approved the holding of a National Sevens Series on 1st December 2009; On 6th May 2010 the following nine sides were designated as Core teams: 1) British Army, 2) Samurai International RFC, 3) Akuma Smurfs, 4) HFW Wailers, 5) Gilbert Pups, 6)

White Hart Marauders RFC, 7) Raging Bull Ronin, 8) Apache and 9) Olorun ID; These nine Core teams participated at every Round of this National Sevens Series alongside three different guest teams each time, which meant that only the Core teams were actually eligible for competition points; The French Pyrenees, Esher and the Irish Raiders were the respective three guest teams at the 2010 RugbyRocks London Sevens; Carl Murray was the tournament captain; Geoff Griffiths and Simon Hunt played in the Samurai team that won the Amsterdam Heineken Sevens on 22nd-23rd May 2010]

[The National Sevens Series used a points system where the Winners, Runners-Up, Semi-Finalists, Quarter-Finalists, Plate Winners, Plate Runners-Up and Plate Semi-Finalists were awarded 20, 16, 12, 10, 8, 6 and 4 points respectively]

[**MANAGER:** *John Elliott*] [**COACH:** *Russ Earnshaw*]

CAPTAIN: *Carl Murray* (NZ)

First Round - Group 'D'

[12th Jun Apache 21 **SAMURAI** 22]

[*Team:* ?, Simon Hunt, ?, Ripol (SP), Mike Davis (2) (NZ), Rhys Jones (WA), Wiley (NZ)]

[*Bench:* G. Dacey (WA), G. Griffiths (rep), ?, ?, ?]

[*Scorers:* **tries** by Simon Hunt, Ripol (SP), ? and G. Griffiths, **conversion** by ?]

[12th Jun Irish Raiders (*IR*) 19 **SAMURAI** 29]

[*Team:* Bright (NZ), ?, ?, Ripol (SP), Rhys Jones (WA), G. Dacey (WA), Simon Hunt]

[*Bench:* Mike Davis (2) (NZ) (rep), G. Griffiths, ?, ?, ?]

[*Scorers:* **tries** by Simon Hunt (2), ?, ? and G. Griffiths, **conversions** by ? (2)]

Quarter-Final

[12th Jun White Hart Marauders 12 **SAMURAI** 21]

[*Team:* ?, Simon Hunt, Carl Murray (NZ), Ripol (SP), Rhys Jones (WA), G. Dacey (WA), Wiley (NZ)]

[*Bench:* Mike Davis (2) (NZ) (rep), G. Griffiths (rep), ?, ?, ?]

[*Scorers:* **tries** by Simon Hunt (2) and G. Dacey (WA), **conversions** by Rhys Jones (WA) (3)]

Semi-Final

[12th Jun HFW Wailers 21 **SAMURAI** 26]

[*Team:* G. Griffiths, Simon Hunt, Bright (NZ), Ripol (SP), Rhys Jones (WA), G. Dacey (WA), Wiley (NZ)]

[*Bench:* Mike Davis (2) (NZ) (rep), Carl Murray (NZ), G. Ryan (SC) (rep), Spiers (SC), Winslade (NZ)]

[*Scorers:* **tries** by Simon Hunt (2), Wiley (NZ) and Mike Davis (NZ), **conversions** by Rhys Jones (WA) (3)]

Final

[12th Jun Esher 31 **SAMURAI** 42]

[*Team:* Bright (NZ), G. Ryan (SC), Winslade (NZ), Ripol (SP), Mike Davis (2) (NZ), Rhys Jones (WA), Simon Hunt]

[*Bench:* G. Dacey (WA) (rep), G. Griffiths (rep), Carl Murray (NZ), Spiers (SC), Wiley (NZ) (rep)]

[*Scorers:* **tries** by Ripol (SP), G. Dacey (WA) (2), G. Griffiths and Simon Hunt (2), **conversions** by Rhys Jones (WA) (6)]

POSITION: WINNERS

[The Samurai scored 20 competition points in this Round of the 2010 National Sevens Series]

WEST COUNTRY SEVENS
NATIONAL SEVENS SERIES 2010 ROUND 2

Keynsham RFC, Crown Field, Bristol Road, Keynsham, Bristol
[*Tournament squad:* J. Rudd, Jake Abbott, G. Griffiths, Jevon Groves (WA) (*forward*), Bright (NZ), Simon Hunt, A. Cheeseman, Rhys Jones (WA), Mike Davis (2) (NZ), Lee Rees (WA) (*scrum half*), D. Norton, Wiley (NZ)]
(squad of 12)
[Paul John won 10 caps for Wales between 1994-98 and was the Coach when Wales won the Rugby World Cup Sevens in Dubai on 7th March 2009; The Trust PA Cavaliers, Shamrock Warriors and Les Bleus were the respective three guest teams at the 2010 West Country Sevens; Mark Bright was the tournament captain; Alex Cheeseman played for English Universities in the BUCS Home Nations Rugby Sevens at the University of Edinburgh on 15th April 2010]
[**MANAGER:** *John Elliott*] [**COACHES:** *Russ Earnshaw* & *Paul John* (WA)]
CAPTAIN: *Mark Bright* (NZ)
First Round - Group 'A'
[19th Jun Raging Bull Ronin 0 **SAMURAI** 56]
[*Team:* Bright (NZ), Jake Abbott, G. Griffiths, L. Rees (WA), Mike Davis (2) (NZ), ?, Simon Hunt]
[*Bench:* A. Cheeseman, Groves (WA), J. Rudd, Wiley (NZ), ?]
[*Scorers:* **tries** by Simon Hunt (3), L. Rees (WA) (2), Jake Abbott, G. Griffiths and ?, **conversions** by ? (8)]
[19th Jun Apache 5 **SAMURAI** 31]
[*Team:* Bright (NZ), A. Cheeseman, Groves (WA), L. Rees (WA), Rhys Jones (WA), D. Norton, Wiley (NZ)]
[*Bench:* Jake Abbott, Mike Davis (2) (NZ), G. Griffiths, Simon Hunt, J. Rudd (rep)]
[*Scorers:* **tries** by Rhys Jones (WA), ?, L. Rees (WA), Groves (WA) and J. Rudd, **conversions** by ? (3)]
Quarter-Final
[19th Jun Gilbert Pups 21 **SAMURAI** 36]
[*Team:* Bright (NZ), Jake Abbott, Simon Hunt, L. Rees (WA), Rhys Jones (WA), A. Cheeseman, J. Rudd]
[*Bench:* Mike Davis (2) (NZ) (rep), G. Griffiths (rep), Groves (WA), D. Norton (rep), Wiley (NZ)]
[*Scorers:* **tries** by Simon Hunt, Jake Abbott, D. Norton, J. Rudd, G. Griffiths and Bright (NZ), **conversions** by Rhys Jones (WA) (3)]
Semi-Final
[19th Jun White Hart Marauders 5 **SAMURAI** 26]
[*Team:* Bright (NZ), Jake Abbott, G. Griffiths, L. Rees (WA), Rhys Jones (WA), D. Norton, J. Rudd]
[*Bench:* A. Cheeseman (rep), Mike Davis (2) (NZ) (rep), Groves (WA), Simon Hunt, Wiley (NZ)]
[*Scorers:* **tries** by G. Griffiths, J. Rudd, Jake Abbott and Bright (NZ), **conversions** by Rhys Jones (WA) (3)]
Final
[19th Jun British Army (*SER*) 33 **SAMURAI** 36]
[*Team:* Bright (NZ), Jake Abbott, G. Griffiths, L. Rees (WA), Rhys Jones (WA), D. Norton, J. Rudd]
[*Bench:* A. Cheeseman, Mike Davis (2) (NZ) (rep), Groves (WA) (rep), Simon Hunt (rep),

Wiley (NZ)]
[*Scorers:* **tries** by G. Griffiths, J. Rudd, L. Rees (WA), Jake Abbott, Rhys Jones (WA) and Mike Davis (NZ), **conversions** by Rhys Jones (WA) (2) and Mike Davis (NZ)]
POSITION: WINNERS
[*The Samurai scored 20 competition points in this Round of the 2010 National Sevens Series*]

MANCHESTER RUGBY SEVENS
NATIONAL SEVENS SERIES 2010 ROUND 3

Heywood Road, Brooklands, Sale
[SAMURAI: [*Tournament squad:* Bright (NZ), M. Purdy (*forward*), H. Paul, Carl Murray (NZ), G. Griffiths, Billy Ngawini (NZ) (*scrum half*), G. Dacey (WA), Wiley (NZ), Thomas 'Tom' Loizides (*centre/wing*), Brake, Jamie Hearn (*wing*), Martyn (SC)]**]**
(squad of 12)
[Simon Hunt was unavailable for this tournament due to injury; Lees Rees unavailable due to club commitments; John Rudd unavailable due to family commitments; The Gameface Pacific Warriors, Great Britain Students and Sale Sharks were the respective three guest teams at the 2010 Manchester Rugby Sevens; Carl Murray was the tournament captain; Jamie Hearn played for the Samurai Barracudas development side at the Safaricom Sevens in Nairobi on 5th-6th June 2010]
[GREAT BRITAIN STUDENTS: [*Tournament squad:* Tom O'Toole (*wing*), Pitfield, Cameron Brown (SC) (*fly half/centre*), David 'Dave' Fenlon (IR) (*forward*), Whittington, David Smith (2), Peter Clarke (1), A. Cheeseman, Richard Ellis (*forward*), Sam Bellhouse (SC) (*wing*), Alex Grodynski (SC) (*fly half/centre*), Sean Morris (*wing*)]**]**
(squad of 12)
[The Gameface Pacific Warriors, Great Britain Students and Sale Sharks were the respective three guest teams at the 2010 Manchester Rugby Sevens; Richard Ellis, Cam Brown, David Smith (2) and Tom O'Toole all played for English Universities in the BUCS Home Nations Rugby Sevens at the University of Edinburgh on 15th April 2010; Andy Grodynski played for Scotland A at Rugby League in June 2008]
[SAMURAI: [MANAGER: *Terry Sands*] **[COACHES:** *Mike Friday* & *Paul John* (WA)]**]**
[GREAT BRITAIN STUDENTS: [**COACH:** *Tim Stevens*]**]**
CAPTAIN: *Carl Murray* (NZ) [Samurai]
CAPTAIN: *??* [Great Britain Students]
First Round - Group 'A'
CAPTAIN: *Carl Murray* (NZ)
[4th July Akuma Smurfs 12 **SAMURAI** 22]
[*Team:* Bright (NZ), H. Paul, G. Dacey (WA)]
[*Bench:*]
[*Scorers:* **tries** by H. Paul, ?, ? and G. Griffiths, **conversion** by ?]
[4th July Raging Bull Ronin 7 **SAMURAI** 19]
[*Team:* M. Purdy, Ngawini (NZ), Hearn]
[*Bench:*]
[*Scorers:* **tries** by M. Purdy, Ngawini (NZ) and Martyn (SC), **conversions** by ? (2)]
First Round - Group 'C'
CAPTAIN: *??*
[4th July HFW Wailers 26 **GREAT BRITAIN STUDENTS*** 19]
[*Team:* A. Cheeseman, Fenlon (IR), R. Ellis, Whittington, ?, ?, David Smith (2)]
[*Bench:* Bellhouse (SC), Sean Morris, Pitfield, T. O'Toole (rep), ?]

[*Scorers:* **tries** by ?, ? and Fenlon (IR), **conversions** by ? (2)]
[4th July Gilbert Pups 39 **GREAT BRITAIN STUDENTS** 0]
[*Team:* A. Cheeseman, Fenlon (IR), R. Ellis, Whittington, Grodynski (SC), Peter Clarke (1), T. O'Toole]
[*Bench:* Bellhouse (SC), Cameron Brown (SC), Sean Morris, Pitfield, David Smith (2)]
[*No scorers*]
Quarter-Final
CAPTAIN: *Carl Murray* (NZ)
[4th July Olorun ID 0 **SAMURAI** 33]
[*Team:* G. Griffiths, Martyn (SC), Bright (NZ), Carl Murray (NZ), H. Paul, G. Dacey (WA), Wiley (NZ)]
[*Bench:* Brake (rep), Hearn (rep), Loizides, Ngawini (NZ) (rep), M. Purdy]
[*Scorers:* **tries** by Martyn (SC) (3), G. Griffiths and Hearn, **conversions** by ? (4)]
[Plate Semi-Final:]
CAPTAIN: *??*
[4th July Apache 17 **GREAT BRITAIN STUDENTS** 26]
[*Team:* A. Cheeseman, Fenlon (IR), R. Ellis, Whittington, Grodynski (SC), Peter Clarke (1), David Smith (2)]
[*Bench:* Bellhouse (SC), Cameron Brown (SC), Sean Morris (rep), Pitfield, T. O'Toole (rep)]
[*Scorers:* **tries** by Whittington, Fenlon (IR), Grodynski (SC) and Sean Morris, **conversions** by ? (2) and Grodynski (SC)]
Semi-Final
CAPTAIN: *Henry Paul*
[4th July HFW Wailers 14 **SAMURAI** 17]
[*Team:* G. Griffiths, Martyn (SC), Bright (NZ), Brake, H. Paul, G. Dacey (WA), Wiley (NZ)]
[*Bench:* Carl Murray (NZ), Hearn, Loizides, Ngawini (NZ) (rep), M. Purdy]
[*Scorers:* **tries** by Martyn (SC) (2) and Wiley (NZ), **conversion** by ?]
[Plate Final:]
CAPTAIN: *??*
[4th July Raging Bull Ronin 31 **GREAT BRITAIN STUDENTS*** 14]
[*Team:* A. Cheeseman, Fenlon (IR), R. Ellis, Whittington, Grodynski (SC), Peter Clarke (1), T. O'Toole]
[*Bench:* Bellhouse (SC) (rep), Cameron Brown (SC), Sean Morris (rep), Pitfield (rep)]
[*Scorers:* **tries** by Peter Clarke and T. O'Toole, **conversions** by ? and T. O'Toole]
Final
CAPTAIN: *Carl Murray* (NZ)
[4th July British Army (*SER*) 26 **SAMURAI*** 15]
[*Team:* G. Griffiths, Bright (NZ), Purdy, Carl Murray (NZ), H. Paul. G. Dacey (WA), Brake]
[*Bench:* Hearn, Loizides, Martyn (SC) (rep), Ngawini (NZ) (rep), Wiley (NZ) (rep)]
[*Scorers:* **tries** by Brake, G. Dacey (WA) and Wiley (NZ)]
POSITION: LOSING FINALISTS [Samurai]
FANTASY: *WINNERS* [Samurai]
POSITION: FIRST ROUND LOSERS [*PLATE FINALISTS*] [Great Britain Students]
[The Samurai scored 16 competition points in this Round of the 2010 National Sevens Series]

NEWQUAY SURF SEVENS
NATIONAL SEVENS SERIES 2010 ROUND 4

Newquay Sports Centre, Tretherras Road, Newquay
[*Tournament squad:* Bright (NZ), Rhys Jones (WA), Gareth Davies (2) (WA), M. Purdy, Rob Lewis (WA) (*scrum half*), Lee Beach (WA) (*forward*), Drauniniu, Shabbo, Errie Claassens (SA) (*wing*), Fedo (SC), G. Dacey (WA) (*hooker*), Wiley (NZ)]
(squad of 12)
[Russ Earnshaw appointed as Coach but withdrew due to being unavailable; Simon Hunt was unavailable for this tournament due to injury; Geoff Griffiths, Carl Murray, Lee Rees and John Brake were all unavailable; The Kamikaze, the Handstand Harlequins and the Force XV French Froggies were the respective three guest teams at the 2010 Newquay Surf Sevens; Mark Bright was the tournament captain]
[MANAGER: *Terry Sands*] **[COACH:** *Mark Hewitt*]
CAPTAIN: *Mark Bright* (NZ)
First Round - Group 'B'
[17th July Kamikaze 7 **SAMURAI** 32]
[*Team:* Fedo (SC), G. Dacey (WA), Bright (NZ), Rob Lewis (WA), Rhys Jones (WA), Shabbo, E. Claassens (SA)]
[*Bench:* Beach (WA), Gareth Davies (2) (WA) (rep), Drauniniu, M. Purdy, Wiley (NZ)]
[*Scorers:* **tries** by Bright (NZ) (3), ?, ? and ?, **conversion** by ?]
[17th July Raging Bull Ronin 0 **SAMURAI** 38]
[*Team:* Beach (WA), G. Dacey (WA), M. Purdy, Rob Lewis (WA), Gareth Davies (2) (WA), Drauniniu, Wiley (NZ)]
[*Bench:* Bright (NZ), E. Claassens (SA) (rep), Fedo (SC), Rhys Jones (WA) (rep)]
[*Scorers:* **tries** by Drauniniu (4), ? and ?, **conversions** by ? (4)]
Quarter-Final
[17th July Akuma Smurfs 19 **SAMURAI** 22]
[*Team:* Beach (WA), Fedo (SC), Bright (NZ), Rob Lewis (WA), Rhys Jones (WA), Drauniniu, Wiley (NZ)]
[*Bench:* E. Claassens (SA) (rep), G. Dacey (WA) (rep), Gareth Davies (2) (WA), M. Purdy (rep)]
[*Scorers:* **tries** by ?, ?, Drauniniu and E. Claassens (SA), **conversion** by ?]
Semi-Final
[17th July White Hart Marauders 12 **SAMURAI*** 7]
[*Team:* Beach (WA), G. Dacey (WA), Bright (NZ), Rob Lewis (WA), Rhys Jones (WA), Drauniniu, E. Claassens (SA)]
[*Bench:* Fedo (SC) (rep), Gareth Davies (2) (WA) (rep), M. Purdy, Wiley (NZ) (rep)]
[*Scorers:* **try** by E. Claassens (SA), **conversion** by Rhys Jones (WA)]
POSITION: LOSING SEMI-FINALISTS
[The Samurai scored 12 competition points in this Round of the 2010 National Sevens Series]
RANKING: 1ST 68 [British Army (*SER*) 68, HFW Wailers 48, White Hart Marauders 48, Gilbert Pups 42, Akuma Smurfs 42, Apache 32, Olorun ID 32, Raging Bull Ronin 20]
[The Samurai won the National Sevens Series because they had a better points difference than the British Army]

WORLD UNIVERSITY RUGBY SEVENS CHAMPIONSHIP

Estádio do Bessa XXI, Porto

[*Tournament squad:* Tom Mitchell (2) (*centre*), Bellhouse (SC) (*forward*), David Smith (2), R. Ellis, Pitfield, Paul Jarvis (*scrum half/fly half*), Whittington, H. Smales (*scrum half/fly half*), Richard de Carpentier (*forward*), Edward 'Ed' Tellwright (WA) (*forward*), A. Cheeseman, Sean Morris]

(squad of 12)

[This tournament was played on a pitch made from artificial grass; This tournament was originally scheduled with a First Round consisting of 5 Groups of four teams, but this structure was changed on 19th July 2010 to 2 Pools of seven teams after the squads from America, Australia, the Ukraine, France, South Africa and Kenya all withdrew from the competition; The Great Britain Students squad arrived in Portugal on 20th July 2010; Paul Jarvis and Tom Mitchell (2) played for English Universities in the BUCS Home Nations Rugby Sevens at the University of Edinburgh on 15th April 2010]

[**MANAGER:** *Tim Stevens*] [**COACH:** *James Farndon*]

CAPTAIN: *David Smith (2)*

First Round - Pool 'D'

[21st July HUNGARY STUDENTS 0 **GREAT BRITAIN STUDENTS** 52]

[*Team:* R. Ellis, Tellwright (WA), Pitfield, P. Jarvis, Whittington, A. Cheeseman, David Smith (2)]

[*Bench:* Bellhouse (SC) (rep), de Carpentier, Tom Mitchell (2), Sean Morris (rep), H. Smales]

[*Scorers:* **tries** by P. Jarvis (3), David Smith (2), Whittington (2) and R. Ellis, **conversions** by Whittington (6)]

[22nd Jul NORWAY STUDENTS 0 **GREAT BRITAIN STUDENTS** 48]

[*Team:* de Carpentier, Bellhouse (SC), Pitfield, H. Smales, P. Jarvis, Tom Mitchell (2), Sean Morris]

[*Bench:* A. Cheeseman (rep), R. Ellis (rep), David Smith (2), Tellwright (WA), Whittington]

[*Scorers:* **tries** by P. Jarvis, de Carpentier, Sean Morris (2), Tom Mitchell, Bellhouse (SC), R. Ellis and H. Smales, **conversions** by H. Smales (4)]

[22nd Jul Canadian Universities (*CAN*) 12 **GREAT BRITAIN STUDENTS** 36]

[*Team:* R. Ellis, Whittington, David Smith (2)]

[*Bench:* Sean Morris (rep)]

[*Scorers:* **tries** by ?, Whittington (2), ?, ? and Sean Morris, **conversions** by ? and Whittington (2)]

[23rd July JAPAN STUDENTS 5 **GREAT BRITAIN STUDENTS** 40]

[*Team:* de Carpentier, Tellwright (WA), Pitfield, P. Jarvis, Whittington, A. Cheeseman, David Smith (2)]

[*Bench:* Bellhouse (SC), R. Ellis, Tom Mitchell (2) (rep), Sean Morris (rep), H. Smales]

[*Scorers:* **tries** by Whittington (2), David Smith, A. Cheeseman and Tom Mitchell (2), **conversions** by Whittington (5)]

[23rd July Moroccan Universities (*MOR*) 7 **GREAT BRITAIN STUDENTS** 43]

[*Team:* R. Ellis, A. Cheeseman, Tellwright (WA), P. Jarvis, H. Smales, Tom Mitchell (2), David Smith (2)]

[*Bench:* de Carpentier, Sean Morris (rep), Pitfield (rep), Tellwright (WA), Whittington (rep)]

[*Scorers:* **tries** by David Smith (3), Tom Mitchell, R. Ellis, Tellwright (WA) and H. Smales, **conversions** by H. Smales (4)]

[23rd July Spanish Universities (*SP*) 10 **GREAT BRITAIN STUDENTS** 12]

[*Team:* de Carpentier, A. Cheeseman, Pitfield, P. Jarvis, Whittington, Tom Mitchell (2), David

Smith (2)]
[*Bench:* Bellhouse (SC), R. Ellis (rep), Sean Morris, H. Smales, Tellwright (WA)]
[*Scorers:* **tries** by David Smith and P. Jarvis, **conversion** by Whittington]

Semi-Final

[24th July RUSSIA STUDENTS 22 **GREAT BRITAIN STUDENTS*** 12]
[*Team:* de Carpentier, A. Cheeseman, R. Ellis, P. Jarvis, Whittington, Tom Mitchell (2), David Smith (2)]
[*Bench:* Bellhouse (SC) (rep), Sean Morris (rep), H. Smales, Tellwright (WA) (rep)]
[*Scorers:* **tries** by David Smith and Sean Morris, **conversion** by Whittington]

Third Place Play-Off

[24th July Spanish Universities (*SP*) 12 **GREAT BRITAIN STUDENTS** 19]
[*Team:* Tellwright (WA), de Carpentier, Pitfield, P. Jarvis, Whittington, A. Cheeseman, Tom Mitchell (2)]
[*Bench:* Bellhouse (SC) (rep), R. Ellis (rep), Sean Morris, H. Smales, David Smith (2) (rep)]
[*Scorers:* **tries** by Tom Mitchell (2) and Whittington, **conversions** by Whittington (2)]

POSITION: 3RD PLACE [*BRONZE MEDALISTS*]

PART 2
ENGLAND PLAYER TOUR MATCH RESULTS, TEAMS & SCORERS
2000-2010

2000

[No tour matches]

2001

PENGUINS TOUR TO GERMANY AND ARGENTINA 2001

[**MANAGER:** *Alan Wright*] [**COACH:** *Craig Brown* (NZ)]

CAPTAIN: *Andre Fox* (SA)

[6th June Argentina Naval Selection (*AR*) 5 **PENGUINS** 103]
Buenos Aires
[*Team:*]
[*Bench:*]
[*Scorers:*]

[10th Jun Combined Western Provinces (*AR*) 18 **PENGUINS** 24]
Neuquén RC, Neuquén
[*Team:*]
[*Bench:*]
[*Scorers:* **try** by ?, **penalty goals** by Fratti (IT) (2)]

ENGLAND TOUR TO CANADA AND AMERICA 2001

[**TEAM MANAGER:** *Clive Woodward*] [**HEAD COACH:** *Brian Ashton*] [**ASSISTANT COACHES:** *John Wells, Ellery Hanley, Paul Grayson & Dave Reddin*]

CAPTAIN: *Alex Sanderson*

5th June British Columbia (*CAN*) 19 **ENGLAND XV** 41
Thunderbird Stadium, Vancouver
[*Team:* Trevor Woodman, C. Fortey, Nebbett, Alex Brown, Tom Palmer (2), White-Cooper, Hazell, A. Sanderson, Benton, Barkley, David Rees (2), Ewens, F. Waters, Sackey, Voyce]
[*Bench:* Flatman (rep), A. King (rep), A. Long (rep), P. Sanderson (rep), S. Shaw (rep), Stimpson (rep), J. Worsley]
[*Scorers:* **tries** by F. Waters (2), Hazell, David Rees, Trevor Woodman and Tom Palmer, **penalty goal** by Barkley, **conversions** by Barkley (2) and Stimpson (2)]

12th June USA A 21 **ENGLAND XV** 83
University of California, Los Angeles
[*Team:* Flatman, M. Regan, Nebbett, Rob Fidler, Tom Palmer (2), A. Sanderson, Hazell, P. Sanderson, Walshe, A. King, David Rees (2), Barkley, F. Waters, Sackey, Voyce]
[*Bench:* C. Fortey (rep), Grayson, Steve Thompson (2) (rep), Martyn Wood, Trevor Woodman (rep)]
[*Scorers:* **tries** by A. Sanderson, David Rees (2), Sackey (2), Flatman, Voyce (3), Walshe, A. King (2) and F. Waters, **conversions** by Barkley (9)]

BRITISH & IRISH LIONS TOUR TO AUSTRALIA 2001

[**MANAGER:** *Donal Lenihan* (IR)] [**COACH:** *Graham Henry* (NZ)] [**ASSISTANT COACHES:** *Andy Robinson & Phil Larder*]

CAPTAIN: *Keith Wood* (IR)

[8th June Western Australia President's XV (*AU*) 10 **BRITISH & IRISH LIONS XV** 116]
WACA Ground, Perth
[*Team:* Darren Morris (WA), K. Wood (IR), Vickery, Grewcock, M. O'Kelly (IR), Richard Hill (2), Back, Scott Quinnell (WA), Howley (WA), O'Gara (IR), Luger, W. Greenwood, M. Taylor (WA), B. Cohen, Brian O'Driscoll (IR)]
[*Bench:* Balshaw (rep), J. Davidson (IR) (rep), Healey (rep), R. Henderson (IR) (rep), J. Leonard (rep), McBryde (WA) (rep), Simon Taylor (2) (SC) (rep)]

[*Scorers:* **tries** by Scott Quinnell (WA) (3), Howley (WA) (2), Luger (3), W. Greenwood, Back (2), Grewcock, M. Taylor (WA), Simon Taylor (SC), Balshaw (2), Healey and Brian O'Driscoll (IR), **conversions** by O'Gara (IR) (13)]

CAPTAIN: *Dai Young* (WA)

[12th Jun Queensland President's XV (*AU*) 6 **BRITISH & IRISH LIONS XV** 83]
Dairy Farmers Stadium, Townsville

[*Team:* Tom Smith (2) (SC), McBryde (WA), D. Young (WA), J. Davidson (IR), S. Murray (SC), Charvis (WA), Martyn Williams (WA), Corry, Matt Dawson, N. Jenkins (WA), Jason Robinson, R. Henderson (IR), W. Greenwood, Dafydd James (WA), Matt Perry]

[*Bench:* G. Bulloch (SC) (rep), Healey (rep), Richard Hill (2), J. Leonard (rep), Luger, M. O'Kelly (IR) (rep), M. Taylor (WA) (rep)]

[*Scorers:* **tries** by D. Young (WA), Charvis (WA) (2), Jason Robinson (5), penalty try, R. Henderson (IR) (3) and M. O'Kelly (IR), **conversions** by N. Jenkins (WA) (5) and Matt Perry (4)]

CAPTAIN: *Martin Johnson*

[16th Jun Queensland Reds (*AU*) 8 **BRITISH & IRISH LIONS XV** 42]
Ballymore Stadium, Brisbane

[*Team:* Tom Smith (2) (SC), K. Wood (IR), Vickery, Martin Johnson, Grewcock, Richard Hill (2), Back, Corry, Howley (WA), Jonny Wilkinson, Luger, R. Henderson (IR), Brian O'Driscoll (IR), Dafydd James (WA), Balshaw]

[*Bench:* G. Bulloch (SC), Charvis (WA) (rep), Matt Dawson (rep), Healey, J. Leonard, S. Murray (SC) (rep), Jason Robinson (rep)]

[*Scorers:* **tries** by Luger, R. Henderson (IR), Dafydd James (WA), Richard Hill and Brian O'Driscoll (IR), **penalty goals** by Jonny Wilkinson (3), **conversions** by Jonny Wilkinson (4)]

CAPTAIN: *Dai Young* (WA) [*Lawrence Dallaglio took over when Dai Young was substituted in the 2nd half; Scott Quinnell* (WA) *took over when Lawrence Dallaglio was temporarily sin-binned in the 2nd half*]

[19th Jun AUSTRALIA A 28 **BRITISH & IRISH LIONS XV*** 25]
North Power Stadium, Gosford

[*Team:* J. Leonard, McBryde (WA), D. Young (WA), S. Murray (SC), M. O'Kelly (IR), Dallaglio, Martyn Williams (WA), Scott Quinnell (WA), Healey, N. Jenkins (WA), Jason Robinson, M. Catt, W. Greenwood, B. Cohen, Matt Perry]

[*Bench:* G. Bulloch (SC) (rep), Charvis (WA) (rep), J. Davidson (IR) (rep), Matt Dawson (rep), Darren Morris (WA) (rep), O'Gara (IR), M. Taylor (WA) (rep)]

[*Scorers:* **tries** by M. Taylor (WA), Matt Perry and Jason Robinson, **penalty goals** by N. Jenkins (WA) (2), **conversions** by Matt Dawson (2)]

CAPTAIN: *Martin Johnson*

[23rd Jun New South Wales Waratahs (*AU*) 24 **BRITISH & IRISH LIONS XV** 41]
Sydney Football Stadium, Sydney

[*Team:* Darren Morris (WA), K. Wood (IR), Vickery, Martin Johnson, Grewcock, Dallaglio, Back, Scott Quinnell (WA), Matt Dawson, Jonny Wilkinson, Jason Robinson, W. Greenwood, Brian O'Driscoll (IR), Dafydd James (WA), Balshaw]

[*Bench:* Corry, Healey (rep), Richard Hill (2) (rep), McBryde (WA) (rep), O'Gara (IR) (rep), Matt Perry (rep), Tom Smith (2) (SC) (rep)]

[*Scorers:* **tries** by Brian O'Driscoll (IR), Jason Robinson (2), Jonny Wilkinson and Dafydd James (WA), **penalty goals** by Jonny Wilkinson (2), **conversions** by Jonny Wilkinson (4) and Matt Dawson]

CAPTAIN: *Dai Young* (WA)

[26th Jun New South Wales Country Cockatoos (*AU*) 3 **BRITISH & IRISH LIONS XV** 46]

Coffs Harbour International Sports Stadium, Coffs Harbour

[*Team:* J. Leonard, G. Bulloch (SC), D. Young (WA), J. Davidson (IR), M. O'Kelly (IR), Charvis (WA), Martyn Williams (WA), Corry, Healey, N. Jenkins (WA), T. Howe (IR), Gibbs (WA), M. Taylor (WA), B. Cohen, Balshaw]

[*Bench:* Matt Dawson, Darren Morris (WA) (rep), S. Murray (SC) (rep), O'Gara (IR) (rep), Matt Perry, D. Wallace (IR) (rep), D. West]

[*Scorers:* **tries** by B. Cohen (2), Charvis (WA), Gibbs (WA), Healey and D. Young (WA), **penalty goals** by N. Jenkins (WA) (2), **conversions** by N. Jenkins (WA) (5)]

CAPTAIN: *Dai Young* (WA) [*Matt Dawson took over when Dai Young was injured in the 2nd half*]

[3rd July ACT Brumbies (*AU*) 28 **BRITISH & IRISH LIONS XV** 30]

Bruce Stadium, Canberra

[*Team:* Darren Morris (WA), D. West, D. Young (WA), J. Davidson (IR), S. Murray (SC), D. Wallace (IR), Martyn Williams (WA), Corry, Matt Dawson, O'Gara (IR), Healey, Gibbs (WA), M. Taylor (WA), B. Cohen, Balshaw]

[*Bench:* G. Bulloch (SC), T. Howe (IR), Dafydd James (WA) (rep), N. Jenkins (WA), J. Leonard (rep), Martin Johnson, M. O'Kelly (IR)]

[*Scorers:* **tries** by Healey (2) and D. Wallace (IR), **penalty goals** by Matt Dawson (3), **conversions** by Matt Dawson (3)]

2002

PENGUINS TOUR TO AMERICA AND CANADA 2002

[**MANAGERS:** *Bill Calcraft* (AU) & *Alan Wright*] [**PLAYER-COACH:** *Craig Brown* (NZ)]

CAPTAIN: *Mark Denney*

[15th Jun New York Athletic Club Select XV (*US*) 17 **PENGUINS** 74]

Travers Island, Shore Road, Pelham, New York

[*Team:*]

[*Bench:*]

[*Scorers:*]

ENGLAND TOUR TO ARGENTINA 2002

[**HEAD COACH:** *Clive Woodward*] [**COACH:** *Andy Robinson*] [**ASSISTANT COACH:** *Phil Larder*]

CAPTAIN: *Hugh Vyvyan*

17th June ARGENTINA A 29 **ENGLAND XV*** 24

Cricket & Rugby Club Stadium, Buenos Aires

[*Team:* Trevor Woodman, M. Regan, R. Morris, Rob Fidler, H. Vyvyan, Balding, D. Danaher, Anglesea, Walshe, Walder, David Rees (2), May, K. Sorrell, Cueto, Beim]

[*Bench:* Codling, Flatman, Gomarsall, C. Hodgson, A. Sanderson (rep), Stimpson (rep), Steve Thompson (2)]

[*Scorers:* **tries** by Cueto, R. Morris and Walder, **penalty goal** by Walder, **conversions** by Walder (3)]

ENGLAND COUNTIES TOUR TO CHILE 2002

[**MANAGER:** *Rob Udwin*] [**ASSISTANT MANAGER:** *Danny Hodgson*] [**COACH:** *Bob Hood*] [**ASSISTANT COACH:** *Tommy Borthwick*]

CAPTAIN: *Tony Windo*

[22nd Jun NORTHERN REGIONAL XV 12 **ENGLAND COUNTIES XV** 38]

Estadio Sausalito, Viña del Mar

[*Team:* Windo, Lawn, L. Fortey, Schofield, J. Winterbottom, Muckalt, L. Jones, G. Wilson, Andy Brown, Mike Scott (1), Kirkby, Mike Davies, Bonney, Strettle, A. Hodgson]

[*Bench:* Botterman, Ricky Pellow, Craig Raymond (rep), ?, ?, ?, ?]

[*Scorers:* **tries** by L. Jones, Muckalt, Strettle (2) and Kirkby (2), **conversions** by Mike Scott (3) and Craig Raymond]

CAPTAIN: *Glen Wilson*

[25th Jun SOUTHERN REGIONAL XV 10 **ENGLAND COUNTIES XV** 69]

Tineo Park, Concepción

[*Team:* R. Moore, Botterman, Sigley, J. Winterbottom, J. Oakes, G. Wilson, John Sewell (2), S. Brady, Ricky Pellow, Craig Raymond, Kerfoot, Bonney, S. Martin, Strettle, I. Kennedy]

[*Bench:* Andy Brown, Lawn, Mike Scott (1) (rep), Windo, ?, ?, ?]

[*Scorers:* **tries** by John Sewell, Bonney, S. Martin, Craig Raymond, S. Brady (2), Sigley, Kerfoot, Botterman (2) and J. Oakes, **conversions** by Craig Raymond (6) and Mike Scott]

2003

ENGLAND TOUR TO NEW ZEALAND AND AUSTRALIA 2003

[**HEAD COACH:** *Clive Woodward*] [**COACH:** *Andy Robinson*] [**ASSISTANT COACH:** *Phil Larder*]

CAPTAIN: *Phil Vickery*

9th June NEW ZEALAND MAORI 9 **ENGLAND XV** 23

Yarrow Stadium, New Plymouth

[*Team:* Trevor Woodman, D. West, Vickery, S. Shaw, S. Borthwick, Corry, Hazell, J. Worsley, K. Bracken, Grayson, J. Simpson-Daniel, S. Abbott, Noon, Luger, Balshaw]

[*Bench:* Gomarsall (rep), A. King (rep), Ben Johnston (rep), Tom Palmer (2) (rep), M. Regan (rep), Volley (rep), M. Worsley (rep)]

[*Scorers:* **tries** by S. Shaw and Gomarsall, **penalty goals** by Grayson (3), **conversions** by Grayson (2)]

ENGLAND COUNTIES TOUR TO ROMANIA AND FRANCE 2003

[**MANAGER:** *Rob Udwin*] [**ASSISTANT MANAGER:** *Danny Hodgson*] [**COACH:** *Bob Hood*] [**ASSISTANT COACH:** *Tommy Borthwick*]

CAPTAIN: *Tony Windo*

[10th Jun ROMANIA A 24 **ENGLAND COUNTIES XV** 26]

Stadionul "Gheorghe Hagi", Constanţa

[*Team:* Windo, M. Armstrong, R. Moore, Paul Arnold (2), Soper, Rossigneux, N. Bland, G. Wilson, Andy Brown, Peter Murphy, Kirkby, Bonney, C. Cooper, Swords, Hitchmough]

[*Bench:* S. Brady (rep), Giraud (rep), D. Knight (rep), Paul Knight (2) (rep), J. Moore (rep), Muckalt (rep), J. Oakes (rep), O'Keefe (rep), P. Price (rep), Sigley (rep), E. Thorpe]

[*Scorers:* **tries** by P. Price and Bonney, **penalty goals** by Peter Murphy (3) and J. Moore, **conversions** by J. Moore (2)]

ENGLAND 'A' TOUR TO JAPAN 2003

[**COACH:** *Jim Mallinder*] [**ASSISTANT COACH:** *Steve Diamond*]

CAPTAIN: *Pete Anglesea*

[3rd July JAPAN SELECT XV 10 **ENGLAND A XV** 37]

Ajinomoto Stadium, Tokyo

[*Team:* Hatley, M. Cairns, Flatman, Chris Jones, Alex Brown, Volley, Hazell, Anglesea, Walshe, Barkley, Christophers, Ben Johnston, F. Waters, Scarbrough, Horak]

[*Bench:* Will Green (1) (rep), D. Hyde (rep), H. Paul (rep), Sheridan (rep), Titterrell (rep), H. Vyvyan (rep), Martyn Wood (rep)]

[*Scorers:* **tries** by Anglesea, Barkley (2), Christophers and Scarbrough, **penalty goals** by Barkley (2), **conversions** by Barkley (3)]

2004

PENGUINS TOUR TO HONG KONG 2004

[**MANAGER:** *Craig Brown* (NZ)] [**COACH:** *Bill Calcraft* (AU)]

CAPTAIN: *Craig de Goldi* (NZ)

[13th Jun Hong Kong Barbarians 18 **PENGUINS** 73]
King's Park Sports Ground, Hong Kong
[*Team:* Brenton, de Goldi (NZ)]
[*Bench:*]
[*Scorers:* **tries** by Dowson, Breeze (WA), Rodan (FIJ), Mark Sweeney (AU) and Brenton (2)]

ENGLAND COUNTIES TOUR TO CANADA 2004

[**MANAGER:** *Rob Udwin*] [**ASSISTANT MANAGER:** *Danny Hodgson*] [**COACH:** *Mark Nelson*] [**ASSISTANT COACH:** *Paul Westgate*]

CAPTAIN: *Craig Hammond*

[12th Jun Vancouver Island Crimson Tide (*CAN*) 0 **ENGLAND COUNTIES XV** 43]
Shawnigan Lake School, Victoria
[*Team:* Wring, Luffman, O'Keefe, Paul Arnold (2), J. Oakes, Craig Hammond, Wilks, E. Thorpe, S. Perry, T. Barlow, Strettle, P. Mooney, Mal Roberts, James Aston, Spragg]
[*Bench:* R. Faulkner (rep), Foden (rep), Fullman (rep), Hyslop (rep), Jess (rep), Craig Jones (rep), Lowrie (rep), J. Moore (rep), P. Price (rep), Senior (rep), Paul Williams (3) (rep)]
[*Scorers:* **tries** by Mal Roberts, Fullman, S. Perry, Lowrie, penalty try and Strettle, **penalty goal** by J. Moore, **conversions** by T. Barlow (2) and J. Moore (3)]

PENGUINS TOUR TO MEXICO 2004

[**MANAGER:** *Craig Brown* (NZ)] [**COACH:** *Steve Hill*]

CAPTAIN: *Dave Gorrie* (NZ)

[30th Jun Mexican Regional Selection (*MEX*) L **PENGUINS** W]
Celaya Rugby Club, Universidad de Celaya
[*Team:*]
[*Bench:*]
[*Scorers:*]
[3rd July MEXICO SELECT XV L **PENGUINS** W]
Acapulco
[*Team:*]
[*Bench:*]
[*Scorers:*]

2005

BRITISH & IRISH LIONS TOUR TO NEW ZEALAND 2005

[**MANAGER:** *Bill Beaumont*] [**HEAD COACH:** *Clive Woodward*] [**ASSISTANT COACHES:** *Eddie O'Sullivan* (IR), *Andy Robinson* & *Phil Larder*]

CAPTAIN: *Brian O'Driscoll* (IR)

[4th June Bay of Plenty (*NZ*) 20 **BRITISH & IRISH LIONS XV** 34]
Rotorua International Stadium

[*Team:* Gethin Jenkins (WA), G. Bulloch (SC), M. Stevens, P. O'Connell (IR), Kay, Richard Hill (2), Martyn Williams (WA), Dallaglio, Peel (WA), O'Gara (IR), Shanklin (WA), Henson (WA), Brian O'Driscoll (IR), Cueto, J. Lewsey]

[*Bench:* Corry (rep), G. D'Arcy (IR) (rep), Matt Dawson (rep), C. Hodgson, D. O'Callaghan (IR), Sheridan (rep), Steve Thompson (2) (rep)]

[*Scorers:* **tries** by J. Lewsey (2), Cueto, Shanklin (WA), Peel (WA) and G. D'Arcy (IR), **conversions** by O'Gara (IR) (2)]

[**MANAGER:** *Bill Beaumont*] [**HEAD COACH:** *Clive Woodward*] [**ASSISTANT COACHES:** *Ian McGeechan* (SC), *Gareth Jenkins* (WA) & *Mike Ford*]

CAPTAIN: *Martin Corry*

[8th June Taranaki (*NZ*) 14 **BRITISH & IRISH LIONS XV** 36]
Yarrow Stadium, New Plymouth

[*Team:* Rowntree, Titterrell, J. Hayes (IR), D. O'Callaghan (IR), Grewcock, Corry, Moody, Michael Owen (WA), Cusiter (SC), C. Hodgson, Hickie (IR), Ollie Smith (2), W. Greenwood, Horgan (IR), G. Murphy (IR)]

[*Bench:* S. Byrne (IR) (rep), Gareth Cooper (WA) (rep), Henson (WA), Gethin Jenkins (WA) (rep), Kay, Jonny Wilkinson, Martyn Williams (WA)]

[*Scorers:* **tries** by Corry, Horgan (IR) and G. Murphy (IR) (2), **penalty goals** by C. Hodgson (4), **conversions** by C. Hodgson (2)]

[**MANAGER:** *Bill Beaumont*] [**HEAD COACH:** *Clive Woodward*] [**ASSISTANT COACHES:** *Eddie O'Sullivan* (IR), *Andy Robinson* & *Phil Larder*]

CAPTAIN: *Brian O'Driscoll* (IR)

[11th Jun NEW ZEALAND MAORI 19 **BRITISH & IRISH LIONS XV*** 13]
Waikato Stadium, Hamilton

[*Team:* Sheridan, Steve Thompson (2), Julian White, S. Shaw, P. O'Connell (IR), Richard Hill (2), Martyn Williams (WA), Michael Owen (WA), Matt Dawson, Stephen Jones (2) (WA), Shane Williams (WA), G. D'Arcy (IR), Brian O'Driscoll (IR), Shanklin (WA), J. Lewsey]

[*Bench:* S. Byrne (IR) (rep), S. Easterby (IR), Gethin Jenkins (WA) (rep), Horgan (IR) (rep), Kay, O'Gara (IR) (rep), Peel (WA)]

[*Scorers:* **try** by Brian O'Driscoll (IR), **penalty goals** by Stephen Jones (WA) (2), **conversion** by Stephen Jones (WA)]

[**MANAGER:** *Bill Beaumont*] [**HEAD COACH:** *Clive Woodward*] [**ASSISTANT COACHES:** *Ian McGeechan* (SC), *Gareth Jenkins* (WA) & *Mike Ford*]

CAPTAIN: *Brian O'Driscoll* (IR)

[15th Jun Wellington (*NZ*) 6 **BRITISH & IRISH LIONS XV** 23]
WestpacTrust Stadium, Wellington

[*Team:* Gethin Jenkins (WA), S. Byrne (IR), Julian White, Grewcock, Kay, S. Easterby (IR), Back, Corry, Peel (WA), Jonny Wilkinson, Gareth Thomas (2) (WA), Henson (WA), Brian O'Driscoll (IR), Jason Robinson, J. Lewsey]

[*Bench:* G. Bulloch (SC), Cusiter (SC) (rep), Richard Hill (2), Horgan (IR) (rep), Stephen Jones (2) (WA) (rep), P. O'Connell (IR), M. Stevens (rep)]

[*Scorers:* **tries** by Gethin Jenkins (WA) and Gareth Thomas (WA), **penalty goals** by Jonny Wilkinson (3), **conversions** by Jonny Wilkinson (2)]
CAPTAIN: *Gordon Bulloch* (SC) [*Will Greenwood took over when Gordon Bulloch was substituted in the 2nd half*]

[18th Jun Otago (*NZ*) 19 **BRITISH & IRISH LIONS XV** 30]
Carisbrook Stadium, Dunedin
[*Team:* Rowntree, G. Bulloch (SC), M. Stevens, S. Shaw, D. O'Callaghan (IR), S. Easterby (IR), Martyn Williams (WA), Ryan Jones (WA), Cusiter (SC), C. Hodgson, Shane Williams (WA), G. D'Arcy (IR), W. Greenwood, Hickie (IR), G. Murphy (IR)]
[*Bench:* Matt Dawson (rep), Grewcock (rep), O'Gara (IR) (rep), Michael Owen (WA) (rep), Sheridan (rep), Ollie Smith (2) (rep), Steve Thompson (2) (rep)]
[*Scorers:* **tries** by W. Greenwood, Ryan Jones (WA) and S. Williams (WA), **penalty goals** by C. Hodgson (3), **conversions** by C. Hodgson (3)]
CAPTAIN: *Michael Owen* (WA) [*Ronan O'Gara* (IR) *took over when Michael Owen was substituted in the 2nd half*]

[21st Jun Southland (*NZ*) 16 **BRITISH & IRISH LIONS XV** 26]
Rugby Park Stadium, Invercargill
[*Team:* M. Stevens, Titterrell, J. Hayes (IR), S. Shaw, D. O'Callaghan (IR), Moody, Martyn Williams (WA), Michael Owen (WA), Gareth Cooper (WA), O'Gara (IR), Hickie (IR), Henson (WA), Ollie Smith (2), Cueto, G. Murphy (IR)]
[*Bench:* G. Bulloch (SC) (rep), Cusiter (SC) (rep), G. D'Arcy (IR) (rep), S. Easterby (IR) (rep), C. Hodgson, Shanklin (WA) (rep), Sheridan (rep)]
[*Scorers:* **tries** by Henson (WA) (2), **penalty goals** by O'Gara (IR) (4), **conversions** by O'Gara (IR) (2)]
CAPTAIN: *Gordon Bulloch* (SC) [*Charlie Hodgson took over when Gordon Bulloch was injured in the 1st half; Michael Owen* (WA) *took over when Charlie Hodgson was substituted in the 2nd half*]

[28th Jun Manawatu (*NZ*) 6 **BRITISH & IRISH LIONS XV** 109]
FMG Stadium, Palmerston North
[*Team:* Sheridan, G. Bulloch (SC), J. Hayes (IR), S. Shaw, D. O'Callaghan (IR), Corry, Martyn Williams (WA), Michael Owen (WA), Cusiter (SC), C. Hodgson, Shane Williams (WA), G. D'Arcy (IR), Ollie Smith (2), Jason Robinson, G. Murphy (IR)]
[*Bench:* Back (rep), Cockbain (WA) (rep), Gareth Cooper (WA) (rep), Cueto (rep), O'Gara (IR) (rep), M. Stevens (rep), Titterrell (rep)]
[*Scorers:* **tries** by Shane Williams (WA) (5), Corry, G. Murphy (IR), Jason Robinson, C. Hodgson, Ollie Smith, Back, G. D'Arcy (IR), O'Gara (IR) (2), Cueto (2) and Gareth Cooper (WA), **conversions** by C. Hodgson (7) and O'Gara (IR) (5)]
CAPTAIN: *Gordon Bulloch* (SC)

[5th July Auckland (*NZ*) 13 **BRITISH & IRISH LIONS XV** 17]
Eden Park, Auckland
[*Team:* Rowntree, G. Bulloch (SC), J. Hayes (IR), S. Shaw, Kay, Jason White (SC), Martyn Williams (WA), Michael Owen (WA), Matt Dawson, C. Hodgson, Hickie (IR), G. D'Arcy (IR), W. Greenwood, Cueto, G. Murphy (IR)]
[*Bench:* Cockbain (WA) (rep), Corry (rep), Cusiter (SC), Horgan (IR) (rep), O'Gara (IR) (rep), M. Stevens (rep), Titterrell]
[*Scorers:* **try** by Martyn Williams (WA), **penalty goals** by C. Hodgson and O'Gara (IR) (3)]

ENGLAND COUNTIES TOUR TO ARGENTINA AND URUGUAY 2005

[**CHAIRMAN OF SELECTORS:** *Peter Hartley*] [**MANAGER:** *Jim Robinson*] [***ASSISTANT MANAGER:*** *Danny Hodgson*] [**COACH:** *Paul Westgate*] [**ASSISTANT COACH:** *Ben Ryan*]

CAPTAIN: *Craig Hammond*

[15th Jun Atlético del Rosario Invitación XV (*AR*) 0 **ENGLAND COUNTIES XV** 38]

Club Atlético del Rosario

[*Team:* P. Price, Glenn Cooper, M. Long, Rouse, Paul Arnold (2), Craig Hammond, Ponton, G. Wilson, D. McCormack, O. Thomas, A. MacRae, Blackett, Malherbe, Jess, B. Thompson]

[*Bench:* C. Bentley (rep), Andy Brown (rep), D. Hughes, D. Parkes (rep), E. Thorpe (rep), Wilks (rep), Johnny Williams (rep)]

[*Scorers:* **tries** by Blackett (2), Glenn Cooper, O. Thomas, M. Long and Paul Arnold, **conversions** by O. Thomas (4)]

PUBLIC SCHOOL WANDERERS TOUR TO SRI LANKA 2005

[**MANAGER:** *Rolph James* (WA)] [**ASSISTANT MANAGER:** *Gavin Holmes*]

CAPTAIN: *Ben Harvey*

[14th Jun Western Province Rugby Union (*SRI*) 13 **PUBLIC SCHOOL WANDERERS** 58]

Ceylon Rugby and Football Club Grounds, Longden Place, Colombo

[*Team:* Nick Baxter]

[*Bench:*]

[*Scorers:* **tries** by ?, ?, ?, ?, ?, ?, ?, ? and ?, **penalty goal** by ?, **conversions** by ? (5)]

CAPTAIN: *Steve White-Cooper*

[19th Jun Central Province Invitation XV (*SRI*) 3 **PUBLIC SCHOOL WANDERERS** 33]

Kandy Sports Club, Nittawela Grounds, Kandy

[*Team:* White-Cooper (*number 8*)]

[*Bench:*]

[*Scorers:* **tries** by ?, ?, ?, ? and ?, **conversions** by ? (4)]

CAPTAIN: *Ben Harvey*

[22nd Jun Combined Defence Services (*SRI*) 6 **PUBLIC SCHOOL WANDERERS** 61]

Army Grounds, Galle Face, Colombo

[*Team:*]

[*Bench:*]

[*Scorers:* **tries** by ?, ?, ?, ?, ?, ?, ?, ? and ?, **conversions** by ? (8)]

2006

WORLD XV TOUR TO SOUTH AFRICA 2006

[**COACH:** *Bob Dwyer* (AU)] [**ASSISTANT COACHES:** *Mike Ruddock* (WA) & *Craig Dowd* (NZ)]

CAPTAIN: *Justin Marshall* (NZ)

[9th June	Western Province Corné Krige XV (*SA*)	31	**WORLD XV**	49]

Norwich Park Newlands, Cape Town

[*Team:* Califano (FR), M. Regan, C. Visagie (SA), Pierre (FR), Samo (AU), Finegan (AU), Magne (FR), Chabal (FR), J. Marshall (NZ), Mercier (FR), Reihana (NZ), Desbrosse (FR), Roff (AU), Nacewa (FIJ), Matt Burke (AU)]

[*Bench:* Drotske (SA) (rep), Sam Harding (NZ) (rep), Hewett (NZ) (rep), Kefu (AU) (rep), Mark Robinson (2) (NZ) (rep), C. Spencer (NZ) (rep), F. Waters (rep)]

[*Scorers:* **tries** by Califano (FR) (2), Samo (AU), Nacewa (FIJ) (2), Roff (AU) and Chabal (FR), **conversions** by Mercier (FR) (6) and C. Spencer (NZ)]

2007

ENGLAND COUNTIES TOUR TO RUSSIA 2007

[**CHAIRMAN OF SELECTORS:** *Peter Hartley*] [**MANAGER:** *Jim Robinson*] [**ASSISTANT MANAGER:** *Danny Hodgson*] [**COACH:** *Harvey Biljon* (SA)] [**ASSISTANT COACH:** *Dave Baldwin*]

CAPTAIN: *Duncan Cormack*

[7th June Krasny-Yar (*RUS*) 19 **ENGLAND COUNTIES XV** 27]

Centralny Stadium, Otdykha Island, Krasnoyarsk, Siberia

[*Team:* D. Cormack, L. Wordley, Tideswell, A. Davidson, Campton, Blakeburn, Rainbow, G. Hayter, Paul Knight (2), M. Woodrow, T. Jarvis, Bedworth, Cruickshanks, H. Smales, Viney]

[*Bench:* Glenn Cooper (rep), T. Mathias, Neale (rep), C. Pilgrim (rep), Rawlings, N. Spence (rep), J. Winterbottom (rep)]

[*Scorers:* **tries** by Tideswell, T. Jarvis, Blakeburn and Bedworth, **penalty goal** by M. Woodrow, **conversions** by M. Woodrow (2)]

CAPTAIN: *James Winterbottom*

[12th Jun VVA Podmoskovje (*RUS*) 35 **ENGLAND COUNTIES XV** 15]

Monino Stadium, Moscow

[*Team:* T. Mathias, Glenn Cooper, C. Rimmer, A. Davidson, J. Winterbottom, Chris Morgan, N. Spence, Blakeburn, C. Pilgrim, M. Leek, H. Smales, Malherbe, Rawlings, Viney, Neale]

[*Bench:* Campton (rep), Cruickshanks (rep), T. Jarvis (rep), Paul Knight (2) (rep), Rainbow (rep), Tideswell (rep), L. Wordley (rep)]

[*Scorers:* **tries** by T. Jarvis and L. Wordley, **penalty goal** by Neale, **conversion** by M. Leek]

2008
[No tour matches]

2009

OXBRIDGE TOUR TO JAPAN 2009

[**MANAGERS:** *Stewart Eru* (NZ) & *Tim Stevens*] [**COACHES:** *Steve Hill* & *Ian Minto*]

CAPTAIN: *Peter Clarke (1)*

[22nd Mar All Kanto Gakuin University (*JAP*) 10 **OXBRIDGE XV** 17]

Mitsuzawa Stadium, Yokohama

[*Team:* Conlon (IR), M. Crockett (WA), A. Daniel, Kench, B. Payne, J. Wheeler, Peter Clarke (1), Peter Wright (2), R. McGuire (WA), T. Henry, T. Catling, T. Gregory, A. Cheeseman, Burdon, Mahony (NZ)]

[*Bench:* W. Browne, J. Burnett (AU), Chris Davies (rep), K. Davis, Lutton (rep), Malaney, McKerchar (SC), Sean Morris, C. O'Keeffe (IR) (rep), Rosen (rep)]

[*Scorers:* **tries** by T. Catling, Mahony (NZ) and Peter Wright, **conversion** by T. Gregory]

BRITISH & IRISH LIONS TOUR TO SOUTH AFRICA 2009

[**MANAGER:** *Gerald Davies* (WA)] [**HEAD COACH:** *Ian McGeechan* (SC)] [**ASSISTANT COACHES:** *Warren Gatland* (NZ), *Rob Howley* (WA), *Shaun Edwards* & *Graham Rowntree*]

CAPTAIN: *Paul O'Connell* (IR)

[30th May Royal XV (*SA*) 25 **BRITISH & IRISH LIONS XV** 37]

Royal Bafokeng Stadium, Rustenburg

[*Team:* Sheridan, M. Rees (WA), Adam Jones (2) (WA), S. Shaw, P. O'Connell (IR), J. Worsley, Martyn Williams (WA), D. Wallace (IR), M. Blair (SC), O'Gara (IR), Shane Williams (WA), J. Roberts (WA), Earls (IR), Bowe (IR), L. Byrne (WA)]

[*Bench:* Flutey (rep), Heaslip (IR) (rep), Alun-Wyn Jones (WA) (rep), Stephen Jones (2) (WA), Mears (rep), Mike Phillips (2) (WA) (rep), Vickery (rep)]

[*Scorers:* **tries** by Bowe (IR), L. Byrne (WA), Alun-Wyn Jones (WA) and O'Gara (IR), **penalty goals** by O'Gara (IR) (3), **conversions** by O'Gara (IR) (4)]

CAPTAIN: *Brian O'Driscoll* (IR) [*Phil Vickery took over when Brian O'Driscoll was substituted in the 2nd half; Alun-Wyn Jones* (WA) *took over when Phil Vickery was then himself substituted in the 2nd half*]

[3rd June Golden Lions (*SA*) 10 **BRITISH & IRISH LIONS XV** 74]

Coca-Cola Park, Johannesburg

[*Team:* Gethin Jenkins (WA), Mears, Vickery, Hines (SC), Alun-Wyn Jones (WA), T. Croft, D. Wallace (IR), Heaslip (IR), Mike Phillips (2) (WA), Stephen Jones (2) (WA), Monye, J. Roberts (WA), Brian O'Driscoll (IR), Bowe (IR), R. Kearney (IR)]

[*Bench:* Harry Ellis (rep), Ferris (IR) (rep), R. Ford (SC) (rep), J. Hook (WA) (rep), E. Murray (SC) (rep), Andy Powell (WA) (rep), Shane Williams (WA) (rep)]

[*Scorers:* **tries** by J. Roberts (WA) (2), Brian O'Driscoll (IR), Monye (2), T. Croft, Bowe (IR) (2), J. Hook (WA) and Ferris (IR), **penalty goals** by Stephen Jones (WA) (2), **conversions** by Stephen Jones (WA) (6) and J. Hook (WA) (3)]

CAPTAIN: *Paul O'Connell* (IR)

[6th June Free State Cheetahs (*SA*) 24 **BRITISH & IRISH LIONS XV** 26]

Vodacom Park Stadium, Bloemfontein

[*Team:* Sheridan, R. Ford (SC), E. Murray (SC), D. O'Callaghan (IR), P. O'Connell (IR), Ferris (IR), J. Worsley, Andy Powell (WA), Harry Ellis, J. Hook (WA), Shane Williams (WA), L. Fitzgerald (IR), Earls (IR), Halfpenny (WA), L. Byrne (WA)]

[*Bench:* M. Blair (SC), G. D'Arcy (IR) (rep), Hines (SC) (rep), Adam Jones (2) (WA) (rep), O'Gara (IR), M. Rees (WA) (rep), S. Shaw]

[*Scorers:* **tries** by Ferris (IR) and Earls (IR), **penalty goals** by J. Hook (WA) (4), **conversions** by J. Hook (WA) (2)]
CAPTAIN: *Paul O'Connell* (IR) [*Brian O'Driscoll* (IR) *took over when Paul O'Connell was substituted in the 2nd half*]
[10th Jun Natal Sharks (*SA*) 3 **BRITISH & IRISH LIONS XV** 39]
ABSA Stadium, Durban
[*Team:* Gethin Jenkins (WA), Mears, Adam Jones (2) (WA), Alun-Wyn Jones (WA), P. O'Connell (IR), T. Croft, D. Wallace (IR), Heaslip (IR), Mike Phillips (2) (WA), O'Gara (IR), L. Fitzgerald (IR), J. Roberts (WA), Brian O'Driscoll (IR), Shane Williams (WA), L. Byrne (WA)]
[*Bench:* M. Blair (SC) (rep), Flutey (rep), J. Hook (WA) (rep), M. Rees (WA) (rep), S. Shaw (rep), Vickery (rep), J. Worsley]
[*Scorers:* **tries** by Mears, Mike Phillips (WA), L. Fitzgerald (IR), L. Byrne (WA) and Heaslip (IR), **penalty goals** by O'Gara (IR) (2), **conversions** by O'Gara (IR) (3) and J. Hook (WA)]
[**MANAGER:** *Gerald Davies* (WA)] [**HEAD COACH:** *Ian McGeechan* (SC)] [**ASSISTANT COACHES:** *Warren Gatland* (NZ), *Rob Howley* (WA), *Shaun Edwards*, *Graham Rowntree* & *Neil Jenkins* (WA)]
CAPTAIN: *Phil Vickery* [*Martyn Williams* (WA) *took over when Phil Vickery was substituted in the 2nd half*]
[13th Jun Western Province (*SA*) 23 **BRITISH & IRISH LIONS XV** 26]
Newlands, Cape Town
[*Team:* Sheridan, M. Rees (WA), Vickery, D. O'Callaghan (IR), Hines (SC), J. Worsley, Martyn Williams (WA), Andy Powell (WA), Harry Ellis, Stephen Jones (2) (WA), Monye, Flutey, Earls (IR), Bowe (IR), R. Kearney (IR)]
[*Bench:* T. Croft (rep), G. D'Arcy (IR), R. Ford (SC) (rep), J. Hook (WA) (rep), E. Murray (SC) (rep), S. Shaw (rep), Shane Williams (WA) (*scrum half*)]
[*Scorers:* **tries** by Bowe (IR), Monye and Martyn Williams (WA), **penalty goals** by Stephen Jones (WA) (2) and J. Hook (WA), **conversion** by Stephen Jones (WA)]
CAPTAIN: *Donncha O'Callaghan* (IR)
[16th Jun Southern Kings (*SA*) 8 **BRITISH & IRISH LIONS XV** 20]
Nelson Mandela Bay Stadium, Port Elizabeth
[*Team:* Sheridan, R. Ford (SC), E. Murray (SC), S. Shaw, D. O'Callaghan (IR), Hines (SC), J. Worsley, Andy Powell (WA), M. Blair (SC), J. Hook (WA), L. Fitzgerald (IR), G. D'Arcy (IR), Flutey, Monye, Earls (IR)]
[*Bench:* T. Croft, Harry Ellis, Adam Jones (2) (WA) (rep), O'Gara (IR) (rep), M. Rees (WA) (rep), D. Wallace (IR), Shane Williams (WA) (rep)]
[*Scorers:* **tries** by Monye and penalty try, **penalty goals** by O'Gara (IR) (2), **conversions** by O'Gara (IR) (2)]
CAPTAIN: *Ronan O'Gara* (IR) [*Donncha O'Callaghan* (IR) *took over when Ronan O'Gara was substituted in the 2nd half*]
[23rd Jun EMERGING SPRINGBOKS 13 **BRITISH & IRISH LIONS XV*** 13]
Newlands, Cape Town
[*Team:* T. Payne, R. Ford (SC), J. Hayes (IR), D. O'Callaghan (IR), Hines (SC), J. Worsley, Martyn Williams (WA), Andy Powell (WA), Harry Ellis, O'Gara (IR), L. Fitzgerald (IR), G. D'Arcy (IR), Flutey, Shane Williams (WA), Earls (IR)]
[*Bench:* M. Blair (SC), J. Hook (WA) (rep), Mears (rep), Monye (rep), S. Shaw (rep), Vickery (rep), D. Wallace (IR) (rep)]
[*Scorers:* **try** by Earls (IR), **penalty goals** by O'Gara (IR) and J. Hook (WA), **conversion** by O'Gara (IR)]

ENGLAND COUNTIES TOUR TO KOREA AND JAPAN 2009

[**MANAGER:** *Danny Hodgson*] [**ASSISTANT MANAGER:** *Mike Old*] [**COACH:** *Dave Baldwin*] [**ASSISTANT COACH:** *Tommy Borthwick*]

CAPTAIN: *Jason Smithson*

[8th June East Japan (*JAP*) 31 **ENGLAND COUNTIES XV** 67]
Edogawa Stadium, Tokyo

[*Team:* Rob O'Donnell, O. Hambly, P. Joyce, M. Howard, P. Ralph, S. Moss, Sprangle, Smithson, Huw Thomas (2), Eaton, James Aston, P. Leach, Dench, Royle, G. Collins]

[*Bench:* Joe Graham (rep), Jack Harrison (rep), Matt Owen, Rainbow (rep), T. Richardson (rep), C. Rowland (rep), M. Woodrow (rep)]

[*Scorers:* **tries** by P. Leach, James Aston, Sprangle, Dench, Rob O'Donnell, M. Woodrow, G. Collins and T. Richardson (2), **penalty goals** by Huw Thomas (2), **conversions** by Huw Thomas (6) and M. Woodrow (2)]

CAPTAIN: *Matt Long*

[12th Jun Yamaha Jubilo (*JAP*) 20 **ENGLAND COUNTIES XV** 36]
Yamaha Stadium, Shizuoka

[*Team:* Rob O'Donnell, Joe Graham, M. Long, M. Howard, Matt Owen, Gesinde, Rainbow, S. Moss, T. Richardson, M. Woodrow, S. Parsons, P. Leach, Jack Harrison, Royle, Bishay]

[*Bench:* Dench (rep), O. Hambly (rep), P. Ralph (rep), C. Rowland (rep), Smithson (rep), Sprangle (rep), Huw Thomas (2) (rep)]

[*Scorers:* **tries** by Royle, T. Richardson and S. Parsons, **penalty goals** by M. Woodrow (5), **conversions** by M. Woodrow (3)]

2010

PENGUINS TOUR TO PORTUGAL 2010

[**MANAGER:** *Ben Dormer* (NZ)] [**ASSISTANT MANAGER:** *Craig Brown* (NZ)] [**COACHES:** *Steve Hill*, *John McKittrick* (NZ) & *Riccardo Franconi* (IT)]

CAPTAIN: *Marcus Di Rollo* (SC)

[26th May Lisbon Selection XV (*POR*) 17 **PENGUINS** 34]

Campo A, Complexo Desportivo da Tapada

[*Team:* Ketchin (SC), Di Rollo (SC)]

[*Bench:*]

[*Scorers:*]

ENGLAND COUNTIES TOUR TO CANADA 2010

[**MANAGER:** *Danny Hodgson*] [**ASSISTANT MANAGER:** *Mike Old*] [**COACH:** *Dave Baldwin*] [**ASSISTANT COACH:** *Jan Bonney*]

CAPTAIN: *Matt Long*

[4th June The Rock (*CAN*) 6 **ENGLAND COUNTIES XV** 20]

Swilers RFC, Swilers Rugby Park, St. John's, Newfoundland

[*Team:* M. Long, Matt Hall, Voisey, L. Collins, H. Spencer, M. Wilson, W. Fraser, Mark Evans, Kessell, Winney, Tincknell, S. Hamilton, Staff, Mulchrone, G. Collins]

[*Bench:* Baines (rep), Cliff (rep), Dench (rep), N. Flynn (rep), T. Jarvis (rep), L. McGowan (rep), Roddam (rep), G. Woods (rep)]

[*Scorers:* **tries** by Kessell, Mulchrone and W. Fraser, **penalty goal** by Winney, **conversion** by Winney]

CAPTAIN: *Kyle Dench*

[8th June Ontario Blues (*CAN*) 26 **ENGLAND COUNTIES XV** 32]

Oakville Crusaders RC, Oakville Crusaders Park, Toronto

[*Team:* G. Woods, Roddam, N. Flynn, L. McGowan, L. Collins, M. Wilson, Baines, Eggleshaw, Kessell, P. Humphries, Ingall, Staff, Dench, Tincknell, T. Jarvis]

[*Bench:* Mark Evans (rep), Matt Hall (rep), S. Hamilton (rep), Mulchrone (rep), H. Spencer (rep), Voisey (rep), Winney (rep)]

[*Scorers:* **tries** by Kessell, G. Woods, T. Jarvis and Baines, **penalty goals** by T. Jarvis and P. Humphries, **conversions** by T. Jarvis and P. Humphries (2)]

ENGLAND TOUR TO AUSTRALIA AND NEW ZEALAND 2010

[**TEAM MANAGER:** *Martin Johnson*] [**COACH:** *Brian Smith* (IR)] [**ASSISTANT COACHES:** *John Wells*, *Mike Ford* & *Graham Rowntree*]

CAPTAIN: *Chris Robshaw*

8th June Australian Barbarians 28 **ENGLAND XV*** 28

ME Bank Stadium, Perth

[*Team:* Flatman, Mears, David Wilson (2), Attwood, Parling, Robshaw, H. Fourie, Ward-Smith, Wigglesworth, C. Hodgson, Monye, Barkley, M. Tait, Banahan, D. Armitage]

[*Bench:* Chuter (rep), Doran-Jones (rep), Geraghty (rep), P. Hodgson (rep), Lawes (rep), Waldouck (rep), J. Worsley (rep)]

[*Scorers:* **tries** by Mears, Ward-Smith and Banahan, **penalty goals** by Barkley (3), **conversions** by Barkley (2)]

CAPTAIN: *Joe Worsley*

15th June Australian Barbarians 9 **ENGLAND XV** 15

Bluetongue Central Coast Stadium, Gosford

[*Team:* J. Golding, Mears, Doran-Jones, Attwood, Ward-Smith, J. Worsley, S. Armitage, Haskell, Wigglesworth, C. Hodgson, Banahan, Barkley, Waldouck, Strettle, D. Armitage]

[*Bench:* Dowson (rep), Flatman (rep), Geraghty (rep), P. Hodgson (rep), Robshaw, M. Tait (rep), R. Webber (rep)]

[*Scorers:* **penalty goals** by C. Hodgson (2) and Barkley (3)]

CAPTAIN: *Chris Robshaw*

23rd June NEW ZEALAND MAORI 35 **ENGLAND XV*** 28

McLean Park, Napier

[*Team:* Flatman, Chuter, Doran-Jones, Attwood, Parling, Robshaw, S. Armitage, Dowson, Care, C. Hodgson, C. Ashton, Barritt, M. Tait, Strettle, D. Armitage]

[*Bench:* D. Cole (rep), Foden (rep), Geraghty (rep), Haskell (rep), Ward-Smith (rep), R. Webber (rep), B. Youngs (rep)]

[*Scorers:* **tries** by S. Armitage, Care and C. Ashton, **penalty goals** by C. Hodgson (3), **conversions** by C. Hodgson (2)]

PART 3
ENGLAND PLAYER MATCH NOTES 2000-2010

2000

STUDENT RUGBY WORLD CUP

Italy

CAPTAIN: *??*

First Round - Pool 'C'

5th Aug WALES STUDENTS 0 **ENGLAND STUDENTS** 22

Campo Tevere, CUS Roma, Stadio degli Eucalipti, Rome

[*This match kicked off at 6.30pm; England Students were originally scheduled to play a First Round match in Group C against Russia Students on 2nd August 2000; Ed Mallett was the brother of John Mallett; James Lofthouse captained England Schools 18 Group on their tour of Australia in August 1997; Simon Amor was capped for England Schools 18 Group in April 1997 and toured Australia with England Schools 18 Group in August 1997*]

(*Ed Mallett scored in the 9th minute; England Students were leading 16-0 at half-time*)

8th Aug JAPAN STUDENTS 14 **ENGLAND STUDENTS** 35

Campo delle Bandiere, CUS Roma, Stadio degli Eucalipti, Rome

[*This match kicked off at 8.30pm; This match was originally scheduled for 5th August 2000, whereas the other First Round game against Wales Students was initially supposed to take place on 8th August 2000!; James Cockle was capped for England Schools 18 Group in January 1995; Phil Christophers was capped for England Schools 18 Group in March 1998*]

(*James Cockle, Phil Christophers and Ayoola Erinle all had a brilliant game*)

CAPTAIN: *Andy Beattie*

Quarter-Final

13th Aug ITALY STUDENTS 11 **ENGLAND STUDENTS** 30

Stadio Comunale, Rieti

[*This match was originally scheduled to start at 6.00pm but the kick-off was delayed until 6.30pm; Craig Mitcherson selected but withdrew being replaced by Haydn Jeffreys; Ed Mallett selected but withdrew, being replaced by James Winterbottom; Richard Protherough was capped for England Schools 18 Group in January 1995; Tony Roques captained England Schools 18 Group for 3 matches during their Grand Slam season in March-April 1997 and then toured Australia with England Schools 18 Group in August 1997; Andy Beattie toured Australia with England Schools 18 Group in August 1997; Simon Brading was capped for England Schools 18 Group in March 1997; Simon Brocklehurst was capped for England Colts in March 1997*]

(*Phil Christophers scored in the 2nd minute!; England Students were leading 14-5 in the 10th minute; England Students were still leading 14-5 midway through the first half; England Students were leading 17-5 in the 29th minute; England Students were leading 17-8 shortly before half-time; England Students were leading 17-11 at half-time; England Students were leading 24-11 in the 43rd minute; England Students were leading 27-11 in the 49th minute; England Students were still leading 27-11 midway through the second half; England Students were leading 30-11 in the 65th minute*)

CAPTAIN: *Ben Cole*
Semi-Final
16th Aug FRANCE STUDENTS 34 **ENGLAND STUDENTS** 15
Stadio Comunale Tommaso Fattori, L'Aquila
[*This match was originally scheduled to start at 6.00pm but the kick-off was delayed until 6.30pm*]
(*Alex Audebert scored in the 4th minute!; England Students were losing 5-3 in the 7th minute; England Students were still losing 5-3 midway through the first half; England Students were leading 9-5 in the 31st minute; England Students were leading 12-5 shortly before half-time when collectively poor tackling allowed Benjamin Boyet to score, thus 7 points were preventable; England Students were drawing 12-12 at half-time; England Students were losing 19-15 in the 43rd minute; England Students were still losing 19-15 in the 55th minute; England Students were losing 25-15 midway through the second half; England Students were still losing 25-15 with 6 minutes of normal time remaining; England Students were losing 31-15 in the fourth minute of injury time; France Students were allowed to score 22 unanswered points to win the match*)
Third Place Play-Off
19th Aug SCOTLAND STUDENTS 25 **ENGLAND STUDENTS** 18
Stadio Comunale Tommaso Fattori, L'Aquila
[*This match was originally scheduled to start at 1.15pm but the kick-off was eventually delayed until 5.30pm; James Winterbottom was capped for England Schools 18 Group in March 1996; Adam Bidwell played for M.R. Steele-Bodger's XV against Cambridge University at Grange Road on 29th November 2000, scoring a try*]
(*Craig Mitcherson was sent off in the final quarter for stamping*)
(*This match was played in 93 degree heat; Phil Graham scored in the early stages; Adam Bidwell went off injured in the 33rd minute, being replaced by Jon Fabian; England Students were losing 9-5 at half-time; Andy Beattie scored early in the second half*)

CWMTAWE SEVENS

Pontardawe RFC, Parc Ynysderw, Ynysderw Road, Pontardawe, Swansea
CAPTAIN: *Dave Scully*
First Round - Pool 'C'
5th Aug Pontardawe (*WA*) 0 **SAMURAI** 59
[No match notes]
5th Aug Cwmgors (*WA*) 0 **SAMURAI** 48
[No match notes]
5th Aug Llandovery (*WA*) 0 **SAMURAI** 47
[No match notes]
Quarter-Final
5th Aug Saracens 0 **SAMURAI** 43
[No match notes]
Semi-Final
5th Aug Bridgend (*WA*) 0 **SAMURAI** 29
[No match notes]
Final
5th Aug Swansea (*WA*) 33 **SAMURAI** 24
[*Gavin Henson and Arwel Thomas played for Swansea in this match; Dave Scully*

***played in the White Hart Marauders team that won the Henley International Sevens on 13th May 2001 and captained M.R. Steele-Bodger's XV against Cambridge University at Grange Road on 26th November 2003*]**

(*The Samurai were leading 17-12 at half-time; The Samurai were losing 26-17 when Russ Earnshaw scored a brilliant try; The Samurai were losing 26-24 in the final minute when Rhodri Jones scored with the last move of the match to clinch the game for Swansea; Russ Earnshaw had a brilliant game*)

EUROBET MIDDLESEX CHARITY SEVENS

Twickenham

CAPTAIN: *??*

First Round

12th Aug London Wasps 12 **SAMURAI** 14

[*This match kicked off at 12.56pm; Mike Friday played for London Wasps in this match*]

Quarter-Final

12th Aug Penguins 26 **SAMURAI** 12

[*This match kicked off at 3.28pm; The Penguins went on to win the Middlesex Sevens but no English players were involved on this occasion*]

GERMAN RUGBY UNION CENTENARY MATCH

CAPTAIN: *Scott Hastings* (SC)

12th Aug GERMANY 19 **BARBARIANS** 47

Eilenriede-Stadion, Hannover

[*Barbarian FC founded 1890; Adrian Garvey, Dion O'Cuinneagain, Nathan Thomas, Ronan O'Gara and Matthew Robinson all in original squad but then withdrew; Jeff Probyn captained M.R. Steele-Bodger's XV against Cambridge University at Grange Road on 29th November 2000; Julian Horrobin was capped for England Schools 18 Group in January 1986; Matt Jones was capped for England Schools 18 Group in March 1994*]

(*The Barbarians were drawing 14-14 at half-time*)

REMEMBRANCE MATCH

CAPTAIN: *No captain appointed*

7th Nov COMBINED SERVICES (*SER*) C **BARBARIANS** C

Kingsholm, Gloucester

[*This match was cancelled on the day of the game due to heavy rain flooding the pitch and most of the surrounding countryside!; John Lawn played for M.R. Steele-Bodger's XV against Cambridge University at Grange Road on 29th November 2000*]

EMIRATES AIRLINE SOUTH AFRICA SEVENS

ABSA Stadium, Durban

CAPTAIN: *Mark Sowerby*

First Round - Pool 'C'

18th Nov AUSTRALIA 43 **ENGLAND** 0

[*This match kicked off at 3.20pm*]

(*This match was played on a wet pitch*)

18th Nov ARGENTINA 24 **ENGLAND** 7

[*This match kicked off at 6.20pm*]

(*This match was played on a wet pitch*)

18th Nov	ZIMBABWE	15	**ENGLAND**	5

[This match kicked off at 8.20pm]
(This match was played on a wet pitch)
[Bowl Quarter-Final:]

[19th Nov	GEORGIA	10	**ENGLAND**	7]

[This match kicked off at 9.20am]
(This match was played on an extremely wet pitch)

AUSTRALIAN TOUR TO FRANCE, SCOTLAND AND ENGLAND 2000

CAPTAIN: *Martin Johnson*

18th Nov	**ENGLAND**	22	AUSTRALIA	19

Twickenham

[This match kicked off at 2.30pm; Trevor Woodman and Alex Sanderson unavailable due to injury; Ben Cohen selected at left wing but withdrew due to bereavement, Austin Healey was moved from the bench to the team, with Dan Luger then moving from right wing to left wing to accommodate Healey while Will Greenwood was now selected for the bench; Julian White, Richard Kirke and Joe Worsley in original training squad of 26 but were not selected for team or bench; Jason Leonard were capped for England Colts in March 1987; Phil Greening captained England Schools 18 Group to a Grand Slam in March-April 1994; Phil Vickery was capped for England Colts in April 1994; Martin Johnson was capped for England Schools 18 Group in April 1987 and toured Australia with both England Schools 18 Group in July-August 1988 and New Zealand Colts in June 1990; Richard Hill (2) was capped for both England Schools 18 Group in March 1991 and England Colts in March 1992; Neil Back was capped for both England Schools 18 Group in January 1986 and England Colts in March 1988 and also played for M.R. Steele-Bodger's XV against Cambridge University at Grange Road on 29th November 1989; Lawrence Dallaglio was capped for England Colts in March 1991; Kyran Bracken captained England Schools 18 Group for 4 matches in March-April 1990; Jonny Wilkinson played as a centre for England Schools 18 Group in their 38-20 win over Australian Schools 18 Group at North Sydney Oval on 27th August 1997, scoring 5 conversions; Mike Tindall, David Flatman, Steve Borthwick and Iain Balshaw all toured Australia with England Schools 18 Group in August 1997; Matt Perry was capped as a fly half for England Colts in March 1996; Mark Regan was capped for England Schools 18 Group in March 1990; Martin Corry was capped as a lock for England Schools 18 Group in April 1992; Matt Dawson was capped as a scrum half for England Schools 18 Group in January 1991; Will Greenwood sat on the bench as a fly half for England Schools 18 Group in January 1991 and March-April 1991; Will Greenwood was the son of Dick Greenwood]

(England were leading 3-0 in the 8th minute; England were leading 6-0 in the 15th minute; England were leading 6-3 midway through the first half; England were leading 9-6 in the 30th minute; England were drawing 9-9 just before half-time; England were leading 12-9 at half-time; England were still leading 12-9 in the 44th minute when Matt Burke scored after Austin Healey missed a tackle on Joe Roff, thus 7 points were preventable; England were losing 19-15 in the 56th minute; England were still losing 19-15 midway through the second half; England were losing 19-15 in the 68th minute when Jonny Wilkinson missed an eminently kickable 25 metre drop goal attempt; Phil Greening went off injured in the fifth minute of injury time, being replaced by Mark Regan; England were still losing 19-15 in the eighth minute of injury time when Iain

Balshaw put in a superb chip ahead and Dan Luger followed up into the in-goal area, where the video referee adjudged that he had correctly grounded the ball to score a try which Jonny Wilkinson then brilliantly converted from the left touchline with the last kick of the match to clinch the game; Iain Balshaw had a brilliant game; Austin Healey had a poor game)

EMIRATES AIRLINE DUBAI RUGBY SEVENS

Dubai Exiles Stadium, Dubai

CAPTAIN: *Mark Sowerby*

First Round - League W

23rd Nov	ARABIAN GULF	0	**ENGLAND**	27

[*This match kicked off at 11.00am; Arabian Gulf also billed as the United Arab Emirates*]

23rd Nov	GEORGIA	12	**ENGLAND**	33

[*This match kicked off at 4.20pm*]

23rd Nov	NEW ZEALAND	40	**ENGLAND**	7

[*This match kicked off at 8.00pm*]

(England were losing 12-7 at half-time; New Zealand were allowed to score 28 unanswered points in the second half to clinch the match)

Quarter-Final

24th Nov	FIJI	43	**ENGLAND**	0

[*This match kicked off at 10.40am*]

[Plate Semi-Final:]

[24th Nov	SOUTH AFRICA	45	**ENGLAND**	0]

[*This match kicked off at 12.40pm; Paul Treu played for South Africa in this match*]

ARGENTINE TOUR TO ENGLAND 2000

CAPTAIN: *Martin Johnson*

25th Nov	**ENGLAND**	19	ARGENTINA	0

Twickenham

[*This match kicked off at 2.30pm; Trevor Woodman, Phil Greening, Richard Kirke and Alex Sanderson all unavailable due to injury; Jason Leonard set a new England record of 86 caps; Ben Cohen was capped for England Colts in March 1997; An Argentine XV beat the Combined Services 44-7 at Portsmouth on 21st November 2000, with Nick Bartlett, Lee Soper, Andy Dawling, Howard Graham and Spencer Brown all playing for the Combined Services*]

(The first half of this match was played in wet conditions; Jonny Wilkinson scored a penalty goal in the 2nd minute!; England were leading 3-0 midway through the first half; England were leading 6-0 in the 28th minute when Jonny Wilkinson missed a speculative 49 metre penalty goal attempt; England were leading 9-0 in the 32nd minute; England were still leading 9-0 shortly before half-time when Jonny Wilkinson missed an eminently kickable drop goal attempt; England were leading 9-0 at half-time; England were leading 12-0 in the 44th minute; England were still leading 12-0 in the 57th minute when Iain Balshaw wasted a great try-scoring opportunity by attempting to make the line himself instead of passing to the unmarked Ben Cohen; England were leading 12-0 midway through the second half; England were still leading 12-0 in the 63rd minute when Mike Catt saved a certain try by tap-tackling Ignacio Corletto; England were leading 12-0 in the 69th minute when Ben Cohen scored under the posts after Jonny Wilkinson put in a brilliant grubber kick; England were leading

19-0 with 4 minutes remaining when Dan Luger had a great try-scoring chance but was tackled into touch at the corner flag by Ignacio Corletto; Jonny Wilkinson became the youngest player to score 300 points in cap international matches; Martin Johnson had a brilliant game)

SOUTH AFRICAN TOUR TO IRELAND, WALES AND ENGLAND 2000

CAPTAIN: *Mike Shelley*

28th Nov	**ENGLISH NATIONAL DIVISIONS XV**	35	SOUTH AFRICA XV	30

Worcester RFC, Sixways Stadium, Pershore Lane, Hindip, Worcester

[This match kicked off at 7.30pm; Blair Foote and Ken O'Connell in match squad of 22 announced on 21st November 2000 but then withdrew, being replaced by Chris Hall and Cameron Mather respectively; Rob Baxter, Nathan Carter, Richard Elliott, Earl Va'a, Trevor Walsh and Steve Swindells all in original squad of 28 but were not selected for team or bench; Julian Hyde captained England Colts in March 1987; Tom Palmer (2) played for Scotland in the U19 World Championship in France in April 1998 and played for Scotland U21 in February 1999, but then switched his allegiance to England in October 2000; Scott Benton was capped by England Colts in March 1994; Richard Le Bas played for New Zealand Colts before 1993, but then qualified for England through residency; Steve Pope came on as a replacement for Major R.V. Stanley's XV against Oxford University at Iffley Road on 18th November 1998; After this match the RFU decreed that only English-qualified players could play for the English National Divisions XV; On 29th November 2000 it was announced that an English National Divisions XV match against a French Second Division XV was provisionally scheduled for May 2001 in Nice, but this idea was eventually abandoned]

(Tom Palmer (2) dominated the lineout in this match; The English National Divisions XV was leading 3-0 in the 10th minute; The English National Divisions XV was losing 5-3 midway through the first half; The English National Divisions XV was leading 6-5 in the 22nd minute; The English National Divisions XV was leading 9-5 in the 31st minute when Dan Scarbrough scored after Richard Le Bas made a brilliant break; The English National Divisions XV was leading 19-5 shortly before half-time; The English National Divisions XV was leading 19-8 at half-time; The English National Divisions XV was leading 19-13 in the 55th minute; The English National Divisions XV was still leading 19-13 midway through the second half when Liam Mooney scored from a rolling maul; The English National Divisions XV was leading 32-13 in the 67th minute; The English National Divisions XV was leading 32-20 with 7 minutes of normal time remaining; Ben Harvey came on as a replacement for Richard Le Bas with 4 minutes of normal time remaining; The South African XV was allowed to score 17 unanswered points; The English National Divisions XV was leading 32-30 in the first minute of injury time when Ben Harvey scored a penalty goal to clinch the match; Richard Le Bas scored 22 points in this match; Ben Hinshelwood had a brilliant game)

THE INVESTEC INTERNATIONAL

CAPTAIN: *Martin Johnson*

2nd Dec	**ENGLAND**	25	SOUTH AFRICA	17

Twickenham

[This match kicked off at 2.30pm; Trevor Woodman and Alex Sanderson unavailable due to injury; Mike Catt selected at inside centre but withdrew due to injury, Will

Greenwood was moved from the bench to the team and Austin Healey was then selected for the bench]
(Jonny Wilkinson made a brilliant 34 metre break in the 2nd minute, but Lawrence Dallaglio then wasted this great try-scoring opportunity by electing to take the ball into contact instead of using an overlap outside him!; England were leading 3-0 in the 8th minute; Martin Corry came on as a temporary blood replacement for Neil Back in the 18th minute, with Lawrence Dallaglio then switching from number 8 to blindside flanker to accommodate Corry; England were leading 6-3 immediately afterwards when Richard Hill (2) saved a certain try by managing to get beneath the ball as Percy Montgomery attempted to ground it; England were still leading 6-3 midway through the first half; Richard Hill (2) had to go off in the 22nd minute after receiving a head injury requiring 9 stitches when he was kneed by Robbie Kempson, being temporarily replaced by Mark Regan with Phil Greening then switching from hooker to blindside flanker to accommodate Mark Regan and Lawrence Dallaglio moving from blindside to openside flanker to accommodate Greening; England were leading 9-6 in the 28th minute; Neil Back came back on as a replacement for Mark Regan in the 34th minute; Will Greenwood scored a brilliant 24 metre solo try immediately afterwards which Jonny Wilkinson then converted to give England a 16-6 lead; Iain Balshaw came on as a replacement for Dan Luger in the second minute of first half injury time; England were leading 19-9 at half-time; Richard Hill (2) came back on as a replacement for Martin Corry at the start of the second half; Mark Regan also came back on as a temporary blood replacement for Phil Greening at the start of the second half; England were still leading 19-9 in the 44th minute when Braam van Straaten scored after a poor tackle by Lawrence Dallaglio, thus 5 points were preventable; England were leading 19-14 midway through the second half; Phil Greening came back on as a replacement for Mark Regan in the 61st minute; England were leading 22-14 in the 67th minute when Phil Greening put in a superb 40 metre clearance kick to touch!; England were leading 22-17 with 3 minutes of normal time remaining when Jonny Wilkinson scored a 41 metre penalty goal to clinch the match; Austin Healey came on as a replacement for Will Greenwood in the first minute of injury time; England were leading 25-17 in the fifth minute of injury time when Jonny Wilkinson missed a kickable 28 metre drop goal attempt; Jonny Wilkinson scored 20 points in this match; Danny Grewcock had a brilliant game)

THE SCOTTISH AMICABLE CHALLENGE

CAPTAIN: *Lawrence Dallaglio*

10th Dec **BARBARIANS*** 31 SOUTH AFRICA XV 41

Millennium Stadium, Cardiff

[This match kicked off at 3.00pm; Lewis Moody and Jonah Lomu in original squad but withdrew due to injury; Greg Somerville in revised squad of 22 but withdrew, being replaced by Peter Clohessy; Jonah Lomu travelled to Cardiff to provide pitchside support for the Barbarians; The Millennium Stadium had its retractable roof closed for this match; Brian O'Driscoll was the nephew of Barry and John O'Driscoll]
(This match took place on a very poor playing surface; Chester Williams followed up and scored in the 2nd minute after Carlos Spencer threw a poor pass to Daniel Herbert and Brian O'Driscoll was then deceived by the bounce of the ball!; The Barbarians were losing 7-3 in the 12th minute when Brian O'Driscoll powered through to score a try which Matt Burke then brilliantly converted from the left touchline; The Barbarians were leading 10-7 in the 16th minute when Agustin Pichot scored after Ron Cribb threw a brilliant reverse pass; The Barbarians were leading 17-7 midway through the

***first half; The Barbarians were leading 24-12 in the 25th minute; The Barbarians were still leading 24-12 in the 39th minute when Christian Cullen scored after Chris Latham broke through and then put up a superb cross-kick; The Barbarians were leading 31-12 just before half-time; The Barbarians were leading 31-17 at half-time; The Barbarians were still leading 31-17 in the 50th minute when Carlos Spencer threw another poor pass to Christian Cullen who was then caught in possession in front of his own 22, which led directly to a try by Breyton Paulse; The Barbarians were leading 31-24 in the 54th minute when Ollie le Roux scored after a poor tackle by Christian Cullen, thus 3 tries and 21 points were preventable; Neil Jenkins came on as a replacement for Carlos Spencer in the 57th minute; The Barbarians were losing 38-31 midway through the second half; Iain Balshaw came on as a replacement for Chris Latham in the 67th minute; The Barbarians were still losing 38-31 in the third minute of injury time; The South African XV was allowed to score 29 unanswered points to win the match; Brian O'Driscoll injured playing in the match*)**

ENGLAND U21 MATCH

CAPTAIN: *Mark Tucker*

20th Dec **ENGLAND U21 A XV** 27 WALES U21 A XV 26

Bridgwater & Albion RFC, College Way, Bath Road, Bridgwater

[*This match kicked off at 7.15pm; Alex Clarke selected but withdrew, Adam Webb was moved from the bench to the team and Ollie Smith (1) was then selected for the bench; Louis Deacon selected but withdrew, Karl Rudzki was moved from the bench to the team; Richard Haughton selected but withdrew, being replaced by James Tapster; Darren Carr selected but withdrew, being replaced by Anthony Elliott; A Combined Midlands & North U21 XV and a Combined London & South West U21 XV lost 34-20 and 53-18 respectively to two French U21 Selection teams at Salon de Provence on 18th November 2000, with Nigel Melville being the Manager of both English U21 teams; Andy Titterrell, Ian Clarke, Alex Page, Anthony Elliott and Ross Winney played for England in the U19 World Championship in France in April 2000; Rob Devonshire and Matt Leek were capped for England Schools 18 Group in January 1999; Declan Danaher played for Ireland in the U19 World Championship in Wales in March-April 1999 but then switched his allegiance to England in October 2000; Phil Murphy (1) was the brother of Chris Murphy; Mark Tucker and Sean Marsden were capped for England Schools 18 Group in March 1998*]

(*Sam Cox scored in the 3rd minute!; The England U21 A XV was leading 8-0 when Chris Thomas scored after Damien Adams intercepted the ball near the halfway line, thus 5 points were preventable; The England U21 A XV was leading 8-5 when Anthony Elliott scored after Sam Cox made a brilliant run; The England U21 A XV was leading 15-12 at half-time; The England U21 A XV was still leading 15-12 when Anthony Elliott scored a superb solo try; The England U21 A XV was leading 27-12 at one point in the second half; The England U21 A XV was leading 27-19 in injury time; Charlie Hodgson and Sam Cox both had a brilliant game*)

2001
RUGBY WORLD CUP SEVENS

Estadio José Maria Minella, Mar del Plata

CAPTAIN: *Joe Worsley*

First Round - Pool 'C'

26th Jan CHILE 7 **ENGLAND** 21

[*This match kicked off at 3.20pm*]

(*This match was played in extremely hot conditions; The England players had insufficient time to shake off their jet lag; England were drawing 0-0 when Paul Sampson gathered a loose ball and ran 20 metres to score; England were leading 7-0 at half-time; England were still leading 7-0 early in the second half when Rob Thirlby scored a brilliant 50 metre solo try; England were leading 14-7 when Josh Lewsey scored to clinch the match*)

CAPTAIN: *Mike Friday*

26th Jan ZIMBABWE 7 **ENGLAND** 28

[*This match kicked off at 7.20pm*]

(*The England players had insufficient time to shake off their jet lag; England monopolised possession in this match; England were drawing 0-0 when collectively poor tackling allowed Karl Mudzamba to score, thus 7 points were preventable; England were losing 7-0 straight after the restart when Paul Sampson scored after Josh Lewsey made a brilliant break!; England were drawing 7-7 at half-time; England were leading 14-7 when Ben Johnston fly-hacked a loose ball on before regathering it to score a brilliant try under the posts; England scored three tries in 3 minutes to win the match*)

26th Jan SPAIN 14 **ENGLAND*** 12

[*This match kicked off at 11.00pm*]

(*The England players had insufficient time to shake off their jet lag; England were leading 5-0 in the early stages; England were losing 7-5 just before half-time when Paul Sackey scored a brilliant 50 metre solo try; England were leading 12-7 at half-time; England wasted a number of great try-scoring opportunities in the second half; England were still leading 12-7 with 2 minutes remaining when a poor defensive alignment allowed Oriol Ripol to score a try which Ferrán Velazco then converted to win the match for Spain*)

CAPTAIN: *Joe Worsley*

27th Jan JAPAN 7 **ENGLAND** 24

[*This match kicked off at 6.20pm*]

(*This match was played in wet conditions*)

CAPTAIN: *Mike Friday*

27th Jan NEW ZEALAND 17 **ENGLAND** 7

[*This match kicked off at 11.00pm; England qualified for the Quarter-Finals because they had a better points difference than Spain*]

(*This match was played in wet conditions; England were drawing 0-0 in the early stages when Rob Thirlby scored a brilliant 49 metre try; England were leading 7-0 at half-time; New Zealand were allowed to score 17 unanswered points to win the match*)

Quarter-Final

28th Jan AUSTRALIA 33 **ENGLAND** 5

[*This match kicked off at 7.00pm*]

(*A poor tackle by Josh Lewsey allowed Brendan Williams to score after just 55*

***seconds had been played!; England were losing 7-5 midway through the first half; England were still losing 7-5 shortly before half-time when they created a 2 man overlap, but Josh Lewsey's intended scoring pass was then intercepted by Brendan Williams who ran 45 metres to score another try; England were losing 14-5 just before half-time; England were losing 21-5 at half-time; England were still losing 21-5 when Brendan Williams scored his third try after another poor tackle by Josh Lewsey, thus 3 tries and 21 points were preventable; Australia were allowed to score 26 unanswered points to clinch the match*)**

6 NATIONS CHAMPIONSHIP

CAPTAIN: *Martin Johnson*

3rd Feb WALES 15 **ENGLAND** 44

Millennium Stadium, Cardiff

[*This match kicked off at 4.00pm; Phil Greening in original training squad of 30 but withdrew on 12th January 2001 due to injury; David Flatman, Simon Shaw, Steve Borthwick, Joe Worsley, Alex Sanderson, Kyran Bracken, Jamie Noon and Leon Lloyd all in original training squad of 30 but were not selected for team or bench; Phil Greening, Simon Shaw and Kyran Bracken later went on to travel with the England squad to Cardiff to provide potential injury cover; Trevor Woodman was capped for England Colts in March 1995*]

(*Dan Luger went off injured in the 7th minute, being replaced by Austin Healey; England were leading 7-0 in the 12th minute; Will Greenwood scored his second try in 3 minutes to give England a 12-0 lead in the 15th minute; England were leading 15-3 midway through the first half; England were still leading 15-3 in the 22nd minute when Richard Hill (2) bought a dummy by Rob Howley who then ran 40 metres to score; England were leading 15-8 in the 31st minute when Matt Dawson took a quick tap penalty and scored; England were leading 22-8 in the 37th minute when Matt Dawson scored another try under the posts after he wrong-footed Stephen Jones (2) with a brilliant sidestep; England were leading 29-8 at half-time; Will Greenwood scored after just 52 seconds of the second half had been played to become the first English player to score a hat-trick of tries in Cardiff!; England were leading 34-8 in the 46th minute when Iain Balshaw put in a superb chip ahead, but he then wasted this great try-scoring opportunity by knocking the ball on over the Welsh line as he attempted to regather it!; England were leading 37-8 in the 58th minute; England were leading 44-8 midway through the second half; England scored 29 unanswered points to clinch the match; England were still leading 44-8 in the 63rd minute when a poor defensive alignment allowed Scott Quinnell to score, thus 2 tries and 12 points were preventable; Jonny Wilkinson had a brilliant game; This was both the highest points total and the widest margin of victory ever achieved by an England team against Wales in Cardiff*)

17th Feb **ENGLAND** 80 ITALY 23

Twickenham

[*This match kicked off at 2.30pm; Phil Greening, Dan Luger and David Rees (2) unavailable due to injury; Jason Leonard broke Rory Underwood's record of 91 caps for England and the British Lions; Jason Robinson was capped 12 times for Great Britain at Rugby League between 1993-99, played for England in the Rugby League World Cup Final at Wembley on 28th October 1995, played Rugby Union for Bath between September 1996 and January 1997 and then returned to Rugby Union in October 2000*]

(*This match took place on a poor playing surface; England were awarded a penalty in*

an eminently kickable position in the 2nd minute, but Martin Johnson unaccountably ordered a kick to the corner in a vain attempt to score a try from the ensuing lineout!; England were drawing 0-0 in the 6th minute when collectively poor tackling allowed Denis Dallan to score; England were drawing 10-10 in the 17th minute; England were leading 17-10 midway through the first half; England were still leading 17-10 in the 24th minute when Carlo Checchinato scored after Iain Balshaw dropped Cristian Stoica's garryowen, thus 2 tries and 14 points were preventable; England were losing 20-17 in the 28th minute; England were drawing 20-20 in the 34th minute; England were leading 30-23 just before half-time; England were leading 33-23 at half-time; The England forwards monopolised possession in the second half; England were leading 40-23 in the 43rd minute; Jason Robinson came on as a replacement for Ben Cohen in the 51st minute; England were still leading 40-23 in the 56th minute; England were leading 47-23 midway through the second half; England were leading 54-23 in the 63rd minute; England were leading 61-23 in the 70th minute; England were still leading 61-23 with 4 minutes of normal time remaining when Iain Balshaw scored a brilliant 78 metre solo try; England scored 50 unanswered points to clinch the match; Joe Worsley had a brilliant game; Jonny Wilkinson set a new 6 Nations Championship record by scoring 35 points in the match, while England set two new 6 Nations Championship records by accumulating 80 points in total and winning the match by a margin of 57 points)

3rd March **ENGLAND** 43 SCOTLAND 3

Twickenham

[*This match kicked off at 2.30pm; Mike Tindall and Dan Luger unavailable due to injury; Steve Borthwick was added to the squad on 27th February 2001 to provide injury cover for Neil Back*]

(*This match was played in extremely cold conditions; England were drawing 0-0 in the 8th minute when Lawrence Dallaglio scored after Iain Balshaw made a brilliant break; England were leading 8-0 in the 12th minute; England were leading 8-3 midway through the first half; England were still leading 8-3 in the 37th minute when some superb handling allowed Richard Hill (2) to score; England were leading 15-3 just before half-time; England were leading 22-3 at half-time; Dorian West went off injured at half-time, being replaced by Mark Regan; England played with the wind in the second half; England were still leading 22-3 in the 46th minute when Will Greenwood threw a superb reverse pass that enabled Iain Balshaw to score a try which Jonny Wilkinson then brilliantly converted from the right touchline; England were leading 29-3 midway through the second half; England were still leading 29-3 in the 63rd minute when Iain Balshaw scored after Mike Catt put up a brilliant cross-kick; Mike Catt went off injured immediately afterwards, being replaced by Jason Robinson with Austin Healey then switching from wing to fly half to accommodate Jason Robinson and Jonny Wilkinson moving from fly half to centre to accommodate Healey; England were leading 36-3 with 2 minutes of normal time remaining when Will Greenwood scored after Jason Robinson made a superb run; England scored 35 unanswered points to clinch the match; Mike Catt and Iain Balshaw both had a brilliant game; England amassed their highest ever points total against Scotland and also achieved their greatest ever margin of victory over Scotland*)

CAPTAIN: *No captain appointed*

24th Mar IRELAND P **ENGLAND** P

Lansdowne Road

**[*This match was postponed by the IRFU on 7th March 2001 due to an outbreak of foot*

***and mouth disease in England; This venue in Dublin was officially called Lansdowne Road Stadium, but it was usually just referred to as Lansdowne Road*]**

CAPTAIN: *Martin Johnson*

7th April **ENGLAND** 48 FRANCE 19

Twickenham

[*This match kicked off at 2.30pm; Phil Vickery, Danny Grewcock and Dan Luger unavailable due to injury; Trevor Woodman selected for bench but withdrew due to injury, being replaced by David Flatman*]

(*England were leading 7-0 in the 6th minute; England were still leading 7-0 in the 7th minute when Iain Balshaw saved a certain try by tackling Philippe Bernat-Salles; England were leading 10-0 in the 13th minute; Dorian West came on as a temporary blood replacement for Phil Greening in the 19th minute; England were drawing 10-10 midway through the first half; England were still drawing 10-10 in the 25th minute when Jonny Wilkinson missed an eminently kickable 22 metre penalty goal attempt; Martin Corry came on as a temporary blood replacement for Steve Borthwick in the 29th minute; England were losing 13-10 in the 32nd minute when Iain Balshaw saved another certain try by tackling Christophe Dominici into touch at the corner flag; France were allowed to score 16 unanswered points; David Flatman came on as a temporary blood replacement for Jason Leonard in the first minute of first half injury time; England were losing 16-10 in the second minute of first half injury time when Jonny Wilkinson scored a 39 metre penalty goal which enabled him to beat Rob Andrew's existing England cap international scoring record of 396 points; England were losing 16-13 at half-time; The England forwards dominated the lineout in the second half; England were still losing 16-13 in the 44th minute when Richard Hill (2) scored a brilliant 39 metre solo try; England were leading 20-16 in the 57th minute; England were leading 20-19 midway through the second half when Iain Balshaw scored after Jonny Wilkinson threw a brilliant long pass; England were leading 27-19 in the 62nd minute when Matt Dawson saved a third certain try by tackling Xavier Garbajosa into touch at the corner flag; England were still leading 27-19 in the 69th minute when Phil Greening scored after Jason Robinson made a superb run; England were leading 34-19 with 4 minutes of normal time remaining when Mike Catt scored after Austin Healey did a brilliant overhead kick; England scored 28 unanswered points to clinch the match; Matt Dawson and Iain Balshaw both had a brilliant game; England recorded their highest ever points total against France*)

CAPTAIN: *No captain appointed*

5th May IRELAND P **ENGLAND** P

Lansdowne Road

[*The Six Nations Committee provisionally arranged this rescheduled match on 13th March 2001, subject to the approval of the Irish Department of Agriculture; This match was then postponed by the Six Nations Committee on 1st April 2001 due to the continuing occurrence of foot and mouth disease in England*]

CAPTAIN: *Matt Dawson* [*Neil Back*]

20th Oct IRELAND 20 **ENGLAND*** 14

Lansdowne Road

[*This match kicked off at 3.00pm; The Six Nations Committee arranged this rescheduled match on 24th April 2001 and in doing so unaccountably changed the running order of Ireland's 3 remaining games from Wales, England and Scotland to Scotland, Wales and England, which meant that Ireland effectively had the advantage of playing 2 warm-up matches before they faced England, who were by contrast*

playing their first match of the 2001-02 season!; Lawrence Dallaglio, Ben Johnston and Leon Lloyd unavailable due to injury; Phil Vickery, Martin Johnson and Josh Lewsey in original training squad of 30 but withdrew due to injury; Ben Kay, Joe Worsley, Alex Sanderson, Dave Walder, Ben Cohen and Mike Tindall all in original training squad of 30 but were not selected for team or bench; Simon Shaw was capped for England Schools 18 Group in March 1991; Graham Rowntree was capped for England Schools 18 Group in March 1989; Lewis Moody was capped for England Schools 18 Group in March 1996]

(Martin Corry played with an injury; Will Greenwood was short of match fitness; The England backs kicked away too much possession in the first half; England were leading 3-0 in the 10th minute; England were drawing 3-3 in the 17th minute when a poor defensive alignment allowed Keith Wood to score directly from an Irish lineout, thus 5 points were preventable; England were losing 8-3 midway through the first half; England were losing 11-3 in the 30th minute; Matt Dawson went off injured in the 37th minute, being replaced by Kyran Bracken; England were still losing 11-3 in the second minute of first half injury time; England were losing 11-6 at half-time; Phil Greening went off injured at half-time, being replaced by Dorian West; England were losing 14-6 in the 49th minute; England were still losing 14-6 in the 54th minute when Jonny Wilkinson scored a brilliant 43 metre penalty goal from a difficult angle; England were losing 14-9 in the 56th minute when Dan Luger broke through, but he then unaccountably failed to go for the line at full speed which allowed Peter Stringer to get back and tap-tackle him, costing England a certain 7 points and the Grand Slam; England were losing 17-9 midway through the second half; Austin Healey came on as a replacement for Dan Luger in the 61st minute; England were still losing 17-9 with 6 minutes of normal time remaining; England were losing 20-9 with 4 minutes of normal time remaining when Austin Healey scored after Kyran Bracken took a quick tap penalty; England were losing 20-14 in the third minute of injury time when Austin Healey inexplicably knocked the ball on when there was an overlap outside him; Iain Balshaw had a poor game; England set a new Six Nations record by scoring 229 points in their 5 matches)

ENGLAND STUDENTS MATCHES

CAPTAIN: *Ed Mallett*

2nd Feb WALES STUDENTS 29 **ENGLAND STUDENTS** 29

Brewery Field, Bridgend

[This match kicked off at 7.00pm; Adam Billig was capped for England Schools 18 Group in March 1999; Dan Taberner was capped for England Colts in March 1998]

(England Students were drawing 0-0 in the early stages when Simon Brading scored a brilliant try; England Students were leading 7-0 when Ben Lewitt scored from a rolling maul; Adam Billig scored after Simon Brading made a brilliant break; England Students were leading 17-13 at half-time; England Students were losing 23-17 at one point in the second half; England Students were losing 29-26 with 5 minutes remaining when Simon Amor scored a penalty goal to draw the match)

CAPTAIN: *Scott Bemand*

2nd Mar **ENGLAND STUDENTS** 33 SCOTLAND STUDENTS 10

Sedgley Park RFC, Park Lane, Whitefield, Manchester

[This match kicked off at 7.30pm]

(This match was played in extremely cold conditions; The England Students forwards monopolised possession in this match; England Students were losing 10-7 at half-

time; England Students scored 26 unanswered points in the second half to win the match)

23rd Mar IRELAND STUDENTS C **ENGLAND STUDENTS** C

Trinity College, Dublin

[This match was postponed by the IRFU on 7th March 2001 due to an outbreak of foot and mouth disease in England and was never rescheduled]

6th April **ENGLAND STUDENTS** 25 FRANCE STUDENTS 14

Worcester RFC, Sixways Stadium, Pershore Lane, Hindip, Worcester

[This match kicked off at 7.30pm; Kieran Roche was capped for England Colts in March 1998; Adam Balding toured Australia with England Schools 18 Group in August 1997]

(Benjamin Lhande scored in the 5th minute!; England Students were leading 7-5 in the 16th minute; England Students were losing 8-7 midway through the first half; England Students were leading 10-8 in the 30th minute; England Students were losing 11-10 shortly before half-time; England Students were losing 14-10 at half-time; James Cockle came on as a replacement for Ben Lewitt in the 57th minute; England Students were still losing 14-10 midway through the second half; England Students were leading 20-14 in the 65th minute; France Students were still losing 20-14 in the sixth minute of injury time when Adam Balding scored after England Students kept the ball for 15 phases of play; England Students scored 15 unanswered points in the second half to win the match)

U21 6 NATIONS CHAMPIONSHIP

CAPTAIN: *Mark Tucker*

2nd Feb WALES U21 27 **ENGLAND U21** 12

Sardis Road, Pwllgwaun, Pontypridd

[This match kicked off at 2.30pm; Johnny Roddam selected for bench but withdrew, being replaced by Matt Williams; Jon Dawson and James Grindal toured Australia with England Schools 18 Group in August 1997; Jon Dunbar and Matt Williams (1) were capped for England Schools 18 Group in March 1998; Tom Voyce played for England in the U19 World Championship in France in April 2000; Gavin Henson played for Wales U21 in this match]

(The England U21 forwards could not win any possession; England U21 were losing 6-0 in the 10th minute; England U21 were losing 9-3 when Mark Tucker saved a certain try by tackling Shaun James; England U21 were still losing 9-3 when Phil Christophers had a great try-scoring chance but was tackled into touch at the corner flag by Hal Luscombe; England U21 were losing 9-3 at half-time; England U21 were losing 9-6 in the 42nd minute; England U21 were losing 19-6 in the 52nd minute; England U21 were losing 22-12 in injury time when Michael Owen scored as the direct consequence of a defensive mistake on the touchline, thus 5 points were preventable; Jon Dawson injured playing in the match)

17th Feb **ENGLAND U21** 47 ITALY U21 18

Stoop Memorial Ground, Langhorn Drive, Twickenham

[This match kicked off at 11.00am; Jon Dawson unavailable due to injury; Ian Clarke selected but withdrew, Alex Alesbrook was moved from the bench to the team; Karl Rudzki selected for bench but withdrew due to injury, being replaced by Alex Hadley; Louis Deacon, Alex Alesbrook and Alex Clarke were all capped for England Schools 18 Group in January 1999; Michael Stephenson was capped for England Schools 18 Group in March 1998]

(Charlie Hodgson scored a penalty goal in the 2nd minute!; England U21 were leading 13-0 in the 13th minute; England U21 were leading 20-3 in the 24th minute; England U21 were leading 23-6 at half-time; England U21 were still leading 23-6 at the start of the second half when Michael Stephenson scored a brilliant try; England U21 were leading 37-13 midway through the second half; England U21 were leading 47-13 in the closing stages; Charlie Hodgson played brilliantly and scored 22 points in this match)

2nd Mar **ENGLAND U21** 62 SCOTLAND U21 29

Webb Ellis Road, Rugby

[This match kicked off at 7.30pm; Rob Devonshire selected but withdrew, Ian Clarke was moved from the bench to the team; Andy Goode was capped for England Schools 18 Group in March 1998]

(This match was played in extremely cold conditions; Andy Goode scored a brilliant try in the 5th minute!; England U21 were leading 23-3 midway through the first half; England U21 were still leading 23-3 when Mark Tucker scored after Andy Goode made a superb break; England U21 were leading 43-3 in the fifth minute of first half injury time when collectively poor tackling allowed Neil Stenhouse to score, thus 7 points were preventable; England U21 were leading 43-10 at half-time; England U21 were leading 43-17 in the 41st minute; Andy Goode went off injured in the 51st minute, being replaced by Charlie Hodgson; England U21 were leading 48-17 in the 59th minute when Tom Voyce made a brilliant break which enabled Sean Marsden to complete a hat-trick of tries; Andy Goode had a brilliant game)

23rd Mar IRELAND U21 C **ENGLAND U21** C

Donnybrook, Dublin

[This match was scheduled to kick off at 7.30pm; This match was postponed by the IRFU on 7th March 2001 due to an outbreak of foot and mouth disease in England and was never rescheduled]

6th April **ENGLAND U21** 10 FRANCE U21 8

Newbury RFC, Monks Lane, Newbury

[This match kicked off at 7.30pm]

(The England U21 scrum was put under severe pressure; Henri-Pierre Vermis scored a penalty goal in the 5th minute!; England U21 were losing 3-0 midway through the first half; England U21 were losing 8-0 in the 24th minute; England U21 were still losing 8-0 shortly afterwards when Andy Goode missed an eminently kickable penalty goal attempt; England U21 were losing 8-0 at half-time; England U21 played with the wind in the second half; England U21 were still losing 8-0 early in the second half when they were awarded 2 penalties in eminently kickable positions, but on each occasion Mark Tucker ordered a kick to the corner in a vain attempt to score a try from the ensuing lineout; England U21 were losing 8-0 midway through the second half; England U21 were losing 8-3 in the 63rd minute; England U21 were still losing 8-3 in the first minute of injury time when Tom Voyce scored a brilliant try which Andy Goode then converted to win the match)

'A' INTERNATIONAL CHAMPIONSHIP

CAPTAIN: *Steve Borthwick*

2nd Feb WALES A 19 **ENGLAND A*** 19

The Racecourse Ground, Wrexham

[This match kicked off at 7.30pm; Ali Hepher retired in April 2006; John Mallett toured Australia with England Schools 18 Group in July-August 1988; Ben Kay was capped for England Schools 18 Group in March 1994; Martyn Wood was capped for England

Schools 18 Group in January 1995; Leon Lloyd was capped for England Colts in March 1997; Rob Hardwick was capped for England Colts in March 1988; Chris Fortey and Lee Fortey were twins; Tom May was capped for England Schools 18 Group in March 1997]

(England A were drawing 0-0 in the 4th minute when Andy Goode missed a 30 metre penalty goal attempt; England A were leading 3-0 midway through the first half; Leon Lloyd went off injured in the 28th minute, being replaced by Tom May; England A were leading 6-3 just before half-time when Andy Goode took too much time over his clearance kick and was charged down by Huw Harries, who went on to score, thus 7 points were preventable; England A were losing 10-6 at half-time; England A were losing 13-6 midway through the second half when Paul Sampson scored a brilliant try; England A were drawing 16-16 with 1 minute of normal time remaining when Andy Goode scored a penalty goal; England A were leading 19-16 in the fifth minute of injury time when Lee Jarvis scored a penalty goal to draw the match for Wales A; David Rees (2) injured playing in the match; Jason Robinson saw very little of the ball in this match)

16th Feb **ENGLAND A** 44 ITALY A 3

Goldington Road, Goldington, Bedford

[This match kicked off at 7.30pm; Ali Hepher and David Rees (2) unavailable due to injury; Steve White-Cooper selected but withdrew due to injury, Grant Seely was moved from the bench to the team and Rob Fidler was then selected for the bench; Andy Long was capped for England Schools 18 Group in March 1996; Will Johnson was the brother of Martin Johnson; Liam Botham was the son of the England cricketer Ian Botham; Rob Fidler was the son of John Fidler and was capped for England Schools 18 Group in February 1993]

(This match took place on a poor playing surface; The England A forwards monopolised possession in this match; England A were losing 3-0 in the 9th minute; England A were still losing 3-0 midway through the first half; England A were drawing 3-3 in the 23rd minute; England A were still drawing 3-3 in the 32nd minute when some superb handling amongst the backs allowed Nnamdi Ezulike to score; England A were leading 11-3 just before half-time; England A were leading 18-3 at half-time; The second half started 20 minutes late due to a floodlight failure!; England A were still leading 18-3 in the 44th minute when Paul Sampson ghosted through to score a brilliant try; Dave Walder came on as a replacement for Andy Goode in the 53rd minute; England A were leading 23-3 midway through the second half; England A were leading 30-3 in the 62nd minute; England A were still leading 30-3 with 5 minutes of normal time remaining when Will Johnson scored from a rolling maul; England A were leading 37-3 in injury time; England A scored 44 unanswered points to win the match; Dave Walder had a brilliant game)

2nd Mar **ENGLAND A** 60 SCOTLAND A 20

Headingley Stadium, Leeds

[This match kicked off at 7.30pm; Tom Palmer (2) was included in an original 8 man bench selection; Kingston Park Stadium, Newcastle was the original venue for this match, but it was declared unplayable on 1st March 2001 due to both frost and an outbreak of foot and mouth disease in England; Alex King was capped for England Colts in March 1994; John Mallett retired in May 2003]

(This match was played in extremely cold conditions; The England A forwards monopolised possession in this match; Paul Sampson scored in the 1st minute!; Some superb handling allowed Steve White-Cooper to score a try which Dave Walder then converted to give England A a 15-0 lead in the 17th minute; Paul Sampson scored

***a brilliant solo try; England A were leading 29-3 in the 37th minute when Paul Sampson dropped Gordon Ross' cross-kick and Jon Steel followed up to score, thus 7 points were preventable; England A were leading 36-10 at half-time; England A were leading 60-15 in the closing stages; Dave Walder had a brilliant game*)**

CAPTAIN: *No captain appointed*

23rd Mar IRELAND A C **ENGLAND A** C

Thomond Park, Limerick

[*This match was scheduled to kick off at 7.30pm; This match was postponed by the IRFU on 7th March 2001 due to an outbreak of foot and mouth disease in England and was never rescheduled*]

CAPTAIN: *Ben Kay*

6th April **ENGLAND A** 23 FRANCE A 22

Recreation Ground, Redruth

[*This match kicked off at 1.30pm; Rob Hardwick and Scott Benton unavailable due to injury; David Flatman selected but withdrew as he was now required to sit on the bench for the full England international team, being replaced by Mike Worsley; Martyn Wood selected but withdrew due to illness, Nick Walshe was moved from the bench to the team and Ricky Pellow was then selected for the bench; Lewis Moody selected for bench but withdrew due to injury, being replaced by Alex Sanderson; Mike Worsley was capped for England Schools 18 Group in January 1995; Alex Sanderson toured Australia with England Schools 18 Group in August 1997; Ricky Pellow was capped for England Schools 18 Group in March 1996; Serge Betsen played for France A in this match*]

(*This match was played on a wet and muddy pitch; England A were losing 3-0 in the 8th minute; England A were losing 8-0 in the 16th minute; England A were still losing 8-0 midway through the first half; England A were losing 8-7 in the 23rd minute; England A were leading 14-8 in the 32nd minute; England A were leading 17-8 shortly before half-time; England A were leading 20-8 at half-time; France A played down the slope towards Hellfire Corner in the second half; The England A forwards could not win any possession in the second half; England A were leading 23-8 in the 43rd minute; England A scored 23 unanswered points to win the match; England A were still leading 23-8 in the 52nd minute when Alex Audebert scored after a poor tackle by Leon Lloyd, thus 7 points were preventable; England A were leading 23-15 midway through the second half; England A were still leading 23-15 with 4 minutes of normal time remaining; France A were allowed to score 14 unanswered points*)

TELECOM 2GO NEW ZEALAND INTERNATIONAL SEVENS

WestpacTrust Stadium, Wellington

CAPTAIN: *Mark Sowerby*

First Round - Pool 'B'

9th Feb CHINA 14 **ENGLAND** 33

[*This match kicked off at 2.00pm*]

(*England scored 28 unanswered points to win the match*)

9th Feb USA 17 **ENGLAND*** 12

[*This match kicked off at 4.40pm*]

(*England were drawing 12-12 in the final minute when Dan Younger intercepted the ball and ran 80 metres to score to win the match for the USA, thus 5 points were preventable*)

9th Feb	FIJI	41	**ENGLAND**	5	

[*This match kicked off at 8.20pm*]
[Bowl Quarter-Final:]

[10th Feb	NIUE	7	**ENGLAND**	22	**]**

[*This match kicked off at 2.00pm*]
[Bowl Semi-Final:]

[10th Feb	SOUTH AFRICA	31	**ENGLAND**	12	**]**

[*This match kicked off at 5.05pm*]

BRISBANE SEVENS

Suncorp Stadium, Lang Park, Brisbane
CAPTAIN: *No captain appointed*

16th Feb	*No opponents named*	C	**ENGLAND**	C

[*This Round was scheduled for 16th-17th February 2001 but was cancelled by the IRB on 14th January 2001 after the Australian government banned Fiji from appearing on 10th January 2001*]

ALASTAIR HIGNELL BENEFIT MATCH

CAPTAIN: *Michael Count* [Cambridge Past and Present]
CAPTAIN: *Phil de Glanville* [AJ Hignell XV]

7th Mar	**CAMBRIDGE PAST AND PRESENT**	55	**AJ HIGNELL XV**	46

University Football Ground, Grange Road, Cambridge
[CAMBRIDGE PAST AND PRESENT: [*This match kicked off at 3.00pm; Rudolf Bosch selected but withdrew, Mike Tweedie was moved from the bench to the team and Ronan Workman was then selected for the bench; Henry Whitford selected but withdrew, Martin Purdy was moved from the bench to the team; Adam Bidwell selected but withdrew, Chris Davis was moved from the bench to the team and Tony Dalwood was then selected for the bench; Cambridge Past & Present originally named a 9 man bench selection; Stuart Moffat was originally selected at right wing with Paul Surridge at full back, but the two swapped positions before the match; Stefan Rodgers was the son of Tony Rodgers and played for M.R. Steele-Bodger's XV against Cambridge University at Grange Road on 26th November 2003; Matt Singer switched his allegiance to Wales in October 1997*]
(*Cambridge Past and Present were leading 5-0 in the 7th minute; Cambridge Past and Present were leading 12-7 midway through the first half; Cambridge Past and Present were leading 19-7 in the 24th minute; Cambridge Past and Present were drawing 19-19 in the 35th minute; Cambridge Past and Present were losing 31-19 at half-time; Cambridge Past and Present were losing 36-19 in the 41st minute; The AJ Hignell XV was allowed to score 29 unanswered points; Cambridge Past and Present were losing 36-24 midway through the second half; Cambridge Past and Present were losing 41-31 in the 67th minute; Cambridge Past and Present were losing 46-31 with 5 minutes of normal time remaining; Cambridge Past and Present were losing 46-45 in the last minute of normal time; Cambridge Past and Present scored 24 unanswered points to win the match*)]
**[AJ HIGNELL XV: [*This match kicked off at 3.00pm; The AJ Hignell XV was also billed as the Alastair Hignell XV; Ramin Mathieson, Karl Rudzki, Adam Jones (1) and Adedayo Adebayo all selected but withdrew, being replaced by Tim Marston, Charlie Simpson, Jim Evans and Nick Drake respectively; Peter Short selected but withdrew,*

being replaced by Peter Scrivener who then himself withdrew, with Ben Cole was moving from the bench to the team to replace him; Richard Nias and Gareth Williams (3) played for M.R. Steele-Bodger's XV against Cambridge University at Grange Road on 29th November 2000, with Nias scoring a try and Gareth Williams (3) scoring 2 tries; Jon Sleightholme was capped for England Colts in March 1991; Rob Ashforth was capped as a full back for England Schools 18 Group in February 1993; Lee Mears toured Australia with England Schools 18 Group in August 1997; Richard Siveter was capped for England Schools 18 Group in April 1997]
(The AJ Hignell XV was losing 5-0 in the 7th minute; The AJ Hignell XV was still losing 5-0 in the 12th minute when Phil de Glanville scored a brilliant try; Andy Craig came on as a temporary blood replacement for Charlie Simpson in the 13th minute; The AJ Hignell XV was losing 12-7 midway through the first half; The AJ Hignell XV was losing 19-7 in the 24th minute; The AJ Hignell XV was drawing 19-19 in the 35th minute; The AJ Hignell XV was leading 31-19 at half-time; The AJ Hignell XV was leading 36-19 in the 41st minute; The AJ Hignell XV scored 29 unanswered points; Gareth Williams (3) came on as a replacement for Phil de Glanville in the 53rd minute; The AJ Hignell XV was leading 36-24 midway through the second half; The AJ Hignell XV was leading 41-31 in the 67th minute; The AJ Hignell XV was leading 46-31 with 5 minutes of normal time remaining; The AJ Hignell XV was leading 46-45 in the last minute of normal time; Cambridge Past and Present were allowed to score 24 unanswered points to win the match)]

CREDIT SUISSE FIRST BOSTON HONG KONG SEVENS

Hong Kong Stadium, Eastern Hospital Road, So Kon Po, Hong Kong
CAPTAIN: *Jon Sleightholme*
First Round - Pool 'D'
30th Mar JAPAN 14 **ENGLAND** 28
[This match kicked off at 8.00pm]
(England were drawing 7-7 at one point in the first half; England were leading 14-7 at half-time)
31st Mar SINGAPORE 5 **ENGLAND** 66
[This match kicked off at 12.00pm]
(England were leading 33-0 at half-time)
31st Mar SAMOA 28 **ENGLAND** 0
[This match kicked off at 6.00pm]
(England were losing 14-0 at half-time)
Quarter-Final
1st April FIJI 22 **ENGLAND** 7
[This match kicked off at 1.30pm]
(England were leading 7-0 in the early stages; England were still leading 7-0 when Nigel Simpson broke through but was then brilliantly tap-tackled by Alifereti Doviverata; England were leading 7-5 at half-time; England were still leading 7-5 in the 10th minute; Fiji were allowed to score 22 unanswered points to win the match)

SHANGHAI SEVENS

Yuanshen Stadium, Pudong, Shanghai

CAPTAIN: *Andy Gomarsall*

First Round - Pool 'B'

7th April	CHINA	14	**ENGLAND**	22

[*This match kicked off at 11.50am*]

7th April	WALES	0	**ENGLAND**	29

[*This match kicked off at 2.40pm*]

7th April	AUSTRALIA	43	**ENGLAND**	0

[*This match kicked off at 5.30pm*]

Quarter-Final

8th April	SOUTH AFRICA	24	**ENGLAND**	7

[*This match kicked off at 10.50am*]

[Plate Semi-Final:]

[8th April	ARGENTINA	17	**ENGLAND**	19]

[*This match kicked off at 1.00pm*]

CAPTAIN: *??*

[Plate Final:]

[8th April	FIJI	45	**ENGLAND**	14]

[*This match kicked off at 2.50pm; Andy Gomarsall played in the White Hart Marauders team that won the Henley International Sevens on 13th May 2001*]

(*Waisake Bole scored in the 1st minute!; Mark Meenan scored a brilliant try straight after the restart!; England were losing 26-7 at half-time; England were losing 45-7 when the full-time hooter sounded, but the ball was still in play and Rob Thirlby was able to score a consolation try*)

TILNEY MELROSE SEVENS

The Greenyards, Melrose

CAPTAIN: *Shaun Longstaff* (SC)

Second Round

14th April	West of Scotland (*SC*)	14	**BARBARIANS**	33

[*This match kicked off at 3.27pm*]

Quarter-Final

14th April	Kirkcaldy (*SC*)	14	**BARBARIANS**	26

[*This match kicked off at 4.57pm*]

Semi-Final

14th April	Glasgow Hawks (*SC*)	12	**BARBARIANS**	24

[*This match kicked off at 5.55pm*]

(*The Barbarians were leading 14-7 at half-time; The Barbarians were leading 24-7 in the closing stages; The Barbarians scored 24 unanswered points to win the match*)

Final

14th April	Nawaka (*FIJ*)	19	**BARBARIANS**	38

[*This match kicked off at 6.35pm*]

(*Conan Sharman scored a brilliant try in the 1st minute!; The Barbarians were leading 7-0 in the 3rd minute when Conan Sharman chipped ahead and regathered the ball to score a superb try; The Barbarians were leading 19-0 when Conan Sharman went off injured, being replaced by David Irving; The Barbarians were leading 26-0 at half-time; Simon Webster intercepted the ball and scored a try which David Irvine then converted*

to give the Barbarians a 38-0 lead with 6 minutes remaining; Alex Page went off injured in the closing stages, which reduced the Barbarians to 6 men because they had already used up their permitted number of replacements; Nawaka were allowed to score 19 unanswered points; Conan Sharman played brilliantly and scored 50 points in the competition)

BANK OF SCOTLAND BORDER LEAGUE CENTENARY MATCH

CAPTAIN: *Graham Shiel* (SC)

16th April Border League Select XV (*SC*) 31 **BARBARIANS*** 24

The Greenyards, Melrose

[*This match kicked off at 6.15pm; Sailosi Nawavu selected but withdrew to sit on the bench, being replaced by Vuniani Derenalagi; Alex Page selected for bench but withdrew due to injury, being replaced by Mark Chapman-Smith*]

(*The Barbarians were leading 5-0 in the 7th minute; Neil Boobyer made a brilliant break that enabled Phil Graham to score a try which Graham Shiel then converted to give the Barbarians a 12-0 lead in the 11th minute; The Border League Select XV was losing 12-7 in the 18th minute when Ian Fairley was able to follow up and score after the Barbarians pack let the ball squirt out of a scrum, thus 7 points were preventable; The Border League Select XV was allowed to score 26 unanswered points to win the match; The Barbarians were losing 26-12 at half-time; The Barbarians were losing 26-19 midway through the second half; The Barbarians were still losing 26-19 in the closing stages of normal time; The Barbarians were losing 31-19 in the first minute of injury time when Alain Studer scored a consolation try; Alain Studer had a brilliant game*)

MALAYSIA SEVENS

MPPJ Stadium, Petaling Jaya, Kelana Jaya

CAPTAIN: *Chris Davis*

First Round - Pool 'A'

21st April MALAYSIA 10 **ENGLAND** 31

[*This match kicked off at 3.50pm*]

(*Malaysia were allowed to score a try in each half*)

21st April WALES 24 **ENGLAND** 14

[*This match kicked off at 7.00pm*]

21st April NEW ZEALAND 33 **ENGLAND** 5

[*This match kicked off at 9.40pm*]

[Bowl Quarter-Final:]

[22nd Apr TAIWAN 0 **ENGLAND** 38]

[*This match kicked off at 2.30pm; Taiwan also billed as Chinese Taipei*]

[Bowl Semi-Final:]

[22nd Apr JAPAN 7 **ENGLAND** 34]

[*This match kicked off at 5.10pm*]

(*Simon Hunt scored 10 tries in the competition*)

[Bowl Final:]

[22nd Apr KOREA 24 **ENGLAND** 12]

[*This match kicked off at 7.30pm*]

(*England were leading 12-0 at half-time; Korea were allowed to score 24 unanswered points in the second half to win the match*)

VOLKSWAGEN JAPAN SEVENS

Chichibunomiya Rugby Stadium, Tokyo

CAPTAIN: *Chris Davis*

First Round - Pool 'B'

29th April MALAYSIA 5 **ENGLAND** 31

[This match kicked off at 12.10pm]

(This match was played in cold and wet conditions)

29th April JAPAN 7 **ENGLAND** 24

[This match kicked off at 2.50pm]

(This match was played in cold and wet conditions)

29th April AUSTRALIA 26 **ENGLAND** 0

[This match kicked off at 5.30pm]

(This match was played in cold and wet conditions)

Quarter-Final

30th April NEW ZEALAND 26 **ENGLAND** 7

[This match kicked off at 12.20pm]

(This match was played on a wet pitch)

[Plate Semi-Final:]

[30th Apr CANADA 5 **ENGLAND** 29 **]**

[This match kicked off at 2.50pm]

(This match was played on a wet pitch; Simon Hunt scored 20 points in this match)

[Plate Final:]

[30th Apr SOUTH AFRICA 38 **ENGLAND** 15 **]**

[This match kicked off at 4.45pm]

(This match was played on a wet pitch; England were leading 15-12 at half-time; South Africa were allowed to score 26 unanswered points in the second half to win the match; Simon Hunt scored 9 tries in the competition)

ENGLAND STUDENTS MATCH

CAPTAIN: *??*

5th May **ENGLAND STUDENTS U21** 32 COMBINED SERVICES U21 (*SER*) 21

Twickenham

[This match kicked off at 12.00pm and was a curtain raiser game for the Army v Navy match; Alan Hubbleday, Seb FitzGerald, Marko Stanojevic, Mark Eastwood, Simon Danielli and Phil Christophers all selected but withdrew, being replaced by John Williams (3), Peter Murphy, Michael Lennon, Alex Cadwallader, Simon Hunt and Jonny Hylton respectively; Chris Brain was capped for England Schools 18 Group in March 1998; Jonny Hylton was capped for England Schools 18 Group in March 1999]

(England Students U21 were leading 8-0 at one point in the first half; England Students U21 were leading 14-7 at half-time; England Students U21 were leading 22-7 early in the second half; England Students U21 were leading 27-14 at one point in the second half; England Students U21 were leading 27-21 in injury time when John Williams (3) scored to clinch the match)

FIRST SCOTTISH AMICABLE TOUR MATCH

CAPTAIN: *Gary Teichmann* (SA)

20th May WALES XV 38 **BARBARIANS** 40

Millennium Stadium, Cardiff

[*This match kicked off at 3.00pm; Bobby Skinstad in original squad but withdrew due to injury; Wales eventually decided not to award caps for this match; Gavin Henson came on as a replacement for the Wales XV in this match*]

(*This match was played in hot conditions; The Barbarians were leading 7-0 in the 8th minute; The Barbarians were still leading 7-0 midway through the first half when Neil Jenkins scored after a poor tackle by Braam van Straaten; The Barbarians were drawing 7-7 in the 25th minute when Joost van der Westhuizen threw a superb reverse pass that enabled Joeli Vidiri to score a try which Braam van Straaten then brilliantly converted from the right touchline; The Barbarians were leading 14-7 in the 32nd minute when Percy Montgomery wasted a great try-scoring opportunity by dropping the ball while the Wales XV line was at his mercy; The Barbarians were leading 14-7 at half-time; Joost van der Westhuizen went off injured in the 44th minute, being replaced by Andy Gomarsall; The Barbarians were drawing 14-14 in the 55th minute; The Barbarians were losing 21-14 midway through the second half; The Barbarians were losing 21-19 in the 63rd minute; The Barbarians were losing 28-19 with 9 minutes of normal time remaining when Naka Drotske scored after Pat Lam broke from the base of a five metre scrum; The Barbarians were losing 28-26 with 5 minutes of normal time remaining when collectively poor tackling allowed Craig Quinnell to score, thus 2 tries and 14 points were preventable; The Barbarians were losing 35-26 with 1 minute of normal time remaining when Percy Montgomery scored after Tim Horan put in a brilliant grubber kick; The Barbarians were losing 38-33 in the third minute of injury time when some superb handling allowed Friedrich Lombard to score a try which Braam van Straaten then brilliantly converted from the right touchline with the last kick of the match to win the game; Joost van der Westhuizen had a brilliant game*)

SECOND SCOTTISH AMICABLE TOUR MATCH

CAPTAIN: *Tim Horan* (AU)

24th May SCOTLAND XV 31 **BARBARIANS** 74

Murrayfield

[*This match kicked off at 7.45pm; This venue in Edinburgh was officially called Murrayfield Stadium, but it was usually just referred to as Murrayfield; Josh Kronfeld selected but withdrew on the day of the match to sit on the bench, being replaced by Angus Gardiner; Cristian Stoica selected but withdrew on the day of the match due to injury, Geordan Murphy was moved from the bench to the team with Percy Montgomery then moving from fly half to full back to accommodate Geordan Murphy, while Braam van Straaten was now selected for the bench; David Wilson (1) selected for bench but withdrew due to injury, being replaced by Josh Kronfeld; Friedrich Lombard was originally selected at left wing with Jonah Lomu at right wing, but the two swapped positions on the day of the match*]

(*Jonah Lomu scored in the 1st minute!; The Barbarians were leading 10-0 in the 8th minute when Friedrich Lombard scored after Geordan Murphy made a superb break; The Barbarians were leading 15-0 shortly afterwards when Robin Brooke had his pass intercepted by Marcus Di Rollo who went on to score, thus 7 points were preventable; John Langford went off injured in the 18th minute, being replaced by Tom Bowman; The Barbarians were losing 21-15 in the 19th minute; Tim Horan went off injured in the*

***20th minute, being replaced by Pat Howard; The Barbarians were leading 22-21 in the 26th minute when Richard Cockerill scored after Jonah Lomu went on a brilliant rampaging run; Jonah Lomu scored 4 tries in the first half!; The Barbarians were leading 34-21 in the 36th minute when James McLaren scored after a poor tackle by Friedrich Lombard, thus 2 tries and 12 points were preventable; The Barbarians were leading 41-26 at half-time; The Barbarians were still leading 41-26 in the 44th minute when Joost van der Westhuizen scored after Jonah Lomu powered through 3 attempted tackles; The Barbarians were leading 62-31 midway through the second half; The Barbarians were still leading 62-31 in the closing stages; Jonah Lomu had a brilliant game*)**

TETLEY'S COUNTY CHALLENGE

CAPTAIN: *Ian Sanders*

26th May **CORNWALL** 19 Yorkshire 47

Twickenham

[*This match kicked off at 4.00pm; This County Challenge match was played between Yorkshire and Cornwall because the former team won the 2000 County Championship, while the latter was the top seeded county side based on the results of the last three seasons; Julian Wilce unavailable due to club commitments; Adam Harris selected but withdrew due to injury, being replaced by Lee Soper; Ben Salt selected but withdrew due to injury, Andy Hymans was moved from the bench to the team and Liam Chapple was then selected for the bench; Simon Griffiths selected for bench but withdrew, being replaced by John Navin; John Lawn, Mark Sowerby, Dave Scully, Rob Liley, Mark Kirkby, Neil Summers, Jon Shepherd, Stuart Dixon and Dan Scarbrough all played for Yorkshire in this match, with Kirkby, Jon Shepherd, Stuart Dixon and Scarbrough all scoring tries while Rob Liley kicked 5 conversions; Ross Winney and Diccon Edwards sat on the bench for Yorkshire in this match; Adryan Winnan toured Canada, New Zealand and Australia with England Schools 18 Group in July-August 2001 and played for England in the U19 World Championship in Italy in March 2002; Jason Hobson played for England in the U19 World Championship in Italy in March 2002*]

(*This match was played in hot conditions; Steve Larkins scored a 40 metre penalty goal in the 3rd minute!; Cornwall were losing 7-6 in the 10th minute; Cornwall were losing 14-9 in the 28th minute when collectively poor tackling allowed Mark Kirkby to score, thus 5 points were preventable; Cornwall were losing 19-9 shortly afterwards when they created an overlap but James Hawken then wasted this great try-scoring opportunity by dropping the ball; Cornwall were losing 19-12 at half-time; Dan Scarbrough scored after just 90 seconds of the second half had been played!; Cornwall were losing 26-12 when James Hendy knocked the ball on 5 metres short of the Yorkshire line; Cornwall were losing 33-12 in the 57th minute; Cornwall were losing 40-12 with 7 minutes remaining when James Hendy scored a consolation try*)

THIRD SCOTTISH AMICABLE TOUR MATCH

CAPTAIN: *Kyran Bracken* [*Josh Lewsey*] [England XV]

CAPTAIN: *Gary Teichmann* (SA) [Barbarians]

27th May **ENGLAND XV*** 29 **BARBARIANS** 43

Twickenham

[ENGLAND XV: [*This match kicked off at 3.15pm; Clive Woodward rested Graham Rowntree, Dorian West, Ben Kay and Martin Corry by relegating them to the bench for*

this match; Martyn Wood played in the White Hart Marauders team that won the Henley International Sevens on 13th May 2001]
(*Dave Walder kicked away too much possession in the first half; Pat Howard scored in the 3rd minute!; The England XV was losing 12-3 in the 12th minute; The England XV was losing 19-3 in the 17th minute; Martyn Wood came on as a temporary blood replacement for Kyran Bracken in the 19th minute; The England XV was losing 19-8 midway through the first half; The England XV was still losing 19-8 in the 28th minute when Jonah Lomu scored after a poor tackle by Paul Sampson, thus 5 points were preventable; Mark Regan went off injured in the 29th minute after being concussed, being replaced by Dorian West; The England XV was losing 24-8 in the 37th minute when Paul Sampson scored after Leon Lloyd made a brilliant break; Josh Lewsey went off injured in the 38th minute, being replaced by Ben Johnston; The England XV was losing 24-15 at half-time; The England XV was still losing 24-15 in the 56th minute; Alex King came on as a temporary blood replacement for Tim Stimpson in the 59th minute, with Dave Walder then switching from fly half to full back to accommodate Alex King; Simon Shaw went off injured at the same time, being replaced by Steve Borthwick; The England XV was losing 29-22 midway through the second half; The England XV was losing 36-22 in the 69th minute; The England XV was losing 36-29 with 8 minutes of normal time remaining; Ben Johnston went off injured with 3 minutes of normal time remaining, being replaced by Tim Stimpson; The England XV was still losing 36-29 in the third minute of injury time when Adrian Garvey scored a try which Braam van Straaten then converted with the last kick of the match to clinch the game for the Barbarians*)]
[BARBARIANS: [*This match kicked off at 3.15pm; Adrian Garvey selected but withdrew to sit on the bench, being replaced by Garry Pagel; Tim Horan selected but withdrew due to injury, Jason Little was moved from the bench to the team and Friedrich Lombard was then selected for the bench; Kevin Yates selected for bench but withdrew, being replaced by Adrian Garvey; John Langford selected for bench but withdrew, being replaced by Tom Bowman; Jeremy Guscott retired after this match*]
(*Pat Howard scored in the 3rd minute!; The Barbarians were leading 7-3 in the 12th minute when Joeli Vidiri scored after Jonah Lomu went on a brilliant rampaging run; Jeremy Guscott came on as a temporary blood replacement for Jason Little in the 13th minute; The Barbarians were leading 12-3 in the 17th minute when Jeremy Guscott scored after Pat Howard put in a superb chip ahead; The Barbarians were leading 19-3 midway through the first half; The Barbarians were leading 24-8 in the 28th minute; The Barbarians were still leading 24-8 in the 37th minute; The Barbarians were leading 24-15 at half-time; Richard Cockerill came on as a replacement for Naka Drotske in the 51st minute; The Barbarians were still leading 24-15 in the 56th minute when Pat Lam scored after Braam van Straaten made a brilliant break; The Barbarians were leading 29-15 midway through the second half when Michael Stephenson scored after a poor tackle by Geordan Murphy, thus 7 points were preventable; The Barbarians were leading 36-22 in the 69th minute; The Barbarians were leading 36-29 with 8 minutes of normal time remaining; The Barbarians were still leading 36-29 in the third minute of injury time when Adrian Garvey scored a try which Braam van Straaten then converted with the last kick of the match to clinch the game*)]

EMIRATES AIRLINE LONDON SEVENS

London

CAPTAIN: *Nigel Simpson*

First Round - Pool 'D'

27th May **ENGLAND** 36 WEST INDIES 5
Stoop Memorial Ground, Langhorn Drive, Twickenham
[*This match kicked off at 2.20pm*]

27th May **ENGLAND** 19 WALES 0
Stoop Memorial Ground, Langhorn Drive, Twickenham
[*This match kicked off at 5.10pm*]
(*Simon Amor scored a brilliant 90 metre solo try in this match*)

27th May **ENGLAND** 22 SAMOA 19
Stoop Memorial Ground, Langhorn Drive, Twickenham
[*This match kicked off at 8.00pm*]
(*England were losing 14-5 at half-time; England were losing 19-5 early in the second half; England were losing 19-17 in the last minute when Simon Hunt scored a match-winning try to complete a hat-trick*)

Quarter-Final

28th May **ENGLAND*** 12 FIJI 14
Twickenham
[*This match kicked off at 1.40pm*]
(*England were losing 14-12 in the final minute when Simon Amor unaccountably took a tap penalty from in front of the posts instead of kicking a penalty goal!*)

[Plate Semi-Final:]

[28th May **ENGLAND** 33 ARGENTINA 14 **]**
Twickenham
[*This match kicked off at 3.30pm*]
(*Simon Hunt scored 6 tries in the competition*)

[Plate Final:]

[28th May **ENGLAND** 7 SOUTH AFRICA 31 **]**
Twickenham
[*This match kicked off at 5.30pm*]

EMIRATES AIRLINE WALES SEVENS

Wales

CAPTAIN: *Nigel Simpson*

First Round - Pool 'C'

2nd June SPAIN 19 **ENGLAND** 19
Rodney Parade, Newport
[*This match kicked off at 12.40pm*]

2nd June GEORGIA 17 **ENGLAND** 12
Rodney Parade, Newport
[*This match kicked off at 3.10pm*]

2nd June FIJI 19 **ENGLAND*** 15
Rodney Parade, Newport
[*This match kicked off at 6.20pm*]
(*England were leading 15-0 at one point in the first half; Fiji were allowed to score 19 unanswered points to win the match*)

[Bowl Quarter-Final:]
[3rd June FRANCE 12 **ENGLAND** 17]
Millennium Stadium, Cardiff
[This match kicked off at 12.40pm]
[Bowl Semi-Final:]
[3rd June CANADA 14 **ENGLAND** 29]
Millennium Stadium, Cardiff
[This match kicked off at 3.10pm]
[Bowl Final:]
[3rd June PORTUGAL 26 **ENGLAND** 35]
Millennium Stadium, Cardiff
[This match kicked off at 5.00pm]
(Tony Roques scored in the last minute to clinch the match)

PENGUINS TOUR TO GERMANY AND ARGENTINA 2001

CAPTAIN: *Andre Fox* (SA)
2nd June GERMANY 8 **PENGUINS** 101
Fritz-Grunebaum-Sportpark, Heidelberg-Kirchheim
[No match notes]

ENGLAND TOUR TO CANADA AND AMERICA 2001

CAPTAIN: *Kyran Bracken*
2nd June CANADA 10 **ENGLAND** 22
Fletcher's Fields, Markham, Toronto
[This match kicked off at 4.30pm; Mark Regan and Steve Thompson (2) unavailable due to injury]
(England played into a strong wind in the first half; England were drawing 0-0 in the 7th minute when Dave Walder badly missed a kickable 35 metre penalty goal attempt; England were losing 3-0 in the 11th minute; Michael Stephenson had to go off in the 15th minute after he was disorientated by an illegal body-check from Scott Stewart straight after the kick-off, being temporarily replaced by Tim Stimpson; England were still losing 3-0 midway through the first half; England were losing 3-0 in the 23rd minute when Kyran Bracken was able to follow up and score after the Canadian pack let the ball squirt out of a scrum in front of their own line; England were leading 5-3 at half-time; Michael Stephenson came back on at the start of the second half; England were still leading 5-3 in the 44th minute when Dorian West scored from a rolling maul; England were leading 15-3 in the 47th minute; England were still leading 15-3 midway through the second half; England were leading 15-3 in the 68th minute when Josh Lewsey scored a brilliant 60 metre solo try; England scored 22 unanswered points to win the match; England were leading 22-3 with 2 minutes remaining; Ben Kay, Lewis Moody and Jamie Noon all had a brilliant game; Dave Walder had a poor game)
CAPTAIN: *Kyran Bracken* [*Ben Kay; Dorian West*]
9th June CANADA 20 **ENGLAND** 59
Swangard Stadium, Burnaby, Toronto
[This match kicked off at 4.00pm; Steve Thompson (2), Alex Brown and Joe Ewens unavailable due to injury; Martin Corry selected but withdrew on 8th June 2001 as he was now required to join the British & Irish Lions tour of Australia, Steve White-Cooper was moved from the bench to the team and Steve Borthwick was then selected for the bench; Rob Fidler joined the tour after this match]

(Simon Shaw scored in the 2nd minute!; England were leading 12-3 in the 8th minute; England were leading 15-6 midway through the first half; England were leading 21-6 in the 34th minute; Kyran Bracken went off injured in the 35th minute, being replaced by Martyn Wood; Paul Sampson went off injured just before half-time having broken his leg, being replaced by Tim Stimpson; England were leading 28-6 at half-time; England were still leading 28-6 in the 42nd minute when Simon Shaw scored after Dave Walder made a brilliant break; Ben Kay went off injured in the 44th minute, being replaced by Steve Borthwick; England were leading 33-13 in the 58th minute when Dave Walder scored two superb solo tries in 2 minutes!; England were leading 47-13 midway through the second half; England were leading 54-13 in the 62nd minute; England were still leading 54-13 with 6 minutes remaining; England were leading 59-13 with 2 minutes remaining; Dave Walder played brilliantly and scored 29 points in this match; England equalled their existing record of 10 consecutive Test match wins)

CAPTAIN: *Kyran Bracken*

16th June USA 19 **ENGLAND** 48

Matthew J. Boxer Stadium, Balboa Park, San Francisco

[This match kicked off at 1.00pm; Alex Brown, Ben Kay, Joe Ewens, Paul Sampson and Tim Stimpson all unavailable due to injury; Olly Barkley was capped for England without playing in a single game of senior club rugby!; On 28th August 2001 Kris Radlinski turned down an offer, reportedly worth over £1 million, from the RFU to play Rugby Union because he preferred to continue playing Rugby League for Wigan Warriors!]

(This match was played in 80 degree heat; Kyran Bracken played with a back injury; Dorian West scored from a rolling maul in the 3rd minute!; England were leading 7-0 in the 11th minute when Pat Sanderson scored while he was on as a temporary blood replacement for Lewis Moody!; England were leading 21-0 in the 16th minute; England were leading 21-5 midway through the first half; England were still leading 21-5 in the 24th minute when Joe Worsley scored after Steve Borthwick made a brilliant 40 metre run; England were leading 33-5 in the 36th minute; England were leading 33-5 at half-time; England were leading 38-5 in the 46th minute; Olly Barkley came on as a replacement for Jamie Noon in the 49th minute; England were leading 38-12 midway through the second half when Pat Sanderson saved a certain try by tackling Jovesa Naivalu; England were leading 38-19 in the 64th minute; England were leading 43-19 with 7 minutes remaining when Dave Walder went off injured, being replaced by Tom Voyce with Leon Lloyd then switching from wing to centre to accommodate Voyce and Olly Barkley moving from centre to fly half to accommodate Leon Lloyd; England were leading 48-19 in the final minute when Olly Barkley badly mishit a conversion attempt, resulting in the ball bouncing across the pitch!; A mistake by the fourth official resulted in England having 16 players on the field for a period of 2 minutes in the second half!; Leon Lloyd injured playing in the match; Lewis Moody had a brilliant game; England broke their previous record by winning their 11th consecutive cap international match!)

GRAND PRIX OF EUROPE INTERNATIONAL SEVENS TOURNAMENT

Fritz-Grunebaum-Sportpark, Heidelberg-Kirchheim

CAPTAIN: *Mike Friday*

First Round - Pool 'A'

3rd June Comite Alpes Maritimes (*FR*) 0 **PENGUINS** 35

[No match notes]

3rd June POLAND 14 **PENGUINS** 33
[No match notes]
Semi-Final
3rd June NETHERLANDS 0 **PENGUINS** 36
[No match notes]
Final
3rd June GERMANY 7 **PENGUINS** 57
[No match notes]

BRITISH & IRISH LIONS TOUR TO AUSTRALIA 2001

CAPTAIN: *Martin Johnson*
30th Jun AUSTRALIA 13 **BRITISH & IRISH LIONS** 29
Wooloongabba Stadium, Brisbane
[This match kicked off at 7.00pm; This venue was officially called the Wooloongabba Stadium but it was usually referred to as the Gabba; Neil Back and Will Greenwood unavailable due to injury; On 1st July 2001 a Queensland Rugby Union hearing found Colin Charvis guilty of illegal use of the knee on an opponent and thus banned him for 2 matches; On the same day an internal British & Irish Lions disciplinary hearing fined Matt Dawson £5,000 for criticising the tour's training regime and management in a newspaper article published on 30th June 2001]
(This match was played on a pitch containing a muddy and slippery area around the centre of the halfway line which had been created when a cricket square had been covered over!; The Lions players decided to ignore Graham Henry's structured game-plan in this match; Jason Robinson beat Chris Latham for pace on the outside to score a brilliant try in the 3rd minute!; The Lions were leading 5-0 in the 8th minute when Jonny Wilkinson missed a kickable 40 metre penalty goal attempt; The Lions were leading 5-3 midway through the first half; The Lions were still leading 5-3 in the 33rd minute when Jonny Wilkinson had an eminently kickable 22 metre penalty goal attempt which hit the top of the left-hand post and then bounced wide!; The Lions were leading 5-3 in the 34th minute when a superb run by Brian O'Driscoll enabled Dafydd James to score a try which Jonny Wilkinson then brilliantly converted from the right touchline; The Lions were leading 12-3 at half-time; Matt Perry went off injured at half-time, being replaced by Iain Balshaw; Brian O'Driscoll scored a superb 56 metre solo try under the posts after just 53 seconds of the second half had been played!; Scott Quinnell powered through to score a try under the posts which Jonny Wilkinson then converted to give the Lions a 29-3 lead in the 52nd minute; The Lions scored 24 unanswered points to clinch the match; The Lions were still leading 29-3 in the 58th minute when Jason Robinson saved a certain try by tackling Matt Burke into touch at the corner flag; The Lions were leading 29-3 midway through the second half; Scott Quinnell went off injured in the 62nd minute, being replaced by Colin Charvis; The Lions were leading 29-3 in the 66th minute when Gordon Bulloch came on as a temporary blood replacement for Keith Wood and immediately afterwards Rob Howley put up a wayward box kick, which led directly to a try by Andrew Walker, thus 5 points were preventable; The Lions were leading 29-13 in the 69th minute; Jason Leonard came on as a replacement for Tom Smith (2) with 7 minutes of normal time remaining; The Lions were still leading 29-13 in the last minute of normal time when Keith Wood missed a speculative 41 metre drop goal attempt!; Keith Wood, Danny Grewcock and Brian O'Driscoll all had a brilliant game; Iain Balshaw had a poor game defensively)

7th July AUSTRALIA 35 **BRITISH & IRISH LIONS** 14

Colonial Stadium, Melbourne

[*This match kicked off at 7.00pm; Dai Young, Scott Murray and Will Greenwood unavailable due to injury; Colin Charvis unavailable due to suspension; Austin Healey selected for bench but withdrew due to injury, being replaced by Neil Jenkins; Darren Morris, Gordon Bulloch, David Wallace and Ben Cohen all in match squad of 27 announced on 4th July 2001 but not were not selected for team or bench; The Colonial Stadium had its retractable roof closed for this match; After this match Jonny Wilkinson was taken to hospital where his bruised left shin was put into plaster, but he then recovered sufficiently to play in the third test!*]

(*Neil Back was short of match fitness; The Lions forwards could not win any lineout ball; The Lions were drawing 0-0 in the 4th minute when Dafydd James broke through but then wasted this great try-scoring opportunity by electing to take the ball into contact instead of waiting for Jason Robinson to arrive in support; The Lions were leading 3-0 in the 9th minute; The Lions were leading 6-0 in the 12th minute; The Lions were leading 6-3 midway through the first half; Brian O'Driscoll injured his neck in the 25th minute but elected to remain on the pitch; The Lions were still leading 6-3 in the 27th minute when Neil Back scored from a rolling maul, with Jonny Wilkinson then missing the eminently kickable conversion attempt; In the 37th minute Martin Corry came on as a temporary blood replacement for Richard Hill (2), who had been concussed by an illegal flying elbow from Nathan Grey; The Lions were leading 11-3 in the 40th minute; The Lions were leading 11-6 in the third minute of first half injury time when Jonny Wilkinson missed a kickable 38 metre penalty goal attempt; The Lions were leading 11-6 at half-time; Graham Henry unaccountably changed the tactical emphasis from the forwards to the backs at half-time; Martin Corry came back on as a permanent replacement for the concussed Richard Hill (2) at the start of the second half; Jonny Wilkinson had his speculative pass to Rob Henderson intercepted by Joe Roff, who then ran 28 metres to score after just 23 seconds of the second half had been played!; Australia were leading 14-11 in the 49th minute when Joe Roff scored another try after the Lions forwards were inexplicably driven off their own ball at a scrum, thus 2 tries and 12 points were preventable; Australia were allowed to score 18 unanswered points to win the match; The Lions were losing 21-11 in the 53rd minute when Jonny Wilkinson had another kickable 44 metre penalty goal attempt go underneath the crossbar; Iain Balshaw came on as a replacement for Matt Perry immediately afterwards; The Lions were losing 21-14 midway through the second half; The Lions were losing 26-14 in the 65th minute; Jason Leonard came on as a replacement for Phil Vickery in the 66th minute; The Lions were losing 29-14 with 6 minutes of normal time remaining; Jonny Wilkinson went off injured with 3 minutes of normal time remaining, being replaced by Neil Jenkins; The Lions were losing 32-14 in the third minute of injury time; Rob Howley went off injured in the sixth minute of injury time, being replaced by Matt Dawson; Neil Back, Scott Quinnell and Rob Henderson all injured playing in the match; Scott Quinnell had a brilliant game; This was Australia's highest ever points total against the Lions*)

14th July AUSTRALIA 29 **BRITISH & IRISH LIONS*** 23

Stadium Australia, Sydney Olympic Park, Homebush Bay, Sydney

[*This match kicked off at 7.00pm; Richard Hill (2), Rob Howley and Neil Jenkins unavailable due to injury; Will Greenwood selected for bench but withdrew due to injury and illness, being replaced by Mark Taylor; Austin Healey selected at right wing but withdrew on the morning of the match due to injury, being replaced by Dafydd James with Mark Taylor then withdrawing from the bench so that Andy Nicol could be*

accommodated; On 6th September 2001 a British & Irish Lions disciplinary committee fined Austin Healey £2000 after finding him guilty of bringing the tour into disrepute by putting his name to an inflammatory newspaper column, which appeared on 13th July 2001 and was actually ghost-written by Eddie Butler!]

(Scott Quinnell and Matt Dawson both played with an injury; The Lions players were exhausted because Graham Henry had over-trained them throughout the tour; The Australians cracked the code for the lineout calls before the game and the Lions forwards were unable to win much lineout ball as a consequence; Matt Burke scored a penalty goal in the 3rd minute!; The Lions were drawing 3-3 in the 8th minute; The Lions were losing 9-3 midway through the first half when some superb handling amongst the forwards allowed Jason Robinson to score a try which Jonny Wilkinson then brilliantly converted from the left touchline; The Lions were leading 10-9 in the 25th minute when Jonny Wilkinson missed a kickable 40 metre penalty goal attempt; The Lions were still leading 10-9 in the 38th minute when Jonny Wilkinson missed an eminently kickable 24 metre penalty goal attempt; The Lions were losing 16-10 just before half-time; The Lions were losing 16-13 at half-time; Scott Quinnell went off injured at half-time, being replaced by Colin Charvis; The Lions were still losing 16-13 in the 42nd minute when Jonny Wilkinson scored after he wrong-footed Toutai Kefu with a brilliant sidestep; The Lions were leading 20-16 in the 50th minute when a poor defensive alignment allowed Daniel Herbert to score, thus 7 points were preventable; The Lions were drawing 23-23 in the 53rd minute; The Lions were still drawing 23-23 midway through the second half when Jonny Wilkinson missed another eminently kickable 24 metre penalty goal attempt; The Lions were drawing 23-23 in the 62nd minute when they created and then squandered an overlap; The Lions were losing 26-23 in the 69th minute; Iain Balshaw came on as a replacement for Dafydd James with 6 minutes of normal time remaining; The Lions were still losing 26-23 in the first minute of injury time; The Lions were losing 29-23 in the third minute of injury time when they were awarded a lineout 10 metres from the Australian line, but Justin Harrison then managed to steal the ball off Martin Johnson; The Lions were still losing 29-23 in the fifth minute of injury time when they created and then squandered another overlap with the last move of the match; Colin Charvis had a poor game; Jason Robinson scored 10 tries on the tour)

RICOH SOUTHERN HEMISPHERE UNDER 21 RUGBY CHAMPIONSHIP

Sydney Showground, Sydney Olympic Park, Homebush Bay, Sydney

CAPTAIN: *Mark Tucker*

First Round - Pool 'A'

20th Jun	IRELAND U21	10	**ENGLAND U21**	15

[This match kicked off at 3.00pm; Nick Cox played for England in the U19 World Championship in Chile in April 2001; Andy Higgins (2) was capped for England Schools 18 Group in January 1999]

(The England U21 players had insufficient time to shake off their jet lag; The England U21 forwards could not win any possession; England U21 were losing 3-0 in the 8th minute; England U21 were leading 5-3 when Sean Marsden saved a certain try by tap-tackling Brian O'Riordan; England U21 were leading 12-3 just before half-time; England U21 were leading 15-3 at half-time; England U21 were leading 15-10 in the 54th minute; England U21 were still leading 15-10 midway through the second half)

23rd Jun NEW ZEALAND U21 63 **ENGLAND U21** 3
[*This match kicked off at 4.00pm; Richie McCaw and Riki Flutey played for New Zealand U21 in this match*]
(*The England U21 forwards could not win any lineout ball; England U21 were losing 32-3 at half-time; New Zealand U21 were allowed to score 31 unanswered points in the second half to seal the match; Charlie Hodgson and Andy Higgins (2) injured playing in the match*)
27th Jun ARGENTINA U21 26 **ENGLAND U21** 42 **BP**
[*This match kicked off at 3.00pm; England's bonus point enabled them to finish second in Pool 'A'*]
(*England U21 were leading 22-0 just before half-time; England U21 were leading 22-7 at half-time; England U21 were leading 22-19 early in the second half*)
Third Place Play-Off
30th Jun FRANCE U21 36 **ENGLAND U21** 6
[*This match kicked off at 1.00pm; Imanol Harinordoquy played for France U21 in this match*]
(*England U21 were losing 14-6 at half-time; France U21 were allowed to score 22 unanswered points in the second half to seal the match*)

TUSKER SAFARI SEVENS

RFU of East Africa Ground, Ngong Road, Nairobi
CAPTAIN: *??*
First Round - Pool 'B'
23rd Jun ZAMBIA L **ENGLAND STUDENTS U21** W
[*This match kicked off at 11.40am; England Students U21 were also billed as England Students, English Universities, England Universities and England Universities Select!*]
23rd Jun TANZANIA L **ENGLAND STUDENTS U21** W
[*This match kicked off at 1.00pm*]
23rd Jun KENYA 10 **ENGLAND STUDENTS U21** 15
[*This match kicked off at 5.00pm*]
Quarter-Final
24th Jun UGANDA 12 **ENGLAND STUDENTS U21** 35
[No match notes]
Semi-Final
24th Jun Bristol University Select 31 **ENGLAND STUDENTS U21** 7
[No match notes]

CWMTAWE SEVENS

Pontardawe RFC, Parc Ynysderw, Ynysderw Road, Pontardawe, Swansea
CAPTAIN: *Howard Graham*
First Round - Pool 'D'
4th Aug Brynamman (*WA*) 0 **SAMURAI** 47
[No match notes]
4th Aug Abercrave (*WA*) 0 **SAMURAI** 45
[No match notes]
4th Aug Llandovery (*WA*) 0 **SAMURAI** 40
[No match notes]

Quarter-Final

4th Aug Neath (*WA*) 10 **SAMURAI** 45

[No match notes]

Semi-Final

4th Aug Swansea (*WA*) 12 **SAMURAI** 33

[No match notes]

Final

4th Aug Samurai-Ecosse 15 **SAMURAI** 28

[*This match kicked off at 6.30pm; Samurai International RFC teamed up with Rugby Ecosse Legends to enter a 2nd VII; Spencer Bromley and Will Kershaw-Naylor both played for Samurai-Ecosse in this match*]

(*Emosi Naisaramaki scored 2 brilliant long-range tries in this match; Emosi Naisaramaki had a brilliant game*)

WORLD GAMES SEVENS

Yabase Stadium, Akita City, Japan

CAPTAIN: *Mark Lee* (SC)

Preliminary League - Pool 'B'

25th Aug AUSTRALIA 31 **GREAT BRITAIN** 0

[*This match kicked off at 10.50am*]

(*Great Britain were losing 10-0 at half-time*)

25th Aug SOUTH AFRICA 43 **GREAT BRITAIN** 5

[*This match kicked off at 1.25pm*]

(*Great Britain were losing 22-0 at half-time*)

25th Aug JAPAN 38 **GREAT BRITAIN** 7

[*This match kicked off at 2.55pm*]

(*Great Britain were losing 14-7 at half-time; Japan were allowed to score 24 unanswered points in the second half to clinch the match*)

First Round

26th Aug FIJI 35 **GREAT BRITAIN** 0

[*This match kicked off at 10.00am*]

(*Great Britain were losing 21-0 at half-time*)

Consolation Match

26th Aug SOUTH AFRICA 22 **GREAT BRITAIN*** 19

[*This match kicked off at 12.10pm*]

(*Great Britain were losing 12-7 at half-time; Great Britain were leading 19-17 in the last minute when Marius Schoeman scored to win the match for South Africa*)

7th/8th Place Play-Off

26th Aug JAPAN 19 **GREAT BRITAIN** 21

[*This match kicked off at 2.05pm*]

(*Great Britain were leading 14-7 at half-time; Great Britain were leading 21-7 at one point in the second half; Great Britain were leading 21-14 in the last minute*)

AUSTRALIAN TOUR TO ENGLAND, SPAIN, FRANCE AND WALES 2001

CAPTAIN: *Dave Sims*

28th Oct	**ENGLISH NATIONAL DIVISIONS XV**	22	AUSTRALIA XV	34

Welford Road, Leicester

[This match kicked off at 2.30pm; Ben Clarke unavailable after he announced that he no longer wished to be considered for selection to England representative teams; Chris Johnson selected (1) as captain in the original squad of 22 but withdrew due to injury, being replaced by Sam Blythe; Jim Thorp, Martin Haag and Charlie Harrison in original squad of 22 but withdrew due to injury, being replaced by Nick Lloyd, Julian Hyde and Alex Birkby respectively; Chris Ritchie played for the White Hart Marauders at the Dubai Rugby Sevens on 4th-5th December 1997; Rob Baxter was the son of John Baxter and was capped for England Colts in April 1990; Richard Baxter was the brother of Rob Baxter and the son of John Baxter; Simon Binns was capped for England Schools 18 Group in February 1993; Harvey Thorneycroft played for M.R. Steele-Bodger's XV against Cambridge University at Grange Road on 27th November 2002; George Truelove was capped for England Schools 18 Group in February 1995; Julian Hyde played for M.R. Steele-Bodger's XV against Cambridge University at Grange Road on 28th November 2001; Phil Greaves was capped for England Colts in April 1997; Leigh Hinton had played for Wales U19 but was now qualified to play for England]

(The English National Divisions XV only had one training session before this match!; The English National Divisions XV forwards could not win any lineout ball; Daniel Herbert scored in the 5th minute!; The English National Divisions XV was losing 7-0 midway through the first half; The English National Divisions XV was losing 14-0 in the 25th minute; The English National Divisions XV was losing 17-6 shortly before half-time; The English National Divisions XV was losing 20-6 at half-time; The English National Divisions XV was losing 27-6 in the 48th minute; The English National Divisions XV was losing 27-9 in the 62nd minute when Simon Binns scored a brilliant drop goal; The English National Divisions XV was losing 27-15 in the 68th minute; The English National Divisions XV was losing 34-15 with 2 minutes remaining when Phil Greaves scored after Simon Binns put in a superb grubber kick; Richard Baxter and Simon Binns both had a brilliant game)

REMEMBRANCE MATCH

CAPTAIN: *Andy Gomarsall*

6th Nov	COMBINED SERVICES (*SER*)	14	**BARBARIANS**	50

United Services Recreation Ground, Burnaby Road, Portsmouth

[This match kicked off at 6.00pm; Martyn Madden selected but withdrew, being replaced by John Davies; Mark Ellis selected but withdrew, being replaced by Hedley Verity who then himself withdrew due to injury and was replaced by Julian Horrobin; Andy Powell selected but withdrew, being replaced by Richard Baxter; Alastair Murdock selected but withdrew, being replaced by Duncan Roke; John Lawn selected for bench but withdrew, being replaced by Andy Cuthbert; Dwayne Peel selected for bench but withdrew, being replaced by Dale Burn; Peter Buxton was capped for England Schools 18 Group in March 1996; Brendon Daniel played for the New Zealand Sevens team in March 1997; Warwick Bullock played for M.R. Steele-Bodger's XV against Cambridge University at Grange Road on 28th November 2001; Lee Soper, Dan

Coen and Mal Roberts played for the Combined Services in this match, with Mal Roberts scoring a try and Coen scoring a conversion]
(***The Barbarians were losing 7-0 in the 13th minute; The Barbarians were leading 17-7 when some superb handling allowed Ian Calder to score; The Barbarians were leading 24-7 at half-time; The Barbarians were still leading 24-7 midway through the second half; The Barbarians were leading 24-7 in the 65th minute when Rory Greenslade-Jones intercepted the ball and went on to score, thus 7 points were preventable; The Barbarians scored 26 unanswered points in the last 10 minutes to seal the match***)

EMIRATES AIRLINE DUBAI RUGBY SEVENS

Dubai Exiles Stadium, Dubai

CAPTAIN: *No captain appointed*

8th Nov *No opponents named* C **ENGLAND** C

[***This Round was scheduled for 8th-9th November 2001 but was cancelled by the IRB on 16th October 2001 due to fears over terrorist activity in the Middle East; Ironically the Dubai Exiles RFC held their annual International Invitation Rugby Sevens at the same venue between 7th-9th November 2001 without any problems!; England withdrew from this International Invitation Rugby Sevens on 21st October 2001***]

ROMANIAN TOUR TO ENGLAND 2001

CAPTAIN: *Howard Quigley*

8th Nov **ENGLAND STUDENTS*** 11 ROMANIA XV 21

University Football Ground, Grange Road, Cambridge

[***This match kicked off at 7.15pm; Peter Short and Adam Balding unavailable for this match due to club commitments; Chris Collins, Ed Mallett, Simon Amor and Alastair Newmarch unavailable due to Varsity Match commitments; Danny Porte played for M.R. Steele-Bodger's XV against Cambridge University at Grange Road on 28th November 2001; Phil Greenaway was capped for England Colts in March 1998; Romania beat the Combined Services 28-15 at Portsmouth on 12th November 2001, with Nick Bartlett, Lee Soper and Matt Cornish all playing for the Combined Services***]
(***This match was played in extremely cold conditions; England Students were drawing 0-0 midway through the first half; England Students were still drawing 0-0 shortly before half-time; England Students were leading 3-0 at half-time; England Students were losing 7-3 in the 42nd minute when Rob Hunt came on as a replacement for Chris Borrett; England Students were losing 14-3 in the 57th minute; Romania were allowed to score 14 unanswered points to win the match; England Students were losing 14-8 midway through the second half; England Students were losing 14-11 in the 68th minute; England Students were losing 21-11 in the 69th minute***)

AUSTRALIAN TOUR TO ENGLAND, SPAIN, FRANCE AND WALES 2001

CAPTAIN: *Neil Back*

10th Nov **ENGLAND** 21 AUSTRALIA 15

Twickenham

[***This match kicked off at 2.30pm; Martin Johnson, Lawrence Dallaglio and Martin Corry unavailable due to injury; Matt Dawson in original training squad of 26 but withdrew due to injury; Julian White, Steve Thompson (2) and Henry Paul in original training squad of 26 but were not selected for team or bench***]
(***Ben Kay and Danny Grewcock dominated the lineout in the first half; Jonny Wilkinson***

***scored a brilliant 49 metre penalty goal in the 4th minute!; England were leading 3-0 in the 6th minute when Jonny Wilkinson missed a difficult 42 metre penalty goal attempt; England were leading 6-0 in the 15th minute when Jonny Wilkinson scored a brilliant 29 metre drop goal; England were leading 12-0 midway through the first half; England were still leading 12-0 in the 23rd minute when George Smith's last-ditch tackle momentarily unbalanced Dan Luger, who then elected to pass to Joe Worsley instead of attempting to create enough momentum to make the nearby line himself; England were leading 12-0 in the 34th minute when Jason Robinson broke through but was then superbly tackled by Nathan Grey; England were still leading 12-0 in the 37th minute when Jonny Wilkinson had a kickable 29 metre drop goal attempt charged down by Stephen Larkham; England were leading 12-0 in the 39th minute when Mike Catt had a speculative 45 metre drop goal attempt charged down by George Smith; England scored 15 unanswered points to win the match; England were leading 15-0 at half-time; England were still leading 15-0 in the 44th minute when Mike Catt missed another speculative 37 metre drop goal attempt; England were leading 15-0 in the 49th minute when Matt Burke scored after a poor tackle by Jason Robinson, thus 7 points were preventable; England were leading 15-10 in the 54th minute; England were leading 18-10 midway through the second half when Jonny Wilkinson missed a kickable 38 metre penalty goal attempt; England were leading 21-10 in the 70th minute when Jason Robinson took a quick lineout and ran 38 metres before he was tackled as he looked in vain for support; Immediately afterwards Mike Catt brilliantly flicked the ball between his legs so that Will Greenwood could put in a clearance kick to touch!; England were leading 21-10 with 5 minutes of normal time remaining; Jonny Wilkinson scored all of England's 21 points in this match; Graham Rowntree, Ben Kay and Kyran Bracken all had a brilliant game*)**

EMIRATES AIRLINE SOUTH AFRICA SEVENS

ABSA Stadium, Durban

CAPTAIN: *Pat Sanderson*

First Round - Pool 'A'

17th Nov	ARABIAN GULF	14	**ENGLAND**	38

[*This match kicked off at 11.22am; Arabian Gulf also billed as the United Arab Emirates*]

17th Nov	GEORGIA	0	**ENGLAND**	34

[*This match kicked off at 2.28pm*]

17th Nov	NEW ZEALAND	28	**ENGLAND**	0

[*This match kicked off at 7.30pm*]

Quarter-Final

18th Nov	AUSTRALIA	7	**ENGLAND**	27

[No match notes]

Semi-Final

18th Nov	SAMOA	24	**ENGLAND**	7

[No match notes]

ROMANIAN TOUR TO ENGLAND 2001

CAPTAIN: *Neil Back* [*Kyran Bracken*]

17th Nov	**ENGLAND**	134	ROMANIA	0

Twickenham

[*This match kicked off at 2.30pm; Lawrence Dallaglio, Martin Corry and Matt Dawson*

***unavailable due to injury; Martin Johnson was rested for this match; David Flatman, Steve Thompson (2), Phil Vickery, Richard Hill (2), Hall Charlton, Harry Ellis, Henry Paul and Matt Perry all in original training squad of 30 but were not selected for team or bench; Tom Palmer (2) was added to the squad on 12th November 2001 to provide injury cover for Steve Borthwick; Jason Leonard set a new world record for a forward by winning his 93rd cap for England and the British & Irish Lions*]**

(*Charlie Hodgson scored a brilliant 40 metre penalty goal in the 3rd minute!; England were leading 6-0 in the 11th minute when Ben Cohen scored after the Romanian forwards were driven off their own ball at a five metre scrum; England were leading 25-0 midway through the first half; England were still leading 25-0 in the 26th minute when Austin Healey took a quick tap penalty and scored; England were leading 51-0 in the 36th minute; England were leading 58-0 in the first minute of first half injury time when Jason Robinson scored a superb 64 metre solo try; England were leading 65-0 just before half-time; England were leading 72-0 at half-time; Alex Sanderson and Kyran Bracken came on as replacements for Neil Back and Austin Healey respectively at the start of the second half; England were leading 82-0 in the 51st minute; England were leading 103-0 midway through the second half; England were still leading 103-0 in the 64th minute when Mark Regan scored from a rolling maul; England were leading 122-0 with 9 minutes remaining; England were leading 129-0 in the final minute when Dan Luger scored in the corner with the last move of the match to give Charlie Hodgson a chance of beating Simon Culhane's existing world record of 45 points in a cap international game, but Charlie Hodgson then had the difficult conversion attempt come back off the left-hand post!; Jason Robinson scored 20 points in this match; Ben Kay had a brilliant game; Charlie Hodgson played brilliantly and set a new England record of 44 points in a cap international match; England achieved their highest ever points total without reply in a cap international match, set a new scoring record of 134 points in an England cap international match and recorded the biggest winning margin in the history of international rugby!*)

FIJIIAN TOUR TO ITALY AND FRANCE 2001

CAPTAIN: *Olivier Roumat* (FR)

17th Nov **FRENCH BARBARIANS*** 15 FIJI XV 17

Stade Félix Mayol, Toulon

[*This match kicked off at 4.00pm; Barbarian RC founded 1979; Cédric Soulette selected but withdrew, Patrice Collazo was moved from the bench to the team and Sylvain Marconnet was then selected for the bench; Waisale Serevi captained the Fiji XV in this match*]

(*This match was played in cold and wet conditions; The French Barbarians were leading 3-0 in the 12th minute; The French Barbarians were still leading 3-0 midway through the first half; The French Barbarians were leading 10-0 in the 22nd minute; The French Barbarians were still leading 10-0 in the 33rd minute when collectively poor tackling allowed Waisale Serevi to score, thus 7 points were preventable; The French Barbarians were leading 10-7 shortly before half-time; The French Barbarians were drawing 10-10 at half-time; Sergei Sergueev came on as a replacement for Olivier Roumat in the 51st minute; The French Barbarians were losing 17-10 in the 54th minute; The French Barbarians were losing 17-15 midway through the second half; The Fiji XV was allowed to score 17 unanswered points to win the match; The French Barbarians were still losing 17-15 in injury time when Yann Delaigue missed a penalty goal attempt from in front of the posts!*)

SOUTH AFRICA 'A' TOUR TO ENGLAND 2001

CAPTAIN: *Dave Sims*

21st Nov **ENGLISH NATIONAL DIVISIONS XV** 9 SOUTH AFRICA A 33

Worcester RFC, Sixways Stadium, Pershore Lane, Hindip, Worcester

[*This match kicked off at 8.00pm; Russ Earnshaw, Dominic Chapman and Duncan Roke selected but withdrew, being replaced by Nathan Carter, Jamie Greenlees and Ed Jennings respectively; Gary Willis selected for bench but withdrew, being replaced by Matt Cornish; Rob Liley selected for bench but withdrew, being replaced by Steve Vile; Richard Davies in original squad of 22 but was withdrawn after he switched his allegiance to Wales; Jim Thorp, Chris Johnson (1) and Neil Spence in original squad of 22 but withdrew due to injury; Matt Cornish was capped for England Schools 18 Group in January 1995; Steve Vile became eligible to play for England in 2000 after qualifying through residency; Chris Ritchie played for M.R. Steele-Bodger's XV against Cambridge University at Grange Road on 27th November 2002; Dave Sims played for Major R.V. Stanley's XV against Oxford University at Iffley Road on both 14th November 2001 and 12th November 2003*]

(*The English National Divisions XV only had two days to prepare for this match; Gaffie du Toit scored a penalty goal in the 3rd minute!; The English National Divisions XV was drawing 3-3 in the 12th minute; The English National Divisions XV was losing 6-3 midway through the first half; The English National Divisions XV was still losing 6-3 in the 26th minute when Simon Binns' attempted clearance kick went straight to Ricardo Loubscher who instigated a counter-attack which led directly to a try by Marius Joubert, thus 5 points were preventable; The English National Divisions XV was losing 11-3 shortly before half-time when Simon Binns missed a penalty goal attempt; The English National Divisions XV was losing 11-3 at half-time; The English National Divisions XV was losing 11-6 in the 43rd minute; The English National Divisions XV was losing 11-9 in the 57th minute; The English National Divisions XV was losing 14-9 midway through the second half; The English National Divisions XV was losing 21-9 in the 69th minute; The English National Divisions XV was losing 28-9 in the second minute of injury time; South Africa A were allowed to score 22 unanswered points to clinch the match*)

SOUTH AFRICAN TOUR TO FRANCE, ITALY AND ENGLAND 2001

CAPTAIN: *Martin Johnson*

24th Nov **ENGLAND** 29 SOUTH AFRICA 9

Twickenham

[*This match kicked off at 2.30pm; Lawrence Dallaglio, Martin Corry and Matt Dawson unavailable due to injury*]

**(*England were leading 3-0 in the 7th minute; England were drawing 3-3 midway through the first half; England were still drawing 3-3 in the 23rd minute when Dorian West wasted a great try-scoring opportunity by cutting back inside when there was an overlap outside him; England were leading 6-3 in the 25th minute; England were still leading 6-3 in the 40th minute; England were drawing 6-6 in the fourth minute of first half injury time; England were leading 9-6 at half-time; England were still leading 9-6 in the 46th minute when Kyran Bracken crossed the tryline but then could not get downward pressure on the ball; England were leading 15-6 in the 53rd minute; Richard Hill (2) went off injured in the 58th minute, being replaced by Lewis Moody; England*

were still leading 15-6 midway through the second half when Mike Catt scored a brilliant 27 metre drop goal; England were leading 21-9 in the 66th minute; England were leading 24-9 with 7 minutes of normal time remaining; Mike Catt went off injured with 2 minutes of normal time remaining, being replaced by Mike Tindall; England were still leading 24-9 in the second minute of injury time when Dan Luger saved a certain try by managing to get beneath the ball as Victor Matfield attempted to ground it; England were leading 24-9 in the sixth minute of injury time when Dan Luger intercepted Bobby Skinstad's pass and ran 93 metres to score in the corner with the last move of the match, with Jonny Wilkinson then hitting the left-hand post with the eminently kickable conversion attempt; Neil Back injured playing in the match; Jonny Wilkinson played brilliantly and scored 21 points in this match; Joe Worsley had a brilliant game; England achieved their greatest ever margin of victory over South Africa!)

AUSTRALIAN TOUR TO ENGLAND, SPAIN, FRANCE AND WALES 2001

CAPTAIN: *Rob Howley* (WA)

28th Nov **BARBARIANS*** 35 AUSTRALIA XV 49

Millennium Stadium, Cardiff

[*This match kicked off at 7.15pm; John Eales chose not to come out of retirement to play for the Barbarians in this match; Neil Back unavailable due to injury; The Millennium Stadium had its retractable roof closed for this match*]

(This match was played in cold conditions; The Barbarians were drawing 0-0 in the 4th minute when Raphäel Ibañez had a great try-scoring chance but was tackled just short of the Australia XV line by Elton Flatley; Stefan Terblanche missed a speculative 39 metre drop goal attempt immediately afterwards!; The Barbarians were still drawing 0-0 in the 9th minute when Breyton Paulse fly-hacked a loose ball on before regathering it to score a brilliant try; The Barbarians were leading 7-0 in the 15th minute when Stéphane Glas scored after Pat Howard threw a brilliant pass; The Barbarians were leading 14-0 midway through the first half; The Barbarians were leading 14-7 in the 24th minute when George Gregan kicked ahead, Percy Montgomery unaccountably allowed the ball to stay infield and Chris Latham then followed up and volleyed it on, which enabled the Australian XV to create an attacking platform that culminated in a try by Elton Flatley, thus 7 points were preventable; The Barbarians were drawing 14-14 in the 30th minute when Breyton Paulse scored after Darren Morris put in a superb chip-kick; The Barbarians were leading 21-14 in the 33rd minute; The Barbarians were losing 28-21 just before half-time; The Barbarians were losing 35-21 at half-time; Richard Cockerill came on as a replacement for Raphäel Ibañez at the start of the second half; The Barbarians were still losing 35-21 in the 49th minute when the referee inexplicably allowed play to continue after Manny Edmonds threw a clear forward pass to Chris Latham and Ben Tune went on to score, thus 7 points were unlawful; Mat Rogers came on as a replacement for Stéphane Glas in the 50th minute; The Barbarians were losing 42-21 in the 58th minute when Rob Howley kicked ahead and followed up unchallenged to the Australian XV 10 metre line, but then mishit the ball as he attempted to fly-hack it on; The Barbarians were losing 49-21 midway through the second half; The Australian XV was allowed to score 35 unanswered points to win the match; The Barbarians were still losing 49-21 with 7 minutes remaining when Pat Lam scored after Craig Dowd brilliantly chipped ahead into space; The Barbarians

***were losing 49-28 with 5 minutes remaining when Breyton Paulse scored a 61 metre interception try to complete a hat-trick*)**

ENGLAND U21 MATCH

CAPTAIN: *Alex Page*

19th Dec WALES U21 A XV 21 **ENGLAND U21 A XV*** 21

Sardis Road, Pwllgwaun, Pontypridd

[*This match kicked off at 7.15pm; James Forrester in original squad of 22 but withdrew due to club commitments, being replaced by Simon Cross; Mark Soden in original squad of 22 but withdrew, being replaced by Matt Styles; Johnny Roddam selected but withdrew to sit on the bench, James Buckland was moved from the bench to the team; Alex Alesbrook selected but withdrew, Matt Styles was moved from the bench to the team and Darren Fox was then selected for the bench; Andy Springgay played for England in the U19 World Championship in France in April 2000; Matt Styles, Michael Holford and Matt Parr played for England in the U19 World Championship in Chile in April 2001; Ed Thrower played for England in the U19 World Championship in Chile in April 2001 and toured Canada, New Zealand and Australia with England Schools 18 Group in July-August 2001*]

(*The England U21 A XV was losing 3-0 in the early stages; Ed Thrower intercepted the ball and ran 50 metres to score a try which he then converted to give the England U21 A XV an 18-3 lead; The England U21 A XV was leading 21-6 at half-time; The England U21 A XV was leading 21-9 early in the second half; The England U21 A XV was leading 21-16 in the closing stages; The Wales U21 A XV was allowed to score 15 unanswered points in the second half to draw the match; The referee allowed 6 minutes of injury time to be played*)

2002

CERVEZA CRISTAL SANTIAGO SEVENS

Estadio San Carlos de Apoquindo, Santiago

CAPTAIN: *Mike Friday*

First Round - Pool 'C'

4th Jan URUGUAY 0 **ENGLAND** 54

[*This match kicked off at 2.52pm*]

4th Jan FRANCE 17 **ENGLAND** 15

[*This match kicked off at 5.58pm*]

(*Mike Friday was sent to the sin-bin in this match*)

4th Jan SOUTH AFRICA 7 **ENGLAND** 12

[*This match kicked off at 10.30pm*]

CAPTAIN: *??*

Quarter-Final

5th Jan FIJI 36 **ENGLAND** 7

[*This match kicked off at 5.50pm; Mike Friday and Richard Haughton unavailable due to injury*]

[Plate Semi-Final:]

[5th Jan AUSTRALIA 7 **ENGLAND** 15 **]**

[*This match kicked off at 8.34pm; Mike Friday and Richard Haughton unavailable due to injury*]

[Plate Final:]

[5th Jan SAMOA 21 **ENGLAND** 12 **]**

[*This match kicked off at 11.30pm; Mike Friday and Richard Haughton unavailable due to injury*]

(*England were leading 12-7 at half-time; Samoa were allowed to score 14 unanswered points in the second half to win the match*)

MAR DEL PLATA SEVENS

Estadio José Maria Minella, Mar del Plata

CAPTAIN: *Mike Friday*

First Round - Pool 'B'

11th Jan PARAGUAY 0 **ENGLAND** 45

[*This match kicked off at 5.04pm*]

11th Jan CHILE 0 **ENGLAND** 43

[*This match kicked off at 8.10pm*]

(*Ben Gollings scored 28 points in this match*)

11th Jan AUSTRALIA 12 **ENGLAND*** 7

[*This match kicked off at 11.36pm*]

(*Australia scored a last-minute try to win the match*)

Quarter-Final

12th Jan NEW ZEALAND 26 **ENGLAND** 5

[*This match kicked off at 4.28pm*]

(*England were losing 7-0 at half-time; England were losing 7-5 at one point in the second half; New Zealand were allowed to score 19 unanswered points to clinch the match*)

[Plate Semi-Final:]

[12th Jan SAMOA 12 **ENGLAND** 19 **]**

[This match kicked off at 7.34pm]

[Plate Final:]

[12th Jan AUSTRALIA 15 **ENGLAND*** 12 aet**]**

[This match kicked off at 10.30pm]

(England were leading 12-7 in the last minute of normal time; England were drawing 12-12 in the sixth minute of sudden death extra time when Tim Walsh scored a 30 metre penalty goal to win the match for Australia; Ben Gollings scored 58 points in the competition)

6 NATIONS CHAMPIONSHIP

CAPTAIN: *Martin Johnson*

2nd Feb SCOTLAND 3 **ENGLAND** 29

Murrayfield

[This match kicked off at 4.00pm; Phil Greening, Lawrence Dallaglio and Matt Dawson unavailable due to injury; Dorian West, Phil Vickery, Lewis Moody and Dan Luger all in original training squad of 30 but withdrew due to injury; Declan Danaher, Nick Walshe, Mike Catt, Henry Paul and Matt Perry all in original training of 30 but were not selected for team or bench; David Flatman and Ricky Nebbett were added to the squad on 16th January 2002]

(This match was played on a wet pitch; England played with the wind in the first half; England were drawing 0-0 in the 9th minute when some superb handling amongst the backs allowed Jason Robinson to score; Jason Robinson scored a superb try which Jonny Wilkinson then brilliantly converted from the left touchline to give England a 12-0 lead in the 14th minute; England were still leading 12-0 midway through the first half; England were leading 12-0 in the 22nd minute when Jonny Wilkinson put up a brilliant cross-kick, but Mike Tindall was then deceived by the bounce of the ball while the Scottish tryline was at his mercy; England were leading 12-3 in the 29th minute; England were leading 12-3 at half-time; Kyran Bracken went off injured at half-time, being replaced by Nick Duncombe; England were still leading 12-3 in the 50th minute when Mike Tindall chipped ahead and followed up to score a superb try; England were leading 19-3 midway through the second half; England were still leading 19-3 in the 67th minute when Jonny Wilkinson scored a brilliant 48 metre penalty goal from a difficult angle; Iain Balshaw came on as a replacement for Mike Tindall with 7 minutes of normal time remaining, with Jason Robinson then switching from full back to centre to accommodate Balshaw; Jonny Wilkinson went off injured in the fifth minute of injury time, being replaced by Charlie Hodgson; England were leading 22-3 in the seventh minute of injury time when Ben Cohen powered through to score a try which Charlie Hodgson then brilliantly converted from the left touchline; England scored 17 unanswered points in the second half to seal the match; Steve Thompson (2) and Will Greenwood both had a brilliant game)

16th Feb **ENGLAND** 45 IRELAND 11

Twickenham

[This match kicked off at 2.30pm; Lawrence Dallaglio, Matt Dawson and Dan Luger unavailable due to injury; Martin Corry in original training squad of 30 but withdrew due to injury; Mark Regan, Julian White, Declan Danaher, Mike Catt, Henry Paul, Mark Cueto and Matt Perry all in original training squad of 30 but were not selected for team

***or bench; Jason Leonard set a new world record for a forward by winning his 100th cap for England and the British & Irish Lions; England moved to the top of the Zurich World Rankings after this match*]**

(*The England forwards monopolised possession in the first half; England were losing 3-0 in the 9th minute; England were drawing 3-3 in the 12th minute; Graham Rowntree went off injured in the 17th minute, being replaced by Jason Leonard; England were still drawing 3-3 midway through the first half; England were drawing 3-3 in the 23rd minute when some superb handling allowed Jonny Wilkinson to score; England were leading 10-3 in the 25th minute when Ben Cohen scored after Austin Healey instigated a brilliant 81 metre counter-attack; England were leading 17-6 in the 29th minute; England were leading 24-6 in the 36th minute when Austin Healey crossed the tryline but then lost the ball in the act of scoring; England were leading 29-6 just before half-time when Jonny Wilkinson scored a brilliant conversion from the left touchline; England were leading 31-6 at half-time; England were still leading 31-6 in the 45th minute when Ben Kay ran 33 metres to score after Jonny Wilkinson threw a superb inside pass; England were leading 38-6 in the 56th minute when Will Greenwood scored a brilliant try; England scored 28 unanswered points to seal the match; England were leading 45-6 midway through the second half when a poor defensive alignment allowed Ronan O'Gara to score, thus 5 points were preventable; Martin Johnson went off due to illness in the 61st minute, being replaced by Danny Grewcock; Nick Duncombe came on as a replacement for Kyran Bracken with 1 minute of normal time remaining; Jonny Wilkinson played brilliantly and scored 20 points in this match; England won their 14th successive cap international match at Twickenham to break the existing record which had been set way back in 1924!*)

2nd Mar FRANCE 20 **ENGLAND*** 15

Stade de France, Paris

[*This match kicked off at 3.00pm; Lewis Moody, Lawrence Dallaglio, Dave Walder, Charlie Hodgson, Mike Catt and Tim Stimpson all unavailable due to injury; On 22nd February 2002 a RFU hearing found Martin Johnson guilty of punching an opponent in a Leicester club game on 9th February 2002 and thus banned him for 3 weeks, but the RFU then allowed Martin Johnson to play in this match after he appealed against this decision on the grounds that the offence had already been dealt with at the time by the referee who gave him a yellow card; Henry Paul had an English grandparent and never played for New Zealand at Rugby Union; Henry Paul won the last of his 23 caps for New Zealand at Rugby League in July 2001 and returned to Rugby Union in October 2001*]

**(*The referee unaccountably allowed Serge Betsen to be consistently offside; England were losing 7-0 in the 10th minute; England were losing 7-0 in the 18th minute when Jason Robinson was famously wrapped up and driven back 10 metres by Aurélien Rougerie, which led directly to a try by Imanol Harinordoquy, thus 7 points were preventable; England were losing 14-0 midway through the first half; England were still losing 14-0 in the 26th minute when Mike Tindall saved a certain try by tackling Pieter de Villiers; England were losing 14-0 in the 34th minute when Jonny Wilkinson missed a difficult 24 metre drop goal attempt; England were losing 17-0 in the 37th minute; France were allowed to score 17 unanswered points to win the match; Mike Tindall went off injured in the 40th minute, being replaced by Henry Paul; England were losing 17-0 in the sixth minute of first half injury time when Jason Robinson scored under the posts after he wrong-footed the French defence with a brilliant sidestep; England were losing 17-7 at half-time; England were losing 17-10 in the 43rd minute; Martin Corry came on as a temporary blood replacement for Neil Back in the*

***47th minute; England were still losing 17-10 in the 51st minute when Will Greenwood made a brilliant break, but his intended scoring pass was then dropped by Kyran Bracken; England were losing 20-10 midway through the second half; Jonny Wilkinson went off injured with 5 minutes of normal time remaining, being replaced by Dan Luger with Austin Healey then switching from wing to fly half to accommodate Luger; England were still losing 20-10 in the sixth minute of injury time when Austin Healey put up a superb cross-kick which enabled Ben Cohen to score a consolation try with the last move of the match; Will Greenwood had a brilliant game; Joe Worsley, Kyran Bracken and Henry Paul all had a poor game*)**

CAPTAIN: *Neil Back*

23rd Mar **ENGLAND** 50 WALES 10

Twickenham

[*This match kicked off at 2.30pm; Mike Catt and Matt Perry unavailable due to injury; Martin Johnson unavailable after his appeal against a 3 week suspension was turned down by a RFU hearing on 5th March 2002; Lawrence Dallaglio was rested for this match; Charlie Hodgson selected for bench but withdrew due to injury, being replaced by Iain Balshaw; Tim Stimpson was added to the squad on 18th March 2002 to provide injury cover for Jason Robinson; Phil Vickery and Jason Robinson in original training squad of 27 but withdrew due to injury; Mark Regan, Steve Borthwick and Nick Duncombe in original training squad of 27 but were not selected for team or bench*]

(*The England forwards monopolised possession in this match; England were leading 3-0 in the 6th minute; England were still leading 3-0 in the 11th minute when Will Greenwood scored after Jonny Wilkinson put in a brilliant chip-kick; England were leading 10-0 midway through the first half; England were leading 13-0 in the 23rd minute; England were leading 13-3 in the 31st minute; England were leading 16-3 just before half-time; England were leading 19-3 at half-time; England were leading 26-3 in the 45th minute; England were leading 29-3 in the 54th minute; England were still leading 29-3 midway through the second half; Tim Stimpson came on as a replacement for Mike Tindall in the 65th minute, with Austin Healey then switching from full back to centre to accommodate Stimpson; England were leading 36-3 in the 66th minute; England scored 30 unanswered points to seal the match; England were leading 43-3 with 7 minutes of normal time remaining; England were leading 43-10 in the sixth minute of injury time when Tim Stimpson powered through 2 attempted tackles to score; Jonny Wilkinson scored 30 points in this match and became the first England player to score 500 points in cap internationals; Danny Grewcock had a brilliant game; England achieved their greatest ever margin of victory over Wales!*)

CAPTAIN: *Neil Back* [*Martin Johnson*]

7th April ITALY 9 **ENGLAND** 45

Stadio Flaminio, Rome

[*This match kicked off at 4.00pm; Phil Vickery, Mike Catt and Matt Perry unavailable due to injury; The England replacements bench had 316 caps between them!*]

(*Jonny Wilkinson scored a penalty goal in the 3rd minute!; England were leading 10-3 in the 8th minute; England were still leading 10-3 in the 17th minute when Lewis Moody crossed the tryline but then lost the ball in the act of scoring; England were leading 10-3 midway through the first half; Martin Johnson came on as a temporary blood replacement for Danny Grewcock in the 20th minute; England were leading 17-3 in the 25th minute; England were still leading 17-3 in the 37th minute when Jason Robinson ghosted through to score a brilliant try; England were leading 24-3 at half-time; England were leading 24-9 in the 52nd minute; Four former England captains,*

***namely Jason Leonard, Martin Johnson, Lawrence Dallaglio and Matt Dawson, came on as replacements for Graham Rowntree, Danny Grewcock, Neil Back and Kyran Bracken respectively in the 56th minute!; England were still leading 24-9 midway through the second half when Lawrence Dallaglio scored with his first proper touch in international rugby for 12 months!; England were leading 31-9 in the 69th minute when Will Greenwood scored after Matt Dawson did a brilliant overhead kick at a tap penalty; Mike Tindall went off injured with 3 minutes of normal time remaining, being replaced by Charlie Hodgson with Jonny Wilkinson then switching from fly half to centre to accommodate Charlie Hodgson; England were leading 38-9 in the fourth minute of injury time when some superb handling amongst the backs allowed Austin Healey to score with the last move of the match; England scored 21 unanswered points to seal the match; Will Greenwood had a brilliant game*)**

ENGLAND STUDENTS MATCHES

CAPTAIN: *Scott Bemand*

1st Feb SCOTLAND STUDENTS 14 **ENGLAND STUDENTS** 19

Stewart's Melville FP RFC, Inverleith, Ferry Road, Edinburgh

[*This match kicked off at 2.00pm*]

(*This match was played on a slippery pitch; England Students were drawing 0-0 in the early stages when Simon Hunt scored after Ian Bulloch had his kick charged down; England Students were leading 7-3 in the 15th minute; England Students were leading 14-3 midway through the first half; England Students were leading 14-3 at half-time; England Students were leading 14-6 in the 49th minute; England Students were leading 14-11 with 8 minutes remaining when Kieran Roche scored to clinch the match*)

15th Feb **ENGLAND STUDENTS** 17 IRELAND STUDENTS 18

Bournemouth RFC, Chapel Gate, Parley Lane, Hurn, Christchurch

[*This match kicked off at 7.15pm*]

(*The England Students forwards could not win any lineout ball; Simon Hunt scored a brilliant try in the 5th minute!; England Students were losing 7-5 at half-time; England Students were still losing 7-5 early in the second half when Danny Porte scored from a rolling maul; England Students were losing 18-10 in the third minute of injury time when Simon Hunt scored a consolation try after James Brown put up a brilliant garryowen*)

CAPTAIN: *Matt Cairns*

1st Mar FRANCE STUDENTS 22 **ENGLAND STUDENTS** 15

Stade Léon Sausset, Tournon

[*This match kicked off at 7.00pm; Jake Niarchos selected but withdrew, being replaced by James Brown; Neil Hallett selected for bench but withdrew, being replaced by Rob Hoadley; Chris Wilkes in original squad of 23 but was not selected for team or bench*]

(*England Students were losing 7-0 in the 6th minute; England Students were losing 10-0 in the 14th minute; England Students were still losing 10-0 midway through the first half; England Students were losing 17-0 in the 23rd minute; France Students were allowed to score 17 unanswered points to win the match; England Students were losing 17-3 in the 31st minute; England Students were losing 17-3 at half-time; England Students were losing 22-3 in the 49th minute; England Students were still losing 22-3 midway through the second half; England Students were losing 22-3 with 1 minute of normal time remaining; England Students were losing 22-10 in the first minute of injury time*)

CAPTAIN: *Scott Bemand*

22nd Mar **ENGLAND STUDENTS** 35 WALES STUDENTS 6

Ashton Gate, Bristol

[This match kicked off at 5.15pm and was a curtain raiser game for the England A v Wales A match; Jonny Barrett played for Major R.V. Stanley's XV against Oxford University at Iffley Road on 12th November 2003]

(England Students were losing 3-0 in the 6th minute; England Students were losing 6-3 in the 15th minute when Alex Cadwallader scored a brilliant try; England Students were leading 10-6 midway through the first half; England Students were leading 13-6 in the 27th minute; England Students were leading 16-6 just before half-time when Ben Lewitt scored from a rolling maul; England Students were leading 21-6 at half-time; England Students were still leading 21-6 early in the second half when Ben Lewitt scored another try from a rolling maul; England Students were leading 28-6 midway through the second half; Ben Lewitt briefly left the field in the 62nd minute after receiving an injury when he was stamped on by Carl Hocking; England Students were leading 35-6 shortly afterwards; England Students scored 32 unanswered points to win the match)

U21 6 NATIONS CHAMPIONSHIP

CAPTAIN: *Mark Soden*

1st Feb SCOTLAND U21 16 **ENGLAND U21** 31

Dunbar RFC, Hallhill Healthy Living Centre, Kellie Road, Dunbar

[This match kicked off at 2.00pm; Poynder Park, Kelso was the original venue for this match but, with less than 12 hours to go before the scheduled 7.30pm kick-off, it was declared unplayable due to flooding; Simon Cross in original training squad of 28 but was not selected for team or bench; Mark Soden was capped for England Schools 18 Group in March 1998 and captained England at the U19 World Championship in France in April 2000; Jim Scaysbrook and Ollie Smith (2) played for England in the U19 World Championship in Chile in April 2001; Phil Davies (3) played for England in the U19 World Championship in France in April 2000; Jon Goodridge was capped as a fly half for England Schools 18 Group in March 1999]

(England U21 were losing 3-0 in the early stages; England U21 were drawing 3-3 in the 14th minute; Andy Higgins (2) went off injured in the 15th minute, being replaced by James Simpson-Daniel; England U21 were leading 10-3 in the 25th minute when Olly Barkley scored a brilliant solo try; England U21 were leading 17-6 at half-time; England U21 were leading 24-16 in the 67th minute; England U21 were still leading 24-16 with 5 minutes remaining when Olly Barkley scored to seal the match; Olly Barkley had a brilliant game)

15th Feb **ENGLAND U21** 28 IRELAND U21 23

Coundon Road, Coventry

[This match kicked off at 5.00pm; This match was switched from its original venue of Banbury RUFC for financial reasons; Michael Holford in original squad of 23 but was not selected for team or bench; Harry Ellis played for England in the U19 World Championship in Chile in April 2001]

(This match was played in extremely cold conditions; England U21 were losing 7-0 in the 12th minute; England U21 were still losing 7-0 midway through the first half; England U21 were losing 7-0 in the 26th minute when Alex Crockett scored a brilliant long-range solo try; England U21 were leading 13-10 at half-time; England U21 were leading 18-16 in the 55th minute; England U21 were losing 23-18 midway through the

second half when James Simpson-Daniel scored a brilliant try; England U21 were leading 25-23 when Olly Barkley scored a penalty goal to clinch the match)

1st Mar FRANCE U21 21 **ENGLAND U21*** 19

Stade de la Vallée du Cher, Tours

[This match kicked off at 7.30pm]

(This match was played in wet conditions; Olly Barkley scored a penalty goal in the 5th minute!; England U21 were drawing 3-3 in the 11th minute; England U21 were losing 6-3 midway through the first half; England U21 were leading 8-6 in the 32nd minute; England U21 were losing 9-8 at half-time; England U21 were leading 13-9 in the 46th minute; England U21 were drawing 16-16 in the 54th minute; England U21 were leading 19-16 midway through the second half; England U21 were still leading 19-16 with 7 minutes of normal time remaining)

22nd Mar **ENGLAND U21*** 35 WALES U21 36

Newbury RFC, Monks Lane, Newbury

[This match kicked off at 7.30pm; James Forrester unavailable due to injury; James Hamilton played for England in the U19 World Championship in Chile in April 2001]

(Michael Hook scored a penalty goal in the 2nd minute!; England U21 were losing 6-3 in the 7th minute; England U21 were leading 10-6 when Tom Voyce scored a brilliant try; England U21 were leading 22-16 at half-time; England U21 were leading 25-19 in the 47th minute; England U21 were leading 32-19 in the 56th minute; England U21 were leading 35-24 in the 68th minute; England U21 were leading 35-29 in the final minute of normal time when they conceded a penalty try after collapsing three successive scrums on their own line, with Michael Hook then kicking the conversion to win the match for Wales U21; England U21 were losing 36-35 in the third minute of injury time when Olly Barkley missed a long-range penalty goal attempt with the last kick of the match; Olly Barkley scored 20 points in this match)

6th April ITALY U21 15 **ENGLAND U21** 50

Stadio Santa Colomba, Benevento

[This match kicked off at 4.00pm]

(England U21 were leading 24-10 at half-time)

'A' INTERNATIONAL CHAMPIONSHIP

CAPTAIN: *Steve Borthwick*

1st Feb SCOTLAND A 6 **ENGLAND A*** 6

Stirling County RFC, Bridgehaugh Park, Stirling

[This match kicked off at 7.30pm; Tom Beim and Tim Stimpson unavailable due to injury; Dave Walder selected but withdrew on the day of the match due to injury, Andy Goode was moved from the bench to the team and Tom May was then selected for the bench; Trevor Woodman in original training squad of 26 but withdrew when he was banned for 6 weeks on 14th January 2002 after being found guilty of stamping in a Gloucester club match; Chris Fortey, Stuart Turner, Adam Eustace, Steve White-Cooper, James Forrester, Nick Duncombe, Harry Ellis, Olly Barkley, Leon Lloyd, Michael Stephenson, Paul Sackey and Tom Voyce all in original training squad of 26 but were not selected for team or bench; Andy Sheridan and Mike Shelley was added to the squad on 18th January 2002; Steve Hanley toured Argentina with England Colts in August 1998; Hall Charlton was capped for England Schools 18 Group in March 1998 and played for England Students]

(This match was played in heavy rain on a very muddy pitch; England A played with a strong wind in the first half; England A were drawing 0-0 in the early stages when

Andy Goode missed 2 penalty goal attempts in succession; England A were leading 3-0 in the 18th minute; England A were still leading 3-0 in the 23rd minute when Andy Goode hit the post with another penalty goal attempt; England A were leading 3-0 just before half-time; England A were leading 6-0 at half-time; England A were leading 6-3 in the 47th minute; England A were still leading 6-3 shortly afterwards when the strong wind prevented Andy Goode's 35 metre penalty goal attempt from actually reaching the posts!; England A were leading 6-3 midway through the second half; England A were drawing 6-6 in the 67th minute when Steve Hanley crossed the tryline but the move was disallowed because he was adjudged to have hit the corner flag before he grounded the ball; England A were still drawing 6-6 in the 69th minute when Andy Goode had a 40 metre penalty goal attempt which clearly went between the posts but the touch judges inexplicably failed to award it; England A were drawing 6-6 with 4 minutes remaining when Andy Goode missed a final penalty goal attempt)

CAPTAIN: *Nick Walshe*

15th Feb **ENGLAND A*** 18 IRELAND A 25

Franklin's Gardens, Northampton

[*This match kicked off at 8.00pm; Tom Beim and Tim Stimpson unavailable due to injury; Trevor Woodman unavailable due to suspension; Steve Borthwick and Dave Walder in original training squad of 23 but withdrew due to injury; Stuart Turner, Andy Long and Jamie Noon in original training squad of 23 but were not selected for team or bench; Andy Sheridan toured Australia with England Schools 18 Group in August 1997*]

(*England A were losing 3-0 in the 6th minute; England A were drawing 3-3 in the 12th minute when Paul Sackey knocked-on after Paul Burke hit the post with a penalty goal attempt, which allowed John Kelly to score from the resulting Ireland A scrum, thus 5 points were preventable; England A were losing 8-6 in the 26th minute; England A were losing 11-6 shortly before half-time when Alex Sanderson crossed the tryline but then could not get downward pressure on the ball; England A were losing 11-9 at half-time; England A were leading 15-11 in the 44th minute; England A were leading 18-14 midway through the second half when Henry Paul and Paul Sackey both saved a certain try by tackling Tyrone Howe; England A were leading 18-17 shortly afterwards when Andy Goode missed 3 penalty goal attempts in succession; England A were losing 22-18 in the 70th minute; England A were still losing 22-18 with 3 minutes remaining when Paul Burke scored a penalty goal to clinch the match for Ireland A*)

CAPTAIN: *Steve Borthwick*

1st Mar FRANCE A 19 **ENGLAND A*** 13

Parc Municipal des Sports de Beaublanc, Limoges

[*This match kicked off at 5.30pm; Dave Walder, Tom Beim and Tim Stimpson unavailable due to injury; Louis Deacon selected but withdrew on the morning of the match due to illness, Tom Palmer (2) was moved from the bench to the team and Andy Sheridan was then selected for the bench; Stuart Turner in original training squad of 24 but was not selected for team or bench; Phil Jones became a Rugby Union player in August 2001 when he joined Orrell; Sébastien Chabal played for France A in this match*]

(*Steve Borthwick dominated the lineout in this match; Andy Goode scored a penalty goal in the 2nd minute!; England A were leading 3-0 in the 11th minute when Olivier Sarramea intercepted the ball and scored, thus 7 points were preventable; England A were losing 7-3 midway through the first half; England A were still losing 7-3 in the 28th minute when they were awarded a penalty try; England A were leading 10-7 at*

half-time; England A were drawing 10-10 in the 49th minute; England A were still drawing 10-10 midway through the second half; England A were drawing 10-10 with 9 minutes of normal time remaining; England A were losing 13-10 with 5 minutes of normal time remaining when Phil Jones scored a penalty goal to bring the scores level; England A were losing 16-13 in the third minute of injury time when Romain Tuelet scored a drop goal to clinch the match for France A; Matt Dawson had a brilliant game)

22nd Mar **ENGLAND A*** 21 WALES A 29

Ashton Gate, Bristol

[*This match kicked off at 7.30pm; Andy Long, Pat Sanderson, Dave Walder, Tom Beim and Matt Perry all unavailable due to injury; Chris Fortey selected for bench but withdrew due to injury, being replaced by Mike Shelley; Louis Deacon and Ollie Smith (2) in original training squad of 24 but withdrew due to injury; Declan Danaher in original training squad of 24 but withdrew as he was now required to join an England Sevens training squad preparing for Hong Kong, being replaced by Paul Gustard; David Flatman, Mike Worsley, Stuart Turner, Alex Brown, Declan Danaher, Tom May, Paul Sackey and Tim Stimpson all in original training squad of 24 but were not selected for team or bench*]

(*The England A forwards dominated the lineout in this match; The England A scrum was put under severe pressure; Lee Jarvis scored a drop goal in the 2nd minute!; Tom Palmer (2) went off injured in the 7th minute having broken his leg and was replaced by Mark Cornwell; England A were leading 5-3 in the 8th minute; England A were losing 10-5 midway through the first half; England A were losing 13-5 in the 33rd minute when Mark Regan scored from a brilliant rolling maul; England A were losing 13-12 at half-time; England A were leading 18-13 in the 51st minute; England A were losing 23-18 in the 58th minute when Phil Jones scored a brilliant penalty goal; England A were losing 26-21 in the 63rd minute; England A were still losing 26-21 with 7 minutes remaining when Lee Jarvis scored a 30 metre penalty goal to clinch the match for Wales A*)

6th April ITALY A 22 **ENGLAND A*** 21

Stadio CUS Napoli, Naples

[*This match kicked off at 4.00pm; Pat Sanderson, Dave Walder and Matt Perry unavailable due to injury; Steve White-Cooper selected but withdrew, Ben Sturnham was moved from the bench to the team and Paul Gustard was then selected for the bench; Rob Hardwick retired in May 2006*]

(*England A were leading 3-0 in the 13th minute; England A were leading 6-0 midway through the first half; England A were still leading 6-0 in the 39th minute; England A were losing 7-6 in the fourth minute of first half injury time; England A were losing 10-6 at half-time; England A were leading 13-10 in the 57th minute when Francesco Mazzariol intercepted the ball and went on to score, thus 7 points were preventable; England A were losing 17-13 midway through the second half; England A were losing 22-13 in the 66th minute; England A were losing 22-16 in the 70th minute; Ben Gollings came on as a replacement for Dan Scarbrough with 6 minutes remaining; England A were losing 22-16 with 5 minutes remaining when Mark Cornwell scored a pushover try*)

BRISBANE WORLD RUGBY SEVENS

Ballymore Stadium, Brisbane

CAPTAIN: *Rob Thirlby*

First Round - Pool 'D'

2nd Feb TONGA 0 **ENGLAND** 33

[*This match kicked off at 1.06pm*]

(*England were leading 21-0 at half-time*)

2nd Feb CANADA 0 **ENGLAND** 29

[*This match kicked off at 4.06pm*]

(*England were leading 19-0 at half-time*)

2nd Feb SOUTH AFRICA 17 **ENGLAND** 5

[*This match kicked off at 8.16pm*]

(*This match was played on a slippery pitch*)

Quarter-Final

3rd Feb AUSTRALIA 29 **ENGLAND*** 12

[*This match kicked off at 1.12pm; Mat Rogers and Wendell Sailor played for Australia in this match*]

(*England were losing 15-5 in the closing stages when James Forrester scored a brilliant solo try under the posts*)

[Plate Semi-Final:]

[3rd Feb FIJI 17 **ENGLAND*** 12 aet]

[*This match kicked off at 4.04pm*]

(*England were leading 12-0 at half-time; Fiji were still losing 12-0 with 2 minutes of normal time remaining when Jope Tuikabe scored directly from a poor England lineout, thus 5 points were preventable; England were leading 12-5 when the full-time hooter sounded, but the ball was still in play and Apenisa Valesu scored a try which Waisale Serevi then converted to send the game into sudden death extra time; Fiji were allowed to score 17 unanswered points to win the match*)

TELECOM MORE MOBILE NEW ZEALAND INTERNATIONAL SEVENS

WestpacTrust Stadium, Wellington

CAPTAIN: *Mike Friday*

First Round - Pool 'A'

8th Feb PAPUA NEW GUINEA 0 **ENGLAND** 36

[*This match kicked off at 3.16pm*]

(*England were leading 14-0 at half-time*)

8th Feb USA 21 **ENGLAND** 26

[*This match kicked off at 6.12pm*]

(*England were losing 14-7 at half-time; England were leading 26-14 in the closing stages*)

8th Feb NEW ZEALAND 50 **ENGLAND** 7

[*This match kicked off at 10.00pm*]

(*England were losing 24-0 at half-time*)

CAPTAIN: *??*
Quarter-Final
9th Feb FIJI 14 **ENGLAND** 19
[This match kicked off at 3.39pm]
(England were losing 7-0 in the early stages; England were losing 14-0 in the 4th minute; England were losing 14-7 at half-time; England were still losing 14-7 midway through the second half; England were losing 14-7 with 2 minutes remaining; England were drawing 14-14 in the last minute when Michael Stephenson brilliantly chipped ahead and then followed up to score a match-winning try)
CAPTAIN: *Mike Friday*
Semi-Final
9th Feb SAMOA 36 **ENGLAND** 5
[This match kicked off at 7.00pm]
(England were losing 17-5 at half-time; Samoa were allowed to score 19 unanswered points in the second half to seal the match)

BEIJING SEVENS

National Olympic Sports Centre, Beijing
CAPTAIN: *Mike Friday*
First Round - Pool 'C'
16th Mar HONG KONG 0 **ENGLAND** 43
[This match kicked off at 9.41am]
(England were leading 24-0 at half-time)
16th Mar CANADA 10 **ENGLAND** 7
[This match kicked off at 12.42pm]
(England were losing 5-0 at half-time)
16th Mar SAMOA 5 **ENGLAND** 7
[This match kicked off at 4.42pm]
(England were leading 7-0 at half-time)
Quarter-Final
17th Mar FIJI 28 **ENGLAND** 14
[This match kicked off at 11.20am]
(This match was played in windy conditions; England were losing 14-7 at half-time; England were losing 28-7 in the closing stages when James Simpson-Daniel scored a consolation try)
[Plate Semi-Final:]
[17th Mar USA 12 **ENGLAND** 21]
[This match kicked off at 1.58pm]
(England were leading 12-7 at half-time)
[Plate Final:]
[17th Mar SAMOA 14 **ENGLAND** 33]
[This match kicked off at 4.45pm]
(England were leading 5-0 in the early stages; England were losing 14-5 just before half-time when Geoff Appleford scored after James Simpson-Daniel threw a brilliant reverse pass; England were losing 14-12 at half-time; Richard Haughton scored after just 18 seconds of the second half had been played!; England scored 28 unanswered points to win the match)

CREDIT SUISSE FIRST BOSTON HONG KONG SEVENS

Hong Kong Stadium, Eastern Hospital Road, So Kon Po, Hong Kong

CAPTAIN: *Phil Greening*

First Round - Pool 'F'

22nd Mar JAPAN 0 **ENGLAND** 47

[This match kicked off at 9.02pm]

(Richard Haughton scored a brilliant 64 metre solo try in the 2nd minute!; Simon Amor scored a brilliant solo try; England were leading 26-0 at half-time; Simon Amor scored 22 points in this match)

23rd Mar THAILAND 5 **ENGLAND** 33

[This match kicked off at 12.36pm]

(This match was played in wet conditions on a slippery pitch; England were leading 21-0 at half-time)

23rd Mar ARGENTINA 5 **ENGLAND** 19

[This match kicked off at 7.12pm]

(This match was played in wet conditions on a slippery pitch; England were leading 5-0 when Richard Haughton brilliantly gathered a bouncing ball and went on to score; England were leading 12-0 at half-time; England were still leading 12-0 when Ben Gollings ran 80 metres to score after Simon Amor took a quick tap penalty; England scored 19 unanswered points to win the match; England were leading 19-0 in injury time when Benjamin Bourse scored after James Simpson-Daniel dropped the ball behind his own line, thus 5 points were preventable; Phil Greening and Henry Paul both had a brilliant game)

Quarter-Final

24th Mar SAMOA 5 **ENGLAND** 19

[This match kicked off at 2.14pm]

(This match was played in wet conditions on a slippery pitch; England were leading 12-5 at half-time)

Semi-Final

24th Mar WALES 12 **ENGLAND** 19

[This match kicked off at 4.48pm; Arwel Thomas played for Wales in this match; After this match the Hong Kong R.F.U. cited Phil Greening for stamping which meant that he was suspended from the Final in accordance with the IRB World Sevens Series rules]

(This match was played in wet conditions on a slippery pitch; England were leading 7-0 in the early stages; Phil Greening was sent to the sin-bin early in the first half; England were leading 12-7 at half-time; England were drawing 12-12 with 2 minutes remaining when Josh Lewsey scored an interception try which Simon Amor then converted to clinch the match)

CAPTAIN: *Simon Amor*

Final

24th Mar FIJI 20 **ENGLAND** 33

[This match kicked off at 6.22pm; Phil Greening unavailable due to suspension; On 25th March 2002 the Hong Kong R.F.U. judicial committee found Phil Greening guilty of stamping and thus duly confirmed his original one game suspension]

(Phil Greening only found out that he was suspended as he was about to walk onto the pitch to play the game!; This match was played in wet conditions on a slippery pitch; England were losing 5-0 in the early stages; England were still losing 5-0 shortly afterwards when Simon Amor took a quick tap penalty and ran 50 metres to score a brilliant solo try; England were losing 10-7 midway through the first half; England were

still losing 10-7 just before half-time when James Simpson-Daniel scored a brilliant 70 metre solo try; England were leading 14-10 at half-time; England were still leading 14-10 early in the second half when James Simpson-Daniel scored another try after Henry Paul put in a superb kick ahead; England were leading 28-10 shortly afterwards; England scored 21 unanswered points to win the match; England were leading 33-15 in the closing stages; Henry Paul had a brilliant game; Simon Amor scored 52 points in the competition)

TILNEY MELROSE SEVENS

The Greenyards, Melrose

CAPTAIN: *??*

Second Round

13th April Selkirk (*SC*) 19 **BARBARIANS** 40

[This match kicked off at 2.44pm]

(The Barbarians scored two tries in the first 2 minutes!; The Barbarians were leading 19-0 at one point in this match; Charlie Keenan had a brilliant game)

Quarter-Final

13th April Melrose (*SC*) 21 **BARBARIANS** 26 aet

[This match kicked off at 4.26pm]

(The Barbarians were leading 14-7 at half-time; The Barbarians were drawing 21-21 in sudden death extra time when Alex Page scored to win the match)

Semi-Final

13th April Boroughmuir (*SC*) 19 **BARBARIANS** 12

[This match kicked off at 5.20pm]

(The Barbarians were losing 12-0 in the early stages; The Barbarians were losing 12-7 at half-time)

SINGAPORE SEVENS

National Stadium, Kallang

CAPTAIN: *Jamie Noon*

First Round - Pool 'D'

20th April CANADA 0 **ENGLAND** 31

[This match kicked off at 11.30am]

(England were leading 7-0 when Ben Gollings chipped ahead and regathered the ball to score a brilliant try; England were leading 14-0 at half-time; England were still leading 14-0 when Ben Gollings scored a superb 60 metre try; England were leading 26-0 when Ben Gollings scored after Dan Luger made a brilliant run; Ben Gollings played brilliantly and scored 26 points in this match)

20th April TAIWAN 7 **ENGLAND** 28

[This match kicked off at 2.26pm; Taiwan also billed as Chinese Taipei]

(England were leading 21-0 at half-time; England scored 28 unanswered points to win the match; England were leading 28-0 in the closing stages)

20th April ARGENTINA 19 **ENGLAND*** 14

[This match kicked off at 7.12pm]

(England were leading 14-0 at half-time; Argentina were allowed to score 19 unanswered points to win the match)

Quarter-Final

21st April SOUTH AFRICA 7 **ENGLAND** 15

[This match kicked off at 1.49pm]

(Dan Luger had to go off after he ruptured the anterior cruciate ligament in his knee)

Semi-Final

21st April NEW ZEALAND 19 **ENGLAND*** 10

[This match kicked off at 5.16pm; Dan Luger unavailable due to injury]

(England were losing 12-0 in the early stages; England were still losing 12-0 midway through the first half; England were losing 12-0 just before half-time when Ben Gollings kicked ahead twice and then regathered the ball to score a brilliant try; England were losing 12-5 at half-time; England were losing 12-10 in the closing stages)

MALAYSIA SEVENS

MPPJ Stadium, Petaling Jaya, Kelana Jaya

CAPTAIN: *Howard Graham*

First Round - Pool 'D'

27th April JAPAN 0 **ENGLAND** 31

[This match was scheduled to kick off at 3.12pm but the kick-off was delayed for 25 minutes due to a tropical storm]

(This match was played on a wet pitch; England were leading 14-0 at half-time)

27th April THAILAND 0 **ENGLAND** 34

[This match was scheduled to kick off at 6.08pm]

(England were leading 22-0 at half-time)

27th April AUSTRALIA 14 **ENGLAND** 7

[This match was scheduled to kick off at 9.46pm]

(England were losing 14-0 at half-time)

Quarter-Final

28th April SOUTH AFRICA 19 **ENGLAND** 0

[This match kicked off at 3.12pm]

(England were losing 19-0 at half-time; England were still losing 19-0 in the final minute when David Rees (2) had a great try-scoring chance but was tackled short of the South African line in the last move of the match)

[Plate Semi-Final:]

[28th Apr WALES 5 **ENGLAND** 22]

[This match kicked off at 5.50pm]

(This match was played on a waterlogged pitch; England were drawing 0-0 when Richard Haughton scored after he wrong-footed the defence with 2 brilliant sidesteps; England were leading 10-0 at half-time; England scored 22 unanswered points to win the match; England were leading 22-0 in the last minute)

[Plate Final:]

[28th Apr ARGENTINA 7 **ENGLAND** 43]

[This match kicked off at 8.15pm]

(This match was played on a waterlogged pitch; England scored 26 unanswered points to win the match; England were leading 26-0 just before half-time; England were leading 26-7 at half-time)

ENGLAND STUDENTS MATCH

CAPTAIN: *??*

4th May	**ENGLAND STUDENTS U21**	23	COMBINED SERVICES U21 (*SER*)	19

Twickenham

[This match kicked off at 12.00pm and was a curtain raiser game for the Army v Navy match; Dan Chesham played for England in the U19 World Championship in Chile in April 2001; Tom Miklausic was capped for England Schools 18 Group in January 1999; Ben Durham toured Canada, New Zealand and Australia with England Schools 18 Group in July-August 2001; Will Kershaw-Naylor played for Wales 7s in December 2002 and for Wales U21 in March 2003; Duncan Murray captained Wales U18 in April 1999; James Gaunt played for Crawshay's Welsh; From 2003-07 the annual Army v Navy curtain raiser game at Twickenham was played between the English Universities team and either Combined Services U21 or Combined Services U23]

(England Students U21 were losing 10-3 in the early stages; England Students U21 were leading 20-10 at half-time)

TETLEY'S COUNTY CHAMPIONSHIP SEMI-FINAL

CAPTAIN: *Steve Larkins* (CO)

18th May	**CORNWALL**	10	Gloucestershire	22 aet

Recreation Ground, Redruth

[This match kicked off at 3.00pm; Joe Bearman and Rocky Newton unavailable due to family commitments; Tony Windo, Lee Fortey, Dave Sims, Paul Knight (2), Steve Thompson (1), Mike Davies, Simon Martin and Dave Knight all played for Gloucestershire in this match, with Sims captaining the side and scoring a try and Dave Knight scoring a try]

(Cornwall played with a strong wind in the first half; The Cornwall forwards could not win any lineout ball; The Cornwall scrum was put under severe pressure; Steve Larkins missed a 22 metre penalty goal attempt in the 1st minute!; Cornwall were drawing 0-0 midway through the first half; Cornwall were awarded 2 penalties in eminently kickable positions in the first half, but on each occasion Steve Larkins chose to run the ball in a vain attempt to score a try; Cornwall were drawing 0-0 at half-time; Cornwall played down the slope towards Hellfire Corner in the second half; Cornwall were losing 3-0 in the 47th minute; Cornwall were still losing 3-0 midway through the second half; Cornwall were losing 3-0 with 4 minutes of normal time remaining; Cornwall were drawing 3-3 in the closing stages of normal time when Steve Larkins missed a difficult penalty goal attempt; Cornwall were drawing 3-3 at the end of normal time; Cornwall were losing 8-3 in the ninth minute of extra time; Cornwall were losing 15-3 with 7 minutes of extra time remaining; Gloucestershire were allowed to score 19 unanswered points to win the match; Cornwall were losing 22-3 in the final minute of extra time when Shane Kirman scored a consolation try with the last move of the match)

EMIRATES AIRLINE LONDON SEVENS

Twickenham

CAPTAIN: *Phil Greening*

First Round - Pool 'B'

24th May **ENGLAND** 40 CANADA 0

[*This match kicked off at 2.22pm*]

(*England were drawing 0-0 in the early stages when Ben Gollings scored a brilliant 68 metre solo try; England were leading 7-0 midway through the first half; England were leading 21-0 at half-time; Richard Haughton came on as a replacement for Paul Sampson at the start of the second half; England were still leading 21-0 early in the second half when Richard Haughton scored after Henry Paul brilliantly created space by getting out of the way of Ben Gollings' pass!; England were leading 28-0 midway through the second half when Richard Haughton scored another superb 46 metre solo try; England were leading 35-0 in the final minute when Richard Haughton scored a brilliant 62 metre solo try with the last move of the match to complete a second half hat-trick!*)

24th May **ENGLAND** 34 SPAIN 14

[*This match kicked off at 5.22pm*]

24th May **ENGLAND** 27 SAMOA 0

[*This match kicked off at 9.00pm*]

(*England were drawing 0-0 in the early stages when Richard Haughton scored a brilliant 50 metre solo try; England were leading 5-0 shortly afterwards when Josh Lewsey scored after Nick Duncombe brilliantly dummied his way through; England were leading 10-0 midway through the first half; England were still leading 10-0 shortly before half-time when Richard Haughton scored another superb 42 metre solo try; England were leading 15-0 at half-time; England were leading 22-0 midway through the second half; England were still leading 22-0 when the full-time hooter sounded, but the ball was still in play and some superb handling allowed Josh Lewsey to score another try; Henry Paul had a brilliant game*)

Quarter-Final

25th May **ENGLAND** 26 AUSTRALIA 14

[*This match kicked off at 1.44pm*]

(*Peter Hewat scored in the 2nd minute!; England were losing 7-0 in the 3rd minute when Tony Roques scored a brilliant 46 metre solo try; England were drawing 7-7 midway through the first half; England were still drawing 7-7 just before half-time when Ben Gollings broke through but he was then superbly chased back and tackled by Scott Barton; England were drawing 7-7 at half-time; Paul Sampson came on as a replacement for Richard Haughton at the start of the second half; England were still drawing 7-7 in the 9th minute when Phil Greening scored after Henry Paul wrong-footed the defence with a brilliant sidestep, with Ben Gollings then missing the eminently kickable conversion attempt; England were leading 12-7 in the 10th minute were a poor defensive alignment allowed Peter Miller to score, thus 7 points were preventable; England were losing 14-12 midway through the second half; England were still losing 14-12 with 2 minutes of normal time remaining when Henry Paul made a superb 44 metre run that enabled Paul Sampson to score a try which Ben Gollings then brilliantly converted from the right touchline; England were leading 19-14 when the full-time hooter sounded, but the ball was still in play and some superb handling allowed Josh Lewsey to score a match-clinching try under the posts; Henry Paul had a brilliant game*)

Semi-Final

25th May **ENGLAND*** 12 SOUTH AFRICA 26

[*This match kicked off at 4.48pm*]

(*The England scrum was put under severe pressure; Jorrie Muller scored in the 1st minute after a poor tackle by Henry Paul!; England were losing 7-0 in the 2nd minute when Josh Lewsey scored a superb 56 metre solo try which Ben Gollings then brilliantly converted from the right touchline; England were drawing 7-7 midway through the first half; South Africa were still drawing 0-0 shortly before half-time when Egon Seconds scored after the England defence bought a dummy by Jean de Villiers; England were losing 14-7 at half-time; England were still losing 14-7 early in the second half when Paul Treu put in a chip-kick and then followed up to score after Nick Duncombe unaccountably allowed the ball to bounce; England were losing 19-7 midway through the second half; England were still losing 19-7 with 2 minutes remaining when Ben Gollings dummied his way through to score a brilliant try, but then missed the eminently kickable conversion attempt!; England were losing 19-12 in the last minute when Tom May lost a strike against the head which led directly to a try by Gaffie du Toit, thus 4 tries and 26 points were preventable*)

FIRST PRUDENTIAL TOUR MATCH

CAPTAIN: *Phil Vickery* [England XV]

CAPTAIN: *Todd Blackadder* (NZ) [Barbarians]

26th May **ENGLAND XV** 53 **BARBARIANS** 29

Twickenham

[ENGLAND XV: [*This match kicked off at 3.00pm; Simon Shaw selected but withdrew due to injury, Alex Codling was moved from the bench to the team and Ed Pearce was then selected for the bench; Steve Thompson (2) was the only survivor from the 22 players who were involved in the previous cap international match against Italy!; Michael Horak played for South Africa U21 before August 1997 and played for South Africa at Rugby League*]

(*Dave Walder scored a penalty goal in the 1st minute!; The England XV was leading 3-0 midway through the first half when James Forrester dummied Jonah Lomu to score a brilliant 65 metre solo try; The England XV was leading 10-0 in the 26th minute when Steve Thompson (2) powered through 3 attempted tackles to score; The England XV was leading 17-5 in the 36th minute when James Simpson-Daniel created space by throwing the ball to himself and then beat Jonah Lomu for pace on the outside to score a brilliant 40 metre solo try; James Simpson-Daniel injured his ankle scoring this try but elected to remain on the pitch; The England XV was leading 22-12 just before half-time when Michael Horak scored after Dave Walder put in a superb grubber kick; The England XV was leading 29-12 at half-time; The England XV was leading 39-12 in the 45th minute; James Forrester went off injured in the 52nd minute, being replaced by Grant Seely; The England XV was leading 39-17 midway through the second half when Dave Walder chipped ahead and regathered the ball to score a brilliant try; The England XV was leading 46-24 in the 65th minute; The England XV was leading 53-24 with 8 minutes of normal time remaining; Geoff Appleford went off injured with 7 minutes of normal time remaining, being replaced by Kevin Sorrell; The England XV was still leading 53-24 in the second minute of injury time; Dave Walder scored 21 points in this match; Andy Gomarsall had a brilliant game*)]

[BARBARIANS: [*This match kicked off at 3.00pm; Abdelatif Benazzi selected but withdrew on the day of the match, Kieran Roche was moved from the bench to the*

team and Josh Kronfeld was then selected for the bench; The Barbarians' starting lineup had 486 caps between them!]
(Dave Walder scored a penalty goal in the 1st minute!; Stéphane Glas went off injured in the 5th minute, being replaced by Thomas Castaignède; Todd Blackadder went off injured in the 13th minute, being replaced by Pat Lam; The Barbarians were losing 10-0 midway through the first half; Thomas Castaignède went off injured in the 21st minute, being replaced by Percy Montgomery; The Barbarians were losing 17-0 in the 26th minute; The Barbarians were losing 22-5 in the 36th minute; The Barbarians were losing 22-12 just before half-time; The Barbarians were losing 29-12 at half-time; The Barbarians were losing 39-12 in the 45th minute; The Barbarians were losing 46-17 midway through the second half; The Barbarians were losing 46-24 in the 65th minute; The Barbarians were losing 53-24 with 8 minutes of normal time remaining; The Barbarians were still losing 53-24 in the second minute of injury time when Pat Lam scored a consolation try; Jonah Lomu had a poor game)]

SECOND PRUDENTIAL TOUR MATCH

CAPTAIN: *Pat Lam* (SAM)

29th May WALES XV 25 **BARBARIANS** 40

Millennium Stadium, Cardiff

[This match kicked off at 7.15pm; Joe Worsley and Austin Healey in original squad but withdrew; Ryan Strudwick selected but withdrew to sit on the bench, Kieran Roche was moved from the bench to the team]
(The Barbarians were losing 3-0 in the 12th minute; The Barbarians were losing 11-0 midway through the first half; The Barbarians were losing 18-0 in the 33rd minute; The Barbarians were losing 25-0 at half-time; The Barbarians were losing 25-7 in the 51st minute when Thinus Delport scored after Ollie Smith (2) threw a brilliant pass; The Barbarians were losing 25-14 midway through the second half; The Barbarians were losing 25-21 in the 65th minute when some superb handling allowed Adrian Garvey to score; Liam Botham also came on as a replacement for Ollie Smith at the same time; The Barbarians were leading 35-25 with 3 minutes of normal time remaining; The Barbarians were still leading 35-25 in the second minute of injury time; The Barbarians scored 40 unanswered points in the second half to win the match)

EMIRATES AIRLINE CARDIFF SEVENS

Millennium Stadium, Cardiff

CAPTAIN: *Phil Greening*

First Round - Pool 'B'

31st May FRANCE 7 **ENGLAND** 10

[This match kicked off at 2.22pm]
(England were drawing 0-0 in the early stages when Sylvian Mottet scored after Richard Haughton failed to fall properly on a loose ball, thus 7 points were preventable; England were losing 7-0 midway through the first half; England were still losing 7-0 shortly afterwards when Richard Haughton scored after Phil Greening took a strike against the head during a French scrum; England were losing 7-5 at half-time; Michael Stephenson dummied his way through to score a brilliant try after just 17 seconds of the second half had been played!; England were leading 10-7 midway through the second half; Michael Stephenson was injured in the final minute but elected to remain on the pitch)

31st May RUSSIA 10 **ENGLAND** 28

[This match kicked off at 5.22pm; Michael Stephenson unavailable due to injury]

(England were losing 5-0 when Paul Sampson scored a brilliant 60 metre solo try; England were leading 14-5 at half-time; England were leading 14-10 early in the second half; England scored 14 unanswered points to clinch the match)

31st May WALES 14 **ENGLAND** 28

[This match kicked off at 9.00pm; Michael Stephenson unavailable due to injury; Arwel Thomas played for Wales in this match]

(England were drawing 0-0 in the early stages when Pat Sanderson powered through 4 attempted tackles to score; England were leading 7-0 midway through the first half; England were still leading 7-0 shortly afterwards when Richard Haughton scored a brilliant 77 metre solo try; England were leading 14-0 at half-time; England were still leading 14-0 early in the second half when Phil Jones scored after Nick Duncombe instigated a brilliant 93 metre counter-attack; England scored 21 unanswered points to win the match; England were leading 21-0 midway through the second half; England were leading 21-7 in the last minute of normal time when Jason Forster scored after a poor tackle by Ben Gollings, thus 7 points were preventable; England were leading 21-14 when the full-time hooter sounded, but the ball was still in play and Tony Roques was able to score a superb 59 metre solo try to clinch the match)

Quarter-Final

1st June SCOTLAND 0 **ENGLAND** 17

[This match kicked off at 12.49pm; Michael Stephenson and Phil Jones unavailable due to injury]

(England were drawing 0-0 in the early stages when Ben Gollings scored after Rob Thirlby threw a brilliant inside pass; England were leading 5-0 midway through the first half; England were still leading 5-0 shortly afterwards when Ben Gollings scored after he took a return pass from Rob Thirlby; England were leading 10-0 at half-time; England were still leading 10-0 in the 8th minute when Rob Thirlby scored a brilliant 83 metre solo try; England were leading 17-0 midway through the second half)

Semi-Final

1st June FIJI 0 **ENGLAND** 24

[This match kicked off at 3.48pm; Michael Stephenson and Phil Jones unavailable due to injury]

(England were drawing 0-0 in the early stages when Paul Sampson scored after Phil Greening threw a brilliant pass; England were leading 5-0 midway through the first half; England were still leading 5-0 just before half-time when Paul Sampson scored another brilliant 79 metre solo try; England were leading 12-0 at half-time; England were still leading 12-0 early in the second half when Paul Sampson saved a certain try by tackling Josefa Uluivuda into touch at the corner flag; England were leading 12-0 shortly afterwards when Richard Haughton scored after Phil Greening threw another superb pass; England were leading 17-0 midway through the second half; England were still leading 17-0 in the final minute when Ben Gollings scored a brilliant 38 solo try with the last move of the match; Nick Duncombe had a brilliant game)

Final

1st June NEW ZEALAND 24 **ENGLAND*** 12

[This match kicked off at 6.00pm; Michael Stephenson and Phil Jones unavailable due to injury]

(England were drawing 0-0 in the 2nd minute when Ben Gollings wasted a great try-scoring opportunity by throwing a poor pass to the unmarked Paul Sampson; England were still drawing 0-0 shortly afterwards when Rob Thirlby had a great try-scoring chance but was tackled short of the New Zealand line; England were drawing 0-0

***midway through the first half when Joe Rokococo scored after a poor tackle by Paul Sampson; England were losing 5-0 shortly afterwards when Rob Thirlby scored a brilliant 50 metre solo try; England were drawing 5-5 just before half-time; England were losing 12-5 at half-time; England were still losing 12-5 early in the second half when a poor defensive alignment allowed Chris Masoe to score; Jamie Noon came on as a replacement for Nick Duncombe immediately afterwards, with Ben Gollings then switching from fly half to scrum half to accommodate Noon; England were losing 17-5 shortly afterwards when collectively poor tackling allowed Brad Fleming to score, 3 tries and 17 points were preventable; England were losing 24-5 midway through the second half; England were still losing 24-5 with 1 minute remaining; England were losing 24-12 in the last minute when Tom May crossed the tryline but then lost the ball in the act of scoring*)**

THIRD PRUDENTIAL TOUR MATCH

CAPTAIN: *Ian Jones (2)* (NZ)

1st June SCOTLAND XV 27 **BARBARIANS** 47

Murrayfield

[*This match kicked off at 3.00pm; Joe Worsley and Austin Healey in original squad but withdrew; Mauricio Reggiardo selected for bench but withdrew, being replaced by Adrian Garvey; Ollie Smith (2) selected for bench but withdrew, being replaced by Christophe Dominici who then himself withdrew and was replaced by Barry Everitt; Liam Botham became a Rugby League player in July 2003 and retired in August 2005 due to injury*]

(*Percy Montgomery saved a certain try in the 1st minute when he tackled Rory Kerr!; Brendan Laney scored a penalty goal in the 2nd minute!; The Barbarians were leading 7-3 in the 11th minute; The Barbarians were still leading 7-3 midway through the first half; The Barbarians were leading 7-3 in the 26th minute when Jim Williams broke from the base of a scrum to score; The Barbarians were leading 21-3 in the 31st minute; The Barbarians were leading 21-13 in the sixth minute of first half injury time when some superb handling allowed Josh Kronfeld to score; The Barbarians were leading 28-13 at half-time; Mark Robinson (2) scored a brilliant try which Braam van Straaten then converted to give the Barbarians a 35-13 lead in the 52nd minute; The Barbarians were leading 35-20 in the 58th minute when Mark Robinson (2) scored from a rolling maul; The Barbarians were leading 40-20 midway through the second half; The Barbarians were still leading 40-20 with 7 minutes remaining when Pieter Muller scored after Thinus Delport put up a superb cross-kick; The Barbarians were leading 47-20 with 1 minute remaining when Liam Botham came on as a replacement for Pieter Rossouw; Ian Jones (2) and Josh Kronfeld both had a brilliant game*)

LISBON SEVENS

Lisbon

CAPTAIN: *Waisale Serevi* (FIJ) [Penguins]

CAPTAIN: *Gerrie Engelbrecht* (SA) [Samurai]

First Round - Group ?

8th June Lousã (*POR*) 0 **PENGUINS** 68

[No match notes]

8th June Belenenses (*POR*) 7 **PENGUINS** 38

[No match notes]

8th June White Hart Marauders 12 **PENGUINS** 35

[No match notes]

First Round - Group ?

8th June	Samurai Sharks	L	**SAMURAI**	W

[*Samurai Sharks were a 2nd VII entered by Samurai International RFC*]

8th June	GDS Cascais (*POR*)	L	**SAMURAI**	W

[No match notes]

8th June	Técnico (*POR*)	L	**SAMURAI**	W

[No match notes]

Quarter Final - Group ?

9th June	GDS Cascais (*POR*)	0	**PENGUINS**	49

[No match notes]

9th June	Euskarians (*FR*)	7	**PENGUINS**	35

[No match notes]

Quarter Final - Group ?

9th June	Direito (*POR*)	L	**SAMURAI**	W

[No match notes]

9th June	<u>White Hart Marauders</u>	L	**SAMURAI**	W

[No match notes]

Semi-Final

9th June	<u>White Hart Marauders</u>	0	**PENGUINS**	47

[No match notes]

9th June	Euskarians (*FR*)	5	**SAMURAI**	15

[No match notes]

Final

9th June	**PENGUINS**	24	**SAMURAI**	38

[PENGUINS: (*The Penguins were losing 28-12 at half-time; Waisale Serevi scored a brilliant try in the second half*)]
[SAMURAI: (*The Samurai were leading 28-12 at half-time*)]

<u>IRB U21 WORLD CHAMPIONSHIP</u>

South Africa
CAPTAIN: *Mark Soden*
First Round - Pool 'D'

14th Jun	NEW ZEALAND U21	67	**ENGLAND U21**	23

Ellis Park Stadium, Johannesburg
[*This match kicked off at 5.00pm; Jon Goodridge injured his shoulder in a pre-tournament training session and thus left the squad injured before this match; Jonny Hylton joined the squad before this match; David Tibbott joined the squad after this match; Phil Davies (3) played for England in the U19 World Championship in France in April 2000; Dan Carter played for New Zealand U21 in this match*]
(*This match was played at high altitude; Sam Tuitupou scored in the 3rd minute!; England U21 were losing 21-0 in the 6th minute!; England U21 were losing 32-3 shortly before half-time when Michael Holford scored after Matt Honeyben put up a brilliant cross-kick; England U21 were losing 35-8 at half-time; Adam Billig scored after Tom Voyce put in a superb chip-kick; Alex Cadwallader dislocated his shoulder in this match; Michael Holford had a brilliant game*)

CAPTAIN: *Martin Purdy*

18th Jun	ITALY U21	12	**ENGLAND U21**	41 **BP**

Rand Afrikaans University Stadium, Johannesburg

[This match kicked off at 7.00pm; Ian Clarke returned home injured after this match; Alex Alesbrook joined the squad after this match; Magnus Lund toured Canada, New Zealand and Australia with England Schools 18 Group in July-August 2001; Magnus Lund and Spencer Davey played for England in the U19 World Championship in Italy in March 2002]

(This match was played at high altitude in cold conditions; Sam Vesty missed a 40 metre penalty goal attempt in the 3rd minute!; England U21 were drawing 3-3 in the 12th minute; England U21 were still drawing 3-3 shortly afterwards when Jonny Hylton scored under the posts after John Rudd made a brilliant run; England U21 were leading 10-3 midway through the second half; England U21 were leading 13-6 just before half-time; England U21 were leading 20-6 at half-time; England U21 were leading 20-9 early in the second half; Ian Clarke went off injured in this match, being replaced by Paul Hodgson; Adam Halsey was concussed during the match)

CAPTAIN: *Mark Soden* [*Martin Purdy*]

21st Jun	ARGENTINA U21	17	**ENGLAND U21**	20

Witts University Stadium, Johannesburg

[This match kicked off at 1.00pm; Jim Scaysbrook selected but withdrew, being replaced by Phil Davies (3); Adam Halsey and Ben Gotting returned home injured after this match; Brett Sturgess and Andrew Kyriacou joined the squad after this match]

(Mark Soden was sent off in the 35th minute for stamping and thus duly banned for 1 match, despite video evidence failing to show any wrongdoing)

(This match was played at high altitude; Tom Voyce missed a penalty goal attempt from in front of the posts in the 5th minute!; England U21 were drawing 0-0 midway through the first half; England U21 were leading 3-0 in the 25th minute; England U21 were leading 6-0 shortly before half-time when David Tibbott had a great try-scoring chance but was tackled just short of the Argentina U21 line; England U21 were leading 6-0 at half-time; The England U21 scrum was put under severe pressure in the second half; England U21 were leading 13-0 in the 50th minute; England U21 were leading 13-3 midway through the second half; England U21 were leading 13-10 with 7 minutes of normal time remaining; England U21 were losing 17-13 with 1 minute of normal time remaining; Argentina U21 were allowed to score 17 unanswered points; England U21 were reduced to 13 players in the closing stages when James Buckland was sent to the sin-bin!; England U21 were still losing 17-13 in the sixth minute of injury time when the full-time hooter sounded, but the ball was still in play and Jonny Hylton was able to score a try under the posts which Sam Vesty then converted with the last kick of the match to clinch the game)

CAPTAIN: *Martin Purdy*

5th/6th/7th/8th Place Semi-Final

25th Jun	IRELAND U21	28	**ENGLAND U21***	15

Rand Afrikaans University Stadium, Johannesburg

[This match kicked off at 3.00pm; Mark Soden unavailable due to suspension; Michael Holford selected but was moved to the bench on the morning of the game due to illness, being replaced by Nick Cox; Paul Hodgson selected but was moved to the bench on the morning of the game due to illness, being replaced by Matt Honeyben with Ben Hampson then moving from fly half to scrum half to accommodate Matt

***Honeyben; Adam Billig selected but withdrew on the morning of the match due to illness, being replaced by John Rudd with Simon Hunt moving from right wing to centre to accommodate John Rudd; Andrew Kyriacou toured Canada, New Zealand and Australia with England Schools 18 Group in July-August 2001 and played for England in the U19 World Championship in Italy in March 2002*]**

(*This match was played at high altitude; David Tibbott played with an illness; England U21 were pressing in attack when they lost the ball and James Norton was able to score a long-range try, thus 5 points were preventable; England U21 were losing 15-0 in the 17th minute; England U21 were losing 15-5 in the 33rd minute; England U21 were still losing 15-5 just before half-time; England U21 were losing 15-10 at half-time; England U21 were losing 22-10 early in the second half; England U21 were losing 25-10 at one point in the second half; David Tibbott went off in the 70th minute due to illness, being replaced by Sam Vesty; England U21 were losing 25-15 in the closing stages*)

CAPTAIN: *Mark Soden*

7th/8th Place Play-Off

28th Jun ARGENTINA U21 14 **ENGLAND U21** 74

Ellis Park Stadium, Johannesburg

[*This match kicked off at 11.00am; Ed Burrill played for England in the U19 World Championship in Italy in March 2002*]

(*This match was played at high altitude; Simon Hunt scored a penalty goal in the 5th minute!; England U21 were leading 10-0 in the 10th minute; England U21 were still leading 10-0 midway through the first half; England U21 were leading 10-0 in the 32nd minute; England U21 were leading 31-0 in the 37th minute; England U21 were leading 31-0 at half-time; England U21 were leading 38-0 in the 45th minute; England U21 scored 38 unanswered points to win the match; England U21 were leading 38-7 in the 47th minute; England U21 were leading 38-14 midway through the second half; England U21 were leading 50-14 with 9 minutes of normal time remaining; England U21 were leading 62-14 with 3 minutes of normal time remaining when John Rudd scored to complete a hat-trick of tries; England U21 were leading 69-14 in the first minute of injury time when Simon Hunt also scored to complete a hat-trick of tries!; Simon Hunt scored 34 points in this match*)

PENGUINS TOUR TO AMERICA AND CANADA 2002

CAPTAIN: *Mark Denney*

18th Jun Toronto Renegades (*CAN*) 7 **PENGUINS** 32

Oakville Crusaders RC, Crusaders Park, Oakville, Ontario

[*This match was played at night under floodlights; The Toronto Renegades were a combined team containing players from various clubs in Toronto; Mark Denney was capped for England Schools 18 Group in April 1992*]

(*The Penguins were leading 14-7 at half-time*)

ENGLAND TOUR TO ARGENTINA 2002

CAPTAIN: *Phil Vickery*

22nd Jun ARGENTINA 18 **ENGLAND** 26

CA Vélez Sársfield, Estadio José Amalfitani, Buenos Aires

[*This match kicked off at 5.45pm*]

(*The England forwards dominated the lineout in this match; The England scrum was put under severe pressure in the first half; England were leading 3-0 in the 7th minute; England were still leading 3-0 in the 9th minute when Charlie Hodgson missed an*

eminently kickable penalty goal attempt; England were drawing 3-3 in the 18th minute when Charlie Hodgson missed another eminently kickable penalty goal attempt; England were losing 6-3 midway through the first half; England were losing 12-3 in the 33rd minute; England were losing 12-3 at half-time; England were still losing 12-3 in the 44th minute when Ben Kay ran 30 metres to score after Andy Gomarsall threw a brilliant reverse pass; England were losing 15-13 in the 58th minute when Phil Christophers scored a superb solo try; England were leading 20-15 midway through the second half; England were still leading 20-15 in the 66th minute when Charlie Hodgson scored a brilliant 45 metre penalty goal; England were leading 23-18 with 4 minutes remaining when Tim Stimpson scored a superb penalty goal from the halfway line to clinch the match; Ben Kay and Alex Sanderson both had a brilliant game)

ENGLAND COUNTIES TOUR TO CHILE 2002

CAPTAIN: *Tony Windo*

29th Jun CHILE 21 **ENGLAND COUNTIES** 33

Centro de Alto Rendimiento de Rugby, La Reina, Santiago

[This match kicked off at 4.00pm; Gregg Botterman played for M.R. Steele-Bodger's XV against Cambridge University at Grange Road on 28th November 2001, scoring a try]

(England Counties were drawing 0-0 in the 13th minute when Craig Raymond scored a brilliant solo try; England Counties were drawing 7-7 in the 15th minute; England Counties were leading 21-7 at half-time; England Counties were still leading 21-7 in the 52nd minute when Mark Kirkby scored a superb solo try; England Counties were leading 26-14 when John Lawn scored from a rolling maul; England Counties were leading 33-14 in the closing stages)

COMMONWEALTH SEVENS

City of Manchester Stadium

CAPTAIN: *Phil Greening*

First Round - Pool 'C'

2nd Aug **ENGLAND** 24 COOK ISLANDS 12

[This match kicked off at 5.00pm]

(This match was played on a wet pitch; Amosa Amosa scored in the 1st minute after Pat Sanderson slipped over and thus created a gap in the defensive line, thus 7 points were preventable!; England were losing 7-0 shortly afterwards when Rob Thirlby scored a brilliant 50 metre solo try; England were losing 12-5 midway through the first half; England were still losing 12-5 just before half-time; England were drawing 12-12 at half-time; England were still drawing 12-12 midway through the second half; England were drawing 12-12 with 3 minutes remaining; England were leading 17-12 with 2 minutes remaining when Josh Lewsey saved a certain try by tackling Darren Robson; England were still leading 17-12 in the last minute when Josh Lewsey scored after Paul Sampson made a brilliant run; England scored 19 unanswered points to win the match)

2nd Aug **ENGLAND** 33 KENYA 12

[This match kicked off at 7.50pm]

(This match was played on a wet pitch; England were losing 12-5 at half-time; England were still losing 12-5 when Henry Paul scored a brilliant try; England scored 28 unanswered points in the second half to win the match; Henry Paul had a brilliant game)

3rd Aug **ENGLAND** 19 SAMOA 7
[This match kicked off at 1.20pm]
(England were drawing 0-0 midway through the first half; England were still drawing 0-0 just before half-time when Phil Greening scored after Henry Paul threw a brilliant long pass; England were leading 5-0 at half-time; England were still leading 5-0 early in the second half when Simon Amor scored after Henry Paul put in a superb kick ahead; England were leading 12-0 midway through the second half when Simon Amor scored a brilliant solo try; England scored 19 unanswered points to win the match; England were leading 19-0 in the closing stages of this match; Henry Paul had a brilliant game)
Quarter-Final
3rd Aug **ENGLAND*** 5 FIJI 7
[This match kicked off at 9.00pm]
(England were drawing 0-0 midway through the first half; England were still drawing 0-0 shortly before half-time when Henry Paul saved a certain try by tackling Norman Ligairi; England were drawing 0-0 at half-time; England were still drawing 0-0 midway through the second half when some superb handling allowed Paul Sampson to score in the right corner; England were leading 5-0 with 1 minute remaining when Rupeni Caucau scored directly from a poor lineout throw by Phil Greening, thus 7 points were preventable)
[Plate Semi-Final:]
[4th Aug **ENGLAND** 29 CANADA 0]
[This match kicked off at 12.00pm]
(England were leading 12-0 at half-time)
[Plate Final:]
[4th Aug **ENGLAND** 36 AUSTRALIA 12]
[This match kicked off at 1.30pm; Rob Thirlby unavailable due to injury; Nick Duncombe died of blood poisoning on 14th February 2003; Simon Amor played for M.R. Steele-Bodger's XV against Cambridge University at Grange Road on 27th November 2002]
(England were leading 5-0 in the early stages; England were leading 17-0 midway through the first half; A brilliant pass by Pat Sanderson enabled Josh Lewsey to score a brilliant try which gave England a 22-0 lead in the 8th minute; England scored 22 unanswered points to win the match; England were leading 22-7 at half-time; England were leading 22-12 early in the second half when Nick Duncombe scored after Josh Lewsey threw a superb pass out of the tackle; England were leading 29-12 midway through the second half; Geoff Appleford came on as a replacement for Phil Greening with 3 minutes remaining; England were still leading 29-12 in the closing stages)

DEREK MORGAN MATCH

CAPTAIN: *??* [British Students]
CAPTAIN: *Tim O'Brien (2)* (AU) [Penguins]
2nd Oct **BRITISH STUDENTS** 17 **PENGUINS** 50
Iffley Road, Oxford
[BRITISH STUDENTS: *[This match kicked off at 6.00pm; England Students were originally scheduled to play this match; Will Kershaw-Naylor selected but withdrew on the day of the match, being replaced by Will Ellerby; British Students were also billed as British Universities; Tom Hayman played for M.R. Steele-Bodger's XV against Cambridge University at Grange Road on 27th November 2002]*
(British Students were losing 26-0 at half-time)]

[PENGUINS: ***[This match kicked off at 6.00pm; England Students were the originally scheduled opponents; Waisale Serevi selected as captain but withdrew on the day of the match due to club commitments; Steve White-Cooper played for Major R.V. Stanley's XV against Oxford University at Iffley Road on 13th November 2002 and 12th November 2003 and played for M.R. Steele-Bodger's XV against Cambridge University at Grange***
Road on 27th November 2002]
(The Penguins were leading 26-0 at half-time)]

NEW ZEALAND TOUR TO ENGLAND, FRANCE AND WALES 2002

CAPTAIN: *Martin Johnson*

9th Nov **ENGLAND** 31 NEW ZEALAND 28
Twickenham

[This match kicked off at 2.30pm; Joe Worsley, Alex Sanderson, Charlie Hodgson, Dan Luger and Iain Balshaw all unavailable due to injury; Julian White unavailable after a RFU hearing on 8th October 2002 found him guilty of head-butting an opponent in a Zurich Premiership match on 29th September 2002 and thus banned him for 10 weeks; England did not select a fly half for the bench after Clive Woodward decided that Austin Healey could provide injury cover for that position; Mike Catt in original training squad of 30 but withdrew due to injury; Graham Rowntree, Dorian West, Simon Shaw, James Forrester, Andy Gomarsall, Phil Christophers and Marcel Garvey all in original training squad of 30 but were not selected for team or bench]
(Jonny Wilkinson scored a penalty goal in the 5th minute!; England were leading 6-0 in the 15th minute when Jonah Lomu scored a try that should not have been given because the scoring pass from Keith Lowen was clearly forward, thus 7 points were unlawful; England were losing 7-6 in the 18th minute when Jonny Wilkinson had a kickable 30 metre drop goal attempt charged down by Marty Holah; England were still losing 7-6 midway through the first half; England were losing 7-6 in the 25th minute when they were awarded a 5 metre penalty in an eminently kickable position, but Matt Dawson unaccountably chose to put in a chip-kick towards Will Greenwood in a vain attempt to score a try; England were leading 9-7 in the 33rd minute when Doug Howlett ran 46 metres to score after Richard Hill (2)'s pass to Will Greenwood was intercepted by Tana Umaga; England were losing 14-9 in the 40th minute when Jonny Wilkinson scored a brilliant 43 metre penalty goal; England were losing 14-12 in the third minute of first half injury time when Jonny Wilkinson missed a speculative 51 metre penalty goal attempt; England were still losing 14-12 in the fifth minute of first half injury time when some superb handling amongst the backs allowed Lewis Moody to score; England were leading 17-14 at half-time; Will Greenwood went off injured at half-time, being replaced by Ben Johnston; England were still leading 17-14 in the 46th minute when Jonny Wilkinson chipped ahead and regathered the ball to score a brilliant try; Ben Cohen scored a superb 50 metre solo try which Jonny Wilkinson then converted to give England a 31-14 lead in the 48th minute; England scored 22 unanswered points to win the match; Neil Back came on as a temporary blood replacement for Richard Hill (2) in the 49th minute; England were still leading 31-14 in the 58th minute when Jonah Lomu scored another try after a poor tackle by Mike Tindall; England were leading 31-21 midway through the second half; England were still leading 31-21 in the 65th minute when Jonny Wilkinson missed a kickable 40 metre penalty goal attempt; England were leading 31-21 in the 68th minute when Phil Vickery saved a certain try by

***tackling Joe McDonnell; England were still leading 31-21 with 9 minutes of normal time remaining when a poor defensive alignment allowed Danny Lee to score, thus 3 tries and 21 points were preventable; England were leading 31-28 with 1 minute of normal time remaining when Ben Cohen saved another certain try by tackling Ben Blair into touch at the corner flag; James Simpson-Daniel saw very little of the ball in the match; Jonny Wilkinson played brilliantly and scored 21 points in this match; Steve Thompson (2) and Lewis Moody both had a brilliant game*)**

REMEMBRANCE MATCH

CAPTAIN: *Doddie Weir* (SC)

12th Nov COMBINED SERVICES (*SER*) 27 **BARBARIANS*** 26

Devonport Services RFC, Rectory Stadium, Second Avenue, Devonport, Plymouth

[*This match kicked off at 7.15pm; Tom Voyce selected but withdrew, Matthew Watkins was moved from the bench to the team and Ross Winney was then selected for the bench; Daren O'Leary selected but withdrew, being replaced by Matt Mostyn; Matt Pini selected but withdrew, Wayne Proctor was moved from the bench to the team and Piran Trethewey was then selected for the bench; Chris Horsman was capped for England Colts in March 1996; Hedley Verity played for M.R. Steele-Bodger's XV against Cambridge University at Grange Road on 29th November 2000; Chris Budgen, Howard Graham, Mal Roberts and Spencer Brown played for the Combined Services in this match, with Mal Roberts captaining the side and scoring a try and Spencer Brown scoring a try*]

(*This match was played in extremely wet conditions; The Barbarians were losing 3-0 in the 6th minute; Some superb handling allowed Doddie Weir to score a try which Killian Keane then converted to give the Barbarians a 14-3 lead in the 18th minute; The Barbarians were still leading 14-3 midway through the first half; The Barbarians were leading 14-10 in the 24th minute; The Barbarians were leading 19-17 in first half injury time when Wayne Proctor scored after Kanogo Njuru made a brilliant break; The Barbarians were leading 26-17 at half-time; The Barbarians were leading 26-22 in the 45th minute; The Barbarians were still leading 26-22 midway through the second half; The Barbarians were awarded seven penalties in kickable positions but Doddie Weir unaccountably ordered a tap penalty to be taken on each occasion!; The Barbarians were leading 26-22 with 6 minutes of normal time remaining when Killian Keane unaccountably dropped the ball as he shaped to put in a clearance kick and Andy Crompton followed up and scored, thus 5 points were preventable; Ross Winney came on as a replacement for Killian Keane immediately afterwards!; Graham Dawe came on as a replacement for Ben Phillips with 2 minutes of normal time remaining; The Barbarians were losing 27-26 in the fifth minute of injury time when Ross Winney missed an eminently kickable penalty goal attempt with the last kick of the match; Doddie Weir and Matt Mostyn both had a brilliant game*)

ENGLAND U21 TRIAL MATCHES

CAPTAIN: *??*

13th Nov FRANCE U21 WEST XV 22 **ENGLAND U21 SOUTH XV** 18

Centre National de Rugby, Domaine de Bellejame, Marcoussis

[*This match kicked off at 12.00pm; Richard Martin-Redman played for Wales in the U19 World Championship in Chile in April 2001*]

(*The England U21 South XV was losing 17-6 at half-time; Pat Sykes was supposed to switch from right wing to centre at the start of the second half but went off injured at half-time instead!*)

CAPTAIN: *??*

13th Nov FRANCE U21 EAST XV 31 **ENGLAND U21 NORTH XV** 20

Centre National de Rugby, Domaine de Bellejame, Marcoussis

[*This match kicked off at 2.00pm; Stuart Brown was capped for England Schools 18 Group in March 1999 and played for England in the U19 World Championship in Chile in April 2001*]

(*The England North U21 XV was losing 21-3 at half-time*)

AUSTRALIAN TOUR TO IRELAND, ENGLAND AND ITALY 2002

CAPTAIN: *Martin Johnson*

16th Nov **ENGLAND** 32 AUSTRALIA 31

Twickenham

[*This match kicked off at 2.30pm; Simon Shaw, Joe Worsley, Alex Sanderson, Charlie Hodgson, Dan Luger and Iain Balshaw all unavailable due to injury; Julian White unavailable due to suspension; Trevor Woodman selected but withdrew due to injury, Jason Leonard was moved from the bench to the team and Robbie Morris was then selected for the bench; England did not select a fly half for the bench after Clive Woodward decided that Austin Healey could provide injury cover for that position*]

**(*This match was played in cold conditions; James Simpson-Daniel played with an illness; England were drawing 0-0 in the 10th minute when some superb handling amongst the backs allowed Ben Cohen to score; England were leading 7-3 in the 14th minute; Jonny Wilkinson scored a brilliant 50 metre penalty goal to give England a 10-6 lead midway through the first half; England were still leading 10-6 in the 35th minute when Matt Dawson broke from a base of a ruck and ran 51 metres before being tackled as he looked in vain for support; Jonny Wilkinson scored another brilliant 46 metre penalty goal to give England a 16-6 lead in the 40th minute; England were still leading 16-6 in the eighth minute of first half injury time when Elton Flatley scored after Jonny Wilkinson slipped over and thus created a gap in the defensive line; England were leading 16-13 at half-time; Lawrence Dallaglio came on as a temporary blood replacement for Richard Hill (2) in the 42nd minute; England were still leading 16-13 in the 43rd minute when collectively poor tackling allowed Wendell Sailor to score, thus 2 tries and 12 points were preventable; England were losing 18-16 in the 46th minute when they were awarded a 30 metre penalty in an eminently kickable position, but Matt Dawson chose to take a quick tap penalty in a vain attempt to score a try; Immediately afterwards the referee unaccountably allowed play to continue after Stephen Larkham handled in a ruck, which allowed Elton Flatley to gather the resulting loose ball and run 80 metres to score, thus 7 points were unlawful; Australia were allowed to score 22 unanswered points; England were losing 28-16 in the 54th minute when Jonny Wilkinson scored a third superb 46 metre penalty goal; England were losing 31-19 in the 56th minute; England were losing 31-22 midway through the second half when Will Greenwood brilliantly created an overlap by chipping the ball to himself, but he then threw a poor pass to Lewis Moody which thus prevented the unmarked Jason Leonard from having to run 70 metres down the right wing to score!; England were losing 31-25 in the 68th minute when Ben Cohen scored after James Simpson-Daniel brilliantly created space by delaying his pass; England scored 13 unanswered points to win the match; England were leading 32-31 with 3 minutes of normal time remaining when Matt Burke missed a kickable 41 metre penalty goal attempt for Australia!; Austin Healey came on as a replacement for Mike Tindall in the fourth minute of injury time; England*

were still leading 32-31 in the fifth minute of injury time when Jason Robinson had a great try-scoring chance, but his attempted chip over the Australian line was then superbly charged down by Stephen Larkham; The referee unaccountably allowed 6 minutes of injury time to be played; Jonny Wilkinson scored 22 points in this match; Matt Dawson had a brilliant game)

SOUTH AFRICAN TOUR TO FRANCE, SCOTLAND AND ENGLAND 2002

CAPTAIN: *Martin Johnson*

23rd Nov **ENGLAND** 53 SOUTH AFRICA 3
Twickenham

[This match kicked off at 2.30pm; Trevor Woodman, Simon Shaw, Joe Worsley, Alex Sanderson, Charlie Hodgson, Dan Luger, Mike Catt and Iain Balshaw all unavailable due to injury; James Simpson-Daniel unavailable due to illness; Julian White unavailable due to suspension; England did not select a fly half for the bench after Clive Woodward decided that Austin Healey could provide injury cover for that position; England moved back to the top of the Zurich World Rugby Rankings after this match; Tim Stimpson retired in January 2006]

(This match was marred by a number of violent off the ball incidents, which were instigated by South Africa; England were leading 3-0 in the 13th minute; Lewis Moody went off injured in the 15th minute, being replaced by Lawrence Dallaglio; England were still leading 3-0 midway through the first half when Ben Cohen scored after Matt Dawson made a brilliant 25 metre break from the base of a scrum; England were leading 8-0 in the 23rd minute when Jannes Labuschagne was sent off for late-tackling Jonny Wilkinson while the latter was in the air; England were still leading 8-0 in the 25th minute when Jonny Wilkinson put up a brilliant cross-kick, but Ben Cohen was adjudged to have knocked the descending ball forward into the hands of Breyton Paulse before he then regathered and grounded it; England were leading 8-0 in the 31st minute when Will Greenwood powered through to score under the posts; England were leading 15-3 in the 39th minute and pressing in attack when Steve Thompson (2) collided with the referee and knocked him over!; England were leading 18-3 at half-time; England were still leading 18-3 in the 42nd minute when Will Greenwood dummied his way through to score another superb try which Matt Dawson then brilliantly converted from the left touchline; Jonny Wilkinson went off injured in the 44th minute, being replaced by Austin Healey; Matt Dawson went off injured in the 58th minute, being replaced by Andy Gomarsall; England were leading 25-3 midway through the second half when the referee awarded a penalty try after Phil Christophers was prevented from scoring by an illegal high tackle from Werner Greeff; England were leading 32-3 in the 70th minute when a rolling maul enabled Neil Back to score a try which Andy Gomarsall then brilliantly converted from the left touchline; Tim Stimpson came on as a replacement for Will Greenwood with 9 minutes of normal time remaining; England were leading 39-3 with 5 minutes of normal time remaining when Austin Healey put up another superb cross-kick which enabled Richard Hill (2) to score a try which Tim Stimpson then brilliantly converted from the right touchline; England were leading 46-3 in the third minute of injury time when Lawrence Dallaglio scored a pushover try with the last move of the match; England scored 38 unanswered points to seal the match; Phil Vickery had a brilliant game; England amassed their highest ever points total against South Africa and won their 18th successive cap

international match at Twickenham to set a new world record for a single venue; This was South Africa's worst ever margin of defeat in a cap international match!)

EMIRATES AIRLINE DUBAI RUGBY SEVENS

Dubai Exiles Stadium, Dubai

CAPTAIN: *Simon Amor*

First Round - Pool 'B'

6th Dec CANADA 5 **ENGLAND** 26

[*This match kicked off at 11.52am*]

(*England monopolised possession in this match*)

6th Dec ARABIAN GULF 5 **ENGLAND** 49

[*This match kicked off at 4.12pm; Arabian Gulf also billed as the United Arab Emirates*]

(*Paul Sampson had to go off after injuring his knee ligaments; England scored 49 unanswered points to win the match; Ben Gollings scored 24 points in this match*)

6th Dec WALES 0 **ENGLAND** 33

[*This match kicked off at 8.10pm; Paul Sampson unavailable due to injury*]

Quarter-Final

7th Dec NEW ZEALAND 19 **ENGLAND*** 7

[*This match kicked off at 11.14am; Paul Sampson unavailable due to injury*]

(*New Zealand were allowed to score 14 unanswered points to win the match; England were losing 14-0 at half-time; England were losing 14-0 early in the second half when Ben Russell (2) scored a brilliant try; England were losing 14-7 midway through the second half; England were still losing 14-7 in the last minute*)

[Plate Semi-Final:]

[7th Dec ARGENTINA 12 **ENGLAND** 19 **]**

[*This match kicked off at 1.26pm; Paul Sampson unavailable due to injury*]

(*England were drawing 0-0 when Richard Haughton scored a brilliant 80 metre solo try; England were losing 7-5 at half-time; England were leading 19-7 in the closing stages of this match*)

[Plate Final:]

[7th Dec FIJI 29 **ENGLAND** 5 **]**

[*This match kicked off at 7.45pm; Paul Sampson unavailable due to injury*]

(*England were losing 5-0 at half-time; Fiji were allowed to score 29 unanswered points to win the match; England were losing 29-0 in the closing stages when Simon Amor scored a consolation try after Ben Russell (2) threw a brilliant pass*)

EMIRATES AIRLINE SOUTH AFRICA SEVENS

Outeniqua Park Stadium, George

CAPTAIN: *Simon Amor*

First Round - Pool 'B'

13th Dec FRANCE 10 **ENGLAND** 19

[*This match kicked off at 10.44am*]

(*Davy Larguet scored in the 3rd minute!; England were losing 5-0 midway through the first half; England were leading 7-5 shortly before half-time; England were losing 10-7 at half-time; England were leading 14-10 in the 9th minute; England were still leading 14-10 midway through the second half; England were leading 14-10 with 1 minute remaining*)

13th Dec NAMIBIA 7 **ENGLAND** 19

[*This match kicked off at 1.50pm*]

(Rob Thirlby scored in the 2nd minute!; England were leading 7-0 midway through the first half; England were leading 12-0 at half-time; England were still leading 12-0 in the 10th minute; England were leading 12-7 midway through the second half)

13th Dec AUSTRALIA 19 **ENGLAND*** 14

[This match kicked off at 6.12pm]

(Rob McDonald scored in the 3rd minute!; England were losing 7-0 midway through the first half; England were drawing 7-7 at half-time; England were leading 14-7 in the 9th minute; England were still leading 14-7 midway through the second half; England were drawing 14-14 with 1 minute remaining)

Quarter-Final

14th Dec NEW ZEALAND 19 **ENGLAND*** 7

[This match kicked off at 11.46am]

(Rob Thirlby scored a brilliant 100 metre solo try in the 2nd minute!; Rob Thirlby went off immediately afterwards having pulled a hamstring, being replaced by Richard Haughton!; England were leading 7-0 midway through the first half; England were still leading 7-0 shortly before half-time; England were leading 7-5 at half-time; England were losing 12-7 in the 9th minute; England were still losing 12-7 midway through the second half; England were losing 12-7 with 2 minutes remaining; New Zealand were allowed to score 19 unanswered points to win the match)

[Plate Semi-Final:]

[14th Dec SAMOA 19 **ENGLAND*** 12]

[This match kicked off at 2.52pm; Rob Thirlby unavailable due to injury]

(Maurie Fa'asavlu scored in the 2nd minute!; England were losing 7-0 midway through the first half; England were losing 14-0 shortly before half-time; Samoa were allowed to score 19 unanswered points to win the match; England were losing 19-0 at half-time; England were losing 19-7 in the 9th minute; England were still losing 19-7 midway through the second half; England were losing 19-12 with 2 minutes remaining)

ENGLAND U21 MATCH

CAPTAIN: *Michael Holford*

18th Dec **ENGLAND U21 A XV** 28 WALES U21 A XV 5

Newbury RFC, Monks Lane, Newbury

[This match kicked off at 2.00pm; Luke Abraham played for England in the U19 World Championship in Italy in March 2002; John Holtby played for England in the U19 World Championship in Chile in April 2001]

(This match was played in cold conditions; The England U21 A XV played with the wind in the first half; The England U21 A XV was drawing 0-0 in the 5th minute when Andrew Jones scored as a direct consequence of a mistake by Andy Frost, thus 5 points were preventable; The England U21 A XV was leading 9-5 at half-time; James Hamilton dominated the lineout in the second half; The England U21 A XV was still leading 9-5 in the 48th minute when Ben Woods scored from a rolling maul; The England U21 A XV was leading 23-5 in the 50th minute; The England U21 A XV was leading 28-5 midway through the second half; The England U21 A XV scored 28 unanswered points to win the match; Dan Hipkiss and Tom Allen both had a brilliant game)

2003
BRISBANE SEVENS

Ballymore Stadium, Brisbane

CAPTAIN: *Simon Amor*

First Round - Pool 'D'

1st Feb COOK ISLANDS 0 **ENGLAND** 21

[This match kicked off at 1.06pm]

(England were drawing 0-0 midway through the first half; England were drawing 0-0 at half-time; Richard Haughton scored after just 30 seconds of the second half had been played!; England were leading 7-0 midway through the second half; England were leading 14-0 when the full-time hooter sounded, but the ball was still in play and Rob Thirlby was able to score to seal the match)

1st Feb JAPAN 19 **ENGLAND** 22

[This match kicked off at 4.06pm]

(Yohei Shinomiya followed up and scored in the 1st minute after Henry Paul failed to deal with a loose ball behind his own line, thus 7 points were preventable!; England were losing 5-0 straight after the restart when Nathan McAvoy scored a brilliant 70 metre solo try; England were leading 10-5 just before half-time; England were leading 15-5 at half-time; England were leading 22-5 early in the second half; England scored 22 unanswered points to win the match; England were leading 22-12 in the closing stages)

1st Feb FIJI 14 **ENGLAND** 19

[This match kicked off at 8.16pm]

(England were drawing 0-0 midway through the first half; England were losing 14-0 just before half-time; England were losing 14-7 at half-time; England scored 19 unanswered points to win the match)

Quarter-Final

2nd Feb SAMOA 5 **ENGLAND** 27

[This match kicked off at 12.50pm]

(England were losing 5-0 in the early stages; England were leading 10-5 at half-time; England were still leading 10-5 early in the second half when Richard Haughton scored after Nathan McAvoy made a brilliant break; England scored 27 unanswered points to win the match)

Semi-Final

2nd Feb NEW ZEALAND 14 **ENGLAND** 19

[This match kicked off at 4.26pm]

(England were losing 7-0 in the early stages; England were losing 7-5 at half-time; England were still losing 7-5 early in the second half when Ugo Monye scored a brilliant 50 metre solo try; England scored 19 unanswered points to win the match; England were leading 19-7 midway through the second half; England were still leading 19-7 with 1 minute remaining)

Final

2nd Feb FIJI 14 **ENGLAND** 28

[This match kicked off at 7.00pm; Phil Dowson unavailable due to injury]

(England were drawing 0-0 midway through the first half; England were still drawing 0-0 in the 7th minute when Tony Roques powered through to score; England were losing 14-7 shortly before half-time when Ugo Monye chipped ahead and followed up to score a brilliant try; England were drawing 14-14 at half-time; England were still drawing 14-

***14 midway through the second half; England were drawing 14-14 with 4 minutes remaining when Ugo Monye ran 60 metres to score another try after Henry Paul put in a superb crossfield kick; England were leading 21-14 in the closing stages when Ben Gollings scored after Simon Amor made a brilliant break*)**

TELECOM NEW ZEALAND INTERNATIONAL SEVENS

WestpacTrust Stadium, Wellington

CAPTAIN: *Tony Roques*

First Round - Pool 'A'

7th Feb	PAPUA NEW GUINEA	0	**ENGLAND**	49

[*This match kicked off at 3.34pm*]

(*Ben Gollings scored 24 points in this match*)

CAPTAIN: *Simon Amor*

7th Feb	TONGA	17	**ENGLAND**	28

[*This match kicked off at 6.30pm*]

(*England were losing 12-7 at half-time*)

7th Feb	NEW ZEALAND	24	**ENGLAND**	0

[*This match kicked off at 9.56pm*]

(*England were losing 19-0 at half-time*)

Quarter-Final

8th Feb	SOUTH AFRICA	7	**ENGLAND**	17

[*This match kicked off at 3.39pm*]

(*England were losing 7-0 at one point in the first half; England were leading 10-7 at half-time; England scored 17 unanswered points to win the match; Henry Paul had a brilliant game*)

Semi-Final

8th Feb	AUSTRALIA	15	**ENGLAND**	21

[*This match kicked off at 7.00pm*]

(*England were losing 10-7 at half-time; England were losing 15-7 at one point in the second half; England scored 14 unanswered points to win the match*)

Final

8th Feb	NEW ZEALAND	38	**ENGLAND**	26

[*This match kicked off at 9.00pm*]

(*This match was played in very windy conditions; England were losing 5-0 in the 3rd minute; England were losing 10-0 midway through the first half when Henry Paul scored a brilliant 60 metre solo try; England were losing 17-7 shortly before half-time; England were losing 17-14 at half-time; Ben Gollings scored after just 30 seconds of the second half had been played!; England were leading 26-24 in the 13th minute; England were still leading 26-24 midway through the second half; England were leading 26-24 with 3 minutes of normal time remaining; England were losing 31-26 when the full-time hooter sounded, but the ball remained in play until Anthony Tuitavake powered through some collectively poor tackling to score to clinch the match for New Zealand, thus 7 points were preventable*)

6 NATIONS CHAMPIONSHIP

CAPTAIN: *Martin Johnson*

15th Feb	**ENGLAND**	25	FRANCE	17

Twickenham

[*This match kicked off at 4.00pm; David Flatman, Trevor Woodman, Austin Healey, Iain*

***Balshaw and Michael Horak all unavailable due to injury; Matt Dawson selected but withdrew due to injury, Andy Gomarsall was moved from the bench to the team and Nick Walshe was then selected for the bench; Phil Vickery and Mike Tindall in original training squad of 27 but withdrew due to injury; Dorian West, Simon Shaw, Joe Worsley and Tim Stimpson all in original training squad of 27 but were not selected for team or bench; Charlie Hodgson was played out of position as a centre; Jason Leonard set a new England record of 100 caps; There was a minute's silence for Nick Duncombe, who had died the day before the match*]**

(*This match was played in cold conditions; England were drawing 0-0 in the 15th minute when Jonny Wilkinson scored a brilliant 45 metre penalty goal where the ball hit the crossbar and then bounced over!; England were leading 3-0 in the 16th minute when Charlie Hodgson took too much time over his clearance kick and was charged down by Olivier Magne, who went on to score from the ensuing rebound, thus 7 points were preventable; England were losing 7-6 midway through the first half; England were leading 9-7 in the 29th minute; Jason Leonard went off injured in the 34th minute, being replaced by Graham Rowntree; England were still leading 9-7 in the 39th minute when Charlie Hodgson broke through, but he then wasted this great try-scoring opportunity by failing to pass to the unmarked Will Greenwood outside him; England were leading 9-7 just before half-time; England were leading 12-7 at half-time; England played with a strong wind in the second half; Lewis Moody injured his shoulder in the 10th minute but unaccountably elected to remain on the pitch until the 45th minute, being replaced by Lawrence Dallaglio with Richard Hill (2) then switching from number 8 to flanker to accommodate Dallaglio; The referee had to briefly order uncontested scrums in the 48th minute after Graham Rowntree went off with a blood injury to leave England with only one fit prop left!; England were still leading 12-7 in the 49th minute when Jason Robinson scored after Will Greenwood threw a superb miss pass; England were leading 22-7 midway through the second half; England were leading 25-7 in the 64th minute; England scored 22 unanswered points to win the match; England were leading 25-12 in the 67th minute; England were still leading 25-12 in the second minute of injury time; The referee allowed 13 minutes of injury time to be played!; Jonny Wilkinson played brilliantly and scored 20 points in this match and became the first England player to score 600 points in cap internationals*)

22nd Feb WALES 9 **ENGLAND** 26

Millennium Stadium, Cardiff

[*This match kicked off at 5.30pm; David Flatman, Trevor Woodman, Jason Leonard, Phil Vickery, Lewis Moody, Matt Dawson, Austin Healey and Iain Balshaw all unavailable due to injury; Julian White selected but withdrew due to injury, being replaced by Robbie Morris; Charlie Hodgson was played out of position as a centre*]

(*England were losing 3-0 in the 9th minute; England were drawing 3-3 midway through the first half when Jonny Wilkinson scored a brilliant 30 metre drop goal from a difficult angle; England were drawing 6-6 in the 27th minute when Jonny Wilkinson missed an eminently kickable 24 metre penalty goal attempt; England were still drawing 6-6 in the 29th minute when Jonny Wilkinson scored another superb 31 metre drop goal; England were leading 9-6 in the 40th minute when a poor tackle by Charlie Hodgson allowed Mark Taylor to break through, but he then unaccountably attempted to make the line himself when there was a 2 man overlap outside him!; Jason Robinson went off injured immediately afterwards, being replaced by Phil Christophers with Ben Cohen then switching from wing to the unfamiliar position of full back to accommodate Christophers; England were leading 9-6 at half-time; Richard Hill (2) went off with a blood injury at half-time, being temporarily replaced by*

***James Simpson-Daniel who played as a wing in the brief absence of the sin-binned Phil Christophers, which ensured that the backline remained at full numerical strength!; England were still leading 9-6 in the 47th minute when Will Greenwood powered through 4 attempted tackles to score; England were leading 16-6 in the 52nd minute when Jonny Wilkinson missed a kickable 26 metre drop goal attempt; Neil Back went off injured in the 56th minute, being replaced by Joe Worsley who scored immediately afterwards with his first touch of the ball!; England scored 17 unanswered points to win the match; England were leading 23-6 midway through the second half; England were leading 26-9 with 8 minutes of normal time remaining; Jonny Wilkinson went off injured with 2 minutes of normal time remaining, being replaced by James Simpson-Daniel with Charlie Hodgson then moving from centre to fly half to accommodate James Simpson-Daniel; Dan Luger went off injured at the same time, being replaced by Andy Gomarsall who had to play out of position as a wing; Ben Cohen injured playing in the match; Lawrence Dallaglio and Will Greenwood both had a brilliant game*)**

CAPTAIN: *Jonny Wilkinson* [*Lawrence Dallaglio*]

9th March **ENGLAND** 40 ITALY 5

Twickenham

[*This match kicked off at 3.00pm; David Flatman, Jason Leonard, Phil Vickery, Julian White, Lewis Moody, Neil Back, Austin Healey, Ben Cohen, Mike Catt, Jason Robinson and Iain Balshaw all unavailable due to injury; Martin Johnson selected as captain in the original training squad of 25 but withdrew due to injury; Phil Christophers and Jamie Noon in original training squad of 25 but were not selected for team or bench*]

(*England played with a swirling wind in the first half; Some superb handling amongst the backs allowed Josh Lewsey to score in the 3rd minute!; England were leading 14-0 in the 13th minute when James Simpson-Daniel scored a brilliant try; England were leading 21-0 in the 16th minute when Josh Lewsey scored a brilliant 72 metre solo try; England were leading 28-0 midway through the first half; Alex Sanderson came on as a temporary blood replacement for Lawrence Dallaglio in the 20th minute; England were leading 33-0 in the 22nd minute!; England scored 33 unanswered points to win the match; England were leading 33-0 at half-time; Jonny Wilkinson went off injured in the 48th minute, being replaced by Charlie Hodgson who then himself had to go off in the 54th minute after he ruptured the anterior cruciate ligament in his knee, being replaced by Ollie Smith (2) with Will Greenwood then having to switch from centre to the unfamiliar position of fly half to accommodate Ollie Smith (2); England were still leading 33-0 midway through the second half; England were leading 33-5 in the 70th minute when Dan Luger scored after Ollie Smith (2) made a superb break; Josh Lewsey went off injured with 8 minutes of normal time remaining, being replaced by Kyran Bracken with James Simpson-Daniel then switching from wing to the unfamiliar position of full back to accommodate Kyran Bracken, who also had to play out of position as a wing!; Josh Lewsey had a brilliant game*)

CAPTAIN: *Martin Johnson*

22nd Mar **ENGLAND** 40 SCOTLAND 9

Twickenham

**[*This match kicked off at 4.00pm; David Flatman, Phil Vickery, Julian White, Lewis Moody, Austin Healey, Charlie Hodgson and Iain Balshaw all unavailable due to injury; Ollie Smith (2) in original training squad of 30 but withdrew due to injury; Mike Worsley, Robbie Morris, Steve Borthwick, Simon Shaw, Alex Sanderson, Kyran Bracken, Jamie Noon and James Simpson-Daniel all in original training squad of 30*

***but were not selected for team or bench; Jason Leonard was added to the squad on 17th March 2003*]**
(*England played into the wind in the first half; Jonny Wilkinson scored a penalty goal in the 2nd minute!; England were leading 6-0 in the 11th minute; England were drawing 6-6 midway through the first half; England were still drawing 6-6 in the 22nd minute when some superb handling amongst the backs allowed Josh Lewsey to score; England were leading 13-6 in the 31st minute when Josh Lewsey saved a certain try by tackling Gordon Bulloch; England were leading 13-9 shortly before half-time; England were leading 16-9 at half-time; England were still leading 16-9 in the 50th minute when Jonny Wilkinson put up a brilliant cross-kick which enabled Ben Cohen to knock the descending ball backwards, regather it and then touch the ball down, but the move was disallowed after he was wrongly adjudged to have knocked the ball on; Immediately afterwards Bryan Redpath dropped the ball in front of his own line after Matt Dawson tap-tackled him as he shaped to kick and Ben Cohen was able to follow up and score; Mike Tindall went off injured in the 57th minute, being replaced by Dan Luger with Jason Robinson then switching from wing to centre to accommodate Luger; England were leading 26-9 midway through the second half; Ben Kay went off injured in the 63rd minute, being replaced by Danny Grewcock; England were still leading 26-9 in the 64th minute when Jason Robinson scored a superb 45 metre solo try after Matt Dawson took a quick tap penalty; England were leading 33-9 with 2 minutes of normal time remaining when Jason Robinson scored another try after Matt Dawson broke from the base of a ruck; England scored 27 unanswered points to clinch the match; Richard Hill (2) had a brilliant game*)

30th Mar IRELAND 6 **ENGLAND** 42
Lansdowne Road
[*This match kicked off at 2.00pm; David Flatman, Phil Vickery, Julian White, Lewis Moody, Austin Healey, Charlie Hodgson and Iain Balshaw all unavailable due to injury; Steve Borthwick was added to the squad on 25th March 2003 to provide potential cover for Danny Grewcock, who was due to appear at a RFU hearing later the same day after he was cited for twice punching an opponent and then tearing up that same opponent's scrum cap in a Zurich Premiership match on 15th March 2003, but ironically Grewcock was merely fined and not suspended!*]
**(*England played into a strong wind in the first half; David Humphreys scored a drop goal in the 5th minute!; England were losing 3-0 in the 9th minute when Lawrence Dallaglio scored under the posts after Richard Hill (2) gathered a loose ball from the base of an Ireland scrum; England were leading 7-3 midway through the first half; Joe Worsley came on as a temporary blood replacement for Richard Hill (2) in the 23rd minute; Kyran Bracken came on as temporary blood replacement for Matt Dawson in the 26th minute; England were leading 10-6 in the 30th minute; Graham Rowntree went off injured in the 38th minute, being replaced by Trevor Woodman; England were still leading 10-6 in the first minute of first half injury time when Jonny Wilkinson scored a brilliant drop goal; England were leading 13-6 at half-time; Jonny Wilkinson injured his shoulder in the 42nd minute but elected to remain on the pitch; England were still leading 13-6 in the 44th minute when Jonny Wilkinson had a brilliant 39 metre drop-goal attempt which the referee awarded, but this decision was then reversed after a touch judge adjudged that Steve Thompson (2) had taken a quick lineout from the wrong position on the touchline!; Danny Grewcock came on as a temporary blood replacement for Ben Kay in the 46th minute; Paul Grayson came on as a temporary blood replacement for Jonny Wilkinson in the 54th minute; England were leading 13-6 midway through the second half when Mike Tindall scored a superb try and injured his*

***ankle in the process!; England were leading 20-6 in the 65th minute when Will Greenwood powered through to score; Mike Tindall went off injured in the 69th minute, being replaced by Dan Luger with Jason Robinson then switching from wing to centre to accommodate Luger; Matt Dawson briefly went off at the same time for further attention to a blood injury and was again replaced by Kyran Bracken; England were leading 30-6 with 8 minutes of normal time remaining; England were still leading 30-6 in the first minute of injury time when Will Greenwood intercepted Geordan Murphy's pass and then ran diagonally to the corner flag to ground the ball for another try!; England were leading 35-6 in the seventh minute of injury time when Dan Luger scored in the last move of the match after Jonny Wilkinson brilliantly flicked the ball on to Jason Leonard; England scored 35 unanswered points to clinch the match and the Grand Slam; Lawrence Dallaglio had a brilliant game*)**

ENGLAND STUDENTS MATCHES

CAPTAIN: *Ben Gerry*

14th Feb	**ENGLAND STUDENTS***	28	FRANCE STUDENTS	30

Sedgley Park RFC, Park Lane, Whitefield, Manchester

[*This match kicked off at 7.30pm*]

(*Matt Honeyben missed two eminently kickable penalty goal attempts in the first half; England Students were losing 16-0 at half-time; Ross Winney came on as a replacement for Matt Honeyben at half-time; England Students were losing 23-14 when Tom Hayman scored a brilliant solo try; England Students were losing 30-21 in the closing stages when Adam Billig scored after Ross Winney put up a brilliant garryowen; France Students scored two interception tries, thus 2 tries and 14 points were preventable; Neil Clark, Tom Hayman and Ross Winney all had a brilliant game*)

21st Feb	WALES STUDENTS	17	**ENGLAND STUDENTS**	23

St. Helen's, Swansea

[*This match kicked off at 7.00pm; Ed Lewsey played for Wales Students in this match*]

(*The England Students forwards dominated the lineout in this match; England Students were leading 5-0 in the 12th minute; England Students were still leading 5-0 midway through the first half; England Students were leading 5-0 in the 26th minute when Tom Hayman scored from a rolling maul; England Students were leading 15-3 in the 31st minute; England Students were leading 15-9 at half-time; England Students were leading 15-14 in the 46th minute; England Students were leading 18-17 with 5 minutes remaining when Ben Gerry scored to clinch the match*)

CAPTAIN: *No captain appointed*

7th Mar	**ENGLAND STUDENTS**	C	ITALY STUDENTS	C

Rectory Field, Charlton Road, Blackheath

[*This match was cancelled on 4th March 2003 after financial difficulties prevented Italy Students from travelling to England*]

21st Mar	**ENGLAND STUDENTS**	C	SCOTLAND STUDENTS	C

?@

[*This match was cancelled on 23rd December 2002 after the SRU announced that the Scotland Students team would not be playing in 2003 for financial reasons*]

U21 6 NATIONS CHAMPIONSHIP

CAPTAIN: *Chris Day*

14th Feb **ENGLAND U21** 26 FRANCE U21 25

Newbury RFC, Monks Lane, Newbury

[*This match kicked off at 7.30pm; Adryan Winnan selected but withdrew due to injury, Andy Frost was moved from the bench to the team and Tim Taylor was then selected for the bench; Alex Gluth, Geoff Parling, Ben Hughes, Magnus Lund, Matt Styles, Chris Mayor and James Bailey all in original training squad of 29 but were not selected for team or bench; Ben Russell (2), Clive Stuart-Smith and Ryan Peacey toured Canada, New Zealand and Australia with England Schools 18 Group in July-August 2001*]

(*England U21 were leading 5-0 in the 6th minute; England U21 were leading 8-3 in the 12th minute; Ben Woods went off injured in the 19th minute, being replaced by Michael Holford; England U21 were losing 10-8 midway through the first half; Andy Frost went off injured in the 22nd minute, being replaced by Tim Taylor; England U21 were leading 11-10 in the 32nd minute when Matt Stevens scored from a rolling maul; England U21 were leading 18-15 at half-time; England U21 were losing 20-18 in the 43rd minute; England U21 were leading 23-18 in the 48th minute; England U21 were leading 23-18 midway through the second half; England U21 were losing 25-23 in the 64th minute; England U21 were still losing 25-23 with 8 minutes remaining when Warren Spragg scored a penalty goal to win the match*)

21st Feb WALES U21 35 **ENGLAND U21** 9

The Gnoll, Neath

[*This match kicked off at 2.30pm; James Hamilton selected but withdrew, Jon Pendlebury was moved from the bench to the team and Geoff Parling was then selected for the bench; Chris Hyndman selected but withdrew, Spencer Davey was moved from the bench to the team; Ugo Monye selected but withdrew to sit on the bench, being replaced by Marcel Garvey; Andy Frost selected but withdrew, being replaced by Chris Mayor; Ryan Peacey selected for bench but withdrew, being replaced by Magnus Lund; Marcel Garvey played for England in the U19 World Championship in Italy in March 2002*]

(*England U21 were losing 3-0 in the 7th minute; England U21 were leading 6-3 in the 18th minute; England U21 were drawing 6-6 when Warren Spragg missed 2 penalty goal attempts in succession; England U21 were still drawing 6-6 shortly before half-time; England U21 were losing 16-6 at half-time; The England U21 forwards could not win any possession in the second half; England U21 were losing 23-6 in the 46th minute; England U21 were losing 23-9 in the 52nd minute; England U21 were still losing 23-9 midway through the second half; England U21 were losing 23-9 with 7 minutes of normal time remaining*)

7th Mar **ENGLAND U21** 34 ITALY U21 3

Newbury RFC, Monks Lane, Newbury

[*This match kicked off at 7.30pm; Chris Bell played for England in the U19 World Championship in Chile in April 2001 and Italy in March 2002*]

(*This match was played in driving rain; England U21 were leading 3-0 in the early stages; England U21 were still leading 3-0 when Chris Mayor scored a brilliant try; England U21 were leading 10-3 in the 26th minute; England U21 were leading 10-3 at half-time; A rolling maul enabled Magnus Lund to score a try which Ed Thrower then converted to give England U21 a 22-3 lead early in the second half; England U21 were leading 27-3 with 2 minutes remaining; England U21 scored 24 unanswered points in the second half to win the match*)

21st Mar **ENGLAND U21** 15 SCOTLAND U21 12

Newbury RFC, Monks Lane, Newbury

[*This match kicked off at 7.30pm; Will Skinner, Chris Mayor and Chris Hyndman in original squad of 24 but were not selected for team or bench; Marcel Garvey was added to the squad on 20th March 2003*]

(*Ed Thrower missed a penalty goal attempt in the 2nd minute!; England U21 were leading 5-0 in the 9th minute; England U21 were drawing 5-5 midway through the first half; England U21 were still drawing 5-5 in the 25th minute when Ed Thrower scored after Magnus Lund made a brilliant break; England U21 were leading 10-5 at half-time; England U21 were still leading 10-5 in the 42nd minute when an attempted clearance kick went straight to Nikki Walker, who instigated a counter-attack which led directly to a try by Paul Boston, thus 7 points were preventable; England U21 were losing 12-10 midway through the second half when Magnus Lund scored after Paul Hodgson made a brilliant blindside break; England U21 were leading 15-12 when Ed Thrower hit the post with a penalty goal attempt; England U21 were leading 15-12 in the last minute when Dan Hipkiss crossed the tryline but the move was disallowed after the referee adjudged that there had been an accidental offside; Magnus Lund had a brilliant game*)

28th Mar IRELAND U21 21 **ENGLAND U21*** 20

Ravenhill Park, Belfast

[*This match kicked off at 7.30pm; Chris Rowland in original squad of 23 but was not selected for team or bench; Tom Williams played for Wales U19 but then switched his allegiance to England in March 2002*]

(*England U21 were losing 3-0 in the 7th minute; England U21 were leading 6-3 midway through the first half; England U21 were leading 13-3 in the 26th minute; England U21 were leading 13-3 at half-time; England U21 were leading 13-6 in the 44th minute; England U21 were still leading 13-6 midway through the second half when Spencer Davey scored a brilliant solo try; England U21 were leading 20-6 in the 68th minute; England U21 were leading 20-16 with 4 minutes of normal time remaining when Ed Thrower missed a penalty goal attempt; England U21 were still leading 20-16 in the third minute of injury time when Tommy Bowe scored to win the match for Ireland U21*)

'A' INTERNATIONAL CHAMPIONSHIP

CAPTAIN: *Dorian West*

14th Feb **ENGLAND A** 30 FRANCE A 13

Franklin's Gardens, Northampton

**[*This match kicked off at 7.35pm; David Flatman, Trevor Woodman, Austin Healey, Nick Duncombe, Dave Walder, Iain Balshaw and Michael Horak all unavailable due to injury; Kyran Bracken selected as captain in the original training squad of 25 but withdrew due to injury; Fraser Waters selected for bench but withdrew due to injury, being replaced by Jamie Noon; Nick Walshe selected but withdrew on the day of the match as he was now required to sit on the bench for the full England international team, Martyn Wood was moved from the bench to the team and Scott Benton was then selected for the bench; Graham Rowntree in original training squad of 25 but withdrew as he was now required to sit on the bench for the full England international team; Kevin Sorrell in original training squad of 25 but withdrew due to injury; Andy Sheridan, Maurice Fitzgerald, James Forrester, Mark Cueto and Matt Perry all in original training squad of 25 but were not selected for team or bench; Mike Shelley and Josh Lewsey were added to the squad on 9th February 2003; Dorian West, Simon*

***Shaw, Joe Worsley and Tim Stimpson were all added to the squad on 10th February 2003*]**
(*Paul Grayson scored a penalty goal in the 3rd minute!; England A were leading 6-0 in the 12th minute; England A were leading 6-3 midway through the first half; England A were leading 9-3 in the 28th minute; England A were still leading 9-3 in the second minute of first half injury time when the referee inexplicably ignored Patrick Tabacco illegally impeding the defence, which created space for Guillaume Bousses to score, thus 7 points were unlawful; England A were losing 10-9 at half-time; England A were leading 12-10 in the 43rd minute; England A were losing 13-12 in the 48th minute; England A were still losing 13-12 midway through the second half; England A were leading 15-13 in the 64th minute; England A were leading 18-13 with 7 minutes of normal time remaining when Joe Worsley scored after Dan Scarbrough made a brilliant break; England A scored 18 unanswered points to win the match; Paul Grayson scored 20 points in this match; Joe Worsley and Jamie Noon both had a brilliant game*)

CAPTAIN: *No captain appointed*

21st Feb WALES A C **ENGLAND A** C

The Racecourse Ground, Wrexham

[*This match was cancelled on 6th January 2003 after Wales A withdrew from the tournament because the WRU could not afford to play the matches!*]

CAPTAIN: *Dorian West*

7th Mar **ENGLAND A** 43 ITALY A 11

Franklin's Gardens, Northampton

[*This match kicked off at 7.35pm; Dave Walder and Kevin Sorrell unavailable due to injury; Paul Grayson selected but withdrew due to injury, Alex King was moved from the bench to the team and Olly Barkley was then selected for the bench; Olly Barkley then himself withdrew due to injury and was replaced by Martyn Wood; Andy Sheridan, Mark Cueto, Hugh Vyvyan, Tim Stimpson and Matt Perry all in original training squad of 25 but were not selected for team or bench; Maurice Fitzgerald was capped for England Colts in March 1995; Adam Vander was capped for England Colts in March 1993*]

(*This match was played on a very wet and muddy pitch; Dorian West scored from a rolling maul in the 3rd minute!; England A were leading 5-0 in the 15th minute when Ben Johnston scored after Alex King put in a brilliant grubber kick; England A were leading 10-3 when Andy Hazell scored after Jamie Noon made a superb break; England A were leading 17-6 at half-time; England A were leading 17-11 in the 44th minute; Jamie Noon was replaced at half-time by Fraser Waters who scored with his first touch of the ball!; Andy Hazell scored a brilliant try in injury time; England A scored 26 unanswered points to clinch the match*)

CAPTAIN: *Kyran Bracken*

21st Mar **ENGLAND A** 78 SCOTLAND A 6

Franklin's Gardens, Northampton

[*This match kicked off at 7.35pm; Dave Walder and Matt Perry unavailable due to injury; Neal Hatley, Mike Shelley, Tom Palmer (2), Andy Hazell, Martyn Wood, Olly Barkley and Marcel Garvey all in original training squad of 22 but were not selected for team or bench*]

(*Alex King scored a penalty goal in the 2nd minute!; England A were leading 17-0 in the 12th minute when Dan Scarbrough scored after James Forrester made a brilliant 40 metre run; Chris Jones made a superb break that enabled Mark Cueto to score a try*

***which Alex King then converted to give England A a 31-0 lead midway through the first half; England A were leading 31-6 in the 31st minute; James Simpson-Daniel went off injured in the 37th minute, being replaced by Ben Johnston; England A were leading 31-6 at half-time; Alex Sanderson went off injured at half-time, being replaced by Martin Corry; England A were leading 38-6 in the 49th minute when James Forrester scored after he stole the ball at a Scotland A lineout on the halfway line; England A were leading 50-6 in the 56th minute when Kyran Bracken scored from a rolling maul; England A were leading 57-6 midway through the second half; England A were leading 64-6 in the 67th minute; England A were leading 71-6 in the second minute of injury time; England A scored 47 unanswered points in the second half to seal the match; Alex King scored 23 points in this match; James Forrester and Dan Scarbrough both had a brilliant game; England A achieved their highest ever points total and margin of victory against an international team!*)**

CAPTAIN: *Martin Corry*

28th Mar IRELAND A 24 **ENGLAND A*** 21

Donnybrook, Dublin

[*This match kicked off at 7.00pm; Joe Lydon missed this match as he was away in Hong Kong with the England Sevens team; Dave Walder, James Simpson-Daniel and Matt Perry unavailable due to injury; Andy Gomarsall selected but withdrew due to injury, Nick Walshe was moved from the bench to the team and Martyn Wood was then selected for the bench*]

(*Paul Shields scored in the 2nd minute!; Olly Barkley came on as a temporary blood replacement for Alex King in the 7th minute; Maurice Fitzgerald came on as a temporary blood replacement for Robbie Morris in the 18th minute; England A were losing 5-3 midway through the first half when Alex King missed an eminently kickable penalty goal attempt; England A were leading 6-5 in the 31st minute when Dan Scarbrough followed up his own grubber kick to score a brilliant try; Adam Vander went off injured just before half-time, being replaced by Hugh Vyvyan; England A were leading 13-8 at half-time; England A were leading 13-11 in the 52nd minute when some superb handling by Mike Worsley allowed Dan Scarbrough to score again; England A were leading 18-14 midway through the second half when they wasted a great try-scoring opportunity by knocking the ball on 10 metres from the tryline; England A were still leading 18-14 with 7 minutes of normal time remaining; England A were losing 21-18 in the third minute of injury time when Alex King kicked a penalty goal to bring the scores level; England A were drawing 21-21 in the sixth minute of injury time when Mark McHugh scored a penalty goal from the halfway line with the last kick of the match to win the game for Ireland A*)

JARROD CUNNINGHAM SALSA FOUNDATION BENEFIT MATCH

CAPTAIN: *Rob Howley* (WA)

6th Mar London Irish All-Stars 33 **BARBARIANS** 66

Stoop Memorial Ground, Langhorn Drive, Twickenham

[*This match kicked off at 7.45pm; Neil Hatley selected but withdrew, Duncan Bell was moved from the bench to the team; Chris Sheasby selected but withdrew, Simon Hepher was moved from the bench to the team; Neil Jenkins selected but withdrew, being replaced by Waisale Serevi; Duncan Bell and Simon Hepher then both withdrew to sit on the bench, being replaced by Kelvin Todd and Roy Winters respectively; Duncan Bell then withdrew from the bench, being replaced by Ian Critchley; Matt Cannon selected for bench but withdrew, being replaced by Lee Starling; Jarrod Cunningham's illness prevented him from being available as a full-time player but he*

***was still able to come onto the pitch at regular intervals to take the London Irish All-Stars' kicks at goal!; Jarrod Cunningham died in July 2007; Roy Winters was capped for England Schools 18 Group in March 1994; Simon Hepher was the brother of Ali Hepher*]**

(*Oriol Ripol scored in the 3rd minute!; The Barbarians were losing 7-5 in the 6th minute; The Barbarians were losing 12-7 midway through the first half; The Barbarians were losing 19-7 in the 30th minute; The Barbarians were leading 28-19 at half-time; The Barbarians were leading 35-26 in the 45th minute; The Barbarians were leading 42-26 midway through the second half; The Barbarians were leading 42-33 in the 68th minute; The Barbarians were leading 54-33 with 2 minutes of normal time remaining when Waisale Serevi scored to complete a hat-trick of tries; The Barbarians scored 24 unanswered points to seal the match; The Barbarians were leading 66-33 in the second minute of injury time when Trevor Leota missed a difficult conversion attempt!; Waisale Serevi played brilliantly and scored 31 points in this match*)

NIG CHALLENGE

CAPTAIN: *Richard Cockerill*

7th Mar	Leicester XV	21	**BARBARIANS**	12

Welford Road, Leicester

[*This match kicked off at 7.45pm; Ben Wheeler was the son of Peter Wheeler*]

(*The Barbarians were leading 12-0 at half-time; The Barbarians were leading 12-7 with 2 minutes remaining; The Barbarians were losing 14-12 in the closing stages when Morgan Williams had his pass intercepted by James Buckland who then ran 40 metres to score, thus 7 points were preventable; The Leicester XV was allowed to score 21 unanswered points to win the match*)

VIÑA DEL MAR SEVENS

Estadio Sausalito, Viña del Mar

CAPTAIN: *No captain appointed*

7th March	*No opponents named*	C	**ENGLAND**	C

[*This Round was rescheduled for 7th-8th March 2003 but was cancelled by the IRB on 12th February 2003 after the tournament sponsor Cerveza Cristal withdrew its funding*]

CREDIT SUISSE FIRST BOSTON HONG KONG SEVENS

Hong Kong Stadium, Eastern Hospital Road, So Kon Po, Hong Kong

CAPTAIN: *Phil Greening*

First Round - Pool 'B'

28th Mar	SINGAPORE	0	**ENGLAND**	52

[*This match kicked off at 5.22pm; England were originally scheduled to play First Round matches in Pool B against Kenya and Italy*]

(*The England players had insufficient time to shake off their jet lag; Jamie Noon scored in the 1st minute!; England were leading 7-0 when Rob Thirlby kicked ahead and followed up to score; England were leading 33-0 at half-time; England were reduced to 5 men at one point in the second half after Geoff Appleford and Johnny Howard were sent to the sin-bin in quick succession!; The majority of England's conversion attempts were taken by the respective try-scorer in an attempt to get as much playing time as possible out of this match's allotted 14 minutes!*)

CAPTAIN: *Simon Amor*

29th Mar	CHINESE TAIPEI	5	**ENGLAND**	43

[This match kicked off at 1.20pm]

(Ugo Monye scored 4 tries in the first half of this match!; Ugo Monye scored 20 points in this match)

29th Mar	TONGA	7	**ENGLAND**	42

[This match kicked off at 5.44pm]

Quarter-Final

30th Mar	AUSTRALIA	14	**ENGLAND**	19

[This match kicked off at 2.21pm]

Semi-Final

30th Mar	FIJI	19	**ENGLAND**	24

[This match kicked off at 4.33pm]

(England were losing 5-0 when Rob Thirlby scored a brilliant solo try; Henry Paul powered through several attempted tackles to score a superb try; England were leading 17-7 at half-time; England were leading 24-7 early in the second half; Henry Paul had a brilliant game)

Final

30th Mar	NEW ZEALAND	17	**ENGLAND**	22

[This match kicked off at 6.31pm]

(England were losing 5-0 when Ugo Monye scored a brilliant solo try; England were drawing 5-5 when Roy Kinikinlau scored after a poor tackle by Ugo Monye, thus 7 points were preventable; England were losing 12-5 at half-time; Richard Haughton came on a replacement for Ugo Monye at the start of the second half; England were still losing 12-5 when Henry Paul scored a superb 35 metre solo try; England were drawing 12-12 when Richard Haughton scored two tries in 3 minutes!; England scored 17 unanswered points to win the match; England were leading 22-12 in the closing stages; Henry Paul had a brilliant game)

BEIJING SEVENS

National Olympic Sports Centre, Beijing

CAPTAIN: *No captain appointed*

5th April	*No opponents named*	C	**ENGLAND**	C

[This Round was scheduled for 5th-6th April 2003 but was cancelled by the IRB on 28th March 2003 due to fears about the spread of the SARS virus]

SINGAPORE SEVENS

National Stadium, Kallang

CAPTAIN: *No captain appointed*

26th April	*No opponents named*	C	**ENGLAND**	C

[This tournament was originally scheduled to take place on 26th-27th April 2003 but was then postponed by the competition organisers on 3rd April 2003 due to fears about the spread of the SARS virus; The organisers initially hoped to reschedule the tournament for the end of May 2003, but they could not guarantee that the SARS virus would have been sufficiently contained by that point so the IRB eventually decided to cancel the competition on 18th April 2003 on the grounds of health and safety]

MALAYSIA SEVENS

MPPJ Stadium, Petaling Jaya, Kelana Jaya

CAPTAIN: *No captain appointed*

3rd May *No opponents named* C **ENGLAND** C

[*This Round was scheduled for 3rd-4th May 2003 but was cancelled by the IRB on 12th February 2003 due to a financial dispute between the Malaysian Rugby Union and the tournament organisers*]

TETLEY'S COUNTY CHAMPIONSHIP SEMI-FINAL

CAPTAIN: *Steve Evans* (CO)

17th May **CORNWALL*** 13 Lancashire 23

Recreation Ground, Redruth

[*This match kicked off at 3.00pm; Joe Bearman unavailable due to injury; Martin O'Keefe, Paul Arnold (2), Richard Senior, Dave McCormack, Rob Hitchmough, Neil Kerfoot and Sean Casey all played for Lancashire in this match, with Richard Senior and Sean Casey both scoring a try*]

(*Cornwall played down the slope towards Hellfire Corner in the first half; Chris Glynn scored a penalty goal in the 1st minute!; Cornwall were drawing 3-3 in the 16th minute; Cornwall were still drawing 3-3 midway through the first half when Rocky Newton scored a brilliant try; Cornwall were leading 8-3 when Rocky Newton missed a difficult penalty goal attempt into the wind; Cornwall were leading 8-3 at half-time; Cornwall played with a strong wind in the second half; The Cornwall scrum was put under severe pressure in the second half; Cornwall were losing 10-8 in the 54th minute; Cornwall were still losing 10-8 midway through the second half; Cornwall were losing 15-8 in the 64th minute; Cornwall were still losing 15-8 with 8 minutes of normal time remaining when Craig Bonds chipped the ball straight to Jalo van der Venter who then ran 70 metres to score, thus 5 points were preventable; Lancashire were allowed to score 17 unanswered points; Cornwall were losing 20-8 with 3 minutes of normal time remaining when James Hawken scored a consolation try; Cornwall were losing 20-13 in the seventh minute of injury time when Chris Glynn scored a penalty goal to clinch the match for Lancashire*)

TETLEY'S NATIONAL COUNTIES SEVEN-A-SIDE TOURNAMENT

Twickenham

CAPTAIN: *Rob Thirlby*

Semi-Final

24th May Eastern Counties 0 **CORNWALL** 47

[*This match kicked off at 10.20am*]

Final

24th May Yorkshire 31 **CORNWALL** 33

[*This match kicked off at 11.40am*]

(*Cornwall were losing 26-7 at half-time; Cornwall were still losing 26-7 early in the second half when Rob Thirlby scored 2 brilliant solo tries in succession; Cornwall were losing 31-26 in injury time when Ian Hambly ran 78 metres to score a try under the posts which Paul Thirlby then converted with the last kick of the match to win the game*)

FIRST LLOYDS TSB TOUR MATCH

CAPTAIN: *Phil Vickery* [England XV]
CAPTAIN: *Taine Randell* (NZ) [Barbarians]
25th May **ENGLAND XV*** 36 **BARBARIANS** 49
Twickenham
[ENGLAND XV: [*This match kicked off at 3.00pm; Michael Lipman played for Australia U21*]
(The England XV scrum was put under severe pressure; Thomas Castaignède scored in the 4th minute!; The England XV was losing 7-3 in the 9th minute when collectively poor tackling allowed Christian Califano to score; The England XV was losing 14-3 in the 11th minute when Dave Walder hit the post with a penalty goal attempt; The England XV was still losing 14-3 midway through the first half; Mike Worsley went off injured in the 23rd minute, being replaced by David Flatman who immediately made a poor tackle which allowed Mark Robinson (2) to score; The England XV was losing 21-3 in the 34th minute when Dave Walder hit the post with another penalty goal attempt, but as the ball rebounded back he brilliantly flicked it into the path of Michael Lipman who went on to score!; The England XV was losing 21-8 in the second minute of first half injury time when some superb handling allowed Jamie Noon to score; The England XV was losing 21-15 at half-time; The England XV was losing 28-15 in the 54th minute when Jamie Noon scored another try after he wrong-footed the Barbarians defence with a brilliant sidestep; The England XV was losing 35-22 midway through the second half when further collectively poor tackling allowed Bruce Reihana to score, thus 3 tries and 21 points were preventable; The England XV was losing 42-22 in the 65th minute when Dave Walder chipped ahead and regathered the ball to score a superb try; Simon Amor came on as a replacement for Phil Christophers with 6 minutes of normal time remaining; The England XV was losing 42-29 with 2 minutes of normal time remaining; Pete Anglesea had to go off in the second minute of injury time after being concussed by an illegal straight arm from Jerry Collins, being replaced by Martin Corry; The England XV was losing 49-29 in the sixth minute of injury time when Nick Walshe scored a consolation try after Alex Codling made a brilliant 40 metre break; Jamie Noon had a brilliant game)]
[BARBARIANS: [*This match kicked off at 3.00pm; Agustin Pichot selected but withdrew on the day of the match due to injury, Mark Robinson (2) was moved from the bench to the team and Darren Edwards was then selected for the bench; Budge Pountney and Scott Quinnell in original squad of 20 but withdrew due to injury*]
(The Barbarians forwards dominated the scrums in this match; Thomas Castaignède scored in the 4th minute!; The Barbarians were leading 14-3 in the 9th minute; The Barbarians were still leading 14-3 midway through the first half when Thomas Castaignède wasted a great try-scoring opportunity by knocking-on while the England XV line was at his mercy; The Barbarians were leading 21-3 in the 24th minute; The Barbarians were leading 21-8 in the 34th minute; The Barbarians were still leading 21-8 in the second minute of first half injury time; The Barbarians were leading 21-15 at half-time; The Barbarians were still leading 21-15 in the 52nd minute when Jonathan Bell scored a brilliant try; The Barbarians were leading 28-22 in the 58th minute when some superb handling amongst the forwards allowed Raphäel Ibañez to score; The Barbarians were leading 35-22 midway through the second half when Bruce Reihana scored after Percy Montgomery made a brilliant run; The Barbarians were leading 42-29 in the 65th minute; The Barbarians were still leading 42-29 with 2 minutes of normal time remaining; The Barbarians were leading 49-29 in the sixth minute of injury time)]

SECOND LLOYDS TSB TOUR MATCH

CAPTAIN: *Mick Galwey* (IR)

28th May SCOTLAND XV 15 **BARBARIANS** 24

Murrayfield

[*This match kicked off at 7.00pm; Agustin Pichot selected but withdrew to sit on the bench, Darren Edwards was moved from the bench to the team*]

(*This match was played on a damp pitch; Scott Staniforth scored in the 2nd minute!; The Barbarians were leading 12-0 in the 11th minute; The Barbarians were leading 12-5 midway through the first half; The Barbarians were leading 12-8 in the 28th minute; The Barbarians were leading 19-8 in the 35th minute; The Barbarians were still leading 19-8 shortly before half-time when Aurélien Rougerie scored a brilliant 40 metre try; The Barbarians were leading 24-8 at half-time; The Barbarians forwards could not win any possession in the second half; Matt Perry came on as a replacement for Conrad Jantjes in the 54th minute; The Barbarians were still leading 24-8 midway through the second half; The Barbarians were leading 24-15 in the 67th minute*)

EMIRATES AIRLINE CARDIFF SEVENS

Cardiff Arms Park

CAPTAIN: *Pat Sanderson*

First Round - Pool 'B'

31st May WALES 26 **ENGLAND*** 14

[*This match kicked off at 10.14am; Simon Amor unavailable due to injury; Ben Breeze played for Wales in this match*]

(*England were drawing 0-0 in the early stages when Tal Selley scored after a poor tackle by Rob Thirlby; England were losing 14-0 midway through the first half; England were still losing 14-0 just before half-time; Wales were allowed to score 19 unanswered points to win the match; England were losing 19-0 at half-time; England were still losing 19-0 early in the second half when Ugo Monye scored a brilliant 100 metre solo try; England were losing 19-7 shortly afterwards when Mark Cueto scored a brilliant 62 metre solo try; England were losing 19-14 midway through the second half; England were still losing 19-14 in the closing stages when Gareth Williams (4) scored after a poor tackle by Magnus Lund, thus 2 tries and 14 points were preventable*)

31st May RUSSIA 0 **ENGLAND** 31

[*This match kicked off at 1.10pm; Simon Amor unavailable due to injury*]

(*England were leading 19-0 at half-time; England were leading 31-0 early in the second half; England were still leading 31-0 midway through the second half*)

31st May FRANCE 12 **ENGLAND** 19

[*This match kicked off at 7.34pm; Simon Amor unavailable due to injury*]

(*England were drawing 0-0 in the early stages when Rob Thirlby scored after James Brooks brilliantly side-footed a loose ball to Ben Gollings; England were leading 7-0 shortly afterwards when Magnus Lund crossed the tryline, but the move was disallowed because the referee adjudged that there had been an earlier forward pass; England were still leading 7-0 midway through the first half and pressing in attack when Pat Sanderson threw a wild pass behind him which allowed Laurent Diaz to fly-hack the ensuing loose ball on and score; England were drawing 7-7 shortly before half-time when Mark Cueto scored a brilliant 42 metre solo try, with Ben Gollings then missing the eminently kickable conversion attempt; England were leading 12-7 at half-time; England were still leading 12-7 early in the second half when a lineout overthrow by James Brooks led directly to a try by Nicolas Carmona, thus 2 tries and 12 points*

were preventable; England were drawing 12-12 midway through the second half; England were still drawing 12-12 in the closing stages when Ben Gollings put in a brilliant grubber kick and then followed up to score a match-winning try)
CAPTAIN: *Simon Amor*
Quarter-Final
1st June NEW ZEALAND 10 **ENGLAND** 14
[*This match kicked off at 12.58pm*]
(*Ben Gollings was sent off in the 3rd minute for kicking Amasio Valence in retaliation and thus duly banned for 3 sevens matches*)
(*England were drawing 0-0 in the 2nd minute when Ben Gollings was prevented from scoring by an illegal high tackle from Eric Rush, but the referee unaccountably ignored this obvious penalty try offence; England were leading 7-0 immediately afterwards; Rob Thirlby played as a fly half in the absence of Ben Gollings, who was sent off in the 3rd minute; England were still leading 7-0 midway through the first half; England were leading 7-5 shortly before half-time when Magnus Lund took a quick tap penalty and scored; England were leading 14-5 at half-time; England were leading 14-10 midway through the second half*)
Semi-Final
1st June SOUTH AFRICA 22 **ENGLAND*** 10
[*This match kicked off at 5.00pm; Ben Gollings unavailable due to suspension*]
(*England were drawing 0-0 in the early stages when Marius Schoeman scored after Pat Sanderson failed to commit himself to a tackle on Eugene Francis; England were losing 7-0 midway through the first half; England were still losing 7-0 shortly before half-time when some superb handling allowed Ugo Monye to score; England were losing 7-5 just before half-time; England were losing 12-5 at half-time; England were losing 12-10 early in the second half when Simon Amor missed an eminently kickable conversion attempt; England were losing 15-10 midway through the second half; South Africa were still leading 15-10 in the final minute when Phil Dowson threw a wild pass behind Mark Cueto, Earl Rose fly-hacked the resulting loose ball on towards the England line where Pat Sanderson then knocked it on, which allowed Rudi Coetzee to follow up and score with the last move of the match, thus 2 tries and 14 points were preventable!*)

THIRD LLOYDS TSB TOUR MATCH

CAPTAIN: *Mark Connors* (AU)
31st May WALES XV 35 **BARBARIANS** 48
Millennium Stadium, Cardiff
[*This match kicked off at 3.00pm*]
(*The Barbarians were leading 5-0 in the 10th minute; The Barbarians were still leading 5-0 midway through the first half; The Barbarians were leading 5-0 in the 28th minute when some superb handling allowed Olivier Magne to score; The Barbarians were leading 10-7 in the 37th minute when Sam Harding scored after Percy Montgomery put up a brilliant garryowen; The Barbarians were leading 17-7 at half-time; The Barbarians were still leading 17-7 in the 42nd minute when collectively poor tackling allowed Iestyn Harris to score, thus 7 points were preventable; The Barbarians were leading 24-14 in the 48th minute; Mick Galwey came on as a temporary blood replacement for A.J. Venter in the 54th minute; Matt Perry came on as a replacement for Percy Montgomery in the 56th minute; The Barbarians were leading 29-14 midway through the second half; The Barbarians were leading 36-21 in the 68th minute; The Barbarians*

***were leading 41-21 with 7 minutes remaining when Mark Robinson (2) scored after Scott Staniforth made a brilliant break and then kicked ahead; The Barbarians scored 19 unanswered points to seal the match; The Barbarians were leading 48-21 with 3 minutes remaining*)**

EMIRATES AIRLINE LONDON SEVENS

Twickenham

CAPTAIN: *Phil Greening*

First Round - Pool 'B'

6th June **ENGLAND** 29 SCOTLAND 5

[*This match kicked off at 2.12pm; Ben Gollings unavailable due to suspension*]

(*England were drawing 0-0 in the early stages when Simon Amor tapped a lineout throw backwards over his own line where Phil Greening then knocked-on after he unaccountably attempted to field the bouncing ball instead of falling on it, which allowed Mark Lee to follow up and score, thus 5 points were preventable; England were losing 5-0 midway through the first half when Richard Haughton scored a brilliant 72 metre solo try; England were drawing 5-5 shortly before half-time; England were leading 10-5 at half-time; England were still leading 10-5 early in the second half when Rob Thirlby scored a brilliant 94 metre solo try; England were leading 15-5 midway through the second half when Ugo Monye chipped ahead and regathered the ball to score a superb try; England were leading 22-5 in the final minute when James Brooks scored after Simon Amor and Phil Greening created space with a brilliant scissors move; England scored 29 unanswered points to win the match; Richard Haughton had a brilliant game*)

6th June **ENGLAND** 19 GEORGIA 7

[*This match kicked off at 5.18pm; Ben Gollings unavailable due to suspension*]

(*England were losing 7-0 in the early stages; England were still losing 7-0 midway through the first half when Ugo Monye scored a brilliant solo try; England were drawing 7-7 at half-time; England were still drawing 7-7 early in the second half when Simon Amor scored a brilliant try; England were leading 14-7 midway through the second half; England scored 19 unanswered points to win the match; Phil Greening injured playing in the match*)

CAPTAIN: *Simon Amor* [*Pat Sanderson*]

6th June **ENGLAND** 35 ARGENTINA 5

[*This match kicked off at 9.00pm*]

(*This match was played in drizzly conditions; England were drawing 0-0 in the early stages when Richard Haughton scored a brilliant 69 metre solo try; England were leading 7-0 shortly afterwards when Henry Paul scored after he wrong-footed Lucio López Fleming with a brilliant sidestep; England were leading 14-0 midway through the first half; England were still leading 14-0 shortly before half-time when Phil Dowson scored after Henry Paul took a return pass from Ben Gollings; England scored 21 unanswered points to win the match; England were leading 21-0 at half-time; James Brooks and Rob Thirlby came on as replacements for Simon Amor and Henry Paul respectively at the start of the second half; England were still leading 21-0 in the 8th minute when collectively poor tackling allowed Santiago Sanz to score, thus 5 points were preventable; England were leading 21-5 midway through the second half when Rob Thirlby scored after Richard Haughton made a superb 41 metre run; England were leading 28-5 shortly afterwards when Ugo Monye made a brilliant 49 metre run but then wasted this great try-scoring opportunity by throwing a poor pass to the*

***unmarked Ben Gollings; England were still leading 28-5 in the final minute when Ben Gollings volleyed Rob Thirlby's pass, fly-hacked the ensuing loose ball on and then regathered it to score under the posts with the last move of the match; Henry Paul had a brilliant game*)**

CAPTAIN: *Simon Amor* [*Pat Sanderson*]

Quarter-Final

7th June **ENGLAND** 50 ITALY 0

[*This match kicked off at 1.49pm; Phil Greening unavailable due to injury*]

(*England were leading 7-0 in the early stages; England were still leading 7-0 shortly afterwards when Rob Thirlby scored a brilliant 44 metre solo try; England were leading 14-0 midway through the first half; England were leading 19-0 shortly before half-time when Tony Roques scored after Phil Dowson threw a brilliant one-handed reverse pass; England were leading 24-0 at half-time; England were still leading 24-0 early in the second half when Rob Thirlby took a quick tap penalty and scored to complete a hat-trick of tries; England were leading 29-0 shortly afterwards when Pat Sanderson slipped over while the tryline was at his mercy, but ironically he still had enough time to regain his feet and score unopposed!; England were leading 36-0 midway through the second half; England were leading 43-0 in the closing stages when James Brooks scored a superb 69 metre solo try*)

CAPTAIN: *Simon Amor* [*Pat Sanderson*]

Semi-Final

7th June **ENGLAND** 26 SOUTH AFRICA 5

[*This match kicked off at 5.22pm; Phil Greening unavailable due to injury*]

(*England were drawing 0-0 midway through the first half when Simon Amor scored after Ben Gollings threw a brilliant pass out of the tackle; England were leading 7-0 shortly before half-time when Tony Roques reached the tryline but then lost the ball in the act of scoring; England were leading 7-0 at half-time; England were still leading 7-0 in the 8th minute when Tony Roques scored after Henry Paul wrong-footed the South African defence with a brilliant sidestep; England scored 14 unanswered points to win the match; England were leading 14-0 shortly afterwards when collectively poor tackling allowed Marius Schoeman to score, thus 5 points were preventable; England were leading 14-5 midway through the second half when Ben Gollings scored after Richard Haughton made a superb 53 metre run; England were leading 21-5 in the final minute when Tony Roques dummied his way through to score a brilliant try with the last move of the match*)

CAPTAIN: *Simon Amor* [*Pat Sanderson*]

Final

7th June **ENGLAND** 31 FIJI 24

[*This match kicked off at 7.15pm; Phil Greening unavailable due to injury*]

(*Nasoni Roko scored in the 1st minute after a poor tackle by Ben Gollings, thus 7 points were preventable!; England were losing 7-0 shortly afterwards when Tony Roques scored a brilliant 49 metre solo try; England were losing 7-5 midway through the first half when Henry Paul ripped the ball from a maul and ran 31 metres to score, with Ben Gollings then missing the eminently kickable conversion attempt!; England were leading 17-7 at half-time; England were still leading 17-7 early in the second half when Simon Amor scored after he made a brilliant blindside break; England scored 24 unanswered points to win the match; England were leading 24-17 midway through the second half when Ugo Monye scored a superb 56 metre solo try; England were leading 31-17 in the last minute; Henry Paul had a brilliant game*)

ENGLAND TOUR TO NEW ZEALAND AND AUSTRALIA 2003

CAPTAIN: *Martin Johnson*

14th June NEW ZEALAND 13 **ENGLAND** 15

WestpacTrust Stadium, Wellington

[This match kicked off at 7.00pm; Simon Shaw unavailable due to injury; Matt Dawson selected but withdrew due to injury, Kyran Bracken was moved from the bench to the team and Andy Gomarsall was then selected for the bench; Jonny Wilkinson's tactical kicking fell below its normal standard in this match after he had trouble with the swirling wind; Simon Shaw returned home injured after this match]

(This match was played in extremely windy conditions; Steve Thompson (2)'s throwing-in was poor and the England lineout suffered accordingly; Jonny Wilkinson scored a penalty goal in the 2nd minute!; England were drawing 3-3 in the 12th minute; England were still drawing 3-3 midway through the first half; England were drawing 3-3 in the 26th minute when Jonny Wilkinson scored a brilliant 30 metre penalty goal from the right touchline; England were leading 6-3 in the 37th minute; England were drawing 6-6 at half-time; England were still drawing 6-6 in the 44th minute when Jonny Wilkinson scored a brilliant 46 metre penalty goal; England were leading 9-6 in the 48th minute when they were briefly reduced to 13 men after Neil Back and Lawrence Dallaglio were both sin-binned in quick succession, but England's temporary six-man scrum then famously prevented the New Zealand forwards from scoring a pushover try immediately afterwards!; England were leading 12-6 in the 56th minute; England were leading 15-6 midway through the second half; England were still leading 15-6 in the 63rd minute when Doug Howlett was awarded a try that should not have been given because he was in front of Carlos Spencer when the latter kicked ahead, thus 7 points were unlawful; England were leading 15-13 with 7 minutes remaining when Jonny Wilkinson had a speculative penalty goal attempt from the halfway line go underneath the crossbar; England were still leading 15-13 with 5 minutes remaining when Phil Vickery made a superb break but then ran out of support!; Josh Lewsey received a head injury requiring 6 stitches when he was stamped on by Ali Williams with 4 minutes remaining; Graham Rowntree injured playing in the match; Phil Vickery and Kyran Bracken both had a brilliant game; England broke their previous record by winning their 12th consecutive cap international match!)

COOK CUP MATCH

CAPTAIN: *Martin Johnson*

21st June AUSTRALIA 14 **ENGLAND** 25

Telstra Dome, Melbourne

[This match kicked off at 7.00pm; The Telstra Dome was previously called the Colonial Stadium; The Telstra Dome had its retractable roof closed for this match]

(The England forwards dominated the lineout in this match; Will Greenwood scored in the 5th minute after England kept the ball for 13 phases of play!; England were leading 7-3 in the 10th minute; England were still leading 7-3 midway through the first half; England were leading 7-3 in the 30th minute when Mike Tindall scored after Will Greenwood brilliantly flicked the ball on to him, with Jonny Wilkinson then hitting the left-hand post with the conversion attempt from the left touchline; England were leading 12-3 in the 36th minute when the forwards created a superb rolling maul which travelled 38 metres before it was illegally collapsed by George Gregan in front of the Australian line, but the referee unaccountably ignored this obvious penalty try offence; England were leading 12-3 at half-time; England were leading 12-9 in the 51st

***minute; England were leading 15-9 midway through the second half; England were still leading 15-9 in the 64th minute when Ben Cohen scored a brilliant 40 metre solo try; England were leading 22-9 with 2 minutes of normal time remaining when a poor defensive alignment allowed Wendell Sailor to score, thus 5 points were preventable; England were leading 22-14 in the last minute of normal time when Josh Lewsey made a famous tackle on Mat Rogers; England were still leading 22-14 in the second minute of injury time when Jonny Wilkinson scored a 25 metre penalty goal with the last kick of the match to seal the game; Steve Thompson (2) and Martin Johnson both had a brilliant game; England broke their previous record by winning their 13th consecutive cap international match and secured their first ever cap international match victory on Australian soil at their 11th attempt since 1963!*)**

ENGLAND COUNTIES TOUR TO ROMANIA AND FRANCE 2003

CAPTAIN: *Tony Windo*

14th Jun	ROMANIA	45	**ENGLAND COUNTIES**	23

Stadionul National "Lia Manoliu", Bucharest

[*This match kicked off at 8.00pm; Stadionul National "Lia Manoliu" was previously called Stadionul "23 August"; Florent Rossigneux played for France 7s and toured Australia with the French Barbarians in June 1994, but qualified for England after have resided there since 1997; John Swords played for Crawshay's Welsh against Cambridge University at Grange Road on 12th February 2003 and played for Major R.V. Stanley's XV against Oxford University at Iffley Road on 12th November 2003*]

(*The England Counties forwards could not win any possession; Petru Balan scored in the 5th minute!; England Counties were losing 8-3 in the 11th minute; England Counties were still losing 8-3 midway through the first half; England Counties were losing 15-3 in the 29th minute; England Counties were losing 15-9 in the 39th minute; England Counties were losing 22-9 in the third minute of first half injury time; England Counties were losing 25-9 at half-time; England Counties were still losing 25-9 in the 46th minute when Lee Soper scored from a rolling maul; England Counties were losing 28-16 in the 48th minute; England Counties were losing 35-16 midway through the second half; England Counties were losing 42-16 in the 65th minute; Romania were allowed to score 17 unanswered points to seal the match; England Counties were still losing 42-16 in the 70th minute when the referee awarded a penalty try after the Romanian forwards illegally collapsed a series of rolling mauls; England Counties were losing 42-23 with 8 minutes remaining*)

24th Jun	FRANCE AMATEURS	26	**ENGLAND COUNTIES***	24

Stade Ernest Argeles, Blagnac

[*This match kicked off at 7.00pm; Dave Knight was the brother of Paul Knight (2)*]

(*England Counties were drawing 0-0 in the 11th minute when James Moore scored after Rob Hitchmough made a brilliant run; England Counties were leading 7-0 midway through the first half; England Counties were drawing 7-7 in the 27th minute when they failed to deal with a drop goal attempt by David Darricarrere which rebounded off the right-hand post and Daral Couturier was able to follow up and score, thus 7 points were preventable; England Counties were losing 14-7 at half-time; England Counties were losing 17-7 in the 52nd minute when Shaun Brady scored a brilliant try; England Counties were losing 20-17 midway through the second half; England Counties were losing 23-17 with 8 minutes of normal time remaining; England Counties were leading 24-23 in the fourth minute of injury time when Laurent Caillat scored a penalty goal to win the match for France Amateurs*)

IRB U21 WORLD CHAMPIONSHIP

England

CAPTAIN: *Chris Day*

First Round - Pool 'C'

13th Jun **ENGLAND U21*** 22 AUSTRALIA U21 52

Iffley Road, Oxford

[*This match kicked off at 7.00pm; Tim Taylor returned home injured after this match; Andy Reay joined the squad after this match; Ben Skirving played for England in the U19 World Championship in Italy in March 2002; Brad Davies toured Canada, New Zealand and Australia with England Schools 18 Group in July-August 2001; Aston Croall played for England in the U19 World Championships in Italy in March 2002 and France in April 2003*]

(*The referee unaccountably ignored a number of forward passes and crooked lineout throws; Collectively poor tackling allowed Mark Gerrard to score in the 3rd minute!; England U21 were losing 7-0 in the 13th minute when Chris Rowland scored after Ugo Monye made a brilliant break; England U21 were losing 7-5 in the 17th minute when Mark Gerrard had a penalty goal attempt which clearly went below the crossbar, but the touch judges inexplicably proceeded to award it!; England U21 were losing 10-5 midway through the first half; England U21 were losing 17-5 in the 30th minute; England U21 were losing 17-8 shortly before half-time when Ugo Monye took too much time over his clearance kick and was charged down by Cameron Shepherd, who went on to score from the ensuing rebound; England U21 were losing 24-15 at half-time; England U21 were losing 31-15 in the 54th minute when Lachlan Mackay scored after a poor tackle by Brad Davies, thus 3 tries and 21 points were preventable; England U21 were losing 38-15 midway through the second half; England U21 were losing 38-22 in the 63rd minute; England U21 were still losing 38-22 with 7 minutes remaining when Rocky Elsom scored a try that should not have been given because he clearly knocked the ball on, thus 1 try and 10 points were unlawful; England U21 were losing 45-22 in the third minute of injury time; Marcel Garvey and Ugo Monye saw very little of the ball in this match*)

CAPTAIN: *Paul Hodgson*

17th Jun **ENGLAND U21** 69 JAPAN U21 3 **BP**

Newbury RFC, Monks Lane, Newbury

[*This match kicked off at 7.30pm; Ben Skirving returned home injured after this match; Richard Martin-Redman joined the squad after this match*]

(*England U21 were leading 5-3 in the 16th minute; England U21 were leading 10-3 midway through the first half; England U21 were still leading 10-3 shortly afterwards when Ed Thrower scored after Adryan Winnan made a brilliant run; England U21 were leading 29-3 at half-time; James Bailey scored two tries in 2 minutes to complete a hat-trick!; England U21 were leading 62-3 in the closing stages; England U21 scored 69 unanswered points to win the match; Ben Skirving injured playing in the match; John Hart (2) had a brilliant game*)

CAPTAIN: *Chris Day*

21st Jun **ENGLAND U21*** 16 FRANCE U21 21 **BP**

Henley RFC, Dry Leas, Marlow Road, Henley-on-Thames

[*This match kicked off at 2.00pm; Michael Holford and Ugo Monye unavailable due to injury; Spencer Davey returned home injured after this match*]

(This match was played in extremely hot conditions; The England U21 forwards could not win any possession in the first half; England U21 were losing 3-0 in the 6th minute; England U21 were leading 6-3 midway through the first half; Spencer Davey went off injured in the 22nd minute, being replaced by Andy Reay; England U21 were losing 8-6 in the 31st minute; England U21 were losing 8-6 at half-time; England U21 were losing 11-6 in the 50th minute; England U21 were losing 14-9 in the 62nd minute when Adryan Winnan had his pass intercepted by Romain Cabannes who went on to score, thus 7 points were preventable; England U21 were losing 21-9 with 6 minutes remaining when James Bailey scored while France U21 were briefly reduced to 12 men after the referee sent three of their players to the sin-bin!)

5th/6th/7th/8th Place Semi-Final

25th Jun	**ENGLAND U21**	27	WALES U21	44

Henley RFC, Dry Leas, Marlow Road, Henley-on-Thames

[This match kicked off at 3.00pm; Jon Pendlebury and Ugo Monye unavailable due to injury; Paul Hodgson and Ugo Monye returned home injured after this match; Harry Ellis, Dan Hipkiss and Tom Williams joined the squad after this match]

(Ed Thrower scored a penalty goal in the 3rd minute!; England U21 were losing 15-3 midway through the first half; England U21 were losing 15-13 in the 27th minute; England U21 were losing 18-13 at half-time; John Hart (2) went off in the 43rd minute for attention to a blood injury, being temporarily replaced by Jason Hobson who had to play out of position as a number 8; England U21 were losing 32-13 in the 48th minute; Paul Hodgson went off injured in the 51st minute, being replaced by Clive Stuart-Smith; England U21 were still losing 32-13 midway through the second half; England U21 were losing 39-13 in the 68th minute; Wales U21 were allowed to score 29 unanswered points to clinch the match; England U21 were losing 44-13 with 5 minutes remaining when Andy Reay scored a brilliant solo consolation try)

7th/8th Place Play-Off

29th Jun	**ENGLAND U21***	22	SCOTLAND U21	33

Newbury RFC, Monks Lane, Newbury

[This match kicked off at 11.00am]

(England U21 were losing 5-0 in the 8th minute; England U21 were leading 7-5 in the 13th minute; England U21 were losing 8-7 midway through the first half; England U21 were still losing 8-7 in the 30th minute when Tom Williams scored after Brad Davies threw a brilliant 20 metre spin pass; Michael Holford scored from a tap penalty to give England U21 a 19-8 lead in the 33rd minute; England U21 were still leading 19-8 just before half-time; England U21 were leading 19-15 at half-time; England U21 played into a strong wind in the second half; England U21 were leading 22-15 early in the second half; England U21 were leading 22-18 midway through the second half; England U21 were losing 23-22 with 9 minutes remaining; England U21 were losing 30-22 in the final minute; Scotland U21 were allowed to score 18 unanswered points to win the match)

CHURCHILL CUP

Canada

CAPTAIN: *Hugh Vyvyan*

First Round

14th Jun	CANADA	7	**ENGLAND A**	43

Thunderbird Stadium, Vancouver

[This match kicked off at 4.00pm; Mike Worsley, Tom Palmer (2), Paul Volley, Andy Hazell, Ben Johnston, James Simpson-Daniel and Iain Balshaw were all unavailable as

they had yet to join the tour; Will Green (1) was capped for England Schools 18 Group in April 1991]
(Dave Walder scored a penalty goal in the 1st minute!; England A were losing 7-3 in the 8th minute; England A were leading 10-7 in the 17th minute; England A were leading 16-7 when Andy Titterrell scored after Hugh Vyvyan instigated a brilliant 60 metre move; England A were leading 21-7 at half-time; England A were still leading 21-7 when Martyn Wood scored a superb try after he took a quick close-range tap penalty; England A were leading 26-7 when Fraser Waters scored after Dave Walder made a brilliant 50 metre run; England A were leading 36-7 in the last minute of normal time when Matt Cairns scored a try which was then converted by the prop David Flatman!; England A scored 40 unanswered points to win the match)

21st Jun USA 10 **ENGLAND A** 36
Thunderbird Stadium, Vancouver
[This match kicked off at 1.00pm; Tom Palmer (2) returned home injured after this match]
(England A were leading 5-0 in the 6th minute; England A were still leading 5-0 when Iain Balshaw scored after James Simpson-Daniel made a brilliant break; Andy Hazell went off injured in the 29th minute, being replaced by Pete Anglesea; England A were leading 12-0 in the 33rd minute; Tom Palmer (2) went off injured in the 38th minute, being replaced by Matt Cairns with Phil Greening then switching from hooker to flanker to accommodate Matt Cairns, Pete Anglesea moving from flanker to number 8 to accommodate Greening and Hugh Vyvyan switching from number 8 to lock to accommodate Anglesea; England A were leading 12-5 just before half-time; England A were leading 19-5 at half-time; England A were still leading 19-5 in the 42nd minute when Michael Horak scored two tries in 3 minutes to complete a hat-trick!; England A scored 19 unanswered points to clinch the match; England A were leading 31-5 in the 53rd minute when Cayo Nicolau scored a try that should not have been given because he clearly knocked the ball on before he touched it down, thus 5 points were unlawful; England A were leading 31-10 midway through the second half; England A were still leading 31-10 in the 66th minute when Michael Horak ran 59 metres to score his fourth try; Dan Scarbrough came on as a replacement for Michael Horak with 8 minutes remaining; Michael Horak scored 20 points in this match)

Final

28th Jun USA 6 **ENGLAND A** 43
Thunderbird Stadium, Vancouver
[This match kicked off at 4.00pm]
(This match was played in hot conditions; England A were losing 3-0 in the early stages; England A were still losing 3-0 midway through the first half; England A were losing 3-0 in the 24th minute when Ben Johnston scored after Dave Walder put in a brilliant chip-kick; England A were leading 10-6 just before half-time; England A were leading 17-6 at half-time; England A were still leading 17-6 early in the second half when Pete Anglesea scored a try that should not have been given because he appeared to hit the corner flag before he grounded the ball; England A were leading 24-6 in the 58th minute when Henry Paul ran 50 metres to score after Dave Walder brilliantly dribbled the ball to himself at a 22 drop-out; England A were leading 31-6 midway through the second half; The USA were still losing 31-6 shortly afterwards when Martyn Wood joined the front of a close-range England A lineout and passed the ball straight back to Phil Greening who went on to score in the corner!; England A were leading 36-6 in the closing stages when Iain Balshaw scored under the posts after James Simpson-Daniel made a superb run; England A scored 33 unanswered

points to clinch the match; Alex Codling injured playing in the match; Dave Walder had a brilliant game)

ENGLAND 'A' TOUR TO JAPAN 2003

CAPTAIN: *Hugh Vyvyan*

6th July JAPAN 20 **ENGLAND A** 55

National Olympic Stadium, Tokyo

[*This match kicked off at 2.10pm; Alex Brown selected but withdrew due to injury, Chris Jones was moved from the bench to the team; Jim Mallinder and Steve Diamond originally named an 8 man bench selection; Alex Codling retired in January 2006 due to injury; Pete Anglesea retired in April 2006 due to injury*]

(*This match was played in high humidity; England A were drawing 0-0 in the 7th minute when Mike Worsley scored after Andy Hazell made a brilliant break; England A were leading 5-0 in the 13th minute when Martyn Wood scored two tries in 7 minutes; England A were leading 17-0 midway through the first half; England A were leading 17-7 in the 24th minute; Alex Codling went off injured in the 27th minute, being replaced by Paul Volley with Pete Anglesea then moving from flanker to number 8 to accommodate Volley and Hugh Vyvyan switching from number 8 to lock to accommodate Anglesea; England A were leading 17-10 in the 35th minute when Iain Balshaw scored a superb try; England A were leading 24-10 at half-time; Chris Jones went off injured in the 58th minute, being replaced by Andy Sheridan; England A played in the last quarter with Andy Sheridan and Hugh Vyvyan as the lineout jumpers; Will Green (1) scored after Iain Balshaw brilliantly chipped the ball ahead twice; Iain Balshaw scored an 80 metre interception try in the 64th minute; Neal Hatley scored a superb 30 metre solo try; England A were leading 55-15 in the closing stages; Iain Balshaw had a brilliant game*)

GREENE KING HENLEY INTERNATIONAL SEVENS

Henley RFC, Dry Leas, Marlow Road, Henley-on-Thames

CAPTAIN: *Rob Thirlby*

First Round

10th Aug **YOUNG ENGLAND** 40 Apache 0

[*Apache RC were an invitational team founded in 2000 by the Old Kelleians from Kelly College in Devon*]

(*This match was played in 100 degree heat*)

Quarter-Final

10th Aug **YOUNG ENGLAND** 5 British Army (*SER*) 17

(*This match was played in 100 degree heat*)

[Shield Qualifying Round:]

[10th Aug **YOUNG ENGLAND** 17 UGANDA CRANES 26]

[*Uganda Cranes were the Ugandan national Sevens team; The Shield Final was contested by the two highest scoring teams from the Shield Qualifying Round*]

(*This match was played in 100 degree heat*)

LONDON PRIDE MIDDLESEX SEVENS

Twickenham

CAPTAIN: *Rob Thirlby*

First Round

16th Aug **YOUNG ENGLAND** 26 London Irish 10

[*This match kicked off at 12.00pm; James Haskell scored 2 tries for M.R. Steele-*

***Bodger's XV against Cambridge University at Grange Road on 26th November 2003 and played for England in the U19 World Championship in South Africa in March-April 2004*]**

Quarter-Final

16th Aug	**YOUNG ENGLAND**	0	Newcastle Falcons	42

[*This match kicked off at 2.20pm*]

FIRST INVESTEC CHALLENGE MATCH

CAPTAIN: *Jason Leonard*

23rd Aug	WALES	9	**ENGLAND**	43

Millennium Stadium, Cardiff

[*This match kicked off at 2.30pm; Dan Luger played at right wing despite wearing the number 11 on his shirt!*]

(*This match was played in extremely hot conditions; The England forwards dominated the scrums; England were drawing 0-0 in the 7th minute when Alex King missed a kickable 40 metre penalty goal attempt; James Simpson-Daniel made a brilliant break immediately afterwards but Lewis Moody then wasted this great try-scoring opportunity by throwing a poor pass to Joe Worsley; England were losing 3-0 in the 12th minute; England were leading 6-3 midway through the first half; A rolling maul enabled Lewis Moody to score a try which Alex King then brilliantly converted from the right touchline to give England a 13-3 lead in the 24th minute; England were leading 13-6 in the 35th minute when Alex King missed a difficult 28 metre penalty goal attempt; Mark Regan went off injured in the 38th minute, being replaced by Dorian West; England were leading 16-6 just before half-time; England were leading 16-9 at half-time; England were still leading 16-9 in the 45th minute when Alex King missed an eminently kickable 22 metre penalty goal attempt; England were leading 16-9 in the 52nd minute when Alex King completed a hat-trick of penalty goal misses in 7 minutes!; England were leading 23-9 in the 56th minute; England were leading 26-9 midway through the second half; England were still leading 26-9 in the 62nd minute when Joe Worsley broke from the base of a scrum to score; England were leading 31-9 with 8 minutes of normal time remaining when Alex King went off injured, being replaced by Dave Walder; England were still leading 31-9 with 5 minutes of normal time remaining when Stuart Abbott scored after Danny Grewcock made a superb run; England were leading 36-9 in the second minute of injury time when Dorian West scored from another rolling maul; England scored 27 unanswered points in the second half to clinch the match; Simon Shaw and Andy Gomarsall both had a brilliant game; Dan Scarbrough had a poor game; England broke their previous record by winning their 14th consecutive cap international match!*)

SECOND WORLD CUP WARM-UP MATCH

CAPTAIN: *Dorian West* [*Paul Grayson*]

30th Aug	FRANCE	17	**ENGLAND***	16

Stade Vélodrome, Marseille

[*This match kicked off at 9.00pm; Joe Worsley selected but withdrew due to injury, Alex Sanderson was moved from the bench to the team and Andy Hazell was then selected for the bench; England wore skin-tight shirts for the first time in this match; Andy Titterrell, Will Green (1), Steve Borthwick, Andy Hazell, Alex Sanderson, Dave Walder, Jamie Noon and Dan Scarbrough were all released from the World Cup training squad on 1st September 2003*]

(*The England scrum was put under severe pressure; Frédéric Michalak scored a*

penalty goal in the 3rd minute!; Jason Leonard came on as a temporary blood replacement for Julian White in the 7th minute; Jamie Noon came on as a blood replacement for Ben Cohen in the 11th minute; England were drawing 3-3 in the 18th minute when Mike Tindall powered through to score a brilliant try; England were leading 10-3 midway through the first half; England were still leading 10-3 in the 24th minute when Paul Grayson put in a brilliant chip-kick which enabled Iain Balshaw to follow up and ground the ball in the corner, but the move was disallowed because Balshaw was adjudged to have been in front of the kicker; France were losing 10-6 in the 36th minute when Nicolas Brusque scored after the England pack unaccountably allowed the ball to squirt out of the side of a ruck, thus 5 points were preventable; Frédéric Michalak missed the subsequent conversion attempt after an England water carrier inexplicably ran in front of him as he was about to start his run up!; England were losing 11-10 straight after the restart when Frédéric Michalak's attempted clearance kick was charged down by Alex Sanderson, who followed up unchallenged as the ball rebounded behind the French line but then unaccountably failed to ground the ball properly as he dived on it!; England were leading 13-11 in the fifth minute of first half injury time; England were losing 14-13 at half-time; England played into the wind in the second half; Steve Thompson (2) came on as a replacement for Dorian West in the 51st minute; England were still losing 14-13 in the 53rd minute when Josh Lewsey put in a superb chip-kick, but Iain Balshaw was unable to gather the bouncing ball while the French tryline was at his mercy; Iain Balshaw went off injured in the 55th minute, being replaced by Jamie Noon with Ollie Smith (2) then switching from centre to right wing to accommodate Noon and Josh Lewsey moving from wing to full back to accommodate Ollie Smith (2); England were losing 14-13 midway through the second half; England were leading 16-14 in the 62nd minute; England were losing 17-16 in the 65th minute; Mike Tindall went off injured with 4 minutes of normal time remaining, being replaced by Andy Gomarsall with Austin Healey then moving from scrum half to right wing to accommodate Gomarsall and Ollie Smith (2) switching from right wing to centre to accommodate Healey; England were still losing 17-16 in the sixth minute of injury time when Paul Grayson had an eminently kickable 20 metre drop goal attempt charged down by Brian Liebenberg; England were losing 17-16 in the seventh minute of injury time when Paul Grayson narrowly missed a speculative 36 metre drop goal attempt with the last kick of the match; Martin Corry had a brilliant game; Alex Sanderson and Austin Healey both had poor games)

SECOND INVESTEC CHALLENGE MATCH

CAPTAIN: *Martin Johnson* [*Neil Back*]

6th Sept **ENGLAND** 45 FRANCE 14

Twickenham

[*This match kicked off at 6.00pm; Dan Luger selected but withdrew due to injury, Iain Balshaw was moved from the bench to the team and Josh Lewsey was then selected for the bench; Jason Leonard won his 111th cap for England and the British & Irish Lions to equal Philippe Sella's world record; Graham Rowntree, Simon Shaw, Austin Healey, Ollie Smith (2) and James Simpson-Daniel were all released from the World Cup training squad on 7th September 2003 as Clive Woodward named his official World Cup squad of 30*]

(*Gérald Merceron scored a penalty goal in the 3rd minute!; England were drawing 3-3 in the 9th minute when Jonny Wilkinson scored a brilliant 45 metre penalty goal; England were leading 9-3 midway through the first half; England were leading 12-3 in the 27th minute; England were still leading 12-3 in the 34th minute when Ben Cohen*

scored under the posts after Jonny Wilkinson put in a superb grubber kick; Kyran Bracken went off injured in the 35th minute, being replaced by Matt Dawson; England were leading 26-3 in the 37th minute; England were still leading 26-3 just before half-time when Jason Robinson scored a brilliant 54 metre solo try; England were leading 33-3 at half-time; Iain Balshaw scored after just 11 seconds of the second half had been played!; England scored 38 unanswered points to win the match; England were leading 38-3 in the 43rd minute when Jason Robinson saved a certain try by tackling Aurélien Rougerie into touch at the corner flag; Simon Shaw and Paul Grayson came on as replacements for Martin Johnson and Jonny Wilkinson respectively in the 44th minute; England were still leading 38-3 in the 52nd minute when Iain Balshaw put in a superb chip into space behind Clément Poitrenaud, but Will Greenwood then wasted this great try-scoring opportunity by fly-hacking the resulting loose ball into touch in-goal; England were leading 38-6 in the 57th minute when Ben Cohen saved another certain try by tackling Raphäel Ibañez; England were still leading 38-6 midway through the second half; Stuart Abbott went off injured in the 61st minute, being replaced by Josh Lewsey; England were leading 38-6 in the 66th minute when Iain Balshaw had a great try-scoring chance but was brilliantly tackled by Aurélien Rougerie; England were still leading 38-6 in the 68th minute when Paul Grayson put in a superb chip-kick, but Iain Balshaw then dropped the ball while the French tryline was at his mercy; England were leading 38-9 with 7 minutes of normal time remaining; England were still leading 38-9 in the first minute of injury time when Josh Lewsey scored a brilliant try; England were leading 45-9 in the sixth minute of injury time when Aurélien Rougerie scored in the last move of the match after a poor tackle by Jason Robinson, thus 5 points were preventable; Steve Thompson (2) and Simon Shaw both had a brilliant game; England won their 22nd successive cap international victory at Twickenham to set a new world record for a single venue)

WORLD CUP

Australia

CAPTAIN: *Martin Johnson*

First Round - Pool 'C'

12th Oct	GEORGIA	6	**ENGLAND**	84 **BP**

Subiaco Oval, Perth

[***This match kicked off at 8.00pm; Iain Balshaw selected for bench but withdrew due to injury, being replaced by Dan Luger; Kyran Bracken selected for bench but withdrew after he injured his back in a warm-up session just before the match, being replaced by Andy Gomarsall; Danny Grewcock also injured himself in this pre-match warm-up session!; Jason Leonard broke Philippe Sella's world record of 111 caps***]

(***This match was played on a wet pitch; The England forwards monopolised possession in this match; Jonny Wilkinson scored a penalty goal in the 4th minute!; England were drawing 3-3 in the 10th minute; Matt Dawson broke from the base of a scrum to score a try which Jonny Wilkinson then converted to give England a 17-3 lead midway through the first half; England were leading 24-3 in the 26th minute when Neil Back was able to follow up and score after the Georgian pack let the ball squirt out of a scrum in front of their own line; Jason Leonard came on as a temporary blood replacement for Trevor Woodman in the 29th minute; England were leading 31-3 in the 35th minute when Trevor Woodman had the ball illegally kicked out of his hands by Bessik Khamashuridze as he attempted to ground it under the posts, but the referee***

***unaccountably ignored this obvious penalty try offence; Matt Dawson and Mike Tindall both went off injured immediately afterwards, being replaced by Andy Gomarsall and Dan Luger respectively; England were still leading 31-3 just before half-time; England were leading 34-3 at half-time; England were still leading 34-3 in the 46th minute when Lawrence Dallaglio scored a pushover try; Richard Hill (2) went off injured in the 51st minute, being replaced by Lewis Moody; England were leading 53-3 in the 54th minute; England scored 50 unanswered points to win the match; England were leading 53-6 midway through the second half when Ben Cohen scored after Paul Grayson put up a brilliant cross-kick; England were leading 65-6 in the 64th minute; England were still leading 65-6 with 8 minutes of normal time remaining when Will Greenwood scored a try and then famously signalled to the crowd that he had not lost a testicle during the grounding of the ball!; England were leading 79-6 with 4 minutes of normal time remaining; England were leading 84-6 in the first minute of injury time when Mark Regan dropped a poor pass from Josh Lewsey while the Georgian tryline was at his mercy; Andy Gomarsall injured playing in the match*)**

18th Oct SOUTH AFRICA 6 **ENGLAND** 25

Subiaco Oval, Perth

[*This match kicked off at 8.00pm; Danny Grewcock unavailable due to injury; Iain Balshaw was rested for this match; Richard Hill (2) selected but withdrew due to injury, Lewis Moody was moved from the bench to the team and Joe Worsley was then selected for the bench; Matt Dawson selected but withdrew due to injury, Kyran Bracken was moved from the bench to the team and Andy Gomarsall was then selected for the bench; Jason Robinson played at full back despite wearing the number 14 on his shirt!; After this match Will Greenwood returned home for family reasons*]

(*The England scrum was put under severe pressure in the first half; Jonny Wilkinson scored a penalty goal in the 4th minute!; England were leading 3-0 in the 11th minute when Mike Tindall broke through but then carried the ball under the wrong arm which allowed Joe van Niekerk to tackle him into touch at the corner flag; England were drawing 3-3 midway through the first half; England were leading 6-3 in the 29th minute; England were still leading 6-3 in the 37th minute when Louis Koen missed a penalty goal attempt and Will Greenwood then famously forgot to touch the ball down behind the tryline before throwing it forward for a 22 drop-out!; England were drawing 6-6 at half-time; England were leading 9-6 in the 46th minute when Jason Robinson saved a certain try by tacking Bakkies Botha into touch at the corner flag; England were leading 12-6 in the 51st minute; England were still leading 12-6 midway through the second half; England were leading 12-6 in the 63rd minute when Lewis Moody brilliantly charged down Louis Koen's kick which allowed Will Greenwood to follow up and dribble through to score; England were leading 22-6 in the 67th minute; England were still leading 22-6 with 5 minutes remaining; England scored 19 unanswered points in the second half to win the match; Jonny Wilkinson scored 20 points in this match; Ben Kay and Kyran Bracken both had a brilliant game*)

26th Oct SAMOA 22 **ENGLAND** 35 **BP**

Telstra Dome, Melbourne

[*This match kicked off at 8.30pm; Danny Grewcock and Richard Hill (2) unavailable due to injury; Will Greenwood unavailable due to family illness; The Telstra Dome had its retractable roof closed for this match; Dan Luger took the field illegally and so did not win a cap!; After this match Martin Corry temporarily returned home due to family*

***reasons; England briefly had 16 players on the field during the game against Samoa after they ignored the instructions of a match official and a subsequent World Cup judicial inquiry on 30th October 2003 found them guilty of misconduct and thus duly fined the RFU £10,000*]**

(*The England forwards could not win any lineout ball in the first half; Earl Va'a scored a penalty goal in the 4th minute!; England were losing 10-0 in the 6th minute; England were still losing 10-0 in the 13th minute when Jonny Wilkinson missed a kickable 45 metre penalty goal attempt to end his sequence of 24 consecutive successful kicks!; England were losing 10-0 midway through the second half; England were still losing 10-0 in the 25th minute when Neil Back scored from a rolling maul; England were drawing 10-10 in the 28th minute; England were losing 16-10 in the 36th minute when Jonny Wilkinson hit the left-hand post with an eminently kickable 21 metre penalty goal attempt; England were losing 16-13 at half-time; England were still losing 16-13 in the 41st minute when Jonny Wilkinson missed a speculative 41 metre drop goal attempt; England were losing 16-13 in the 51st minute when they were awarded a 5 metre penalty in an eminently kickable position, but Ben Cohen unaccountably chose to take a quick tap penalty in a vain attempt to score a try; England were still losing 16-13 in the 52nd minute when the referee awarded a penalty try after the Samoan forwards collapsed a scrum as they were being driven backwards over their own line; England were leading 20-19 midway through the second half; England were losing 22-20 in the 62nd minute; England were leading 23-22 in the 70th minute when Iain Balshaw scored after Jonny Wilkinson put up a brilliant cross-kick; Mike Catt came on as a replacement for Stuart Abbott with 9 minutes of normal time remaining; Phil Vickery scored a brilliant try which Jonny Wilkinson then converted to give England a 35-22 lead with 6 minutes of normal time remaining; England scored 15 unanswered points to win the match; Mike Tindall went to the non-playing side of the touchline for attention to a leg injury in the last minute of normal time and then returned to the playing area in the first minute of injury time, by which time Dan Luger had taken the field without waiting for the match officials to give him the necessary authorisation, which meant that England famously had 16 players on the pitch for a period of 34 seconds!; Joe Worsley and Matt Dawson both had poor games*)

CAPTAIN: *Phil Vickery* [*Martin Johnson*]

2nd Nov	URUGUAY	13	**ENGLAND**	111
				BP

Suncorp Stadium, Lang Park, Brisbane

[*This match kicked off at 5.30pm; Richard Hill (2) unavailable due to injury; Trevor Woodman selected but withdrew due to injury, being replaced by Jason Leonard; Neil Back selected for bench but withdrew due to injury, being replaced by Ben Kay; Ben Cohen selected for bench but withdrew due to injury, being replaced by Jason Robinson; Danny Grewcock returned home injured after this match; Simon Shaw joined the squad after this match*]

(*Lewis Moody scored in the 3rd minute!; England were leading 7-3 in the 5th minute!; England were leading 14-3 midway through the first half when Iain Balshaw scored a brilliant 50 metre solo try; England were leading 28-3 in the 34th minute when some superb handling amongst the backs allowed Mike Catt to score; England were leading 42-3 just before half-time when Juan Menchaca scored a penalty goal for Uruguay despite his boot coming off as he took the kick!; England were leading 42-6 at half-time; England were still leading 42-6 in the 41st minute when Josh Lewsey scored after Joe Worsley threw a brilliant one-handed pass; Martin Corry and Iain Balshaw both went off injured in the 45th minute, being replaced by Martin Johnson and Jason*

***Robinson respectively; England were leading 52-6 in the 47th minute when Pablo Lemoine scored after a poor tackle by Danny Grewcock, thus 7 points were preventable; England were leading 52-13 in the 49th minute when Stuart Abbott scored after he wrong-footed the Uruguayan defence with 2 superb sidesteps; England were leading 59-13 in the 52nd minute when Josh Lewsey scored to complete a hat-trick of tries; Julian White came on as a replacement for Phil Vickery in the 53rd minute; England were leading 87-13 midway through the second half; Will Greenwood came on as a replacement for Paul Grayson in the 62nd minute, with Mike Catt then switching from centre to fly half to accommodate Will Greenwood; England were leading 94-13 in the 70th minute when Jason Robinson scored a brilliant 78 metre solo try; England were leading 106-13 with 5 minutes remaining when Josh Lewsey scored to equal Daniel Lambert and Rory Underwood's joint England record of 5 tries in a cap international match; England scored 59 unanswered points to seal the match; Joe Worsley infamously applauded the crowd when he was sent to the sin-bin with 2 minutes remaining!; Danny Grewcock broke his hand in this match but elected to remain on the pitch; Paul Grayson scored 22 points in this match; Mike Catt and Iain Balshaw both had a brilliant game; England amassed their highest ever points total in the World Cup*)**

CAPTAIN: *Martin Johnson*

Quarter-Final

9th Nov WALES 17 **ENGLAND** 28

Suncorp Stadium, Lang Park, Brisbane

[*This match kicked off at 8.00pm; Richard Hill (2), Martin Corry and Paul Grayson unavailable due to injury; Iain Balshaw selected for bench but withdrew due to injury, being replaced by Dan Luger; Josh Lewsey selected at full back but withdrew due to injury, Dan Luger was moved from the bench to the team with Jason Robinson then moving from wing to full back to accommodate Luger, while Stuart Abbott was now selected for the bench*]

(*The England players were exhausted because Clive Woodward had over-trained them in the week before the match; The England forwards could not win any lineout ball in the first half; Jonny Wilkinson hit the left-hand post with an eminently kickable 22 metre penalty goal attempt in the 3rd minute!; England were drawing 0-0 in the 18th minute when Jonny Wilkinson scored a brilliant 45 metre penalty goal; England were leading 3-0 midway through the first half; England were still leading 3-0 in the 22nd minute when Jonny Wilkinson missed a speculative 38 metre drop goal attempt; England were leading 3-0 in the 24th minute when they were awarded a 5 metre penalty in front of the posts, but Ben Cohen unaccountably chose to put in a chip-kick to Neil Back who was then unable to prevent Mark Jones (2) from catching the ball; England were still leading 3-0 in the 30th minute when Mike Tindall inexplicably chose to put up a cross-kick to Ben Kay, which allowed Shane Williams to instigate a counter-attack that led directly to a try by Stephen Jones (2); England were losing 5-3 in the 35th minute when Colin Charvis was allowed to score from a rolling maul; England were losing 10-3 at half-time; Dan Luger had a poor game and was replaced by Mike Catt at half-time, with Mike Tindall then moving from inside centre to wing to accommodate Mike Catt; England were still losing 10-3 in the 44th minute when Jason Robinson made a superb 59 metre diagonal run that enabled Will Greenwood to score a try which Jonny Wilkinson then brilliantly converted from the right touchline; England were leading 16-10 in the 52nd minute; Will Greenwood went off injured in the 53rd minute, being replaced by Stuart Abbott; England were leading 22-10 midway through the second half; England scored 22 unanswered points to win the match;*

***England were leading 25-10 with 9 minutes of normal time remaining when Lawrence Dallaglio dropped Ceri Sweeney's cross-kick and Martyn Williams followed up to score, thus 3 tries and 17 points were preventable; England were leading 25-17 in the first minute of injury time when Jonny Wilkinson scored a superb 39 metre drop goal with the last kick of the match to seal the game; Jonny Wilkinson scored 23 points in this match; Mike Catt had a brilliant game*)**

Semi-Final

16th Nov FRANCE 7 **ENGLAND** 24

Telstra Stadium, Sydney Olympic Park, Homebush Bay, Sydney

[*This match kicked off at 8.00pm; The Telstra Stadium was previously called Stadium Australia; Jason Leonard set a new England record of 112 caps*]

(*This match was played in extremely wet conditions; England played into a strong wind in the first half; Jason Leonard came on as a temporary blood replacement for Phil Vickery in the 4th minute!; England were drawing 0-0 in the 9th minute when Jonny Wilkinson scored a brilliant 21 metre drop goal; France were losing 3-0 in the 10th minute when Serge Betsen was awarded a try by the video referee that should not have been given because Richard Hill (2) also appeared to have his hand on the ball when it was grounded, thus 7 points were unlawful; England were losing 7-3 midway through the first half; England were still losing 7-3 in the 23rd minute when Christophe Dominici famously injured himself tripping Jason Robinson, with Jonny Wilkinson then missing the resulting kickable 42 metre penalty goal attempt!; England were losing 7-6 in the 30th minute; England were still losing 7-6 in the 38th minute; England were leading 9-7 just before half-time when Jonny Wilkinson scored a brilliant 42 metre penalty goal; England were leading 12-7 at half-time; The England forwards monopolised possession in the second half; England were still leading 12-7 in the 50th minute when Jonny Wilkinson missed another kickable 36 metre penalty goal attempt; England were leading 15-7 in the 58th minute when Jonny Wilkinson completed a superb hat-trick of drop goals!; England were leading 18-7 midway through the second half; England were leading 21-7 in the 64th minute; Mike Tindall came on as a replacement for Mike Catt in the 69th minute; England were leading 24-7 with 7 minutes remaining; England scored 21 unanswered points to win the match; England were still leading 24-7 with 3 minutes remaining when Mike Tindall crossed the tryline but then could not get downward pressure on the ball; Jonny Wilkinson scored all of England's 24 points in this match; Neil Back had a brilliant game*)

Final

22nd Nov AUSTRALIA 17 **ENGLAND** 20 aet

Telstra Stadium, Sydney Olympic Park, Homebush Bay, Sydney

[*This match kicked off at 8.00pm; Martin Johnson retired from international rugby on 17th January 2004*]

(*This match was played in wet conditions; England played with the wind in the first half; The referee unaccountably kept penalising Trevor Woodman and Phil Vickery at the scrums; England created and then squandered an overlap in the 1st minute!; England were losing 5-0 in the 6th minute; England were still losing 5-0 in the 12th minute when Jonny Wilkinson scored a brilliant 47 metre penalty goal; England were leading 6-5 midway through the first half; England were still leading 6-5 in the 23rd minute when Jonny Wilkinson badly missed a speculative 39 metre drop goal attempt; Jonny Wilkinson injured his neck tackling Matt Giteau in the 25th minute but elected to remain on the pitch; England were leading 6-5 immediately afterwards when Ben Kay*

wasted a great try-scoring opportunity by dropping the ball while the Australian line was at his mercy; England were leading 9-5 in the 28th minute; England were still leading 9-5 in the 37th minute when Mike Tindall made a famous tackle on George Gregan; England were leading 9-5 in the 38th minute when some superb handling allowed Jason Robinson to score; England were leading 14-5 at half-time; England were leading 14-8 in the 48th minute; England were leading 14-11 midway through the second half; England were still leading 14-11 in the 68th minute when Mike Tindall put in a brilliant grubber kick, but Mat Rogers managed to kick the ball into touch as Will Greenwood was about to dribble through and score!; England were leading 14-11 with 8 minutes of normal time remaining when Jonny Wilkinson missed a kickable 30 metre drop goal attempt; Mike Tindall went off injured with 1 minute of normal time remaining, being replaced by Mike Catt; England were still leading 14-11 in the last minute of normal time when Elton Flatley scored a penalty goal for Australia to send the match into extra time; Jason Leonard came on as a replacement for Phil Vickery at the start of extra time; England were still drawing 14-14 in the second minute of extra time when Jonny Wilkinson scored a superb 46 metre penalty goal; Josh Lewsey went off injured in the sixth minute of extra time, being replaced by Iain Balshaw with Jason Robinson then switching from wing to full back to accommodate Balshaw; England were leading 17-14 in the tenth minute of extra time when Jonny Wilkinson missed another kickable 30 metre drop goal attempt; England were leading 17-14 at the end of the first period of extra time; Richard Hill (2) went off injured in the fourteenth minute of extra time, being replaced by Lewis Moody; England were still leading 17-14 immediately afterwards when Jason Robinson and Ben Cohen both saved a certain try by tackling Lote Tuqiri (1); England were drawing 17-17 with 27 seconds of extra time remaining when Jonny Wilkinson scored a brilliant 25 metre drop goal to win the match and the World Cup; Martin Johnson and Lawrence Dallaglio both had a brilliant game; Jonny Wilkinson scored 113 points in the competition and set a new England cap international career scoring record of 817 points)

ESS REMEMBRANCE MATCH

CAPTAIN: *Dan Baugh* (CAN)

11th Nov COMBINED SERVICES (*SER*) 8 **BARBARIANS** 26

Army Rugby Stadium, Queen's Avenue, Aldershot

[*This match kicked off at 6.30pm; The Army Rugby Stadium was previously called Aldershot Military Stadium; Simon Shaw selected as captain but withdrew as he was now required to join the England squad in the World Cup; Pete Taylor and Danny Porte played for M.R. Steele-Bodger's XV against Cambridge University at Grange Road on 26th November 2003; Ben Whetstone played for M.R. Steele-Bodger's XV against Cambridge University at Grange Road on both 27th November 2002 and 26th November 2003; Paul Evans was converted from a back row player to a lock by his new club Wharfedale; Mattie Stewart, Lee Soper, Andy Dawling, Dan Coen and Mal Roberts all played for the Combined Services in this match*]

(*This match was played in intermittent drizzle; The Barbarians scrum was put under severe pressure; The Barbarians were losing 3-0 when Dan Baugh scored a brilliant 30 metre solo try; The Barbarians were losing 8-7 midway through the first half; The Barbarians were leading 19-8 at half-time; The Barbarians were still leading 19-8 when Gonçalo Malheiro scored a brilliant try; The Barbarians scored 19 unanswered points to win the match*)

ENGLAND SEVENS TRAINING MATCH

CAPTAIN: *Simon Amor* [England VII]

CAPTAIN: *??* [Samurai]

2nd Dec **ENGLAND VII** 35 **SAMURAI** 30

Rashid School, Dubai

[ENGLAND VII: (*Both sides agreed to allow unlimited substitutions in this match; No conversions were attempted in this match!*)]

[SAMURAI: [*Mike Friday played for Major R.V. Stanley's XV against Oxford University at Iffley Road on 12th November 2003*]

(*Both sides agreed to allow unlimited substitutions in this match; Mike Friday came on as a replacement in the closing stages; No conversions were attempted in this match!*)]

ENGLAND U21 TRIAL MATCH

CAPTAIN: *Geoff Parling* [England U21 North XV]

CAPTAIN: *Nils Mordt* [England U21 South XV]

2nd Dec **ENGLAND U21 NORTH XV** 26 **ENGLAND U21 SOUTH XV** 26

Broadstreet RFC, Ivor Preece Field, Binley Woods, Coventry

[ENGLAND U21 NORTH XV: [*Stuart Friswell played for England in the U19 World Championship in Italy in March 2002; Matt Hampson, Mark Hopley, Iyran Clunis and Tom Ryder played for England in the U19 World Championship in France in April 2003; Rhodri McAtee played for England in the U19 World Championship in France in April 2003, played for Wales U21 in February 2005 and played for Wales 7s in December 2005; Ben Russell (1) captained England in the U19 World Championship in France in April 2003; Jon Clarke played for England in the U19 World Championships in Italy in March 2002; Nathan Jones played for England in the U19 World Championships in Italy in March 2002 and France in April 2003; James Wellwood played for England in the U19 World Championship in France in April 2003 and played for Wales U21 in March 2004*]

(*The England U21 North XV was losing 12-0 in the 13th minute; The England U21 North XV was leading 14-12 at half-time; The England U21 North XV was leading 19-14 in the 44th minute; The England U21 North XV scored 19 unanswered points; The England U21 North XV was drawing 19-19 when Tom Allen scored after Jon Clarke made a brilliant run; The England U21 North XV was drawing 26-26 in the 68th minute*)]

[ENGLAND U21 SOUTH XV: [*James Graham, James Greenwood, Will Bowley, Richard Thorpe, Joe Bedford, Andy Buist and Simon Whatling played for England in the U19 World Championship in France in April 2003; Mike Guess and Greg Nicholls played for England in the U19 World Championship in Italy in March 2002; Nils Mordt was the nephew of Ray Mordt*]

(*The England U21 South XV was leading 12-0 in the 13th minute; The England U21 South XV was losing 14-12 at half-time; The England U21 South XV was losing 19-14 in the 44th minute; The England U21 North XV was allowed to score 19 unanswered points; The England U21 South XV was losing 19-14 when Tom Williams scored after Luke Narraway made a brilliant run; The England U21 South XV was drawing 26-26 in the 68th minute*)]

EMIRATES AIRLINE DUBAI RUGBY SEVENS

Dubai Exiles Stadium, Dubai

CAPTAIN: *Ben Gollings*

First Round - Pool 'A'

4th Dec MOROCCO 0 **ENGLAND** 45

[*This match kicked off at 9.40am*]

(*England were leading 21-0 at half-time; Ben Gollings scored 25 points in this match*)

CAPTAIN: *Simon Amor*

4th Dec SRI LANKA 0 **ENGLAND** 75

[*This match kicked off at 1.56pm*]

(*England monopolised possession in this match; England were leading 40-0 at half-time; Ben Gollings came on as a replacement for Simon Amor in the 8th minute*)

4th Dec FRANCE 0 **ENGLAND** 40

[*This match kicked off at 6.20pm*]

(*England were leading 19-0 at half-time; England scored 160 unanswered points in their three Pool matches!*)

Quarter-Final

5th Dec ARGENTINA 5 **ENGLAND** 14

[*This match kicked off at 9.48am*]

(*England were leading 14-0 at half-time; Simon Amor went off injured with 2 minutes remaining, being replaced by James Brooks*)

CAPTAIN: *Ben Gollings*

Semi-Final

5th Dec SOUTH AFRICA 13 **ENGLAND*** 12

[*This match kicked off at 6.00pm; Simon Amor unavailable due to injury*]

(*England were losing 5-0 when Richard Haughton scored after Geoff Appleford made a brilliant run; England were leading 7-5 at half-time; England were leading 12-5 early in the second half; England were leading 12-10 in the final minute when South Africa were awarded a penalty under the posts which Earl Rose duly kicked to win the match; Ben Gollings scored 57 points in the competition*)

EMIRATES AIRLINE SOUTH AFRICA SEVENS

Outeniqua Park Stadium, George

CAPTAIN: *Tony Roques*

First Round - Pool 'A'

12th Dec CANADA 0 **ENGLAND** 38

[*This match kicked off at 10.00am*]

(*Ugo Monye scored in the 2nd minute!; England were leading 14-0 midway through the first half; England were still leading 14-0 just before half-time; England were leading 21-0 at half-time; England were leading 26-0 in the 9th minute; England were leading 33-0 midway through the second half*)

12th Dec ZAMBIA 0 **ENGLAND** 33

[*This match kicked off at 1.06pm*]

(*Phil Dowson scored in the 2nd minute!; England were leading 14-0 midway through the first half; England were leading 21-0 at half-time; England were leading 26-0 midway through the second half; England were still leading 26-0 in the last minute*)

12th Dec ARGENTINA 5 **ENGLAND** 26

[*This match kicked off at 5.50pm*]

(Rob Thirlby was sin-binned in the 1st minute!; England were losing 5-0 in the 3rd minute; England were still losing 5-0 midway through the first half; England were leading 7-5 just before half-time; England were leading 12-5 at half-time; England were leading 19-5 in the 10th minute; England were still leading 19-5 midway through the second half; England were leading 19-5 in the last minute; England scored 26 unanswered points to win the match)

CAPTAIN: *Geoff Appleford*

Quarter-Final

13th Dec FRANCE 0 **ENGLAND** 50

[This match kicked off at 11.45am; After this match Dan Hipkiss was suspended for one game for punching an opponent]

(Rob Thirlby scored in the 2nd minute!; England were leading 10-0 midway through the first half; England were leading 15-0 just before half-time; England were leading 22-0 at half-time; England were leading 29-0 in the 9th minute; England were leading 36-0 midway through the second half; England were leading 43-0 in the last minute; Ben Gollings had a brilliant game)

CAPTAIN: *Tony Roques*

Semi-Final

13th Dec SOUTH AFRICA 7 **ENGLAND** 19

[This match kicked off at 3.35pm; Dan Hipkiss unavailable due to suspension]

(England were drawing 0-0 midway through the first half; England were leading 7-0 in the 5th minute; England were still leading 7-0 just before half-time; England were drawing 7-7 at half-time; England were leading 14-7 in the 10th minute; England were still leading 14-7 midway through the second half; Tony Roques went off injured with 1 minute remaining, being replaced by Tom Rees; Ben Gollings had a brilliant game)

CAPTAIN: *Geoff Appleford*

Final

13th Dec NEW ZEALAND 14 **ENGLAND** 38

[This match kicked off at 6.00pm; Tony Roques unavailable due to injury]

(Rob Thirlby scored in the 2nd minute!; England were leading 14-0 midway through the first half; England were still leading 14-0 in the 6th minute; England were leading 14-7 at half-time; England were leading 21-7 in the 12th minute; England were leading 26-14 midway through the second half; England were still leading 26-14 with 1 minute remaining when Ben Gollings scored a brilliant solo try; England scored 17 unanswered points to clinch the match; Ben Gollings and Rob Thirlby both had a brilliant game; Ben Gollings scored 70 points in the competition)

ZURICH WORLD CHAMPIONS CHALLENGE

CAPTAIN: *Richard Hill (2)* [*Andy Gomarsall*]

20th Dec **ENGLAND XV** 42 New Zealand Barbarians 17

Twickenham

[This match kicked off at 5.00pm; Steve Thompson (2) selected but withdrew due to injury, Mark Regan was moved from the bench to the team and Andy Titterrell was then selected for the bench; Charlie Hodgson selected for bench but withdrew due to injury, being replaced by Ben Gollings; Mark Regan then himself withdrew due to injury, Andy Titterrell was moved from the bench to the team and Andy Long was then selected for the bench]

(This match was played in cold conditions on a wet pitch; Paul Grayson scored a penalty goal in the 4th minute!; Pat Sanderson came on as a temporary blood

***replacement for Richard Hill (2) in the 7th minute; The England XV was losing 7-3 in the 9th minute; The England XV was losing 10-3 midway through the first half when it was awarded an 11 metre penalty in an eminently kickable position and Paul Grayson then famously told the referee to move out of his way before putting up a brilliant cross-kick which enabled Ben Cohen to score!; The England XV was losing 10-8 in the 29th minute when Paul Grayson scored a brilliant try but then missed the eminently kickable conversion attempt!; The England XV was leading 13-10 at half-time; The England XV was leading 16-10 in the 47th minute when Ben Cohen scored another try after Andy Gomarsall took a quick tap penalty; The England XV was leading 28-10 midway through the second half; Richard Hill (2) had to go off in the 61st minute after his nose was broken by an illegal straight arm from Troy Flavell, being replaced by Hugh Vyvyan; The England XV was leading 28-10 in the 64th minute when James Simpson-Daniel scored after Paul Grayson put up another superb cross-kick; The England XV scored 32 unanswered points to win the match; The England XV was leading 35-10 with 6 minutes remaining when Keith Lowen scored after a poor tackle by Mike Tindall, thus 7 points were preventable; Stuart Abbott went off injured with 1 minute remaining, being replaced by Ben Gollings; The England XV was leading 35-17 in the final minute; Ben Cohen had a brilliant game*)**

JEAN-CLAUDE BAQUÉ SHIELD MATCH

CAPTAIN: *Jamie Hamilton*

28th Dec **ENGLAND COUNTIES*** 18 FRANCE AMATEURS 27

Henley RFC, Dry Leas, Marlow Road, Henley-on-Thames

[*This match kicked off at 2.00pm; Craig Hammond played for New Zealand U19*]

(*The England Counties forwards dominated the lineout in this match; England Counties were drawing 0-0 in the first quarter when Lee Cholewa wasted a great try-scoring opportunity by throwing a poor pass 5 metres from the France Amateurs line; England Counties were still drawing 0-0 midway through the first half; England Counties were losing 3-0 in the 22nd minute; England Counties were losing 10-3 shortly before half-time when Jan Bonney wasted another great try-scoring opportunity by throwing a poor pass to the unmarked Lee Soper; England Counties were losing 10-3 at half-time; England Counties were losing 10-6 early in the second half; England Counties were losing 15-6 midway through the second half when Lee Soper scored from a rolling maul; England Counties were losing 20-13 in the final quarter when James Moore scored after Jamie Hamilton made a brilliant break; England Counties were losing 20-18 with 2 minutes remaining when James Moore missed a 40 metre penalty goal attempt; England Counties were still losing 20-18 in the final minute when Christophe Gasperi scored a try which Laurent Caillat then converted with the last kick of the match to clinch the game for France Amateurs*)

2004

AXA NEW ZEALAND INTERNATIONAL SEVENS

WestpacTrust Stadium, Wellington

CAPTAIN: *Simon Amor*

First Round - Pool 'A'

6th Feb KENYA 17 **ENGLAND** 26

[This match kicked off at 2.28pm]

(Ben Gollings scored after he made a brilliant blindside break; England scored 26 unanswered points to win the match; England were leading 26-0 at half-time; England were still leading 26-0 midway through the second half; Kenya were allowed to score 17 unanswered points in the second half)

6th Feb PAPUA NEW GUINEA 0 **ENGLAND** 26

[This match kicked off at 5.24pm]

(England were leading 7-0 at half-time; Rob Thirlby, James Brooks and Nils Mordt were all sent to the sin-bin in this match!)

6th Feb AUSTRALIA 17 **ENGLAND** 26

[This match kicked off at 9.34pm]

(England were leading 7-0 in the early stages; England were losing 12-7 at half-time; England were still losing 12-7 when Ben Gollings scored after Tony Roques made a brilliant run; England were leading 21-12 when some superb handling allowed Ben Gollings to score another try)

Quarter-Final

7th Feb SAMOA 7 **ENGLAND** 19

[This match kicked off at 2.33pm]

(Gaolo Elisara scored in the 3rd minute!; England were losing 7-0 midway through the first half; England were still losing 7-0 just before half-time when Rob Thirlby scored a brilliant 40 metre solo try; England were drawing 7-7 at half-time; England scored 19 unanswered points to win the match)

Semi-Final

7th Feb FIJI 15 **ENGLAND*** 10 aet

[This match kicked off at 6.35pm]

(England were drawing 5-5 at half-time; England were losing 10-5 when Nnamdi Obi wasted a great try-scoring opportunity by dropping the ball while the Fijian line was at his mercy; England were still losing 10-5 in the last minute of normal time when Nnamdi Obi ran 50 metres to score a try to bring the scores level, with the game then going into sudden death extra time after Ben Gollings missed the difficult conversion attempt; England were drawing 10-10 in sudden death extra time when Temesia Kaumaia scored to win the match for Fiji)

TEAM ROC USA SEVENS

Home Depot Center, Carson City, Los Angeles

CAPTAIN: *Simon Amor*

First Round - Pool 'A'

14th Feb USA 0 **ENGLAND** 40

[This match kicked off at 12.12pm]

14th Feb TRINIDAD & TOBAGO 0 **ENGLAND** 50

[This match kicked off at 3.18pm]

14th Feb	SAMOA	19	**ENGLAND***	17	

[This match kicked off at 6.56pm]
(*England were losing 12-0 at one point in this match; England scored 17 unanswered points; England were leading 17-12 with 2 minutes remaining*)
Quarter-Final

15th Feb	NEW ZEALAND	22	**ENGLAND**	0	

(*England were losing 12-0 at half-time*)
[Plate Semi-Final:]

[15th Feb	SOUTH AFRICA	7	**ENGLAND**	33	]

[No match notes]
[Plate Final:]

[15th Feb	CANADA	0	**ENGLAND**	55	]

(*Ben Gollings scored 61 points in the competition*)

6 NATIONS CHAMPIONSHIP

CAPTAIN: *Lawrence Dallaglio*

15th Feb	ITALY	9	**ENGLAND**	50

Stadio Flaminio, Rome
[This match kicked off at 4.00pm; Andy Sheridan, Julian White, Lewis Moody, Alex Sanderson, Jonny Wilkinson, Charlie Hodgson, Mike Catt, Mike Tindall and Stuart Abbott all unavailable due to injury; Andy Titterrell unavailable due to suspension; Steve Borthwick originally selected for bench but had to withdraw in accordance with the 6 Nations Championship rules because he was cited after a club game the previous weekend, being replaced by Simon Shaw; Matt Stevens, Dorian West, Alex King, Ollie Smith (2) and James Simpson-Daniel all in original training squad of 28 but were not selected for team or bench; Will Greenwood played at inside centre despite wearing the number 13 on his shirt!; Jason Leonard established a new England record of 114 caps and, thanks to his 5 appearances for the British & Irish Lions, set a new world record of 119 caps]
(*Paul Grayson scored a penalty goal in the 2nd minute!; England were drawing 3-3 in the 6th minute; England were still drawing 3-3 in the 15th minute when Iain Balshaw dummied his way through to score a brilliant try; England were leading 13-3 midway through the first half; England were leading 13-6 in the 22nd minute when Jason Robinson wrong-footed Rima Wakarua to score a superb solo try; England were leading 18-9 in the 28th minute; Simon Shaw came on as a temporary blood replacement for Danny Grewcock in the 38th minute; England were leading 21-9 just before half-time; England were leading 26-9 at half-time; Henry Paul came on as a temporary blood replacement for Jason Robinson in the 53rd minute; England were still leading 26-9 in the 58th minute when Josh Lewsey scored a brilliant solo try; Jason Robinson came back on as a replacement for Iain Balshaw in the 59th minute; England were leading 33-9 midway through the second half; England were still leading 33-9 in the 63rd minute when Jason Robinson scored to complete a hat-trick of tries; England were leading 38-9 in the 68th minute when Paul Grayson chipped ahead and regathered the ball to score a superb try; England were leading 45-9 in the last minute; England scored 24 unanswered points in the second half to seal the match; Paul Grayson played brilliantly and scored 20 points in this match; Jason Robinson had a brilliant game*)

21st Feb	SCOTLAND	13	**ENGLAND**	35

Murrayfield

[This match kicked off at 5.30pm; Julian White, Joe Worsley, Lewis Moody, Jonny Wilkinson, Mike Catt, Mike Tindall and James Simpson-Daniel all unavailable due to injury; Steve Borthwick unavailable due to suspension; Will Greenwood played at inside centre despite wearing the number 13 on his shirt!; Alex Sanderson retired due to injury in November 2005]

(This match was played in cold and wet conditions; Chris Paterson scored a penalty goal in the 3rd minute!; England were losing 3-0 in the 11th minute when Ben Cohen scored after Jason Robinson put in a brilliant chip-kick; England were leading 10-3 midway through the first half; England were leading 13-6 in the 29th minute when Iain Balshaw was awarded a try which should not have been given because Danny Grewcock clearly knocked the ball on earlier in the movement; England were leading 20-6 at half-time; England played with the wind in the second half; England were still leading 20-6 in the 47th minute when Josh Lewsey charged down a kick by Chris Paterson and followed up to score; England were leading 25-6 in the 57th minute when Simon Danielli kicked ahead and followed up to score after Iain Balshaw was deceived by the bounce of the ball, thus 7 points were preventable; England were leading 25-13 midway through the second half; England were leading 28-13 in the 65th minute when Danny Grewcock powered through to score under the posts; Henry Paul came on as a replacement for Will Greenwood with 4 minutes remaining; Danny Grewcock and Chris Jones both had a brilliant game)

6th March	**ENGLAND***	13	IRELAND	19

Twickenham

[This match kicked off at 4.00pm; Lewis Moody, Alex Sanderson, Danny Grewcock, Simon Shaw and Jonny Wilkinson all unavailable due to injury; Jason Leonard and Stuart Abbott in original training squad of 26 but were not selected for team or bench; Will Greenwood played at inside centre despite wearing the number 13 on his shirt!; Neil Back retired from international rugby on 15th March 2004 but then changed his mind in April 2005]

(This match was played on a wet pitch; Steve Thompson (2)'s throwing-in was poor and the England lineout suffered accordingly; England were losing 3-0 in the 17th minute; England were still losing 3-0 midway through the first half; England were losing 3-0 in the 22nd minute when Jason Robinson broke through but was then brilliantly tap-tackled by Peter Stringer; England were losing 6-0 in the 26th minute when Matt Dawson scored after Peter Stringer was caught in possession by Lawrence Dallaglio at the base of an Ireland scrum; England were leading 10-6 in the 31st minute; England were leading 10-9 just before half-time; England were losing 12-10 at half-time; England were still losing 12-10 at the start of the second half when Paul Grayson brilliantly chipped ahead and regathered the ball which enabled Ben Cohen to reach the tryline despite carrying the ball under the wrong arm, but the move was disallowed after the video referee adjudged that he had made a double movement; England were losing 19-10 in the 51st minute; Ireland were allowed to score 13 unanswered points to win the match; Iain Balshaw went off injured in the 53rd minute, being replaced by James Simpson-Daniel with Josh Lewsey then switching from wing to full back to accommodate James Simpson-Daniel; Olly Barkley came on as a temporary blood replacement for Paul Grayson in the 55th minute; Mark Regan came on as a replacement for Steve Thompson (2) in the 59th minute; England were still losing 19-10 midway through the second half when Mark Regan crossed the tryline but the move was disallowed after the video referee adjudged that he hit the touch flag

***before he grounded the ball; England were losing 19-13 in the 67th minute; England were still losing 19-13 with 2 minutes remaining when Paul Grayson put in a superb chip-kick, but the ball went over the dead ball line before Will Greenwood could touch it down; Steve Thompson (2) and Iain Balshaw both had a poor game; This was the first time since 1999 that England had lost a cap international match at Twickenham!*)**

20th Mar **ENGLAND** 31 WALES 21
Twickenham

[*This match kicked off at 4.00pm; Lewis Moody, Jonny Wilkinson and Iain Balshaw unavailable due to injury; Paul Grayson selected but withdrew due to injury, being replaced by Olly Barkley; Jason Leonard, Matt Stevens, Andy Titterrell and Neil Back all in original training squad of 28 but were not selected for team or bench; Will Greenwood played at inside centre despite wearing the number 13 on his shirt!*]

(*England were drawing 0-0 in the 6th minute when Ben Cohen powered through 2 attempted tackles to score; England were leading 7-6 in the 14th minute; England were leading 13-6 midway through the first half; England were leading 13-9 in the 27th minute when Chris Jones wasted a great try-scoring opportunity by throwing a poor pass over Will Greenwood's head 5 metres from the Welsh line; England were still leading 13-9 just before half-time; England were leading 16-9 at half-time; Chris Jones went off injured at half-time, being replaced by Joe Worsley; England played with a swirling wind in the second half; England were drawing 16-16 in the 42nd minute; England were still drawing 16-16 in the 50th minute when Mark Taylor scored a try which should not have been given because the scoring pass from Shane Williams was clearly forward, thus 5 points were unlawful; Wales were allowed to score 12 unanswered points; England were losing 21-16 midway through the second half; England were still losing 21-16 in the 64th minute when Ben Cohen powered round the fringes of a ruck to score another try; England were leading 23-21 with 7 minutes of normal time remaining when Olly Barkley scored a penalty goal despite Ceri Sweeney unaccountably attempting to charge down the kick!; England were leading 26-21 with 1 minute of normal time remaining; England scored 15 unanswered points to win the match*)

27th Mar FRANCE 24 **ENGLAND*** 21
Stade de France, Paris

[*This match kicked off at 9.00pm; Lewis Moody, Jonny Wilkinson and Iain Balshaw unavailable due to injury; Paul Grayson selected but withdrew due to injury, being replaced by Olly Barkley; Will Greenwood played at inside centre despite wearing the number 13 on his shirt!*]

**(*Olly Barkley missed a kickable 45 metre penalty goal attempt in the 3rd minute!; England were drawing 0-0 in the 7th minute when Phil Vickery made a famous tackle on Olivier Magne; England were losing 3-0 midway through the first half; Danny Grewcock went off injured in the 23rd minute, being replaced by Steve Borthwick; England were still losing 3-0 immediately afterwards when Ben Cohen unaccountably left his defensive position on the wing and consequently Dimitri Yachvili put up a cross-kick which enabled Imanol Harinordoquy to score unopposed in the right corner; England were losing 8-0 in the 31st minute when the referee inexplicably allowed play to continue after Imanol Harinordoquy raised his left leg backwards to illegally obstruct Matt Dawson at the base of a French scrum and Dimitri Yachvili went on to score a penalty goal, thus 3 points were unlawful; England were losing 14-0 in the 36th minute; France were allowed to score 14 unanswered points to win the match; England were losing 14-3 shortly before half-time when Josh Lewsey unaccountably failed to defend the fringes of a ruck and Dimitri Yachvili was able to kick through and*

***score, thus 2 tries and 12 points were preventable; England were losing 21-3 at half-time; Mike Catt came on as a replacement for Will Greenwood in the 49th minute; England were losing 24-6 in the 52nd minute when Ben Cohen scored after Mike Catt threw a brilliant long pass; England were losing 24-11 midway through the second half; England were still losing 24-11 with 8 minutes of normal time remaining; England were losing 24-14 with 5 minutes of normal time remaining when Josh Lewsey scored a brilliant consolation try; England were losing 24-21 in the first minute of injury time when they created and then squandered an overlap with the last move of the match; Will Greenwood had a poor game*)**

ENGLAND STUDENTS MATCHES

CAPTAIN: *Ross Winney*

14th Feb ITALY U25 25 **ENGLAND STUDENTS*** 21

Stadio Comunale di Telese Terme, Benevento

[*Dan Parkes selected but withdrew, being replaced by Dan Chesham; Ollie Smith (1) in original bench squad but was not selected for bench; Haydn Thomas toured Canada, New Zealand and Australia with England Schools 18 Group in July-August 2001*]

(*England Students were losing 3-0 in the 10th minute; England Students were drawing 3-3 midway through the first half; England Students were drawing 6-6 in the 25th minute; England Students were drawing 6-6 at half-time; The England Students scrum was put under severe pressure in the second half; England Students were losing 13-6 in the 50th minute; England Students were losing 18-6 midway through the second half; England Students were losing 18-14 in the 70th minute; England Students were leading 21-18 with 4 minutes of normal time remaining; England Students were still leading 21-18 in the first minute of injury time when Pietro Travagli scored a try which David Bortolussi then converted with the last kick of the match to clinch the game for Italy U25*)

19th Mar **ENGLAND STUDENTS** 48 WALES STUDENTS 12

Clifton RFC, Station Road, Cribbs Causeway, Henbury, Bristol

[*This match kicked off at 7.30pm; James Hudson and John Chance selected but withdrew due to injury, being replaced by Tom Skelding and Simon Gibbons respectively; Dan Parkes and Craig Cooper selected for bench but withdrew due to injury, being replaced by Wayne Thompson and Mark Foster respectively; Wayne Thompson played for England in the U19 World Championship in France in April 2003*]

(*England Students were leading 3-0 in the early stages; England Students were leading 10-0 midway through the second half; England Students were still leading 10-0 in the 28th minute when Haydn Thomas followed up a kick ahead to score a brilliant try; England Students were leading 17-0 in the 35th minute; England Students were leading 24-0 at half-time; England Students were leading 24-5 early in the second half; Ross Winney scored a superb solo try; England Students were leading 48-5 with 5 minutes remaining; England Students were still leading 48-5 in the last minute*)

26th Mar FRANCE STUDENTS 43 **ENGLAND STUDENTS** 8

Stade Municipal Georges Vuillermet, Lyon

[*This match kicked off at 8.00pm; Matt Street and Craig Cooper unavailable due to injury; Ben Woods unavailable due to club commitments*]

(*England Students were losing 17-0 at one point in the first half; England Students were losing 31-3 at half-time; England Students were losing 43-3 in injury time when James Jones scored a consolation try*)

U21 6 NATIONS CHAMPIONSHIP

CAPTAIN: *Clive Stuart-Smith*

14th Feb ITALY U21 3 **ENGLAND U21** 57

Stadio Leone, Pomigliano D'Arco, Naples

[*This match kicked off at 2.30pm; Brad Davies was selected but withdrew due to injury, Adrian Jarvis was moved from the bench to the team and Nils Mordt was then selected for the bench; Nick Wood toured Canada, New Zealand and Australia with England Schools 18 Group in July-August 2001*]

(*The England U21 forwards monopolised possession in this match; Marcel Garvey scored in the 5th minute!; England U21 were leading 14-0 in the 16th minute; England U21 were leading 19-0 midway through the first half; England U21 were leading 31-0 in the 32nd minute; England U21 were leading 31-0 at half-time; England U21 were leading 38-0 in the 43rd minute; England U21 were leading 45-0 in the 48th minute; England U21 scored 45 unanswered points to win the match; England U21 were leading 45-3 midway through the second half; England U21 were leading 57-3 with 8 minutes remaining*)

20th Feb SCOTLAND U21 9 **ENGLAND U21** 27

Stirling County RFC, Bridgehaugh Park, Stirling

[*This match kicked off at 7.30pm; Jon Pendlebury and Andy Frost in original training squad of 24 but were not selected for team or bench*]

(*Adrian Jarvis scored a penalty goal in the 2nd minute!; Ben Skirving ran 30 metres to score a try which Adrian Jarvis then converted to give England U21 a 10-0 lead in the 5th minute; England U21 were leading 10-3 in the 17th minute when Ben Skirving scored another try after Rob Hawkins took a strike against the head during a Scotland U21 scrum; England U21 were leading 15-6 midway through the first half; England U21 were leading 15-9 in the 25th minute; England U21 were leading 22-9 in the 37th minute; England U21 were leading 22-9 at half-time; England U21 were still leading 22-9 midway through the second half; England U21 were leading 22-9 with 1 minute of normal time remaining when Ben Russell (2) scored a pushover try to seal the match*)

5th Mar **ENGLAND U21** 27 IRELAND U21 19

Kingsholm, Gloucester

[*This match kicked off at 7.30pm; David Wilson (2) played for England in the U19 World Championship in South Africa in March-April 2004*]

(*Gareth Steenson scored a penalty goal in the 4th minute!; England U21 were leading 5-3 in the 8th minute when Adrian Jarvis had his conversion attempt charged down from in front of the posts!; England U21 were still leading 5-3 midway through the first half; England U21 were leading 5-3 in the 23rd minute when Ben Russell (2) scored a brilliant try, with Adrian Jarvis then having the conversion attempt come back off the post; England U21 were drawing 10-10 in the 30th minute; England U21 were drawing 10-10 at half-time; England U21 were losing 13-10 early in the second half when Chris Bell scored after Adrian Jarvis put in a brilliant grubber kick; England U21 were leading 20-19 midway through the second half; England U21 were still leading 20-19 in the last minute when Chris Bell scored another try which Brad Davies then converted to clinch the match*)

19th Mar **ENGLAND U21** 22 WALES U21 19

Kingsholm, Gloucester

[*This match kicked off at 7.05pm; Gavin Quinnell played for Wales U21 in this match*]

**(*England U21 were leading 7-0 in the 7th minute; England U21 were drawing 7-7 in the 18th minute; England U21 were leading 12-7 midway through the first half; England*

U21 were drawing 12-12 shortly afterwards; England U21 were still drawing 12-12 in the 36th minute; England U21 were losing 19-12 at half-time; Adrian Jarvis went off injured at half-time, being replaced by Brad Davies; England U21 were drawing 19-19 early in the second half; Will Skinner went off injured in the 46th minute, being replaced by Tom Parker (1); England U21 were still drawing 19-19 midway through the second half; England U21 were drawing 19-19 with 9 minutes of normal time remaining when Brad Davies scored a 40 metre penalty goal to win the match; England U21 were leading 22-19 in the seventh minute of injury time when James Wellwood dropped the ball in the act of scoring for Wales U21!)

26th Mar FRANCE U21 18 **ENGLAND U21** 25

Parc Municipal des Sports, Brive-la-Gaillarde

[*This match kicked off at 7.30pm; Will Skinner selected but withdrew due to injury, being replaced by Tom Rees; Adrian Jarvis selected but withdrew due to injury, being replaced by Brad Davies*]

(*England U21 were losing 3-0 in the 15th minute; England U21 were still losing 3-0 midway through the first half; England U21 were leading 14-3 in the 31st minute; England U21 scored 14 unanswered points to win the match; England U21 were leading 14-8 in the 33rd minute; England U21 were leading 14-8 at half-time; England U21 were leading 14-11 in the 47th minute; Richard Wigglesworth came on as a temporary blood replacement for Clive Stuart-Smith in the 54th minute; England U21 were leading 19-11 midway through the second half; England U21 were still leading 19-11 with 7 minutes of normal time remaining; England U21 were leading 22-11 with 1 minute of normal time remaining; England U21 were leading 22-18 in the second minute of injury time when Ross Laidlaw scored a penalty goal to clinch the match and the Grand Slam*)

'A' INTERNATIONAL MATCHES

CAPTAIN: *Mike Catt*

6th Mar FRANCE A 26 **ENGLAND A*** 22

Stade Aimé Giral, Perpignan

[*This match kicked off at 7.30pm; Duncan Bell selected for bench but withdrew as he erroneously believed that he was due to qualify to play for Wales on residency grounds in May 2004, being replaced by Perry Freshwater; David Flatman in original training squad of 23 but withdrew due to injury, being replaced by Duncan Bell; Dan Richmond, Alex King, Andy Higgins (2) and Jamie Noon all in original training squad of 23 but were not selected for team or bench; Mike Catt was added to the squad on 27th February 2004; Perry Freshwater played for New Zealand U21 in 1993 but qualified to play for England in 1998 after completing a residency period of 3 years*]

(*England A played with a strong wind in the first half; England A were losing 7-0 in the 6th minute; England A were losing 7-6 in the 15th minute; England A were losing 10-6 midway through the first half; England A were losing 13-6 in the 26th minute; England A were losing 20-6 in the 37th minute; England A were losing 20-9 at half-time; Martyn Wood came on as a replacement for Harris Ellis at the start of the second half; James Forrester had to go off in the 44th minute after he dislocated his shoulder, being replaced by Pat Sanderson; England A were losing 23-9 in the 47th minute; England A were losing 23-15 midway through the second half; England A were losing 26-15 in the 67th minute; England A wasted 6 great try-scoring opportunities in the final quarter!; England A were still losing 26-15 with 4 minutes remaining when Pat Sanderson scored a brilliant consolation try; Henry Paul had a brilliant game*)

CAPTAIN: *No captain appointed*

19th Mar ITALY A C **ENGLAND A** C

Stadio Comunale, Pomezia

[This match was cancelled on 27th February 2004 after a number of Zurich Premiership matches were rearranged for 20th-21st March 2004, which meant that England A would be unable to raise a sufficiently competitive team]

CATHAY PACIFIC/CREDIT SUISSE HONG KONG SEVENS

Hong Kong Stadium, Eastern Hospital Road, So Kon Po, Hong Kong

CAPTAIN: *Simon Amor*

First Round - Pool 'B'

26th Mar CHINA 0 **ENGLAND** 49

[This match kicked off at 5.22pm]

(This match was played in wet conditions; England were leading 7-0 just before half-time; England were leading 14-0 at half-time; Neil Baxter came on as a replacement early in the second half; Ben Gollings scored 24 points in this match; Geoff Appleford had a brilliant game)

27th Mar SCOTLAND 12 **ENGLAND** 38

[This match kicked off at 1.20pm]

(England were leading 7-5 at half-time)

27th Mar GEORGIA 0 **ENGLAND** 42

[This match kicked off at 5.44pm]

(Richard Haughton scored two tries early in the second half to complete a hat-trick)

Quarter-Final

28th Mar FIJI 12 **ENGLAND** 17

[This match kicked off at 2.21pm]

(Richard Haughton wasted 2 great try-scoring opportunities in the first half by dropping the ball; England were losing 7-5 at half-time; England were leading 12-7 when Rob Thirlby scored a brilliant 30 metre solo try)

Semi-Final

28th Mar SOUTH AFRICA 7 **ENGLAND** 15

[This match kicked off at 4.33pm]

(England were leading 5-0 at half-time; England were losing 7-5 when Richard Haughton scored a brilliant solo try; England were leading 10-7 when the full-time hooter sounded, but the ball was still in play and Peter Richards was able to score a try to clinch the match)

Final

28th Mar ARGENTINA 12 **ENGLAND** 22

[This match kicked off at 6.31pm]

(England were losing 5-0 when Simon Amor scored after Peter Richards made a brilliant run; England were drawing 5-5 just before half-time when Peter Richards scored a superb solo try; England were leading 12-5 at half-time; Richard Haughton scored a brilliant 77 metre solo try to give England a 17-5 lead midway through the second half; England were still leading 17-5 when Matias Albina scored as a direct consequence of a mistake by Ben Gollings, thus 7 points were preventable; England were leading 17-12 when Rob Thirlby scored a brilliant try from a tap penalty to clinch the match)

STANDARD CHARTERED SEVENS, SINGAPORE

National Stadium, Kallang

CAPTAIN: *Simon Amor*

First Round - Pool 'B'

3rd April JAPAN 0 **ENGLAND** 28

[This match kicked off at 12.58pm]

(This match was played in hot and humid conditions; England were leading 14-0 at half-time; England were leading 21-0 in the closing stages)

3rd April HONG KONG 5 **ENGLAND** 26

[This match kicked off at 3.54pm]

(Some of the England team played with an illness; This match was played in hot and humid conditions; England were losing 5-0 in the early stages; England were leading 7-5 at half-time; England scored 26 unanswered points to win the match)

3rd April FRANCE 14 **ENGLAND** 14

[This match kicked off at 7.46pm]

(This match was played in hot and humid conditions; England were losing 7-0 in the early stages; France were allowed to score 14 unanswered points; England were losing 14-7 in the last minute)

Quarter-Final

4th April ARGENTINA 21 **ENGLAND** 0

[This match kicked off at 1.05pm]

(Some of the England team played with an illness; Andrés Romagnoli scored in the 1st minute!; England were losing 14-0 in the 4th minute; Argentina were allowed to score 21 unanswered points to win the match; England were losing 21-0 at half-time; England were still losing 21-0 early in the second half when Rob Thirlby wasted a great try-scoring opportunity by dropping the ball when there was a 2 man overlap outside him)

[Plate Semi-Final:]

[4th April FIJI 19 **ENGLAND** 5 **]**

[This match kicked off at 4.10pm]

(This match was played in torrential rain; Filimone Bolavucu scored in the 3rd minute!; England were losing 14-0 at half-time; England were still losing 14-0 midway through the second half when Ben Gollings scored a brilliant solo try; England were losing 14-5 in the last minute)

ROSSLYN PARK 125TH ANNIVERSARY MATCH

CAPTAIN: *Stewart Eru* (NZ)

2nd May Rosslyn Park 48 **OXBRIDGE XV** 53

Rosslyn Park FC, Priory Lane, Upper Richmond Road, Roehampton

[This match kicked off at 2.30pm; Gavin Webster was capped for England Colts in March 1992; Mike Friday and James Lofthouse played for Rosslyn Park in this match]

(The Oxbridge XV was leading in the early stages; The Oxbridge XV was leading 29-17 at half-time; The lead frequently changed hands in the second half!; The Oxbridge XV was drawing 48-48 in injury time when Stewart Eru scored a match-winning try)

FIRST STAFFWARE CHALLENGE TOUR MATCH

CAPTAIN: *Taine Randell* (NZ)

22nd May SCOTLAND XV 33 **BARBARIANS** 40

Murrayfield

[*This match kicked off at 3.00pm; Bruce Reihana selected for bench but withdrew, being replaced by Stefan Terblanche; The Barbarians' starting lineup had 612 caps between them!*]

(*The Barbarians were drawing 0-0 in the 9th minute when Vilimoni Delasau ran 50 metres to score after Mark Robinson (2) threw a brilliant inside pass; The Barbarians were leading 7-0 midway through the first half; The Barbarians were still leading 7-0 in the 25th minute when Mark Robinson (2) scored after Brian O'Driscoll threw a brilliant pass to Shane Horgan; The Barbarians were leading 14-0 straight after the restart when David Humphreys' pass was intercepted by Dan Parks who then went on to score, thus 7 points were preventable; The Barbarians were leading 14-7 in the 34th minute when Shane Horgan scored after Christian Cullen made a superb break; The Barbarians were leading 21-7 in the 36th minute when Shane Horgan scored another try after Bobby Skinstad instigated a brilliant counter-attack; The Barbarians were leading 28-7 at half-time; Vilimoni Delasau went off injured at half-time, being replaced by Stefan Terblanche; The Barbarians were leading 28-14 in the 44th minute; Eric Miller came on as a temporary blood replacement for Bobby Skinstad in the 49th minute; The Barbarians were leading 33-14 midway through the second half; The Barbarians were leading 33-26 in the 64th minute; The Barbarians were still leading 33-26 with 8 minutes remaining; The Barbarians were leading 40-26 with 6 minutes remaining; Mark Robinson (2) and Bobby Skinstad both had a brilliant game*)

SECOND STAFFWARE CHALLENGE TOUR MATCH

CAPTAIN: *Matt Burke* (AU)

26th May WALES XV 42 **BARBARIANS** 0

Ashton Gate, Bristol

[*This match kicked off at 7.45pm; The original venue for this match was the Racecourse Ground, Wrexham; Stefan Terblanche unavailable due to injury; Paul Sackey selected but withdrew on the evening of the match as he was now required to play for the England XV on the following Sunday; Dafydd James thus replaced Paul Sackey; Cobus Visagie selected for bench but withdrew, being replaced by Jason Leonard*]

**(*The Barbarians made a number of handling errors in this match; The Barbarians were drawing 0-0 in the 13th minute when collectively poor tackling allowed Ceri Sweeney to score; The Barbarians were losing 7-0 midway through the first half; The Barbarians were losing 10-0 in the 28th minute; The Barbarians were losing 13-0 shortly before half-time when Breyton Paulse made a brilliant break but Dafydd James' intended scoring pass was then intercepted by Colin Charvis; The Barbarians were losing 13-0 at half-time; Thomas Castaignède came on as a replacement for Bruce Reihana at half-time; The Barbarians were losing 20-0 in the 44th minute; The Barbarians were losing 25-0 in the 49th minute; The Barbarians were still losing 25-0 shortly afterwards when Thomas Castaignède wasted a great try-scoring opportunity by dropping the ball while the Wales XV line was at his mercy; Jason Leonard came on as a replacement for Richard Bands in the 54th minute; The Barbarians were losing 25-0 midway through the second half; The Barbarians were losing 30-0 in the 66th minute; The Barbarians were still losing 30-0 with 9 minutes of normal time remaining when further collectively*

***poor tackling allowed Gavin Henson to score, thus 2 tries and 12 points were preventable; The Barbarians were losing 35-0 with 6 minutes of normal time remaining when Hal Luscombe scored a try that should not have been given because the scoring pass from Sonny Parker was clearly forward, thus 7 points were unlawful; Matt Burke had a poor game; The was the first time in 26 years that the Barbarians had failed to score any points in a match!*)**

EMIRATES AIRLINE BORDEAUX SEVENS

Stade Jacques Chaban-Delmas, Bordeaux

CAPTAIN: *Simon Amor*

First Round - Pool 'B'

28th May	KENYA	5	**ENGLAND**	31

[*This match kicked off at 1.28pm*]

(*England were leading 19-0 at half-time*)

CAPTAIN: *Ben Gollings*

28th May	SPAIN	12	**ENGLAND**	36

[*This match kicked off at 4.24pm*]

(*England were leading 19-5 at half-time; England were leading 36-5 in the closing stages*)

CAPTAIN: *Simon Amor*

28th May	AUSTRALIA	12	**ENGLAND**	19

[*This match kicked off at 8.44pm*]

(*Ugo Monye scored after just 30 seconds had been played!; England were drawing 7-7 at half-time; Simon Amor scored a brilliant 60 metre solo try in the second half; England were leading 19-7 in the last minute*)

Quarter-Final

29th May	CANADA	0	**ENGLAND**	36

[*This match kicked off at 2.34pm*]

(*This match was played in hot conditions; England were leading 19-0 at half-time*)

Semi-Final

29th May	SOUTH AFRICA	14	**ENGLAND**	17

[*This match kicked off at 6.36pm*]

(*England were losing 7-0 in the early stages; England were losing 14-7 at half-time; James Brooks came on as a replacement for Ben Gollings in the second half; England were drawing 14-14 when the full-time hooter sounded, but the ball was still in play and they were then awarded a 40 metre penalty which Simon Amor duly kicked to win the match*)

Final

29th May	NEW ZEALAND	28	**ENGLAND**	19

[*This match kicked off at 9.35pm*]

(*England were drawing 0-0 in the early stages when Simon Amor brilliantly chipped ahead and followed up to score; England were losing 14-5 just before half-time; England were losing 14-12 at half-time; England were still losing 14-12 early in the second half when Liam Messam scored after a poor tackle by Henry Paul, thus 7 points were preventable; England were losing 28-12 in the closing stages when Kai Horstmann scored a consolation try*)

THIRD STAFFWARE CHALLENGE TOUR MATCH

CAPTAIN: *Hugh Vyvyan* [England XV]
CAPTAIN: *Anton Oliver* (NZ) [*Mark Andrews* (SA)] [Barbarians]

30th May **ENGLAND XV** 12 **BARBARIANS** 32
Twickenham

[ENGLAND XV: [*This match kicked off at 3.00pm*]
(*The England XV forwards could not win any lineout ball in the first half; Jason Leonard scored in the 4th minute!; The England XV was losing 7-0 in the 8th minute when a lack of communication between Michael Horak and Nick Walshe saw them both attempt to deal with a speculative kick by Brian O'Driscoll which allowed Shane Horgan to follow up and score; The England XV was losing 12-3 midway through the first half when Dave Walder missed a kickable 35 metre drop goal attempt; The England XV was losing 17-6 in the 25th minute; The England XV was losing 17-12 in the 33rd minute; Robbie Morris went off injured in the 39th minute, being replaced by Jon Dawson; The England XV was still losing 17-12 just before half-time; The England XV was losing 20-12 at half-time; The England XV was still losing 20-12 in the 48th minute when Dave Walder missed an eminently kickable 25 metre penalty goal attempt; The England XV was losing 20-12 in the 54th minute when it created and then squandered an overlap; The England XV was still losing 20-12 midway through the second half when Dave Walder's pass was intercepted by Bobby Skinstad who then ran 32 metres to score, thus 2 tries and 12 points were preventable; The final quarter of this match was played in wet conditions; The England XV was losing 27-12 in the 64th minute when Dan Hyde had a great try-scoring chance but was tackled into touch at the corner flag by Matt Burke; Andy Hazell went off injured with 8 minutes of normal time remaining, being replaced by Peter Buxton; The England XV was still losing 27-12 with 5 minutes of normal time remaining; Jamie Noon had a brilliant game*)]

[BARBARIANS: [*This match kicked off at 3.00pm; Mark Andrews retired after this match*]
(*The Barbarians forwards dominated the lineout in the first half; Jason Leonard ran 3 metres to score a try in the 4th minute!; The Barbarians were leading 12-0 in the 8th minute; The Barbarians were leading 12-3 midway through the first half; The Barbarians were leading 17-6 in the 25th minute; The Barbarians were leading 17-12 in the 33rd minute; The Barbarians were still leading 17-12 just before half-time; The Barbarians were leading 20-12 at half-time; Bobby Skinstad came on as a replacement for Taine Randell at the start of the second half; The Barbarians were still leading 20-12 midway through the second half when Bobby Skinstad scored a 32 metre interception try; The final quarter of this match was played in wet conditions; The Barbarians were leading 27-12 in the 64th minute when Matt Burke saved a certain try by tackling Dan Hyde into touch at the corner flag; Jason Leonard was substituted in the 67th minute, being replaced by Greg Feek; The Barbarians were still leading 27-12 with 5 minutes of normal time remaining when Malcolm O'Kelly scored from a rolling maul, with acting captain Mark Andrews then badly mishitting the conversion attempt from the right touchline, resulting in the ball bouncing sideways across the pitch!*)]

EMIRATES AIRLINE LONDON SEVENS

Twickenham

CAPTAIN: *Simon Amor*

First Round - Pool 'B'

5th June **ENGLAND** 12 SCOTLAND 7

[*This match kicked off at 12.42pm*]

(*Simon Amor scored in the 2nd minute after Ugo Monye threw a brilliant pass out of the tackle!; England were leading 5-0 midway through the first half when Peter Richards scored after Geoff Appleford threw a brilliant reverse pass; England were leading 12-0 at half-time; Rob Thirlby came on as a replacement for Peter Richards at the start of the second half; England were still leading 12-0 midway through the second half; England were leading 12-0 in the last minute when Andrew Turnbull scored after a poor tackle by Rob Thirlby, thus 5 points were preventable; Ugo Monye injured playing in the match*)

5th June **ENGLAND** 40 ITALY 0

[*This match kicked off at 4.02pm; Ugo Monye unavailable due to injury*]

(*England were drawing 0-0 in the 3rd minute when Henry Paul jinked through to score a brilliant 40 metre try; England were leading 5-0 midway through the first half; England were leading 19-0 at half-time; England were still leading 19-0 early in the second half when Rob Thirlby scored a brilliant 93 metre solo try; England were leading 26-0 midway through the second half when Ben Gollings scored a superb long-range solo try; England were leading 33-0 in the closing stages when Rob Thirlby scored to complete a hat-trick of tries*)

5th June **ENGLAND** 40 FRANCE 7

[*This match kicked off at 7.20pm; Ugo Monye unavailable due to injury*]

(*England were drawing 0-0 in the early stages when Ben Gollings scored after Rob Thirlby made a brilliant 32 metre run; England were leading 7-0 midway through the first half when Ben Gollings scored another try after Peter Richards threw a brilliant pass out of the tackle; England were leading 14-0 shortly before half-time when Peter Richards crossed the French tryline but then allowed Simon Amor to score instead!; England were leading 19-0 at half-time; England were still leading 19-0 early in the second half when Peter Richards scored after he took a return pass from Tony Roques; England were leading 26-0 shortly afterwards when Rob Thirlby scored after Ben Gollings threw a superb long reverse pass; England were leading 33-0 midway through the second half; England were still leading 33-0 shortly afterwards when Rob Thirlby scored another brilliant 63 metre solo try; England scored 40 unanswered points to win the match; England were leading 40-0 in the closing stages; Ben Gollings scored 20 points in this match*)

Quarter-Final

6th June **ENGLAND** 14 AUSTRALIA 5

[*This match kicked off at 2.04pm; Ugo Monye unavailable due to injury*]

(*England were losing 5-0 in the early stages; England were still losing 5-0 midway through the first half; England were losing 5-0 shortly before half-time; England were leading 7-5 at half-time; England were still leading 7-5 early in the second half when Rob Thirlby scored after he wrong-footed Peter Owens with a brilliant sidestep; England were leading 14-5 midway through the second half; England were still leading 14-5 in the closing stages when Simon Amor reached the tryline but then could not get downward pressure on the ball*)

Semi-Final

6th June	**ENGLAND**	14	FIJI	12

[This match kicked off at 5.24pm; Ugo Monye unavailable due to injury]

(England were drawing 0-0 midway through the first half; England were still drawing 0-0 just before half-time; England were leading 7-0 at half-time; England were still leading 7-0 in the 8th minute when collectively poor tackling allowed Saula Roko to score; England were leading 7-5 in the 9th minute when Rob Thirlby scored a brilliant 68 metre solo try; England were leading 14-5 midway through the second half; England were still leading 14-5 when the full-time hooter sounded, but the ball was still in play and further collectively poor tackling allowed Tuidriva Bainivalu to score, thus 2 tries and 12 points were preventable)

Final

6th June	**ENGLAND**	22	NEW ZEALAND	19

[This match kicked off at 7.10pm; Ugo Monye unavailable due to injury]

(England were drawing 0-0 in the 2nd minute when Ben Gollings wasted a great try-scoring opportunity by electing to kick when Tony Roques was unmarked outside him; England were losing 5-0 in the 3rd minute; England were still losing 5-0 midway through the first half when Rob Thirlby powered through 2 attempted tackles to score; England were drawing 5-5 shortly before half-time when Ben Gollings scored after Henry Paul put in a brilliant grubber kick; England were leading 10-5 at half-time; England were still leading 10-5 early in the second half when Henry Paul scored after Ben Gollings made a superb 32 metre break; England scored 17 unanswered points to win the match; England were leading 17-5 midway through the second half when Orene Ai'i scored after Simon Amor missed a tackle on Liam Messam, thus 7 points were preventable; England were leading 17-12 with 2 minutes remaining when Simon Amor brilliantly chipped ahead and followed up to score; England were leading 22-12 in the last minute; Ben Gollings scored 55 points in the competition)

BATTLE OF THE CENTURIONS - TRIBUTE TO RUGBY LEGENDS MATCH

CAPTAIN: *Jason Leonard*

6th June	NEIL JENKINS XV	80	**JASON LEONARD XV**	80

Millennium Stadium, Cardiff

[This match was originally scheduled to start at 3.00pm but the kick-off was delayed for 15 minutes due to crowd congestion; Kris Chesney selected but withdrew, being replaced by Steve Williams (2); Matt Perry selected but withdrew, being replaced by Kenny Logan; The Millennium Stadium had its retractable roof closed for this match; The Jason Leonard XV all wore number 1 on their shirts whereas the Neil Jenkins XV all wore number 10; Jason Leonard, Jon Sleightholme, Nick Beal and Andy Deacon retired after this match; John Leslie was the son of Andy Leslie, who won 10 caps for New Zealand between 1974-76; Nick Greenstock was capped for England Schools 18 Group in April 1992]

(Neil Boobyer scored after just 61 seconds had been played!; The Jason Leonard XV was losing 12-0 when John Leslie scored after Neil Back made a brilliant break; The Jason Leonard XV was drawing 19-19 midway through the first half; The Jason Leonard XV was leading 40-38 at half-time; The Jason Leonard XV was leading 75-73 with 9 minutes remaining; The Jason Leonard XV was drawing 80-80 in the final minute when Jason Leonard himself missed a difficult conversion attempt with the last

***kick of the match!*)**
[*There was a combined bench of 15 replacements available for both teams*]

PORTUGUESE NATIONAL DAY MATCH

CAPTAIN: *Rob Baxter*

10th Jun PORTUGAL 34 **BARBARIANS** 66

Estádio de Honra, Estádio Universitário, Lisbon

[*This match kicked off at 5.00pm; Portugal awarded caps for this match; Gonçalo Malheiro played for Portugal in this match; Mark Mapletoft was capped for England Schools 18 Group in March 1990; Matt Allen was capped for England Schools 18 Group in April 1992; Dorian West retired after this match; Mark Mapletoft retired in May 2005*]

(*The Barbarians scored in the 1st minute!; The Barbarians were leading 7-3 in the 5th minute!; The Barbarians were leading 14-3 in the 16th minute when Gonçalo Malheiro scored after an interception, thus 7 points were preventable; The Barbarians were leading 14-10 midway through the first half; The Barbarians were leading 21-10 in the 30th minute; The Barbarians were leading 28-17 shortly before half-time; The Barbarians were leading 35-24 at half-time; The Barbarians were leading 42-24 in the 42nd minute; The Barbarians were leading 42-27 in the 50th minute; The Barbarians were leading 56-27 midway through the second half; The Barbarians were leading 61-27 with 6 minutes of normal time remaining; The Barbarians scored 19 unanswered points to seal the match; The Barbarians were leading 61-34 in the second minute of injury time*)

PENGUINS TOUR TO HONG KONG 2004

CAPTAIN: *Craig de Goldi* (NZ)

10th Jun HONG KONG 0 **PENGUINS** 86

King's Park Sports Ground, Hong Kong

[*This match kicked off at 7.30pm; This match was played on a pitch made from artificial grass*]

(*The Penguins forwards monopolised possession in this match; The Penguins were drawing 0-0 when Laurent Gomez scored from a rolling maul; The Penguins scored 13 tries in this match!; Stu Wilson (2) had a brilliant game*)

IRB U21 WORLD CHAMPIONSHIP

Scotland

CAPTAIN: *Clive Stuart-Smith*

First Round - Pool 'D'

11th Jun NEW ZEALAND U21 42 **ENGLAND U21** 13

Gala RFC, Netherdale, Nether Road, Galashiels

[*This match kicked off at 7.30pm; Ugo Monye unavailable due to injury*]

(*Luke McAlister scored a penalty goal in the 4th minute!; England U21 were losing 13-0 midway through the first half; England U21 were still losing 13-0 when Andy Reay scored after Adrian Jarvis threw a brilliant pass; England U21 were losing 13-7 just before half-time; England U21 were losing 13-10 at half-time; England U21 were losing 20-13 at one point in the second half; New Zealand U21 were allowed to score 22 unanswered points in the last 15 minutes to clinch the match; Ben Russell (2) injured playing in the match*)

15th Jun SCOTLAND U21 14 **ENGLAND U21** 25

Gala RFC, Netherdale, Nether Road, Galashiels

[*This match kicked off at 7.30pm; Ugo Monye unavailable due to injury; Ugo Monye and Ben Russell (2) returned home injured after this match; Luke Myring and Chris Goodman joined the squad after this match*]

(*The England U21 forwards dominated the lineout in this match; England U21 were drawing 0-0 in the 18th minute when Ben Russell (2) went off injured, being replaced by Luke Narraway; England U21 were losing 3-0 midway through the first half; England U21 were leading 13-6 at half-time; England U21 were leading 13-9 early in the second half; England U21 were still leading 13-9 when Tom Rees scored after Marvel Garvey threw a brilliant pass; England U21 were leading 20-9 when Richard Thorpe scored from a rolling maul; England U21 were leading 25-9 midway through the second half; England U21 were still leading 25-9 with 4 minutes remaining; Tom Rees and Delon Armitage both had a brilliant game*)

19th Jun WALES U21 14 **ENGLAND U21** 23

Raeburn Place, Stockbridge, Edinburgh

[*This match kicked off at 4.00pm and was played at the home ground of Edinburgh Academicals, the third oldest rugby club in the world after Guy's Hospital and Dublin University*]

(*This match was played in extremely wet conditions; England U21 were leading 8-3 when Luke Myring missed 2 penalty goal attempts in succession; England U21 were losing 9-8 at half-time; England U21 were leading 11-9 in the 51st minute; England U21 were leading 16-14 when Marcel Garvey scored a brilliant solo try which Adrian Jarvis then converted to clinch the match; Nick Wood had a brilliant game*)

CAPTAIN: *Chris Bell*

5th/6th/7th/8th Place Semi-Final

23rd Jun ARGENTINA U21 13 **ENGLAND U21** 39

Gala RFC, Netherdale, Nether Road, Galashiels

[*This match kicked off at 7.30pm; James Percival selected but withdrew, Chris Day was moved from the bench to the team and Aston Croall was then selected for the bench; Chris Goodman played for England in the U19 World Championship in South Africa in March-April 2004*]

(*This match was played in wet and windy conditions; Mauro Comuzzi scored after just 68 seconds had been played!; England U21 were leading 20-8 at half-time; England U21 were still leading 20-8 early in the second half when Harry Barratt scored after Chris Bell made a brilliant break; England U21 were leading 25-13 midway through the second half; England U21 scored 3 tries from rolling mauls in this match!; Joe Bedford had a brilliant game*)

CAPTAIN: *Clive Stuart-Smith*

5th/6th Place Play-Off

27th Jun WALES U21 19 **ENGLAND U21** 26

Cartha Queens Park RFC, Dumbreck Road, Dumbreck, Glasgow

[*This match kicked off at 1.00pm; Cameron Dott selected for bench but withdrew, being replaced by Aston Croall; Stuart Friswell retired due to injury in January 2009*]

**(*Tom Rees scored in the 3rd minute!; England U21 were leading 8-0 shortly afterwards; A brilliant run by Marcel Garvey enabled Chris Bell to score a try which Adrian Jarvis then converted to give England U21 a 15-0 lead; England U21 were leading 15-7 at half-time; England U21 were leading 15-12 early in the second half when Geoff Parling scored from a rolling maul; England U21 were leading 23-12 at one*

point in the second half; England U21 were leading 23-19 in the closing stages when Adrian Jarvis scored a penalty goal to clinch the match)

ENGLAND TOUR TO NEW ZEALAND AND AUSTRALIA 2004

CAPTAIN: *Lawrence Dallaglio*

12th June NEW ZEALAND 36 **ENGLAND** 3

Carisbrook Stadium, Dunedin

[This match kicked off at 7.35pm; Tom Voyce selected for bench but was withdrawn on the morning of match in order to accommodate Olly Barkley]

(This match was played in cold conditions; The England forwards could not win any lineout ball; The England forwards were outplayed in the loose by their New Zealand counterparts; England were losing 3-0 in the 6th minute; England were drawing 3-3 in the 15th minute when Matt Dawson took too much time over his clearance kick and was charged down by Chris Jack, which led directly to a try by Carlos Spencer, thus 7 points were preventable; England were losing 10-3 midway through the first half; Stuart Abbott came on as a temporary blood replacement for Josh Lewsey in the 22nd minute, with Mike Catt briefly switching from centre to full back to accommodate Stuart Abbott; England were still losing 10-3 in the 25th minute when the referee unaccountably allowed play to continue after Justin Marshall threw a clear forward pass to Richie McCaw and Joe Rokocoko went on to score after a poor tackle by Charlie Hodgson, thus 7 points were unlawful; England were losing 17-3 in the 29th minute when they were awarded a 10 metre penalty in front of the posts by the referee, who then immediately reversed his decision because Ben Cohen swore in front of him when he went to complain that he had been tackled in an off the ball incident by Tana Umaga!; England were losing 24-3 in the 33rd minute; England were losing 30-3 at half-time; England were still losing 30-3 midway through the second half; Andy Gomarsall came on as a replacement for Matt Dawson in the 65th minute; England were losing 36-3 in the 67th minute; New Zealand were allowed to score 33 unanswered points to win the match; Chris Jones had a poor game)

19th June NEW ZEALAND 36 **ENGLAND** 12

Eden Park, Auckland

[This match kicked off at 7.35pm; After this match Danny Grewcock was banned for 6 weeks after being found guilty of reckless use of the boot on Dan Carter's head, while Simon Shaw was actually cleared of any wrongdoing because the video referee had been illegally used to identify him!; Stuart Abbott left the tour injured after this match; Trevor Woodman retired due to injury in August 2005]

(Simon Shaw was sent off in the 11th minute for kneeing Keith Robinson in the back)

(England were leading 3-0 in the 6th minute; New Zealand were losing 6-0 in the 11th minute when they conceded a penalty on the halfway line, but this decision was then reversed after a touch judge intervened to draw the referee's attention to a knee in the back on Keith Robinson by an England player, who the video referee subsequently identified as Simon Shaw; Lawrence Dallaglio played in the unfamiliar position of lock in the absence of Simon Shaw; England were leading 6-0 in the 13th minute when Tom Voyce crossed the tryline but the move was disallowed because Mark Regan had tackled Justin Marshall in an off the ball incident; England were leading 6-3 midway through the first half; England were still leading 6-3 in the 24th minute when Charlie Hodgson missed a kickable 30 metre drop goal attempt; Stuart Abbott went off injured in the 27th minute, being replaced by Fraser Waters; England were leading 6-3 in the 32nd minute when collectively poor tackling allowed Dan Carter to score, thus 7 points were preventable; Mike Tindall went off injured immediately afterwards, being replaced

by Olly Barkley; England were losing 10-6 at half-time; England were losing 17-6 in the 46th minute; England were losing 24-6 in the 55th minute; England were losing 24-9 midway through the second half; England were losing 24-12 in the 62nd minute; England were losing 31-12 in the 66th minute; England were still losing 31-12 with 6 minutes remaining; Matt Stevens injured playing in the match; Tom Voyce had a poor game defensively)

FIRST COOK CUP MATCH

CAPTAIN: *Lawrence Dallaglio*

26th June AUSTRALIA 51 **ENGLAND** 15

Suncorp Stadium, Lang Park, Brisbane

[This match kicked off at 6.30pm; Trevor Woodman and Matt Stevens unavailable due to injury; Lawrence Dallaglio retired from international rugby on 31st August 2004 but then changed his mind in April 2005]

(Joe Roff scored a penalty goal in the 5th minute!; England were losing 6-3 in the 18th minute when the referee unaccountably allowed play to continue after Matt Giteau threw a clear forward pass to Lote Tuqiri (1) and Clyde Rathbone went on to score, thus 7 points were unlawful; England were losing 13-3 midway through the first half; England were losing 16-3 in the 29th minute when Richard Hill (2) scored a brilliant try; England were losing 16-8 just before half-time when Clyde Rathbone scored after Ben Cohen bought a dummy by Joe Roff; England were losing 21-8 at half-time; England were losing 24-8 in the 49th minute when Lawrence Dallaglio scored after Matt Dawson took a quick tap penalty; Joe Worsley went off injured in the 56th minute, being replaced by Martin Corry; England were losing 29-15 in the 57th minute when collectively poor tackling allowed Jeremy Paul to score; England were losing 36-15 midway through the second half; England were losing 41-15 in the 69th minute when further collectively poor tackling allowed Lote Tuqiri (1) to score, thus 3 tries and 19 points were preventable; Richard Hill (2) went off injured with 3 minutes of normal time remaining, being replaced by Michael Lipman; England were losing 48-15 in the first minute of injury time; Australia were allowed to score 27 unanswered points to seal the match)

ENGLAND COUNTIES TOUR TO CANADA 2004

CAPTAIN: *Craig Hammond*

18th Jun RUGBY CANADA SUPER LEAGUE ALL-STARS 17 **ENGLAND COUNTIES** 38

Ellerslie Rugby Park, Edmonton

[This match kicked off at 7.00pm; The Rugby Canada Super League All-Stars were effectively the Canada A team; Justin Wring played for Ireland U25 before 1998; Tom Barlow (2) was capped for England Schools 18 Group in February 1995; Craig Jones played for Wales Students against England Students in March 2004]

(Justin Wring was sent off in the 70th minute for punching and thus duly banned for 1 match)

(The England Counties forwards monopolised possession in this match; England Counties were losing 6-0 in the 25th minute when Kris Fullman scored from a rolling maul; Paul Mooney powered through several attempted tackles to score; England Counties were leading 17-12 at half-time; James Moore chipped ahead and then fly-hacked the loose ball over the line to score a brilliant try)

CHURCHILL CUP

Canada

CAPTAIN: *Hugh Vyvyan*

First Round

13th Jun CANADA 23 **ENGLAND A** 48

Rugby Park, Calgary

[*This match kicked off at 6.00pm; Micky Ward toured Argentina with England Colts in August 1998*]

(*England A were leading 5-0 in the 9th minute; England A were still leading 5-0 in the 13th minute when Mark Cueto scored after Hugh Vyvyan made a brilliant break; England A were leading 12-3 midway through the first half when Stirling Richmond scored after Henry Paul missed a tackle on Quentin Fyffe; England A were leading 12-8 in the 24th minute when Jamie Noon powered through to score; England A were leading 24-8 in the 36th minute; England A were still leading 24-8 just before half-time; England A were leading 24-11 at half-time; England A played with a strong wind in the second half; Alex King went off injured in the 46th minute, being replaced by Dave Walder; England A were still leading 24-11 in the 54th minute when Hugh Vyvyan scored after Dave Walder brilliantly created space; England A were leading 31-11 in the 57th minute when Ryan Smith scored after a poor tackle by Henry Paul; England A were leading 31-16 midway through the second half when collectively poor tackling allowed Quentin Fyffe to score, thus 3 tries and 17 points were preventable; Pat Sanderson went off injured in the 63rd minute, being replaced by Will Johnson; England A were leading 31-23 in the 67th minute when Andy Hazell powered through to score; England A were leading 38-23 in the third minute of injury time; England A were leading 43-23 in the eighth minute of injury time when Dan Scarbrough scored in the last move of the match; England A scored 17 unanswered points to seal the match*)

Final

19th Jun NEW ZEALAND MAORI 26 **ENGLAND A*** 19 aet

Commonwealth Stadium, Edmonton

[*This match kicked off at 6.00pm; Alex King unavailable due to injury; Martyn Wood retired due to injury in November 2006*]

(*Dave Walder scored a penalty goal in the 5th minute!; England A were losing 5-3 in the 15th minute when some superb handling amongst the backs allowed Jamie Noon to score; England A were leading 10-5 midway through the first half; England A were leading 19-5 at half-time; Alex Brown went off injured at half-time, being replaced by Richard Birkett; Andy Hazell went off injured early in the second half, being replaced by Pat Sanderson; England A were leading 19-12 in the 49th minute when Henry Paul had his pass intercepted by Glen Jackson who went on to score, thus 7 points were preventable; England A were drawing 19-19 midway through the second half; England A were still drawing 19-19 in the 71st minute when Dave Walder had a penalty goal attempt which clearly went between the posts but the touch judges inexplicably failed to award it; England A were drawing 19-19 in the first period of extra time when Dave Walder missed a drop goal attempt; England A were drawing 19-19 at the end of the first period of extra time; England A were still drawing 19-19 in the second period of extra time when Dave Walder missed a 44 metre penalty goal attempt; England A were drawing 19-19 with 2 minutes of extra time remaining; The New Zealand Maori were allowed to score 21 unanswered points to win the match; Dan Scarbrough had a brilliant game*)

PENGUINS TOUR TO MEXICO 2004

CAPTAIN: *Dave Gorrie* (NZ)

27th Jun MEXICO XV 0 **PENGUINS** 92

Las Caballerizas, Dos Rios

[*The Mexican national team were known as the Serpents*]

(*This match was played at high altitude on a wet pitch*)

HENLEY INTERNATIONAL SEVENS

Henley RFC, Dry Leas, Marlow Road, Henley-on-Thames

CAPTAIN: *No captain appointed*

1st Aug **YOUNG ENGLAND** C *No opponents named* C

[*This tournament was cancelled on 31st May 2004 after it became clear that the planned new artificial grass pitch was not going to be ready in time*]

COMPASS GROUP INTERNATIONAL SEVENS

Stoop Memorial Ground, Langhorn Drive, Twickenham

CAPTAIN: *Joe Bedford*

First Round - Pool Four

6th Aug **YOUNG ENGLAND** L Samurai W

[*This match kicked off at 2.00pm; The Samurai went on to reach the final but no English players were involved*]

6th Aug **YOUNG ENGLAND** L Gloucester W

[*This match kicked off at 6.00pm*]

6th Aug **YOUNG ENGLAND** W Pacific Coast Grizzlies (*US*) L

[*This match kicked off at 8.40pm; Pacific Coast Grizzlies also billed as a USA Pacific Coast Select*]

[Bowl Quarter-Final:]

[7th Aug **YOUNG ENGLAND** 12 Saracens 15]

[*This match kicked off at 12.00pm*]

(*This match was played in extremely hot conditions*)

[Jug Semi-Final:]

[7th Aug **YOUNG ENGLAND** L Australian Legends (*AU*) W]

[*This match kicked off at 2.00pm; Australian Legends RC founded 1995; After this tournament Young England's role as a development side for the full England Sevens team was taken over by Samurai St George who duly won their first ever competition, namely the Harpenden Sevens, on 6th September 2004!*]

(*This match was played in extremely hot conditions*)

KBR REMEMBRANCE MATCH

CAPTAIN: *Ed Orgee*

9th Nov COMBINED SERVICES (*SER*) 38 **BARBARIANS*** 36

Army Rugby Stadium, Queen's Avenue, Aldershot

[*This match kicked off at 6.30pm; Simon Shaw selected as captain but withdrew due to injury; Rob Baxter selected but withdrew, being replaced by Matt Veater; Ian Boobyer selected but withdrew, being replaced by Ioan Cunningham; Ricky Nebbett selected for bench but withdrew, being replaced by Richard Liddington; Andy Cuthbert selected for bench but withdrew, being replaced by Dave Addleton; George Davis was capped for England Schools 18 Group in March 1998; Stephen Ward played for England Students but was also capped for Wales Schools 18 Group in February 1996*

***and his declared allegiance was to Wales; Ian Humphreys was the brother of David Humphreys; Chris Budgen, Mattie Stewart, Andy Dawling and Mal Roberts played for the Combined Services in this match, with Mal Roberts captaining the side and scoring a conversion*]**

(*This match was played in driving rain; The Barbarians were drawing 0-0 when Nick Baxter scored a 40 metre solo try; Nick Baxter injured playing in the match; The Barbarians were losing 7-5 at one point in the first half; The Barbarians were leading 24-14 at half-time; The Barbarians were leading 36-26 in the 66th minute; The Barbarians were leading 36-31 in injury time when Isoa Damu scored a try which Mal Roberts then converted to win the match for the Combined Services*)

CANADIAN TOUR TO ENGLAND 2004

CAPTAIN: *Jason Robinson* [*Mike Tindall*]

13th Nov **ENGLAND** 70 CANADA 0

Twickenham

[*This match kicked off at 2.30pm; Trevor Woodman, David Flatman, Phil Vickery, Alex Brown, Louis Deacon, Richard Hill (2), Harry Ellis, Stuart Abbott, Ollie Smith (2) and James Simpson-Daniel all unavailable due to injury; George Chuter unavailable due to suspension; Jonny Wilkinson was made England captain on 4th October 2004 but was unavailable for this match due to injury; Joe Worsley selected at blindside flanker but withdrew due to injury, Andy Hazell was moved from the bench to the team, with Lewis Moody then moving from openside to blindside flanker to accommodate Hazell while Hugh Vyvyan was now selected for the bench; Matt Stevens, Mark Regan, Chris Jones, Alex King, Jamie Noon and Iain Balshaw all in original training squad of 30 but were not selected for team or bench; Henry Paul played at inside centre despite wearing the number 13 on his shirt!*]

(*This match was played in cold conditions; England were drawing 0-0 in the 9th minute when Jason Robinson powered through 3 attempted tackles to score; England were leading 5-0 in the 14th minute when Josh Lewsey scored after Andy Gomarsall made a brilliant break; England were leading 10-0 midway through the first half when Josh Lewsey scored after Charlie Hodgson put up a superb cross-kick; England were leading 15-0 in the 31st minute when Mike Tindall scored after Henry Paul brilliantly dummied his way through; England were leading 27-0 in the 34th minute when Charlie Hodgson hit the left-hand post with an eminently kickable conversion attempt; England were still leading 27-0 in the 36th minute when some superb handling allowed Jason Robinson to score; Charlie Hodgson missed 5 conversion attempts in the first half!; England were leading 32-0 at half-time; England were still leading 32-0 in the 44th minute when Charlie Hodgson scored a brilliant 27 metre solo try; England were leading 39-0 in the 49th minute when Jason Robinson completed a hat-trick by scoring a superb solo try which Henry Paul then brilliantly converted from the left touchline; Ben Cohen came on as a replacement for Jason Robinson in the 50th minute, with Josh Lewsey then switching from wing to full back to accommodate Ben Cohen; Will Greenwood came on as a replacement for Charlie Hodgson in the 55th minute, with Henry Paul then moving from inside centre to fly half to accommodate Will Greenwood; England were leading 46-0 midway through the second half; England were still leading 46-0 in the 62nd minute when Will Greenwood scored after Henry Paul put in a superb grubber kick; Hugh Vyvyan came on as a replacement for Steve Borthwick in the 68th minute; England were leading 60-0 with 8 minutes remaining when Lewis Moody scored from a rolling maul, with Henry Paul then missing the eminently kickable conversion attempt; England were leading 65-0 with 2 minutes*

remaining when Hugh Vyvyan scored to seal the match; Will Greenwood injured playing in the match; Henry Paul and Jason Robinson both had a brilliant game; Mike Tindall had a poor game)

SOUTH AFRICAN TOUR TO WALES, IRELAND, ENGLAND AND SCOTLAND 2004

CAPTAIN: *Jason Robinson*

20th Nov **ENGLAND** 32 SOUTH AFRICA 16

Twickenham

[This match kicked off at 2.30pm; Trevor Woodman, David Flatman, Phil Vickery, Richard Hill (2), Jonny Wilkinson, Ollie Smith and James Simpson-Daniel all unavailable due to injury; George Chuter unavailable due to suspension; Henry Paul played at inside centre despite wearing the number 13 on his shirt!]

(This match was played in cold and wet conditions; Danny Grewcock and Steve Borthwick dominated the lineout in this match; Charlie Hodgson scored a penalty goal in the 2nd minute!; Andy Hazell came on as a temporary blood replacement for Lewis Moody in the 7th minute; England were drawing 3-3 in the 16th minute when Charlie Hodgson scored a brilliant solo try; England were leading 10-3 midway through the first half; Henry Paul put up a brilliant cross-kick that allowed Mark Cueto to score a try which Charlie Hodgson then converted to give England a 17-3 lead in the 26th minute; England were leading 17-6 in the 32nd minute when Charlie Hodgson scored a superb 43 metre penalty goal; England were leading 20-6 at half-time; England were leading 20-9 in the 46th minute; England were leading 23-9 in the 54th minute when Charlie Hodgson scored a brilliant 30 metre drop goal; England were leading 29-9 midway through the second half; Harry Ellis came on as a replacement for Andy Gomarsall in the 67th minute; England were still leading 29-9 in the 71st minute; England were leading 32-9 in the 73rd minute when Bryan Habana scored after Charlie Hodgson missed a tackle on Jaco van der Westhuyzen, thus 7 points were preventable; The referee unaccountably blew for full-time after only 39 minutes of the second half had been played!; Charlie Hodgson scored 27 points in this match; Joe Worsley had a brilliant game)

ENGLAND U21 DEVELOPMENT MATCHES

CAPTAIN: *??*

24th Nov FRANCE U21 WEST XV 17 **ENGLAND U21 SOUTH XV** 7

Stade de l'Etang Neuf, Centre National de Rugby, Domaine de Bellejame, Marcoussis

[This match kicked off at 1.30pm; Laurence Ovens and Richard Blaze played for England in the U19 World Championship in South Africa in March-April 2004; Steffon Armitage was the brother of Delon Armitage; Shane Geraghty played for England in the U19 World Championship in South Africa in April 2005; Topsy Ojo played for England in the U19 World Championships in France in April 2003 and South Africa in March-April 2004]

(The England U21 South XV was leading 7-0 at one point in the first half; The England U21 South XV was drawing 7-7 at half-time; The France U21 West XV was allowed to score 17 unanswered points to win the match)

CAPTAIN: *??*

24th Nov FRANCE U21 EAST XV 22 **ENGLAND U21 NORTH XV** 25

Stade de l'Etang Neuf, Centre National de Rugby, Domaine de Bellejame, Marcoussis

[This match kicked off at 3.30pm; Stuart Mackie, Sean Cox, Paul Diggin and Kieron

***Lewitt played for England in the U19 World Championship in South Africa in March-April 2004; Tom Ryder captained England in the U19 World Championship in South Africa in March-April 2004; Lee Dickson played for Scotland in the U19 World Championship in South Africa in March-April 2004 but subsequently switched his allegiance to England; Toby Flood was the grandson of the actor Gerald Flood; Thom Evans played for England in the U19 World Championship in France in April 2003*]**
(*The England U21 North XV was leading 10-0 at one point in the first half; The England U21 North XV was drawing 10-10 at half-time; The France U21 East XV was allowed to score 17 unanswered points; The England U21 North XV was drawing 22-22 when Toby Flood scored a penalty goal to win the match*)

AUSTRALIAN TOUR TO SCOTLAND, FRANCE AND ENGLAND 2004

CAPTAIN: *Jason Robinson*

27th Nov **ENGLAND*** 19 AUSTRALIA 21
Twickenham

[*This match kicked off at 2.30pm; Trevor Woodman, David Flatman, Phil Vickery, Richard Hill (2), Jonny Wilkinson, Ollie Smith and James Simpson-Daniel all unavailable due to injury; George Chuter unavailable due to suspension; Henry Paul played at inside centre despite wearing the number 13 on his shirt!*]
(*England were drawing 0-0 in the 16th minute when collectively poor tackling allowed Jeremy Paul to score; England were losing 7-0 midway through the first half; Henry Paul had a poor first quarter and was unaccountably substituted in the 25th minute before he had a chance to redeem himself, being replaced by Will Greenwood; England were still losing 7-0 in the 28th minute when further collectively poor tackling allowed Chris Latham to score; England were losing 12-0 in the 33rd minute when Charlie Hodgson missed two eminently kickable penalty goal attempts in 4 minutes; England were losing 12-0 at half-time; Charlie Hodgson injured his thigh in the 45th minute but inexplicably elected to remain on the pitch after Andy Gomarsall and then Mike Tindall took over the goal-kicking; England were losing 15-0 in the 49th minute when Lewis Moody scored from a rolling maul, with Andy Gomarsall then missing the eminently kickable conversion attempt; England were losing 15-5 midway through the second half when Josh Lewsey peeled away from another rolling maul to score; England were losing 15-12 in the 64th minute when some superb handling amongst the backs allowed Mark Cueto to score; England scored 19 unanswered points; England were leading 19-15 in the 68th minute; Charlie Hodgson eventually went off injured in the 70th minute, being replaced by Harry Ellis with Andy Gomarsall then switching to the unfamiliar position of fly half to accommodate Harry Ellis; England were leading 19-18 with 8 minutes remaining when Andy Gomarsall unaccountably hit Matt Giteau with a late shoulder-charge and Australia were awarded a 44 metre penalty, which Giteau duly kicked to win the match, thus 2 tries and 15 points were preventable; Jason Robinson had a brilliant game*)

EMIRATES AIRLINE DUBAI RUGBY SEVENS

Dubai Exiles Stadium, Dubai

CAPTAIN: *Simon Amor*

First Round - Pool 'B'

2nd Dec SCOTLAND 19 **ENGLAND** 24
[*This match kicked off at 11.08am*]

(England were leading 5-0 in the early stages; England were losing 12-10 at half-time; England were losing 19-10 when Ugo Monye scored a brilliant long-range try; England were losing 19-17 when Ugo Monye wasted a great try-scoring opportunity by dropping the ball while the Scottish line was at his mercy; England were still losing 19-17 when the full-time hooter sounded, but the ball was still in play and Peter Richards was able to score a try which Simon Amor then converted with the last kick of the match to clinch the game)

2nd Dec UGANDA 7 **ENGLAND** 34

[This match kicked off at 3.24pm]

(England were drawing 0-0 in the early stages when Ugo Monye scored a brilliant long-range solo try; England were leading 19-7 at half-time; England were still leading 19-7 when Simon Amor started a brilliant attack and then took a return pass to finish the move with a try; England scored 21 unanswered points to clinch the match)

2nd Dec FRANCE 14 **ENGLAND** 26

[This match kicked off at 7.04pm]

(England were losing 7-0 in the early stages; England were drawing 7-7 when Simon Amor scored after Matt Tait made a brilliant run; England were leading 14-7 at half-time; England were still leading 14-7 when Rob Thirlby scored the 70th try of his IRB World Sevens career; England were leading 21-14 when Rob Thirlby scored a brilliant solo try)

Quarter-Final

3rd Dec AUSTRALIA 5 **ENGLAND** 24

[This match kicked off at 12.14pm]

(Peter Richards scored in the 1st minute!; England were leading 10-0 when Matt Tait crossed the tryline but instead of grounding the ball immediately he tried to make the conversion easier by passing infield to Geoff Appleford, who promptly knocked-on!; England were still leading 10-0 when Simon Amor crossed the tryline but the move was disallowed because the referee adjudged that there had been an earlier forward pass; England were leading 10-0 at half-time; England were leading 10-5 when Ugo Monye scored after he wrong-footed the defence with a brilliant series of sidesteps; England were leading 17-5 in the closing stages when Simon Amor scored to seal the match)

Semi-Final

3rd Dec SOUTH AFRICA 5 **ENGLAND** 14

[This match kicked off at 7.02pm]

(Tony Roques scored in the 1st minute after Matt Tait threw a brilliant pass!; England were leading 7-5 at half-time; Ugo Monye went off injured in the second half, being replaced by Rob Thirlby; England were still leading 7-5 when Peter Richards scored after he wrong-footed the defence with a brilliant sidestep)

Final

3rd Dec FIJI 21 **ENGLAND** 26

[This match kicked off at 8.54pm]

(England were losing 7-0 in the early stages; England were still losing 7-0 when Pat Sanderson scored after Paul Sampson made a brilliant run; England were drawing 7-7 when Peter Richards crossed the tryline but the move was disallowed as he was adjudged to have put a foot into touch; Simon Amor went off injured in the first half, being replaced by Neil Starling; England were leading 14-7 just before half-time; England were leading 19-7 at half-time; England were leading 26-7 midway through the second half; Fiji were allowed to score 14 unanswered points; England were leading

26-21 in the closing stages when Rob Thirlby missed a penalty goal attempt; Pat Sanderson had a brilliant game)

NEW ZEALAND TOUR TO ITALY, WALES AND FRANCE 2004

CAPTAIN: *Justin Marshall* (NZ)

4th Dec **BARBARIANS** 19 NEW ZEALAND XV 47

Twickenham

[This match kicked off at 3.00pm]

(Marty Holah scored in the 5th minute!; The Barbarians were losing 7-0 in the 15th minute when Xavier Rush scored from a brilliant rolling maul; The Barbarians were drawing 7-7 in the 18th minute when Rico Gear scored after a poor tackle by Mat Rogers; The Barbarians were losing 12-7 midway through the first half; The Barbarians were still losing 12-7 shortly before half-time when Ma'a Nonu scored after a poor tackle by Bill Young; The Barbarians were losing 19-7 at half-time; The Barbarians were losing 26-7 in the 43rd minute; The New Zealand XV was allowed to score 19 unanswered points to win the match; The Barbarians were still losing 26-7 in the 47th minute when Andrea Lo Cicero peeled away from another rolling maul to score; The Barbarians were losing 26-12 in the 50th minute when the referee unaccountably allowed play to continue after Jimmy Cowan brought down Mat Rogers with an illegal high tackle and Casey Laulala went on to score, thus 7 points were unlawful; The Barbarians were losing 33-12 midway through the second half; The Barbarians were losing 40-12 in the 63rd minute; The Barbarians were still losing 40-12 in the 70th minute when Albert van den Berg intercepted the ball and ran 64 metres to score; The Barbarians were losing 40-19 in the last minute when collectively poor tackling allowed Piri Weepu to score, thus 3 tries and 19 points were preventable; Mat Rogers had a poor game)

EMIRATES AIRLINE SOUTH AFRICA SEVENS

Outeniqua Park Stadium, George

CAPTAIN: *Tony Roques*

First Round - Pool 'B'

10th Dec KENYA 0 **ENGLAND** 26

[This match kicked off at 10.44am]

(Neil Starling scored in the 3rd minute!; England were leading 7-0 midway through the first half; England were leading 14-0 in the 5th minute; England were leading 14-0 at half-time; Paul Sampson came on as a replacement for Richard Haughton at the start of the second half; England were still leading 14-0 in the 9th minute when Neil Starling scored to complete a hat-trick of tries; England were leading 19-0 midway through the second half; England were still leading 19-0 with 1 minute remaining)

CAPTAIN: *Ben Gollings*

10th Dec IRELAND 19 **ENGLAND** 31

[This match kicked off at 1.50pm]

(Peter Richards scored in the 2nd minute!; England were leading 14-0 midway through the first half; England scored 14 unanswered points to win the match; England were leading 14-5 shortly before half-time; England were leading 19-5 at half-time; England were leading 26-5 in the 9th minute; England were still leading 26-5 midway through the second half when Ian Humphreys scored as a direct consequence of a defensive mistake; England were leading 26-12 with 2 minutes of normal time remaining when James Norton scored as a direct consequence of another defensive mistake, thus 2

tries and 14 points were preventable; England were leading 26-19 when the full-time hooter sounded, but the ball was still in play and Peter Richards was able to score another try to clinch the match)

CAPTAIN: *Tony Roques*

10th Dec AUSTRALIA 12 **ENGLAND** 24

[This match kicked off at 6.02pm]

(Richard Haughton scored in the 2nd minute!; England were drawing 7-7 midway through the first half; England were drawing 7-7 at half-time; England were leading 19-7 in the 9th minute; England were still leading 19-7 midway through the second half; England were leading 19-12 with 1 minute remaining; Kai Horstmann had a brilliant game)

Quarter-Final

11th Dec TUNISIA 0 **ENGLAND** 52

[This match kicked off at 12.19pm]

(Paul Sampson scored in the 2nd minute!; England were leading 26-0 at half-time; Ben Gollings scored his 1000th IRB World Sevens point in this match; Ollie Phillips had a brilliant game)

Semi-Final

11th Dec FIJI 19 **ENGLAND** 12

[This match kicked off at 3.38pm; Paul Sampson played for Samurai St George in the Dubai International Invitation Rugby Sevens on 30th November-2nd December 2005]

(Kai Horstmann was sin-binned in the 6th minute and then sent off in the 11th minute after receiving his second yellow card)

(This match was played in extremely hot conditions; England were drawing 0-0 midway through the first half; England were still drawing 0-0 shortly before half-time; England were losing 5-0 at half-time; England were losing 12-0 in the 10th minute when Matt Tait scored a brilliant 59 metre solo try; England were losing 12-5 midway through the second half; England were still losing 12-5 with 2 minutes of normal time remaining; England were losing 19-5 when the full-time hooter sounded, but the ball was still in play and Neil Starling was able to score a consolation try)

2005

AXA NEW ZEALAND INTERNATIONAL SEVENS

WestpacTrust Stadium, Wellington

CAPTAIN: *Ben Gollings*

First Round - Pool 'A'

4th Feb CANADA 5 **ENGLAND** 31

[This match kicked off at 2.28pm; Simon Amor was selected for the bench because he was not match fit]

(England were losing 5-0 in the early stages; England were leading 14-5 at half-time; James Bailey scored a brilliant long-range solo try; England scored 31 unanswered points to win the match)

CAPTAIN: *Simon Amor*

4th Feb NIUE 7 **ENGLAND** 41

[This match kicked off at 5.24pm]

(Simon Amor played with an injury; England were leading 5-0 in the early stages; England were losing 7-5 in the 5th minute when Ben Gollings scored a try which enabled him to beat Waisale Serevi's existing IRB World Sevens points scoring record of 1033; England were leading 17-7 at half-time; England scored 36 unanswered points to win the match)

4th Feb SAMOA 10 **ENGLAND** 21

[This match kicked off at 9.34pm]

(Simon Amor played with an injury; England were drawing 0-0 when Ben Gollings scored the 100th try of his IRB World Sevens career; England were leading 14-0 at half-time)

Quarter-Final

5th Feb FIJI 24 **ENGLAND** 19

[This match kicked off at 2.33pm]

(Simon Amor played with an injury; England were losing 12-0 when Rob Thirlby scored a brilliant solo try; England were losing 12-7 at half-time; England were losing 24-12 when the full-time hooter sounded, but the ball was still in play and James Bailey was able to score a consolation try)

CAPTAIN: *Ben Gollings*

[Plate Semi-Final:]

[5th Feb SCOTLAND 19 **ENGLAND*** 17]

[This match kicked off at 5.38pm; Simon Amor was relegated to the bench because he was not match fit]

(England were losing 12-0 in the early stages; England were drawing 12-12 at half-time; England were leading 17-12 in the final minute when 2 defensive errors in succession led directly to a try by Clark Laidlaw, which he then converted with the last kick of the match to win the game for Scotland; Ben Gollings finished the tournament with a new IRB World Sevens record of 1060 points)

6 NATIONS CHAMPIONSHIP

CAPTAIN: *Jason Robinson*

5th Feb WALES 11 **ENGLAND*** 9

Millennium Stadium, Cardiff

[This match kicked off at 5.30pm; Trevor Woodman, David Flatman, Richard Hill (2), Martin Corry, Jonny Wilkinson, Will Greenwood, Mike Tindall, Stuart Abbott and James

***Simpson-Daniel all unavailable due to injury; Lewis Moody selected but withdrew due to injury, being replaced by Chris Jones; Andy Sheridan, George Chuter, Simon Shaw, Hugh Vyvyan, Andy Gomarsall, Henry Paul, Ollie Smith (2) and Iain Balshaw all in original training squad of 30 but were not selected for team or bench; The Millennium Stadium had its retractable roof closed for this match*]**

(*This match took place on a very poor playing surface; England were drawing 0-0 in the 10th minute when a lineout overthrow by Steve Thompson (2) led directly to a try by Shane Williams, thus 5 points were preventable; England were losing 5-3 midway through the first half when Charlie Hodgson hit the left-hand post with an eminently kickable 22 metre drop goal attempt; England were losing 8-3 in the 24th minute; England were still losing 8-3 shortly before half-time when Charlie Hodgson missed a kickable 38 metre penalty goal attempt; England were losing 8-3 at half-time; James Forrester came on as a temporary blood replacement for Joe Worsley in the 41st minute; England were still losing 8-3 in the 46th minute and pressing in attack when Matt Tait was famously tackled by Gavin Henson!; England were losing 8-6 in the 49th minute; England were still losing 8-6 midway through the second half; Olly Barkley came on as a replacement for Matt Tait in the 60th minute; England were leading 9-8 in the 70th minute; Julian White went off injured with 7 minutes remaining, being replaced by Graham Rowntree; England were still leading 9-8 with 3 minutes remaining when Gavin Henson kicked a difficult 44 metre penalty goal to win the match for Wales*)

13th Feb **ENGLAND*** 17 FRANCE 18

Twickenham

[*This match kicked off at 3.00pm; Trevor Woodman, David Flatman, Julian White, Richard Hill (2), Jonny Wilkinson, Will Greenwood, Mike Tindall and Stuart Abbott all unavailable due to injury; Matt Stevens, Simon Shaw and Matt Tait in original training squad of 25 but were not selected for team or bench*]

(*This match was played on a wet pitch; England played with a swirling wind in the first half; Charlie Hodgson missed a kickable 43 metre penalty goal attempt in the 3rd minute!; Dimitri Yachvili scored a penalty goal in the 5th minute!; England were losing 3-0 midway through the first half when Olly Barkley scored after Jamie Noon made a brilliant break; England were leading 10-6 in the 31st minute when Charlie Hodgson missed an eminently kickable 22 metre penalty goal attempt; England were still leading 10-6 in the 36th minute when Josh Lewsey scored a brilliant try; England were leading 17-6 in the 39th minute when Olly Barkley missed a speculative penalty goal attempt from the halfway line; England were still leading 17-6 just before half-time when Olly Barkley missed another speculative 49 metre penalty goal attempt; England were leading 17-6 at half-time; England were still leading 17-6 in the 48th minute when Charlie Hodgson missed another kickable 43 metre penalty goal attempt; England were leading 17-6 in the 52nd minute when Lewis Moody unaccountably committed a series of infringements which allowed Dimitri Yachvili to score three penalty goals in 11 minutes; England were leading 17-12 midway through the second half; England were leading 17-15 in the 66th minute when Olly Barkley missed a third kickable 45 metre penalty goal attempt; England were losing 18-17 in the 70th minute; England were still losing 18-17 with 2 minutes remaining when Charlie Hodgson badly missed a 23 metre drop goal attempt from in front of the posts*)

27th Feb IRELAND 19 **ENGLAND*** 13

Lansdowne Road

[*This match kicked off at 3.00pm; Trevor Woodman, David Flatman, Julian White, Richard Hill (2), Jonny Wilkinson, Will Greenwood, Mike Tindall and Stuart Abbott all*

***unavailable due to injury; Phil Vickery and Andy Sheridan in original training squad of 30 but withdrew due to injury; George Chuter, Simon Shaw, Chris Jones, Andy Gomarsall, Henry Paul, Matt Tait and Ben Cohen all in original training squad of 30 but were not selected for team or bench; Duncan Bell was capped for England Schools 18 Group in April 1993*]**
(*England played with the wind in the first half; Ronan O'Gara scored a drop goal in the 4th minute!; England were losing 3-0 in the 7th minute when Martin Corry broke from the base of a ruck and ran 35 metres to score; England were losing 9-7 midway through the first half; England were still losing 9-7 in the 25th minute when Charlie Hodgson scored a brilliant penalty goal from the halfway line; England were losing 12-10 shortly before half-time when Charlie Hodgson put up a brilliant cross-kick which enabled Mark Cueto to catch the ball unopposed and ground it, but the move was unaccountably disallowed because Cueto was wrongly adjudged to have been in front of the kicker; England were losing 12-10 at half-time; England were still losing 12-10 in the 56th minute when Charlie Hodgson scored a superb 22 metre drop goal into the wind; England were leading 13-12 in the 58th minute when the referee inexplicably allowed play to continue after Shane Horgan entered a maul from an offside position and Brian O'Driscoll went on to score, thus 7 points were unlawful; England were losing 19-13 midway through the second half; England were still losing 19-13 with 6 minutes remaining when they were awarded a 10 metre penalty in an eminently kickable position, but Jason Robinson ordered a kick to the corner in an attempt to score a try from the ensuing lineout; Immediately afterwards England set up a rolling maul that reached the Irish tryline where Josh Lewsey claimed to have grounded the ball, but the unsighted referee unaccountably elected not to consult the video referee and awarded a scrum to Ireland; England were losing 19-13 with 3 minutes remaining when Jamie Noon wasted a great try-scoring opportunity by electing to take the ball into contact instead of using an overlap outside him; Jason Robinson injured playing in the match*)

CAPTAIN: *Martin Corry*

12th Mar **ENGLAND** 39 ITALY 7
Twickenham

[*This match kicked off at 4.00pm; Trevor Woodman, David Flatman, Julian White, Phil Vickery, Richard Hill (2), Jonny Wilkinson, Will Greenwood, Mike Tindall, Stuart Abbott and Jason Robinson all unavailable due to injury; Ben Cohen in original squad of 30 but withdrew due to injury; Andy Sheridan, George Chuter, Simon Shaw, Chris Jones, Andy Gomarsall, Leon Lloyd and James Simpson-Daniel all in original training squad of 30 but were not selected for team or bench*]
**(*England were leading 3-0 in the 7th minute; England were still leading 3-0 in the 9th minute when Mark Cueto scored after Iain Balshaw made a brilliant break; England were leading 10-0 in the 14th minute when Josh Lewsey wasted a great try-scoring opportunity by failing to pass to the unmarked Martin Corry outside him; England were still leading 10-0 midway through the first half; England were leading 10-0 in the 35th minute when Charlie Hodgson missed a kickable 42 metre penalty goal attempt; England were still leading 10-0 in the 37th minute when Steve Thompson (2) powered through to score; England were leading 17-0 just before half-time when some superb handling allowed Mark Cueto to score another try; England scored 22 unanswered points to win the match; England were leading 22-0 at half-time; England were still leading 22-0 in the 45th minute when Alessandro Troncon scored after a poor tackle by Graham Rowntree, thus 7 points were preventable; Matt Dawson came on as a replacement for Harry Ellis in the 51st minute; The referee had to order uncontested*

scrums in the 58th minute after Giorgio Intoppa went off injured; England were leading 27-7 midway through the second half; England were still leading 27-7 in the 64th minute when some superb handling amongst the backs allowed Mark Cueto to score to complete a hat-trick of tries; Ollie Smith (2) came on as a replacement for Jamie Noon in the 65th minute; Duncan Bell and Andy Goode came on as replacements for Graham Rowntree and Charlie Hodgson respectively with 6 minutes of normal time remaining; England were leading 32-7 in the last minute of normal time when Iain Balshaw kicked ahead into space and followed up unchallenged, but then dropped the ball on the Italian tryline as he attempted to regather it!; Martin Corry had a brilliant game)

19th Mar	**ENGLAND**	43	SCOTLAND	22

Twickenham

[*This match kicked off at 6.00pm; Trevor Woodman, David Flatman, Julian White, Phil Vickery, Richard Hill (2), Jonny Wilkinson, Will Greenwood, Mike Tindall, Stuart Abbott, Ben Cohen and Jason Robinson all unavailable due to injury; Graham Rowntree selected but withdrew on the morning of the match due to injury, Duncan Bell was moved from the bench to the team, with Matt Stevens then moving from tight-head to loose-head prop to accommodate Duncan Bell while Mike Worsley was now selected for the bench*]

(*England were drawing 0-0 in the 12th minute when Charlie Hodgson missed a 40 metre penalty goal attempt from in front of the posts!; England were still drawing 0-0 in the 13th minute when Jamie Noon scored after Charlie Hodgson made a brilliant break; Ben Kay went off injured in the 14th minute, being replaced by Steve Borthwick; England were leading 7-0 midway through the first half; England were leading 7-3 in the 22nd minute when Jamie Noon powered through 4 attempted tackles to score another try; England were leading 19-3 in the 26th minute; Iain Balshaw went off injured in the 32nd minute, being replaced by Ollie Smith (2) with Josh Lewsey then switching from wing to full back to accommodate Ollie Smith (2); England were still leading 19-3 in the 34th minute when Josh Lewsey scored after Charlie Hodgson threw a superb long pass; England were leading 26-3 just before half-time; England were leading 26-10 at half-time; Lewis Moody went off injured at half-time, being replaced by Andy Hazell; England were leading 26-17 in the 47th minute when Harry Ellis scored a brilliant try; England were leading 33-17 in the 51st minute when Harry Ellis had his pass intercepted by Simon Taylor (2) who then ran 40 metres to score, thus 5 points were preventable; England were leading 33-22 midway through the second half; Matt Dawson came on as a replacement for Harry Ellis in the 63rd minute; England were still leading 33-22 in the 67th minute when Jamie Noon scored to complete a hat-trick of tries; England were leading 38-22 in the 70th minute when Mark Cueto scored after Olly Barkley made a superb break; Jamie Noon had a brilliant game; England equalled their highest ever points total against Scotland!*)

U21 6 NATIONS CHAMPIONSHIP

CAPTAIN: *Tom Rees*

4th Feb	WALES U21	32	**ENGLAND U21**	21

Rodney Parade, Newport

[*This match kicked at 7.05pm; Tom Ryder and Richard Thorpe unavailable due to injury; David Seymour, Lee Dickson, Matt Jess and Tom Biggs all in original training squad of 26 but were not selected for team or bench; Ross Broadfoot played for England in the U19 World Championships in France in April 2003 and South Africa in March-April 2004*]

(England U21 were leading 3-0 in the 11th minute; England U21 were losing 13-3 midway through the first half; Wales U21 were still leading 13-3 in the 32nd minute when Rhys Shellard was able to follow up and score after the England U21 pack let the ball squirt out of a scrum in front of their own line, thus 7 points were preventable; Wales U21 were allowed to score 27 unanswered points to win the match; England U21 were losing 27-3 just before half-time; England U21 were losing 27-6 at half-time; England U21 were losing 32-6 in the 44th minute; England U21 were losing 32-11 in the 51st minute; England U21 were still losing 32-11 midway through the second half; England U21 were losing 32-11 with 7 minutes of normal time remaining when James Haskell scored from a rolling maul)

11th Feb **ENGLAND U21*** 17 FRANCE U21 20

Franklin's Gardens, Northampton

[This match kicked off at 7.30pm; Martin Halsall, Neil Briggs and Olly Morgan unavailable due to injury]

(England U21 were drawing 0-0 in the 6th minute when Matt Cornwell scored after Benjamin Dambielle's kick was charged down by David Seymour; England U21 were leading 7-0 shortly afterwards when Richard Blaze scored after Ryan Davis put in a brilliant chip ahead; England U21 were leading 17-0 midway through the first half; England U21 were leading 17-5 in the 31st minute; England U21 were leading 17-10 at half-time; England U21 were leading 17-13 midway through the second half; England U21 were still leading 17-13 in the sixth minute of injury time when Sylvain Mirande scored a try which Regis Lespinas then converted with the last kick of the match to clinch the game for France U21; David Seymour had a brilliant game)

CAPTAIN: *Ryan Davis*

25th Feb IRELAND U21 6 **ENGLAND U21** 28

Donnybrook, Dublin

[This match kicked off at 4.00pm; Chris Goodman, Ross Broadfoot and Paul Diggin unavailable due to injury]

(This match was played on a muddy pitch; Toby Flood missed a penalty goal attempt in the 1st minute!; Michael Cusack scored in the 4th minute!; England U21 were leading 15-3 in the 16th minute; England U21 were still leading 15-3 midway through the first half; England U21 were leading 15-6 in the 31st minute when Toby Flood missed an eminently kickable penalty goal attempt; England U21 were leading 15-6 at half-time; England U21 were leading 20-6 midway through the second half; England U21 were leading 23-6 in the 67th minute; England U21 were still leading 23-6 in injury time when Olly Morgan scored to seal the match; Toby Flood missed 8 out of 9 kicks at goal!)

11th Mar **ENGLAND U21** 31 ITALY U21 14

Franklin's Gardens, Northampton

[This match kicked off at 7.30pm; Aston Croall unavailable due to injury; Mark Lambert and Will Matthews in original training squad of 24 but were not selected for team or bench; Matt Hampson suffered a severe neck injury during an England U21 training session at Franklin's Gardens on 15th March 2005]

(England U21 were leading 3-0 in the 10th minute; England U21 were leading 8-0 midway through the first half; England U21 were leading 8-7 in the 25th minute when Toby Flood took too much time over his clearance kick and was charged down by Valerio Bernabo, who went on to score from the ensuing rebound, thus 7 points were preventable; England U21 were losing 14-11 in the 27th minute; England U21 were still losing 14-11 shortly before half-time; England U21 were drawing 14-14 at half-time;

England U21 were still drawing 14-14 in the 56th minute when Tom Varndell scored a brilliant try; England U21 were leading 24-14 midway through the second half; England U21 were still leading 24-14 with 4 minutes remaining when David Seymour scored from a rolling maul)

CAPTAIN: *Tom Rees*

18th Mar **ENGLAND U21*** 17 SCOTLAND U21 19

Franklin's Gardens, Northampton

[This match kicked off at 7.30pm; Matt Hampson unavailable due to injury]

(Scotland U21 were drawing 0-0 in the 10th minute when Ben Addison scored after the England U21 defence failed to deal with Alasdhair McFarlane's kick ahead, thus 7 points were preventable; England U21 were losing 10-8 in the 34th minute; England U21 were still losing 10-8 in the seventh minute of first half injury time; England U21 were leading 11-10 at half-time; England U21 were losing 16-14 midway through the second half; England U21 were leading 17-16 with 2 minutes of normal time remaining when Scotland U21 were awarded a penalty which David Blair duly kicked to win the match; England U21 were losing 19-17 in the fifth minute of injury time when Toby Flood missed a drop goal attempt)

ENGLAND STUDENTS MATCHES

CAPTAIN: *Tom Hayman*

11th Feb **ENGLAND STUDENTS** 10 FRANCE STUDENTS 6

Rectory Field, Charlton Road, Blackheath

[This match kicked off at 7.30pm]

(This match was played on a wet pitch; England Students were losing 3-0 in the 7th minute; Jonan Boto went off injured in the 10th minute, being replaced by Chris Wyles; England Students were drawing 3-3 in the 13th minute; England Students were still drawing 3-3 midway through the first half; England Students were losing 6-3 in the 30th minute; James Whittingham missed 2 speculative long-range penalty goal attempts in the first half; England Students were losing 6-3 at half-time; England Students were still losing 6-3 in the 51st minute when the referee awarded a penalty try against France Students for persistent infringement; England Students were leading 10-6 midway through the second half; Mark Irish went off injured in the 61st minute, being replaced by Wayne Thompson)

25th Feb FRANCE STUDENTS 23 **ENGLAND STUDENTS** 6

Stade Henri Desgranges, La Roche-sur-Yon

[This match kicked off at 7.30pm; Jonan Boto unavailable due to injury; George Davis and Robin Scothern unavailable due to personal commitments; Brad Davies unavailable as his club Gloucester required him to fulfil his Zurich Premiership commitments; Mark Irish selected but withdrew due to injury, being replaced by Dave Bassett; Simon Carter in original training squad of 23 but withdrew due to injury; Ben Wheeler was capped for Singapore in November 2008]

(Julien Salellas scored in the 4th minute!; England Students were losing 5-3 in the 6th minute; England Students were still losing 5-3 midway through the first half; England Students were leading 6-5 in the 27th minute; England Students were losing 8-6 shortly before half-time; England Students were losing 11-6 at half-time; England Students were still losing 11-6 midway through the second half; England Students were losing 16-6 in the 64th minute; England Students were still losing 16-6 with 6 minutes remaining; France Students were allowed to score 18 unanswered points to win the match)

CAPTAIN: *Andy Dalgleish*

11th Mar	**ENGLAND STUDENTS***	27	ITALY U25	27

Iffley Road, Oxford

[*This match kicked off at 6.00pm; Rory Teague played for England in the U19 World Championship in South Africa in March-April 2004; Rob Jewell was capped for England Colts in March 1998; Rory Teague was the cousin of Mike Teague*]

(*James Whittingham scored a penalty goal in the 3rd minute!; England Students were drawing 3-3 in the 5th minute!; England Students were still drawing 3-3 midway through the first half; England Students were drawing 3-3 in the 26th minute when a poor defensive alignment allowed Michele Rizzo to score; England Students were losing 10-3 in the 36th minute when Joseph Ajuwa scored after James Whittingham brilliantly kicked ahead into space; England Students were drawing 10-10 shortly before half-time; England Students were losing 17-10 at half-time; England Students were still losing 17-10 in the 55th minute when Mark Foster scored a superb 50 metre solo try; England Students were losing 17-15 midway through the second half when another poor defensive alignment allowed Martin Lopez-Facundo to score from a rolling maul, thus 2 tries and 12 points were preventable; England Students were losing 22-20 in the 70th minute; England Students were losing 27-20 in the second minute of injury time; England Students were still losing 27-20 in the eighth minute of injury time when Mark Foster scored a brilliant 80 metre solo try which James Whittingham then converted to draw the match*)

'A' INTERNATIONAL MATCH

CAPTAIN: *Hugh Vyvyan*

11th Feb	**ENGLAND A**	30	FRANCE A	20

Recreation Ground, Bath

[*This match kicked off at 7.45pm; Michael Lipman in original training squad of 28 but withdrew due to injury; Matt Stevens in original training squad of 28 but withdrew as he was now required to join the full England international squad; Andy Sheridan, Adam Balding, Alex King, Henry Paul, Andy Higgins (2), Ugo Monye, Steve Hanley, James Simpson-Daniel and Michael Horak all in original training squad of 28 but were not selected for team or bench*]

(*This match was played in driving rain on a muddy pitch; England A were leading 3-0 in the 11th minute; England A were still leading 3-0 midway through the first half; England A were leading 6-0 in the 23rd minute; England A were still leading 6-0 in the 30th minute when Duncan Bell scored from a rolling maul; Andy Goode put in a brilliant chip-kick that enabled Ollie Smith (2) to score a try which Andy Goode then converted to give England A an 18-0 lead in the 38th minute; England A were leading 18-3 at half-time; Louis Deacon scored after just 33 seconds of the second half had been played to give England A a 23-3 lead!; England A were still leading 23-3 in the 44th minute when Anthony Forest scored a try which should not have been given because the scoring pass from Nicolas Durand was clearly forward, thus 7 points were unlawful; England A were leading 23-10 in the 47th minute when Andy Goode missed a difficult 39 metre penalty goal attempt into the wind; England A were leading 23-15 in the 52nd minute; England A were still leading 23-15 midway through the second half; Nick Walshe came on as a replacement for Andy Gomarsall in the 67th minute; England A were leading 23-15 with 6 minutes remaining when Iain Balshaw scored after Ollie Smith (2) made a superb run; England A were leading 30-15 in the last minute; Duncan Bell and Magnus Lund both had a brilliant game*)

JEAN-CLAUDE BAQUÉ SHIELD MATCH

CAPTAIN: *Craig Hammond*

12th Feb **ENGLAND COUNTIES** 38 FRANCE AMATEURS 0

Newbury RFC, Monks Lane, Newbury

[*This match kicked off at 6.00pm; Martin O'Keefe and Jimmy Rule in original training squad of 22 but were not selected for team or bench; Dan Cook was capped for England Schools 18 Group in April 1993; Russ Earnshaw played in the Samurai team that won the Amsterdam Heineken Sevens on 21st-22nd May 2005; Joe Clark was capped for England Colts in April 1996*]

(*This match was played in extremely cold conditions; England Counties played with the wind in the first half; England Counties were leading 7-0 in the 7th minute; England Counties were leading 12-0 midway through the first half when Craig Hammond scored after an interception; England Counties were leading 19-0 shortly before half-time; England Counties were leading 26-0 at half-time; England Counties were still leading 26-0 at the start of the second half when Dave Wilks scored from a rolling maul; England Counties were leading 33-0 midway through the second half; England Counties were still leading 33-0 in the closing stages when Warren Spragg scored after Shaun Perry made a brilliant break; Mal Roberts had a brilliant game*)

TEAM ROC USA SEVENS

Home Depot Center, Carson City, Los Angeles

CAPTAIN: *Peter Richards*

First Round - Pool 'A'

12th Feb TONGA 12 **ENGLAND** 19

[*This match kicked off at 12.12pm*]

(*England were losing 5-0 in the early stages; England were still losing 5-0 just before half-time when James Brooks scored after James Bailey made a brilliant break; England were drawing 5-5 at half-time; Ben Gollings came on as a replacement for Peter Richards at half-time; England were leading 19-5 at one point in the second half; England scored 19 unanswered points to win the match; England were still leading 19-5 when the referee unaccountably allowed play to continue after a clear forward pass and Alipate Fatafehi went on to score, thus 7 points were unlawful*)

CAPTAIN: *Ben Gollings*

12th Feb WEST INDIES 7 **ENGLAND** 52

[*This match kicked off at 3.18pm*]

(*England were leading 26-0 at half-time; England scored 38 unanswered points to win the match; England were leading 45-7 when James Bailey scored to complete a hat-trick of tries in the second half!*)

CAPTAIN: *Peter Richards*

12th Feb FIJI 10 **ENGLAND** 14

[*This match kicked off at 6.46pm*]

(*England were losing 5-0 in the early stages; England were leading 7-5 at half-time; England were still leading 7-5 early in the second half when Geoff Appleford scored after Rob Thirlby made a brilliant break; England were leading 14-5 midway through the second half; England were still leading 14-5 in the last minute*)

Quarter-Final

13th Feb SAMOA 7 **ENGLAND** 28

[*This match kicked off at 11.28am*]

(*England were losing 7-0 in the early stages; England were leading 14-7 at half-time;*

England were leading 21-7 early in the second half; England scored 28 unanswered points to win the match)

Semi-Final

13th Feb	ARGENTINA	17	**ENGLAND**	0

[This match kicked off at 3.28pm; After this tournament the IRB presented Ben Gollings with a special trophy in recognition of his achievement in breaking Waisale Serevi's IRB World Sevens points scoring record]

(The England players kicked away too much possession in this match; England were drawing 0-0 when collectively poor tackling allowed Juan Martín Berberian to score, thus 7 points were preventable; England were losing 12-0 at half-time; Ben Gollings increased his IRB World Sevens record to 1094 points in this tournament)

IRB RUGBY AID MATCH

CAPTAIN: *Lawrence Dallaglio*

5th Mar	**NORTH**	19	SOUTH	54

Twickenham

[This match kicked off at 2.30pm; Brian O'Driscoll selected as captain in the original squad of 22 but withdrew due to injury; Andrea Lo Cicero, Pieter de Villiers, Gordon Bulloch, Fabien Pelous, Paul O'Connell, Sergio Parisse, Chris Cusiter, Dwayne Peel, Aurélien Rougerie and Rhys Williams all in original squad of 22 but then withdrew due to injury or unavailability; Damien Traille selected but withdrew, Ceri Sweeney was moved from the bench to the team and Mark Taylor was then selected for the bench; Olivier Brouzet selected for bench but withdrew, being replaced by Eric Miller; Brian O'Driscoll travelled to London to provide pitchside support for the North; Chris Paterson was the nephew of Duncan Paterson; Shane Drahm came on as a replacement for the South in this match; Chris Horsman qualified to play for Wales in September 2005 after completing a residency period of 3 years and was capped for Wales in November 2005]

(This match was played on a wet pitch; The North were drawing 0-0 in the 13th minute when Tana Umaga scored a try that should not have been given because the scoring pass from Brian Lima was clearly forward, thus 7 points were unlawful; The North were losing 7-0 midway through the first half when Andy Titterrell scored after Lawrence Dallaglio made a brilliant run; The North were drawing 7-7 in the 25th minute when collectively poor tackling allowed Brian Lima to score; The North were losing 14-7 in the 27th minute when Pat Sanderson scored after David Humphreys put up a brilliant cross-kick; The North were losing 14-12 in the 35th minute; The North were losing 21-12 just before half-time; The North were losing 28-12 at half-time; Gareth Cooper went off injured in the 42nd minute, being replaced by Mike Phillips (2); Clive Woodward famously caught the ball when it was cleared to touch in the 47th minute!; Cédric Soulette came on as a temporary blood replacement for John Yapp in the 50th minute; The North were losing 35-12 in the 52nd minute; The South were allowed to score 21 unanswered points to clinch the match; Mark Taylor came on as a replacement for David Humphreys in the 53rd minute, with Ceri Sweeney then switching from centre to fly half to accommodate Mark Taylor; Matt Tait came on as a replacement for Chris Paterson in the 57th minute; The North were losing 35-19 midway through the second half; The North were still losing 35-19 in the 64th minute when Andrew Mehrtens put up a cross-kick and Ben Cohen was deceived by the bounce of the ball, which allowed Chris Latham to follow up and score, thus 2 tries and 14 points were preventable; The North were losing 42-19 in the 69th minute when Ben Cohen crossed the tryline but then dropped the ball in the act of scoring; Ben

***Cohen went off injured with 5 minutes of normal time remaining, being replaced by Simon Taylor (2) who had to play out of position as a wing; The North were losing 54-19 in the first minute of injury time when Eric Miller kicked ahead in the last move of the match, but the ball went over the dead ball line before Marco Bortolami could touch it down; Matt Tait injured playing in the match; Ollie Smith (2) had a brilliant game*)**

RUGBY WORLD CUP SEVENS

Hong Kong Stadium, Eastern Hospital Road, So Kon Po, Hong Kong

CAPTAIN: *Simon Amor*

First Round - Pool 'B'

18th Mar GEORGIA 0 **ENGLAND** 47

[*This match kicked off at 11.55am*]

(*The England players had insufficient time to shake off their jet lag; England were drawing 0-0 when Ben Gollings scored after Phil Dowson made a brilliant break; England were leading 21-0 at half-time; Neil Starling scored a brilliant solo try in the second half*)

CAPTAIN: *Ben Gollings*

18th Mar ITALY 0 **ENGLAND** 41

[*This match kicked off at 4.19pm*]

(*The England players had insufficient time to shake off their jet lag; Richard Haughton scored a hat-trick of tries in the first half!; England were leading 22-0 at half-time; England were still leading 22-0 when some superb handling allowed Peter Richards to score*)

CAPTAIN: *Simon Amor*

18th Mar FRANCE 28 **ENGLAND*** 17

[*This match kicked off at 8.58pm*]

(*The England players had insufficient time to shake off their jet lag; England were losing 7-0 in the early stages; England were still losing 7-0 in the 3rd minute when Jérôme Naves scored after a poor tackle by Pat Sanderson; England were losing 14-0 just before half-time when Ugo Monye scored a brilliant 56 metre solo try; England were losing 14-7 at half-time; England were losing 14-12 early in the second half; England were losing 21-17 in the final minute and pressing in attack when Henry Paul had his pass intercepted by Jérôme Naves, who then ran 58 metres to score another try to clinch the match for France, thus 2 tries and 14 points were preventable*)

19th Mar CHINESE TAIPEI 0 **ENGLAND** 41

[*This match kicked off at 1.01pm*]

(*England were leading 5-0 in the early stages; England were still leading 5-0 when Ben Gollings scored a brilliant 90 metre solo try; England were leading 15-0 at half-time; England were still leading 15-0 early in the second half when Henry Paul scored another brilliant 83 metre solo try; Richard Haughton went off injured, being replaced by Ugo Monye; England were leading 27-0 when Ugo Monye scored a superb 52 metre solo try; England were leading 34-0 in the final minute*)

19th Mar SAMOA 7 **ENGLAND** 12

[*This match kicked off at 6.53pm; Richard Haughton selected but withdrew due to injury, being replaced by Ugo Monye*]

(*England were drawing 0-0 in the 3rd minute when Ugo Monye had a great try-scoring chance but was brilliantly tap-tackled by Sailosi Tagicakibau; England were still drawing 0-0 immediately afterwards when Ben Gollings wasted a great try-scoring*

***opportunity by throwing a poor pass to the unmarked Ugo Monye; England were drawing 0-0 midway through the first half; England were still drawing 0-0 in the 4th minute when Ugo Monye broke through but then carried the ball under the wrong arm which allowed Sailosi Tagicakibau to get back and dislodge it; England were drawing 0-0 in the 6th minute when Ugo Monye powered through to score; England were leading 7-0 just before half-time; England were drawing 7-7 at half-time; England were still drawing 7-7 in the 10th minute when Simon Amor made a brilliant 67 metre run down the left wing to score a match-winning try; England were leading 12-7 midway through the second half; Henry Paul injured playing in the match*)**

Quarter-Final

20th Mar	SCOTLAND	0	**ENGLAND**	36

[*This match kicked off at 3.11pm; Henry Paul unavailable due to injury*]

(*England were leading 5-0 in the 4th minute; England were still leading 5-0 midway through the first half; England were leading 5-0 in the 6th minute when Peter Richards jinked through to score a brilliant try; England were leading 17-0 just before half-time when Ben Gollings missed an eminently kickable conversion attempt; England were leading 17-0 at half-time; England were still leading 17-0 in the 10th minute when Ben Gollings scored after Richard Haughton made a superb 62 metre break; England were leading 24-0 midway through the second half; England were still leading 24-0 with 2 minutes remaining when Rob Thirlby scored a brilliant 60 metre solo try*)

Semi-Final

20th Mar	FIJI	24	**ENGLAND***	19 aet

[*This match kicked off at 5.23pm; Henry Paul and Ugo Monye unavailable due to injury*]

(*Richard Haughton played with an injury; Sireli Bobo scored after just 34 seconds had been played when Richard Haughton failed to fall properly on a loose ball!; England were losing 7-0 midway through the first half; England were still losing 7-0 in the 6th minute when Richard Haughton had a great try-scoring chance but was brilliantly tap-tackled by William Ryder; England were losing 7-0 just before half-time when Ben Gollings kicked ahead and then followed up to score under the posts after he gathered the ball when Sireli Bobo made it available at a tackle situation!; England were drawing 7-7 at half-time; Richard Haughton went off injured at half-time, being replaced by Rob Thirlby; England were still drawing 7-7 in the 10th minute when Ifereimi Rawaqa scored after a poor tackle by Rob Thirlby; England were losing 19-7 midway through the second half; England were still losing 19-7 with 1 minute of normal time remaining when Tony Roques scored under the posts after Rob Thirlby threw a brilliant reverse pass; England were losing 19-14 in the last minute of normal time when Simon Amor dummied his way through to score a brilliant try to bring the scores level, with the game then going into sudden death extra time after Ben Gollings narrowly missed the difficult conversion attempt; England were still drawing 19-19 in the second minute of sudden death extra time when they allowed the ball to go loose at a ruck situation in front of their own 22 and Waisale Serevi was able to gather it and score in the corner to win the match for Fiji, thus 3 tries and 17 points were preventable*)

STANDARD CHARTERED SEVENS, SINGAPORE

National Stadium, Kallang

CAPTAIN: *Ben Gollings*

First Round - Pool 'B'

16th April	KENYA	7	**ENGLAND**	24

[This match kicked off at 2.08pm]

(This match was played in extreme heat and high humidity; England were leading 12-0 at half-time; England were leading 24-0 in the closing stages of this match)

16th April	HONG KONG	0	**ENGLAND**	38

[This match kicked off at 5.04pm]

(This match was played in extreme heat and high humidity)

16th April	SCOTLAND	5	**ENGLAND**	21

[This match kicked off at 9.16pm]

(This match was played in extreme heat and high humidity; England were leading 7-5 at half-time; England were still leading 7-5 when they were reduced to 5 men after Rob Thirlby and Ben Gollings were both sent to the sin-bin; Peter Richards scored a brilliant solo try shortly afterwards)

Quarter-Final

17th April	AUSTRALIA	14	**ENGLAND**	17

[This match kicked off at 4.02pm]

(This match was played in extreme heat and high humidity; England were leading 5-0 when Andrew Brown scored after a poor tackle by Ben Gollings; England were losing 7-5 just before half-time when Geoff Appleford scored after Ben Gollings threw a brilliant pass; England were leading 10-7 at half-time)

Semi-Final

17th April	FIJI	12	**ENGLAND**	14

[This match kicked off at 7.38pm]

(This match was played in extreme heat and high humidity; England were losing 12-0 at one point in this match; England were losing 12-7 with 30 seconds remaining when Ben Gollings scored a try to bring the scores level and then kicked the conversion to win the match!)

Final

17th April	NEW ZEALAND	26	**ENGLAND**	5

[This match kicked off at 9.30pm]

(This match was played in extreme heat and high humidity; England were drawing 0-0 when Ben Gollings wasted a great try-scoring opportunity by dropping the ball near the New Zealand line; England were losing 21-0 at half-time; England were losing 26-0 in the 13th minute; Ben Gollings increased his IRB World Sevens record to 1120 points in this tournament)

NEW ZEALAND ARMY TOUR TO ENGLAND AND WALES 2005

CAPTAIN: *??*

5th May	**PUBLIC SCHOOL WANDERERS**	24	New Zealand Army (*NZ*)	48

Iffley Road, Oxford

[This match kicked off at 3.00pm; Public School Wanderers RFC founded 1940; Adam Slade played for M.R. Steele-Bodger's XV against Cambridge University at Grange Road on 27th November 2002]

ZURICH TEST

CAPTAIN: *Michael Owen* (WA)

23rd May **BRITISH & IRISH LIONS*** 25 ARGENTINA 25

Millennium Stadium, Cardiff

[This match was originally scheduled to start at 7.45pm but the kick-off was delayed for 15 minutes due to traffic congestion; Matt Stevens, Richard Hill (2), Tom Shanklin, Gavin Henson and Will Greenwood all unavailable due to injury; Andy Sheridan, Andy Titterrell, Stephen Jones (2), Charlie Hodgson, Jason Robinson, Gareth Thomas (2) and Mark Cueto all unavailable due to club commitments; Neil Back unavailable due to suspension; Malcolm O'Kelly selected but withdrew due to injury, Donncha O'Callaghan was moved from the bench to the team and Ben Kay was then selected for the bench; Simon Taylor (2) selected at blindside flanker but withdrew due to injury, Martin Corry was moved from the bench to the team and Lawrence Dallaglio was then selected for the bench; The Millennium Stadium had its retractable roof closed for this match]

(The Lions made a number of handling errors in this match; The Lions scrum was put under severe pressure in the first half; Federico Todeschini scored a penalty goal in the 4th minute!; The Lions were losing 3-0 in the 7th minute when a poor defensive alignment allowed José Núñez Piossek to score, thus 7 points were preventable; The Lions were losing 13-0 in the 17th minute when Ollie Smith (2) scored after Jonny Wilkinson brilliantly created space; The Lions were losing 13-7 midway through the first half; The Lions were losing 16-7 in the 22nd minute; The Lions were losing 19-10 in the 35th minute; The Lions were losing 19-13 just before half-time; The Lions were losing 19-16 at half-time; The Lions were drawing 19-19 in the 50th minute; Chris Cusiter came on as a replacement for Gareth Cooper in the 59th minute; The Lions were losing 25-19 midway through the second half; The Lions conceded too many needless penalties within Federico Todeschini's kicking range; Ollie Smith (2) went off injured in the 62nd minute, being replaced by Shane Horgan; The Lions were losing 25-22 in the 67th minute; Steve Thompson (2) came on as a replacement for Shane Byrne in the 70th minute; Ben Kay came on as a replacement at the same time, with Donncha O'Callaghan then briefly leaving the field by mistake instead of Danny Grewcock!; The Lions were still losing 25-22 with 2 minutes of normal time remaining when they were awarded a 22 metre penalty in an eminently kickable position, but Michael Owen ordered a kick to the corner in a vain attempt to score a try from the ensuing lineout; The Lions were losing 25-22 in the fifth minute of injury time when Gordon D'Arcy wasted a great try-scoring opportunity by dropping the ball while the Argentine line was at his mercy; The Lions were still losing 25-22 in the ninth minute of injury time when Jonny Wilkinson scored a 26 metre penalty goal with the last kick of the match to draw the game; Jonny Wilkinson scored 20 points in this match; Chris Cusiter had a brilliant game)

BARBARIANS MATCH

CAPTAIN: *David Humphreys* (IR)

24th May SCOTLAND XV 38 **BARBARIANS** 7

Pittodrie Stadium, Aberdeen

[This match kicked off at 7.30pm]

(This match was played in cold conditions; Raphäel Ibañez came on as a temporary blood replacement for Frankie Sheahan in the 6th minute; The Barbarians were drawing 0-0 in the 10th minute when Andy Henderson scored after a poor tackle by

***Darren Morris; The Barbarians were losing 7-0 midway through the first half; The Barbarians were still losing 7-0 in the 22nd minute when Andrea Lo Cicero scored from a rolling maul; The Barbarians were drawing 7-7 in the 37th minute; The Barbarians were losing 10-7 at half-time; Kenny Logan came on as a replacement for Brian Lima in the 47th minute; Thomas Castaignède came on as a replacement for Matt Burke in the 54th minute; The Barbarians were still losing 10-7 in the 58th minute when Dougie Hall scored after Owen Finegan missed a tackle on Mike Blair; The Barbarians were losing 17-7 midway through the second half; The Barbarians were losing 24-7 in the 63rd minute; The Barbarians were still losing 24-7 with 7 minutes of normal time remaining; The Barbarians were losing 31-7 with 2 minutes of normal time remaining and pressing in attack when Hugo Southwell scored after Graeme Beveridge intercepted the ball, thus 2 tries and 14 points were preventable; The Scotland XV was allowed to score 31 unanswered points to win the match*)**

TIBCO CHALLENGE

CAPTAIN: *Pat Sanderson* [England XV]
CAPTAIN: *Corné Krige* (SA) [Barbarians]

28th May **ENGLAND XV*** 39 **BARBARIANS** 52
Twickenham

[ENGLAND XV: [*This match kicked off at 3.00pm*]
(*Andy Goode kicked away too much possession in the first half; Andy Goode scored a penalty goal in the 5th minute!; The England XV was losing 5-3 in the 7th minute; Micky Ward went off injured in the 16th minute, being replaced by Robbie Morris; The England XV was still losing 5-3 midway through the first half; The England XV was losing 12-6 in the 33rd minute when collectively poor tackling allowed Carlos Spencer to score, thus 5 points were preventable; The England XV was losing 17-6 in the 37th minute when Paul Sackey scored a brilliant 60 metre solo try; The England XV was losing 17-13 at half-time; A brilliant break by Andy Goode enabled Ayoola Erinle to score a try which Andy Goode then converted to give the England XV a 20-17 lead in the 42nd minute; The England XV was losing 24-20 in the 46th minute when Trevor Halstead scored after Tom Voyce missed a tackle on Brent Russell; The England XV was losing 31-20 in the 53rd minute when the referee unaccountably allowed play to continue after Sébastien Chabal knocked the ball on and Wendell Sailor went on to score, thus 7 points were unlawful; The referee had to order uncontested scrums in the 56th minute after Mike Worsley went off injured to leave the England XV with only one fit prop left!; The Barbarians were allowed to score 28 unanswered points to win the match; The England XV was losing 45-20 midway through the second half; The England XV was still losing 45-20 in the 64th minute when some superb handling amongst the forwards allowed Paul Sackey to score another try; The England XV was losing 45-27 in the 68th minute when Brent Russell scored after a poor tackle by Pat Sanderson, thus 3 tries and 19 points were preventable; The England XV was losing 52-27 with 7 minutes remaining when James Forrester scored after James Simpson-Daniel made a brilliant run; The England XV was losing 52-32 in the final minute when Pat Sanderson scored from a rolling maul with the last move of the match*)]
[BARBARIANS: [*This match kicked off at 3.00pm; Girvan Dempsey selected for bench but withdrew, being replaced by Matt Burke*]
(*Andy Goode scored a penalty goal in the 5th minute!; The Barbarians were losing 3-0 in the 7th minute when Bruce Reihana scored after Wendell Sailor went on a brilliant rampaging run; The Barbarians were leading 5-3 midway through the first half; The Barbarians were losing 6-5 in the 30th minute when Wendell Sailor scored after Carlos*

***Spencer brilliantly created space by throwing the ball to himself!; The Barbarians were leading 12-6 in the 33rd minute when Carlos Spencer dummied his way through to score a superb try; The Barbarians were leading 17-13 at half-time; The Barbarians were losing 20-17 in the 43rd minute when Bruce Reihana scored another try after Carlos Spencer made a brilliant break; The Barbarians were leading 24-20 in the 46th minute when Trevor Halstead scored after Brent Russell made a superb run; The Barbarians were leading 38-20 in the 53rd minute; The referee had to order uncontested scrums in the 56th minute after Mike Worsley went off injured to leave the England XV with only one fit prop left!; The Barbarians were leading 45-20 midway through the second half; The Barbarians scored 28 unanswered points to win the match; The Barbarians were leading 52-27 in the 68th minute; The Barbarians were leading 52-32 in the last minute; Carlos Spencer had a brilliant game*)]**

EMIRATES AIRLINE LONDON SEVENS

Twickenham

CAPTAIN: *Simon Amor*

First Round - Pool 'B'

4th June	**ENGLAND**	29	FRANCE	0

[*This match kicked off at 11.42am*]

(*Phil Dowson scored in the 1st minute!; England were leading 12-0 when Richard Haughton scored a brilliant solo try; England were leading 17-0 at half-time; England were still leading 17-0 when Richard Haughton scored another try after Phil Dowson made a brilliant run*)

4th June	**ENGLAND**	33	GEORGIA	5

[*This match kicked off at 3.00pm*]

(*England were drawing 0-0 when Dan Hipkiss scored after he wrong-footed the defence with a brilliant sidestep; England were leading 12-0 at half-time; England were leading 26-5 in the closing stages when Matt Tait scored a brilliant 60 metre solo try*)

4th June	**ENGLAND***	15	SAMOA	19

[*This match kicked off at 6.18pm*]

(*Richard Haughton injured his shoulder in the 1st minute but elected to remain on the pitch; David Lemi scored immediately afterwards!; England were drawing 5-5 midway through the first half when Ben Gollings missed an eminently kickable conversion attempt; England were still drawing 5-5 in the 6th minute when Matt Tait scored a brilliant 35 metre solo try, with Ben Gollings then missing the eminently kickable conversion attempt; England were leading 10-5 just before half-time; England were losing 12-10 at half-time; England were still losing 12-10 midway through the second half; England were losing 12-10 with 1 minute remaining when Mikaele Senio scored after a poor tackle by Simon Amor, thus 7 points were preventable; England were losing 19-10 in the third minute of injury time when Rob Thirlby scored a brilliant consolation try with the last move of the match*)

Quarter-Final

5th June	**ENGLAND**	40	SCOTLAND	7

[*This match kicked off at 1.59pm*]

(*Richard Haughton scored in the 2nd minute!; England were leading 21-0 at half-time; England were leading 28-0 early in the second half; England scored 28 unanswered points to win the match; England were leading 28-7 when Rob Thirlby scored a brilliant 70 metre solo try*)

Semi-Final

5th June **ENGLAND** 33 ARGENTINA 7

[This match kicked off at 5.28pm]

(Phil Dowson powered through 3 attempted tackles to score after just 34 seconds had been played!; England were losing 7-5 in the 3rd minute; England were still losing 7-5 midway through the first half; England were losing 7-5 in the 6th minute when Ben Gollings chipped ahead and regathered the ball to score a brilliant try; England were leading 12-7 at half-time; England were still leading 12-7 in the 9th minute when Simon Amor scored a superb try; England were leading 19-7 midway through the second half; England were leading 26-7 in the final minute when Matt Tait scored a brilliant 78 metre solo try with the last move of the match; England scored 28 unanswered points to win the match)

Final

5th June **ENGLAND*** 12 SOUTH AFRICA 21

[This match kicked off at 7.14pm]

(England made a number of handling errors in this match; Richard Haughton scored a 62 metre solo try after just 80 seconds had been played!; England were leading 7-0 in the 4th minute when Jaco Pretorius scored after a poor tackle by Richard Haughton; England were drawing 7-7 midway through the first half; England were losing 14-7 in the 7th minute; England were still losing 14-7 just before half-time when Fabien Juries scored after Peter Richards failed to commit himself to a tackle, thus 2 tries and 14 points were preventable; South Africa were allowed to score 21 unanswered points to win the match; England were losing 21-7 at half-time; England were losing 21-12 in the 12th minute when Ben Gollings missed an eminently kickable conversion attempt; England were still losing 21-12 in the 14th minute when Phil Dowson crossed the tryline but then could not get downward pressure on the ball; England were losing 21-12 in the 15th minute when both Simon Amor and Phil Dowson were unable to ground the ball after crossing the tryline in quick succession; England were still losing 21-12 midway through the second half; England were losing 21-12 in the 16th minute when Peter Richards reached the tryline but the move was disallowed as he was adjudged to have made a double movement; Ben Gollings increased his IRB World Sevens record to 1166 points in this tournament)

NOBOK CHALLENGE - JONNO V JONAH

CAPTAIN: *Martin Johnson*

4th June **MARTIN JOHNSON XV** 33 JONAH LOMU XV 29

Twickenham

[This match kicked off at 7.30pm; Andrea Lo Cicero and Alessandro Troncon in original squad of 22 but then withdrew, being replaced by Perry Freshwater and Morgan Williams respectively; Simon Shaw selected but withdrew as he was now required to go on the British & Irish Lions tour of New Zealand, being replaced by Chris Jones; Perry Freshwater selected for bench but withdrew as he was now required to play for England A in the Churchill Cup, being replaced by Will Green (1); Austin Healey was originally selected at left wing with Ayoola Erinle at right wing, but the two swapped positions on the day of the match; Pat Howard was added to the original 8 man bench selection; Martin Johnson retired after this match; A Jonah Lomu VII beat a Martin Johnson VII 25-10 at Twickenham on 5th June 2005; Austin Healey retired in May 2006; Anthony Foley was the son of Brendan Foley]

(This match was played on a pitch where the in-goal areas were shorter than normal because Twickenham was simultaneously hosting the London Sevens; The Martin

Johnson XV was losing 5-0 in the 6th minute; The Martin Johnson XV was still losing 5-0 in the 18th minute when Austin Healey scored after Jamie Noon made a brilliant run; The Martin Johnson XV was leading 7-5 midway through the first half; The Martin Johnson XV was still leading 7-5 in the 24th minute when Andy Goode threw a superb reverse pass to Ayoola Erinle, who then powered through Jonah Lomu's attempted tackle to score; The Martin Johnson XV was leading 14-5 in the 28th minute when Austin Healey scored in the corner after Andy Goode put in a brilliant chip-kick to Jamie Noon, with Andy Goode then having the difficult conversion attempt come back off the left-hand post; The Martin Johnson XV was leading 19-5 in the 34th minute when Jonah Lomu was awarded a try that should not have been given because he put a foot into touch before he grounded the ball, thus 5 points were unlawful; The Martin Johnson XV was leading 19-10 just before half-time; The Martin Johnson XV was leading 19-15 at half-time; Leon Lloyd came on as a replacement for Gregor Townsend in the 44th minute, with Austin Healey then switching from wing to full back to accommodate Leon Lloyd; The Martin Johnson XV was losing 22-19 in the 55th minute; The Martin Johnson XV was still losing 22-19 midway through the second half; The Martin Johnson XV was losing 22-19 in the 65th minute when Austin Healey's pass was intercepted by Matt Burke who then went on to score, thus 7 points were preventable; The Jonah Lomu XV was allowed to score 24 unanswered points; Pat Howard came on as a replacement for Rob Henderson in the 67th minute; The Martin Johnson XV was losing 29-19 in the 69th minute when Austin Healey intercepted the ball and ran 60 metres to score to complete a hat-trick; The Martin Johnson XV was losing 29-26 with 2 minutes remaining when Leon Lloyd scored a match-winning try after Pat Howard threw a superb pass; Andy Goode had a brilliant game)

BRITISH & IRISH LIONS TOUR TO NEW ZEALAND 2005

CAPTAIN: *Brian O'Driscoll* (IR) [*Martin Corry*]

25th Jun NEW ZEALAND 21 **BRITISH & IRISH LIONS** 3

Jade Stadium, Christchurch

[*This match kicked off at 7.10pm; The Jade Stadium was previously called Lancaster Park; After this match Danny Grewcock was banned for 2 months after being found guilty of biting Kevin Mealamu; Richard Hill (2) and Tom Shanklin returned home injured after this match; Brent Cockbain joined the tour after this match; Richard Hill (2) retired in May 2008; Neil Back retired in July 2005*]

**(*This match was played in driving rain and then hailstones in extremely cold conditions; Andy Robinson unaccountably changed the lineout calls the day before the match and the Lions lineout suffered accordingly; Jason Robinson played with an injury and consequently had a poor game; The Lions backs kicked away too much possession; Brian O'Driscoll had to go off in the 2nd minute after he dislocated his shoulder when he was illegally upended and then dropped to the ground by both Kevin Mealamu and Tana Umaga in an off the ball incident, being replaced by Will Greenwood; The Lions were drawing 0-0 in the 5th minute when they were awarded a 45 metre penalty in a kickable position, but Dwayne Peel inexplicably chose to take a quick tap penalty in a vain attempt to score a try; The Lions were still drawing 0-0 in the 7th minute when the referee unaccountably ignored Justin Marshall being in front of Aaron Mauger when the latter kicked ahead and awarded New Zealand a 17 metre penalty which Dan Carter duly kicked, thus 3 points were unlawful; The Lions were losing 6-0 in the 13th minute; Richard Hill (2) had to go off in the 18th minute after he ruptured the anterior cruciate ligament in his knee attempting to tackle Ali Williams, being replaced by Ryan Jones; The Lions were still losing 6-0 midway through the first*

half; The Lions were losing 6-0 in the 24th minute when Shane Byrne's lineout throw went straight to Ali Williams who then powered through some collectively poor tackling to score; The Lions were losing 11-0 in the 38th minute when Jonny Wilkinson missed a kickable 42 metre penalty goal attempt; The Lions were losing 11-0 at half-time; The Lions were losing 14-0 in the 47th minute when Dwayne Peel inexplicably knocked-on as he took a quick tap penalty, which allowed Sitiveni Sivivatu to score from the resulting New Zealand scrum, thus 2 tries and 12 points were preventable; New Zealand were allowed to score 21 unanswered points to win the match; The Lions were losing 21-0 in the 56th minute when Jonny Wilkinson scored a 28 metre consolation penalty goal; Steve Thompson (2), Danny Grewcock and Shane Horgan came on as replacements for Shane Byrne, Ben Kay and Jason Robinson respectively in the 57th minute, with Gareth Thomas (2) then switching from wing to full back to accommodate Horgan; The Lions were losing 21-3 midway through the second half; Matt Dawson came on as a replacement for Dwayne Peel with 6 minutes remaining)

CAPTAIN: *Gareth Thomas (2)* (WA)

2nd July NEW ZEALAND 48 **BRITISH & IRISH LIONS** 18

WestpacTrust Stadium, Wellington

[This match kicked off at 7.10pm; Brian O'Driscoll and Ollie Smith (2) unavailable due to injury; Jason Robinson retired from international rugby on 24th September 2005 but then changed his mind in January 2007]

(Jason Robinson played with an injury; Gareth Thomas (2) scored a brilliant solo try in the 2nd minute!; The Lions were leading 7-0 in the 5th minute when Jonny Wilkinson hit the left-hand post with a kickable 34 metre penalty goal attempt; The Lions were leading 7-6 in the 18th minute when Tana Umaga scored after Gavin Henson missed a tackle on Dan Carter, thus 7 points were preventable; The Lions were losing 13-7 midway through the first half; The Lions were losing 13-10 in the 27th minute; The Lions were losing 16-13 in the 32nd minute when the referee unaccountably ignored Byron Kelleher holding onto the ball in the tackle, which allowed Sitiveni Sivivatu to score from the resulting New Zealand scrum; The Lions were losing 21-13 at half-time; The Lions were losing 24-13 in the 43rd minute when the referee inexplicably ignored Rodney So'oialo tackling Shane Williams without the ball, which duly created a gap for Dan Carter to run through and score, thus 2 tries and 14 points were unlawful; The Lions were losing 31-13 in the 48th minute when they were awarded an 8 metre penalty in an eminently kickable position, but Gareth Thomas (2) ordered a kick to the corner in a vain attempt to score a try from the ensuing lineout; Jonny Wilkinson went off injured in the 60th minute, being replaced by Stephen Jones (2); The Lions were losing 34-13 midway through the second half; The Lions were losing 34-18 in the 66th minute; The Lions were losing 41-18 in the 70th minute; Gavin Henson went off injured with 9 minutes of normal time remaining, being replaced by Shane Horgan; The Lions were losing 48-18 in the last minute of normal time when Shane Horgan was driven over the New Zealand line and claimed to have scored, but the referee was unsighted and the video referee could not award the try because it was unclear whether the ball had indeed been grounded; Gavin Henson only received one pass in the entire match!; Shane Williams had a poor game defensively; This was New Zealand's highest ever points total against the Lions)

CAPTAIN: *Gareth Thomas (2)* (WA) [*Paul O'Connell* (IR)]

9th July NEW ZEALAND 38 **BRITISH & IRISH LIONS*** 19

Eden Park, Auckland

[*This match kicked off at 7.10pm; Andy Sheridan, Simon Shaw, Ben Kay, Jonny Wilkinson, Charlie Hodgson, Gavin Henson, Gordon D'Arcy, Brian O'Driscoll and Ollie Smith (2) all unavailable due to injury; Steve Thompson (2) selected but withdrew on the morning of the match due to illness, Shane Byrne was moved from the bench to the team and Gordon Bulloch was then selected for the bench*]

(*This match was played in wet conditions; Stephen Jones (2) scored a penalty goal in the 3rd minute!; The Lions were leading 3-0 in the 8th minute when Donncha O'Callaghan wasted a great try-scoring opportunity by attempting to make the line himself instead of using a 4 man overlap outside him!; The Lions were leading 6-0 in the 10th minute when Conrad Smith scored after a poor tackle by Geordan Murphy; New Zealand were leading 7-6 in the 13th minute when Luke McAlister put in a grubber kick over the Lions line where Dwayne Peel dropped the ball and was then unable to regather it because Rodney So'oialo trod on his ankle, which in turn allowed Ali Williams to follow up and score, thus 7 points were unlawful; The Lions were losing 17-9 midway through the first half; The Lions were losing 17-12 in the 23rd minute; The Lions were still losing 17-12 in the 34th minute when Stephen Jones (2) hit the right-hand post with a kickable 40 metre penalty goal attempt; The Lions were losing 17-12 shortly before half-time; The Lions were losing 24-12 at half-time; The Lions were losing 31-12 in the 48th minute; Dwayne Peel went off injured in the 49th minute, being replaced by Matt Dawson; The Lions were still losing 31-12 in the 51st minute when they were awarded a 22 metre penalty in an eminently kickable position, but Gareth Thomas (2) ordered a kick to the corner in a vain attempt to score a try from the ensuing lineout; Gareth Thomas (2) went off due to illness immediately afterwards, being replaced by Shane Horgan; The Lions were losing 31-12 midway through the second half when Lewis Moody scored from a rolling maul; Geordan Murphy went off injured in the 66th minute, being replaced by Ronan O'Gara with Stephen Jones (2) then switching from fly half to centre to accommodate O'Gara, Shane Horgan moving from centre to wing to accommodate Stephen Jones (2) and Josh Lewsey switching from wing to full back to accommodate Horgan; Gordon Bulloch came on as a replacement for Shane Byrne in the 70th minute; Martyn Williams came on as a replacement for Lewis Moody with 4 minutes remaining; The Lions were losing 31-19 in the final minute and pressing in attack when Will Greenwood had his pass to Shane Horgan intercepted by Rico Gear who then kicked ahead to score in the corner with the last move of the match, thus 2 tries and 14 points were preventable*)

TRIBUTE TO RUGBY'S LEGENDS

CAPTAIN: *Scott Quinnell* (WA)

5th June **BRITAIN AND IRELAND XV** 57 THE WORLD XV 67

Millennium Stadium, Cardiff

**[*This match kicked off at 3.00pm; Dai Young selected but withdrew, Darren Morris was moved from the bench to the team; Mick Galwey selected but withdrew to sit on the bench, Craig Quinnell was moved from the bench to the team; Gregor Townsend selected but withdrew to sit on the bench, being replaced by John Devereux; Barry Williams, Matt Dawson and Bryan Redpath in original squad but were not selected for team or bench; Jason Leonard and Neil Jenkins both came out of retirement to play in this match; The Millennium Stadium had its retractable roof closed for this match; The Britain and Ireland XV all wore number 8 on their shirts whereas the World XV all wore*

number 9; Tony Diprose was capped for England Schools 18 Group in January 1991; Scott Quinnell retired after this match; Tony Diprose and Kyran Bracken retired in May 2006; Bobby Skinstad played for the World XV in this match; Rob Howley's long-standing wrist injury prevented him from being available as a full-time player but he was still able to come onto the pitch at regular intervals to take the World XV's kicks at goal!]

(The Britain and Ireland XV was losing 40-31 at half-time; Ally McCoist came on as a replacement at half-time; Ally McCoist played as a hooker in one scrum!; Scott Quinnell's father Derek and 6 year old son Steele came on as special replacements with 2 minutes remaining, with Steele Quinnell then being driven over the World XV's line to score the final try of the match which was then converted by a ball girl called Charmian Martin!; Rob Howley scored 6 conversions for the World XV in this match; The referee was persuaded to blow for full-time after only 30 minutes of the second half had been played!)

[Ally McCoist was added to the original 12 man bench selection; Ally McCoist won 61 caps for Scotland at football between 1985-98]

IRB U21 WORLD CHAMPIONSHIP

Argentina

CAPTAIN: *Matt Cornwell*

First Round - Pool 'B'

9th June SAMOA U21 22 **ENGLAND U21** 52 **BP**

Maristas RC, Mendoza

[This match kicked off at 1.00pm; Michael Cusack unavailable due to injury; Dylan Hartley played for England in the U19 World Championships in South Africa in March-April 2004 and April 2005]

(England U21 were leading 7-0 in the 8th minute; England U21 were leading 14-0 in the 12th minute; England U21 were leading 14-3 midway through the first half; England U21 were leading 21-3 in the 26th minute; England U21 were leading 21-8 in the 31st minute; Olly Morgan went off injured in the 39th minute, being replaced by Ben Russell (1); England U21 were leading 28-8 at half-time; Will Bowley came on as a temporary blood replacement for Sean Cox in the 41st minute; England U21 were leading 28-15 in the 42nd minute; England U21 were leading 35-15 in the 50th minute; England U21 were still leading 35-15 midway through the second half; England U21 were leading 40-15 in the 64th minute; England U21 were leading 45-15 with 7 minutes remaining; England U21 scored 17 unanswered points to seal the match; England U21 were leading 45-22 with 3 minutes remaining when Dylan Hartley scored after Shane Geraghty put in a brilliant kick ahead; Simon Whatling injured playing in the match; Matt Cornwell had a brilliant game)

13th Jun SOUTH AFRICA U21 34 **ENGLAND U21** 16

Liceo RC, Mendoza

[This match kicked off at 1.00pm; Simon Whatling and Olly Morgan unavailable due to injury]

(This match was played in extremely cold conditions; England U21 were losing 3-0 in the 6th minute; England U21 were still losing 3-0 shortly afterwards when Toby Flood had 2 penalty goal attempts in succession come back off the post; England U21 were drawing 3-3 in the 12th minute; England U21 were losing 10-3 midway through the first half; England U21 were losing 10-6 in the 29th minute; England U21 were losing 17-6 in the 33rd minute; England U21 were losing 17-9 at half-time; England U21 played into

***the wind in the second half; England U21 were losing 22-9 in the 46th minute; England U21 were still losing 22-9 midway through the second half; England U21 were losing 34-9 in the 70th minute; South Africa U21 were allowed to score 17 unanswered points to seal the match; England U21 were still losing 34-9 with 5 minutes remaining when Mark Hopley scored a consolation try*)**

17th Jun FRANCE U21 37 **ENGLAND U21** 27 **BP**

Mendoza RC, Mendoza

[*This match kicked off at 1.00pm*]

(*<u>Sean Cox was sent off in the 77th minute and thus duly banned for 1 match</u>*)

(*England U21 were losing 3-0 in the 11th minute; England U21 were losing 8-3 midway through the first half; England U21 were losing 11-10 in the 30th minute; England U21 were losing 14-10 shortly before half-time; England U21 were losing 21-10 at half-time; England U21 were losing 21-15 in the 43rd minute; England U21 were losing 24-15 in the 52nd minute; England U21 were losing 24-22 midway through the second half; England U21 were losing 31-22 in the 66th minute; England U21 were losing 34-22 with 5 minutes of normal time remaining; France U21 were allowed to score 13 unanswered points to clinch the match; England U21 were losing 37-22 in the first minute of injury time when James Haskell scored a consolation try*)

CAPTAIN: *Simon Whatling*

5th/6th/7th/8th Place Semi-Final

21st Jun ARGENTINA U21 20 **ENGLAND U21** 6

Mendoza RC, Mendoza

[*This match kicked off at 1.00pm; Sean Cox unavailable due to suspension*]

(*England U21 were leading 3-0 in the 11th minute; England U21 were still leading 3-0 midway through the first half; England U21 were leading 3-0 shortly afterwards when they were awarded 2 penalties in eminently kickable positions, but on each occasion Simon Whatling chose to run the ball in a vain attempt to score a try; England U21 were losing 7-3 in the 31st minute; England U21 were losing 7-3 at half-time; England U21 were losing 10-3 in the 52nd minute; England U21 were losing 10-6 midway through the second half; England U21 were losing 20-6 in the 67th minute; The referee had to order uncontested scrums after Wayne Thompson was sin-binned in the 70th minute; England U21 were still losing 20-6 in the closing stages when Tom Biggs wasted a great try-scoring opportunity by failing to gather a bouncing ball while the Argentina U21 line was at his mercy; England U21 were losing 20-6 shortly afterwards when Tom Varndell made a brilliant 40 metre break but then ran out of support*)

CAPTAIN: *Matt Cornwell*

7th/8th Place Play-Off

25th Jun WALES U21 32 **ENGLAND U21** 57

Liceo RC, Mendoza

[*This match kicked off at 11.00am*]

(*The England U21 forwards dominated the lineout in this match; Aled Thomas scored in the 3rd minute!; Olly Morgan went off injured in the 4th minute, being replaced by Shane Geraghty; England U21 were losing 10-0 in the 10th minute; England U21 were drawing 10-10 midway through the first half; England U21 were still drawing 10-10 in the 27th minute when Toby Flood scored a brilliant solo try; England U21 were drawing 17-17 in the 31st minute; England U21 were still drawing 17-17 just before half-time; England U21 were leading 24-17 at half-time; England U21 were leading 31-20 in the 44th minute; England U21 were leading 36-20 midway through the second*

half when Tom Varndell scored to complete a hat-trick of tries; England U21 were leading 57-20 in the 68th minute; England U21 scored 33 unanswered points to clinch the match; England U21 were leading 57-25 with 6 minutes remaining)

GMF PARIS SEVENS

Stade Jean Bouin, Paris

CAPTAIN: *Simon Amor*

First Round - Pool 'B'

10th June CANADA 5 **ENGLAND** 42

[This match kicked off at 1.28pm]

(Simon Amor played with a hamstring injury; Simon Amor had to go off in the 3rd minute after he aggravated his hamstring injury, being replaced by Geoff Appleford; England were leading 28-0 at half-time; Will Matthews was replaced by Rob Vickerman, who scored with his first touch of the ball!; Ben Gollings scored 22 points in this match)

CAPTAIN: *Ben Gollings*

10th June PORTUGAL 0 **ENGLAND** 29

[This match kicked off at 4.24pm; Simon Amor unavailable due to injury]

(England were drawing 0-0 when Andy Vilk scored a brilliant 80 metre solo try; England were leading 5-0 when some superb handling between Rob Thirlby and Tony Roques allowed Geoff Appleford to score; England were leading 12-0 at half-time; England were leading 19-0 when Will Matthews scored after James Bailey made a brilliant run)

10th June SCOTLAND 5 **ENGLAND** 26

[This match kicked off at 8.44pm; Simon Amor unavailable due to injury; Geoff Appleford retired due to injury in January 2007]

(England were losing 5-0 in the early stages; England were still losing 5-0 when Ben Gollings scored a brilliant long-range solo try; England were leading 7-5 when Richard Haughton scored after Ben Gollings instigated a counter-attack from behind his own line; England were leading 12-5 at half-time; England were leading 19-5 early in the second half; England scored 26 unanswered points to win the match; Geoff Appleford injured playing in the match)

Quarter-Final

11th June SAMOA 21 **ENGLAND*** 14

[This match kicked off at 11.34am; Geoff Appleford unavailable due to injury]

(David Lemi scored in the 2nd minute!; England were drawing 7-7 just before half-time; England were losing 14-7 at half-time; England were losing 21-7 early in the second half; England were losing 21-14 in the closing stages when James Bailey had a great try-scoring chance but was brilliantly tackled by Uale Mai)

CAPTAIN: *Simon Amor*

[Plate Semi-Final:]

[11th Jun AUSTRALIA 0 **ENGLAND** 24]

[This match kicked off at 2.40pm; Geoff Appleford unavailable due to injury]

(Simon Amor played with an injury; England were drawing 0-0 when Ben Gollings made a brilliant break and then took a return pass from Andy Vilk to score; England were leading 14-0 at half-time; England were still leading 14-0 when Ben Gollings scored a brilliant solo try; England were leading 19-0 when Richard Haughton scored the 100th try of his IRB World Sevens career)

CAPTAIN: *Ben Gollings*
[Plate Final:]
[11th Jun SOUTH AFRICA 26 **ENGLAND*** 19]
[This match kicked off at 4.46pm; Simon Amor and Geoff Appleford unavailable due to injury]
(England were losing 7-0 in the early stages; England were drawing 7-7 just before half-time; England were losing 12-7 at half-time; England were losing 19-7 early in the second half; England were still losing 19-7 when Rob Thirlby scored a brilliant long-range solo try; England were losing 19-12 with 1 minute remaining; England were drawing 19-19 in the last minute when Danwel Demas scored to win the match for South Africa; Ben Gollings scored 59 points in this tournament and thus increased his overall IRB World Sevens record to 1225)

ENGLAND COUNTIES TOUR TO ARGENTINA AND URUGUAY 2005

CAPTAIN: *Craig Hammond*
12th Jun ARGENTINA XV 36 **ENGLAND COUNTIES** 10
Club de Rugby Ateneo Inmaculada, Santa Fe
[This match kicked off at 3.00pm]
(Genaro Fessia scored in the 5th minute!; England Counties were drawing 7-7 in the 22nd minute; England Counties were leading 10-7 in the 32nd minute; England Counties were leading 10-7 at half-time; England Counties were losing 21-10 in the 48th minute; England Counties were losing 26-10 in the 53rd minute; England Counties were losing 33-10 midway through the second half; England Counties were losing 36-10 in the 70th minute; The Argentine XV was allowed to score 29 unanswered points in the second half to win the match)
18th Jun URUGUAY 9 **ENGLAND COUNTIES** 29
British School, Montevideo
[This match kicked off at 2.00pm; Both sides agreed to select an 8 man bench containing an extra front row player who could only be used if there was an injury, with Stewart Pearl duly being named as this additional replacement; Chris Wyles played for USA 7s in March 2007 and was capped for the USA in June 2007; Chris Bentley played for England U21]
(This match was played in wet conditions; England Counties were leading 5-0 in the 10th minute; England Counties were leading 5-3 midway through the first half; England Counties were losing 6-5 in the 26th minute; England Counties were still losing 6-5 in the 36th minute when Glenn Cooper scored from a rolling maul; England Counties were leading 10-6 at half-time; England Counties were leading 10-9 in the 50th minute; England Counties were still leading 10-9 in the 56th minute when Matt Long scored from another rolling maul; England Counties were leading 15-9 midway through the second half; England Counties were leading 22-9 in the 64th minute; Glenn Cooper went off injured in the 69th minute, being replaced by Stewart Pearl; England Counties were still leading 22-9 with 5 minutes remaining; England Counties scored 19 unanswered points to seal the match)

PUBLIC SCHOOL WANDERERS TOUR TO SRI LANKA 2005

CAPTAIN: *Steve White-Cooper*

16th Jun	SRI LANKAN RFU PRESIDENT'S XV	7	**PUBLIC SCHOOL WANDERERS**	63

Colombo Hockey & Football Club Grounds, Maitland Crescent, Colombo

[*This match kicked off at 5.00pm; Dan Leek was played out of position as a prop; The Sri Lankan RFU President's XV was also billed as Sri Lanka A; Dan Leek was the brother of Matt Leek; Dan Leek toured Canada, New Zealand and Australia with England Schools 18 Group in July-August 2001; Jim Jenner played for Major R.V. Stanley's XV against Oxford University at Iffley Road on 12th November 2003 and played for the Samurai in the Hong Kong Tens at Hong Kong Football Club on 24th-25th March 2004; The Public School Wanderers were scheduled to tour Kenya in June 2008 but the idea was eventually abandoned*]

(*This match was played in extreme heat; The Public School Wanderers forwards monopolised possession; Andrew Harrison scored in the 4th minute!; Simon Granger scored after Richard Smith made a brilliant break; The Public School Wanderers were leading 17-0 midway through the first half; The Public School Wanderers were leading 32-0 at half-time; The referee allowed a water break midway through both the first and second halves; The referee blew for full-time after only 30 minutes of the second half had been played!; Nick Baxter was the top try scorer on the tour*)

TUSKER SAFARI SEVENS

RFU of East Africa Ground, Ngong Road, Nairobi

CAPTAIN: *Ben Harvey*

First Round - Pool 'D'

17th Jun	TANZANIA	5	**PUBLIC SCHOOL WANDERERS**	47

[*This match kicked off at 11.18am*]

17th Jun	Shujaa (*KEN*)	14	**PUBLIC SCHOOL WANDERERS**	10

[*This match kicked off at 3.30pm; Waisale Serevi played for Shujaa in this match*]

(*The Public School Wanderers were losing 14-0 at half-time*)

18th Jun	SWAZILAND	0	**PUBLIC SCHOOL WANDERERS**	40

[*This match kicked off at 10.32am*]

18th Jun	NAMIBIA	7	**PUBLIC SCHOOL WANDERERS**	31

[*This match kicked off at 3.36pm*]

Quarter-Final

19th Jun	Western Province (*SA*)	17	**PUBLIC SCHOOL WANDERERS***	14

[*This match kicked off at 11.48am*]

(*The Public School Wanderers were leading in injury time*)

[Plate Quarter-Final:]

[19th Jun	Bristol University Select	21	**PUBLIC SCHOOL WANDERERS**	19]

[No match notes]

CHURCHILL CUP

Canada

CAPTAIN: *Pat Sanderson*

First Round

19th Jun CANADA 5 **ENGLAND A** 29

Commonwealth Stadium, Edmonton

[*This match kicked off at 3.00pm; Matt Tait unavailable due to injury; Andy Goode's goal-kicking fell below its normal standard in this match after he had trouble with the feel of the Canadian KooGa ball*]

(*This match was played in 75 degree heat; England A were drawing 0-0 midway through the first half when Andy Goode missed a kickable 33 metre penalty goal attempt; England A were still drawing 0-0 in the 24th minute when Paul Sackey scored after James Simpson-Daniel threw a brilliant pass; England A were leading 5-0 in the 31st minute when Sam Vesty scored after Andy Goode put up a brilliant cross-kick; England A were leading 12-0 just before half-time when Andy Goode missed another kickable 44 metre penalty goal attempt; England A were leading 12-0 at half-time; Ugo Monye went off injured at half-time, being replaced by Ayoola Erinle with James Simpson-Daniel then switching from outside centre to right wing to accommodate Erinle; Tom Voyce came on as a replacement for Sam Vesty in the 49th minute; England A were still leading 12-0 in the 53rd minute when Tom Voyce jinked through to score a superb 42 metre try under the posts; Peter Richards came on as a replacement for Andy Gomarsall in the 54th minute; England A were leading 19-0 midway through the second half; England A were still leading 19-0 in the 69th minute when Pat Sanderson wasted a great try-scoring opportunity by attempting to make the line himself instead of using a 3 man overlap outside him; England A were briefly reduced to 13 men with 9 minutes of normal time remaining when Louis Deacon and Andy Goode were both sin-binned in quick succession for fighting!; James Simpson-Daniel played as a fly half in the absence of Andy Goode; James Forrester came on as a replacement for Phil Dowson with 6 minutes of normal time remaining and then played out of position as a centre to ensure that the backline remained at full numerical strength; England A were leading 19-0 with 4 minutes of normal time remaining when James Simpson-Daniel scored a brilliant 40 metre solo try; England A scored 24 unanswered points to win the match; England A were leading 24-0 with 2 minutes of normal time remaining when James Forrester wasted another great try-scoring opportunity by dropping the ball when he was tackled by Kris Witkowski in front of the Canadian line; England A were leading 24-5 in the second minute of injury time; Chris Jones went off injured in the seventh minute of injury time, which reduced England A to 14 men because they had already used up their permitted seven replacements; Andy Goode briefly played as a flanker in the absence of Chris Jones!; England A were leading 24-5 in the tenth minute of injury time when Pat Sanderson scored a superb try with the last move of the match; Phil Dowson, James Simpson-Daniel and Tom Voyce all had a brilliant game*)

Final

26th Jun ARGENTINA A 16 **ENGLAND A** 45

Commonwealth Stadium, Edmonton

[*This match kicked off at 3.10pm; Ugo Monye and Sam Vesty unavailable due to injury*]

(*England A were leading 3-0 in the 9th minute; England A were still leading 3-0 in the 17th minute when James Simpson-Daniel ghosted through to score a brilliant try; England A were leading 13-0 midway through the first half; England A were leading 13-*

6 in the 32nd minute; England A were leading 18-6 just before half-time; England A were leading 21-6 at half-time; England A were leading 21-9 in the 47th minute when Miguel Avramovic scored after a poor tackle by Pat Sanderson, thus 7 points were preventable; James Simpson-Daniel played as a fly half in the absence of Andy Goode, who was sent to the sin-bin in the 51st minute; England A were leading 21-16 in the 56th minute when Peter Richards scored a penalty goal while Andy Goode was in the sin-bin!; Andy Gomarsall came on as a replacement for Peter Richards immediately afterwards; England A were leading 24-16 midway through the second half when Tom Voyce scored after Paul Sackey made a brilliant run; England A were leading 31-16 with 2 minutes of normal time remaining when some superb handling amongst the backs allowed Paul Sackey to score; England A were leading 38-16 in the second minute of injury time when Andy Gomarsall scored in the last move of the match; England A scored 24 unanswered points to clinch the match; Perry Freshwater played brilliantly in the scrums; James Simpson-Daniel had a brilliant game)

WORLD GAMES SEVENS

MSV-Arena, Duisburg

CAPTAIN: *??*

First Round - Pool 'A'

22nd Jul	GERMANY	7	**GREAT BRITAIN**	24

[*This match kicked off at 2.25pm*]

(*Great Britain were leading 7-0 in the early stages; Great Britain were drawing 7-7 just before half-time; Great Britain were leading 12-7 at half-time; Dave Strettle came on as a replacement for Cameron Johnston at the start of the second half; Great Britain scored 17 unanswered points to win the match*)

22nd Jul	JAPAN	7	**GREAT BRITAIN**	26

[*This match kicked off at 4.35pm*]

(*Great Britain were leading 7-0 in the early stages; Great Britain were drawing 7-7 at half-time; Great Britain were leading 19-7 at one point in the second half; Great Britain were still leading 19-7 when the full-time hooter sounded, but the ball was still in play and Andrew Turnbull was able to score a try which Rory Lawson then converted with the last kick of the match to seal the game*)

22nd Jul	FIJI	33	**GREAT BRITAIN**	17

[*This match kicked off at 6.30pm*]

(*Great Britain were losing 21-0 at one point in the first half; Fiji were allowed to score 21 unanswered points to win the match; Great Britain were still losing 21-0 just before half-time; Great Britain were losing 21-5 at half-time; Great Britain were still losing 21-5 early in the second half and pressing in attack when Fiji scored an interception try, thus 7 points were preventable; Dave Strettle went off injured in this match, being replaced by Cameron Johnston; Great Britain were losing 28-17 at one point in the second half*)

Semi-Final

23rd July	SOUTH AFRICA	52	**GREAT BRITAIN**	0

[*This match kicked off at 3.30pm; Dave Strettle unavailable due to injury*]

(*The Great Britain players could not win any possession; James Mathias was sin-binned at the start of the second half!*)

Third Place Play-Off

23rd July ARGENTINA 22 **GREAT BRITAIN** 10

[This match kicked off at 5.45pm; Dave Strettle unavailable due to injury; Great Britain were not invited to take part in the 2009 World Games Sevens at Kaohsiung on 24th-25th July 2009]

(Great Britain were losing 7-0 in the early stages; Great Britain were losing 7-5 at one point in the first half; Great Britain were losing 12-5 when Ali Warnock fly-hacked a loose ball down the touchline and followed up to score a brilliant try; Great Britain were losing 12-10 in the closing stages)

LLOYDS TSB CWMTAWE SEVENS

Pontardawe RFC, Parc Ynysderw, Ynysderw Road, Pontardawe, Swansea

CAPTAIN: *??*

First Round - Pool 'A'

6th Aug Gorseinion (*WA*) 0 **SAMURAI** 38

[No match notes]

6th Aug Bath Bandits 7 **SAMURAI** 24

[The Bath Bandits were an invitational team consisting of current and former players from Bath University]

6th Aug Llangennech (*WA*) 5 **SAMURAI** 41

[No match notes]

Quarter-Final

6th Aug Neath (*WA*) 10 **SAMURAI** 17

[No match notes]

Semi-Final

6th Aug Welsh Wizards 19 **SAMURAI*** 12

(Dave Strettle scored a brilliant try in this match; The Samurai were leading 12-5 at one point in this match)

AUSTRALIAN TOUR TO FRANCE, ENGLAND, IRELAND AND WALES 2005

CAPTAIN: *Martin Corry*

12th Nov **ENGLAND** 26 AUSTRALIA 16

Twickenham

[This match kicked off at 2.30pm; Tom Palmer (2), Alex Brown, Joe Worsley, Jonny Wilkinson and Iain Balshaw all unavailable due to injury; Julian White unavailable after a RFU hearing on 18th October 2005 found him guilty of striking an opponent in a Guinness Premiership match on 14th October 2005 and thus banned him for 8 weeks; Simon Shaw in original training squad of 30 but withdrew due to injury; Perry Freshwater, Andy Hazell, James Forrester, Peter Richards, Andy Goode, Ollie Smith (2) and Tom Voyce all in original training squad of 30 but were not selected for team or bench; Mark Van Gisbergen qualified to play for England on 1st September 2005 after completing a residency period of 3 years]

(Mark Van Gisbergen came on as a temporary blood replacement for Mark Cueto in the 2nd minute, with Josh Lewsey then switching from full back to wing to accommodate Van Gisbergen!; Mat Rogers scored a penalty goal in the 3rd minute!; England were losing 3-0 in the 7th minute when Charlie Hodgson saved a certain try by tackling Drew Mitchell; England were losing 6-3 midway through the first half; England were still losing 6-3 in the 28th minute when some superb handling amongst the backs

allowed Ben Cohen to score; England were leading 10-6 shortly before half-time when Charlie Hodgson missed a kickable 39 metre penalty goal attempt; England were leading 10-6 at half-time; England were still leading 10-6 in the 41st minute when Charlie Hodgson scored a brilliant 26 metre drop goal; England were leading 16-9 in the 55th minute when a lineout overthrow by Steve Thompson (2) led directly to a try by Drew Mitchell, thus 7 points were preventable; Charlie Hodgson went off injured in the 57th minute, being replaced by Olly Barkley; England were drawing 16-16 midway through the second half when Olly Barkley scored a superb 50 metre penalty goal; The referee had to order uncontested scrums in the 70th minute after Matt Dunning went off injured; England were leading 19-16 with 8 minutes of normal time remaining when Olly Barkley missed another kickable 34 metre penalty goal attempt; England were still leading 19-16 with 5 minutes of normal time remaining when Mark Cueto powered through to score a try which Olly Barkley then brilliantly converted from the left touchline to clinch the match; Andy Sheridan played brilliantly in the scrums)

ATKINS REMEMBRANCE RUGBY MATCH

CAPTAIN: *Bobby Skinstad* (SA)

15th Nov COMBINED SERVICES (*SER*) 6 **BARBARIANS** 45

Newbury RFC, Monks Lane, Newbury

[This match kicked off at 7.30pm; Tom Beim selected but withdrew due to injury, being replaced by Marcel Garvey who then himself withdrew and was replaced by Kenny Bingham; The Barbarians named a 6 man bench selection; Chris Budgen, Ben Hughes, Andrew Smith, Matt Cornish, Apolosi Satala, Mal Roberts and Tim Barlow played for the Combined Services in this match, with Matt Cornish captaining the side and Mal Roberts scoring 2 penalty goals; Nick Baxter retired in April 2007]

(The Barbarians front row dominated the scrums in this match; The Barbarians were drawing 0-0 in the 12th minute when Bobby Skinstad scored after Chris Malherbe made a brilliant break; The Barbarians were leading 12-0 in the 15th minute; The Barbarians were still leading 12-0 midway through the first half; The Barbarians were leading 12-3 at half-time; The Barbarians were leading 12-6 in the 44th minute; The Barbarians were still leading 12-6 when Gonçalo Malheiro scored after Richard McCarter made a brilliant break; The Barbarians were leading 26-6 in the 65th minute; The Barbarians were leading 33-6 in the closing stages when Kenny Bingham scored a superb try; The Barbarians scored 33 unanswered points to clinch the match; Craig Hammond had a brilliant game)

NEW ZEALAND TOUR TO WALES, IRELAND, ENGLAND AND SCOTLAND 2005

CAPTAIN: *Martin Corry*

19th Nov **ENGLAND*** 19 NEW ZEALAND 23

Twickenham

[This match kicked off at 2.30pm; Tom Palmer (2) and Jonny Wilkinson unavailable due to injury; Julian White unavailable due to suspension; Perry Freshwater, Simon Shaw, Andy Hazell, James Forrester, Peter Richards, Andy Goode, Ollie Smith (2) and Tom Voyce all in original training squad of 30 but were not selected for team or bench]

(This match was played in cold conditions; Martin Corry scored from a rolling maul in the 3rd minute!; England were leading 7-0 in the 16th minute when Tana Umaga scored a try which should not have been given because the scoring pass from Dan Carter was clearly forward, thus 7 points were unlawful; England were drawing 10-10 midway

***through the first half; England were losing 13-10 in the 30th minute; England were still losing 13-10 in the 34th minute when Charlie Hodgson missed an eminently kickable 28 metre penalty goal attempt; England were losing 13-10 at half-time; England were losing 20-10 in the 45th minute; England were losing 23-13 in the 53rd minute; England were still losing 23-13 midway through the second half; England were losing 23-13 in the 63rd minute when Charlie Hodgson scored a brilliant 48 metre penalty goal; England were losing 23-19 in the 67th minute; Matt Stevens came on as a replacement for Andy Sheridan with 6 minutes of normal time remaining; England were still losing 23-19 in the first minute of injury time when Charlie Hodgson decided not to try a cross-kick towards Mark Cueto on the right touchline and instead moved the ball down his backline to Ben Cohen, who was then tackled into touch in the last move of the match*)**

SAMOAN TOUR TO SCOTLAND AND ENGLAND 2005

CAPTAIN: *Martin Corry*

26th Nov **ENGLAND** 40 SAMOA 3
Twickenham

[*This match kicked off at 2.30pm; Jonny Wilkinson unavailable due to injury; Julian White unavailable due to suspension; Matt Dawson selected for bench but withdrew due to injury, being replaced by Peter Richards; Phil Vickery, Danny Grewcock, Andy Hazell, Chris Jones, Ben Cohen, Jamie Noon and Mark Van Gisbergen all in original training squad of 30 but were not selected for team or bench*]

(Lewis Moody was sent off in the 77th minute for fighting Alesana Tuilagi and thus duly banned for 9 weeks)

(*This match was played in cold conditions on a wet pitch; England were leading 3-0 in the 8th minute; England were drawing 3-3 in the 16th minute when Charlie Hodgson scored a brilliant 49 metre penalty goal; England were leading 6-3 midway through the first half; Andy Sheridan went off injured in the 21st minute, being replaced by Perry Freshwater; England were still leading 6-3 in the 24th minute when some superb handling allowed Tom Voyce to score; England were leading 13-3 in the 31st minute when Mark Cueto crossed the tryline but then lost the ball in the act of scoring; England were still leading 13-3 shortly before half-time; England were leading 16-3 at half-time; James Simpson-Daniel went off injured at half-time, being replaced by Olly Barkley with Mike Tindall then switching from inside to outside centre to accommodate Barkley; England were leading 23-3 in the 53rd minute; England were still leading 23-3 midway through the second half; Tom Varndell came on as a replacement for Josh Lewsey in the 61st minute, with Tom Voyce then moving from wing to full back to accommodate Varndell; England were leading 28-3 in the 70th minute when Harry Ellis scored a brilliant 24 metre solo try; James Forrester came on as a replacement for Martin Corry with 9 minutes remaining; Immediately afterwards Eliota Fuimaono-Sapolu famously used a volleyed kick for a restart!; England were leading 35-3 with 1 minute remaining when Tom Varndell scored with his second ever touch in cap international rugby!; England scored 37 unanswered points to win the match; Charlie Hodgson played brilliantly and scored 20 points in this match*)

EMIRATES AIRLINE DUBAI RUGBY SEVENS

Dubai Exiles Stadium, Dubai

CAPTAIN: *Simon Amor*

First Round - Pool 'C'

1st Dec KENYA 7 **ENGLAND** 52

[This match kicked off at 11.52am]

(This match was played in 90 degree heat; Tom Varndell scored in the 1st minute!; Tom Varndell scored another try straight after the restart!; England were leading 26-7 at half-time; Matt Tait came on as a replacement for Tom Varndell in the second half; England scored 26 unanswered points in the second half to seal the match)

CAPTAIN: *Ben Gollings*

1st Dec UGANDA 0 **ENGLAND** 48

[This match kicked off at 4.38pm]

(This match was played in 90 degree heat; Jonny Hylton scored in the 1st minute!; England were leading 17-0 at half-time; England were still leading 17-0 when Tom Varndell managed to pass the ball after his shirt had been pulled over his head and Andy Vilk went on to score!)

CAPTAIN: *Simon Amor*

1st Dec AUSTRALIA 5 **ENGLAND** 33

[This match kicked off at 7.56pm]

(This match was played in 90 degree heat; England were losing 5-0 in the early stages; England were leading 7-5 just before half-time; England were leading 14-5 at half-time; England were still leading 14-5 early in the second half when Simon Amor scored after Tom Varndell made a brilliant blindside break; Ben Foden scored a brilliant try in the second half; England scored 33 unanswered points to clinch the match)

Quarter-Final

2nd Dec ARGENTINA 12 **ENGLAND** 24

[This match kicked off at 11.52am]

(This match was played in 90 degree heat; England were losing 7-0 at one point in the first half; England were leading 12-7 at half-time; England were drawing 12-12 early in the second half; Matt Tait came on a replacement for Tom Varndell in the second half; Simon Amor had a brilliant game)

Semi-Final

2nd Dec SAMOA 5 **ENGLAND** 7

[This match kicked off at 6.42pm]

(This match was played in 90 degree heat; England were drawing 0-0 midway through the first half; England were drawing 0-0 at half-time; England were losing 5-0 in the 8th minute; England were still losing 5-0 midway through the second half; England were losing 5-0 with 2 minutes remaining when Andy Vilk crossed the tryline but the move was disallowed as he was adjudged to have put a foot into touch; England were still losing 5-0 in the final minute when Tom Varndell scored a try which Simon Amor then converted with the last kick of the match to win the game)

Final

2nd Dec FIJI 26 **ENGLAND** 28

[This match kicked off at 8.34pm; England wore navy blue shirts for this match]

(This match was played in 90 degree heat; England were losing 7-0 in the early stages; England were still losing 7-0 when Tom Varndell scored a brilliant 70 metre solo try; England were losing 12-7 when Ben Gollings powered through 2 attempted tackles to

score; England were leading 14-12 at half-time; England were leading 21-12 early in the second half; England were leading 21-19 midway through the second half; England were still leading 21-19 with 2 minutes remaining; England were leading 28-19 in the last minute; Tom Varndell scored 10 tries in the competition; Ben Gollings increased his IRB World Sevens record to 1277 points in this tournament)

EMIRATES AIRLINE SOUTH AFRICA SEVENS

Outeniqua Park Stadium, George

CAPTAIN: *Ben Gollings*

First Round - Pool 'C'

9th Dec CANADA 0 **ENGLAND** 40

[This match kicked off at 1.20pm]

(Jonny Hylton scored in the 2nd minute!; England were leading 12-0 midway through the first half; England were leading 19-0 just before half-time; England were leading 26-0 at half-time; Dan Luger came on as a replacement for Will Matthews in the 10th minute; England were leading 33-0 midway through the second half; England were still leading 33-0 with 1 minute remaining; Ben Gollings scored 20 points in this match)

CAPTAIN: *Simon Amor*

9th Dec PORTUGAL 0 **ENGLAND** 36

[This match kicked off at 4.26pm]

(Ben Gollings scored in the 3rd minute!; England were leading 7-0 midway through the first half; England were leading 12-0 just before half-time; Ben Gollings scored his 1300th IRB World Sevens point in the first half; England were leading 19-0 at half-time; Ben Foden came on as a replacement for Ben Gollings at the start of the second half; England were leading 24-0 in the 10th minute; England were still leading 24-0 midway through the second half; England were leading 24-0 with 2 minutes remaining)

9th Dec SAMOA 21 **ENGLAND** 22

[This match kicked off at 8.16pm]

(Nils Mordt scored in the 2nd minute!; England were leading 7-0 midway through the first half; England were drawing 7-7 just before half-time; England were leading 12-7 at half-time; England were losing 14-12 in the 10th minute; England were losing 21-12 midway through the second half; England were still losing 21-12 with 1 minute remaining; England were losing 21-19 in the final minute when Simon Amor scored a penalty goal with the last kick of the match to win the game)

Quarter-Final

10th Dec FRANCE 5 **ENGLAND** 26

[This match kicked off at 12.50pm]

(Andy Vilk scored a brilliant 60 metre solo try in the 3rd minute!; England were leading 12-0 midway through the first half; England were still leading 12-0 just before half-time; England were leading 12-5 at half-time; England were leading 19-5 midway through the second half; England were still leading 19-5 in the final minute; England scored 14 unanswered points to clinch the match)

Semi-Final

10th Dec FIJI 28 **ENGLAND** 22

[This match kicked off at 4.43pm]

(Ben Gollings scored in the 2nd minute which enabled him to beat Santiago Gómez Cora's existing IRB World Sevens record of 121 tries!; England were leading 5-0 midway through the first half; England were losing 7-5 shortly before half-time; Fiji were allowed to score 14 unanswered points to win the match; England were losing

***14-5 at half-time; England were still losing 14-5 in the 9th minute when Matt Tait scored a brilliant long-range solo try; England were losing 21-10 midway through the second half; England were losing 28-15 in the last minute when Luke Narraway scored a consolation try; Ben Gollings increased his IRB World Sevens record to 1322 points in this tournament*)**

2006
AXA NEW ZEALAND INTERNATIONAL SEVENS

WestpacTrust Stadium, Wellington

CAPTAIN: *Simon Amor*

First Round - Pool 'A'

3rd Feb SCOTLAND 5 **ENGLAND** 12

[*This match kicked off at 2.28pm*]

(*The England players could not win any possession; England were losing 5-0 in the early stages; England were drawing 5-5 at half-time; England were still drawing 5-5 midway through the second half; England were drawing 5-5 in the closing stages when Henry Paul scored after he wrong-footed the Scottish defence with a brilliant sidestep*)

CAPTAIN: *Ben Gollings*

3rd Feb PAPUA NEW GUINEA 0 **ENGLAND** 64

[*This match kicked off at 5.24pm*]

(*England monopolised possession in this match; Dave Strettle scored in the 1st minute!; Dave Strettle scored 5 tries in the first half!; England were leading 38-0 at half-time; Dave Strettle set a new IRB World Sevens record by scoring 5 tries in his first ever match!*)

CAPTAIN: *Simon Amor*

3rd Feb AUSTRALIA 7 **ENGLAND** 19

[*This match kicked off at 9.34pm*]

(*This match was played in wet conditions; England were drawing 0-0 in the early stages when Matt Tait scored a brilliant try; England were losing 7-5 at half-time; England were leading 12-7 in the 8th minute; England were still leading 12-7 midway through the second half; England were leading 12-7 in the last minute when Ben Gollings scored to clinch the match*)

Quarter-Final

4th Feb FRANCE 19 **ENGLAND*** 14

[*This match kicked off at 2.33pm*]

(*The England players could not win any possession; Jérôme Naves scored in the 3rd minute!; England were losing 5-0 when Matt Tait scored after Henry Paul threw a brilliant reverse pass; England were losing 12-7 at half-time; England were still losing 12-7 early in the second half when collectively poor tackling allowed Julien Patey to score, thus 7 points were preventable; England were losing 19-7 with 2 minutes remaining when Dave Strettle scored a brilliant 60 metre solo try*)

[Plate Semi-Final:]

[4th Feb SAMOA 17 **ENGLAND** 21]

[*This match kicked off at 5.38pm*]

(*England were leading 7-0 in the early stages; England were leading 7-5 when Nils Mordt scored a brilliant solo try under the posts; England were leading 14-5 at half-time; England were leading 14-10 when Luke Narraway scored after Danny Care made a brilliant break*)

[Plate Final:]

[4th Feb ARGENTINA 10 **ENGLAND** 14]

[*This match kicked off at 8.30pm*]

(*England were leading 7-0 in the early stages; Matt Tait powered through to score a try which Simon Amor then converted to give England a 14-0 lead shortly afterwards; England scored 14 unanswered points to win the match; England were leading 14-5 at

half-time; England were leading 14-10 in the last minute when Dave Strettle had a great try-scoring chance but was tackled just short of the Argentine line; Ben Gollings increased his IRB World Sevens record to 1343 points in this tournament)

6 NATIONS CHAMPIONSHIP

CAPTAIN: *Martin Corry*

4th Feb **ENGLAND** 47 WALES 13

Twickenham

[This match kicked off at 3.30pm; Phil Vickery, George Chuter, Pat Sanderson, Jonny Wilkinson, Olly Barkley and Mark Van Gisbergen all unavailable due to injury; Alex Brown, Chris Jones, James Forrester, Peter Richards and James Simpson-Daniel all in original training squad of 27 but were not selected for team or bench]

(This match was played in cold conditions; Lawrence Dallaglio came on as a temporary blood replacement for Joe Worsley in the 7th minute; England were drawing 0-0 in the 14th minute when Mark Cueto scored after Jamie Noon made a brilliant run; England were leading 7-3 midway through the first half; Josh Lewsey went off injured in the 21st minute, being replaced by Tom Voyce; England were leading 10-3 in the 30th minute when Lewis Moody scored from a rolling maul; England were leading 15-3 in the 34th minute when a poor defensive alignment allowed Martyn Williams to score, thus 7 points were preventable; England were leading 15-10 at half-time; England were leading 18-10 in the 51st minute when Mike Tindall wasted a great try-scoring opportunity by mistiming his pass while there was a 2 man overlap outside him; England were leading 21-13 midway through the second half when Charlie Hodgson missed a kickable 39 metre penalty goal attempt; England were leading 26-13 in the 63rd minute; Lawrence Dallaglio came on as a replacement for Martin Corry in the 64th minute; England were still leading 26-13 with 9 minutes of normal time remaining when Lawrence Dallaglio broke from the base of a scrum to score; Matt Dawson came on as a replacement for Harry Ellis with 7 minutes of normal time remaining; England were leading 33-13 with 5 minutes of normal time remaining when Matt Dawson was awarded a try which should not have been given because he clearly knocked the ball forward out of Michael Owen's hands and then regathered it!; England scored 29 unanswered points to clinch the match; Matt Stevens had a brilliant game)

11th Feb ITALY 16 **ENGLAND** 31

Stadio Flaminio, Rome

[This match kicked off at 5.00pm; Phil Vickery, Pat Sanderson, Jonny Wilkinson, Olly Barkley and Josh Lewsey all unavailable due to injury; Perry Freshwater, George Chuter, Alex Brown, Chris Jones, Magnus Lund, James Forrester, Shaun Perry, Stuart Abbott and Tom Varndell all in original training squad of 31 but were not selected for team or bench]

(England were drawing 0-0 in the 16th minute when Mark Cueto wasted a great try-scoring opportunity by electing to take the ball into contact instead of using an overlap outside him; England were still drawing 0-0 midway through the first half when Martin Corry crossed the line and claimed to have scored, but the referee was unsighted and the video referee could not award the try because it was unclear whether the ball had indeed been grounded; England were leading 7-0 in the 26th minute; England were leading 7-3 in the 33rd minute; England were leading 7-6 shortly before half-time when Charlie Hodgson missed a 21 metre drop goal attempt from in front of the posts!; England were leading 7-6 at half-time; England were losing 9-7 in

the 42nd minute; England were leading 10-9 in the 50th minute; Matt Dawson came on as a replacement for Harry Ellis in the 55th minute; England were leading 17-9 midway through the second half; England were still leading 17-9 in the 64th minute when Charlie Hodgson hit the left-hand post with a speculative 50 metre penalty goal attempt; England were leading 22-9 in the 66th minute when Charlie Hodgson scored a brilliant conversion from the right touchline; England scored 17 unanswered points to win the match; England were leading 24-9 with 2 minutes of normal time remaining when collectively poor tackling allowed Mirco Bergamasco to score, thus 7 points were preventable; England were leading 24-16 in the third minute of injury time when James Simpson-Daniel gathered a loose ball and scored in the last move of the match)

CAPTAIN: *Martin Corry* [*Mike Tindall*]

25th Feb SCOTLAND 18 **ENGLAND*** 12

Murrayfield

[This match kicked off at 5.30pm; Phil Vickery, Matt Stevens, Pat Sanderson, Jonny Wilkinson and Olly Barkley all unavailable due to injury; Stuart Abbott in original training squad of 31 but withdrew due to injury; Jon Clarke was added to the squad on 20th February 2006]

(This match was played in wet and windy conditions; Chris Paterson scored a penalty goal in the 3rd minute!; England were drawing 3-3 in the 10th minute when Charlie Hodgson chipped ahead towards the corner and was then body-checked by Hugo Southwell as he attempted to follow up, but the referee unaccountably ignored this infringement and awarded Scotland a 22 drop-out after the ball went into touch in-goal; England were still drawing 3-3 midway through the first half; England were drawing 3-3 in the 28th minute when Charlie Hodgson missed a kickable 43 metre penalty goal attempt; England were still drawing 3-3 in the 29th minute when Charlie Hodgson wasted a great try-scoring opportunity by electing to take the ball into contact instead of using an overlap outside him; England were drawing 3-3 shortly before half-time when Martin Corry wasted the chance of a pushover try by losing control at the base of a scrum as the Scottish forwards were being driven backwards over their own line, with Ben Cohen then wasting another great try-scoring opportunity immediately afterwards by dropping the ball in front of the Scottish line; England were drawing 3-3 at half-time; England were losing 9-6 in the 48th minute; Matt Dawson came on as a temporary blood replacement for Harry Ellis in the 51st minute; England were losing 12-6 midway through the second half; England were losing 12-9 in the 62nd minute; The England captain Martin Corry was inexplicably substituted in the 64th minute, being replaced by Lawrence Dallaglio; England were still losing 12-9 with 8 minutes of normal time remaining; England were losing 15-12 with 2 minutes of normal time remaining)

CAPTAIN: *Martin Corry*

12th Mar FRANCE 31 **ENGLAND** 6

Stade de France, Paris

[This match kicked off at 4.00pm; Phil Vickery, Pat Sanderson, Jonny Wilkinson and Olly Barkley all unavailable due to injury]

(This match was played in cold conditions; Steve Thompson (2), Matt Dawson and Mike Tindall were unaccountably allowed to play with an illness and consequently had poor games; Florian Fritz scored after just 41 seconds had been played when a lack of communication between Jamie Noon and Josh Lewsey saw them both attempting to deal with Frédéric Michalak's garryowen, which resulted in the ball bouncing into the hands of Damien Traille!; England were losing 10-0 in the 7th minute; England were

losing 13-0 in the 12th minute; England were still losing 13-0 midway through the first half; England were losing 13-0 in the 27th minute when Mark Cueto wasted a great try-scoring opportunity by electing to take the ball into contact instead of using an overlap outside him; England were still losing 13-0 in the 29th minute when Charlie Hodgson hit the right-hand post with an eminently kickable 22 metre penalty goal attempt; England were losing 16-0 in the 33rd minute; France were allowed to score 16 unanswered points to win the match; England were still losing 16-0 shortly before half-time; England were losing 16-3 at half-time; Charlie Hodgson went off injured at half-time, being replaced by Andy Goode; England were losing 16-6 in the 43rd minute; England were still losing 16-6 midway through the second half; England were losing 16-6 in the 67th minute when Damien Traille kicked ahead and then followed up and scored after Harry Ellis failed to fall properly on the ensuing loose ball; England were losing 24-6 with 8 minutes remaining; England were still losing 24-6 with 1 minute remaining when Andy Goode had his pass intercepted by Christophe Dominici who then ran 25 metres to score under the posts, thus 3 tries and 19 points were preventable; This was England's heaviest defeat against France since 1972!)

18th Mar	**ENGLAND***	24	IRELAND	28

Twickenham

[This match kicked off at 5.30pm; Phil Vickery, Pat Sanderson, Jonny Wilkinson and Olly Barkley all unavailable due to injury; Matt Stevens selected but withdrew due to injury, Julian White was moved from the bench to the team and Perry Freshwater was then selected for the bench; Steve Thompson (2) retired due to injury in April 2007 but then changed his mind in October 2007; Matt Dawson retired in May 2006]

(This match was played in cold conditions; Jamie Noon powered through to score a try after just 74 seconds had been played!; England were leading 5-0 in the 7th minute when Brian O'Driscoll put in a grubber kick, Ben Cohen slipped as he attempted to gather the ball and Shane Horgan was able to follow up and score a try that should not have been given because the ball clearly hit the touchline as he fly-hacked it on; England were losing 8-5 midway through the first half when Andy Goode missed a kickable 39 metre penalty goal attempt; England were still losing 8-5 in the 22nd minute when Andy Goode missed an eminently kickable 29 metre penalty goal attempt; England were losing 11-5 in the 33rd minute; England were losing 11-8 at half-time; England played into a strong wind in the second half; England were losing 14-8 in the 43rd minute; Ireland were losing 18-14 in the 57th minute when Ben Cohen was wrongly adjudged to have been on the field of play when he threw the ball in for a quick lineout, with Denis Leamy then scoring directly from the new England lineout ordered by the referee, thus 2 tries and 12 points were unlawful; England were losing 21-18 midway through the second half; Matt Dawson came on as a replacement for Harry Ellis in the 67th minute; England were still losing 21-18 in the 69th minute when Andy Goode scored a brilliant 46 metre penalty goal to bring the scores level; England were drawing 21-21 with 5 minutes of normal time remaining when Andy Goode scored another brilliant 27 metre penalty goal from a difficult angle; England were leading 24-21 with 2 minutes of normal time remaining when Ronan O'Gara put in a chip-kick and Ben Cohen was deceived by the bounce of the ball, which enabled Brian O'Driscoll to instigate a counter-attack that culminated in a try by Shane Horgan which O'Gara then converted to clinch the match and the Triple Crown for Ireland, thus 7 points were preventable)

U21 6 NATIONS CHAMPIONSHIP

CAPTAIN: *Matt Cornwell*

3rd Feb **ENGLAND U21** 26 WALES U21 18

Worcester RFC, Sixways Stadium, Pershore Lane, Hindip, Worcester

[*This match kicked off at 8.05pm; Toby Flood and Nick Abendanon unavailable due to injury; Alex Rogers and Thom Evans in original training squad of 24 but were not selected for team or bench; Chris Brooker and Ryan Lamb played for England in the U19 World Championship in South Africa in April 2005; Michael Hills and Mark Lambert played for England in the U19 World Championship in South Africa in March-April 2004; Jordan Crane captained England in the U19 World Championship in South Africa in April 2005; Anthony Allen played for England in the U19 World Championship in South Africa in March-April 2004, captained the England team that reached the Final of the Commonwealth Youth Games Rugby Sevens at Bendigo, Victoria on 2nd-3rd December 2004 and played for England in the U19 World Championship in South Africa in April 2005; James Hook played for Wales U21 in this match*]

(*This match was played in extremely cold conditions; England U21 were leading 3-0 in the 10th minute; England U21 were leading 6-5 midway through the first half; England U21 were still leading 6-5 in the 26th minute when Ryan Lamb missed a speculative 49 metre penalty goal attempt; England U21 were leading 6-5 in the 38th minute when Olly Morgan scored after Ryan Lamb put in a brilliant chip-kick; England U21 were leading 13-5 at half-time; England U21 were leading 16-5 in the 51st minute; England U21 were leading 16-11 midway through the second half; England U21 were still leading 16-11 in the 67th minute when Ryan Lamb missed an eminently kickable 28 metre penalty goal attempt; England U21 were leading 16-11 in the 68th minute when Mike Brown scored after Tom Croft threw a brilliant one-handed pass; England U21 were leading 21-18 with 8 minutes of normal time remaining; Olly Morgan went off injured with 2 minutes of normal time remaining, being replaced by Shane Geraghty; England U21 were still leading 21-18 in the sixth minute of injury time when Jordan Crane scored with the last move of the match to clinch the game*)

9th Feb ITALY U21 3 **ENGLAND U21** 48

Stadio Alessandro Lamarmora, Biella

[*This match kicked off at 8.00pm; Toby Flood, Nick Abendanon and Olly Morgan unavailable due to injury*]

(*Topsy Ojo scored in the 4th minute!; England U21 were leading 10-0 in the 9th minute; England U21 were still leading 10-0 midway through the first half; England U21 were leading 17-0 in the 32nd minute when Topsy Ojo intercepted the ball and scored to complete a hat-trick of tries; England U21 were leading 24-0 shortly before half-time; England U21 were leading 24-3 at half-time; England U21 were leading 31-3 in the 44th minute; England U21 were leading 36-3 in the 50th minute; England U21 were still leading 36-3 midway through the second half; England U21 were leading 48-3 in the 70th minute; England U21 scored 24 unanswered points in the second half to seal the match; Topsy Ojo scored 20 points in this match*)

24th Feb SCOTLAND U21 22 **ENGLAND U21** 49

Falkirk Stadium

[*This match kicked off at 7.30pm; Shane Geraghty unavailable due to injury; Chris Brooker in original training squad of 23 but withdrew due to injury; Alex Rogers played for England in the U19 World Championship in South Africa in April 2005; Nick Abendanon played for England in the U19 World Championship in South Africa in April*

2005 and played for Samurai St George in the Dubai International Invitation Rugby Sevens on 30th November-2nd December 2005]
(This match was played in cold conditions; England U21 played into a strong wind in the first half; England U21 were drawing 0-0 in the 7th minute when Ben Foden scored after Mike Brown made a brilliant 70 metre break; England U21 were losing 10-7 midway through the first half; England U21 were drawing 10-10 in the 23rd minute; England U21 were losing 15-10 in the 25th minute; England U21 were still losing 15-10 just before half-time; England U21 were leading 17-15 at half-time; England U21 were leading 20-15 in the 43rd minute; England U21 were leading 27-15 in the 48th minute; England U21 were leading 34-22 in the 53rd minute; England U21 were leading 37-22 midway through the second half; England U21 were leading 44-22 shortly afterwards when Ben Foden scored after Topsy Ojo made a brilliant break; England U21 scored 22 unanswered points to clinch the match; England U21 were leading 49-22 in the 70th minute)

11th Mar FRANCE U21 17 **ENGLAND U21** 30
Stade Municipal, Périgueux
[This match kicked off at 5.30pm; Chris Robshaw unavailable due to injury; Alex Rae played for England in the U19 World Championship in South Africa in April 2005]
(England U21 played with the wind in the first half; Toby Flood scored a penalty goal in the 4th minute!; England U21 were leading 10-0 in the 10th minute; England U21 were leading 13-7 midway through the first half; England U21 were leading 20-7 in the 35th minute; Sean Cox came on as a temporary blood replacement for Jordan Crane in the 36th minute; England U21 were leading 23-7 at half-time; England U21 were leading 23-14 in the 43rd minute; England U21 were still leading 23-14 midway through the second half; Toby Flood went off injured in the 61st minute, being replaced by Ryan Lamb; England U21 were leading 30-14 in the 62nd minute; England U21 were leading 30-17 in the 67th minute)

17th Mar **ENGLAND U21** 40 IRELAND U21 5
Worcester RFC, Sixways Stadium, Pershore Lane, Hindip, Worcester
[This match kicked off at 8.00pm; Thom Evans played for Scotland A in November 2006, played for Scotland 7s in February 2007 and was capped for Scotland in June 2008]
(This match was played in cold and windy conditions; Toby Flood scored a penalty goal in the 1st minute!; England U21 were leading 6-0 in the 5th minute; England U21 were still leading 6-0 midway through the first half when James Haskell scored after Anthony Allen made a brilliant break; England U21 were leading 14-0 in the 34th minute; England U21 were leading 21-0 at half-time; England U21 were still leading 21-0 in the 42nd minute when Nick Abendanon scored a superb solo try; England U21 were leading 33-0 in the 48th minute; England U21 were still leading 33-0 in the 57th minute when Nick Abendanon scored another try after James Haskell made a brilliant break; England U21 were leading 40-0 midway through the second half; England U21 scored 40 unanswered points to win the match and the Grand Slam; England U21 were leading 40-5 in the 62nd minute; David Wilson (2) injured playing in the match)

'A' INTERNATIONAL MATCHES

CAPTAIN: *Perry Freshwater*

3rd Feb ITALY A 13 **ENGLAND A** 57
Stadio Maurizio Natali, Colleferro
[This match kicked off at 6.30pm; Andy Beattie, Tom Rees and Chris Bell unavailable due to injury; Michael Lipman selected but withdrew due to injury, Hugh Vyvyan was

moved from the bench to the team and James Forrester was then selected for the bench; Tim Payne and Nick Wood in original training squad of 27 but were not selected for team or bench; Shane Drahm played for the Australian Barbarians in June 1998 (at a time when they were officially recognised as Australia's A team), played for Australia U21 in the SANZAR/UAR U21 Tournament in July 1998 and played for Australia 7s in the Dubai Rugby Sevens at Dubai in December 1999, but then qualified to play for England in August 2004 after completing a residency period of 3 years]

(This match took place on a very poor playing surface; Luciano Orquera scored a penalty goal in the 3rd minute!; England A were losing 3-0 in the 15th minute when Stuart Abbott scored after Shane Drahm put in a brilliant chip-kick; England A were leading 7-6 midway through the first half; England A were still leading 7-6 shortly before half-time; England A were leading 10-6 at half-time; England A were losing 13-10 in the 46th minute when Tom Varndell scored two tries in 3 minutes; England A were leading 22-13 midway through the second half when Hugh Vyvyan scored from a rolling maul; England A were leading 36-13 with 7 minutes remaining; England A were leading 43-13 with 5 minutes remaining when Tom Varndell brilliantly chipped over the last defender and regathered the descending ball to score his fourth try; England A were leading 50-13 in the last minute; England A scored 47 unanswered points to win the match; Tom Varndell scored 20 points in this match)

CAPTAIN: *Shaun Perry* [*Nick Walshe*]

17th Mar **ENGLAND A** 18 IRELAND A 33

Kingsholm, Gloucester

[This match kicked off at 7.45pm; This was the last ever England A international match; Alex Brown, Peter Richards and James Simpson-Daniel unavailable due to injury; Duncan Bell and Hugh Vyvyan in original training squad but were not selected for team or bench]

(This match was played in extremely cold conditions; England A were drawing 0-0 in the 12th minute when Mark Van Gisbergen created an overlap but then wasted this great try-scoring opportunity by throwing a poor pass to the unmarked Paul Sackey; England A were leading 3-0 in the 15th minute when some superb handling allowed Paul Sackey to score; England A were leading 8-3 midway through the first half; England A were leading 8-6 in the 25th minute; England A were losing 11-8 in the 36th minute; Ollie Smith (2) went off injured in the 38th minute, being replaced by Delon Armitage with Chris Bell then switching from wing to centre to accommodate Delon Armitage; England A were drawing 11-11 just before half-time; England A were losing 18-11 at half-time; England A played with a strong wind in the second half; England A were still losing 18-11 in the 49th minute when Jon Clarke wasted another great try-scoring opportunity by dropping the ball when there was an overlap outside him; England A were losing 18-11 in the 50th minute when Shane Drahm missed a kickable 43 metre penalty goal attempt; England A were still losing 18-11 in the 55th minute when Jeremy Staunton missed a penalty goal attempt into the wind, but Mark Van Gisbergen then unaccountably allowed the ball to bounce which enabled Kieran Lewis to follow up and score, thus 7 points were preventable; Ireland A were allowed to score 14 unanswered points to win the match; England A were losing 25-11 midway through the second half when Michael Lipman powered through 2 attempted tackles to score; Dan Ward-Smith came on as a replacement for Tom Palmer (2) in the 60th minute, with Chris Jones then moving from number 8 to lock to accommodate Ward-Smith; England A were losing 28-18 in the 62nd minute; England A were losing 33-18 with 9 minutes of normal time remaining; Nick Walshe came on as a replacement for Shaun Perry with 1 minute of normal time remaining; England A were still losing 33-18

in the fourth minute of injury time when Delon Armitage was tackled into touch at the corner flag by Tommy Bowe in the last move of the match)

ENGLAND STUDENTS MATCHES

CAPTAIN: *Kevin Brennan*

4th Feb **ENGLAND STUDENTS** 6 FRANCE STUDENTS 41

Twickenham

[This match kicked off at 6.00pm; This was the first time that England Students had played at Twickenham; Tom Gregory played for England in the U19 World Championship in South Africa in March-April 2004; Jon Pritchard had switched his allegiance back to England before this match]

(Fabien Gengenbacher scored a penalty goal in the 2nd minute!; England Students were drawing 3-3 in the 5th minute!; England Students were losing 8-3 in the 9th minute; England Students were losing 15-3 in the 15th minute; England Students were still losing 15-3 midway through the first half; England Students were losing 15-3 shortly before half-time; England Students were losing 15-6 at half-time; England Students were still losing 15-6 early in the second half when Jamie Lennard had a penalty goal attempt come back off the post; England Students were losing 15-6 in the 50th minute; England Students were losing 34-6 midway through the second half; England Students were still losing 34-6 with 2 minutes remaining; France Students were allowed to score 26 unanswered points in the second half to seal the match)

10th Feb ITALY U25 44 **ENGLAND STUDENTS** 31

Stadio Comunale, Nuoro, Sardinia

[This match kicked off at 2.30pm; Steve Pape in original training squad of 23 but were not selected for team or bench]

(Luciano Orquera scored a penalty goal in the 1st minute!; England Students were drawing 3-3 in the 3rd minute!; England Students were losing 9-3 in the 12th minute; Chris Lowrie went off injured in the 14th minute, being replaced by Tom Yellowlees; England Students were losing 9-8 midway through the first half; England Students were losing 16-8 in the 22nd minute; England Students were losing 16-11 in the 27th minute; England Students were losing 16-14 shortly before half-time; England Students were losing 23-14 at half-time; England Students were losing 30-14 in the 45th minute; England Students were losing 37-14 in the 54th minute; Italy U25 were allowed to score 21 unanswered points to clinch the match; England Students were still losing 37-14 midway through the second half when Tom Gregory scored after Richard Vasey put in a brilliant chip-kick; England Students were losing 44-24 in the 67th minute; England Students were still losing 44-24 with 2 minutes remaining when Jon Pritchard scored a superb consolation try; Greg Irvin and Jon Pritchard both had a brilliant game)

CAPTAIN: *Andy Dalgleish*

10th Mar FRANCE STUDENTS 17 **ENGLAND STUDENTS** 3

Stade Marcel Tribut, Dunkirk

[This match kicked off at 6.30pm; Lille was the original venue for this match; James Jones, Kevin Brennan and Ali James unavailable due to injury; James Hanks unavailable due to exam commitments]

(This match was played in wet conditions; Robin Janisson scored in the 3rd minute!; England Students were losing 5-3 in the 7th minute; England Students were still losing 5-3 midway through the first half; England Students were losing 5-3 at half-time; England Students played into the wind in the second half; England Students were

losing 10-3 in the 47th minute; England Students were losing 17-3 in the 50th minute; France Students were allowed to score 12 unanswered points to clinch the match; England Students were still losing 17-3 midway through the second half)

USA SEVENS

Home Depot Center, Carson City, Los Angeles

CAPTAIN: *Henry Paul*

First Round - Pool 'A'

11th Feb KENYA 5 **ENGLAND** 26

[*This match kicked off at 12.12pm*]

(*England were leading 7-0 in the early stages; England were leading 14-0 midway through the first half; England were leading 19-0 at half-time; Will Matthews came on as a replacement for Luke Narraway at the start of the second half; England were leading 26-0 early in the second half; England scored 26 unanswered points to win the match; England were still leading 26-0 midway through the second half; Will Matthews went off injured in the closing stages, which reduced England to 6 men because they had already used up their permitted three replacements*)

11th Feb USA 0 **ENGLAND** 45

[*This match kicked off at 3.18pm; Will Matthews unavailable due to injury; England wore navy blue shirts for this match*]

(*England were drawing 0-0 in the 4th minute when Andy Vilk powered through to score; England were leading 21-0 at half-time; Dave Strettle scored a hat-trick of tries before he was substituted by Ollie Phillips!; England were leading 33-0 when Nils Mordt scored from a tap penalty; England were leading 40-0 when Ben Gollings kicked ahead and followed up to score a brilliant try; Ben Gollings scored 20 points in this match*)

11th Feb FRANCE 19 **ENGLAND** 24

[*This match kicked off at 6.46pm; Will Matthews unavailable due to injury*]

(*England were losing 7-0 in the early stages; England were losing 12-0 when Luke Narraway scored after Dave Strettle made a brilliant break; England were losing 12-7 when Dave Strettle scored after he wrong-footed the French defence with a brilliant sidestep; England were leading 14-12 at half-time; England were leading 19-12 early in the second half; England were leading 24-12 in the last minute when they conceded their second penalty try of the match!*)

Quarter-Final

12th Feb ARGENTINA 15 **ENGLAND** 19

[*This match kicked off at 11.28am; Will Matthews unavailable due to injury*]

(*England were losing 5-0 in the early stages; England were leading 7-5 when Matt Tait scored a brilliant 56 metre solo try; England were leading 12-5 just before half-time; England were leading 12-10 at half-time; England were losing 15-12 early in the second half; England were still losing 15-12 when Matt Tait had a great try-scoring chance but was tackled short of the Argentine line; England were losing 15-12 when Matt Tait scored under the posts after he wrong-footed the Argentine defence with a brilliant sidestep; England were leading 19-15 when Dave Strettle had another great try-scoring chance but was tackled into touch at the corner flag; England were still leading 19-15 in the final minute when Ben Gollings saved a certain try by managing to get beneath the ball as Nicolás Fernández Lobbe attempted to ground it in the last move of the match*)

Semi-Final

12th Feb SOUTH AFRICA 0 **ENGLAND** 38

[This match kicked off at 3.38pm; Will Matthews unavailable due to injury]

(Dave Strettle scored in the 1st minute!; England were leading 21-0 midway through the first half; England were leading 26-0 at half-time; England were still leading 26-0 early in the second half when Andy Vilk scored to complete a hat-trick of tries; England were leading 33-0 midway through the second half)

Final

12th Feb FIJI 5 **ENGLAND** 38

[This match kicked off at 5.45pm; Will Matthews unavailable due to injury; England wore navy blue shirts for this match]

(Dave Strettle scored a brilliant 69 metre solo try in the early stages!; A brilliant 48 metre run by Dave Strettle enabled Andy Vilk to score a try which Ben Gollings then converted to give England a 14-0 lead shortly afterwards; England were leading 14-5 when Matt Tait saved a certain try by tackling William Ryder; England were leading 14-5 at half-time; England were leading 21-5 in the 8th minute; England were still leading 21-5 shortly afterwards when Matt Tait saved another certain try by tackling Timoci Volavola into touch at the corner flag; England were leading 21-5 midway through the second half when Andy Vilk scored a superb 47 metre solo try; Nils Mordt scored straight after the restart!; England were leading 33-5 in the closing stages when Ben Gollings put in a brilliant grubber kick and followed up to score; England scored 24 unanswered points in the second half to seal the match; Matt Tait had a brilliant game; Ben Gollings scored 59 points in this tournament and thus increased his overall IRB World Sevens record to 1402)

JEAN-CLAUDE BAQUÉ SHIELD MATCH

CAPTAIN: *James Winterbottom*

11th Mar FRANCE AMATEURS 16 **ENGLAND COUNTIES** 29

Stade Jean Guiral, Beaune

[This match kicked off at 3.00pm; Paul Price, Glen Townson and Chris Wilkins in original training squad of 25 but were not selected for team or bench; Stean Williams toured Australia with England Schools 18 Group in August 1997]

(England Counties were leading 3-0 in the 7th minute; England Counties were drawing 3-3 in the 15th minute; England Counties were still drawing 3-3 midway through the first half; England Counties were drawing 3-3 in the 32nd minute when Wayne Reed scored from a rolling maul; England Counties were leading 10-6 in the first minute of first half injury time when Oliver Viney scored after Chris Briers threw a brilliant pass; England Counties were leading 15-6 at half-time; England Counties were leading 15-11 in the 44th minute; England Counties were still leading 15-11 in the 54th minute when Chris Malherbe scored after Ollie Thomas made a superb break; England Counties were leading 22-11 midway through the second half; England Counties were still leading 22-11 with 9 minutes remaining; England Counties were leading 22-16 with 3 minutes remaining when Hamish Smales gathered a loose ball and ran 68 metres to score a brilliant match-clinching try)

COMMONWEALTH SEVENS

Telstra Dome, Melbourne

CAPTAIN: *Simon Amor*

Preliminary Round - Pool 'C'

16th Mar COOK ISLANDS 5 **ENGLAND** 35

[This match kicked off at 12.52pm]

(England were drawing 0-0 midway through the first half when Tom Varndell scored a brilliant 58 metre solo try; England were leading 7-0 in the 6th minute when Henry Paul scored after he wrong-footed Rangi Vallance with a brilliant sidestep; England were leading 14-0 at half-time; David Seymour scored after just 26 seconds of the second half had been played!; England were leading 21-0 in the 10th minute when Magnus Lund scored after Henry Paul made a brilliant run; England scored 28 unanswered points to win the match; England were leading 28-0 midway through the second half; England were still leading 28-0 with 2 minutes of normal time remaining; England were leading 28-5 when the full-time hooter sounded, but the ball was still in play and Danny Care was able to score)

CAPTAIN: *Ben Gollings*

16th Mar SRI LANKA 0 **ENGLAND** 61

[This match kicked off at 6.44pm]

(David Seymour scored a brilliant 63 metre solo try in the 2nd minute!; England were leading 7-0 in the 4th minute when Matt Tait scored another brilliant 34 metre solo try; England were leading 14-0 midway through the first half; England were still leading 14-0 in the 7th minute when Richard Haughton charged down a kick by Saliya Kumara and then regathered the ball to score; David Seymour scored another try straight after the restart!; England were leading 26-0 at half-time; England were leading 33-0 in the 9th minute; England were leading 40-0 midway through the second half when Tom Varndell scored after Ben Gollings made a superb 42 metre break; England were leading 54-0 when the full-time hooter sounded, but the ball was still in play and Matt Tait was able to dummy his way through and score to complete a hat-trick of tries)

CAPTAIN: *Simon Amor*

16th Mar AUSTRALIA 12 **ENGLAND** 14

[This match kicked off at 10.12pm]

(Chris Latham scored in the 2nd minute!; England were losing 7-0 midway through the first half; England were losing 7-0 at half-time; England were still losing 7-0 in the 9th minute when Simon Amor beat Chris Latham for pace on the outside to score a brilliant solo try; England were drawing 7-7 midway through the second half; England were still drawing 7-7 with 1 minute of normal time remaining when Tom Varndell scored a brilliant 95 metre solo try; England were leading 14-7 when the full-time hooter sounded, but the ball was still in play and Cameron Shepherd was able to score for Australia, with Brendan Williams then badly missing the difficult conversion attempt which would have drawn the match!)

Quarter-Final

17th Mar SAMOA 14 **ENGLAND** 17

[This match kicked off at 2.22pm]

(Matt Tait powered through 2 attempted tackles after just 85 seconds had been played!; England were leading 7-0 midway through the first half when Tom Varndell brilliantly kicked ahead into space but then dropped the ball as he attempted to regather it while the Samoan tryline was at his mercy; England were leading 12-0 in the 5th minute; England were leading 12-0 at half-time; England were leading 12-7 in the

9th minute; England were losing 14-12 midway through the second half; England were still losing 14-12 in the final minute when Matt Tait scored a brilliant 52 metre solo try with the last move of the match to complete a hat-trick and win the game)

Semi-Final

17th Mar FIJI 14 **ENGLAND** 21

[This match kicked off at 7.50pm; England wore navy blue shirts for this match]

(Filimone Bolavucu ran 21 metres to score in the 1st minute after he intercepted Simon Amor's pass, thus 7 points were preventable!; England were losing 7-0 midway through the first half; England were still losing 7-0 in the 4th minute when Simon Amor scored a brilliant 65 metre solo try; England were drawing 7-7 just before half-time; England were leading 14-7 at half-time; England were still leading 14-7 in the 10th minute when Matt Tait scored a brilliant 95 metre solo try; England scored 21 unanswered points to win the match; England were leading 21-7 midway through the second half; Tom Varndell went off injured with 1 minute remaining, being replaced by Richard Haughton; England were still leading 21-7 in the final minute)

Final

17th Mar NEW ZEALAND 29 **ENGLAND*** 21

[This match kicked off at 9.52pm]

(Tom Varndell played with an injury; Cory Jane scored in the 2nd minute!; England were losing 5-0 in the 4th minute when Matt Tait scored a brilliant 79 metre solo try; England were leading 7-5 midway through the first half; England were losing 10-7 in the 6th minute; England were still losing 10-7 just before half-time; England were losing 15-7 at half-time; Andy Vilk came on as a replacement for Ben Russell (2) in the 12th minute, with David Seymour then switching from hooker to loose-head prop to accommodate Vilk and Magnus Lund moving from loose-head to tight-head prop to accommodate David Seymour; England were losing 15-14 in the 14th minute; Ben Gollings came on as a replacement for Tom Varndell in the 15th minute, with Henry Paul then switching from fly half to centre to accommodate Gollings and Matt Tait moving from centre to wing to accommodate Henry Paul; New Zealand were leading 22-14 midway through the second half when Josh Blackie scored after a poor tackle by Ben Gollings, thus 7 points were preventable; New Zealand were allowed to score 14 unanswered points to clinch the match; England were losing 29-14 with 1 minute remaining when Simon Amor followed up his own kick ahead and crossed the tryline but then could not get downward pressure on the ball; England were still losing 29-14 in the last minute when Ben Gollings powered through to score a try which he then converted, but the full-time hooter sounded just as Gollings attempted to restart the match!)

CATHAY PACIFIC/CREDIT SUISSE HONG KONG SEVENS

Hong Kong Stadium, Eastern Hospital Road, So Kon Po, Hong Kong

CAPTAIN: *Ben Gollings*

First Round - Pool 'B'

31st Mar HONG KONG 0 **ENGLAND** 52

[This match kicked off at 4.52pm]

(England were leading 7-0 midway through the first half; England were leading 21-0 just before half-time; England were leading 28-0 at half-time; England were leading 33-0 early in the second half; Dave Strettle scored his third try with 3 minutes remaining after Ben Russell (2) made a brilliant run; Dave Strettle scored 20 points in this match)

CAPTAIN: *Simon Amor*

1st April USA 5 **ENGLAND** 40

[*This match kicked off at 1.04pm*]

(*England were drawing 0-0 when Ben Gollings scored after Tom Varndell made a brilliant break; England were leading 14-0 at half-time; England scored 40 unanswered points to win the match; Ben Gollings scored 20 points in this match*)

1st April CANADA 12 **ENGLAND** 36

[*This match kicked off at 5.56pm*]

(*Dave Strettle scored a brilliant 74 metre solo try in the 3rd minute!; England were leading 19-0 at half-time; Tom Varndell scored a brilliant solo try in the second half*)

Quarter-Final

2nd April SAMOA 10 **ENGLAND** 14

[*This match kicked off at 2.26pm*]

(*Uale Mai scored in the 1st minute!; England were losing 10-0 when Simon Amor scored a brilliant 63 metre solo try; England were losing 10-7 at half-time; England were still losing 10-7 early in the second half when Andy Vilk scored after Ben Gollings brilliantly created space; England scored 14 unanswered points to win the match; England were leading 14-10 midway through the second half*)

Semi-Final

2nd April SOUTH AFRICA 0 **ENGLAND** 24

[*This match kicked off at 4.38pm*]

(*England were drawing 0-0 when Matt Tait scored a brilliant 90 metre solo try; England were leading 7-0 when Simon Amor scored after Andy Vilk went on a brilliant rampaging run; England were leading 12-0 at half-time; England were still leading 12-0 early in the second half when Tom Varndell scored a superb 47 metre solo try; England were leading 19-0 when Dave Strettle ran 47 metres to score with his first touch of the ball!; Ben Foden came on as a temporary blood replacement*)

Final

2nd April FIJI 24 **ENGLAND** 26

[*This match kicked off at 6.20pm; England wore navy blue shirts for this match*]

(*Tom Varndell scored in the early stages after Ben Gollings made a brilliant 60 metre run; England were leading 5-0 when collectively poor tackling allowed Jone Daunivucu to score, thus 7 points were preventable; England were losing 7-5 when Ben Gollings scored a brilliant 33 metre solo try; England were leading 12-7 when Matt Tait scored a superb 59 metre solo try; England were leading 19-7 at half-time; England were leading 19-14 in the 13th minute; Tom Varndell went off injured after he was bitten by Jone Daunivucu, being replaced by Dave Strettle; England were drawing 19-19 with 2 minutes of normal time remaining; Fiji were allowed to score 17 unanswered points; England were losing 24-19 when the full-time hooter sounded, but the ball was still in play and Ben Gollings was able to score a brilliant try which he then converted with the last kick of the match to win the game and the competition!; Ben Gollings scored 65 points in this tournament and thus increased his overall IRB World Sevens record to 1467*)

QINETIQ CHALLENGE MATCH

CAPTAIN: *Bobby Skinstad* (SA)

4th April Royal Navy (*SER*) 10 **BARBARIANS** 31

Plymouth Albion RFC, Brickfields Recreation Ground, Madden Road, Plymouth

[*This match kicked off at 7.00pm; Tom Beim selected but withdrew, Nat Saumi was*

***moved from the bench to the team; Richard Baxter selected for bench but withdrew, being replaced by Nick Burnett; The Barbarians originally named a 7 man bench selection; Greig Laidlaw was the nephew of Roy Laidlaw; Jon Ufton was the son of the England footballer Derek Ufton and was capped for England Schools 18 Group in April 1992; Alex Page played for the Samurai Barracudas development side at the Safaricom Sevens in Nairobi on 5th-6th June 2010*]**
(*Dave Pascoe scored a penalty goal in the 4th minute!; The Barbarians were losing 3-0 in the 11th minute when Dafydd Lewis scored after Kenny Bingham made a brilliant break; The Barbarians were leading 5-3 in the 16th minute when Danny Thomas scored after Wayne Reed went on a brilliant rampaging run; The Barbarians were leading 12-3 midway through the first half when Nat Saumi scored after Jon Ufton threw a superb overhead pass; The Barbarians were leading 26-3 in the 23rd minute; The Barbarians scored 26 unanswered points to win the match; The Barbarians were leading 26-3 at half-time; The Barbarians were still leading 26-3 midway through the second half; The Barbarians were leading 26-3 with 7 minutes remaining; The Barbarians were leading 26-10 with 2 minutes remaining when Ian Humphreys started a brilliant attack from inside his own 22 and then took a return pass to finish the move with a try in the corner*)

STANDARD CHARTERED SEVENS, SINGAPORE

National Stadium, Kallang
CAPTAIN: *Simon Amor*
First Round - Pool 'B'
8th April KENYA 12 **ENGLAND** 26
[*This match kicked off at 1.28pm*]
(*This match was played in high humidity; Teddy Omondi scored in the 3rd minute!; England were losing 7-0 midway through the first half; England were still losing 7-0 just before half-time when Henry Paul dummied his way through to score a brilliant try; England were drawing 7-7 at half-time; Dave Strettle went off injured at half-time, being replaced by Tom Varndell; England scored 26 unanswered points to win the match; England were leading 26-7 in the closing stages*)
CAPTAIN: *Ben Gollings*
8th April KOREA 5 **ENGLAND** 47
[*This match kicked off at 4.24pm; England wore navy blue shirts for this match*]
(*This match was played in high humidity; England were leading 26-0 at half-time; Dave Strettle scored a brilliant 61 metre solo try in the second half*)
CAPTAIN: *Simon Amor*
8th April SAMOA 14 **ENGLAND*** 12
[*This match kicked off at 8.16pm*]
(*This match was played in high humidity; England were losing 7-0 in the early stages; England were still losing 7-0 midway through the first half; England were losing 7-0 at half-time; England were losing 14-0 with 3 minutes remaining; England were losing 14-7 with 1 minute remaining; England were still losing 14-7 in the final minute when Tom Varndell scored in the corner, but Henry Paul then missed the difficult conversion attempt that would have drawn the match*)
Quarter-Final
9th April AUSTRALIA 14 **ENGLAND** 26
[*This match kicked off at 2.42pm*]
(*This match was played in 95 degree heat and high humidity; Tom Varndell scored*

***after just 32 seconds had been played!; England were leading 14-0 at one point in the first half; England were leading 14-7 when Simon Amor brilliantly chipped ahead and followed up to score; England were leading 21-7 at half-time; England were leading 26-7 in the last minute*)

Semi-Final

9th April	SOUTH AFRICA	14	**ENGLAND**	33

[***This match kicked off at 6.08pm***]

(***This match was played in 95 degree heat and high humidity; England were leading 7-0 in the 4th minute; England were drawing 7-7 when Ben Gollings chipped ahead and regathered the ball to score a brilliant try; England were leading 14-7 at half-time; England were still leading 14-7 when Andy Vilk scored after Ben Gollings instigated a brilliant 95 metre counter-attack; England were leading 21-14 with 2 minutes of normal time remaining when Simon Amor scored after Ben Russell (2) made a superb 30 metre run; England were leading 26-14 when the full-time hooter sounded, but the ball was still in play and Matt Tait was able to score to seal the match; Ben Russell (2) had a brilliant game***)

Final

9th April	FIJI	40	**ENGLAND**	19

[***This match kicked off at 8.00pm; England wore navy blue shirts for this match***]

(***This match was played in 95 degree heat and high humidity; The England players could not win any possession; Sireli Naqelevuki scored in the 1st minute!; England were drawing 7-7 in the 4th minute; England were leading 14-7 midway through the first half; England were still leading 14-7 when collectively poor tackling allowed Norman Ligairi to score; England were drawing 14-14 just before half-time; England were losing 19-14 at half-time; England were still losing 19-14 in the 13th minute when William Ryder scored after a poor tackle by David Seymour, thus 2 tries and 14 points were preventable; England were losing 40-14 midway through the second half; Fiji were allowed to 34 unanswered points to win the match; England were still losing 40-14 with 2 minutes remaining when Andy Vilk powered through 2 attempted tackles to score a consolation try; Ben Gollings increased his IRB World Sevens record to 1519 points in this tournament***)

MATT HAMPSON CHALLENGE MATCH

CAPTAIN: *Jordan Crane*

16th May	Leicester Tigers Development XV	17	**ENGLAND U21 XV**	36

Welford Road, Leicester

[***This match kicked off at 7.00pm; Matt Cornwell originally intended to play the first half for the Leicester Tigers Development XV and the second half for the England U21 XV but he eventually decided to play the whole match for the former team, with Jamie Lennard then taking his place in the England U21 XV squad; Ben Foden selected but withdrew on the day of the match, Nick Runciman was moved from the bench to the team and James Honeyben was then selected for the bench; Tom Mercey played for England in the U19 World Championships in South Africa in April 2005 and Dubai in April 2006; Iain Grieve played for England in the U19 World Championship at Dubai in April 2006; Tom Croft, Brett Deacon, Will Skinner, Scott Bemand and Matt Cornwell played for the Leicester Tigers Development XV in this match, with Matt Cornwell captaining the side***]

(***The England U21 XV was losing 5-0 in the 13th minute; Nick Abendanon went off injured in the 18th minute, being replaced by Jamie Lennard; The England U21 XV was***

losing 5-3 midway through the first half; The England U21 XV was still losing 5-3 in the 27th minute when Michael Hills scored after Sam Robinson made a brilliant break; The England U21 XV was leading 10-5 in the 34th minute when Paul Diggin scored after Mike Brown made a superb run; The England U21 XV was leading 15-5 just before half-time; The England U21 XV scored 22 unanswered points to win the match; The England U21 XV was leading 22-5 at half-time; The England U21 XV was leading 22-12 in the 52nd minute; The England U21 XV was leading 22-17 midway through the second half; The England U21 XV was still leading 22-17 in the 68th minute when Mike Brown scored a brilliant solo try; The England U21 XV was leading 29-17 in the last minute when James Haskell scored after Will Matthews made a superb break)

RICHARD HILL TESTIMONIAL SPECIAL

CAPTAIN: *Lawrence Dallaglio*

21st May Saracens 14 **WORLD XV** 64

Vicarage Road, Watford

[This match kicked off at 3.00pm; Simon Shaw selected but withdrew, Daniel Leo was moved from the bench to the team and Toutai Kefu was then selected for the bench; De Wet Barry selected for bench but withdrew, being replaced by Isa Nacewa; Andrea Lo Cicero and Radike Samo in original squad but were not selected for team or bench; David Flatman, Kris Chesney, Ben Russell (2), Tony Diprose, Dan Luger and Kyran Bracken all played for Saracens in this match; Richard Hill (2) became the Saracens' team Manager for the day after his long-standing knee injury prevented him from being available as a player!]

(This match was played in extremely wet conditions; The World XV was leading 12-0 in the early stages when Matt Burke scored a brilliant solo try; The World XV was leading 40-7 at half-time; Bruce Reihana scored a superb solo try in the second half; The World XV was leading 57-14 in the final minute when Isa Nacewa scored a try which the referee Wayne Barnes then converted with the last kick of the match!)

GMF PARIS SEVENS

Stade Sébastien Charléty, Paris

CAPTAIN: *Simon Amor*

First Round - Pool 'B'

27th May SCOTLAND 7 **ENGLAND** 24

[This match kicked off at 2.12pm]

(Richard Haughton scored a brilliant 27 metre solo try in the second half; England scored 3 tries in the second half)

27th May RUSSIA 7 **ENGLAND** 26

[This match kicked off at 5.20pm]

(England were losing 7-5 at half-time)

27th May FRANCE 12 **ENGLAND** 19

[This match kicked off at 8.38pm]

(Julien Candelon scored in the 2nd minute!; England were losing 7-0 in the 3rd minute when Dave Strettle scored a brilliant 79 metre try; England were drawing 7-7 midway through the first half; England were still drawing 7-7 just before half-time; England were leading 14-7 at half-time; England were still leading 14-7 midway through the second half; England were leading 14-12 with 2 minutes remaining; England were still leading 14-12 in the final minute when Richard Haughton scored with the last move of the match to clinch the game)

Quarter-Final

28th May	AUSTRALIA	29	**ENGLAND***	17

[This match kicked off at 1.34pm]

(England were leading 5-0 when Andy Vilk scored a brilliant 90 metre solo try; England were leading 10-0 shortly before half-time; England were leading 10-5 at half-time; England were losing 15-10 early in the second half; England were still losing 15-10 when Rob Thirlby scored a brilliant 37 metre solo try; England were leading 17-15 in the closing stages when A.J. Gilbert scored as a direct consequence of a mistake by Rob Thirlby; England were losing 22-17 in the final minute when Tim Atkinson scored after a poor tackle by Ben Russell (2), thus 2 tries and 14 points were preventable; Australia were allowed to score 14 unanswered points to win the match)

[Plate Semi-Final:]

[28th May	ARGENTINA	14	**ENGLAND***	12]

[This match kicked off at 3.58pm]

(England were leading 12-7 in the closing stages; Ben Gollings increased his IRB World Sevens record to 1538 points in this tournament)

<u>GARTMORE CHALLENGE</u>

CAPTAIN: *Pat Sanderson* [England XV]

CAPTAIN: *Raphäel Ibañez* (FR) [Barbarians]

28th May	**ENGLAND XV**	46	**BARBARIANS**	19

Twickenham

[ENGLAND XV: [*This match kicked off at 3.00pm; James Haskell played in the Samurai team that won the Amsterdam Heineken Sevens on 20th-21st May 2006*]

(Both sides agreed to allow unlimited substitutions in this match; Olly Barkley scored a penalty goal in the 4th minute!; The England XV was leading 6-0 in the 11th minute when James Simpson-Daniel saved a certain try by tackling Joe Roff; The England XV was still leading 6-0 midway through the first half; James Simpson-Daniel intercepted the ball and ran 80 metres to score a try which Olly Barkley then converted to give the England XV a 13-0 lead in the 22nd minute; The England XV was losing 14-13 in the 30th minute; The England XV was still losing 14-13 just before half-time when James Simpson-Daniel scored another try after Peter Richards instigated a superb counter-attack; The England XV was leading 18-14 at half-time; The England XV was still leading 18-14 in the 42nd minute when Iain Balshaw crossed the tryline, but the move was disallowed because the scoring pass from Matt Tait was adjudged to have been forward; The England XV was leading 18-14 in the 53rd minute when Thomas Castaignède threw a clear forward pass to Matt Burke who went on to score after the referee unaccountably allowed play to continue, thus 5 points were unlawful; David Paice came on as a replacement for Lee Mears in the 54th minute; The England XV was losing 19-18 midway through the second half when Olly Barkley caught Carlos Spencer's chip-kick and ran 32 metres to score; The England XV was leading 25-19 in the 62nd minute when James Forrester scored after Iain Balshaw brilliantly chipped ahead and regathered the ball; The England XV was leading 32-19 with 2 minutes of normal time remaining; The England XV scored 28 unanswered points to win the match; James Forrester injured playing in the match; Olly Barkley scored 21 points in this match; Pat Sanderson and David Paice both had a brilliant game)]

[BARBARIANS: [*This match kicked off at 3.00pm; Dave Hewett, Owen Finegan and David Humphreys in original squad but were not selected for team or bench*]

(Both sides agreed to allow unlimited substitutions in this match; Olly Barkley scored

a penalty goal in the 4th minute!; The Barbarians were losing 6-0 in the 11th minute when Joe Roff had a great try-scoring chance but was brilliantly tackled by James Simpson-Daniel; The Barbarians were still losing 6-0 midway through the first half; The Barbarians were losing 6-0 in the 22nd minute and pressing in attack when Bruce Reihana had his intended scoring pass intercepted by James Simpson-Daniel who then ran 80 metres to score, thus 7 points were preventable; The Barbarians were losing 13-7 in the 30th minute when Bruce Reihana scored after Toutai Kefu made a superb run; The Barbarians were leading 14-13 just before half-time; The Barbarians were losing 18-14 at half-time; The Barbarians were leading 19-18 in the 53rd minute; The Barbarians were still leading 19-18 midway through the second half when Carlos Spencer chipped the ball straight to Olly Barkley who then ran 32 metres to score; The Barbarians were losing 32-19 in the 62nd minute; Mark Regan and Fraser Waters came on as a replacement for Raphäel Ibañez and Dominic Feau'nati respectively in the 64th minute; The Barbarians were still losing 32-19 with 2 minute of normal time remaining when Thomas Castaignède threw a wild pass in front of his own line which allowed David Barnes to follow up and score, thus 2 tries and 14 points were preventable; The England XV was allowed to score 28 unanswered points to win the match)]

BARBARIANS MATCH

CAPTAIN: *Will Greenwood*

31st May SCOTLAND XV 66 **BARBARIANS** 19
Murrayfield

[This match kicked off at 7.30pm; Tony Marsh was added to the original 7 man bench selection; Darren Crompton was capped for England Schools 18 Group in March 1990; Will Greenwood retired after this match]

(Both sides agreed to allow unlimited substitutions in this match; Chris Paterson scored a penalty goal in the 3rd minute!; The Barbarians were losing 3-0 in the 6th minute when Kieron Dawson charged down Mike Blair's attempted clearance kick and followed up to score a try which Chris Malone then brilliantly converted from the left touchline; The Barbarians were losing 10-7 in the 15th minute when Will Greenwood dropped a pass from Leon Lloyd in his own 22 and Andy Henderson gathered the loose ball and scored; The Barbarians were losing 17-7 midway through the first half; The Barbarians were still losing 17-7 in the 23rd minute when some superb handling amongst the backs allowed Steve Hanley to score; The Barbarians were losing 24-12 in the 30th minute; The Barbarians were still losing 24-12 shortly before half-time when Kevin Tkachuk crossed the tryline but then dropped the ball in the act of scoring; The Barbarians were losing 24-12 at half-time; The Barbarians were losing 31-12 in the 45th minute; Ugo Monye came on as a replacement for Steve Hanley in the 46th minute; Bobby Skinstad came on as a replacement for Jason Forster in the 51st minute; The Scotland XV was leading 38-12 in the 58th minute when Sam Pinder scored after Donnie Macfadyen intercepted Dan Browne's pass from the base of a Barbarians scrum, thus 2 tries and 14 points were preventable; The Scotland XV was allowed to score 28 unanswered points to clinch the match; Will Greenwood was substituted in the 59th minute, being replaced by Tony Marsh; The Barbarians were losing 45-12 midway through the second half when Tony Marsh scored after Chris Malone made a brilliant break; The Barbarians were losing 45-19 with 9 minutes remaining when Mike Blair scored a try that should not have been given because the scoring pass was clearly forward, thus 7 points were unlawful; The Barbarians were losing 52-19 with 4 minutes remaining)

TUNISIAN TOUR TO ENGLAND 2006

CAPTAIN: *Duncan Cormack*

3rd June **ENGLAND COUNTIES** 35 TUNISIA 7

Broadstreet RFC, Ivor Preece Field, Binley Woods, Coventry

[*This match kicked off at 2.00pm; Ed Lewsey in original squad but withdrew due to injury, being replaced by Kenny Bingham; Neil Hallett in original squad but withdrew due to his Barbarians commitments, being replaced by Dave Knight; Matt Jess in original squad but withdrew due to club commitments, being replaced by Neil Kerfoot*]

(*England Counties were drawing 0-0 when James Rodwell scored a pushover try; England Counties were drawing 7-7 at half-time; England Counties were leading 14-7 in the 45th minute when Duncan Cormack scored from a rolling maul; England Counties were leading 21-7 midway through the second half; England Counties were leading 21-7 with 8 minutes remaining when Ed Barnes scored a brilliant solo try; England Counties were leading 28-7 in injury time; England Counties scored 28 unanswered points in the second half to win the match*)

WORLD XV TOUR TO SOUTH AFRICA 2006

CAPTAIN: *Justin Marshall* (NZ)

3rd June SOUTH AFRICA XV 30 **WORLD XV*** 27

Ellis Park Stadium, Johannesburg

[*This match kicked off at 3.00pm; Toutai Kefu unavailable due to injury; The World XV's starting lineup had 501 caps between them!; Andrea Lo Cicero, Raphäel Ibañez and Thomas Castaignède left the tour after this match; Naka Drotske joined the tour after this match*]

(*This match was played at high altitude; The World XV players had insufficient time to shake off their jet lag; Matt Burke scored a penalty goal in the 5th minute!; The World XV was drawing 3-3 in the 10th minute when Justin Marshall scored after Sébastien Chabal broke from the base of a five metre scrum; The World XV was leading 8-6 midway through the first half; The World XV was leading 11-6 in the 29th minute; The World XV was losing 12-11 just before half-time; The World XV was losing 15-11 at half-time; In the 43rd minute Justin Marshall famously sat down on the pitch while he was waiting for Bruce Reihana to put in a clearance kick from his own 22!; The World XV was still losing 15-11 in the 45th minute when Isa Nacewa scored after Carlos Spencer put up a brilliant cross-kick; Carlos Spencer went off injured in the 48th minute, being replaced by Ludovic Mercier; The World XV was drawing 18-18 in the 53rd minute; Mark Regan came on a replacement for Raphäel Ibañez in the 57th minute; The World XV was losing 24-21 midway through the second half; The World XV was still losing 24-21 in the 66th minute when Matt Burke scored a superb 30 metre penalty goal from the right touchline; The World XV was drawing 24-24 with 8 minutes remaining; The World XV was drawing 27-27 with 3 minutes remaining; The World XV was still drawing 27-27 in the last minute when Percy Montgomery scored a penalty goal to win the match for the South African XV; The World XV won the game's try-count 2-0; Sébastien Chabal had a brilliant game*)

EMIRATES AIRLINE LONDON SEVENS

Twickenham

CAPTAIN: *Simon Amor*

First Round - Pool 'B'

3rd June **ENGLAND** 26 KENYA 0

[This match kicked off at 1.12pm]

(Simon Amor pulled his abdominal muscles taking a lineout throw in the early stages, but elected to remain on the pitch; England were drawing 0-0 midway through the first half; England were still drawing 0-0 just before half-time when Ben Gollings jinked through to score a brilliant try; England were leading 7-0 at half-time; England were leading 14-0 early in the second half; England were leading 21-0 when Dave Strettle scored a brilliant 68 metre solo try)

CAPTAIN: *Ben Gollings*

3rd June **ENGLAND** 51 GERMANY 0

[This match kicked off at 4.22pm; Simon Amor unavailable due to injury]

(Dave Strettle scored after just 36 seconds had been played!; England were leading 26-0 at half-time; Ben Foden went off injured in this match)

3rd June **ENGLAND*** 19 AUSTRALIA 24

[This match kicked off at 8.08pm; Simon Amor and Ben Foden unavailable due to injury]

(Australia were allowed to score 17 unanswered points to win the match; England were losing 17-0 at half-time; Jonny Hylton had to go off after he pulled a hamstring, being replaced by Richard Haughton; Will Matthews had to go off after he also pulled a hamstring, being replaced by Luke Narraway; England were still losing 17-0 early in the second half when Andy Vilk powered through 2 attempted tackles to score under the posts; James Bailey went off injured, being replaced by Ollie Phillips; England were losing 17-12 in the 10th minute; England were still losing 17-12 midway through the second half; England were losing 17-12 with 2 minutes remaining when Mark Gilbride scored after Andy Vilk missed a tackle on Julian Huxley, thus 7 points were preventable; England were losing 24-12 in the last minute when Dave Strettle scored a brilliant consolation try)

Quarter-Final

4th June **ENGLAND** 14 FRANCE 7

[This match kicked off at 1.34pm; Simon Amor, Ben Foden, Jonny Hylton and Will Matthews all unavailable due to injury; England only had 8 fit players]

(England were losing 7-0 in the 4th minute; England were losing 7-0 at half-time; England were still losing 7-0 when Richard Haughton scored a brilliant 91 metre solo try; England were leading 14-7 with 2 minutes remaining)

Semi-Final

4th June **ENGLAND** 7 SAMOA 15

[This match kicked off at 5.01pm; Simon Amor, Ben Foden, Jonny Hylton and Will Matthews all unavailable due to injury; England only had 8 fit players]

(England were drawing 0-0 when Ofisa Treviranus scored after a poor tackle by James Bailey, thus 5 points were preventable; England were losing 5-0 at half-time; Richard Haughton went off injured early in the second half, being replaced by Ollie Phillips; Samoa were allowed to score 15 unanswered points to win the match; England were losing 15-0 with 2 minutes remaining when a brilliant long lineout throw by James Bailey allowed Dave Strettle to score a consolation try; Ben Gollings increased his IRB World Sevens record to 1568 points in this tournament)

BARCLAYS CHURCHILL CUP

Canada & USA

CAPTAIN: *Paul Hodgson*

First Round - Pool 'B'

3rd June SCOTLAND A 13 **ENGLAND SAXONS*** 7 **BP**

York University Stadium, Toronto

[This match kicked off at 2.45pm; Clive Stuart-Smith unavailable due to injury; Ayoola Erinle selected but withdrew on the morning of the match due to injury, Chris Bell was moved from the bench to the team and Kieran Roche was then selected for the bench; Luke Narraway, Andy Higgins (2) and Richard Haughton joined the squad after this match]

(This match was played in wet and windy conditions; Calum MacRae scored a penalty goal in the 4th minute!; The England Saxons were losing 3-0 in the 5th minute when Sam Vesty put in a brilliant grubber kick which allowed Chris Bell to follow up and catch the ball on the bounce, but he then dived too early and lost the ball in the act of scoring before he actually slid across the tryline!; The England Saxons were still losing 3-0 in the 16th minute when Sam Vesty put in another superb grubber kick but Delon Armitage then wasted this great try-scoring opportunity by fly-hacking the ball over the dead ball line; The England Saxons were losing 3-0 midway through the first half; The England Saxons were still losing 3-0 in the 26th minute when Delon Armitage saved a certain try by tackling Craig Hamilton; The England Saxons were losing 3-0 just before half-time when Dave Walder missed a 34 metre penalty goal attempt from in front of the posts; The England Saxons were losing 3-0 at half-time; The England Saxons were losing 6-0 in the 53rd minute; Scotland A were still leading 6-0 midway through the second half when the England Saxons forwards set up a rolling maul which enabled David Seymour to clearly ground the ball for a try but the referee was unsighted; The England Saxons were losing 6-0 in the 63rd minute when the referee awarded a penalty try after the Scotland A forwards collapsed a scrum as they were being driven backwards over their own line; The England Saxons were losing 13-7 in the 69th minute; Ben Woods came on as a replacement for David Seymour in the fourth minute of injury time; The England Saxons were still losing 13-7 in the thirteenth minute of injury time when Ben Woods crossed the tryline in the last move of the match, but then could not get downward pressure on the ball; David Seymour had a brilliant game)

CAPTAIN: *Ben Johnston* [*David Barnes*]

10th Jun CANADA 11 **ENGLAND SAXONS** 41 **BP**

York University Stadium, Toronto

[This match kicked off at 2.45pm; Andy Higgins (2) selected but withdrew due to injury, Alex Crockett was moved from the bench to the team and Ayoola Erinle was then selected for the bench; Robbie Morris retired due to injury in November 2010]

(The England Saxons played with a strong wind in the first half; Richard Haughton scored in the 4th minute!; The England Saxons were leading 8-0 in the 15th minute; The England Saxons were still leading 8-0 midway through the first half when Chris Bell crossed the tryline, but the move was disallowed because the scoring pass from Luke Narraway was adjudged to have been forward; The England Saxons were leading 8-0 in the 27th minute when Delon Armitage scored two tries in 3 minutes; The England Saxons scored 20 unanswered points to win the match; The England Saxons

***were leading 20-0 in the 33rd minute; The England Saxons were leading 20-5 at half-time; The England Saxons were leading 20-8 in the 49th minute when Kai Horstmann scored after Richard Haughton wrong-footed the Canadian defence with a brilliant sidestep; The England Saxons were leading 27-8 midway through the second half; The England Saxons were still leading 27-8 in the 63rd minute when Chris Bell scored after Richard Haughton made a superb break; Luke Narraway played as a centre in the absence of Ben Johnston, who was sent to the sin-bin in the 65th minute; The England Saxons were leading 34-11 in the 67th minute; The England Saxons were still leading 34-11 in the fifth minute of injury time when Dave Walder made a brilliant break but Chris Bell then wasted this great try-scoring opportunity by throwing a poor pass to Ayoola Erinle; The England Saxons were leading 34-11 in the eighth minute of injury time when Ben Woods scored in the last move of the match after Dave Walder put in a superb grubber kick; David Seymour had a brilliant game*)**

CAPTAIN: *Clive Stuart-Smith*

[Plate Final:]

[17th Jun IRELAND A 30 **ENGLAND SAXONS*** 27]

Commonwealth Stadium, Edmonton

[*This match kicked off at 12.00pm; Alex Crockett and Andy Higgins (2) unavailable due to injury; Chris Bell selected but withdrew due to injury, being replaced by Sam Vesty*]

(*The England Saxons forwards could not win any lineout ball; The England Saxons were leading 3-0 in the 9th minute; The England Saxons were still leading 3-0 in the 17th minute when Dave Walder missed an eminently kickable 22 metre penalty goal attempt; The England Saxons were leading 3-0 midway through the first half; The England Saxons were drawing 3-3 in the 25th minute; The England Saxons were losing 6-3 in the 32nd minute; The England Saxons were still losing 6-3 in the 38th minute when Kai Horstmann scored a try which Dave Walder then converted from the left touchline despite falling over as he took the kick!; The England Saxons were losing 13-10 in the fourth minute of first half injury time when Ayoola Erinle scored after Dave Walder put in a brilliant grubber kick; The England Saxons were leading 17-13 at half-time; The England Saxons were leading 22-13 in the 48th minute when Dave Walder missed an eminently kickable conversion attempt; The England Saxons were leading 22-18 in the 51st minute; The England Saxons were still leading 22-18 midway through the second half; David Seymour went off injured in the 60th minute, being replaced by Ben Woods; The England Saxons were leading 22-18 with 5 minutes of normal time remaining; Ireland A were allowed to score 2 unanswered tries from rolling mauls; The England Saxons were losing 23-22 in the first minute of injury time when Sam Vesty put in a chip-kick which rebounded into the arms of Ben Johnston who went on to score, with Dave Walder then missing the eminently kickable conversion attempt; The England Saxons were leading 27-23 in the seventh minute of injury time when Ronnie McCormack scored from a third rolling maul to win the match for Ireland A; The England Saxons were briefly reduced to 12 players immediately afterwards when David Paice joined David Barnes and Andy Beattie in the sin-bin!; Richard Haughton saw very little of the ball in this match*)

BARBARIANS TOUR TO GEORGIA 2006

CAPTAIN: *Bobby Skinstad* (SA)

4th June GEORGIA 19 **BARBARIANS** 28

FC Lokomotivi Tbilisi, Mikheil Meshki Stadium, Vake, Tbilisi

[*This match kicked off at 6.00pm; Georgia allowed the Barbarians to add John Davies, Jason Forster and Pat Howard to their original 7 man bench selection one hour before*

the kick-off; Georgia awarded caps for this match; James Hamilton was capped for Scotland in November 2006; Leon Lloyd retired due to injury in August 2008; Steve Hanley retired due to injury in July 2008]

(This match was played in 85 degree heat; Georgia allowed the Barbarians to have unlimited substitutions in this match; The referee divided the first half into 2 periods of 25 and 15 minutes respectively with a water break in between; The Barbarians were drawing 0-0 midway through the first half; The Barbarians were still drawing 0-0 in the 23rd minute when some superb handling amongst the backs allowed Ugo Monye to score; The Barbarians were leading 14-0 in the 29th minute; The Barbarians were still leading 14-0 shortly before half-time; The Barbarians were leading 14-7 at half-time; The Barbarians were still leading 14-7 in the 49th minute when Irakli Machkhaneli intercepted the ball and ran 60 metres to score, thus 7 points were preventable; The Barbarians were drawing 14-14 in the 58th minute when Steve Hanley scored after Jake Rauluni put up a brilliant garryowen; The Barbarians were leading 21-14 midway through the second half; The Barbarians were leading 28-14 in the 68th minute; The Barbarians were still leading 28-14 in the last minute of normal time)

IRB U21 WORLD CHAMPIONSHIP

France

CAPTAIN: *Matt Cornwell*

First Round - Pool 'B'

9th June FIJI U21 8 **ENGLAND U21** 34 **BP**

Stade Louis Darragon, Vichy

[This match kicked off at 5.00pm; Rob Webber played for England in the U19 World Championship in South Africa in March-April 2004; Matt Cornwell played for England in the U19 World Championship at Dubai in April 2006, Tom Croft played for Samurai St George in the Dubai International Invitation Rugby Sevens on 30th November-2nd December 2005]

(This match was played in hot and windy conditions; The England U21 forwards dominated the lineout in this match; Toby Flood scored a penalty goal in the 4th minute!; England U21 were losing 5-3 midway through the first half; England U21 were leading 6-5 in the 24th minute; England U21 were leading 6-5 in the 31st minute when Toby Flood scored a brilliant solo try; England U21 were leading 13-5 at half-time; Matt Cornwell went off injured at half-time, being replaced by Anthony Allen; England U21 were leading 13-8 in the 43rd minute; England U21 were leading 20-8 midway through the second half; England U21 were leading 27-8 with 8 minutes of normal time remaining; England U21 were still leading 27-8 in the first minute of injury time; England U21 scored 21 unanswered points to clinch the match; Toby Flood had a brilliant game)

CAPTAIN: *Jordan Crane*

13th Jun NEW ZEALAND U21 29 **ENGLAND U21** 14

Stade Louis Darragon, Vichy

[This match kicked off at 7.00pm; Matt Cornwell selected for bench but withdrew due to injury, being replaced by Matt Riley; Michael Hills played in the Samurai team that won the Amsterdam Heineken Sevens on 20th-21st May 2006]

(Toby Flood missed a penalty goal attempt in the 5th minute!; England U21 were losing 3-0 in the 16th minute; England U21 were still losing 3-0 midway through the first half; England U21 were losing 3-0 in the 23rd minute when Ryan Lamb missed a

penalty goal attempt; England U21 were losing 13-0 in the 29th minute; England U21 were losing 16-0 in the 38th minute when Ryan Lamb missed another penalty goal attempt; England U21 were still losing 16-0 just before half-time when Jordan Crane missed a further penalty goal attempt; England U21 were losing 16-0 at half-time; England U21 were losing 21-0 in the 47th minute; England U21 were losing 26-0 midway through the second half; England U21 were losing 29-0 in the 66th minute; New Zealand U21 were allowed to score 29 unanswered points to win the match; England U21 were still losing 29-0 with 8 minutes remaining when James Haskell scored after Ben Foden made a brilliant break; England U21 were losing 29-7 with 1 minute remaining when Topsy Ojo scored a consolation try after he wrong-footed the defence with a brilliant sidestep)

CAPTAIN: *Matt Cornwell*

17th Jun SCOTLAND U21 12 **ENGLAND U21** 31 **BP**

Stade Emile Pons, Riom

[*This match kicked off at 6.00pm; England U21 failed to score enough bonus points to get into the top 4 teams and thus did not have a chance of playing for a place in the final*]

(*England U21 were losing 3-0 in the 6th minute; England U21 were still losing 3-0 midway through the first half; England U21 were losing 9-0 in the 28th minute; England U21 were losing 9-0 at half-time; The second half of this match was played in torrential rain; England U21 were still losing 9-0 in the 53rd minute; England U21 were losing 9-5 in the 58th minute when Jordan Crane scored after Ben Foden made a brilliant break; England U21 were leading 12-9 midway through the second half; England U21 were leading 17-9 in the 63rd minute; England U21 were leading 17-12 with 8 minutes of normal time remaining when James Haskell scored after Michael Hills made a superb break; England U21 were leading 24-12 in the second minute of injury time; England U21 scored 14 unanswered points to clinch the match*)

5th/6th/7th/8th Place Semi-Final

21st Jun WALES U21 11 **ENGLAND U21** 13

Stade Louis Darragon, Vichy

[*This match kicked off at 5.00pm*]

(*Nick Griffiths scored in the 3rd minute!; England U21 were losing 8-0 in the 8th minute; England U21 were losing 8-3 in the 13th minute; Iain Grieve went off injured in the 18th minute, being replaced by Jordan Crane; England U21 were still losing 8-3 midway through the first half; England U21 were losing 8-3 shortly before half-time when Ben Foden chipped ahead and Matt Riley followed up and grounded the ball, but the move was disallowed because Riley was adjudged to have been in front of the kicker; England U21 were losing 8-3 at half-time; England U21 were losing 8-6 in the 54th minute; England U21 were still losing 8-6 midway through the second half; England U21 were losing 11-6 in the 69th minute; England U21 were still losing 11-6 with 6 minutes remaining when David Wilson (2) scored a try which Ryan Lamb then converted to win the match*)

5th/6th Place Play-Off

25th Jun IRELAND U21 8 **ENGLAND U21** 32

Stade Maurice Couturier, Cournon d'Auvergne

[*This match kicked off at 2.30pm*]

**(*The first half of this match was played in high humidity; Ryan Lamb scored a penalty goal in the 5th minute!; England U21 were losing 5-3 in the 11th minute; England U21*

were drawing 8-8 midway through the first half; England U21 were leading 15-8 in the 24th minute; Chris Robshaw came on as a temporary blood replacement for Jordan Crane in the 30th minute; The first half finished in a thunderstorm; England U21 were leading 15-8 at half-time; The start of the second half was delayed after the thunderstorm created a waterlogged pitch; England U21 were still leading 15-8 in the 44th minute when Anthony Allen scored after Ryan Lamb made a brilliant break; England U21 were leading 27-8 in the 55th minute; England U21 were still leading 27-8 midway through the second half; England U21 were leading 27-8 in the fifth minute of injury time when Michael Hills scored while playing out of position as a centre due to a number of injuries!; England U21 scored 24 unanswered points to win the match)

ANDY MULLIGAN TROPHY MATCH

CAPTAIN: *Rod Moore* (AU)

10th Jun	Paris Université Club Past & Present (*FR*)	7	**PENGUINS**	40

Stade Sébastien Charléty, Paris

[*This match kicked off at 1.00pm; The Penguins were provisionally scheduled to play the Czech Republic on either 14th or 15th June 2006, but this idea was eventually abandoned*]

(*This match was played in 82 degree heat; The Penguins were leading 7-0 when Craig de Goldi scored a brilliant try; The Penguins were leading 14-0 at half-time*)

ENGLAND TOUR TO AUSTRALIA 2006

CAPTAIN: *Pat Sanderson*

11th June	AUSTRALIA	34	**ENGLAND**	3

Telstra Stadium, Sydney Olympic Park, Homebush Bay, Sydney

[*This match kicked off at 8.05pm; James Simpson-Daniel unavailable due to injury*]

**(*This match was played in windy conditions on a wet pitch; Magnus Lund was played out of position as a blindside flanker; England were drawing 0-0 in the 9th minute when Iain Balshaw brilliantly created an overlap for Tom Varndell, who then wasted this great try-scoring opportunity by putting in a poor grubber kick which allowed Stephen Larkham to fly-hack the ball into touch; England were losing 3-0 midway through the first half; England were still losing 3-0 in the 25th minute when some superb handling amongst the backs created space for Tom Varndell, who then threw a poor pass to the unmarked Tom Voyce to waste another great try-scoring opportunity; England were losing 6-0 in the 28th minute when Tom Varndell beat Lote Tuqiri (1) for pace on the outside and was then body-checked by Chris Latham after he chipped the ball ahead into the corner, but the referee unaccountably ignored this infringement; England were still losing 6-0 in the 29th minute when Iain Balshaw crossed the tryline after Olly Barkley chipped ahead, but the video referee could not award the try because George Gregan managed to get beneath the ball as Balshaw attempted to ground it; England were losing 6-0 in the 31st minute when Olly Barkley missed an eminently kickable 21 metre penalty goal attempt; England were still losing 6-0 in the 33rd minute when Pat Sanderson broke through but then inexplicably ignored the unmarked Tom Voyce on his immediate right and threw a poor speculative pass in the direction of Tom Varndell; England were losing 6-0 just before half-time; England were losing 9-0 at half-time; England were losing 9-3 in the 44th minute; England were losing 12-3 in the 54th minute when Chris Latham scored after a poor tackle by Mike Catt, thus 7 points were preventable; Magnus Lund went off injured in the 57th minute, being replaced by Joe Worsley; England were losing 19-3 midway through the second*

***half; England were losing 22-3 in the 68th minute; England were still losing 22-3 with 7 minutes remaining; England were losing 29-3 with 4 minutes remaining; Australia were allowed to score 25 unanswered points to clinch the match*)**

17th June AUSTRALIA 43 **ENGLAND** 18

Telstra Dome, Melbourne

[*This match kicked off at 8.05pm; James Simpson-Daniel unavailable due to injury; Lewis Moody selected but withdrew on the day of the match due to injury, being replaced by Michael Lipman; The Telstra Dome had its retractable roof closed for this match; Graham Rowntree retired in February 2007; Stuart Abbott retired due to injury in October 2007*]

(*Chris Jones and Ben Kay dominated the lineout in this match; Andy Goode scored a drop goal in the 4th minute!; England were leading 3-0 in the 6th minute when George Smith scored after he fly-hacked a loose ball on and then regathered it when the ball rebounded off Tom Varndell's head!; England were losing 7-3 in the 11th minute when they awarded a 15 metre penalty in an eminently kickable position but Andy Goode unaccountably chose to take a quick tap penalty in a vain attempt to score a try; England were losing 12-3 in the 14th minute; England were still losing 12-3 midway through the first half; England were losing 12-6 in the 26th minute; England were still losing 12-6 in the 38th minute when Lote Tuqiri (1) scored after Chris Latham powered through 4 attempted tackles, thus 2 tries and 14 points were preventable; England were losing 19-6 at half-time; The referee had to order uncontested scrums after Graham Rowntree and Julian White both went off injured at half-time; Tim Payne and Magnus Lund came on as replacements for Graham Rowntree and Julian White respectively at the start of the second half, with Joe Worsley then switching from flanker to prop to accommodate Lund; Andy Goode delivered an inch-perfect pass to the referee in the 42nd minute!; England were losing 26-6 in the 48th minute when George Chuter dummied his way through to score a brilliant try; Stuart Abbott came on as a replacement for Matt Tait in the 55th minute, with Jamie Noon then switching from centre to wing to accommodate Stuart Abbott; England were losing 26-11 midway through the second half; England were losing 36-11 in the 66th minute; England were still losing 36-11 with 2 minutes of normal time remaining; Australia were allowed to score 17 unanswered points to seal the match; England were losing 43-11 in the first minute of injury time when a superb break by Nick Walshe enabled Tom Varndell to score a consolation try with the last move of the match; Chris Jones had a brilliant game; This was the first time since 1984 that England had lost 5 cap international matches in a row!*)

WORLD UNIVERSITY RUGBY SEVENS CHAMPIONSHIP

CUS Roma, Stadio degli Eucalipti, Rome

CAPTAIN: *John Houston* (SC)

First Round - Pool 'B'

4th Aug Ukrainian Universities (*UKR*) 0 **GREAT BRITAIN STUDENTS** 38

[*This match kicked off at 9.30am in an attempt to play in cooler conditions*]

(*This match was played in 90 degree heat*)

4th Aug Moroccan Universities (*MOR*) 0 **GREAT BRITAIN STUDENTS** 45

[*This match kicked off at 6.40pm in an attempt to attempt to play in cooler conditions*]

(*This match was played in 90 degree heat*)

Quarter-Final

5th Aug ITALY STUDENTS 12 **GREAT BRITAIN STUDENTS** 24

[*This match kicked off before 12 noon in an attempt to play in cooler conditions*]
(*This match was played in extremely hot conditions*)

Semi-Final

5th Aug Spanish Universities (*SP*) 19 **GREAT BRITAIN STUDENTS** 24

[*This match kicked off before 12 noon in an attempt to play in cooler conditions*]
(*This match was played in extremely hot conditions*)

Final

5th Aug FRANCE STUDENTS 33 **GREAT BRITAIN STUDENTS** 10

[*This match kicked off after 5.00pm in an attempt to attempt to play in cooler conditions*]
(*This match was played in extremely hot conditions*)

LAWRENCE HAMBLIN HENLEY INTERNATIONAL SEVENS

Henley RFC, Dry Leas, Marlow Road, Henley-on-Thames

CAPTAIN: *Jamie Murray* (SC)

First Round

6th Aug Henley Hawks 0 **SAMURAI** 34

[*This match kicked off at 10.20am; Kirk King missed this match after his train was delayed!*]
(*The Samurai were drawing 0-0 midway through the first half; The Samurai were leading 10-0 at half-time; The Samurai were leading 17-0 early in the second half; The Samurai were leading 22-0 shortly afterwards when Matt Vaughan dummied his way through to score a brilliant try; The Samurai were leading 29-0 in the closing stages*)

Quarter-Final

6th Aug British Army (*SER*) 12 **SAMURAI** 19

[*This match kicked off at 1.20pm*]
(*The Samurai were losing 7-0 in the 3rd minute!; The Samurai were still losing 7-0 just before half-time when Gert De Kock scored after Kirk King made a brilliant run; The Samurai were losing 7-5 at half-time; The Samurai were losing 12-5 in the 10th minute; The Samurai were still losing 12-5 shortly afterwards when Angus Martyn scored after he wrong-footed the defence with a brilliant sidestep; The Samurai were drawing 12-12 with 2 minutes remaining when Angus Martyn scored another try after Kirk King made a superb run down the left touchline; Kirk King injured playing in the match*)

Semi-Final

6th Aug Hartpury College 12 **SAMURAI** 17

(*Ross Blake scored in the 3rd minute!; The Samurai were leading 12-0 in the 6th minute; The Samurai were leading 12-5 at half-time; The Samurai were leading 17-5 early in the second half; The Samurai were still leading 17-5 midway through the second half; The Samurai were leading 17-5 with 2 minutes remaining*)

Final

6th Aug <u>Scorpions</u> 24 **SAMURAI** 19

[*This match kicked off at 7.00pm; The Scorpions were an invitational team founded by Ian Davies at University College Chichester*]
(*The Samurai were losing 7-0 midway through the first half; The Samurai were losing 12-7 shortly before half-time; The Samurai were drawing 12-12 at half-time; Kirk King came on as a replacement at the start of the second half but had to go off injured immediately afterwards with a knee injury!; The Samurai were still drawing 12-12*

shortly afterwards when they wasted a great try-scoring opportunity by dropping the ball while the Scorpions line was at their mercy; The Scorpions were allowed to score 12 unanswered points to win the match; The Samurai were losing 24-12 in the last minute when Jamie Murray scored a consolation try; Jamie Murray had a brilliant game)

NEW ZEALAND TOUR TO ENGLAND, FRANCE AND WALES 2006

CAPTAIN: *Martin Corry*

5th Nov **ENGLAND*** 20 NEW ZEALAND 41

Twickenham

[This match kicked off at 3.30pm; Matt Stevens, Steve Borthwick, Richard Hill (2), Jonny Wilkinson, Olly Barkley and Stuart Abbott all unavailable due to injury; Mark Cueto selected but withdrew due to injury, being replaced by Paul Sackey; Perry Freshwater, James Forrester, Tom Rees, Matt Tait, Josh Lewsey and Olly Morgan all in original training squad of 30 but withdrew due to injury; Tom Palmer (2) and Toby Flood in original training squad of 30 but were not selected for team or bench; Dan Ward-Smith, Phil Christophers and Mark Van Gisbergen were added to the squad on 31st October 2006; On 7th November 2006 the IRB admitted that Jamie Noon's disallowed try should actually have been given!]

(Dan Carter scored a penalty goal in the 3rd minute!; England were losing 3-0 in the 5th minute when Jamie Noon ignored the unmarked Danny Grewcock outside him and powered across the New Zealand line himself with the ball clearly in his arms, but the referee was unsighted and the video referee could not award the try because no camera angle actually showed the grounding of the ball; England were losing 6-0 in the 14th minute; England were still losing 6-0 midway through the first half; England were losing 6-0 in the 22nd minute when Aaron Mauger scored after Jamie Noon missed a tackle on Rico Gear; England were losing 13-0 in the 30th minute when Jamie Noon scored after Anthony Allen made a brilliant break; England were losing 16-5 in the 39th minute when Anthony Allen's pass was intercepted by Joe Rokocoko, who then ran 50 metres to score; England were losing 28-5 at half-time; England were still losing 28-5 in the 45th minute when some superb handling amongst the forwards allowed Ben Cohen to score; England were losing 28-12 in the 49th minute when Charlie Hodgson missed a kickable 43 metre penalty goal attempt; England were still losing 28-12 in the 55th minute when Charlie Hodgson overhit a 22 drop-out and Dan Carter went on to score after a poor tackle by Anthony Allen, thus 3 tries and 21 points were preventable; England were losing 35-12 midway through the second half when Shaun Perry caught a chip by Aaron Mauger and ran 60 metres to score a brilliant try; England were losing 35-20 in the 65th minute; England were losing 38-20 with 5 minutes remaining; England lost by 21 points to record their worst ever margin of defeat in a cap international match at Twickenham)

ARGENTINE TOUR TO ENGLAND AND ITALY 2006

CAPTAIN: *Martin Corry*

11th Nov **ENGLAND*** 18 ARGENTINA 25

Twickenham

[This match kicked off at 2.30pm; Matt Stevens, Steve Borthwick, Richard Hill (2), James Forrester, Jonny Wilkinson, Olly Barkley, Stuart Abbott and Olly Morgan all unavailable due to injury; Andy Sheridan and Mark Cueto in original training squad of

***30 but withdrew due to injury; Chris Jones, Tom Rees, Dan Ward-Smith, Andy Goode, Ben Johnston and Mark van Gisbergen all in original training squad of 30 but were not selected for team or bench*]

(***Charlie Hodgson scored a penalty goal in the 4th minute!; England were drawing 3-3 in the 7th minute; Magnus Lund came on as a temporary blood replacement for Lewis Moody in the 8th minute; England were still drawing 3-3 midway through the second half; England were drawing 3-3 in the 32nd minute when Paul Sackey scored a brilliant 41 metre solo try; England were leading 10-6 just before half-time; England were leading 10-9 at half-time; England were losing 12-10 in the 44th minute; Charlie Hodgson was unaccountably substituted in the 52nd minute, being replaced by Toby Flood; Paul Sackey went off injured in the 54th minute, being replaced by Josh Lewsey; England were still losing 12-10 in the 55th minute when Toby Flood's pass was intercepted by Federico Todeschini, who then ran 60 metres to score, thus 7 points were preventable; England were losing 19-13 midway through the second half when Iain Balshaw scored a brilliant 50 metre solo try, with Toby Flood then missing the eminently kickable conversion attempt; England were losing 22-18 in the 69th minute; England were losing 25-18 with 6 minutes remaining; England conceded too many needless penalties within Federico Todeschini's kicking range; England were booed off the pitch at the end of the match!; Shaun Perry had a poor game; This was the first time since 1972 that England had lost 7 cap international matches in a row!***)

ATKINS REMEMBRANCE RUGBY MATCH

CAPTAIN: *Andy Dalgleish*

14th Nov COMBINED SERVICES (*SER*) 25 **BARBARIANS** 33

Newbury RFC, Monks Lane, Newbury

[***This match kicked off at 7.30pm; Dai Maddocks selected but withdrew due to injury, Tom Davies was moved from the bench to the team and Steve Pope was then selected for the bench; Jason Forster selected but withdrew due to injury, being replaced by Iain Dick; Andy Dalgleish played for Major R.V. Stanley's XV against Oxford University at Iffley Road on 22nd November 2006; Chris Budgen, Ben Hughes, Lee Soper and Mal Roberts played for the Combined Services in this match***]

(***The Barbarians were drawing 0-0 midway through the first half when Richard Morris scored after Tyrone Howe made a brilliant run; The Barbarians were drawing 5-5 in the 29th minute when Kenny Bingham scored a brilliant solo try; The Barbarians were leading 12-10 shortly before half-time; The Barbarians were losing 13-12 at half-time; The Barbarians were leading 19-13 in the 42nd minute; The Barbarians were leading 19-18 in the 50th minute; The Barbarians were losing 25-19 midway through the second half; The Barbarians were leading 26-25 in the 64th minute; Dafydd Lewis came on as a replacement for Arwel Thomas in the 65th minute; The Barbarians were still leading 26-25 in the fifth minute of injury time when Richard Morris powered through 3 attempted tackles to score another try which Dafydd Lewis then converted with the last kick of the match to clinch the game***)

SOUTH AFRICAN TOUR TO IRELAND AND ENGLAND 2006

CAPTAIN: *Martin Corry*

18th Nov **ENGLAND** 23 SOUTH AFRICA 21

Twickenham

[***This match kicked off at 2.30pm; Matt Stevens, Steve Borthwick, Richard Hill (2), James Forrester, Jonny Wilkinson, Stuart Abbott and Paul Sackey all unavailable due to injury; Iain Balshaw selected but withdrew due to injury, being replaced by Ben***

***Cohen with Josh Lewsey then moving from wing to full back to accommodate Ben Cohen; Perry Freshwater in original training squad of 30 but withdrew due to injury; Stuart Turner, Danny Grewcock, Magnus Lund, Tom Rees, Anthony Allen and Ben Johnston all in original training squad of 30 but were not selected for team or bench*]**
(*Charlie Hodgson scored a penalty goal in the 2nd minute!; England were drawing 3-3 in the 7th minute when Charlie Hodgson missed a kickable 40 metre penalty goal attempt; England were still drawing 3-3 in the 13th minute when Josh Lewsey saved a certain try by getting across to brilliantly tackle Jean de Villiers into touch at the corner flag; England were leading 6-3 midway through the first half; England were still leading 6-3 in the 22nd minute when they were awarded a 10 metre penalty in an eminently kickable position, but Martin Corry ordered a kick to the corner in a vain attempt to score a try from the ensuing lineout; England were leading 6-3 in the 27th minute when Francois Steyn scored a 45 metre drop goal after Josh Lewsey failed to find touch; England were drawing 6-6 in the 37th minute when Ben Cohen's attempted clearance kick went straight to Ricky Januarie, who instigated a counter-attack that led directly to a try by Butch James, thus 1 try and 10 points were preventable; Charlie Hodgson went off injured immediately afterwards, being replaced by Andy Goode; England were losing 13-6 at half-time; England were losing 18-6 in the 43rd minute; Andy Sheridan went off injured in the 49th minute, being replaced by Phil Vickery; England were still losing 18-6 immediately afterwards when Mark Cueto reacted superbly to gather a loose ball on the South African line and score; England were losing 21-13 in the 57th minute; England were still losing 21-13 midway through the second half; England were losing 21-16 in the 68th minute; England were still losing 21-16 with 7 minutes remaining when a rolling maul enabled Phil Vickery to score a try which Andy Goode then converted to win the match*)

FOURTH INVESTEC CHALLENGE MATCH

CAPTAIN: *Martin Corry*

25th Nov **ENGLAND** 14 SOUTH AFRICA 25
Twickenham

[*This match kicked off at 2.30pm; Perry Freshwater, Matt Stevens, Richard Hill (2), Tom Rees, James Forrester, Jonny Wilkinson, Charlie Hodgson, Stuart Abbott and Iain Balshaw all unavailable due to injury; Andy Sheridan in original training squad of 28 but withdrew due to injury; Stuart Turner in original training squad of 28 but withdrew after a RFU hearing on 21st November 2006 found him guilty of kneeing an opponent in a Guinness Premiership match on 17th November 2006 and thus banned him for 1 week; Danny Grewcock, Magnus Lund, Tom Rees, Ben Johnston, Anthony Allen and Paul Sackey all in original training squad of 28 but were not selected for team or bench; Tim Payne and Mark Van Gisbergen were added to the squad on 20th November 2006*]
(*Phil Vickery was played out of position as a loose-head prop; The England forwards dominated the lineout in the first half; England were leading 3-0 in the 6th minute; England were leading 6-0 in the 12th minute; England were leading 9-3 midway through the first half when Andy Goode missed a kickable 30 metre drop goal attempt; England were leading 14-3 in the 30th minute; England were leading 14-9 just before half-time; England were losing 16-14 at half-time; England were losing 19-14 in the 47th minute; England were still losing 19-14 in the 57th minute when Andy Goode missed 2 speculative long-range penalty goal attempts in 2 minutes; England were losing 19-14 midway through the second half when Andy Goode put up a brilliant cross-kick, but Mark Cueto then wasted this great try-scoring opportunity by dropping*

the ball while the South African line was at his mercy; England were still losing 19-14 with 5 minutes remaining; Andre Pretorius scored a hat-trick of drop goals in the second half!; South Africa were allowed to score 22 unanswered points to win the match; England failed to score a single point in the final 50 minutes of this match!; England were booed off the pitch at the end of the match!)

AUSTRALIAN TOUR TO WALES, ITALY, IRELAND AND SCOTLAND 2006

CAPTAIN: *No captain appointed*

29th Nov **BARBARIANS** C AUSTRALIA XV C
Twickenham

[*The Barbarians cancelled this match on 5th September 2006 when it became clear that they would be unable to raise a sufficiently competitive team because many potential players had extensive club and international commitments in the period in question*]

EMIRATES AIRLINE DUBAI RUGBY SEVENS

Dubai Exiles Stadium, Dubai

CAPTAIN: *Simon Amor*

First Round - Pool 'B'

1st Dec SCOTLAND 0 **ENGLAND** 38

[*This match kicked off at 11.52am*]

(*This match was played in hot conditions; England were leading 12-0 shortly before half-time; England were leading 19-0 at half-time; Nick Abendanon came on as a replacement for Simon Amor early in the second half; England were leading 26-0 early in the second half; Tom Croft scored after James Haskell threw a brilliant pass*)

1st Dec ZIMBABWE 0 **ENGLAND** 29

[*This match kicked off at 4.38pm*]

(*This match was played in drizzly conditions; England were leading 12-0 at half-time*)

1st Dec FRANCE 10 **ENGLAND** 19

[*This match kicked off at 7.56pm*]

(*This match was played in very wet and windy conditions; England were drawing 0-0 midway through the first half; England were still drawing 0-0 in the 6th minute when Ben Gollings brilliantly chipped ahead and followed up to score; England were leading 5-0 shortly before half-time when Ben Gollings scored another superb try; England were leading 12-0 at half-time; Nick Abendanon scored after Marcel Garvey went on a brilliant rampaging run*)

Quarter-Final

2nd Dec AUSTRALIA 5 **ENGLAND** 21

[*This match kicked off at 12.14pm*]

(*This match was played in heavy rain on a muddy pitch; David Dillon scored in the 2nd minute!; England were losing 5-0 midway through the first half; England were still losing 5-0 in the 6th minute; England were leading 7-5 at half-time; A superb long pass by Nick Abendanon enabled Dave Strettle to score a try which Ben Gollings then brilliantly converted from the left touchline to give England a 14-5 lead in the 9th minute; England were still leading 14-5 midway through the second half; England were leading 21-5 with 2 minutes remaining; England scored 21 unanswered points to win the match*)

Semi-Final

2nd Dec SOUTH AFRICA 19 **ENGLAND** 0

[This match kicked off at 6.42pm]

(This match was played in heavy rain on a very muddy pitch; England were drawing 0-0 midway through the first half; England were drawing 0-0 just before half-time when Philip Burger scored after a poor tackle by Andy Vilk, thus 7 points were preventable; England were losing 7-0 at half-time; England were losing 14-0 in the 9th minute; England were still losing 14-0 midway through the second half; England were losing 14-0 in the last minute; Ben Gollings increased his IRB World Sevens record to 1603 points in this tournament)

SOUTH AFRICAN TOUR TO IRELAND AND ENGLAND 2006

CAPTAIN: *Lawrence Dallaglio*

3rd Dec **WORLD XV** 7 SOUTH AFRICA XV 32

Walkers Stadium, Filbert Way, Leicester

[This match kicked off at 3.00pm; Kabamba Floors unavailable due to his Sevens commitments; Gaffie du Toit in original squad but withdrew for personal reasons; Breyton Paulse and Morgan Turinui in original squad but were not selected for team or bench; Scott Staniforth in revised squad of 22 but withdrew, being replaced by Clinton Schiscofske; Ben Tune in revised squad of 22 but withdrew due to injury; The World XV's starting lineup had 523 caps between them!; Andy Farrell was capped 34 times for Great Britain at Rugby League between 1993-2004 (including 29 in a row as captain), played for England in the Rugby League World Cup Final at Wembley on 28th October 1995, played Rugby League for Great Britain in the Super League World Nines in January-February 1997, captained England at the Rugby League World Sevens in February 2003 and then became a Rugby Union player in March 2005 when he joined Saracens; Matt Perry retired due to injury in March 2007]

(This match was played in cold conditions; The World XV forwards could not win any possession in the first half; The World XV was losing 7-0 in the 11th minute; The World XV was still losing 7-0 midway through the first half; The World XV was losing 10-0 in the 26th minute when Andy Farrell missed a kickable 42 metre penalty goal attempt; The World XV was still losing 10-0 shortly before half-time when Andy Farrell missed an eminently kickable 24 metre penalty goal attempt; The World XV was losing 10-0 at half-time; The World XV was losing 13-0 in the 48th minute when they were awarded a 20 metre penalty in an eminently kickable position, but Lawrence Dallaglio ordered a kick to the corner in a vain attempt to score a try from the ensuing lineout; The World XV was still losing 13-0 in the 52nd minute when they were awarded a 23 metre penalty in another eminently kickable position, but Lawrence Dallaglio again ordered a kick to the corner in a vain attempt to score a try from the ensuing lineout; Pablo Gómez Cora came on as a replacement for Matt Perry in the 54th minute, with Clinton Schiscofske then switching from wing to full back to accommodate Pablo Gómez Cora; The World XV was losing 13-0 in the 57th minute when a poor defensive alignment allowed Albert van den Berg to score, thus 7 points were preventable; The World XV was losing 20-0 midway through the second half; The final quarter was played in wet conditions; The World XV was still losing 20-0 with 8 minutes of normal time remaining; The South African XV was allowed to score 27 unanswered points to win the match; The World XV was losing 27-0 with 4 minutes of normal time remaining when some superb handling amongst the backs allowed Drew Mitchell to score; The World XV was losing 27-7 in the last minute of normal time)

EMIRATES AIRLINE SOUTH AFRICA SEVENS

Outeniqua Park Stadium, George

CAPTAIN: *Simon Amor*

First Round - Pool 'B'

8th Dec WALES 14 **ENGLAND*** 14

[*This match kicked off at 12.36pm*]

(*The England players monopolised possession in the first half; England were leading 7-0 midway through the first half; England were leading 7-0 at half-time; David Doherty scored a brilliant 65 metre solo try which Ben Gollings then converted to give England a 14-0 lead in the 9th minute; England were still leading 14-0 midway through the second half; England were leading 14-7 in the last minute when Tal Selley scored after a poor tackle by Ben Gollings, thus 7 points were preventable; Wales were allowed to score 14 unanswered points to draw the match; England were drawing 14-14 when the full-time hooter sounded, but the ball remained in play until Ben Gollings was tackled two metres short of the Welsh line*)

8th Dec PORTUGAL 5 **ENGLAND** 58

[*This match kicked off at 3.42pm*]

(*Andy Vilk scored after just 27 seconds had been played!; Marcel Garvey scored after Simon Amor made a brilliant run; England were leading 27-0 at half-time; Marcel Garvey scored to complete a hat-trick of tries after just 16 seconds of the second half had been played!; England scored 58 unanswered points to win the match; England were leading 58-0 in the last minute*)

8th Dec ARGENTINA 7 **ENGLAND** 26

[*This match kicked off at 7.54pm*]

(*England were drawing 0-0 midway through the first half; England were leading 7-0 in the 5th minute; England were leading 14-0 at half-time; England were leading 21-0 in the 9th minute; England were leading 26-0 midway through the second half; England scored 26 unanswered points to win the match; England were still leading 26-0 in the final minute*)

Quarter-Final

9th Dec SAMOA 0 **ENGLAND** 24

[*This match kicked off at 1.37pm; Marcel Garvey unavailable due to injury*]

(*This match was played on a wet pitch; England were drawing 0-0 in the 2nd minute when Charlie Amesbury crossed the tryline but was then pushed into touch in-goal by both Faitio Sione and Lolo Lui before he could ground the ball!; Rob Thirlby went off injured in the 3rd minute, being replaced by Ben Gollings; England were drawing 0-0 midway through the first half when Michael Hills scored from a tap penalty; England were leading 5-0 just before half-time; England were leading 12-0 at half-time; England were still leading 12-0 in the 9th minute when James Haskell powered through 3 attempted tackles to score; England were leading 17-0 midway through the second half; England were still leading 17-0 with 2 minutes remaining when Dom Shabbo scored after Danny Gray put in a crossfield kick from behind his own line!*)

Semi-Final

9th Dec SOUTH AFRICA 10 **ENGLAND*** 7

[*This match kicked off at 5.03pm; Rob Thirlby and Marcel Garvey unavailable due to injury*]

(*Charlie Amesbury broke through in the 1st minute but was then brilliantly tackled by Stefan Basson!; England were drawing 0-0 in the 3rd minute when Kabamba Floors scored after a poor tackle by Andy Vilk, thus 5 points were preventable; England were

***losing 5-0 midway through the first half; England were still losing 5-0 in the 6th minute when Michael Hills scored after Danny Gray threw a brilliant long pass; England were leading 7-5 at half-time; England were still leading 7-5 midway through the second half; England were leading 7-5 with 2 minutes remaining; Ben Gollings increased his IRB World Sevens record to 1613 points in this tournament*)**

2007

NEW ZEALAND INTERNATIONAL SEVENS

WestpacTrust Stadium, Wellington

CAPTAIN: *Simon Amor*

First Round - Pool 'C'

2nd Feb SCOTLAND 12 **ENGLAND** 33

[This match kicked off at 1.00pm]

(England were leading 7-5 in the 5th minute; England were leading 19-5 at half-time; England were leading 19-12 early in the second half; England scored 14 unanswered points to win the match; Simon Amor had a brilliant game)

2nd Feb PAPUA NEW GUINEA 7 **ENGLAND** 22

[This match kicked off at 3.56pm]

(England were drawing 0-0 in the early stages when Alistair McLay scored after Andy Vilk missed a tackle on Willie Rikis, thus 7 points were preventable; England were losing 7-0 when David Smith (2) scored after Rob Thirlby made a brilliant run; England were losing 7-5 when Rob Thirlby dummied his way through to score a superb try; England were leading 12-7 at half-time; England were leading 17-7 when Charlie Amesbury scored a brilliant solo try; England scored 22 unanswered points to win the match)

2nd Feb SAMOA 19 **ENGLAND*** 12

[This match kicked off at 8.50pm]

(The England players could not win any possession in the first half; Samoa were allowed to score 19 unanswered points to win the match; England were losing 19-0 at half-time; England were still losing 19-0 when Andy Vilk had a great try-scoring chance but was tackled short of the Samoan line; England were losing 19-0 when Danny Gray brilliantly chipped ahead but Rob Thirlby was unable to gather the bouncing ball while the Samoan tryline was at his mercy; England were losing 19-7 in the closing stages)

Quarter-Final

3rd Feb NEW ZEALAND 14 **ENGLAND*** 7

[This match kicked off at 2.55pm]

(England were drawing 0-0 in the 2nd minute when Andy Vilk lost a strike against the head which led directly to a try by Lote Raikabula, thus 7 points were preventable!; England were losing 7-0 midway through the first half; England were still losing 7-0 when the half-time hooter sounded, but the ball was still in play and Danny Gray was able to dummy his way through to score a brilliant try; England were drawing 7-7 at half-time; England were losing 14-7 early in the second half; England were still losing 14-7 midway through the second half)

[Plate Semi-Final:]

[3rd Feb CANADA 7 **ENGLAND** 29]

[This match kicked off at 5.38pm]

(England were losing 7-0 in the early stages; Rob Thirlby powered through several attempted tackles to score a brilliant try; England were leading 19-7 at half-time; England scored 29 unanswered points to win the match)

[Plate Final:]

[3rd Feb FRANCE 12 **ENGLAND** 21]

[This match kicked off at 8.30pm]

(England were losing 12-0 in the early stages; England were still losing 12-0 when Simon Amor scored after Rob Thirlby made a brilliant run; England were leading 14-12

at half-time; England were still leading 14-12 early in the second half when Danny Gray dummied his way through to score a superb try; England scored 21 unanswered points to win the match; England were leading 21-12 when Charlie Amesbury made a brilliant break but Simon Amor then wasted this great try-scoring opportunity by dropping the ball)

6 NATIONS CHAMPIONSHIP

CAPTAIN: *Phil Vickery*

3rd Feb **ENGLAND** 42 SCOTLAND 20

Twickenham

[*This match kicked off at 4.00pm; Andy Sheridan, Steve Thompson (2), Dan Ward-Smith, Charlie Hodgson, Mark Cueto and Paul Sackey all unavailable due to injury; Iain Balshaw selected but withdrew due to injury, being replaced by Olly Morgan; Lewis Moody selected for bench but withdrew due to injury, being replaced by Tom Rees; Tim Payne, Shane Geraghty, Mike Catt and Jamie Noon all in final training squad of 29 but were not selected for team or bench*]

(*England were leading 3-0 in the 11th minute; England were drawing 3-3 midway through the first half when Jonny Wilkinson scored a brilliant 25 metre drop goal; England were leading 6-3 in the 25th minute when a lineout overthrow by George Chuter led directly to a try Simon Taylor (2), thus 7 points were preventable; England were leading 12-10 in the 37th minute when Jason Robinson dummied his way through to score a superb try; England were leading 17-10 at half-time; England were leading 17-13 in the 43rd minute; England were leading 23-13 in the 55th minute when Harry Ellis kicked ahead and while Sean Lamont reached the ball first he failed to get any downward pressure on it, which allowed Jason Robinson to follow up and score another try; England were leading 30-13 midway through the second half when the video referee unaccountably awarded Jonny Wilkinson a try that should not have been given because his right foot landed in touch before he grounded the ball; Joe Worsley went off injured in the 62nd minute, being replaced by Tom Rees; England were leading 37-13 with 8 minutes of normal time match remaining; England were leading 42-13 with 3 minutes of normal time remaining; Jonny Wilkinson played brilliantly and scored 27 points in this match; Harry Ellis had a brilliant game*)

10th Feb **ENGLAND** 20 ITALY 7

Twickenham

[*This match kicked off at 1.30pm, which was the earliest time that an international had ever started at Twickenham; Andy Sheridan, Steve Thompson (2), Joe Worsley, Lewis Moody, Dan Ward-Smith, Charlie Hodgson and Paul Sackey all unavailable due to injury*]

(*This match was played on a wet pitch; Jonny Wilkinson kicked away too much possession in the first half; Jonny Wilkinson scored a brilliant 47 metre penalty goal in the 4th minute!; England were leading 6-0 in the 15th minute; England were still leading 6-0 midway through the first half; England were leading 9-0 in the 25th minute; Iain Balshaw went off injured in the 38th minute, being replaced by Matt Tait with Josh Lewsey then switching from wing to full back to accommodate Matt Tait; England were still leading 9-0 shortly before half-time when Jason Robinson scored a superb try; England were leading 14-0 at half-time; England were still leading 14-0 in the 56th minute; England were leading 17-0 midway through the second half; England were still leading 17-0 in the 65th minute when they unaccountably failed to defend the fringes of a maul and Andrea Scanavacca was able to break through and score, thus 7 points*

were preventable; Mike Tindall went off injured immediately afterwards, being replaced by Toby Flood with Josh Lewsey then moving from full back to wing to accommodate Toby Flood and Matt Tait switching from wing to centre to accommodate Josh Lewsey; England were leading 17-7 in the 69th minute when they were awarded a 27 metre penalty in an eminently kickable position, but Josh Lewsey inexplicably chose to take a quick tap penalty in a vain attempt to score a try; England were still leading 17-7 with 9 minutes remaining when Jonny Wilkinson had a speculative 37 metre drop goal attempt go underneath the crossbar!; England were leading 17-7 with 5 minutes remaining when Jonny Wilkinson scored a brilliant 43 metre penalty goal to seal the match; Iain Balshaw had a poor game)

24th Feb IRELAND 43 **ENGLAND** 13

Croke Park, Dublin

[*This match kicked off at 5.30pm; Andy Sheridan, Steve Thompson (2), Lewis Moody, Dan Ward-Smith, Charlie Hodgson, Paul Sackey and Iain Balshaw all unavailable due to injury; Jason Robinson selected but withdrew due to injury, being replaced by Dave Strettle; Mike Catt was added to the squad on 22nd February 2007 to provide injury cover for Jonny Wilkinson*]

(This match was played in cold and very wet conditions; The England scrum was put under severe pressure; The England forwards could not win any lineout ball in the first half; Jonny Wilkinson scored a penalty goal in the 2nd minute!; England were drawing 3-3 in the 6th minute; England were losing 6-3 midway through the first half; England were losing 9-3 in the 26th minute; Olly Morgan went off injured in the 30th minute, being replaced by Matt Tait; England were losing 16-3 in the 36th minute when Matt Tait saved a certain try by tackling Shane Horgan; England were still losing 16-3 shortly before half-time; England were losing 23-3 at half-time; Magnus Lund went off injured at half-time after being concussed, being replaced by Tom Rees; England were losing 26-3 in the 43rd minute; Ireland were allowed to score 26 unanswered points to win the match; Julian White came on as a replacement for Perry Freshwater in the 44th minute, with Phil Vickery then switching from tight-head to loose-head prop to accommodate Julian White; England were still losing 26-3 in the 47th minute when some superb handling amongst the backs allowed Dave Strettle to score a try which Jonny Wilkinson then brilliantly converted from the left touchline; England were losing 26-10 in the 53rd minute when Jonny Wilkinson had a speculative 50 metre penalty goal attempt go underneath the crossbar; England were losing 26-13 in the 57th minute; England were losing 29-13 midway through the second half; England were losing 36-13 in the 65th minute; Shaun Perry came on as a replacement for Harry Ellis in the 68th minute; England were still losing 36-13 with 1 minute remaining when Shaun Perry had his pass intercepted by Isaac Boss who then ran 41 metres to score, thus 7 points were preventable; England lost by 30 points to record their worst ever margin of defeat against Ireland, who achieved their highest ever points total against England)

CAPTAIN: *Mike Catt*

11th Mar **ENGLAND** 26 FRANCE 18

Twickenham

[*This match kicked off at 3.00pm; Andy Sheridan, Phil Vickery, Steve Thompson (2), Lewis Moody, Dan Ward-Smith, Charlie Hodgson, Paul Sackey, Iain Balshaw and Olly Morgan all unavailable due to injury; Steve Borthwick, Jonny Wilkinson and Andy Farrell in original training squad of 28 but withdrew due to injury; Perry Freshwater, James Haskell and Mark Cueto in original training squad of 28 but were not selected*

***for team or bench; Chris Jones was added to the squad on 5th March 2007 to provide injury cover for Steve Borthwick*]**
(*David Skréla scored a penalty goal in the 4th minute!; England were drawing 3-3 in the 8th minute; England were losing 9-3 midway through the first half; England were losing 9-6 in the 31st minute; England were losing 12-9 in the 35th minute; England were still losing 12-9 shortly before half-time when Toby Flood had a speculative 51 metre penalty goal attempt go underneath the crossbar!; England were losing 12-9 at half-time; England were still losing 12-9 in the 48th minute when Toby Flood scored after Mike Catt made a brilliant break; England were leading 16-15 in the 53rd minute; Toby Flood went off injured in the 59th minute, being replaced by Shane Geraghty; England were losing 18-16 midway through the second half; England were leading 19-18 in the 68th minute; England were still leading 19-18 with 7 minutes of normal time remaining when Mike Tindall scored after Shane Geraghty made a superb 64 metre run; Shaun Perry came on as a replacement for Mike Catt with 2 minutes of normal time remaining, with Harry Ellis then switching from scrum half to wing to accommodate Shaun Perry and Matt Tait moving from wing to centre to accommodate Harry Ellis; Tom Rees had a brilliant game*)

CAPTAIN: *Mike Catt* [*Jason Robinson*]

17th Mar WALES 27 **ENGLAND*** 18

Millennium Stadium, Cardiff

[*This match kicked off at 5.30pm; Andy Sheridan, Phil Vickery, Steve Thompson (2), Lewis Moody, Dan Ward-Smith, Charlie Hodgson, Jonny Wilkinson, Andy Farrell, Mike Tindall, Paul Sackey, Iain Balshaw and Olly Morgan all unavailable due to injury; Nick Easter selected but withdrew due to injury, being replaced by James Haskell with Joe Worsley then moving from blindside flanker to number 8 to accommodate Haskell; The Millennium Stadium had its retractable roof closed for this match*]
(*England were drawing 0-0 in the 2nd minute when Toby Flood took too much time over his clearance kick and was charged down by James Hook who went on to score from the ensuing rebound, thus 7 points were preventable; Joe Worsley went off injured in the 9th minute, being replaced by Magnus Lund; England were losing 10-0 in the 11th minute; England were losing 15-0 midway through the first half; England were still losing 15-0 in the 32nd minute when Harry Ellis followed up and scored after Mike Catt made a brilliant break and then kicked ahead; England were losing 15-10 in the 35th minute; England were losing 18-10 just before half-time when Jason Robinson scored after Harry Ellis made a brilliant break; England were losing 18-15 at half-time; Mike Catt went off injured in the 42nd minute, being replaced by Shane Geraghty; England were still losing 18-15 in the 45th minute when they created and then squandered a 2 man overlap; England were drawing 18-18 in the 46th minute; England were still drawing 18-18 midway through the second half; England were losing 21-18 in the 65th minute; England were losing 24-18 in the 68th minute; England were still losing 24-18 with 6 minutes of normal time remaining*)

U21 6 NATIONS CHAMPIONSHIP

CAPTAIN: *Danny Care*

2nd Feb **ENGLAND U20** 31 SCOTLAND U20 5

Recreation Ground, Bath

[*This match kicked off at 7.30pm; Jordan Turner-Hall unavailable due to injury; David Doherty selected but withdrew due to illness, being replaced by Frankie Neale; Andy Saull, Danny Cipriani and Dom Waldouck in original training squad of 23 but withdrew due to injury; Dan Cole, Matt Mullan, Dave Attwood, Alex Shaw, Ollie Dodge, Ross*

McMillan and Hugo Ellis all played for England in the U19 World Championship at Dubai in April 2006; Selorm Kuadey played for England in the U19 World Championship at Dubai in April 2006 and played in the Samurai team that won the Amsterdam Heineken Sevens on 20th-21st May 2006; David Tait played in the England team that reached the Final of the Commonwealth Youth Games Rugby Sevens at Bendigo, Victoria on 2nd-3rd December 2004 and played for England in the U19 World Championships in South Africa in April 2005 and Dubai in April 2006; Adam Powell played in the England team that reached the Final of the Commonwealth Youth Games Rugby Sevens at Bendigo, Victoria on 2nd-3rd December 2004, played for England in the U19 World Championship in South Africa in April 2005 and captained England in the U19 World Championship at Dubai in April 2006; Ollie Dodge was the son of Paul Dodge]

(Danny Care threw a brilliant inside pass which enabled David Tait to score in the 2nd minute!; England U20 were leading 7-0 midway through the first half; England U20 were leading 7-0 at half-time; Frankie Neale missed a penalty goal attempt either side of half-time; England U20 were still leading 7-0 in the 48th minute when Danny Care went off injured, being replaced by Tom Parker (2) who then scored with his second touch of the ball!; A rolling maul enabled David Tait to score a try which Frankie Neale then converted to give England U20 a 21-0 lead in the 56th minute; England U20 scored 21 unanswered points to win the match; England U20 were still leading 21-0 midway through the second half; England U20 were leading 21-5 in the final quarter when Matt Cox scored from another rolling maul)

9th Feb **ENGLAND U20** 30 ITALY U21 10

Recreation Ground, Bath

[This match kicked off at 8.00pm; Danny Cipriani, Jordan Turner-Hall and Dom Waldouck unavailable due to injury; Tom Youngs played for England in the U19 World Championships in South Africa in April 2005 and Dubai in April 2006; Tom Youngs was the son of Nick Youngs]

(This match was played in extremely cold conditions on a muddy pitch; Ollie Dodge scored in the 4th minute!; England U20 were leading 12-0 in the 18th minute when David Doherty missed an eminently kickable conversion attempt; England U20 were still leading 12-0 midway through the first half; England U20 were leading 19-3 in the 26th minute; England U20 were still leading 19-3 in the 36th minute when David Doherty had a kickable 33 metre penalty goal attempt come back off the right-hand post; England U20 were still leading 19-3 just before half-time; England U20 were leading 22-3 at half-time; England U20 were still leading 22-3 in the 43rd minute when Seb Jewell dummied his way through to score a brilliant try; England U20 were leading 27-3 midway through the second half; Danny Care scored a brilliant 23 metre drop goal to give England U20 a 30-3 lead in the 62nd minute; England U20 were still leading 30-3 in the second minute of injury time)

23rd Feb IRELAND U20 13 **ENGLAND U20** 6

Dubarry Park, Athlone

[This match kicked off at 7.30pm; Tom Parker (2), Danny Cipriani and Dom Waldouck unavailable due to injury; Tom Mercey selected but withdrew to sit on the bench due to illness, Dan Cole was moved from the bench to the team; David Tait played for Scotland 7s in December 2009; Richard Bolt and Jordan Turner-Hall played for England in the U19 World Championship at Dubai in April 2006]

(This match was played in wet conditions; David Doherty scored a penalty goal in the 5th minute!; England U20 were leading 3-0 shortly afterwards when Chevvy Pennycook crossed the tryline but the move was disallowed because the scoring pass

from Alex Shaw was adjudged to have been forward; England U20 were still leading 3-0 midway through the first half; England U20 were leading 3-0 shortly before half-time; Dave Attwood and Seb Jewell both went off injured just before half-time, being replaced by Matt Cox and Frankie Neale respectively; England U20 were losing 7-3 at half-time; Frankie Neale went off injured in the 48th minute, being replaced by Jordan Turner-Hall with Adam Powell then switching from centre to fly half to accommodate Turner-Hall; England U20 were losing 7-6 shortly afterwards when David Doherty missed a penalty goal attempt; England U20 were still losing 7-6 midway through the second half; England U20 were losing 7-6 in the second minute of injury time; England U20 were losing 10-6 in the ninth minute of injury time)

9th Mar **ENGLAND U20** 13 FRANCE U21 32

Franklin's Gardens, Northampton

[This match kicked off at 7.30pm; Danny Cipriani unavailable due to injury; Andy Saull played for England in the U19 World Championship at Dubai in April 2006; Dom Waldouck played for England in the U19 World Championship in South Africa in April 2005]

(This match took place on a poor playing surface; David Doherty hit the left-hand post with an eminently kickable 23 metre penalty goal attempt in the 2nd minute!; Mathieu Nicolas scored in the 4th minute!; England U20 were losing 5-3 in the 15th minute; England U20 were still losing 5-3 midway through the first half when Dan Cole wasted a great try-scoring opportunity by dropping the ball as a rolling maul reached the France U21 line; England U20 were leading 6-5 in the 22nd minute; England U20 were still leading 6-5 in the 32nd minute when the referee awarded a penalty try after the France U21 forwards illegally wheeled a close-range defensive scrum; England U20 were leading 13-5 in the seventh minute of first half injury time; England U20 were leading 13-8 at half-time; England U20 were losing 15-13 in the 47th minute; France U21 were still leading 15-13 in the 52nd minute when Louis Picamoles scored after Danny Care was caught in possession at the base of an England U20 scrum, thus 7 points were preventable; England U20 were losing 22-13 midway through the second half; England U20 were still losing 22-13 with 2 minutes of normal time remaining; England U20 were losing 25-13 in the third minute of injury time; France U21 were allowed to score 27 unanswered points to win the match)

16th Mar WALES U20 21 **ENGLAND U20*** 21

Rodney Parade, Newport

[This match kicked off at 7.40pm; Danny Cipriani unavailable due to injury; Miles Benjamin in original training squad but withdrew the day before the match due to illness; Andy Saull, Hugo Ellis, David Smith (2) and Matt Cox all played for England in the U19 World Championship in Ireland in April 2007; Ben Thomas played for England in the U19 World Championship at Dubai in April 2006]

(Rhys Priestland scored a penalty goal in the 4th minute!; England U20 were losing 9-0 in the 13th minute; England U20 were losing 9-3 midway through the first half; England U20 were still losing 9-3 in the 30th minute when David Smith (2) saved a certain try by brilliantly tackling Jimmy Norris; England U20 were losing 12-3 in the 36th minute; England U20 were losing 12-6 in the first minute of first half injury time when Hugo Ellis made a brilliant break from the base of a scrum but then wasted this great try-scoring opportunity by throwing a poor pass to David Doherty; England U20 were losing 12-6 at half-time; England U20 were still losing 12-6 in the 47th minute when David Doherty scored after Andy Saull threw a superb one-handed pass, with Luke Cozens then missing the eminently kickable conversion attempt; England U20 were losing 15-11 in the 53rd minute; England U20 were losing 18-11 midway through the

second half; England U20 were losing 21-11 in the 64th minute; England U20 were losing 21-14 in the 66th minute; England U20 were still losing 21-14 in the ninth minute of injury time when Tom Youngs scored a try which Luke Cozens then converted with the last kick of the match to draw the game)

ENGLAND SAXONS INTERNATIONAL MATCHES

CAPTAIN: *Jamie Noon*

2nd Feb **ENGLAND SAXONS** 34 ITALY A 5

Sandy Park Stadium, Sandy Park Way, Exeter

[This match kicked off at 8.00pm; David Wilson (2), James Forrester, Ryan Lamb and James Simpson-Daniel all unavailable due to injury; Tom Rees selected but withdrew as he was now required to play for the full England international team the next day, being replaced by Jim Scaysbrook; Mike Catt selected but withdrew due to injury, Olly Barkley was moved from the bench to the team and Tom Varndell was then selected for the bench; Olly Morgan selected but withdrew as he was now required to play for the full England international team the next day, Mike Brown was moved from the bench to the team and Chev Walker was then selected for the bench; Pat Barnard, Will Skinner, Anthony Allen and Ollie Smith (2) all in final training squad of 23 but were not selected for team or bench; Chev Walker played for the combined Leeds Rugby Union and Rugby League team at the Middlesex Sevens at Twickenham on 12th August 2000, was capped for England at Rugby League in October 2000, was jailed for violent disorder in July 2003, was capped for Great Britain at Rugby League in October 2004 and became a Rugby Union player in November 2006 when he joined Bath]

(This match was played in cold conditions; Shane Geraghty missed a kickable 37 metre penalty goal attempt in the 5th minute!; The England Saxons were drawing 0-0 in the 6th minute when Nick Abendanon made a brilliant run down the left touchline and then gave a scoring pass to James Haskell, but the move was unaccountably disallowed after a touch judge wrongly adjudged that Abendanon had put a foot into touch; The England Saxons were still drawing 0-0 midway through the first half; The England Saxons were drawing 0-0 in the 23rd minute when Shane Geraghty missed another kickable 38 metre penalty goal attempt; The England Saxons were leading 3-0 in the 28th minute when Nick Abendanon scored after Dave Strettle made a brilliant run; The England Saxons were leading 8-0 just before half-time; The England Saxons were leading 13-0 at half-time; The England Saxons were still leading 13-0 in the 42nd minute when Dean Schofield powered through 4 attempted tackles to score; The England Saxons scored 20 unanswered points to win the match; The England Saxons were leading 20-0 in the 57th minute when Shane Geraghty took too much time over his clearance kick and was charged down by Fabio Staibano who went on to score from the ensuing rebound, thus 5 points were preventable; The England Saxons were leading 20-5 midway through the second half; Chev Walker came on as a replacement for Jamie Noon in the 68th minute; The England Saxons were still leading 20-5 in the 69th minute when Dave Strettle had a great try-scoring chance but was tackled into touch at the corner flag by Matteo Pratichetti; Tom Varndell came on as a replacement for Dave Strettle with 9 minutes remaining; The England Saxons were leading 20-5 with 8 minutes remaining when Mike Brown scored a superb 40 metre solo try; Dave Strettle came back on as a temporary blood replacement for Mike Brown with 3 minutes remaining, with Nick Abendanon then switching from wing to full back to accommodate Strettle; The England Saxons were leading 27-5 immediately afterwards when Dylan Hartley powered through to score; Shaun Perry and Dave Strettle both had a brilliant game)

CAPTAIN: *Mike Catt*

9th Feb IRELAND A 5 **ENGLAND SAXONS** 32

Ravenhill Park, Belfast

[*This match kicked off at 7.45pm; On 24th April 2007 a RFU hearing found Dylan Hartley guilty of gouging the eyes of two separate opponents in a Guinness Premiership match on 15th April 2007 and thus banned him for 26 weeks; Chev Walker returned to Rugby League in September 2007*]

(*The England Saxons played into the wind in the first half; England Saxons were leading 3-0 in the 16th minute; The England Saxons were still leading 3-0 midway through the first half; The England Saxons were leading 3-0 in the 32nd minute when Dylan Hartley scored after he went on a brilliant rampaging run down the blindside; The England Saxons were leading 8-0 in the 34th minute when Rob Kearney scored after a poor tackle by Chev Walker, thus 5 points were preventable; The England Saxons were leading 8-5 at half-time; The England Saxons were still leading 8-5 in the 56th minute; The England Saxons were leading 11-5 in the 58th minute when Shane Geraghty missed an eminently kickable 27 metre penalty goal attempt; The England Saxons were still leading 11-5 midway through the second half; The England Saxons were leading 11-5 in the 65th minute when James Haskell scored after Mike Catt threw a superb inside pass; The England Saxons were leading 18-5 with 9 minutes of normal time remaining when Dave Strettle scored after Mark Cueto threw a brilliant long pass; The England Saxons were leading 25-5 with 4 minutes of normal time remaining when Richard Wigglesworth scored a superb 22 metre solo try under the posts; The England Saxons scored 24 unanswered points in the second half to clinch the match*)

ENGLAND STUDENTS MATCHES

CAPTAIN: *No captain appointed*

10th Feb SPAIN A C **ENGLAND STUDENTS** C

Campo Central de la Ciudad Universitaria, Madrid

[*Dylan Alexander, Ross Blake, Richard Vasey and Peter Fisher in original training squad of 22 announced on 16th January 2007; This match was eventually cancelled*]

CAPTAIN: *Greg Irvin*

23rd Feb FRANCE STUDENTS 6 **ENGLAND STUDENTS** 8

Stade Lucien Desprats, Cahors

[*This match kicked off at 7.00pm; Peter Fisher in original training squad of 22 but withdrew, being replaced by David Tibbott; Ross Blake in original training squad of 22 but withdrew, being replaced by Chris Pilgrim; Kevin Davis played for England in the U19 World Championship in South Africa in April 2005; Jack Smales was the brother of Hamish Smales*]

(*England Students were drawing 0-0 in the 6th minute when Aaron Liffchak crossed the tryline but then could not get downward pressure on the ball; England Students were still drawing 0-0 midway through the first half; England Students were losing 3-0 in the 28th minute; England Students were losing 3-0 at half-time; England Students were losing 6-0 in the 46th minute; England Students were losing 6-3 in the 56th minute; England Students were still losing 6-3 midway through the second half; England Students were losing 6-3 with 5 minutes of normal time remaining when Jack Smales saved a certain try; England Students were still losing 6-3 with 1 minute of normal time remaining when Alastair Simmie charged down an attempted clearance and then followed up to score a match-winning try; Kevin Davis, Joe Clark and Aaron Liffchak all had a brilliant game*)

9th Mar **ENGLAND STUDENTS** 19 FRANCE STUDENTS 10
Iffley Road, Oxford
[*This match kicked off at 7.00pm; Dan James was paralysed on 12th March 2007 when a scrum collapsed during a club training session and then died from his injuries on 12th September 2008*]
(*England Students were losing 7-0 in the 11th minute; England Students were still losing 7-0 midway through the first half when some superb handling amongst the forwards allowed Ryan Owen to run 40 metres and score; England Students were drawing 10-10 in the 30th minute; England Students were drawing 10-10 at half-time; England Students were leading 13-10 midway through the second half; England Students were still leading 13-10 in the 66th minute when Alastair Simmie scored a brilliant penalty goal from the right touchline; England Students were leading 16-10 with 5 minutes remaining when Alastair Simmie scored a 40 metre penalty goal to clinch the match*)

STEINLAGER USA SEVENS

PETCO Park, San Diego
CAPTAIN: *Simon Amor*
First Round - Pool 'C'
10th Feb KENYA 14 **ENGLAND** 26
[*This match kicked off at 10.00am*]
(*Rob Thirlby scored in the 3rd minute!; England were leading 19-0 in the 5th minute; England scored 19 unanswered points to win the match; England were leading 19-0 at half-time; England were leading 19-7 early in the second half; England were still leading 19-7 midway through the second half; England were leading 19-7 with 1 minute remaining when Dom Shabbo scored after Danny Gray made a brilliant run; England were leading 26-7 in the last minute*)
10th Feb USA 10 **ENGLAND** 26
[*This match kicked off at 1.06pm*]
(*Simon Amor scored in the 2nd minute after John Brake made a brilliant run!; England were leading 7-0 midway through the first half when Charlie Amesbury scored a brilliant 33 metre solo try; England were leading 14-10 at half-time; England were leading 19-10 early in the second half; England were still leading 19-10 midway through the second half when Simon Amor saved a certain try by tackling Jason Pye; England were leading 19-10 in the last minute when Simon Amor scored to seal the match*)
10th Feb AUSTRALIA 19 **ENGLAND** 14
[*This match kicked off at 5.40pm*]
(*England were drawing 0-0 in the early stages when Dom Shabbo had a great try-scoring chance but was tackled into touch at the corner flag; England were losing 5-0 when Corey Niwa scored after a poor tackle by Michael Hills, thus 7 points were preventable; England were losing 12-0 at half-time; England were losing 19-0 early in the second half; Australia were allowed to score 19 unanswered points to win the match; England were losing 19-7 in the 10th minute; England were still losing 19-7 in the closing stages of normal time when Nils Mordt wasted a great try-scoring opportunity; England were losing 19-7 when the full-time hooter sounded, but the ball was still in play and Rob Thirlby was able to score a consolation try*)

Quarter-Final

11th Feb NEW ZEALAND 19 **ENGLAND*** 7

[This match kicked off at 11.50am]

(Rob Thirlby went off injured in the early stages, being replaced by Charlie Amesbury; England were drawing 0-0 midway through the first half; England were still drawing 0-0 in the 5th minute; England were losing 5-0 at half-time; Dom Shabbo came on as a replacement for Michael Hills at the start of the second half; England were losing 12-0 early in the second half; England were still losing 12-0 shortly afterwards when Charlie Amesbury scored after Dom Shabbo made a brilliant 53 metre break; England were losing 12-7 midway through the second half; England were still losing 12-7 in the closing stages when collectively poor tackling allowed Tomasi Cama (2) to score, thus 7 points were preventable)

[Plate Semi-Final:]

[11th Feb SOUTH AFRICA 21 **ENGLAND*** 14]

[This match kicked off at 2.34pm; Rob Thirlby unavailable due to injury]

(Gcobani Bobo scored in the 2nd minute!; England were losing 14-0 shortly afterwards; England were still losing 14-0 when Danny Gray had a great try-scoring chance but was tackled into touch at the corner flag; England were losing 14-7 at half-time; England were drawing 14-14 early in the second half; England were still drawing 14-14 midway through the second half; England were drawing 14-14 with 1 minute remaining)

AIB CLUB INTERNATIONAL MATCH

CAPTAIN: *Duncan Cormack*

23rd Feb IRELAND CLUB XV 20 **ENGLAND COUNTIES*** 17

Donnybrook, Dublin

[This match kicked off at 7.35pm; Alastair Bressington also played cricket for Gloucestershire; Bevon Armitage was the brother of Delon and Steffon Armitage]

(Neil Hallett missed a 40 metre penalty goal attempt in the 3rd minute!; England Counties were drawing 0-0 in the 7th minute when Matt Crockett was allowed to score from a rolling maul; England Counties were losing 7-3 in the 12th minute; England Counties were still losing 7-3 midway through the first half; England Counties were losing 7-3 in the 31st minute and pressing in attack when Tom Hayman's intended scoring pass was intercepted by Glen Telford; England Counties were still losing 7-3 in the second minute of first half injury time; England Counties were losing 10-3 at half-time; The second half of this match was played in wet conditions; England Counties were losing 13-3 in the 49th minute; England Counties were still losing 13-3 in the 56th minute when Neil Hallett took too much time over his clearance kick and was charged down by Niall O'Brien, who went on to score from the ensuing rebound, thus 2 tries and 14 points were preventable; England Counties were losing 20-3 midway through the second half; England Counties were still losing 20-3 in the 69th minute when Chris Malherbe powered through 2 attempted tackles to score; England Counties were losing 20-10 in the third minute of injury time when Mark Bedworth scored a consolation try)

JEAN-CLAUDE BAQUÉ SHIELD MATCH

CAPTAIN: *Duncan Cormack*

10th Mar **ENGLAND COUNTIES** 41 FRANCE AMATEURS 10

Rectory Field, Charlton Road, Blackheath

[This match kicked off at 3.00pm; Frankie Neale was added to the squad to provide

injury cover]
(Neil Hallett scored a penalty goal in the 4th minute!; England Counties were leading 10-0 in the 11th minute; England Counties were still leading 10-0 midway through the first half; England Counties were leading 10-0 in the 23rd minute when Mark Bedworth scored a brilliant 32 metre solo try; Some superb handling amongst the backs allowed Alastair Bressington to score a try which Neil Hallett then converted to give England Counties a 24-0 lead in the 28th minute; England Counties scored 24 unanswered points to win the match; England Counties were still leading 24-0 shortly before half-time; England Counties were leading 24-3 at half-time; England Counties were still leading 24-3 in the 46th minute when Wayne Reed scored from a rolling maul; England Counties were leading 29-3 in the 49th minute when a handling error led directly to a try by Rachid Ourak, thus 7 points were preventable; England Counties were leading 29-10 midway through the second half; England Counties were still leading 29-10 with 8 minutes remaining; Neil Hallett scored 21 points in this match)

FIRST ARMY CENTENARY MATCH

CAPTAIN: *John Blaikie* (NZ)

21st Mar Army (*SER*) 48 **OXBRIDGE XV** 24

Army Rugby Stadium, Queen's Avenue, Aldershot

[This match kicked off at 7.15pm; Tom Tombleson played in the Penguins team that reached the Final of the Hong Kong Tens at Hong Kong Football Club on 28th-29th March 2007; Tim Catling was the cousin of Chris Catling]

(Apolosi Satala scored in the 2nd minute!; The Army was allowed to score 4 unanswered tries in the first quarter; Tom Tombleson scored a brilliant try shortly before half-time; The Oxbridge XV was losing at half-time; Jon Chance scored from a rolling maul; The Oxbridge XV scored 14 points in the second half)

CATHAY PACIFIC/CREDIT SUISSE HONG KONG SEVENS

Hong Kong Stadium, Eastern Hospital Road, So Kon Po, Hong Kong

CAPTAIN: *Simon Amor*

First Round - Pool 'E'

30th Mar HONG KONG 7 **ENGLAND** 38

[This match kicked off at 5.58pm]

(This match was played in 82 degree heat and very high humidity; Tom Williams scored in the 1st minute!; England were leading 7-0 shortly afterwards when Simon Amor brilliantly chipped ahead and followed up to score; England were leading 14-7 just before half-time; England were leading 21-7 at half-time; England were still leading 21-7 early in the second half when Danny Care scored 2 tries in quick succession; England scored 24 unanswered points to clinch the match)

31st Mar KOREA 14 **ENGLAND** 38

[This match kicked off at 2.10pm]

(This match was played in extreme heat and very high humidity; Charlie Amesbury scored in the 1st minute!; England were leading 19-7 at half-time; Charlie Amesbury scored four tries in the first 10 minutes!; Charlie Amesbury scored 20 points in this match)

31st Mar ARGENTINA 14 **ENGLAND** 19

[This match kicked off at 6.34pm]

(This match was played in extreme heat and very high humidity; Simon Amor scored in the 2nd minute!; England were leading 5-0 shortly afterwards when James Brooks scored after Simon Amor threw a brilliant long reverse pass; England were leading 12-

0 midway through the first half; England were still leading 12-0 just before half-time; England were leading 12-7 at half-time; England were still leading 12-7 early in the second half when James Brooks scored after Jack Adams made a brilliant break; Danny Care came on as a replacement for David Doherty with Jack Adams then switching from centre to wing to accommodate Care who had to play out of position as a centre; England were leading 19-7 midway through the second half; England were still leading 19-7 with 2 minutes of normal time remaining when Mariano Dobal scored after a poor tackle by David Seymour, thus 7 points were preventable; England were leading 19-14 when the full-time hooter sounded, but the ball remained in play for over a minute as Argentina vainly attempted to score a try)

Quarter-Final

1st April NEW ZEALAND 26 **ENGLAND** 0

[*This match kicked off at 1.42pm*]

(*This match was played in extreme heat and very high humidity; The England players could not win any possession; Afeleke Pelenise scored in the 1st minute!; England were losing 5-0 midway through the first half when Nigel Hunt scored after Jack Adams missed a tackle on Afeleke Pelenise; England were losing 12-0 just before half-time when Steven Yates scored after a poor tackle by James Brooks; England were losing 19-0 at half-time; England were still losing 19-0 midway through the second half when David Doherty broke through but was then brilliantly tackled by Nigel Hunt; England were losing 19-0 in the last minute and pressing in attack when they allowed the ball to go loose at a ruck situation and D.J. Forbes was able to gather it and instigate a counter-attack that culminated in a try by Solomon King, thus 3 tries and 21 points were preventable*)

SECOND ARMY CENTENARY MATCH

CAPTAIN: *Joe Roff* (AU)

4th April Army (*SER*) 0 **BARBARIANS** 14

Stoop Memorial Ground, Langhorn Drive, Twickenham

[*This match kicked off at 7.45pm; Adam Thompstone was originally selected at left wing with Joe Roff at right wing, but the two swapped positions before the match; Kevin Brennan played in the Penguins team that reached the Final of the Hong Kong Tens at Hong Kong Football Club on 28th-29th March 2007*]

(*This match was played in extremely cold conditions; The Barbarians were drawing 0-0 midway through the first half; The Barbarians were still drawing 0-0 in the 25th minute when Adam Thompstone scored after Gonzalo Quesada put in a brilliant diagonal kick; The Barbarians were leading 7-0 at half-time; The Barbarians made a number of handling errors in the second half; The Barbarians were still leading 7-0 in the 51st minute when George Robson scored from a rolling maul; The Barbarians were leading 14-0 midway through the second half*)

ADELAIDE SEVENS

Adelaide Oval, Adelaide

CAPTAIN: *Simon Amor*

First Round - Pool 'A'

7th April TONGA 12 **ENGLAND** 5

[*This match kicked off at 12.15pm*]

**(*England made a number of handling errors in the first half; England were drawing 0-0 midway through the first half; England were still drawing 0-0 in the 5th minute; England were losing 7-0 at half-time; England were losing 12-0 early in the second*

half; England were still losing 12-0 when Simon Amor scored but then hit the post with his conversion attempt!)

CAPTAIN: *Tony Roques*

7th April CANADA 12 **ENGLAND** 31

[*This match kicked off at 3.21pm*]

(*England were leading 5-0 early in the first half; England were drawing 12-12 at half-time; Danny Care scored a brilliant long-range solo try; Isoa Damu scored a brilliant solo try in the closing stages*)

CAPTAIN: *Simon Amor*

7th April FIJI 12 **ENGLAND** 20

[*This match kicked off at 7.26pm; England wore navy blue shirts for this match*]

(*Danny Care scored after just 30 seconds had been played!; England were leading 7-0 when Charlie Amesbury powered through 2 attempted tackles to score; England were leading 12-0 just before half-time; England scored 17 unanswered points to win the match; England were leading 17-0 at half-time; England were leading 17-12 with 1 minute remaining when Simon Amor scored an 18 metre penalty goal to clinch the match*)

Quarter-Final

8th April KENYA 17 **ENGLAND*** 12

[*This match kicked off at 12.06pm*]

(*Collectively poor tackling allowed Teddy Omondi to score in the 2nd minute!; England were losing 7-0 midway through the first half when Isoa Damu scored after Simon Amor threw a brilliant long pass; England were drawing 7-7 in the 6th minute when Innocent Simiyu scored after a poor tackle by Andy Vilk; England were losing 12-7 just before half-time when they created and then squandered a 2 man overlap; England were losing 12-7 at half-time; England were losing 12-7 in the 9th minute when Innocent Simiyu scored again after a poor tackle by Charlie Amesbury, thus 3 tries and 17 points were preventable; England were losing 17-7 midway through the second half; England were still losing 17-7 with 1 minute remaining when Isoa Damu powered through to score another try; England were losing 17-12 in the final minute and pressing in attack when Andy Vilk unaccountably failed to make the ball available at a tackle situation in the last move of the match!*)

[Plate Semi-Final:]

[8th April AUSTRALIA 26 **ENGLAND** 21]

[*This match kicked off at 3.12pm*]

(*Danny Care scored after just 49 seconds had been played!; England were leading 7-0 in the 4th minute when James Lew scored after a poor tackle by Simon Amor; England were drawing 7-7 midway through the first half; England were still drawing 7-7 in the 6th minute when Shawn Mackay scored as a direct consequence of a mistake by Jack Adams; England were losing 14-7 just before half-time when collectively poor tackling allowed Anthony Sauer to score, thus 3 tries and 21 points were preventable; Australia were allowed to score 21 unanswered points to win the match; England were losing 21-7 at half-time; England were losing 21-14 in the 9th minute; England were losing 26-14 midway through the second half; England were still losing 26-14 with 1 minute remaining when Danny Care wasted a great try-scoring opportunity by throwing a poor pass to the unmarked Simon Amor; England were losing 26-14 in the last minute when Danny Care scored a consolation try*)

BARCLAYS CHURCHILL CUP

England

CAPTAIN: *Neal Hatley* [*Phil Dowson*]

First Round - Pool 'A'

18th May **ENGLAND SAXONS** 51 USA 3 **BP**

Edgeley Park, Hardcastle Road, Edgeley, Stockport

[This match kicked off at 7.45pm; Tom Croft, James Haskell, Olly Barkley, Danny Cipriani, Nick Abendanon, Tom Voyce, Ayoola Erinle and Paul Sackey were all unavailable for this match due to club commitments; Chris Brooker, Kieran Roche, David Seymour, Adrian Jarvis and Paul Diggin were all included in an original 12 man bench selection; Shane Geraghty left the squad on 21st May 2007 due to injury; Ryan Lamb left the squad on 21st May 2007 due to club commitments; The squad was reduced from 36 to 28 on 21st May 2007, with Kieran Roche, Michael Lipman, David Seymour, Paul Diggin, Topsy Ojo and Delon Armitage all being released; Dan Scarbrough left the squad on 25th May 2007 as he was now required to join the England tour of South Africa as a replacement]

(The England Saxons played into a swirling wind in the first half; The England Saxons were losing 3-0 in the 8th minute; The England Saxons were leading 7-3 midway through the first half; The England Saxons were still leading 7-3 in the 23rd minute when Jordan Crane scored a pushover try; Shane Geraghty went off injured in the 29th minute, being replaced by Nils Mordt; The England Saxons were leading 19-3 in the 32nd minute; Tom Mercey came on as a replacement for Neal Hatley in the 37th minute; The England Saxons were still leading 19-3 just before half-time when Jordan Crane scored another pushover try; The England Saxons were leading 24-3 at half-time; The England Saxons were still leading 24-3 in the 46th minute when Jim Evans scored from a rolling maul; The England Saxons were leading 29-3 midway through the second half when Delon Armitage scored after Ryan Lamb made a brilliant break; The England Saxons were leading 34-3 in the 66th minute when Jack Forster scored from another rolling maul; The England Saxons were leading 39-3 with 4 minutes remaining; The England Saxons were leading 44-3 with 2 minutes remaining when Lee Dickson scored after Dan Scarbrough made a superb run; The England Saxons scored 51 unanswered points to win the match; This match finished in extremely wet conditions; Ryan Lamb had a brilliant game)

CAPTAIN: *Neal Hatley* [*Phil Dowson*]

28th May **ENGLAND SAXONS** 18 SCOTLAND A 3

Twickenham

[This match kicked off at 3.00pm; Danny Cipriani played for England in the U19 World Championships in South Africa in April 2005 and Dubai in April 2006; Nick Abendanon left the squad on 30th May 2007 as he was now required to join the England tour of South Africa as a replacement]

(This match was played in wet conditions; Olly Barkley scored a penalty goal in the 4th minute!; The England Saxons were leading 3-0 midway through the first half; The England Saxons were still leading 3-0 just before half-time when David Paice powered through to score after Nick Abendanon made 2 brilliant runs in quick succession; The England Saxons were leading 10-0 at half-time; The England Saxons were still leading 10-0 in the 43rd minute when Nick Abendanon scored after Danny Cipriani put in a superb grubber kick; Jordan Crane came on as a replacement for James Haskell in the 51st minute, with Phil Dowson then switching from number 8 to blindside flanker to

***accommodate Jordan Crane; David Paice went off injured in the 55th minute, being replaced by Matt Thompson; The England Saxons were leading 15-0 midway through the second half when Olly Barkley missed a kickable 35 metre penalty goal attempt; Tom Mercey came on as a replacement for Neal Hatley in the 60th minute; The England Saxons were leading 15-3 in the 66th minute; The England Saxons were still leading 15-3 in the first minute of injury time when Nils Mordt scored a 24 metre penalty goal with the last kick of the match to seal the game; Phil Dowson and Nick Abendanon both had a brilliant game*)**

CAPTAIN: *Neal Hatley* [*Phil Dowson*]

Final

2nd June **ENGLAND SAXONS** 17 NEW ZEALAND MAORI 13
Twickenham

[*This match kicked off at 4.30pm; This was the first time since 1926 that the New Zealand Maori had played at Twickenham!; Neal Hatley retired after this match; Jim Evans retired due to injury in December 2009*]

(*Olly Barkley missed a speculative 49 metre penalty goal attempt in the 5th minute!; The England Saxons were drawing 0-0 in the 18th minute when Paul Sackey scored after Olly Barkley made a brilliant run; The England Saxons were leading 7-0 midway through the first half; Neal Hatley went off injured in the 28th minute, being replaced by Tom Mercey; The England Saxons were still leading 7-0 in the 36th minute when collectively poor tackling allowed Anthony Tahana to score, thus 5 points were preventable; The England Saxons were leading 7-5 at half-time; The England Saxons were losing 8-7 in the 44th minute when some superb handling amongst the backs allowed Tom Voyce to score; Nils Mordt went off injured in the 53rd minute, being replaced by Ayoola Erinle; The England Saxons were leading 12-8 in the 58th minute; The England Saxons were losing 13-12 midway through the second half; Lee Dickson came on as a temporary blood replacement for Richard Wigglesworth in the 66th minute; The England Saxons were still losing 13-12 with 7 minutes remaining when Tom Croft scored a brilliant 60 metre solo try to win the match; Will Skinner and Danny Cipriani both had a brilliant game*)

BARBARIANS TOUR TO TUNISIA AND SPAIN 2007

CAPTAIN: *Hugh Vyvyan*

19th May TUNISIA 10 **BARBARIANS** 33
El Menzah Olympic Stadium, Tunis

[*This match kicked off at 5.00pm; Guy Easterby withdrew after being selected for the England A bench against Otago in January 1997, played for Ireland A in November 1997, played for an Ireland XV in May 2000 and was capped for Ireland in June 2000; Guy Easterby was the brother of Simon Easterby*]

(*The Barbarians were drawing 0-0 in the 14th minute when Rhys Williams (2) scored after Nick Macleod threw a brilliant long pass; The Barbarians were leading 7-0 midway through the first half; Lee Robinson came on as a temporary blood replacement for Stuart Moffat in the 25th minute; The Barbarians were still leading 7-0 in the 30th minute when Tyrone Howe scored from a quick tap penalty; The Barbarians were leading 14-0 just before half-time when John Davies scored from a rolling maul; The Barbarians scored 21 unanswered points to win the match; The Barbarians were leading 21-0 at half-time; The Barbarians were leading 21-7 in the 43rd minute; Jon Mills came on as a replacement for Hugh Vyvyan in the 48th minute; The Barbarians were still leading 21-7 midway through the second half; The Barbarians were leading*

28-7 in the 67th minute; The Barbarians were leading 33-7 with 8 minutes remaining; The Barbarians were still leading 33-7 in the last minute)

23rd May SPAIN 26 **BARBARIANS** 52

Estadio Manuel Martinez Valero, Elche

[***This match kicked off at 7.30pm; Ged Glynn was the Coach for Spain in this match; Andy Dalgleish played for Major R.V. Stanley's XV against Oxford University at Iffley Road on 17th November 2009***]

(***Esteban Roqué scored a penalty goal in the 2nd minute!; The Barbarians were leading 7-3 in the 4th minute!; The Barbarians were losing 13-7 in the 18th minute; The Barbarians were leading 14-13 midway through the first half; The Barbarians were leading 21-13 in the 31st minute; The Barbarians were still leading 21-13 in the 35th minute when Lee Robinson scored to complete a hat-trick of tries in the first half!; The Barbarians were leading 33-16 shortly before half-time; The Barbarians were leading 40-19 at half-time; The Barbarians were leading 45-19 in the 50th minute when Rhys Williams intercepted the ball and ran 75 metres to score; The Barbarians were leading 52-19 midway through the second half; Craig Hammond came on as a replacement for Hugh Vyvyan in the 65th minute; Spain were still losing 52-19 with 1 minute remaining when a Barbarians chip-kick was charged down by Iván Criado who then regathered the ball and ran 20 metres to score, thus 7 points were preventable***)

ENGLAND TOUR TO SOUTH AFRICA 2007

CAPTAIN: *Jason Robinson*

26th May SOUTH AFRICA 58 **ENGLAND** 10

Vodacom Park Stadium, Bloemfontein

[***This match kicked off at 3.00pm; The Vodacom Park Stadium was previously called the Free State Stadium; Nick Wood selected but withdrew due to injury, being replaced by Kevin Yates; Dave Strettle selected but withdrew due to illness, Iain Balshaw was moved from the bench to the team and James Simpson-Daniel was then selected for the bench; Peter Richards selected but withdrew on the day of the match due to illness, Andy Gomarsall was moved from the bench to the team and Shaun Perry was then selected for the bench; Andy Farrell selected but withdrew on the day of the match due to illness, Toby Flood was moved from the bench to the team and Anthony Allen was then selected for the bench; Dave Strettle left the tour to go to hospital on 23rd May 2007; Nick Wood left the tour injured on 25th May 2007; Matt Stevens and Dan Scarbrough joined the tour on 25th May 2007; Dave Strettle was discharged from hospital on the day of the match and thus rejoined the tour; Iain Balshaw left the tour injured on 27th May 2007; Dave Strettle left the tour due to illness on 29th May 2007; Nick Abendanon joined the tour on 30th May 2007; Topsy Ojo joined the tour on 31st May 2007; Pat Sanderson retired due to injury in August 2011***]

(***This match was played at high altitude; Dean Schofield and Alex Brown both played with an illness; The England scrum was put under severe pressure in the first half; Percy Montgomery scored a penalty goal in the 3rd minute!; England were losing 3-0 in the 8th minute when Jonny Wilkinson missed a kickable 35 metre penalty goal attempt; England were losing 6-0 midway through the first half; England were still losing 6-0 in the 23rd minute when a lineout overthrow by Mark Regan led directly to a try by Ashwin Willemse; England were losing 13-0 in the 26th minute when Matt Tait made a brilliant break but Chris Jones then wasted this great try-scoring opportunity by throwing a poor pass behind Nick Easter which enabled Bryan Habana to gather the loose ball and run 70 metres to score; England were losing 20-0 in the 30th minute when Jonny Wilkinson scored a brilliant 52 metre penalty goal; England were losing***

23-3 shortly before half-time when collectively poor tackling allowed Jean de Villiers to score; England were losing 30-3 at half-time; Andy Hazell went off injured at half-time, being replaced by Pat Sanderson; Iain Balshaw went off injured in the 58th minute, being replaced by James Simpson-Daniel; England were still losing 30-3 midway through the second half; England were losing 30-3 in the 62nd minute when some superb handling amongst the backs allowed James Simpson-Daniel to score; England were losing 30-10 in the 70th minute; England were losing 37-10 with 7 minutes remaining when Jonny Wilkinson went off injured, being replaced by Shaun Perry with Andy Gomarsall then switching from scrum half to fly half to accommodate Shaun Perry; England were losing 44-10 with 4 minutes remaining when Bryan Habana scored another try after Pat Sanderson missed a tackle on Percy Montgomery, thus 4 tries and 28 points were preventable; South Africa were allowed to score 28 unanswered points in the last 11 minutes; Jason Robinson injured playing in the match; This was South Africa's highest ever points total against England)

CAPTAIN: *Jonny Wilkinson*

2nd June SOUTH AFRICA 55 **ENGLAND*** 22

Loftus Versfeld Stadium, Pretoria

[*This match kicked off at 3.00pm; Andy Hazell and Jason Robinson unavailable due to injury; Andy Farrell and James Simpson-Daniel unavailable due to illness*]

(This match was played at high altitude; Percy Montgomery scored a penalty goal in the 5th minute!; England were drawing 3-3 in the 10th minute; England were still drawing 3-3 midway through the first half; England were drawing 3-3 in the 23rd minute when Ricky Januarie kicked ahead and then followed up to score after Jamie Noon was deceived by the bounce of the ball; England were losing 17-6 in the 30th minute; England were losing 17-12 just before half-time when Dan Scarbrough scored a 55 metre interception try; England were leading 19-17 at half-time; England were losing 22-19 in the 44th minute; England were drawing 22-22 in the 53rd minute when collectively poor tackling allowed Pierre Spies (2) to score; England were losing 29-22 in the 56th minute and pressing in attack when Ben Skirving's pass was intercepted by Bryan Habana, who then ran 78 metres to score; Stuart Turner came on as a replacement for Kevin Yates in the 58th minute, with Matt Stevens then switching from tight-head to loose-head prop to accommodate Stuart Turner; England were losing 36-22 midway through the second half; England were losing 43-22 in the 65th minute; England were still losing 43-22 with 6 minutes remaining when Bryan Habana scored another try after a poor tackle by Toby Flood; England were losing 48-22 with 3 minutes remaining when Pierre Spies (2) also scored another try after Jonny Wilkinson dropped the ball out of the tackle, thus 5 tries and 33 points were preventable; South Africa were allowed to score 33 unanswered points to win the match)

EMIRATES AIRLINE LONDON SEVENS

Twickenham

CAPTAIN: *Simon Amor*

First Round - Pool 'D'

26th May **ENGLAND** 19 PORTUGAL 14

[*This match kicked off at 11.34am*]

(Pedro Cabral scored in the 3rd minute!; England were losing 7-0 midway through the first half; England were still losing 7-0 shortly before half-time; England were drawing 7-7 at half-time; England were still drawing 7-7 in the 9th minute when Rob Thirlby scored a brilliant 42 metre solo try; England were leading 14-7 in the 10th minute when

***Rob Thirlby followed up his own grubber kick to score; England scored 19 unanswered points to win the match; England were leading 19-7 midway through the second half; England were still leading 19-7 with 1 minute remaining when Adérito Esteves scored after a poor tackle by Michael Hills, thus 7 points were preventable*)**

26th May **ENGLAND** 0 WALES 22

[*This match kicked off at 2.40pm*]

(*England were drawing 0-0 in the 2nd minute when Isoa Damu crossed the tryline but then unaccountably delayed grounding the ball which allowed Aled Thomas to get back and illegally kick the ball out of his hand, but the referee inexplicably ignored this obvious penalty try offence and awarded Wales a 22 drop-out!; England were still drawing 0-0 midway through the first half; England were losing 5-0 in the 6th minute; England were still losing 5-0 just before half-time; England were losing 10-0 at half-time; England could not win any possession in the second half; England were still losing 10-0 midway through the second half when Isoa Damu was dispossessed in the tackle by Dafydd Hewitt who then went on to score; England were losing 15-0 with 1 minute remaining when collectively poor tackling allowed Jonathan Edwards to score, thus 2 tries and 12 points were preventable; Isoa Damu had a poor game*)

26th May **ENGLAND** 17 SOUTH AFRICA 14

[*This match kicked off at 5.58pm*]

(*This match was played in wet conditions; England were drawing 0-0 in the 3rd minute when Danny Care dummied his way through to score a brilliant try; England were leading 7-0 midway through the first half when Simon Amor and Tony Roques both saved a certain try by tackling Dusty Noble; England were still leading 7-0 in the 5th minute when Rob Thirlby broke through, but he was superbly chased back and tackled by Mzwandile Stick; England were leading 7-0 just before half-time; England were drawing 7-7 at half-time; England were still drawing 7-7 midway through the second half when collectively poor tackling allowed Vuyo Zangqa to score, thus 7 points were preventable; England were losing 14-7 in the last minute; England were losing 14-12 with 18 seconds of normal time remaining when Danny Care ran 37 metres to score a match-winning try to complete a hat-trick*)

[Bowl Quarter-Final:]

[27th May **ENGLAND** 19 KENYA 0 **]**

[*This match kicked off at 11.22am*]

(*This match was played in wet conditions; England were drawing 0-0 in the 3rd minute when Ben Foden followed up his own grubber kick to score; England were leading 5-0 midway through the first half; England were still leading 5-0 in the 7th minute when Ben Foden scored another try after Simon Amor brilliantly flicked the ball between his legs at a scrum; England were leading 12-0 at half-time; England were still leading 12-0 in the 11th minute when Rob Thirlby wasted a great try-scoring opportunity by knocking the ball on; England were leading 12-0 midway through the second half; England were still leading 12-0 with 2 minutes remaining when Tom Williams scored after Ben Foden made a superb 38 metre break; Ben Foden had a brilliant game*)

[Bowl Semi-Final:]

[27th May **ENGLAND** 17 FRANCE 7 **]**

[*This match kicked off at 2.50pm*]

(*This match was played on a wet pitch; England were drawing 0-0 in the 3rd minute when collectively poor tackling allowed Khrist Kopetzky to score, thus 7 points were preventable; England were losing 7-0 midway through the first half; England were still losing 7-0 in the 6th minute when Isoa Damu scored after Rob Thirlby made a brilliant*

48 metre run, with Simon Amor then missing the eminently kickable conversion attempt; England were losing 7-5 at half-time; England were still losing 7-5 in the 9th minute when Isoa Damu powered through to score under the posts; England were leading 12-7 midway through the second half; England were still leading 12-7 with 1 minute remaining when Ben Foden scored after Rob Thirlby threw a brilliant reverse pass; England scored 17 unanswered points to win the match)

[Bowl Final:]

[27th May **ENGLAND** 10 PORTUGAL 0]

[*This match kicked off at 5.56pm*]

(*This match was played in drizzly conditions on a wet pitch; England were drawing 0-0 midway through the first half; England were still drawing 0-0 when the half-time hooter sounded, but the ball was still in play and Isoa Damu was able to score, with Simon Amor then missing the eminently kickable conversion attempt; England were leading 5-0 at half-time; Ben Foden went off injured in the 10th minute, being replaced by Charlie Amesbury with Rob Thirlby then switching from wing to centre to accommodate Amesbury; England were still leading 5-0 midway through the second half; England were leading 5-0 with 1 minute remaining when Rob Thirlby had a great try-scoring chance but was tackled into touch at the corner flag by Gonçalo Foro; England were still leading 5-0 in the final minute when Michael Hills scored with the last move of the match to clinch the game*)

EMIRATES AIRLINE EDINBURGH SEVENS

Murrayfield

CAPTAIN: *Tony Roques*

First Round - Pool 'D'

2nd June GEORGIA 0 **ENGLAND** 24

[*This match kicked off at 11.02am; England wore navy blue shirts for this match*]

(*England were drawing 0-0 midway through the first half; England were still drawing 0-0 in the 6th minute when Isoa Damu powered through to score, with Danny Care then missing the eminently kickable conversion attempt; England were leading 5-0 at half-time; England were leading 10-0 in the 8th minute when Danny Care scored a brilliant conversion from the right touchline; England were leading 12-0 in the 10th minute when Danny Care took a quick tap penalty and scored; England were leading 19-0 midway through the second half; England were still leading 19-0 when the full-time hooter sounded, but the ball was still in play and Tony Roques was able to score to seal the match*)

2nd June ARGENTINA 19 **ENGLAND*** 14

[*This match kicked off at 2.08pm*]

(*England were drawing 0-0 in the 3rd minute when Rob Thirlby kicked ahead and followed up to score a brilliant 89 metre solo try; England were leading 7-0 midway through the first half; England were still leading 7-0 in the 5th minute and pressing in attack when Ben Foden threw a poor pass out of the tackle which enabled Ramiro del Busto to gather the loose ball, kick ahead and then follow up to score, thus 7 points were preventable; England were drawing 7-7 just before half-time; England were losing 14-7 at half-time; England were losing 19-7 in the 8th minute; Argentina were allowed to score 19 unanswered points to win the match; England were still losing 19-7 midway through the second half; England were losing 19-7 with 1 minute remaining*)

2nd June NEW ZEALAND 38 **ENGLAND** 0

[*This match kicked off at 5.36pm*]

(Tomasi Cama (2) scored in the 1st minute!; England were losing 10-0 in the 3rd minute; England were still losing 10-0 midway through the first half; Isoa Damu went off injured in the 6th minute, being replaced by Michael Hills; England were losing 10-0 in the 7th minute when Ben Foden had a great try-scoring chance but was tackled by Lote Raikabula 2 metres short of the New Zealand line; England were losing 10-0 at half-time; England were still losing 10-0 in the 8th minute when Afeleke Pelenise scored after a poor tackle by Charlie Amesbury; England were losing 24-0 in the 10th minute; England were still losing 24-0 midway through the second half; England were losing 24-0 with 2 minutes remaining; England were losing 31-0 in the last minute when collectively poor tackling allowed Afeleke Pelenise to score another try, thus 2 tries and 14 points were preventable)

[Bowl Quarter-Final:]

[3rd June CANADA 7 **ENGLAND** 29]

[This match kicked off at 11.07am; Isoa Damu unavailable due to injury]

(England were drawing 0-0 midway through the first half when Ben Foden scored a brilliant 33 metre solo try; England were leading 5-0 in the 6th minute; England were losing 7-5 when the half-time hooter sounded, but the ball was still in play and Noah Cato was able to score; England were leading 10-7 at half-time; England were still leading 10-7 in the 9th minute when Rob Thirlby scored the 100th try of his IRB World Sevens career; England were leading 17-7 midway through the second half; England were leading 24-7 in the last minute when Noah Cato ran 72 metres to score to seal the match; Rob Thirlby injured playing in the match)

[Bowl Semi-Final:]

[3rd June AUSTRALIA 19 **ENGLAND** 24 aet]

[This match kicked off at 2.55pm; Isoa Damu and Rob Thirlby unavailable due to injury]

(Anthony Sauer scored in the 2nd minute!; England were losing 5-0 midway through the first half; England were leading 7-5 in the 6th minute when Danny Care dummied his way through to score a brilliant try; England were leading 12-5 when the half-time hooter sounded, but the ball was still in play and Danny Care was able to chip ahead and then regather the ball to score another superb try; England were leading 19-5 at half-time; England were still leading 19-5 in the 8th minute when Nathan Trist scored after a poor tackle by Ben Foden, thus 7 points were preventable; England were leading 19-12 midway through the second half; England were still leading 19-12 in the last minute of normal time; England were drawing 19-19 in the first minute of sudden death extra time when Michael Hills scored to win the match; Danny Care had a brilliant game)

[Bowl Final:]

[3rd June PORTUGAL 0 **ENGLAND** 31]

[This match kicked off at 5.50pm; Isoa Damu and Rob Thirlby unavailable due to injury; England wore navy blue shirts for this match]

(This match was played in drizzly conditions; Tom Williams chipped ahead and followed up to score a brilliant try after just 64 seconds had been played, with Danny Care then missing the eminently kickable conversion attempt!; David Seymour went off injured immediately afterwards, being replaced by Michael Hills; England were leading 5-0 midway through the first half when Tom Williams scored another try after Danny Care made a brilliant 34 metre run; England were leading 12-0 in the 6th minute when Michael Hills dummied his way through to score a superb try; England were

***leading 19-0 just before half-time when Danny Care wasted a great try-scoring opportunity by dropping the ball while the Portuguese line was at his mercy; England were leading 19-0 at half-time; England were still leading 19-0 midway through the second half; England were leading 19-0 with 2 minutes of normal time remaining when Noah Cato scored a brilliant 102 metre solo try; England were leading 26-0 when the full-time hooter sounded, but the ball was still in play and Noah Cato was able to score a superb 95 metre solo try to seal the match*)**

ENGLAND COUNTIES TOUR TO RUSSIA 2007

CAPTAIN: *Duncan Cormack*

16th Jun RUSSIA 21 **ENGLAND COUNTIES** 23

Slava Stadium, Moscow

[*This match kicked off at 3.00pm; Chris Rainbow and Frankie Neale unavailable due to injury; England Counties named a 6 man bench selection*]

(*England Counties were leading 3-0 in the 16th minute; England Counties were still leading 3-0 midway through the first half; England Counties were leading 3-0 in the 27th minute when Chris Malherbe scored after Mark Bedworth made a brilliant break; England Counties were leading 13-6 at half-time; England Counties were drawing 13-13 early in the second half; England Counties were leading 16-13 midway through the second half; England Counties were still leading 16-13 in the 67th minute; England Counties were drawing 16-16 with 6 minutes of normal time remaining when Chris Malherbe scored another try to win the match; England Counties were leading 23-16 in the eighth minute of injury time*)

FALKLANDS 25 TASK FORCE TROPHY MATCH

CAPTAIN: *Howard Graham*

16th Jun Falklands Task Force XV (*SER*) 33 **PENGUINS*** 33

Stoop Memorial Ground, Langhorn Drive, Twickenham

[*This match kicked off at 4.00pm; Mark Lee selected but withdrew on the day of the match, Ken Aseme was moved from the bench to the team with James Bucknall then moving from number 8 to blindside flanker to accommodate Aseme while Jamie Fleming was now selected for the bench; Tal Selley selected but withdrew on the day of the match, being replaced by Felise Ah-Ling; Graham Barr selected at full back but withdrew on the day of the match to sit on the bench, being replaced by Andy Wright with Jack Smales then switching from right wing to full back to accommodate Andy Wright while Mark Smith stood down from the bench to accommodate Barr; Bill Calcraft selected for bench but withdrew after he injured his back in the pre-match warm-up session shortly before the game; The Falklands Task Force XV originally allowed the Penguins to name a 10 man bench selection; Kevin Brennan in original squad but was not selected for team or bench; James Bucknall was the son of Tony Bucknall; Bill Calcraft was due to come out of retirement to play in this match at the age of 48!; Josh Drauniniu played for the Falklands Task Force XV in this match, scoring 2 tries; Howard Graham played for Major R.V. Stanley's XV against Oxford University at Iffley Road on 19th November 2008 and captained the White Hart Marauders in the Middlesex Sevens at Twickenham on 15th August 2009*]

(*Both sides agreed to allow unlimited substitutions in this match; This match was kicked-off by the television presenter Ken Hames, a Falklands veteran and former Combined Services player, who promptly fell over as his foot made contact with the ball!; The first half of this match was played on a wet pitch; The Penguins were leading 7-0 in the 15th minute; The Penguins were losing 14-7 midway through the first half;*

***The Penguins were losing 19-7 in the 27th minute; The Penguins were still losing 19-7 in the 37th minute when James Gaunt powered through to score; The Penguins were losing 19-14 in the fourth minute of first half injury time; The Penguins were losing 26-14 at half-time; The Penguins were still losing 26-14 in the 55th minute; The Penguins were losing 26-21 midway through the second half; The Penguins were still losing 26-21 with 9 minutes of normal time remaining when Peceli Nacamavuto intercepted the ball and scored, thus 7 points were preventable; The Penguins were losing 33-21 with 4 minutes of normal time remaining when Nicky Griffiths scored but then had his eminently kickable conversion attempt charged down!; The Penguins were losing 33-26 with 1 minute of normal time remaining when Rory Greenslade-Jones scored a try which Nicky Griffiths then converted to draw the match*)**

CWMTAWE SEVENS

Pontardawe RFC, Parc Ynysderw, Ynysderw Road, Pontardawe, Swansea

CAPTAIN: *??*

First Round - Pool 'H'

4th Aug	Glamorgan Young Farmers (*WA*)	7	**SAMURAI**	28

[No match notes]

4th Aug	Brammers International (*FR*)	0	**SAMURAI**	33

[No match notes]

Quarter-Final

4th Aug	Llanelli Scarlets (*WA*)	24	**SAMURAI***	19

(*The Samurai were leading 5-0 in the 5th minute; The Samurai were losing 7-5 at half-time; The Samurai were leading 19-12 at one point in the second half; The Samurai were drawing 19-19 with 1 minute remaining*)

FIRST INVESTEC CHALLENGE MATCH

CAPTAIN: *Phil Vickery* [*Martin Corry; Jonny Wilkinson*]

4th Aug	**ENGLAND**	62	WALES	5

Twickenham

[*This match kicked off at 4.00pm; Peter Richards selected for bench but withdrew on the morning of the match due to injury, being replaced by Andy Gomarsall; Mark Cueto selected but withdrew after he injured his groin in the pre-match warm-up session shortly before the game, Matt Tait was moved from the bench to the team and England were forced to use a 6 man bench selection as there was insufficient time to name a new replacement*]

(*This match was played in 86 degree heat; The England forwards dominated the lineout in this match; Toby Flood came on as a temporary blood replacement for Andy Farrell in the 4th minute; England were drawing 0-0 in the 9th minute when Jonny Wilkinson missed a kickable 45 metre penalty goal attempt; England were still drawing 0-0 in the 14th minute when Nick Easter scored after Shaun Perry made a brilliant blindside break; England were leading 5-0 midway through the first half when Nick Easter scored from a rolling maul; England were leading 19-0 in the 30th minute; England were leading 22-0 at half-time; Phil Vickery went off injured at half-time, being replaced by Matt Stevens; England were still leading 22-0 in the 44th minute when Joe Worsley wasted a great try-scoring opportunity by attempting to make the line himself instead of using an overlap outside him; England were leading 29-0 in the 50th minute when Shaun Perry claimed the try that was later officially credited to Nick Easter!; England scored 36 unanswered points to win the match; Lawrence Dallaglio came on as a replacement for Nick Easter in the 58th minute; England were leading 36-5*

midway through the second half; England were still leading 36-5 in the 66th minute when Lawrence Dallaglio broke from the base of a scrum to score; Lewis Moody came on as a replacement for Martin Corry in the 70th minute; England were leading 50-5 with 6 minutes remaining; England were still leading 50-5 with 2 minutes remaining when Jason Robinson kicked ahead and followed up to score a brilliant try; England were leading 55-5 in the final minute when Matt Tait scored in the last move of the match after Jonny Wilkinson put in a superb kick ahead; Shaun Perry had a brilliant game; England amassed their highest ever points total against Wales and also achieved their greatest ever margin of victory over Wales)

SECOND INVESTEC CHALLENGE MATCH

CAPTAIN: *Mike Catt*

11th Aug **ENGLAND*** 15 FRANCE 21
Twickenham

[*This match kicked off at 5.00pm; Lewis Moody selected but withdrew due to injury, Joe Worsley was moved from the bench to the team and Steve Borthwick was then selected for the bench; Kevin Yates, Tom Palmer (2), James Haskell, Richard Wigglesworth, Danny Cipriani, Charlie Hodgson, Toby Flood, Mike Tindall and Nick Abendanon were released from the World Cup training squad on 13th August 2007 as Brian Ashton named his official World Cup squad of 30*]

(*This match was played in hot conditions; The England forwards won plenty of ball but the backs were unable to turn this ample possession into points; England were leading 3-0 in the 10th minute; England were losing 8-3 midway through the first half; England were losing 8-6 in the 23rd minute; England were leading 9-8 in the 33rd minute; England were losing 11-9 shortly before half-time; England were leading 12-11 at half-time; England were still leading 12-11 in the 56th minute when Andy Gomarsall scored a brilliant 12 metre drop goal; England were leading 15-11 midway through the second half; England were leading 15-14 in the 67th minute when they created a 3 man overlap but Lee Mears then wasted this great try-scoring opportunity by electing to pass to Phil Vickery instead of using his own momentum to make the nearby line himself; England were still leading 15-14 with 9 minutes remaining when collectively poor tackling allowed Sébastien Chabal to score, thus 7 points were preventable; England were losing 21-15 with 3 minutes remaining when Olly Barkley wasted a great try-scoring opportunity by attempting to make the line himself instead of using an overlap outside him; Jonny Wilkinson came on as a replacement for Mike Catt with 2 minutes remaining, with Olly Barkley then switching from fly half to centre to accommodate Jonny Wilkinson; Ben Kay had a brilliant game; This was France's biggest win at Twickenham since 1975!*)

THIRD INVESTEC CHALLENGE MATCH

CAPTAIN: *Phil Vickery* [*Martin Corry*]

18th Aug FRANCE 22 **ENGLAND** 9
Stade Vélodrome, Marseille

[*This match kicked off at 9.00pm; George Chuter selected but withdrew due to injury, being replaced by Mark Regan; For this match England wore red shirts with a white right sleeve, red shorts and socks that were red at the front and white at the back!*]

**(*England were leading 3-0 in the 14th minute; England were drawing 3-3 midway through the first half; England were still drawing 3-3 in the 28th minute when Jonny Wilkinson missed a speculative 46 metre penalty goal attempt; England were drawing 3-3 in the 33rd minute; England were losing 9-3 just before half-time; England were*

losing 12-3 at half-time; Phil Vickery went off injured at half-time after being concussed, being replaced by Matt Stevens; England were losing 12-6 in the 47th minute when Tom Rees and Jonny Wilkinson both saved a certain try by tackling Yannick Nyanga; England were losing 19-9 in the 57th minute; England were still losing 19-9 midway through the second half; England were losing 19-9 in the 65th minute when Paul Sackey slipped over which allowed Imanol Harinordoquy to break through, but he then unaccountably attempted to make the line himself when there was an overlap outside him!; England were losing 22-9 with 9 minutes of normal time remaining; Martin Corry went off injured with 8 minutes of normal time remaining, being replaced by Olly Barkley with Andy Farrell then moving from centre to flanker to accommodate Barkley; Shaun Perry went off injured with 2 minutes of normal time remaining, being replaced by Andy Gomarsall)

FIRA-AER EUROPEAM' FESTIVAL

France

CAPTAIN: *Jim Jenner*

6th Sept RUSSIA 10 **ENGLAND COUNTIES** 76

Stade Municipal Marius-Lacoste, Fleurance

[*This match kicked off at 5.00pm*]

(*This match was played in hot conditions; Nick Royle scored in the 2nd minute!; England Counties were leading 19-0 in the 9th minute; England Counties were still leading 19-0 when Craig Aikman scored to complete a hat-trick of tries; England Counties were leading 26-0 when Craig Aikman had a great try-scoring chance but was brilliantly tackled by Evgeny Matveev; England Counties were still leading 26-0 when Jim Jenner scored a pushover try; England Counties scored 40 unanswered points to win the match; England Counties were leading 40-0 at half-time; England Counties were leading 40-10 at one point in the second half; Nick Royle and Tom Jarvis saw very little of the ball in this match; Tristan Roberts had a brilliant game*)

CAPTAIN: *Tom Bason*

10th Sep SPAIN XV 15 **ENGLAND COUNTIES** 21

Stade des Cordeliers, Morlaàs

[*This match kicked off at 5.00pm; Alastair Simmie selected but withdrew due to injury, Tristan Roberts was moved from the bench to the team and Frankie Neale was then selected for the bench; Jim Jenner was included in an original 8 man bench selection; Ged Glynn was the Coach for Spain in this match*]

(*England Counties made a number of handling errors in the first half; England Counties were leading 3-0 in the 12th minute; England Counties were still leading 3-0 midway through the first half; England Counties were losing 6-3 in the 30th minute; England Counties were losing 9-3 in the 35th minute; England Counties were losing 9-6 at half-time; England Counties were losing 12-6 in the 65th minute; England Counties were losing 15-9 in the 68th minute; Tristan Roberts missed a number of penalty goal attempts; England Counties were still losing 15-9 with 4 minutes of normal time remaining when Glenn Cooper scored from a rolling maul; England Counties were leading 16-15 in the third minute of injury time when Nick Royle powered through 3 attempted tackles to score a match-clinching try*)

CAPTAIN: *Jim Jenner*

13th Sep FRANCE AMATEURS 21 **ENGLAND COUNTIES*** 21

Stade Municipal, Saint-Paul-lès-Dax

[*This match kicked off at 6.00pm; Alastair Simmie unavailable due to injury; Dean Bick*

***selected for bench but withdrew, being replaced by Peter Joyce*]**
(*England Counties played down a slope in the first half; Philippe Lafue scored a penalty goal in the 4th minute!; England Counties were drawing 6-6 in the 33rd minute; Frankie Neale went off injured, being replaced by Jack Smales; England Counties were losing 13-6 in first half injury time when Jim Jenner scored from a tap penalty; England Counties were losing 13-11 at half-time; England Counties were losing 18-11 in the 51st minute; England Counties were losing 21-14 in the closing stages of normal time when Nick Royle wasted 2 great try-scoring opportunities in succession; England Counties were still losing 21-14 in the sixth minute of injury time when Nick Royle scored a brilliant 41 metre diagonal try which Tristan Roberts then converted to draw the match*)

WORLD CUP

France
CAPTAIN: *Phil Vickery* [*Martin Corry*]
First Round - Pool 'A'
8th Sept USA 10 **ENGLAND** 28
Stade Félix Bollaert, Lens
[*This match kicked off at 6.00pm; Jonny Wilkinson unavailable due to injury; On 11th September 2007 a World Cup judicial inquiry found Phil Vickery guilty of deliberately tripping an opponent and thus banned him for 2 games*]
(*Mark Cueto played with an injury and consequently had a poor game; England were leading 3-0 in the 7th minute; England were drawing 3-3 in the 9th minute; England were still drawing 3-3 midway through the first half; England were leading 6-3 in the 27th minute when Olly Barkley put in a brilliant grubber kick but Mike Catt was unable to gather the bouncing ball while the American tryline was at his mercy; England were leading 9-3 in the 35th minute when Jason Robinson scored after Josh Lewsey made a brilliant run; England were leading 14-3 just before half-time; England were leading 21-3 at half-time; The England forwards could not win any lineout ball in the second half; Tom Rees scored a try from a quick tap penalty which Olly Barkley then converted to give England a 28-3 lead in the 49th minute; England scored 25 unanswered points to win the match; England were still leading 28-3 midway through the second half; Matt Tait came on as a replacement for Jason Robinson in the 66th minute, with Mark Cueto then switching from full back to wing to accommodate Matt Tait; England were leading 28-3 with 6 minutes of normal time remaining; England were leading 28-10 in the second minute of injury time when Andy Farrell made a superb break, but Josh Lewsey then wasted this great try-scoring opportunity by throwing a poor return pass*)
CAPTAIN: *Martin Corry*
14th Sept SOUTH AFRICA 36 **ENGLAND** 0
Stade de France, Paris
[*This match kicked off at 9.00pm; Jonny Wilkinson and Mark Cueto unavailable due to injury; Dan Hipkiss and Matt Tait unavailable due to illness; Phil Vickery selected as captain but withdrew due to suspension, Matt Stevens was moved from the bench to the team and Perry Freshwater was then selected for the bench; Olly Barkley selected at fly half but withdrew due to injury, Andy Farrell was moved from the bench to the team and Peter Richards was then selected for the bench; On 13th September 2007 Andy Farrell and Mike Catt swapped positions to inside centre and fly half respectively; Jamie Noon returned home injured after this match; Toby Flood joined the squad after this match*]

(The England backs kicked away too much possession in this match; England were drawing 0-0 in the 6th minute when Juan Smith scored after Shaun Perry missed a tackle on J.P. Pietersen; England were losing 10-0 in the 14th minute when Mike Catt missed a 34 metre drop goal attempt from in front of the posts!; England were still losing 10-0 midway through the first half when Josh Lewsey saved a certain try by tackling Jaque Fourie; England were losing 10-0 in the 28th minute when Jason Robinson made a brilliant break but then ran out of support; England were losing 13-0 shortly before half-time when J.P. Pietersen scored after Paul Sackey missed a tackle on Fourie du Preez; England were losing 20-0 at half-time; Shaun Perry had a poor game and was replaced by Andy Gomarsall at half-time; England were losing 23-0 in the 46th minute and pressing in attack when Ben Kay unaccountably elected to put in a chip-kick instead of passing to Paul Sackey!; Steve Borthwick came on as a temporary blood replacement for Simon Shaw in the 55th minute; England were losing 26-0 in the 57th minute and again pressing in attack when Jason Robinson pulled his left hamstring; Jason Robinson went off injured immediately afterwards, being replaced by Matt Tait with Josh Lewsey then switching from wing to full back to accommodate Matt Tait; England were still losing 26-0 midway through the second half; England were losing 26-0 in the 64th minute when a poor blindside defensive alignment allowed J.P. Pietersen to score another try, thus 3 tries and 21 points were preventable; Jamie Noon went off injured with 2 minutes remaining, being replaced by Peter Richards; England were losing 33-0 with 1 minute remaining; Jason Robinson had a brilliant game; England lost by 36 points to record their worst ever margin of defeat in a World Cup match)

22nd Sep SAMOA 22 **ENGLAND** 44 **BP**

Stade de la Beaujoire, Nantes

[This match kicked off at 4.00pm; Jason Robinson unavailable due to injury; Phil Vickery unavailable due to suspension; Jonny Wilkinson's goal-kicking fell below its normal standard in this match after he had trouble with the feel of the new World Cup Gilbert ball]

(Jonny Wilkinson played with an ankle injury; The England backs kicked away too much possession in this match; Martin Corry scored in the 2nd minute!; England were leading 10-0 in the 6th minute; England were leading 13-6 midway through the first half; England were leading 16-6 in the 26th minute when Jonny Wilkinson missed a 39 metre penalty goal attempt from in front of the posts!; Jonny Wilkinson put in a brilliant grubber kick and Paul Sackey followed up to score a try which Jonny Wilkinson then converted to give England a 23-6 lead in the 32nd minute; England were leading 23-12 at half-time; England were leading 26-15 in the 47th minute when Josh Lewsey's attempted clearance kick went straight to David Lemi who instigated a counter-attack which led directly to a try by Junior Polu, thus 7 points were preventable; England were leading 26-22 in the 56th minute when Jonny Wilkinson missed an eminently kickable 23 metre penalty goal attempt; England were still leading 26-22 midway through the second half; England were leading 29-22 with 8 minutes of normal time remaining when Jonny Wilkinson scored a brilliant 51 metre penalty goal; England were leading 32-22 with 4 minutes of normal time remaining when Martin Corry scored another try after Paul Sackey made a superb run; England were leading 39-22 in the third minute of injury time when Paul Sackey scored a brilliant try with the last move of the match; Jonny Wilkinson scored 24 points in this match; Andy Gomarsall had a brilliant game)

CAPTAIN: *Martin Corry [Phil Vickery]*

28th Sept TONGA 20 **ENGLAND** 36 **BP**

Parc des Princes

[*This match kicked off at 9.00pm; This venue in Paris was officially called the Stade du Parc des Princes, but it was usually just referred to as Parc des Princes; Tom Rees and Jason Robinson unavailable due to injury; Simon Shaw and Joe Worsley were rested for this match; Andy Farrell retired in May 2009*]

(*Jonny Wilkinson played with an ankle injury; England were losing 3-0 in the 10th minute; England were drawing 3-3 in the 17th minute when collectively poor tackling allowed Suka Hufanga to score, thus 7 points were preventable; England were losing 10-3 midway through the first half when Paul Sackey scored after Jonny Wilkinson put up a brilliant cross kick; England were losing 10-8 in the 29th minute when Olly Barkley missed a 15 metre drop goal attempt from in front of the posts!; England were leading 14-10 shortly before half-time when Paul Sackey scored a superb 83 metre solo try; England were leading 19-10 at half-time; The second half of this match was played in wet conditions; England were still leading 19-10 in the 43rd minute when Jonny Wilkinson missed a kickable 40 metre penalty goal attempt; Andy Farrell came on as a replacement for Olly Barkley in the 52nd minute; England were leading 19-13 in the 55th minute; Phil Vickery came on as a replacement for Matt Stevens in the 57th minute; England were leading 26-13 midway through the second half; England were still leading 26-13 in the 66th minute when Andy Farrell scored a brilliant solo try under the posts; England scored 17 unanswered points to clinch the match; Mark Cueto went off injured with 7 minutes remaining, being replaced by Peter Richards with Matt Tait then switching from centre to wing to accommodate Peter Richards; England were leading 36-13 in the last minute; Jonny Wilkinson scored his 1000th cap international point in this match*)

CAPTAIN: *Phil Vickery [Martin Corry]*

Quarter-Final

6th Oct AUSTRALIA 10 **ENGLAND** 12

Stade Vélodrome, Marseille

[*This match kicked off at 3.00pm; Andy Farrell selected but withdrew due to injury, being replaced by Mike Catt; Olly Barkley selected for bench but withdrew due to injury, being replaced by Toby Flood; Jonny Wilkinson's goal-kicking fell below its normal standard in this match because the World Cup Gilbert balls were excessively inflated*]

**(*This match was played in extremely hot conditions; Jonny Wilkinson played with an ankle injury; England were losing 3-0 in the 7th minute; England were still losing 3-0 midway through the first half; Peter Richards came on as a temporary blood replacement for Andy Gomarsall in the 22nd minute; England were drawing 3-3 in the 23rd minute; England were leading 6-3 in the 29th minute when Jonny Wilkinson missed a kickable 35 metre penalty goal attempt; England were still leading 6-3 in the 33rd minute when Lote Tuqiri (1) scored after a poor tackle by Josh Lewsey, thus 7 points were preventable; England were losing 10-6 shortly before half-time when Jonny Wilkinson missed an eminently kickable 23 metre penalty goal attempt; England were losing 10-6 at half-time; England were still losing 10-6 in the 47th minute when the ball went loose at the base of a close-range Australian defensive scrum after Andy Gomarsall brilliantly tackled Wycliff Palu, but Jonny Wilkinson then wasted this great try-scoring opportunity by throwing a poor pass to Mike Catt; England were losing 10-*

9 in the 52nd minute; Matt Stevens came on as a replacement for Phil Vickery in the 59th minute; England were leading 12-10 midway through the second half; England were still leading 12-10 in the 63rd minute when Paul Sackey saved a certain try by tackling Chris Latham after Australia had created a 3 man overlap; Mike Catt went off injured in the 64th minute, being replaced by Toby Flood; Lewis Moody went off injured in the 66th minute, being replaced by Joe Worsley; England were leading 12-10 in the 67th minute when Jonny Wilkinson missed a kickable 33 metre drop goal attempt; England were still leading 12-10 with 5 minutes remaining when Jonny Wilkinson missed a speculative penalty goal attempt from the halfway line; England were leading 12-10 with 2 minutes remaining when Stirling Mortlock missed a difficult 46 metre penalty goal attempt for Australia; Andy Sheridan played brilliantly in the scrums; Jonny Wilkinson broke Gavin Hastings' record of 227 World Cup points)

CAPTAIN: *Phil Vickery* [*Martin Corry*]

Semi-Final

13th Oct FRANCE 9 **ENGLAND** 14

Stade de France, Paris

[*This match kicked off at 9.00pm; Josh Lewsey left the squad injured after this match; Nick Abendanon joined the squad after this match*]

(*Jonny Wilkinson played with an ankle injury; Andy Gomarsall put up a brilliant box kick which enabled Josh Lewsey to score after just 77 seconds had been played!; England were leading 5-3 in the 8th minute; England were losing 6-5 midway through the first half; England were still losing 6-5 in the 26th minute when Jonny Wilkinson missed a speculative 43 metre drop goal attempt; England were losing 6-5 in the 29th minute when Jonny Wilkinson missed a speculative 52 metre penalty goal attempt; Josh Lewsey had to go off in the 40th minute after he pulled a hamstring, being replaced by Dan Hipkiss with Matt Tait then switching from centre to wing to accommodate Hipkiss; England were losing 6-5 at half-time; England were losing 9-5 in the 44th minute; England were losing 9-8 in the 47th minute; Matt Stevens came on as a replacement for Phil Vickery in the 56th minute; England were still losing 9-8 midway through the second half when Jonny Wilkinson hit the left-hand post with a kickable 28 metre drop goal attempt; England were losing 9-8 in the 68th minute when Joe Worsley saved a certain try by brilliantly tap-tackling Vincent Clerc; Mike Catt went off injured in the 69th minute, being replaced by Toby Flood; England were still losing 9-8 with 7 minutes of normal time remaining when Toby Flood badly mishit a speculative 40 metre drop goal attempt, resulting in the ball bouncing across the pitch!; England were leading 11-9 with 5 minutes of normal time remaining; England were still leading 11-9 with 2 minutes of normal time remaining when Jonny Wilkinson scored a superb 39 metre drop goal to clinch the match; Jason Robinson had a brilliant game*)

CAPTAIN: *Phil Vickery* [*Martin Corry*]

Final

20th Oct SOUTH AFRICA 15 **ENGLAND*** 6

Stade de France, Paris

[*This match kicked off at 9.00pm; Lawrence Dallaglio retired in May 2008*]

(*Jonny Wilkinson played with an ankle injury; The England forwards allowed Victor Matfield to dominate the lineout in this match; England were losing 3-0 in the 7th minute; England were still losing 3-0 in the 13th minute when Jonny Wilkinson scored a brilliant 23 metre penalty goal from the right touchline; England were drawing 3-3 in the 15th minute when Lewis Moody unaccountably tripped Butch James and South Africa were awarded a 30 metre penalty which Percy Montgomery duly kicked;*

England were losing 6-3 midway through the first half; England were still losing 6-3 just before half-time; England were losing 9-3 at half-time; Matt Stevens came on as a replacement for Phil Vickery at the start of the second half; England were still losing 9-3 in the 43rd minute when Matt Tait made a brilliant 48 metre break which enabled Mark Cueto to cross the tryline, but the move was disallowed after the video referee adjudged that Cueto had put a foot into touch before he grounded the ball; Jason Robinson had to go off in the 47th minute after he dislocated his shoulder, being replaced by Dan Hipkiss with Matt Tait then switching from centre to full back to accommodate Hipkiss; England were losing 9-6 in the 50th minute when Martin Corry inexplicably handled the ball in a ruck and the referee awarded a 23 metre penalty to South Africa that Percy Montgomery duly kicked, thus 6 points were preventable; Mike Catt went off injured immediately afterwards, being replaced by Toby Flood; England were losing 12-6 midway through the second half; England were losing 15-6 in the 62nd minute; Lawrence Dallaglio came on as a replacement for Nick Easter in the 65th minute; Joe Worsley went off injured with 9 minutes remaining, being replaced by Peter Richards who had to play out of position as a flanker; England were still losing 15-6 immediately afterwards when Jonny Wilkinson had a speculative 43 metre drop goal attempt go underneath the crossbar)

ATKINS REMEMBRANCE RUGBY MATCH

CAPTAIN: *Jannie Bornman* (SA)

14th Nov COMBINED SERVICES (*SER*) 27 **BARBARIANS*** 24

Plymouth Albion RFC, Brickfields Recreation Ground, Madden Road, Plymouth

[*This match kicked off at 7.15pm; Guy Easterby selected but withdrew, being replaced by Gareth Williams (6); Steve Martin selected but withdrew, being replaced by Rob McCusker; Paul Sampson selected but withdrew on the day of the match due to illness, Andy Birkett was moved from the bench to the team and Wihan Neethling was then selected for the bench; Chris Budgen, Ben Hughes and Isoa Damu played for the Combined Services in this match, with Ben Hughes and Damu scoring a try apiece*]

(*This match was played in drizzly conditions; The Barbarians were losing 7-0 in the 14th minute; The Barbarians were losing 12-0 midway through the first half when some superb handling allowed Matt Moore to score; The Barbarians were losing 12-5 shortly before half-time when Diego Zarzosa scored from a rolling maul; The Barbarians were losing 12-10 at half-time; The Barbarians were losing 15-10 in the 52nd minute; The Barbarians were losing 20-10 midway through the second half; The Barbarians were still losing 20-10 in the 65th minute when Nic Sestaret scored after Rhodri McAtee made a brilliant break; The Barbarians were losing 20-17 in the 67th minute when Nic Sestaret scored another try after Brad Davies put up a brilliant cross-kick; The Barbarians were leading 24-20 in the sixth minute of injury time when Isoa Damu scored a superb try which Rob Lloyd then converted with the last kick of the match to clinch the game for the Combined Services*)

EMIRATES AIRLINE DUBAI RUGBY SEVENS

Dubai Exiles Stadium, Dubai

CAPTAIN: *Andy Vilk*

First Round - Pool 'D'

30th Nov TUNISIA 12 **ENGLAND** 27

[*This match kicked off at 12.04pm*]

(*England were leading 12-0 midway through the first half; England were leading 12-7 shortly before half-time; England were leading 17-7 at half-time; England were leading*

***17-12 in the 8th minute*)**

30th Nov	CANADA	24	**ENGLAND***	24

[*This match kicked off at 5.00pm*]

(*Daniel van der Merwe scored in the 2nd minute!; England were leading 12-5 at half-time; Isoa Damu scored after just 11 seconds of the second half had been played!; Jack Adams scored a brilliant try which Ben Foden then converted to give England a 24-5 lead in the 10th minute; England were leading 24-17 in injury time when Jordan Kozina scored after a poor tackle by Jack Adams, thus 7 points were preventable; Canada were allowed to score 19 unanswered points to draw the match*)

30th Nov	SOUTH AFRICA	22	**ENGLAND**	10

[*This match kicked off at 7.56pm*]

(*Anthony Elliott scored in the 2nd minute!; England were losing 7-5 midway through the first half; England were still losing 7-5 in the 6th minute; England were losing 12-5 at half-time; England were losing 17-5 early in the second half; England were losing 17-10 in the closing stages*)

Quarter-Final

1st Dec	SAMOA	19	**ENGLAND**	26

[*This match kicked off at 11.52am*]

(*Anthony Elliott scored after just 35 seconds had been played!; England were drawing 7-7 midway through the first half; England were still drawing 7-7 in the 5th minute when Jack Adams saved a certain try by tackling Roger Warren into touch at the corner flag; England were losing 12-7 just before half-time when Tom Guest scored a brilliant try; England were leading 14-12 at half-time; Anthony Elliott took a quick tap penalty and scored after just 36 seconds of the second half had been played!; England were leading 19-12 midway through the second half; England were drawing 19-19 with 3 minutes remaining; England were still drawing 19-19 in the final minute when Simon Hunt scored a brilliant try with the last move of the match to win the game*)

Semi-Final

1st Dec	FIJI	22	**ENGLAND***	21

[*This match kicked off at 6.42pm; England wore navy blue shirts for this match*]

(*The referee awarded a penalty try after just 34 seconds been played when Simon Hunt was impeded by Etonia Naba as he attempted to support Tom Guest's break!; England were leading 7-0 midway through the first half; England were leading 7-5 in the 5th minute when Ben Foden scored after Tom Guest threw a brilliant reverse pass; England were leading 14-5 in the 6th minute when Vereniki Goneva scored after Ben Foden missed a tackle on Setefano Cakau, thus 7 points were preventable; England were leading 14-12 just before half-time; England were losing 17-14 at half-time; England were losing 22-14 in the 8th minute; Fiji were allowed to score 17 unanswered points to win the match; England were still losing 22-14 midway through the second half; England were losing 22-21 with 2 minutes remaining when Ben Foden kicked ahead and while Neumi Nanuku reached the ball first he failed to get any downward pressure on it, which allowed Foden to follow up his own kick, rip the ball off Nanuku and clearly ground the ball for a try, but the referee unaccountably awarded Fiji a five metre scrum instead*)

GARTMORE CHALLENGE

CAPTAIN: *Mark Regan* [*Justin Marshall* (NZ)]

1st Dec **BARBARIANS** 22 SOUTH AFRICA XV 5

Twickenham

[*This match kicked off at 3.00pm; Brian O'Driscoll selected as captain in the original squad but withdrew due to his Magners League commitments; Paul O'Connell in original squad but withdrew due to his Magners League commitments; Sébastien Chabal in original squad but withdrew due to club commitments; Mauro Ledesma, Juan Martín Hernández, Sitiveni Sivivatu and Chris Latham in original squad but withdrew; Andy Sheridan in training squad of 22 but withdrew due to club commitments; Luke Charteris in training squad of 22 but withdrew; Rocky Elsom was originally selected at blindside flanker with Jerry Collins at number 8, but the two swapped positions before the match; Matt Giteau acted as scrum half cover for Justin Marshall; Jason Robinson retired after this match, changed his mind in July 2010 and then retired for a second and final time in July 2011; Ben Cohen retired in May 2011 but then came out of retirement to play for a H4H Northern Hemisphere XV against a Southern Hemisphere XV at Twickenham on 3rd December 2011*]

(*Matt Giteau scored a penalty goal in the 3rd minute!; The Barbarians were leading 3-0 in the 14th minute when Joe Rokocoko saved a certain try by tackling Ryan Kankowski into touch at the corner flag; The Barbarians were still leading 3-0 in the 18th minute when Matt Giteau scored after Ma'a Nonu fly-hacked a loose ball on from his own 22; The Barbarians were leading 8-0 midway through the first half; The Barbarians were still leading 8-0 in the 28th minute when Ma'a Nonu broke through but then slipped over as he tried to beat Ruan Pienaar; The Barbarians were leading 8-0 in the 32nd minute when Matt Giteau broke through but then wasted this great try-scoring opportunity by slipping over while Jason Robinson was unmarked outside him; The Barbarians were leading 8-5 just before half-time when Jason Robinson made a brilliant run which allowed Martyn Williams to chip ahead and then take a pass from Federico Pucciariello to score; The Barbarians were leading 15-5 at half-time; The second half of this match was played in wet conditions; The Barbarians were leading 22-5 in the 42nd minute; The Barbarians scored 14 unanswered points to clinch the match; Mark Regan was substituted in the 51st minute, being replaced by Schalk Brits; The Barbarians were still leading 22-5 midway through the second half; Ben Cohen came on as a replacement for Isoa Neivua in the 63rd minute; Jason Robinson was substituted in the 68th minute, being replaced by Peter Grant; The Barbarians were leading 22-5 with 4 minutes remaining when Tom Shanklin saved a certain try by tackling Juan Smith; Martyn Williams and Jason Robinson both had a brilliant game*)

EMIRATES AIRLINE SOUTH AFRICA SEVENS

Outeniqua Park Stadium, George

CAPTAIN: *Andy Vilk*

First Round - Pool 'A'

7th Dec ZIMBABWE 7 **ENGLAND** 24

[*This match kicked off at 12.24pm*]

(*Joe Simpson scored in the 3rd minute!; England were leading 7-0 midway through the first half; England were leading 14-0 shortly before half-time when Tom Youngs powered through 2 attempted tackles to score; England scored 19 unanswered points to win the match; England were leading 19-0 at half-time; England were still leading 19-0 midway through the second half; England were leading 19-0 with 3 minutes*

remaining when collectively poor tackling allowed Tangai Nemadire to score, thus 7 points were preventable; England were leading 19-7 with 2 minutes remaining)

7th Dec KENYA 17 **ENGLAND** 7

[*This match kicked off at 3.30pm*]

(Innocent Simiyu scored in the 2nd minute!; England were losing 5-0 midway through the first half; England were leading 7-5 in the 4th minute; England were still leading 7-5 shortly before half-time; England were losing 12-7 at half-time; England were still losing 12-7 in the 9th minute when collectively poor tackling allowed Innocent Simiyu to score another try, thus 5 points were preventable; England were losing 17-7 midway through the second half)

7th Dec NEW ZEALAND 26 **ENGLAND*** 24

[*This match kicked off at 7.46pm*]

(Israel Dagg scored in the 1st minute!; England were losing 7-0 in the 3rd minute when Simon Hunt crossed the New Zealand line in a diving position where he held the ball off the ground and then got to his feet in an attempt to get nearer the posts, only to find that the referee had already awarded a try at the point where he had first crossed the line!; England were losing 7-5 midway through the first half; England were still losing 7-5 in the 4th minute when Ben Foden scored after he wrong-footed Lote Raikabula with a brilliant sidestep; England scored 17 unanswered points; England were leading 17-7 just before half-time when Israel Dagg scored a try which should not have been given because the scoring pass from Zar Lawrence was clearly forward, thus 7 points were unlawful; England were leading 17-14 at half-time; England were still leading 17-14 in the 9th minute; England were losing 21-17 midway through the second half; England were still losing 21-17 with 2 minutes remaining when Isoa Damu scored from a tap penalty; England were leading 24-21 in the final minute when Israel Dagg scored with the last move of the match to complete a hat-trick and win the game for New Zealand)

[Bowl Quarter-Final:]

[8th Dec CANADA 5 **ENGLAND** 35]

[*This match kicked off at 10.14am*]

(Joe Simpson scored in the 1st minute!; England were leading 14-0 midway through the first half; England were leading 21-0 at half-time; England were leading 28-0 in the 8th minute; England were leading 35-0 midway through the second half; England scored 35 unanswered points to win the match; England were still leading 35-0 with 1 minute remaining)

[Bowl Semi-Final:]

[8th Dec AUSTRALIA 14 **ENGLAND** 29]

[*This match kicked off at 2.29pm*]

(Anthony Elliott scored in the 1st minute!; England were leading 12-0 midway through the first half; England were leading 19-0 in the 4th minute; England scored 19 unanswered points to win the match; England were still leading 19-0 shortly before half-time; England were leading 19-7 at half-time; England were leading 19-14 in the 8th minute; England were still leading 19-14 in the 10th minute when Ben Foden kicked ahead and followed up to score a brilliant 93 metre solo try; Ben Foden injured his shoulder scoring this try and had to go off, being replaced by Simon Hunt; England were leading 24-14 midway through the second half; England were still leading 24-14 with 3 minutes remaining when Simon Hunt scored to seal the match)

[Bowl Final:]

[8th Dec WALES 21 **ENGLAND*** 19]

[***This match kicked off at 5.40pm; Ben Foden unavailable due to injury***]

(***Lee Williams scored in the 1st minute!; England were losing 7-0 in the 2nd minute when Anthony Elliott scored after he wrong-footed Gareth Owen with a brilliant sidestep; England were drawing 7-7 midway through the first half; England were still drawing 7-7 just before half-time; England were leading 12-7 at half-time; Anthony Elliott scored a brilliant 78 metre solo try which Joe Simpson then converted to give England a 19-7 lead in the 8th minute; England were still leading 19-7 in the 9th minute when Richard Pugh scored after Jack Adams missed a tackle on Aled Brew, thus 7 points were preventable; England were leading 19-14 midway through the second half when James Lewis scored after Isoa Damu dropped Martin Roberts (2)'s restart into the hands of Jonathan Edwards, thus 2 tries and 14 points were preventable; Wales were allowed to score 14 unanswered points to win the match***)

2008

NEW ZEALAND INTERNATIONAL SEVENS

Westpac Stadium, Wellington

CAPTAIN: *Andy Vilk*

First Round - Pool 'B'

1st Feb COOK ISLANDS 21 **ENGLAND*** 17

[*This match kicked off at 2.50pm*]

(Isoa Damu scored after just 67 seconds had been played!; England were leading 5-0 midway through the first half; England were still leading 5-0 in the 6th minute; England were losing 7-5 when the half-time hooter sounded, but the ball was still in play and collectively poor tackling allowed Nathan Robinson to score; England were losing 14-5 at half-time; England were still losing 14-5 midway through the second half when further collectively poor tackling allowed Ashley Drake to score, thus 2 tries and 14 points were preventable; The Cook Islands were allowed to score 21 unanswered points to win the match; England were losing 21-5 with 1 minute remaining when Matt Banahan came on as a temporary blood replacement for 2 seconds of play!)

1st Feb WALES 15 **ENGLAND** 5

[*This match kicked off at 5.46pm*]

(England were drawing 0-0 midway through the first half; England were losing 5-0 just before half-time; England were losing 10-0 at half-time; England were losing 15-0 in the 10th minute; Wales were allowed to score 15 unanswered points to win the match; England were still losing 15-0 midway through the second half; England were losing 15-0 in the second minute of injury time when Ben Gollings scored a consolation try)

1st Feb FIJI 17 **ENGLAND** 7

[*This match kicked off at 9.34pm; England wore navy blue shirts for this match*]

(Emosi Vucago scored after just 73 seconds had been played!; England were losing 10-0 midway through the first half; England were still losing 10-0 just before half-time; Fiji were allowed to score 17 unanswered points to win the match; England were losing 17-0 at half-time; England were still losing 17-0 midway through the second half; England were losing 17-0 with 2 minutes remaining when Ben Gollings scored a consolation try)

[Bowl Quarter-Final:]

[2nd Feb CANADA 17 **ENGLAND** 33]

[*This match kicked off at 1.00pm*]

(Dom Shabbo scored after just 76 seconds had been played!; England were leading 7-0 midway through the first half; England were leading 14-7 just before half-time; England were leading 14-12 at half-time; Anthony Elliott scored after just 40 seconds of the second half had been played!; England were leading 28-12 midway through the second half; England scored 19 unanswered points to clinch the match; England were leading 33-12 in the last minute)

[Bowl Semi-Final:]

[2nd Feb FRANCE 5 **ENGLAND** 14]

[*This match kicked off at 4.54pm*]

(Florent Gibouin scored after just 35 seconds had been played!; England were losing 5-0 midway through the first half; England were leading 7-5 in the 4th minute; England were leading 7-5 at half-time; England were leading 14-5 midway through the second half; England scored 14 unanswered points to win the match)

[Bowl Final:]

[2nd Feb ARGENTINA 7 **ENGLAND** 12]

[This match kicked off at 8.00pm; England wore navy blue shirts for this match]

(England were drawing 0-0 midway through the first half; England were still drawing 0-0 just before half-time; England were losing 7-0 at half-time; England were still losing 7-0 midway through the second half when Anthony Elliott scored a try which Ben Gollings then converted to beat Waisale Serevi's existing IRB World Sevens record of 457 conversions; England were drawing 7-7 with 2 minutes remaining; Ben Gollings increased his IRB World Sevens record to 1651 points in this tournament)

6 NATIONS CHAMPIONSHIP

CAPTAIN: *Phil Vickery* [*Jonny Wilkinson*]

2nd Feb **ENGLAND*** 19 WALES 26

Twickenham

[This match kicked off at 4.30pm; Dan Ward-Smith, Harry Ellis, Shaun Perry, Ben Foden and Olly Morgan all unavailable due to injury; Olly Barkley unavailable for personal reasons; Josh Lewsey made himself available for this match but was not selected!; Louis Deacon, Tom Croft, Joe Worsley, Nick Easter and Peter Richards all in original training squad of 32 but withdrew due to injury; Tim Payne, George Chuter, Charlie Hodgson, Jamie Noon, Matt Tait and Mark Cueto all in original training squad of 32 but were not selected for team or bench; Michael Lipman, Luke Narraway and Paul Hodgson were added to the squad on 25th January 2008 to provide injury cover; Lesley Vainikolo was born in Tonga, won 12 caps for New Zealand at Rugby League between 1998-2005, played in the Bradford Bulls team that won the Middlesex Sevens at Twickenham on 17th August 2002 and became a Rugby Union player in May 2007 when he joined Gloucester, having already qualified for England in January 2005 after completing a residency period of 3 years]

(Jonny Wilkinson scored a penalty goal in the 2nd minute!; England were drawing 3-3 in the 7th minute when Dave Strettle broke through but then wasted this great try-scoring opportunity by electing to kick instead of waiting for Paul Sackey to arrive in support; Dave Strettle and Lewis Moody went off injured in the 13th and 14th minute, being replaced by Lesley Vainikolo and Tom Rees respectively; England were leading 9-3 midway through the first half; Jonny Wilkinson put up a brilliant cross-kick which enabled Lesley Vainikolo to catch the ball and pass to Toby Flood who scored a try which Jonny Wilkinson then converted to give England a 16-3 lead in the 23rd minute; England were leading 16-6 in the 37th minute when Jonny Wilkinson missed an eminently kickable 25 metre penalty goal attempt; England were still leading 16-6 in the 38th minute when Paul Sackey reached the tryline, but the video referee adjudged that the ball had hit Huw Bennett's arm rather than the ground; England were leading 16-6 at half-time; Tom Rees himself went off injured at half-time after he ruptured the medial ligament in his knee, being replaced by Ben Kay with Luke Narraway then switching from number 8 to the unfamiliar position of openside flanker to accommodate Kay, with the performance of the England back row being badly affected as a result; England were leading 19-6 in the 45th minute; England were still leading 19-6 in the 58th minute; England were leading 19-9 midway through the second half when Luke Narraway saved a certain try by intercepting Ian Gough's pass; England were leading 19-12 in the 64th minute when Mike Tindall had to go off after he suffered both a punctured lung and a torn liver during a tackle, being replaced by Danny Cipriani; England were still leading 19-12 in the 67th minute when Jonny Wilkinson threw a wild pass to Danny Cipriani which allowed James Hook to instigate an attack

***that culminated in a try by Lee Byrne; The England captain Phil Vickery was unaccountably substituted in the 69th minute, being replaced by Matt Stevens; England were drawing 19-19 in the 70th minute when Iain Balshaw took too much time over his clearance kick and was charged down by Mike Phillips (2) who eventually went on to score, thus 2 tries and 14 points were preventable; England conceded 20 unanswered points in 13 minutes to give Wales their first win at Twickenham since 1988!*)**

CAPTAIN: *Steve Borthwick*

10th Feb ITALY 19 **ENGLAND** 23

Stadio Flaminio, Rome

[*This match kicked off at 3.30pm; Louis Deacon, Joe Worsley, Lewis Moody, Tom Rees, Dan Ward-Smith, Harry Ellis, Shaun Perry, Peter Richards, Dave Strettle, Andy Farrell, Mike Tindall and Olly Morgan all unavailable due to injury; Olly Barkley unavailable for personal reasons; Josh Lewsey made himself available for this match but was not selected!; Phil Vickery selected as captain but withdrew on the morning of the match due to illness, Matt Stevens was moved from the bench to the team and Jason Hobson was then selected for the bench; Andy Sheridan in original training squad of 30 but withdrew due to illness; George Chuter, Tom Croft, Magnus Lund, Lee Dickson, Charlie Hodgson, Shane Geraghty and Mark Cueto all in original training squad of 30 but were not selected for team or bench; Jason Hobson was added to the squad on 7th February 2008 to provide injury cover for Phil Vickery*]

(*Paul Sackey scored in the 3rd minute after Jonny Wilkinson chipped ahead into space, regathered the ball and then threw a brilliant reverse pass!; England were leading 7-3 in the 6th minute; Jamie Noon charged down David Bortolussi's kick which allowed Toby Flood to score a try that Jonny Wilkinson then converted to give England a 14-6 lead in the 15th minute; England were still leading 14-6 midway through the first half; England were leading 14-6 in the 23rd minute when Jonny Wilkinson missed a difficult 22 metre penalty goal attempt; England were leading 17-6 in the 32nd minute; England were leading 20-6 at half-time; The England forwards could not win any possession in the second half; England were leading 20-9 in the 44th minute; Matt Tait came on as a temporary blood replacement for Jamie Noon in the 52nd minute; England were leading 20-12 in the 55th minute; England were leading 23-12 midway through the second half; Nick Easter went off injured in the 65th minute, being replaced by Luke Narraway; Danny Cipriani came on as a replacement for Jonny Wilkinson in the 67th minute; England were still leading 23-12 in the 70th minute when they created and then squandered an overlap; England were leading 23-12 with 9 minutes remaining when Jamie Noon saved a certain try by tap-tackling Kane Robertson; England were still leading 23-12 with 4 minutes remaining when Danny Cipriani's chip-kick was charged down by Simon Picone who went on to score from the ensuing rebound, thus 7 points were preventable; Lesley Vainikolo saw very little of the ball in this match; Jonny Wilkinson became the first player to score 1000 cap international points for England; Iain Balshaw had a poor game*)

CAPTAIN: *Phil Vickery*

23rd Feb FRANCE 13 **ENGLAND** 24

Stade de France, Paris

[*This match kicked off at 9.00pm; Lewis Moody, Tom Rees, Dan Ward-Smith, Harry Ellis, Shaun Perry, Peter Richards, Dave Strettle, Andy Farrell, Mike Tindall and Olly Morgan all unavailable due to injury; Olly Barkley unavailable for personal reasons; Josh Lewsey made himself available for this match but was not selected!; Shane*

Geraghty in original training squad of 31 but withdrew due to injury; Tim Payne, George Chuter, Louis Deacon, Joe Worsley, Luke Narraway, Andy Gomarsall, Charlie Hodgson and Mark Cueto all in original training squad of 31 but were not selected for team or bench; On 5th March 2008 the IRB retrospectively ruled that the game between the British & Irish Lions and Argentina at the Millennium Stadium on 23rd May 2005 was in fact a cap international match, which meant that Jonny Wilkinson had now officially equalled Neil Jenkins' world record of 1090 points!]
(Paul Sackey scored in the 5th minute!; England were leading 10-0 in the 14th minute; England were still leading 10-0 midway through the first half; James Haskell went off injured in the 21st minute, being replaced by Tom Croft; England were leading 13-7 in the 29th minute; England were leading 13-7 at half-time; England were leading 13-10 in the 49th minute; England were still leading 13-10 in the 55th minute when Jonny Wilkinson missed a kickable 41 metre penalty goal attempt; England were leading 13-10 in the 58th minute when Jonny Wilkinson had another kickable 42 metre penalty goal attempt go underneath the crossbar; England were still leading 13-10 midway through the second half; England were leading 13-10 in the 64th minute when Jonny Wilkinson scored a brilliant 28 metre drop goal to break Hugo Porta's existing world record of 28 drop goals; England were leading 16-10 in the 68th minute when Jonny Wilkinson scored a superb 50 metre penalty goal; England were leading 19-13 with 1 minute remaining when Richard Wigglesworth scored to clinch the match; Nick Easter had a brilliant game)
CAPTAIN: *Phil Vickery* [*Steve Borthwick*]

8th March SCOTLAND 15 **ENGLAND** 9
Murrayfield
[This match kicked off at 3.15pm; Lewis Moody, Tom Rees, Dan Ward-Smith, Shaun Perry, Peter Richards, Dave Strettle, Andy Farrell, Shane Geraghty, Mike Tindall and Olly Morgan all unavailable due to injury; Olly Barkley unavailable for personal reasons; Josh Lewsey made himself available for this match but was not selected!; Danny Cipriani selected at full back but was unaccountably withdrawn for disciplinary reasons, Iain Balshaw was moved from the bench to the team and Charlie Hodgson was then selected for the bench; James Haskell in original training squad of 30 but withdrew due to injury; Tim Payne, Mark Regan, Louis Deacon, Joe Worsley, Danny Care and Mark Cueto all in original training squad of 30 but were not selected for team or bench; James Simpson-Daniel was added to the squad on 2nd March 2008]
(This match was played in wet and windy conditions on a slippery pitch; The England backs kicked away too much possession; England were losing 3-0 in the 9th minute; England were still losing 3-0 midway through the first half; England were drawing 3-3 in the 27th minute; England were losing 6-3 in the 39th minute when Jonny Wilkinson had a speculative 48 metre penalty goal attempt go underneath the crossbar; England were still losing 6-3 just before half-time; England were losing 9-3 at half-time; England were losing 12-3 in the 41st minute; England conceded too many needless penalties within Chris Paterson's kicking range; England were losing 15-3 in the 48th minute; England were losing 15-9 in the 53rd minute; England were still losing 15-9 midway through the second half; Charlie Hodgson came on as a replacement for Jonny Wilkinson in the 70th minute; Jonny Wilkinson set a new world record of 1099 cap international points in this match; England collectively played poorly)
CAPTAIN: *Phil Vickery* [*Steve Borthwick*]

15th Mar **ENGLAND** 33 IRELAND 10
Twickenham
[This match kicked off at 3.00pm; Lewis Moody, Tom Rees, Peter Richards, Dave

***Strettle, Shane Geraghty, Mike Tindall and Olly Morgan all unavailable due to injury; Olly Barkley unavailable for personal reasons; Josh Lewsey made himself available for this match but was not selected!; James Simpson-Daniel in original training squad of 31 but withdrew due to injury; Tim Payne, Mark Regan, Louis Deacon, Joe Worsley, Luke Narraway, Danny Care, Charlie Hodgson and Mark Cueto all in original training squad of 31 but were not selected for team or bench*]**

(*Rob Kearney scored in the 4th minute!; England were losing 10-0 in the 7th minute; England were losing 10-3 midway through the first half when some superb handling amongst the backs allowed Paul Sackey to score; England were drawing 10-10 in the 24th minute when Jamie Noon had a great try-scoring chance but was tackled just short of the Irish line by both Tommy Bowe and Geordan Murphy; England were leading 13-10 in the 30th minute; England were leading 13-10 at half-time; England were leading 16-10 in the 45th minute; Matt Tait came on as a temporary blood replacement for Paul Sackey in the 48th minute; Jonny Wilkinson came on as a replacement for Toby Flood in the 53rd minute; England were still leading 16-10 in the 57th minute when Matt Tait scored a brilliant try; England were leading 23-10 midway through the second half; Matt Stevens came on as a replacement for Phil Vickery in the 61st minute; England were leading 28-10 in the 69th minute when Danny Cipriani scored a superb conversion from the left touchline; England were leading 33-10 with 6 minutes remaining; England scored 33 unanswered points to win the match; This match finished in wet conditions; Danny Cipriani and Jamie Noon both had a brilliant game*)

U20 6 NATIONS CHAMPIONSHIP

CAPTAIN: *Hugo Ellis*

1st Feb **ENGLAND U20** 28 WALES U20 15

Kingsholm, Gloucester

[*This match kicked off at 7.45pm; Graham Kitchener, Courtney Lawes, Carl Fearns and Alex Tait unavailable due to injury; Joe Simpson selected but withdrew due to injury, Ben Youngs was moved from the bench to the team and Jonny Arr was then selected for the bench; Andy Saull selected but withdrew on the day of the match due to injury, Matt Cox was moved from the bench to the team and Tom Sargent was then selected for the bench; Nathan Catt, Alex Corbisiero, Gregor Gillanders, Scott Hobson, Jon Fisher, Alex Goode, Miles Benjamin, Greig Tonks and Scott Freer all played for England in the U19 World Championship in Ireland in April 2007; Ben Youngs was the brother of Tom Youngs and the son of Nick Youngs; Luke Eves, Tom Sargeant and Seb Stegmann toured Australia with England U18 in August 2007; Luke Eves was the son of Derek Eves*]

(*England U20 were drawing 0-0 midway through the first half; England U20 were still drawing 0-0 in the 25th minute when Noah Cato scored a brilliant solo try; England U20 were leading 7-0 in the 33rd minute when Miles Benjamin powered through to score; England U20 were leading 17-3 at half-time; England U20 were leading 22-3 in the 50th minute; England U20 were leading 25-3 in the 57th minute; England U20 were leading 25-8 midway through the second half; England U20 were still leading 25-8 with 5 minutes remaining*)

9th Feb ITALY U20 13 **ENGLAND U20** 22

Stadio Sciorba, Genoa

[*This match kicked off at 3.00pm; Courtney Lawes, Carl Fearns and Joe Simpson unavailable due to injury; Gregor Gillanders and Miles Benjamin unavailable due to club commitments; Seb Stegmann was originally selected at left wing with Noah Cato*

at right wing, but the two swapped positions before the match; Rob Miller toured Australia with England U18 in August 2007]
(England U20 played into a strong wind in the first half; England U20 were losing 3-0 in the 9th minute; England U20 were still losing 3-0 midway through the first half when Alex Corbisiero scored from a rolling maul; England U20 were leading 7-3 in the 37th minute; England U20 were leading 7-6 shortly before half-time when Alex Goode hit the right-hand post with a kickable 33 metre penalty goal attempt; England U20 were leading 7-6 at half-time; Greig Tonks went off injured at half-time, being replaced by Dan Norton; England U20 were still leading 7-6 in the 49th minute when Noah Cato scored after Ben Youngs made a brilliant blindside break; England U20 were leading 15-6 midway through the second half; England U20 were still leading 15-6 in the 67th minute when Andy Saul scored from another rolling maul; England U20 were leading 22-6 in the final minute)

22nd Feb FRANCE U20 6 **ENGLAND U20** 24
Stade des Alpes, Grenoble
[This match kicked off at 7.00pm; Courtney Lawes, Carl Fearns and Greig Tonks unavailable due to injury; Gregor Gillanders in original training squad of 22 but withdrew due to club commitments, being replaced by Tom Sargeant; Charlie Sharples toured Australia with England U18 in August 2007]
(England U20 were drawing 0-0 midway through the first half; England U20 were leading 3-0 in the 24th minute; England U20 were leading 6-0 in the 29th minute; England U20 were leading 6-3 in the 31st minute when Noah Cato scored a brilliant try; England U20 were leading 14-3 at half-time; England U20 were leading 14-6 in the 48th minute; England U20 were still leading 14-6 midway through the second half; England U20 were leading 14-6 with 2 minutes of normal time remaining when Alex Corbisiero scored from a rolling maul; England U20 were leading 21-6 in the last minute of normal time when Rob Miller scored a brilliant 50 metre penalty goal to seal the match)

7th Mar SCOTLAND U20 15 **ENGLAND U20** 41
Falkirk Stadium
[This match kicked off at 7.30pm; Courtney Lawes, Carl Fearns and Jordan Turner-Hall unavailable due to injury; Gregor Gillanders, Calum Clark, Miles Benjamin, Charlie Sharples, Dan Norton and Alex Tait all unavailable due to club commitments; Mike Stanley in original training squad of 23 but was not selected for team or bench; Greg King played for England in the U19 World Championship in Ireland in April 2007]
(Ben Thomas was sent off just before half-time for allegedly head-butting an opponent)
(England U20 were leading 3-0 in the early stages; England U20 were drawing 3-3 in the 7th minute when Seb Stegmann scored a brilliant try; England U20 were leading 10-3 midway through the first half; England U20 were leading 17-3 in the 27th minute when Hugo Ellis scored from a rolling maul; England U20 were leading 22-3 at half-time; England U20 were leading 22-8 early in the second half; England U20 were still leading 22-8 shortly afterwards when Joe Simpson scored a superb 40 metre solo try; England U20 scored 19 unanswered points in 5 minutes to seal the match; England U20 were leading 41-8 midway through the second half; England U20 were still leading 41-8 in the last minute; Alex Goode had a brilliant game)

CAPTAIN: *Hugo Ellis* [*Nathan Catt*]

14th Mar **ENGLAND U20** 43 IRELAND U20 14
Kingsholm, Gloucester
[This match kicked off at 7.35pm; Courtney Lawes and Carl Fearns unavailable due to

***injury; Rob Miller and Jordan Turner-Hall unavailable due to club commitments; Ben Thomas unavailable due to suspension; Adam Greendale played for England in the U19 World Championships in Dubai in April 2006 and Ireland in April 2007; James Cannon was the son of Vince Cannon*]**

(*This match was played in cold conditions; David Kearney scored in the 4th minute!; England U20 were leading 7-5 in the 7th minute; England U20 were losing 8-7 midway through the first half; England U20 were still losing 8-7 in the 27th minute when some superb handling allowed Hugo Ellis to score; England U20 were leading 14-11 in the 35th minute when Luke Eves scored a brilliant try; England U20 were leading 19-11 shortly before half-time; England U20 were leading 19-14 at half-time; Hugo Ellis went off injured at half-time, being replaced by Andy Saull with Jon Fisher then switching from flanker to number 8 to accommodate Saull; England U20 were still leading 19-14 in the 45th minute when Matt Cox scored after Jon Fisher made a brilliant run; England U20 were leading 26-14 midway through the second half when Noah Cato scored a superb 45 metre solo try; England U20 were leading 31-14 in the 66th minute when Nathan Catt scored after Adam Greendale made a brilliant break; England U20 were leading 38-14 with 5 minutes remaining when Mark Odejobi scored after Alex Goode instigated a superb 80 metre counter-attack; England U20 scored 24 unanswered points in the second half to clinch the match and the Grand Slam; Jon Fisher had a brilliant game*)

ENGLAND SAXONS INTERNATIONAL MATCHES

CAPTAIN: *Jordan Crane*

1st Feb **ENGLAND SAXONS** 31 IRELAND A 13

Welford Road, Leicester

[*This match kicked off at 7.45pm; Michael Lipman, Luke Narraway and Paul Hodgson in original training squad of 32 but withdrew as they were now required to join the full England international squad, being replaced by Will Skinner, George Skivington and James Grindal respectively; Magnus Lund and James Simpson-Daniel in original training squad of 32 but withdrew due to injury; Alex Clarke, Andy Titterrell, Richard Blaze, Alex Brown, Danny Care, Dan Hipkiss, Tom Arscott and Chris Ashton all in original training squad of 32 but were not selected for team or bench; Ben Skirving was added to the squad on 23rd January 2008; On 6th February 2008 the Six Nations Disciplinary Committee found David Wilson (2) guilty of entering a ruck in a dangerous manner and thus banned him for 1 week*]

**(*This match was played in extremely cold conditions; Andrew Dunne scored a penalty goal in the 4th minute!; The England Saxons were losing 3-0 in the 6th minute when Ryan Lamb scored a brilliant 41 metre penalty goal; The England Saxons were drawing 3-3 in the 16th minute when David Paice scored from a rolling maul; Ryan Lamb went off injured in the 18th minute, being replaced by Anthony Allen with Shane Geraghty then switching from centre to fly half to accommodate Anthony Allen; The England Saxons were leading 8-3 midway through the first half; The England Saxons were losing 10-8 in the 26th minute; The England Saxons were losing 10-8 at half-time; The England Saxons were leading 11-10 in the 43rd minute; The England Saxons were still leading 11-10 in the 48th minute when Delon Armitage saved a certain try after he got back to tackle Tommy Bowe; The England Saxons were losing 13-11 in the 54th minute when Tom Varndell scored after Shane Geraghty put up a brilliant cross-kick; The England Saxons were leading 19-13 midway through the second half; The England Saxons were still leading 19-13 with 9 minutes of normal time remaining when Tom Varndell scored another try after Dylan Hartley threw a superb reverse pass; The*

England Saxons were leading 29-13 in the second minute of injury time when Delon Armitage scored a brilliant conversion from the left touchline with the last kick of the match to seal the game; Jordan Crane and Shane Geraghty both had a brilliant game)

CAPTAIN: *Phil Dowson*

9th Feb ITALY A 15 **ENGLAND SAXONS** 38

Stadio Aldo Campo, Ragusa, Sicily

[This match kicked off at 6.00pm; Ryan Lamb unavailable due to injury; Nick Wood, Dylan Hartley, Andy Titterrell, Tom Palmer (2), George Skivington, Jordan Crane, Ollie Smith (2), Anthony Allen, James Simpson-Daniel, Tom Varndell and Chris Ashton all unavailable due to club commitments; David Wilson (2) selected for bench but withdrew due to suspension, being replaced by Jon Golding; Jason Hobson selected but withdrew as he was now required to sit on the bench for the full England international team the next day, Jon Golding was moved from the bench to the team and John Brooks was then selected for the bench; Dave Attwood, James Grindal and Paul Hodgson in original training squad of 24 but were not selected for team or bench; Lee Dickson was added to the squad on 6th February 2008; Tom Biggs was originally selected at left wing with John Rudd at right wing, but the two swapped positions before the match; John Rudd played in the Samurai team that won the Amsterdam Heineken Sevens on 19th-20th May 2007; Alex Crockett failed to take drugs tests on both 13th May and 14th May 2009 and a subsequent RFU Disciplinary Panel on 3rd August 2009 found Crockett guilty of 'conduct prejudicial to the interests of the game' and thus banned him for 9 months, with the ban running from 1st June 2009 until 28th February 2010]

(The England Saxons were losing 3-0 in the 14th minute; The England Saxons were drawing 3-3 midway through the first half; The England Saxons were still drawing 3-3 in the 32nd minute when Tom Guest broke from the base of a scrum to score in the corner; The England Saxons were leading 10-3 just before half-time when Jacobus Erasmus scored after a poor tackle by Nick Abendanon, thus 5 points were preventable; The England Saxons were leading 10-8 at half-time; The England Saxons were still leading 10-8 in the 46th minute when some superb handling amongst the forwards allowed Delon Armitage to score; The England Saxons were leading 24-8 in the 58th minute when Nick Kennedy ran 27 metres to score a brilliant try; The England Saxons were leading 31-8 midway through the second half; The England Saxons were leading 38-8 in the 69th minute; The England Saxons scored 28 unanswered points to clinch the match; The England Saxons were still leading 38-8 in the last minute; Adrian Jarvis had a brilliant game)

USA SEVENS

PETCO Park, San Diego

CAPTAIN: *Andy Vilk*

First Round - Pool 'D'

9th Feb MEXICO 0 **ENGLAND** 48

[This match kicked off at 11.06am]

(The England players monopolised possession in this match; England were leading 26-0 at half-time)

9th Feb USA 21 **ENGLAND** 28

[This match kicked off at 2.12pm]

(England were leading 14-0 in the early stages; England were still leading 14-0 when Anthony Elliott scored a brilliant solo try; England scored 21 unanswered points to

win the match; England were leading 21-0 at half-time; Chris Wyles scored after just 20 seconds of the second half had been played!; England were leading 28-7 with 2 minutes remaining; Isoa Damu had a brilliant game)

9th Feb SOUTH AFRICA 10 **ENGLAND** 14

[This match kicked off at 6.02pm]

(Isoa Damu had to go off in the early stages after he dislocated his shoulder, being replaced by Simon Hunt; England were drawing 0-0 shortly afterwards when Ben Gollings kicked ahead and followed up to score a brilliant try; England were leading 7-5 at half-time; England were losing 10-7 in the closing stages when Ben Gollings scored a brilliant 40 metre solo try to win the match)

Quarter-Final

10th Feb KENYA 17 **ENGLAND*** 7

[This match kicked off at 11.50am; Isoa Damu unavailable due to injury]

(England were drawing 0-0 in the early stages and pressing in attack when Kevin Barrett had his pass intercepted by Collins Injera, who instigated a counter-attack that culminated in a try by Dennis Mwanja, thus 7 points were preventable; England were losing 12-0 at half-time; England were losing 12-7 midway through the second half; England were still losing 12-7 with 1 minute remaining)

[Plate Semi-Final:]

[10th Feb FIJI 21 **ENGLAND*** 14 **]**

[This match kicked off at 2.34pm; Isoa Damu unavailable due to injury; England wore navy blue shirts for this match]

(Uche Oduoza scored a brilliant 95 metre solo try straight after the kick-off!; England were drawing 7-7 at half-time; England were leading 14-7 early in the second half; England were still leading 14-7 midway through the second half; England were drawing 14-14 with 3 minutes remaining; England were losing 21-14 in the final minute when Tom Tombleson was tackled into touch near the corner flag in the last move of the match; Ben Gollings increased his IRB World Sevens record to 1702 points in this tournament)

<u>ENGLAND STUDENTS MATCH</u>

CAPTAIN: *Ian Kench*

23rd Feb FRANCE STUDENTS 45 **ENGLAND STUDENTS** 9

Stade Léon Sausset, Tournon

[This match kicked off at 3.00pm; This match was originally scheduled for 22nd February 2008]

(England Students were leading 3-0 in the 6th minute; England Students were still leading 3-0 midway through the first half; England Students were losing 12-3 in the 24th minute; England Students were losing 12-6 in the 30th minute; England Students were losing 19-6 at half-time; England Students were losing 26-9 in the 42nd minute; England Students were losing 33-9 in the 54th minute; England Students were still losing 33-9 midway through the second half; England Students were losing 40-9 in the 65th minute; Peter Wackett and Tom Jarvis both went off injured in this match; England Students were still losing 40-9 in the third minute of injury time; France Students were allowed to score 26 unanswered points to seal the match; Richard Vasey had a brilliant game)

FOUR NATIONS COLLEGES STUDENT RUGBY TOURNAMENT

CAPTAIN: *Michael Rickner*

7th Mar Scottish Universities (*SC*) 0 **ENGLAND STUDENTS** 42

Lasswade RFC, Hawthornden, Polton, Bonnyrigg

[This match kicked off at 7.30pm; Scott Armstrong in original squad of 21 but withdrew due to injury, being replaced by Drew Locke; Peter Clarke (1) played for a Wales U21 A XV in December 2002]

(This match was played in wet conditions; England Students were drawing 0-0 in the 7th minute when Andy Wright scored after Tristan Roberts made a brilliant break; England Students were leading 7-0 midway through the first half; England Students were leading 14-0 in the 29th minute; England Students were leading 14-0 at half-time; England Students played with a strong wind in the second half; England Students were still leading 14-0 in the 51st minute; England Students were leading 21-0 in the 56th minute when Peter Clarke (1) scored a pushover try; England Students were leading 28-0 midway through the second half; England Students were leading 35-0 with 2 minutes remaining; Mike Denbee had a brilliant game)

CAPTAIN: *Ian Kench*

14th Mar **ENGLAND STUDENTS** 30 Irish Colleges (*IR*) 14

Henley RFC, Dry Leas, Marlow Road, Henley-on-Thames

[This match kicked off at 8.00pm; Tristan Roberts and Giles Pryor unavailable due to injury; Aaron Liffchak played in the Great Britain team that reached the Final of the Rugby Union tournament at the 2009 Maccabiah Games in Netanya on 12th-22nd July 2009]

(Adrian Griffiths scored in the 4th minute!; England Students were leading 10-0 in the 13th minute; England Students were leading 10-3 in the 18th minute when John Nicol scored after Phil Ellis missed a tackle on Dave Rowan, thus 5 points were preventable; England Students were leading 10-8 midway through the first half; England Students were still leading 10-8 in the 38th minute; England Students were leading 13-8 at half-time; Andries Pretorius went off injured in the 49th minute, being replaced by James Lumby; England Students were losing 14-13 in the 50th minute; England Students were still losing 14-13 midway through the second half when Tom Hockedy scored a brilliant try; England Students were leading 30-14 in the 68th minute; England Students scored 17 unanswered points to win the match)

CAPTAIN: *Phil Ellis*

3rd May **ENGLAND STUDENTS** 38 COMBINED SERVICES U23 (*SER*) 26

Twickenham

[This match kicked off at 12.00pm and was a curtain raiser game for the Army v Navy match; England Students were also billed as England Students U23; Toby Henry in original squad of 22 but withdrew due to injury, being replaced by Jamie Hood; Scott Armstrong in original squad of 22 but withdrew due to his Guinness Premiership commitments, being replaced by Mike Coady]

(England Students conceded a penalty try after just 65 seconds had been played when they illegally collapsed a rolling maul!; England Students were losing 7-5 in the 4th minute; England Students were losing 13-8 midway through the first half; England Students were still losing 13-8 in the 26th minute when Phil Ellis scored a brilliant try; England Students were leading 15-13 in the 36th minute; England Students were losing 16-15 just before half-time; England Students were leading 18-16 at half-time; England Students were still leading 18-16 in the 46th minute when Mike Denbee scored

from a rolling maul; England Students were leading 30-16 in the 50th minute; England Students were still leading 30-16 midway through the second half; England Students were leading 33-26 in injury time when Peter Browne scored a pushover try to clinch the match)

CATHAY PACIFIC/CREDIT SUISSE HONG KONG SEVENS

Hong Kong Stadium, Eastern Hospital Road, So Kon Po, Hong Kong

CAPTAIN: *Andy Vilk*

First Round - Pool 'B'

28th Mar	CANADA	12	**ENGLAND**	24

[This match kicked off at 8.38pm]

(England were losing 7-0 in the 3rd minute; England were still losing 7-0 midway through the first half when John Brake scored a brilliant 50 metre solo try; England were drawing 7-7 at half-time; Chris Mayor scored after just 30 seconds of the second half had been played!; England were leading 19-7 midway through the second half; England scored 24 unanswered points to win the match; England were leading 24-7 in the last minute)

29th Mar	SRI LANKA	7	**ENGLAND**	47

[This match kicked off at 11.58am]

(Ben Gollings scored a brilliant 60 metre solo try in the 2nd minute!; England were leading 14-0 midway through the first half; England were leading 21-0 in the 4th minute; England were still leading 21-0 just before half-time when Ben Gollings intercepted the ball and ran 90 metres to score; England were leading 28-0 at half-time; England were still leading 28-0 in the 9th minute when Noah Cato scored a brilliant 50 metre solo try; England scored 33 unanswered points to win the match; England were leading 33-0 midway through the second half; England were leading 33-7 with 3 minutes remaining; Ben Gollings scored 22 points in this match)

29th Mar	SAMOA	5	**ENGLAND**	7

[This match kicked off at 6.34pm]

(England were losing 5-0 midway through the first half; England were losing 5-0 at half-time; England were still losing 5-0 midway through the second half; England were losing 5-0 with 1 minute of normal time remaining when Simon Hunt powered through 2 attempted tackles to score a try which Ben Gollings then converted to win the match; England were leading 7-5 when the full-time hooter sounded, but the ball remained in play until Noah Cato and John Brake both saved a certain try by tackling Mikaele Pesamino into touch in-goal)

Quarter-Final

30th Mar	SAMOA	17	**ENGLAND***	12

[This match kicked off at 1.47pm]

(England were drawing 0-0 midway through the first half; England were still drawing 0-0 shortly before half-time when Anthony Elliott scored after Ben Gollings put in a brilliant chip-kick; England were leading 5-0 just before half-time; England were losing 7-5 at half-time; England were still losing 7-5 in the 8th minute when Andy Vilk ran 55 metres to score under the posts after Ben Gollings made a brilliant break; England were leading 12-7 midway through the second half when Alatasi Tupou scored after a poor tackle by Simon Hunt, thus 5 points were preventable; England were drawing 12-12 with 2 minutes remaining when Alafoti Fa'osiliva was awarded a try that should not have been given because it was unclear whether he had grounded the ball properly,

***thus 5 points were unlawful; Ben Gollings increased his IRB World Sevens record to 1737 points in this tournament*)**

ADELAIDE SEVENS

Adelaide Oval, Adelaide

CAPTAIN: *Andy Vilk*

First Round - Pool 'D'

5th April FIJI 31 **ENGLAND*** 12

[*This match kicked off at 11.09am; James Collins unavailable due to injury; England wore navy blue shirts for this match*]

(*Setefano Cakau scored in the 2nd minute!; England were losing 5-0 shortly afterwards when Simon Hunt kicked ahead and followed up to score a brilliant try; England were losing 12-7 at half-time; England were still losing 12-7 early in the second half when collectively poor tackling allowed William Ryder to score, thus 7 points were preventable; England were losing 19-7 midway through the second half; England were still losing 19-7 with 2 minutes remaining when Kevin Barrett scored an interception try; Ben Gollings increased his IRB World Sevens record to 1739 points in this tournament*)

5th April KENYA 17 **ENGLAND** 10

[*This match kicked off at 2.37pm; James Collins and Ben Gollings unavailable due to injury*]

(*England were leading 5-0 in the early stages; England were losing 12-5 at half-time; Kenya were allowed to score 17 unanswered points to win the match; England were losing 17-5 in the closing stages*)

5th April FRANCE 19 **ENGLAND*** 12

[*This match kicked off at 5.21pm; James Collins and Ben Gollings unavailable due to injury*]

(*Ben Youngs scored in the 1st minute!; England were leading 7-0 midway through the first half when collectively poor tackling allowed Anthony Poujol to score, thus 5 points were preventable; England were leading 12-5 at half-time; England were still leading 12-5 in the 9th minute when Vincent Roux scored a try that should not have been given because the scoring pass from Eddy Labarthe was clearly forward, thus 7 points were unlawful; England were drawing 12-12 midway through the second half; England were still drawing 12-12 with 3 minutes remaining*)

[Bowl Quarter-Final:]

[6th April USA 26 **ENGLAND*** 19 aet]

[*This match kicked off at 11.22am; James Collins and Ben Gollings unavailable due to injury; England wore navy blue shirts for this match; The USA originally won the match 19-17 after the scorekeepers failed to add on an England conversion because it was unclear whether the ball actually went between the posts, but the IRB retrospectively changed the result to a 19-19 draw which meant that the players then had to be recalled to the pitch 5 minutes after the final whistle so that sudden death extra time could be played!; Tom Tombleson played for Major R.V. Stanley's XV against Oxford University at Iffley Road on 19th November 2008*]

(*Chris Wyles scored in sudden death extra time to win the match for the USA*)

[Shield Semi-Final:]

[6th April WALES 19 **ENGLAND*** 14]

[*This match kicked off at 2.06pm; James Collins and Ben Gollings unavailable due to*

***injury*]**
(*England were drawing 14-14 in the last minute; England lost their 5th consecutive match at this competition!*)

EDINBURGH ACADEMICALS 150TH ANNIVERSARY MATCH

CAPTAIN: *Gordon Bulloch* (SC)

9th April Edinburgh Academicals (*SC*) 0 **BARBARIANS** 43

Raeburn Place, Stockbridge, Edinburgh

[*This match kicked off at 6.00pm; Nigel Hall selected but withdrew, Ngalu Taufo'ou was moved from the bench to the team and Ben Evans was then selected for the bench; Dan Norton selected for bench but withdrew due to club commitments, being replaced by Lee Best; Tyrone Howe selected but withdrew on the day of the match to sit on the bench, Lee Best was moved from the bench to the team; Lee Best toured Australia with England Schools 18 Group in August 1997; Ross Blake switched his allegiance to England in January 2007*]

(*This match was played in cold conditions; Both sides agreed to allow unlimited substitutions in this match; The Barbarians were drawing 0-0 in the 6th minute when Nick Macleod scored a brilliant solo try; The Barbarians were leading 7-0 midway through the first half; The Barbarians were still leading 7-0 in the 30th minute; The Barbarians were leading 12-0 in the 32nd minute when Genaro Fessia scored a brilliant try; The Barbarians were leading 19-0 at half-time; The Barbarians were still leading 19-0 in the 43rd minute when Stuart Moffat scored after Tyrone Howe made a superb run; The Barbarians were leading 38-0 midway through the second half; The Barbarians were still leading 38-0 in the 62nd minute when Lee Best scored a brilliant 78 metre solo try*)

EMIRATES AIRLINE LONDON SEVENS

Twickenham

CAPTAIN: *Ben Gollings*

First Round - Pool 'B'

24th May **ENGLAND** 29 SPAIN 7

[*This match kicked off at 11.34am*]

(*Tom Biggs scored in the 2nd minute!; England were leading 5-0 midway through the first half; England were leading 10-0 in the 4th minute; England were still leading 10-0 shortly before half-time; England were leading 10-7 at half-time; England were still leading 10-7 midway through the second half; England were leading 10-7 with 3 minutes remaining when Tom Biggs scored to complete a hat-trick of tries; England were leading 22-7 in the last minute; England scored 19 unanswered points in the second half to clinch the match*)

CAPTAIN: *Andy Vilk*

24th May **ENGLAND** 33 FRANCE 5

[*This match kicked off at 2.40pm*]

(*Ben Foden crossed the tryline in the 1st minute but the move was disallowed because the referee adjudged that there had been an earlier knock-on!; England were drawing 0-0 shortly afterwards when Ben Gollings jinked through to score a brilliant try; England were leading 7-0 midway through the first half when Ben Foden scored a brilliant 54 metre solo try; England were leading 14-0 just before half-time; England were leading 19-0 at half-time; England were still leading 19-0 early in the second half when Uche Oduoza scored a superb 61 metre solo try which Ben Gollings then*

***brilliantly converted from the right touchline; England scored 26 unanswered points to win the match; England were leading 26-0 midway through the second half when collectively poor tackling allowed Anthony Poujol to score, thus 5 points were preventable; England were leading 26-5 in the last minute when Ben Foden scored another superb 61 metre solo try*)**

24th May **ENGLAND** 7 SOUTH AFRICA 22

[*This match kicked off at 5.58pm*]

(*England were losing 7-0 in the 3rd minute; England were still losing 7-0 shortly afterwards when Ollie Phillips scored a brilliant 35 metre solo try; England were leading 7-5 at half-time; England were losing 17-7 early in the second half; England were still losing 17-7 midway through the second half; South Africa were allowed to score 17 unanswered points to clinch the match*)

Quarter-Final

25th May **ENGLAND** 17 NEW ZEALAND 12

[*This match kicked off at 12.28pm*]

(*Nigel Hunt was awarded a try in the 1st minute that should not have been given because he put a foot into touch before he grounded the ball, thus 5 points were unlawful!; England were losing 5-0 midway through the first half; England were still losing 5-0 shortly before half-time when collectively poor tackling allowed Chad Tuoro to score, thus 7 points were preventable; England were losing 12-0 at half-time; England were losing 12-5 in the 8th minute; England were still losing 12-5 midway through the second half; England were losing 12-5 with 2 minutes of normal time remaining; England were drawing 12-12 when the full-time hooter sounded, but the ball was still in play and Tom Biggs was able to score a brilliant 54 metre diagonal try to win the match*)

Semi-Final

25th May **ENGLAND*** 12 SAMOA 14

[*This match kicked off at 4.44pm*]

(*England were drawing 0-0 midway through the first half; England were still drawing 0-0 just before half-time; England were losing 7-0 at half-time; England were still losing 7-0 midway through the second half; Samoa were allowed to score 14 unanswered points to win the match; England were losing 14-0 with 1 minute of normal time remaining when Tom Biggs unaccountably chose to score in the corner instead of committing Lolo Lui to a tackle which would have allowed an unmarked Ben Gollings to score under the posts, with Gollings consequently missing the difficult conversion attempt from the right touchline; England were losing 14-5 when the full-time hooter sounded, but the ball was still in play and Ben Foden was able to score a brilliant 38 metre consolation try; Ben Gollings increased his IRB World Sevens record to 1760 points in this tournament*)

BARBARIANS TOUR TO BELGIUM 2008

CAPTAIN: *Mark Regan*

24th May BELGIUM XV 10 **BARBARIANS** 84

Stade Roi Baudouin, Brussels

[*This match kicked off at 4.00pm*]

(*This match was played on a pitch where the in-goal areas were shorter than normal; The Barbarians were drawing 0-0 in the 9th minute when Kris Chesney powered through to score under the posts; The Barbarians were leading 12-0 in the 16th minute; The Barbarians were leading 17-0 midway through the second half when Glen*

Jackson scored a brilliant conversion from the left touchline; The Barbarians were leading 19-0 in the 24th minute when Morgan Turinui scored after Lesley Vainikolo instigated a superb counter-attack from in front of his own line; The Barbarians were leading 26-0 in the 34th minute when Gareth Thomas (2) scored after Glen Jackson put up a brilliant cross-kick; The Barbarians were leading 31-0 at half-time; The Barbarians were leading 38-0 in the 42nd minute; The Barbarians scored 38 unanswered points to win the match; The Barbarians were still leading 38-0 in the 47th minute when Andy Gomarsall took too much time over his clearance kick and was charged down by Dirk Haghedooren, who went on to score from the ensuing rebound; The Barbarians were leading 38-5 in the 51st minute when Gareth Thomas (2) scored to complete a hat-trick of tries; The Barbarians were leading 52-5 midway through the second half when a superb break by Stephen Larkham allowed Gareth Thomas (2) to score a fourth try which Iain Balshaw then brilliantly converted from the right touchline; The Barbarians were leading 59-5 in the 63rd minute when Gareth Thomas (2) reached the Belgian line for what would have been a fifth try but he then allowed Pedrie Wannenburg to score instead!; The Barbarians were leading 64-5 in the 66th minute when Ma'ama Molitika crossed the tryline where the referee adjudged that he had correctly grounded the ball before he was tackled into touch in-goal; The Barbarians were leading 69-5 in the 68th minute when Sébastien Bruno's attempted clearance kick was charged down by Thibaut André who then went on to score, thus 2 tries and 10 points were preventable; The Barbarians were leading 74-10 with 6 minutes of normal time remaining when Lesley Vainikolo powered through 2 attempted tackles to score; The Barbarians were leading 79-10 with 2 minutes of normal time remaining when Iain Balshaw jinked through to complete his own hat-trick of tries!; Gareth Thomas (2) scored 20 points in this match)

FIRST GARTMORE CHALLENGE MATCH

CAPTAIN: *Morgan Turinui* (AU)

27th May **BARBARIANS** 14 IRELAND XV 39

Kingsholm, Gloucester

[This match kicked off at 7.45pm; Jerry Collins and Seilala Mapusua in original training squad of 24 but were not selected for team or bench]

(A poor tackle by Sosene Anesi allowed Tommy Bowe to score in the 5th minute!; The Barbarians were losing 10-0 in the 10th minute; The Barbarians were losing 17-0 midway through the first half; The Barbarians were still losing 17-0 in the 24th minute when Michael Claassen's pass was intercepted by Rob Kearney, who instigated a 95 metre counter-attack that culminated in a try by Shane Horgan; The Ireland XV was allowed to score 24 unanswered points to win the match; The Barbarians were losing 24-0 in the 38th minute when Craig Newby injured his neck ligaments scoring a try and had to go off, being replaced by Mitch Chapman; The Barbarians were losing 24-7 at half-time; The Barbarians were still losing 24-7 in the 53rd minute; The Barbarians were losing 27-7 in the 56th minute when Jamie Heaslip scored after another poor tackle by Sosene Anesi, thus 3 tries and 21 points were preventable; The Barbarians were losing 34-7 midway through the second half; The Barbarians were still losing 34-7 in the 65th minute when Pedrie Wannenburg scored after he wrong-footed the Ireland XV defence with a brilliant sidestep; The Barbarians were losing 34-14 with 6 minutes remaining)

EMIRATES AIRLINE EDINBURGH SEVENS

Murrayfield

CAPTAIN: *Andy Vilk*

First Round - Pool 'A'

31st May PORTUGAL 0 **ENGLAND** 22

[*This match kicked off at 9.34am*]

(*Uche Oduoza scored a brilliant 77 metre solo try after just 36 seconds had been played!; England were leading 7-0 midway through the first half; England were still leading 7-0 just before half-time when Uche Oduoza scored another brilliant 38 metre solo try, with Ben Gollings then missing the eminently kickable conversion attempt; England were leading 12-0 at half-time; Portugal were still losing 12-0 in the 10th minute when Sebastião da Cunha dropped the ball while the England tryline was at his mercy!; England were leading 12-0 midway through the second half; England were still leading 12-0 with 2 minutes remaining when Ollie Phillips chipped ahead and regathered the ball to score a superb try, with Ben Gollings then missing the eminently kickable conversion attempt; England were leading 17-0 in the last minute when Tom Biggs scored after Jack Adams threw a brilliant long pass, with Ben Gollings then missing the eminently kickable conversion attempt*)

31st May RUSSIA 17 **ENGLAND*** 17

[*This match kicked off at 12.40pm*]

(*Micky Young saved a certain try in the 1st minute after he got back to tackle Andrei Kuzin!; England were losing 5-0 in the 3rd minute; England were still losing 5-0 midway through the first half; England were losing 5-0 just before half-time when Nikolay Shugay scored a try which should not have been given because the scoring pass from Andrei Kuzin was clearly forward, thus 7 points were unlawful; England were losing 12-0 at half-time; Ollie Phillips chipped ahead and regathered the ball to score a brilliant try after just 28 seconds of the second half had been played!; England were losing 12-7 in the 10th minute when Micky Young took a quick tap penalty and scored, with Ben Gollings then missing the eminently kickable conversion attempt; England scored 17 unanswered points; England were leading 17-12 midway through the second half when Ben Gollings had a difficult conversion attempt which clearly went between the posts but the touch judge inexplicably failed to award it; Russia were still losing 17-12 when the full-time hooter sounded, but ball was still in play and Kevin Barrett was caught in possession by Alexander Shakirov at the base of an England scrum which allowed Igor Galinovskiy to score, thus 5 points were preventable, with Yury Kushnarev then missing the eminently kickable conversion attempt which would have won the match for Russia!*)

31st May NEW ZEALAND 21 **ENGLAND*** 12

[*This match kicked off at 4.20pm*]

(*England were drawing 0-0 midway through the first half when Solomon King scored after Uche Oduoza missed a tackle on Chad Tuoro; England were losing 7-0 in the 6th minute when Ben Gollings scored after Andy Vilk made a brilliant 35 metre run; England were drawing 7-7 at half-time; Jack Adams scored after just 48 seconds of the second half had been played!; England were leading 12-7 in the 10th minute when Uche Oduoza saved a certain try by tackling Kendrick Lynn into touch at the corner flag; England were still leading 12-7 midway through the second half; England were leading 12-7 with 2 minutes remaining when Chad Tuoro scored after Ben Gollings missed a tackle on David Smith (3), thus 2 tries and 14 points were preventable;*

England were losing 14-12 in the last minute; New Zealand were allowed to score 14 unanswered points to win the match)

Quarter-Final

1st June	SOUTH AFRICA	0	**ENGLAND**	10

[This match kicked off at 12.49pm]

(Jack Adams scored after just 94 seconds had been played!; England were leading 5-0 in the 4th minute when Kevin Barrett scored after Ben Gollings threw a brilliant reverse pass, with Gollings then missing the eminently kickable conversion attempt; England were leading 10-0 midway through the first half; England were leading 10-0 at half-time; The second half of this match was played in wet conditions; England were still leading 10-0 midway through the second half)

Semi-Final

1st June	WALES	0	**ENGLAND**	7

[This match kicked off at 4.30pm]

(This match was played in very wet conditions; England were drawing 0-0 midway through the first half; England were still drawing 0-0 in the 6th minute when Ben Gollings scored a brilliant 26 metre solo try; England were leading 7-0 at half-time; England were still leading 7-0 midway through the second half; Ollie Phillips came on as a replacement for Tom Youngs with 2 minutes remaining)

Final

1st June	NEW ZEALAND	24	**ENGLAND***	14

[This match kicked off at 6.16pm]

(This match was played on a wet pitch; England were drawing 0-0 in the 4th minute when Solomon King scored after Jack Adams slipped over and thus created a gap in the defensive line; England were losing 7-0 midway through the first half; England were still losing 7-0 in the 7th minute when collectively poor tackling allowed David Smith (3) to score, thus 2 tries and 14 points were preventable; New Zealand were allowed to score 19 unanswered points to win the match; England were losing 19-0 when the half-time hooter sounded, but the ball was still in play and Uche Oduoza was able to score a brilliant 52 metre solo try; England were losing 19-7 at half-time; England were losing 19-14 in the 12th minute; England were still losing 19-14 midway through the second half; England were losing 19-14 in the final minute when Nigel Hunt scored to clinch the match for New Zealand; Ben Gollings increased his IRB World Sevens record to 1782 points in this tournament)

SECOND GARTMORE CHALLENGE MATCH

CAPTAIN: *Nick Easter* [England XV]

CAPTAIN: *Mark Regan* [*Andy Gomarsall*] [Barbarians]

1st June	**ENGLAND XV**	17	**BARBARIANS**	14

Twickenham

[ENGLAND XV: *[This match kicked off at 3.00pm]*

(The England XV was leading 3-0 in the 7th minute; The England XV was still leading 3-0 in the 14th minute when Nick Easter scored from a rolling maul; The England XV was leading 10-0 midway through the first half; Charlie Hodgson went off injured in the 34th minute, being replaced by Peter Richards with Toby Flood then switching from centre to fly half to accommodate Peter Richards; The England XV was leading 10-0 at half-time; The England XV was still leading 10-0 in the 50th minute when Chris Jones' pass to Toby Flood was intercepted by Seilala Mapusua who then ran 35 metres to score, thus 7 points were preventable; Toby Flood went off injured in the 59th minute,

***being replaced by Ugo Monye with Peter Richards then having to move from centre to the unfamiliar position of fly half to accommodate Monye; The England XV was leading 10-7 midway through the second half when Mike Brown missed a kickable 42 metre penalty goal attempt; The England XV was still leading 10-7 in the 64th minute when Matt Tait scored after he wrong-footed the Barbarians defence with a brilliant sidestep; The England XV was leading 17-7 with 1 minute remaining; Nick Easter injured playing in the match*)]**

[BARBARIANS: [*This match kicked off at 3.00pm; Mitch Chapman was included in an original 8 man bench selection; Lawrence Dallaglio unavailable due to club commitments*]

(*Andy Gomarsall missed a kickable 37 metre penalty goal attempt in the 5th minute!; The Barbarians were losing 10-0 in the 14th minute; The Barbarians were still losing 10-0 midway through the first half; The Barbarians were losing 10-0 at half-time; The Barbarians were still losing 10-0 in the 50th minute when Seilala Mapusua intercepted the ball and ran 35 metres to score; The Barbarians were losing 10-7 midway through the second half; Glen Jackson came on as a replacement for Thinus Delport in the 63rd minute, with Stephen Larkham then switching from fly half to full back to accommodate Glen Jackson; The Barbarians were still losing 10-7 in the 64th minute when collectively poor tackling allowed Matt Tait to score, thus 7 points were preventable; The Barbarians were losing 17-7 with 1 minute remaining when Gareth Thomas (2) scored a brilliant consolation try*)]

IRB JUNIOR WORLD CHAMPIONSHIP

Wales

CAPTAIN: *Hugo Ellis*

First Round - Pool 'C'

6th June FIJI U20 17 **ENGLAND U20** 41 **BP**

Rodney Parade, Newport

[*This match kicked off at 7.00pm; England wore navy blue shirts for this match; Calum Clark toured Australia with England U18 in August 2007; Alex Tait played for England in the U19 World Championship in Ireland in April 2007; Alex Tait was the brother of Matt Tait*]

(*England U20 were leading 7-0 in the 8th minute; England U20 were leading 12-0 in the 13th minute; England U20 were leading 15-0 midway through the first half; England U20 were still leading 15-0 in the 22nd minute when Alex Goode scored after Joe Simpson took a quick tap penalty; England U20 were leading 22-0 in the 27th minute when Miles Benjamin scored after Seb Stegmann made a brilliant break; England U20 were leading 27-0 in the 33rd minute when Seb Stegmann scored after Noah Cato instigated a brilliant 80 metre counter-attack; England U20 were leading 34-0 in the 36th minute when Jordan Turner-Hall scored a superb solo try; England U20 scored 41 unanswered points in the first half to win the match; England U20 were leading 41-0 at half-time; England U20 were still leading 41-0 midway through the second half; England U20 were leading 41-12 in the 68th minute; England U20 were still leading 41-12 with 1 minute of normal time remaining*)

10th Jun CANADA U20 18 **ENGLAND U20** 60 **BP**

Rodney Parade, Newport

[*This match kicked off at 5.00pm; Courtney Lawes and James Clark toured Australia*

with England U18 in August 2007]
(Jon Fisher scored in the 5th minute after Charlie Sharples made a brilliant break!; England U20 were leading 14-0 in the 15th minute; England U20 were leading 17-0 midway through the first half; England U20 were leading 17-3 in the 27th minute when Mark Odejobi scored after Alex Tait brilliantly chipped ahead into space; England U20 were leading 29-3 in the 34th minute when Ben Youngs scored a superb 70 metre solo try; England U20 were leading 41-3 shortly before half-time when Hugo Ellis scored after Alex Tait instigated a brilliant counter-attack from inside his own 22; England U20 scored 31 unanswered points to clinch the match; England U20 were leading 48-3 at half-time; England U20 were still leading 48-3 in the 52nd minute; England U20 were leading 53-6 midway through the second half; England U20 were still leading 53-6 with 6 minutes of normal time remaining; England U20 were leading 60-11 in the first minute of injury time when Ben Thomas' pass was intercepted by Thyssen de Goede who then went on to score, thus 7 points were preventable; Rob Miller scored 20 points in this match; Ben Youngs had a brilliant game)

14th Jun AUSTRALIA U20 13 **ENGLAND U20** 18
Rodney Parade, Newport
[This match was originally scheduled to start at 3.00pm but the kick-off was brought forward to 2.30pm]
(England U20 played with a swirling wind in the first half; The England U20 forwards dominated the lineout in this match; England U20 were drawing 0-0 in the 14th minute when Miles Benjamin scored after Luke Eves intercepted Quade Cooper's pass; England U20 were leading 8-3 midway through the first half; England U20 were leading 8-6 in the 34th minute when Alex Goode missed a kickable 39 metre penalty goal attempt; England U20 were still leading 8-6 in the second minute of first half injury time; England U20 were leading 11-6 at half-time; The second half of this match was played in wet conditions; England U20 were still leading 11-6 in the 48th minute when Miles Benjamin crossed the tryline, but the move was disallowed because the scoring pass from Joe Simpson was adjudged to have been forward; England U20 were losing 13-11 midway through the second half; England U20 were still losing 13-11 with 9 minutes of normal time remaining when Alex Goode missed a difficult 21 metre penalty goal attempt; England U20 were losing 13-11 with 2 minutes of normal time remaining when Jordan Turner-Hall charged down Dane Haylett-Petty's kick and Miles Benjamin followed up to score a match-winning try)

Semi-Final

18th Jun SOUTH AFRICA U20 18 **ENGLAND U20** 26
Cardiff Arms Park
[This match was originally scheduled to start at 9.10pm but the kick-off was delayed for 15 minutes because the curtain raising 9th/10th/11th/12th Place Play-Off game between Ireland U20 and Italy U20 went into sudden death extra time]
(This match was played in cold conditions; England U20 played into the wind in the first half; Joe Simpson scored a brilliant solo try in the 5th minute!; England U20 were leading 7-3 in the 16th minute; England U20 were leading 10-3 midway through the first half; England U20 were still leading 10-3 in the 22nd minute when Francois Hougaard put up a box kick and Gerrit-Jan van Velze followed up and scored after both Joe Simpson and Miles Benjamin were deceived by the bounce of the ball; England U20 were leading 10-8 in the 24th minute and pressing in attack when Alex Goode had his kick charged down by Francois Brummer which led directly to a try by Cecil Afrika, thus 2 tries and 12 points were preventable; England U20 were losing 15-10 in the 38th minute when Noah Cato intercepted the ball and ran 60 metres to score, with Alex

Goode then missing the eminently kickable conversion attempt; England U20 were drawing 15-15 at half-time; The second half of this match was played in wet conditions; England U20 were leading 18-15 in the 44th minute; England U20 were still leading 18-15 in the 58th minute when Alex Goode missed a speculative 46 metre penalty goal attempt; England U20 were leading 18-15 midway through the second half; Alex Goode scored a brilliant 23 metre penalty goal from a difficult angle to give England U20 a 21-15 lead in the 64th minute; Alex Tait went off injured immediately afterwards, being replaced by Mark Odejobi; England U20 were leading 21-18 with 8 minutes remaining; England U20 were still leading 21-18 with 1 minute remaining when Alex Corbisiero scored from a rolling maul to clinch the match)

CAPTAIN: *Hugo Ellis* [*Nathan Catt*]

Final

22nd Jun NEW ZEALAND U20 38 **ENGLAND U20** 3

Liberty Stadium, Swansea

[*This match kicked off at 7.00pm; Alex Tait unavailable due to injury*]

(*Calum Clark was sent off in the 67th minute for head-butting an opponent and thus duly banned for 5 matches*)

(Some members of the team were exhausted after playing three games against southern hemisphere opponents in 8 days; Trent Renata scored a penalty goal in the 5th minute!; England U20 was losing 3-0 in the 8th minute when Alex Goode missed an eminently kickable 22 metre penalty goal attempt; England U20 were still losing 3-0 in the 11th minute when Alex Goode missed another eminently kickable 22 metre penalty goal attempt; England U20 were losing 3-0 in the 17th minute when a poor defensive alignment allowed Kade Poki to score; England U20 were losing 10-0 midway through the first half; England U20 were losing 10-3 in the 26th minute; England U20 were still losing 10-3 just before half-time; England U20 were losing 13-3 at half-time; England U20 were losing 19-3 in the 50th minute; England U20 were losing 24-3 in the 61st minute when Matt Cox came on as a replacement for Hugo Ellis; New Zealand U20 were still leading 24-3 in the 66th minute when the England U20 forwards set up a close-range rolling maul, but Calum Clark then wasted this great try-scoring opportunity by unaccountably head-butting Nasi Manu twice!; England U20 were losing 24-3 with 4 minutes remaining when Andre Taylor scored after he followed up his own chip ahead and ripped the descending ball out of Noah Cato's grasp; England U20 were losing 31-3 in the last minute when collectively poor tackling allowed Ryan Crotty to score, thus 3 tries and 21 points were preventable; New Zealand U20 were allowed to score 28 unanswered points to clinch the match)

ENGLAND COUNTIES TOUR TO AMERICA AND CANADA 2008

CAPTAIN: *Liam Wordley*

6th June USA SELECT XV 3 **ENGLAND COUNTIES** 27

Baker Field Athletics Complex, Columbia University, New York

[*This match kicked off at 7.00pm; This match was played on a pitch made from artificial grass; Johnny Williams unavailable due to injury; Dan Hyde was rested for this match; The USA Select XV was also billed as USA A*]

(The England Counties players had insufficient time to shake off their jet lag; England Counties made a number of handling errors in this match; England Counties were drawing 0-0 midway through the first half; England Counties were leading 5-0 in the 22nd minute; England Counties were still leading 5-0 in the 37th minute when some superb handling allowed Andrew Fenby to score; England Counties were leading 12-0 at half-time; England Counties were leading 27-0 midway through the second half;

England Counties scored 27 unanswered points to win the match; England Counties were leading 27-3 in the 62nd minute)

CAPTAIN: *Dan Hyde*

9th June USA SELECT XV 16 **ENGLAND COUNTIES** 31

Baker Field Athletics Complex, Columbia University, New York

[This match kicked off at 7.00pm; This match was played on a pitch made from artificial grass; The USA Select XV was also billed as USA A]

(This match was played in 90 degree heat; England Counties were leading 3-0 in the early stages; England Counties were still leading 3-0 in the 14th minute; England Counties were drawing 3-3 midway through the first half; England Counties were still drawing 3-3 shortly before half-time when James Doherty scored after Tom Jarvis made a brilliant run; England Counties were leading 10-9 at half-time; England Counties were still leading 10-9 early in the second half when collectively poor tackling allowed James Gillenwater to score, thus 7 points were preventable; England Counties were losing 16-10 midway through the second half; England Counties were still losing 16-10 in the 64th minute when Steve Pape scored from a rolling maul; England Counties were leading 17-16 shortly afterwards when Richard Wainwright scored a brilliant solo try; England Counties were leading 24-16 in the closing stages when Liam Wordley scored from another rolling maul; England Counties scored 21 unanswered points to win the match)

TEKSAVVY KENT CUP

CAPTAIN: *Liam Wordley*

13th Jun CANADA SELECT XV 6 **ENGLAND COUNTIES** 31

Chatham-Kent Community Athletic Complex, Chatham, South Ontario

[This match was originally scheduled to start at 6.30pm but the kick-off was delayed due to a thunderstorm, which meant that the national anthem had to be sung in the dressing room!; Johnny Williams selected for bench but withdrew due to injury, being replaced by Petrus du Plessis]

(The delayed start meant that the game had to be divided into 2 periods of 30 minutes each; This match was played in heavy rain on a waterlogged pitch; Mark Evans scored a pushover try in the first half; England Counties were losing 6-5 at half-time; England Counties were still losing 6-5 when Ollie Winter scored after Mark Evans broke from the base of a scrum; Ben Coulbeck scored after Gavin Beasley put up a brilliant garryowen; England Counties scored 25 unanswered points in the second half to win the match)

BARCLAYS CHURCHILL CUP

USA & Canada

CAPTAIN: *Will Skinner* [*Jordan Crane*]

First Round - Pool 'B'

7th June USA 10 **ENGLAND SAXONS** 64 **BP**

Twin Elm Rugby Park, Nepean, Ottawa

[This match kicked off at 2.05pm; Nick Lloyd returned home injured after this match; Tom French (2) joined the squad after this match]

(This match was played in 93 degree heat and a swirling wind on a pitch with very long grass; Ryan Lamb scored a penalty goal in the 3rd minute!; Nick Lloyd had to go off in the 7th minute after injuring the medial ligament in his knee, being replaced by Jack Forster; The England Saxons were leading 3-0 in the 16th minute when Matt Banahan

powered through 3 attempted tackles to score; The England Saxons were leading 10-0 midway through the first half; The England Saxons were still leading 10-0 in the 32nd minute when Ollie Smith (2)'s pass was intercepted by Gavin DeBartolo who then ran 50 metres to score, thus 7 points were preventable; The England Saxons were leading 10-7 in the 39th minute when Matt Banahan scored after Ryan Lamb put up a brilliant cross-kick; The England Saxons were leading 17-7 just before half-time when some superb handling allowed George Skivington to score; The England Saxons were leading 24-7 at half-time; The England Saxons were leading 24-10 in the 45th minute when Anthony Allen scored after George Skivington made a brilliant break; The England Saxons were leading 31-10 in the 51st minute when Matt Banahan scored to complete a hat-trick of tries; Chris Robshaw came on as a replacement for Richard Blaze in the 53rd minute, with Chris Jones then switching from flanker to lock to accommodate Robshaw; The England Saxons were leading 38-10 in the 54th minute when Ben Foden scored after Paul Hodgson made a brilliant break; Steffon Armitage came on as a replacement for Will Skinner in the 58th minute; The England Saxons were leading 45-10 midway through the second half; The England Saxons were still leading 45-10 in the 70th minute when the referee awarded a penalty try after the American forwards collapsed a scrum as they were being driven backwards over their own line; The England Saxons were leading 52-10 with 7 minutes of normal time remaining when Tom Biggs dribbled a loose ball on twice and then followed up to score; The England Saxons were leading 57-10 with 2 minutes of normal time remaining when Ugo Monye scored a superb 77 metre solo try; The England Saxons scored 40 unanswered points to seal the match; Jordan Crane had a brilliant game)

CAPTAIN: *George Chuter* [*Jordan Crane*]

14th Jun	IRELAND A	12	**ENGLAND SAXONS**	34 **BP**

Fletcher's Fields, Markham, Toronto

[This match kicked off at 2.05pm; David Wilson (2) left the squad on 15th June 2008 as he was now required to join the simultaneous England tour of New Zealand; Tom Mercey joined the tour after this match; Richard Blaze retired due to injury in October 2010]

(This match was played in hot and humid conditions; The England Saxons were drawing 0-0 in the 10th minute when the referee unaccountably allowed play to continue after both Mike Ross and Bob Casey failed to retreat 10 metres from their offside position in front of Johnny Sexton's kick ahead and Keith Earls went on to score, thus 5 points were unlawful; The England Saxons were leading 7-5 midway through the first half; The England Saxons were still leading 7-5 in the 27th minute when Ryan Lamb missed a speculative 49 metre penalty goal attempt; The England Saxons were leading 7-5 in the 33rd minute when Matt Banahan scored after Nick Abendanon made a brilliant break; Tom Guest went off injured in the second minute of first half injury time, being replaced by Chris Robshaw with Jordan Crane then switching from flanker to number 8 to accommodate Robshaw; The England Saxons were drawing 12-12 just before half-time; The England Saxons were leading 17-12 at half-time; The England Saxons were leading 22-12 in the 46th minute; The England Saxons were still leading 22-12 midway through the second half; The England Saxons were leading 22-12 in the 62nd minute when they were awarded a penalty and Anthony Allen was able to follow up and score after Carl Fogarty deflected Ryan Lamb's subsequent kick for touch back into the field of play!; Andy Titterrell came on as a replacement for George Chuter with 4 minutes of normal time remaining; The England Saxons were leading 27-12 in the seventh minute of injury time when Nick Abendanon

kicked ahead, Keith Earls tapped the descending ball backwards to Frank Murphy who inexplicably responded by fly-hacking it straight towards Earls' head, which allowed Abendanon to follow up and score from the ensuing rebound!; The England Saxons scored 22 unanswered points to win the match; Nick Abendanon had a brilliant game)

CAPTAIN: *Will Skinner*

Final

21st Jun SCOTLAND A 19 **ENGLAND SAXONS** 36

Toyota Park, Bridgeview, Chicago

[This match kicked off at 2.05pm; Tom Guest unavailable due to injury]

(This match was played in extremely hot conditions; Ryan Lamb had a 22 metre drop goal attempt charged down in the 2nd minute!; The England Saxons were losing 3-0 in the 10th minute; The England Saxons were drawing 6-6 midway through the first half; The England Saxons were still drawing 6-6 in the 25th minute when Matt Banahan scored a brilliant 25 metre diagonal try; The England Saxons were leading 13-9 in the 33rd minute; The England Saxons were still leading 13-9 in the first minute of first half injury time when Ryan Lamb scored a brilliant 47 metre penalty goal; The England Saxons were leading 16-9 at half-time; The England Saxons were still leading 16-9 in the 44th minute when collectively poor tackling allowed Colin Gregor to score, thus 7 points were preventable; The England Saxons were losing 19-16 in the 48th minute; The England Saxons were drawing 19-19 in the 57th minute when Nick Abendanon scored after Ryan Lamb threw a superb long pass; The England Saxons were leading 26-19 midway through the second half; The England Saxons were still leading 26-19 with 5 minutes of normal time remaining when Jordan Crane scored a brilliant 45 metre solo try; The England Saxons were leading 31-19 in the last minute of normal time when Ugo Monye scored after Ryan Lamb put up a superb cross-kick; The England Saxons scored 17 unanswered points to win the match)

ENGLAND TOUR TO NEW ZEALAND 2008

CAPTAIN: *Steve Borthwick*

14th June NEW ZEALAND 37 **ENGLAND*** 20

Eden Park, Auckland

[This match kicked off at 7.35pm; In January 2008 the England Elite Player Squad (EPS) had been issued with a Code of Conduct which stated that a high standard of behaviour was expected during off the field activities, but despite this Mike Brown and Topsy Ojo stayed out all night after the match and on 10th July 2008 a RFU Disciplinary Inquiry found them both guilty of misconduct and duly fined them £1000 and £500 respectively; Andy Sheridan left the tour injured after this match; David Wilson (2) joined the tour after this match]

(Olly Barkley missed an eminently kickable 26 metre penalty goal attempt in the 2nd minute!; England were leading 3-0 in the 11th minute; England were drawing 3-3 in the 18th minute when Dave Strettle had a great try-scoring chance but was brilliantly tackled into touch at the corner flag by Jerome Kaino; England were leading 6-3 midway through the first half; England were losing 20-6 in the 29th minute; New Zealand were allowed to score 20 unanswered points to win the match; England were losing 23-6 in the 37th minute when Olly Barkley missed a difficult 36 metre penalty goal attempt; England were still losing 23-6 shortly before half-time when Topsy Ojo intercepted Dan Carter's intended scoring pass and ran 85 metres to score a try which Olly Barkley then brilliantly converted from the right touchline; England were losing 23-13 at half-time; New Zealand were still leading 23-13 in the 43rd minute when a poor

***tackle by Charlie Hodgson allowed Ma'a Nonu to break through to the England 22 where he then threw a clear forward pass to Mils Muliaina, who went on to score after the referee unaccountably allowed play to continue, thus 7 points were unlawful; England were losing 30-13 in the 47th minute when Steve Borthwick dropped a poor pass from Luke Narraway which allowed Andy Ellis to instigate a move that culminated in a try by Sitiveni Sivivatu, thus 7 points were preventable; Jamie Noon came on as a replacement for Charlie Hodgson in the 50th minute, with Olly Barkley then switching from centre to fly half to accommodate Noon; England were losing 37-13 midway through the second half; Andy Sheridan went off injured in the 63rd minute, being replaced by Tim Payne; England were still losing 37-13 with 7 minutes remaining when Topsy Ojo scored another try after Danny Care put in a brilliant kick ahead; Topsy Ojo scored 2 tries on his cap international debut*)**

21st June NEW ZEALAND 44 **ENGLAND** 12
AMI Stadium, Christchurch

[*This match kicked off at 7.35pm; The AMI Stadium was previously called the Jade Stadium; Dave Strettle selected for bench but withdrew on the day of the match due to injury, being replaced by Tom Croft; Peter Richards retired due to injury in May 2010*]

(*This match was played in cold conditions; Dan Carter scored a penalty goal in the 3rd minute!; England were losing 3-0 in the 12th minute when Richard Kahui scored after Jamie Noon missed a tackle on Dan Carter; England were losing 10-0 midway through the first half when Toby Flood saved a certain try by tackling Richard Kahui; England were losing 13-0 in the 25th minute when Tom Varndell had a great try-scoring chance but was brilliantly tackled into touch at the corner flag by Leon MacDonald; England were still losing 13-0 in the 28th minute when Matt Tait saved a certain try by managing to get beneath the ball as Dan Carter attempted to ground it; Toby Flood went off injured in the 29th minute, being replaced by Olly Barkley; England were losing 20-0 in the 34th minute when Matt Tait made a superb run, chipped ahead and then wasted this great try-scoring opportunity by knocking the ball on over the New Zealand line as he attempted to regather it!; England were losing 20-0 at half-time; England were still losing 20-0 in the 42nd minute when Olly Barkley missed a 23 metre penalty goal attempt from in front of the posts; England were losing 23-0 in the 49th minute when Danny Care took a quick tap penalty and scored; England were losing 23-7 in the 52nd minute when the referee unaccountably allowed play to continue after Dan Carter threw a clear forward pass to Sitiveni Sivivatu and Ma'a Nonu went on to score, thus 7 points were unlawful; England were losing 30-7 midway through the second half; England were losing 37-7 in the 67th minute when some superb handling amongst the backs allowed Tom Varndell to score; Matt Tait went off injured with 7 minutes of normal time remaining, being replaced by Peter Richards who had to play out of position as a full back; England were losing 37-12 and defending their own line when the full-time hooter sounded, but the ball remained in play for over a minute until Jimmy Cowan powered through some collectively poor tackling to score after Steve Borthwick inexplicably ordered a tap penalty move instead of a kick to touch, thus 2 tries and 14 points were preventable!; Olly Barkley injured playing in the match*)

BACK TO BALLYMORE MATCH

CAPTAIN: *Ben Gollings*

13th July Queensland XV (*AU*) 61 **AUSTRALIAN BARBARIANS** 17
Ballymore Stadium, Brisbane

**[*This match kicked off at 3.30pm; Australian Barbarians founded 1956; Nathan Williams was included in an original 8 man bench selection; Justin Marshall in original*

squad but withdrew due to injury, being replaced by Sam Cordingley; Chris Latham was a water boy in this match!]
(The Australian Barbarians used an overhead kick at a tap penalty in the first half!; The Australian Barbarians were losing 21-17 at half-time; Toutai Kefu saved a certain try by tackling Digby Ioane; Aidan Toua broke through for the Queensland XV but then dropped the ball 15 metres short of the tryline while he was 20 metres clear of the nearest Australian Barbarians player!; The Australian Barbarians were losing 33-17 in the 52nd minute; The Australian Barbarians were losing 40-17 in the 70th minute; The Australian Barbarians were losing 59-17 in the closing stages when David Croft scored a conversion for the Queensland XV despite being squirted with water by Chris Latham!; The Queensland XV was allowed to score 40 unanswered points in the second half to clinch the match; Sitaleki Timani and Toutai Kefu both had a brilliant game)

WORLD UNIVERSITY RUGBY SEVENS CHAMPIONSHIP

Estadio Universitario Monte Cronos, Campus de Rabanales, Córdoba

CAPTAIN: *??*

First Round - Pool 'B'

17th July	ROMANIA STUDENTS	12	**GREAT BRITAIN STUDENTS**	19

[This match kicked off at 10.40am]

17th July	Portuguese Universities (*POR*)	0	**GREAT BRITAIN STUDENTS**	17

[This match kicked off at 12.20pm]

17th July	CHINESE TAIPEI STUDENTS	0	**GREAT BRITAIN STUDENTS**	36

[This match kicked off at 7.50pm]

18th July	Spanish Universities (*SP*)	12	**GREAT BRITAIN STUDENTS**	5

[This match kicked off at 10.20am]

18th July	Canadian Universities (*CAN*)	0	**GREAT BRITAIN STUDENTS**	5

[This match kicked off at 12.20pm]
(Great Britain Students were drawing 0-0 midway through the first half; Great Britain Students were drawing 0-0 at half-time; Great Britain Students were still drawing 0-0 midway through the second half; Great Britain Students were drawing 0-0 in the last minute)

Quarter-Final

19th July	RUSSIA STUDENTS	12	**GREAT BRITAIN STUDENTS**	0

[This match kicked off at 10.00am]
[Plate Semi-Final:]

[19th July	CHINESE TAIPEI STUDENTS	14	**GREAT BRITAIN STUDENTS**	21]

[This match kicked off at 11.20am]
[Plate Final:]

[19th July	ROMANIA STUDENTS	10	**GREAT BRITAIN STUDENTS**	14]

[This match kicked off at 6.30pm]
(This competition was played in temperatures as high as 107 degrees!; Great Britain Students were losing 5-0 in the early stages)

TONGA CORONATION MATCH

CAPTAIN: *Colin Charvis* (WA)

31st July	TONGA XV	60	**CORONATION WORLD XV**	26

Teufaiva Stadium, Nuku'alofa
[This match was originally scheduled to start at 3.00pm but the kick-off was delayed

***for 15 minutes to allow time for the king of Tonga to arrive at the stadium!*]**
(*The Coronation World XV only had one training session to prepare for this match; The Coronation World XV was losing 33-14 at half-time; The second half of this match was played in wet conditions; Ratu Nasiganiyavi scored a brilliant solo try in this match*)

CWMTAWE SEVENS

Pontardawe RFC, Parc Ynysderw, Ynysderw Road, Pontardawe, Swansea
CAPTAIN: *Rob Thirlby*
First Round - Pool 'E'

2nd Aug CSG Old Boys (*WA*) 0 **SAMURAI** 28
[No match notes]
2nd Aug Old Breconians (*WA*) 12 **SAMURAI** 35
[No match notes]
Quarter-Final
2nd Aug Covenant Brothers (*FIJ*) 5 **SAMURAI** 24
[No match notes]
Semi-Final
2nd Aug KooGa Wailers 28 **SAMURAI** 7
[*The Wailers were founded in 2005 as an invitational side*]
(*The Samurai were drawing 0-0 midway through the first half; The KooGa Wailers were allowed to score 21 unanswered points to win the match; The Samurai were losing 21-0 at half-time; The Samurai were losing 21-7 at one point in the second half*)

HELP FOR HEROES RUGBY CHALLENGE MATCH

CAPTAIN: *Lawrence Dallaglio* [Help for Heroes XV]
CAPTAIN: *Scott Gibbs* (WA) [*Gareth Llewellyn* (WA)] [International Select XV]
20th Sep **HELP FOR HEROES XV** 29 **INTERNATIONAL SELECT XV** 10
Twickenham
**[HELP FOR HEROES XV: [*This match was originally scheduled to start at 2.30pm but the kick-off was delayed for 15 minutes; Noah Cato selected but withdrew to sit on the bench, Mark Odejobi was moved from the bench to the team; Noah Cato then withdrew from the bench due to injury, being replaced by Dom Shabbo; The Help for Heroes XV named a 9 man bench selection; Richard Hill (2), Lawrence Dallaglio, Will Greenwood, Jason Robinson and Martin Johnson all came out of retirement for this match; Martin Offiah came out of retirement to play in this match at the age of 41!; Will Greenwood played at inside centre despite wearing the number 13 on his shirt!; Martin Offiah played for the Penguins at the Hong Kong Sevens on 28th-29th March 1987, toured France with the Combined England Students in April 1987, scored 4 tries for the Barbarians on their Easter Tour of Wales in April 1987, played in the Rosslyn Park II team that reached the Final of the Middlesex Sevens at Twickenham on 9th May 1987 and then turned professional on 25th June 1987; Martin Offiah was capped 33 times for Great Britain at Rugby League between 1988-94, played for Great Britain in the Rugby League World Cup Final at Wembley on 24th October 1992 and played for England in the Rugby League World Cup Final at Wembley on 28th October 1995; Martin Offiah initially returned to Rugby Union on 5th August 1996 when he joined Bedford, went back to being a full-time Rugby League player on 15th August 1997 and then came back for a final stint in Rugby Union in October 2001 when he joined Wasps, where he remained until he retired in May 2002; Dan Luger briefly became a Bobsleigh competitor in November 2008!; Will Greenwood again came out of*

retirement to play for a H4H Northern Hemisphere XV against a Southern Hemisphere XV at Twickenham on 3rd December 2011]
(*This match was played in 80 degree heat; Both sides agreed to allow unlimited substitutions in this match; The Help for Heroes XV was drawing 0-0 in the 8th minute when Kristian Phillips scored after Mark Regan bought a dummy by Scott Gibbs, thus 5 points were preventable; The Help for Heroes XV was losing 5-0 midway through the first half; The Help for Heroes XV was still losing 5-0 in the 23rd minute when Joe Simpson had a great try-scoring chance but was brilliantly tackled by Joe Kava just short of the International Select XV line; The Help for Heroes XV was losing 5-3 in the 31st minute; The Help for Heroes XV was still losing 5-3 in the 36th minute when Richard Hill (2) powered through 2 attempted tackles to score; Paul Volley came on as a replacement for Richard Hill (2) in the 38th minute; The Help for Heroes XV was leading 10-5 shortly before half-time; The Help for Heroes XV was leading 15-5 at half-time; The Help for Heroes XV was leading 15-10 in the 48th minute when Martin Johnson and Martin Offiah came on as replacements for Scott Hobson and Mark Odejobi respectively; The Help for Heroes XV was still leading 15-10 midway through the second half; The Help for Heroes XV was leading 15-10 in the 65th minute when Will Greenwood dummied his way through to score a brilliant try; The Help for Heroes XV was leading 22-10 with 8 minutes remaining when Harry Barratt kicked ahead but the ball went over the dead ball line before Martin Offiah could touch it down; The Help for Heroes XV was still leading 22-10 in the final minute when Joe Simpson dummied his way through to score a try under the posts in the last move of the match, with Lawrence Dallaglio then using a drop kick to score the conversion!; Will Greenwood had a brilliant game*)]
[INTERNATIONAL SELECT XV: [*This match was originally scheduled to start at 2.30pm but the kick-off was delayed for 15 minutes; Marsh Cormack selected but withdrew to sit on the bench, Howard Parr was moved from the bench to the team; Jonah Lomu selected but withdrew to sit on the bench, Kenny Logan was moved from the bench to the team; Jonah Lomu then withdrew from the bench due to injury, being replaced by Michael Stephenson; The International Select XV named a 9 man bench selection; Guy Easterby, Kenny Logan and Scott Gibbs came out of retirement to play in this match*]
(*This match was played in 80 degree heat; Both sides agreed to allow unlimited substitutions in this match; Rhys Priestland missed a kickable 45 metre penalty goal attempt in the 4th minute!; The International Select XV was drawing 0-0 in the 8th minute when Kristian Phillips scored after Scott Gibbs brilliantly dummied his way through; The International Select XV was leading 5-0 midway through the first half; The International Select XV was still leading 5-0 in the 23rd minute when Joe Kava saved a certain try by tackling Joe Simpson; Kristian Phillips went off injured in the 29th minute, being replaced by Michael Stephenson; The International Select XV was leading 5-3 in the 31st minute; The International Select XV was losing 10-5 just before half-time; The International Select XV was losing 15-5 at half-time; Shane Byrne came on as a replacement for Gordon Bulloch in the 42nd minute; The International Select XV was losing 15-10 in the 45th minute when Rhys Priestland hit the left hand post with a difficult conversion attempt; The International Select XV was still losing 15-10 in the 55th minute when it created and then squandered a 2 man overlap; The International Select XV was losing 15-10 midway through the second half; The International Select XV was still losing 15-10 in the 65th minute when Kenny Logan bought a dummy by Will Greenwood who then went on to score, thus 7 points were preventable; The International Select XV was losing 22-10 in the last minute*)]

ATKINS REMEMBRANCE RUGBY MATCH

CAPTAIN: *Danny Thomas*

4th Nov COMBINED SERVICES (*SER*) 14 **BARBARIANS** 33

Plymouth Albion RFC, Brickfields Recreation Ground, Madden Road, Plymouth

[This match kicked off at 7.15pm; John Yapp selected but withdrew due to injury, being replaced by Ryan Hopkins; Rhodri Gomer-Davies selected but withdrew, being replaced by Tal Selley; Rhys Williams selected for bench but withdrew due to injury, being replaced by Wihan Neethling; Mat Hocken was capped for Belgium in August 2006; Will Runciman was the brother of Nick Runciman; Rhys Jones was the son of Kingsley Jones; Mark Davies was the brother of Brad Davies; Chris Budgen, Ben Hughes, Marsh Cormack, Mark Lee, Joe Kava, Dave Pascoe, Matt Rhodes, Josh Drauniniu, Apolosi Satala, Mal Roberts, Robin Scothern and Gareth Leonard all played for the Combined Services in this match, with Dave Pascoe captaining the side and scoring 2 conversions and Rhodes and Drauniniu scoring a try apiece; Tony Windo retired after this match]

(This match was played in cold conditions; Vasco Uva scored in the 4th minute!; The Barbarians were drawing 7-7 in the 10th minute when Rhodri McAtee scored a brilliant 50 metre solo try; The Barbarians were leading 14-7 midway through the first half; The Barbarians were still leading 14-7 in the 22nd minute when Josh Drauniniu scored after a poor tackle by Dougie Flockhart, thus 7 points were preventable; Rhys Jones went off injured in the 37th minute, being replaced by Mark Davies; The Barbarians were drawing 14-14 at half-time; Wihan Neethling came on as a replacement for Rhodri McAtee at the start of the second half, with Dougie Flockhart then moving from full back to right wing to accommodate Neethling; The Barbarians were still drawing 14-14 in the 50th minute when they created and then squandered a 2 man overlap; The Barbarians were drawing 14-14 midway through the second half when Dougie Flockhart scored after Mark Davies put in a brilliant chip-kick; The Barbarians were leading 26-7 with 5 minutes of normal time remaining when Mark Davies scored a superb conversion from the right touchline; The Barbarians were leading 28-14 in the fifth minute of injury time when Dougie Flockhart gathered a loose ball and scored in the last move of the match; The Barbarians scored 19 unanswered points in the second half to win the match)

PACIFIC ISLANDERS TOUR TO ENGLAND, FRANCE AND ITALY 2008

CAPTAIN: *Steve Borthwick*

8th Nov **ENGLAND** 39 PACIFIC ISLANDERS 13

Twickenham

[This match kicked off at 2.30pm; Dave Strettle unavailable due to injury; Lewis Moody, Luke Narraway, Jonny Wilkinson, James Simpson-Daniel and Matt Tait all in original training squad of 32 but then withdrew due to injury, being replaced by Michael Lipman, Nick Easter, Danny Cipriani, Ugo Monye and Delon Armitage respectively; Tom Varndell in original training squad of 32 but was released on 21st October 2008 as he was not match fit, being replaced by Nick Abendanon who then himself withdrew due to injury on 29th October 2008; David Paice was added to the squad on 3rd November 2008 to provide injury cover for George Chuter; Tim Payne, George Chuter, Simon Shaw, Jordan Crane, Peter Richards, Olly Barkley, Shane Geraghty, Dan Hipkiss and Josh Lewsey all in original training squad of 32 but were not selected for team or bench; Riki Flutey played for New Zealand in the U19 World

***Championship in Wales in March-April 1999, played for New Zealand U21 in June 2000, played for the New Zealand Maori in June 2002 and then qualified for England in September 2008 after completing a residency period of 3 years; England wore red shirts with a white right sleeve for this match; The Pacific Islands Rugby Alliance (PIRA) was a joint organisation incorporating Fiji, Tonga, Samoa, the Cook Islands and Niue*]**

(*England were leading 3-0 in the 10th minute; A brilliant inside pass by Delon Armitage allowed Paul Sackey to score a try which Danny Cipriani then converted to give England a 10-0 lead in the 14th minute; Immediately afterwards Danny Cipriani took too much time over his clearance kick and was charged down by Seru Rabeni, who went on to score from the ensuing rebound, thus 7 points were preventable; England were leading 10-7 midway through the first half; England were still leading 10-7 in the 27th minute when Danny Care wasted a great try-scoring opportunity by knocking-on while the Pacific Islanders line was at his mercy; England were leading 13-7 in the 37th minute when Danny Cipriani scored after Ugo Monye made a brilliant 55 metre break; England were leading 20-7 just before half-time; England were leading 20-10 at half-time; The second half of this match was played in wet conditions; The England forwards dominated the lineout in the second half; James Haskell came on as a temporary blood replacement for Tom Croft at the start of the second half; England were still leading 20-10 in the 44th minute when Nick Kennedy scored after Danny Care made a superb break through the tail of a lineout; England were leading 27-10 in the 56th minute; England were leading 27-13 midway through the second half; England were leading 34-13 in the 68th minute; England were still leading 34-13 with 5 minutes remaining when Paul Sackey scored another try in the right corner despite an illegal high tackle by Semisi Naevo; Dylan Hartley came on as a replacement for Lee Mears with 4 minutes remaining; Delon Armitage had a brilliant game*)

AUSTRALIAN TOUR TO ITALY, ENGLAND, FRANCE AND WALES 2008

CAPTAIN: *Steve Borthwick*

15th Nov	**ENGLAND***	14	AUSTRALIA	28
Twickenham				

[*This match kicked off at 2.30pm; Lewis Moody, Luke Narraway, Jonny Wilkinson, Dave Strettle, James Simpson-Daniel and Nick Abendanon all unavailable due to injury; Tim Payne, George Chuter, David Paice, Nick Kennedy, Jordan Crane, Peter Richards, Olly Barkley, Shane Geraghty, Dan Hipkiss, Josh Lewsey and Matt Tait all in original training squad of 33 but were not selected for team or bench*]

(*The England scrum was put under severe pressure; Lee Mears' throwing-in was poor and the England lineout suffered accordingly; Matt Giteau scored a penalty goal in the 3rd minute!; England were losing 6-0 in the 7th minute; England were still losing 6-0 in the 15th minute when Danny Cipriani missed a kickable 43 metre penalty goal attempt; England were losing 6-0 midway through the first half; England were still losing 6-0 in the 22nd minute when Delon Armitage scored a brilliant 38 metre drop goal; England were losing 9-3 in the 28th minute; Matt Stevens came on as a temporary blood replacement for Andy Sheridan in the 34th minute; England were losing 12-3 in the 35th minute when Nick Easter scored from a rolling maul, with Danny Cipriani then missing the eminently kickable conversion attempt; England were losing 12-11 at half-time; England were still losing 12-11 in the 49th minute when Danny Cipriani badly missed an eminently kickable 14 metre drop goal attempt; England were leading 14-12*

in the 52nd minute; Matt Stevens came on as a replacement for Phil Vickery in the 55th minute; England were losing 18-14 midway through the second half; Andy Sheridan went off injured in the 67th minute, being replaced by Phil Vickery; England were losing 28-14 in the 69th minute; Australia were allowed to score 16 unanswered points to win the match; England were still losing 28-14 with 2 minutes remaining when Phil Vickery wasted a great try-scoring opportunity by cutting back inside when there was an overlap outside him; England conceded too many needless penalties within Matt Giteau's kicking range)

SOUTH AFRICAN TOUR TO WALES, SCOTLAND AND ENGLAND 2008

CAPTAIN: *Steve Borthwick*

22nd Nov **ENGLAND** 6 SOUTH AFRICA 42

Twickenham

[This match kicked off at 2.30pm; Lewis Moody, Luke Narraway, Jonny Wilkinson, Dave Strettle, James Simpson-Daniel and Nick Abendanon all unavailable due to injury; Andy Sheridan selected but withdrew due to injury, being replaced by Tim Payne; George Chuter, David Paice, Nick Kennedy, Michael Lipman, Peter Richards, Olly Barkley, Shane Geraghty, Dan Hipkiss, Josh Lewsey and Matt Tait all in original training squad of 33 but were not selected for team or bench]

(This match was played in cold conditions; Danny Cipriani started the match with a grubber kick!; Danny Cipriani scored a penalty goal in the 2nd minute!; England were drawing 3-3 in the 10th minute when Danny Cipriani missed a speculative 50 metre penalty goal attempt; England were still drawing 3-3 in the 15th minute when collectively poor tackling allowed Danie Rossouw to score; England were losing 10-3 in the 19th minute when Danny Cipriani took too much time over his clearance kick and was charged down by Ruan Pienaar, who went on to score from the ensuing rebound; England were losing 17-3 midway through the first half when Delon Armitage broke through but then carried the ball under the wrong arm which allowed Bakkies Botha to tackle him into touch at the corner flag; England were losing 20-3 in the 25th minute; England were losing 20-6 in the 28th minute; Riki Flutey went off injured in the 30th minute, being replaced by Toby Flood; Tom Palmer (2) went off injured in the 32nd minute, being replaced by Simon Shaw; England were losing 20-6 at half-time; England were losing 27-6 in the 51st minute; England were still losing 27-6 in the 58th minute when Danny Cipriani wasted a great try-scoring opportunity by throwing a poor pass to the unmarked Toby Flood; England were losing 27-6 midway through the second half; England were losing 30-6 in the 63rd minute; Jordan Crane came on as a replacement for Nick Easter in the 69th minute; England were still losing 30-6 with 3 minutes of normal time remaining when Jaque Fourie scored after a poor tackle by Delon Armitage; England were losing 37-6 in the first minute of injury time when the front row inexplicably delayed their engagement at a scrum and the referee awarded a free kick to South Africa which led directly to a try by Bryan Habana in the last move of the match, thus 4 tries and 26 points were preventable; South Africa were allowed to score 22 unanswered points to seal the game; England were booed off the pitch at the end of the match!; Steve Borthwick's leadership was conspicuous by its absence in this match; Danny Cipriani had a poor game; England lost by 36 points to record their worst ever margin of defeat in a cap international match at Twickenham)

EMIRATES AIRLINE DUBAI RUGBY SEVENS

The Sevens, Dubai

CAPTAIN: *Ollie Phillips*

First Round - Pool 'D'

28th Nov PORTUGAL 7 **ENGLAND** 31

[This match kicked off at 12.04pm; Ben Gollings unavailable due to injury]

(Josh Drauniniu scored after just 29 seconds had been played!; England were leading 14-0 in the 3rd minute; England were still leading 14-0 midway through the first half; England were leading 21-0 in the 6th minute; England scored 21 unanswered points to win the match; England were still leading 21-0 just before half-time; England were leading 21-7 at half-time; England were still leading 21-7 in the 8th minute when Uche Oduoza scored after Rob Vickerman threw a brilliant pass out of the tackle, with Ollie Phillips then missing the eminently kickable conversion attempt; England were leading 26-7 midway through the second half; England were still leading 26-7 in the last minute when Greg Barden scored to seal the match)

28th Nov USA 10 **ENGLAND** 24

[This match kicked off at 5.00pm; Ben Gollings unavailable due to injury]

(Ollie Phillips scored after just 59 seconds had been played!; England were leading 7-5 in the 3rd minute; England were still leading 7-5 midway through the first half; England were leading 7-5 just before half-time; England were leading 12-5 at half-time; England were leading 12-10 in the 8th minute; England were still leading 12-10 midway through the second half; England were leading 12-10 with 2 minutes remaining; England were leading 19-10 in the final minute when Isoa Damu scored a brilliant 92 metre solo try to seal the match)

28th Nov FIJI 5 **ENGLAND** 28

[This match kicked off at 7.56pm; Ben Gollings unavailable due to injury]

(England were drawing 0-0 in the 3rd minute when Isoa Damu scored after Kevin Barrett threw a brilliant pass; England were leading 7-0 midway through the first half; England were still leading 7-0 in the 5th minute when both Josh Drauniniu and Uche Oduoza claimed the try that was later officially credited to Uche Oduoza!; England were leading 14-0 at half-time; England were leading 21-0 in the 9th minute; England scored 21 unanswered points to win the match; England were still leading 21-0 midway through the second half; England were leading 21-5 with 2 minutes remaining when Lepani Nabuliwaqa hit the crossbar with a conversion attempt for Fiji from in front of the posts!; England were still leading 21-5 in the final minute when Isoa Damu kicked ahead and followed up to score a brilliant try to seal the match)

Quarter-Final

29th Nov ARGENTINA 5 **ENGLAND** 15

[This match kicked off at 11.30am; Ben Gollings unavailable due to injury]

(This match was played in a sandstorm!; A brilliant break by Rob Vickerman enabled Josh Drauniniu to score after just 60 seconds had been played, with Ollie Phillips then missing the eminently kickable conversion attempt!; England were leading 5-0 midway through the first half; England were still leading 5-0 just before half-time; England were leading 10-0 at half-time; England were still leading 10-0 in the 10th minute when Tom Biggs scored after Ollie Phillips put in a brilliant kick ahead; England scored 15 unanswered points to win the match; England were leading 15-0 midway through the second half; England were still leading 15-0 in the last minute)

Semi-Final

29th Nov NEW ZEALAND 19 **ENGLAND** 21

[This match kicked off at 6.20pm; Ben Gollings unavailable due to injury]

(England monopolised possession in the first half; England were drawing 0-0 midway through the first half when Rob Vickerman scored after Josh Drauniniu threw a brilliant reverse pass; Uche Oduoza went off injured immediately afterwards, being replaced by Tom Biggs; England were leading 7-0 in the 6th minute when Ollie Phillips scored after he wrong-footed Solomon King with a brilliant sidestep; England were leading 14-0 just before half-time when Josh Drauniniu powered through Nafi Tuitavake's attempted tackle to score a superb try; England scored 21 unanswered points to win the match; England were leading 21-0 at half-time; England were leading 21-7 in the 10th minute when Nafi Tuitavake scored after a poor tackle by Tom Biggs; England were leading 21-12 midway through the second half; England were still leading 21-12 in the last minute when collectively poor tackling allowed Solomon King to score, thus 2 tries and 12 points were preventable)

Final

29th Nov SOUTH AFRICA 19 **ENGLAND*** 12

[This match kicked off at 8.34pm; Ben Gollings unavailable due to injury]

(Uche Oduoza played with a knee injury; England were drawing 0-0 in the 4th minute when Robert Ebersohn scored after a poor tackle by Josh Drauniniu; England were losing 7-0 midway through the first half; England were losing 12-0 in the 10th minute when Ollie Phillips had to go off after he dislocated his elbow, being replaced by Micky Young; Uche Oduoza aggravated his knee injury and had to go off in first half injury time, being replaced by Tom Biggs; England were losing 12-0 at half-time; England were still losing 12-0 in the 12th minute when Tom Biggs dummied his way through to score a brilliant try; England were drawing 12-12 midway through the second half; England were still drawing 12-12 in the last minute and pressing in attack when they allowed the ball to go loose at a ruck situation and Ryno Benjamin went on to score to win the match for South Africa, thus 2 tries and 14 points were preventable; Josh Drauniniu injured playing in the match)

NEW ZEALAND TOUR TO SCOTLAND, IRELAND WALES AND ENGLAND 2008

CAPTAIN: *Steve Borthwick*

29th Nov **ENGLAND** 6 NEW ZEALAND 32

Twickenham

[This match kicked off at 2.30pm; Lewis Moody, Luke Narraway, Jonny Wilkinson, Dave Strettle, James Simpson-Daniel and Nick Abendanon all unavailable due to injury; Andy Sheridan and Tom Palmer (2) in original training squad of 33 but withdrew due to injury; George Chuter, David Paice, Simon Shaw, Jordan Crane, Peter Richards, Olly Barkley, Shane Geraghty, Josh Lewsey and Matt Tait all in original training squad of 33 but were not selected for team or bench; Ben Kay was added to the squad on 24th November 2008 to provide injury cover for Tom Palmer (2); Nick Wood was added to the squad on 25th November 2008 to provide injury cover for Andy Sheridan; Michael Lipman failed to take drugs tests on both 13th May and 14th May 2009 and a subsequent RFU Disciplinary Panel on 3rd August 2009 found Lipman guilty of 'conduct prejudicial to the interests of the game' and thus banned him for 9 months, with the ban running from 1st June 2009 until 28th February 2010]

(This match was played in cold conditions; The England backs kicked away too much

possession; England were drawing 0-0 in the 6th minute when Toby Flood missed a kickable 42 metre penalty goal attempt; England were still drawing 0-0 in the 10th minute when Riki Flutey wasted a great try-scoring opportunity by electing to cut back inside when there was a 2 man overlap outside him; England were drawing 3-3 midway through the first half; England were losing 6-3 in the 29th minute when Toby Flood badly missed a speculative 40 metre drop goal attempt; Michael Lipman took a lineout throw in the 30th minute while Lee Mears was in the sin-bin!; England were briefly reduced to 13 men in the 32nd minute when James Haskell joined Lee Mears in the sin-bin; England were losing 9-3 shortly before half-time; England were losing 12-3 at half-time; England were still losing 12-3 at the start of the second half when Nick Easter had a great try-scoring chance but was brilliantly tap-tackled by Mils Muliaina; Riki Flutey playing as a fly half in the absence of Toby Flood, who was also sent to the sin-bin in the 43rd minute; England were losing 12-3 in the 49th minute when Delon Armitage scored a brilliant 35 metre penalty goal from the left touchline; New Zealand were leading 12-6 in the 58th minute when Mils Muliaina scored after the England forwards were unaccountably driven off their own ball at a scrum, thus 5 points were preventable; England were losing 17-6 midway through the second half; England were losing 25-6 in the 69th minute when Tom Croft saved a certain try by getting back and grounding the ball before Mils Muliaina could reach it; England were still losing 25-6 with 8 minutes remaining; New Zealand were allowed to score 20 unanswered points to clinch the match; Paul Sackey went off injured with 7 minutes remaining, being replaced by Dan Hipkiss with Jamie Noon then switching from centre to wing to accommodate Hipkiss; Danny Cipriani came on as a replacement for Jamie Noon with 5 minutes remaining, with Delon Armitage then moving from full back to wing to accommodate Cipriani; New Zealand were leading 32-6 with 4 minutes remaining when Tom Rees became the fourth England player to be sent to the sin-bin by the referee!; This match finished in wet conditions)

AUSTRALIAN TOUR TO ITALY, ENGLAND, FRANCE AND WALES 2008

CAPTAIN: *John Smit* (SA)

3rd Dec	**BARBARIANS***	11	AUSTRALIA XV	18

Wembley Stadium

[This match kicked off at 7.45pm; This match was originally scheduled for 6th December 2008 but the date was changed when it became clear that the Barbarians would be unable to raise a sufficiently competitive team because many potential players had extensive club commitments in the period in question; Phil Vickery unavailable due to club commitments; Gurthro Steenkamp, Carl Hayman and François Trinh-Duc in original squad of 22 but withdrew due to injury, being replaced by Federico Pucciariello, Cencus Johnston and Francois Steyn respectively; Steve Borthwick in original squad of 22 but withdrew due to club commitments, being replaced Johann Muller; The Barbarians players broke with tradition by wearing Cornwall socks rather than their own individual club ones; The Australian XV and Barbarians players were awarded Gold and Silver commemorative medals respectively after this match]

(This match was played in extremely cold conditions on a pitch where the in-goal areas were shorter than normal; The Barbarians only had two training sessions to prepare for this match; The Barbarians were drawing 0-0 in the 13th minute when Lote Tuqiri (1) scored after Jean de Villiers missed a tackle on Ryan Cross, thus 7 points

were preventable; The Barbarians were losing 10-0 midway through the first half; The Australian XV was allowed to score 13 unanswered points to win the match; The Barbarians were losing 13-0 in the 25th minute when Francois Steyn had a speculative drop goal attempt from the halfway line go underneath the crossbar!; The Barbarians were still losing 13-0 in the 31st minute when Francois Steyn missed another speculative 51 metre drop goal attempt; Rodney Blake came on as a replacement for Federico Pucciariello in the 33rd minute; The Barbarians were losing 13-3 shortly before half-time; The Barbarians were losing 13-6 at half-time; Shane Williams came on as a replacement for Percy Montgomery at the start of the second half, with Bryan Habana then switching from wing to full back to accommodate Shane Williams; The referee had to order uncontested scrums in the 47th minute after both Matt Dunning and Sekope Kepu went off injured; The Barbarians were still losing 13-6 in the 49th minute when Fourie de Preez saved a certain try by rolling Adam Ashley-Cooper onto his back as he attempted to ground the ball; Ollie Smith (2) came on as a replacement for Rico Gear in the 51st minute; The Barbarians were losing 13-6 in the 60th minute when Mark Regan came on as a replacement for Rodney Blake, with John Smit then moving from hooker to loose-head prop to accommodate Mark Regan; The Barbarians were still losing 13-6 in the 62nd minute when Jerry Collins scored after Shane Williams made a brilliant run; The Barbarians were losing 13-11 with 7 minutes of normal time remaining when Francois Steyn missed an eminently kickable 30 metre penalty goal attempt; The Barbarians were still losing 13-11 with 4 minutes of normal time remaining when Francois Steyn missed a third speculative 40 metre drop goal attempt)

EMIRATES AIRLINE SOUTH AFRICA SEVENS

Outeniqua Park Stadium, George

CAPTAIN: *Ben Gollings*

First Round - Pool 'A'

5th Dec TUNISIA 7 **ENGLAND** 42

[*This match kicked off at 1.27pm*]

(Ben Gollings scored in the 3rd minute!; England were leading 7-0 midway through the first half; England were still leading 7-0 in the 4th minute when Micky Young caught the ball at the tail of a Tunisian lineout and ran 38 metres to score a brilliant solo try; England were leading 14-0 just before half-time; England were leading 21-0 at half-time; England were leading 28-0 in the 9th minute when Micky Young scored to complete a hat-trick of tries after Ben Gollings threw a brilliant long pass; England were leading 35-0 midway through the second half; England scored 42 unanswered points to win the match; England were leading 42-0 in the last minute)

5th Dec FRANCE 7 **ENGLAND** 21

[*This match kicked off at 4.33pm*]

(England were drawing 0-0 midway through the first half; England were still drawing 0-0 in the 5th minute when Chris Cracknell scored after Micky Young made a brilliant break; England were leading 7-0 at half-time; England were still leading 7-0 in the 8th minute when Ben Gollings scored after Kevin Barrett made a brilliant 30 metre break; England were leading 21-0 midway through the second half; England scored 21 unanswered points to win the match; England were still leading 21-0 in the last minute)

5th Dec NEW ZEALAND 19 **ENGLAND*** 7

[*This match kicked off at 8.16pm*]

(Rob Vickerman scored in the 2nd minute after Tom Biggs threw a brilliant overhead

***pass!; England were leading 7-0 midway through the second half; England were still leading 7-0 in the 6th minute; England were drawing 7-7 at half-time; England were still drawing 7-7 midway through the second half when Nafi Tuitavake scored after a poor tackle by Mat Turner, thus 7 points were preventable; England were losing 14-7 with 1 minute remaining; New Zealand were allowed to score 19 unanswered points to win the match*)**

Quarter-Final

6th Dec SOUTH AFRICA 17 **ENGLAND** 12

[*This match kicked off at 1.05pm*]

(*Robert Ebersohn scored in the 1st minute!; England were losing 12-0 midway through the first half; England were losing 12-0 at half-time; England were still losing 12-0 in the 9th minute when Micky Young scored after Rob Vickerman threw a brilliant pass, with Ben Gollings then missing the eminently kickable conversion attempt; James Rodwell came on as a temporary blood replacement for Isoa Damu in the 10th minute; England were losing 17-5 midway through the second half; England were losing 17-5 in the last minute when Isoa Damu followed up and scored just before the dead ball line after Micky Young put up a brilliant cross-kick*)

[Plate Semi-Final:]

[6th Dec SAMOA 19 **ENGLAND** 20]

[*This match kicked off at 3.54pm*]

(*Micky Young scored in the 1st minute!; England were losing 7-5 midway through the first half when Reupena Levasa scored after a poor tackle by Tom Biggs; England were losing 14-10 shortly before half-time when Ben Gollings missed an eminently kickable conversion attempt; England were losing 14-10 at half-time; England were losing 19-10 in the 8th minute; England were losing 19-15 midway through the second half; England were still losing 19-15 when the full-time hooter sounded, but the ball was still in play and Mat Turner was able to kick ahead and follow up to score a brilliant match-winning try*)

[Plate Final:]

[6th Dec PORTUGAL 7 **ENGLAND** 24]

[*This match kicked off at 6.05pm*]

(*England were drawing 0-0 midway through the first half; England were still drawing 0-0 in the 4th minute when Isoa Damu scored a superb 70 metre solo try which Ben Gollings then brilliantly converted from the right touchline; England were leading 7-0 just before half-time when Micky Young's attempted clearance kick went straight to Alberto Esteves who then ran 31 metres to score, thus 7 points were preventable; England were drawing 7-7 at half-time; England were still drawing 7-7 in the 8th minute when Micky Young followed up his own grubber kick to score a superb try; England were leading 12-7 midway through the first half; England were still leading 12-7 with 2 minutes remaining when Mat Turner scored a brilliant 77 metre solo try; England scored 17 unanswered points to win the match; Ben Gollings increased his IRB World Sevens record to 1823 points in this tournament*)

2009

ENGLAND SAXONS INTERNATIONAL MATCH

CAPTAIN: *Phil Dowson*

30th Jan **ENGLAND SAXONS** 66 PORTUGAL 0

Edgeley Park, Hardcastle Road, Edgeley, Stockport

[This match kicked off at 8.00pm; Lesley Vainikolo unavailable due to injury; Michael Lipman and Dan Hipkiss in original training squad of 32 but withdrew due to injury; Julian White and Steffon Armitage in original training squad of 32 but withdrew as they were now required to join the full England international squad, being replaced by Alex Corbisiero and Will Skinner respectively; Joe Worsley in original training squad of 32 but withdrew as he was now required to join the full England international squad; Nick Wood, Matt Mullan, David Paice, Tom Guest, Chris Robshaw, Peter Richards, Richard Wigglesworth, Paul Hodgson, Ryan Lamb, Olly Barkley, Stephen Myler, Dave Strettle, Jordan Turner-Hall, James Simpson-Daniel, Topsy Ojo and Mike Brown all in original training squad of 32 but withdrew due to club commitments; Louis Deacon, Ben Kay, Richard Blaze and Matt Banahan all in original training squad of 32 but were not selected for team or bench; Ben Woods in revised squad of 21 but withdrew due to injury, being replaced by Jon Fisher; Tom Varndell was added to the revised squad of 21 on 23rd January 2009; Joe Ward played for New Zealand U21 in June 2001 and then qualified for England in October 2008 after completing a residency period of 3 years; Matt Smith (1) was the son of Ian Smith (2)]

(This match was played in cold conditions; The England Saxons forwards dominated the scrums; Ed Barnes missed a 20 metre penalty goal attempt from in front of the posts in the 4th minute!; The England Saxons were drawing 0-0 in the 11th minute when they were awarded a 23 metre penalty in an eminently kickable position, but Phil Dowson ordered a kick to the corner in a vain attempt to score a try from the ensuing lineout; The England Saxons were drawing 0-0 in the 18th minute when Harry Ellis scored a pushover try; The England Saxons were leading 7-0 midway through the first half; The England Saxons were still leading 7-0 in the 24th minute when Adam Powell scored after Ed Barnes put in a brilliant grubber kick; The England Saxons were leading 14-0 in the 27th minute when Tom Varndell scored after Nick Abendanon put up a brilliant cross-kick; The England Saxons were leading 26-0 shortly before half-time when some superb handling allowed Noah Cato to score; The England Saxons were leading 33-0 at half-time; Joe Ward and Alex Goode came on as replacements for Rob Webber and Ed Barnes respectively in the 49th minute; The England Saxons were still leading 33-0 in the 53rd minute when Noah Cato wasted a great try-scoring opportunity by dropping the ball while the Portuguese line was at his mercy; Matt Smith (1) came on as a replacement for Dom Waldouck in the 56th minute; Joe Simpson came on as a replacement for Harry Ellis in the 61st minute; The England Saxons were leading 40-0 midway through the second half when Matt Smith powered through to score; The England Saxons were leading 52-0 in the 68th minute; The England Saxons were leading 59-0 with 2 minutes remaining when Adam Powell scored from a quick tap penalty; Nick Abendanon had a brilliant game)

PARC Y SCARLETS OPENING CELBRATION MATCH

CAPTAIN: *Anton Oliver* (NZ) [*Mark Regan*]

31st Jan Llanelli Scarlets (*WA*) 40 **BARBARIANS*** 24

Parc y Scarlets, Llanelli

[This match kicked off at 2.30pm; Kevin Sorrell in original squad of 22 but withdrew

due to injury, being replaced by Marius Goosen; Mark Regan retired in April 2009]
(The Barbarians only had one day to prepare for this match; This match was played in cold conditions; Matthew Jacob scored in the 3rd minute!; The Barbarians were losing 7-0 in the 7th minute when Ben Blair made a brilliant break, but his intended scoring pass was then dropped by Federico Pucciariello; The Barbarians were still losing 7-0 in the 15th minute when Jon Davies scored after a poor tackle by Ben Blair; The Barbarians were losing 14-0 midway through the first half when a poor defensive alignment allowed Morgan Stoddart to score; The Llanelli Scarlets were allowed to score 21 unanswered points to win the match; The Barbarians were losing 21-0 in the 38th minute when some superb handling amongst the backs allowed Brian Carney to score; The Barbarians were losing 21-5 just before half-time and pressing in attack when Brian Carney chipped the ball straight to Morgan Stoddart who then ran 70 metres to score another try; The Barbarians were losing 26-5 at half-time; The Barbarians played with the wind in the second half; Mark Robinson (2) and Jeremy Staunton came on as replacements for Mike Petri and Jamie Robinson respectively at the start of the second half; The Barbarians were still losing 26-5 in the 48th minute when Mark Robinson (2) put in a wayward clearance kick which led directly to a try by Martin Roberts (2), thus 4 tries and 26 points were preventable; Mark Regan, Ben Evans and Colin Charvis came on replacements for Anton Oliver, Jon Dawson and Steve Tandy respectively in the 50th minute; The Barbarians were losing 40-5 midway through the second half; Gavin Quinnell came on as a replacement for Daniel Vickerman in the 59th minute; The Barbarians were still losing 40-5 in the 62nd minute when Ben Blair ran 26 metres to score a brilliant solo try; The Barbarians were losing 40-17 in the 68th minute when Ben Blair hit the right-hand post with a conversion attempt from the right touchline; The Barbarians were losing 40-24 in the 70th minute; The Barbarians scored 19 unanswered points in the final quarter)

NEW ZEALAND INTERNATIONAL SEVENS

Westpac Stadium, Wellington

CAPTAIN: *Ollie Phillips*

First Round - Pool 'C'

6th Feb FRANCE 10 **ENGLAND** 26

[This match kicked off at 1.00pm; Charlie Simpson-Daniel unavailable due to injury]
(Eddie Labarthe scored in the 1st minute!; England were losing 5-0 midway through the first half; England were still losing 5-0 just before half-time when Kevin Barrett scored a brilliant 75 metre solo try; England were leading 7-5 at half-time; England were losing 10-7 in the 8th minute; England were still losing 10-7 in the 10th minute when some superb handling allowed Ollie Phillips to score; England were leading 14-10 midway through the second half; England were leading 21-10 with 1 minute remaining when Andy Vilk powered through to score; England scored 19 unanswered points to win the match)

6th Feb CANADA 7 **ENGLAND** 34

[This match kicked off at 3.56pm; Charlie Simpson-Daniel unavailable due to injury]
(Ollie Phillips ran 42 metres to score after just 81 seconds had been played!; England were leading 7-0 midway through the first half; England were leading 12-0 just before half-time; England were leading 17-0 at half-time; Ben Jones came on as a replacement for Kevin Barrett at the start of the second half; Rob Vickerman scored after just 27 seconds of the second half had been played!; England scored 22 unanswered points to win the match; England were leading 22-0 midway through the second half; England were still leading 22-0 with 3 minutes remaining; England were

leading 22-7 with 2 minutes remaining when Ben Gollings scored a brilliant 52 metre solo try)

6th Feb ARGENTINA 13 **ENGLAND** 5

[This match kicked off at 8.50pm; Charlie Simpson-Daniel unavailable due to injury]

(Pablo Gómez Cora scored in the 3rd minute!; England were losing 5-0 midway through the first half; England were still losing 5-0 shortly before half-time; England were losing 10-0 at half-time; England were still losing 10-0 in the 9th minute when Kevin Barrett scored a brilliant 24 metre solo try; England were losing 10-5 midway through the second half; England were still losing 10-5 in the last minute when Martín Rodríguez Gurruchaga scored a penalty goal to clinch the match for Argentina)

Quarter-Final

7th Feb FIJI 10 **ENGLAND** 31

[This match kicked off at 2.55pm; Charlie Simpson-Daniel unavailable due to injury; England wore red shirts for this match]

(Peni Rokodiva scored in the 2nd minute!; England were losing 5-0 in the 3rd minute when Rupeni Nasiga scored after Kevin Barrett slipped over, thus 5 points were preventable; England were losing 10-0 midway through the first half; England were still losing 10-0 in the 5th minute when Tom Biggs scored after Isoa Damu threw a brilliant pass out of the tackle; England were losing 10-5 shortly before half-time when Ben Gollings crossed the Fijian tryline under the posts but was then superbly dispossessed by Peni Rokodiva; England were losing 10-5 at half-time; England were leading 12-10 in the 9th minute; England were still leading 12-10 midway through the second half when Ollie Phillips chipped ahead and regathered the ball to score a brilliant try; England were leading 19-10 with 2 minutes remaining when some superb handling allowed Chris Cracknell to score; England were leading 26-10 in the last minute when Ben Gollings chipped ahead and followed up to score a brilliant try; England scored 31 unanswered points to win the match)

Semi-Final

7th Feb KENYA 0 **ENGLAND** 24

[This match kicked off at 6.35pm; Charlie Simpson-Daniel unavailable due to injury; After this match the IRB retrospectively disallowed Ben Gollings' conversion of Chris Cracknell's try because Gollings had allegedly taken more than the permitted 40 seconds to line up and then kick the ball!]

(Kenya were drawing 0-0 in the 3rd minute when Lavin Asego dropped the ball while the England tryline was at his mercy!; England were still drawing 0-0 midway through the first half; England were drawing 0-0 shortly before half-time; England were leading 7-0 at half-time; England were still leading 7-0 in the 9th minute when Ollie Phillips chipped ahead and regathered the ball to score a brilliant try; England were leading 12-0 midway through the second half; England were still leading 12-0 with 3 minutes remaining when Ollie Phillips powered through to complete a hat-trick of tries; England were leading 19-0 in the final minute when Kevin Barrett had the Kenyan tryline at his mercy, but he then allowed Chris Cracknell to score instead!)

Final

7th Feb NEW ZEALAND 17 **ENGLAND** 19

[This match kicked off at 9.00pm; Charlie Simpson-Daniel unavailable due to injury]

(Paul Grant (2) scored in the 3rd minute!; England were losing 5-0 midway through the first half; England were still losing 5-0 in the 6th minute when Tom Biggs had a great try-scoring chance but was brilliantly tackled by Tu Umaga-Marshall; England were losing 5-0 in the 7th minute when Zar Lawrence scored after a poor tackle by Kevin

***Barrett; England were losing 10-0 in the 9th minute when Ollie Phillips was caught in possession in front of his own line by D.J. Forbes who then went on to score, thus 2 tries and 12 points were preventable; New Zealand were allowed to score 17 unanswered points; England were losing 17-0 just before half-time when Ollie Phillips scored a brilliant 59 metre solo try; England were losing 17-5 at half-time; England were still losing 17-5 in the 13th minute when Rob Vickerman intercepted the ball and ran 55 metres to score; England were losing 17-12 midway through the second half; England were still losing 17-12 when the full-time hooter sounded, but the ball was still in play and Isoa Damu was able to score a try under the posts which Ben Gollings then converted with the last kick of the match to win the game and the competition!; Ben Gollings increased his IRB World Sevens record to 1857 points in this tournament*)**

6 NATIONS CHAMPIONSHIP

CAPTAIN: *Steve Borthwick*

7th Feb **ENGLAND** 36 ITALY 11

Twickenham

[*This match kicked off at 3.00pm; Michael Lipman and Jonny Wilkinson unavailable due to injury; Danny Care selected but withdrew due to injury, being replaced by Harry Ellis; Mike Tindall selected but withdrew due to injury, being replaced by Jamie Noon; Lewis Moody, Tom Rees and Toby Flood in original training squad of 32 but withdrew due to injury, being replaced by Steffon Armitage, Joe Worsley and Andy Goode respectively; Matt Stevens in original training squad of 32 but was withdrawn by the RFU on 20th January 2009 after he failed an ERC drugs test, being replaced by Julian White; Tim Payne, Tom Palmer (2) and Ugo Monye in original training squad of 32 but were unavailable for this match due to injury; George Chuter, Simon Shaw, Luke Narraway, Danny Cipriani and Olly Morgan all in original training squad of 32 but were not selected for team or bench; Tom Mercey and James Simpson-Daniel were added to the squad on 2nd February 2009 to provide injury cover for Tim Payne and Ugo Monye respectively*]

(*This match was played in cold conditions; Nick Kennedy dominated the lineout in this match; The England backs kicked away too much possession; Andy Goode followed up his own grubber kick to score a brilliant try after just 92 seconds had been played!; England were leading 7-0 in the 5th minute when Andy Goode missed a speculative 46 metre penalty goal attempt; England were leading 12-0 in the 18th minute; England were still leading 12-0 midway through the first half; England were leading 12-0 in the 28th minute when Riki Flutey scored after Andy Goode fly-hacked a loose ball on; England scored 19 unanswered points to win the match; England were leading 19-0 in the 34th minute; England were leading 22-6 at half-time; England were still leading 22-6 in the 49th minute when Andy Goode missed a speculative 42 metre drop goal attempt; England were leading 22-6 in the 54th minute when Harry Ellis scored a brilliant 49 metre solo try; Dylan Hartley came on as a replacement for Lee Mears in the 56th minute; England were leading 29-6 midway through the second half; Ben Foden came on as a replacement for Harry Ellis in the 60th minute; England were still leading 29-6 with 8 minutes of normal time remaining; Matt Tait came on as a replacement for Jamie Noon with 6 minutes of normal time remaining; England were leading 29-11 with 2 minutes of normal time remaining when some superb handling amongst the backs allowed Mark Cueto to score a try which Andy Goode then brilliantly converted from the left touchline; Steffon and Delon Armitage became the first brothers to play for England in a cap international match since 1995!*)

14th Feb WALES 23 **ENGLAND*** 15

Millennium Stadium, Cardiff

[*This match kicked off at 5.30pm; Michael Lipman, Lewis Moody, Tom Rees and Jonny Wilkinson all unavailable due to injury; Matt Stevens unavailable due to suspension; Danny Care in original training squad of 35 but withdrew due to injury, being replaced by Paul Hodgson; Tom Palmer (2) in original training squad of 35 but was unavailable for this match due to injury; Tim Payne, George Chuter, Tom Mercey, Simon Shaw, Steffon Armitage, Ben Foden, Danny Cipriani, Shane Geraghty, Ugo Monye, Jamie Noon, James Simpson-Daniel and Olly Morgan all in original training squad of 35 but were not selected for team or bench; David Wilson (2) and Jordan Crane were added to the squad on 9th February 2009 to provide injury cover; On 26th February 2009 an ERC hearing found Matt Stevens guilty of taking recreational drugs and thus banned him for 2 years*]

(*Delon Armitage missed a speculative 41 metre drop goal attempt in the 1st minute!; Stephen Jones (2) scored a penalty goal in the 4th minute!; England were losing 6-0 in the 16th minute; England were still losing 6-0 midway through the first half; England were losing 9-0 in the 24th minute when Paul Sackey scored after Andy Goode put in a brilliant chip-kick, with Andy Goode then missing the eminently kickable conversion attempt; England were losing 9-5 in the 30th minute when Andy Goode scored a superb 36 metre drop goal; England were losing 9-8 at half-time; Riki Flutey played as a fly half in the absence of Andy Goode, who was sent to the sin-bin in the 42nd minute; England were losing 17-8 in the 48th minute when Delon Armitage missed a speculative 48 metre penalty goal attempt; Toby Flood came on as a replacement for Andy Goode in the 52nd minute; England were losing 20-8 in the 57th minute when Delon Armitage dummied his way through to score a brilliant 30 metre try; England were losing 20-15 midway through the second half when Paul Sackey wasted a great try-scoring opportunity by mishitting a loose ball as he attempted to fly-hack it on over the Welsh line!; Matt Tait came on as a replacement for Paul Sackey in the 65th minute; England were still losing 20-15 with 8 minutes of normal time remaining; England were losing 23-15 with 6 minutes of normal time remaining when Toby Flood missed an eminently kickable 23 metre penalty goal attempt; Joe Worsley had a brilliant game*)

28th Feb IRELAND 14 **ENGLAND*** 13

Croke Park, Dublin

[*This match kicked off at 5.30pm; Michael Lipman, Lewis Moody, Tom Rees and Jonny Wilkinson all unavailable due to injury; Matt Stevens unavailable due to suspension; Tom Palmer (2) in original training squad of 35 but was unavailable for this match due to injury; Tim Payne, George Chuter, Tom Mercey, Simon Shaw, Steffon Armitage, Ben Foden, Danny Cipriani, Ugo Monye, Shane Geraghty, Jamie Noon, James Simpson-Daniel and Olly Morgan all in original training squad of 35 but were not selected for team or bench*]

(*England were drawing 0-0 midway through the first half; England were still drawing 0-0 in the 28th minute when they created an overlap, but Toby Flood's pass was then intercepted by Brian O'Driscoll; England were losing 3-0 in the 29th minute; England were still losing 3-0 shortly before half-time; England were drawing 3-3 at half-time; England were losing 6-3 in the 45th minute; England were losing 11-3 in the 57th minute; Paul Sackey went off injured in the 58th minute, being replaced by Matt Tait; England were still losing 11-3 midway through the second half when Matt Tait made a brilliant break but then wasted this great try-scoring opportunity by not passing to Riki Flutey, who was unmarked outside him; England were losing 11-6 in the 66th minute;*

***Toby Flood went off injured immediately afterwards, being replaced by Andy Goode; Andy Goode played as a scrum half in the absence of Danny Care, who was sent to the sin-bin in the 70th minute; England were losing 14-6 with 9 minutes of normal time remaining; England were still losing 14-6 with 1 minute of normal time remaining when Delon Armitage scored a consolation try after Andy Goode put in a brilliant grubber kick*)**

15th Mar	**ENGLAND**	34	FRANCE	10

Twickenham

[*This match kicked off at 3.00pm; Michael Lipman, Lewis Moody and Jonny Wilkinson unavailable due to injury; Matt Stevens unavailable due to suspension; Tom Palmer (2) and Shane Geraghty in original training squad of 35 but withdrew due to injury, being replaced by Louis Deacon and Olly Barkley respectively; James Simpson-Daniel and Paul Sackey in original training squad of 35 but were unavailable for this match due to injury; Tim Payne, George Chuter, Tom Mercey, Steffon Armitage, Luke Narraway, Ben Foden, Danny Cipriani, Jamie Noon and Olly Morgan all in original training squad of 35 but were not selected for team or bench; David Strettle was added to the squad on 9th March 2009 to provide injury cover for Paul Sackey; David Wilson (2) was also added to the squad on 9th March 2009 to provide injury cover*]

(*A brilliant break by Riki Flutey enabled Mark Cueto to score after just 69 seconds had been played!; England were leading 10-0 in the 18th minute; England were still leading 10-0 midway through the first half; Riki Flutey scored a superb try which Toby Flood then converted to give England a 17-0 in the 23rd minute; England were still leading 17-0 in the 38th minute; England were reduced to 14 men just before half-time when Toby Flood went off injured; England were leading 29-0 at half-time; Andy Goode came on as a replacement for Toby Flood at the start of the second half; England were still leading 29-0 in the 42nd minute when a brilliant break by Delon Armitage enabled Riki Flutey to score another try, with Andy Goode then missing the eminently kickable conversion attempt; England scored 34 unanswered points to win the match; Julian White came on as a temporary blood replacement for Phil Vickery in the 43rd minute; England were leading 34-0 in the 56th minute; James Haskell came on as a replacement for Simon Shaw in the 57th minute, with Tom Croft then switching from flanker to lock to accommodate Haskell; England were leading 34-5 midway through the second half; England were still leading 34-5 in the 64th minute when a poor defensive alignment allowed Julien Malzieu to score, thus 5 points were preventable; Joe Worsley went off injured in the 68th minute, being replaced by Nick Kennedy with Tom Croft then moving from lock to flanker to accommodate Nick Kennedy; Tom Croft had a brilliant game*)

21st Mar	**ENGLAND**	26	SCOTLAND	12

Twickenham

[*This match kicked off at 3.30pm; Tom Palmer (2), Lewis Moody, Jonny Wilkinson, Shane Geraghty, James Simpson-Daniel and Paul Sackey all unavailable due to injury; Matt Stevens unavailable due to suspension; Tim Payne, Tom Rees, Olly Barkley and Ben Foden were all added to the original training squad of 22 on 17th March 2009 to provide injury cover*]

(*England were losing 3-0 in the 9th minute; England were still losing 3-0 in the 11th minute when Ugo Monye saved a certain try by getting across to tackle Thom Evans; Phil Vickery went off injured in the 14th minute, being replaced by Julian White; Harry Ellis went off injured in the 17th minute, being replaced by Danny Care; England were losing 3-0 midway through the first half; England were leading 5-3 in the 23rd minute; England were leading 12-3 in the 30th minute; England were still leading 12-3 in the*

35th minute when Nick Easter clearly grounded the ball for a try but the referee was unsighted; England were leading 12-3 just before half-time; England were leading 15-3 at half-time; England were leading 18-3 in the 42nd minute; England scored 18 unanswered points to win the match; Ugo Monye went off injured in the 48th minute, being replaced by Matt Tait; England were leading 18-9 in the 51st minute; England were still leading 18-9 midway through the second half when Toby Flood missed an eminently kickable 22 metre penalty goal attempt; England were leading 18-12 in the 67th minute; England were still leading 18-12 with 7 minutes of normal time remaining when Danny Care scored a brilliant 35 metre drop goal; Toby Flood went off injured immediately afterwards, being replaced by Andy Goode; The referee had to order uncontested scrums with 4 minutes of normal time remaining when England were reduced to 14 men after Julian White went off injured; England were leading 21-12 with 2 minutes of normal time remaining when some superb handling amongst the backs allowed Matt Tait to score; Riki Flutey had a brilliant game)

U20 6 NATIONS CHAMPIONSHIP

CAPTAIN: *Calum Clark*

6th Feb **ENGLAND U20** 17 ITALY U20 0

Worcester RFC, Sixways Stadium, Pershore Lane, Hindip, Worcester

[***This match was originally scheduled to start at 8.00pm but the kick-off was brought forward to 5.30pm to prevent the pitch from becoming unplayable due to frost; Phil Swainston, Rob Milligan, Mike Stanley and Sam Smith all in original training squad of 32 but withdrew due to injury, being replaced by Shaun Knight, Josh Ovens, Tom Homer and Greig Tonks respectively; Joe Marler in original training squad of 32 but was unavailable for this match due to injury; Tom Collett, Jacob Rowan, Tom Sargeant, Carl Fearns, Tom Casson, James Short and Freddie Burns all in original training squad of 32 but were not selected for team or bench; Dave Lewis in revised squad of 22 but withdrew due to injury, being replaced by Dan White; The extreme cold caused this match to be played behind closed doors for health and safety reasons!; Ben Moon, Rory Clegg, Henry Trinder, Dan Williams and Dan White all toured Australia with England U18 in August 2007; Jamie George toured Argentina with England U18 in July-August 2008 and played for M.R. Steele-Bodger's XV against Cambridge University at Grange Road on 26th November 2008; James Gaskell and Will Hurrell toured Argentina with England U18 in July-August 2008; Jamie George was the son of Ian George***]

(***This match was played in extremely cold conditions on an icy pitch; England U20 were leading 5-0 midway through the first half; England U20 were still leading 5-0 just before half-time; England U20 were leading 12-0 at half-time; England U20 were still leading 12-0 in the 51st minute when Seb Stegmann scored after he wrong-footed the Italy U20 defence with a brilliant sidestep; England U20 were leading 17-0 midway through the second half***)

13th Feb WALES U20 16 **ENGLAND U20** 28

Brewery Field, Bridgend

[***This match kicked off at 7.05pm; Courtney Lawes, Ben Youngs, Rory Clegg, Luke Eves and Charlie Sharples all in original training squad of 32 but withdrew due to club commitments; Joe Marler and Dave Lewis in original training squad of 32 but were unavailable for this match due to injury; Tom Collett, Jacob Rowan, Carl Fearns, Dan Williams, Tom Casson and James Short all in original training squad of 32 but were not selected for team or bench; Peter Elder, Sam Harrison (2) and Mike Stanley were added to the squad on 12th February 2009; Freddie Burns toured Argentina with***

England U18 in July-August 2008; Mike Stanley toured Australia with England U18 in August 2007]
(This match was played in cold and drizzly conditions; England U20 were drawing 0-0 in the 11th minute when some superb handling allowed Chris York to score; England U20 were leading 7-3 midway through the first half; England U20 were still leading 7-3 in the 32nd minute when Henry Trinder took a quick tap penalty and scored; England U20 were leading 14-3 in the 35th minute when Rob Miller made a brilliant break, but his intended scoring pass to James Gaskell was then intercepted by Josh Navidi; England U20 were still leading 14-3 shortly before half-time time when Calum Clark scored after Seb Stegmann made a brilliant run; England U20 were leading 21-3 at half-time; England U20 were leading 21-6 in the 44th minute; England U20 were leading 21-13 in the 55th minute when Rob Miller ghosted through to score a superb try; England U20 were leading 28-16 midway through the second half; England U20 were still leading 28-16 in the 62nd minute when Calum Clark crossed the tryline, but the move was disallowed after a touch judge wrongly adjudged that Will Hurrell was outside the field of play when he threw the scoring pass; Henry Trinder went off injured in the 70th minute, being replaced by Freddie Burns with Tom Homer then switching from full back to centre to accommodate Freddie Burns; Calum Clark had a brilliant game)

27th Feb IRELAND U20 19 **ENGLAND U20*** 18

Dubarry Park, Athlone

[This match kicked off at 6.15pm; Joe Marler and Dave Lewis in original training squad of 33 but were unavailable for this match due to injury; James Clark, Tom Collett, Graham Kitchener, Jacob Rowan, Rob Miller, Mike Stanley, Henry Trinder and Tom Homer all in original training squad of 33 but were not selected for team or bench; Arthur Ellis, Rory Clegg and George Lowe were added to the original training squad of 33 on 23rd February 2009; Dan Williams in revised squad of 22 but withdrew due to club commitments, being replaced by Carl Fearns; Arthur Ellis was the brother of Hugo Ellis; Carl Fearns captained England U18 on their tour of Australia in August 2007; On 5th March 2009 Josh Ovens was banned for 3 weeks after being cited for a dangerous tackle on Peter O'Mahony]
(Rory Clegg played with an illness; The England U20 backs made a number of handling errors in this match; The England U20 forwards dominated the lineout in the first half; England U20 were drawing 0-0 midway through the first half; England U20 were still drawing 0-0 in the 22nd minute when Josh Ovens scored directly from an Ireland U20 lineout; England U20 were leading 5-3 in the 25th minute; England U20 were still leading 5-3 shortly afterwards when Rory Clegg missed a speculative long-range penalty goal attempt; England U20 were leading 5-3 shortly before half-time; England U20 were losing 6-5 at half-time; England U20 were leading 8-6 in the 52nd minute when Michael Keating scored after Ian McKinley intercepted the ball, thus 7 points were preventable; England U20 were losing 16-8 midway through the second half; England U20 were losing 16-13 in the 65th minute; England U20 were still losing 16-13 with 5 minutes of normal time remaining when George Lowe scored after Seb Stegmann made a brilliant run; England U20 were leading 18-16 in the seventh minute of injury time when Ian Madigan scored a 35 metre drop goal with the last kick of the match to win the game for Ireland U20)

CAPTAIN: *Luke Eves*

13th Mar **ENGLAND U20*** 11 FRANCE U20 31

Worcester RFC, Sixways Stadium, Pershore Lane, Hindip, Worcester

[This match kicked off at 8.00pm; Dave Lewis unavailable due to injury; Josh Ovens

unavailable due to suspension; Graham Kitchener, Courtney Lawes, Carl Fearns, Ben Youngs, Rob Miller, Henry Trinder, Tom Homer and Charlie Sharples all unavailable due to club commitments; Calum Clark selected as captain in the original training squad of 23 but withdrew due to injury; George Lowe was originally selected at left wing with Seb Stegmann at right wing, but the two swapped positions before the match; Jacob Rowan toured Australia with England U18 in August 2007]

(The England U20 forwards could not win any lineout ball; The England U20 scrum was put under severe pressure; England U20 were drawing 0-0 in the 8th minute when George Lowe saved a certain try by managing to get beneath the ball as Leo Griffoul attempted to ground it; England U20 were losing 7-0 in the 9th minute; England U20 were losing 7-3 midway through the first half when Rory Clegg made a brilliant break but Tom Casson then wasted this great try-scoring opportunity by knocking the ball on; England U20 were losing 7-6 in the 23rd minute; England U20 were still losing 7-6 shortly before half-time when Pierre Bernard kicked ahead and Djibril Camara followed up and scored after both Seb Stegmann and Greig Tonks were deceived by the bounce of the ball; England U20 were losing 14-6 at half-time; England U20 were still losing 14-6 in the 44th minute when Pierre Bernard's 20 metre drop goal attempt was deflected under the crossbar by Chris York, which allowed Djibril Camara to fall on the resulting loose ball to score another try, thus 2 tries and 14 points were preventable; England U20 were losing 21-6 in the 49th minute when they were awarded an 11 metre penalty in an eminently kickable position, but Luke Eves ordered a kick to the corner in a vain attempt to score a try; Freddie Burns came on as a replacement for Tom Casson in the 50th minute, with Greig Tonks then switching from full back to centre to accommodate Freddie Burns; England U20 were still losing 21-6 midway through the second half when they were awarded a 14 metre penalty in front of the posts, but Luke Eves took the option of a scrum in a vain attempt to score a try; England U20 were losing 21-6 in the 63rd minute when George Lowe made a brilliant 50 metre break, but he then wasted this great try-scoring opportunity by attempting to make the line himself instead of using a 2 man overlap outside him; England U20 were losing 21-11 in the 66th minute when Rory Clegg missed an eminently kickable conversion attempt; England U20 were losing 24-11 with 9 minutes of normal time match remaining)

20th Mar **ENGLAND U20** 20 SCOTLAND U20 6

Worcester RFC, Sixways Stadium, Pershore Lane, Hindip, Worcester

[This match kicked off at 8.00pm; Calum Clark and Dave Lewis unavailable due to injury; Josh Ovens unavailable due to suspension; Courtney Lawes, Carl Fearns, Ben Youngs, Seb Stegmann, Tom Homer and Charlie Sharples all unavailable due to club commitments; James Gaskell selected but withdrew on the day of the match due to club commitments, Peter Elder was moved from the bench to the team and Danny Wright was then selected for the bench; Jordi Pasqualin toured Argentina with England U18 in July-August 2008]

(This match was played in cold conditions; Robbie McGowan scored a penalty goal in the 5th minute!; England U20 were losing 3-0 in the 8th minute when Henry Trinder scored after he wrong-footed Robbie McGowan with a brilliant sidestep; England U20 were leading 7-3 in the 16th minute when Rob Miller missed a speculative 46 metre penalty goal attempt; England U20 were still leading 7-3 in the 17th minute when Jamie Gibson scored after Chris York threw a superb reverse pass, with Rob Miller then missing the eminently kickable conversion attempt; England U20 were leading 12-3 midway through the first half; England U20 were leading 15-3 in the 34th minute; England U20 scored 15 unanswered points to win the match; England U20 were still leading 15-3 shortly before half-time; England U20 were leading 15-6 at half-time;

***England U20 were leading 20-6 in the 45th minute when Rob Miller missed an eminently kickable conversion attempt; The referee had to order uncontested scrums in the 54th minute after David Morton went off injured; England U20 were still leading 20-6 midway through the second half; Jordi Pasqualin went off injured in the 62nd minute, being replaced by Dan White; Chris York had a brilliant game*)**

ENGLAND SAXONS INTERNATIONAL MATCH

CAPTAIN: *George Skivington*

6th Feb	IRELAND A	C	**ENGLAND SAXONS**	C

Donnybrook, Dublin

[*This match was scheduled to kick off at 7.35pm; Match cancelled just before kick-off after the pitch was declared unplayable due to frost; Alex Corbisiero, Louis Deacon, Michael Lipman, Lesley Vainikolo and Dan Hipkiss unavailable due to injury; Harry Ellis selected but withdrew as he was now required to play for the full England international team against Italy, Paul Hodgson was moved from the bench to the team and Joe Simpson was then selected for the bench; Mike Brown in original training squad of 24 but withdrew due to injury; Nick Wood in original training squad of 24 but was not selected for team or bench*]

USA SEVENS

PETCO Park, San Diego

CAPTAIN: *Ollie Phillips*

First Round - Pool 'C'

14th Feb	SCOTLAND	12	**ENGLAND**	22

[*This match kicked off at 10.02am*]

(*Kevin Barrett scored after just 31 seconds had been played!; England were leading 12-0 midway through the first half; England were still leading 12-0 shortly before half-time; England were leading 12-7 at half-time; England were leading 17-7 in the 9th minute; England were still leading 17-7 midway through the second half; England were leading 17-12 in the last minute*)

14th Feb	JAPAN	12	**ENGLAND**	35

[*This match kicked off at 12.55pm*]

(*England were drawing 0-0 midway through the first half; England were leading 5-0 in the 5th minute when Ben Gollings scored a brilliant conversion from the left touchline; England were leading 21-0 at half-time; England were leading 28-0 in the 8th minute; England scored 28 unanswered points to win the match; England were leading 28-7 midway through the second half; England were leading 28-12 when the full-time hooter sounded, but the ball was still in play and Ben Jones was able to score; Isoa Damu injured playing in the match*)

14th Feb	SAMOA	15	**ENGLAND***	12

[*This match kicked off at 5.06pm; Isoa Damu unavailable due to injury*]

(*Apelu Fa'aiuga scored in the 3rd minute!; England were losing 5-0 midway through the first half; England were losing 10-0 shortly before half-time when Kevin Barrett chipped ahead and followed up to score a brilliant try; England were losing 10-7 at half-time; England were still losing 10-7 in the 8th minute when Ofisa Treviranus scored after a poor tackle by Ollie Phillips, thus 5 points were preventable; England were losing 15-7 midway through the second half; England were still losing 15-7 with 2 minutes remaining*)

Quarter-Final

15th Feb FIJI 10 **ENGLAND** 12

[This match kicked off at 11.20am; Isoa Damu unavailable due to injury; England wore red shirts for this match]

(Peni Rokodiva scored in the 2nd minute!; England were losing 5-0 midway through the first half; England were still losing 5-0 in the 6th minute when the referee awarded a penalty try after Tom Biggs was illegally tackled without the ball by Osea Kolinisau as he chased Ollie Phillips' kick ahead; England were leading 7-5 just before half-time when some superb handling allowed Rob Vickerman to score; England were leading 12-5 at half-time; England were still leading 12-5 midway through the second half; England were leading 12-5 in the last minute)

Semi-Final

15th Feb SOUTH AFRICA 19 **ENGLAND** 22

[This match kicked off at 3.08pm; Isoa Damu unavailable due to injury; England wore red shirts for this match]

(Gio Aplon scored in the 1st minute!; England were losing 5-0 in the 3rd minute when Mpho Mbiyozo scored after a poor tackle by Kevin Barrett, thus 7 points were preventable; England were losing 12-0 midway through the first half; England were still losing 12-0 in the 5th minute when Ben Gollings scored a brilliant 60 metre solo try; England were losing 12-10 shortly before half-time when Ben Gollings scored a brilliant conversion from the right touchline; England were drawing 12-12 at half-time; England were still drawing 12-12 in the 8th minute when Tom Biggs followed up and scored after Ben Gollings put in a superb chip-kick; England were leading 17-12 midway through the second half; England scored 22 unanswered points to win the match; England were leading 22-12 in the last minute)

Final

15th Feb ARGENTINA 19 **ENGLAND*** 14

[This match kicked off at 5.22pm; Isoa Damu unavailable due to injury; England wore red shirts for this match]

(Tom Biggs scored in the 3rd minute!; England were leading 7-0 midway through the first half when collectively poor tackling allowed Santiago Gómez Cora to score; England were leading 7-5 in the 6th minute when Ben Gollings chipped ahead and regathered the ball to score a brilliant try; England were leading 14-5 at half-time; England were still leading 14-5 in the 11th minute when Lucas González Amorosino scored after a poor tackle by James Rodwell, thus 2 tries and 12 points were preventable; England were leading 14-12 in the 13th minute; Argentina were allowed to score 14 unanswered points to win the match; England were losing 19-14 midway through the second half; Ben Gollings increased his IRB World Sevens record to 1889 points in this tournament)

AIB CLUB INTERNATIONAL MATCH

CAPTAIN: *Liam Wordley*

27th Feb IRELAND CLUB XV 13 **ENGLAND COUNTIES*** 13

Donnybrook, Dublin

[This match kicked off at 5.00pm; Mike Myerscough, Alex Page and Rickie Aley in original training squad of 22 but withdrew due to injury, being replaced by Luke Collins, Paul Knight (2) and Gavin Beasley respectively; Darren Fox in original training squad of 22 but withdrew, being replaced by Jason Smithson; Ben Gerry was converted from a flanker to a hooker by his club Leicester in 2003]

(Mark Bedworth missed a penalty goal attempt in the 3rd minute!; England Counties were losing 7-0 in the 8th minute; England Counties were losing 10-0 in the 14th minute; England Counties were still losing 10-0 midway through the first half; England Counties were losing 10-3 in the 29th minute; Rob Baldwin went off injured in the 30th minute, being replaced by Jason Smithson; England Counties were losing 10-3 at half-time; England Counties were still losing 10-3 in the 50th minute when James Doherty powered through to score; England Counties were drawing 10-10 midway through the second half; England Counties were leading 13-10 in the 69th minute; England Counties were still leading 13-10 with 3 minutes remaining)

ENGLAND STUDENTS MATCHES

CAPTAIN: *Phil Ellis*

27th Feb Irish Colleges (*IR*) 10 **ENGLAND STUDENTS** 13

City of Derry RFC, Judge's Road, Strathfoyle, Derry

[This match kicked off at 7.30pm; Tom Hockedy unavailable due to injury; Ed Pickles, Jason Phipps, Joe Horn-Smith, Ricky Lutton, Barney Purbrook, Jon Aston, Jamie Fleming, Matt Gilbert, Andries Pretorius, Alex Waddingham, Phil Burgess, Will Chudleigh, Simon Humberstone, Gareth Wynne, Chris Lewis, James Sharples, Dave Vincent, Andrew Henderson and Peter Clarke (2) all in original training squad of 39 but were not selected for team or bench; James Hall and Alan Awcock were not part of the original training squad; David Butler was the son of John Butler]

(This match was played in windy conditions; Grant Pointer scored a penalty goal in the 2nd minute!; England Students were leading 3-0 in the 7th minute when collectively poor tackling allowed Paul Harte to score, thus 7 points were preventable; England Students were losing 7-3 midway through the first half; England Students were still losing 7-3 in the 22nd minute when Grant Pointer hit the post with a penalty goal attempt; England Students were losing 7-3 at half-time; Tom Malaney and Toby Henry came on as replacements for Andy Bridgeman and Rob Springall respectively at the start of the second half; England Students were still losing 7-3 midway through the second half when Drew Locke scored a brilliant try; England Students were losing 10-8 in the 67th minute; England Students were still losing 10-8 in the second minute of injury time when Grant Pointer scored a superb try to win the match)

13th Mar **ENGLAND STUDENTS** 15 French Universities (*FR*) 13

Clifton RFC, Station Road, Cribbs Causeway, Henbury, Bristol

[This match kicked off at 2.00pm; Tom Hockedy unavailable due to injury]

(England Students were losing 3-0 in the 7th minute; England Students were losing 10-0 in the 13th minute; England Students were still losing 10-0 midway through the first half; England Students were losing 10-0 in the 23rd minute when Grant Pointer scored a brilliant penalty goal; England Students were losing 13-3 shortly before half-time when Grant Pointer ghosted through to score a superb try; England Students were losing 13-10 at half-time; James Hall came on as a replacement for Tom Fidler at the start of the second half; England Students were still losing 13-10 early in the second half when Drew Locke missed a drop goal attempt; England Students were leading 15-13 in the 55th minute; England Students scored 15 unanswered points to win the match; England Students were still leading 15-13 midway through the second half; James Hall and Grant Pointer both had a brilliant game)

RUGBY WORLD CUP SEVENS

The Sevens, Dubai

CAPTAIN: *Ollie Phillips*

First Round - Pool 'E'

5th March HONG KONG 5 **ENGLAND** 42

[This match kicked off at 7.30pm]

(England were drawing 0-0 midway through the first half; Ben Gollings played as a scrum half in the absence of Kevin Barrett, who was sent to the sin-bin in the 4th minute; England were still drawing 0-0 immediately afterwards when a lineout overthrow by Ben Gollings led directly to a try by Marc Goosen, thus 5 points were preventable; England were losing 5-0 in the 6th minute when Tom Biggs scored a brilliant 70 metre solo try; England were leading 7-5 just before half-time when Tom Biggs had a great try-scoring chance but was brilliantly tackled into touch at the corner flag by Rowan Varty; England were leading 7-5 at half-time; Tom Varndell came on as a replacement for Tom Biggs at the start of the second half; England were still leading 7-5 in the 9th minute when Tom Varndell scored a superb 86 metre solo try with his first touch of the ball!; England were leading 21-5 midway through the second half; England were still leading 21-5 with 2 minutes remaining when Ben Gollings scored after he wrong-footed the Hong Kong defence with a brilliant sidestep; England were leading 28-5 with 1 minute remaining when Josh Drauniniu scored a superb 47 metre solo try; England scored 42 unanswered points to win the match; Ben Gollings scored 22 points in this match)

6th March TUNISIA 24 **ENGLAND** 26

[This match kicked off at 11.22am]

(Tom Varndell scored in the 1st minute!; England scored 19 unanswered points to win the match; England were leading 19-0 just before half-time; England were leading 19-7 at half-time; England were leading 26-7 early in the second half; England were leading 26-17 in the last minute; Tunisia were allowed to score 17 unanswered points)

6th March KENYA 7 **ENGLAND** 26

[This match kicked off at 7.04pm]

(England were drawing 0-0 in the 3rd minute when Ben Gollings put up a brilliant cross-kick, but Tom Varndell was then deceived by the bounce of the ball while the Kenyan line was at his mercy; England were still drawing 0-0 immediately afterwards when Kevin Barrett scored after Ben Gollings threw a brilliant reverse pass; England were leading 7-0 midway through the first half; England were still leading 7-0 in the 6th minute when collectively poor tackling allowed Humphrey Kayange to score, thus 7 points were preventable; England were drawing 7-7 just before half-time when Tom Varndell scored a superb 71 metre solo try; England were leading 12-7 at half-time; England were still leading 12-7 in the 9th minute when Isoa Damu scored a brilliant 42 metre solo try; England were leading 19-7 midway through the second half when Isoa Damu powered through 4 attempted tackles to score another try under the posts)

Quarter-Final

7th March SAMOA 31 **ENGLAND*** 26 aet

[This match kicked off at 1.50pm]

(England made a number of handling errors in this match; Lolo Lui scored a try in the 1st minute that should not have been given because Uale Mai knocked the ball forward from the base of an England scrum!; England were losing 7-0 in the 3rd minute when Tom Varndell scored a brilliant 63 metre solo try; England were drawing 7-7 midway

***through the second half when Alatasi Tupou scored after Ben Gollings missed a tackle on Lolo Lui; England were losing 14-7 in the 5th minute when Rob Vickerman threw a poor pass out of the tackle which enabled Alafoti Fa'osiliva to instigate an attack that culminated in a try by Uale Mai, thus 2 tries and 14 points were preventable; England were losing 21-7 at half-time; England were still losing 21-7 in the 10th minute when Tom Varndell scored another brilliant 47 metre solo try; England were losing 21-12 midway through the second half; England were still losing 21-12 with 2 minutes of normal time remaining when Ollie Phillips chipped ahead and followed up to clearly ground the ball on the tryline, but the referee unaccountably awarded Samoa a scrum instead; Ollie Phillips scored immediately afterwards from the aforementioned Samoan scrum!; England were losing 21-19 with 1 minute of normal time remaining when Uale Mai kicked ahead and then illegally prevented Kevin Barrett from regaining his feet with the ball, but the referee inexplicably ignored this infringement and penalised Kevin Barrett for not releasing the ball after the tackle, which allowed Uale Mai to take a quick tap penalty and pass to Alafoti Fa'osiliva who then went on to score, thus 2 tries and 12 points were unlawful; England were losing 26-19 when the full-time hooter sounded, but the referee wrongly adjudged that the ball was still in play and Josh Drauniniu was able to score a superb 37 metre solo try under the posts which Ben Gollings then converted to send the game into sudden death extra time; England were drawing 26-26 in the first minute of sudden death extra time and pressing in attack when they unaccountably twice kicked away possession in a vain attempt to score a try; England were still drawing 26-26 in the second minute of sudden death extra time when Ben Gollings inexplicably encroached offside at a ruck in front of his own line and the referee consequently signalled an advantage to Samoa, at which point the England defence momentarily stopped which allowed Jerry Meafou to gather a loose ball and instigate a move that led directly to a match-winning try by Simaika Mikaele!*)**

JEAN-CLAUDE BAQUÉ SHIELD MATCH

CAPTAIN: *Liam Wordley*

15th Mar **ENGLAND COUNTIES*** 19 FRANCE AMATEURS 27

Twickenham

[*This match kicked off at 5.30pm; Sam Smith was the son of Simon Smith (1)*]

(*The England Counties forwards could not win any lineout ball; England Counties were losing 3-0 in the 10th minute; England Counties were still losing 3-0 in the 15th minute when some superb handling amongst the backs allowed Adam Billig to score; England Counties were leading 7-6 midway through the first half; England Counties were losing 13-7 in the 22nd minute; England Counties were losing 13-7 at half-time; England Counties were still losing 13-7 early in the second half when Luke Collins scored after James Kellard made a brilliant break; England Counties were losing 13-12 in the 57th minute; England Counties were losing 16-12 in the 58th minute when Rob Baldwin scored after Jack Harrison made a superb break; England Counties were leading 19-16 midway through the second half; England Counties were drawing 19-19 in the 66th minute; England Counties were still drawing 19-19 with 3 minutes remaining; France Amateurs were leading 22-19 with 2 minutes remaining when Guillaume Dulay scored as a direct consequence of an England Counties mistake, thus 5 points were preventable*)

BLACKHEATH 150TH ANNIVERSARY MATCH

CAPTAIN: *Paul Volley* [*Gordon Bulloch* (SC)]

18th Mar Blackheath 45 **BARBARIANS** 57

Rectory Field, Charlton Road, Blackheath

[*This match kicked off at 8.00pm; Simon Legg, Liam Wordley, James Honeyben, Matt Leek, Mark Odejobi, Sam Smith and Joe Simpson all played for Blackheath in this match, with Odejobi, Sam Smith and Joe Simpson scoring tries; Paul Volley captained Major R.V. Stanley's XV against Oxford University at Iffley Road on 17th November 2009; Nick Walshe retired in August 2011*]

(*John Dalziel scored in the 4th minute!; The Barbarians were leading 5-0 shortly afterwards when Tom White intercepted the ball and ran 80 metres to score, thus 7 points were preventable; The Barbarians were losing 14-12 midway through the first half; The Barbarians were losing 21-12 in the 25th minute; The Barbarians were leading 31-21 shortly before half-time; The Barbarians were leading 31-28 at half-time; James Lumby and Ollie Dodge came on as replacements for Paul Volley and Simon Hunt respectively at the start of the second half; The Barbarians were leading 38-28 in the 43rd minute; The Barbarians were leading 43-40 in the 52nd minute; The Barbarians were still leading 43-40 midway through the second half; The Barbarians were leading 57-40 in the 67th minute; The Barbarians were still leading 57-40 with 8 minutes remaining; Mark Lee had a brilliant game*)

OXBRIDGE TOUR TO JAPAN 2009

CAPTAIN: *Peter Clarke (1)*

28th Mar All Keio University (*JAP*) 25 **OXBRIDGE XV*** 19

Mitsuzawa Stadium, Yokohama

[*This match kicked off at 2.00pm; The Oxbridge XV named a 10 man bench selection; Chris Davies and Will Browne played for English Universities in the BUCS Home Nations Rugby Sevens at the University of Edinburgh on 15th April 2010; Joe Wheeler was the brother of Ben Wheeler and the son of Peter Wheeler; Alex Cheeseman played for Major R.V. Stanley's XV against Oxford University at Iffley Road on 19th November 2008*]

(*The Oxbridge XV was losing 3-0 in the 10th minute; The Oxbridge XV was still losing 3-0 midway through the first half; The Oxbridge XV was losing 8-0 in the 22nd minute; The Oxbridge XV was still losing 8-0 in the 38th minute when some superb handling amongst the backs allowed Chris Mahony to score; The Oxbridge XV was losing 8-5 at half-time; The Oxbridge XV was losing 13-5 in the 46th minute; The Oxbridge XV was losing 18-5 shortly afterwards; The Oxbridge XV was still losing 18-5 midway through the second half; The Oxbridge XV was losing 18-5 in the 68th minute; The Oxbridge XV was losing 18-12 with 7 minutes remaining when Sean Morris gathered a loose ball, chipped over Ryuji Oda and then followed up to score a superb 78 metre solo try; The Oxbridge XV was leading 19-18 in the closing stages*)

CATHAY PACIFIC/CREDIT SUISSE HONG KONG SEVENS

Hong Kong Stadium, Eastern Hospital Road, So Kon Po, Hong Kong

CAPTAIN: *Ben Gollings*

First Round - Pool 'B'

27th Mar CHINA 0 **ENGLAND** 54

[*This match kicked off at 5.58pm*]

(*This match was played on a wet pitch; England were drawing 0-0 in the early stages*

when Josh Drauniniu scored after Tom Varndell made a brilliant break; England were leading 28-0 at half-time; England were leading 35-0 early in the second half; England were leading 42-0 midway through the second half when Dan Caprice scored a brilliant 48 metre solo try; England were leading 47-0 with 1 minute remaining when Dan Caprice powered through to complete a hat-trick of tries on his debut)

CAPTAIN: *Ollie Phillips*

28th Mar JAPAN 0 **ENGLAND** 50

[This match kicked off at 2.10pm; England wore red shirts for this match]

(This match was played on a wet pitch; Isoa Damu scored in the 2nd minute!; England were leading 12-0 midway through the second half; England were leading 24-0 at half-time; Tom Varndell scored after just 24 seconds of the second half had been played!; England were leading 43-0 when the full-time hooter sounded, but the ball was still in play and Isoa Damu was able to score a try which Ollie Phillips then brilliantly converted to seal the match)

28th Mar WALES 19 **ENGLAND** 26

[This match kicked off at 6.34pm]

(This match was played on a wet pitch; Isoa Damu scored in the 2nd minute!; England were leading 12-0 when Ollie Phillips chipped ahead and regathered the ball to score a brilliant try; England were leading 19-0 just before half-time when some superb handling allowed Chris Cracknell to score; England scored 26 unanswered points to win the match; England were leading 26-0 at half-time; England were leading 26-7 early in the second half; England were still leading 26-7 midway through the second half; England were leading 26-12 shortly afterwards when Tom Biggs had a great try-scoring chance but was tackled into touch at the corner flag by Ifan Evans; England were still leading 26-12 in the last minute; Wales were allowed to score 19 unanswered points)

CAPTAIN: *Ben Gollings*

Quarter-Final

29th Mar FIJI 10 **ENGLAND*** 7

[This match kicked off at 1.47pm; England wore red shirts for this match]

(This match was played on a slippery pitch; Emosi Vucago scored in the 2nd minute!; England were losing 5-0 midway through the first half; England were still losing 5-0 in the 5th minute when Josh Drauniniu had a great try-scoring chance but was brilliantly tackled by Vereniki Goneva; England were losing 5-0 at half-time; England were still losing 5-0 in the 10th minute when Rob Vickerman scored after Isoa Damu made a brilliant 50 metre run; Isoa Damu had to go off shortly afterwards after he dislocated his shoulder, being replaced by James Rodwell; England were leading 7-5 midway through the second half; England were still leading 7-5 in the 12th minute when Kevin Barrett saved a certain try by tackling Orisi Sareki; England were leading 7-5 when the full-time hooter sounded, but the ball was still in play and a lack of communication between James Rodwell and Chris Cracknell saw them both attempting to tackle Vereniki Goneva, which enabled Pio Tuwai to score a match-winning try for Fiji, thus 5 points were preventable; England unaccountably failed to utilise Tom Varndell's pace on the outside; Ben Gollings increased his IRB World Sevens record to 1905 points in this tournament)

ADELAIDE SEVENS

Adelaide Oval, Adelaide

CAPTAIN: *Ollie Phillips*

First Round - Pool 'A'

3rd April AUSTRALIA 21 **ENGLAND*** 17

[This match kicked off at 8.04pm]

(Dominic Shipperley scored in the 2nd minute!; England were losing 7-0 midway through the first half when Luke Morahan scored after a poor tackle by Tom Varndell; England were losing 14-0 in the 5th minute when Tom Varndell scored a brilliant 57 metre solo try; England were losing 14-12 shortly before half-time when Ben Gollings missed an eminently kickable conversion attempt; England were losing 14-12 at half-time; Kevin Barrett went off injured in the second half, being replaced by Josh Drauniniu; England were still losing 14-12 midway through the second half; England were losing 14-12 with 2 minutes remaining when Ollie Phillips scored after Dan Caprice threw a brilliant pass out of the tackle; England scored 17 unanswered points; England were leading 17-14 in the final minute when collectively poor tackling allowed Shaun Foley to score, thus 2 tries and 14 points were preventable)

4th April PORTUGAL 0 **ENGLAND** 29

[This match kicked off at 12.59pm; Kevin Barrett unavailable due to injury; England only had 9 fit players; Mika Taufaao was drafted in as emergency bench cover]

(England were leading 12-0 at half-time; England were leading 24-0 with 1 minute remaining when James Rodwell scored a brilliant 51 metre solo try)

4th April SAMOA 24 **ENGLAND*** 24

[This match kicked off at 5.04pm; Kevin Barrett unavailable due to injury; England only had 9 fit players; After this match Tom Varndell was found guilty of a dangerous tackle on Alafoti Fa'osiliva and thus duly banned for 1 game]

(England were losing 5-0 in the early stages; England were drawing 5-5 midway through the first half; England were still drawing 5-5 in the 7th minute when Afa Aiono scored after Josh Drauniniu missed a tackle on Lolo Lui, thus 7 points were preventable; England were losing 12-5 just before half-time when Tom Varndell scored a brilliant 23 metre solo try; England were losing 12-10 at half-time; England were still losing 12-10 in the 8th minute when Ollie Phillips chipped ahead and regathered the ball to score a brilliant try; England were leading 17-12 midway through the second half; England were losing 19-17 with 1 minute of normal time remaining; England were drawing 24-24 in the first minute of injury time when Lolo Lui missed a difficult conversion attempt for Samoa with the last kick of the match!)

Quarter-Final

5th April FIJI 40 **ENGLAND** 0

[This match kicked off at 1.12pm; Kevin Barrett unavailable due to injury; Tom Varndell unavailable due to suspension; England only had 8 players available!]

(England were drawing 0-0 in the 2nd minute and pressing in attack when Josh Drauniniu's grubber kick rebounded off the boot of Osea Kolinisau, who gathered the resulting loose ball and instigated a counter-attack that led directly to a try by Nasoni Roko!; England were losing 7-0 midway through the first half; England were still losing 7-0 in the 6th minute when Josh Drauniniu dropped the ball into the arms of Vereniki Goneva who then ran 30 metres to score; England were losing 14-0 just before half-time and pressing in attack when they allowed the ball to go loose at a ruck situation which allowed Waqa Kotobalavu to instigate another counter-attack that led directly to a try by Seremaia Burotu, thus 3 tries and 19 points were preventable; England were

***losing 19-0 at half-time; Dan Caprice came on as a replacement for Josh Drauniniu at the start of the second half; England were still losing 19-0 in the 9th minute; England were losing 33-0 midway through the second half; England were still losing 33-0 in the last minute; This was England's heaviest defeat against Fiji since 2000!*)**

[Plate Semi-Final:]

[5th April NEW ZEALAND 14 **ENGLAND** 21]

[*This match kicked off at 3.34pm; Kevin Barrett unavailable due to injury; England only had 9 fit players*]

(*England were drawing 7-7 in the 3rd minute; England were losing 14-7 midway through the first half; England were still losing 14-7 in the 5th minute when some superb handling allowed Chris Cracknell to score; England were drawing 14-14 at half-time; England were still drawing 14-14 midway through the first half; England were drawing 14-14 with 3 minutes remaining when Dan Caprice scored a brilliant 97 metre solo try to win the match*)

[Plate Final:]

[5th April AUSTRALIA 19 **ENGLAND** 24 aet]

[*This match kicked off at 5.50pm; Kevin Barrett unavailable due to injury; England only had 9 fit players*]

(*Henry Vanderglas scored after just 10 seconds had been played, with Richard Kingi then missing the eminently kickable conversion attempt for Australia!; Dan Caprice went off injured in the first quarter, being replaced by Josh Drauniniu; England were losing 5-0 midway through the first half; England were still losing 5-0 in the 5th minute when Tom Varndell scored a brilliant 77 metre solo try; England were leading 14-5 just before half-time when some superb handling allowed James Rodwell to score; England were leading 19-5 at half-time; England were still leading 19-5 in the 10th minute; England were leading 19-12 midway through the second half; England were still leading 19-12 with 2 minutes of normal time remaining when Richard Kingi scored after a poor tackle by Ben Gollings, thus 7 points were preventable; England were drawing 19-19 in the first minute of sudden death extra time when a brilliant run by Tom Varndell enabled Ben Gollings to score a match-winning try; Ben Gollings increased his IRB World Sevens record to 1935 points in this tournament*)

ENGLAND STUDENTS MATCHES

CAPTAIN: *Phil Ellis*

11th April NETHERLANDS 7 **ENGLAND STUDENTS** 68

Nationaal Rugby Centrum, Sportpark "De Eendracht", Bok de Korverweg, Amsterdam

[*This match kicked off at 2.30pm; Tom Hockedy unavailable due to injury*]

(*England Students were leading 3-0 in the early stages; England Students were leading 20-0 midway through the first half; Grant Pointer went off injured in the 21st minute, being replaced by David Butler; England Students were leading 32-0 at half-time; England Students were leading 37-0 early in the second half; England Students were leading 49-0 midway through the second half; England Students were leading 68-0 in the last minute of normal time; England Students scored 68 unanswered points to win the match*)

2nd May **ENGLAND STUDENTS** 65 COMBINED SERVICES U23 (*SER*) 8

Twickenham

[*This match kicked off at 12.00pm and was a curtain raiser game for the Army v Navy*

match; Tom Hockedy unavailable due to injury; Toby Henry played for Major R.V. Stanley's XV against Oxford University at Iffley Road on 17th November 2009]
(Phil Burgess scored in the 3rd minute!; Some superb handling allowed Phil Burgess to score another try just before half-time; England Students were leading 20-3 at half-time; England Students were still leading 20-3 early in the second half when Alan Awcock scored a brilliant solo try; England Students were leading 27-8 in the 55th minute; England Students scored 38 unanswered points to seal the match)

LONDON FLOODLIT SEVENS

Rosslyn Park FC, Priory Lane, Upper Richmond Road, Roehampton
CAPTAIN: *Ollie Phillips*
First Round - Pool 'D'

6th May	Loughborough University	14	**HELP FOR HEROES VII**	31

[This match kicked off at 7.20pm]

6th May	British Army (*SER*)	7	**HELP FOR HEROES VII**	31

[This match kicked off at 8.40pm]
Semi-Final

6th May	Saracens	7	**HELP FOR HEROES VII**	26

[This match kicked off at 9.20pm; Dan Caprice played for Saracens in this match]
Final

6th May	Harlequins	10	**HELP FOR HEROES VII**	31

[This match kicked off at 10.30pm; Gus Qasevakatini was drafted in from the British Army team as emergency bench cover; Seb Jewell, Sam Smith and George Lowe played for Harlequins in this match]
(Ollie Phillips scored a brilliant 50 metre solo try in the early stages!; The Help for Heroes VII was leading 7-0 midway through the first half; The Help for Heroes VII was leading 19-5 at half-time; The Help for Heroes VII was leading 19-10 early in the second half; Josh Drauniniu went off injured in this match, being replaced by Gus Qasevakatini)

DAN JAMES MEMORIAL MATCH

CAPTAIN: *Calum Clark*

13th May	Loughborough University	23	**ENGLAND U20 XV***	20

Loughborough Students RFC, Loughborough University, Loughborough
[This match kicked off at 7.30pm; Tom Casson and Seb Stegmann in original squad of 26 but withdrew due to injury; The England U20 XV named a 9 man bench selection; Courtney Lawes, Josh Ovens, Ben Youngs and Tom Homer all in original squad of 26 but withdrew; Jacob Rowan, Jordi Pasqualin, Jack Cobden and Will Hurrell were not part of the original 26 man squad; Jason Phipps, Jon Aston, Rob Wood, Simon Pitfield, Phil Burgess, Will Chudleigh, Dave Vincent, Grant Pointer and Paul Trendell all played for Loughborough University in this match, with Pointer scoring 2 penalty goals]
(Both sides agreed to allow unlimited substitutions in this match; The England U20 XV only had one training session to prepare for this match!; The England U20 XV made a number of handling errors; The England U20 XV was losing 3-0 in the early stages; The England U20 XV was leading 7-3 midway through the first half; The England U20 XV was still leading 7-3 shortly afterwards when a poor defensive alignment allowed James Golledge to score, thus 7 points were preventable; Loughborough University were allowed to score 14 unanswered points to win the match; The England U20 XV was losing 17-10 in the 30th minute; The England U20 XV was still losing 17-10 shortly

***before half-time when it was awarded a close-range penalty in front of the posts, but Calum Clark took the option of a scrum in a vain attempt to score a try; The England U20 XV was losing 17-10 at half-time; Rory Clegg came on as a replacement for Rob Miller at the start of the second half; The England U20 XV was losing 17-13 early in the second half; The England U20 XV was losing 20-13 midway through the second half; The England U20 XV was losing 23-13 with 4 minutes of normal time remaining; The England U20 XV was still losing 23-13 in the sixth minute of injury time when Luke Eves scored a consolation try with the last move of the match*)**

EMIRATES AIRLINE LONDON SEVENS

Twickenham

CAPTAIN: *Ollie Phillips*

First Round - Pool 'B'

23rd May **ENGLAND** 20 FRANCE 14

[*This match kicked off at 1.47pm*]

(*Kevin Barrett scored after just 58 seconds had been played, with Ollie Phillips then missing the eminently kickable conversion attempt!; England were leading 5-0 in the 4th minute when Thomas Combezou scored after a poor tackle by Ollie Phillips; England were losing 7-5 midway through the first half; England were still losing 7-5 in the 5th minute when Chris Cracknell managed to pass the ball after his shorts had been pulled down and Ollie Phillips went on to score, but then hit the left-hand post with the eminently kickable conversion attempt!; England were leading 10-7 shortly before half-time when they created and then squandered an overlap; England were leading 10-7 at half-time; England were leading 15-7 in the 8th minute when Ollie Phillips missed an eminently kickable conversion attempt; England were still leading 15-7 midway through the second half; England were leading 15-7 with 2 minutes remaining when Ben Gollings scored a brilliant try but then missed the eminently kickable conversion attempt!; England were leading 20-7 in the last minute when Paul Albaladejo scored after a poor tackle by Greg Barden, thus 2 tries and 14 points were preventable; Kevin Barrett went off injured in the final seconds, which reduced England to 6 men because they had already used up their permitted three replacements*)

CAPTAIN: *Ben Gollings*

23rd May **ENGLAND** 61 GEORGIA 0

[*This match kicked off at 4.53pm*]

(*England were drawing 0-0 midway through the first half when Ben Gollings broke from the base of a maul to score; England were leading 7-0 in the 5th minute when Tom Biggs chipped ahead and regathered the ball to score a brilliant try; England were leading 12-0 in the 6th minute when Micky Young followed up his own grubber kick to score a superb try; England were leading 19-0 just before half-time when James Rodwell scored after Micky Young created an overlap; England were leading 26-0 at half-time; England were leading 31-0 in the 8th minute when Ben Gollings scored a brilliant conversion from the left touchline; England were leading 40-0 in the 10th minute; England were leading 47-0 midway through the second half; England were leading 59-0 in the last minute when Ben Gollings scored a brilliant conversion from the left touchline; Ben Gollings scored 21 points in this match*)

CAPTAIN: *Ollie Phillips*

23rd May **ENGLAND** 31 SAMOA 14

[*This match kicked off at 8.33pm*]

(Kevin Barrett scored in the 2nd minute after Ben Gollings threw a brilliant reverse pass!; England were leading 5-0 midway through the first half when collectively poor tackling allowed Reupena Levasa to score; England were losing 7-5 in the 6th minute when Ben Gollings scored a brilliant try; England were leading 12-7 just before half-time when some superb handling allowed Rob Vickerman to score; England were leading 17-7 at half-time; England were still leading 17-7 in the 8th minute when Mikaele Pesamino scored after a poor tackle by Kevin Barrett, thus 2 tries and 14 points were preventable; England were leading 17-14 in the 10th minute when Micky Young scored after he wrong-footed Uale Mai with a brilliant sidestep; England were leading 24-14 midway through the second half; England were still leading 24-14 with 2 minutes remaining; England scored 14 unanswered points to clinch the match)

Quarter-Final

24th May **ENGLAND** 26 AUSTRALIA 12

[*This match kicked off at 1.34pm*]

(James Rodwell scored in the 2nd minute!; England were leading 7-0 midway through the first half when James Rodwell crossed the tryline but the move was disallowed after the referee adjudged that there had been an accidental offside; England were still leading 7-0 in the 5th minute when Tom Biggs scored after he wrong-footed Francis Fainifo with a brilliant sidestep; England were leading 14-0 just before half-time when Ben Gollings chipped ahead and followed up to score a brilliant try but then missed the eminently kickable conversion attempt!; England scored 19 unanswered points to win the match; England were leading 19-0 at half-time; England were still leading 19-0 in the 9th minute when Kevin Barrett saved a certain try by tackling Henry Vanderglas into touch; England were leading 19-0 in the 10th minute when Kevin Barrett saved another certain try by getting back and grounding the ball before Francis Fainifo could reach it; England were leading 19-7 midway through the second half; England were leading 26-7 in the final minute when Shaun Foley scored after a poor tackle by Neil Starling, thus 5 points were preventable)

Semi-Final

24th May **ENGLAND** 26 SCOTLAND 12

[*This match kicked off at 5.06pm*]

(Ollie Phillips scored a brilliant 45 metre solo try after just 71 seconds had been played!; England were leading 7-0 in the 3rd minute when Kevin Barrett wasted a great try-scoring opportunity by dropping the ball while the Scottish line was at his mercy; Tom Biggs wrong-footed the Scottish defence with a brilliant sidestep to score a try which Ben Gollings then converted to give England a 14-0 lead midway through the first half; England were still leading 14-0 in the 6th minute; England were leading 14-5 just before half-time; England were leading 14-12 at half-time; Rob Vickerman went off injured at half-time, being replaced by Greg Barden; England were still leading 14-12 in the 9th minute when Ollie Phillips reached the Scottish tryline but then allowed Greg Barden to score instead!; England were leading 21-12 midway through the second half; England were still leading 21-12 with 2 minutes remaining when Greg Barden had a great try-scoring chance but was superbly tackled into touch at the corner flag by Colin Gregor; England were leading 26-12 with 1 minute remaining when Ben Gollings hit the left-hand post with an eminently kickable conversion attempt)

CAPTAIN: *Ollie Phillips* [*Ben Gollings*]
Final

24th May **ENGLAND** 31 NEW ZEALAND 26 aet

[This match kicked off at 6.52pm]
(Kurt Baker scored in the 2nd minute!; England were losing 7-0 midway through the first half when Julian Savea scored after a poor tackle by Ollie Phillips; England were losing 14-0 in the 7th minute when Julian Savea scored another try after James Rodwell put Kevin Barrett under severe pressure by tapping the ball back at the restart, thus 2 tries and 12 points were preventable; New Zealand were allowed to score 19 unanswered points; England were losing 19-0 at half-time; England were still losing 19-0 in the 11th minute when Tom Biggs broke through but was then brilliantly tackled by Tomasi Cama (2); Micky Young came on as a replacement for Ollie Phillips in the 12th minute, with Ben Gollings then switching from fly half to centre to accommodate Micky Young; Uche Oduoza came on as a replacement for Tom Biggs in the 13th minute and scored immediately afterwards with his first touch of the ball!; England were losing 19-7 midway through the second half when Micky Young powered through 2 attempted tackles to score; England were drawing 19-19 with 2 minutes of normal time remaining; Dan Norton came on as a replacement for Kevin Barrett in the last minute of normal time, with Ben Gollings then moving from centre to fly half to accommodate Dan Norton and Micky Young switching from fly half to scrum half to accommodate Gollings; England were losing 26-19 when the full-time hooter sounded, but the ball was still in play and Dan Norton was able to score a brilliant 61 metre solo try which Ben Gollings then converted to send the game into sudden death extra time; England were drawing 26-26 in the fourth minute of sudden death extra time when Micky Young scored after Rob Vickerman took a strike against the head during a New Zealand five metre scrum!; Ben Gollings scored 65 points in this tournament and thus increased his overall IRB World Sevens record to 2000)

EMIRATES AIRLINE EDINBURGH SEVENS

Murrayfield
CAPTAIN: *Ollie Phillips*
First Round - Pool 'C'

30th May SCOTLAND 33 **ENGLAND*** 17

[This match kicked off at 12.09pm]
(John Houston scored in the 2nd minute after a poor tackle by James Rodwell!; England were losing 7-0 midway through the first half when collectively poor tackling allowed Greig Laidlaw to score; Scotland were allowed to score 21 unanswered points to win the match; England were losing 21-0 just before half-time; England were losing 21-5 at half-time; England were losing 21-10 in the 8th minute; England were still losing 21-10 in the 10th minute when Ben Gollings took a quick tap penalty and ran 76 metres to score a brilliant solo try; England were losing 21-17 midway through the second half when further collectively poor tackling allowed Roddy Grant to score; England were losing 28-17 in the last minute when Andrew Turnbull scored after a poor tackle by Dan Norton, thus 4 tries and 26 points were preventable)

30th May CANADA 12 **ENGLAND** 26

[This match kicked off at 3.35pm]
(England were leading 5-0 midway through the first half; England were still leading 5-0 in the 5th minute; England were losing 7-5 at half-time; England were leading 12-7

***early in the second half; England were still leading 12-7 midway through the second half; England were leading 19-7 with 2 minutes remaining when Ben Gollings scored a brilliant 57 metre solo try; England scored 21 unanswered points to win the match; England were leading 26-7 in the final minute; Rob Vickerman injured playing in the match*)**

30th May KENYA 21 **ENGLAND*** 14

[*This match kicked off at 5.50pm; Rob Vickerman unavailable due to injury*]

(*England were drawing 0-0 in the 4th minute when collectively poor tackling allowed Collins Injera to score; England were losing 7-0 midway through the second half; England were still losing 7-0 in the 5th minute when Biko Adema scored after a poor tackle by Ben Gollings; Kenya were allowed to score 14 unanswered points to win the match; England were losing 14-0 in the 7th minute when Greg Barden scored after Micky Young made a brilliant 40 metre break; England were losing 14-7 immediately afterwards when both Uche Oduoza and Micky Young dropped the ball in the act of scoring in quick succession; England were losing 14-7 at half-time; England were still losing 14-7 in the 8th minute when Ollie Phillips put in a brilliant chip-kick, but he was then deceived by the bounce of the ball while the Kenyan line was at his mercy; England were losing 14-7 midway through the second half; England were still losing 14-7 in the 11th minute and pressing in attack when James Rodwell's pass was intercepted by Lavin Asego who then ran 47 metres to score, thus 3 tries and 21 points were preventable; Dan Norton came on as a replacement for Neil Starling with 2 minutes of normal time remaining, with Ollie Phillips then switching from centre to hooker to accommodate Dan Norton and Greg Barden moving from hooker to tight-head prop to accommodate Ollie Phillips; England were losing 21-7 in the last minute of normal time when Tom Biggs crossed the tryline, but the move was disallowed as he was adjudged to have put a knee into touch; England were still losing 21-7 when the full-time hooter sounded, but the ball was still in play and Ollie Phillips was able to power through 3 attempted tackles to score a consolation try*)

CAPTAIN: *Ben Gollings* [*Ollie Phillips*]

[Bowl Quarter-Final:]

[31st May GEORGIA 7 **ENGLAND** 31]

[*This match kicked off at 10.49am; Chris Cracknell and Rob Vickerman unavailable due to injury*]

(*England were drawing 0-0 midway through the first half when Alexander Nizharadze was awarded a try which should not have been given because it was unclear whether he had grounded the ball properly, thus 7 points were unlawful; England were losing 7-0 in the 6th minute when Dan Norton scored a brilliant 81 metre solo try; England were drawing 7-7 in the 7th minute when James Rodwell scored a superb 55 metre solo try; England were leading 14-7 at half-time; England were still leading 14-7 in the 11th minute; England were leading 19-7 midway through the second half; Ollie Phillips came on as a replacement for Ben Gollings with 2 minutes remaining; England were leading 26-7 with 1 minute remaining when Uche Oduoza scored after Ollie Phillips brilliantly created space, with Ollie Phillips then hitting the right-hand post with the difficult conversion attempt; England scored 31 unanswered points to win the match*)

CAPTAIN: *Ollie Phillips*

[Bowl Semi-Final:]

[31st May PORTUGAL 7 **ENGLAND** 31]

[*This match kicked off at 2.37pm; Chris Cracknell and Rob Vickerman unavailable due to injury*]

(England were drawing 0-0 in the 4th minute when Uche Oduoza scored a brilliant 41 metre solo try; England were leading 7-0 midway through the first half; England were still leading 7-0 in the 6th minute when Uche Oduoza powered through 3 attempted tackles to score another try; England scored 17 unanswered points to win the match; England were leading 17-0 just before half-time when Ben Gollings hit the left-hand post with a difficult conversion attempt; England were leading 17-0 at half-time; England were still leading 17-0 midway through the second half when Pedro Silva scored after a poor tackle by Ben Gollings, thus 7 points were preventable; England were leading 17-7 with 1 minute remaining when Ben Gollings scored after Tom Biggs made a brilliant 66 metre run; Ben Gollings went off injured after kicking the subsequent conversion, being replaced by Micky Young; England were leading 24-7 immediately afterwards when Tom Biggs scored after he intercepted a long pass from Sergio Franco)

[Bowl Final:]

[31st May FRANCE 15 **ENGLAND** 26]

[This match kicked off at 5.25pm; Chris Cracknell and Rob Vickerman unavailable due to injury]

(Paul Dabrin scored in the 2nd minute!; England were leading 7-5 midway through the first half; England were still leading 7-5 in the 5th minute when collectively poor tackling allowed Joffrey Michel to score, thus 5 points were preventable; England were losing 10-7 at half-time; England were leading 14-10 in the 8th minute; England were losing 15-14 midway through the second half when Uche Oduoza scored a brilliant 80 metre solo try under the posts, with Ollie Phillips then having the eminently kickable conversion attempt go underneath the crossbar!; Tom Biggs came on as a replacement for Neil Starling with 2 minutes remaining, with Uche Oduoza then switching from wing to prop to accommodate Biggs; England were leading 19-15 in the final minute when some superb handling allowed Ollie Phillips to score a try to clinch the match; Ben Gollings increased his IRB World Sevens record to 2042 points in this tournament)

BRITISH & IRISH LIONS TOUR TO SOUTH AFRICA 2009

CAPTAIN: *Paul O'Connell* (IR)

20th Jun SOUTH AFRICA 26 **BRITISH & IRISH LIONS*** 21

ABSA Stadium, Durban

[This match kicked off at 3.00pm; Andy Sheridan and James Hook unavailable due to injury; John Hayes and Tim Payne joined the tour after this match]

(The Lions scrum was put under severe pressure in the first half; Stephen Jones (2) missed a 36 metre penalty goal attempt from the left touchline in the 3rd minute!; The Lions were losing 7-0 in the 5th minute; The Lions were still losing 7-0 in the 8th minute when Ugo Monye reached the tryline and appeared to score but the video referee adjudged that the ball had hit Jean de Villiers' arm rather than the ground; The Lions were losing 10-0 in the 11th minute; The Lions were still losing 10-0 in the 16th minute when Stephen Jones (2) missed an eminently kickable 26 metre penalty goal attempt; The Lions were losing 13-0 midway through the first half; The Lions were still losing 13-0 in the 23rd minute when some superb handling allowed Tom Croft to score; The Lions were losing 13-7 in the 26th minute when Tommy Bowe crossed the tryline but the move was disallowed after the referee adjudged that Lee Byrne had illegally obstructed Bryan Habana; The Lions were losing 16-7 in the 33rd minute; Lee Byrne went off injured in the 38th minute, being replaced by Rob Kearney; The Lions were losing 19-7 at half-time; Adam Jones (2) came on as a replacement for Phil

Vickery in the 45th minute; The Lions were still losing 19-7 in the 46th minute when Heinrich Brussow was allowed to score from a rolling maul, thus 7 points were preventable; The Lions were losing 26-7 in the 50th minute when Mike Phillips (2) reached the tryline but then lost the ball in the act of scoring; Matthew Rees came on as a replacement for Lee Mears immediately afterwards; The Lions were still losing 26-7 in the 55th minute when Tommy Bowe broke through but then ran out of support; The Lions were losing 26-7 midway through the second half; Martyn Williams came on as a replacement for David Wallace in the 67th minute; The Lions were still losing 26-7 in the 68th minute; The Lions were losing 26-14 with 8 minutes remaining when Ugo Monye had a great try-scoring chance but was brilliantly dispossessed by Morné Steyn in front of the South African line; The Lions were still losing 26-14 with 5 minutes remaining when Mike Phillips (2) dummied his way through to score a superb try; The Lions were losing 26-21 with 3 minutes remaining when Jamie Roberts' intended scoring pass to Tommy Bowe was intercepted by Jaque Fourie)

27th Jun SOUTH AFRICA 28 **BRITISH & IRISH LIONS*** 25

Loftus Versfeld Stadium, Pretoria

[*This match kicked off at 3.00pm; Nathan Hines unavailable due to suspension; Gethin Jenkins, Adam Jones (2) and Brian O'Driscoll returned home injured after this match*]

(This match was played at high altitude; The referee unaccountably decided not to send off Schalk Burger after he gouged Luke Fitzgerald's eyes after just 20 seconds had been played!; The Lions were leading 3-0 in the 3rd minute; A superb pass out of the tackle by Stephen Jones (2) enabled Rob Kearney to score a try in the right corner which Stephen Jones (2) then brilliantly converted to give the Lions a 10-0 lead in the 7th minute; The Lions were still leading 10-0 in the 12th minute when a poor defensive alignment allowed J.P. Pietersen to score; The Lions were leading 13-5 midway through the first half; The Lions were still leading 13-5 in the 22nd minute when they created and then squandered an overlap; Andy Sheridan came on as a temporary blood replacement for Gethin Jenkins in the 23rd minute; The Lions were still leading 13-5 in the 26th minute when Rob Kearney missed a speculative 51 metre drop goal attempt; The Lions were leading 16-5 in the 36th minute; The Lions were still leading 16-5 just before half-time; The Lions were leading 16-8 at half-time; Gethin Jenkins went off injured in the 46th minute, being replaced by Andy Sheridan; Adam Jones (2) had to go off at the same time after he dislocated his shoulder when Bakkies Botha entered a ruck in a dangerous manner, being replaced by Alun-Wyn Jones with the referee subsequently ordering uncontested scrums in the 51st minute; The Lions were leading 19-8 midway through the second half; The Lions were leading 19-15 in the 63rd minute; Brian O'Driscoll went off injured in the 65th minute after being concussed, being replaced by Shane Williams with Tommy Bowe then switching from right wing to centre to accommodate Shane Williams; Jamie Roberts went off injured in the 68th minute, being replaced by Ronan O'Gara with Stephen Jones (2) then switching from fly half to centre to accommodate O'Gara; The Lions were leading 19-18 in the 70th minute; Ronan O'Gara was concussed attempting to tackle Pierre Spies (2) with 6 minutes of normal time remaining but elected to remain on the pitch; The Lions were leading 22-18 immediately afterwards when Jaque Fourie scored after a poor tackle by Ronan O'Gara, thus 2 tries and 12 points were preventable; The Lions were losing 25-22 with 2 minutes of normal time remaining when Stephen Jones (2) scored a superb 33 metre penalty goal; The Lions were drawing 25-25 in the first minute of injury time when Morné Steyn scored a brilliant 53 metre penalty goal with the last kick of the match to win the game and the series for South Africa; Tommy Bowe injured playing in

the match; Stephen Jones (2) scored 20 points in this match; Simon Shaw had a brilliant game)

4th July SOUTH AFRICA 9 **BRITISH & IRISH LIONS** 28

Coca-Cola Park, Johannesburg

[*This match kicked off at 3.00pm; The Coca-Cola Stadium was previously called Ellis Park Stadium; Ronan O'Gara and Jamie Roberts unavailable due to injury; After this match Simon Shaw was found guilty of kneeing Fourie du Preez and thus duly banned for 2 weeks; Phil Vickery retired due to injury in October 2010; Harry Ellis retired due to injury in July 2010*]

(*This match was played at high altitude; Stephen Jones (2) missed a kickable 45 metre penalty goal attempt in the 4th minute!; The Lions were leading 3-0 in the 9th minute; The Lions were drawing 3-3 midway through the first half; The Lions were still drawing 3-3 in the 25th minute when Jamie Heaslip made a brilliant run which enabled Shane Williams to score, with Stephen Jones (2) then missing the conversion attempt from in front of the posts after he was forced to try a drop-kick when the ball fell off the kicking tee as he began his original run up!; Tom Croft came on as a temporary blood replacement for Joe Worsley in the 31st minute; Riki Flutey followed up his own chip-kick and brilliantly flicked the ball to Shane Williams who then went on to score another try which Stephen Jones (2) then converted to give the Lions a 15-3 lead in the 33rd minute; The Lions scored 12 unanswered points to win the match; Matthew Rees went off injured in the 37th minute, being replaced by Ross Ford; The Lions were still leading 15-3 just before half-time; The Lions were leading 15-6 at half-time; The Lions were still leading 15-6 in the 52nd minute when Tommy Bowe saved a certain try by dislodging the ball as he tackled Zane Kirchner; The Lions were leading 15-6 in the 54th minute when Ugo Monye scored a 77 metre interception try; Riki Flutey went off injured in the 55th minute, being replaced by Harry Ellis with Mike Phillips (2) then switching from scrum half to the unfamiliar position of centre to accommodate Harry Ellis; John Hayes came on as a replacement for Phil Vickery in the 56th minute; The Lions were leading 22-6 midway through the second half; The Lions were still leading 22-6 in the 62nd minute when Rob Kearney missed a speculative 53 metre penalty goal attempt; The Lions were leading 22-6 in the 66th minute when Francois Steyn missed a speculative 61 metre drop goal attempt for South Africa!; Tom Croft came on as a replacement for Joe Worsley immediately afterwards; The Lions were leading 22-9 in the 68th minute; The Lions were leading 28-9 with 4 minutes of normal time remaining when Tommy Bowe saved another certain try by tackling Odwa Ndungane into touch at the corner flag; The Lions equalled their highest ever points total against South Africa!*)

BARBARIANS MATCH

CAPTAIN: *Steve Borthwick* [England XV]

CAPTAIN: *Martin Corry* [Barbarians]

30th May **ENGLAND XV*** 26 **BARBARIANS** 33

Twickenham

[ENGLAND XV: [*This match kicked off at 4.15pm; Matt Tait and Mark Cueto unavailable due to injury*]

(*Andy Goode missed a kickable 40 metre penalty goal attempt in the 2nd minute!; The England XV was losing 0-0 in the 14th minute when Iain Balshaw was awarded a try which should not have been given as he was in front of Josh Lewsey when the latter kicked ahead, thus 7 points were unlawful; The England XV was losing 7-0 in the 17th*

minute when Jamie Noon broke through but was then brilliantly tap-tackled by Glen Jackson; The England XV was still losing 7-0 midway through the first half; The England XV was losing 14-0 in the 22nd minute; The England XV was still losing 14-0 in the 32nd minute when Ben Foden powered through 2 attempted tackles to score; The England XV was losing 14-5 in the 37th minute and pressing in attack when Danny Care juggled the ball and then volleyed it into the arms of Delon Armitage, but the move was disallowed after the referee adjudged that the ball had consequently been knocked-on!; The England XV was losing 14-5 at half-time; Jamie Noon went off injured at half-time, being replaced by Tom May; The England XV was losing 19-5 in the 46th minute when Iain Balshaw scored another try after Gordon D'Arcy powered through some collectively poor tackling; The England XV was losing 26-5 in the 51st minute when Danny Care had a great try-scoring chance but was superbly tap-tackled by Schalk Brits; The England XV was still losing 26-5 immediately afterwards when a poor defensive alignment allowed Gordon D'Arcy to score, thus 2 tries and 14 points were preventable; The Barbarians were allowed to score 19 unanswered points to seal the match; Danny Care went off injured in the 53rd minute, being replaced by Paul Hodgson; The England XV was losing 33-5 immediately afterwards when Delon Armitage saved a certain try by brilliantly tackling Schalk Brits into touch in-goal; Steffon Armitage came on as a replacement for Lewis Moody in the 54th minute; The England XV was still losing 33-5 in the 57th minute when Jordan Turner-Hall scored after Andy Goode put in a superb chip-kick; The England XV was losing 33-12 midway through the second half; Steve Thompson (2) came on as a replacement for Dylan Hartley in the 61st minute; The England XV was still losing 33-12 in the 70th minute when Tom May scored after Andy Goode put in a brilliant grubber kick; The England XV was losing 33-19 with 7 minutes remaining when Matt Banahan scored after Andy Goode put up a superb cross-kick; The England XV scored 21 unanswered points)]
[BARBARIANS: [*This match kicked off at 4.15pm; Iestyn Thomas (2) in original squad of 24 but withdrew due to injury, being replaced by Clarke Dermody; Justin Harrison in original squad of 24 but withdrew on 21st May 2009 after he announced his retirement, being replaced by Phil Waugh; Dimitri Yachvili in original squad of 24 but withdrew as he was now required to join the French tour of New Zealand and Australia, being replaced by Chris Whitaker; Luke McAlister in original squad of 24 but withdrew due to injury, being replaced by Glen Jackson; Peter Grant in original squad of 24 but withdrew as he was now required to join the South African squad for the match against Namibia, being replaced by Ratu Nasiganiyavi; Mike Catt was added to the squad on 22nd May 2009; Seilala Mapusua, Sonny Bill Williams and Geordan Murphy in original squad of 24 but were not selected for team or bench; The Barbarians' starting lineup had 632 caps between them!; Mike Catt retired in May 2010*]
(*The Barbarians were leading 7-0 in the 14th minute; The Barbarians were still leading 7-0 in the 17th minute when Glen Jackson saved a certain try by tap-tackling Jamie Noon; The Barbarians were leading 7-0 midway through the first half; The Barbarians were still leading 7-0 in the 22nd minute when Chris Jack scored after Martin Corry made a brilliant 34 metre run; The Barbarians were leading 14-0 in the 32nd minute; The Barbarians were leading 14-5 at half-time; The Barbarians were still leading 14-5 in the 42nd minute when some superb handling allowed Rocky Elsom to score, with Ben Blair then missing the eminently kickable conversion attempt; The Barbarians were leading 24-5 in the 47th minute when Ben Blair scored a brilliant conversion from the left touchline; Ratu Nasiganiyavi came on as a replacement for Iain Balshaw in the 50th minute; The Barbarians were leading 26-5 in the 51st minute when Gordon D'Arcy scored after Josh Lewsey made a superb 32 metre break; The Barbarians scored 19*

unanswered points to seal the match; The Barbarians were leading 33-5 in the 53rd minute when Schalk Brits had a great try-scoring chance but was brilliantly tackled into touch in-goal by Delon Armitage; The Barbarians were leading 33-12 midway through the second half; Mike Catt came on as a replacement for Josh Lewsey in the 65th minute; The Barbarians were leading 33-19 in the 70th minute; The England XV was allowed to score 21 unanswered points; Schalk Brits had a brilliant game)]

IRB TOSHIBA JUNIOR WORLD CHAMPIONSHIP

Japan

CAPTAIN: *Luke Eves* [*Carl Fearns*]

First Round - Pool 'B'

5th June JAPAN U20 0 **ENGLAND U20** 43 **BP**

Chichibunomiya Rugby Stadium, Tokyo

[*This match kicked off at 7.00pm; Calum Clark unavailable due to injury*]

(*Joe Marler was sent off in the 41st minute for punching and thus duly banned for 2 matches*)

(This match was played in very wet conditions; England U20 were drawing 0-0 in the 7th minute when they were awarded a 40 metre penalty in a kickable position, but Luke Eves ordered a kick to the corner in a vain attempt to score a try from the ensuing lineout; England U20 were leading 7-0 in the 15th minute; England U20 were leading 10-0 midway through the first half; England U20 were still leading 10-0 in the 26th minute when Chris York scored after Carl Fearns broke from the base of a scrum; England U20 were leading 17-0 shortly before half-time when Luke Eves scored after Rory Clegg threw a brilliant inside pass; England U20 were leading 24-0 at half-time; Henry Trinder came on as a replacement for Luke Eves at the start of the second half; Ben Moon came on as a replacement for Chris York in the 43rd minute; England U20 were still leading 24-0 in the 47th minute when George Lowe scored a superb 49 metre solo try which Tom Homer then brilliantly converted from the right touchline; England U20 were leading 31-0 in the 54th minute when Carl Fearns broke from the base of a five metre scrum to score, with Tom Homer then missing the eminently kickable conversion attempt; England U20 were leading 36-0 midway through the second half; The referee had to temporarily order uncontested scrums in the 61st minute while Bob Baker was in the sin-bin; Courtney Lawes came on as a replacement for Carl Fearns in the 64th minute; England U20 were still leading 36-0 with 9 minutes of normal time remaining; England U20 were leading 43-0 with 1 minute of normal time remaining when Greig Tonks had a great try-scoring chance but was tackled into touch at the corner flag by Kota Yamashita; Carl Fearns had a brilliant game)

CAPTAIN: *Luke Eves*

9th June SCOTLAND U20 7 **ENGLAND U20** 30 **BP**

Chichibunomiya Rugby Stadium, Tokyo

[*This match kicked off at 5.00pm; Calum Clark unavailable due to injury; Joe Marler unavailable due to suspension*]

(England U20 made a number of handling errors in this match; Tom Homer scored a brilliant 46 metre penalty goal in the 3rd minute!; England U20 were leading 8-0 in the 14th minute when Charlie Sharples scored a superb 70 metre solo try; England U20 were leading 10-0 midway through the first half; England U20 were still leading 10-0 in the 37th minute when Henry Trinder scored after Rob Miller put in a superb grubber

kick; England U20 were leading 17-0 just before half-time; England U20 were leading 20-0 at half-time; England U20 were still leading 20-0 in the 42nd minute when Luke Eves scored a brilliant try; Rory Clegg came on as a replacement for Luke Eves in the 50th minute; England U20 were leading 25-0 midway through the second half; England U20 were still leading 25-0 with 2 minutes remaining; England U20 scored 30 unanswered points to win the match; England U20 were leading 30-0 in the last minute)

CAPTAIN: *Calum Clark* [*Luke Eves*]

13th Jun SAMOA U20 7 **ENGLAND U20** 52 **BP**

Chichibunomiya Rugby Stadium, Tokyo

[*This match kicked off at 1.00pm; Joe Marler unavailable due to suspension*]

(This match was played in 87 degree heat and high humidity; The England U20 front row dominated the scrums in this match; Henry Trinder scored a brilliant try in the 3rd minute!; England U20 were leading 7-0 in the 8th minute when Henry Trinder scored another try after Ben Youngs put in a brilliant chip-kick; England U20 were leading 15-0 in the 13th minute; The referee allowed a water break midway through both the first and second halves; England U20 were leading 18-0 midway through the first half; England U20 were still leading 18-0 in the 26th minute when George Lowe scored after Henry Trinder made a superb break; England U20 were leading 25-0 in the 31st minute when Carl Fearns scored a pushover try; England U20 were leading 32-0 just before half-time when Ben Youngs scored after Carl Fearns broke from the base of a five metre scrum; England U20 were leading 39-0 at half-time; England U20 were leading 42-0 in the 44th minute; England U20 scored 42 unanswered points to win the match; England U20 were leading 42-7 in the 49th minute; England U20 were still leading 42-7 midway through the second half when Carl Fearns scored another pushover try; England U20 were leading 47-7 with 9 minutes remaining when Charlie Sharples jinked through to score a brilliant try)

CAPTAIN: *Calum Clark*

Semi-Final

17th Jun SOUTH AFRICA U20 21 **ENGLAND U20** 40

Chichibunomiya Rugby Stadium, Tokyo

[*This match kicked off at 7.00pm*]

(England U20 played with the wind in the first half; The England U20 scrum was put under severe pressure in the first half; Ben Youngs had a speculative 37 metre drop goal attempt charged down by David Bulbring in the 2nd minute!; England U20 were leading 3-0 in the 3rd minute; England U20 were leading 6-0 in the 11th minute when Sampie Mastriet unaccountably attempted to charge down a 30 metre penalty goal attempt by Tom Homer that subsequently hit the right-hand post, at which point the referee ordered the kick to be retaken with Homer duly scoring a penalty goal at the second time of asking!; England U20 were leading 9-3 in the 16th minute when Ben Youngs took too much time over his clearance kick and was charged down by Christiaan Stander, who went on to score from the ensuing rebound; England U20 were leading 9-8 midway through the first half; England U20 were still leading 9-8 in the 31st minute when Tom Homer missed a speculative 51 metre penalty goal attempt; James Clark went off injured in the 34th minute, being replaced by Jamie George; England U20 were leading 9-8 in the 37th minute when Charlie Sharples put in a brilliant chip-kick but then inexplicably attempted to gather the resulting loose ball instead of fly-hacking it on over the South Africa U20 line; England U20 were still

***leading 9-8 just before half-time; England U20 were losing 11-9 at half-time; England U20 were still losing 11-9 in the 42nd minute when Ben Youngs scored after he made a brilliant break through the middle of a lineout; England U20 were leading 16-11 in the 55th minute when both Charlie Sharples and Tom Homer failed to deal with Lionel Cronje's grubber kick and Nicolaas Hanekom was able to follow up and score, thus 2 tries and 12 points were preventable; England U20 were losing 21-16 midway through the second half when James Gaskell powered through 3 attempted tackles to score; England U20 were leading 26-21 in the 66th minute; England U20 were still leading 26-21 with 9 minutes remaining when Courtney Lawes scored from a rolling maul; England U20 were leading 33-21 in the last minute when Henry Trinder scored a superb try; England U20 scored 24 unanswered points to win the match; Tom Homer scored 20 points in this match*)**

Final

21st Jun	NEW ZEALAND U20	44	**ENGLAND U20***	28

Chichibunomiya Rugby Stadium, Tokyo

[*This match kicked off at 3.00pm*]

(*This match was played on a wet pitch; The England U20 forwards were outplayed in the loose by their New Zealand U20 counterparts; England U20 were leading 3-0 in the 7th minute; England U20 were still leading 3-0 in the 12th minute when Ben Youngs had a great try-scoring chance but was brilliantly dispossessed by Robbie Robinson behind the New Zealand U20 line; England U20 were leading 6-0 in the 13th minute; England U20 were leading 6-5 in the 17th minute; England U20 were leading 11-5 midway through the second half; England U20 were leading 11-10 in the 26th minute; England U20 were losing 13-11 in the 28th minute when collectively poor tackling allowed Aaron Cruden to score; Ben Youngs went off injured in the 29th minute, being replaced by Dave Lewis; England U20 were losing 25-11 in the 31st minute; New Zealand U20 were allowed to score 20 unanswered points to win the match; England U20 were losing 25-14 in the 38th minute when they created and then squandered an overlap; England U20 were still losing 25-14 shortly before half-time when Tom Homer missed a speculative 47 metre penalty goal attempt; England U20 were losing 25-14 at half-time; England U20 made a number of handling errors in the second half; England U20 were still losing 25-14 in the 44th minute when a poor defensive alignment allowed Shaun Treeby to score; England U20 were losing 32-14 in the 50th minute when Carl Fearns took a quick tap penalty and scored; England U20 were losing 32-21 in the 55th minute when Charlie Sharples had another great try-scoring chance but he could not get downward pressure on the ball after he followed up a kick ahead by Rob Miller; England U20 were losing 37-21 midway through the second half; England U20 were still losing 37-21 with 8 minutes of normal time remaining when Brayden Mitchell scored after Dave Lewis bought a dummy by Alex Ryan, thus 3 tries and 19 points were preventable; England U20 were losing 44-21 with 2 minutes of normal time remaining when Dave Lewis scored a consolation try after he brilliantly picked up a loose ball at the base of a New Zealand U20 scrum*)

ENGLAND COUNTIES TOUR TO KOREA AND JAPAN 2009

CAPTAIN: *Matt Long*

5th Jun	KOREA RUGBY UNION PRESIDENT'S XV	10	**ENGLAND COUNTIES**	108

Seongnam Stadium, Seoul

[*This match kicked off at 7.00pm*]

(*The England Counties forwards monopolised possession in this match; England*

***Counties were leading 61-0 at half-time; England Counties scored 87 unanswered points to win the match; England Counties were leading 87-7 midway through the second half; England Counties were leading 101-10 with 5 minutes remaining; Steve Parsons scored 20 points in this match; Mark Woodrow played brilliantly and scored 29 points in this match*)**

CHURCHILL CUP

USA

CAPTAIN: *Stuart Hooper*

First Round - Pool 'B'

6th June ARGENTINA JAGUARS 20 **ENGLAND SAXONS** 28

Infinity Park, Glendale

[*This match kicked off at 2.15pm; Joe Ward, Dean Schofield and Nick Kennedy unavailable due to injury; Tom Varndell played at left wing despite wearing the number 14 on his shirt!*]

(*This match was played at high altitude in 103 degree heat; The England Saxons forwards were outplayed in the loose by their Argentina Jaguars counterparts in the first half; Danny Cipriani badly missed a kickable 44 metre penalty goal attempt in the 5th minute!; The England Saxons were drawing 0-0 in the 9th minute when Danny Cipriani missed another kickable 32 metre penalty goal attempt; The England Saxons were still drawing 0-0 in the 10th minute when Danny Cipriani scored a brilliant 48 metre penalty goal; The England Saxons were drawing 3-3 midway through the first half when Shane Geraghty made a brilliant 29 metre break, but he then wasted this great try-scoring opportunity by electing to kick instead of waiting for Dom Waldouck to arrive in support; The England Saxons were still drawing 3-3 in the 23rd minute when they were awarded a 40 metre penalty in a kickable position, but Stuart Hooper ordered a kick to the corner in a vain attempt to score a try from the ensuing lineout; The England Saxons were drawing 3-3 in the 37th minute; The Argentina Jaguars were leading 6-3 just before half-time when Peter Short saved a certain try by tackling Tomás Leonardi in front of the England Saxons line; The England Saxons were losing 6-3 at half-time; Phil Dowson came on as a replacement for Peter Short in the 45th minute, with Chris Jones then switching from blindside flanker to lock to accommodate Dowson; The England Saxons were still losing 6-3 in the 46th minute when some superb handling amongst the backs allowed Matt Smith (1) to score; The England Saxons were leading 10-9 in the 50th minute; The England Saxons were leading 13-12 in the 56th minute when Joe Simpson broke from the base of a scrum to score; The England Saxons were leading 20-12 in the 58th minute when Matt Smith (1) had a great try-scoring chance but was tackled into touch at the corner flag by Ignacio Mieres; The England Saxons were still leading 20-12 midway through the second half; The referee allowed a water break midway through both the first and second halves; The England Saxons were leading 20-12 in the 64th minute when collectively poor tackling allowed Tomás Roan to score, thus 7 points were preventable; Stephen Myler came on as a replacement for Danny Cipriani in the 65th minute; The England Saxons were leading 20-17 in the 67th minute when Stephen Myler hit the right-hand post with a speculative 49 metre penalty goal attempt; The England Saxons were still leading 20-17 immediately afterwards when Tom Varndell kicked the ball 77 metres!; The England Saxons were leading 20-17 in the 70th minute when Tom Varndell broke from the base of a ruck to score; The England Saxons were leading 25-17 with 1 minute of normal time remaining; The England Saxons were leading 25-20 in the first minute of injury*

time when Stephen Myler scored a brilliant 27 metre drop goal with the last kick of the match to clinch the game; Joe Simpson had a brilliant game)

CAPTAIN: *Phil Dowson*

14th Jun USA 17 **ENGLAND SAXONS** 56 **BP**

Infinity Park, Glendale

[*This match kicked off at 1.00pm; Joe Ward, Dean Schofield and Shane Geraghty unavailable due to injury; Tom Mercey selected but withdrew on the day of the match due to injury, Dan Cole was moved from the bench to the team and Mark Lambert was then selected for the bench; Brad Barritt played for South Africa in the IRB U21 World Championship in France in June 2006 and played for the Emerging Springboks in June 2007; Tom Varndell was originally selected at left wing with Noah Cato at right wing, but the two swapped positions before the match; A rocket man delivered the match ball just before the 2 teams took the field!*]

(*This match was played at high altitude in 81 degree heat; The England Saxons front row dominated the scrums; Stephen Myler scored a penalty goal in the 5th minute!; The England Saxons were leading 3-0 in the 6th minute when a poor defensive alignment allowed Mike Petri to score, thus 7 points were preventable; The England Saxons were losing 7-3 in the 9th minute when Phil Dowson deflected Alipate Tuilevuka's attempted clearance straight to Nick Kennedy who powered through to score, with Stephen Myler then missing the eminently kickable conversion attempt!; The England Saxons were leading 14-7 midway through the first half; The referee allowed a water break midway through both the first and second halves; The England Saxons were leading 14-10 in the 27th minute when Micky Young broke from the base of a ruck to score; The England Saxons were leading 21-10 shortly before half-time; The England Saxons were leading 28-10 at half-time; The second half of this match was played in drizzly conditions; The England Saxons were still leading 28-10 in the 46th minute when Tom Guest scored a brilliant 52 metre solo try; The England Saxons were leading 35-10 in the 50th minute when some superb handling amongst the backs allowed Tom Varndell to score; Nick Abendanon went off injured in the on the 52nd minute, being replaced by Danny Cipriani ; The England Saxons scored 46 unanswered points to win the match; The England Saxons were leading 49-10 midway through the second half; Neil Briggs came on as a replacement for Nick Kennedy in the 60th minute, with Chris Jones then switching from number 8 to lock to accommodate Neil Briggs; The England Saxons were leading 49-17 in the 67th minute; The England Saxons were still leading 49-17 with 6 minutes of normal time remaining when Noah Cato scored after he wrong-footed Paul Emerick with a brilliant sidestep; The England Saxons were leading 56-17 with 1 minute of normal time remaining when Mike Hercus kicked the ball 95 metres!; Stephen Myler played brilliantly and scored 21 points in this match; The England Saxons recorded their 13th consecutive match win!*)

Final

21st Jun IRELAND A 49 **ENGLAND SAXONS*** 22

Dick's Sporting Goods Park, Commerce City

[*This match kicked off at 2.30pm; Tom Varndell was originally selected at left wing with Noah Cato at right wing, but the two swapped positions before the match*]

(*This match was played at high altitude in 115 degree heat; The England Saxons forwards were outplayed in the loose by their Ireland A counterparts; Stephen Myler scored a penalty goal in the 3rd minute!; The England Saxons were leading 6-0 in the 5th minute; The England Saxons were losing 10-6 in the 14th minute; The England*

Saxons were losing 10-9 midway through the first half; The referee allowed a water break midway through both the first and second halves; The England Saxons were still losing 10-9 in the 22nd minute when Stephen Myler missed a difficult 24 metre penalty goal attempt; The England Saxons were losing 10-9 in the 24th minute when collectively poor tackling allowed Isaac Boss to score; The England Saxons were losing 17-12 in the 30th minute; The England Saxons were losing 20-12 just before half-time when Stephen Myler missed a speculative 50 metre penalty goal attempt; The England Saxons were losing 20-12 at half-time; Further collectively poor tackling allowed Sean Cronin to score after just 22 seconds of the second half had been played!; The England Saxons were losing 27-12 in the 45th minute when some superb handling allowed Ben Woods to score in the corner despite an Ireland A physio getting in the way!; The England Saxons were losing 27-17 in the 54th minute when Stephen Myler kicked the ball 95 metres from inside his own 22 to touch in-goal, which allowed Felix Jones to score from the resulting Ireland A scrum, thus 3 tries and 19 points were preventable; The England Saxons were losing 39-17 midway through the second half; Danny Cipriani and Shane Geraghty came on as replacements for Stephen Myler and Brad Barritt respectively in the 61st minute; The England Saxons were losing 42-17 in the 65th minute; The England Saxons were still losing 42-17 with 5 minutes remaining when John Muldoon broke from the base of a scrum and scored a try which should not have been given because the Ireland A forwards engaged their counterparts before the referee instructed them to do so, thus 7 points were unlawful; Ireland A were allowed to score 22 unanswered points to seal the match; David Flatman went off injured with 1 minute remaining, being replaced by Dan Cole; The England Saxons were losing 49-17 in the final minute when Tom Varndell dummied his way through to score a brilliant consolation try with the last move of the match)

ENGLAND TOUR TO ARGENTINA 2009

CAPTAIN: *Steve Borthwick*

6th June	ARGENTINA	15	**ENGLAND**	37
Old Trafford				

[*This match kicked off at 4.00pm; Argentina were regarded as the home team after they received permission from the IRB to play this match at Old Trafford and thus raise money for the UAR; Jamie Noon unavailable due to injury*]

(*This match was played on a wet pitch containing in-goal areas which were only 5 metres long; The England backs kicked away too much possession in the first half; Juan Martín Hernández scored a drop goal in the 2nd minute!; England were drawing 3-3 in the 11th minute when Andy Goode missed a speculative 49 metre penalty goal attempt; England were still drawing 3-3 in the 18th minute when Andy Goode scored a brilliant 38 metre drop goal; England were leading 6-3 midway through the first half; Delon Armitage put in a brilliant chip-kick which enabled Matt Banahan to follow up and score a try which Andy Goode then converted to give England a 16-3 lead in the 26th minute; England scored 16 unanswered points to win the match; England were leading 16-6 in the 37th minute when Andy Goode scored another superb 32 metre drop goal; England were leading 19-9 at half-time; England were leading 22-9 in the 47th minute when Andy Goode missed another speculative 47 metre penalty goal attempt; England were leading 22-15 in the 54th minute when they were awarded a 41 metre penalty and Steve Borthwick ordered a shot at goal, which led to Andy Goode being slow hand-clapped by the crowd as he lined up the subsequently successful kick!; England were leading 32-15 midway through the second half; Julian White came on as a replacement for David Wilson (2) in the 64th minute; England were still leading*

***32-15 in the 66th minute when Andy Goode missed a kickable 34 metre penalty goal attempt; Sam Vesty came on as a replacement for Tom May with 7 minutes remaining; Matt Tait came on as a replacement for Matt Banahan with 4 minutes remaining; Steve Thompson (2) played as a flanker after coming on as a replacement for Steffon Armitage with 1 minute remaining; England were leading 32-15 in the final minute when Andy Goode put in a chip-kick, Mark Cueto volleyed the ball on and Delon Armitage followed up to score in the last move of the match, with Andy Goode then missing the eminently kickable conversion attempt; Andy Goode scored 22 points in this match; Matt Banahan had a brilliant game*)**

QUILMES MATCH

CAPTAIN: *Steve Borthwick*

13th June ARGENTINA 24 **ENGLAND*** 22

Estadio Padre Ernesto Martearena, Salta

[*This match kicked off at 4.10pm*]

(*This match was played at high altitude; Andy Goode kicked away too much possession in the first half; A poor defensive alignment allowed Juan Manuel Leguizamón to score in the 3rd minute!; England were losing 5-0 in the 7th minute when Andy Goode scored a brilliant 48 metre penalty goal; England were losing 7-3 in the 11th minute when Danny Care wasted a great try-scoring opportunity by electing to take the ball into contact instead of using a 2 man overlap outside him; Dan Hipkiss went off injured in the 17th minute, being replaced by Matt Tait; England were losing 11-3 midway through the first half; England were losing 14-3 in the 24th minute; England were still losing 14-3 in the 31st minute when Dylan Hartley crossed the tryline but the move was disallowed because the referee adjudged that Andy Goode had thrown an earlier forward pass to Matt Banahan; England were losing 14-3 in the 38th minute when Andy Goode missed a speculative 47 metre drop goal attempt; England were still losing 14-3 just before half-time when Andy Goode missed an eminently kickable 24 metre penalty goal attempt; England were losing 14-3 at half-time; England played with a swirling wind in the second half; England were still losing 14-3 in the 43rd minute when another poor defensive alignment allowed to Gonzalo Camacho to score; Argentina were allowed to score 16 unanswered points to win the match; Ben Kay came on as a temporary blood replacement for Steve Borthwick in the 46th minute; England were losing 21-3 in the 47th minute; England were losing 21-9 in the 51st minute; England were losing 21-12 midway through the second half; England were losing 21-15 with 9 minutes remaining when Dylan Hartley kicked the ball 87 metres from inside his own 22 to touch in-goal, which allowed Juan Martín Hernández to score a 30 metre drop goal from the resulting Argentine scrum, thus 2 tries and 15 points were preventable; England were losing 24-15 with 3 minutes remaining when Matt Banahan powered through to score under the posts after Delon Armitage threw a brilliant pass out of the tackle*)

BARBARIANS TOUR TO AUSTRALIA 2009

CAPTAIN: *Phil Waugh* (AU)

6th June AUSTRALIA XV 55 **BARBARIANS** 7

Sydney Football Stadium, Sydney

[*This match kicked off at 7.30pm; Rocky Elsom selected but withdrew on the afternoon of the match due to injury, being replaced by David Lyons; Martin Corry and Josh Lewsey both retired after this match*]

(*The Barbarians forwards could not win any possession; The Barbarians were drawing*

***0-0 in the 3rd minute when Sonny Bill Williams had a great try-scoring chance but was brilliantly tackled by Luke Burgess just short of the Australian XV line; The Barbarians were still drawing 0-0 in the 7th minute when a poor defensive alignment allowed James Horwill to score; The Barbarians were losing 8-0 in the 16th minute when Drew Mitchell scored after a poor tackle by Seilala Mapusua; The Barbarians were losing 13-0 midway through the first half when Geordan Murphy saved a certain try by getting across to tackle Lachie Turner into touch at the corner flag; The Barbarians were still losing 13-0 in the 23rd minute when another poor defensive alignment allowed Matt Giteau to score; The Australian XV was losing 20-0 in the 27th minute when Geordan Murphy saved another certain try by brilliantly dislodging the ball as he tackled Stirling Mortlock on the Barbarians line; Seilala Mapusua went off injured in the 31st minute, being replaced by Glen Jackson; The Barbarians were still losing 20-0 just before half-time when Iain Balshaw scored after David Lyons instigated a brilliant 78 metre counter-attack; The Barbarians were losing 20-7 at half-time; Luke McAlister and Glen Jackson swapped positions at half-time; Geordan Murphy went off injured in the 46th minute, being replaced by Ben Blair; The Barbarians were still losing 20-7 in the 57th minute when the referee unaccountably allowed play to continue after George Smith threw a clear forward pass to Josh Valentine and Stephen Moore went on to score, thus 7 points were unlawful; The Barbarians were losing 27-7 midway through the second half; Serge Betsen and Martin Corry came on as replacements for Phil Waugh and Chris Jack respectively in the 65th minute; The Barbarians were losing 34-7 in the 66th minute; The Barbarians were losing 41-7 with 3 minutes of normal time remaining; The Barbarians were losing 48-7 with 1 minute of normal time remaining when James O'Connor scored after a poor tackle by Josh Lewsey, thus 4 tries and 24 points were preventable; The Australian XV was allowed to score 35 unanswered points to seal the match*)**

TUSKER SAFARI SEVENS

RFU of East Africa Ground, Ngong Road, Nairobi

CAPTAIN: *Angus Martyn* (SC)

First Round - Pool 'C'

20th Jun	Shujaa (*KEN*)	5	**SAMURAI**	22

[*This match kicked off at 10.40am*]

20th Jun	MOROCCO	0	**SAMURAI**	29

[*This match kicked off at 1.40pm*]

20th Jun	EMERGING BOKS	26	**SAMURAI**	24

[*This match kicked off at 4.40pm*]

Quarter-Final

21st Jun	ZIMBABWE	0	**SAMURAI**	17

[*This match kicked off at 12.00pm*]

Semi-Final

21st Jun	KENYA	24	**SAMURAI**	0

[*This match kicked off at 4.20pm*]

(*The Samurai were losing 19-0 at half-time*)

MIDDLESEX CHARITY SEVENS

Twickenham

CAPTAIN: *Simon Amor* [Samurai]

CAPTAIN: *Greg Barden* [Help for Heroes VII]

First Round

CAPTAIN: *Humphrey Kayange* (KEN) [*Simon Amor*]

15th Aug Northampton Saints 12 **SAMURAI** 17

[This match was scheduled to kick off at 11.20am but the kick-off was delayed for 7 minutes due to a serious injury in the White Hart Marauders game against the Harlequins; The Samurai were also billed as Samurai Internationals; John Brake played for Northampton Saints in this match]

(Marius Schoeman scored a brilliant 79 metre solo try after just 42 seconds had been played!; The Samurai were leading 7-0 midway through the first half; The Samurai were drawing 7-7 in the 4th minute; The Samurai were still drawing 7-7 just before half-time; The Samurai were leading 12-7 at half-time; Tony Roques and Simon Amor came on as replacements for Julien Palmer and Tim Walsh respectively at the start of the second half; The Samurai were leading 17-7 in the 10th minute; The Samurai were still leading 17-7 midway through the second half; Nick Wakley came on as a replacement for Marius Schoeman in the 11th minute, with Willie Bishop then switching from centre to fly half to accommodate Wakley and Humphrey Kayange moving from fly half to forward to accommodate Willie Bishop; The Samurai were leading 17-7 in the final minute)

CAPTAIN: *Greg Barden*

15th Aug Sale Sharks 21 **HELP FOR HEROES VII** 29

[This match was scheduled to kick off at 12.20pm but the kick-off was delayed for 7 minutes due to a serious injury in the White Hart Marauders game against the Harlequins]

(Collectively poor tackling allowed Matt Williams (2) to score in the 1st minute!; The Help for Heroes VII was losing 7-0 in the 2nd minute when Greg Barden scored after Chris Brightwell put in a brilliant grubber kick; The Help for Heroes VII was losing 7-5 midway through the first half; The Help for Heroes VII was still losing 7-5 in the 5th minute when Peter Jericevich scored after Rory Hutton made a brilliant 42 metre run; The Help for Heroes VII was leading 12-7 in the 6th minute when Rory Hutton broke from the base of a ruck to score; The Help for Heroes VII was leading 17-7 when the half-time hooter sounded, but the ball was still in play and Ed Styles was able to score after a poor tackle by Tal Selley, thus 2 tries and 14 points were preventable; The Help for Heroes VII was leading 17-14 at half-time; The Help for Heroes VII was losing 21-17 in the 8th minute; The Help for Heroes VII was still losing 21-17 in the 10th minute when Peter Jericevich scored another try after he wrong-footed Ed Styles with a superb sidestep; The Help for Heroes VII was leading 22-21 midway through the second half; The Help for Heroes VII was still leading 22-21 with 1 minute of normal time remaining when Uche Oduoza brilliantly chipped the ball to himself which enabled Mat Turner to score a match-clinching try)

Quarter-Final

CAPTAIN: *Simon Amor* [*Humphrey Kayange* (KEN)]

15th Aug Leeds Carnegie 17 **SAMURAI** 33

[This match was scheduled to kick off at 2.40pm but the kick-off was delayed for 7 minutes due to a serious injury in the White Hart Marauders game against the Harlequins; Andy Gomarsall and Scott Armstrong played for Leeds Carnegie in this match]

(Humphrey Kayange scored in the 2nd minute!; The Samurai were leading 7-0 in the 3rd minute when Collins Injera gathered a loose ball and ran 53 metres to score; The Samurai were leading 12-0 midway through the first half; The Samurai were still

***leading 12-0 in the 6th minute; The Samurai were leading 12-7 just before half-time when Tony Roques scored after Collins Injera threw a brilliant reverse pass out of the tackle; The Samurai were leading 19-7 at half-time; Julien Palmer came on as a replacement for Tony Roques at the start of the second half; The Samurai were still leading 19-7 in the 9th minute when Collins Injera scored a brilliant 57 metre solo try; The Samurai scored 14 unanswered points to win the match; Willie Bishop came on as a replacement for Simon Amor in the 10th minute, with Tim Walsh then switching from fly half to scrum half to accommodate Willie Bishop; The Samurai were leading 26-7 midway through the second half; The Samurai were still leading 26-7 with 2 minutes remaining when Oli Stedman scored after a poor tackle by Willie Bishop; The Samurai were leading 26-12 with 1 minute remaining when Tim Walsh tried a cross-kick from inside his own 22, but the ball went straight to Scott Armstrong who then went on to score, thus 2 tries and 10 points were preventable!; The Samurai were leading 26-17 in the final minute when Chase Minnaar powered through 2 attempted tackles to score with the last move of the match*)**

CAPTAIN: *Greg Barden*

15th Aug Newcastle Falcons 34 **HELP FOR HEROES VII** 5

[*This match was scheduled to kick off at 3.00pm but the kick-off was delayed for 7 minutes due to a serious injury in the White Hart Marauders game against the Harlequins; Rob Vickerman, Rob Miller and Charlie Amesbury played for the Newcastle Falcons in this match*]

(*The Help for Heroes VII could not win any possession in the first half; Charlie Amesbury scored in the 1st minute!; The Help for Heroes VII was losing 10-0 in the 3rd minute; The Help for Heroes VII was still losing 10-0 midway through the first half; The Help for Heroes VII was losing 10-0 in the 4th minute when Rob Miller scored after Andy Titterrell slipped over and thus created a gap in the defensive line; The Help for Heroes VII was losing 22-0 in the 6th minute; Mat Turner came on as a replacement for Andy Titterrell immediately afterwards, with Tal Selley then switching from centre to forward to accommodate Mat Turner and Greg Barden then moving from forward to hooker to accommodate Selley; The Help for Heroes VII was losing 22-0 at half-time; Newcastle Falcons were allowed to score 29 unanswered points to win the match; David Akinluyi came on as a replacement for Chris Brightwell in the 9th minute, with Uche Oduoza then switching from wing to forward to accommodate Akinluyi; The Help for Heroes VII was losing 29-0 midway through the second half when Mat Turner powered through 2 attempted tackles to score; The Help for Heroes VII was losing 29-5 with 1 minute remaining when collectively poor tackling allowed Josh Afu to score, thus 2 tries and 12 points were preventable*)

CAPTAIN: *Simon Amor*

Semi-Final

15th Aug Newcastle Falcons 17 **SAMURAI** 28

[*This match was scheduled to kick off at 4.20pm but the kick-off was delayed for 7 minutes due to a serious injury in the White Hart Marauders game against the Harlequins; Rob Vickerman, Rob Miller and Charlie Amesbury played for the Newcastle Falcons in this match*]

(*Rob Miller scored in the 3rd minute!; The Samurai were losing 5-0 midway through the first half; The Samurai were still losing 5-0 in the 6th minute; The Samurai were leading 7-5 just before half-time when Julien Palmer powered through to score under the posts; The Samurai scored 14 unanswered points to win the match; The Samurai were leading 14-5 at half-time; The Samurai were still leading 14-5 in the 8th minute when*

Charlie Amesbury scored after Collins Injera missed a tackle on Rob Vickerman; The Samurai were leading 14-12 in the 10th minute when Collins Injera scored after Humphrey Kayange brilliantly created space by cutting back inside; The Samurai were leading 21-12 midway through the second half when Aaron Myers scored after a poor tackle by Chase Minnaar, thus 2 tries and 12 points were preventable; The Samurai were leading 21-17 with 1 minute of normal time remaining when Willie Bishop scored a match-clinching try after Collins Injera wrong-footed Charlie Amesbury with a brilliant sidestep)

Final

15th Aug London Irish 26 **SAMURAI*** 19

[This match was scheduled to kick off at 5.30pm but the kick-off was delayed for 7 minutes due to a serious injury in the White Hart Marauders game against the Harlequins; Steffon Armitage, Peter Richards, Nick Kennedy, Paul Hodgson and Delon Armitage all played for London Irish in this match]

(The Samurai only had one day to prepare for this tournament!; Delon Armitage scored in the 3rd minute!; The Samurai were losing 7-0 midway through the first half; The Samurai were still losing 7-0 in the 6th minute when Chase Minnaar accidentally tripped up Humphrey Kayange, which duly created a gap for Marcus Watson to run through and score!; The Samurai were losing 12-0 in the 8th minute when Tim Walsh wasted a great try-scoring opportunity by throwing a forward pass to the unmarked Collins Injera; The Samurai were still losing 12-0 just before half-time when Paul Hodgson scored a try that should not have been given because the scoring pass from Peter Richards was clearly forward, thus 7 points were unlawful; The Samurai were losing 19-0 at half-time; Peceli Nacamavuto came on as a replacement for Chase Minnaar at the start of the second half, with Humphrey Kayange then moving from centre to forward to accommodate Nacamavuto; The Samurai were still losing 19-0 in the 13th minute when Nick Kennedy's chip-kick hit Simon Amor's head and rebounded into touch!; The Samurai were losing 19-0 in the 14th minute when collectively poor tackling allowed Sailosi Tagicakibau to score, thus 2 tries and 12 points were preventable; London Irish were allowed to score 26 unanswered points to win the match; The Samurai were losing 26-0 midway through the second half; Michael Fedo came on as a replacement for Tony Roques with 2 minutes of normal time remaining; The Samurai were losing 26-7 with 1 minute of normal time remaining when Willie Bishop scored a brilliant 74 metre solo try; The Samurai were losing 26-12 when the full-time hooter sounded, but the ball was still in play and Peceli Nacamavuto was able to score a consolation try)

AUSTRALIAN TOUR TO ENGLAND, IRELAND, SCOTLAND AND WALES 2009

CAPTAIN: *Steve Borthwick*

7th Nov **ENGLAND*** 9 AUSTRALIA 18

Twickenham

[This match kicked off at 2.30pm; This match replaced the originally scheduled game against Fiji on 28th November 2009; Andy Sheridan, Lee Mears, Phil Vickery, Julian White, Simon Shaw, Tom Rees, Nick Easter, Harry Ellis, Toby Flood, Danny Cipriani, Olly Barkley, Riki Flutey, Delon Armitage and Olly Morgan all unavailable due to injury; Matt Stevens and Michael Lipman unavailable due to suspension; James Simpson-Daniel made himself available for this match but was not selected!; Richard Blaze and Mike Tindall in original training squad of 32 but were unavailable for this match due to

injury; David Barnes, George Chuter, Ben Kay, Joe Worsley, Steffon Armitage, Richard Wigglesworth, Matt Tait, Dave Strettle and Ben Foden all in original training squad of 32 but were not selected for team or bench; Nick Kennedy and Ayoola Erinle were added to the squad on 1st November 2009 to provide injury cover for Richard Blaze and Mike Tindall respectively]

(*Jonny Wilkinson scored a brilliant 33 metre drop goal in the 3rd minute!; England were leading 6-0 in the 10th minute; England were still leading 6-0 in the 15th minute when Jonny Wilkinson hit the left-hand post with a speculative 52 metre penalty goal attempt; England were leading 6-0 midway through the first half when they unaccountably failed to defend the fringes of a ruck in front of their own line and Will Genia was able to break through and score; England were leading 6-5 in the 26th minute when Danny Care put up a superb cross kick, but Lewis Moody was unable to catch the descending ball; England were leading 9-5 in the 27th minute; England were leading 9-5 at half-time; England were still leading 9-5 in the 45th minute when Matt Banahan saved a certain try by tackling Rocky Elsom; England were leading 9-8 in the 47th minute; David Wilson (2) went off injured in the 58th minute, being replaced by Duncan Bell; England were still leading 9-8 immediately afterwards when Duncan Bell was wrongly adjudged to have collapsed a five metre scrum in a situation where Ben Robinson was actually infringing and Australia were inexplicably awarded a penalty which Matt Giteau duly kicked, thus 3 points were unlawful; England were losing 11-9 midway through the second half; England were still losing 11-9 in the 64th minute when Jonny Wilkinson badly missed a speculative 39 metre drop goal attempt; Ayoola Erinle came on as a replacement for Dan Hipkiss in the 67th minute; Courtney Lawes came on as a replacement for Louis Deacon in the 69th minute; England were losing 11-9 with 9 minutes of normal time remaining when collectively poor tackling allowed Adam Ashley-Cooper to score, thus 2 tries and 12 points were preventable; England failed to score a single point in the final 54 minutes of this match!; Jonny Wilkinson was brilliant in defence*)

ATKINS REMEMBRANCE RUGBY MATCH

CAPTAIN: *Craig Hammond*

11th Nov COMBINED SERVICES (*SER*) 22 **BARBARIANS*** 19

Army Rugby Stadium, Queen's Avenue, Aldershot

[*This match kicked off at 7.15pm; Ben Johnston unavailable due to injury; Tom Youngs was converted from a centre to a hooker by his club Nottingham in August 2009; Rob and James Lewis were the twin sons of Steve Lewis; David Blair was the brother of Mike Blair; Chris Budgen, Apolosi Satala, Mark Lee, Greg Barden and Mal Roberts all played for the Combined Services in this match, with Mark Lee captaining the side, Apolosi Satala and Greg Barden scoring a try apiece and Mal Roberts scoring a penalty goal and 2 conversions; Chris Ritchie played for Major R.V. Stanley's XV against Oxford University at Iffley Road on 17th November 2009; The Barbarians beat a New Zealand XV 25-18 at Twickenham on 5th December 2009 but no English players were involved in the game*]

(*This match was played in cold conditions; Rhys Shellard scored in the 2nd minute!; Steven Turnbull went off injured in the 15th minute, being replaced by Henry Head; The Barbarians were leading 7-0 in the 17th minute; The Barbarians were leading 7-3 midway through the first half; The Barbarians were still leading 7-3 in the 25th minute when collectively poor tackling allowed Apolosi Satala to score, thus 7 points were preventable; Sean-Michael Stephen came on as a temporary blood replacement for Rhys Shellard in the 38th minute; The Barbarians were losing 10-7 at half-time; The*

***Barbarians were still losing 10-7 in the 56th minute; Chris Pilgrim came on as a replacement for Rob Lewis in the 58th minute; The Barbarians were losing 17-7 midway through the second half; The Barbarians were losing 22-7 in the 69th minute; The Combined Services were allowed to score 22 unanswered points to win the match; Frankie Neale came on as a replacement for Craig Morgan with 9 minutes of normal time remaining; The Barbarians were still losing 22-7 with 6 minutes of normal time remaining when Henry Head scored from a tap penalty; The Barbarians were losing 22-14 in the last minute of normal time; This match finished in wet conditions; Rob and James Lewis became the first twins to play for the Barbarians!*)**

ARGENTINE TOUR TO ENGLAND, WALES AND SCOTLAND 2009

CAPTAIN: *Steve Borthwick*

14th Nov **ENGLAND** 16 ARGENTINA 9

Twickenham

[*This match kicked off at 2.30pm; Andy Sheridan, Lee Mears, Phil Vickery, Julian White, Tom Rees, Nick Easter, Harry Ellis, Toby Flood, Danny Cipriani, Olly Barkley, Riki Flutey, James Simpson-Daniel, Delon Armitage and Olly Morgan all unavailable due to injury; Matt Stevens and Michael Lipman unavailable due to suspension; David Barnes, David Wilson (2), Richard Blaze and Mike Tindall all in original training squad of 34 but were unavailable for this match due to injury; George Chuter, Ben Kay, Nick Kennedy, Steffon Armitage, Jordan Crane, Richard Wigglesworth, Matt Tait, Dave Strettle and Ben Foden all in original training squad of 34 but were not selected for team or bench; Paul Doran-Jones was added to the squad on 9th November 2009 to provide injury cover for David Wilson (2); Paul Doran-Jones played for Ireland in the IRB U21 World Championship in France in June 2006; England wore purple shirts and purple shorts for this match*]

(*This match was played on a wet pitch; The England backs kicked away too much possession in the first half; England were drawing 0-0 in the 6th minute when Jonny Wilkinson scored a brilliant 35 metre drop goal; England were leading 3-0 in the 7th minute when Mark Cueto had a great try-scoring chance but was tackled 8 metres short of the Argentine line by Horacio Agulla; England were drawing 3-3 in the 14th minute; England were drawing 3-3 midway through the first half when Jonny Wilkinson scored a superb 47 metre penalty goal; England were drawing 6-6 in the 26th minute; England were losing 9-6 shortly before half-time; England were drawing 9-9 at half-time; England were booed off the pitch at half-time!; Mark Cueto and Ugo Monye swapped positions at half-time; England played with a swirling wind in the second half; England were still drawing 9-9 in the 45th minute when Jonny Wilkinson missed a kickable 40 metre penalty goal attempt; England were drawing 9-9 midway through the second half when they created and then squandered an overlap; England were still drawing 9-9 in the 63rd minute when Jonny Wilkinson missed a speculative 49 metre penalty goal attempt; Paul Doran-Jones came on as a replacement for Tim Payne immediately afterwards; England were drawing 9-9 in the 68th minute when Jonny Wilkinson missed another kickable 39 metre penalty goal attempt; England were still drawing 9-9 in the 70th minute when Matt Banahan scored after Lewis Moody brilliantly created space by delaying his pass; Andy Goode came on as a replacement for Jonny Wilkinson with 5 minutes of normal time remaining; Steve Borthwick's leadership was conspicuous by its absence in this match; Lewis Moody had a brilliant game; Ugo Monye had a poor game*)

FIRA-AER 75TH ANNIVERSARY MATCH

CAPTAIN: *Matthew Clarkin*

14th Nov French Barbarians 39 **XV EUROPE*** 26

Stade Roi Baudouin, Brussels

[This match kicked off at 3.00pm; The XV Europe named an 8 man bench selection; Mamuka Magrakvelidze, Jean-Philippe Genevois, Benjamin Noirot, Andrey Ostrikov and Alex Manta in original squad of 23 but withdrew, being replaced by Olivier Tissot, Joan Caudullo, Rémy Bonfils, Damien Godefroy and Benjamin Goze respectively; Damien Godefroy and Benjamin Goze then both withdrew, being replaced by Gonçalo Uva and Pierre Hendrickx respectively; Matthew Clarkin was originally selected at blindside flanker with Magnus Lund at openside flanker, but the two swapped positions before the match; Gonçalo Uva was the brother of Vasco Uva; Matthew Clarkin played a Ringwraith in his brief career as an actor in New Zealand!; Pablo Feijoo was the son of Alfonso Feijoo; No English players were involved with the French Barbarians on this occasion; Dimitri Yachvili played for the French Barbarians in this match]

(This match was played on a pitch where the in-goal areas were shorter than normal; The XV Europe played with a swirling wind in the first half; The XV Europe was losing 7-0 in the 6th minute; The XV Europe was losing 12-0 in the 18th minute when Phil Christophers wasted a great try-scoring opportunity by electing to pass to Robert Mohr instead of using his own momentum to make the nearby line himself; The XV Europe was still losing 12-0 midway through the first half when collectively poor tackling allowed Jérôme Porical to score; The French Barbarians were allowed to score 19 unanswered points to win the match; The XV Europe was losing 19-0 in the 33rd minute when Nicolas Laharrague scored a brilliant try; The XV Europe was losing 19-7 in the 35th minute when Phil Christophers made a brilliant break but then wasted this great try-scoring opportunity by throwing a poor pass to the unmarked Gonçalo Uva; The referee blew for half-time after only 39 minutes of the first half had been played!; The XV Europe was losing 24-7 at half-time; César Sempere came on as a replacement for Samuele Pace at the start of the second half, with Sepp Visser then switching from left to right wing to accommodate Sempere; Luis Pissarra came on as a replacement for Pablo Feijoo in the 46th minute; Mathieu Verschelden came on as a replacement for Robert Mohr in the 56th minute, with Gonçalo Uva then moving from lock to number 8 to accommodate Verschelden; The XV Europe was still losing 24-7 in the 57th minute when Marc Andrieu scored after a poor tackle by Luis Pissarra; The XV Europe was losing 29-7 midway through the second half; The XV Europe was losing 34-7 in the 65th minute when Rémy Bonfils scored under the posts after he gathered a bouncing ball straight after a restart!; The XV Europe was losing 34-14 in the 69th minute when further collectively poor tackling allowed Pierre-Manuel Garcia to score, thus 3 tries and 17 points were preventable; The XV Europe was losing 39-14 with 9 minutes of normal time remaining when Tiberius Dimofte dummied his way through to score a superb try; The XV Europe was losing 39-21 with 5 minutes of normal time remaining when Sepp Visser scored after Magnus Lund threw a brilliant pass out of the tackle, with David Chartier then missing the conversion attempt from the right touchline after he was forced to try a drop-kick when the ball fell off the kicking tee as he began his original run up!; The XV Europe was losing 39-26 with 4 minutes of normal time remaining when Matthew Clarkin performed an acrobat's roll after he lost his balance!; The XV Europe was still losing 39-26 in the last minute of normal time when Magnus Lund crossed the tryline but then could not get downward

pressure on the ball; The XV Europe was losing 39-26 in the first minute of injury time when David Chartier tap-tackled Marc Andrieu who responded by performing another acrobat's roll, at which point the referee blew the final whistle because there had been an earlier forward pass!)

NEW ZEALAND TOUR TO WALES, ITALY, ENGLAND AND FRANCE 2009

CAPTAIN: *Steve Borthwick*

21st Nov **ENGLAND*** 6 NEW ZEALAND 19

Twickenham

[This match kicked off at 2.30pm; Andy Sheridan, Lee Mears, Phil Vickery, Julian White, Tom Rees, Nick Easter, Harry Ellis, Toby Flood, Danny Cipriani, Olly Barkley, Riki Flutey, James Simpson-Daniel, Delon Armitage and Olly Morgan all unavailable due to injury; Matt Stevens and Michael Lipman unavailable due to suspension; David Barnes, Richard Blaze, Mike Tindall and Dave Strettle all in original training squad of 35 but were unavailable for this match due to injury; Paul Doran-Jones, George Chuter, Ben Kay, Nick Kennedy, Courtney Lawes, Steffon Armitage, Jordan Crane, Richard Wigglesworth, Andy Goode and Ben Foden all in original training squad of 35 but were not selected for team or bench; David Flatman, Simon Shaw and Paul Sackey were added to the squad on 15th November 2009 to provide injury cover for David Wilson (2), Richard Blaze and Dave Strettle respectively]

(This match was played on a slippery pitch; Jonny Wilkinson was unaccountably told to play with a deep alignment which meant that the England backs had less attacking options; Joe Worsley had to go off in the 3rd minute after he ruptured the medial ligament in his knee; England were drawing 0-0 in the 12th minute when Ugo Monye reached the tryline and grounded the ball, but the move was disallowed as he was adjudged to have made an earlier knock-on when he tackled Zac Guildford; England were leading 3-0 in the 17th minute; England were still leading 3-0 midway through the first half when Ugo Monye saved a certain try by tackling Mils Muliaina into touch at the corner flag; England were leading 6-3 in the 26th minute; England were drawing 6-6 in the 30th minute; England were drawing 6-6 at half-time; England were losing 9-6 in the 47th minute; Steve Thompson (2) came on as a replacement for Dylan Hartley in the 49th minute; England were still losing 9-6 in the 57th minute when a lack of communication between Paul Hodgson and Matt Banahan saw them both attempting to tackle Sitiveni Sivivatu, which enabled Jimmy Cowan to score, thus 7 points were preventable; England were losing 16-6 midway through the second half; England were still losing 16-6 in the 63rd minute when Jonny Wilkinson missed an eminently kickable 14 metre drop goal attempt; Ayoola Erinle went off injured immediately afterwards, being replaced by Shane Geraghty; England were losing 16-6 in the 64th minute when Shane Geraghty put in a brilliant cross-kick to the unmarked Matt Banahan, who then wasted this great try-scoring opportunity by dropping the ball; Tim Payne went off injured in the 65th minute, being replaced by Duncan Bell; England were still losing 16-6 in the 66th minute when Paul Hodgson saved another certain try after he got back to prevent Conrad Smith's intended scoring pass from reaching Sitiveni Sivivatu; England were losing 19-6 in the 68th minute; Matt Tait came on as a replacement for Matt Banahan with 8 minutes remaining; England were still losing 19-6 with 7 minutes remaining when Tom Croft had a great try-scoring chance but was tackled 5 metres short of the New Zealand line by Dan Carter; England were losing 19-6 with 5 minutes remaining when Ugo Monye wasted a second great try-scoring

opportunity by failing to make contact with a loose ball as he attempted to fly-hack it on over the New Zealand line!; England failed to score a single point in the final 54 minutes of this match!; Shane Geraghty had a brilliant game)

FIJIAN TOUR TO SCOTLAND, IRELAND AND ENGLAND 2009

CAPTAIN: *No captain appointed*

28th Nov **ENGLAND** C FIJI C

Twickenham

[This match was scheduled to kick off at 2.30pm; This match was cancelled by the RFU on 17th June 2009 after they received permission from the IRB to play Australia on 7th November 2009 instead and thus raise money for the FRU]

EMIRATES AIRLINE DUBAI RUGBY SEVENS

The Sevens, Dubai

CAPTAIN: *Kevin Barrett*

First Round - Pool 'C'

4th Dec USA 12 **ENGLAND** 40

[This match kicked off at 10.04am; England wore red shirts for this match]

(Dan Norton scored after just 48 seconds had been played!; England were leading 14-0 midway through the first half; England were still leading 14-0 in the 5th minute when Dan Norton scored to complete a hat-trick of tries in the first half!; England scored 21 unanswered points to win the match; England were leading 21-0 at half-time; England were still leading 21-0 at the start of the second half when Nick Edwards scored after a poor tackle by Dan Norton, thus 7 points were preventable; England were leading 21-7 in the 9th minute when Kevin Barrett scored after Jake Abbott made a brilliant 65 metre run; England were leading 28-7 in the 11th minute when Ben Gollings fly-hacked a loose ball on and then followed up to score; England were leading 33-7 midway through the second half; England were leading 33-12 in the final minute)

4th Dec RUSSIA 0 **ENGLAND** 28

[This match kicked off at 1.40pm]

(England were drawing 0-0 in the 3rd minute when Ben Gollings followed up his own grubber kick to score a brilliant try; England were leading 7-0 midway through the first half; England were leading 7-0 at half-time; England were still leading 7-0 in the 9th minute when Isoa Damu scored a superb 70 metre solo try; England were leading 14-0 midway through the second half; England were still leading 14-0 with 1 minute remaining when Dan Caprice scored after Kevin Barrett took a quick tap penalty; Dan Caprice had a brilliant game)

4th Dec KENYA 10 **ENGLAND** 27

[This match kicked off at 6.52pm]

(Collins Injera scored in the 1st minute!; England were losing 7-0 midway through the first half; England were still losing 7-0 in the 4th minute when Nick Royle scored a brilliant 35 metre solo try; England were leading 7-5 in the 7th minute; England were losing 10-7 just before half-time when Nick Royle scored another brilliant 69 metre solo try; England were leading 12-10 at half-time; England were leading 17-10 in the 9th minute when Ben Gollings hit the post with an eminently kickable conversion attempt; England were still leading 17-10 in the 10th minute when Ben Gollings fly-hacked a loose ball on twice and then regathered it to score; England were leading 22-10 midway through the second half; England were still leading 22-10 in the final minute; England scored 20 unanswered points to win the match)

Quarter-Final

5th Dec	ARGENTINA	12	**ENGLAND**	17 aet

[This match kicked off at 11.32am; England wore red shirts for this match]

(England were drawing 0-0 midway through the first half; England were still drawing 0-0 in the 6th minute; England were losing 7-0 at half-time; Nick Royle scored after just 37 seconds of the second half had been played, with Ben Gollings then missing the eminently kickable conversion attempt!; England were losing 7-5 in the 10th minute when Dan Norton scored a brilliant 83 metre solo try; England were leading 12-7 midway through the second half; England were still leading 12-7 in the last minute of normal time; England were drawing 12-12 in the second minute of sudden death extra time when Ben Gollings scored a brilliant try in the left corner to win the match)

Semi-Final

5th Dec	SAMOA	28	**ENGLAND***	19

[This match kicked off at 6.52pm]

(Lolo Lui scored in the 1st minute after Nick Royle bought a dummy by Timoteo Iosua!; England were losing 7-0 in the 3rd minute when Jake Abbott unaccountably tapped a restart backwards into the arms of Simaika Mikaele who instigated a move that culminated in a try by Alafoti Fa'osiliva; England were losing 14-0 midway through the first half; Samoa were still leading 14-0 in the 4th minute when Mikaele Pesamino was awarded a try which should not have been given because Lolo Lui knocked the ball on as he attempted to ground it over the England line, thus 7 points were unlawful; Samoa were allowed to score 21 unanswered points to win the match; England were losing 21-0 in the 6th minute; England were losing 21-7 at half-time; Nick Royle went off injured in the 10th minute, being replaced by Dan Caprice; England were still losing 21-7 midway through the second half when Kevin Barrett took a quick tap penalty that enabled Chris Cracknell to score a try which Ben Gollings then brilliantly converted from the right touchline; England were losing 21-14 with 2 minutes remaining when collectively poor tackling allowed Mikaele Pesamino to score, thus 3 tries and 21 points were preventable; England were losing 28-14 in the final minute when Chris Cracknell scored a brilliant consolation try with the last move of the match; Ben Gollings increased his IRB World Sevens record to 2088 points in this tournament)

EMIRATES AIRLINE SOUTH AFRICA SEVENS

Outeniqua Park Stadium, George

CAPTAIN: *Kevin Barrett* [*Ben Gollings*]

First Round - Pool 'D'

11th Dec	TUNISIA	0	**ENGLAND**	45

[This match kicked off at 12.04pm]

(Jake Abbott scored after just 29 seconds had been played!; England were leading 12-0 midway through the first half; England were still leading 12-0 in the 4th minute when Christian Wade scored a brilliant 88 metre solo try; England were leading 26-0 just before half-time when Christian Wade scored another try after Kevin Barrett brilliantly flicked the ball on to him; England were leading 33-0 at half-time; Dan Caprice came on as a replacement for Kevin Barrett in the 8th minute; England were still leading 33-0 in the 10th minute; England were leading 40-0 midway through the second half; England were leading 45-0 with 1 minute remaining when Ben Gollings missed an eminently kickable conversion attempt)

CAPTAIN: *Kevin Barrett*

11th Dec ARGENTINA 7 **ENGLAND** 17

[*This match kicked off at 3.10pm*]

(*Tomas Passerotti scored in the 2nd minute!; Nick Royle went off injured in the 3rd minute, being replaced by Christian Wade; England were losing 7-0 midway through the first half; England were still losing 7-0 in the 6th minute when Christian Wade scored a brilliant try; James Rodwell came on as a temporary blood replacement for Isoa Damu shortly before half-time; England were drawing 7-7 at half-time; England were still drawing 7-7 in the 9th minute when Isoa Damu powered through 2 attempted tackles to score; England were leading 12-7 midway through the second half; England were leading still 12-7 in the final minute when Christian Wade scored to clinch the match*)

CAPTAIN: *Ben Gollings*

11th Dec SCOTLAND 19 **ENGLAND** 29

[*This match kicked off at 7.32pm; Nick Royle unavailable due to injury*]

(*Dan Norton scored after just 28 seconds had been played!; England were leading 12-0 in the 3rd minute; England were still leading 12-0 midway through the first half; England were leading 12-7 just before half-time; England were leading 19-7 at half-time; England were still leading 19-7 in the 8th minute when Mike Adamson scored after Dan Norton dropped the ball out of the tackle; England were leading 18-12 in the 9th minute when Ben Gollings scored after Isoa Damu threw a brilliant pass; England were leading 24-12 midway through the second half; England were still leading 24-12 with 2 minutes remaining when Dan Caprice had his pass intercepted by Mike Adamson who then ran 37 metres to score, thus 2 tries and 12 points were preventable; England were leading 24-19 when the full-time hooter sounded, but the ball was still in play and Dan Norton was able to score a try to clinch the match*)

CAPTAIN: *Kevin Barrett*

Quarter-Final

12th Dec NEW ZEALAND 22 **ENGLAND*** 19

[*This match kicked off at 2.13pm; Nick Royle unavailable due to injury*]

(*This match was played in 95 degree heat; Ben Gollings scored a brilliant 28 metre solo try after just 24 seconds had been played, but then missed the eminently kickable conversion attempt!; England were leading 5-0 in the 3rd minute when Ben Gollings scored another superb solo try which he then brilliantly converted from the left touchline; England were leading 12-0 midway through the first half; England were still leading 12-0 in the 6th minute; England were leading 12-5 just before half-time when Kevin Barrett scored after Chris Cracknell brilliantly flicked the ball on; England were leading 19-5 at half-time; England were leading 19-10 in the 9th minute; England were leading 19-17 midway through the second half; England were still leading 19-17 with 1 minute remaining when Zar Lawrence scored after a poor tackle by Christian Wade, thus 5 points were preventable; New Zealand were allowed to score 17 unanswered points in the second half to win the match*)

[Plate Semi-Final:]

[12th Dec AUSTRALIA 5 **ENGLAND** 24]

[*This match kicked off at 5.07pm; Nick Royle unavailable due to injury*]

(*Pat McCutcheon scored in the 3rd minute!; England were losing 5-0 midway through the first half; England were still losing 5-0 in the 5th minute when Christian Wade scored a brilliant 94 metre solo try; England were drawing 5-5 in the 7th minute; England were leading 10-5 at half-time; England were leading 17-5 in the 9th minute;*

England were still leading 17-5 midway through the second half when Christian Wade scored another try after he wrong-footed the Australian defence with 2 brilliant sidesteps; England scored 24 unanswered points to win the match; England were leading 24-5 in the final minute when Dan Norton wasted a great try-scoring opportunity by knocking the ball on while the Australian line was at his mercy)

CAPTAIN: *Kevin Barrett* [*Ben Gollings*]

[Plate Final:]

[12th Dec SOUTH AFRICA 7 **ENGLAND** 21]

[*This match kicked off at 7.35pm; Nick Royle unavailable due to injury*]

(*Dan Norton scored in the 3rd minute after Ben Gollings made a brilliant break!; England were leading 7-0 midway through the first half; England were still leading 7-0 in the 7th minute; England were leading 14-0 at half-time; England were still leading 14-0 in the 9th minute when Isoa Damu scored after Christian Wade made a brilliant 40 metre run; England scored 21 unanswered points to win the match; England were leading 21-0 midway through the second half; Dan Caprice came on as a replacement for Kevin Barrett with 1 minute remaining; England were still leading 21-0 in the last minute when Christian Wade bought a dummy by Shaun Venter who then went on to score, thus 7 points were preventable; Ben Gollings scored 55 points in this tournament and thus increased his overall IRB World Sevens record to 2143*)

2010

ENGLAND U20 TRAINING MATCH

CAPTAIN: *Jacob Rowan*

21st Jan Cambridge University 7 **ENGLAND U20 XV** 61

University Football Ground, Grange Road, Cambridge

[This match kicked off at 7.15pm; The England U20 XV named a 10 man bench selection; James Gaskell, Jamie Gibson, Jordi Pasqualin, Rory Clegg, Tom Casson, Freddie Burns, Marcus Watson and Tom Homer all in original training squad of 32 but were not selected for team or bench; Owen Farrell was not part of the original squad; Will Welch, Tom Catterick and Lee Imiolek toured Argentina with England U18 in July-August 2008; Alex Gray captained England U18 on their tour of Argentina in July-August 2008; Jake Sharp, Jonathan Joseph, Charlie Matthews and Sam Stuart all toured South Africa with England U18 in July-August 2009; Kieran Brookes played for an Ireland U20 Development XV in April 2009; Mako Vunipola toured Argentina and South Africa with England U18 in July-August 2008 and July-August 2009 respectively; Jackson Wray played for Major R.V. Stanley's XV against Oxford University at Iffley Road on 17th November 2009; Owen Farrell toured Argentina and South Africa with England U18 in July-August 2008 and July-August 2009 respectively, played for Major R.V. Stanley's XV against Oxford University at Iffley Road on 17th November 2009 and played for M.R. Steele-Bodger's XV against Cambridge University at Grange Road on 25th November 2009; Mako Vunipola was the son of Fe'ao Vunipola, who won 32 caps for Tonga between 1988-2001; Owen Farrell was the son of Andy Farrell]

(The England U20 XV was losing 7-0 in the early stages; The England U20 XV was drawing 7-7 midway through the first half; The England U20 XV was still drawing 7-7 in the 26th minute; The England U20 XV was leading 26-7 at half-time; The England U20 XV scored 61 unanswered points to win the match)

ENGLAND STUDENTS MATCH

CAPTAIN: *Phil Burgess*

30th Jan PORTUGAL XV 21 **ENGLAND STUDENTS*** 18

Estádio Universitário, Lisbon

[This match kicked off at 3.00pm; Tom Peddie, Nic Carter, Matt Smith (2), Evan Stewart, Dave Hughes, Henry Pyrgos, Jimmy Fouracre, Sam Dimmick, Tim Streather, Richard Coskie, Kristian Cook, Tom Shiel, Nick Barrett and Geraint Walsh all in original training squad of 36 but were not selected for team or bench; Derek Salisbury, George Thomas, Will Warden and Louis Messer all in revised squad of 26 but were not selected for team or bench; Will Chudleigh, Louis Messer, Sean Morris and John Bordiss were all not part of the original squad]

(This match was played in hot conditions; England Students were leading 3-0 in the early stages; England Students were still leading 3-0 midway through the first half; England Students were leading 3-0 in the 32nd minute; England Students missed 2 penalty goal attempts in the first half; England Students were drawing 3-3 just before half-time when some superb handling allowed Matt Humphries to score; England Students were leading 10-3 at half-time; England Students were leading 10-6 in the 49th minute; England Students were leading 15-6 midway through the second half; England Students were leading 18-6 in the 65th minute; England Students were leading 18-9 with 4 minutes remaining; England Students were leading 18-14 with 2 minutes remaining; The Portugal XV was allowed to score 15 unanswered points to win the match)

ENGLAND SAXONS INTERNATIONAL MATCH

CAPTAIN: *George Skivington*

31st Jan **ENGLAND SAXONS** 17 IRELAND A 13

Recreation Ground, Bath

[This match kicked off at 2.00pm; Anthony Allen unavailable due to injury; Tom Varndell made himself available for this match but was not selected!; Dan Cole, Matt Mullan, Chris Robshaw, Dan Ward-Smith and Chris Ashton all in original training squad of 32 but withdrew as they were now required to join the full England international squad, being replaced by Tom Mercey, Paul Doran-Jones, Luke Narraway, Tom Wood and Noah Cato respectively; Alex Corbisiero, Nick Kennedy, Paul Sackey and Olly Morgan all in original training squad of 32 but withdrew due to injury, being replaced by David Flatman, Geoff Parling, Miles Benjamin and Alex Goode respectively; Danny Cipriani in original training squad of 32 but withdrew due to bereavement, being replaced by Jon Clarke; Tom Rees and Joe Simpson in original training squad of 32 but were unavailable for this match due to injury; George Chuter, Duncan Bell, Ben Kay, Ben Woods, Richard Wigglesworth, Charlie Hodgson and Stephen Myler all in original training squad of 32 but were not selected for team or bench; The Ireland A team was officially renamed as the Ireland Wolfhounds on 5th February 2010]

(This match was played in cold conditions on a muddy pitch; Paddy Wallace scored a penalty goal in the 3rd minute!; The England Saxons were losing 3-0 in the 14th minute when Ben Youngs made a superb run that enabled Dave Strettle to score a try which Shane Geraghty then brilliantly converted from the right touchline; The England Saxons were leading 7-3 midway through the first half; The England Saxons were leading 7-6 in the 30th minute when some superb handling allowed Shane Geraghty to score; The England Saxons were leading 14-6 at half-time; Andy Saull went off injured in the 47th minute, being replaced by Luke Narraway; David Paice went off injured in the 58th minute, being replaced by Rob Webber; The England Saxons were still leading 14-6 midway through the second half; The England Saxons were leading 14-6 in the 64th minute when a poor defensive alignment allowed Chris Henry to score, thus 7 points were preventable; The England Saxons were leading 14-13 in the 69th minute when Shane Geraghty missed a speculative 47 metre penalty goal attempt; The England Saxons were leading 14-13 in the first minute of injury time when Shane Geraghty scored a 23 metre penalty goal with the last kick of the match to clinch the game; Phil Dowson had a brilliant game)

NEW ZEALAND INTERNATIONAL SEVENS

Westpac Stadium, Wellington

CAPTAIN: *Kevin Barrett*

First Round - Pool 'C'

5th Feb USA 7 **ENGLAND** 31

[This match kicked off at 1.44pm]

(Ben Gollings scored in the 2nd minute!; England were leading 5-0 midway through the first half; England were still leading 5-0 in the 6th minute when Jake Abbott saved a certain try by tackling Nick Edwards; England were leading 5-0 just before half-time when Mat Turner scored a brilliant 53 metre solo try, with Ben Gollings then missing the eminently kickable conversion attempt; England were leading 10-0 at half-time; Jake Abbott scored after just 35 seconds of the second half had been played!; England were leading 17-0 in the 10th minute when Mat Turner scored another try after

***Christian Wade made a superb 45 metre run; England were leading 24-0 midway through the second half; England were still leading 24-0 with 2 minutes remaining when Kevin Barrett scored after Ben Gollings made a brilliant 42 metre run; England scored 31 unanswered points to win the match; England were leading 31-0 in the final minute when collectively poor tackling allowed Leonard Peters to score, thus 7 points were preventable*)**

CAPTAIN: *Kevin Barrett* [*Ben Gollings*]

5th Feb TONGA 19 **ENGLAND** 24

[*This match kicked off at 4.40pm*]

(*Christian Wade scored in the 2nd minute!; England were leading 7-0 midway through the first half; England were still leading 7-0 in the 6th minute when Siaosi Iongi scored after a poor tackle by Christian Wade; England were drawing 7-7 just before half-time when a poor defensive alignment allowed Etisoni Hefa to score, thus 2 tries and 14 points were preventable; England were losing 14-7 at half-time; Kevin Barrett went off injured in the 9th minute, being replaced by Dan Caprice; England were still losing 14-7 in the 10th minute when Dan Norton scored a brilliant 51 metre solo try, with Ben Gollings then missing the eminently kickable conversion attempt; England were losing 14-12 midway through the second half; England were leading 19-14 with 1 minute of normal time remaining when the referee unaccountably allowed play to continue after Josateki Veikune threw a clear forward pass and Charles Mateo went on to score, thus 7 points were unlawful; England were drawing 19-19 when the full-time hooter sounded, but the ball was still in play and Dan Caprice was able to score a match-winning try*)

CAPTAIN: *Ben Gollings*

5th Feb KENYA 10 **ENGLAND** 24

[*This match kicked off at 9.12pm; Kevin Barrett unavailable due to injury*]

(*Gibson Weru Kahuthia scored in the 2nd minute!; England were losing 5-0 midway through the first half when Dan Caprice scored a brilliant 80 metre solo try; England were leading 12-5 in the 5th minute; England were leading 12-5 just before half-time; England were leading 17-5 at half-time; England were still leading 17-5 midway through the second half; England were leading 17-5 with 1 minute remaining when Dan Caprice gathered the ball behind his own line, kicked ahead and then followed up to score after Lavin Asego failed to fall on the ball properly!; England scored 24 unanswered points to win the match; England were leading 24-5 in the final minute*)

Quarter-Final

6th Feb CANADA 0 **ENGLAND** 31

[*This match kicked off at 3.17pm; Kevin Barrett unavailable due to injury*]

(*Dan Caprice and Ben Gollings alternated between scrum half and fly half throughout this match; England were drawing 0-0 midway through the first half when Dan Norton saved a certain try by tackling Sean Duke; England were still drawing 0-0 just before half-time when Dan Caprice scored after he took a return pass from James Rodwell; England were leading 7-0 at half-time; Don Barrell came on as a replacement for Jake Abbott at the start of the second half; England were still leading 7-0 in the 9th minute when Ben Gollings caught the ball at the tail of a Canadian lineout and ran 68 metres to score a brilliant solo try, but then missed the eminently kickable conversion attempt!; England were leading 12-0 in the 10th minute when Ben Gollings powered through to score another try; England were leading 19-0 midway through the second half; Christian Wade came on as a replacement for Dan Norton with 3 minutes*

remaining; England were still leading 19-0 with 2 minutes remaining when Mat Turner broke from the base of a ruck to score)

Semi-Final

6th Feb	FIJI	28	**ENGLAND***	19

[This match kicked off at 7.00pm; Kevin Barrett unavailable due to injury]

(Christian Wade scored a brilliant 43 metre solo try after just 55 seconds had been played!; England were leading 7-0 in the 3rd minute when Emosi Vucago scored after a poor tackle by Ben Gollings; England were drawing 7-7 midway through the first half; England were still drawing 7-7 in the 4th minute when collectively poor tackling allowed Seremaia Burotu to score; England were losing 14-7 in the 6th minute when Don Barrell crossed the tryline and appeared to score but the referee adjudged that the ball had hit Waisale Beci's knee rather than the ground; England were losing 14-7 just before half-time when Osea Kolinisau scored after a poor tackle by James Rodwell; Fiji were allowed to score 21 unanswered points to win the match; England were losing 21-7 at half-time; England were still losing 21-7 midway through the second half when Mat Turner scored a brilliant 58 metre solo try; England were losing 21-14 with 1 minute remaining when a poor defensive alignment allowed William Ryder to score from a tap penalty, thus 4 tries and 28 points were preventable; England were losing 28-14 in the final minute when Ben Gollings broke from the base of a ruck to score a consolation try; Ben Gollings increased his IRB World Sevens record to 2187 points in this tournament)

6 NATIONS CHAMPIONSHIP

CAPTAIN: *Steve Borthwick*

6th Feb	**ENGLAND**	30	WALES	17

Twickenham

[This match kicked off at 5.00pm; This match commemorated the Centenary of the first cap international rugby match being played at Twickenham, with England wearing special white shirts based on the ones they wore in the aforementioned game against Wales on 15th January 1910; Phil Vickery, Olly Barkley and Mike Tindall unavailable due to injury; Matt Stevens and Michael Lipman unavailable due to suspension; James Simpson-Daniel made himself available for this match but was not selected!; Joe Worsley was rested as he was not match-fit; Riki Flutey selected but withdrew due to injury, Toby Flood was moved from the bench to the team and Shontayne Hape was then selected for the bench; Shontayne Hape then himself withdrew on the day of the match due to illness, being replaced by Dan Hipkiss; Andy Sheridan, Julian White, Tom Croft and Harry Ellis all in original training squad of 32 but withdrew due to injury, being replaced by Matt Mullan, Dan Cole, Dan Ward-Smith and Ben Youngs respectively; Courtney Lawes in original training squad of 32 but was unavailable for this match due to injury; Lee Mears, Jordan Crane, Matt Banahan and Chris Ashton all in original training squad of 32 but were not selected for team or bench; Tom Palmer (2) and Chris Robshaw were added to the squad on 24th January 2010]

(This match was played in cold conditions; The England forwards dominated the lineout in the first half; England were drawing 0-0 in the 8th minute when Jonny Wilkinson was caught in possession by both Shane Williams and James Hook, who then proceeded to carry him into touch!; England were leading 3-0 in the 12th minute; England were still leading 3-0 in the 18th minute when Nick Easter crossed the tryline but then could not get downward pressure on the ball; England were leading 3-0 midway through the first half; England were drawing 3-3 in the 28th minute; England

***were leading 6-3 just before half-time when James Haskell powered through to score; England were leading 13-3 at half-time; Danny Care scored a try which Jonny Wilkinson then converted to give England a 20-3 lead in the 45th minute; England scored 17 unanswered points to win the match; England were leading 20-10 in the 49th minute; England were still leading 20-10 midway through the second half; Dan Cole came on as a replacement for David Wilson (2) in the 60th minute; England were leading 20-10 with 9 minutes remaining when a poor defensive alignment allowed James Hook to score, thus 7 points were preventable; England were leading 20-17 with 5 minutes remaining when James Haskell scored another try after Matt Tait threw a brilliant reverse pass; England were leading 27-17 with 1 minute remaining*)**

14th Feb ITALY 12 **ENGLAND** 17

Stadio Flaminio, Rome

[*This match kicked off at 3.30pm; Andy Sheridan, Phil Vickery, Julian White, Tom Croft, Harry Ellis, Olly Barkley and Mike Tindall all unavailable due to injury; Matt Stevens and Michael Lipman unavailable due to suspension; James Simpson-Daniel made himself available for this match but was not selected!; Joe Worsley was rested as he was not match-fit; Lee Mears, Courtney Lawes, Chris Robshaw, Jordan Crane, Dan Ward-Smith, Ben Youngs, Matt Banahan, Dan Hipkiss, Shontayne Hape, Chris Ashton and Ben Foden all in original training squad of 33 but were not selected for team or bench*]

(*The England backs kicked away too much possession; England were drawing 0-0 in the 1st minute when Delon Armitage put in a brilliant grubber kick, but Tito Tebaldi managed to kick the ball over the dead ball line!; England were leading 3-0 in the 10th minute; England were drawing 3-3 in the 18th minute when Jonny Wilkinson missed a kickable 43 metre penalty goal attempt; England were still drawing 3-3 midway through the first half; England were drawing 3-3 in the 23rd minute when Jonny Wilkinson missed an eminently kickable 18 metre penalty goal attempt; England were still drawing 3-3 in the 35th minute; England were losing 6-3 in the 40th minute when Riki Flutey broke through and ran 50 metres before he was tackled as he looked in vain for support; England were still losing 6-3 just before half-time; England were drawing 6-6 at half-time; England were still drawing 6-6 in the 45th minute when some superb handling allowed Matt Tait to score, with Jonny Wilkinson then missing the eminently kickable conversion attempt; England were leading 11-6 in the 56th minute when Ugo Monye wasted a great try-scoring opportunity by failing to pass to the unmarked Mark Cueto; England were leading 14-6 midway through the second half; Matt Mullan came on as a replacement for Tim Payne in the 59th minute; England were leading 14-9 in the 64th minute; England were leading 14-12 with 6 minutes remaining when Jonny Wilkinson scored a brilliant 22 metre drop goal to clinch the match*)

27th Feb **ENGLAND*** 16 IRELAND 20

Twickenham

[*This match kicked off at 4.00pm; Andy Sheridan, Phil Vickery, Julian White, Tom Croft, Harry Ellis and Mike Tindall all unavailable due to injury; Matt Stevens and Michael Lipman unavailable due to suspension; James Simpson-Daniel made himself available for this match but was not selected!; Dan Hipkiss in original training squad of 33 but was unavailable for this match due to injury; Matt Mullan, Steve Thompson (2), Courtney Lawes, Chris Robshaw, Steffon Armitage, Jordan Crane, Dan Ward-Smith, Ben Youngs, Matt Banahan, Shontayne Hape and Chris Ashton all in original training squad of 33 but were not selected for team or bench; Charlie Hodgson and Jamie Noon were added to the squad on 22nd February 2010 to provide injury cover*

for Jonny Wilkinson and Dan Hipkiss respectively; Joe Worsley was added to the squad on 22nd February 2010]

(*The first half of this match was played in wet conditions; The England forwards were outplayed in the loose by their Irish counterparts; A poor defensive alignment allowed Tommy Bowe to score in the 4th minute!; Simon Shaw went off injured in the 5th minute, being replaced by Louis Deacon; England were losing 5-0 in the 10th minute when they created and then squandered an overlap; England were still losing 5-0 in the 12th minute when Jonny Wilkinson hit the right-hand post with an eminently kickable 28 metre penalty goal attempt; England were losing 5-3 in the 16th minute; England were still losing 5-3 midway through the first half; England were losing 8-3 in the 32nd minute when Danny Care saved a certain try by getting back and grounding the ball before Jamie Heaslip could reach it; England were still losing 8-3 shortly before half-time; England were losing 8-6 at half-time; England were still losing 8-6 in the 43rd minute when they awarded a 52 metre penalty in a position where Ireland had a poor defensive alignment, but Danny Care then wasted this great try-scoring opportunity by electing not to take a quick tap; Jonny Wilkinson duly missed the resulting speculative kick at goal!; Delon Armitage went off injured in the 49th minute, being replaced by Ben Foden; England were losing 8-6 in the 54th minute when Danny Care unaccountably threw Tomás O'Leary to the ground after Ireland had been penalised at a scrum, at which point a touch judge intervened to draw the referee's attention to this aforementioned infringement and the penalty was therefore reversed, which allowed Keith Earls to score from the resulting lineout; England were losing 13-6 midway through the second half when the video referee adjudged that Dan Cole had correctly grounded the ball to score; England were drawing 13-13 in the 67th minute when Jonny Wilkinson missed a kickable 31 metre penalty goal attempt; England were still drawing 13-13 with 9 minutes of normal time remaining when Jonny Wilkinson scored a brilliant 33 metre drop goal; England were leading 16-13 with 6 minutes of normal time remaining when another poor defensive alignment allowed Tommy Bowe to score again, thus 3 tries and 17 points were preventable*)

13th Mar SCOTLAND 15 **ENGLAND*** 15

Murrayfield

[*This match kicked off at 5.00pm; Andy Sheridan, Phil Vickery, Julian White, Tom Croft and Harry Ellis all unavailable due to injury; Matt Stevens and Michael Lipman unavailable due to suspension; James Simpson-Daniel made himself available for this match but was not selected!; Dan Hipkiss in original training squad of 34 but withdrew due to injury, being replaced by Mike Tindall; Simon Shaw and Dan Ward-Smith in original training squad of 34 but were unavailable for this match due to injury; Matt Mullan, Lee Mears, Chris Robshaw, Steffon Armitage, Jordan Crane, Paul Hodgson, Matt Banahan, Shontayne Hape and Chris Ashton all in original training squad of 34 but were not selected for team or bench; Tom Palmer (2), Hendre Fourie, Shane Geraghty and Olly Morgan were added to the squad on 8th March 2010 to provide injury cover for Simon Shaw, Dan Ward-Smith, Toby Flood and Delon Armitage respectively*]

(*This match took place on a poor playing surface; The England forwards could not win any possession in the first half; England were losing 3-0 in the 7th minute; England were still losing 3-0 in the 12th minute when they created an overlap, but Jonny Wilkinson then wasted this great try-scoring opportunity by throwing a poor miss pass to Dylan Hartley; England were losing 6-3 midway through the first half; England were drawing 6-6 in the 32nd minute; England were still drawing 6-6 shortly before half-time; England were losing 9-6 at half-time; England were drawing 9-9 in the 42nd*

***minute; Jonny Wilkinson went off injured in the 45th minute, being replaced by Toby Flood; England were leading 12-9 in the 52nd minute; England were drawing 12-12 in the 56th minute when Dan Cole saved a certain try by tackling Chris Cusiter; Ugo Monye went off injured immediately afterwards, being replaced by Ben Youngs who had to play out of position as a wing; England were still drawing 12-12 midway through the second half when Toby Flood missed a speculative 47 metre penalty goal attempt; England were drawing 12-12 in the 64th minute when they created and then squandered an overlap; England were leading 15-12 in the 65th minute; England were drawing 15-15 in the 69th minute; England were still drawing 15-15 with 2 minutes of normal time remaining when Toby Flood hit the padding at the foot of the left-hand post with another speculative 48 metre penalty goal attempt; England were drawing 15-15 in the second minute of injury time when Toby Flood had a speculative 41 metre drop goal attempt charged down by Rory Lawson; Steve Borthwick injured his knee in this match but elected to remain on the pitch*)**

CAPTAIN: *Lewis Moody*

20th Mar FRANCE 12 **ENGLAND*** 10

Stade de France, Paris

[*This match kicked off at 8.45pm; Andy Sheridan, Phil Vickery, Julian White, Tom Croft, Harry Ellis and Dan Hipkiss all unavailable due to injury; Matt Stevens and Michael Lipman unavailable due to suspension; James Simpson-Daniel made himself available for this match but was not selected!; Steve Borthwick selected as captain but withdrew due to injury, Louis Deacon was moved from the bench to the team and Tom Palmer (2) was then selected for the bench; Dan Ward-Smith and Ugo Monye in original training squad of 34 but were unavailable for this match due to injury; Matt Mullan, Lee Mears, Courtney Lawes, Chris Robshaw, Steffon Armitage, Jordan Crane, Paul Hodgson, Matt Banahan, Shontayne Hape and Delon Armitage all in original training squad of 34 but were not selected for team or bench; Charlie Hodgson was added to the squad on 15th March 2010 to provide injury cover for Jonny Wilkinson; Tom Palmer (2) was added to the squad on 17th March 2010 to provide injury cover for Steve Borthwick; David Flatman and Hendre Fourie were added to the squad on 19th March 2010; Chris Ashton played for England A at Rugby League in October 2006, became a Rugby Union player in August 2007 when he joined Northampton and played in the Samurai team that won the Amsterdam Heineken Sevens on 16th-17th May 2009*]

**(*This match was played in intermittent heavy rain on a poor playing surface; The England scrum was put under severe pressure in the first half; François Trinh-Duc scored a drop goal in the 4th minute!; England were losing 3-0 in the 5th minute when some superb handling amongst the backs allowed Ben Foden to score a try which Toby Flood then brilliantly converted from the left touchline; Simon Shaw went off injured in the 15th minute, being replaced by Tom Palmer (2); England were leading 7-6 midway through the first half; England were losing 9-7 in the 25th minute; England were losing 12-7 in the 34th minute; England were losing 12-7 at half-time; Steve Thompson (2) and David Wilson (2) came on as replacements for Dylan Hartley and Dan Cole respectively at the start of the second half; England were still losing 12-7 in the 48th minute when Toby Flood missed a speculative 39 metre drop goal attempt; England were losing 12-7 immediately afterwards when Chris Ashton wasted a great try-scoring opportunity by electing to kick when there was an overlap outside him; Matt Tait came on as a replacement for Mike Tindall in the 53rd minute; England were still losing 12-7 midway through the second half when Mark Cueto broke through but then ran out of support; Jonny Wilkinson came on as a replacement for Riki Flutey in the 61st minute, with Toby Flood then switching from fly half to inside centre to*

accommodate Jonny Wilkinson; Dan Cole came back on as a temporary blood replacement for Tim Payne in the 64th minute, with David Wilson (2) then moving from tight-head to loose-head prop to accommodate Dan Cole; England were losing 12-7 in the 68th minute when Jonny Wilkinson scored a brilliant 43 metre penalty goal from the right touchline; Nick Easter injured playing in the match)

U20 6 NATIONS CHAMPIONSHIP

CAPTAIN: *Jacob Rowan*

5th Feb **ENGLAND U20** 41 WALES U20 14

Kingsholm, Gloucester

[This match kicked off at 7.45pm; Arthur Ellis selected for bench but withdrew on the day of the match due to injury, being replaced by Rob Buchanan; Jordi Pasqualin and Marcus Watson in original training squad of 32 but were unavailable for this match due to injury; Christian Wade in original training squad of 32 but withdrew due to his England Sevens commitments; Kieran Brooks, Mako Vunipola, Peter Elder, Danny Wright, Jamie Gibson, Jake Sharp and Tom Casson all in original training squad of 32 but were not selected for team or bench; Rob Buchanan toured South Africa with England U18 in July-August 2009]

(Alex Gray was sent off in the 64th minute for stamping and thus duly banned for 2 weeks)

(This match was played in cold conditions on a muddy pitch; Matthew Jarvis scored a penalty goal in the 2nd minute!; England U20 were drawing 3-3 in the 13th minute; England U20 were losing 8-3 midway through the first half; England U20 were still losing 8-3 in the 37th minute; England U20 were losing 8-6 at half-time; England U20 were still losing 8-6 in the 42nd minute when Joe Marler scored a brilliant 33 metre solo try; England U20 were leading 13-11 in the 47th minute when Rory Clegg put up a superb cross-kick that allowed Jamie George to score a try which Freddie Burns then brilliantly converted from the right touchline; Jonathan Joseph came on as a replacement for Tom Catterick in the 52nd minute, with Tom Homer then switching from centre to full back to accommodate Jonathan Joseph; England U20 were leading 20-14 in the 56th minute when some superb handling amongst the forwards allowed Jacob Rowan to score; Jonny May came on as a replacement for Freddie Burns in the 58th minute, with Rory Clegg then moving from centre to fly half to accommodate Jonny May; England U20 were leading 27-14 midway through the second half; England U20 were still leading 27-14 in the 66th minute when Joe Marler powered through 2 attempted tackles to score another try; England U20 were leading 34-14 with 7 minutes of normal time remaining; England U20 scored 21 unanswered points to seal the match; Jamie George had a brilliant game)

12th Feb ITALY U20 10 **ENGLAND U20** 16

Stadio Mario e Romolo Pacifici, San Donà di Piave

[This match kicked off at 7.00pm; Jordi Pasqualin and Marcus Watson in original training squad of 32 but were unavailable for this match due to injury; Alex Gray in original training squad of 32 but withdrew due to suspension; Christian Wade in original training squad of 32 but withdrew due to his England Sevens commitments; Calum Green, James Gaskell, Jamie Gibson, Sam Smith, Rory Clegg and Tom Homer all in original training squad of 32 but withdrew due to club commitments; Kieran Brooks and Mako Vunipola in original training squad of 32 but were not selected for team or bench; Sam Edgerley and George Kruis were not part of the original squad; Sam Edgerley toured Argentina and South Africa with England U18 in July-August 2008 and July-August 2009 respectively]

(England U20 made a number of handling errors in this match; Jonny May scored a brilliant try in the 3rd minute!; England U20 were leading 7-0 midway through the first half; England U20 were still leading 7-0 just before half-time; England U20 were leading 7-3 at half-time; Jake Sharp came on as a replacement for Tom Catterick at the start of the second half, with Freddie Burns then switching from fly half to full back to accommodate Jake Sharp; England U20 were still leading 7-3 midway through the second half; England U20 were leading 13-3 in the 70th minute; England U20 were leading 16-3 in the last minute of normal time; England U20 were still leading 16-3 in the sixth minute of injury time)

26th Feb **ENGLAND U20*** 10 IRELAND U20 25

Kingsholm, Gloucester

[This match kicked off at 7.45pm; Mako Vunipola, Calum Green, Jamie Gibson, Will Welch, Sam Smith, Rory Clegg, Tom Homer and Marcus Watson all in original training squad of 34 but withdrew due to club commitments; James Gaskell, Peter Elder, Sam Stuart, Sam Edgerley and Tom Catterick all in original training squad of 34 but were not selected for team or bench; Jack Wallace was not part of the original squad; Jack Wallace toured Argentina and South Africa with England U18 in July-August 2008 and July-August 2009 respectively]

(The England U20 forwards won plenty of ball but the backs were unable to turn this ample possession into points; England U20 were leading 3-0 in the 15th minute; England U20 were still leading 3-0 midway through the first half when Andrew Conway scored after Freddie Burns dropped the ball out of the tackle 5 metres short of the Ireland U20 tryline; England U20 were losing 10-3 in the 29th minute; England U20 were still losing 10-3 shortly afterwards when Brendan Macken knocked Jonny May's chip-kick on into the arms of Darren Hudson, who then ran 35 metres to score after the referee unaccountably allowed play to continue, thus 7 points were unlawful; Ireland U20 were allowed to score 17 unanswered points to win the match; England U20 were losing 17-3 in the 35th minute when the referee awarded a penalty try after the Ireland U20 forwards collapsed a scrum as they were being driven backwards over their own line; England U20 were losing 17-10 shortly before half-time when Jack Wallace slipped over as he attempted to get back and gather Darren Hudson's grubber kick, which allowed Andrew Conway to follow up and score another try, thus 2 tries and 12 points were preventable; England U20 were losing 22-10 at half-time; Joe Marler came on as a replacement for Lee Imiolek in the 50th minute; Christian Wade came on as a replacement for Jonny May in the 58th minute; England U20 were still losing 22-10 midway through the second half; England U20 were losing 22-10 with 5 minutes remaining)

12th Mar SCOTLAND U20 6 **ENGLAND U20** 27

Firhill, Glasgow

[This match kicked off at 7.30pm; Will Hurrell in original training squad of 34 but was unavailable for this match due to injury; Shaun Knight, Kieran Brooks, James Gaskell, Peter Elder, George Kruis, Alex Gray, Sam Stuart, Freddie Burns, Jake Sharp, Christian Wade, Sam Edgerley, Jonny May and Tom Homer all in original training squad of 34 but were not selected for team or bench; Andy Forsyth and Mark Atkinson were not part of the original squad; Andy Forsyth toured Argentina with England U18 in July-August 2008; Marcus Watson toured Argentina and South Africa with England U18 in July-August 2008 and July-August 2009 respectively]

(Andy Forsyth scored in the 4th minute after Rory Clegg put in a brilliant grubber kick!; England U20 were leading 10-0 in the 9th minute; Rory Clegg threw a superb miss pass which enabled Marcus Watson to score a try that Rory Clegg then brilliantly

converted from the right touchline to give England U20 a 17-3 lead midway through the first half; England U20 were leading 17-6 in the 25th minute; England U20 were still leading 17-6 in the 38th minute; England U20 were leading 20-6 just before half-time when Charlie Matthews scored after Sam Smith made a superb 25 metre break; England U20 were leading 27-6 at half-time; Mako Vunipola came on as a replacement for Lee Imiolek in the 54th minute; Scotland U20 were still losing 27-6 midway through the second half when Alex Blair crossed the England U20 line but then dropped the ball in the act of scoring!; Mark Atkinson came on as a replacement for Tom Casson in the 62nd minute; England U20 were leading 27-6 in the closing stages when Jonathan Joseph had a great try-scoring chance but was tackled short of the Scotland U20 line; Rory Clegg had a brilliant game)

21st Mar FRANCE U20 33 **ENGLAND U20** 47

Stade du Préhembert, St Nazaire

[This match kicked off at 3.00pm; Will Hurrell unavailable due to injury; Mako Vunipola and Jonathan Joseph in original training squad of 24 but were not selected for team or bench]

(England U20 were drawing 0-0 in the 1st minute when Jamie Gibson charged down a kick by Jean-Marc Doussain and then regathered the ball to score!; England U20 were leading 14-5 in the 8th minute; England U20 were leading 14-12 midway through the first half; England U20 were leading 20-12 in the 30th minute; England U20 were leading 20-19 in the 35th minute; England U20 were leading 23-19 at half-time; England U20 were still leading 23-19 in the 43rd minute when Marcus Watson scored a brilliant try; England U20 were leading 30-19 in the 46th minute when Tom Casson scored a superb try; Charlie Davies came on as a replacement for Sam Harrison (2) in the 50th minute; England U20 were leading 37-19 in the 54th minute when Sam Smith scored after Rory Clegg put up a brilliant cross-kick; England U20 scored 24 unanswered points to clinch the match; England U20 were leading 44-19 midway through the second half; England U20 were leading 44-26 in the 63rd minute; England U20 were leading 47-26 with 4 minutes remaining; Tom Homer played brilliantly and scored 22 points in this match)

ENGLAND SAXONS INTERNATIONAL MATCH

CAPTAIN: *George Skivington*

7th Feb ITALY A 5 **ENGLAND SAXONS** 31

Stadio Comunale, Mogliano Veneto

[This match kicked off at 2.30pm; Anthony Allen unavailable due to injury; Luke Narraway and Ben Youngs in original training squad of 32 but withdrew due to club commitments, being replaced by Chris Robshaw and Danny Cipriani respectively; David Paice and Andy Saull in original training squad of 32 but withdrew due to injury, being replaced by Rob Vickers and Hendre Fourie respectively; Tom Rees and Joe Simpson in original training squad of 32 but were unavailable for this match due to injury; Nick Wood, George Chuter, Duncan Bell, Ben Kay, Ben Woods, Charlie Hodgson, Stephen Myler and Noah Cato all in original training squad of 32 but were not selected for team or bench; Hendre Fourie qualified for England in September 2009 after completing a residency period of 3 years]

(Tom Mercey came on as a blood replacement for David Flatman in the 19th minute; The England Saxons were drawing 0-0 midway through the first half; The England Saxons were still drawing 0-0 in the 30th minute when collectively poor tackling allowed Pablo Canavosio to score, thus 5 points were preventable; The England Saxons were losing 5-0 at half-time; Richard Wigglesworth came on as a replacement

for Micky Young at the start of the second half; The England Saxons were losing 5-3 in the 48th minute; The England Saxons were still losing 5-3 in the 58th minute when Miles Benjamin scored after Dave Strettle made a brilliant run; The England Saxons were leading 10-5 midway through the second half; The England Saxons were leading 17-5 in the 67th minute; The England Saxons were still leading 17-5 with 4 minutes of normal time remaining; The England Saxons were leading 24-5 in the second minute of injury time when Dave Strettle scored a brilliant solo try; The England Saxons scored 31 unanswered points in the second half to win the match)

USA SEVENS

Sam Boyd Stadium, Las Vegas

CAPTAIN: *Ben Gollings*

First Round - Pool 'D'

13th Feb WALES 10 **ENGLAND** 26

[This match kicked off at 1.12pm]

(Collectively poor tackling allowed Lloyd Williams to score in the 2nd minute, thus 5 points were preventable!; England were losing 10-0 in the 4th minute; England were still losing 10-0 midway through the first half; England were losing 10-0 when the half-time hooter sounded, but the ball was still in play and Ben Gollings was able to gather a loose ball and score under the posts; England were losing 10-7 at half-time; England were still losing 10-7 in the 11th minute when Dan Norton scored a brilliant 65 metre solo try, with Ben Gollings then missing the eminently kickable conversion attempt; England were leading 12-10 midway through the second half; England were leading 17-10 with 1 minute of normal time remaining when Ben Gollings scored a brilliant conversion from the right touchline; England were leading 19-10 when the full-time hooter sounded, but the ball was still in play and Ben Gollings was able to score a superb try; England scored 26 unanswered points to win the match)

13th Feb JAPAN 5 **ENGLAND** 24

[This match kicked off at 4.18pm]

(Collectively poor tackling allowed Kaoru Matsushita to score in the 2nd minute, thus 5 points were preventable!; England were losing 5-0 midway through the first half; England were still losing 5-0 in the 5th minute when some superb handling allowed Jake Abbott to score; England were drawing 5-5 at half-time; England were leading 12-5 in the 9th minute; England were still leading 12-5 midway through the second half when Christian Wade scored a brilliant 30 metre solo try, with Ben Gollings then missing the eminently kickable conversion attempt; England were leading 17-5 with 1 minute remaining; England scored 24 unanswered points to win the match; England were leading 24-5 in the final minute when Don Barrell saved a certain try by tackling Takashi Toyomae into touch at the corner flag in the last move of the match)

13th Feb ARGENTINA 12 **ENGLAND*** 12

[This match kicked off at 7.58pm; England wore red shirts for this match]

(England were drawing 0-0 in the 2nd minute when Nick Royle kicked ahead and followed up to score a superb try which Ben Gollings then brilliantly converted from the right touchline!; England were leading 7-0 midway through the first half; England were still leading 7-0 in the 6th minute; England were leading 7-5 when the half-time hooter sounded, but the ball was still in play and Nick Royle was able to break from the base of a ruck to score; England were leading 12-5 at half-time; Dan Caprice came on as a replacement for Ben Gollings in the 8th minute, with Ollie Lindsay-Hague then switching from scrum half to fly half to accommodate Caprice; England were still

***leading 12-5 midway through the second half; England were leading 12-5 with 1 minute remaining when Ollie Lindsay-Hague bought a dummy by Hernan Olivari who then went on to score, thus 7 points were preventable*)**

Quarter-Final

14th Feb KENYA 26 **ENGLAND*** 21 aet

[*This match kicked off at 12.50pm*]

(*Christian Wade scored a brilliant 45 metre solo try in the 3rd minute!; England were leading 7-0 midway through the first half; England were still leading 7-0 in the 5th minute when a poor defensive alignment allowed Gibson Weru Kahuthia to score, thus 7 points were preventable; England were drawing 7-7 just before half-time when Ben Gollings scored after Christian Wade threw a brilliant one-handed pass; England were leading 14-7 at half-time; England were drawing 14-14 in the 9th minute; England were still drawing 14-14 midway through the second half; England were drawing 14-14 with 2 minutes of normal time remaining when Dan Norton scored a brilliant try; England were leading 21-14 in the last minute of normal time; England were drawing 21-21 in the third minute of sudden death extra time when the ball came straight back out of the tunnel at a scrum, but the unsighted referee failed to have the scrum re-set and Benedict Nyambu went on to score after a poor tackle by Dan Caprice, thus 5 points were unlawful*)

[Plate Semi-Final:]

[14th Feb SOUTH AFRICA 27 **ENGLAND*** 14 **]**

[*This match kicked off at 3.38pm*]

(*Collectively poor tackling allowed Kyle Brown to score in the 1st minute!; England were losing 12-0 in the 3rd minute; England were losing 12-0 midway through the first half when Kyle Brown scored another try after Jake Abbott missed a tackle on Branco du Preez; South Africa were allowed to score 17 unanswered points to win the match; England were losing 17-0 just before half-time when Ben Gollings put in a brilliant grubber kick and followed up to score; England were losing 17-7 at half-time; England were still losing 17-7 in the 9th minute when further collectively poor tackling allowed Steven Hunt to score; England were losing 22-7 midway through the second half; England were still losing 22-7 in the 11th minute when Don Barrell lost a strike against the head which led directly to a try by Cecil Afrika, thus 4 tries and 22 points were preventable; England were losing 27-7 when the full-time hooter sounded, but the ball was still in play and Dan Norton was able to score a consolation try; Ben Gollings increased his IRB World Sevens record to 2229 points in this tournament*)

ENGLAND COUNTIES MATCH

CAPTAIN: *Tom Bason*

26th Feb **ENGLAND COUNTIES** 29 IRELAND CLUB XV 25

Stourbridge RFC, Stourton Park, Bridgnorth Road, Stourbridge

[*This match kicked off at 7.30pm; Matt Johnson, Nick Sharpe, Ross Laidlaw, Kyle Dench, Rob Kitching and Peter Hodgkinson all in original training squad of 30 but were not selected for team or bench; This squad of 30 was named on 8th January 2010, with one position initially being listed as 'A.N. Other' until Nick Flynn was selected to fill the vacant place on 12th January 2010; Ben Gerry, James Inglis and Sam Stitcher in revised squad of 22 but withdrew due to injury, being replaced by Matt Hall, Tom Bason and Alex Nash respectively*]

(*This match was played in very cold conditions; England Counties were drawing 0-0 in*

the 2nd minute when both David Howells and Frankie Neale claimed the try that was later officially credited to Frankie Neale!; Sam Ulph scored a brilliant conversion from the left touchline immediately afterwards; England Counties were leading 7-0 in the 5th minute when Luke Baldwin scored a superb 60 metre solo try which Sam Ulph also brilliantly converted from the left touchline!; England Counties scored 14 unanswered points to win the match; England Counties were leading 14-3 in the 8th minute; England Counties were still leading 14-3 midway through the first half; England Counties were leading 14-3 in the 24th minute when some superb handling amongst the backs allowed Frankie Neale to score another try; England Counties were leading 19-3 just before half-time when Frankie Neale scored to complete a hat-trick try after Seb Jewell made a brilliant break; England Counties were leading 26-3 at half-time; England Counties played into a strong wind in the second half; England Counties were still leading 26-3 in the 46th minute when Michael Essex was allowed to score from a rolling maul; England Counties were leading 26-8 in the 54th minute when a poor defensive alignment allowed Stephen Kelly to fly-hack a loose ball 50 metres to score; England Counties were leading 26-15 in the 57th minute when Luke Baldwin broke through but he was then superbly chased back and tackled by John Cleary; England Counties were still leading 26-15 in the 58th minute when Tom Powell saved a certain try by tackling John Cleary; Seb Jewell went off injured in the 59th minute, being replaced by Matt Riley; England Counties were leading 26-15 midway through the second half; Sam Heard went off injured in the 65th minute, being replaced by Tom Warren; England Counties were leading 26-20 in the 66th minute; The Ireland Club XV was allowed to score 17 unanswered points; England Counties were leading 29-20 with 9 minutes of normal time remaining when Matt Riley put in a wayward kick ahead which led directly to another try by Stephen Kelly, thus 3 tries and 17 points were preventable; England Counties were leading 29-25 with 4 minutes of normal time remaining when Steve Parsons saved another certain try by getting back and gathering the ball before Stephen Kelly could reach it; Seb Jewell had a brilliant game)

ENGLAND STUDENTS MATCHES

CAPTAIN: *Phil Burgess*

26th Feb **ENGLAND STUDENTS** 42 Irish Colleges (*IR*) 9

Gosforth RFC, Druid Park, Ponteland Road, Woolsington

[This match kicked off at 7.30pm; Kingston Park Stadium, Newcastle was the original venue for this match, but it was declared unplayable on the day of the game due to snow; Jon Aston, Alex Waddingham and John Bordiss unavailable due to injury]

(This match was played in driving snow in extremely cold conditions; Conor Murphy scored a penalty goal in the 5th minute!; England Students were losing 3-0 in the 7th minute when Phil Burgess broke from the base of a scrum to score; England Students were losing 6-5 in the 15th minute when Phil Burgess scored another try after the Irish Colleges forwards were driven off their own ball at a scrum; England Students were leading 10-9 midway through the first half; England Students were still leading 10-9 just before half-time; Greg Nicholls went off injured in the first half, being replaced by Will Chudleigh; England Students were leading 13-9 at half-time; England Students were leading 16-9 in the 45th minute when some superb handling allowed Evan Stewart to score; England Students were leading 23-9 in the 48th minute when Mark Wilson scored after Phil Burgess made a brilliant break; England Students were leading 30-9 in the 54th minute when Matt Humphries scored a brilliant try; England Students were leading 35-9 midway through the second half; England Students were still leading 35-9 in the 65th minute when some further superb handling allowed Sean

***Morris to score; England Students scored 32 unanswered points to clinch the match; Phil Burgess had a brilliant game*)**

19th Mar French Universities (*FR*) 35 **ENGLAND STUDENTS*** 22

Stade Émile Pons, Riom

[*This match kicked off at 6.30pm; Greg Nicholls unavailable due to injury*]

(*This match was played in wet conditions; England Students were losing 3-0 in the 8th minute; England Students were losing 10-0 in the 16th minute when Sean Morris scored a brilliant 75 metre solo try; England Students were losing 10-7 midway through the first half; Sean Morris went off injured in the 25th minute, being replaced by James Crozier; England Students were still losing 10-7 in the 32nd minute; England Students were losing 13-7 in the 37th minute when some superb handling allowed Louis Messer to score; England Students were losing 13-12 at half-time; England Students played with a strong wind in the second half; England Students were losing 20-12 in the 49th minute; England Students were losing 23-12 midway through the second half; England Students were losing 23-15 in the 64th minute; England Students were losing 28-20 with 3 minutes of normal time remaining when James Crozier scored a brilliant conversion from the left touchline; England Students were losing 28-22 in the fifth minute of injury time and pressing in attack when the ball went loose which allowed the French Universities to instigate a counter-attack that culminated in a try by Clément Albaladejo, thus 7 points were preventable*)

JEAN-CLAUDE BAQUÉ SHIELD MATCH

CAPTAIN: *Tom Bason*

19th Mar FRANCE AMATEURS 29 **ENGLAND COUNTIES** 11

Stade Vélodrome, Roubaix

[*This match kicked off at 8.00pm; The original venue for this match was the Stade Lille Métropole, Villeneuve d'Ascq; Sam Heard and Tom Warren unavailable due to injury; Jonny Hylton played for Major R.V. Stanley's XV against Oxford University at Iffley Road on 17th November 2009; Graham Barr played for Major R.V. Stanley's XV against Oxford University at Iffley Road on both 19th November 2008 and 17th November 2009*]

(*This match was played in wet conditions; The England Counties scrum was put under severe pressure; Frankie Neale scored a brilliant long-range penalty goal in the 5th minute!; England Counties were leading 3-0 midway through the first half; England Counties were losing 14-3 in the 25th minute; England Counties were losing 17-3 in the 30th minute; France Amateurs were allowed to score 17 unanswered points to win the match; England Counties were still losing 17-3 shortly before half-time; England Counties were losing 17-6 at half-time; England Counties were losing 20-6 in the 43rd minute; England Counties were losing 23-6 in the 54th minute when Darren Fox scored from a rolling maul; England Counties were losing 26-11 midway through the second half; Dan Baines came on as a replacement for Dan Legge with 8 minutes of normal time remaining; England Counties were still losing 26-11 in the second minute of injury time; England Counties conceded too many needless penalties within Bertrand Artero's kicking range*)

ADELAIDE SEVENS

Adelaide Oval, Adelaide

CAPTAIN: *Ben Gollings*

First Round - Pool 'D'

19th Mar USA 24 **ENGLAND*** 21

[*This match kicked off at 8.12pm*]

(Mat Turner scored a brilliant 40 metre solo try after just 38 seconds had been played!; England were drawing 7-7 in the 2nd minute; England were still drawing 7-7 midway through the first half; England were losing 12-7 in the 6th minute; England were still losing 12-7 when the half-time hooter sounded, but the ball was still in play and Matt Hawkins was able to score after Christian Wade threw a poor pass out of the tackle in front of his own 22; The USA were allowed to score 17 unanswered points to win the match; England were losing 17-7 at half-time; Ben Gollings chipped ahead and followed up to score a superb try after just 32 seconds of the second half had been played!; England were losing 17-14 in the 10th minute when collectively poor tackling allowed Kevin Swiryn to score, thus 2 tries and 12 points were preventable; England were losing 24-14 midway through the second half; England were still losing 24-14 with 2 minutes of normal time remaining when Nick Royle scored a brilliant 86 metre solo try; England were losing 24-21 when the full-time hooter sounded, but the ball remained in play until Nick Royle wasted a great try-scoring opportunity by electing to kick when there was an overlap outside him)

20th Mar NIUE 0 **ENGLAND** 38

[This match kicked off at 4.27pm]

(Tom Powell scored in the 2nd minute!; England were leading 14-0 midway through the first half; England were still leading 14-0 just before half-time when Nick Royle scored a brilliant 39 metre solo try; England were leading 21-0 at half-time; England were leading 28-0 in the 10th minute; England were still leading 28-0 midway through the second half; England were leading 28-0 with 2 minutes remaining; England were leading 33-0 with 1 minute remaining when Oliver Lindsay-Hague scored a brilliant 47 metre solo try)

20th Mar AUSTRALIA 17 **ENGLAND*** 12

[This match kicked off at 8.10pm]

(Mat Turner scored a brilliant 26 metre solo in the 2nd minute!; England were leading 7-0 midway through the first half when collectively poor tackling allowed Kimami Sitauti to score; England were drawing 7-7 just before half-time; England were leading 12-7 at half-time; England were still leading 12-7 in the 8th minute when a poor defensive alignment allowed Kimami Sitauti to score another try, thus 2 tries and 12 points were preventable; England were drawing 12-12 midway through the second half; England were still drawing 12-12 in the final minute of normal time when the referee unaccountably allowed play to continue after Brackin Karauria-Henry threw a clear forward pass to Kimami Sitauti and Liam Gill went on to score, thus 5 points were unlawful; Dan Caprice injured playing in the match)

[Bowl Quarter-Final:]

[21st Mar PAPUA NEW GUINEA 0 **ENGLAND** 47]

[This match kicked off at 11.00am; Dan Caprice unavailable due to injury]

(Ben Gollings scored in the 3rd minute!; England were leading 7-0 midway through the first half; England were leading 14-0 in the 5th minute; England were leading 21-0 just before half-time; England were leading 26-0 at half-time; James Rodwell scored after just 30 seconds of the second half had been played!; England were leading 33-0 midway through the second half; England were still leading 33-0 with 1 minute of normal time remaining; Ben Gollings scored 22 points in this match)

[Bowl Semi-Final:]

[21st Mar FRANCE 0 **ENGLAND** 19]

[This match kicked off at 2.28pm; Dan Caprice unavailable due to injury]

(England were drawing 0-0 midway through the first half; England were still drawing 0

***-0 in the 6th minute; England were leading 7-0 when the half-time hooter sounded, but the ball was still in play and Chris Brightwell was able to power through 2 attempted tackles to score; England were leading 14-0 at half-time; England were still leading 14-0 in the 10th minute when Ollie Lindsay-Hague scored a brilliant 41 metre solo try; England were leading 19-0 midway through the second half*)**

[Bowl Final:]

[21st Mar KENYA 12 **ENGLAND** 33]

[*This match kicked off at 5.20pm; Dan Caprice unavailable due to injury*]

(*Christian Wade scored in the 2nd minute!; England were leading 7-5 midway through the first half; England were still leading 7-5 in the 6th minute; England were leading 14-5 when the half-time hooter sounded, but the ball was still in play and Tom Powell was able to score a brilliant 50 metre solo try; England were leading 19-5 at half-time; England were leading 26-5 in the 10th minute; England scored 19 unanswered points to clinch the match; England were still leading 26-5 midway through the second half when collectively poor tackling allowed Humphrey Kayange to score, thus 7 points were preventable; England were leading 26-12 with 2 minutes remaining when Jake Abbott scored a brilliant 60 metre solo try; Ben Gollings scored 60 points in this tournament and thus increased his overall IRB World Sevens record to 2289*)

CATHAY PACIFIC/CREDIT SUISSE HONG KONG SEVENS

Hong Kong Stadium, Eastern Hospital Road, So Kon Po, Hong Kong

CAPTAIN: *Ben Gollings* [*Mat Turner*]

First Round - Pool 'E'

26th Mar HONG KONG 0 **ENGLAND** 45

[*This match kicked off at 5.58pm; Dan Caprice unavailable due to injury*]

(*Ollie Lindsay-Hague scored in the 2nd minute!; England were leading 7-0 midway through the first half; England were still leading 7-0 in the 5th minute when Christian Wade scored a brilliant 95 metre solo try; England were leading 14-0 in the 6th minute when some superb handling amongst the forwards allowed James Rodwell to score; England were leading 21-0 at half-time; Josh Drauniniu came on as a replacement for Ben Gollings at the start of the second half, with Mat Turner then switching from centre to fly half to accommodate Drauniniu; England were still leading 21-0 in the 9th minute when Ollie Lindsay-Hague scored a brilliant 45 metre solo try; England were leading 28-0 in the 10th minute when Nick Royle scored after Mat Turner made a superb run; England were leading 33-0 midway through the second half; England were leading 38-0 when the full-time hooter sounded, but the ball was still in play and Nick Royle was able to score another try after Josh Drauniniu put in a brilliant kick ahead*)

CAPTAIN: *Ben Gollings* [*Mat Turner*]

27th Mar JAPAN 0 **ENGLAND** 45

[*This match kicked off at 2.10pm; Dan Caprice unavailable due to injury*]

(*A brilliant 55 metre break by Mat Turner enabled Ben Gollings to score after just 22 seconds had been played!; England were leading 7-0 in the 2nd minute when Ben Gollings jinked past Kenji Shomen which enabled Nick Royle to score a try which Gollings then brilliantly converted from the left touchline; England were leading 14-0 midway through the first half; England were leading 19-0 in the 6th minute when Mat Turner saved a certain try by tackling Alisi Tupuailei into touch at the corner flag; Immediately afterwards James Rodwell took a quick lineout to instigate a counter-attack which culminated in Nick Royle running 59 metres to score another superb try; England were leading 26-0 at half-time; Josh Drauniniu came on as a replacement for Ben Gollings at the start of the second half; England were still leading 26-0 in the 11th*

minute when Nick Royle put in a brilliant chip-kick, but he was then unable to gather the bouncing ball while the Japanese line was at his mercy; England were leading 26-0 midway through the second half; England were still leading 26-0 with 2 minutes of normal time remaining when Josh Drauniniu powered through to score under the posts; England were leading 33-0 in the last minute of normal time; England were leading 40-0 when the full-time hooter sounded, but the ball was still in play and Ollie Lindsay-Hague was able to score a superb 70 metre solo try)

CAPTAIN: *Ben Gollings*

27th Mar WALES 5 **ENGLAND** 26

[This match kicked off at 6.34pm; Dan Caprice unavailable due to injury]

(James Rodwell scored after just 34 seconds had been played!; England were leading 7-0 in the 3rd minute when Christian Wade broke from the base of a ruck to score; England scored 14 unanswered points to win the match; England were leading 14-0 midway through the first half; England were leading 14-0 at half-time; Jevon Groves scored after just 11 seconds of the second half had been played when James Rodwell unaccountably tapped the restart backwards into space behind the England defence!; England were leading 14-5 in the 10th minute when Ollie Lindsay-Hague scored a brilliant 62 metre solo try; England were leading 21-5 midway through the second half when Ben Gollings crossed the tryline, but the move was disallowed after he was adjudged to have got to his feet with the ball after being tackled by Alex Cuthbert; England were still leading 21-5 with 1 minute of normal time remaining when Nick Royle scored after Ben Gollings made a brilliant 50 metre run; England were leading 26-5 in the last minute of normal time when Jake Abbott had a great try-scoring chance but was tackled into touch at the corner flag by both Lee Rees and Nicky Thomas)

Quarter-Final

28th Mar AUSTRALIA 19 **ENGLAND** 26

[This match kicked off at 12.33pm; Dan Caprice unavailable due to injury]

(Christian Wade scored after just 29 seconds had been played!; England were leading 5-0 in the 4th minute; England were drawing 5-5 midway through the first half; England were still drawing 5-5 in the 6th minute when Christian Wade scored a brilliant 94 metre solo try; England were leading 12-5 just before half-time when collectively poor tackling allowed Ed Stubbs to score, thus 7 points were preventable; England were drawing 12-12 at half-time; England were losing 19-12 in the 8th minute; England were still losing 19-12 in the 10th minute when James Rodwell scored a brilliant 79 metre solo try; England were drawing 19-19 midway through the second half; England were still drawing 19-19 in the final minute when some superb handling allowed Tom Powell to score a match-winning try)

Semi-Final

28th Mar SAMOA 28 **ENGLAND*** 24

[This match kicked off at 4.30pm; Dan Caprice unavailable due to injury]

(Mikaele Pesamino scored in the 2nd minute!; England were losing 7-0 midway through the first half when Chris Brightwell powered through 3 attempted tackles to score; England were drawing 7-7 in the 6th minute when Alafoti Fa'osiliva scored after Ben Gollings missed a tackle on Ofisa Treviranus; England were losing 14-7 when the half-time hooter sounded, but the ball was still in play and Ollie Lindsay-Hague was able to take a quick tap penalty and score, with Ben Gollings then missing the eminently kickable conversion attempt; England were losing 14-12 at half-time; A brilliant grubber kick by Ben Gollings enabled Mat Turner to score after just 47

***seconds of the second half had been played!; England were leading 19-14 in the 10th minute when a poor defensive alignment allowed Mikaele Pesamino to score another try; England were losing 21-19 midway through the second half; Christian Wade came on as a replacement for Nick Royle in the 11th minute; England were still losing 21-19 with 2 minutes of normal time remaining when Lolo Lui scored after a poor tackle by James Rodwell, thus 3 tries and 21 points were preventable; Samoa were allowed to score 14 unanswered points to win the match; England were losing 28-19 when the full-time hooter sounded, but the ball was still in play and James Rodwell was able to power through 2 attempted tackles to score a consolation try; Christian Wade did not receive a single pass!; Ben Gollings increased his IRB World Sevens record to 2322 points in this tournament*)**

LONDON FLOODLIT SEVENS

Rosslyn Park FC, Priory Lane, Upper Richmond Road, Roehampton

CAPTAIN: *Mat Turner*

First Round - Pool 'C'

6th May **DIG DEEP ENGLAND** 38 Esher 7

[*This match kicked off at 5.40pm; Dig Deep England also billed as an England VII*]

6th May **DIG DEEP ENGLAND** 40 Loughborough University 7

[*This match kicked off at 7.00pm; Loughborough University also billed as Loughborough Students*]

Semi-Final

6th May **DIG DEEP ENGLAND** 24 Wasps 10

[*This match kicked off at 9.20pm; Mark Odejobi played for Wasps in this match*]

Final

6th May **DIG DEEP ENGLAND** 17 Saracens 5

[*This match kicked off at 10.30pm; Justin Marshall and Noah Cato played for Saracens in this match*]

(*Dig Deep England were losing 5-0 in the early stages; Dig Deep England were leading 12-5 at half-time; Dig Deep England scored 17 unanswered points to win the match; Dig Deep England were reduced to 5 men at one point in the second half when Simon Hunt joined James Rodwell in the sin-bin!; Dig Deep England were leading 17-5 in the closing stages when Mat Turner saved a certain try by tackling Noah Cato*)

DAN JAMES MEMORIAL MATCH

CAPTAIN: *Jacob Rowan*

19th May Loughborough University 11 **ENGLAND U20 XV** 29
ab

Loughborough Students RFC, Loughborough University, Loughborough

[*This match kicked off at 7.30pm; James Gaskell unavailable due to injury; Will Hurrell in original training squad of 26 but withdrew due to injury, being replaced by Marcus Watson; The England U20 XV named a 9 man bench selection; Lee Imiolek, Mako Vunipola and Jamie Gibson in original training squad of 26 but were not selected for team or bench; Alex Waller was not part of the original squad*]

(*The England U20 XV forwards monopolised possession in this match; The England U20 XV was drawing 0-0 in the early stages when Freddie Burns missed a penalty goal attempt; The England U20 XV was losing 3-0 shortly afterwards; The England U20 XV was losing 6-3 midway through the first half when Christian Wade powered through to score; The England U20 XV was leading 17-6 in the 30th minute; The England U20 XV*

***was still leading 17-6 shortly afterwards when Joe Marler scored from a rolling maul; The England U20 XV scored 21 unanswered points to win the match; The England U20 XV was leading 24-6 shortly before half-time when Marcus Watson crossed the tryline but then lost the ball in the act of scoring; The England U20 XV was leading 24-6 at half-time; The England U20 XV was still leading 24-6 early in the second half when Jacob Rowan also lost the ball in the act of scoring; The England U20 XV was leading 24-11 shortly afterwards; The England U20 XV was still leading 24-11 midway through the second half; The England U20 XV was leading 24-11 in the 63rd minute when Jonny May scored a brilliant try; This match was abandoned in the 64th minute when the floodlights failed; Tom Catterick injured playing in the match*)**

EMIRATES AIRLINE LONDON SEVENS

Twickenham

CAPTAIN: *Ben Gollings* [*Kevin Barrett*]

First Round - Pool 'D'

22nd May **ENGLAND** 29 RUSSIA 5

[*This match kicked off at 1.04pm*]

(*This match was played in 80 degree heat; Collectively poor tackling allowed Vladimir Ostroushko to score in the 1st minute, thus 5 points were preventable!; England were losing 5-0 midway through the first half; England were still losing 5-0 in the 4th minute when Tom Powell dummied his way through to score a brilliant try; England were drawing 5-5 just before half-time when Ben Gollings scored after Mat Turner made a brilliant break; England were leading 12-5 at half-time; England were still leading 12-5 in the 9th minute when James Rodwell scored a superb 79 metre solo try; England were leading 17-5 midway through the second half; Ben Gollings had to go off with 2 minutes remaining when he aggravated a hamstring injury, being replaced by Micky Young; England were leading 24-5 in the last minute when Mat Turner scored a brilliant 51 metre solo try; England scored 29 unanswered points to win the match*)

CAPTAIN: *Ben Gollings* [*Kevin Barrett*]

22nd May **ENGLAND** 36 SCOTLAND 10

[*This match kicked off at 4.10pm*]

**(*This match was played in 80 degree heat; England were drawing 0-0 in the 3rd minute when the referee unaccountably allowed play to continue after Mark Robertson threw a clear forward pass and Colin Shaw went on to score, thus 5 points were unlawful; England were losing 5-0 midway through the first half; England were losing 10-0 in the 6th minute when Christian Wade was awarded a try that should not have been given because the scoring pass from James Rodwell was clearly forward!; England were losing 10-5 when the half-time hooter sounded, but the ball was still in play and Ben Gollings was able to score the 200th try of his IRB World Sevens career; England were drawing 10-10 at half-time; A brilliant chip-kick by Ben Gollings enabled James Rodwell to score after just 56 seconds of the second half had been played!; England were leading 17-10 in the 10th minute when Mat Turner scored a superb 36 metre solo try in the right corner which Ben Gollings then brilliantly converted; England were leading 24-10 midway through the second half; England were still leading 24-10 with 3 minutes of normal time remaining when Tom Varndell scored a brilliant 40 metre solo try; Micky Young came on as a replacement for Ben Gollings with 2 minutes of normal time remaining; England were leading 29-10 with 1 minute of normal time remaining when Kevin Barrett's flick pass legally went backwards in its initial flight and then bounced forward, which allowed Tom Varndell to gather the resulting loose ball and score another try after the Scottish defence momentarily stopped!; England 36*

***unanswered points to win the match; England were leading 36-10 when the full-time hooter sounded, but the ball remained in play until Tom Varndell saved a certain try by tackling Alex Blair into touch*)**

CAPTAIN: *Kevin Barrett*

22nd May **ENGLAND** 5 AUSTRALIA 38

[*This match kicked off at 7.28pm; Ben Gollings was rested for this match*]

(*England could not win any possession in this match; Clinton Sills scored in the 1st minute!; England were losing 5-0 in the 3rd minute when a poor defensive alignment allowed James Stannard to score; England were losing 12-0 midway through the first half; England were still losing 12-0 in the 5th minute when collectively poor tackling allowed James Stannard to score another try; England were losing 19-0 at half-time; England were losing 24-0 in the 8th minute; England were still losing 24-0 in the 10th minute when further collectively poor tackling allowed Brackin Karauria-Henry to score; Australia were allowed to score 31 unanswered points to win the match; England were losing 31-0 midway through the second half; England were still losing 31-0 with 2 minutes remaining with Micky Young scored directly from an Australian lineout; England were losing 31-5 in the last minute when a lack of communication between Tom Powell and James Rodwell allowed Samisoni Latunipulu to break through and score, thus 4 tries and 28 points were preventable*)

CAPTAIN: *Ben Gollings* [*Kevin Barrett*]

Quarter-Final

23rd May **ENGLAND*** 12 SOUTH AFRICA 17

[*This match kicked off at 12.42pm*]

(*This match was played in 80 degree heat; England were drawing 0-0 midway through the first half when Ben Gollings was sent to the sin-bin after the referee adjudged that he had deliberately knocked the ball on; Mat Turner played as a fly half in the absence of Ben Gollings; England were still drawing 0-0 in the 5th minute when a poor defensive alignment allowed M.J. Mentz to score; England were losing 7-0 in the 6th minute when Rob Vickerman took a strike against the head during a South African scrum, but the ball then squirted between the unsighted Kevin Barrett's legs which allowed Frankie Horne to gather it and pass to Ryno Benjamin who duly went on to score, thus 2 tries and 12 points were preventable!; England were losing 12-0 when the half-time hooter sounded, but the ball remained in play until Mat Turner set up a maul inside his own 22 which Chris Dry then illegally entered from the side, but the referee unaccountably ignored this infringement and penalised Mat Turner for not releasing the ball when the aforementioned maul went to ground, which allowed Cecil Afrika to score from the resulting tap penalty, thus 5 points were unlawful; South Africa were allowed to score 17 unanswered points to win the match; England were losing 17-0 at half-time; England were still losing 17-0 in the 9th minute when they created and then squandered an overlap; England were losing 17-7 in the 10th minute; England were still losing 17-7 midway through the second half; England were losing 17-7 with 51 seconds remaining when Ben Gollings inexplicably decided not to try a miss pass to the unmarked Christian Wade and instead threw a forward pass to James Rodwell; England were still losing 17-7 when Tom Powell scored a consolation try just as the full-time hooter sounded!*)

CAPTAIN: *Ben Gollings*

[Plate Semi-Final:]

[23rd May **ENGLAND*** 19 NEW ZEALAND 22]

[*This match kicked off at 3.26pm*]

(This match was played in 80 degree heat; Tim Mikkelson scored in the 1st minute!; England were losing 5-0 in the 2nd minute when the referee unaccountably allowed play to continue after Lote Raikabula clearly knocked the ball on and Kurt Baker went on to power through some collectively poor tackling to score, thus 7 points were unlawful; England were losing 12-0 midway through the first half; England were still losing 12-0 in the 5th minute; England were losing 12-7 at half-time; Mat Turner made a brilliant 25 metre run which enabled Ben Gollings to score after just 57 seconds of the second half had been played!; England were leading 14-12 in the 10th minute when Christian Wade scored after he wrong-footed Tim Mikkelson with a brilliant sidestep; England scored 19 unanswered points; England were leading 19-12 midway through the second half; England were still leading 19-12 with 57 seconds of normal time remaining when they inexplicably failed to defend the fringes of a ruck and Toby Arnold was able to break through and score; Ben Ryan tried to bring on a substitute before the restart, but the match officials unaccountably failed to give him the necessary authorisation in time; England were leading 19-17 straight after the aforementioned restart when Ben Gollings broke through, ran 40 metres and then, with only 10 seconds of normal time remaining, inexplicably chose to grubber the ball towards the New Zealand line in a vain attempt to score a try instead of kicking it over the dead ball line, which meant that the ball was still in play when the full-time hooter sounded and as a consequence Kurt Baker was able to run 93 metres and score a match-winning try for New Zealand after a poor tackle by Christian Wade, thus 2 tries and 10 points were preventable; Ben Gollings increased his IRB World Sevens record to 2351 points in this tournament)

PENGUINS TOUR TO PORTUGAL 2010

CAPTAIN: *Marcus Di Rollo* (SC)

29th May AEIS Agronomia (*POR*) 17 **PENGUINS** 30

Campo A, Complexo Desportivo da Tapada

[This match kicked off at 5.00pm]

(This match was played in hot conditions; The Penguins conceded 2 tries in the early stages; The outcome of this match was still uncertain in the 70th minute)

EMIRATES AIRLINE EDINBURGH SEVENS

Murrayfield

CAPTAIN: *Ben Gollings*

First Round - Pool 'C'

29th May PORTUGAL 5 **ENGLAND** 17

[This match kicked off at 11.25am]

(This match was played on a wet pitch; England were drawing 0-0 in the 3rd minute when Mat Turner scored a brilliant 62 metre solo try; England were leading 7-0 midway through the first half; England were still leading 7-0 in the 6th minute when Gonçalo Foro scored after a poor tackle by Mat Turner, thus 5 points were preventable; Nick Royle came on as a replacement for Uche Oduoza in the 7th minute; England were leading 7-5 at half-time; Ben Gollings put in a brilliant grubber kick which enabled Nick Royle to score after just 44 seconds of the second half had been played!; Mat Turner went off injured in the 11th minute, being replaced by Ollie Lindsay-Hague; England were leading 12-5 midway through the second half when Ollie Lindsay-Hague scored after Nick Royle threw a superb reverse pass)

29th May CANADA 26 **ENGLAND*** 19

[This match kicked off at 2.51pm]

(England used a 2 man lineout in the absence of Rob Vickerman, who was sent to the sin-bin in the 3rd minute; England were drawing 0-0 midway through the first half; England were still drawing 0-0 in the 5th minute when Conor Trainor scored after a poor tackle by James Rodwell; England were losing 7-0 in the 6th minute when Uche Oduoza scored after he went on a brilliant 69 metre rampaging run!; England were losing 7-5 at half-time; Nick Royle came on as a replacement for Uche Oduoza at the start of the second half; England were still losing 7-5 straight after the restart when Chris Brightwell chipped the ball straight to Neil Meechan who then gave a scoring pass to Sean Duke, thus 2 tries and 14 points were preventable; England were losing 14-5 in the 9th minute when Nick Royle brilliantly gathered a loose ball and ran 33 metres to score; England were losing 14-12 in the 11th minute; England scored 14 unanswered points; England were leading 19-14 midway through the second half; England were still leading 19-14 with 2 minutes remaining; England were drawing 19-19 in the final minute when Justin Mensah-Coker scored a try that should not have been given because the scoring pass from Phil Mack was clearly forward, thus 7 points were unlawful)

29th May AUSTRALIA 21 **ENGLAND*** 21

[This match was originally scheduled to start at 6.39pm but the kick-off was brought forward to 6.19pm]

(England were drawing 0-0 in the 1st minute when Micky Young had the Australian tryline at his mercy, but he then allowed Ben Gollings to score instead!; England were leading 14-0 in the 3rd minute; England were still leading 14-0 midway through the first half; England were leading 14-0 in the 5th minute when some superb handling allowed Mat Turner to score; England scored 21 unanswered points; England were leading 21-0 in the 7th minute; England were leading 21-7 at half-time; England were still leading 21-7 in the 8th minute when collectively poor tackling allowed James Stannard to score; England were leading 21-14 midway through the second half; England were still leading 21-14 when the full-time hooter sounded, but the ball was still in play and Samisoni Latunipulu was able to score after a poor tackle by Ben Gollings, with James Stannard then kicking the conversion to draw the match for Australia, thus 2 tries and 14 points were preventable)

Quarter-Final

30th May SCOTLAND 7 **ENGLAND** 19

[This match kicked off at 11.55am]

(This match was played in cold and drizzly conditions; Ben Gollings broke through in the 1st minute but was then brilliantly tap-tackled by Greig Laidlaw!; England were drawing 0-0 in the 3rd minute when James Rodwell bought a dummy by Roddy Grant, who then went on to score after the referee inadvertently got in the way of Ben Gollings' attempted tackle, thus 7 points were preventable!; England were losing 7-0 midway through the first half; Rob Vickerman went off injured in the 6th minute, being replaced by Greg Barden; England were losing 7-0 at half-time; Mat Turner scored a brilliant 31 metre solo try after just 15 seconds of the second half had been played!; Nick Royle came on as a replacement for Uche Oduoza in the 11th minute; England were drawing 7-7 midway through the second half; England were still drawing 7-7 with 1 minute of normal time remaining; England were leading 12-7 when the full-time hooter sounded, but the ball was still in play and Nick Royle was able to score a try to clinch the match)

Semi-Final

30th May SAMOA 15 **ENGLAND*** 12
aet

[*This match kicked off at 3.43pm; Rob Vickerman unavailable due to injury*]
(*This match was played on a wet pitch; England were drawing 0-0 in the 3rd minute when Afa Aiono scored after Micky Young slipped over and thus created a gap in the defensive line, thus 7 points were preventable; England were losing 7-0 midway through the first half; Uche Oduoza went off injured just before half-time, being replaced by Nick Royle; England were losing 7-0 at half-time; England were still losing 7-0 midway through the second half; England were drawing 7-7 with 2 minutes of normal time remaining; England were losing 12-7 when the full-time hooter sounded, but the ball was still in play and Greg Barden was able to score a try to bring the scores level, with the game then going into sudden death extra time after Ben Gollings hit the right-hand post with the eminently kickable conversion attempt; Ben Gollings played as a hooker in the absence of James Rodwell, who was sent to the sin-bin in the third minute of sudden death extra time; England were drawing 12-12 in the fourth minute of sudden death extra time when Kevin Barrett and Nick Royle both saved a certain try by tackling Ofisa Treviranus into touch at the corner flag; England were still drawing 12-12 when the hooter sounded at the end of the first period of sudden death extra time, but the ball remained in play until Nick Royle wasted a great try-scoring opportunity by mishitting a loose ball as he attempted to fly-hack it on over the Samoan line; England were drawing 12-12 at the end of the first period of sudden death extra time; England were still drawing 12-12 with 3 minutes of sudden death extra time remaining when Nick Royle had a great try-scoring chance, but his attempted chip in space was then brilliantly charged down by Fautua Otto; England were drawing 12-12 when the hooter sounded at the end of the second period of sudden death extra time, but the ball remained in play until Lolo Lui scored a 29 metre penalty goal to win the match and the IRB World Sevens Series for Samoa; Ben Gollings increased his IRB World Sevens record to 2374 points in this tournament*)

FIRST MASTERCARD TROPHY MATCH

CAPTAIN: *Nick Easter* [England XV]
CAPTAIN: *Xavier Rush* (NZ) [Barbarians]

30th May **ENGLAND XV** 35 **BARBARIANS*** 26
Twickenham

[ENGLAND XV: [*This match kicked off at 5.00pm; Jonny Wilkinson unavailable due to injury; George Chuter, Dan Cole, Geoff Parling, Tom Croft, Lewis Moody, Ben Youngs and Toby Flood all unavailable due to club commitments; Shontayne Hape won 14 caps for New Zealand at Rugby League between 2004-07, became a Rugby Union player in May 2008 when he joined Bath and qualified for England in December 2009 after completing a residency period of 3 years*]
(*Charlie Hodgson missed a kickable 44 metre penalty goal attempt in the 5th minute!; The England XV was drawing 0-0 in the 8th minute when Danny Care's intended scoring pass to the unmarked Steffon Armitage was deliberately knocked-on by Xavier Rush but the referee unaccountably ignored this obvious penalty try offence and merely awarded a penalty, which Charlie Hodgson duly kicked; The England XV was leading 6-0 in the 14th minute when James Haskell scored a brilliant 65 metre solo try; The England XV was leading 13-0 midway through the first half; The England XV was still leading 13-0 in the 23rd minute when Mark Cueto made a brilliant 46 metre break*

but then ran out of support; The England XV was leading 13-0 in the 24th minute when Shontayne Hape scored a superb 32 metre solo try; The England XV scored 20 unanswered points to win the match; The England XV was leading 20-0 in the 31st minute when Shontayne Hape saved a certain try by tackling Rodney So'oialo; Charlie Hodgson went off injured in the 36th minute, being replaced by Olly Barkley; The England XV was leading 20-7 on the 37th minute when Ben Foden scored after Steve Thompson (2) threw a brilliant long pass; The England XV was leading 25-7 at half-time; Jon Golding went off injured in the 45th minute, being replaced by Tim Payne; Immediately afterwards Mike Tindall ran 43 metres to score a try which Olly Barkley then converted to give the England XV a 32-7 lead; The England XV was still leading 32-7 in the 48th minute when it was awarded a 12 metre penalty in an eminently kickable position, but Nick Easter took the option of a scrum in a vain attempt to score a try; The England XV was leading 32-7 in the 50th minute when it was awarded a 42 metre penalty in a kickable position, but Nick Easter ordered a kick to the corner in a vain attempt to score a try from the ensuing lineout; Dan Ward-Smith came on as a replacement for Dave Attwood in the 51st minute; The England XV was leading 32-14 in the 58th minute when it was awarded a 29 metre penalty in another eminently kickable position, but Nick Easter again ordered a kick to the corner in a vain attempt to score a try from the ensuing lineout; The England XV was still leading 32-14 midway through the second half; Matt Tait came on as a replacement for Shontayne Hape in the 61st minute; The England XV was leading 32-19 in the 65th minute; Joe Worsley came on as a replacement for Steffon Armitage in the 66th minute; Joe Simpson had to play out of position as a wing after he came on as a replacement for Dave Strettle with 8 minutes of normal time remaining; The England XV was still leading 32-19 with 4 minutes of normal time remaining; The Barbarians were allowed to score 19 unanswered points; The England XV was leading 32-26 in the first minute of injury time; Joe Simpson injured his hamstring in the closing stages but elected to remain on the pitch; Mark Cueto had a brilliant game)]

[BARBARIANS: [*This match kicked off at 5.00pm; Danny Cipriani in original squad but withdrew due to injury; Carl Hayman, Jerry Collins, Jean de Villiers and Doug Howlett all in original squad but withdrew; Sébastien Bruno, Jannie du Plessis and Napolioni Nalaga in training squad but withdrew, being replaced by Ken Owens, Julian White and Seru Rabeni respectively; David Barnes in training squad but was not selected for team or bench; Jean-Baptiste Élissalde was the son of Jean-Pierre Élissalde; Paul Sackey decided to wear one sock from Wasps and one sock from Toulon because he was changing clubs in the close season!; Ben Kay retired after this match*]

(*Jean-Baptiste Élissalde missed a difficult 36 metre penalty goal attempt in the 3rd minute!; The Barbarians were losing 3-0 in the 9th minute; The Barbarians were losing 6-0 in the 14th minute when collectively poor tackling allowed James Haskell to score; The Barbarians were losing 13-0 midway through the first half; The Barbarians were still losing 13-0 in the 24th minute when Shontayne Hape scored after a poor tackle by Ben Kay; The England XV was allowed to score 20 unanswered points to win the match; The Barbarians were losing 20-0 in the 35th minute when Paul Sackey scored after Jean-Baptiste Élissalde brilliantly chipped the ball to himself; The Barbarians were losing 25-7 at half-time; The Barbarians were still losing 25-7 in the 45th minute when a poor defensive alignment allowed Mike Tindall to score, thus 3 tries and 21 points were preventable; Cencus Johnston and George Smith came on as replacements for Julian White and Ben Kay respectively in the 49th minute, with Xavier Rush then switching from number 8 to lock to accommodate George Smith; The Barbarians were losing 32-7 in the 56th minute when David Smith (3) scored after*

***Byron Kelleher threw a brilliant reverse pass; The Barbarians were losing 32-14 midway through the second half; Paul Sackey injured his hamstring in the 61st minute but elected to remain on the pitch; The Barbarians were still losing 32-14 in the 65th minute when Cencus Johnston powered through 3 attempted tackles to score; The Barbarians were losing 32-19 with 9 minutes of normal time remaining when they created and then squandered an overlap; The Barbarians were still losing 32-19 with 4 minutes of normal time remaining when Paul Sackey scored another try after Cédric Heymans threw a superb one-handed pass; The Barbarians scored 19 unanswered points; The Barbarians were losing 32-26 in the first minute of injury time*)]**

SECOND MASTERCARD TROPHY MATCH

CAPTAIN: *Xavier Rush* (NZ) [*George Smith* (AU)]

4th June IRELAND XV 23 **BARBARIANS** 29

Thomond Park, Limerick

[*This match kicked off at 7.45pm; Paul Sackey selected for bench but withdrew on the day of the match due to injury, being replaced by Fabrice Estebanez; Malcolm O'Kelly retired after this match*]

(*The Barbarians were leading 3-0 in the 12th minute; The Barbarians were leading 6-0 midway through the first half; The Barbarians were leading 9-3 in the 31st minute when Pierre Mignoni brilliantly chipped the ball to himself but was then tackled by Andrew Trimble 6 meters from the Ireland XV line; The Barbarians were still leading 9-3 in the 34th minute when Xavier Rush scored after he broke from the base of a scrum and then took a return pass from Pierre Mignoni; The Barbarians were leading 14-3 in the 37th minute when George Smith scored after Casey Laulala gathered a loose ball and then went on a brilliant 72 metre run; The Barbarians scored 15 unanswered points to clinch the match; The Barbarians were leading 21-3 just before half-time; The Barbarians were leading 21-10 at half-time; The Barbarians were leading 21-13 in the 48th minute when Cédric Heymans scored after Brock James threw a brilliant long pass; Rodney So'oialo came on as a replacement for Malcolm O'Kelly in the 52nd minute, with Alan Quinlan then switching from blindside flanker to lock to accommodate So'oialo; The Barbarians were leading 26-13 in the 55th minute when Cédric Heymans had a great try-scoring chance but was tackled by Johne Murphy 2 metres from the Ireland XV line; The Barbarians were leading 29-13 in the 57th minute; The Barbarians were leading 29-20 midway through the second half; Martyn Williams came on as a replacement for Xavier Rush in the 61st minute, with George Smith then moving from openside to blindside flanker to accommodate Martyn Williams and Rodney So'oialo moving from blindside flanker to number 8 to accommodate George Smith; The Barbarians were leading 29-23 in the 64th minute; Julian White came on as a replacement for Cencus Johnston in the 66th minute; The Barbarians were still leading 29-23 with 1 minute of normal time remaining when George Smith saved a certain try by getting back to deflect Paddy Wallace's chip-kick away from Johne Murphy*)

ENGLAND COUNTIES TOUR TO CANADA 2010

CAPTAIN: *Matt Long*

12th Jun British Columbia Bears (*CAN*) 7 **ENGLAND COUNTIES XV** 46

Capilano RFC, Klahanie Park, West Vancouver

[*This match kicked off at 3.00pm; The England Counties XV named an 8 man bench selection; James Tincknell was originally selected at left wing with Tom Jarvis at right wing, but the two swapped positions before the match*]

(This match was played in hot and humid conditions; The England Counties XV was drawing 0-0 in the early stages when Henry Staff scored a brilliant 43 metre solo try; The England Counties XV was leading 10-0 when Paul Humphries scored a brilliant conversion from the right touchline; The England Counties XV was leading 19-0 when Louis McGowan powered through to score; The England Counties XV scored 24 unanswered points to win the match; The England Counties XV was leading 24-7 at half-time; The England Counties XV was leading 27-7 midway through the second half; The England Counties XV was still leading 27-7 in the closing stages)

IRB JUNIOR WORLD CHAMPIONSHIP

Argentina

CAPTAIN: *Jacob Rowan*

First Round - Pool 'B'

5th June ARGENTINA U20 22 **ENGLAND U20** 48 **BP**

Estadio El Coloso del Parque, Rosario

[This match kicked off at 4.10pm; England U20 wore purple shirts for this match]

(England U20 played into a low overhead sun in the first half; England U20 were leading 3-0 in the 7th minute; England U20 were still leading 3-0 in the 8th minute when collectively poor tackling allowed Ramiro Moyano to score; Ignacio Rodríguez Muedra scored the subsequent conversion using a drop kick which the England U20 players unaccountably failed to charge!; England U20 were losing 7-6 midway through the first half; England U20 were still losing 7-6 in the 23rd minute when Tom Homer missed a speculative 50 metre penalty goal attempt; England U20 were losing 7-6 in the 27th minute when further collectively poor tackling allowed Emiliano Coria to score, thus 2 tries and 14 points were preventable; England U20 were losing 14-6 in the 31st minute when Jonny May scored after he wrong-footed Ramiro Moyano with a brilliant sidestep; England U20 were leading 16-14 in the 40th minute when Jonny May scored another try after Tom Homer instigated a brilliant 80 metre counter-attack; Tom Homer scored the ensuing conversion after the ball hit the top of the left-hand post and then bounced in!; Marcus Watson went off in the second minute of first half injury time having injured his hamstring, being replaced by Rory Clegg with Freddie Burns then switching from fly half to full back to accommodate Rory Clegg and Tom Homer moving from full back to wing to accommodate Freddie Burns; England U20 were leading 23-14 just before half-time; England U20 were leading 23-19 at half-time; England U20 were leading 23-22 in the 43rd minute; Back row player Alex Gray inexplicably wore the number 11 on his shirt when he came on as a replacement for Jackson Wray in the 52nd minute!; England U20 were leading 26-22 midway through the second half when some superb handling amongst the backs allowed Jonny May to score to complete a hat-trick of tries; England U20 were leading 34-22 in the 64th minute; Andy Forsyth came on as a replacement for Freddie Burns in the 68th minute, with Tom Homer then switching from wing to full back to accommodate Forsyth; England U20 were still leading 34-22 with 3 minutes of normal time remaining when Jacob Rowan scored from a rolling maul; England U20 were leading 41-22 in the ninth minute of injury time when Christian Wade scored a brilliant 37 metre solo try with the last move of the match; England U20 scored 25 unanswered points to clinch the match; Tom Homer scored 23 points in this match)

9th June IRELAND U20 21 **ENGLAND U20** 36

Estadio El Coloso del Parque, Rosario

[This match kicked off at 2.10pm; Marcus Watson unavailable due to injury]

(England U20 played into a low overhead sun in the first half; James McKinney scored a penalty goal in the 3rd minute!; England U20 were leading 6-3 in the 12th minute; England U20 were drawing 6-6 in the 18th minute when Jamie Gibson powered through 3 attempted tackles to score; England U20 were leading 13-6 midway through the first half; England U20 were still leading 13-6 in the 26th minute when Tom Homer kicked a penalty goal to score his 100th IRB Junior World Championship point; England U20 were leading 16-6 in the first minute of first half injury time; England U20 were leading 16-11 at half-time; The start of the second half was briefly delayed while a stray dog was removed!; England U20 were leading 19-11 in the 50th minute; Sam Harrison (2) came on as a replacement for Charlie Davies in the 54th minute; England U20 were leading 19-14 midway through the second half; England U20 were still leading 19-14 in the 62nd minute when Lee Imiolek wasted a great try-scoring opportunity by throwing a poor pass to the unmarked Christian Wade; Freddie Burns came on as a replacement for Rory Clegg immediately afterwards; England U20 were leading 19-14 in the 66th minute when Freddie Burns dummied his way through to score a brilliant try; England U20 were leading 26-14 in the 70th minute when Tom Homer missed a kickable 43 metre penalty goal attempt; Rob Buchanan came on as a replacement for Jamie George with 1 minute of normal time remaining; England U20 were leading 29-14 in the second minute of injury time when Freddie Burns intercepted the ball and ran 77 metres to score another try; England U20 scored 17 unanswered points to clinch the match; England U20 were leading 36-14 in the sixth minute of injury time when Tom Casson and Jonny May both bought a dummy by Eoin Griffin who then went on to score, thus 7 points were preventable; Tom Homer scored 21 points in this match)

CAPTAIN: *Jamie George*

13th Jun FRANCE U20 9 **ENGLAND U20** 17

Estadio El Coloso del Parque, Rosario

[This match kicked off at 2.10pm; Jacob Rowan was rested for this match]

(This match was played in cold conditions; England U20 made a number of handling errors in the first half; England U20 were losing 3-0 in the 13th minute; England U20 were still drawing 0-0 midway through the first half; England U20 were losing 6-3 in the 24th minute; England U20 were still losing 6-3 in the 38th minute when Andy Forsyth saved a certain try by managing to get beneath the ball as Remi Lamerat attempted to ground it; England U20 were losing 6-3 at half-time; Charlie Matthews, Jackson Wray and Jonny May came on as replacements for George Kruis, Alex Gray and Tom Casson respectively at the start of the second half; Tom Homer came on as a replacement for Marcus Watson in the 47th minute; England U20 were still losing 6-3 in the 55th minute; England U20 were drawing 6-6 in the 56th minute when Jamie Gibson powered through 3 attempted tackles to score; England U20 were leading 11-6 midway through the second half; England U20 were still leading 11-6 in the 63rd minute when Tom Homer missed a 27 metre penalty goal attempt from in front of the posts; England U20 were leading 11-6 in the 65th minute when Tom Homer missed a difficult 28 metre penalty goal attempt; England U20 were still leading 11-6 in the 69th minute when Jean Marc Doussain missed an eminently kickable 20 metre penalty goal attempt!; England U20 were leading 11-6 with 5 minutes of normal time remaining when Rory Clegg scored a brilliant 22 metre drop goal; England U20 were leading 14-9 in the first minute of injury time when Freddie Burns scored a 21 metre penalty goal to clinch the match)

CAPTAIN: *Jacob Rowan*

Semi-Final

17th Jun AUSTRALIA U20 28 **ENGLAND U20*** 16

Estadio El Coloso del Parque, Rosario

[This match kicked off at 2.10pm]

(Matt Toomua scored a penalty goal in the 5th minute!; England U20 were losing 3-0 in the 9th minute when Sam Smith scored after Andy Forsyth threw a brilliant long pass; England U20 were leading 5-3 in the 16th minute when Aidan Toua scored after a lack of communication between Tom Casson and Andy Forsyth saw them both attempting to tackle Robbie Coleman; England U20 were losing 10-3 midway through the first half; England U20 were still losing 10-3 in the 22nd minute when they created and then squandered an overlap; England U20 were losing 10-3 in the 24th minute and pressing in attack when Jamie George broke through, but the move was disallowed because he had accidentally collided with the referee!; England U20 were losing 10-8 in the 26th minute; England U20 were losing 17-8 in the 34th minute; England U20 were still losing 17-8 just before half-time; England U20 were losing 20-8 at half-time; Lee Imiolek, Sam Harrison (2) and Jonny May came on as replacements for Joe Marler, Charlie Davies and Andy Forsyth respectively at the start of the second half; England U20 were still losing 20-8 in the 47th minute when Tom Homer missed a 37 metre penalty goal attempt from the left touchline; Will Welch came on as a replacement for Jackson Wray in the 49th minute, with Jamie Gibson then switching from blindside flanker to number 8 to accommodate Will Welch; Freddie Burns came on as replacement for Rory Clegg in the 53rd minute; George Kruis came on as a temporary blood replacement for Will Welch in the 56th minute; England U20 were losing 20-8 midway through the second half when Freddie Burns followed up his own chip kick and was about to gather the bouncing ball and touch it down for a try when Kimami Sitauti got back and deliberately knocked the ball into touch in-goal, but the referee unaccountably ignored this obvious penalty try offence and merely awarded a penalty, which Tom Homer duly kicked to set a new IRB Junior World Championship record of 118 points; Joe Marler came back on to replace the injured Shaun Knight in the 67th minute; England U20 were losing 23-11 with 5 minutes of normal time remaining when Christian Wade chipped ahead into the 22 and was then body-checked by Nick White as he attempted to follow up, but the referee inexplicably ignored this infringement; England U20 were still losing 23-11 in the last minute of normal time when collectively poor tackling allowed Kimami Sitauti to score, thus 2 tries and 12 points were preventable; England U20 were losing 28-11 in the third minute of injury time when Jonny May managed to score a consolation try with the last move of the match after his shorts had been pulled down!; Christian Wade saw very little of the ball in this match)

Third Place Play-Off

21st Jun SOUTH AFRICA U20 27 **ENGLAND U20*** 22

Estadio El Coloso del Parque, Rosario

[This match kicked off at 4.45pm]

(England U20 played with a low overhead sun in the first half; England U20 were drawing 0-0 in the 6th minute when Christian Wade saved a certain try after he got back to prevent Patrick Lambie's intended scoring pass from reaching Wandile Mjekevu; England U20 were losing 7-0 in the 9th minute; England U20 were still losing 7-0 in the 13th minute when Marcus Watson scored after Tom Homer threw a brilliant long pass to Jonny May; Jamie Gibson played as a lock in the absence of Calum

Green, who was sent to the sin-bin in the 18th minute; England U20 were drawing 7-7 midway through the first half when Freddie Burns missed a difficult 40 metre penalty goal attempt; England U20 were still drawing 7-7 in the 24th minute when Freddie Burns broke through down the blindside and scored a try which he then brilliantly converted from the left touchline; England U20 were leading 14-7 in the 27th minute when collectively poor tackling allowed Sibusiso Sithole to score; England U20 were leading 14-12 in the 30th minute when Jonny May put in a superb grubber kick, but he then wasted this great try-scoring opportunity by knocking the ball on while the South Africa U20 line was at his mercy; England U20 were still leading 14-12 in the 39th minute when Joe Marler powered through 2 attempted tackles to score; England U20 were leading 19-12 at half-time; Shaun Knight came on as a replacement for Mako Vunipola at the start of the second half; England U20 were still leading 14-12 in the 42nd minute when further collectively poor tackling allowed Patrick Lambie to score, thus 2 tries and 10 points were preventable; Rory Clegg came on as a replacement for Tom Casson in the 49th minute; England U20 were leading 19-17 in the 52nd minute when Freddie Burns missed a kickable 43 metre penalty goal attempt; Charlie Davies came on as a replacement for Sam Harrison (2) immediately afterwards; England U20 were losing 24-19 midway through the second half; Freddie Burns went off injured in the 62nd minute, being replaced by Sam Smith with Marcus Watson then switching from wing to full back to accommodate Sam Smith, Tom Homer moving from full back to centre to accommodate Marcus Watson and Rory Clegg switching from centre to fly half to accommodate Homer; Alex Gray came on as a replacement for Will Welch in the 65th minute, with Jamie Gibson then moving from number 6 to blindside flanker to accommodate Alex Gray; England U20 were losing 24-22 with 9 minutes of normal time remaining; England U20 were losing 27-22 with 1 minute of normal time remaining when Sam Smith saved another certain try after he got across to prevent Patrick Lambie's intended scoring pass from reaching Wandile Mjekevu; England U20 were still losing 27-22 in the third minute of injury time when Tom Homer made a brilliant 54 metre break, but he then inexplicably ignored the unmarked Jonny May on his immediate left and threw a poor pass to Christian Wade)

ENGLAND TOUR TO AUSTRALIA AND NEW ZEALAND 2010

CAPTAIN: *Lewis Moody* [*Nick Easter*]

12th June AUSTRALIA 27 **ENGLAND*** 17

Subiaco Oval, Perth

[*This match kicked off at 6.00pm; Hendre Fourie unavailable due to injury; Hendre Fourie left the tour injured after this match*]

(The England forwards dominated the scrums in this match; England were drawing 0-0 in the 13th minute when Mark Cueto wasted a great try-scoring opportunity by electing to kick when there was an overlap outside him; England were still drawing 0-0 in the 15th minute when Chris Ashton saved a certain try by tackling Drew Mitchell; England were losing 7-0 in the 17th minute; England were still losing 7-0 midway through the first half; England were losing 7-0 in the 26th minute when Toby Flood missed a kickable 44 metre penalty goal attempt; England were still losing 7-0 in the 31st minute when Quade Cooper scored after Shontayne Hape missed a tackle on Luke Burgess; Australia were allowed to score 14 unanswered points to win the match; England were losing 14-0 in the 33rd minute when they were awarded a 29 metre penalty in an eminently kickable position, but Lewis Moody ordered a kick to the corner in a vain attempt to score a try from the ensuing lineout; England were losing 14-0 at half-time; Lewis Moody was concussed straight after the restart but elected to remain on the

pitch; England were losing 14-3 in the 47th minute when Nick Easter put in a brilliant 44 metre kick out of defence!; England were still losing 14-3 in the 50th minute when Mike Tindall broke through but was then tackled by both James O'Connor and Digby Ioane 2 metres short of the Australian line; England were losing 14-3 in the 51st minute when Tom Croft crossed the tryline but then could not get downward pressure on the ball; England were still losing 14-3 in the 53rd minute when the referee awarded a penalty try after the Australian front row stood up as they were being driven backwards towards their own line at a five metre scrum; England were losing 14-10 in the 57th minute when collectively poor tackling allowed Quade Cooper to score another try, thus 2 tries and 14 points were preventable; Ben Youngs came on as a replacement for Danny Care in the 59th minute; England were losing 21-10 midway through the second half when Mike Tindall reached the tryline by crawling through the legs of Courtney Lawes, at which point the referee adjudged that there had been an accidental offside!; England were still losing 21-10 in the 66th minute when Chris Ashton wasted another great try-scoring opportunity by throwing a poor pass out of the tackle to the unmarked Tom Croft; James Haskell came on as a replacement for Lewis Moody immediately afterwards; George Chuter came on as a replacement for Steve Thompson (2) in the 69th minute; England were losing 21-10 in the 70th minute when the referee awarded another penalty try after the Australian forwards collapsed a scrum as they were being driven backwards towards their own line; England were losing 21-17 with 7 minutes of normal time remaining; England were losing 24-17 with 1 minute of normal time remaining)

CAPTAIN: *Lewis Moody*

19th June AUSTRALIA 20 **ENGLAND** 21

ANZ Stadium, Sydney Olympic Park, Homebush Bay, Sydney

[This match kicked off at 8.00pm; ANZ Stadium was previously called the Telstra Stadium; Ugo Monye and Dom Waldouck unavailable due to injury; Matt Banahan unavailable due to suspension; England wore black armbands on their tracksuits in memory of Andy Ripley, who died two days before the match; Steve Thompson (2) retired due to injury for a second and final time in December 2011]

(Toby Flood scored a penalty goal in the 3rd minute!; David Wilson (2) came on as a temporary blood replacement for Dan Cole in the 5th minute; England were drawing 3-3 in the 8th minute; England were losing 6-3 in the 18th minute when Ben Youngs scored a brilliant 31 metre solo try; England were leading 10-6 midway through the first half; England were losing 13-10 in the 25th minute when Toby Flood missed a speculative penalty goal attempt from the halfway line; England were still losing 13-10 in the 27th minute when Chris Ashton scored after Tom Palmer (2) threw a superb inside pass, with Toby Flood then missing the eminently kickable conversion attempt; England were leading 15-13 at half-time; England were losing 20-15 in the 43rd minute; Toby Flood went off injured in the 51st minute, being replaced by Jonny Wilkinson; England were leading 21-20 in the 53rd minute; England were still leading 21-20 midway through the second half; Danny Care came on as a replacement for Ben Youngs in the 66th minute; Delon Armitage came on as a replacement for Mike Tindall in the 68th minute; England were leading 21-20 with 9 minutes remaining when Matt Giteau missed an 18 metre penalty goal attempt from in front of the posts!; England were still leading 21-20 with 1 minute remaining when Jonny Wilkinson had an eminently kickable 25 metre penalty goal attempt which went over the top of the left-hand post; Ben Youngs had a brilliant game)

CHURCHILL CUP

USA

CAPTAIN: *George Skivington*

First Round - Pool 'B'

9th June RUSSIA 17 **ENGLAND SAXONS** 49 **BP**

Infinity Park, Glendale

[This match kicked off at 3.00pm; Phil Dowson selected as captain but withdrew the day before the match as he was now required to join the simultaneous England tour of Australia and New Zealand, Andy Saull was moved from the bench to the team and Brad Barritt was then selected for the bench; Steve Diamond and Henry Paul were Head Coach and Assistant Coach respectively for Russia in this match]

(This match was played at high altitude in 85 degree heat; James Simpson-Daniel brilliantly created space by delaying his pass which enabled Andy Saull to score after just 94 seconds had been played!; The England Saxons were leading 7-3 in the 9th minute when some superb handling allowed Nick Abendanon to score; The England Saxons were leading 14-3 in the 11th minute when Luke Narraway scored from a rolling maul; The England Saxons were leading 21-3 midway through the first half; The referee allowed a water break midway through both the first and second halves; The England Saxons were leading 21-6 in the 24th minute when Stephen Myler used an overhead kick to clear the ball from his own 22!; The England Saxons were leading 21-9 in the 35th minute when some superb handling amongst the backs allowed Tom Varndell to score; The England Saxons were leading 28-9 in the 38th minute when James Simpson-Daniel's pass out of the tackle hit Micky Young's head and rebounded forwards, at which point the referee adjudged that the ball had been knocked-on!; The England Saxons were still leading 28-9 just before half-time when Vasily Artemyev scored after a poor tackle by Stephen Myler, thus 5 points were preventable; The England Saxons were leading 28-14 at half-time; Alex Corbisiero came on as a replacement for Duncan Bell at the start of the second half; The England Saxons were leading 35-14 in the 43rd minute; James Simpson-Daniel went off injured in the 46th minute, being replaced by Brad Barritt; The England Saxons were still leading 35-14 in the 49th minute when Micky Young scored after Nick Wood threw a brilliant pass out of the tackle; Nick Wood went off injured in the 54th minute, being replaced by Nathan Catt; The England Saxons were leading 42-14 in the 57th minute when Stephen Myler scored a superb try; The England Saxons were leading 49-14 midway through the second half when Micky Young put in a brilliant grubber kick, but the ball went over the dead ball line before he could touch it down; The England Saxons were still leading 49-14 in the 64th minute when they were awarded a 25 metre penalty in an eminently kickable position, but George Skivington ordered a kick to the corner in a vain attempt to score a try from the ensuing lineout; The England Saxons were leading 49-14 with 7 minutes remaining; Lee Dickson came on as a replacement for Micky Young with 6 minutes remaining)

13th Jun USA 9 **ENGLAND SAXONS** 32 **BP**

Infinity Park, Glendale

[This match kicked off at 1.00pm; James Simpson-Daniel unavailable due to injury; Brad Barritt left the squad on 17th June 2010 as he was now required to join the simultaneous England tour of Australia and New Zealand]

(This match was played at high altitude; Alex Goode scored a brilliant 47 metre penalty

goal in the 4th minute!; The England Saxons were leading 6-0 in the 8th minute when some superb handling allowed Tom Varndell to score; The England Saxons were leading 11-3 in the 16th minute when some superb handling amongst the backs allowed Anthony Allen to score a try in the right corner which Alex Goode then brilliantly converted; The England Saxons were leading 18-3 midway through the first half; The England Saxons were still leading 18-3 in the 33rd minute; The England Saxons were leading 18-6 just before half-time when Alex Goode missed a kickable 43 metre penalty goal attempt; The England Saxons were leading 18-6 at half-time; Duncan Bell came on as a replacement for Nick Wood in the 42nd minute, with Alex Corbisiero then switching from tight-head to loose-head prop to accommodate Duncan Bell; The England Saxons were leading 18-9 in the 49th minute when Alex Goode missed a speculative 47 metre penalty goal attempt; The England Saxons were still leading 18-9 in the 53rd minute when some further superb handling allowed Tom Varndell to score another try which Alex Goode then brilliantly converted from the left touchline; Stephen Myler came on as a replacement for Alex Goode in the 55th minute; The England Saxons were leading 25-9 midway through the second half when Luke Narraway scored a pushover try; Graham Kitchener came on as a replacement for George Skivington in the 60th minute; Tom Lindsay came on as a replacement for Andy Titterrell in the 68th minute; The England Saxons were leading 32-9 in the 69th minute when Tom Varndell kicked the ball 70 metres!; Micky Young came on as a replacement for Lee Dickson with 6 minutes remaining; The England Saxons were still leading 32-9 with 4 minutes remaining when Nick Abendanon made a brilliant 33 metre break but his intended scoring pass to Anthony Allen was then intercepted by Paul Emerick)

Final

19th Jun CANADA 18 **ENGLAND SAXONS** 38

Red Bull Arena, Harrison, New Jersey

[This match kicked off at 2.45pm]

(This match was played in 85 degree heat on a pitch where the in-goal areas were shorter than normal; Stephen Myler scored a penalty goal in the 4th minute!; The England Saxons were leading 3-0 in the 6th minute when Nick Abendanon powered through 3 attempted tackles to score; Alex Goode dummied his way through to score a brilliant try which Alex Goode then converted to give the England Saxons a 17-0 lead in the 11th minute; The England Saxons scored 17 unanswered points to win the match; The England Saxons were still leading 17-0 in the 15th minute when collectively poor tackling allowed Matt Evans (2) to score; The England Saxons were leading 17-5 midway through the first half when the referee unaccountably allowed play to continue after Justin Mensah-Coker illegally obstructed Alex Goode and Chauncey O'Toole went on to score, thus 5 points were unlawful; The referee allowed a water break midway through both the first and second halves; The England Saxons were leading 20-10 in the 32nd minute; Canada were losing 23-13 just before half-time when Luke Narraway saved a certain try by tackling Adam Kleeberger in front of the England Saxons line; The England Saxons were leading 23-13 at half-time; The England Saxons were leading 26-13 in the 46th minute when Jon Clarke scored a brilliant try; Duncan Bell came on as a replacement for Alex Corbisiero in the 50th minute; Canada were losing 33-13 immediately afterwards when the England Saxons scrum went forwards so quickly that Luke Narraway slipped over as he attempted to control the ball at the base!; The England Saxons were still leading 33-13 in the 54th minute when Anthony Allen broke through but then wasted this great try-scoring opportunity by throwing a poor pass to the unmarked Jon Clarke; Alex Corbisiero

came back on to replace the injured Nick Wood in the 59th minute; The England Saxons were leading 33-13 midway through the second half when Luke Narraway scored after Jon Clarke threw a superb long pass to Graham Kitchener; Tom Varndell came on as a replacement for James Simpson-Daniel in the 61st minute; The England Saxons were leading 38-13 in the 68th minute when Tom Varndell wasted another great try-scoring opportunity by dropping a pass from Alex Corbisiero while the Canadian line was at his mercy; The England Saxons were still leading 38-13 in the 69th minute when Ollie Smith (2) had a great try-scoring chance but was tackled by D.T.H. van der Merwe 2 metres short of the Canadian line; The England Saxons were leading 38-13 with 6 minutes of normal time remaining when Stephen Myler wasted a third great try-scoring opportunity by attempting to make the line himself instead of using an overlap outside him; The England Saxons were still leading 38-13 with 5 minutes of normal time remaining when Ryan Smith powered through a poor tackle by Nick Abendanon to score after Tom Varndell chipped the ball straight to Ryan Hamilton, thus 2 tries and 10 points were preventable; The England Saxons were leading 38-18 with 1 minute of normal time remaining when they were awarded a 31 metre penalty in a kickable position, but George Skivington ordered a kick to the corner in a vain attempt to score a try from the ensuing lineout; Luke Narraway had a brilliant game)

RUGBYROCKS LONDON SEVENS

Athletic Ground, Kew Foot Road, Richmond

CAPTAIN: *Carl Murray* (NZ)

First Round - Group 'D'

12th Jun Apache 21 **SAMURAI** 22

[This match kicked off at 11.00am]

(The Samurai were losing 21-17 in the final minute when Geoff Griffiths scored a match-winning try with the last move of the game)

12th Jun Irish Raiders (*IR*) 19 **SAMURAI** 29

[This match kicked off at 12.20pm]

(Collectively poor tackling allowed Massey Tuhakaraina to score in the second half, thus 5 points were preventable)

Quarter-Final

12th Jun White Hart Marauders 12 **SAMURAI** 21

[This match kicked off at 3.20pm; Rhys Crane played for the White Hart Marauders in this match]

(The Samurai were leading 5-0 in the early stages when Rhys Jones scored a brilliant conversion from the left touchline; The Samurai were leading 7-0 shortly afterwards when Simon Hunt kicked ahead and followed up to score a brilliant try; The Samurai scored 14 unanswered points to win the match; The Samurai were leading 14-0 midway through the first half; The Samurai were still leading 14-0 just before half-time when Carl Murray saved a certain try by managing to get beneath the ball as Adam Bishop attempted to ground it; The Samurai were leading 14-0 at half-time; The Samurai were still leading 14-0 early in the second half when collectively poor tackling allowed Rhys Crane to score, thus 7 points were preventable; The Samurai were leading 21-7 in the closing stages)

Semi-Final

12th Jun HFW Wailers 21 **SAMURAI** 26

[This match kicked off at 4.40pm; Steve Parsons played for the HFW Wailers in this match]

(The Samurai were losing 7-0 in the early stages; The Samurai were still losing 7-0 shortly afterwards when Simon Hunt scored a try in the right corner which Rhys Jones then brilliantly converted; The Samurai were drawing 7-7 midway through the first half; The Samurai were still drawing 7-7 shortly before half-time when Tom Wiley scored after Geoff Griffiths threw a superb long pass; The Samurai were leading 12-7 at half-time; The Samurai were still leading 12-7 early in the second half when collectively poor tackling allowed Steve Parsons to score, thus 7 points were preventable; The Samurai were losing 14-12 midway through the second half when Simon Hunt scored after Mike Davis (2) brilliantly flicked the ball between his legs at a ruck; The Samurai were losing 21-19 in the closing stages when Mike Davis (2) scored a superb 78 metre solo try to win the match)

Final

12th Jun	Esher	31	**SAMURAI**	42

[This match kicked off at 6.30pm; Jonny Hylton and Mark Odejobi played for Esher in this match]

(Collectively poor tackling allowed Mark Odejobi to score in the 1st minute, thus 5 points were preventable!; The Samurai were losing 17-0 shortly afterwards; Esher were allowed to score 17 unanswered points; The Samurai were still losing 17-0 midway through the first half when Oriol Ripol scored after Rhys Jones threw a brilliant reverse pass; The Samurai were losing 17-14 just before half-time; The Samurai were losing 24-14 at half-time; The Samurai were losing 24-21 early in the second half when Geoff Griffiths scored a superb 52 metre solo try; The Samurai were leading 28-24 midway through the second half when Geoff Griffiths saved a certain try by tap-tackling Mark Odejobi; The Samurai were losing 31-28 in the closing stages when Simon Hunt scored a brilliant 54 metre solo try; The Samurai were leading 35-31 in the last minute when Simon Hunt scored to seal the match; Simon Hunt scored 9 tries in the competition)

WEST COUNTRY SEVENS

Keynsham RFC, Crown Field, Bristol Road, Keynsham, Bristol

CAPTAIN: *Mark Bright* (NZ)

First Round - Group 'A'

19th Jun	Raging Bull Ronin	0	**SAMURAI**	56

[This match kicked off at 10.00am]

(The Samurai were leading 7-0 in the early stages when Simon Hunt dummied his way through to score a brilliant try; Simon Hunt scored a brilliant 79 metre solo try to complete a hat-trick)

19th Jun	Apache	5	**SAMURAI**	31

[This match kicked off at 11.20am]

(The Samurai were drawing 0-0 in the early stages when Rhys Jones scored after Lee Rees threw a brilliant long pass; The Samurai were leading at half-time; Dan Connolly scored early in the second half after a poor tackle by Jevon Groves, thus 5 points were preventable; Lee Rees dummied his way through to score a brilliant try shortly afterwards)

Quarter-Final

19th Jun	Gilbert Pups	21	**SAMURAI**	36

[This match kicked off at 2.20pm]

(Simon Hunt scored after just 29 seconds had been played!; The Samurai were losing 7-5 midway through the first half; The Samurai were leading 10-7 at half-time; Dan Norton came on as a replacement for Alex Cheeseman at the start of the second half;

***Dan Norton scored a brilliant 77 metre solo try after just 25 seconds of the second half had been played!; The Samurai were leading 31-7 midway through the second half when Simon Hunt brilliantly fly-hacked Lee Rees' overhead pass which enabled Mark Bright to score; The Samurai scored 31 unanswered points to win the match; The Samurai were leading 36-7 in the closing stages when James Stephenson scored after a poor tackle by Simon Hunt, thus 7 points were preventable; The Gilbert Pups were allowed to score 14 unanswered points*)**

Semi-Final

19th Jun White Hart Marauders 5 **SAMURAI** 26

[*This match kicked off at 4.20pm; The Samurai wore green shirts for this match*]

(*The Samurai monopolised possession in this match; The Samurai were leading 5-0 midway through the first half; The Samurai were still leading 5-0 shortly afterwards when John Rudd scored a brilliant 50 metre solo try; The Samurai were leading 12-0 just before half-time; The Samurai were leading 19-0 at half-time; The Samurai were leading 26-0 early in the second half; The Samurai scored 26 unanswered points to win the match; The Samurai were still leading 26-0 midway through the second half*)

Final

19th Jun British Army (*SER*) 33 **SAMURAI** 36

[*This match kicked off at 6.30pm; The Samurai wore green shirts for this match; John Rudd retired after this match*]

(*Collectively poor tackling allowed Gus Qasevakatini to score in the 1st minute!; The Samurai were losing 7-0 shortly afterwards when further collectively poor tackling allowed Malakai Magnus to score; The Army were allowed to score 14 unanswered points; The Samurai were losing 14-0 midway through the first half when Geoff Griffiths scored after Lee Rees made a brilliant run; The Samurai were losing 14-7 shortly afterwards when John Rudd powered through to score, with Rhys Jones then missing the eminently kickable conversion attempt; The Samurai were losing 14-12 at half-time; Lee Rees chipped ahead and regathered the ball to score a brilliant try after just 26 seconds of the second half had been played!; The Samurai were leading 24-14 shortly afterwards when Rhys Jones missed an eminently kickable conversion attempt; The Samurai scored 29 unanswered points to win the match; The Samurai were leading 29-14 midway through the second half; The Samurai were still leading 29-14 with 4 minutes remaining when Bunny Burenivalu scored after Dan Norton bought a dummy by Malakai Magnus, thus 3 tries and 21 points were preventable; The Samurai were leading 36-21 with 2 minutes remaining; The Samurai were leading 36-28 with 1 minute remaining when Jack Prasad used a grubber kick to restart the match!; Simon Hunt injured playing in the match*)

MANCHESTER RUGBY SEVENS

Heywood Road, Brooklands, Sale

CAPTAIN: *Carl Murray* (NZ) [Samurai]

CAPTAIN: *??* [Great Britain Students]

First Round - Group 'A'

CAPTAIN: *Carl Murray* (NZ)

4th July Akuma Smurfs 12 **SAMURAI** 22

[*This match kicked off at 10.20am*]

(*The Samurai were leading 17-0 in the early stages; The Samurai were leading 17-12 when Geoff Griffiths scored to clinch the match*)

4th July Raging Bull Ronin 7 **SAMURAI** 19
[This match kicked off at 11.40am]
(The Samurai were losing 7-0 in the first half; The Samurai scored 19 unanswered points to win the match)
First Round - Group 'C'
CAPTAIN: *??*
4th July HFW Wailers 26 **GREAT BRITAIN STUDENTS*** 19
[This match kicked off at 12.20pm]
(Great Britain Students were leading 12-7 at half-time; Great Britain Students were leading 19-7 early in the second half; Great Britain Students were drawing 19-19 in the final minute when Tom O'Toole bought a dummy by Scott Riddell who then went on to score, thus 7 points were preventable; The HFW Wailers were allowed to score 19 unanswered points to win the match)
4th July Gilbert Pups 39 **GREAT BRITAIN STUDENTS** 0
[This match kicked off at 1.40pm; Mark Odejobi played for the Gilbert Pups in this match]
(Collectively poor tackling allowed Neil Chivers to score, thus 7 points were preventable)
Quarter-Final
CAPTAIN: *Carl Murray* (NZ)
4th July Olorun ID 0 **SAMURAI** 33
[This match kicked off at 2.40pm]
(The Samurai were leading 14-0 when Angus Martyn took a quick tap penalty and scored to complete a hat-trick of tries; The Samurai were leading 19-0 at half-time; Geoff Griffiths scored a brilliant 76 metre solo try after just 35 seconds of the second half had been played!; The Samurai were leading 26-0 when Jamie Hearn scored after Billy Ngawini threw a brilliant reverse pass)
[Plate Semi-Final:]
CAPTAIN: *??*
[4th July Apache 17 **GREAT BRITAIN STUDENTS** 26]
[This match kicked off at 4.20pm; Gareth Collins played for the Apache in this match]
(Collectively poor tackling allowed Gareth Collins to score after just 13 seconds had been played!; Great Britain Students were losing 5-0 midway through the first half when further collectively poor tackling allowed Dan Connolly to score; Great Britain Students were losing 12-0 shortly before half-time when Harry Whittington scored a brilliant 72 metre solo try; Great Britain Students were losing 12-5 at half-time; Great Britain Students were still losing 12-5 in the 8th minute when Dave Fenlon scored after Andy Grodynski threw a brilliant one-handed reverse pass; Great Britain Students were drawing 12-12 in the 10th minute when David Smith (2) had the Apache tryline at his mercy, but he then allowed Andy Grodynski to score instead!; Great Britain Students were leading 19-12 midway through the second half when Sean Morris scored a superb 40 metre solo try; Great Britain Students scored 26 unanswered points to win the match; Great Britain Students were leading 26-12 in the closing stages when Will Woodward scored after a poor tackle by Dave Fenlon, thus 3 tries and 17 points were preventable; David Smith (2) injured playing in the match)

Semi-Final
CAPTAIN: *Henry Paul*
4th July HFW Wailers 14 **SAMURAI** 17
[*This match kicked off at 4.40pm; The Samurai wore white shirts with different player numbers for this match!; Hamish Smales and Steve Parsons both played for the HFW Wailers in this match*]
(*The Samurai were leading 5-0 in the early stages; The Samurai were still leading 5-0 shortly afterwards when Tom Wiley dummied his way through to score a brilliant try; The Samurai were leading 12-0 midway through the second half; The Samurai were leading 12-0 at half-time; The Samurai were leading 12-7 early in the second half; The Samurai were leading 17-7 midway through the second half; The Samurai were still leading 17-7 in the closing stages*)
[Plate Final:]
CAPTAIN: *??*
[4th July Raging Bull Ronin 31 **GREAT BRITAIN STUDENTS*** 14]
[*This match kicked off at 6.00pm; David Smith (2) unavailable due to injury*]
(*Great Britain Students were losing 5-0 in the early stages when Tom O'Toole kicked the ball straight through a hole in the pitch boundary boards!; Great Britain Students were losing 12-0 midway through the first half; Raging Bull Ronin were allowed to score 17 unanswered points to win the match; Great Britain Students were losing 17-0 at half-time; Simon Pitfield came on as a replacement for Alex Cheeseman at the start of the second half; Richard Ellis wasted a great try-scoring chance straight after the restart by throwing a poor pass behind the unmarked Harry Whittington and into touch; Great Britain Students were still losing 17-0 shortly afterwards when Peter Clarke (1) scored from a tap penalty; Great Britain Students were losing 17-7 straight after the restart when collectively poor tackling allowed Ashley Kalnins to score; Great Britain Students were losing 24-7 midway through the second half; Great Britain Students were still losing 24-7 with 2 minutes remaining when Tom O'Toole scored after Sean Morris made a brilliant 58 metre run; Great Britain Students were losing 24-14 in the final minute when Ashley Kalnins scored to complete a hat-trick after Harry Whittington missed a tackled on Matt Goode, thus 2 tries and 14 points were preventable*)
Final
CAPTAIN: *Carl Murray* (NZ)
4th July British Army (*SER*) 26 **SAMURAI*** 15
[*This match kicked off at 6.30pm; The Samurai wore white shirts with different player numbers for this match!; Apolosi Satala played for the British Army in this match*]
**(*Geoff Griffiths saved a certain try in the 1st minute by getting across to tackle Gus Qasevakatini!; The Samurai were drawing 0-0 shortly afterwards when John Brake scored a brilliant 60 metre solo try; The Samurai were leading 5-0 midway through the first half when Gavin Dacey scored after Henry Paul threw a brilliant pass; The Samurai were leading 10-0 just before half-time when Gus Qasevakatini scored just before the dead ball line; The Samurai were leading 10-5 at half-time; The Samurai were losing 12-10 in the 12th minute; The Samurai were still losing 12-10 shortly afterwards when Tom Wiley dummied his way through to score a superb try; The Samurai were leading 15-12 midway through the second half; The Samurai were still leading 15-12 in the closing stages when Gus Qasevakatini scored another try after Angus Martyn bought a dummy by Apolosi Satala; The Samurai were losing 19-15 in*

the final minute when collectively poor tackling allowed Gus Qasevakatini to score to complete a hat-trick, thus 2 tries and 14 points were preventable)

NEWQUAY SURF SEVENS

Newquay Sports Centre, Tretherras Road, Newquay

CAPTAIN: *Mark Bright* (NZ)

First Round - Group 'B'

17th July <u>Kamikaze</u> 7 **SAMURAI** 32

[This match kicked off at 10.20am]

(Mark Bright scored after Gareth Davies (2) brilliantly dummied his way through; Dom Shabbo injured his hamstring in this match)

17th July <u>Raging Bull Ronin</u> 0 **SAMURAI** 38

[This match kicked off at 11.40am; Dom Shabbo unavailable due to injury]

(Josh Drauniniu jinked through to score a brilliant try; Josh Drauniniu scored 20 points in this match)

Quarter-Final

17th July <u>Akuma Smurfs</u> 19 **SAMURAI** 22

[This match kicked off at 3.00pm; Dom Shabbo unavailable due to injury]

(The Samurai were leading 10-0 midway through the first half; The Samurai were still leading 10-0 shortly afterwards when Josh Drauniniu scored after he wrong-footed the Akuma Smurfs defence with 2 brilliant sidesteps; The Samurai scored 17 unanswered points; The Samurai were leading 17-0 at half-time; The Samurai were leading 17-14 midway through the second half; The Samurai were still leading 17-14 with 2 minutes remaining when Owen Broad scored after he put in a grubber kick and then regathered the ball when it rebounded off Josh Drauniniu!; The Akuma Smurfs were allowed to score 19 unanswered points; The Samurai were losing 19-17 in the final minute when Errie Claassens took a return pass from Josh Drauniniu to score a match-winning try with the last move of the game)

Semi-Final

17th July <u>White Hart Marauders</u> 12 **SAMURAI*** 7

[This match kicked off at 4.40pm; Dom Shabbo unavailable due to injury; Simon Pitfield, Paul Jarvis and Tom Mitchell (2) played for the White Hart Marauders in this match]

(The Samurai were losing 7-0 in the early stages; The Samurai were still losing 7-0 midway through the first half; The Samurai were losing 7-0 shortly afterwards when a poor defensive alignment allowed Paul Jarvis to take a quick tap penalty and score, thus 5 points were preventable; The Samurai were losing 12-0 at half-time; The Samurai were still losing 12-0 midway through the second half; The Samurai were losing 12-0 with 3 minutes remaining when Errie Claassens powered through to score)

WORLD UNIVERSITY RUGBY SEVENS CHAMPIONSHIP

Estádio do Bessa XXI, Porto

CAPTAIN: *David Smith (2)*

First Round - Pool 'D'

21st July HUNGARY STUDENTS 0 **GREAT BRITAIN STUDENTS** 52

[This match kicked off at 11.15am; Great Britain Students were originally scheduled to play First Round matches in Pool F against Moroccan Universities, Chinese Taipei Students and Poland Students]

(Great Britain Students monopolised possession in the first half; Paul Jarvis scored after just 40 seconds had been played!; Great Britain Students were leading 12-0

***midway through the first half; Great Britain Students were still leading 12-0 in the 5th minute when Paul Jarvis scored another brilliant 65 metre solo try; Great Britain Students were leading 26-0 just before half-time when David Smith (2) scored after Harry Whittington instigated a superb counter-attack from in front of his own line; Great Britain Students were leading 33-0 at half-time; Great Britain Students were leading 40-0 in the 9th minute; Great Britain Students were still leading 40-0 midway through the second half when Harry Whittington scored a brilliant 90 metre solo try; Great Britain Students were leading 47-0 with 1 minute remaining when Paul Jarvis scored to complete a hat-trick of tries; Harry Whittington scored 22 points in this match*)**

22nd Jul NORWAY STUDENTS 0 **GREAT BRITAIN STUDENTS** 48

[*This match kicked off at 10.15am*]

(*Paul Jarvis powered through 3 attempted tackles to score in the 2nd minute!; Great Britain Students were leading 5-0 in the 4th minute when Richard de Carpentier scored after he took a return pass from Tom Mitchell (2); Great Britain Students were leading 12-0 midway through the first half; Great Britain Students were leading 19-0 just before half-time when Tom Mitchell (2) scored a brilliant 89 metre solo try; Great Britain Students were leading 24-0 at half-time; Norway attempted to restart the match before the referee had blown his whistle!; Great Britain Students were still leading 24-0 in the 9th minute when Sam Bellhouse scored after Richard de Carpentier threw a brilliant reverse pass; Richard Ellis came on as a replacement for Sam Bellhouse in the 11th minute; Great Britain Students were leading 31-0 midway through the second half; Great Britain Students were leading 36-0 with 1 minute remaining*)

22nd Jul Canadian Universities (*CAN*) 12 **GREAT BRITAIN STUDENTS** 36

[*This match kicked off at 7.15pm; Great Britain Students wore red shirts for this match*]

(*Great Britain Students were leading 12-0 in the 3rd minute; Great Britain Students were still leading 12-0 midway through the first half; Great Britain Students were leading 12-0 just before half-time; Great Britain Students were leading 12-7 at half-time; Great Britain Students were leading 17-7 in the 8th minute; Great Britain Students were leading 17-12 midway through the second half; Great Britain Students were leading 24-12 with 1 minute of normal time remaining when Harry Whittington scored a brilliant 40 metre solo try; Great Britain Students were leading 29-12 when the full-time hooter sounded, but the ball was still in play and Sean Morris was able to score; Great Britain Students scored 19 unanswered points to clinch the match*)

23rd July JAPAN STUDENTS 5 **GREAT BRITAIN STUDENTS** 40

[*This match kicked off at 10.15am*]

(*Harry Whittington caught the ball at a Japan Students quick lineout and ran 63 metres to score a brilliant solo try after just 30 seconds had been played!; Great Britain Students were leading 14-0 midway through the first half; Great Britain Students were leading 21-0 in the 6th minute; Great Britain Students scored 21 unanswered points to win the match; Great Britain Students were still leading 21-0 just before half-time when Shohei Toyoshima scored a try that should not have been given because the scoring pass was clearly forward, thus 5 points were unlawful; Great Britain Students were leading 21-5 at half-time; Great Britain Students were still leading 21-5 midway through the second half when they instigated a brilliant 92 metre counter-attack that culminated in another try by Harry Whittington; Great Britain Students were leading 28-5 with 1 minute remaining; Harry Whittington scored 20 points in this match*)

23rd July Moroccan Universities (*MOR*) 7 **GREAT BRITAIN STUDENTS** 43

[This match kicked off at 3.40pm]

(This match was played in 80 degree heat; David Smith (2) scored a brilliant 85 metre solo try after just 23 seconds had been played!; Great Britain Students were leading 7-0 in the 4th minute when Tom Mitchell (2) scored a brilliant 91 metre solo try, with Hamish Smales then missing the eminently kickable conversion attempt; Great Britain Students were leading 12-0 midway through the first half; Great Britain Students were leading 12-7 just before half-time when David Smith (2) gathered a loose ball and ran 62 metres to score another try; Great Britain Students were leading 19-7 at half-time; Great Britain Students were still leading 19-7 in the 9th minute when David Smith (2) gathered another loose ball and ran 26 metres to score to complete a hat-trick of tries, with Hamish Smales then missing the eminently kickable conversion attempt; Great Britain Students were leading 31-7 midway through the second half; Great Britain Students were still leading 31-7 with 2 minutes remaining when Ed Tellwright scored after Hamish Smales took a quick tap penalty; Great Britain Students were leading 36-7 when the full-time hooter sounded, but the ball was still in play and Hamish Smales was able to score; Great Britain Students scored 31 unanswered points to clinch the match)

23rd July Spanish Universities (*SP*) 10 **GREAT BRITAIN STUDENTS** 12

[This match kicked off at 8.15pm]

(Simon Pitfield was sent off in the 8th minute for punching)

(Victor Gomez scored in the 1st minute!; Great Britain Students were losing 5-0 midway through the first half; Great Britain Students were still losing 5-0 in the 5th minute when David Smith (2) had a great try-scoring chance but was pushed into touch in-goal before he could ground the ball; Great Britain Students were drawing 5-5 when the half-time hooter sounded, but the ball was still in play and Paul Jarvis was able to score after Tom Mitchell (2) took a quick tap penalty; Great Britain Students were leading 12-5 at half-time; Great Britain Students were still leading 12-5 in the 8th minute when Tom Mitchell (2) crossed the tryline, but the move was disallowed after a touch judge intervened to draw the referee's attention to earlier foul play by Simon Pitfield; Great Britain Students were leading 12-5 midway through the second half; Great Britain Students were still leading 12-5 with 3 minutes of normal time remaining when David Smith (2) saved a certain try by getting back to tackle Izko Armental into touch in-goal; Great Britain Students were leading 12-5 with 1 minute of normal time remaining)

Semi-Final

24th July RUSSIA STUDENTS 22 **GREAT BRITAIN STUDENTS*** 12

[This match kicked off at 11.05am; Simon Pitfield unavailable due to suspension; Great Britain Students wore red shirts for this match]

(This match was played in 80 degree heat; Great Britain Students were drawing 0-0 in the 3rd minute when Vladimir Ostroushko scored after a poor tackle by Tom Mitchell (2); Great Britain Students were losing 7-0 midway through the first half; Great Britain Students were losing 12-0 in the 6th minute when David Smith (2) scored a brilliant 63 metre solo try; Great Britain Students were losing 12-7 just before half-time when David Smith (2) had a great try-scoring chance but was brilliantly tackled; Great Britain Students were losing 12-7 at half-time; Great Britain Students were still losing 12-7 in the 9th minute when Dmitriy Perov scored after David Smith (2) failed to commit himself to a tackle, thus 2 tries and 12 points were preventable; Great Britain Students were losing 17-7 midway through the second half; Great Britain Students were losing

***22-7 with 2 minutes of normal time remaining; Great Britain Students were still losing 22-7 in the last minute of normal time when Sean Morris grubbered ahead and followed up to score a superb try*)**

Third Place Play-Off

24th July Spanish Universities (*SP*) 12 **GREAT BRITAIN STUDENTS** 19

[*This match kicked off at 5.05pm*]

(*This match was played in 86 degree heat; Tom Mitchell (2) scored a brilliant 80 metre solo try after just 28 seconds had been played!; Great Britain Students were leading 7-0 midway through the first half; Great Britain Students were still leading 7-0 in the 5th minute when Harry Whittington scored a superb 86 metre solo try; Great Britain Students were leading 12-0 at half-time; Richard Ellis came on as a replacement for Ed Tellwright in the 9th minute; Great Britain Students were still leading 12-0 in the 11th minute when Tom Mitchell (2) scored another try after he wrong-footed the Spanish Universities defence with a brilliant sidestep; Great Britain Students scored 19 unanswered points to win the match; Great Britain Students were leading 19-0 midway through the second half; David Smith (2) came on as a replacement for Harry Whittington with 1 minute, with Tom Mitchell (2) then switching from wing to centre to accommodate David Smith (2) and Alex Cheeseman moving from centre to fly half to accommodate Tom Mitchell (2); Great Britain Students were leading 19-5 in the last minute*)

PART 4
ENGLAND PLAYER TOUR MATCH NOTES 2000-2010

2000

[No tour matches]

2001

PENGUINS TOUR TO GERMANY AND ARGENTINA 2001

CAPTAIN: *Andre Fox* (SA)

6th June Argentina Naval Selection (*AR*) 5 **PENGUINS** 103
Buenos Aires
[*This match was played at night under floodlights*]

10th Jun Combined Western Provinces (*AR*) 18 **PENGUINS** 24
Neuquén RC, Neuquén
[*This match was originally scheduled to be played at Estadio José Rosas y Perito Moreno, Neuquén but the local football team Club Atlético Independiente wanted to use it instead on the day in question!*]
(*The Penguins were losing 18-13 in the 70th minute; The Penguins were drawing 18-18 with 3 minutes remaining*)

ENGLAND TOUR TO CANADA AND AMERICA 2001

CAPTAIN: *Alex Sanderson*

5th June British Columbia (*CAN*) 19 **ENGLAND XV** 41
Thunderbird Stadium, Vancouver
[*This match kicked off at 7.30pm; This match replaced the originally scheduled game against Canada A; Steve Thompson (2) unavailable due to injury; Martyn Wood selected for bench but withdrew on the day of the match due to illness, being replaced by Joe Worsley; Scott Benton left the tour injured after this match; Nick Walshe joined the tour after this match*]
(*This match was played on a very hard pitch; John Graf scored a penalty goal in the 2nd minute!; The England XV was drawing 3-3 in the 12th minute; The England XV was losing 6-3 when Fraser Walters scored after Olly Barkley put in a brilliant chip-kick; The England XV was leading 10-6 when Olly Barkley hit the post with an eminently kickable 20 metre penalty goal attempt; Alex Brown went off injured in the 31st minute, being replaced by Simon Shaw; The England XV was leading 17-9 at half-time; Scott Benton went off injured at half-time, being replaced by Alex King with Olly Barkley then switching from fly half to the unfamiliar position of scrum half to accommodate Alex King; Joe Ewens went off injured in the 45th minute, being replaced by Tim Stimpson with Tom Voyce then moving from full back to centre to accommodate Stimpson; The England XV was leading 22-12 in the 58th minute; The England XV was leading 22-19 midway through the second half; Trevor Woodman scored after Alex Sanderson threw a superb pass; The England XV was leading 34-19 in the closing stages; The England XV scored 19 unanswered points to win the match; Paul Sackey saw very little of the ball in this match; Olly Barkley and Fraser Waters both had a brilliant game*)

12th June USA A 21 **ENGLAND XV** 83
University of California, Los Angeles
[*This match kicked off at 3.00pm; Alex Brown, Joe Ewens and Paul Sampson unavailable due to injury; Ellery Hanley selected for bench but withdrew due to injury; England only named a 5 man bench selection due to a series of injuries; Jason Keyter played for USA A in this match*]
**(*This match was played in extremely hot conditions; Link Wilfley scored a penalty goal in the 4th minute!; The England XV was leading 33-3 at one point in the first quarter; The England XV was leading 33-10 midway through the first half when Pat Sanderson*

had his pass intercepted by Jovesa Naivalu who then ran 70 metres to score, thus 5 points were preventable; Tom Voyce scored after Olly Barkley made a brilliant break; The England XV was leading 40-15 at half-time; The England XV was leading 40-21 early in the second half; Steve Thompson (2) played as a flanker after coming on as a replacement for Pat Sanderson in the 57th minute; Alex King scored after Steve Thompson (2) went on a brilliant rampaging run; Clive Woodward threatened to take the England XV off the field in the 66th minute because a touch judge was not following the game properly!; The England XV scored 43 unanswered points to seal the match; Fraser Waters had a brilliant game)

BRITISH & IRISH LIONS TOUR TO AUSTRALIA 2001

CAPTAIN: *Keith Wood* (IR)

8th June	Western Australia President's XV (*AU*)	10	**BRITISH & IRISH LIONS XV**	116

WACA Ground, Perth

[This match kicked off at 6.30pm; This match was originally scheduled for 9th June 2001; Lawrence Dallaglio, Jonny Wilkinson, Neil Jenkins and Mike Catt all unavailable due to injury; Martin Johnson was rested for this match; Phil Greening ruptured the medial ligament in his knee in a training session the day before this match; Will Greenwood played at inside centre despite wearing the number 13 on his shirt!; Simon Taylor (2) returned home injured after this match; Gordon Bulloch and Martin Corry joined the tour after this match]

(This match was played in wet conditions; Scott Quinnell scored in the 3rd minute!; The Lions XV was leading 7-0 in the 9th minute when Rob Howley dummied his way through to score a brilliant try; The Lions XV was leading 19-0 in the 16th minute when Will Greenwood scored after Brian O'Driscoll made a brilliant 49 metre run; The Lions XV was leading 24-0 midway through the first half; The Lions XV was still leading 24-0 in the 26th minute when Neil Back scored from a rolling maul; The Lions XV was leading 31-0 in the 29th minute when Neil Back scored another try from a rolling maul!; The Lions XV was leading 50-0 shortly before half-time when Dan Luger scored a superb 29 metre solo try; The Lions XV was leading 57-0 at half-time; Richard Hill (2) went off injured at half-time, being replaced by Simon Taylor (2); The Lions XV was leading 64-0 in the 45th minute; The Lions XV scored 69 unanswered points to win the match; The Lions XV was leading 69-0 in the 52nd minute when Brent Becroft scored after a poor tackle by Ben Cohen, thus 5 points were preventable; Iain Balshaw came on as a replacement for Will Greenwood in the 57th minute, with Brian O'Driscoll then switching from full back to centre to accommodate Balshaw; The Lions XV was leading 76-5 midway through the second half when Simon Taylor (2) injured his knee but unaccountably elected to remain on the pitch; The Lions XV was leading 83-5 in the 67th minute; The Lions XV was leading 83-10 in the 70th minute when Iain Balshaw scored a superb 61 metre solo try; The Lions XV was leading 90-10 with 7 minutes remaining when Scott Quinnell scored to complete a hat-trick of tries; The Lions XV was leading 97-10 with 5 minutes remaining when Austin Healey scored a brilliant 62 metre solo try; Iain Balshaw went off injured with 3 minutes remaining, being replaced by Rob Howley; Ronan O'Gara scored 26 points in this match; Keith Wood, Scott Quinnell and Will Greenwood all had a brilliant game; Ben Cohen had a poor game; The Lions XV achieved their highest ever score against an international or non-international team and set a new record for a team from the British Isles playing overseas by scoring 18 tries in the match)

CAPTAIN: *Dai Young* (WA)
12th Jun Queensland President's XV (*AU*) 6 **BRITISH & IRISH LIONS XV** 83
Dairy Farmers Stadium, Townsville
[This match kicked off at 7.30pm; Phil Greening, Lawrence Dallaglio, Jonny Wilkinson and Mike Catt all unavailable due to injury; Martin Johnson was rested for this match; Shane Drahm played for the Queensland President's XV in this match]
(The Lions XV forwards could not win any lineout ball in the first half; Robin McBryde went off injured in the 8th minute, being replaced by Gordon Bulloch; The Lions XV was drawing 0-0 in the 9th minute when Dai Young scored from a rolling maul; The Lions XV was leading 5-0 in the 16th minute when Colin Charvis powered through to score; The Lions XV was leading 10-3 midway through the first half; The Queensland President's XV was losing 10-6 in the 30th minute when Will Greenwood saved a certain try by intercepting the ball 9 metres from the Lions XV line; The Lions XV was leading 10-6 at half-time; Colin Charvis scored after just 27 seconds of the second half had been played!; The Lions XV was leading 17-6 in the 47th minute when some superb handling amongst the backs allowed Jason Robinson to score; The Lions XV was leading 22-6 in the 50th minute when the referee awarded a penalty try after the Queensland President's XV forwards illegally collapsed a rolling maul; The Lions XV was leading 36-6 midway through the second half when Jason Robinson scored a brilliant try; The Lions XV was leading 43-6 in the 62nd minute when Rob Henderson followed up his own grubber kick to score a brilliant try; Austin Healey came on as a replacement for Neil Jenkins in the 63rd minute; The Lions XV was leading 50-6 in the 64th minute when Jason Robinson scored to complete a hat-trick of tries; The Lions XV was leading 55-6 in the 69th minute when Malcolm O'Kelly scored after Jason Leonard threw a superb pass out of the tackle; The Lions XV was leading 69-6 with 9 minutes remaining; Jason Robinson scored 5 tries in the second half on his Lions debut!; The Lions XV scored 73 unanswered points to clinch the match; Colin Charvis had a brilliant game; Neil Jenkins had a poor game)

CAPTAIN: *Martin Johnson*
16th Jun Queensland Reds (*AU*) 8 **BRITISH & IRISH LIONS XV** 42
Ballymore Stadium, Brisbane
[This match kicked off at 7.30pm; Phil Greening, Robin McBryde, Lawrence Dallaglio and Mike Catt all unavailable due to injury; Scott Quinnell selected but withdrew due to injury, Martin Corry was moved from the bench to the team and Scott Murray was then selected for the bench; Phil Greening left the tour after this match so that he could see an Australian knee specialist]
(The Lions XV forwards dominated the lineout in this match; The Lions XV scrum was put under severe pressure; The Lions XV was losing 3-0 in the 11th minute; The Lions XV was still losing 3-0 in the 14th minute when Dan Luger scored after Jonny Wilkinson put up a brilliant cross-kick; The Lions XV was leading 5-3 in the 17th minute when Jonny Wilkinson put up another brilliant cross-kick, but Iain Balshaw then wasted this great try-scoring opportunity by dropping the ball while the Queensland Reds line was at his mercy; The Lions XV was leading 8-3 midway through the first half; The Lions XV was still leading 8-3 in the 24th minute when Martin Corry charged down Elton Flatley's kick and Rob Henderson followed up to score; The Lions XV was leading 18-3 in the 34th minute when Dafydd James followed up and scored after Keith Wood put in a superb chip-kick; The Lions XV was leading 25-3 just before half-time when Richard Hill (2) scored after Jonny Wilkinson threw a brilliant inside pass; The Lions XV was leading 32-3 at half-time; The Lions XV was still

leading 32-3 in the 43rd minute when Brian O'Driscoll scored a superb try; The Lions XV was leading 39-3 shortly afterwards when it created and then squandered a 6 man overlap!; Rob Howley played brilliantly in this match but then went off injured in the 47th minute, being replaced by Matt Dawson; The Lions XV scored 42 unanswered points to win the match; The Lions XV was leading 42-3 midway through the second half; The Lions XV was still leading 42-3 in the 64th minute when Matt Dawson took too much time over his clearance kick and was charged down by Sam Cordingley, who went on to score from the ensuing rebound, thus 5 points were preventable; Martin Corry, Jonny Wilkinson and Rob Henderson all had a brilliant game)

CAPTAIN: *Dai Young* (WA) [*Lawrence Dallaglio; Scott Quinnell* (WA)]

19th Jun AUSTRALIA A 28 **BRITISH & IRISH LIONS XV*** 25

North Power Stadium, Gosford

[This match kicked off at 7.30pm; Rob Howley unavailable due to injury; Mike Catt left the tour injured after this match; Scott Gibbs joined the tour after this match]

(Neil Jenkins and Mike Catt both played with an injury; The Lions XV only had one training session to prepare for this match; This match was played in cold conditions; The Lions XV scrum was put under severe pressure; The Lions XV forwards could not win any lineout ball in the first half; The Lions XV was drawing 0-0 in the 8th minute when Neil Jenkins hit the left-hand post with a kickable 38 metre penalty goal attempt; The Lions XV was leading 3-0 in the 10th minute; The Lions XV was drawing 3-3 in the 14th minute; The Lions XV was drawing 3-3 midway through the first half; The Lions XV was drawing 6-6 in the 25th minute; Colin Charvis came on as a temporary blood replacement for Scott Quinnell in the 30th minute; Austin Healey was kneed in the buttocks in the 31st minute but elected to remain on the pitch!; The Lions XV was losing 12-6 in the 33rd minute; Mike Catt had to go off in the 39th minute after he aggravated his calf injury, being replaced by Mark Taylor; The Lions XV was losing 15-6 at half-time; The Lions XV was still losing 15-6 in the 45th minute when they were awarded a 5 metre penalty in an eminently kickable position, but Dai Young ordered a kick to the corner in a vain attempt to score a try from the ensuing lineout; The Lions XV was losing 15-6 in the 50th minute when Matt Perry broke through but then ran out of support; The Lions XV was still losing 15-6 in the 54th minute when Scott Staniforth scored after Ben Cohen missed a tackle on Graeme Bond, thus 7 points were preventable; Australia A were allowed to score 16 unanswered points to win the match; Matt Dawson came on a replacement for Neil Jenkins in the 55th minute, with Austin Healey then switching from scrum half to fly half to accommodate Matt Dawson; The Lions XV was losing 22-6 in the 58th minute when Mark Taylor scored after Matt Dawson took a quick tap penalty; The Lions XV was losing 25-13 midway through the second half; Darren Morris came on as a replacement for Dai Young in the 64th minute; The Lions XV was losing 28-13 in the 69th minute; The Lions XV conceded too many needless penalties within Manny Edmonds' kicking range; The Lions XV was still losing 28-13 with 8 minutes of normal time remaining when Matt Dawson missed a 33 metre penalty goal attempt from in front of the posts; The Lions XV was losing 28-18 with 6 minutes of normal time remaining; The Lions XV was still losing 28-18 with 1 minute of normal time remaining when some superb handling allowed Jason Robinson to score; The Lions XV missed 20 tackles in this match!; Scott Quinnell and Mark Taylor both had a brilliant game; Scott Murray, Martyn Williams and Neil Jenkins all had a poor game)

CAPTAIN: *Martin Johnson*

23rd Jun New South Wales Waratahs (*AU*) 24 **BRITISH & IRISH LIONS XV** 41

Sydney Football Stadium, Sydney

[*This match kicked off at 7.30pm; Rob Howley unavailable due to injury; Dan Luger selected but withdrew due to injury, Jason Robinson was moved from the bench to the team and Ben Cohen was then selected for the bench; Ben Cohen then himself withdrew from the bench so that Matt Perry could be accommodated; Dan Luger left the tour injured after he fractured his cheekbone in a training session 3 days before this match; Lawrence Dallaglio left the tour injured after this match; Tyrone Howe joined the tour after this match*]

(*This match was marred by extreme violence; Tom Bowman was sent to the sin-bin after just 18 seconds had been played!; The Lions XV was drawing 0-0 in the 3rd minute when Brian O'Driscoll scored a brilliant try; The New South Wales Waratahs were losing 7-0 in the 6th minute when Jonny Wilkinson inexplicably threw the ball into space behind the Lions XV defence and Stu Pinkerton was able to follow up and score; The Lions XV was leading 14-5 midway through the first half when Manny Edmonds' 40 metre penalty goal attempt was tapped forwards in mid-air by Danny Grewcock, who had been lifted above the crossbar by his team-mates!; Will Greenwood went off injured in the 22nd minute, being replaced by Ronan O'Gara with Jonny Wilkinson then switching from fly half to centre to accommodate O'Gara; The Lions XV was leading 17-5 in the 34th minute when Jason Robinson dummied his way through to score a superb try; The Lions XV scored 17 unanswered points to clinch the match; Lawrence Dallaglio injured the cruciate ligament in his knee shortly before half-time but unaccountably elected to remain on the pitch; The Lions XV was leading 24-5 at half-time; The Lions XV was still leading 24-5 in the 45th minute when the referee unaccountably allowed play to continue after Manny Edmonds threw a clear forward pass to Duncan McRae and Francis Cullimore went on to score, thus 5 points were unlawful; The Lions XV was leading 24-17 in the 51st minute; Ronan O'Gara had to go off in the 55th minute after receiving an eye injury requiring 8 stitches when he was repeatedly punched in the head by Duncan McRae, being replaced by Matt Perry with Jonny Wilkinson then moving back to fly half from centre to accommodate Matt Perry; Cameron Blades, Brendan Cannon, Phil Vickery and Danny Grewcock were all sent to the sin-bin in the 56th minute for fighting, which meant that the referee had to temporarily order uncontested scrums!; The Lions XV was leading 27-17 midway through the second half; The Lions XV was leading 34-17 in the 65th minute; Neil Back went off injured with 8 minutes remaining, being replaced by Richard Hill (2); The Lions XV was still leading 34-17 with 6 minutes remaining; The Lions XV was leading 41-17 with 4 minutes remaining when a poor defensive alignment allowed Manny Edmonds to score, thus 2 tries and 12 points were preventable; Keith Wood went off injured with 2 minutes remaining, being replaced by Robin McBryde who in turn aggravated a thigh injury before the end of the game!; Phil Vickery injured planning in the match; Danny Grewcock, Scott Quinnell and Jason Robinson all had a brilliant game; Iain Balshaw had a poor game*)

CAPTAIN: *Dai Young* (WA)

26th Jun New South Wales Country Cockatoos (*AU*) 3 **BRITISH & IRISH LIONS XV** 46

Coffs Harbour International Sports Stadium, Coffs Harbour

**[*This match kicked off at 3.00pm; Robin McBryde, Phil Vickery, Neil Back and Will Greenwood unavailable due to injury; Rob Howley was rested for this match; Dorian*

***West and David Wallace joined the tour 5 hours before this match kicked off; Robin McBryde returned home injured after this match*]**
(*Austin Healey played after being given a pain-killing injection; The referee unaccountably allowed the New South Wales Country Cockatoos players to be offside at the breakdown throughout the match; The Lions XV was leading 3-0 in the 8th minute; The Lions XV was still leading 3-0 midway through the first half; The Lions XV was drawing 3-3 in the 26th minute when some superb handling amongst the backs allowed Ben Cohen to score; The Lions XV was leading 8-3 in the 32nd minute when Colin Charvis powered through to score; The Lions XV was leading 15-3 in the 37th minute when Scott Gibbs scored a brilliant try; The Lions XV was leading 22-3 just before half-time; The Lions XV was leading 29-3 at half-time; The Lions XV was leading 32-3 in the 46th minute when Dai Young scored from a rolling maul; Ronan O'Gara came on as a temporary blood replacement for Scott Gibbs in the 49th minute; David Wallace came on as replacement for Martin Corry in the 57th minute, which enabled Richard, Paul and David Wallace to become the first trio of brothers to play for the Lions!; The Lions XV was leading 39-3 midway through the second half; The Lions XV was still leading 39-3 in the 62nd minute when Ben Cohen scored a superb 52 metre solo try; The Lions XV scored 43 unanswered points to win the match; Martin Corry had a brilliant game; Iain Balshaw had a poor game*)

CAPTAIN: *Dai Young* (WA) [*Matt Dawson*]

3rd July ACT Brumbies (*AU*) 28 **BRITISH & IRISH LIONS XV** 30
Bruce Stadium, Canberra

[*This match kicked off at 7.30pm; Neil Back, Will Greenwood and Matt Perry unavailable due to injury; Colin Charvis unavailable due to suspension*]
(*The Lions XV was drawing 0-0 in the 7th minute when Mark Bartholomeusz scored a try that should not have been given because the scoring pass from Damien McInally was clearly forward; The Lions XV was losing 7-0 in the 10th minute when Willy Gordon scored a try which should not have been given because he put a knee into touch, thus 2 tries and 14 points were unlawful; Dafydd James came on as a temporary blood replacement for Mark Taylor in the 14th minute; The Lions XV was losing 14-3 midway through the first half; The Lions XV was losing 19-3 in the 26th minute when Matt Dawson missed an eminently kickable 22 metre penalty goal attempt; The Lions XV was still losing 19-3 shortly afterwards when Scott Murray wasted a great try-scoring opportunity by knocking-on while the ACT Brumbies line was at his mercy; The Lions XV was losing 19-3 in the 33rd minute when Austin Healey scored a 51 metre interception try; The Lions XV was losing 22-10 at half-time; The Lions XV was losing 22-17 in the 44th minute; The Lions XV was losing 22-20 in the 56th minute; The Lions XV was still losing 22-20 midway through the second half; The Lions XV was losing 25-20 in the 62nd minute; The Lions XV was losing 25-23 with 9 minutes of normal time remaining; Dai Young went off injured with 8 minutes of normal time remaining, being replaced by Jason Leonard; The Lions XV was losing 28-23 with 5 minutes of normal time remaining; Dorian West, Scott Murray and Martyn Williams were all injured in this match but elected to remain on the pitch; The Lions XV was still losing 28-23 when the full time hooter sounded, but the ball remained in play for a minute until Austin Healey scored a brilliant try which Matt Dawson then converted with the last kick of the match to win the game; Austin Healey injured his thigh as he grounded the ball for his second try; Austin Healey had a brilliant game*)

2002

PENGUINS TOUR TO AMERICA AND CANADA 2002

CAPTAIN: *Mark Denney*

15th Jun	New York Athletic Club Select XV (*US*)	17	**PENGUINS**	74

Travers Island, Shore Road, Pelham, New York

[Eric Peters left the tour after this match]

ENGLAND TOUR TO ARGENTINA 2002

CAPTAIN: *Hugh Vyvyan*

17th June	ARGENTINA A	29	**ENGLAND XV***	24

Cricket & Rugby Club Stadium, Buenos Aires

[This match kicked off at 8.00pm]

(The England XV scrum was put under severe pressure; The England XV was drawing 0-0 in the 8th minute when Pablo Bouza scored after Tom Beim dropped a garryowen, thus 7 points were preventable; The England XV was losing 7-0 in the 15th minute when Mark Cueto scored a brilliant try; The England XV was losing 10-7 midway through the first half when the referee unaccountably allowed play to continue after a clear forward pass and Gonzalo Quesada put in a grubber kick which enabled Diego Giannantonio to follow up and score, thus 7 points were unlawful; Tim Stimpson came on as a temporary blood replacement for Tom Beim in the 23rd minute; Alex Sanderson came on as a temporary blood replacement for Pete Anglesea in the 27th minute; The England XV was losing 20-7 in the 28th minute; The England XV was losing 20-14 in the 31st minute; Dave Walder missed 2 eminently kickable penalty goal attempts in the first half; The England XV was losing 20-14 at half-time; The England XV was losing 23-14 in the 43rd minute; The England XV was losing 23-17 in the 57th minute when Dave Walder dummied his way through to score a brilliant try under the posts; The England XV was leading 24-23 midway through the second half; The England XV was losing 26-24 in the 69th minute when Juan Fernández Miranda scored a penalty goal to clinch the match for Argentina A; Mark Cueto only received one pass in the second half!)

ENGLAND COUNTIES TOUR TO CHILE 2002

CAPTAIN: *Tony Windo*

22nd Jun	NORTHERN REGIONAL XV	12	**ENGLAND COUNTIES XV**	38

Estadio Sausalito, Viña del Mar

[This match kicked off at 5.00pm]

(The England Counties XV players had insufficient time to shake off their jet lag; The England Counties XV was drawing 0-0 in the 13th minute when Jan Bonney wasted a great try-scoring opportunity by dropping the ball while the Northern Regional XV line was at his mercy; The England Counties XV was leading 7-0 in the 18th minute when Dave Muckalt crossed the tryline but the move was disallowed because the referee adjudged that there had been an earlier forward pass; The England Counties XV was leading 19-0 at half-time; The England Counties XV was still leading 19-0 midway through the second half when Mark Kirkby scored after Mike Davies made a brilliant break; The England Counties XV was leading 26-12 at one point in the final quarter)

CAPTAIN: *Glen Wilson*

25th Jun SOUTHERN REGIONAL XV 10 **ENGLAND COUNTIES XV** 69

Tineo Park, Concepción

[*This match kicked off at 3.00pm*]

(Jon Sewell (2) scored in the 1st minute!; The England Counties XV was leading 17-0 in the 11th minute; José Sariego scored after Ian Kennedy had his pass intercepted by Diego Valderrama, thus 7 points were preventable; The England Counties XV was leading 29-10 at half-time; Gregg Botterman scored two tries in 4 minutes midway through the second half; The England Counties XV scored 40 unanswered points in the second half to seal the match; Shaun Brady had a brilliant game)

2003

ENGLAND TOUR TO NEW ZEALAND AND AUSTRALIA 2003

CAPTAIN: *Phil Vickery*

9th June NEW ZEALAND MAORI 9 **ENGLAND XV** 23

Yarrow Stadium, New Plymouth

[This match kicked off at 7.35pm; Mike Worsley, Tom Palmer (2), Paul Volley, Andy Hazell, Ben Johnston, James Simpson-Daniel and Iain Balshaw all left the tour after this match as they were now required to join the England A squad in Canada]

(This match was played in extremely wet conditions; Simon Shaw and Steve Borthwick dominated the lineout in this match; The England XV was drawing 0-0 in the 2nd minute when Paul Grayson put up a brilliant cross-kick, but Dan Luger was then deceived by the bounce of the ball while the New Zealand Maori tryline was at his mercy!; The England XV was losing 3-0 in the 6th minute; The England XV was still losing 3-0 in the 10th minute when Simon Shaw scored from a rolling maul; The England XV was leading 10-3 midway through the first half; The England XV was leading 10-6 in the 27th minute; The England XV was still leading 10-6 just before half-time when Iain Balshaw wasted a great try-scoring opportunity by fly-hacking a loose ball into touch in-goal while the New Zealand Maori line was at his mercy; The England XV was leading 10-6 at half-time; The England XV played with a very strong wind in the second half; The England XV was leading 13-6 in the 45th minute when Paul Grayson missed an eminently kickable 25 metre drop goal attempt; The England XV was still leading 13-6 in the 46th minute when Iain Balshaw missed a kickable 30 metre drop goal attempt!; Iain Balshaw went off injured in the 48th minute, being replaced by Ben Johnston who had to play out of position as a full back; The England XV was leading 13-6 in the 52nd minute when Ben Johnston saved a certain try by getting back and grounding the ball before Rico Gear could reach it; Andy Gomarsall came on as a replacement for Kyran Bracken in the 53rd minute; The England XV was leading 13-9 in the 54th minute; The England XV was still leading 13-9 midway through the second half; The England XV was leading 13-9 in the 69th minute when Paul Grayson missed a kickable 40 metre penalty goal attempt; Simon Shaw injured his neck in the 70th minute but elected to remain on the pitch; Stuart Abbott went off injured at the same time, being replaced by Alex King with Ben Johnston then switching from full back to centre to accommodate Alex King; The England XV was leading 16-9 with 4 minutes remaining when Andy Gomarsall broke from the base of a five metre scrum to score a match-clinching try; Andy Gomarsall had a brilliant game)

ENGLAND COUNTIES TOUR TO ROMANIA AND FRANCE 2003

CAPTAIN: *Tony Windo*

10th Jun ROMANIA A 24 **ENGLAND COUNTIES XV** 26

Stadionul "Gheorghe Hagi", Constanţa

[This match kicked off at 5.00pm; Stadionul "Gheorghe Hagi" was previously called Stadionul "Farul"; Sean Casey selected but withdrew due to injury, Jan Bonney was moved from the bench to the team; The England Counties XV was allowed to select a bench containing 11 replacements]

(The England Counties XV scrum was put under severe pressure in the first half; Peter Murphy scored a penalty goal in the 4th minute!; The England Counties XV was leading 3-0 midway through the first half; The England Counties XV was leading 6-0 in the 25th minute; The England Counties XV was still leading 6-0 in the 37th minute; The England Counties XV was losing 7-6 at half-time; The England Counties XV was

leading 9-7 in the 43rd minute; The England Counties XV was losing 14-9 in the 47th minute; Peter Murphy went off injured in the second half; The England Counties XV was still losing 14-9 midway through the second half; The England Counties XV was losing 17-9 in the 63rd minute; The England Counties XV was still losing 17-9 with 7 minutes of normal time remaining when Paul Price scored from a rolling maul; The England Counties XV was losing 17-16 with 2 minutes of normal time remaining when James Moore scored a brilliant 45 metre penalty goal; The England Counties XV was leading 19-17 in the last minute of normal time when its defence failed to deal with a missed penalty goal attempt by Iulia Andrei and Constantin Gheara was able to follow up and score, thus 7 points were preventable; The England Counties XV was losing 24-19 in the second minute of injury time when Jan Bonney scored a try which James Moore then converted with the last kick of the match to win the game)

ENGLAND 'A' TOUR TO JAPAN 2003

CAPTAIN: *Pete Anglesea*

3rd July	JAPAN SELECT XV	10	**ENGLAND A XV**	37

Ajinomoto Stadium, Tokyo

[This match kicked off at 7.00pm; Alex Codling selected but withdrew due to injury, Alex Brown was moved from the bench to the team and Hugh Vyvyan was then selected for the bench]

(This match was played in wet conditions and high humidity; The England A XV players had insufficient time to shake off their jet lag; The England A XV was leading 3-0 in the 10th minute; The England A XV was losing 7-3 midway through the first half; The England A XV was losing 10-3 in the 23rd minute; The England A XV was losing 10-6 in the 37th minute; The England A XV was still losing 10-6 in the second minute of first half injury time when Pete Anglesea intercepted the ball and ran 22 metres to score; The England A XV was leading 11-10 at half-time; Alex Brown went off injured at half-time, being replaced by Hugh Vyvyan; The England A XV was leading 18-10 in the 44th minute; The England A XV was leading 25-10 in the 58th minute; The England A XV was still leading 25-10 with 3 minutes remaining when Olly Barkley fly-hacked a loose ball on the halfway line and Dan Scarbrough followed up and scored; The England A XV scored 34 unanswered points to win the match; Olly Barkley scored 22 points in this match; Neal Hatley had a brilliant game)

2004

PENGUINS TOUR TO HONG KONG 2004

CAPTAIN: *Craig de Goldi* (NZ)

13th Jun Hong Kong Barbarians 18 **PENGUINS** 73
King's Park Sports Ground, Hong Kong
[This match kicked off at 4.30pm; This match was played on a pitch made from artificial grass; Michael Holford and Martin Leslie played for the Hong Kong Barbarians in this match]
(This match was played in extremely hot conditions; The Penguins were losing 5-0 in the 9th minute; The Penguins were leading midway through the first half; The Penguins were leading 35-11 at half-time; Arthur Brenton had a brilliant game)

ENGLAND COUNTIES TOUR TO CANADA 2004

CAPTAIN: *Craig Hammond*

12th Jun Vancouver Island Crimson Tide (*CAN*) 0 **ENGLAND COUNTIES XV** 43
Shawnigan Lake School, Victoria
[This match kicked off at 3.00pm]
(This match was played in wet conditions; Both sides agreed to a relaxation of the rule about the maximum number of substitutions in this match; The England Counties XV players had insufficient time to shake off their jet lag; The England Counties XV was drawing 0-0 in the 15th minute when Mal Roberts scored after Tom Barlow (2) made a brilliant break; The England Counties XV was leading 7-0 midway through the first half; The England Counties XV was still leading 7-0 in the 27th minute; The England Counties XV was leading 19-0 at half-time; The England Counties XV was leading 22-0 midway through the second half; The England Counties XV was leading 29-0 in the 63rd minute; The England Counties XV was still leading 29-0 shortly afterwards when the referee awarded a penalty try after James Moore was impeded as he chased a kick ahead; The England Counties XV was leading 36-0 in the closing stages when Dave Strettle scored to seal the match; James Moore had a brilliant game)

PENGUINS TOUR TO MEXICO 2004

CAPTAIN: *Dave Gorrie* (NZ)

30th Jun Mexican Regional Selection (*MEX*) L **PENGUINS** W
Celaya Rugby Club, Universidad de Celaya
[No match notes]

3rd July MEXICO SELECT XV L **PENGUINS** W
Acapulco
[The Penguins included some Mexican players in their team for this match]

2005

BRITISH & IRISH LIONS TOUR TO NEW ZEALAND 2005

CAPTAIN: *Brian O'Driscoll* (IR)

4th June Bay of Plenty (*NZ*) 20 **BRITISH & IRISH LIONS XV** 34

Rotorua International Stadium

[This match kicked off at 7.10pm; Gareth Thomas (2) and Jason Robinson unavailable as they had yet to join the tour; Simon Taylor (2) unavailable due to injury; Neil Back unavailable due to suspension; Malcolm O'Kelly selected for bench but withdrew due to injury, being replaced by Donncha O'Callaghan; Malcolm O'Kelly left the tour injured two days before this match; Simon Shaw joined the tour on the day of this match; Lawrence Dallaglio left the tour injured after this match; Simon Easterby joined the tour after this match]

(This match was played on a wet pitch; Josh Lewsey scored in the 2nd minute!; The Lions XV was leading 10-0 in the 6th minute; Ronan O'Gara put up a brilliant cross-kick which enabled Mark Cueto to score a try which O'Gara then converted to give the Lions XV a 17-0 lead in the 11th minute; The Lions XV was still leading 17-0 in the 15th minute when Colin Bourke scored after Ronan O'Gara missed a tackle on Nili Latu, thus 7 points were preventable; The Lions XV was leading 17-7 midway through the first half; Lawrence Dallaglio had to go off in the 20th minute after he fractured and dislocated his ankle, being replaced by Martin Corry; The Lions XV was leading 17-10 in the 31st minute; Bay of Plenty were allowed to score 17 unanswered points; The Lions XV was drawing 17-17 at half-time; The Lions XV was still drawing 17-17 in the 52nd minute when Tom Shanklin powered through to score; The Lions XV was drawing 22-20 midway through the second half; Andy Sheridan came on as a replacement for Matt Stevens in the 65th minute; The Lions XV was leading 27-20 with 9 minutes remaining when Ronan O'Gara missed an eminently kickable conversion attempt; Tom Shanklin went off injured with 3 minutes remaining, being replaced by Matt Dawson with Dwayne Peel then switching from scrum half to the unfamiliar position of wing to accommodate Matt Dawson; The Lions XV was still leading 27-20 immediately afterwards when Gordon D'Arcy scored after Josh Lewsey made a superb break; Andy Sheridan played brilliantly in the scrums)

CAPTAIN: *Martin Corry*

8th June Taranaki (*NZ*) 14 **BRITISH & IRISH LIONS XV** 36

Yarrow Stadium, New Plymouth

[This match kicked off at 7.10pm; Jason Robinson unavailable as he had yet to join the tour; Neil Back unavailable due to suspension; Gareth Thomas (2) joined the tour the day before this match; Jason Robinson joined the tour after this match; Martin Corry forgot to take the traditional Lions mascot with him as he took the field to play the game!]

(This match was played in cold conditions; The Lions XV was drawing 0-0 in the 10th minute when Geordan Murphy crossed the tryline, but the move was disallowed as the scoring pass from Shane Horgan was adjudged to have been forward; The Lions XV was leading 3-0 midway through the first half; The Lions XV was still leading 3-0 in the 31st minute when Chris Cusiter's attempted pass to Charlie Hodgson went over the dead ball line, which allowed Chris Masoe to score from the resulting Taranaki five metre scrum; The Lions XV was losing 7-6 at half-time; The Lions XV was leading 11-7 in the 48th minute; The Lions XV was leading 17-7 midway through the second half; The Lions XV was leading 24-7 in the 66th minute; The Lions XV was still leading 24-7

with 8 minutes of normal time remaining when Geordan Murphy scored after Michael Owen threw a brilliant long pass; The Lions XV was leading 31-7 with 5 minutes of normal time remaining when Geordan Murphy scored another try after Charlie Hodgson put up a brilliant cross-kick to Shane Horgan; The Lions XV scored 30 unanswered points to win the match; The Lions XV was leading 36-7 in the second minute of injury time when collectively poor tackling allowed Brendon Watt to score, thus 2 tries and 14 points were preventable; Charlie Hodgson and Geordan Murphy both had a brilliant game)

CAPTAIN: *Brian O'Driscoll* (IR)

11th Jun NEW ZEALAND MAORI 19 **BRITISH & IRISH LIONS XV*** 13
Waikato Stadium, Hamilton

[This match kicked off at 7.10pm; Neil Back unavailable due to suspension; Simon Taylor (2) selected but withdrew due to injury, Michael Owen was moved from the bench to the team and Simon Easterby was then selected for the bench; The Lions XV's starting front row was, at 54 stone, the heaviest ever to take the field!; Simon Taylor (2) left the tour injured after this match; Ryan Jones joined the tour after this match]

(This match was played in cold conditions; The Lions XV was leading 3-0 in the 14th minute; The Lions XV was drawing 3-3 midway through the first half; The Lions XV was losing 6-3 in the 29th minute when Stephen Jones (2) missed a speculative penalty goal from the halfway line; The Lions XV was still losing 6-3 shortly before half-time; The Lions XV was drawing 6-6 at half-time; The Lions XV forwards could not win any lineout ball in the second half; The Lions XV was losing 9-6 in the 51st minute; The Lions XV was still losing 9-6 midway through the second half when collectively poor tackling allowed Leon MacDonald to score, thus 7 points were preventable; The Lions XV was losing 19-6 in the 69th minute when they were awarded a 28 metre penalty in an eminently kickable position, but Brian O'Driscoll ordered a kick to the corner in a vain attempt to score a try from the ensuing lineout; The Lions XV was still losing 19-6 with 5 minutes remaining when Brian O'Driscoll scored after he wrong-footed the New Zealand Maori defence with a brilliant sidestep; The Lions XV was losing 19-13 with 3 minutes remaining when Josh Lewsey was impeded by Piri Weepu as he attempted to support Martyn Williams' brilliant break, but the referee unaccountably ignored this infringement; Martyn Williams was outplayed by Marty Holah at the breakdown)

CAPTAIN: *Brian O'Driscoll* (IR)

15th Jun Wellington (*NZ*) 6 **BRITISH & IRISH LIONS XV** 23
WestpacTrust Stadium, Wellington

[This match kicked off at 7.10pm; Michael Owen unavailable due to family commitments; Lewis Moody selected for bench but withdrew due to injury, being replaced by Richard Hill (2); Riki Flutey played for Wellington in this match]

(This match was played in wet and windy conditions; Jason Robinson played with an injury; The Lions XV forwards monopolised possession in this match; Jonny Wilkinson missed an eminently kickable 23 metre drop goal attempt in the 1st minute!; The Lions XV was leading 3-0 in the 9th minute; The Lions XV was still leading 3-0 in the 16th minute when Jonny Wilkinson missed a kickable 38 metre penalty goal attempt; The Lions XV was leading 3-0 midway through the first half; The Lions XV was leading 6-0 in the 24th minute; The Lions XV was leading 6-3 in the 30th minute when Martin Corry wasted a great try-scoring opportunity by attempting to make the line himself instead of using a 3 man overlap outside him; A brilliant break by Dwayne

Peel enabled Gethin Jenkins to score a try which Jonny Wilkinson then converted to give the Lions XV a 13-3 lead in the 36th minute; The Lions XV was leading 13-6 at half-time; The Lions XV was leading 16-6 in the 44th minute; The Lions XV was still leading 16-6 in the 58th minute when Jonny Wilkinson missed another kickable 34 metre kickable penalty goal attempt; The Lions XV was leading 16-6 midway through the second half; Stephen Jones (2) came on as a replacement for Gavin Henson in the 63rd minute, with Jonny Wilkinson then switching from fly half to centre to accommodate Stephen Jones (2); The Lions XV was still leading 16-6 with 3 minutes of normal time remaining when Gareth Thomas (2) chipped ahead and regathered the ball to score a brilliant try; Gethin Jenkins and Neil Back both had a brilliant game)

CAPTAIN: *Gordon Bulloch* (SC) [*Will Greenwood*]

18th Jun Otago (*NZ*) 19 **BRITISH & IRISH LIONS XV** 30

Carisbrook Stadium, Dunedin

[*This match kicked off at 7.10pm; Lewis Moody selected but withdrew due to injury, Simon Easterby was moved from the bench to the team and Michael Owen was then selected for the bench*]

(This match was played in cold conditions; The Lions XV was losing 3-0 in the 6th minute; The Lions XV was losing 6-0 in the 16th minute; The Lions XV was losing 6-3 midway through the first half; The Lions XV was drawing 6-6 in the 22nd minute; The Lions XV was still drawing 6-6 in the 33rd minute when Danny Lee scored after Denis Hickie and Charlie Hodgson both missed a tackle on Neil Brew, thus 7 points were preventable; The Lions XV was losing 13-6 just before half-time when Charlie Hodgson put up a brilliant cross-kick and Will Greenwood followed up and scored; The Lions XV was drawing 13-13 at half-time; The Lions XV was losing 16-13 in the 44th minute; The Lions XV was still losing 16-13 in the 53rd minute when Ryan Jones powered through to score; The Lions XV was leading 20-16 midway through the second half; Steve Thompson (2) came on as a replacement for Gordon Bulloch in the 62nd minute; The Lions XV was leading 23-19 in the 68th minute when Shane Williams wrong-footed Glen Horton with a superb sidestep to score under the posts; Graham Rowntree played brilliantly in the scrums; Ryan Jones had a brilliant game)

CAPTAIN: *Michael Owen* (WA) [*Ronan O'Gara* (IR)]

21st Jun Southland (*NZ*) 16 **BRITISH & IRISH LIONS XV** 26

Rugby Park Stadium, Invercargill

[*This match kicked off at 7.10pm*]

(The Lions XV made a number of handling errors; Andy Titterrell's throwing-in was poor and the Lions XV lineout suffered accordingly; The Lions XV was leading 3-0 in the 6th minute; The Lions XV was still leading 3-0 in the 13th minute when Gavin Henson powered through 2 attempted tackles to score; The Lions XV was leading 10-3 midway through the first half; The Lions XV was still leading 10-3 in the 23rd minute when Ollie Smith (2) wasted a great try-scoring opportunity by knocking-on when there an overlap outside him; The Lions XV was leading 10-3 in the 26th minute when Ronan O'Gara missed a speculative penalty goal attempt from the halfway line; The Lions XV was leading 10-3 at half-time; The Lions XV was drawing 10-10 in the 46th minute; The Lions XV was still drawing 10-10 in the 53rd minute when Gavin Henson powered through to score another try; The Lions XV was leading 20-10 midway through the second half; The Lions XV was leading 20-13 in the 64th minute when Simon Easterby came on as a replacement for Michael Owen; The Lions XV was leading 23-13 with 8 minutes remaining; The Lions XV was leading 23-16 in the last minute when Ronan O'Gara scored a penalty goal to clinch the match; Gavin Henson had a brilliant game)

CAPTAIN: *Gordon Bulloch* (SC) [*Charlie Hodgson; Michael Owen* (WA)]

28th Jun Manawatu (*NZ*) 6 **BRITISH & IRISH LIONS XV** 109

FMG Stadium, Palmerston North

[*This match kicked off at 7.10pm; Gethin Jenkins, Ben Kay, Stephen Jones (2), Gavin Henson and Brian O'Driscoll all unavailable due to injury; Jason White joined the tour after this match*]

(*Jason Robinson played with an injury; Shane Williams scored in the 3rd minute!; The Lions XV was leading 12-0 in the 11th minute; The Lions XV was still leading 12-0 midway through the first half; The Lions XV was leading 19-0 in the 28th minute when Geordan Murphy scored after he wrong-footed the Manawatu defence with 2 brilliant sidesteps; The Lions XV was leading 26-0 in the 31st minute when Jason Robinson scored after Chris Cusiter took a quick tap penalty; The Lions XV was leading 31-3 in the 36th minute when a brilliant reverse pass by Ollie Smith (2) enabled Shane Williams to score to complete a hat-trick of tries in the first half!; Gordon Bulloch went off injured in the 39th minute, being replaced by Andy Titterrell; The Lions XV was leading 38-6 at half-time; Charlie Hodgson scored after just 69 seconds of the second half had been played!; The Lions XV was leading 57-6 in the 49th minute when Neil Back scored after Simon Shaw made a superb 55 metre run; Ronan O'Gara came on as a replacement for Charlie Hodgson in the 51st minute; The Lions XV was leading 64-6 in the 53rd minute when Gordon D'Arcy scored after Ronan O'Gara threw a brilliant long pass; The Lions XV was leading 74-6 midway through the second half; The Lions XV was leading 88-6 in the 66th minute; The Lions XV was leading 95-6 with 4 minutes of normal time remaining when some superb handling allowed Shane Williams to score his fifth try of the match!; The Lions XV was leading 102-6 when the full-time hooter sounded, but the ball was still in play and Mark Cueto was able to score in the corner; The Lions XV scored 71 unanswered points in the second half to seal the match; Ollie Smith (2) injured playing in the match; Shane Williams played brilliantly and scored 25 points in this match; Andy Sheridan played brilliantly in the scrums; This was the Lions' biggest-ever win over a New Zealand provincial side!*)

CAPTAIN: *Gordon Bulloch* (SC)

5th July Auckland (*NZ*) 13 **BRITISH & IRISH LIONS XV** 17

Eden Park, Auckland

[*This match kicked off at 7.10pm; Brian O'Driscoll and Ollie Smith (2) unavailable due to injury; Andy Sheridan selected but withdrew due to injury, being replaced by Graham Rowntree*]

(*This match was played in wet conditions; Charlie Hodgson scored a penalty goal in the 5th minute!; The Lions XV was leading 3-0 midway through the first half; Charlie Hodgson went off injured in the 21st minute, being replaced by Ronan O'Gara; The Lions XV was still leading 3-0 immediately afterwards when Martyn Williams and Matt Dawson both saved a certain try by managing to get beneath the ball as John Afoa attempted to ground it; The Lions XV was leading 6-0 in the 28th minute; The Lions XV was leading 9-3 just before half-time when Martyn Williams scored after Mark Cueto made a brilliant 49 metre run; The Lions XV was leading 14-3 at half-time; The Lions XV was still leading 14-3 in the 54th minute; The Lions XV was leading 14-6 midway through the second half; The Lions XV was leading 14-13 in the 62nd minute; The Lions XV was still leading 14-13 with 3 minutes remaining when Ronan O'Gara scored a 22 metre penalty goal to clinch the match; Gordon D'Arcy injured playing in the match; Gordon Bulloch, Matt Dawson and Mark Cueto all had a brilliant game*)

ENGLAND COUNTIES TOUR TO ARGENTINA AND URUGUAY 2005

CAPTAIN: *Craig Hammond*

15th June	Atlético del Rosario Invitación XV (*AR*)	0	**ENGLAND COUNTIES XV**	38

Club Atlético del Rosario

[This match kicked off at 7.00pm]

(This match was played on a damp and slippery pitch; The England Counties XV was drawing 0-0 in the 7th minute when Lee Blackett scored after Chris Malherbe made a brilliant break; The England Counties XV was leading 12-0 in the 14th minute; The England Counties XV was still leading 12-0 midway through the first half; Craig Hammond saved a certain try when he tackled Leopoldo Gosmana; The England Counties XV was leading 12-0 at half-time; The England Counties XV was leading 19-0 in the 43rd minute; The England Counties XV was leading 26-0 in the 48th minute; The England Counties XV was leading 31-0 midway through the second half; The England Counties XV was still leading 31-0 in the 69th minute when Paul Arnold scored from a rolling maul)

PUBLIC SCHOOL WANDERERS TOUR TO SRI LANKA 2005

CAPTAIN: *Ben Harvey*

14th Jun	Western Province Rugby Union (*SRI*)	13	**PUBLIC SCHOOL WANDERERS**	58

Ceylon Rugby and Football Club Grounds, Longden Place, Colombo

[This match kicked off at 4.30pm]

(This match was played in extreme heat; The Public School Wanderers forwards monopolised possession; The Public School Wanderers were leading 39-13 at half-time; The referee allowed a water break midway through both the first and second halves; The referee blew for full-time after only 30 minutes of the second half had been played!)

CAPTAIN: *Steve White-Cooper*

19th Jun	Central Province Invitation XV (*SRI*)	3	**PUBLIC SCHOOL WANDERERS**	33

Kandy Sports Club, Nittawela Grounds, Kandy

[This match kicked off at 5.00pm]

(This match was played in extreme heat; The Public School Wanderers forwards monopolised possession; The referee allowed a water break midway through both the first and second halves; The referee blew for full-time after only 30 minutes of the second half had been played!)

CAPTAIN: *Ben Harvey*

22nd Jun	Combined Defence Services (*SRI*)	6	**PUBLIC SCHOOL WANDERERS**	61

Army Grounds, Galle Face, Colombo

[This match kicked off at 5.00pm]

(This match was played in extreme heat; The Public School Wanderers forwards monopolised possession)

2006

WORLD XV TOUR TO SOUTH AFRICA 2006

CAPTAIN: *Justin Marshall* (NZ)

9th June	Western Province Corné Krige XV (*SA*)	31	**WORLD XV**	49

Norwich Park Newlands, Cape Town

[*This match kicked off at 7.10pm; Carlos Spencer selected but withdrew to sit on the bench, Ludovic Mercier was moved from the bench to the team; Bobby Skinstad came on as a replacement for the Western Province Corné Krige XV in this match*]

(*The World XV was losing 7-0 in the 9th minute; The World XV was drawing 7-7 midway through the first half; The World XV was leading 21-7 in the 30th minute; The World XV scored 21 unanswered points to win the match; The World XV was leading 21-7 at half-time; The World XV was leading 21-12 in the 46th minute when Isa Nacewa scored after Justin Marshall put in a brilliant grubber kick; The World XV was leading 35-12 in the 51st minute; The World XV was leading 35-24 midway through the second half; The World XV was leading 42-24 in the 67th minute; The World XV was still leading 42-24 with 9 minutes remaining when Zhahier Ryland intercepted the ball and went on to score, thus 7 points were preventable; The World XV was leading 42-31 with 4 minutes remaining when Sébastien Chabal powered through to score a brilliant 40 metre solo try*)

2007

ENGLAND COUNTIES TOUR TO RUSSIA 2007

CAPTAIN: *Duncan Cormack*

7th June Krasny-Yar (*RUS*) 19 **ENGLAND COUNTIES XV** 27

Centralny Stadium, Otdykha Island, Krasnoyarsk, Siberia

[This match kicked off at 7.00pm]

(The England Counties XV players had insufficient time to shake off their jet lag; The England Counties XV was drawing 3-3 when James Tideswell scored after Mark Woodrow put up a brilliant cross-kick; The England Counties XV was leading 8-3 when Tom Jarvis scored after Paul Knight (2) took a quick tap penalty; The England Counties XV was leading 13-3 at half-time; The England Counties XV was drawing 13-13 in the 58th minute; Chris Rainbow went off injured in the 61st minute, being replaced by Neil Spence; The England Counties XV was still drawing 13-13 when Mike Blakeburn scored after Gregor Hayter made a brilliant 36 metre run; Gregor Hayter went off injured in the last minute of normal time, being replaced by Glenn Cooper; The England Counties XV was leading 20-19 in injury time when Mark Bedworth scored under the posts to clinch the match; Mike Blakeburn and Chris Rainbow both had a brilliant game)

CAPTAIN: *James Winterbottom*

12th Jun VVA Podmoskovje (*RUS*) 35 **ENGLAND COUNTIES XV** 15

Monino Stadium, Moscow

[This match kicked off at 6.00pm; Gregor Hayter unavailable due to injury; The England Counties squad had to fly from Siberia to Moscow to play in this match!]

(The England Counties XV players had insufficient time to shake off their jet lag; The England Counties XV forwards could not win any lineout ball; Frankie Neale scored a penalty goal in the early stages; A lack of communication between Chris Pilgrim and Matt Leek allowed Yury Kushnarev to break through and score, thus 5 points were preventable; The England Counties XV was losing 22-3 at half-time; The England Counties XV was losing 29-3 early in the second half; The England Counties XV was losing 32-8 midway through the second half; The England Counties XV was still losing 32-8 when Liam Wordley scored a brilliant try; Frankie Neale went off injured in this match, being replaced by Arran Cruickshanks; Chris Morgan had a brilliant game)

2008

[No tour matches]

2009

OXBRIDGE TOUR TO JAPAN 2009

CAPTAIN: *Peter Clarke (1)*

22nd Mar All Kanto Gakuin University (*JAP*) 10 **OXBRIDGE XV** 17

Mitsuzawa Stadium, Yokohama

[This match kicked off at 2.00pm; This game commemorated the 125th Anniversary of the foundation of Kanto Gakuin University in 1884; The Oxbridge XV named a 10 man bench selection]

(This match was played in wet conditions; The Oxbridge XV played into the wind in the first half; The Oxbridge XV was losing 3-0 in the 18th minute; Andy Daniel went off injured immediately afterwards, being replaced by Ricky Lutton; The Oxbridge XV was still losing 3-0 midway through the first half; The Oxbridge XV was losing 3-0 in the 29th minute when Tom Gregory missed a penalty goal attempt; The Oxbridge XV was still losing 3-0 in the 37th minute when a handling error led directly to a try by Hiroshi Mizuno, thus 7 points were preventable; The Oxbridge XV was losing 10-0 at half-time; The Oxbridge XV was still losing 10-0 in the 56th minute when Tom Gregory missed another penalty goal attempt; The Oxbridge XV was losing 10-0 midway through the second half when Toby Henry missed a drop goal attempt; The Oxbridge XV was still losing 10-0 in the 64th minute when Tim Catling scored a 40 metre interception try; The Oxbridge XV was losing 10-7 in the 67th minute when Chris Mahony started a superb counter-attack and then took a return pass to finish the move with a try; The Oxbridge XV was leading 12-10 with 8 minutes remaining when Peter Wright (2) broke from the base of a scrum to score; The Oxbridge XV scored 17 unanswered points in the second half to win the match)

BRITISH & IRISH LIONS TOUR TO SOUTH AFRICA 2009

CAPTAIN: *Paul O'Connell* (IR)

30th May Royal XV (*SA*) 25 **BRITISH & IRISH LIONS XV** 37

Royal Bafokeng Stadium, Rustenburg

[This match kicked off at 3.00pm; This match replaced the originally scheduled game against a Highveld XV; Leigh Halfpenny unavailable as he had yet to join the tour; Andy Powell selected but withdrew on the morning of the match due to illness, being replaced by David Wallace; Stephen Ferris selected for bench but withdrew on the morning of the match due to injury, being replaced by Jamie Heaslip; Euan Murray, Tom Croft, Harry Ellis, Luke Fitzgerald, Brian O'Driscoll and Rob Kearney were all rested for this match; Leigh Halfpenny joined the tour after this match]

(This match was played at high altitude in 80 degree heat on a narrow pitch; The Lions XV was leading 3-0 in the 8th minute; The Lions XV was drawing 3-3 in the 17th minute when a poor defensive alignment allowed Wilhelm Koch to score; The Lions XV was losing 10-3 midway through the first half; The Lions XV was losing 13-3 in the 27th minute when Ryno Barnes was allowed to score from a rolling maul; The Royal XV was allowed to score 18 unanswered points; The Lions XV was losing 18-3 in the 30th minute when Mike Blair charged down Sarel Pretorius' kick but then unaccountably attempted to gather the resulting loose ball instead of fly-hacking it on over the Royal XV line; The Lions XV was still losing 18-3 in the 33rd minute when it was awarded a 33 metre penalty in a kickable position, but Paul O'Connell ordered a kick to the corner in a vain attempt to score a try from the ensuing lineout; The Lions XV was losing 18-3 shortly before half-time when Tommy Bowe scored after Ronan O'Gara threw a brilliant inside pass; Keith Earls had a poor first half; The Lions XV was losing 18-10 at

half-time; The Lions XV forwards monopolised possession in the second half; The Lions XV was losing 18-13 in the 43rd minute; The Lions XV was still losing 18-13 in the 52nd minute when Shane Williams wasted a great try-scoring opportunity by throwing a poor pass behind the unmarked Tommy Bowe; The Lions XV was losing 18-13 in the 53rd minute when Shane Williams reached the tryline but then dropped the ball in the act of scoring; The Lions XV was still losing 18-13 in the 57th minute when it was awarded another 35 metre penalty in a kickable position, but Paul O'Connell again ordered a kick to the corner in a vain attempt to score a try from the ensuing lineout; The Lions XV was losing 18-13 midway through the second half; The Lions XV was still losing 18-13 in the 65th minute when Bees Roux scored after Simon Shaw missed a tackle on Devon Raubenheimer, thus 3 tries and 19 points were preventable; Keith Earls went off injured in the 66th minute, being replaced by Riki Flutey; The Lions XV was losing 25-13 in the 67th minute when Lee Byrne kicked ahead and followed up to score a superb 75 metre solo try; The Lions XV was losing 25-20 with 9 minutes remaining when Riki Flutey broke through but was then brilliantly tackled by Russell Jeacocks; The Lions XV was losing 25-23 with 4 minutes remaining when Alun-Wyn Jones scored from a rolling maul; The Lions XV was leading 30-25 in the last minute when Ronan O'Gara scored after Martyn Williams threw a superb inside pass; The Lions XV scored 24 unanswered points to win the match; Riki Flutey injured playing in the match; Ronan O'Gara scored 22 points in this match; Lee Byrne had a brilliant game)

CAPTAIN: *Brian O'Driscoll* (IR) [*Phil Vickery; Alun-Wyn Jones* (WA)]

3rd June Golden Lions (*SA*) 10 **BRITISH & IRISH LIONS XV** 74

Coca-Cola Park, Johannesburg

[*This match kicked off at 7.10pm; The Gauteng Lions changed their name to the Golden Lions in 1998; Riki Flutey and Keith Earls unavailable due to injury; Gordon D'Arcy joined the tour after this match*]

(*This match was played at high altitude; The Lions XV was drawing 0-0 in the 6th minute when Jamie Roberts scored a brilliant try; The Lions XV was leading 7-0 in the 10th minute when some superb handling amongst the backs allowed Brian O'Driscoll to score; The Lions XV was leading 17-0 in the 13th minute; The Lions XV was leading 25-3 midway through the first half; Tom Croft scored a brilliant try which Stephen Jones (2) then converted to give the Lions XV a 32-3 lead in the 31st minute; The Lions XV was still leading 32-3 in the 37th minute when a poor defensive alignment allowed Shandre Frolick to score, thus 7 points were preventable; The Lions XV was leading 32-10 when the half-time hooter sounded, but the ball was still in play and Jamie Roberts was able to score; The Lions XV was leading 39-10 at half-time; The Lions XV was still leading 39-10 in the 47th minute when Stephen Jones (2) superbly flicked the ball on to Tommy Bowe who scored a try which Stephen Jones (2) then brilliantly converted from the right touchline; James Hook came on as a replacement for Jamie Roberts in the 53rd minute; Tommy Bowe scored a 57 metre interception try which Stephen Jones (2) then converted to give the Lions XV a 53-10 lead midway through the second half; Shane Williams came on as a replacement for Brian O'Driscoll in the 61st minute, with Tommy Bowe then switching from wing to centre to accommodate Shane Williams; Harry Ellis came on as a replacement for Stephen Jones (2) in the 62nd minute, with Mike Phillips (2) then moving from scrum half to the unfamiliar position of centre to accommodate Harry Ellis and James Hook switching from centre to fly half to accommodate Mike Phillips (2); The Lions XV was leading 60-10 in the 69th minute; The Lions XV was reduced to 14 men with 8 minutes of normal time remaining when Ugo Monye went off injured; The Lions XV was still leading 60-10 with*

***6 minutes of normal time remaining when James Hook scored another 60 metre interception try; The Lions XV was leading 67-10 when the full-time hooter sounded, but the ball was still in play and Stephen Ferris was able to score a superb 77 metre solo try; The Lions XV scored 42 unanswered points to seal the match; Tom Croft had a brilliant game*)**

CAPTAIN: *Paul O'Connell* (IR)

6th June Free State Cheetahs (*SA*) 24 **BRITISH & IRISH LIONS XV** 26

Vodacom Park Stadium, Bloemfontein

[*This match kicked off at 3.00pm; Riki Flutey unavailable due to injury; Martyn Williams selected but withdrew due to injury, being replaced by Joe Worsley; Stephen Ferris left the tour injured after this match*]

(*This match was played at high altitude; The Lions XV was leading 3-0 in the 7th minute; The Lions XV was still leading 3-0 in the 10th minute when Stephen Ferris gathered a loose ball and ran 35 metres to score; The Lions XV was leading 10-0 in the 16th minute when Keith Earls scored after James Hook put in a brilliant chip-kick; The Lions XV was leading 20-0 midway through the first half; The Lions XV scored 20 unanswered points to win the match; The Lions XV was leading 20-7 in the 26th minute; The Lions XV was leading 20-14 in the 34th minute; The Free State Cheetahs were allowed to score 14 unanswered points; The Lions XV was leading 23-14 at half-time; The Lions XV was leading 23-17 in the 42nd minute; The Lions XV was leading 26-17 in the 51st minute; The Lions XV was still leading 26-17 midway through the second half; The Lions XV was leading 26-17 in the 66th minute when Keith Earls wasted a great try-scoring opportunity by electing to take the ball into contact instead of using a 2 man overlap outside him; The Lions XV was still leading 26-17 with 8 minutes of normal time remaining and pressing in attack when Shane Williams had his pass to James Hook intercepted by Corné Uys who then ran 88 metres to score, thus 7 points were preventable; The Lions XV was leading 26-24 with 1 minute of normal time remaining when Louis Strydom narrowly missed a speculative 44 metre drop goal attempt for the Free State Cheetahs!*)

CAPTAIN: *Paul O'Connell* (IR) [*Brian O'Driscoll* (IR)]

10th Jun Natal Sharks (*SA*) 3 **BRITISH & IRISH LIONS XV** 39

ABSA Stadium, Durban

[*This match kicked off at 7.10pm; Martyn Williams unavailable due to injury; Leigh Halfpenny selected for bench but withdrew due to injury, being replaced by James Hook; Leigh Halfpenny left the tour injured after this match; Ryan Jones joined the tour on 11th June but then had to leave the next day because he had suffered concussion in the Wales match against the USA in Chicago on 6th June 2009!*]

(*The Lions XV played into a swirling wind in the first half; The Lions XV forwards monopolised possession in this match; The referee unaccountably kept penalising Gethin Jenkins at the scrums; The Lions XV was drawing 0-0 in the 11th minute when Jamie Heaslip crossed the tryline but then could not get downward pressure on the ball; The Lions XV was still drawing 0-0 midway through the first half when Brian O'Driscoll intercepted the ball in front of his own 22, but he was then superbly chased back and tackled 1 metre short of the tryline by Lwazi Mvovo; The Lions XV was drawing 0-0 in the 23rd minute when Lee Mears powered through to score; The Lions XV was leading 7-3 in the 30th minute; The Lions XV was still leading 7-3 shortly before half-time when Ronan O'Gara put up a brilliant cross-kick, but Shane Williams then wasted this great try-scoring opportunity by dropping the ball while the Natal Sharks line was at his mercy; The Lions XV was leading 7-3 at half-time; Mike Phillips*

(2) dummied his way through to score a brilliant try after just 71 seconds of the second half had been played!; The Lions XV was leading 15-3 in the 49th minute; The Lions XV was leading 18-3 midway through the second half when some superb handling allowed Luke Fitzgerald to score; Simon Shaw came on as a replacement for Paul O'Connell in the 64th minute; Jamie Roberts went off injured at the same time, being replaced by Riki Flutey; The Lions XV was leading 25-3 in the 68th minute when Lee Byrne scored a brilliant 51 metre solo try; The Lions XV was leading 32-3 when the full-time hooter sounded, but the ball was still in play and Jamie Heaslip was able to power through 3 attempted tackles to score; The Lions XV scored 32 unanswered points to clinch the match; Jamie Heaslip had a brilliant game)

CAPTAIN: *Phil Vickery* [*Martyn Williams* (WA)]

13th Jun Western Province (*SA*) 23 **BRITISH & IRISH LIONS XV** 26

Newlands, Cape Town

[*This match kicked off at 3.00pm; Jamie Roberts unavailable due to injury; Mike Blair selected for bench but withdrew on the morning of the match due to injury, being replaced by Shane Williams who acted as scrum half cover for Harry Ellis*]

(*This match was played in wet conditions; Willem De Waal scored a penalty goal in the 4th minute!; The Lions XV was leading 6-3 in the 14th minute when Stephen Jones (2) had a kickable 43 metre penalty goal attempt go underneath the crossbar; The Lions XV was drawing 6-6 midway through the first half; The Lions XV was losing 9-6 in the 28th minute when some superb handling allowed Tommy Bowe to score; The Lions XV was leading 11-9 in the 35th minute when Tommy Bowe made a brilliant 27 metre break which enabled Ugo Monye to score a try which Stephen Jones (2) then brilliantly converted from the left touchline; The Lions XV was leading 18-9 just before half-time; The Lions XV was leading 18-12 at half-time; The Lions XV played with a swirling wind in the second half; The Lions XV was leading 18-15 in the 48th minute; The Lions XV was still leading 18-15 in the 56th minute when Martyn Williams scored from a rolling maul; Euan Murray came on as a replacement for Phil Vickery in the 57th minute; The Lions XV was leading 23-18 midway through the second half; Rob Kearney went off injured in the 64th minute, being replaced by James Hook; The Lions XV was drawing 23-23 in the 67th minute when James Hook missed a speculative 47 metre penalty goal attempt; The Lions XV was still drawing 23-23 with 3 minutes remaining when James Hook scored a superb 47 metre penalty goal to win the match; Tommy Bowe had a brilliant game*)

CAPTAIN: *Donncha O'Callaghan* (IR)

16th Jun Southern Kings (*SA*) 8 **BRITISH & IRISH LIONS XV** 20

Nelson Mandela Bay Stadium, Port Elizabeth

[*This match kicked off at 3.00pm; This match replaced the originally scheduled game against a SA Coastal XV; Rob Kearney unavailable due to injury; Shane Williams selected but withdrew on the morning of the match to sit on the bench due to illness, Ugo Monye was moved from the bench to the team; Euan Murray left the tour injured after this match*]

**(*This match took place on a poor playing surface; Jaco van der Westhuyzen scored a penalty goal in the 2nd minute!; Euan Murray went off injured in the 8th minute, being replaced by Adam Jones (2); James Hook went off injured in the 13th minute, being replaced by Ronan O'Gara; The Lions XV was losing 3-0 midway through the first half when it was awarded a 44 metre penalty in a kickable position, but Donncha O'Callaghan ordered a kick to the corner in a vain attempt to score a try from the ensuing lineout; The Lions XV was still losing 3-0 in the 24th minute when Keith Earls*

***made a brilliant 46 metre run but then wasted this great try-scoring opportunity by throwing a forward pass to the unmarked Luke Fitzgerald; The Lions XV was drawing 3-3 in the 27th minute; The Lions XV was still drawing 3-3 in the 36th minute when Ronan O'Gara saved a certain try by tackling Wylie Human; The Lions XV was drawing 3-3 at half-time; The Lions XV was leading 6-3 in the 50th minute when Ugo Monye scored after Ronan O'Gara put up a brilliant cross-kick; The Lions XV was leading 13-3 midway through the second half; Shane Williams came on as a replacement for Ugo Monye in the 64th minute; The Lions XV was still leading 13-3 immediately afterwards when Ronan O'Gara hit the left-hand post with a speculative 48 metre penalty goal attempt; The Lions XV was leading 13-3 in the 69th minute when the referee awarded a penalty try after the Southern Kings forwards collapsed two successive scrums in front of their own line; The Lions XV scored 20 unanswered points to win the match; The Lions XV was leading 20-3 with 8 minutes of normal time remaining; Andrew Sheridan injured playing in the match; Simon Shaw had a brilliant game*)**

CAPTAIN: *Ronan O'Gara* (IR) [*Donncha O'Callaghan* (IR)]

23rd Jun EMERGING SPRINGBOKS 13 **BRITISH & IRISH LIONS XV*** 13

Newlands, Cape Town

[*This match kicked off at 7.10pm; Andrew Sheridan and Lee Byrne unavailable due to injury; On 24th June 2009 Nathan Hines was banned for 1 week after being cited for a dangerous tackle on Wilhelm Steenkamp; Lee Byrne left the tour injured after this match*]

(*This match was played on a wet pitch with intermittent torrential rain; Ronan O'Gara missed a 23 metre penalty goal attempt from in front of the posts in the 4th minute!; The Lions XV was leading 3-0 in the 9th minute; The Lions XV was still leading 3-0 in the 15th minute when Keith Earls scored after he wrong-footed Janno Vermaak with a brilliant sidestep; The Lions XV was leading 10-0 midway through the first half; The Lions XV was still leading 10-0 in the 37th minute; The Lions XV was leading 10-3 at half-time; James Hook came on as a replacement for Ronan O'Gara in the 45th minute; The Lions XV was leading 10-6 in the 50th minute; The Lions XV was still leading 10-6 midway through the second half; Ugo Monye came on as a replacement for Luke Fitzgerald in the 65th minute, with Shane Williams then switching from right to left wing to accommodate Monye; Phil Vickery came on as a replacement for John Hayes in the 67th minute; The Lions XV was leading 10-6 with 3 minutes remaining; The Lions XV was leading 13-6 in the last minute when Danwel Demas scored a try which Willem de Waal then brilliantly converted from the right touchline with the last kick of the match to draw the game for the Emerging Springboks; Shane Williams saw very little of the ball in this match*)

ENGLAND COUNTIES TOUR TO KOREA AND JAPAN 2009

CAPTAIN: *Jason Smithson*

8th June East Japan (*JAP*) 31 **ENGLAND COUNTIES XV** 67

Edogawa Stadium, Tokyo

[*This match kicked off at 7.00pm; Matt Long selected for bench but withdrew, being replaced by Chris Rowland*]

(*The England Counties XV was leading 3-0 in the 7th minute; The England Counties XV was losing 7-3 in the 14th minute; The England Counties XV was leading 10-7 midway through the first half; The England Counties XV was losing 14-10 in the 23rd minute; The England Counties XV was still losing 14-10 in the 36th minute when James Aston powered through to score; The England Counties XV was leading 22-14 at half-time; The England Counties XV was leading 25-14 in the 42nd minute; The England Counties*

XV was leading 39-14 in the 55th minute; The England Counties XV was still leading 39-14 midway through the second half when Mark Woodrow dummied his way through to score a brilliant try; The England Counties XV was leading 46-14 in the 64th minute when Gareth Collins chipped ahead and followed up to score a superb 70 metre solo try; The England Counties XV scored 43 unanswered points to win the match; The England Counties XV was leading 53-19 with 5 minutes of normal time remaining; The England Counties XV was leading 67-24 in the fourth minute of injury time; Patrick Leach and Kyle Dench both had a brilliant game)

CAPTAIN: *Matt Long*

12th Jun Yamaha Jubilo (*JAP*) 20 **ENGLAND COUNTIES XV** 36
Yamaha Stadium, Shizuoka

[This match kicked off at 6.00pm]

(The England Counties XV was losing 5-0 in the early stages; The England Counties XV was losing 10-0 midway through the first half; The England Counties XV was losing 17-6 in the 36th minute; The England Counties XV was losing 17-9 just before half-time; The England Counties XV was losing 20-9 at half-time; The England Counties XV was still losing 20-9 in the 46th minute when Nick Royle scored a 70 metre interception try; The England Counties XV was losing 20-16 in the 57th minute when Mark Woodrow scored a brilliant penalty goal from a difficult angle; The England Counties XV was losing 20-19 midway through the second half; The England Counties XV was still losing 20-19 in the 63rd minute when Tom Richardson scored a superb try; The England Counties XV was leading 33-20 in the 70th minute; The England Counties XV scored 27 unanswered points to win the match; Mark Woodrow played brilliantly and scored 21 points in this match)

2010

PENGUINS TOUR TO PORTUGAL 2010

CAPTAIN: *Marcus Di Rollo* (SC)

26th May Lisbon Selection XV (*POR*) 17 **PENGUINS** 34

Campo A, Complexo Desportivo da Tapada

[This match kicked off at 7.00pm]

ENGLAND COUNTIES TOUR TO CANADA 2010

CAPTAIN: *Matt Long*

4th June The Rock (*CAN*) 6 **ENGLAND COUNTIES XV** 20

Swilers RFC, Swilers Rugby Park, St. John's, Newfoundland

[This match kicked off at 6.15pm; The England Counties XV named an 8 man bench selection]

(This match was played in cold and wet conditions; The England Counties XV was drawing 0-0 in the early stages when Ross Winney missed 2 penalty goal attempts in succession; The England Counties XV was still drawing 0-0 midway through the first half; The England Counties XV was leading 5-0 in the 30th minute; The England Counties XV was leading 8-3 shortly before half-time when Fergus Mulchrone scored a superb solo try which Ross Winney then brilliantly converted from the right touchline; The England Counties XV was leading 15-3 at half-time; The England Counties XV played into the wind in the second half; The England Counties XV was leading 15-6 in the 51st minute; The England Counties XV was still leading 15-6 midway through the second half; The England Counties XV was leading 15-6 in the 66th minute when Will Fraser scored from a rolling maul; Will Fraser injured his knee in the closing stages; Will Cliff injured playing in the match; Will Fraser had a brilliant game)

CAPTAIN: *Kyle Dench*

8th June Ontario Blues (*CAN*) 26 **ENGLAND COUNTIES XV** 32

Oakville Crusaders RC, Oakville Crusaders Park, Toronto

[This match kicked off at 7.00pm; Will Fraser unavailable due to injury; Will Cliff selected but withdrew on the day of the match due to injury, Tom Kessell was moved from the bench to the team and Ross Winney was then selected for the bench; Will Fraser left the tour injured after this match]

(Tom Kessell scored in the 2nd minute after Paul Humphries made a brilliant break!; The England Counties XV was leading 10-0 in the 6th minute; The England Counties XV was still leading 10-0 midway through the first half; The Ontario Blues were allowed to score 16 unanswered points; The England Counties XV was losing 16-10 at half-time; The England Counties XV played with the wind in the second half; The England XV was still losing 16-10 early in the second half when Gavin Woods scored from a rolling maul; The England Counties XV was leading 17-16 in the 50th minute when Tom Jarvis scored after Paul Humphries put in a brilliant kick ahead; The England Counties XV was losing 23-22 midway through the second half when Dan Baines scored after Paul Humphries threw a superb pass; The England Counties XV was leading 32-26 in the 66th minute; Paul Humphries had a brilliant game)

ENGLAND TOUR TO AUSTRALIA AND NEW ZEALAND 2010

CAPTAIN: *Chris Robshaw*

8th June Australian Barbarians 28 **ENGLAND XV*** 28

ME Bank Stadium, Perth

[*This match kicked off at 7.00pm; Jon Golding and Jonny Wilkinson unavailable due to injury; No English players were involved with the Australian Barbarians on this occasion; Dave Attwood was cited after this match for stamping on two opponents, but the charges were dropped on 9th June 2010 because Australia had broken the Tour Agreement by appointing a local citing commissioner instead of one from a neutral country!; Phil Dowson joined the tour after this match*]

(*The England XV made a number of handling errors in this match; Olly Barkley scored a penalty goal in the 2nd minute!; The England XV was leading 6-0 in the 12th minute; The England XV was still leading 6-0 in the 18th minute when Hendre Fourie saved a certain try by brilliantly tackling Berrick Barnes; The England XV was leading 6-0 midway through the first half; The England XV was still leading 6-0 in the 22nd minute when collectively poor tackling allowed James O'Connor to score; The England XV was losing 8-5 in the 30th minute when Olly Barkley bought a dummy by James O'Connor who then went on to score another try; The England XV was losing 15-6 in the 33rd minute when Olly Barkley missed an eminently kickable 28 metre penalty goal attempt; The England XV was losing 15-13 just before half-time; The England XV was losing 18-13 at half-time; Hendre Fourie went off injured at half-time, being replaced by Joe Worsley; The England XV was still losing 18-13 in the 44th minute when Matt Banahan unaccountably moved infield from his defensive position on the wing and consequently Josh Valentine put in a grubber kick which allowed James O'Connor to score to complete a hat-trick of tries, thus 3 tries and 19 points were preventable; The England XV was losing 25-13 in the 50th minute when it was awarded a 31 metre penalty in a kickable position, but Chris Robshaw ordered a kick to the corner in a vain attempt to score a try from the ensuing lineout; The England XV was losing 25-16 midway through the second half; The Australian Barbarians were still leading 25-16 in the 62nd minute when Lachie Turner dropped the ball while the England XV tryline was at his mercy!; Paul Hodgson came on as a replacement for Richard Wigglesworth immediately afterwards; Dom Waldouck came on as a replacement for Delon Armitage in the 64th minute, with Matt Tait then switching from centre to full back to accommodate Waldouck; The England XV was losing 25-16 in the 67th minute when Matt Banahan inexplicably knocked the ball on as he attempted to take a quick tap penalty 6 metres from the Australian Barbarians line!; The England XV was still losing 25-16 in the 69th minute when the Australian Barbarians forwards collapsed a scrum as they were being driven backwards over their own line, but the referee unaccountably ignored this obvious penalty try offence and merely awarded a penalty; The England XV was losing 25-16 with 8 minutes of normal time remaining when Dan Ward-Smith powered through to score; Shane Geraghty came on as a replacement for Charlie Hodgson with 7 minutes of normal time remaining; The England XV was losing 25-23 with 6 minutes of normal time remaining when some superb handling amongst the backs allowed Matt Banahan to score; The England XV was leading 28-25 with 3 minutes of normal time remaining; The England XV was drawing 28-28 in the first minute of injury time when Berrick Barnes missed a kickable 45 metre penalty goal attempt for the Australian Barbarians with the last kick of the match!*)

CAPTAIN: *Joe Worsley*
15th June Australian Barbarians 9 **ENGLAND XV** 15
Bluetongue Central Coast Stadium, Gosford
[This match kicked off at 7.30pm; Bluetongue Central Coast Stadium, Gosford was previously called Grahame Park, Gosford; Geoff Parling and Ugo Monye unavailable due to injury; No English players were involved with the Australian Barbarians on this occasion; On 16th June 2010 an Australian Rugby Union (ARU) judicial hearing found Matt Banahan guilty of making a dangerous tackle on Berrick Barnes and thus banned him for 2 weeks; Brad Barritt joined the tour after this match]
(This match was played in cold conditions; Charlie Hodgson scored a penalty goal in the 3rd minute!; The England XV was leading 3-0 in the 11th minute when Charlie Hodgson missed an eminently kickable 24 metre penalty goal attempt; The England XV was still leading 3-0 in the 12th minute when Dom Waldouck broke through, but Richard Wigglesworth then wasted this great-scoring opportunity by knocking the ball on 5 metres from the Australian Barbarians line; The England XV was leading 6-0 in the 17th minute when Delon Armitage crossed the tryline, but the move was disallowed because the scoring pass from Charlie Hodgson was adjudged to have been forward; The England XV was still leading 6-0 midway through the first half; The England XV was leading 6-0 in the 23rd minute when Dom Waldouck saved a certain try by tackling Kurtley Beale; The England XV was leading 6-3 in the 30th minute; Dom Waldouck went off injured immediately afterwards, being replaced by Matt Tait; The England XV was drawing 6-6 at half-time; Phil Dowson came on as a replacement for James Haskell in the 49th minute; The England XV was losing 9-6 in the 50th minute; Paul Hodgson came on as a replacement for Richard Wigglesworth in the 53rd minute; The England XV was drawing 9-9 midway through the second half; Shane Geraghty came on as a replacement for Charlie Hodgson in the 63rd minute; The England XV was still drawing 9-9 with 8 minutes remaining; The England XV was leading 12-9 with 6 minutes remaining when Shane Geraghty badly missed a speculative 37 metre drop goal attempt; The England XV was still leading 12-9 with 3 minutes remaining when Olly Barkley scored a 44 metre penalty goal to clinch the match; Dom Waldouck had a brilliant game; Richard Wigglesworth had a poor game)
CAPTAIN: *Chris Robshaw*
23rd June NEW ZEALAND MAORI 35 **ENGLAND XV*** 28
McLean Park, Napier
[This match kicked off at 7.35pm; This game commemorated the Centenary of the first rugby match being played by the New Zealand Maori in 1910; Ugo Monye unavailable due to injury; Matt Banahan unavailable due to suspension; Dom Waldouck selected at outside centre but withdrew due to injury, being replaced by Chris Ashton with Matt Tait then switching from wing to centre to accommodate Chris Ashton; Olly Barkley in original training squad of 28 but withdrew due to injury; Tim Payne, Lee Mears, Courtney Lawes and Richard Wigglesworth all in original training squad of 28 but were not selected for team or bench]
(This match was played in cold conditions; The England XV forwards dominated the scrums; Charlie Hodgson scored a penalty goal in the 3rd minute!; The England XV was leading 3-0 in the 5th minute when Charlie Hodgson put in a superb grubber kick that enabled Steffon Armitage to score a try which Charlie Hodgson then brilliantly converted from the left touchline; The England XV was leading 13-0 in the 10th minute; The England XV was leading 13-3 in the 14th minute when Charlie Hodgson hit the right-hand post with a kickable 41 metre penalty goal attempt and Robbie Robinson

instigated a counter-attack that culminated in Hosea Gear powering through some collectively poor tackling to score; The England XV was leading 13-10 midway through the first half when a lack of communication between Phil Dowson and Danny Care saw the ball go loose at the base of a scrum which allowed Aaron Smith to instigate a move that culminated in a try by Liam Messam; The England XV was losing 17-13 in the 35th minute; The England XV was losing 17-16 in the 39th minute when Danny Care took a quick tap penalty and scored; The England XV was leading 23-17 just before half-time when Chris Ashton scored after Charlie Hodgson intercepted Luke McAlister's pass, with Charlie Hodgson then missing the eminently kickable conversion attempt; The England XV scored 15 unanswered points; The England XV was leading 28-17 at half-time; The England XV was still leading 28-17 in the 43rd minute when a poor defensive alignment allowed Hosea Gear to score another try, thus 3 tries and 21 points were preventable; The England XV was losing 29-28 in the 46th minute; Shane Geraghty came on as a replacement for Charlie Hodgson in the 48th minute; The England XV was still losing 29-28 in the 54th minute when it was awarded a 41 metre penalty in a kickable position, but Chris Robshaw ordered a kick to the corner in a vain attempt to score a try from the ensuing lineout; The England XV was losing 29-28 midway through the second half when Chris Ashton saved a certain try by tackling Luke McAlister; Ben Youngs came on as a replacement for Danny Care in the 60th minute; The England XV was still losing 29-28 in the 65th minute when Delon Armitage missed a speculative 47 metre penalty goal attempt; The England XV was losing 29-28 in the 67th minute when Delon Armitage wasted a great try-scoring opportunity by electing to kick when there was an overlap outside him; Ben Foden came on as a replacement for Matt Tait immediately afterwards, with Delon Armitage then switching from full back to outside centre to accommodate Foden; The England XV was still losing 29-28 with 6 minutes of normal time remaining; The New Zealand Maori were allowed to score 18 unanswered points to win the match; The England XV was losing 35-28 with 1 minute of normal time remaining when Ben Foden broke through but then wasted this second great try-scoring opportunity by chipping the ball into touch in-goal)

PART 5
ENGLAND TEAM AND PLAYER RECORDS SINCE 1969

A) ACHIEVEMENTS

1) INTERNATIONAL / 5 NATIONS / HOME INTERNATIONAL / 5 NATIONS / 6 NATIONS CHAMPIONSHIP RESULTS 1883-2010:

RANK	TEAM	WINNERS	GRAND SLAMS	TRIPLE CROWNS	NOTES
1=	**ENGLAND**	35*	12	23	*Includes 10 shared titles
1=	WALES	35*	10	19	*Includes 11 shared titles
3	FRANCE	25*	9	-	*Includes 8 shared titles
4	SCOTLAND	22*	3	10	*Includes 8 shared titles
5	IRELAND	19*	2	10	*Includes 8 shared titles
6	ITALY	0	0	-	

2) COMPETITION RESULTS 1969-2010:

Winners

Five Nations Championship 1973, 1980, 1991, 1992, 1995, 1996
Six Nations Championship 2000, 2001, 2003
Grand Slam 1980, 1991, 1992, 1995, 2003
Triple Crown 1980, 1991, 1992, 1995, 1996, 1997, 1998, 2002, 2003
Calcutta Cup 1969, 1973, 1975, 1977, 1978, 1979, 1980, 1981, 1982, 1985, 1987, 1988, 1989, 1991, 1992, 1993, 1994, 1995, 1996, 1997, 1998, 1999, 2001, 2002, 2003, 2004, 2005, 2007, 2009, 2010
Millennium Trophy 1988, 1989, 1990, 1991, 1992, 1995, 1996, 1997, 1998, 1999, 2000, 2002, 2003, 2008
International Seven-A-Side Tournament 1973
International Students Festival of Rugby 1982
Student Five Nations Championship 1992
Student Triple Crown 1992
Harlequins Lord's Taverners Sevens 1992
Rugby World Cup Sevens 1993
U21 Five Nations Championship 1998
Cook Cup 2000, 2001, 2002, 2003, 2005
Hong Kong Sevens 2002, 2003, 2004, 2006
Shell Cup 2002
Brisbane Sevens 2003
'A' International Championship 2003
London Sevens 2003, 2004, 2009
Churchill Cup 2003, 2005, 2007, 2008, 2010
World Cup 2003
South Africa Sevens 2003
U21 Six Nations Championship 2004, 2006

U21 Grand Slam 2004, 2006
U21 Triple Crown 2004, 2006
Dubai Rugby Sevens 2004, 2005
Jean-Claude Baqué Shield 2005, 2006, 2007
USA Sevens 2006
U20 Six Nations Championship 2008
U20 Grand Slam 2008
U20 Triple Crown 2008
Four Nations Colleges Student Rugby Tournament 2008
Teksavvy Kent Cup 2008
New Zealand International Sevens 2009
Standard Bank Cup 2009
[London Floodlit Sevens 2010 [as 'Dig Deep England']]

Finalists

International Sevens 1986 [as the 'English Bulldogs']
World Cup 1991, 2007
Melun Sevens 1995
Cardiff Sevens 2002
New Zealand International Sevens 2003
Bordeaux Sevens 2004
Churchill Cup 2004, 2009
Singapore Sevens 2005, 2006
London Sevens 2005
Commonwealth Sevens 2006 [***Silver Medallists***]
Edinburgh Sevens 2008
Junior World Championship 2008, 2009
Dubai Rugby Sevens 2008
USA Sevens 2009

Semi-Finalists

Paris Rugby Sevens 1980 [as the 'Sandy Sanders VII']
[Old Belvedere International Seven-A-Side 1992 [as 'Dick Best's Selection']]
Dubai International Rugby Sevens 1992
World Cup 1995
Hong Kong Sevens 1996, 2000, 2010
Madrid Sevens 1996 [as the 'RFU President's VII']
Student Rugby World Cup 2000
Safari Sevens 2001 [as 'England Students U21']
South Africa Sevens 2001, 2004, 2005, 2006
New Zealand International Sevens 2002, 2004, 2010
Singapore Sevens 2002
London Sevens 2002, 2006, 2008
Cardiff Sevens 2003
Dubai Rugby Sevens 2003, 2006, 2007, 2009
USA Sevens 2005
Rugby World Cup Sevens 2005
Edinburgh Sevens 2010
Junior World Championship 2010

3rd Place

Paris Rugby Sevens 1980 [as the 'Sandy Sanders VII']

4th Place

World Cup 1995
Southern Hemisphere Alliance U21 Tournament 2000
Student Rugby World Cup 2000
Ricoh Southern Hemisphere Under 21 Rugby Championship 2001
Junior World Championship 2010

Quarter-Finalists

World Cup 1987, 1999
Student Rugby World Cup 1992
Hong Kong Sevens 1995, 2001, 2007, 2008, 2009
Rugby World Cup Sevens 1997, 2001, 2009
Commonwealth Sevens 1998, 2002
[Dubai International Rugby Sevens 1998 [as an 'England Select VII']]
Dubai Rugby Sevens 2000, 2002
Air France Sevens 1999, 2000
Shanghai Sevens 2001
Japan Sevens 2001
London Sevens 2001, 2010
Santiago Sevens 2002
Mar del Plata Sevens 2002
Brisbane Sevens 2002
Beijing Sevens 2002
Malaysia Sevens 2002
South Africa Sevens 2002, 2009
Henley International Sevens 2003 [as 'Young England']
Middlesex Sevens 2003 [as 'Young England']
USA Sevens 2004, 2007, 2008, 2010
Singapore Sevens 2004
New Zealand International Sevens 2005, 2006, 2007
Paris Sevens 2005, 2006
Adelaide Sevens 2007, 2009

5th Place

Student Rugby World Cup 1988, 1992
SANZAR/UAR U21 Tournament 1998
U21 World Championship 2004, 2006

6th Place

SANZAR U21 Tournament 1999

7th Place

U21 World Championship 2002, 2005

8th Place

U21 World Championship 2003

Plate Winners

Beijing Sevens 2002

Malaysia Sevens 2002
Commonwealth Sevens 2002
USA Sevens 2004
New Zealand International Sevens 2006, 2007
South Africa Sevens 2008, 2009
Adelaide Sevens 2009

Plate Finalists

Shanghai Sevens 2001
Japan Sevens 2001
London Sevens 2001
Santiago Sevens 2002
Mar del Plata Sevens 2002
Dubai Rugby Sevens 2002
Paris Sevens 2005
Churchill Cup 2006

Plate Semi-Finalists

Paris Sevens 2000, 2006
Dubai Rugby Sevens 2000
Brisbane Sevens 2002
South Africa Sevens 2002
Singapore Sevens 2004
New Zealand International Sevens 2005
USA Sevens 2007, 2008, 2010
Adelaide Sevens 2007
London Sevens 2010

Bowl Winners

Wales Sevens 2001
London Sevens 2007
Edinburgh Sevens 2007, 2009
New Zealand International Sevens 2008
Adelaide Sevens 2010

Bowl Finalists

Paris Sevens 1999
Malaysia Sevens 2001
South Africa Sevens 2007

Bowl Semi-Finalists

New Zealand International Sevens 2001

Bowl Quarter-Finalists

South Africa Sevens 2000
Compass Group International Sevens 2004 [as 'Young England']
Adelaide Sevens 2008

B) CAPS

1) ENGLAND CAP HOLDERS 1969-2010:

[In numerical order; current players in italics; data up to and including Australia v England 19th June 2010]

Rank	Caps	Surname	Forename	Position	Period
1	114	Leonard	Jason	**Prop**	1990-2004
Notes: 5 Lions caps (2 in 1993, 1 in 1997 and 2 in 2001)					
2=	85	Underwood	Rory	**Wing**	1984-1996
Notes: 6 Lions caps (3 in 1989 and 3 in 1993)					
2=	85	Dallaglio	Lawrence	Flanker/**Number 8**	1995-2007
Notes: 3 Lions caps 1997					
4	84	Johnson	Martin	**Lock**	1993-2003
Notes: 8 Lions caps (2 in 1993, 3 in 1997 and 3 in 2001)					
5	80	*Wilkinson*	Jonny	**Fly half**/Centre	1998-2010
Notes: 6 Lions caps (3 in 2001 and 3 in 2005)					
6=	77	Dawson	Matt	**Scrum half**	1995-2006
Notes: 7 Lions caps (3 in 1997, 2 in 2001 and 2 in 2005)					
6=	77	Worsley	Joe	Flanker/Number 8	1999-2010
Notes: 1 Lions cap 2009					
8	75	Catt	Mike	Fly half/Centre/Full back	1994-2007
Notes: 1 cap at wing v Ireland 1998; 1 Lions cap 1997					
9	73	Vickery	Phil	Prop	1998-2009
Notes: 4 Lions caps (3 in 2001 and 1 in 2009)					
10	72	Carling	Will	**Centre**	1988-1997
Notes: 1 Lions cap 1993					
11=	71	Andrew	Rob	Fly half	1985-1997
Notes: 1 cap at full back v Fiji 1988; 5 Lions caps (2 in 1989 and 3 in 1993)					
11=	71	Hill (2)	Richard	Flanker/Number 8	1997-2004
Notes: 5 Lions caps (2 in 1997, 2 in 2001 and 1 in 2005)					
13	69	Grewcock	Danny	Lock	1997-2007
Notes: 5 Lions caps (3 in 2001 and 2 in 2005)					
14	66	Back	Neil	**Flanker**	1994-2003
Notes: Played for an England XV v an Italy XV in 1990; 5 Lions caps (2 in 1997, 2 in 2001 and 1 in 2005)					
15	65	Guscott	Jeremy	Centre	1989-1999
Notes: 8 Lions caps (2 in 1989, 3 in 1993 and 3 in 1997)					
16=	64	Moore	Brian	**Hooker**	1987-1995
Notes: 1 cap at flanker v W. Samoa 1995; 5 Lions caps (3 in 1989 and 2 in 1993)					
16=	64	Corry	Martin	Lock/Flanker/Number 8	1997-2007
Notes: 7 Lions caps (3 in 2001 and 4 in 2005)					
18=	63	*Tindall*	Mike	Centre	2000-2010
18=	63	*Moody*	Lewis	Flanker	2001-2010
Notes: 3 Lions caps 2005					
20	62	Kay	Ben	Lock	2001-2009
Notes: 2 Lions caps 2005					

Rank	Caps	Surname	Forename	Position	Period
21	59	*Shaw*	Simon	Lock	1996-2010
Notes:	2 Lions caps 2009				
22	58	Winterbottom	Peter	Flanker	1982-1993
Notes:	7 Lions caps (4 in 1983 and 3 in 1993)				
23=	57	Cohen	Ben	Wing	2000-2006
23=	57	*Borthwick*	Steve	Lock	2001-2010
23=	57	Thompson (2)	Steve	Hooker	2002-2010
Notes:	3 Lions caps 2005				
26=	55	Dooley	Wade	Lock	1985-1993
Notes:	2 Lions caps 1989				
26=	55	Greenwood	Will	Centre	1997-2004
Notes:	2 Lions caps 2005				
26=	55	Lewsey	Josh	Fly half/Centre/Wing/Full back	1998-2007
Notes:	3 Lions caps 2005				
29	54	Rowntree	Graham	Prop	1995-2006
Notes:	3 Lions caps 2005				
30=	51	Bracken	Kyran	Scrum half	1993-2003
30=	51	Healey	Austin	Scrum half/Fly half/Wing	1997-2003
Notes:	1 cap at full back v Wales 2002; 2 Lions caps 1997				
30=	51	*White*	Julian	Prop	2000-2009
Notes:	4 Lions caps 2005				
30=	51	Robinson	Jason	Wing/Full back	2001-2007
Notes:	3 caps at centre v Italy, Scotland and Ireland 2004; 5 Lions caps (3 in 2001 and 2 in 2005)				
34	48	Richards	Dean	Number 8	1986-1996
Notes:	6 Lions caps (3 in 1989 and 3 in 1993)				
35	46	Regan	Mark	Hooker	1995-2008
Notes:	1 Lions cap 1997				
36	44	Rodber	Tim	Lock/Flanker/Number 8	1992-1999
Notes:	Captained England in 1997 Rugby World Cup Sevens; 2 Lions caps 1997				
37	43	Neary	Tony	Flanker	1971-1980
Notes:	1 Lions cap 1977				
38	42	Pullin	John	Hooker	1966-1976
Notes:	**[5 England caps 1966-68]**; 7 Lions caps (**3 in 1968** and 4 in 1971)				
39=	41	Wheeler	Peter	Hooker	1975-1984
Notes:	7 Lions caps (3 in 1977 and 4 in 1980)				
39=	41	*Cueto*	Mark	Wing/Full back	2004-2010
Notes:	1 Lions cap 2005				
41	40	Clarke	Ben	Flanker/Number 8	1992-1999
Notes:	3 Lions caps 1993				
42=	38	de Glanville	Phil	Centre	1992-1999
42=	38	Luger	Dan	Wing	1998-2003
42=	38	*Noon*	Jamie	Centre	2001-2009
42=	38	*Tait*	Matt	Centre/Wing/Full back	2005-2010

Rank	Caps	Surname	Forename	Position	Period
46	37	Probyn	Jeff	Prop	1988-1993
47=	36	Duckham	David	Centre/Wing	1969-1976
Notes:	3 Lions caps 1971				
47=	36	Pearce (1)	Gary	Prop	1979-1991
47=	36	Perry	Matt	Centre/**Full back**	1997-2001
Notes:	3 Lions caps 2001				
50=	35	*Gomarsall*	Andy	Scrum half	1996-2008
50=	35	*Balshaw*	Iain	Wing/Full back	2000-2008
Notes:	3 Lions caps 2001				
50=	35	*Mears*	Lee	Hooker	2005-2010
Notes:	1 Lions cap 2009				
53=	34	Rogers	Budge	Flanker	1961-1969
Notes:	**[30 England caps 1961-68; 2 Lions caps 1962]**				
53=	34	Beaumont	Bill	Lock	1975-1982
Notes:	7 Lions caps (3 in 1977 and 4 in 1980)				
53=	34	Scott	John	Lock/Number 8	1978-1984
53=	34	*Easter*	Nick	Flanker/Number 8	2007-2010
57	33	Webb	Jonathan	Full back	1987-1993
58=	32	Dodge	Paul	Centre	1978-1985
Notes:	2 Lions caps 1980				
58=	32	Grayson	Paul	Fly half	1995-2004
58=	32	*Stevens*	Matt	Prop	2004-2008
58=	32	*Sheridan*	Andy	Prop/Lock	2004-2009
Notes:	2 Lions caps 2009				
62=	31	Cotton	Fran	Prop	1971-1981
Notes:	Captained England to victory in 1973 International Seven-A-Side Tournament; 7 Lions caps (4 in 1974 and 3 in 1977)				
62=	31	Slemen	Mike	Wing	1976-1984
Notes:	1 Lions cap 1980				
62=	31	Bayfield	Martin	Lock	1991-1996
Notes:	3 Lions caps 1993				
62=	31	*Hodgson*	Charlie	Fly half	2001-2008
62=	31	*Flood*	Toby	Fly half/Centre	2006-2010
67=	29	Squires	Peter	Wing	1973-1979
Notes:	1 Lions cap 1977				
67=	29	Hill (1)	Richard	Scrum half	1984-1991
69=	28	Smith (1)	Steve	Scrum half	1973-1983
69=	28	Rendall	Paul	Prop	1984-1991
69=	28	*Haskell*	James	Flanker/Number 8	2007-2010
72=	27	Teague	Mike	Flanker/Number 8	1985-1993
Notes:	3 Lions caps (2 in 1989 and 1 in 1993)				
72=	27	Underwood	Tony	Wing	1992-1998
Notes:	1 Lions cap 1997				
72=	27	Cockerill	Richard	Hooker	1997-1999

Rank	Caps	Surname	Forename	Position	Period
72=	27	Ellis	Harry	Scrum half	2004-2009

Notes: 1 Lions cap 2009

Rank	Caps	Surname	Forename	Position	Period
76=	26	Carleton	John	Wing	1979-1984

Notes: 6 Lions caps (3 in 1980 and 3 in 1983)

Rank	Caps	Surname	Forename	Position	Period
76=	26	Morris	Dewi	Scrum half	1988-1995

Notes: Captained England in 1992 Harlequin Lord's Taverners Invitation Sevens; 3 Lions caps 1993

Rank	Caps	Surname	Forename	Position	Period
78=	25	Stevens	Stack	Prop	1969-1975
78=	25	Hare	Dusty	Full back	1974-1984
78=	25	Colclough	Maurice	Lock	1978-1986

Notes: 8 Lions caps (4 in 1980 and 4 in 1983)

Rank	Caps	Surname	Forename	Position	Period
78=	25	Garforth	Darren	Prop	1997-2000
82=	24	Larter	Peter	Lock	1967-1973

Notes: **[6 England caps 1967-68, 1 Lions cap 1968]**

Rank	Caps	Surname	Forename	Position	Period
82=	24	Ripley	Andy	Number 8	1972-1976

Notes: Captained England in 1986 International Sevens

Rank	Caps	Surname	Forename	Position	Period
82=	24	Ubogu	Victor	Prop	1992-1999
82=	24	Greening	Phil	Hooker	1996-2001

Notes: Captained England in 2002 Commonwealth Sevens

Rank	Caps	Surname	Forename	Position	Period
82=	24	*Chuter*	George	Hooker	2006-2010
87=	23	Uttley	Roger	Lock/Flanker/Number 8	1973-1980

Notes: 4 Lions caps 1974

Rank	Caps	Surname	Forename	Position	Period
87=	23	Rees	Gary	Flanker	1984-1991
87=	23	Halliday	Simon	Centre	1986-1992

Notes: Played for an England XV against Canada in 1983

Rank	Caps	Surname	Forename	Position	Period
87=	23	*Barkley*	Olly	Fly half/Centre	2001-2008
91=	22	Ralston	Chris	Lock	1971-1975

Notes: The 1000th player to be capped by England; Scored England's first 4 point try; 1 Lions cap 1974

Rank	Caps	Surname	Forename	Position	Period
91=	22	Dixon	Peter	Flanker/Number 8	1971-1978

Notes: 3 Lions caps 1971

Rank	Caps	Surname	Forename	Position	Period
91=	22	Ackford	Paul	Lock	1988-1991

Notes: Played for England B v France B in 1979; 3 Lions caps 1989

Rank	Caps	Surname	Forename	Position	Period
91=	22	Woodman	Trevor	Prop	1999-2004
91=	22	*Payne*	Tim	Prop	2004-2010
91=	22	*Sackey*	Paul	Wing	2006-2009
97=	21	Woodward	Clive	Centre	1980-1984

Notes: 2 Lions caps 1980; Was the Head Coach when England won the World Cup in 2003

Rank	Caps	Surname	Forename	Position	Period
97=	21	Davies (1)	Huw	Fly half/Centre/Full back	1981-1986
97=	21	Hall	Jon	Flanker	1984-1994
97=	21	Skinner	Mickey	Flanker	1988-1992
97=	21	Archer	Garath	Lock	1996-2000
97=	21	West	Dorian	Hooker	1998-2003
97=	21	*Care*	Danny	Scrum half	2008-2010

Rank	Caps	Surname	Forename	Position	Period
104=	20	Horton	Nigel	Lock	1969-1980
Notes:	Played for England in 3 separate decades!				
104=	20	Redman	Nigel	Lock	1984-1997
106=	19	Hiller	Bob	Full back	1968-1972
Notes:	**[4 England caps 1968]**				
106=	19	Blakeway	Phil	Prop	1980-1985
106=	19	Stimpson	Tim	Full back	1996-2002
Notes:	3 caps at wing against New Zealand at Dunedin in 1998, South Africa at Pretoria in 2000 and Argentina in 2002; 1 Lions cap 1997				
106=	19	*Hartley*	Dylan	Prop/Hooker	2008-2010
110=	18	Old	Alan	Fly half/Centre	1972-1978
110=	18	Bainbridge	Steve	Lock	1982-1987
Notes:	2 Lions caps 1983				
110=	18	*Deacon*	Louis	Lock	2005-2010
110=	18	*Croft*	Tom	Lock/Flanker/Number 8	2008-2010
Notes:	3 Lions caps 2009				
114=	17	Burton	Mike	Prop	1972-1978
114=	17	Rafter	Mike	Flanker	1977-1981
114=	17	Smart	Colin	Prop	1979-1983
114=	17	*Goode*	Andy	Fly half	2005-2009
118=	16	Davis (1)	Mike	Lock	1963-1970
Notes:	**[12 England caps 1963-67]**; Was the Coach when England won the 5 Nations Grand Slam in 1980				
118=	16	Taylor	Bob	Flanker/Number 8	1966-1971
Notes:	**[6 England caps 1966-68; 4 Lions caps 1968]**				
118=	16	*Sanderson*	Pat	Flanker	1998-2007
118=	16	*Palmer (2)*	Tom	Lock	2001-2010
118=	16	*Armitage*	Delon	Centre/Wing/Full back	2008-2010
123=	15	Simms	Kevin	Centre	1985-1988
123=	15	Harrison	Mike	Wing	1985-1988
123=	15	Beal	Nick	Centre/Wing/Full back	1996-1999
123=	15	*Rees*	Tom	Flanker	2007-2008
127=	14	Spencer	John	Centre	1969-1971
127=	14	Hignell	Alastair	Full back	1975-1979
127=	14	Jeavons	Nick	Flanker	1981-1983
127=	14	Chilcott	Gareth	Prop	1984-1989
127=	14	Orwin	John	Lock	1985-1988
127=	14	Hodgkinson	Simon	Full back	1989-1991
127=	14	*Perry*	Shaun	Scrum half	2006-2007
134=	13	Finlan	John	Fly half	1967-1973
Notes:	**[7 England caps 1967-68]**				
134=	13	Horton	John	Fly half	1978-1984
134=	13	Brain	Steve	Hooker	1984-1986
134=	13	Melville	Nigel	Scrum half	1984-1988

Rank	Caps	Surname	Forename	Position	Period
134=	13	Oti	Chris	Wing	1988-1991
134=	13	Richards	Peter	Scrum half/Centre	2006-2008
134=	13	*Hipkiss*	Dan	Centre	2007-2010
134=	13	*Monye*	Ugo	Centre/Wing	2008-2010

Notes: 2 Lions caps 2009

Rank	Caps	Surname	Forename	Position	Period
134=	13	*Flutey*	Riki	Fly Half/Centre	2008-2010

Notes: 1 Lions cap 2009

Rank	Caps	Surname	Forename	Position	Period
143=	12	Webb	Rod	Wing	1967-1972

Notes: **[6 England caps 1967-68]**; Played in all 7 games when an England XV toured the Far East in 1971

Rank	Caps	Surname	Forename	Position	Period
143=	12	Fairbrother	Keith	Prop	1969-1971
143=	12	Janion	Jeremy	Centre/Wing	1971-1975
143=	12	Preece	Peter	Centre	1972-1976
143=	12	Cusworth	Les	Fly half	1979-1988
143=	12	Cooke (2)	David	Flanker	1981-1985
143=	12	Harding	Richard	Scrum half	1985-1988
143=	12	Salmon	Jamie	Centre	1985-1987
143=	12	Ojomoh	Steve	Flanker/Number 8	1994-1998
143=	12	Sleightholme	Jon	Wing	1996-1997
143=	12	*Jones*	Chris	Lock/Flanker/Number 8	2004-2007
154=	11	Powell	David	Prop	1966-1971

Notes: **[2 England caps 1966]**

Rank	Caps	Surname	Forename	Position	Period
154=	11	Rollitt	Dave	Number 8	1967-1975

Notes: **[4 England caps 1967]**

Rank	Caps	Surname	Forename	Position	Period
154=	11	Webster	Jan	Scrum half	1972-1975
154=	11	Cooper	Martin	Fly half	1973-1977
154=	11	Rees (2)	David	Wing	1997-1999
154=	11	*Wilson (2)*	David	Prop	2009-2010
160=	10	Fielding	Keith	Wing	1969-1972
160=	10	Bucknall	Tony	Flanker	1969-1971
160=	10	Corless	Barrie	Centre	1976-1978
160=	10	Young	Malcolm	Scrum half	1977-1979
160=	10	Hesford	Bob	Number 8	1981-1985
160=	10	Rose	Marcus	Full back	1981-1987
160=	10	Barnes	Stuart	Fly half/Full back	1984-1993
160=	10	Heslop	Nigel	Wing	1990-1992
160=	10	Diprose	Tony	Number 8	1997-1998
160=	10	*Simpson-Daniel*	James	Centre/Wing	2002-2007
160=	10	*Lipman*	Michael	Flanker	2004-2008
160=	10	*Freshwater*	Perry	Prop/Hooker	2005-2007
160=	10	*Lund*	Magnus	Flanker	2006-2007
173=	9	Evans (2)	Geoff	Centre	1972-1974
173=	9	Smith (1)	Simon	Wing	1985-1986
173=	9	*Voyce*	Tom	Wing/Full back	2001-2006

Rank	Caps	Surname	Forename	Position	Period
173=	9	Abbott	Stuart	Centre	2003-2006
173=	9	*Hodgson*	Paul	Scrum half	2008-2010
178=	8	West	Bryan	Flanker	1968-1970

Notes: [4 England caps 1968]

Rank	Caps	Surname	Forename	Position	Period
178=	8	Cowling	Robin	Prop	1977-1979
178=	8	Robinson	Andy	Flanker	1988-1995
178=	8	*Flatman*	David	Prop	2000-2002
178=	8	Farrell	Andy	Centre/Flanker	2007-2007
183=	7	Starmer-Smith	Nigel	Scrum half	1969-1971

Notes: Later became a rugby author, journalist, broadcaster and commentator for the BBC and IRB

Rank	Caps	Surname	Forename	Position	Period
183=	7	Jorden	Tony	Full back	1970-1975
183=	7	Rossborough	Peter	Full back	1971-1975
183=	7	Watkins (1)	John	Flanker	1972-1975
183=	7	Morley	Alan	Wing	1972-1975
183=	7	Bennett	Neil	Fly half	1975-1979
183=	7	Maxwell (1)	Andy	Centre	1975-1978
183=	7	Barley	Bryan	Centre	1984-1988
183=	7	Bailey	Mark	Wing	1984-1990
183=	7	Egerton	Dave	Number 8	1988-1990
183=	7	Hunter	Ian	Wing/Full back	1992-1995
183=	7	Sheasby	Chris	Flanker/Number 8	1996-1997

Notes: Captained England in 1998 Commonwealth Sevens

Rank	Caps	Surname	Forename	Position	Period
183=	7	*Hazell*	Andy	Flanker	2004-2007
183=	7	*Narraway*	Luke	Flanker/Number 8	2008-2009
183=	7	*Cipriani*	Danny	Fly half/Full back	2008-2008
183=	7	*Kennedy*	Nick	Lock	2008-2009
183=	7	*Cole*	Dan	Prop	2010-2010
200=	6	Wardlow	Chris	Centre	1969-1971
200=	6	Warfield	Peter	Centre	1973-1975
200=	6	Nelmes	Barry	Prop	1975-1978
200=	6	Wilkinson	Bob	Lock	1975-1976
200=	6	Bond	Tony	Centre	1978-1982
200=	6	Swift	Tony	Wing	1981-1984
200=	6	Youngs	Nick	Scrum half	1983-1984
200=	6	Adebayo	Adedayo	Wing	1996-1998
200=	6	*Paul*	Henry	Fly half/Centre	2002-2004
200=	6	*Strettle*	Dave	Wing	2007-2008
200=	6	*Geraghty*	Shane	Fly half/Centre	2007-2009
200=	6	*Foden*	Ben	Scrum half/Wing/Full back	2009-2010
212=	5	Greenwood	Dick	Flanker	1966-1969

Notes: [4 England caps 1966-67]; Scored his only try for England on his debut against Ireland in 1966]

Rank	Caps	Surname	Forename	Position	Period
212=	5	Wintle	Trevor	Scrum half	1966-1969
Notes:	**[1 England cap 1966]**				
212=	5	Page	Jacko	Scrum half	1971-1975
212=	5	Cowman	Dick	Fly half	1971-1973
212=	5	Kingston	Peter	Scrum half	1975-1979
212=	5	Kent	Charles	Centre	1977-1978
212=	5	Mills	Steve	Hooker	1981-1984
212=	5	Stringer	Nick	Full back	1982-1985
212=	5	Dawe	Graham	Hooker	1987-1995
212=	5	Callard	Jon	Full back	1993-1995
212=	5	*King*	Alex	Fly half	1997-2003
212=	5	Lloyd	Leon	Centre/Wing	2000-2001
212=	5	Sanderson	Alex	Flanker/Number 8	2001-2003
212=	5	*Smith (1)*	Ollie	Centre/Wing	2003-2005
Notes:	1 Lions cap 2005				
212=	5	*Titterrell*	Andy	Hooker	2004-2007
212=	5	*Bell*	Duncan	Prop	2005-2009
212=	5	*Vainikolo*	Lesley	Wing	2008-2008
212=	5	*Wigglesworth*	Richard	Scrum half	2008-2008
212=	5	*Armitage*	Steffon	Flanker	2009-2010
212=	5	*Banahan*	Matt	Centre/Wing	2009-2009
232=	4	Barton	John	Lock/Number 8	1967-1972
Notes:	**[3 England caps 1967; Scored 2 tries in 1967]**				
232=	4	Plummer	Ken	Wing	1969-1976
Notes:	Played 52 times for Cornwall				
232=	4	Shackleton	Roger	Fly half	1969-1970
232=	4	Wright	Ian	Fly half	1971-1971
232=	4	Smith	Keith	Centre	1974-1975
232=	4	Keyworth	Mark	Flanker	1976-1976
232=	4	Lampkowski	Mike	Scrum half	1976-1976
232=	4	Cooke (1)	David	Centre	1976-1976
232=	4	Fidler	John	Lock	1981-1984
232=	4	White	Colin	Prop	1983-1984
232=	4	Martin	Chris	Full back	1985-1985
232=	4	Clough	Fran	Centre	1986-1987
232=	4	Williams	Peter	Fly half/Full back	1987-1987
232=	4	Bentley	John	Wing	1988-1997
Notes:	2 Lions caps 1997				
232=	4	Ryan	Dean	Number 8	1990-1998
232=	4	Pears	David	Fly half/Full back	1990-1994
232=	4	Hull	Paul	Fly half/Full back	1994-1994
232=	4	*Yates*	Kevin	Prop	1997-2007
Notes:	Holds the England record for the longest time between caps, namely 9 years and 353 days				

Rank	Caps	Surname	Forename	Position	Period
232=	4	Greenstock	Nick	Centre	1997-1997
232=	4	Green (1)	Will	Prop	1997-2003
232=	4	*Walder*	Dave	Fly half	2001-2003
232=	4	*Varndell*	Tom	Wing	2005-2008
232=	4	*Lawes*	Courtney	Lock/Flanker	2009-2010
255=	3	Glover	Peter	Wing	1967-1971

Notes: [1 England cap 1967]; Played in all 7 games when an England XV toured the Far East in 1971

Rank	Caps	Surname	Forename	Position	Period
255=	3	Hale	Peter	Wing	1969-1970
255=	3	Novak	John	Wing	1970-1970
255=	3	Hannaford	Charlie	Number 8	1971-1971
255=	3	Brinn	Alan	Lock	1972-1972
255=	3	Beese	Mike	Centre	1972-1972
255=	3	Knight (1)	Peter	Wing/Full back	1972-1972
255=	3	Doble	Sam	Full back	1972-1973
255=	3	Roughley	Dave	Centre	1973-1974
255=	3	Preston	Nick	Centre	1979-1980
255=	3	Boyle	Steve	Lock	1983-1983
255=	3	Simpson	Paul	Flanker	1983-1987
255=	3	Butcher	Chris	Number 8	1984-1984
255=	3	Palmer	John	Centre	1984-1986
255=	3	Buckton	John	Centre	1988-1990
255=	3	Olver	John	Hooker	1990-1992
255=	3	Hopley	Damian	Centre/Wing	1995-1995
255=	3	Sturnham	Ben	Flanker	1998-1998
255=	3	Sims	Dave	Lock	1998-1998
255=	3	*Sampson*	Paul	Wing/Full back	1998-2001
255=	3	McCarthy	Neil	Hooker	1999-2000
255=	3	*Stephenson*	Michael	Wing/Full back	2001-2001
255=	3	*Waters*	Fraser	Centre	2001-2004
255=	3	*Christophers*	Phil	Wing	2002-2003
255=	3	Worsley	Mike	Prop	2003-2005
255=	3	*Brown*	Alex	Lock	2006-2007
255=	3	*Turner*	Stuart	Prop	2007-2007
255=	3	*Brown*	Mike	Wing/Full back	2007-2008
255=	3	*Crane*	Jordan	Number 8	2008-2009
255=	3	*Youngs*	Ben	Scrum half	2010-2010
255=	3	*Ashton*	Chris	Wing	2010-2010
286=	2	Jackson	Barry	Prop	1970-1970
286=	2	Weston	Lionel	Scrum half	1972-1972
286=	2	Butler	Peter	Full back	1975-1976
286=	2	Adey	Garry	Number 8	1976-1976
286=	2	Caplan	David	Full back	1978-1978
286=	2	Cardus	Richard	Centre	1979-1979

Rank	Caps	Surname	Forename	Position	Period
286=	2	Syddall	Jim	Lock	1982-1984
286=	2	Trick	David	Wing	1983-1984
286=	2	Huntsman	Paul	Prop	1985-1985
286=	2	Robbins	Graham	Number 8	1986-1986
286=	2	Evans	Barry	Wing	1988-1988
286=	2	Haag	Martin	Lock	1997-1997
286=	2	Mallinder	Jim	Full back	1997-1997
286=	2	*Long*	Andy	Hooker	1997-2001
286=	2	Ravenscroft	Steve	Centre	1998-1998
286=	2	Brown	Spencer	Wing	1998-1998
286=	2	Beim	Tom	Wing	1998-1998
286=	2	Fidler	Rob	Lock	1998-1998
286=	2	Baxendell	Jos	Fly half/Centre	1998-1998
286=	2	White-Cooper	Steve	Lock/Flanker	2001-2001
286=	2	Wood	Martyn	Scrum half	2001-2001
286=	2	Duncombe	Nick	Scrum half	2002-2002
286=	2	*Johnston*	Ben	Centre	2002-2002
286=	2	Morris	Robbie	Prop	2003-2003
286=	2	*Scarbrough*	Dan	Wing/Full back	2003-2007
286=	2	Forrester	James	Flanker	2005-2005
286=	2	Walshe	Nick	Scrum half	2006-2006
286=	2	*Allen*	Anthony	Centre	2006-2006
286=	2	*Morgan*	Olly	Full back	2007-2007
286=	2	*Schofield*	Dean	Lock	2007-2007
286=	2	*Winters*	Roy	Lock/Flanker/Number 8	2007-2007
Notes:	Played for England A v a New Zealand XV in 1997; Toured South Africa with England in 2000				
286=	2	*Abendanon*	Nick	Wing/Full back	2007-2007
286=	2	*Ojo*	Topsy	Wing	2008-2008
286=	2	*Paice*	David	Prop/Hooker	2008-2008
286=	2	*May*	Tom	Fly half/Centre/Wing/Full back	2009-2009
286=	2	*Vesty*	Sam	Fly half/Centre/Full back	2009-2009
286=	2	*Erinle*	Ayoola	Centre	2009-2009
286=	2	*Hape*	Shontayne	Centre/Wing	2010-2010
324=	1	Dalton	Tim	Wing	1969
Notes:	The first player to be used by England as an injury replacement, namely against Scotland in 1969				
324=	1	Bulpitt	Mike	Wing	1970
324=	1	Leadbetter	Mike	Lock	1970
324=	1	Redmond	Gerry	Number 8	1970
324=	1	Ninnes	Barry	Lock	1971
Notes:	Played 24 times for Cornwall				
324=	1	Creed	Roger	Flanker	1971
324=	1	Martin	Nick	Lock	1972

Rank	Caps	Surname	Forename	Position	Period
324=	1	Anderson	Frank	Prop	1973
324=	1	Mantell	Neil	Lock	1975
324=	1	Wordsworth	Nellie	Fly half	1975
324=	1	Wyatt	Derek	Wing	1976
324=	1	Williams (2)	Chris	Fly half	1976
324=	1	Mordell	Bob	Flanker	1978
324=	1	Sheppard	Austin	Prop	1981
324=	1	Sargent	Gordon	Prop	1981
324=	1	Redfern	Steve	Prop	1984
324=	1	Dun	Andy	Flanker	1984
324=	1	Preedy	Malcolm	Prop	1984
324=	1	Lozowski	Rob	Centre	1984
324=	1	Cusani	Dave	Lock/Number 8	1987
Notes:	Played for an England XV v an Italy XV in 1990				
324=	1	Harriman	Andy	Wing	1988
Notes:	Captained England to victory in 1993 Rugby World Cup Sevens				
324=	1	Bates	Steve	Scrum half	1989
324=	1	Linnett	Mark	Prop	1989
324=	1	Mullins	Andy	Prop	1989
324=	1	Mallett	John	Prop	1995
324=	1	Hardwick	Rob	Prop	1996
324=	1	Mapletoft	Mark	Fly half/Full back	1997
324=	1	Pool-Jones	Richard	Flanker	1998
324=	1	*Benton*	Scott	Scrum half	1998
324=	1	Potter	Stuart	Centre	1998
324=	1	Chapman	Dominic	Wing	1998
324=	1	Hanley	Steve	Wing	1999
324=	1	Mather	Barrie-Jon	Centre	1999
324=	1	Codling	Alex	Lock	2002
324=	1	Appleford	Geoff	Centre	2002
324=	1	*Horak*	Michael	Full back	2002
324=	1	*Vyvyan*	Hugh	Lock/Number 8	2004
Notes:	Formed a sevens team with his 6 brothers!; Captained England A to victory in 2003 Churchill Cup				
324=	1	*Van Gisbergen*	Mark	Full back	2005
324=	1	*Cairns*	Matt	Hooker	2007
324=	1	*Crompton*	Darren	Prop	2007
324=	1	*Skirving*	Ben	Number 8	2007
324=	1	*Hobson*	Jason	Prop	2008
324=	1	*Robshaw*	Chris	Flanker/Number 8	2009
324=	1	*Doran-Jones*	Paul	Prop	2009
324=	1	*Mullan*	Matt	Prop/Hooker	2010

2) ENGLAND UNUSED BENCH REPLACEMENTS (CAP MATCHES) 1969-2010:

[In numerical order; restricted to uncapped players only; current players in italics; data up to and including Australia v England 19th June 2010]

Rank	Benches	Surname	Forename	Position	Period
1	16	**Simpson**	Andy	Hooker	1981-1986
Notes:	Bench England XV v President's XV 1984				
2	13	**Raphael**	Jon	Hooker	1975-1979
Notes:	Bench England XV v Fiji 1979				
3	7	**Harris**	Roger	Hooker	1969-1970
Notes:	Played 62 times for Cornwall				
4	6	**Orum**	Ian	Scrum half	1975-1978
5=	5	**Johnson**	Andy	Hooker	1971-1971
5=	5	**Peck**	Ian	Scrum half	1979-1980
7=	4	**Boddy**	Tony	Hooker	1972-1972
7=	4	**Gray**	John	Hooker	1973-1973
Notes:	Played for England in 1973 International Seven-A-Side Tournament				
7=	4	**French**	Nigel	Centre	1977-1977
7=	4	**Doubleday**	John	Prop	1979-1979
7=	4	**Robson**	Simon	Scrum half	1988-1988
7=	4	**Hynes**	Martin	Prop	1992-1992
13=	3	**Hayward**	Phil	Flanker	1969-1970
13=	3	**Palmer (1)**	Tom	Fly half	1972-1972
13=	3	**McGregor**	Clint	Prop	1979-1981
13=	3	**Adamson**	Ray	Full back	1988-1988
17=	2	**White (1)**	John	Hooker	1973-1973
17=	2	**Pryor**	Terry	Prop	1978-1978
Notes:	Captained England B to victory v Romania B 1978				
17=	2	**Cannon**	Vince	Lock	1982-1982
17=	2	**Simmons**	Alan	Hooker	1986-1987
17=	2	**Cook (1)**	Peter	Lock/Flanker	1986-1986
17=	2	**Buttimore**	Tim	Centre	1988-1988
17=	2	**Dunn**	Kevin	Hooker	1988-1992
17=	2	**Thompson**	Adrian	Fly half/Centre	1988-1989
25=	1	**Trickey**	Richard	Lock	1970
25=	1	**Broderick**	Jim	Prop	1971
25=	1	**Richardson**	Keith	Prop	1974
25=	1	**Ashton**	Brian	Scrum half	1975
Notes:	Was the Head Coach when England reached the World Cup Final in 2007				
25=	1	**Elliott**	John	Hooker	1976
25=	1	**Gifford**	Chris	Scrum half	1978
Notes:	Bench England XV v Fiji 1979				
25=	1	**Cutter**	Andy	Prop	1978
Notes:	Bench England XV v Argentina 1978				
25=	1	**Metcalfe**	Ian	Full back	1979

Rank	Benches	Surname	Forename	Position	Period
25=	1	**Moss**	Phil	Flanker/Number 8	1981
25=	1	**Thomas**	Steve	Scrum half	1982
Notes:	Bench England XV v Fiji 1982				
25=	1	**Dixon**	Mike	Hooker	1983
25=	1	**Holmes**	David	Scrum half	1987
25=	1	**Buzza**	Alan	Full back	1990
25=	1	**Liley**	John	Full back	1990
25=	1	**Thompson**	Gavin	Centre/Wing	1990
25=	1	**Botterman**	Gregg	Hooker	1995
25=	1	**Allen**	Matt	Centre	1997
25=	1	**Diamond**	Steve	Hooker	1997
25=	1	***Balding***	Adam	Lock	2002
25=	1	***Sorrell***	Kevin	Centre	2002
25=	1	***Charlton***	Hall	Scrum half	2004

3) ENGLAND NON-CAP MATCH APPEARANCES 1969-2010:

[In numerical order; current players in italics; uncapped players in bold or bold italics; data up to and including an England XV v Barbarians 30th May 2010]

Rank Matches Surname Forename Position Period

1 19 Wheeler Peter **Hooker** 1971-1983

Matches: Japan (Osaka) 1971, Singapore 1971, Ceylon (Colombo I) 1971, The Rest (Twickenham) 1974, The Rest 1975, The Rest 1977, The Rest 1978, Argentina 1978, The Rest 1979, Japan (Osaka) 1979, Japan (Tokyo) 1979, Fiji 1979, Tonga 1979, The Rest (Twickenham I) 1981, Canada 1982, USA 1982, Fiji 1982, The Rest 1982, Canada 1983

2 15 Scott John Lock/**Number 8** 1977-1984

Matches: USA 1977, The Rest 1978 (rep), Argentina 1978, Japan (Osaka) 1979, Japan (Tokyo) 1979, Fiji 1979, Tonga 1979, The Rest (Twickenham I) 1981, Canada 1982, USA 1982, Fiji 1982, The Rest 1982, Canada 1983, The Rest 1984, President's XV 1984

3 14 Cotton Fran **Prop** 1971-1981

Matches: The Rest 1971, Japan (Osaka) 1971, Japan (Tokyo) 1971, Hong Kong 1971, Ceylon (Colombo I) 1971, Ceylon (Colombo II) 1971, The Rest (Twickenham II) 1972, Fiji 1973, The Rest (Burton-on-Trent) 1974, France XV 1974, The Rest (Twickenham) 1974, The Rest 1975, Argentina 1978, The Rest (Twickenham I) 1981

4= 13 Dodge Paul **Centre** 1977-1983

Matches: USA 1977, The Rest 1978 (rep), Argentina 1978, The Rest 1979, Japan (Osaka) 1979, Japan (Tokyo) 1979, Fiji 1979, Tonga 1979, The Rest (Twickenham I) 1981, The Rest (Twickenham II) 1981, Fiji 1982, The Rest 1982, Canada 1983

4= 13 Carleton John **Wing** 1977-1986

Matches: USA 1977, The Rest 1978, Japan (Tokyo) 1979, Tonga 1979, The Rest 1980, The Rest (Twickenham II) 1981, Canada 1982, USA 1982, The Rest 1982, Canada 1983, The Rest 1984, President's XV 1984, Portugal XV 1986

4= 13 Pearce (1) Gary Prop 1979-1991

Matches: Japan (Osaka) 1979, Japan (Tokyo) 1979, Fiji 1979 (rep), Tonga 1979, The Rest (Twickenham I) 1981, The Rest (Twickenham II) 1981, USA 1982, The Rest 1982, Canada 1983, The Rest 1984, Japan 1986, Portugal XV 1987 (rep), Gloucester 1991

7= 12 Hare Dusty **Full back** 1974-1984

Matches: France XV 1974, USA 1977, The Rest 1979, Japan 1979 (Osaka), The Rest 1980, The Rest (Twickenham I) 1981, Canada 1982, USA 1982, Fiji 1982, The Rest 1982, Canada 1983, The Rest 1984

7= 12 Beaumont Bill **Lock** 1975-1981

Matches: The Rest 1975, The Rest 1977 (rep), USA 1977, The Rest 1978, Argentina 1978, The Rest 1979, Japan (Osaka) 1979, Japan (Tokyo) 1979, Fiji 1979, The Rest 1980, The Rest (Twickenham I) 1981, The Rest (Twickenham II) 1981

9= 11 Neary Tony **Flanker** 1971-1979

Matches: The Rest 1971, Japan (Osaka) 1971, Japan (Tokyo) 1971, Ceylon (Colombo I) 1971, The Rest (Twickenham I) 1972, The Rest (Twickenham II) 1972, Fiji 1973, The Rest (Burton-on-Trent) 1974, France XV 1974, The Rest 1975, The Rest 1979

9= 11 Uttley Roger Lock/Flanker/Number 8 1971-1980

Matches: Japan (Osaka) 1971, Japan (Tokyo) 1971, Ceylon (Colombo I) 1971, Ceylon (Colombo II) 1971, Fiji 1973, The Rest (Burton-on-Trent) 1974, France XV 1974, The Rest (Twickenham) 1974, The Rest 1977, The Rest 1979, The Rest 1980

Rank **Matches** **Surname** **Forename** **Position** **Period**

9= 11 Slemen Mike Wing 1977-1984
Matches: The Rest 1977, Argentina 1978, The Rest 1979, Japan (Osaka) 1979, Japan (Tokyo) 1979, Fiji 1979, Tonga 1979, The Rest 1980, The Rest (Twickenham I) 1981, Canada 1983, The Rest 1984

9= 11 Winterbottom Peter **Flanker** 1982-1991
Matches: Canada 1982, USA 1982, The Rest 1982, Canada 1983, The Rest 1984, Portugal XV 1986, Portugal XV 1987, England B XV 1988, Barbarians 1990, Gloucester 1991, England Students 1991

13= 10 Squires Peter Wing 1973-1979
Matches: Fiji 1973, France XV 1974, The Rest (Twickenham) 1974, The Rest 1975, The Rest 1977, The Rest 1978, Argentina 1978, The Rest 1979, Japan 1979 (Osaka), Fiji 1979

13= 10 Colclough Maurice Lock 1978-1984
Matches: Argentina 1978, Tonga 1979, The Rest 1980, The Rest (Twickenham I) 1981, The Rest (Twickenham II) 1981, Canada 1982, USA 1982, Fiji 1982, The Rest 1982, The Rest 1984

13= 10 Rendall Paul Prop 1981-1991
Matches: The Rest (Twickenham II) 1981, Canada 1982, USA 1982, Canada 1983, Portugal XV 1986, The Rest 1987, Portugal XV 1987, England B XV 1988, Gloucester 1991, England Students 1991 (rep)

16= 9 Duckham David Centre/Wing 1970-1975
Matches: The Rest 1970, The Rest 1971, The Rest (Twickenham I) 1972, The Rest (Twickenham II) 1972, Fiji 1973, The Rest (Burton-on-Trent) 1974, France XV 1974, The Rest (Twickenham) 1974, The Rest 1975

16= 9 Janion Jeremy Centre/Wing 1971-1972
Matches: The Rest 1971, Japan (Osaka) 1971, Japan (Tokyo) 1971, Hong Kong 1971, Singapore 1971, Ceylon (Colombo I) 1971, Ceylon (Colombo II) 1971, The Rest (Twickenham I) 1972, The Rest (Twickenham II) 1972

16= 9 Smith (1) Steve **Scrum half** 1973-1982
Matches: Fiji 1973, The Rest (Burton-on-Trent) 1974, The Rest 1980, The Rest (Twickenham I) 1981, The Rest (Twickenham II) 1981, Canada 1982, USA 1982, Fiji 1982, The Rest 1982

16= 9 Rafter Mike Flanker 1977-1980
Matches: The Rest 1977, USA 1977, The Rest 1978, Argentina 1978, The Rest 1979, Japan (Osaka) 1979, Japan (Tokyo) 1979, Fiji 1979, The Rest 1980

20= 8 Larter Peter Lock 1969-1972
Matches: The Rest 1969, The Rest 1970, The Rest 1971, Japan (Tokyo) 1971, Hong Kong 1971, Singapore 1971, Ceylon (Colombo I) 1971, The Rest (Twickenham II) 1972

20= 8 Ralston Chris Lock 1971-1974
Matches: Japan (Osaka) 1971, Hong Kong 1971, Singapore 1971, Ceylon (Colombo II) 1971, The Rest (Twickenham II) 1972, Fiji 1973, The Rest (Burton-on-Trent) 1974, France XV 1974

20= 8 Davies (1) Huw Fly half/Centre/Full back 1979-1984
Matches: Japan (Osaka) 1979, Japan (Tokyo) 1979, Fiji 1979, Tonga 1979, The Rest (Twickenham II) 1981, The Rest 1982, Canada 1983, The Rest 1984

20= 8 Hill (1) Richard Scrum half 1984-1992
Matches: President's XV 1984, Japan 1986, The Rest 1987, Portugal XV 1987, Barbarians 1990, USSR 1991, Gloucester 1991, Leicester 1992

Rank	Matches	Surname	Forename	Position	Period
20=	8	Underwood	Rory	Wing	1984-1991

Matches: President's XV 1984, Japan 1986, The Rest 1987, Portugal XV 1987, England B XV 1988, Barbarians 1990, USSR 1991, England Students 1991

20=	8	Dooley	Wade	Lock	1986-1991

Matches: Portugal XV 1986, Portugal XV 1987, England B XV 1988, Italy 1990, Barbarians 1990, USSR 1991, Gloucester 1991, England Students 1991

20=	8	Probyn	Jeff	Prop	1986-1992

Matches: Portugal XV 1986 (rep), Portugal XV 1987, England B XV 1988, Italy XV 1990, Barbarians 1990, USSR 1991, England Students 1991, Leicester 1992

27=	7	Webb	Rod	Wing	1969-1971

Matches: The Rest 1969, Japan (Osaka) 1971, Japan (Tokyo) 1971, Hong Kong 1971, Singapore 1971, Ceylon (Colombo I) 1971, Ceylon (Colombo II) 1971

27=	7	Pullin	John	Hooker	1970-1974

Matches: The Rest 1970, The Rest 1971, The Rest (Twickenham I) 1972, The Rest (Twickenham II) 1972, Fiji 1973, The Rest (Burton-on-Trent) 1974, France XV 1974

27=	7	Hannaford	Charlie	Number 8	1971-1974

Matches: The Rest 1971, Japan (Osaka & Tokyo) 1971, Hong Kong 1971, Ceylon (Colombo I) 1971, Ceylon (Colombo II) 1971, The Rest (Burton-on-Trent) 1974

27=	7	Webster	Jan	Scrum half	1971-1974

Matches: Japan (Tokyo) 1971, Singapore 1971, Ceylon (Colombo II) 1971, The Rest (Twickenham I) 1972, The Rest (Twickenham II) 1972, France XV 1974, The Rest (Twickenham) 1974

27=	7	Old	Alan	Fly half/Centre	1972-1978

Matches: The Rest (Twickenham I) 1972, The Rest (Twickenham II) 1972, Fiji 1973, The Rest (Burton-on-Trent) 1974, France XV 1974, The Rest (Twickenham) 1974, The Rest 1978

27=	7	Woodward	Clive	Centre	1980-1984

Matches: The Rest 1980, The Rest (Twickenham I) 1981, The Rest (Dec) 1981, Canada 1982, USA 1982, The Rest 1984, President's XV 1984

27=	7	Bainbridge	Steve	Lock	1982-1986

Matches: Canada 1982, USA 1982, Fiji 1982, The Rest 1982, Canada 1983, The Rest 1984, Japan 1986

27=	7	Rees	Gary	Flanker	1984-1991

Matches: The Rest 1984 (rep), President's XV 1984, Japan 1986, The Rest 1987, Portugal XV 1987, Barbarians 1990 (rep), USSR 1991

27=	7	Andrew	Rob	**Fly half**	1986-1992

Matches: Portugal XV 1986, Portugal XV 1987, Italy XV 1990, Barbarians 1990, USSR 1991, England Students 1991, Leicester 1992

27=	7	Carling	Will	Centre	1988-1996

Matches: England B XV 1988, Italy XV 1990, Barbarians 1990, USSR 1991, Gloucester 1991, Leicester 1992, New Zealand Barbarians 1996

37=	6	Lloyd	Bob	Centre	1969-1971

Matches: The Rest 1969, Japan (Osaka) 1971, Hong Kong 1971, Singapore 1971 (rep), Ceylon (Colombo I) 1971, Ceylon (Colombo II) 1971 **[Also won 5 England caps 1967-68]**

37=	6	Cowman	Dick	Fly half	1971-1971

Matches: Japan (Osaka) 1971, Japan (Tokyo) 1971 (rep), Hong Kong 1971 (played at full back), Singapore 1971, Ceylon (Colombo I) 1971 (played at full back), Ceylon (Colombo II) 1971

Rank Matches Surname Forename Position Period

37= 6 Glover Peter Wing 1971-1971
Matches: Japan (Osaka) 1971, Japan (Tokyo) 1971, Hong Kong 1971, Singapore 1971, Ceylon (Colombo I) 1971, Ceylon (Colombo II) 1971

37= 6 Ripley Andy Number 8 1972-1975
Matches: The Rest (Twickenham I) 1972, The Rest (Twickenham II) 1972, Fiji 1973, France XV 1974, The Rest (Twickenham) 1974, The Rest 1975

37= 6 Swift Tony Wing 1981-1982
Matches: The Rest (Twickenham I) 1981, The Rest (Twickenham II) 1981, Canada 1982, USA 1982, Fiji 1982, The Rest 1982

37= 6 Cusworth Les Fly half 1982-1988
Matches: Canada 1982, USA 1982, Fiji 1982, The Rest 1982, The Rest 1984, England B XV 1988

37= 6 Halliday Simon Centre 1983-1991
Matches: Canada 1983, Japan 1986, The Rest 1987, USSR 1991 (rep), Gloucester 1991, England Students 1991

37= 6 Moore Brian Hooker 1986-1992
Matches: Japan 1986, The Rest 1987, Italy XV 1990, USSR 1991, England Students 1991, Leicester 1992

37= 6 Redman Nigel Lock 1986-1992
Matches: Japan 1986, Portugal XV 1986, Portugal XV 1987, England B XV 1988, Gloucester 1991, Leicester 1992

37= 6 Leonard Jason Prop 1991-1999
Matches: USSR 1991, Gloucester 1991 (rep), England Students 1991, New Zealand Barbarians 1996, Premiership All Stars (Anfield) 1999, Premiership All Stars (Twickenham) 1999

47= 5 Horton Nigel Lock 1969-1979
Matches: The Rest 1969, The Rest (Twickenham II) 1972 (rep), The Rest (Twickenham) 1974, The Rest 1978, The Rest 1979 (rep)

47= 5 Stevens Stack Prop 1970-1974
Matches: The Rest 1970, The Rest (Twickenham II) 1972, Fiji 1973, The Rest (Burton-on-Trent) 1974, France XV 1974

47= 5 Starmer-Smith Nigel Scrum half 1970-1971
Matches: The Rest 1970, Japan (Osaka) 1971, Hong Kong 1971, Singapore 1971 (played at full back), Ceylon (Colombo I) 1971

47= 5 **Gray** John Hooker 1971-1971
Matches: Japan (Tokyo) 1971, Hong Kong 1971, Singapore 1971 (played at prop), Ceylon (Colombo I) 1971 (played at prop), Ceylon (Colombo II) 1971

47= 5 Rogers Budge Flanker 1971-1971
Matches: Japan (Tokyo) 1971, Hong Kong 1971, Singapore 1971, Ceylon (Colombo I) 1971, Ceylon (Colombo II) 1971

47= 5 Dixon Peter Flanker/Number 8 1972-1978
Matches: The Rest (Twickenham I) 1972, France XV 1974, The Rest 1977, USA 1977, The Rest 1978

47= 5 Hignell Alastair Full back 1975-1979
Matches: The Rest 1975, The Rest 1979 (rep), Japan (Tokyo) 1979, Fiji 1979, Tonga 1979

47= 5 **Butler** John Lock 1979-1979
Matches: The Rest 1979, Japan (Osaka) 1979, Japan (Tokyo) 1979, Fiji 1979, Tonga 1979

Rank	Matches	Surname	Forename	Position	Period
47=	5	Regan	Mark	Hooker	1996-2004

Matches: New Zealand Barbarians 1996, Barbarians 2001, Barbarians 2002 (rep), Barbarians 2003, Barbarians 2004

47=	5	Worsley	Joe	Flanker/Number 8	1999-2010

Matches: Premiership All Stars (Anfield) 1999, Barbarians 2001, Barbarians 2002, New Zealand Barbarians 2003, Barbarians 2010 (rep)

47=	5	Corry	Martin	Lock/Flanker/Number 8	1999-2003

Matches: Premiership All Stars (Anfield) 1999 (rep), Premiership All Stars (Twickenham) 1999 (rep), Barbarians 2001 (rep), Barbarians 2003, New Zealand Barbarians 2003

47=	5	*Vyvyan*	Hugh	Lock/Number 8	2002-2005

Matches: Barbarians 2002, Barbarians 2003 (rep), New Zealand Barbarians 2003 (rep), Barbarians 2004, Barbarians 2005

59=	4	Fairbrother	Keith	Prop	1969-1972

Matches: The Rest 1969, The Rest 1970, The Rest 1971, The Rest (Twickenham I) 1972

59=	4	Rossborough	Peter	Full back	1971-1974

Matches: The Rest 1971, Japan (Osaka) 1971, Japan (Tokyo) 1971, The Rest (Burton-on-Trent) 1974

59=	4	**Robinson**	David	Flanker	1971-1971

Matches: Japan (Osaka) 1971, Hong Kong 1971, Singapore 1971, Ceylon (Colombo II) 1971

59=	4	**Hannell**	Mike	Prop	1971-1971

Matches: Japan (Tokyo) 1971, Hong Kong 1971, Singapore 1971, Ceylon (Colombo II) 1971

59=	4	Finlan	John	Fly half	1971-1971

Matches: Japan (Tokyo) 1971, Hong Kong 1971, Ceylon (Colombo I) 1971, Ceylon (Colombo II) 1971 (played at full back)

59=	4	Evans (2)	Geoff	Centre	1971-1974

Matches: Singapore 1971, Fiji 1973, The Rest (Burton-on-Trent) 1974, France XV 1974

59=	4	Watkins (1)	John	Flanker	1972-1974

Matches: The Rest (Twickenham II) 1972, The Rest (Burton-on-Trent) 1974, France XV 1974 (rep), The Rest (Twickenham) 1974

59=	4	Preece	Peter	Centre	1972-1974

Matches: The Rest (Twickenham II) 1972, Fiji 1973, The Rest (Burton-on-Trent) 1974, The Rest (Twickenham) 1974

59=	4	Horton	John	Fly half	1977-1981

Matches: USA 1977, Argentina 1978, The Rest 1980, The Rest (Twickenham I) 1981

59=	4	**Doubleday**	John	Prop	1979-1979

Matches: The Rest 1979 (rep), Japan (Tokyo) 1979, Fiji 1979, Tonga 1979

59=	4	**McMillan**	Alan	Centre	1979-1979

Matches: The Rest 1979 (rep), Japan (Tokyo) 1979, Fiji 1979 (rep), Tonga 1979

59=	4	Smart	Colin	Prop	1979-1982

Matches: Japan (Osaka) 1979, Fiji 1979, Fiji 1982, The Rest 1982

59=	4	Jeavons	Nick	Flanker	1981-1984

Matches: The Rest (Twickenham II) 1981, Canada 1982, USA 1982, President's XV 1984

59=	4	Rose	Marcus	Full back	1981-1987

Matches: The Rest (Twickenham II) 1981, Japan 1986, The Rest 1987, Portugal XV 1987

59=	4	**McDowell**	Neil	Centre	1982-1982

Matches: Canada 1982, USA 1982, Fiji 1982, The Rest 1982 (rep)

Rank Matches Surname Forename Position Period

59= 4 Bailey Mark Wing 1986-1987
Matches: Japan 1986, Portugal XV 1986, The Rest 1987, Portugal XV 1987

59= 4 Webb Jonathan Full back 1987-1992
Matches: Portugal XV 1987, Gloucester 1991, England Students 1991, Leicester 1992

59= 4 Richards Dean Number 8 1988-1991
Matches: England B XV 1988, Barbarians 1990, Gloucester 1991, England Students 1991

59= 4 Hodgkinson Simon Full back 1988-1991
Matches: England B XV 1988, Italy XV 1990, Barbarians 1990, USSR 1991

59= 4 Back Neil Flanker 1990-1999
Matches: Italy XV 1990, Leicester 1992, Premiership All Stars (Anfield) 1999, Premiership All Stars (Twickenham) 1999

59= 4 Heslop Nigel Wing 1990-1992
Matches: Italy XV 1990, Gloucester 1991, England Students 1991, Leicester 1992

59= 4 Teague Mike Flanker/Number 8 1990-1991
Matches: Barbarians 1990, USSR 1991, Gloucester 1991, England Students 1991

59= 4 Guscott Jeremy Centre 1990-1992
Matches: Barbarians 1990, USSR 1991, England Students 1991, Leicester 1992

59= 4 de Glanville Phil Centre 1992-1999
Matches: Leicester 1992 (rep), New Zealand Barbarians 1996, Premiership All Stars (Anfield) 1999, Premiership All Stars (Twickenham) 1999

59= 4 Rowntree Graham Prop 1996-2001
Matches: New Zealand Barbarians 1996, Premiership All Stars (Anfield) 1999 (rep), Premiership All Stars (Twickenham) 1999 (rep), Barbarians 2001 (rep)

59= 4 *Gomarsall* Andy Scrum half 1996-2005
Matches: New Zealand Barbarians 1996, Barbarians 2002, New Zealand Barbarians 2003, Barbarians 2005

59= 4 Catt Mike Fly half/Centre/Full back 1996-2006
Matches: New Zealand Barbarians 1996, Premiership All Stars (Anfield) 1999 (rep), Premiership All Stars (Twickenham) 1999 (rep), Barbarians 2006

59= 4 Vickery Phil Prop 1999-2003
Matches: Premiership All Stars (Anfield) 1999, Premiership All Stars (Twickenham) 1999, Barbarians 2002, Barbarians 2003

59= 4 *Walder* Dave Fly half 2001-2004
Matches: Barbarians 2001, Barbarians 2002, Barbarians 2003, Barbarians 2004

59= 4 *Simpson-Daniel* James Centre/Wing 2002-2006
Matches: Barbarians 2002, New Zealand Barbarians 2003, Barbarians 2005, Barbarians 2006

59= 4 *Noon* Jamie Centre 2003-2009
Matches: Barbarians 2003, Barbarians 2004, Barbarians 2005, Barbarians 2009

59= 4 *Tait* Matt Centre/Wing/Full back 2005-2010
Matches: Barbarians 2005 (rep), Barbarians 2006, Barbarians 2008, Barbarians 2010 (rep)

91= 3 Hiller Bob Full back 1969-1972
Matches: The Rest 1969, The Rest 1970, The Rest (Twickenham I) 1972

91= 3 Burton Mike Prop 1972-1977
Matches: The Rest (Twickenham I) 1972, The Rest 1975, The Rest 1977

91= 3 Cooper Martin Fly half 1974-1977
Matches: France XV 1974, The Rest 1975, The Rest 1977

Rank Matches Surname Forename Position Period

91= 3 Corless Barrie Centre 1975-1978
Matches: The Rest 1975, The Rest 1977, The Rest 1978

91= 3 Kent Charles Centre 1975-1978
Matches: The Rest 1975 (rep), The Rest 1977, The Rest 1978

91= 3 Cowling Robin Prop 1977-1979
Matches: The Rest 1977, The Rest 1978, The Rest 1979

91= 3 Young Malcolm Scrum half 1977-1979
Matches: The Rest 1977, The Rest 1978, The Rest 1979

91= 3 **Gifford** Chris Scrum half 1978-1979
Matches: Argentina 1978, Japan (Osaka) 1979, Tonga 1979

91= 3 **Pomphrey** Nigel Lock/Flanker 1979-1979
Matches: Japan (Tokyo) 1979, Fiji 1979, Tonga 1979

91= 3 Mills Steve Hooker 1980-1984
Matches: The Rest 1980, The Rest (Twickenham II) 1981, President's XV 1984

91= 3 Cooke (2) David Flanker 1981-1982
Matches: The Rest (Twickenham I) 1981, The Rest (Twickenham II) 1981, Fiji 1982

91= 3 **Gadd** John Flanker 1982-1983
Matches: Fiji 1982, The Rest 1982, Canada 1983

91= 3 Stringer Nick Full back 1982-1984
Matches: USA 1982 (rep), Canada 1983 (rep), President's XV 1984

91= 3 Hall Jon Flanker 1984-1987
Matches: President's XV 1984, Japan 1986, The Rest 1987

91= 3 Barnes Stuart Fly half/Full back 1984-1987
Matches: President's XV 1984, Japan 1986, The Rest 1987

91= 3 Dawe Graham Hooker 1986-1988
Matches: Portugal XV 1986 (rep), Portugal XV 1987, England B XV 1988

91= 3 Oti Chris Wing 1990-1991
Matches: Italy XV 1990, USSR 1991, Gloucester 1991

91= 3 Olver John Hooker 1990-1991
Matches: Italy XV 1990 (rep), Barbarians 1990, Gloucester 1991

91= 3 Ackford Paul Lock 1990-1991
Matches: Barbarians 1990, USSR 1991, England Students 1991

91= 3 Pears David Fly half/Full back 1991-1992
Matches: USSR 1991 (rep), Gloucester 1991, Leicester 1992

91= 3 *Shaw* Simon Lock 1996-2003
Matches: New Zealand Barbarians 1996, Barbarians 2001, New Zealand Barbarians 2003

91= 3 Dallaglio Lawrence Flanker/Number 8 1996-1999
Matches: New Zealand Barbarians 1996, Premiership All Stars (Anfield) 1999, Premiership All Stars (Twickenham) 1999

91= 3 Grewcock Danny Lock 1999-2003
Matches: Premiership All Stars (Anfield) 1999 (rep), Premiership All Stars (Twickenham) 1999, New Zealand Barbarians 2003

91= 3 Woodman Trevor Prop 2001-2003
Matches: Barbarians 2001, Barbarians 2002, New Zealand Barbarians 2003

91= 3 Bracken Kyran Scrum half 2001-2003
Matches: Barbarians 2001, Barbarians 2003, New Zealand Barbarians 2003 (rep)

Rank Matches Surname Forename Position Period

91= 3 *Johnston* Ben Centre 2001-2003
Matches: Barbarians 2001 (rep), Barbarians 2002, Barbarians 2003

91= 3 Thompson (2) Steve Hooker 2002-2010
Matches: Barbarians 2002, Barbarians 2009 (rep), Barbarians 2010

91= 3 Forrester James Flanker 2002-2006
Matches: Barbarians 2002, Barbarians 2005 (rep), Barbarians 2006

91= 3 Walshe Nick Scrum half 2002-2004
Matches: Barbarians 2002 (rep), Barbarians 2003 (rep), Barbarians 2004

91= 3 ***Sorrell*** Kevin Centre 2002-2004
Matches: Barbarians 2002 (rep), Barbarians 2003 (rep), Barbarians 2004

91= 3 Worsley Mike Prop 2003-2005
Matches: Barbarians 2003, Barbarians 2004, Barbarians 2005

91= 3 *Brown* Alex Lock 2003-2006
Matches: Barbarians 2003, Barbarians 2004, Barbarians 2006

91= 3 *Jones* Chris Lock/Flanker/Number 8 2003-2008
Matches: Barbarians 2003, Barbarians 2005, Barbarians 2008

91= 3 Sanderson Pat Flanker 2003-2006
Matches: New Zealand Barbarians 2003 (rep), Barbarians 2005, Barbarians 2006

91= 3 *Mears* Lee Hooker 2005-2010
Matches: Barbarians 2005 (rep), Barbarians 2006, Barbarians 2010 (rep)

91= 3 Richards Peter Scrum half/Centre 2005-2008
Matches: Barbarians 2005 (rep), Barbarians 2006, Barbarians 2008 (rep)

91= 3 *Payne* Tim Prop 2006-2010
Matches: Barbarians 2006, Barbarians 2009, Barbarians 2010 (rep)

91= 3 *Haskell* James Flanker/Number 8 2006-2010
Matches: Barbarians 2006 (rep), Barbarians 2009 (rep), Barbarians 2010

91= 3 *Easter* Nick Flanker/Number 8 2008-2010
Matches: Barbarians 2008, Barbarians 2009, Barbarians 2010

91= 3 *Care* Danny Scrum half 2008-2010
Matches: Barbarians 2008 (rep), Barbarians 2009, Barbarians 2010

131= 2 West Bryan Flanker 1969-1970
Matches: The Rest 1969, The Rest 1970

131= 2 Shackleton Roger Fly half 1969-1970
Matches: The Rest 1969, The Rest 1970

131= 2 Spencer John Centre 1969-1970
Matches: The Rest 1969, The Rest 1970

131= 2 Fielding Keith Wing 1969-1972
Matches: The Rest 1969, The Rest (Twickenham I) 1972

131= 2 Bucknall Tony Flanker 1970-1971
Matches: The Rest 1970, The Rest 1971

131= 2 Wardlow Chris Centre 1971-1971
Matches: The Rest 1971, Japan (Tokyo) 1971

131= 2 Morley Alan Wing 1972-1974
Matches: The Rest (Twickenham II) 1972, France XV 1974 (rep)

131= 2 **Hendy** Peter Flanker 1973-1974
Matches: Fiji 1973, The Rest (Twickenham) 1974

Rank	Matches	Surname	Forename	Position	Period
131=	2	White	Colin	Prop	1974-1984

Matches: The Rest (Twickenham) 1974, The Rest 1984

131=	2	Wilkinson	Bob	Lock	1975-1977

Matches: The Rest 1975, The Rest 1977

131=	2	Caplan	David	Full back	1977-1978

Matches: The Rest 1977, The Rest 1978

131=	2	Nelmes	Barry	Prop	1977-1978

Matches: USA 1977, Argentina 1978

131=	2	Bond	Tony	Centre	1979-1980

Matches: The Rest 1979, The Rest 1980

131=	2	Cardus	Richard	Centre	1979-1979

Matches: Japan (Osaka) 1979, Fiji 1979

131=	2	**Peck**	Ian	Scrum half	1979-1979

Matches: Japan (Tokyo) 1979, Fiji 1979

131=	2	**Cook (1)**	Peter	Lock/Flanker	1981-1986

Matches: The Rest (Twickenham I) 1981, Portugal XV 1986

131=	2	Blakeway	Phil	Prop	1982-1982

Matches: Canada 1982, Fiji 1982

131=	2	Syddall	Jim	Lock	1983-1984

Matches: Canada 1983, President's XV 1984

131=	2	Youngs	Nick	Scrum half	1983-1984

Matches: Canada 1983, The Rest 1984

131=	2	Simpson	Paul	Flanker	1984-1986

Matches: The Rest 1984, Portugal XV 1986

131=	2	Salmon	Jamie	Centre	1986-1987

Matches: Japan 1986, The Rest 1987

131=	2	Simms	Kevin	Centre	1986-1988

Matches: Portugal XV 1986, England B XV 1988

131=	2	Harrison	Mike	Wing	1986-1988

Matches: Portugal XV 1986, England B XV 1988

131=	2	Cusani	Dave	Lock/Number 8	1987-1990

Matches: The Rest 1987, Italy XV 1990

131=	2	Egerton	Dave	Number 8	1987-1987

Matches: The Rest 1987, Portugal XV 1987

131=	2	Clough	Fran	Centre	1987-1990

Matches: Portugal XV 1987, Italy XV 1990 (rep)

131=	2	**Wells**	John	Flanker	1988-1990

Matches: England B XV 1988, Italy XV 1990

131=	2	Underwood	Tony	Wing	1990-1992

Matches: Barbarians 1990, Leicester 1992

131=	2	Johnson	Martin	Lock	1996-1999

Matches: New Zealand Barbarians 1996, Premiership All Stars (Twickenham) 1999

131=	2	Rodber	Tim	Lock/Flanker/Number 8	1996-1999

Matches: New Zealand Barbarians 1996, Premiership All Stars (Anfield) 1999

131=	2	Stimpson	Tim	Full back	1996-2001

Matches: New Zealand Barbarians 1996, Barbarians 2001

Rank Matches Surname Forename Position Period

131= 2 Cockerill Richard Hooker 1999-1999
Matches: Premiership All Stars (Anfield) 1999, Premiership All Stars (Twickenham) 1999
131= 2 Dawson Matt Scrum half 1999-1999
Matches: Premiership All Stars (Anfield) 1999, Premiership All Stars (Twickenham) 1999
131= 2 Grayson Paul Fly half 1999-2003
Matches: Premiership All Stars (Anfield) 1999, New Zealand Barbarians 2003
131= 2 Greenwood Will Centre 1999-1999
Matches: Premiership All Stars (Anfield) 1999, Premiership All Stars (Twickenham) 1999
131= 2 Healey Austin Scrum half/Fly half/Wing 1999-1999
Matches: Premiership All Stars (Anfield) 1999, Premiership All Stars (Twickenham) 1999
131= 2 Perry Matt Centre/Full back 1999-1999
Matches: Premiership All Stars (Anfield) 1999, Premiership All Stars (Twickenham) 1999
131= 2 Garforth Darren Prop 1999-1999
Matches: Premiership All Stars (Anfield) 1999 (rep), Premiership All Stars (Twickenham) 1999 (rep)
131= 2 Luger Dan Wing 1999-1999
Matches: Premiership All Stars (Anfield) 1999 (rep), Premiership All Stars (Twickenham) 1999
131= 2 Hill (2) Richard Flanker/Number 8 1999-2003
Matches: Premiership All Stars (Twickenham) 1999, New Zealand Barbarians 2003
131= 2 *Borthwick* Steve Lock 2001-2009
Matches: Barbarians 2001, Barbarians 2009
131= 2 *Hazell* Andy Flanker 2001-2004
Matches: Barbarians 2001, Barbarians 2004
131= 2 Codling Alex Lock 2002-2003
Matches: Barbarians 2002, Barbarians 2003
131= 2 *Christophers* Phil Wing 2002-2003
Matches: Barbarians 2002, Barbarians 2003
131= 2 *Horak* Michael Full back 2002-2004
Matches: Barbarians 2002, Barbarians 2004
131= 2 *Flatman* David Prop 2002-2003
Matches: Barbarians 2002 (rep), Barbarians 2003 (rep)
131= 2 *Lipman* Michael Flanker 2003-2006
Matches: Barbarians 2003, Barbarians 2006
131= 2 *Cueto* Mark Wing 2003-2010
Matches: Barbarians 2003, Barbarians 2010
131= 2 *Scarbrough* Dan Full back 2003-2004
Matches: Barbarians 2003, Barbarians 2004 (rep)
131= 2 *Titterrell* Andy Hooker 2003-2003
Matches: Barbarians 2003 (rep), New Zealand Barbarians 2003
131= 2 Abbott Stuart Centre 2003-2006
Matches: New Zealand Barbarians 2003, Barbarians 2006 (rep)
131= 2 *Tindall* Mike Centre 2003-2010
Matches: New Zealand Barbarians 2003 (rep), Barbarians 2010
131= 2 *Sackey* Paul Wing 2004-2005
Matches: Barbarians 2004, Barbarians 2005

Rank Matches Surname Forename Position Period

131= 2 *Deacon* Louis Lock 2005-2009
Matches: Barbarians 2005, Barbarians 2009

131= 2 *Palmer (2)* Tom Lock 2005-2010
Matches: Barbarians 2005, Barbarians 2010

131= 2 *Goode* Andy Fly half 2005-2009
Matches: Barbarians 2005, Barbarians 2009

131= 2 ***Hooper*** Stuart Lock 2005-2008
Matches: Barbarians 2005 (rep), Barbarians 2008 (rep)

131= 2 *Barkley* Olly Fly half/Centre 2006-2010
Matches: Barbarians 2006, Barbarians 2010 (rep)

131= 2 *Paice* David Prop/Hooker 2006-2008
Matches: Barbarians 2006 (rep), Barbarians 2008

131= 2 *Armitage* Delon Centre/Wing/Full back 2006-2009
Matches: Barbarians 2006 (rep), Barbarians 2009

131= 2 *Hodgson* Charlie Fly half 2008-2010
Matches: Barbarians 2008, Barbarians 2010

131= 2 *Strettle* Dave Wing 2008-2010
Matches: Barbarians 2008, Barbarians 2010

131= 2 *Wilson (2)* David Prop 2008-2009
Matches: Barbarians 2008 (rep), Barbarians 2009

131= 2 *Hartley* Dylan Prop/Hooker 2008-2009
Matches: Barbarians 2008 (rep), Barbarians 2009

131= 2 *Foden* Ben Scrum half/Wing/Full back 2009-2010
Matches: Barbarians 2009, Barbarians 2010

131= 2 *Armitage* Steffon Flanker 2009-2010
Matches: Barbarians 2009 (rep), Barbarians 2010

197= 1 Powell David Prop 1969
Matches: The Rest 1969

197= 1 **Harris** Roger Hooker 1969
Matches: The Rest 1969

197= 1 Greenwood Dick Flanker 1969
Matches: The Rest 1969

197= 1 **Tennick** Ron Number 8 1969
Matches: The Rest 1969

197= 1 Wintle Trevor Scrum half 1969
Matches: The Rest 1969

197= 1 **Briggs** Pat Fly half 1969
Matches: The Rest 1969 (rep)

197= 1 Davis (1) Mike Lock 1970
Matches: The Rest 1970

197= 1 Taylor Bob Flanker/Number 8 1970
Matches: The Rest 1970

197= 1 Hale Peter Wing 1970
Matches: The Rest 1970

197= 1 Novak John Wing 1970
Matches: The Rest 1970

Rank Matches Surname Forename Position Period

197= 1 Ninnes Barry Lock 1971
Matches: The Rest 1971

197= 1 Page Jacko Scrum half 1971
Matches: The Rest 1971

197= 1 Wright Ian Fly half 1971
Matches: The Rest 1971

197= 1 **Kirkpatrick** George Centre 1971
Matches: The Rest 1971

197= 1 **Broderick** Jim Prop 1971
Matches: Japan (Osaka) 1971

197= 1 Martin Nick Lock 1972
Matches: The Rest (Twickenham I) 1972

197= 1 Watt Dave Lock 1972
Matches: The Rest (Twickenham I) 1972 **[4 England caps 1967]**

197= 1 Beese Mike Centre 1972
Matches: The Rest (Twickenham I) 1972

197= 1 Doble Sam Full back 1972
Matches: The Rest (Twickenham II) 1972

197= 1 Jorden Tony Full back 1973
Matches: Fiji 1973

197= 1 **Carr** Dave Wing 1974
Matches: The Rest (Burton-on-Trent) 1974

197= 1 Smith Keith Centre 1974
Matches: The Rest (Twickenham) 1974

197= 1 **Richards** Geoff Full back 1974
Matches: The Rest (Twickenham) 1974

197= 1 Keyworth Mark Flanker 1975
Matches: The Rest 1975

197= 1 Lampkowski Mike Scrum half 1975
Matches: The Rest 1975

197= 1 Maxwell (1) Andy Centre 1975
Matches: The Rest 1975

197= 1 **Powell** Roger Lock 1977
Matches: The Rest 1977

197= 1 **Ayres** Barry Lock 1977
Matches: The Rest 1977 (rep)

197= 1 **Cox** Gary Hooker 1977
Matches: USA 1977

197= 1 **Bell** Jeff Prop 1977
Matches: USA 1977

197= 1 Mantell Neil Lock 1977
Matches: USA 1977 (played at number 8)

197= 1 **Carfoot** David Scrum half 1977
Matches: USA 1977

197= 1 Wyatt Derek Wing 1977
Matches: USA 1977

Rank	Matches	Surname	Forename	Position	Period
197=	1	**French**	Nigel	Centre	1977

Matches: USA 1977

197=	1	**Greaves**	Bert	Prop	1978

Matches: The Rest 1978

197=	1	**Bignell**	Eric	Number 8	1978

Matches: The Rest 1978

197=	1	**Sorrell**	David	Fly half/Full back	1978

Matches: The Rest 1978 (rep)

197=	1	**Demming**	Bob	Wing	1978

Matches: The Rest 1978 (rep)

197=	1	Warfield	Peter	Centre	1978

Matches: Argentina 1978

197=	1	**Bushell**	Billy	Full back	1978

Matches: Argentina 1978

197=	1	**Dickinson**	Willie	Prop	1979

Matches: The Rest 1979

197=	1	Bennett	Neil	Fly half	1979

Matches: The Rest 1979

197=	1	Mordell	Bob	Flanker	1979

Matches: Japan (Osaka) 1979

197=	1	**Allchurch**	Toby	Flanker	1979

Matches: Tonga 1979

197=	1	Sargent	Gordon	Prop	1980

Matches: The Rest 1980

197=	1	**McGregor**	Clint	Prop	1980

Matches: The Rest 1980

197=	1	**Cheeseman**	Trevor	Flanker/Number 8	1980

Matches: The Rest 1980

197=	1	**Field**	Russ	Lock	1980

Matches: The Rest 1980 (rep)

197=	1	**Morris**	Terry	Flanker	1981

Matches: The Rest (Twickenham I) 1981 (rep)

197=	1	Hesford	Bob	Number 8	1981

Matches: The Rest (Twickenham II) 1981

197=	1	Trick	David	Wing	1982

Matches: Fiji 1982

197=	1	**Simpson**	Andy	Hooker	1984

Matches: The Rest 1984

197=	1	**Redfern**	Stuart	Prop	1984

Matches: President's XV 1984

197=	1	**Bell**	Eddie	Prop	1984

Matches: President's XV 1984

197=	1	Lozowski	Rob	Centre	1984

Matches: President's XV 1984

197=	1	Chilcott	Gareth	Prop	1986

Matches: Japan 1986

Rank	Matches	Surname	Forename	Position	Period
197=	1	Brain	Steve	Hooker	1986

Matches: Portugal XV 1986

197=	1	**Lee**	Richard	Prop	1986

Matches: Portugal XV 1986

197=	1	Harding	Richard	Scrum half	1986

Matches: Portugal XV 1986

197=	1	Williams	Peter	Fly half/Full back	1986

Matches: Portugal XV 1986

197=	1	**Pinnegar**	Colin	Lock	1986

Matches: Portugal XV 1986 (rep)

197=	1	**Smith (2)**	Simon	Fly half	1986

Matches: Portugal XV 1986 (rep)

197=	1	**Morrison**	John	Lock	1987

Matches: The Rest 1987

197=	1	Melville	Nigel	Scrum half	1988

Matches: England B XV 1988

197=	1	**MacFarlane**	Andy	Number 8	1988

Matches: England B XV 1988 (rep)

197=	1	Linnett	Mark	Prop	1990

Matches: Italy XV 1990

197=	1	**Kimmins**	Bob	Lock	1990

Matches: Italy XV 1990

197=	1	Bates	Steve	Scrum half	1990

Matches: Italy XV 1990

197=	1	Buckton	John	Centre	1990

Matches: Italy XV 1990

197=	1	Skinner	Mickey	Flanker	1991

Matches: USSR 1991

197=	1	Morris	Dewi	Scrum half	1991

Matches: England Students 1991

197=	1	**Hynes**	Martin	Prop	1992

Matches: Leicester 1992

197=	1	Bayfield	Martin	Lock	1992

Matches: Leicester 1992

197=	1	Ojomoh	Steve	Flanker/Number 8	1992

Matches: Leicester 1992

197=	1	Clarke	Ben	Flanker/Number 8	1992

Matches: Leicester 1992

197=	1	**Pepper**	Martin	Flanker	1992

Matches: Leicester 1992 (rep)

197=	1	Sheasby	Chris	Flanker/Number 8	1996

Matches: New Zealand Barbarians 1996

197=	1	Adebayo	Adedayo	Wing	1996

Matches: New Zealand Barbarians 1996

197=	1	Sleightholme	Jon	Wing	1996

Matches: New Zealand Barbarians 1996

Rank	Matches	Surname	Forename	Position	Period
197=	1	Archer	Garath	Lock	1999
Matches: Premiership All Stars (Anfield) 1999					
197=	1	Beal	Nick	Centre/Wing/Full back	1999
Matches: Premiership All Stars (Anfield) 1999					
197=	1	McCarthy	Neil	Hooker	1999
Matches: Premiership All Stars (Anfield) 1999 (rep)					
197=	1	*Wilkinson*	Jonny	Fly half/Centre	1999
Matches: Premiership All Stars (Twickenham) 1999					
197=	1	Rees (2)	David	Wing	1999
Matches: Premiership All Stars (Twickenham) 1999 (rep)					
197=	1	*White*	Julian	Prop	2001
Matches: Barbarians 2001					
197=	1	Sanderson	Alex	Flanker/Number 8	2001
Matches: Barbarians 2001					
197=	1	*Stephenson*	Michael	Wing/Full back	2001
Matches: Barbarians 2001					
197=	1	Lewsey	Josh	Fly half/Centre/Wing/Full back	2001
Matches: Barbarians 2001					
197=	1	Lloyd	Leon	Centre/Wing	2001
Matches: Barbarians 2001					
197=	1	*Sampson*	Paul	Wing/Full back	2001
Matches: Barbarians 2001					
197=	1	West	Dorian	Hooker	2001
Matches: Barbarians 2001 (rep)					
197=	1	Kay	Ben	Lock	2001
Matches: Barbarians 2001 (rep)					
197=	1	Wood	Martyn	Scrum half	2001
Matches: Barbarians 2001 (rep)					
197=	1	*King*	Alex	Fly half	2001
Matches: Barbarians 2001 (rep)					
197=	1	***Gustard***	Paul	Flanker/Number 8	2002
Matches: Barbarians 2002					
197=	1	Appleford	Geoff	Centre	2002
Matches: Barbarians 2002					
197=	1	***Pearce***	Ed	Lock	2002
Matches: Barbarians 2002 (rep)					
197=	1	***Seely***	Grant	Number 8	2002
Matches: Barbarians 2002 (rep)					
197=	1	***Jones***	Phil	Fly half	2002
Matches: Barbarians 2002 (rep)					
197=	1	**Anglesea**	Pete	Flanker/Number 8	2003
Matches: Barbarians 2003 (rep)					
197=	1	***Amor***	Simon	Scrum half/Fly half	2003
Matches: Barbarians 2003 (rep)					
197=	1	*Stevens*	Matt	Prop	2003
Matches: New Zealand Barbarians 2003					

Rank	Matches	Surname	Forename	Position	Period
197=	1	Cohen	Ben	Wing	2003
Matches: New Zealand Barbarians 2003					
197=	1	*Smith (1)*	Ollie	Centre/Wing	2003
Matches: New Zealand Barbarians 2003					
197=	1	Robinson	Jason	Wing/Full back	2003
Matches: New Zealand Barbarians 2003					
197=	1	*Sheridan*	Andy	Prop/Lock	2003
Matches: New Zealand Barbarians 2003 (rep)					
197=	1	***Gollings***	Ben	Fly half/Full back	2003
Matches: New Zealand Barbarians 2003 (rep)					
197=	1	Morris	Robbie	Prop	2004
Matches: Barbarians 2004					
197=	1	***Cornwell***	Mark	Lock	2004
Matches: Barbarians 2004					
197=	1	***Hyde***	Dan	Flanker	2004
Matches: Barbarians 2004					
197=	1	***Garvey***	Marcel	Wing	2004
Matches: Barbarians 2004					
197=	1	***Dawson***	Jon	Prop	2004
Matches: Barbarians 2004 (rep)					
197=	1	***Buxton***	Peter	Flanker	2004
Matches: Barbarians 2004 (rep)					
197=	1	***Ward***	Micky	Prop	2005
Matches: Barbarians 2005					
197=	1	*Chuter*	George	Hooker	2005
Matches: Barbarians 2005					
197=	1	*Erinle*	Ayoola	Centre	2005
Matches: Barbarians 2005					
197=	1	*Voyce*	Tom	Wing/Full back	2005
Matches: Barbarians 2005					
197=	1	*Vesty*	Sam	Fly half/Centre/Full back	2005
Matches: Barbarians 2005 (rep)					
197=	1	*Bell*	Duncan	Prop	2006
Matches: Barbarians 2006					
197=	1	***Hudson***	James	Lock	2006
Matches: Barbarians 2006					
197=	1	*Balshaw*	Iain	Wing/Full back	2006
Matches: Barbarians 2006					
197=	1	*Van Gisbergen*	Mark	Full back	2006
Matches: Barbarians 2006					
197=	1	***Barnes***	David	Prop	2006
Matches: Barbarians 2006 (rep)					
197=	1	***Roche***	Kieran	Lock/Flanker/Number 8	2006
Matches: Barbarians 2006 (rep)					
197=	1	***Bemand***	Scott	Scrum half	2006
Matches: Barbarians 2006 (rep)					

Rank	Matches	Surname	Forename	Position	Period
197=	1	***Lloyd***	Nick	Prop	2008

Matches: Barbarians 2008

Rank	Matches	Surname	Forename	Position	Period
197=	1	*Hobson*	Jason	Prop	2008

Matches: Barbarians 2008

Rank	Matches	Surname	Forename	Position	Period
197=	1	*Kennedy*	Nick	Lock	2008

Matches: Barbarians 2008

Rank	Matches	Surname	Forename	Position	Period
197=	1	*Narraway*	Luke	Flanker/Number 8	2008

Matches: Barbarians 2008

Rank	Matches	Surname	Forename	Position	Period
197=	1	***Skinner***	Will	Flanker/Number 8	2008

Matches: Barbarians 2008

Rank	Matches	Surname	Forename	Position	Period
197=	1	*Wigglesworth*	Richard	Scrum half	2008

Matches: Barbarians 2008

Rank	Matches	Surname	Forename	Position	Period
197=	1	*Flood*	Toby	Fly half/Centre	2008

Matches: Barbarians 2008

Rank	Matches	Surname	Forename	Position	Period
197=	1	*Ojo*	Topsy	Wing	2008

Matches: Barbarians 2008

Rank	Matches	Surname	Forename	Position	Period
197=	1	*Brown*	Mike	Wing/Full back	2008

Matches: Barbarians 2008

Rank	Matches	Surname	Forename	Position	Period
197=	1	***Guest***	Tom	Flanker/Number 8	2008

Matches: Barbarians 2008 (rep)

Rank	Matches	Surname	Forename	Position	Period
197=	1	*Monye*	Ugo	Centre/Wing	2008

Matches: Barbarians 2008 (rep)

Rank	Matches	Surname	Forename	Position	Period
197=	1	*Robshaw*	Chris	Flanker/Number 8	2009

Matches: Barbarians 2009

Rank	Matches	Surname	Forename	Position	Period
197=	1	*Moody*	Lewis	Flanker	2009

Matches: Barbarians 2009

Rank	Matches	Surname	Forename	Position	Period
197=	1	*Banahan*	Matt	Centre/Wing	2009

Matches: Barbarians 2009

Rank	Matches	Surname	Forename	Position	Period
197=	1	***Turner-Hall***	Jordan	Centre	2009

Matches: Barbarians 2009

Rank	Matches	Surname	Forename	Position	Period
197=	1	*Hodgson*	Paul	Scrum half	2009

Matches: Barbarians 2009 (rep)

Rank	Matches	Surname	Forename	Position	Period
197=	1	*May*	Tom	Fly half/Centre/Wing/Full back	2009

Matches: Barbarians 2009 (rep)

Rank	Matches	Surname	Forename	Position	Period
197=	1	***Wood***	Nick	Prop	2009

Matches: Barbarians 2009 (rep)

Rank	Matches	Surname	Forename	Position	Period
197=	1	***Golding***	Jon	Prop	2010

Matches: Barbarians 2010

Rank	Matches	Surname	Forename	Position	Period
197=	1	*Doran-Jones*	Paul	Prop	2010

Matches: Barbarians 2010

Rank	Matches	Surname	Forename	Position	Period
197=	1	***Attwood***	Dave	Lock	2010

Matches: Barbarians 2010

Rank	Matches	Surname	Forename	Position	Period
197=	1	*Hape*	Shontayne	Centre/Wing	2010

Matches: Barbarians 2010

Rank	Matches	Surname	Forename	Position	Period
197=	1	**Ward-Smith**	Dan	Lock/Flanker/Number 8	2010

Matches: Barbarians 2010 (rep)

Rank	Matches	Surname	Forename	Position	Period
197=	1	***Simpson***	Joe	Scrum half	2010

Matches: Barbarians 2010 (rep)

4) ENGLAND UNUSED BENCH REPLACEMENTS (NON-CAP MATCHES) 1969-2010:

[In numerical order; restricted to uncapped players only; current players in italics; data up to and including an England XV v Barbarians 30th May 2010]

Rank	Benches	Surname	Forename	Position	Period
1=	3	**Raphael**	Jon	Hooker	1979-1979
Benches: Japan (Osaka) 1979, Japan (Tokyo) 1979, Fiji 1979					
2=	2	**George**	Ian	Scrum half	1977-1983
Benches: USA 1977, Canada 1983					
2=	2	**Gifford**	Chris	Scrum half	1979-1979
Benches: Japan (Tokyo) 1979, Fiji 1979					
4=	1	**Pearn**	Alan	Scrum half	1971
Benches: The Rest 1971					
4=	1	**Coley**	David	Fly half	1971
Benches: The Rest 1971					
4=	1	**Grant**	Paul	Centre	1971
Benches: The Rest 1971					
4=	1	**Palmer (1)**	Tom	Fly half	1972
Benches: The Rest (Twickenham I) 1972					
4=	1	**Richards**	Tony	Wing	1972
Benches: The Rest (Twickenham I) 1972					
4=	1	**Codd**	Ray	Full back	1972
Benches: The Rest (Twickenham I) 1972					
4=	1	**White (2)**	John	Hooker	1973
Benches: Fiji 1973					
4=	1	**Corless**	Trevor	Prop	1977
Benches: USA 1977					
4=	1	**Tabern**	Ray	Hooker	1977
Benches: USA 1977					
4=	1	**Cutter**	Andy	Prop	1978
Benches: Argentina 1978					
4=	1	**Gadd**	John	Flanker	1982
Benches: Canada 1982					
4=	1	**Thomas**	Steve	Scrum half	1982
Benches: Fiji 1982					
4=	1	**Simpson**	Andy	Hooker	1984
Benches: President's XV 1984					
4=	1	**Moon**	Richard	Scrum half	1986
Benches: Portugal XV 1986					
4=	1	**Knibbs**	Ralph	Centre/Wing	1986
Benches: Portugal XV 1986					
4=	1	**Pegler**	David	Flanker/Number 8	1990
Benches: Italy XV 1990					
4=	1	***Fox***	Darren	Flanker	2004
Benches: Barbarians 2004					

5) ENGLAND TOUR MATCH APPEARANCES 1969-2010:

[In numerical order; current players in italics; uncapped players in bold or bold italics; data up to and including an England XV v New Zealand Maori 23rd June 2010]

Rank	Matches	Surname	Forename	Position	Period
1	22	Pearce (1)	Gary	**Prop**	1979-1991

Matches: Kyushu 1979, Fiji Juniors 1979, Northern Region XV 1981, Buenos Aires Selection 1981, Southern Region XV 1981, Littoral Region XV 1981, Eastern Canada 1982, US Cougars 1982, Western Rugby Football Union 1982, Eastern Rugby Union 1982, Currie Cup 'B' Section 1984, South African Rugby Association 1984, South African Country Districts 1984, North Auckland 1985, Auckland 1985, Queensland Country Invitation XV 1988, Queensland B 1988, South Australia Invitation XV 1988, New South Wales B 1988, Queensland 1991, Fiji B 1991, Emerging Wallabies 1991

Rank	Matches	Surname	Forename	Position	Period
2	15	Redman	Nigel	**Lock**	1988-1997

Matches: Queensland Country Invitation XV 1988, Queensland B 1988, South Australia Invitation XV 1988, New South Wales 1988, New South Wales B 1988, Tucumán Selection 1990, Buenos Aires Selection 1990, Victorian President's XV 1991, Fiji B 1991, Emerging Wallabies 1991, Natal 1994, Western Transvaal 1994, Transvaal 1994, Córdoba 1997, Buenos Aires 1997

Rank	Matches	Surname	Forename	Position	Period
3	14	Scott	John	Lock/**Number 8**	1979-1984

Matches: Japan Select 1979, Kyushu 1979, San Isidro Club 1981, Northern Region XV 1981, Buenos Aires Selection 1981, US Cougars 1982, Pacific Coast Grizzlies 1982, Western Rugby Football Union 1982, Mid-Western Rugby Football Union 1982, Currie Cup 'B' Section 1984, Proteas 1984, Western Province 1984, South African Rugby Association 1984, South African Country Districts 1984

Rank	Matches	Surname	Forename	Position	Period
4=	13	Dodge	Paul	**Centre**	1979-1985

Matches: Japan Select 1979, Kyushu 1979 (rep), Fiji Juniors 1979, San Isidro Club 1981, Northern Region XV 1981, Buenos Aires Selection 1981, Southern Region XV 1981, Littoral Region XV 1981, Currie Cup 'B' Section 1984, Proteas 1984, North Auckland 1985, Poverty Bay 1985, Auckland 1985

Rank	Matches	Surname	Forename	Position	Period
4=	13	Carleton	John	**Wing**	1979-1982

Matches: Japan Select 1979, Kyushu 1979, Fiji Juniors 1979, San Isidro Club 1981, Northern Region XV 1981, Buenos Aires Selection 1981, Southern Region XV 1981, Littoral Region XV 1981, Eastern Canada 1982, Pacific Coast Grizzlies 1982, Western Rugby Football Union 1982, Mid-Western Rugby Football Union 1982, Eastern Rugby Union 1982

Rank	Matches	Surname	Forename	Position	Period
6=	12	Rendall	Paul	Prop	1981-1991

Matches: Northern Region XV 1981, Eastern Canada 1982, Pacific Coast Grizzlies 1982, Mid-Western Rugby Football Union 1982, Currie Cup 'B' Section 1984, South African Rugby Association 1984, South African Country Districts 1984, Queensland 1988, New South Wales 1988, Victorian President's XV 1991, Fiji B 1991, Emerging Wallabies 1991

Rank	Matches	Surname	Forename	Position	Period
6=	12	Barnes	Stuart	**Fly half**/Full back	1985-1994

Matches: North Auckland 1985, Auckland 1985, Otago 1985, Queensland Country Invitation XV 1988, Queensland B 1988, South Australia Invitation XV 1988, New South Wales 1988, New South Wales B 1988, Orange Free State 1994, Natal 1994 (rep), Western Transvaal 1994, South Africa A 1994

Rank	Matches	Surname	Forename	Position	Period
8=	11	Neary	Tony	**Flanker**	1971-1975

Matches: Waseda University Past and Present 1971, Natal 1972, Western Province 1972, Bantu XV 1972, Northern Transvaal 1972, Taranaki 1973, Canterbury 1973, Western Australia 1975, Sydney 1975, New South Wales 1975, New South Wales Country 1975

Rank	Matches	Surname	Forename	Position	Period
8=	11	Burton	Mike	Prop	1972-1975

Matches: Western Province 1972, Proteas 1972, Bantu XV 1972, Griqualand West 1972, Taranaki 1973, Wellington 1973, Sydney 1975, New South Wales 1975, New South Wales Country 1975, Queensland 1975, Queensland Country 1975

8= 11 Bainbridge Steve Lock 1981-1985

Matches: Northern Region XV 1981, Buenos Aires Selection 1981, Southern Region XV 1981, Littoral Region XV 1981, US Cougars 1982, Pacific Coast Grizzlies 1982, Mid-Western Rugby Football Union 1982, Poverty Bay 1985, Auckland 1985, Otago 1985, Southland 1985

8= 11 Cooke (2) David **Flanker** 1981-1985

Matches: Northern Region XV 1981, Buenos Aires Selection 1981, Littoral Region XV 1981, Eastern Canada 1982, US Cougars 1982, Western Rugby Football Union 1982, Eastern Rugby Union 1982, North Auckland 1985, Poverty Bay 1985, Auckland 1985, Southland 1985

8= 11 Rees Gary **Flanker** 1984-1991

Matches: Currie Cup 'B' Section 1984, South African Rugby Association 1984, South African Country Districts 1984, Poverty Bay 1985, Otago 1985, Southland 1985, Queensland 1988, New South Wales 1988, New South Wales B 1988, Victorian President's XV 1991, Fiji B 1991

8= 11 Skinner Mickey **Flanker** 1988-1991

Matches: Queensland Country Invitation XV 1988 (rep), Queensland 1988, Queensland B 1988, South Australia Invitation XV 1988, New South Wales 1988, Banco Nación 1990, Cuyo Selection 1990, New South Wales 1991 (rep), Victorian President's XV 1991, Fiji B 1991, Emerging Wallabies 1991

14= 10 Beaumont Bill Lock 1975-1981

Matches: Sydney 1975, New South Wales Country 1975, Queensland 1975, Japan Select 1979, Kyushu 1979, Fiji Juniors 1979, San Isidro Club 1981, Northern Region XV 1981, Buenos Aires Selection 1981, Littoral Region XV 1981

14= 10 Davies (1) Huw Fly half/Centre/Full back 1979-1985

Matches: Japan Select 1979 (rep), Kyushu 1979, Northern Region XV 1981, Buenos Aires Selection 1981, Proteas 1984, Western Province 1984, South African Rugby Association 1984, Poverty Bay 1985, Otago 1985, Southland 1985

14= 10 Swift Tony Wing 1981-1984

Matches: San Isidro Club 1981, Buenos Aires Selection 1981, Eastern Canada 1982, US Cougars 1982, Pacific Coast Grizzlies 1982, Mid-Western Rugby Football Union 1982, Eastern Rugby Union 1982, Proteas 1984, South African Rugby Association 1984, South African Country Districts 1984

14= 10 Hill (1) Richard **Scrum half** 1984-1991

Matches: Currie Cup 'B' Section 1984, Western Province 1984, Poverty Bay 1985, Otago 1985, Southland 1985, Banco Nación 1990, Buenos Aires Selection 1990, Cuyo Selection 1990, New South Wales 1991, Queensland 1991

14= 10 Barley Bryan Centre 1984-1988

Matches: South African Rugby Association 1984, South African Country Districts 1984, Poverty Bay 1985, Auckland 1985, Otago 1985, Southland 1985, Queensland Country Invitation XV 1988, Queensland B 1988, New South Wales 1988, New South Wales B 1988

14= 10 Dooley Wade Lock 1985-1991

Matches: North Auckland 1985, Poverty Bay 1985, Auckland 1985, Southland 1985, Queensland 1988, South Australia Invitation XV 1988, Tucumán Selection 1990, Buenos Aires Selection 1990, New South Wales 1991, Queensland 1991

Rank	Matches	Surname	Forename	Position	Period
14=	10	Ojomoh	Steve	Flanker/Number 8	1994-1998

Matches: Orange Free State 1994, Natal 1994 (rep), Western Transvaal 1994, South Africa A 1994, Eastern Province 1994, Buenos Aires 1997, Argentina A 1997 (rep), Cuyo 1997, New Zealand A 1998, New Zealand Maori 1998 (rep)

21=	9	Cotton	Fran	Prop	1971-1975

Matches: Waseda University Past and Present 1971, Natal 1972, Proteas 1972, Bantu XV 1972, Northern Transvaal 1972, Wellington 1973, Canterbury 1973, Western Australia 1975, Sydney 1975

21=	9	Ripley	Andy	Number 8	1972-1975

Matches: Natal 1972, Western Province 1972, Bantu XV 1972, Northern Transvaal 1972, Taranaki 1973, Canterbury 1973, Sydney 1975, New South Wales 1975, Queensland 1975

21=	9	Preece	Peter	Centre	1972-1975

Matches: Natal 1972, Western Province 1972, Proteas 1972, Northern Transvaal 1972, Taranaki 1973, Western Australia 1975, Sydney 1975, New South Wales 1975, Queensland Country 1975

21=	9	Janion	Jeremy	Centre/Wing	1972-1975

Matches: Western Province 1972, Proteas 1972, Bantu XV 1972, Griqualand West 1972, Taranaki 1973, Wellington 1973, New South Wales Country 1975, Queensland 1975, Queensland Country 1975

21=	9	Morley	Alan	Wing	1972-1975

Matches: Western Province 1972, Bantu XV 1972, Northern Transvaal 1972, Griqualand West 1972, Western Australia 1975, New South Wales 1975, New South Wales Country 1975, Queensland 1975 (rep), Queensland Country 1975

21=	9	Blakeway	Phil	Prop	1975-1984

Matches: Western Australia 1975, Sydney 1975 (rep), New South Wales 1975, Queensland 1975 (rep), Queensland Country 1975, Pacific Coast Grizzlies 1982, Mid-Western Rugby Football Union 1982, Proteas 1984, Western Province 1984

21=	9	Winterbottom	Peter	Flanker	1982-1991

Matches: Pacific Coast Grizzlies 1982, Mid-Western Rugby Football Union 1982, Proteas 1984, Western Province 1984, Tucumán Selection 1990, Buenos Aires Selection 1990, New South Wales 1991, Queensland 1991, Emerging Wallabies 1991

21=	9	Moore	Brian	**Hooker**	1988-1994

Matches: Queensland Country Invitation XV 1988 (rep), Queensland 1988, New South Wales 1988, Banco Nación 1990, Cuyo Selection 1990, New South Wales 1991, Queensland 1991, Natal 1994, Transvaal 1994

29=	8	Uttley	Roger	Lock/Flanker/Number 8	1971-1975

Matches: Waseda University Past and Present 1971, Wellington 1973, Canterbury 1973, Western Australia 1975, Sydney 1975, New South Wales 1975, New South Wales Country 1975, Queensland 1975

29=	8	Pullin	John	Hooker	1972-1975

Matches: Natal 1972, Western Province 1972, Northern Transvaal 1972, Taranaki 1973, Canterbury 1973, Western Australia 1975, New South Wales 1975, Queensland 1975

29=	8	Old	Alan	Fly half/Centre	1972-1975

Matches: Natal 1972, Western Province 1972, Bantu XV 1972, Northern Transvaal 1972, Griqualand West 1972, Wellington 1973, Canterbury 1973, Queensland Country 1975

Rank	Matches	Surname	Forename	Position	Period
29=	8	Squires	Peter	Wing	1973-1979

Matches: Wellington 1973, Canterbury 1973, Western Australia 1975, Sydney 1975, New South Wales 1975, New South Wales Country 1975 (rep), Queensland 1975, Fiji Juniors 1979

29=	8	Jeavons	Nick	Flanker	1981-1982

Matches: San Isidro Club 1981, Buenos Aires Selection 1981, Southern Region XV 1981, Littoral Region XV 1981, Eastern Canada 1982, US Cougars 1982 (rep), Pacific Coast Grizzlies 1982, Eastern Rugby Union 1982

29=	8	Mills	Steve	Hooker	1981-1984

Matches: Northern Region XV 1981, Buenos Aires Selection 1981, Eastern Canada 1982, US Cougars 1982, Western Rugby Football Union 1982, Eastern Rugby Union 1982, Currie Cup 'B' Section 1984, Western Province 1984

29=	8	Melville	Nigel	Scrum half	1981-1985

Matches: Northern Region XV 1981, Southern Region XV 1981, Littoral Region XV 1981, US Cougars 1982, Western Rugby Football Union 1982, Eastern Rugby Union 1982, North Auckland 1985, Auckland 1985

29=	8	Stringer	Nick	**Full back**	1982-1984

Matches: Eastern Canada 1982, US Cougars 1982, Western Rugby Football Union 1982, Mid-Western Rugby Football Union 1982 (rep), Eastern Rugby Union 1982, Currie Cup 'B' Section 1984, South African Rugby Association 1984, South African Country Districts 1984

29=	8	Preedy	Malcolm	Prop	1982-1985

Matches: US Cougars 1982, Western Rugby Football Union 1982, Eastern Rugby Union 1982, Proteas 1984, Western Province 1984, Poverty Bay 1985, Auckland 1985, Southland 1985

29=	8	Hall	Jon	Flanker	1984-1991

Matches: Currie Cup 'B' Section 1984, Western Province 1984, South African Rugby Association 1984, North Auckland 1985, Auckland 1985, Otago 1985, New South Wales 1991, Fiji B 1991

29=	8	Teague	Mike	Flanker/Number 8	1984-1991

Matches: Proteas 1984, South African Rugby Association 1984, South African Country Districts 1984, Poverty Bay 1985, Auckland 1985, New South Wales 1991, Queensland 1991, Emerging Wallabies 1991

29=	8	Dawe	Graham	Hooker	1988-1994

Matches: Queensland Country Invitation XV 1988, Queensland B 1988, South Australia Invitation XV 1988, New South Wales B 1988, Orange Free State 1994, Western Transvaal 1994, South Africa A 1994, Eastern Province 1994

29=	8	Underwood	Rory	Wing	1988-1994

Matches: Queensland B 1988, South Australia Invitation XV 1988, New South Wales 1988, New South Wales 1991, Queensland 1991, Natal 1994, Transvaal 1994, Eastern Province 1994 (rep)

29=	8	Carling	Will	Centre	1988-1994

Matches: New South Wales B 1988, Banco Nación 1990, Buenos Aires Selection 1990, New South Wales 1991, Queensland 1991, Natal 1994, Western Transvaal 1994, Transvaal 1994

29=	8	Clarke	Ben	Flanker/Number 8	1994-2000

Matches: Natal 1994, Western Transvaal 1994, Transvaal 1994, Córdoba 1997, Buenos Aires 1997, New Zealand A 1998, North West Leopards 2000, Griqualand West 2000

Rank Matches Surname Forename Position Period

29= 8 *King* Alex Fly half 1997-2003

Matches: Buenos Aires 1997, Argentina A 1997, Cuyo 1997, New Zealand Academy 1998, New Zealand Maori 1998, British Columbia 2001 (rep), USA A 2001, New Zealand Maori 2003 (rep)

45= 7 Webster Jan Scrum half 1971-1973

Matches: Waseda University Past and Present 1971, Natal 1972, Western Province 1972, Bantu XV 1972 (rep), Northern Transvaal 1972, Taranaki 1973, Canterbury 1973

45= 7 Watkins (1) John Flanker 1972-1973

Matches: Natal 1972, Proteas 1972, Northern Transvaal 1972, Griqualand West 1972, Taranaki 1973, Wellington 1973, Canterbury 1973

45= 7 Ralston Chris Lock 1972-1973

Matches: Western Province 1972, Proteas 1972, Bantu XV 1972, Griqualand West 1972, Taranaki 1973, Wellington 1973, Canterbury 1973

45= 7 Smith (1) Steve Scrum half 1972-1982

Matches: Griqualand West 1972, Wellington 1973, San Isidro Club 1981, Buenos Aires Selection 1981, Easter Canada 1982, Pacific Coast Grizzlies 1982, Mid-Western Rugby Football Union 1982

45= 7 Colclough Maurice Lock 1979-1982

Matches: Japan Select 1979, Fiji Juniors 1979, Eastern Canada 1982, Pacific Coast Grizzlies 1982, Western Rugby Football Union 1982, Mid-Western Rugby Football Union 1982, Eastern Rugby Union 1982

45= 7 Hare Dusty Full back 1979-1984

Matches: Fiji Juniors 1979, San Isidro Club 1981, Buenos Aires Selection 1981, Pacific Coast Grizzlies 1982, Mid-Western Rugby Football Union 1982, Proteas 1984, Western Province 1984

45= 7 Hesford Bob Number 8 1981-1985

Matches: Northern Region XV 1981, Buenos Aires Selection 1981 (rep), Southern Region XV 1981, Littoral Region XV 1981, North Auckland 1985, Otago 1985, Southland 1985

45= 7 Trick David Wing 1981-1984

Matches: Northern Region XV 1981, Southern Region XV 1981, Littoral Region XV 1981, Currie Cup 'B' Section 1984, Western Province 1984, South African Rugby Association 1984, South African Country Districts 1984

45= 7 Orwin John Lock 1985-1988

Matches: North Auckland 1985, Otago 1985, Queensland Country Invitation XV 1988, Queensland 1988, Queensland B 1988, New South Wales 1988, New South Wales B 1988

45= 7 Richards Dean Number 8 1988-1994

Matches: Queensland Country Invitation XV 1988, Queensland 1988, New South Wales 1988, Victorian President's XV 1991, Queensland 1991, Natal 1994, Transvaal 1994

45= 7 Robinson Andy Flanker 1988-1990

Matches: Queensland Country Invitation XV 1988, Queensland B 1988, South Australia Invitation XV 1988, New South Wales B 1988, Banco Nación 1990, Cuyo Selection 1990, Córdoba 1990

45= 7 Egerton Dave Number 8 1988-1990

Matches: Queensland Country Invitation XV 1988, Queensland B 1988, South Australia Invitation XV 1988, New South Wales B 1988, Banco Nación 1990, Buenos Aires Selection 1990, Córdoba 1990

Rank Matches Surname Forename Position Period

45= 7 Andrew Rob Fly half 1988-1994
Matches: Queensland 1988, South Australia Invitation XV 1988, New South Wales 1988, New South Wales 1991, Queensland 1991, Natal 1994, Transvaal 1994

45= 7 Ubogu Victor Prop 1990-1999
Matches: Banco Nación 1990, Buenos Aires Selection 1990, Córdoba 1990, Natal 1994, Transvaal 1994, Eastern Province 1994 (rep), Queensland Reds 1999 (rep)

45= 7 Pears David Fly half/Full back 1990-1994
Matches: Banco Nación 1990, Tucumán Selection 1990, Buenos Aires Selection 1990, Victorian President's XV 1991, Fiji B 1991, Emerging Wallabies 1991, Natal 1994

45= 7 Leonard Jason Prop 1990-1999
Matches: Tucumán Selection 1990, Buenos Aires Selection 1990, New South Wales 1991, Queensland 1991, Natal 1994, Transvaal 1994, Queensland Reds 1999

45= 7 Rodber Tim Lock/Flanker/Number 8 1990-1999
Matches: Tucumán Selection 1990, Cuyo Selection 1990, Córdoba 1990, Natal 1994, Transvaal 1994, Eastern Province 1994 (rep), Queensland Reds 1999

45= 7 Underwood Tony Wing 1990-1994
Matches: Tucumán Selection 1990, Cuyo Selection 1990, Córdoba 1990, Orange Free State 1994 (rep), Natal 1994, Western Transvaal 1994, Transvaal 1994

45= 7 Hull Paul Fly half/Full back 1990-1994
Matches: Buenos Aires Selection 1990, Cuyo Selection 1990, Córdoba 1990, Orange Free State 1994, Western Transvaal 1994, Transvaal 1994, Eastern Province 1994

45= 7 Hopley Damian Centre/Wing 1991-1994
Matches: Victorian President's XV 1991, Fiji B 1991, Emerging Wallabies 1991, Orange Free State 1994, Western Transvaal 1994, South Africa A 1994, Eastern Province 1994

45= 7 Corry Martin Lock/Flanker/Number 8 1997-2003
Matches: Buenos Aires 1997 (rep), Argentina A 1997, Cuyo 1997 (rep), Queensland Reds 1999, Griqualand West 2000 (rep), Gauteng Falcons 2000, New Zealand Maori 2003

45= 7 Worsley Joe Flanker/Number 8 1999-2010
Matches: Queensland Reds 1999 (rep), North West Leopards 2000, Griqualand West 2000, Gauteng Falcons 2000, New Zealand Maori 2003, Australian Barbarians (Perth) 2010 (rep), Australian Barbarians (Gosford) 2010

45= 7 *Flatman* David Prop 2000-2010
Matches: North West Leopards 2000, Gauteng Falcons 2000 (rep), British Columbia 2001 (rep), USA A 2001, Australian Barbarians (Perth) 2010, Australian Barbarians (Gosford) 2010 (rep), New Zealand Maori 2010

68= 6 Stevens Stack Prop 1972-1973
Matches: Natal 1972, Western Province 1972, Northern Transvaal 1972, Griqualand West 1972, Taranaki 1973, Canterbury 1973

68= 6 **Raphael** Jon Hooker 1975-1979
Matches: Sydney 1975, New South Wales Country 1975, Queensland Country 1975, Japan Select 1979, Kyushu 1979, Fiji Juniors 1979

68= 6 **Simpson** Andy Hooker 1981-1985
Matches: San Isidro Club 1981, Southern Region XV 1981, Littoral Region XV 1981, Poverty Bay 1985, Otago 1985, Southland 1985

68= 6 Horton John Fly half 1981-1984
Matches: San Isidro Club 1981, Southern Region XV 1981, Littoral Region XV 1981, Currie Cup 'B' Section 1984, Western Province 1984, South African Country Districts 1984

Rank Matches Surname Forename Position Period

68= 6 Woodward Clive Centre 1981-1982
Matches: San Isidro Club 1981, Buenos Aires Selection 1981, Eastern Canada 1982, US Cougars 1982, Pacific Coast Grizzlies 1982, Mid-Western Rugby Football Union 1982

68= 6 **Poole** Matt Lock 1990-1994
Matches: Banco Nación 1990, Cuyo Selection 1990, Córdoba 1990, Orange Free State 1994, South Africa A 1994, Eastern Province 1994

68= 6 Oti Chris Wing 1990-1991
Matches: Banco Nación 1990, Tucumán Selection 1990, Buenos Aires Selection 1990, Córdoba 1990, Victorian President's XV 1991, Queensland 1991

68= 6 Olver John Hooker 1990-1991
Matches: Tucumán Selection 1990, Buenos Aires Selection 1990, Córdoba 1990, Victorian President's XV 1991, Fiji B 1991, Emerging Wallabies 1991

68= 6 Ryan Dean Number 8 1990-1994
Matches: Tucumán Selection 1990, Buenos Aires Selection 1990, Orange Free State 1994, Western Transvaal 1994, South Africa A 1994, Eastern Province 1994

68= 6 Morris Dewi Scrum half 1990-1994
Matches: Tucumán Selection 1990, Victorian President's XV 1991, Fiji B 1991, Emerging Wallabies 1991, Natal 1994, Transvaal 1994

68= 6 Hodgkinson Simon Full back 1990-1991
Matches: Tucumán Selection 1990, Cuyo Selection 1990, Victorian President's XV 1991, Queensland 1991, Fiji B 1991 (rep), Emerging Wallabies 1991

68= 6 Bates Steve Scrum half 1990-1994
Matches: Córdoba 1990, Orange Free State 1994, Western Transvaal 1994, Transvaal 1994 (rep), South Africa A 1994, Eastern Province 1994

68= 6 Rowntree Graham Prop 1994-2000
Matches: Orange Free State 1994, Western Transvaal 1994, South Africa A 1994, Eastern Province 1994, Griqualand West 2000, Gauteng Falcons 2000

68= 6 Catt Mike Fly half/Centre/Full back 1994-1999
Matches: Orange Free State 1994, South Africa A 1994, Eastern Province 1994, Córdoba 1997, Argentina A 1997 (rep), Queensland Reds 1999

68= 6 *Shaw* Simon Lock 1994-2003
Matches: South Africa A 1994, Eastern Province 1994, North West Leopards 2000, Gauteng Falcons 2000 (rep), British Columbia 2001 (rep), New Zealand Maori 2003

68= 6 Garforth Darren Prop 1997-2000
Matches: Córdoba 1997, Argentina A 1997, Queensland Reds 1999, North West Leopards 2000, Griqualand West 2000 (rep), Gauteng Falcons 2000

68= 6 Baxendell Jos Fly half/Centre 1997-1998
Matches: Buenos Aires 1997 (rep), Argentina A 1997, Cuyo 1997, New Zealand A 1998, New Zealand Academy 1998, New Zealand Maori 1998

85= 5 Larter Peter Lock 1971-1972
Matches: Waseda University Past and Present 1971, Natal 1972, Western Province 1972, Bantu XV 1972, Northern Transvaal 1972

85= 5 Knight (1) Peter Wing/Full back 1972-1973
Matches: Natal 1972, Western Province 1972, Northern Transvaal 1972, Taranaki 1973, Wellington 1973

Rank	Matches	Surname	Forename	Position	Period
85=	5	Wilkinson	Bob	Lock	1973-1975

Matches: Wellington 1973, Western Australia 1975, New South Wales Country 1975, Queensland 1975, Queensland Country 1975

85=	5	Bennett	Neil	Fly half	1975-1979

Matches: Western Australia 1975, New South Wales 1975, New South Wales Country 1975, Japan Select 1979, Fiji Juniors 1979

85=	5	Hignell	Alastair	Full back	1975-1979

Matches: Western Australia 1975, New South Wales Country 1975, Queensland 1975, Japan Select 1979, Kyushu 1979

85=	5	Smart	Colin	Prop	1979-1981

Matches: Japan Select 1979, Kyushu 1979 (rep), San Isidro Club 1981, Northern Region XV 1981 (rep), Buenos Aires Selection 1981

85=	5	**Gadd**	John	Flanker	1982-1982

Matches: Eastern Canada 1982, US Cougars 1982, Western Rugby Football Union 1982, Mid-Western Rugby Football Union 1982, Eastern Rugby Union 1982

85=	5	**McDowell**	Neil	Centre	1982-1982

Matches: US Cougars 1982, Pacific Coast Grizzlies 1982, Western Rugby Union 1982, Mid-Western Rugby Football Union 1982, Eastern Rugby Union 1982

85=	5	Brain	Steve	Hooker	1984-1985

Matches: Proteas 1984, South African Rugby Association 1984, South African Country Districts 1984, North Auckland 1985, Auckland 1985

85=	5	Chilcott	Gareth	Prop	1988-1988

Matches: Queensland Country Invitation XV 1988, Queensland B 1988, South Australia Invitation XV 1988, New South Wales 1988, New South Wales B 1988

85=	5	Evans	Barry	Wing	1988-1988

Matches: Queensland Country Invitation XV 1988, Queensland 1988, Queensland B 1988, South Australia Invitation XV 1988, New South Wales 1988

85=	5	Buckton	John	Centre	1988-1990

Matches: Queensland Country Invitation XV 1988, Queensland 1988, Banco Nación 1990, Tucumán Selection 1990, Cuyo Selection 1990

85=	5	Probyn	Jeff	Prop	1988-1991

Matches: Queensland 1988, Tucumán Selection 1990, Cuyo Selection 1990, New South Wales 1991, Victorian President's XV 1991

85=	5	Halliday	Simon	Centre	1988-1991

Matches: Queensland 1988, Queensland B 1988, Victorian President's XV 1991, Fiji B 1991, Emerging Wallabies 1991

85=	5	Heslop	Nigel	Wing	1990-1991

Matches: Banco Nación 1990, Buenos Aires Selection 1990, New South Wales 1991, Fiji B 1991, Emerging Wallabies 1991

85=	5	Mallett	John	Prop	1994-1997

Matches: Orange Free State 1994, Western Transvaal 1994, South Africa A 1994, Eastern Province 1994, Buenos Aires 1997

85=	5	Adebayo	Adedayo	Wing	1994-1997

Matches: Orange Free State 1994, South Africa A 1994, Eastern Province 1994, Córdoba 1997, Cuyo 1997

Rank	Matches	Surname	Forename	Position	Period
85=	5	Potter	Stuart	Centre	1994-1998

Matches: Orange Free State 1994, Western Transvaal 1994, South Africa A 1994, Eastern Province 1994, New Zealand Academy 1998

85=	5	Greening	Phil	Hooker	1997-2000

Matches: Córdoba 1997, New Zealand A 1998, New Zealand Maori 1998, Queensland Reds 1999 (rep), North West Leopards 2000

85=	5	Diprose	Tony	Number 8	1997-1998

Matches: Córdoba 1997 (rep), Buenos Aires 1997, Argentina A 1997, New Zealand Academy 1998, New Zealand Maori 1998

85=	5	Rees (2)	David	Wing	1997-2002

Matches: Buenos Aires 1997, Argentina A 1997, British Columbia 2001, USA A 2001, Argentina A 2002

85=	5	Fidler	Rob	Lock	1998-2002

Matches: New Zealand A 1998, New Zealand Academy 1998, New Zealand Maori 1998, USA A 2001, Argentina A 2002

85=	5	Lewsey	Josh	Fly half/Centre/Wing/Full back	1998-2000

Matches: New Zealand A 1998, New Zealand Academy 1998 (rep), North West Leopards 2000 (rep), Griqualand West 2000 (rep), Gauteng Falcons 2000

85=	5	Stimpson	Tim	Full back	1998-2002

Matches: New Zealand Academy 1998, New Zealand Maori 1998, North West Leopards 2000, British Columbia 2001 (rep), Argentina A 2002 (rep)

85=	5	Walshe	Nick	Scrum half	2000-2002

Matches: North West Leopards 2000 (rep), Griqualand West 2000 (rep), Gauteng Falcons 2000, USA A 2001, Argentina A 2002

85=	5	Regan	Mark	Hooker	2000-2003

Matches: Griqualand West 2000, Gauteng Falcons 2000 (rep), USA A 2001, Argentina A 2002, New Zealand Maori 2003 (rep)

111=	4	Wheeler	Peter	Hooker	1971-1982

Matches: Waseda University Past and Present 1971, Eastern Canada 1982 (rep), Pacific Coast Grizzlies 1982, Mid-Western Rugby Football Union 1982

111=	4	Watt	Dave	Lock	1972-1972

Matches: Natal 1972, Proteas 1972, Northern Transvaal 1972, Griqualand West 1972

111=	4	**Richards**	Tony	Wing	1972-1972

Matches: Natal 1972, Proteas 1972, Bantu XV 1972, Griqualand West 1972

111=	4	Doble	Sam	Full back	1972-1972

Matches: Natal 1972, Western Province 1972, Bantu XV 1972, Northern Transvaal 1972

111=	4	Mantell	Neil	Lock	1975-1975

Matches: Western Australia 1975, Sydney 1975 (rep), New South Wales 1975, Queensland Country 1975

111=	4	Rollitt	Dave	Number 8	1975-1975

Matches: Western Australia 1975, New South Wales 1975, Queensland 1975, Queensland Country 1975

111=	4	Maxwell (1)	Andy	Centre	1975-1975

Matches: Western Australia 1975, New South Wales 1975, New South Wales Country 1975, Queensland 1975

Rank	Matches	Surname	Forename	Position	Period
111=	4	Wyatt	Derek	Wing	1975-1975

Matches: Sydney 1975, New South Wales Country 1975, Queensland 1975, Queensland Country 1975

111=	4	Fidler	John	Lock	1981-1984

Matches: San Isidro Club 1981, Southern Region XV 1981, Currie Cup 'B' Section 1984, Western Province 1984

111=	4	Syddall	Jim	Lock	1982-1982

Matches: Eastern Canada 1982, US Cougars 1982, Western Rugby Football Union 1982, Eastern Rugby Union 1982

111=	4	Cusworth	Les	Fly half	1982-1982

Matches: Eastern Canada 1982, Pacific Coast Grizzlies 1982, Mid-Western Rugby Football Union 1982, Eastern Rugby Union 1982 (rep)

111=	4	Butcher	Chris	Number 8	1984-1984

Matches: Currie Cup 'B' Section 1984, Proteas 1984, Western Province 1984, South African Country Districts 1984

111=	4	Smith (1)	Simon	Wing	1985-1985

Matches: North Auckland 1985, Poverty Bay 1985 (rep), Auckland 1985, Otago 1985 (rep)

111=	4	**Robson**	Simon	Scrum half	1988-1988

Matches: Queensland Country Invitation XV 1988, Queensland B 1988, South Australia Invitation XV 1988, New South Wales B 1988

111=	4	**Adamson**	Ray	Full back	1988-1988

Matches: Queensland Country Invitation XV 1988, Queensland B 1988, South Australia Invitation XV 1988, New South Wales B 1988

111=	4	Webb	Jonathan	Full back	1988-1991

Matches: Queensland 1988, New South Wales 1988, New South Wales 1991, Fiji B 1991

111=	4	**Liley**	John	Full back	1990-1990

Matches: Banco Nación 1990, Tucumán Selection 1990 (rep), Cuyo Selection 1990, Córdoba 1990

111=	4	Guscott	Jeremy	Centre	1991-1999

Matches: New South Wales 1991, Queensland 1991, Fiji B 1991 (rep), Queensland Reds 1999

111=	4	Bayfield	Martin	Lock	1991-1994

Matches: Victorian President's XV 1991, Fiji B 1991, Orange Free State 1994, Western Transvaal 1994

111=	4	de Glanville	Phil	Centre	1994-1997

Matches: Natal 1994, Transvaal 1994, Córdoba 1997, Buenos Aires 1997

111=	4	Cockerill	Richard	Hooker	1997-1999

Matches: Buenos Aires 1997, Argentina A 1997, New Zealand Academy 1998 (rep), Queensland Reds 1999

111=	4	*Gomarsall*	Andy	Scrum half	1997-2003

Matches: Buenos Aires 1997, Argentina A 1997, Cuyo 1997, New Zealand Maori 2003 (rep)

111=	4	Green (1)	Will	Prop	1997-2000

Matches: Cuyo 1997, New Zealand A 1998, North West Leopards 2000 (rep), Griqualand West 2000

111=	4	Lloyd	Leon	Centre/Wing	1999-2000

Matches: Queensland Reds 1999, North West Leopards 2000, Griqualand West 2000, Gauteng Falcons 2000 (rep)

Rank	Matches	Surname	Forename	Position	Period
111=	4	*Borthwick*	Steve	Lock	2000-2003

Matches: North West Leopards 2000, Griqualand West 2000, Gauteng Falcons 2000, New Zealand Maori 2003

111=	4	***Volley***	Paul	Flanker	2000-2003

Matches: North West Leopards 2000, Griqualand West 2000 (rep), Gauteng Falcons 2000, New Zealand Maori 2003 (rep)

111=	4	*Long*	Andy	Hooker	2000-2001

Matches: North West Leopards 2000 (rep), Griqualand West 2000 (rep), Gauteng Falcons 2000, British Columbia 2001 (rep)

111=	4	Woodman	Trevor	Prop	2001-2003

Matches: British Columbia 2001, USA A 2001 (rep), Argentina A 2002, New Zealand Maori 2003

111=	4	*Barkley*	Olly	Fly half/Centre	2001-2010

Matches: British Columbia 2001, USA A 2001, Australian Barbarians (Perth) 2010, Australian Barbarians (Gosford) 2010

140=	3	Rossborough	Peter	Full back	1971-1973

Matches: Waseda University Past and Present 1971, Taranaki 1973, Canterbury 1973

140=	3	Spencer	John	Centre	1972-1972

Matches: Natal 1972, Proteas 1972, Griqualand West 1972

140=	3	**Cowell**	Tim	Flanker	1972-1972

Matches: Western Province 1972, Proteas 1972, Griqualand West 1972

140=	3	**Boddy**	Tony	Hooker	1972-1972

Matches: Proteas 1972, Bantu XV 1972, Griqualand West 1972

140=	3	Barton	John	Lock/Number 8	1972-1972

Matches: Proteas 1972, Bantu XV 1972, Griqualand West 1972

140=	3	**Palmer (1)**	Tom	Fly half	1972-1972

Matches: Proteas 1972, Bantu XV 1972, Northern Transvaal 1972

140=	3	Evans (2)	Geoff	Centre	1973-1973

Matches: Taranaki 1973 (rep), Wellington 1973, Canterbury 1973

140=	3	**Callum**	Steve	Flanker	1975-1975

Matches: Sydney 1975, New South Wales Country 1975, Queensland Country 1975

140=	3	Kingston	Peter	Scrum half	1975-1975

Matches: Sydney 1975, New South Wales 1975, Queensland Country 1975

140=	3	Butler	Peter	Full back	1975-1975

Matches: Sydney 1975, New South Wales 1975, Queensland Country 1975

140=	3	**Doubleday**	John	Prop	1979-1979

Matches: Japan Select 1979, Kyushu 1979, Fiji Juniors 1979

140=	3	**Allchurch**	Toby	Flanker	1979-1979

Matches: Japan Select 1979, Kyushu 1979, Fiji Juniors 1979

140=	3	**Butler**	John	Lock	1979-1979

Matches: Japan Select 1979 (rep), Kyushu 1979, Fiji Juniors 1979

140=	3	**McGregor**	Clint	Prop	1981-1981

Matches: San Isidro Club 1981, Southern Region XV 1981, Littoral Region XV 1981

140=	3	Preston	Nick	Centre	1981-1981

Matches: Northern Region XV 1981, Southern Region XV 1981, Littoral Region XV 1981

140=	3	**Patrick**	Brian	Full back	1981-1981

Matches: Northern Region XV 1981, Southern Region XV 1981, Littoral Region XV 1981

Rank	Matches	Surname	Forename	Position	Period
140=	3	Williams	Peter	Fly half/Full back	1982-1982

Matches: US Cougars 1982, Western Rugby Football Union 1982, Eastern Rugby Union 1982

140=	3	**Holdstock**	Steve	Wing	1982-1982

Matches: US Cougars 1982, Western Rugby Football Union 1982, Eastern Rugby Union 1982

140=	3	Bailey	Mark	Wing	1984-1984

Matches: Currie Cup 'B' Section 1984, Proteas 1984, Western Province 1984

140=	3	Palmer	John	Centre	1984-1984

Matches: Currie Cup 'B' Section 1984, Proteas 1984 (rep), Western Province 1984

140=	3	Cusani	Dave	Lock/Number 8	1984-1984

Matches: Proteas 1984, South African Rugby Association 1984, South African Country Districts 1984

140=	3	Youngs	Nick	Scrum half	1984-1984

Matches: Proteas 1984, South African Rugby Association 1984, South African Country Districts 1984

140=	3	**Burnhill**	Steve	Centre	1984-1984

Matches: Proteas 1984, South African Rugby Association 1984, South African Country Districts 1984

140=	3	**Goodwin**	John	Wing	1985-1985

Matches: North Auckland 1985, Poverty Bay 1985, Southland 1985

140=	3	Salmon	Jamie	Centre	1985-1985

Matches: North Auckland 1985, Otago 1985, Southland 1985

140=	3	Martin	Chris	Full back	1985-1985

Matches: North Auckland 1985, Otago 1985, Southland 1985

140=	3	Sheppard	Austin	Prop	1985-1985

Matches: Poverty Bay 1985, Otago 1985, Southland 1985

140=	3	Harrison	Mike	Wing	1985-1985

Matches: Poverty Bay 1985, Auckland 1985, Otago 1985

140=	3	**Metcalfe**	Ian	Full back	1985-1985

Matches: Poverty Bay 1985, Auckland 1985, Southland 1985

140=	3	Bentley	John	Wing	1988-1988

Matches: Queensland Country Invitation XV 1988, Queensland 1988, New South Wales B 1988

140=	3	Linnett	Mark	Prop	1990-1990

Matches: Banco Nación 1990, Cuyo Selection 1990, Córdoba 1990

140=	3	**Kimmins**	Bob	Lock	1990-1990

Matches: Banco Nación 1990, Cuyo Selection 1990, Córdoba 1990

140=	3	**Thompson**	Gavin	Centre/Wing	1990-1990

Matches: Tucumán Selection 1990, Buenos Aires Selection 1990, Córdoba 1990

140=	3	Ackford	Paul	Lock	1991-1991

Matches: New South Wales 1991, Queensland 1991, Emerging Wallabies 1991

140=	3	Hunter	Ian	Wing/Full back	1991-1991

Matches: Victorian President's XV 1991, Fiji B 1991, Emerging Wallabies 1991

140=	3	Dallaglio	Lawrence	Flanker/Number 8	1994-1994

Matches: Orange Free State 1994, South Africa A 1994, Eastern Province 1994

Rank	Matches	Surname	Forename	Position	Period
140=	3	Johnson	Martin	Lock	1994-1999

Matches: Natal 1994, Transvaal 1994, Queensland Reds 1999

140=	3	Callard	Jon	Full back	1994-1994

Matches: Western Transvaal 1994 (rep), South Africa A 1994, Eastern Province 1994

140=	3	Hardwick	Rob	Prop	1997-1997

Matches: Córdoba 1997, Argentina A 1997 (rep), Cuyo 1997

140=	3	**Jenkins**	Rory	Flanker	1997-1997

Matches: Córdoba 1997, Argentina A 1997, Cuyo 1997

140=	3	Bracken	Kyran	Scrum half	1997-2003

Matches: Córdoba 1997, Queensland Reds 1999, New Zealand Maori 2003

140=	3	Greenstock	Nick	Centre	1997-1997

Matches: Córdoba 1997, Buenos Aires 1997, Cuyo 1997 (rep)

140=	3	Mallinder	Jim	Full back	1997-1997

Matches: Córdoba 1997, Buenos Aires 1997, Cuyo 1997 (rep)

140=	3	Mapletoft	Mark	Fly half/Full back	1997-1997

Matches: Buenos Aires 1997 (rep), Argentina A 1997, Cuyo 1997

140=	3	Grewcock	Danny	Lock	1997-1999

Matches: Argentina A 1997, Cuyo 1997, Queensland Reds 1999 (rep)

140=	3	**Windo**	Tony	Prop	1998-1998

Matches: New Zealand A 1998, New Zealand Academy 1998, New Zealand Maori 1998

140=	3	Sanderson	Pat	Flanker	1998-2001

Matches: New Zealand A 1998, British Columbia 2001 (rep), USA A 2001

140=	3	**Moore**	Matt	Wing	1998-1998

Matches: New Zealand A 1998, New Zealand Academy 1998, New Zealand Maori 1998

140=	3	Beim	Tom	Wing	1998-2002

Matches: New Zealand A 1998, New Zealand Maori 1998 (rep), Argentina A 2002

140=	3	*Crompton*	Darren	Prop	1998-1998

Matches: New Zealand A 1998 (rep), New Zealand Academy 1998, New Zealand Maori 1998

140=	3	*Chuter*	George	Hooker	1998-2010

Matches: New Zealand Academy 1998, Australian Barbarians (Perth) 2010 (rep), New Zealand Maori 2010

140=	3	*Benton*	Scott	Scrum half	1998-2001

Matches: New Zealand Academy 1998, New Zealand Maori 1998 (rep), British Columbia 2001

140=	3	Luger	Dan	Wing	1999-2003

Matches: Queensland Reds 1999, North West Leopards 2000, New Zealand Maori 2003

140=	3	**Hepher**	Ali	Fly half	2000-2000

Matches: North West Leopards 2000, Griqualand West 2000, Gauteng Falcons 2000

140=	3	*Johnston*	Ben	Centre	2000-2003

Matches: North West Leopards 2000, Gauteng Falcons 2000, New Zealand Maori 2003 (rep)

140=	3	*Sheridan*	Andy	Prop/Lock	2000-2000

Matches: North West Leopards 2000 (rep), Griqualand West 2000, Gauteng Falcons 2000

140=	3	***Thirlby***	Rob	Wing/Full back	2000-2000

Matches: North West Leopards 2000 (rep), Griqualand West 2000, Gauteng Falcons 2000

Rank **Matches** **Surname** **Forename** **Position** **Period**

140= 3 *Palmer (2)* Tom Lock 2001-2003
Matches: British Columbia 2001, USA A 2001, New Zealand Maori 2003 (rep)

140= 3 *Hazell* Andy Flanker 2001-2003
Matches: British Columbia 2001, USA A 2001, New Zealand Maori 2003

140= 3 Sanderson Alex Flanker/Number 8 2001-2002
Matches: British Columbia 2001, USA A 2001, Argentina A 2002 (rep)

140= 3 ***Attwood*** Dave Lock 2010-2010
Matches: Australian Barbarians (Perth) 2010, Australian Barbarians (Gosford) 2010, New Zealand Maori 2010

140= 3 **Ward-Smith** Dan Lock/Flanker/Number 8 2010-2010
Matches: Australian Barbarians (Perth) 2010, Australian Barbarians (Gosford) 2010, New Zealand Maori 2010 (rep)

140= 3 *Hodgson* Charlie Fly half 2010-2010
Matches: Australian Barbarians (Perth) 2010, Australian Barbarians (Gosford) 2010, New Zealand Maori 2010

140= 3 *Tait* Matt Centre/Wing/Full back 2010-2010
Matches: Australian Barbarians (Perth) 2010, Australian Barbarians (Gosford) 2010 (rep), New Zealand Maori 2010

140= 3 *Armitage* Delon Centre/Wing/Full back 2010-2010
Matches: Australian Barbarians (Perth) 2010, Australian Barbarians (Gosford) 2010, New Zealand Maori 2010

140= 3 *Doran-Jones* Paul Prop 2010-2010
Matches: Australian Barbarians (Perth) 2010 (rep), Australian Barbarians (Gosford) 2010, New Zealand Maori 2010

140= 3 *Geraghty* Shane Fly half/Centre 2010-2010
Matches: Australian Barbarians (Perth) 2010 (rep), Australian Barbarians (Gosford) 2010 (rep), New Zealand Maori 2010 (rep)

207= 2 Weston Lionel Scrum half 1972-1972
Matches: Proteas 1972, Bantu XV 1972

207= 2 **Whibley** Dave Full back 1972-1972
Matches: Proteas 1972, Griqualand West 1972

207= 2 Cooper Martin Fly half 1973-1973
Matches: Taranaki 1973, Canterbury 1973

207= 2 Duckham David Centre/Wing 1973-1973
Matches: Taranaki 1973, Canterbury 1973

207= 2 Wordsworth Nellie Fly half 1975-1975
Matches: Sydney 1975, Queensland 1975

207= 2 Nelmes Barry Prop 1975-1975
Matches: New South Wales Country 1975, Queensland 1975

207= 2 **Orum** Ian Scrum half 1975-1975
Matches: New South Wales Country 1975, Queensland 1975

207= 2 Mordell Bob Flanker 1979-1979
Matches: Japan Select 1979, Fiji Juniors 1979

207= 2 **Peck** Ian Scrum half 1979-1979
Matches: Japan Select 1979, Kyushu 1979

207= 2 Slemen Mike Wing 1979-1979
Matches: Japan Select 1979, Kyushu 1979

Rank	Matches	Surname	Forename	Position	Period
207=	2	**McMillan**	Alan	Centre	1979-1979

Matches: Japan Select 1979, Kyushu 1979

207=	2	Cardus	Richard	Centre	1979-1979

Matches: Kyushu 1979, Fiji Juniors 1979

207=	2	Rafter	Mike	Flanker	1981-1981

Matches: San Isidro Club 1981, Southern Region XV 1981

207=	2	Bond	Tony	Centre	1982-1982

Matches: Eastern Canada 1982, Western Rugby Union 1982

207=	2	Huntsman	Paul	Prop	1985-1985

Matches: North Auckland 1985, Otago 1985

207=	2	Harding	Richard	Scrum half	1988-1988

Matches: Queensland 1988, New South Wales 1988

207=	2	**Buttimore**	Tim	Centre	1988-1988

Matches: South Australia Invitation XV 1988, New South Wales B 1988

207=	2	**Childs**	Graham	Centre	1990-1990

Matches: Cuyo Selection 1990, Córdoba 1990

207=	2	Haag	Martin	Lock	1997-1997

Matches: Córdoba 1997, Argentina A 1997

207=	2	Sheasby	Chris	Flanker/Number 8	1997-1997

Matches: Córdoba 1997, Cuyo 1997

207=	2	Sleightholme	Jon	Wing	1997-1997

Matches: Córdoba 1997, Buenos Aires 1997

207=	2	*Yates*	Kevin	Prop	1997-1997

Matches: Buenos Aires 1997, Argentina A 1997

207=	2	**Baldwin**	Dave	Lock	1997-1997

Matches: Buenos Aires 1997, Cuyo 1997

207=	2	**O'Leary**	Daren	Wing	1997-1997

Matches: Argentina A 1997, Cuyo 1997

207=	2	**Allen**	Matt	Centre	1997-1997

Matches: Argentina A 1997, Cuyo 1997

207=	2	Sims	Dave	Lock	1998-1998

Matches: New Zealand A 1998, New Zealand Academy 1998

207=	2	Dawson	Matt	Scrum half	1998-1999

Matches: New Zealand A 1998, Queensland Reds 1999 (rep)

207=	2	Chapman	Dominic	Wing	1998-1998

Matches: New Zealand A 1998, New Zealand Academy 1998

207=	2	Sturnham	Ben	Flanker	1998-1998

Matches: New Zealand Academy 1998, New Zealand Maori 1998

207=	2	*Moody*	Lewis	Flanker	1998-1998

Matches: New Zealand Academy 1998, New Zealand Maori 1998

207=	2	Pool-Jones	Richard	Flanker	1998-1998

Matches: New Zealand Academy 1998 (rep), New Zealand Maori 1998

207=	2	Richards	Peter	Scrum half/Centre	1998-1998

Matches: New Zealand Academy 1998 (rep), New Zealand Maori 1998

207=	2	Ravenscroft	Steve	Centre	1998-1998

Matches: New Zealand Academy 1998 (rep), New Zealand Maori 1998

Rank Matches Surname Forename Position Period

207= 2 Wood Martyn Scrum half 2000-2000
Matches: North West Leopards 2000, Griqualand West 2000

207= 2 **Botham** Liam Centre/Wing/Full back 2000-2000
Matches: North West Leopards 2000, Griqualand West 2000 (rep)

207= 2 *Winters* Roy Lock/Flanker/Number 8 2000-2000
Matches: North West Leopards 2000 (rep), Griqualand West 2000

207= 2 Greenwood Will Centre 2000-2000
Matches: Griqualand West 2000, Gauteng Falcons 2000

207= 2 Hanley Steve Wing 2000-2000
Matches: Griqualand West 2000, Gauteng Falcons 2000

207= 2 ***Fortey*** Chris Hooker 2001-2001
Matches: British Columbia 2001, USA A 2001 (rep)

207= 2 ***Nebbett*** Ricky Prop 2001-2001
Matches: British Columbia 2001, USA A 2001

207= 2 *Waters* Fraser Centre 2001-2001
Matches: British Columbia 2001, USA A 2001

207= 2 *Sackey* Paul Wing 2001-2001
Matches: British Columbia 2001, USA A 2001

207= 2 *Voyce* Tom Wing/Full back 2001-2001
Matches: British Columbia 2001, USA A 2001

207= 2 *Mears* Lee Hooker 2010-2010
Matches: Australian Barbarians (Perth) 2010, Australian Barbarians (Gosford) 2010

207= 2 ***Parling*** Geoff Lock 2010-2010
Matches: Australian Barbarians (Perth) 2010, New Zealand Maori 2010

207= 2 *Robshaw* Chris Flanker/Number 8 2010-2010
Matches: Australian Barbarians (Perth) 2010, New Zealand Maori 2010

207= 2 *Wigglesworth* Richard Scrum half 2010-2010
Matches: Australian Barbarians (Perth) 2010, Australian Barbarians (Gosford) 2010

207= 2 *Banahan* Matt Centre/Wing 2010-2010
Matches: Australian Barbarians (Perth) 2010, Australian Barbarians (Gosford) 2010

207= 2 *Hodgson* Paul Scrum half 2010-2010
Matches: Australian Barbarians (Perth) 2010 (rep), Australian Barbarians (Gosford) 2010 (rep)

207= 2 ***Waldouck*** Dom Centre 2010-2010
Matches: Australian Barbarians (Perth) 2010 (rep), Australian Barbarians (Gosford) 2010

207= 2 *Armitage* Steffon Flanker 2010-2010
Matches: Australian Barbarians (Gosford) 2010, New Zealand Maori 2010

207= 2 *Haskell* James Flanker/Number 8 2010-2010
Matches: Australian Barbarians (Gosford) 2010, New Zealand Maori 2010 (rep)

207= 2 *Strettle* Dave Wing 2010-2010
Matches: Australian Barbarians (Gosford) 2010, New Zealand Maori 2010

207= 2 ***Webber*** Rob Hooker 2010-2010
Matches: Australian Barbarians (Gosford) 2010 (rep), New Zealand Maori 2010 (rep)

207= 2 ***Dowson*** Phil Flanker/Number 8 2010-2010
Matches: Australian Barbarians (Gosford) 2010 (rep), New Zealand Maori 2010

Rank	Matches	Surname	Forename	Position	Period
262=	1	**Broderick**	Jim	Prop	1971

Matches: Waseda University Past and Present 1971

262=	1	Rogers	Budge	Flanker	1971

Matches: Waseda University Past and Present 1971

262=	1	Hannaford	Charlie	Number 8	1971

Matches: Waseda University Past and Present 1971

262=	1	Finlan	John	Fly half	1971

Matches: Waseda University Past and Present 1971

262=	1	Webb	Rod	Wing	1971

Matches: Waseda University Past and Present 1971

262=	1	Wardlow	Chris	Centre	1971

Matches: Waseda University Past and Present 1971

262=	1	Lloyd	Bob	Centre	1971

Matches: Waseda University Past and Present 1971

262=	1	Glover	Peter	Wing	1971

Matches: Waseda University Past and Present 1971

262=	1	Martin	Nick	Lock	1973

Matches: Taranaki 1973

262=	1	**White (2)**	John	Hooker	1973

Matches: Wellington 1973

262=	1	**Hendy**	Peter	Flanker	1973

Matches: Wellington 1973

262=	1	Jorden	Tony	Full back	1973

Matches: Wellington 1973

262=	1	**Ashton**	Brian	Scrum half	1975

Matches: Western Australia 1975

262=	1	Smith	Keith	Centre	1975

Matches: Sydney 1975

262=	1	Dixon	Peter	Flanker/Number 8	1975

Matches: Queensland Country 1975

262=	1	**Pomphrey**	Nigel	Lock/Flanker	1979

Matches: Kyushu 1979

262=	1	**Gifford**	Chris	Scrum half	1979

Matches: Fiji Juniors 1979

262=	1	**Diamond**	Steve	Hooker	1997

Matches: Cuyo 1997

262=	1	Beal	Nick	Centre/Wing/Full back	1998

Matches: New Zealand A 1998

262=	1	*Bell*	Duncan	Prop	1998

Matches: New Zealand Academy 1998 (rep)

262=	1	Brown	Spencer	Wing	1998

Matches: New Zealand Maori 1998

262=	1	Hill (2)	Richard	Flanker/Number 8	1999

Matches: Queensland Reds 1999

262=	1	Back	Neil	Flanker	1999

Matches: Queensland Reds 1999

Rank	Matches	Surname	Forename	Position	Period
262=	1	*Wilkinson*	Jonny	Fly half/Centre	1999
Matches: Queensland Reds 1999					
262=	1	Perry	Matt	Centre/Full back	1999
Matches: Queensland Reds 1999					
262=	1	Healey	Austin	Scrum half/Fly half/Wing	1999
Matches: Queensland Reds 1999 (rep)					
262=	1	*Tindall*	Mike	Centre	1999
Matches: Queensland Reds 1999 (rep)					
262=	1	Cohen	Ben	Wing	2000
Matches: Griqualand West 2000					
262=	1	*Brown*	Alex	Lock	2001
Matches: British Columbia 2001					
262=	1	White-Cooper	Steve	Lock/Flanker	2001
Matches: British Columbia 2001					
262=	1	**Ewens**	Joe	Centre	2001
Matches: British Columbia 2001					
262=	1	Thompson (2)	Steve	Hooker	2001
Matches: USA A 2001 (rep)					
262=	1	Morris	Robbie	Prop	2002
Matches: Argentina A 2002					
262=	1	*Vyvyan*	Hugh	Lock/Number 8	2002
Matches: Argentina A 2002					
262=	1	***Balding***	Adam	Lock	2002
Matches: Argentina A 2002					
262=	1	***Danaher***	Declan	Flanker/Number 8	2002
Matches: Argentina A 2002					
262=	1	**Anglesea**	Pete	Flanker/Number 8	2002
Matches: Argentina A 2002					
262=	1	*Walder*	Dave	Fly half	2002
Matches: Argentina A 2002					
262=	1	*May*	Tom	Fly half/Centre/Wing/Full back	2002
Matches: Argentina A 2002					
262=	1	***Sorrell***	Kevin	Centre	2002
Matches: Argentina A 2002					
262=	1	*Cueto*	Mark	Wing	2002
Matches: Argentina A 2002					
262=	1	West	Dorian	Hooker	2003
Matches: New Zealand Maori 2003					
262=	1	Vickery	Phil	Prop	2003
Matches: New Zealand Maori 2003					
262=	1	Grayson	Paul	Fly half	2003
Matches: New Zealand Maori 2003					
262=	1	*Simpson-Daniel*	James	Centre/Wing	2003
Matches: New Zealand Maori 2003					
262=	1	Abbott	Stuart	Centre	2003
Matches: New Zealand Maori 2003					

Rank Matches Surname Forename Position Period

262= 1 *Noon* Jamie Centre 2003
Matches: New Zealand Maori 2003

262= 1 *Balshaw* Iain Wing/Full back 2003
Matches: New Zealand Maori 2003

262= 1 Worsley Mike Prop 2003
Matches: New Zealand Maori 2003 (rep)

262= 1 *Wilson (2)* David Prop 2010
Matches: Australian Barbarians (Perth) 2010

262= 1 ***Fourie*** Hendre Flanker 2010
Matches: Australian Barbarians (Perth) 2010

262= 1 *Monye* Ugo Centre/Wing 2010
Matches: Australian Barbarians (Perth) 2010

262= 1 *Lawes* Courtney Lock/Flanker 2010
Matches: Australian Barbarians (Perth) 2010 (rep)

262= 1 ***Golding*** Jon Prop 2010
Matches: Australian Barbarians (Gosford) 2010

262= 1 *Care* Danny Scrum half 2010
Matches: New Zealand Maori 2010

262= 1 *Ashton* Chris Wing 2010
Matches: New Zealand Maori 2010

262= 1 ***Barritt*** Brad Fly half/Centre 2010
Matches: New Zealand Maori 2010

262= 1 *Cole* Dan Prop 2010
Matches: New Zealand Maori 2010 (rep)

262= 1 *Youngs* Ben Scrum half 2010
Matches: New Zealand Maori 2010 (rep)

262= 1 *Foden* Ben Scrum half/Wing/Full back 2010
Matches: New Zealand Maori 2010 (rep)

6) ENGLAND UNUSED TOUR SQUAD MEMBERS 1969-2010:

[In numerical order; restricted to uncapped players only; current players in italics; data up to and including an England XV v New Zealand Maori 23rd June 2010]

Rank	Tours	Surname	Forename	Position	Period
1	2	***Wood***	Nick	Prop	2007-2009
Tours: Tour of South Africa 2007, Tour of Argentina 2009					
2=	1	**Catt**	Richard	Scrum half	1994
Tours: [Tour of South Africa 1994]					
2=	1	***Bemand***	Scott	Scrum half	2006
Tours: Tour of Australia 2006					
2=	1	***Turner-Hall***	Jordan	Centre	2009
Tours: Tour of Argentina 2009					

7) ENGLAND SEVENS COMPETITION APPEARANCES* 1973-2009:

[In numerical order; current players in italics; uncapped players in bold or bold italics; data up to and including Rugby World Cup Sevens 5th-7th March 2009]
[*excludes IRB World Sevens competition]

Rank Comps Surname Forename Position Period

1 7 Sheasby Chris **Forward** 1992-1998
Competitions: Selkirk 1992, Harlequin 1992, Dubai 1992, Rugby World Cup 1993, Hong Kong 1996, Rugby World Cup 1997, Commonwealth 1998

2= 5 **Scully** Dave **Scrum half** 1992-1997
Competitions: Selkirk 1992, Rugby World Cup 1993, Hong Kong 1995, Hong Kong 1996, Rugby World Cup 1997

2= 5 Beal Nick **Fly half** 1992-1997
Competitions: Harlequin 1992, Dubai 1992, Rugby World Cup 1993, Hong Kong 1996, Rugby World Cup 1997

4= 4 Rodber Tim Forward 1992-1997
Competitions: Selkirk 1992, Rugby World Cup 1993, Hong Kong 1996, Rugby World Cup 1997

4= 4 Hopley Damian **Hooker**/Centre 1992-1996
Competitions: Selkirk 1992, Harlequin 1992, Rugby World Cup 1993, Hong Kong 1996

4= 4 Adebayo Adedayo **Centre** 1993-1997
Competitions: Rugby World Cup 1993, Hong Kong 1995, Hong Kong 1996, Rugby World Cup 1997

4= 4 ***Thirlby*** Rob **Back**/Forward 1999-2005
Competitions: Air France 1999, Rugby World Cup 2001, Commonwealth 2002, Rugby World Cup 2005

4= 4 ***Gollings*** Ben Fly half/Centre 2002-2009
Competitions: Commonwealth 2002, Rugby World Cup 2005, Commonwealth 2006, Rugby World Cup 2009

9= 3 **Cassell** Justyn Forward 1992-1993
Competitions: Selkirk 1992, Harlequin 1992, Rugby World Cup 1993

9= 3 Healey Austin Fly half 1995-1997
Competitions: Hong Kong 1995, Hong Kong 1996, Rugby World Cup 1997

9= 3 *Sampson* Paul Scrum half/Fly half/**Wing** 1999-2002
Competitions: Air France 1999, Rugby World Cup 2001, Commonwealth 2002

9= 3 *Paul* Henry Back/Forward 2002-2006
Competitions: Commonwealth 2002, Rugby World Cup 2005, Commonwealth 2006

9= 3 ***Amor*** Simon Scrum half/Fly half 2002-2006
Competitions: Commonwealth 2002, Rugby World Cup 2005, Commonwealth 2006

14= 2 Ripley Andy **Prop** 1973-1986
Competitions: International 1973, International 1986

14= 2 Clarke Ben Forward 1992-1992
Competitions: Selkirk 1992, Harlequin 1992

14= 2 Dallaglio Lawrence Forward 1992-1993
Competitions: Dubai 1992, Rugby World Cup 1993

14= 2 Hill (2) Richard Forward 1995-1997
Competitions: Hong Kong 1995, Rugby World Cup 1997

Rank	Comps	Surname	Forename	Position	Period
14=	2	Back	Neil	Hooker	1996-1997
Competitions:	Hong Kong 1996, Rugby World Cup 1997				
14=	2	Stimpson	Tim	Back/Forward	1996-1999
Competitions:	Hong Kong 1996, Air France 1999				
14=	2	Sleightholme	Jon	Wing	1996-1997
Competitions:	Hong Kong 1996, Rugby World Cup 1997				
14=	2	**Earnshaw**	Russ	Forward	1998-1999
Competitions:	Commonwealth 1998, Air France 1999				
14=	2	**Williams**	Jamie	Back	1998-1999
Competitions:	Commonwealth 1998, Air France 1999				
14=	2	**Friday**	Mike	Scrum half	1998-2001
Competitions:	Commonwealth 1998, Rugby World Cup 2001				
14=	2	***Chesney***	Kris	Forward	1999-2001
Competitions:	Air France 1999, Rugby World Cup 2001				
14=	2	Worsley	Joe	Forward	1999-2001
Competitions:	Air France 1999, Rugby World Cup 2001				
14=	2	Lewsey	Josh	Back/Forward	2001-2002
Competitions:	Rugby World Cup 2001, Commonwealth 2002				
14=	2	***Roques***	Tony	Forward	2002-2005
Competitions:	Commonwealth 2002, Rugby World Cup 2005				
14=	2	Sanderson	Pat	Forward	2002-2005
Competitions:	Commonwealth 2002, Rugby World Cup 2005				
14=	2	Appleford	Geoff	Back/Forward	2002-2005
Competitions:	Commonwealth 2002, Rugby World Cup 2005				
14=	2	***Haughton***	Richard	Wing	2005-2006
Competitions:	Rugby World Cup 2005, Commonwealth 2006				
14=	2	***Vilk***	Andy	Back/Forward	2006-2009
Competitions:	Commonwealth 2006, Rugby World Cup 2009				
14=	2	*Varndell*	Tom	Wing	2006-2009
Competitions:	Commonwealth 2006, Rugby World Cup 2009				
33=	1	Cotton	Fran	Prop	1973
Competitions:	International 1973				
33=	1	Uttley	Roger	Prop	1973
Competitions:	International 1973				
33=	1	**Gray**	John	Hooker	1973
Competitions:	International 1973				
33=	1	Smith (1)	Steve	Scrum half	1973
Competitions:	International 1973				
33=	1	Rossborough	Peter	Fly half	1973
Competitions:	International 1973				
33=	1	Preece	Peter	Fly half/Centre	1973
Competitions:	International 1973				
33=	1	Duckham	David	Centre	1973
Competitions:	International 1973				
33=	1	Fielding	Keith	Wing	1973
Competitions:	International 1973				

Rank	Comps	Surname	Forename	Position	Period
33=	1	Bond	Tony	Forward	1986
Competitions: International 1986					
33=	1	**Buckton**	Peter	Forward	1986
Competitions: International 1986					
33=	1	Winterbottom	Peter	Forward	1986
Competitions: International 1986					
33=	1	**Simpson**	Andy	Hooker	1986
Competitions: International 1986					
33=	1	Hill (1)	Richard	Scrum half	1986
Competitions: International 1986					
33=	1	**Jermyn**	Mark	Fly half	1986
Competitions: International 1986					
33=	1	Williams	Peter	Fly half	1986
Competitions: International 1986					
33=	1	Clough	Fran	Centre	1986
Competitions: International 1986					
33=	1	Simms	Kevin	Centre	1986
Competitions: International 1986					
33=	1	**Thomas (1)**	Huw	Wing	1986
Competitions: International 1986					
33=	1	**Buzza**	Alan	Fly half	1992
Competitions: Selkirk 1992					
33=	1	**Strett**	Martin	Fly half	1992
Competitions: Selkirk 1992					
33=	1	de Glanville	Phil	Centre	1992
Competitions: Selkirk 1992					
33=	1	Hunter	Ian	Wing	1992
Competitions: Selkirk 1992					
33=	1	**Snow**	Alex	Forward	1992
Competitions: Harlequin 1992					
33=	1	Morris	Dewi	Scrum half	1992
Competitions: Harlequin 1992					
33=	1	Pears	David	Fly half	1992
Competitions: Harlequin 1992					
33=	1	Underwood	Tony	Wing	1992
Competitions: Harlequin 1992					
33=	1	**Adams**	Gareth	Forward	1992
Competitions: Dubai 1992					
33=	1	Haag	Martin	Forward	1992
Competitions: Dubai 1992					
33=	1	Ojomoh	Steve	Forward	1992
Competitions: Dubai 1992					
33=	1	Mapletoft	Mark	Fly half	1992
Competitions: Dubai 1992					
33=	1	Hull	Paul	Fly half	1992
Competitions: Dubai 1992					

Rank Comps Surname Forename Position Period

33= 1 **Thompson** Adrian Fly half/Centre 1992
Competitions: Dubai 1992

33= 1 **Bibby** Carl Centre/Wing 1992
Competitions: [Dubai 1992]

33= 1 **Knibbs** Ralph Centre/Wing 1992
Competitions: Dubai 1992

33= 1 Dawson Matt Scrum half 1993
Competitions: Rugby World Cup 1993

33= 1 Harriman Andy Wing 1993
Competitions: Rugby World Cup 1993

33= 1 **Dods [SCO]** Michael Wing 1993
Competitions: [Rugby World Cup 1993]

33= 1 **Scrivener** Peter Forward 1995
Competitions: Hong Kong 1995

33= 1 Diprose Tony Forward 1995
Competitions: Hong Kong 1995

33= 1 **Eves** Derek Hooker 1995
Competitions: Hong Kong 1995

33= 1 Greenstock Nick Fly half/Centre 1995
Competitions: Hong Kong 1995

33= 1 **Yates** Chris Centre 1995
Competitions: Hong Kong 1995

33= 1 **Hackney** Steve Wing 1995
Competitions: Hong Kong 1995

33= 1 **Kitchin** Rob Scrum half 1995
Competitions: Melun 1995

33= 1 Catt Mike Fly half/Centre 1997
Competitions: Rugby World Cup 1997

33= 1 ***Jenner*** Jim Prop 1998
Competitions: Commonwealth 1998

33= 1 **Cockle** James Forward 1998
Competitions: Commonwealth 1998

33= 1 **Davis** Chris Forward 1998
Competitions: Commonwealth 1998

33= 1 **Harvey** Ben Scrum half/Fly half 1998
Competitions: Commonwealth 1998

33= 1 **Baxter** Nick Wing 1998
Competitions: Commonwealth 1998

33= 1 **Griffiths** Matt Wing 1998
Competitions: Commonwealth 1998

33= 1 Sturnham Ben Forward 1999
Competitions: Air France 1999

33= 1 **Vander** Adam Forward 1999
Competitions: Air France 1999

33= 1 *Balshaw* Iain Wing 1999
Competitions: Air France 1999

Rank	Comps	Surname	Forename	Position	Period
33=	1	Brown	Spencer	Wing	1999
Competitions: Air France 1999					
33=	1	Cohen	Ben	Wing	1999
Competitions: Air France 1999					
33=	1	*Johnston*	Ben	Forward	2001
Competitions: Rugby World Cup 2001					
33=	1	***Seely***	Grant	Forward	2001
Competitions: Rugby World Cup 2001					
33=	1	**Simpson**	Nigel	Back/Forward	2001
Competitions: Rugby World Cup 2001					
33=	1	*Sackey*	Paul	Wing	2001
Competitions: Rugby World Cup 2001					
33=	1	Greening	Phil	Hooker	2002
Competitions: Commonwealth 2002					
33=	1	Duncombe	Nick	Scrum half	2002
Competitions: Commonwealth 2002					
33=	1	**St. Hilaire**	Marcus	Wing	2002
Competitions: Commonwealth 2002					
33=	1	***Dowson***	Phil	Forward	2005
Competitions: Rugby World Cup 2005					
33=	1	*Monye*	Ugo	Back/Forward	2005
Competitions: Rugby World Cup 2005					
33=	1	Richards	Peter	Scrum half/Hooker	2005
Competitions: Rugby World Cup 2005					
33=	1	***Starling***	Neil	Fly half/Centre	2005
Competitions: Rugby World Cup 2005					
33=	1	*Lund*	Magnus	Forward	2006
Competitions: Commonwealth 2006					
33=	1	***Russell (2)***	Ben	Forward	2006
Competitions: Commonwealth 2006					
33=	1	***Seymour***	David	Forward	2006
Competitions: Commonwealth 2006					
33=	1	***Mordt***	Nils	Back/Forward	2006
Competitions: Commonwealth 2006					
33=	1	*Care*	Danny	Scrum half	2006
Competitions: Commonwealth 2006					
33=	1	*Tait*	Matt	Centre	2006
Competitions: Commonwealth 2006					
33=	1	***Cracknell***	Chris	Forward	2009
Competitions: Rugby World Cup 2009					
33=	1	***Damu***	Isoa	Forward	2009
Competitions: Rugby World Cup 2009					
33=	1	***Rodwell***	James	Forward	2009
Competitions: Rugby World Cup 2009					
33=	1	***Vickerman***	Rob	Forward/Back	2009
Competitions: Rugby World Cup 2009					

Rank	Comps	Surname	Forename	Position	Period
33=	1	***Barrett***	Kevin	Scrum half	2009

Competitions: Rugby World Cup 2009

Rank	Comps	Surname	Forename	Position	Period
33=	1	***Simpson-Daniel***	Charlie	Scrum half	2009

Competitions: Rugby World Cup 2009

Rank	Comps	Surname	Forename	Position	Period
33=	1	***Drauniniu***	Josh	Centre/Wing	2009

Competitions: Rugby World Cup 2009

Rank	Comps	Surname	Forename	Position	Period
33=	1	***Phillips***	Ollie	Centre/Wing	2009

Competitions: Rugby World Cup 2009

Rank	Comps	Surname	Forename	Position	Period
33=	1	***Biggs***	Tom	Wing	2009

Competitions: Rugby World Cup 2009

8) ENGLAND IRB WORLD SEVENS COMPETITION APPEARANCES 2000-2010:

[In numerical order; current players in italics; uncapped players in bold or bold italics; data up to and including Edinburgh Sevens 29th-30th May 2010]

Rank Comps Surname Forename Position Period

1 62 ***Gollings*** Ben **Fly half**/Centre 2000-2010

Competitions: Air France 2000, Shanghai 2001, Santiago 2002, Mar del Plata 2002, Brisbane 2002, New Zealand 2002, Hong Kong 2002, Singapore 2002, London 2002, Cardiff 2002, Dubai 2002, South Africa 2002, Brisbane 2003, New Zealand 2003, Cardiff 2003, London 2003, Dubai 2003, South Africa 2003, New Zealand 2004, USA 2004, Hong Kong 2004, Singapore 2004, Bordeaux 2004, London 2004, South Africa 2004, New Zealand 2005, USA 2005, Singapore 2005, London 2005, Paris 2005, Dubai 2005, South 2005, New Zealand 2006, USA 2006, Hong Kong 2006, Singapore 2006, Paris 2006, London 2006, Dubai 2006, South Africa 2006, New Zealand 2008, USA 2008, Hong Kong 2008, Adelaide 2008, London 2008, Edinburgh 2008, Dubai 2008, South Africa 2008, New Zealand 2009, USA 2009, Hong Kong 2009, Adelaide 2009, London 2009, Edinburgh 2009, Dubai 2009, South Africa 2009, New Zealand 2010, USA 2010, Adelaide 2010, Hong Kong 2010, London 2010, Edinburgh 2010

2 43 ***Amor*** Simon **Scrum half**/Fly half 2001-2007

Competitions: Malaysia 2001, Japan 2001, London 2001, South Africa 2001, Santiago 2002, Mar del Plata 2002, Brisbane 2002, New Zealand 2002, Beijing 2002, Hong Kong 2002, Dubai 2002, South Africa 2002, Brisbane 2003, New Zealand 2003, Hong Kong 2003, Cardiff 2003, London 2003, Dubai 2003, New Zealand 2004, USA 2004, Hong Kong 2004, Singapore 2004, Bordeaux 2004, London 2004, Dubai 2004, New Zealand 2005, Singapore 2005, London 2005, Paris 2005, Dubai 2005, South Africa 2005, New Zealand 2006, Hong Kong 2006, Singapore 2006, Paris 2006, London 2006, Dubai 2006, South Africa 2006, New Zealand 2007, USA 2007, Hong Kong 2007, Adelaide 2007, London 2007

3 36 ***Thirlby*** Rob **Back**/Forward 2001-2007

Competitions: Shanghai 2001, London 2001, South Africa 2001, Brisbane 2002, New Zealand 2002, Singapore 2002, Cardiff 2002, Dubai 2002, South Africa 2002, Brisbane 2003, New Zealand 2003, Hong Kong 2003, Cardiff 2003, London 2003, Dubai 2003, South Africa 2003, New Zealand 2004, USA 2004, Hong Kong 2004, Singapore 2004, Bordeaux 2004, London 2004, Dubai 2004, South Africa 2004, New Zealand 2005, USA 2005, Singapore 2005, London 2005, Paris 2005, Paris 2006, Dubai 2006, South Africa 2006, New Zealand 2007, USA 2007, London 2007, Edinburgh 2007

4 32 ***Haughton*** Richard **Wing** 2001-2006

Competitions: New Zealand 2001, Shanghai 2001, London 2001, Wales 2001, Santiago 2002, Mar del Plata 2002, Brisbane 2002, New Zealand 2002, Beijing 2002, Hong Kong 2002, Singapore 2002, Malaysia 2002, London 2002, Cardiff 2002, Dubai 2002, South Africa 2002, Brisbane 2003, New Zealand 2003, Hong Kong 2003, London 2003, Dubai 2003, South Africa 2003, USA 2004, Hong Kong 2004, Singapore 2004, Bordeaux 2004, South Africa 2004, Singapore 2005, London 2005, Paris 2005, Paris 2006, London 2006

Rank	Comps	Surname	Forename	Position	Period
5	29	***Vilk***	Andy	Back/**Forward**	2005-2009

Competitions: New Zealand 2005, USA 2005, Paris 2005, Dubai 2005, South Africa 2005, New Zealand 2006, USA 2006, Hong Kong 2006, Singapore 2006, Paris 2006, London 2006, Dubai 2006, South Africa 2006, New Zealand 2007, USA 2007, Hong Kong 2007, Adelaide 2007, London 2007, Edinburgh 2007, Dubai 2007, South Africa 2007, New Zealand 2008, USA 2008, Hong Kong 2008, Adelaide 2008, London 2008, Edinburgh 2008, New Zealand 2009, USA 2009

Rank	Comps	Surname	Forename	Position	Period
6	28	***Roques***	Tony	Forward	2001-2007

Competitions: London 2001, Wales 2001, Hong Kong 2002, London 2002, Cardiff 2002, Brisbane 2003, New Zealand 2003, Hong Kong 2003, London 2003, Dubai 2003, South Africa 2003, New Zealand 2004, USA 2004, Bordeaux 2004, London 2004, Dubai 2004, South Africa 2004, New Zealand 2005, USA 2005, Singapore 2005, London 2005, Paris 2005, New Zealand 2007, USA 2007, Hong Kong 2007, Adelaide 2007, London 2007, Edinburgh 2007

Rank	Comps	Surname	Forename	Position	Period
7	21	Appleford	Geoff	Back/Forward	2001-2005

Competitions: South Africa 2001, Santiago 2002, Mar del Plata 2002, Brisbane 2002, New Zealand 2002, Beijing 2002, Hong Kong 2002, Hong Kong 2003, Dubai 2003, South Africa 2003, USA 2004, Hong Kong 2004, Bordeaux 2004, London 2004, Dubai 2004, South Africa 2004, New Zealand 2005, USA 2005, Singapore 2005, London 2005, Paris 2005

Rank	Comps	Surname	Forename	Position	Period
8	20	***Barrett***	Kevin	Scrum half	2002-2010

Competitions: Malaysia 2002, London 2002, USA 2008, Hong Kong 2008, Adelaide 2008, London 2008, Edinburgh 2008, Dubai 2008, South Africa 2008, New Zealand 2009, USA 2009, Hong Kong 2009, Adelaide 2009, London 2009, Edinburgh 2009, Dubai 2009, South Africa 2009, New Zealand 2010, London 2010, Edinburgh 2010

Rank	Comps	Surname	Forename	Position	Period
9=	17	***Phillips***	Ollie	**Centre**/Wing	2004-2009

Competitions: Dubai 2004, South Africa 2004, New Zealand 2005, USA 2005, New Zealand 2006, USA 2006, Paris 2006, London 2006, London 2008, Edinburgh 2008, Dubai 2008, New Zealand 2009, USA 2009, Hong Kong 2009, Adelaide 2009, London 2009, Edinburgh 2009

Rank	Comps	Surname	Forename	Position	Period
9=	17	***Rodwell***	James	Forward	2008-2010

Competitions: Edinburgh 2008, Dubai 2008, South Africa 2008, New Zealand 2009, USA 2009, Hong Kong 2009, Adelaide 2009, London 2009, Edinburgh 2009, Dubai 2009, South Africa 2009, New Zealand 2010, USA 2010, Adelaide 2010, Hong Kong 2010, London 2010, Edinburgh 2010

Rank	Comps	Surname	Forename	Position	Period
11=	15	***Brooks***	James	Scrum half/Fly half	2001-2007

Competitions: New Zealand 2001, Wales 2001, Cardiff 2003, London 2003, Dubai 2003, South Africa 2003, New Zealand 2004, USA 2004, Bordeaux 2004, London 2004, New Zealand 2005, USA 2005, Singapore 2005, Hong Kong 2007, Adelaide 2007

Rank	Comps	Surname	Forename	Position	Period
11=	15	***Dowson***	Phil	Forward	2003-2005

Competitions: Brisbane 2003, New Zealand 2003, Hong Kong 2003, Cardiff 2003, London 2003, Dubai 2003, South Africa 2003, New Zealand 2004, USA 2004, Hong Kong 2004, Singapore 2004, Bordeaux 2004, London 2004, USA 2005, London 2005

Rank	Comps	Surname	Forename	Position	Period
13=	14	**Simpson**	Nigel	Back/Forward	2000-2002

Competitions: Hong Kong 2000, Air France 2000, New Zealand 2001, Hong Kong 2001, Shanghai 2001, Malaysia 2001, Japan 2001, London 2001, Wales 2001, South Africa 2001, Santiago 2002, Mar del Plata 2002, Singapore 2002, Malaysia 2002

Rank	Comps	Surname	Forename	Position	Period
13=	14	*Paul*	Henry	Back/Forward	2002-2006

Competitions: Hong Kong 2002, London 2002, Brisbane 2003, New Zealand 2003, Hong Kong 2003, London 2003, Bordeaux 2004, London 2004, Dubai 2005, South Africa 2005, New Zealand 2006, USA 2006, Hong Kong 2006, Singapore 2006

13=	14	***Russell (2)***	Ben	Forward	2002-2007

Competitions: Dubai 2002, South Africa 2002, New Zealand 2005, USA 2005, Dubai 2005, New Zealand 2006, Hong Kong 2006, Singapore 2006, Paris 2006, London 2006, New Zealand 2007, Hong Kong 2007, Adelaide 2007, London 2007

13=	14	***Damu***	Isoa	Forward	2007-2009

Competitions: Adelaide 2007, London 2007, Edinburgh 2007, Dubai 2007, South Africa 2007, New Zealand 2008, USA 2008, Dubai 2008, South Africa 2008, New Zealand 2009, USA 2009, Hong Kong 2009, Dubai 2009, South Africa 2009

17	13	Sanderson	Pat	Forward	2000-2004

Competitions: Hong Kong 2000, Air France 2000, South Africa 2001, Cardiff 2002, Cardiff 2003, London 2003, Dubai 2003, South Africa 2003, USA 2004, Hong Kong 2004, Bordeaux 2004, London 2004, Dubai 2004

18	12	***Cracknell***	Chris	Forward	2008-2009

Competitions: London 2008, Edinburgh 2008, Dubai 2008, South Africa 2008, New Zealand 2009, USA 2009, Hong Kong 2009, Adelaide 2009, London 2009, Edinburgh 2009, Dubai 2009, South Africa 2009

19=	11	***Elliott***	Anthony	Wing	2001-2008

Competitions: New Zealand 2001, Shanghai 2001, Malaysia 2001, Japan 2001, South Africa 2001, Dubai 2007, South Africa 2007, New Zealand 2008, USA 2008, Hong Kong 2008, Adelaide 2008

19=	11	***Hunt***	Simon	Back/Forward	2001-2008

Competitions: Malaysia 2001, Japan 2001, London 2001, Wales 2001, New Zealand 2002, Dubai 2007, South Africa 2007, New Zealand 2008, USA 2008, Hong Kong 2008, Adelaide 2008

19=	11	*Monye*	Ugo	Back/Forward	2003-2004

Competitions: Brisbane 2003, New Zealand 2003, Hong Kong 2003, Cardiff 2003, London 2003, Dubai 2003, South Africa 2003, USA 2004, Bordeaux 2004, London 2004, Dubai 2004

22=	10	*Hipkiss*	Dan	Back/Forward	2003-2006

Competitions: Dubai 2003, South Africa 2003, New Zealand 2004, USA 2004, New Zealand 2005, USA 2005, Singapore 2005, London 2005, Paris 2005, Paris 2006

22=	10	***Mordt***	Nils	Back/Forward	2004-2007

Competitions: New Zealand 2004, Dubai 2005, South Africa 2005, New Zealand 2006, USA 2006, Hong Kong 2006, Singapore 2006, New Zealand 2007, USA 2007, Hong Kong 2007

22=	10	***Vickerman***	Rob	Forward/Back	2005-2010

Competitions: Paris 2005, Dubai 2008, South Africa 2008, New Zealand 2009, USA 2009, Hong Kong 2009, London 2009, Edinburgh 2009, London 2010, Edinburgh 2010

22=	10	*Foden*	Ben	Scrum half/Centre	2005-2008

Competitions: Dubai 2005, South Africa 2005, Hong Kong 2006, Singapore 2006, London 2006, London 2007, Edinburgh 2007, Dubai 2007, South Africa 2007, London 2008

26=	9	Richards	Peter	Scrum half/**Hooker**	2004-2005

Competitions: Hong Kong 2004, Singapore 2004, London 2004, Dubai 2004, South Africa 2004, New Zealand 2005, USA 2005, Singapore 2005, London 2005

Rank Comps Surname Forename Position Period

26= 9 *Tait* Matt Centre 2004-2006
Competitions: Dubai 2004, South Africa 2004, London 2005, Dubai 2005, South Africa 2005, New Zealand 2006, USA 2006, Hong Kong 2006, Singapore 2006

26= 9 ***Biggs*** Tom Wing 2008-2009
Competitions: London 2008, Edinburgh 2008, Dubai 2008, South Africa 2008, New Zealand 2009, USA 2009, Hong Kong 2009, London 2009, Edinburgh 2009

26= 9 ***Turner*** Mat Centre/Wing 2008-2010
Competitions: South Africa 2008, USA 2009, Dubai 2009, New Zealand 2010, USA 2010, Adelaide 2010, Hong Kong 2010, London 2010, Edinburgh 2010

30= 8 *Noon* Jamie Back/Forward 2000-2003
Competitions: Hong Kong 2000, Air France 2000, Brisbane 2002, Beijing 2002, Hong Kong 2002, Singapore 2002, Cardiff 2002, Hong Kong 2003

30= 8 **Friday** Mike Scrum half 2000-2002
Competitions: Hong Kong 2000, Air France 2000, New Zealand 2001, South Africa 2001, Santiago 2002, Mar del Plata 2002, New Zealand 2002, Beijing 2002

30= 8 ***Matthews*** Will Forward 2005-2006
Competitions: Singapore 2005, London 2005, Paris 2005, Dubai 2005, South Africa 2005, USA 2006, Paris 2006, London 2006

30= 8 ***Brake*** John Back/Forward 2007-2008
Competitions: USA 2007, Adelaide 2007, Dubai 2007, South Africa 2007, New Zealand 2008, USA 2008, Hong Kong 2008, Adelaide 2008

30= 8 ***Oduoza*** Uche Forward/Wing 2008-2010
Competitions: New Zealand 2008, USA 2008, London 2008, Edinburgh 2008, Dubai 2008, London 2009, Edinburgh 2009, Edinburgh 2010

30= 8 ***Norton*** Dan Centre/Wing 2009-2010
Competitions: New Zealand 2009, USA 2009, London 2009, Edinburgh 2009, Dubai 2009, South Africa 2009, New Zealand 2010, USA 2010

30= 8 ***Caprice*** Dan Centre/Wing 2009-2010
Competitions: Hong Kong 2009, Adelaide 2009, Dubai 2009, South Africa 2009, New Zealand 2010, USA 2010, Adelaide 2010, Hong Kong 2010

30= 8 ***Brightwell*** Chris Forward 2009-2010
Competitions: Dubai 2009, South Africa 2009, New Zealand 2010, USA 2010, Adelaide 2010, Hong Kong 2010, London 2010, Edinburgh 2010

38= 7 *Stephenson* Michael Centre/Wing 2001-2002
Competitions: South Africa 2001, Brisbane 2002, New Zealand 2002, Hong Kong 2002, Singapore 2002, London 2002, Cardiff 2002

38= 7 *Sampson* Paul Scrum half/Fly half/Wing 2002-2004
Competitions: Singapore 2002, London 2002, Cardiff 2002, Dubai 2002, Singapore 2004, Dubai 2004, South Africa 2004

38= 7 ***Horstmann*** Kai Forward 2004-2004
Competitions: New Zealand 2004, Hong Kong 2004, Singapore 2004, Bordeaux 2004, London 2004, Dubai 2004, South Africa 2004

38= 7 ***Bailey*** James Wing 2005-2006
Competitions: New Zealand 2005, USA 2005, London 2005, Paris 2005, South Africa 2005, Paris 2006, London 2006

Rank Comps Surname Forename Position Period

38= 7 ***Seymour*** David Forward 2006-2007
Competitions: New Zealand 2006, USA 2006, Hong Kong 2006, Singapore 2006, Paris 2006, Hong Kong 2007, Edinburgh 2007

38= 7 *Care* Danny Scrum half 2006-2008
Competitions: New Zealand 2006, USA 2006, Hong Kong 2007, Adelaide 2007, London 2007, Edinburgh 2007, New Zealand 2008

38= 7 *Strettle* Dave Wing 2006-2006
Competitions: New Zealand 2006, USA 2006, Hong Kong 2006, Singapore 2006, Paris 2006, London 2006, Dubai 2006

38= 7 ***Hills*** Michael **Prop** 2006-2007
Competitions: Dubai 2006, South Africa 2006, New Zealand 2007, USA 2007, Adelaide 2007, London 2007, Edinburgh 2007

38= 7 ***Amesbury*** Charlie Wing 2006-2007
Competitions: South Africa 2006, New Zealand 2007, USA 2007, Hong Kong 2007, Adelaide 2007, London 2007, Edinburgh 2007

38= 7 ***Young*** Micky Scrum half 2008-2010
Competitions: Edinburgh 2008, Dubai 2008, South Africa 2008, London 2009, Edinburgh 2009, London 2010, Edinburgh 2010

38= 7 ***Royle*** Nick Wing 2009-2010
Competitions: Dubai 2009, South Africa 2009, New Zealand 2010, USA 2010, Adelaide 2010, Hong Kong 2010, Edinburgh 2010

38= 7 ***Wade*** Christian Wing 2009-2010
Competitions: Dubai 2009, South Africa 2009, New Zealand 2010, USA 2010, Adelaide 2010, Hong Kong 2010, London 2010

50= 6 Luger Dan Wing 2000-2006
Competitions: Air France 2000, Singapore 2002, South Africa 2005, USA 2006, Hong Kong 2006, Singapore 2006

50= 6 Greening Phil Hooker 2002-2003
Competitions: Beijing 2002, Hong Kong 2002, London 2002, Cardiff 2002, Hong Kong 2003, London 2003

50= 6 *Narraway* Luke Forward 2005-2007
Competitions: Dubai 2005, South Africa 2005, New Zealand 2006, USA 2006, London 2006, New Zealand 2007

50= 6 *Varndell* Tom Wing 2005-2010
Competitions: Dubai 2005, Hong Kong 2006, Singapore 2006, Hong Kong 2009, Adelaide 2009, London 2010

50= 6 ***Adams*** Jack Fly half/Centre 2007-2008
Competitions: Hong Kong 2007, Adelaide 2007, Dubai 2007, South Africa 2007, London 2008, Edinburgh 2008

50= 6 ***Barden*** Greg Forward/Centre 2008-2010
Competitions: Dubai 2008, South Africa 2008, London 2009, Edinburgh 2009, London 2010, Edinburgh 2010

50= 6 ***Abbott*** Jake Hooker 2009-2010
Competitions: Dubai 2009, South Africa 2009, New Zealand 2010, USA 2010, Adelaide 2010, Hong Kong 2010

Rank Comps Surname Forename Position Period

50= 6 ***Powell*** Tom Forward 2010-2010
Competitions: New Zealand 2010, USA 2010, Adelaide 2010, Hong Kong 2010, London 2010, Edinburgh 2010

58= 5 ***Stewart (2)*** Rob Scrum half 2000-2001
Competitions: South Africa 2000, Dubai 2000, Hong Kong 2001, Malaysia 2001, Japan 2001

58= 5 **Earnshaw** Russ Forward 2001-2002
Competitions: New Zealand 2001, Hong Kong 2001, Santiago 2002, Mar del Plata 2002, Malaysia 2002

58= 5 *Simpson-Daniel* James Centre/Wing 2001-2002
Competitions: South Africa 2001, Santiago 2002, Mar del Plata 2002, Beijing 2002, Hong Kong 2002

58= 5 Lewsey Josh Back/Forward 2002-2002
Competitions: Santiago 2002, Mar del Plata 2002, Beijing 2002, Hong Kong 2002, London 2002

58= 5 **Shaw** Joe Back/Forward 2002-2002
Competitions: Brisbane 2002, New Zealand 2002, Beijing 2002, Hong Kong 2002, Malaysia 2002

58= 5 *Lund* Magnus Forward 2002-2003
Competitions: Dubai 2002, South Africa 2002, Brisbane 2003, New Zealand 2003, Cardiff 2003

58= 5 ***Hylton*** Jonny Forward/Back 2002-2006
Competitions: Dubai 2002, South Africa 2002, Dubai 2005, South Africa 2005, London 2006

58= 5 *Rees* Tom Forward 2003-2004
Competitions: Dubai 2003, South Africa 2003, New Zealand 2004, USA 2004, Singapore 2004

58= 5 ***Williams*** Tom Back 2004-2007
Competitions: Hong Kong 2004, Singapore 2004, Hong Kong 2007, London 2007, Edinburgh 2007

58= 5 ***Starling*** Neil Fly half/Centre 2004-2009
Competitions: Dubai 2004, South Africa 2004, Adelaide 2009, London 2009, Edinburgh 2009

58= 5 ***Shabbo*** Dom Forward 2006-2008
Competitions: Dubai 2006, South Africa 2006, USA 2007, New Zealand 2008, USA 2008

58= 5 ***Drauniniu*** Josh Centre/Wing 2008-2010
Competitions: Dubai 2008, Hong Kong 2009, Adelaide 2009, Adelaide 2010, Hong Kong 2010

58= 5 ***Lindsay-Hague*** Ollie Back 2010-2010
Competitions: USA 2010, Adelaide 2010, Hong Kong 2010, London 2010, Edinburgh 2010

71= 4 ***Vass*** Ian Scrum half 2000-2002
Competitions: Hong Kong 2000, South Africa 2001, Santiago 2002, Mar del Plata 2002

71= 4 **Brownrigg** Jim Forward 2001-2001
Competitions: New Zealand 2001, Shanghai 2001, Malaysia 2001, Japan 2001

71= 4 **Davis** Chris Forward 2001-2001
Competitions: Hong Kong 2001, Shanghai 2001, Malaysia 2001, Japan 2001

71= 4 *Cueto* Mark Wing 2001-2003
Competitions: Hong Kong 2001, Santiago 2002, Mar del Plata 2002, Cardiff 2003

Rank Comps Surname Forename Position Period

71= 4 ***Howard*** Johnny Scrum half 2001-2003
Competitions: Wales 2001, Brisbane 2003, New Zealand 2003, Hong Kong 2003

71= 4 Duncombe Nick Scrum half 2001-2002
Competitions: South Africa 2001, Singapore 2002, London 2002, Cardiff 2002

71= 4 ***Mayor*** Chris Back 2002-2008
Competitions: Dubai 2002, South Africa 2002, Hong Kong 2008, Adelaide 2008

71= 4 ***Cannon*** Matt Fly half/Centre 2002-2003
Competitions: Dubai 2002, South Africa 2002, Hong Kong 2003, Cardiff 2003

71= 4 ***Doherty*** David Wing 2006-2007
Competitions: Dubai 2006, South Africa 2006, Hong Kong 2007, Adelaide 2007

71= 4 ***Gray*** Danny Fly half 2006-2007
Competitions: South Africa 2006, New Zealand 2007, USA 2007, Edinburgh 2007

71= 4 ***Cato*** Noah Wing 2007-2008
Competitions: London 2007, Edinburgh 2007, Hong Kong 2008, Adelaide 2008

71= 4 ***Youngs*** Tom Forward/Back 2007-2008
Competitions: Dubai 2007, South Africa 2007, London 2008, Edinburgh 2008

71= 4 *Banahan* Matt Forward/Centre/Wing 2007-2008
Competitions: Dubai 2007, South Africa 2007, New Zealand 2008, USA 2008

71= 4 ***Collins*** James Forward 2008-2009
Competitions: New Zealand 2008, USA 2008, Hong Kong 2008, Adelaide 2008

71= 4 ***Jones*** Ben Scrum half 2009-2009
Competitions: New Zealand 2009, USA 2009, Hong Kong 2009, Adelaide 2009

71= 4 ***Barrell*** Don Forward 2010-2010
Competitions: New Zealand 2010, USA 2010, Adelaide 2010, Hong Kong 2010

87= 3 ***Gustard*** Paul Forward 2000-2001
Competitions: Hong Kong 2000, London 2001, Wales 2001

87= 3 ***Drake*** Nick Wing 2000-2001
Competitions: Air France 2000, Malaysia 2001, Japan 2001

87= 3 **Sowerby** Mark Forward 2000-2001
Competitions: South Africa 2000, Dubai 2000, New Zealand 2001

87= 3 *Erinle* Ayoola Centre 2000-2008
Competitions: South Africa 2000, Dubai 2000, New Zealand 2008

87= 3 **Miall** Simon Forward 2001-2001
Competitions: Hong Kong 2001, Malaysia 2001, Japan 2001

87= 3 ***Meenan*** Mark Fly half 2001-2001
Competitions: Hong Kong 2001, Shanghai 2001, London 2001

87= 3 ***Jones*** Phil Fly half/Centre 2002-2002
Competitions: Singapore 2002, Malaysia 2002, Cardiff 2002

87= 3 *Scarbrough* Dan Back/Forward 2002-2004
Competitions: Malaysia 2002, Hong Kong 2004, Singapore 2004

87= 3 ***McAvoy*** Nathan Centre/Wing 2003-2003
Competitions: Brisbane 2003, New Zealand 2003, London 2003

96= 2 **Vander** Adam Forward 2000-2000
Competitions: Hong Kong 2000, Air France 2000

96= 2 *Gomarsall* Andy Scrum half/Fly half 2000-2001
Competitions: Hong Kong 2000, Shanghai 2001

Rank	Comps	Surname	Forename	Position	Period
96=	2	***Chesney***	Kris	Forward	2000-2001
Competitions: Air France 2000, Shanghai 2001					
96=	2	***Dewdney***	Dean	Scrum half/Wing	2000-2001
Competitions: Air France 2000, New Zealand 2001					
96=	2	**Ezulike**	Nnamdi	Wing	2000-2002
Competitions: Air France 2000, Beijing 2002					
96=	2	**Harrison**	Will	Forward	2000-2000
Competitions: South Africa 2000, Dubai 2000					
96=	2	**Stacey**	Simon	Forward	2000-2000
Competitions: South Africa 2000, Dubai 2000					
96=	2	***Fabian***	Jon	Back/Forward	2000-2000
Competitions: South Africa 2000, Dubai 2000					
96=	2	**Graham**	Phil	Back/Forward	2000-2000
Competitions: South Africa 2000, Dubai 2000					
96=	2	***Brown***	James	Fly half	2000-2000
Competitions: South Africa 2000, Dubai 2000					
96=	2	***Pritchard***	Jon	Fly half/Centre	2000-2000
Competitions: South Africa 2000, Dubai 2000					
96=	2	**Cripps**	Henry	Centre	2000-2000
Competitions: South Africa 2000, Dubai 2000					
96=	2	**Breeze**	Ben	Wing	2000-2000
Competitions: South Africa 2000, Dubai 2000					
96=	2	***Greenlees***	Jamie	Wing	2000-2000
Competitions: South Africa 2000, Dubai 2000					
96=	2	***FitzGerald***	Seb	Fly half	2001-2001
Competitions: Hong Kong 2001, Shanghai 2001					
96=	2	***Dunkley***	Paul	Fly half	2001-2001
Competitions: Malaysia 2001, Japan 2001					
96=	2	***Tapster***	James	Wing	2001-2001
Competitions: Malaysia 2001, Japan 2001					
96=	2	***Roche***	Kieran	Forward	2001-2001
Competitions: London 2001, Wales 2001					
96=	2	***Seely***	Grant	Forward	2001-2001
Competitions: London 2001, Wales 2001					
96=	2	**Rudd**	John	Wing	2001-2001
Competitions: London 2001, Wales 2001					
97=	2	Forrester	James	Forward	2001-2002
Competitions: South Africa 2001, Brisbane 2002					
96=	2	***Balding***	Adam	Forward	2002-2002
Competitions: Santiago 2002, Mar del Plata 2002					
96=	2	*Jones*	Chris	Forward	2002-2002
Competitions: Brisbane 2002, New Zealand 2002					
96=	2	Ellis	Harry	Scrum half	2002-2002
Competitions: Brisbane 2002, New Zealand 2002					
96=	2	**Dawling**	Andy	Forward	2002-2002
Competitions: New Zealand 2002, Malaysia 2002					

Rank	Comps	Surname	Forename	Position	Period
96=	2	***Lewitt***	Ben	Forward	2002-2002
Competitions: Singapore 2002, Malaysia 2002					
96=	2	*May*	Tom	Back/Forward	2002-2002
Competitions: London 2002, Cardiff 2002					
96=	2	***Peacey***	Ryan	Forward	2002-2002
Competitions: Dubai 2002, South Africa 2002					
96=	2	***Laird***	Rob	Back	2002-2002
Competitions: Dubai 2002, South Africa 2002					
96=	2	***Skinner***	Will	Forward	2003-2003
Competitions: Brisbane 2003, New Zealand 2003					
96=	2	***Baxter***	Neil	Wing	2004-2004
Competitions: Hong Kong 2004, Singapore 2004					
96=	2	*Armitage*	Delon	Centre/Wing	2005-2005
Competitions: Singapore 2005, Paris 2005					
96=	2	*Croft*	Tom	Prop	2006-2006
Competitions: Dubai 2006, South Africa 2006					
96=	2	*Haskell*	James	Prop	2006-2006
Competitions: Dubai 2006, South Africa 2006					
96=	2	***Garvey***	Marcel	Wing	2006-2006
Competitions: Dubai 2006, South Africa 2006					
96=	2	***Foster***	Mark	Centre/Wing	2007-2007
Competitions: New Zealand 2007, USA 2007					
96=	2	***Smith (2)***	David	Wing	2007-2007
Competitions: New Zealand 2007, USA 2007					
96=	2	***Guest***	Tom	Forward	2007-2007
Competitions: Dubai 2007, South Africa 2007					
96=	2	***Simpson***	Joe	Scrum half	2007-2007
Competitions: Dubai 2007, South Africa 2007					
96=	2	***Gibson***	Liam	Wing	2007-2007
Competitions: Dubai 2007, South Africa 2007					
96=	2	***Tombleson***	Tom	Wing	2008-2008
Competitions: USA 2008, Adelaide 2008					
96=	2	***Cox***	Matt	Forward	2008-2008
Competitions: Hong Kong 2008, Adelaide 2008					
96=	2	*Youngs*	Ben	Scrum half/Fly half	2008-2008
Competitions: Hong Kong 2008, Adelaide 2008					
96=	2	***Simpson-Daniel***	Charlie	Scrum half	2008-2009
Competitions: South Africa 2008, New Zealand 2009					
140=	1	**Gallacher**	Rob	Forward	2000
Competitions: Hong Kong 2000					
140=	1	Worsley	Joe	Forward	2000
Competitions: Hong Kong 2000					
140=	1	Hanley	Steve	Wing	2000
Competitions: Hong Kong 2000					
140=	1	***King***	Kirk	Wing	2000
Competitions: Hong Kong 2000					

Rank	Comps	Surname	Forename	Position	Period
140=	1	*Cairns*	Matt	Hooker	2000
Competitions: Air France 2000					
140=	1	**Bellinger**	Stuart	Forward	2001
Competitions: New Zealand 2001					
140=	1	***Booth***	Steve	Wing	2001
Competitions: New Zealand 2001					
140=	1	***Carr***	Darren	Wing	2001
Competitions: New Zealand 2001					
140=	1	***Sherriff***	Luke	Prop	2001
Competitions: Hong Kong 2001					
140=	1	**Hamilton**	Jamie	Scrum half	2001
Competitions: Hong Kong 2001					
140=	1	**Marsh**	Nick	Wing	2001
Competitions: Hong Kong 2001					
140=	1	Sleightholme	Jon	Wing	2001
Competitions: Hong Kong 2001					
140=	1	Stimpson	Tim	Back/Forward	2001
Competitions: Shanghai 2001					
140=	1	***Bainbridge-Kay***	Toby	Scrum half	2001
Competitions: Malaysia 2001					
140=	1	Sanderson	Alex	Forward	2001
Competitions: Japan 2001					
140=	1	***Bramhall***	James	Scrum half	2001
Competitions: London 2001					
140=	1	**Carrington**	Matt	Fly half	2001
Competitions: Wales 2001					
140=	1	***Arasa***	Gerald	Centre/Wing	2001
Competitions: Wales 2001					
140=	1	Lloyd	Leon	Centre/Wing	2002
Competitions: Brisbane 2002					
140=	1	*Waters*	Fraser	Centre	2002
Competitions: Singapore 2002					
140=	1	***Graham***	Howard	Back/Forward	2002
Competitions: Malaysia 2002					
140=	1	Rees (2)	David	Wing	2002
Competitions: Malaysia 2002					
140=	1	White-Cooper	Steve	Forward	2002
Competitions: London 2002					
140=	1	***Russell (1)***	Ben	Fly half	2002
Competitions: South Africa 2002					
140=	1	*Hodgson*	Paul	Scrum half	2003
Competitions: Cardiff 2003					
140=	1	**Roke**	Duncan	Centre	2003
Competitions: Cardiff 2003					
140=	1	***Rhodes***	Matt	Scrum half	2003
Competitions: South Africa 2003					

Rank	Comps	Surname	Forename	Position	Period
140=	1	***Penney***	Rodd	Centre	2004

Competitions: New Zealand 2004

140=	1	**Obi**	Nnamdi	Wing	2004

Competitions: New Zealand 2004

140=	1	*Skirving*	Ben	Forward	2005

Competitions: Singapore 2005

140=	1	*Abendanon*	Nick	Centre/Wing	2006

Competitions: Dubai 2006

140=	1	***Fisher***	Jon	Forward	2008

Competitions: Hong Kong 2008

140=	1	***Webber***	Rob	Forward	2008

Competitions: London 2008

140=	1	***Dickson***	Lee	Scrum half	2008

Competitions: London 2008

140=	1	***Cook***	Ollie	Forward	2008

Competitions: Edinburgh 2008

140=	1	***Crane***	Rhys	Wing	2008

Competitions: South Africa 2008

140=	1	***Taufaao*** [***TON***]	Mika	Fly half	2009

Competitions: [Adelaide 2009]

C) POINTS

1) ENGLAND CAP MATCH POINTS SCORERS 1969-2010:

[In numerical order; current players in italics; stated period refers to when matches were played not when points were scored; data up to and including Australia v England 19th June 2010]

Rank	Total	Surname	Forename	Period	Tries	Pens	Drops	Cons	Marks
1	1111	*Wilkinson*	Jonny	1998-2010	6	**228**	**33**	**149**	-
Notes: 67 Lions points (36 in 2001 and 31 in 2005)									
2	400	Grayson	Paul	1995-2004	2	72	6	78	-
3	396	Andrew	Rob	1985-1997	2	86	21	33	-
Notes: 1 Lions XV try 1989									
4	296	Webb	Jonathan	1987-1993	4	66	0	41	-
5	259	*Hodgson*	Charlie	2001-2008	6	44	3	44	-
6	240	Hare	Dusty	1974-1984	2	67	1	14	0
7	210	Underwood	Rory	1984-1996	**49**	0	0	0	-
Notes: 1 Lions try 1993									
8	203	Hodgkinson	Simon	1989-1991	1	43	0	35	-
9=	155	Greenwood	Will	1997-2004	31	0	0	0	-
9=	155	Cohen	Ben	2000-2006	31	0	0	0	-
11	143	Guscott	Jeremy	1989-1999	30	0	2	0	-
Notes: 1 Lions try 1989, 1 Lions drop goal 1997									
12	142	Catt	Mike	1994-2007	7	22	3	16	-
13	140	Robinson	Jason	2001-2007	28	0	0	0	-
Notes: 2 Lions tries 2001									
14	138	Hiller	Bob	1968-1972	3	33	2	12	0
15	120	Luger	Dan	1998-2003	24	0	0	0	-
16	110	Lewsey	Josh	1998-2007	22	0	0	0	-
17	107	*Goode*	Andy	2005-2009	1	20	4	15	-
18	101	Dawson	Matt	1995-2006	16	3	0	6	-
Notes: 2 Lions tries 1997									
19	98	Old	Alan	1972-1978	1	23	3	8	0
20=	85	Dallaglio	Lawrence	1995-2007	17	0	0	0	-
20=	85	*Flood*	Toby	2006-2010	3	15	1	11	-
22	83	Back	Neil	1994-2003	16	0	1	0	-
Notes: 1 Lions try 2001									
23=	82	Rose	Marcus	1981-1987	2	22	0	4	-
23=	82	*Barkley*	Olly	2001-2008	2	18	0	9	-
25=	75	Healey	Austin	1997-2003	15	0	0	0	-
25=	75	*Cueto*	Mark	2004-2010	15	0	0	0	-
27	72	Try	Penalty	1969-2010	15	-	-	-	-
28=	69	Callard	Jon	1993-1995	0	21	0	3	-
28=	69	*Tindall*	Mike	2000-2010	13	0	0	2	-
30=	65	Underwood	Tony	1992-1998	13	0	0	0	-
30=	65	*Balshaw*	Iain	2000-2008	13	0	0	0	-
32	60	Hill (2)	Richard	1997-2004	12	0	0	0	-

Rank	Total	Surname	Forename	Period	Tries	Pens	Drops	Cons	Marks
33	55	*Sackey*	Paul	2006-2009	11	0	0	0	-
34	54	Carling	Will	1988-1997	12	0	0	0	-
35=	50	Perry	Matt	1997-2001	10	0	0	0	-
35=	50	Worsley	Joe	1999-2010	10	0	0	0	-
37	49	*Cipriani*	Danny	2008-2008	1	10	0	7	-
38	48	Hignell	Alastair	1975-1979	0	14	0	3	0
39	45	*Moody*	Lewis	2001-2010	9	0	0	0	-
Notes: 1 Lions try 2005									
40	41	*Walder*	Dave	2001-2003	2	3	0	11	-
41	40	de Glanville	Phil	1992-1999	8	0	0	0	-
42	37	*Gomarsall*	Andy	1996-2008	6	0	1	2	-
43	36	Duckham	David	1969-1976	10	0	0	0	0
44=	35	Stimpson	Tim	1996-2002	2	5	0	5	-
44=	35	*Noon*	Jamie	2001-2009	7	0	0	0	-
46=	34	Rossborough	Peter	1971-1975	1	7	1	3	0
46=	34	Barnes	Stuart	1984-1993	0	7	1	5	-
46=	34	*Armitage*	Delon	2008-2010	5	2	1	0	-
49=	32	Slemen	Mike	1976-1984	8	0	0	0	0
49=	32	Harrison	Mike	1985-1988	8	0	0	0	-
49=	32	Oti	Chris	1988-1991	8	0	0	0	-
52=	30	Greening	Phil	1996-2001	6	0	0	0	-
52=	30	Corry	Martin	1997-2007	6	0	0	0	-
54	28	Carleton	John	1979-1984	7	0	0	0	-
55=	25	Rodber	Tim	1992-1999	5	0	0	0	-
55=	25	Ellis	Harry	2004-2009	5	0	0	0	-
55=	25	*Tait*	Matt	2005-2010	5	0	0	0	-
55=	25	*Easter*	Nick	2007-2010	5	0	0	0	-
59=	24	Squires	Peter	1973-1979	6	0	0	0	0
59=	24	Richards	Dean	1986-1996	6	0	0	0	-
61=	23	Bennett	Neil	1975-1979	2	5	0	0	0
61=	23	*King*	Alex	1997-2003	1	3	1	3	-
63	22	Jorden	Tony	1970-1975	0	4	0	5	0
64	21	Morris	Dewi	1988-1995	5	0	0	0	-
65=	20	Doble	Sam	1972-1973	0	6	0	1	0
65=	20	Sleightholme	Jon	1996-1997	4	0	0	0	-
65=	20	*Flutey*	Riki	2008-2010	4	0	0	0	-
68	19	Neary	Tony	1971-1980	5	0	0	0	0
69=	16	Dixon	Peter	1971-1978	4	0	0	0	0
Notes: 1 Lions try 1971									
69=	16	Woodward	Clive	1980-1984	4	0	0	0	-
69=	16	Davies (1)	Huw	1981-1986	4	0	0	0	-
72=	15	Young	Malcolm	1977-1979	1	1	0	4	0
72=	15	Dodge	Paul	1978-1985	1	3	0	1	-
72=	15	Hunter	Ian	1992-1995	3	0	0	0	-

Rank	Total	Surname	Forename	Period	Tries	Pens	Drops	Cons	Marks
72=	15	Clarke	Ben	1992-1999	3	0	0	0	-
72=	15	Bracken	Kyran	1993-2003	3	0	0	0	-
72=	15	Regan	Mark	1995-2008	3	0	0	0	-
72=	15	Beal	Nick	1996-1999	3	0	0	0	-
72=	15	Cockerill	Richard	1997-1999	3	0	0	0	-
72=	15	Rees (2)	David	1997-1999	3	0	0	0	-
72=	15	West	Dorian	1998-2003	3	0	0	0	-
72=	15	*Voyce*	Tom	2001-2006	3	0	0	0	-
72=	15	Thompson (2)	Steve	2002-2010	3	0	0	0	-
72=	15	*Simpson-Daniel*	James	2002-2007	3	0	0	0	-
72=	15	*Varndell*	Tom	2005-2008	3	0	0	0	-
72=	15	*Banahan*	Matt	2009-2009	3	0	0	0	-
87=	13	Winterbottom	Peter	1982-1993	3	0	0	0	-
87=	13	*Care*	Danny	2008-2010	2	0	1	0	-
89=	12	Horton	John	1978-1984	0	0	4	0	-
89=	12	Cusworth	Les	1979-1988	0	0	4	0	-
89=	12	Dooley	Wade	1985-1993	3	0	0	0	-
89=	12	Smith (1)	Simon	1985-1986	3	0	0	0	-
89=	12	Teague	Mike	1985-1993	3	0	0	0	-
89=	12	Probyn	Jeff	1988-1993	3	0	0	0	-
89=	12	Skinner	Mickey	1988-1992	3	0	0	0	-
89=	12	Heslop	Nigel	1990-1992	3	0	0	0	-
97=	10	Butler	Peter	1975-1976	0	2	0	2	0
97=	10	Johnson	Martin	1993-2003	2	0	0	0	-
97=	10	*Shaw*	Simon	1996-2010	2	0	0	0	-
97=	10	Adebayo	Adedayo	1996-1998	2	0	0	0	-
97=	10	Greenstock	Nick	1997-1997	2	0	0	0	-
97=	10	Grewcock	Danny	1997-2007	2	0	0	0	-
97=	10	Vickery	Phil	1998-2009	2	0	0	0	-
97=	10	Lloyd	Leon	2000-2001	2	0	0	0	-
97=	10	*Borthwick*	Steve	2001-2010	2	0	0	0	-
97=	10	Kay	Ben	2001-2009	2	0	0	0	-
97=	10	Abbott	Stuart	2003-2006	2	0	0	0	-
97=	10	*Perry*	Shaun	2006-2007	2	0	0	0	-
97=	10	*Ojo*	Topsy	2008-2008	2	0	0	0	-
97=	10	*Haskell*	James	2007-2010	2	0	0	0	-
111=	9	Rogers	Budge	1961-1969	3	0	0	0	0
111=	9	Finlan	John	1967-1973	0	0	3	0	0
113=	8	Stevens	Stack	1969-1975	2	0	0	0	0
113=	8	Ripley	Andy	1972-1976	2	0	0	0	0
113=	8	Morley	Alan	1972-1975	2	0	0	0	0
113=	8	Uttley	Roger	1973-1980	2	0	0	0	0
Notes: 1 Lions try 1974									
113=	8	Smith (1)	Steve	1973-1983	2	0	0	0	0

Rank	Total	Surname	Forename	Period	Tries	Pens	Drops	Cons	Marks
113=	8	Hall	Jon	1984-1994	2	0	0	0	-
113=	8	Hill (1)	Richard	1984-1991	2	0	0	0	-
113=	8	Rees	Gary	1984-1991	2	0	0	0	-
113=	8	Halliday	Simon	1986-1992	2	0	0	0	-
122	7	Evans (2)	Geoff	1972-1974	1	0	1	0	0
123=	6	Taylor	Bob	1966-1971	2	0	0	0	0
123=	6	Larter	Peter	1967-1973	1	1	0	0	0
123=	6	Webb	Rod	1967-1972	2	0	0	0	0
123=	6	Spencer	John	1969-1971	2	0	0	0	0
123=	6	Cowman	Dick	1971-1973	0	0	2	0	0
123=	6	*Paul*	Henry	2002-2004	0	0	0	3	-
129=	5	Leonard	Jason	1990-2004	1	0	0	0	-
129=	5	Ubogu	Victor	1992-1999	1	0	0	0	-
129=	5	Sheasby	Chris	1996-1997	1	0	0	0	-
129=	5	Diprose	Tony	1997-1998	1	0	0	0	-
129=	5	Sanderson	Pat	1998-2007	1	0	0	0	-
129=	5	Beim	Tom	1998-1998	1	0	0	0	-
129=	5	Hanley	Steve	1999	1	0	0	0	-
129=	5	Wood	Martyn	2001-2001	1	0	0	0	-
129=	5	Sanderson	Alex	2001-2003	1	0	0	0	-
129=	5	*Christophers*	Phil	2002-2003	1	0	0	0	-
129=	5	*Jones*	Chris	2004-2007	1	0	0	0	-
129=	5	*Hazell*	Andy	2004-2007	1	0	0	0	-
129=	5	*Vyvyan*	Hugh	2004	1	0	0	0	-
129=	5	*Mears*	Lee	2005-2010	1	0	0	0	-
129=	5	*Chuter*	George	2006-2010	1	0	0	0	-
129=	5	*Lund*	Magnus	2006-2007	1	0	0	0	-
129=	5	*Strettle*	Dave	2007-2008	1	0	0	0	-
129=	5	*Geraghty*	Shane	2007-2009	0	1	0	1	-
129=	5	*Scarbrough*	Dan	2003-2007	1	0	0	0	-
129=	5	Farrell	Andy	2007-2007	1	0	0	0	-
129=	5	*Kennedy*	Nick	2008-2009	1	0	0	0	-
129=	5	*Wigglesworth*	Richard	2008-2008	1	0	0	0	-
129=	5	*Monye*	Ugo	2008-2010	1	0	0	0	-
Notes: 1 Lions try 2009									
129=	5	*Foden*	Ben	2009-2010	1	0	0	0	-
129=	5	*Cole*	Dan	2010-2010	1	0	0	0	-
129=	5	*Ashton*	Chris	2010-2010	1	0	0	0	-
129=	5	*Youngs*	Ben	2010-2010	1	0	0	0	-
156=	4	Horton	Nigel	1969-1980	1	0	0	0	0
156=	4	Cotton	Fran	1971-1981	1	0	0	0	0
156=	4	Ralston	Chris	1971-1975	1	0	0	0	0
156=	4	Beese	Mike	1972-1972	1	0	0	0	0
156=	4	Cooper	Martin	1973-1977	1	0	0	0	0

Rank	Total	Surname	Forename	Period	Tries	Pens	Drops	Cons	Marks
156=	4	Nelmes	Barry	1975-1978	1	0	0	0	0
156=	4	Maxwell (1)	Andy	1975-1978	1	0	0	0	0
156=	4	Lampkowski	Mike	1976-1976	1	0	0	0	0
156=	4	Corless	Barry	1976-1978	1	0	0	0	0
156=	4	Kent	Charles	1977-1978	1	0	0	0	0
156=	4	Scott	John	1978-1984	1	0	0	0	-
156=	4	Colclough	Maurice	1978-1986	1	0	0	0	-
156=	4	Preston	Nick	1979-1980	1	0	0	0	-
156=	4	Jeavons	Nick	1981-1983	1	0	0	0	-
156=	4	Barley	Bryan	1984-1988	1	0	0	0	-
156=	4	Bailey	Mark	1984-1990	1	0	0	0	-
156=	4	Redman	Nigel	1984-1997	1	0	0	0	-
156=	4	Harding	Richard	1985-1988	1	0	0	0	-
156=	4	Simms	Kevin	1985-1988	1	0	0	0	-
156=	4	Salmon	Jamie	1985-1987	1	0	0	0	-
156=	4	Moore	Brian	1987-1995	1	0	0	0	-
156=	4	Egerton	Dave	1988-1990	1	0	0	0	-
156=	4	Bentley	John	1988-1997	1	0	0	0	-
156=	4	Robinson	Andy	1988-1995	1	0	0	0	-
156=	4	Ackford	Paul	1988-1991	1	0	0	0	-
156=	4	Linnett	Mark	1989	1	0	0	0	-
156=	4	Ryan	Dean	1990-1998	1	0	0	0	-
183=	3	Pullin	John	1966-1976	1	0	0	0	0
183=	3	Rollitt	Dave	1967-1975	1	0	0	0	0
183=	3	Fielding	Keith	1969-1972	1	0	0	0	0
183=	3	Shackleton	Roger	1969-1970	1	0	0	0	0
183=	3	Novak	John	1970-1970	1	0	0	0	0
183=	3	Hannaford	Charlie	1971-1971	1	0	0	0	0
183=	3	Mapletoft	Mark	1997	0	1	0	0	-

2) ENGLAND NON-CAP MATCH POINTS SCORERS 1969-2010:

[In numerical order; current players in italics; uncapped players in bold or bold italics; stated period refers to when matches were played not when points were scored; data up to and including an England XV v Barbarians 30th May 2010]

Rank	Total	Surname	Forename	Period	Tries	Pens	Drops	Cons	Marks
1	152	Hare	Dusty	1974-1984	2	**22**	0	**39**	0
2	58	*Walder*	Dave	2001-2004	2	7	1	12	-
3=	54	Cowman	Dick	1971-1971	5	2	0	15	0
3=	54	Webb	Jonathan	1987-1992	4	4	0	13	-
5	50	Davies (1)	Huw	1979-1988	3	6	0	10	-
6	48	Underwood	Rory	1984-1991	**12**	0	0	0	-
7	44	Carleton	John	1977-1986	11	0	0	0	-
8	40	Hodgkinson	Simon	1988-1991	1	6	0	9	-
9	36	Squires	Peter	1973-1979	9	0	0	0	0
10	34	Grayson	Paul	1999-2003	1	3	0	10	-
11	30	Andrew	Rob	1986-1992	2	0	**2**	8	-
12	32	Swift	Tony	1981-1982	8	0	0	0	-
13=	27	Hignell	Alastair	1975-1979	1	5	0	4	0
13=	27	Webb	Rod	1969-1971	8	0	0	0	0
13=	27	*Wilkinson*	Jonny	1999	0	1	0	12	-
16=	26	Duckham	David	1970-1975	7	0	0	0	0
16=	26	*Barkley*	Olly	2006-2010	1	3	0	6	-
18=	25	Janion	Jeremy	1971-1972	7	0	0	0	0
18=	25	Old	Alan	1972-1978	1	5	0	3	0
18=	25	Rose	Marcus	1986-1986	0	3	0	8	-
18=	25	Healey	Austin	1999-1999	5	0	0	0	-
22=	24	Smith (1)	Steve	1973-1982	6	0	0	0	0
22=	24	Scott	John	1977-1984	6	0	0	0	-
24	23	Hiller	Bob	1969-1972	0	3	0	7	0
25=	20	Dodge	Paul	1977-1983	5	0	0	0	-
25=	20	*Simpson-Daniel*	James	2002-2006	4	0	0	0	-
27	19	Catt	Mike	1996-2006	2	3	0	0	-
28	18	Cusworth	Les	1982-1988	3	0	**2**	0	-
29=	16	Wheeler	Peter	1971-1983	4	0	0	0	0
29=	16	Slemen	Mike	1977-1984	4	0	0	0	0
29=	16	Wyatt	Derek	1977	4	0	0	0	-
29=	16	Winterbottom	Peter	1982-1991	4	0	0	0	-
29=	16	Bailey	Mark	1986-1987	4	0	0	0	-
29=	16	Oti	Chris	1990-1991	4	0	0	0	-
29=	16	*Goode*	Andy	2005-2009	0	2	0	5	-
36=	15	Rossborough	Peter	1971-1974	1	2	0	3	0
36=	15	Dallaglio	Lawrence	1996-1999	3	0	0	0	-
36=	15	Luger	Dan	1999-1999	3	0	0	0	-

Rank	Total	Surname	Forename	Period	Tries	Pens	Drops	Cons	Marks
36=	15	Forrester	James	2002-2006	3	0	0	0	-
40=	14	Glover	Peter	1971-1971	4	0	0	0	0
40=	14	Heslop	Nigel	1990-1992	3	0	0	0	-
42=	12	Ripley	Andy	1972-1975	3	0	0	0	0
42=	12	Beaumont	Bill	1975-1981	3	0	0	0	0
42=	12	**Gadd**	John	1982-1983	3	0	0	0	-
42=	12	Trick	David	1982	3	0	0	0	-
42=	12	Guscott	Jeremy	1990-1992	3	0	0	0	-
47	11	Doble	Sam	1972	0	3	0	1	0
48=	10	**Gray**	John	1971-1971	3	0	0	0	0
48=	10	Hannaford	Charlie	1971-1974	3	0	0	0	0
48=	10	Horton	John	1977-1981	1	0	**2**	0	-
48=	10	**Smith (2)**	Simon	1986	0	0	0	5	-
48=	10	Corry	Martin	1999-2003	2	0	0	0	-
48=	10	*Sampson*	Paul	2001	2	0	0	0	-
48=	10	*Christophers*	Phil	2002-2003	2	0	0	0	-
48=	10	*Noon*	Jamie	2003-2009	2	0	0	0	-
48=	10	Cohen	Ben	2003	2	0	0	0	-
48=	10	*Tindall*	Mike	2003-2010	2	0	0	0	-
48=	10	*Sackey*	Paul	2004-2005	2	0	0	0	-
48=	10	*Hodgson*	Charlie	2008-2010	0	2	0	2	-
48=	10	*Foden*	Ben	2009-2010	2	0	0	0	-
61	9	Back	Neil	1990-1999	2	0	0	0	-
62=	8	Fielding	Keith	1969-1972	2	0	0	0	0
62=	8	Neary	Tony	1971-1979	2	0	0	0	0
62=	8	Evans (2)	Geoff	1971-1974	2	0	0	0	0
62=	8	Caplan	David	1977-1978	0	2	0	1	0
62=	8	**Pomphrey**	Nigel	1979-1979	2	0	0	0	-
62=	8	Hall	Jon	1984-1987	2	0	0	0	-
62=	8	Harrison	Mike	1986-1988	2	0	0	0	-
62=	8	Williams	Peter	1986	2	0	0	0	-
62=	8	Richards	Dean	1988-1991	2	0	0	0	-
62=	8	Skinner	Mickey	1991	2	0	0	0	-
72=	7	**Robinson**	David	1971-1971	2	0	0	0	0
72=	7	Webster	Jan	1971-1974	2	0	0	0	0
74=	6	Starmer-Smith	Nigel	1970-1971	0	0	2	0	0
74=	6	Wright	Ian	1971	0	0	0	3	0
76=	5	Jorden	Tony	1973	0	1	0	1	0
76=	5	de Glanville	Phil	1992-1999	1	0	0	0	-
76=	5	Sleightholme	Jon	1996	1	0	0	0	-
76=	5	Stimpson	Tim	1996-2001	1	0	0	0	-
76=	5	Cockerill	Richard	1999-1999	1	0	0	0	-
76=	5	Worsley	Joe	1999-2010	1	0	0	0	-
76=	5	Beal	Nick	1999	1	0	0	0	-

Rank	Total	Surname	Forename	Period	Tries	Pens	Drops	Cons	Marks
76=	5	Perry	Matt	1999-1999	1	0	0	0	-
76=	5	Garforth	Darren	1999-1999	1	0	0	0	-
76=	5	Rees (2)	David	1999	1	0	0	0	-
76=	5	*Stephenson*	Michael	2001	1	0	0	0	-
76=	5	*Johnston*	Ben	2001-2003	1	0	0	0	-
76=	5	Thompson (2)	Steve	2002-2010	1	0	0	0	-
76=	5	*Horak*	Michael	2002-2004	1	0	0	0	-
76=	5	Walshe	Nick	2002-2004	1	0	0	0	-
76=	5	*Lipman*	Michael	2003-2006	1	0	0	0	-
76=	5	*Stevens*	Matt	2003	1	0	0	0	-
76=	5	Sanderson	Pat	2003-2006	1	0	0	0	-
76=	5	*Erinle*	Ayoola	2005	1	0	0	0	-
76=	5	*Tait*	Matt	2005-2010	1	0	0	0	-
76=	5	***Barnes***	David	2006	1	0	0	0	-
76=	5	*Haskell*	James	2006-2010	1	0	0	0	-
76=	5	*Armitage*	Delon	2006-2009	1	0	0	0	-
76=	5	*Easter*	Nick	2008-2010	1	0	0	0	-
76=	5	*Flood*	Toby	2008	0	1	0	1	-
76=	5	*Banahan*	Matt	2009	1	0	0	0	-
76=	5	***Turner-Hall***	Jordan	2009	1	0	0	0	-
76=	5	*May*	Tom	2009	1	0	0	0	-
76=	5	*Hape*	Shontayne	2010	1	0	0	0	-
105=	4	Try	Penalty	1969-2010	1	-	-	-	-
105=	4	Fairbrother	Keith	1969-1972	1	0	0	0	0
105=	4	Ralston	Chris	1971-1974	1	0	0	0	0
105=	4	Preece	Peter	1972-1974	1	0	0	0	0
105=	4	Cooper	Martin	1974-1977	1	0	0	0	0
105=	4	Smith	Keith	1974	1	0	0	0	0
105=	4	Keyworth	Mark	1975	1	0	0	0	0
105=	4	Maxwell (1)	Andy	1975	1	0	0	0	0
105=	4	Colclough	Maurice	1978-1984	1	0	0	0	-
105=	4	**Gifford**	Chris	1978-1979	1	0	0	0	-
105=	4	Bennett	Neil	1979	1	0	0	0	-
105=	4	Pearce (1)	Gary	1979-1991	1	0	0	0	-
105=	4	Cardus	Richard	1979-1979	1	0	0	0	-
105=	4	**Allchurch**	Toby	1979	1	0	0	0	-
105=	4	Rendall	Paul	1981-1991	1	0	0	0	-
105=	4	Youngs	Nick	1983-1984	1	0	0	0	-
105=	4	Simpson	Paul	1984-1986	1	0	0	0	-
105=	4	Rees	Gary	1984-1991	1	0	0	0	-
105=	4	Salmon	Jamie	1986-1987	1	0	0	0	-
105=	4	Dooley	Wade	1986-1991	1	0	0	0	-
105=	4	Harding	Richard	1986	1	0	0	0	-
105=	4	Dawe	Graham	1986-1988	1	0	0	0	-

Rank	Total	Surname	Forename	Period	Tries	Pens	Drops	Cons	Marks
105=	4	Clough	Fran	1987-1990	1	0	0	0	-
105=	4	Buckton	John	1990	1	0	0	0	-
105=	4	Teague	Mike	1990-1991	1	0	0	0	-
105=	4	Pears	David	1991-1992	1	0	0	0	-
105=	4	*Vesty*	Sam	2005	0	0	0	2	-
132=	3	Greenwood	Dick	1969	1	0	0	0	0
132=	3	Bucknall	Tony	1970-1971	1	0	0	0	0
132=	3	Hale	Peter	1970	1	0	0	0	0
132=	3	**Kirkpatrick**	George	1971	1	0	0	0	0
132=	3	Uttley	Roger	1971-1980	1	0	0	0	0
132=	3	Rogers	Budge	1971-1971	1	0	0	0	0
132=	3	Finlan	John	1971-1971	1	0	0	0	0
139=	2	**Bushell**	Billy	1978	0	0	0	1	-
139=	2	Stringer	Nick	1982-1984	0	0	0	1	-
139=	2	*Gomarsall*	Andy	1996-2005	0	0	0	1	-
139=	2	*Brown*	Mike	2008	0	0	0	1	-

3) ENGLAND TOUR MATCH POINTS SCORERS 1969-2010:

[In numerical order; current players in italics; uncapped players in bold or bold italics; stated period refers to when matches were played not when points were scored; data up to and including an England XV v New Zealand Maori 23rd June 2010]

Rank	Total	Surname	Forename	Period	Tries	Pens	Drops	Cons	Marks
1	99	Hare	Dusty	1979-1984	2	**18**	1	17	-
2	98	Stringer	Nick	1982-1984	1	16	0	**23**	-
3	76	Carleton	John	1979-1982	**19**	0	0	0	-
4	66	Davies (1)	Huw	1979-1985	3	8	0	15	-
5	61	Barnes	Stuart	1985-1994	2	12	**3**	4	-
6	55	Bennett	Neil	1975-1979	3	6	1	11	0
7=	47	**Adamson**	Ray	1988-1988	0	9	0	10	-
7=	47	Hodgkinson	Simon	1990-1991	0	11	0	7	-
7=	47	*Barkley*	Olly	2001-2010	0	7	0	13	-
10	43	Webb	Jonathan	1988-1991	1	11	0	3	-
11	41	**Patrick**	Brian	1981-1981	2	5	0	9	-
12	37	Stimpson	Tim	1998-2002	0	5	0	11	-
13=	36	Morley	Alan	1972-1975	9	0	0	0	0
13=	36	Trick	David	1981-1984	9	0	0	0	-
15=	33	Doble	Sam	1972-1972	0	6	1	6	0
15=	33	Catt	Mike	1994-1999	2	3	0	7	-
17=	32	Old	Alan	1972-1975	1	1	1	11	0
17=	32	Scott	John	1979-1984	8	0	0	0	-
19	31	**Hepher**	Ali	2000-2000	0	3	0	11	-
20	30	Mapletoft	Mark	1997-1997	1	3	0	8	-
21=	28	Squires	Peter	1973-1979	7	0	0	0	0
21=	28	Melville	Nigel	1981-1985	7	0	0	0	-
23=	25	Andrew	Rob	1988-1994	1	5	1	1	-
23=	25	Pears	David	1990-1994	1	4	1	3	-
23=	25	Rees (2)	David	1997-2002	5	0	0	0	-
23=	25	Lloyd	Leon	1999-2000	5	0	0	0	-
27	22	Hignell	Alastair	1975-1979	2	2	0	4	0
28=	20	Preece	Peter	1972-1975	5	0	0	0	0
28=	20	Slemen	Mike	1979-1979	5	0	0	0	-
28=	20	Dodge	Paul	1979-1985	5	0	0	0	-
28=	20	Swift	Tony	1981-1984	5	0	0	0	-
32	19	*Hodgson*	Charlie	2010-2010	0	5	0	2	-
33	18	Hopley	Damian	1991-1994	4	0	0	0	-
34=	17	Underwood	Rory	1988-1994	4	0	0	0	-
34=	17	Callard	Jon	1994-1994	0	5	0	1	-
36=	16	Knight (1)	Peter	1972-1973	4	0	0	0	0
36=	16	**Richards**	Tony	1972-1972	4	0	0	0	0
36=	16	**Holdstock**	Steve	1982-1982	4	0	0	0	-
36=	16	Hill (1)	Richard	1984-1991	4	0	0	0	-

Rank	Total	Surname	Forename	Period	Tries	Pens	Drops	Cons	Marks
36=	16	*King*	Alex	1997-2003	2	2	0	0	-
41=	15	**Liley**	John	1990-1990	1	3	0	1	-
41=	15	Clarke	Ben	1994-2000	3	0	0	0	-
41=	15	Mallinder	Jim	1997-1997	3	0	0	0	-
41=	15	*Gomarsall*	Andy	1997-2003	3	0	0	0	-
41=	15	Baxendell	Jos	1997-1998	3	0	0	0	-
41=	15	Luger	Dan	1999-2003	3	0	0	0	-
41=	15	Worsley	Joe	1999-2010	3	0	0	0	-
41=	15	*Waters*	Fraser	2001-2001	3	0	0	0	-
41=	15	*Voyce*	Tom	2001-2001	3	0	0	0	-
50=	14	*Wilkinson*	Jonny	1999	0	2	0	4	-
50=	14	*Walder*	Dave	2002	1	1	0	3	-
52	13	Grayson	Paul	2003	0	3	0	2	-
53=	12	Hannaford	Charlie	1971	3	0	0	0	0
53=	12	Wardlow	Chris	1971	3	0	0	0	0
53=	12	Ripley	Andy	1972-1975	3	0	0	0	0
53=	12	Janion	Jeremy	1972-1975	3	0	0	0	0
53=	12	Wyatt	Derek	1975-1975	3	0	0	0	0
53=	12	Woodward	Clive	1981-1982	3	0	0	0	-
53=	12	Hesford	Bob	1981-1985	3	0	0	0	-
53=	12	Hall	Jon	1984-1991	3	0	0	0	-
53=	12	Rees	Gary	1984-1991	3	0	0	0	-
53=	12	Teague	Mike	1984-1991	3	0	0	0	-
53=	12	Smith (1)	Simon	1985-1985	3	0	0	0	-
53=	12	Harrison	Mike	1985-1985	3	0	0	0	-
53=	12	Robinson	Andy	1988-1990	3	0	0	0	-
53=	12	Evans	Barry	1988-1988	3	0	0	0	-
53=	12	Heslop	Nigel	1990-1991	3	0	0	0	-
68=	10	Cusworth	Les	1982-1982	1	0	2	0	-
68=	10	Underwood	Tony	1990-1994	2	0	0	0	-
68=	10	Hull	Paul	1990-1994	2	0	0	0	-
68=	10	de Glanville	Phil	1994-1997	2	0	0	0	-
68=	10	Bracken	Kyran	1997-2003	2	0	0	0	-
68=	10	Lewsey	Josh	1998-2000	1	1	0	1	-
68=	10	*Benton*	Scott	1998-2001	2	0	0	0	-
68=	10	*Borthwick*	Steve	2000-2003	2	0	0	0	-
68=	10	*Johnston*	Ben	2000-2003	2	0	0	0	-
68=	10	Greenwood	Will	2000-2000	2	0	0	0	-
68=	10	*Sackey*	Paul	2001-2001	2	0	0	0	-
79=	9	Redman	Nigel	1988-1997	2	0	0	0	-
79=	9	Guscott	Jeremy	1991-1999	2	0	0	0	-
81=	8	Cotton	Fran	1971-1975	2	0	0	0	0
81=	8	Neary	Tony	1971-1975	2	0	0	0	0
81=	8	Watkins (1)	John	1972-1973	2	0	0	0	0

Rank	Total	Surname	Forename	Period	Tries	Pens	Drops	Cons	Marks
81=	8	Spencer	John	1972-1972	2	0	0	0	0
81=	8	Wilkinson	Bob	1973-1975	2	0	0	0	0
81=	8	Jorden	Tony	1973	0	2	0	1	0
81=	8	Rollitt	Dave	1975-1975	2	0	0	0	0
81=	8	Beaumont	Bill	1975-1981	2	0	0	0	0
81=	8	Butler	Peter	1975-1975	0	0	0	4	0
81=	8	**Pomphrey**	Nigel	1979	2	0	0	0	-
81=	8	Cardus	Richard	1979-1979	2	0	0	0	-
81=	8	Jeavons	Nick	1981-1982	2	0	0	0	-
81=	8	**Gadd**	John	1982-1982	2	0	0	0	-
81=	8	Youngs	Nick	1984-1984	2	0	0	0	-
81=	8	Richards	Dean	1988-1994	2	0	0	0	-
81=	8	Egerton	Dave	1988-1990	2	0	0	0	-
81=	8	Skinner	Mickey	1988-1991	2	0	0	0	-
81=	8	**Kimmins**	Bob	1990-1990	2	0	0	0	-
81=	8	Morris	Dewi	1990-1994	2	0	0	0	-
81=	8	Hunter	Ian	1991-1991	2	0	0	0	-
101=	7	Rossborough	Peter	1971-1973	1	1	0	0	0
101=	7	Horton	John	1981-1984	1	0	1	0	-
103=	6	Wheeler	Peter	1971-1982	0	0	0	3	0
103=	6	Larter	Peter	1971-1972	1	0	0	1	0
105=	5	Haag	Martin	1997-1997	1	0	0	0	-
105=	5	Ubogu	Victor	1990-1999	1	0	0	0	-
105=	5	Bates	Steve	1990-1994	1	0	0	0	-
105=	5	*Shaw*	Simon	1994-2003	1	0	0	0	-
105=	5	Diprose	Tony	1997-1998	1	0	0	0	-
105=	5	Grewcock	Danny	1997-1999	1	0	0	0	-
105=	5	**O'Leary**	Daren	1997-1997	1	0	0	0	-
105=	5	Chapman	Dominic	1998-1998	1	0	0	0	-
105=	5	Fidler	Rob	1998-2002	1	0	0	0	-
105=	5	*Chuter*	George	1998-2010	1	0	0	0	-
105=	5	Brown	Spencer	1998	1	0	0	0	-
105=	5	*Flatman*	David	2000-2010	1	0	0	0	-
105=	5	***Thirlby***	Rob	2000-2000	1	0	0	0	-
105=	5	Hanley	Steve	2000-2000	1	0	0	0	-
105=	5	Walshe	Nick	2000-2002	1	0	0	0	-
105=	5	Woodman	Trevor	2001-2003	1	0	0	0	-
105=	5	*Palmer (2)*	Tom	2001-2003	1	0	0	0	-
105=	5	*Hazell*	Andy	2001-2003	1	0	0	0	-
105=	5	Sanderson	Alex	2001-2002	1	0	0	0	-
105=	5	Morris	Robbie	2002	1	0	0	0	-
105=	5	*Cueto*	Mark	2002	1	0	0	0	-
105=	5	*Mears*	Lee	2010-2010	1	0	0	0	-
105=	5	**Ward-Smith**	Dan	2010-2010	1	0	0	0	-

Rank	Total	Surname	Forename	Period	Tries	Pens	Drops	Cons	Marks
105=	5	*Banahan*	Matt	2010-2010	1	0	0	0	-
105=	5	*Armitage*	Steffon	2010-2010	1	0	0	0	-
105=	5	*Care*	Danny	2010	1	0	0	0	-
105=	5	*Ashton*	Chris	2010	1	0	0	0	-
132=	4	Try	Penalty	1969-2010	1	-	-	-	-
132=	4	Rogers	Budge	1971	1	0	0	0	0
132=	4	Webb	Rod	1971	1	0	0	0	0
132=	4	Lloyd	Bob	1971	1	0	0	0	0
132=	4	Glover	Peter	1971	1	0	0	0	0
132=	4	Stevens	Stack	1972-1973	1	0	0	0	0
132=	4	Burton	Mike	1972-1975	1	0	0	0	0
132=	4	Ralston	Chris	1972-1973	1	0	0	0	0
132=	4	**Cowell**	Tim	1972-1972	1	0	0	0	0
132=	4	**Boddy**	Tony	1972-1972	1	0	0	0	0
132=	4	**Palmer (1)**	Tom	1972-1972	1	0	0	0	0
132=	4	Mantell	Neil	1975-1975	1	0	0	0	0
132=	4	Smart	Colin	1979-1981	1	0	0	0	-
132=	4	Colclough	Maurice	1979-1982	1	0	0	0	-
132=	4	**Allchurch**	Toby	1979-1979	1	0	0	0	-
132=	4	**Peck**	Ian	1979-1979	1	0	0	0	-
132=	4	Pearce (1)	Gary	1979-1991	1	0	0	0	-
132=	4	**Simpson**	Andy	1981-1985	1	0	0	0	-
132=	4	Preston	Nick	1981-1981	1	0	0	0	-
132=	4	Syddall	Jim	1982-1982	1	0	0	0	-
132=	4	Preedy	Malcolm	1982-1985	1	0	0	0	-
132=	4	Williams	Peter	1982-1982	1	0	0	0	-
132=	4	Bailey	Mark	1984-1984	1	0	0	0	-
132=	4	Brain	Steve	1984-1985	1	0	0	0	-
132=	4	Cusani	Dave	1984-1984	1	0	0	0	-
132=	4	Orwin	John	1985-1988	1	0	0	0	-
132=	4	**Goodwin**	John	1985-1985	1	0	0	0	-
132=	4	**Metcalfe**	Ian	1985-1985	1	0	0	0	-
132=	4	**Robson**	Simon	1988-1988	1	0	0	0	-
132=	4	Buckton	John	1988-1990	1	0	0	0	-
132=	4	Bentley	John	1988-1988	1	0	0	0	-
132=	4	Probyn	Jeff	1988-1991	1	0	0	0	-
132=	4	Buttimore	Tim	1988-1988	1	0	0	0	-
132=	4	Carling	Will	1988-1994	1	0	0	0	-
132=	4	Oti	Chris	1990-1991	1	0	0	0	-
132=	4	Olver	John	1990-1991	1	0	0	0	-
132=	4	Ryan	Dean	1990-1994	1	0	0	0	-
169	3	**Whibley**	Dave	1972-1972	0	1	0	0	0

4) ENGLAND SEVENS COMPETITION POINTS* 1973-1999:

[In numerical order; current players in italics; uncapped players in bold or bold italics; stated period refers to when matches were played not when points were scored; data up to and including Air France Sevens 29th-30th May 1999]

[*excludes Rugby World Cup Sevens, Commonwealth Sevens and IRB World Sevens competitions]

Rank	Total	Surname	Forename	Period	Tries	Pens	Drops	Cons	Marks
1	57	Beal	Nick	1992-1996	5	0	0	16	-
2	36	Fielding	Keith	1973	9	0	0	0	0
3	25	Sleightholme	Jon	1996	5	0	0	0	-
4	22	Hopley	Damian	1992-1996	4	0	0	1	-
5	20	Sheasby	Chris	1992-1996	4	0	0	0	-
6	18	**Gray**	John	1973	0	0	0	9	0
7	16	Ripley	Andy	1973-1986	4	0	0	0	0
8=	15	Underwood	Tony	1992	3	0	0	0	-
8=	15	Healey	Austin	1995-1996	1	0	0	5	-
8=	15	Adebayo	Adedayo	1995-1996	3	0	0	0	-
8=	15	Back	Neil	1996	3	0	0	0	-
8=	15	Cohen	Ben	1999	3	0	0	0	-
13=	12	Rossborough	Peter	1973	1	0	0	4	0
13=	12	Preece	Peter	1973	3	0	0	0	0
13=	12	Hill (1)	Richard	1986	1	0	0	4	-
16	11	*Sampson*	Paul	1999	1	0	0	3	-
17=	10	Haag	Martin	1992	2	0	0	0	-
17=	10	**Eves**	Derek	1995	2	0	0	0	-
17=	10	Hill (2)	Richard	1995	2	0	0	0	-
17=	10	Greenstock	Nick	1995	2	0	0	0	-
17=	10	*Balshaw*	Iain	1999	2	0	0	0	-
22	7	**Scully**	Dave	1992-1996	1	0	0	1	-
23=	5	**Cassell**	Justyn	1992-1992	1	0	0	0	-
23=	5	Dallaglio	Lawrence	1992	1	0	0	0	-
23=	5	**Hackney**	Steve	1995	1	0	0	0	-
23=	5	Stimpson	Tim	1996-1999	1	0	0	0	-
23=	5	Brown	Spencer	1999	1	0	0	0	-
28=	4	Smith (1)	Steve	1973	1	0	0	0	0
28=	4	Winterbottom	Peter	1986	1	0	0	0	-
28=	4	Williams	Peter	1986	1	0	0	0	-
28=	4	Clough	Fran	1986	1	0	0	0	-
28=	4	**Thomas (1)**	Huw	1986	1	0	0	0	-
33	2	Hull	Paul	1992	0	0	0	1	-

5) ENGLAND RUGBY WORLD CUP SEVENS COMPETITION POINTS SCORERS 1993-2009:

[In numerical order; current players in italics; uncapped players in bold or bold italics; stated period refers to when matches were played not when points were scored; data up to and including Rugby World Cup Sevens 5th-7th March 2009]

Rank	Total	Surname	Forename	Period	Tries	Pens	Drops	Cons	Marks
1	98	***Gollings***	Ben	2005-2009	8	0	0	29	-
2	84	Beal	Nick	1993-1997	6	0	0	27	-
3	62	Harriman	Andy	1993	12	0	0	1	-
4	42	*Sampson*	Paul	2001	4	0	0	11	-
5=	35	***Thirlby***	Rob	2001-2005	7	0	0	0	-
5=	35	***Haughton***	Richard	2005	7	0	0	0	-
5=	35	*Varndell*	Tom	2009	7	0	0	0	-
8	31	Healey	Austin	1997	5	0	0	3	-
9=	30	Sheasby	Chris	1993-1997	6	0	0	0	-
9=	30	Hopley	Damian	1993	6	0	0	0	-
9=	30	*Monye*	Ugo	2005	6	0	0	0	-
12	24	**Scully**	Dave	1993-1997	4	0	0	2	-
13=	20	Dallaglio	Lawrence	1993	4	0	0	0	-
13=	20	***Amor***	Simon	2005	2	0	0	5	-
15=	15	Rodber	Tim	1993-1997	3	0	0	0	-
15=	15	***Roques***	Tony	2005	3	0	0	0	-
17	14	Catt	Mike	1997	2	0	0	2	-
18=	10	Back	Neil	1997	2	0	0	0	-
18=	10	Sleightholme	Jon	1997	2	0	0	0	-
18=	10	*Johnston*	Ben	2001	2	0	0	0	-
18=	10	Lewsey	Josh	2001	2	0	0	0	-
18=	10	*Sackey*	Paul	2001	2	0	0	0	-
18=	10	Appleford	Geoff	2005	2	0	0	0	-
18=	10	Richards	Peter	2005	2	0	0	0	-
18=	10	***Starling***	Neil	2005	2	0	0	0	-
18=	10	*Paul*	Henry	2005	2	0	0	0	-
18=	10	***Damu***	Isoa	2009	2	0	0	0	-
18=	10	***Drauniniu***	Josh	2009	2	0	0	0	-
29=	5	**Cassell**	Justyn	1993	1	0	0	0	-
29=	5	Dawson	Matt	1993	1	0	0	0	-
29=	5	Adebayo	Adedayo	1993-1997	1	0	0	0	-
29=	5	Hill (2)	Richard	1997	1	0	0	0	-
29=	5	***Chesney***	Kris	2001	1	0	0	0	-
29=	5	***Dowson***	Phil	2005	1	0	0	0	-
29=	5	***Cracknell***	Chris	2009	1	0	0	0	-
29=	5	***Barrett***	Kevin	2009	1	0	0	0	-
29=	5	***Phillips***	Ollie	2009	1	0	0	0	-
29=	5	***Biggs***	Tom	2009	1	0	0	0	-

6) ENGLAND COMMONWEALTH SEVENS COMPETITION POINTS SCORERS 1998-2006:

[In numerical order; current players in italics; uncapped players in bold or bold italics; stated period refers to when matches were played not when points were scored; data up to and including Commonwealth Sevens 16th-17th March 2006]

Rank	Total	Surname	Forename	Period	Tries	Pens	Drops	Cons	Marks
1	54	***Gollings***	Ben	2002-2006	4	0	0	17	-
2	48	***Amor***	Simon	2002-2006	4	0	0	14	-
3	45	*Tait*	Matt	2006	9	0	0	0	-
4	30	**Baxter**	Nick	1998	6	0	0	0	-
5	24	*Paul*	Henry	2002-2006	4	0	0	2	-
6=	20	Greening	Phil	2002	4	0	0	0	-
6=	20	Lewsey	Josh	2002	4	0	0	0	-
6=	20	Sampson	Paul	2002	4	0	0	0	-
6=	20	*Varndell*	Tom	2006	4	0	0	0	-
10=	15	Sheasby	Chris	1998	3	0	0	0	-
10=	15	*Seymour*	David	2006	3	0	0	0	-
12	14	**Harvey**	Ben	1998	2	0	0	2	-
13=	10	**Earnshaw**	Russ	1998	2	0	0	0	-
13=	10	***Williams***	Jamie	1998	2	0	0	0	-
15	9	**Davis**	Chris	1998	1	0	0	2	-
16=	7	***Mordt***	Nils	2006	1	0	0	1	-
16=	7	*Care*	Danny	2006	1	0	0	1	-
18=	5	***Jenner***	Jim	1998	1	0	0	0	-
18=	5	**Friday**	Mike	1998	1	0	0	0	-
18=	5	***Griffiths***	Matt	1998	1	0	0	0	-
18=	5	***Roques***	Tony	2002	1	0	0	0	-
18=	5	Sanderson	Pat	2002	1	0	0	0	-
18=	5	Duncombe	Nick	2002	1	0	0	0	-
18=	5	***Thirlby***	Rob	2002	1	0	0	0	-
18=	5	*Lund*	Magnus	2006	1	0	0	0	-
18=	5	***Vilk***	Andy	2006	1	0	0	0	-
18=	5	***Haughton***	Richard	2006	1	0	0	0	-

7) ENGLAND IRB WORLD SEVENS COMPETITION POINTS SCORERS 2000-2010:

[In numerical order; current players in italics; uncapped players in bold or bold italics; stated period refers to when matches were played not when points were scored; data up to and including Edinburgh Sevens 29th-30th May 2010]

Rank	Total	Surname	Forename	Period	Tries	Pens	Drops	Cons	Marks
1	2374	***Gollings***	Ben	2000-2010	202	0	0	682	-
Notes: 98 Rugby World Cup Sevens points; 54 Commonwealth Sevens points									
2	721	***Amor***	Simon	2001-2007	72	3	0	176	-
3	538	***Haughton***	Richard	2001-2006	106	0	0	4	-
4	527	***Thirlby***	Rob	2001-2007	101	0	0	11	-
5	241	***Phillips***	Ollie	2004-2009	39	0	0	23	-
6	235	*Monye*	Ugo	2003-2004	47	0	0	0	-
7	205	***Vilk***	Andy	2005-2009	41	0	0	0	-
8	170	***Hunt***	Simon	2001-2008	34	0	0	0	-
9=	165	*Varndell*	Tom	2005-2010	33	0	0	0	-
9=	165	*Strettle*	Dave	2006-2006	33	0	0	0	-
9=	165	***Damu***	Isoa	2007-2009	33	0	0	0	-
12	156	***Brooks***	James	2001-2007	24	0	0	18	-
13	153	*Foden*	Ben	2005-2008	23	0	0	19	-
14	150	***Roques***	Tony	2001-2007	30	0	0	0	-
15=	145	Appleford	Geoff	2001-2005	29	0	0	0	-
15=	145	*Tait*	Matt	2004-2006	29	0	0	0	-
17	141	**Simpson**	Nigel	2000-2002	27	0	0	3	-
18	120	*Care*	Danny	2006-2008	16	0	0	20	-
19	115	***Oduoza***	Uche	2008-2010	23	0	0	0	-
20=	112	*Paul*	Henry	2002-2006	18	0	0	11	-
20=	112	***Barrett***	Kevin	2002-2010	22	0	0	1	-
22=	110	Sanderson	Pat	2000-2004	22	0	0	0	-
22=	110	***Wade***	Christian	2009-2010	22	0	0	0	-
24	105	***Rodwell***	James	2008-2010	21	0	0	0	-
25=	100	Richards	Peter	2004-2005	20	0	0	0	-
25=	100	***Biggs***	Tom	2008-2009	20	0	0	0	-
27	99	***Turner***	Mat	2008-2010	19	0	0	2	-
28	95	***Royle***	Nick	2009-2010	19	0	0	0	-
29	91	***Young***	Micky	2008-2010	17	0	0	3	-
30	90	***Dowson***	Phil	2003-2005	18	0	0	0	-
31	89	*Sampson*	Paul	2002-2004	17	0	0	2	-
32=	85	***Elliott***	Anthony	2001-2008	17	0	0	0	-
32=	85	*Hipkiss*	Dan	2003-2006	17	0	0	0	-
32=	85	***Vickerman***	Rob	2005-2010	17	0	0	0	-
35	84	*Simpson-Daniel*	James	2001-2002	14	0	0	7	-
36	80	***Norton***	Dan	2009-2010	16	0	0	0	-
37	69	*Gomarsall*	Andy	2000-2001	6	1	0	18	-

Rank	Total	Surname	Forename	Period	Tries	Pens	Drops	Cons	Marks
38	65	***Caprice***	Dan	2009-2010	13	0	0	0	-
39	64	Lewsey	Josh	2002-2002	12	0	0	2	-
40=	60	***Jones***	Phil	2002-2002	10	0	0	5	-
40=	60	***Amesbury***	Charlie	2006-2007	12	0	0	0	-
42=	55	***Bailey***	James	2005-2006	11	0	0	0	-
42=	55	***Cracknell***	Chris	2008-2009	11	0	0	0	-
44	50	***Meenan***	Mark	2001-2001	4	0	0	15	-
45	47	*Noon*	Jamie	2000-2003	9	0	0	1	-
46=	45	*Cueto*	Mark	2001-2003	9	0	0	0	-
46=	45	*Stephenson*	Michael	2001-2002	9	0	0	0	-
46=	45	***Mordt***	Nils	2004-2007	9	0	0	0	-
46=	45	***Brake***	John	2007-2008	9	0	0	0	-
46=	45	***Powell***	Tom	2010-2010	9	0	0	0	-
46=	45	***Lindsay-Hague***	Ollie	2010-2010	9	0	0	0	-
52	44	***Drauniniu***	Josh	2008-2010	8	0	0	2	-
53=	40	***Russell (2)***	Ben	2002-2007	8	0	0	0	-
53=	40	***Starling***	Neil	2004-2009	8	0	0	0	-
53=	40	*Narraway*	Luke	2005-2007	8	0	0	0	-
53=	40	***Hills***	Michael	2006-2007	8	0	0	0	-
53=	40	***Adams***	Jack	2007-2008	8	0	0	0	-
53=	40	***Abbott***	Jake	2009-2010	8	0	0	0	-
59=	35	*Scarbrough*	Dan	2002-2004	7	0	0	0	-
59=	35	***Shabbo***	Dom	2006-2008	7	0	0	0	-
59=	35	***Doherty***	David	2006-2007	7	0	0	0	-
62	32	Luger	Dan	2000-2006	6	0	0	1	-
63=	30	**Rudd**	John	2001-2001	6	0	0	0	-
63=	30	*Rees*	Tom	2003-2004	6	0	0	0	-
63=	30	*Banahan*	Matt	2007-2008	6	0	0	0	-
63=	30	***Simpson***	Joe	2007-2007	4	0	0	5	-
63=	30	***Brightwell***	Chris	2009-2010	6	0	0	0	-
68=	27	***Stewart (2)***	Rob	2000-2001	5	0	0	1	-
68=	27	***Gray***	Danny	2006-2007	5	0	0	1	-
70=	25	***King***	Kirk	2000	5	0	0	0	-
70=	25	***Tapster***	James	2001-2001	5	0	0	0	-
70=	25	***Garvey***	Marcel	2006-2006	5	0	0	0	-
70=	25	***Cato***	Noah	2007-2008	5	0	0	0	-
70=	25	***Barden***	Greg	2008-2010	5	0	0	0	-
75=	22	Greening	Phil	2002-2003	4	0	0	1	-
75=	22	*Armitage*	Delon	2005-2005	4	0	0	1	-
77=	20	Try	Penalty	2000-2010	4	-	-	-	-
77=	20	***Fabian***	Jon	2000-2000	2	0	0	5	-
77=	20	*Erinle*	Ayoola	2000-2008	4	0	0	0	-
77=	20	**Brownrigg**	Jim	2001-2001	4	0	0	0	-
77=	20	**Earnshaw**	Russ	2001-2002	4	0	0	0	-

Rank	Total	Surname	Forename	Period	Tries	Pens	Drops	Cons	Marks
77=	20	***Graham***	Howard	2002	0	0	0	10	-
77=	20	*Lund*	Magnus	2002-2003	4	0	0	0	-
77=	20	***Hylton***	Jonny	2002-2006	4	0	0	0	-
77=	20	***Mayor***	Chris	2002-2008	4	0	0	0	-
77=	20	***Williams***	Tom	2004-2007	4	0	0	0	-
77=	20	***Matthews***	Will	2005-2006	4	0	0	0	-
77=	20	***Guest***	Tom	2007-2007	4	0	0	0	-
89=	15	Worsley	Joe	2000	3	0	0	0	-
89=	15	Sleightholme	Jon	2001	3	0	0	0	-
89=	15	***Seely***	Grant	2001-2001	3	0	0	0	-
89=	15	Forrester	James	2001-2002	3	0	0	0	-
89=	15	**Shaw**	Joe	2002-2002	3	0	0	0	-
89=	15	Rees (2)	David	2002	3	0	0	0	-
89=	15	***McAvoy***	Nathan	2003-2003	3	0	0	0	-
89=	15	***Baxter***	Neil	2004-2004	3	0	0	0	-
89=	15	***Seymour***	David	2006-2007	3	0	0	0	-
89=	15	*Haskell*	James	2006-2006	3	0	0	0	-
99	14	**Carrington**	Matt	2001	0	0	0	7	-
100	13	*Youngs*	Ben	2008-2008	1	0	0	4	-
101=	12	***Gustard***	Paul	2000-2001	2	0	0	1	-
101=	12	***Howard***	Jonny	2001-2003	2	0	0	1	-
103	11	***Booth***	Steve	2001	1	0	0	3	-
104=	10	Hanley	Steve	2000	2	0	0	0	-
104=	10	***Drake***	Nick	2000-2001	2	0	0	0	-
104=	10	**Ezulike**	Nnamdi	2000-2002	2	0	0	0	-
104=	10	**Sowerby**	Mark	2000-2001	2	0	0	0	-
104=	10	**Greenlees**	Jamie	2000-2000	2	0	0	0	-
104=	10	**Davis**	Chris	2001-2001	2	0	0	0	-
104=	10	**Hamilton**	Jamie	2001	2	0	0	0	-
104=	10	***Roche***	Kieran	2001-2001	2	0	0	0	-
104=	10	***Balding***	Adam	2002-2002	2	0	0	0	-
104=	10	*Jones*	Chris	2002-2002	2	0	0	0	-
104=	10	*Waters*	Fraser	2002	2	0	0	0	-
104=	10	***Peacey***	Ryan	2002-2002	2	0	0	0	-
104=	10	***Horstmann***	Kai	2004-2004	2	0	0	0	-
104=	10	**Obi**	Nnamdi	2004	2	0	0	0	-
104=	10	*Abendanon*	Nick	2006	2	0	0	0	-
104=	10	***Youngs***	Tom	2007-2008	2	0	0	0	-
104=	10	***Jones***	Ben	2009-2009	2	0	0	0	-
121	9	***Brown***	James	2000-2000	1	0	0	2	-
122	8	***FitzGerald***	Seb	2001-2001	0	0	0	4	-
123	6	***Bramhall***	James	2001	0	0	0	3	-
124=	5	**Vander**	Adam	2000-2000	1	0	0	0	-
124=	5	**Friday**	Mike	2000-2002	1	0	0	0	-

Rank	Total	Surname	Forename	Period	Tries	Pens	Drops	Cons	Marks
124=	5	***Vass***	Ian	2000-2002	1	0	0	0	-
124=	5	***Chesney***	Kris	2000-2001	1	0	0	0	-
124=	5	**Graham**	Phil	2000-2000	1	0	0	0	-
124=	5	***Pritchard***	Jon	2000-2000	1	0	0	0	-
124=	5	Duncombe	Nick	2001-2002	1	0	0	0	-
124=	5	Ellis	Harry	2002-2002	1	0	0	0	-
124=	5	Lloyd	Leon	2002	1	0	0	0	-
124=	5	**Dawling**	Andy	2002-2002	1	0	0	0	-
124=	5	White-Cooper	Steve	2002	1	0	0	0	-
124=	5	*May*	Tom	2002-2002	1	0	0	0	-
124=	5	***Laird***	Rob	2002-2002	1	0	0	0	-
124=	5	***Cannon***	Matt	2002-2003	1	0	0	0	-
124=	5	*Skirving*	Ben	2005	1	0	0	0	-
124=	5	*Croft*	Tom	2006-2006	1	0	0	0	-
124=	5	***Smith (2)***	David	2007-2007	1	0	0	0	-
124=	5	***Tombleson***	Tom	2008-2008	1	0	0	0	-
124=	5	***Cox***	Matt	2008-2008	1	0	0	0	-
124=	5	***Dickson***	Lee	2008	1	0	0	0	-
124=	5	***Barrell***	Don	2010-2010	1	0	0	0	-
145	2	***Dunkley***	Paul	2001-2001	0	0	0	1	-

D) CAPTAINCY

1) ENGLAND CAP MATCHES 1969-2010:

[In numerical order; current players in italics; Acting captains shown in brackets; data up to and including Australia v England 19th June 2010]

Rank Matches Surname Forename Position Captaincy

1 59 Carling Will **Centre** 1988-1996

Matches: Australia (Twickenham) 1988, Scotland 1989, Ireland 1989, France 1989, Wales 1989, Fiji 1989, Ireland 1990, France 1990, Wales 1990, Scotland 1990, Argentina (Buenos Aires I) 1990, Argentina (Buenos Aires II) 1990, Argentina (Twickenham) 1990, Wales 1991, Scotland (Twickenham) 1991, Ireland 1991, France (Twickenham) 1991, Fiji 1991, Australia (Sydney) 1991, New Zealand 1991, Italy 1991, USA 1991, France (Paris) 1991, Scotland (Murrayfield) 1991, Australia (Twickenham) 1991, Scotland 1992, Ireland 1992, France 1992, Wales 1992, Canada 1992, South Africa 1992, France 1993, Wales 1993, Scotland 1993, Ireland 1993, New Zealand 1993, Scotland 1994, Ireland 1994, France 1994, Wales 1994, South Africa (Pretoria) 1994, South Africa (Cape Town) 1994, Romania 1994, Canada 1994, Ireland 1995, France (Twickenham) 1995, Wales 1995, Scotland 1995, Argentina 1995, Western Samoa (Durban) 1995, Australia 1995, New Zealand 1995, France (Pretoria) 1995, South Africa 1995, Western Samoa (Twickenham) 1995, France 1996, Wales 1996, Scotland 1996, Ireland 1996

2 39 (2) Johnson Martin **Lock** 1998-2003

Matches: Netherlands 1998, Italy 1998, Australia 1999, USA 1999, Canada 1999, Italy 1999, New Zealand 1999, Tonga 1999, Fiji 1999, South Africa 1999, South Africa (Pretoria) 2000, South Africa (Bloemfontein) 2000, Australia 2000, Argentina 2000, South Africa (Twickenham) 2000, Wales 2001, Italy 2001, Scotland 2001, France 2001, South Africa 2001, Scotland 2002, Ireland 2002, France 2002, (Italy 2002), New Zealand 2002, Australia 2002, South Africa 2002, France (Twickenham I) 2003, Wales (Cardiff I) 2003, Scotland 2003, Ireland 2003, New Zealand 2003, Australia (Melbourne) 2003, France (Twickenham II) 2003, Georgia 2003, South Africa 2003, Samoa 2003, (Uruguay 2003), Wales (Brisbane) 2003, France (Sydney) 2003, Australia (Sydney) 2003

3 22 (3) Dallaglio Lawrence **Flanker**/Number 8 1997-2004

Matches: Australia (Twickenham) 1997, New Zealand (Old Trafford) 1997, South Africa 1997, New Zealand (Twickenham) 1997, France 1998, Wales 1998, Scotland 1998, Ireland 1998, Australia (Twickenham) 1998, South Africa (Twickenham) 1998, Scotland 1999, Ireland 1999, France 1999, Wales 1999, (Tonga 1999), (South Africa [Pretoria] 2000), (Italy 2003), Italy 2004, Scotland 2004, Ireland 2004, Wales 2004, France 2004, New Zealand (Dunedin) 2004, New Zealand (Auckland) 2004, Australia (Brisbane) 2004

4 21 (2) *Borthwick* Steve Lock 2008-2010

Matches: Italy 2008, (Scotland 2008), (Ireland 2008), New Zealand (Auckland) 2008, New Zealand (Christchurch) 2008, Pacific Islanders 2008, Australia 2008, South Africa 2008, New Zealand (Twickenham) 2008, Italy 2009, Wales 2009, Ireland 2009, France 2009, Scotland 2009, Argentina (Old Trafford) 2009, Argentina (Salta) 2009, Australia 2009, Argentina (Twickenham) 2009, New Zealand 2009, Wales 2010, Italy 2010, Ireland 2010, Scotland 2010

Rank	Matches	Surname	Forename	Position	Captaincy
5	21 (1)	Beaumont	Bill	Lock	1978-1982

Matches: France 1978, Wales 1978, Scotland 1978, Ireland 1978, New Zealand 1978, (Scotland 1979), Ireland 1979, France 1979, Wales 1979, New Zealand 1979, Ireland 1980, France 1980, Wales 1980, Scotland 1980, Wales 1981, Scotland 1981, Ireland 1981, France 1981, Argentina (Buenos Aires I) 1981, Argentina (Buenos Aires II) 1981, Australia 1982, Scotland 1982

6	17 (6)	Corry	Martin	Lock/Flanker/**Number 8**	2005-2007

Matches: Italy 2005, Scotland 2005, Australia 2005, New Zealand 2005, Samoa 2005, Wales 2006, Italy 2006, Scotland 2006, France 2006, Ireland 2006, New Zealand 2006, Argentina 2006, South Africa (Twickenham I) 2006, South Africa (Twickenham II) 2006, (Wales [Twickenham] 2007), (France [Marseille] 2007), (USA 2007), South Africa (Paris I) 2007, Samoa 2007, Tonga 2007, (Australia 2007), (France [Paris] 2007), (South Africa [Paris II] 2007)

7	15 (1)	Vickery	Phil	**Prop**	2002-2008

Matches: Argentina 2002, Uruguay 2003, Scotland 2007, Italy 2007, Ireland 2007, Wales (Twickenham) 2007, France (Marseille) 2007, USA 2007, (Tonga 2007), Australia 2007, France [Paris] 2007, South Africa (Paris II) 2007, Wales 2008, France 2008, Scotland 2008, Ireland 2008

8	13 (1)	Pullin	John	**Hooker**	1972-1975

Matches: South Africa 1972, New Zealand (Twickenham) 1973, Wales 1973, Ireland 1973, France 1973, Scotland 1973, New Zealand (Auckland) 1973, Australia 1973, Scotland 1974, Ireland 1974, France 1974, Wales 1974, (Australia [Sydney] 1975), Australia (Brisbane) 1975

9	9 (1)	Dawson	Matt	**Scrum half**	1998-2001

Matches: New Zealand (Dunedin) 1998, New Zealand (Auckland) 1998, South Africa (Cape Town) 1998, (Canada 1999), Ireland 2000, France 2000, Wales 2000, Italy 2000, Scotland 2000, Ireland 2001

10	8	de Glanville	Phil	Centre	1996-1997

Matches: Italy 1996, Scotland 1997, Ireland 1997, France 1997, Wales 1997, Argentina (Buenos Aires I) 1997, Argentina (Buenos Aires II) 1997, Australia (Sydney) 1997

11	7 (1)	Robinson	Jason	Wing/Full back	2004-2007

Matches: Canada 2004, South Africa 2004, Australia (Twickenham) 2004, Wales 2005, France 2005, Ireland 2005, (Wales [Cardiff] 2007), South Africa (Bloemfontein) 2007

12=	7	Hiller	Bob	**Full back**	1969-1972

Matches: South Africa 1969, Ireland 1970, Wales 1970, Scotland 1970, France 1971, Wales 1972, Ireland 1972

12=	7	Neary	Tony	Flanker	1975-1976

Matches: Scotland 1975, Australia (Sydney) 1975, Australia 1976, Wales 1976, Scotland 1976, Ireland 1976, France 1976

12=	7	Melville	Nigel	Scrum half	1984-1988

Matches: Australia 1984, Wales 1986, Scotland 1986, Ireland 1986, France 1986, Scotland 1988, Ireland (Twickenham) 1988

12=	7	Dodge	Paul	Centre	1985-1985

Matches: Romania 1985, France 1985, Scotland 1985, Ireland 1985, Wales 1985, New Zealand (Christchurch) 1985, New Zealand (Wellington) 1985

Rank Matches Surname Forename Position Captaincy

12= 7 Harrison Mike **Wing** 1987-1988
Matches: Scotland 1987, Australia 1987, Japan 1987, USA 1987, Wales (Brisbane) 1987, France 1988, Wales 1988

17= 5 Uttley Roger Lock/Flanker/Number 8 1977-1979
Matches: Scotland 1977, Ireland 1977, France 1977, Wales 1977, Scotland 1979

17= 5 Smith (1) Steve Scrum half 1982-1983
Matches: Ireland 1982, France 1982, Wales 1982, France 1983, Wales 1983

17= 5 Wheeler Peter Hooker 1983-1984
Matches: New Zealand 1983, Scotland 1984, Ireland 1984, France 1984, Wales 1984

20 4 (2) Back Neil Flanker 2001-2003
Matches: (Ireland 2001), Australia 2001, Romania 2001, Wales 2002, Italy 2002, (France [Twickenham II] 2003)

21= 4 Spencer John Centre 1971-1971
Matches: Ireland 1971, Scotland (Twickenham) 1971, Scotland (Murrayfield) 1971, President's Overseas XV 1971

21= 4 Scott John Lock/Number 8 1983-1984
Matches: Scotland 1983, Ireland 1983, South Africa (Port Elizabeth) 1984, South Africa (Johannesburg) 1984

23= 3 (1) Orwin John Lock 1988-1988
Matches: (Ireland [Twickenham] 1988), Ireland (Dublin) 1988, Australia (Brisbane) 1988, Australia (Sydney) 1988

23= 3 (1) Bracken Kyran Scrum half 2001-2001
Matches: Canada (Ontario) 2001, Canada (Toronto) 2001, USA 2001, (Romania 2001)

25= 3 Rogers Budge Flanker 1969-1969
Matches: France 1969, Scotland 1969, Wales 1969

25= 3 Cotton Fran Prop 1975-1975
Matches: Ireland 1975, France 1975, Wales 1975

25= 3 Hill (1) Richard Scrum half 1987-1987
Matches: Ireland 1987, France 1987, Wales (Cardiff) 1987

25= 3 Catt Mike Fly half/Centre/Full back 2007-2007
Matches: France (Twickenham I) 2007, Wales (Cardiff) 2007, France (Twickenham II) 2007

25= 3 *Moody* Lewis Flanker 2010-2010
Matches: France 2010, Australia (Perth) 2010, Australia (Sydney) 2010

30 2 (2) *Wilkinson* Jonny **Fly half**/Centre 2003-2008
Matches: Italy 2003, South Africa (Pretoria) 2007, (Wales [Twickenham] 2007), (Wales 2008)

31 2 (1) Andrew Rob **Fly half** 1989-1995
Matches: Romania 1989, (Wales 1992), Italy 1995

32= 2 Dixon Peter Flanker/Number 8 1972-1972
Matches: France 1972, Scotland 1972

32= 2 Leonard Jason Prop 1996-2003
Matches: Argentina 1996, Wales (Cardiff II) 2003

32= 2 Sanderson Pat Flanker 2006-2006
Matches: Australia (Sydney) 2006, Australia (Melbourne) 2006

35 1 (1) West Dorian Hooker 2001-2003
Matches: (Canada [Toronto] 2001), France (Marseille) 2003

Rank	Matches	Surname	Forename	Position	Captaincy
36=	1	Greenwood	Dick	Flanker	1969
Matches: Ireland 1969					
36=	1	Taylor	Bob	Flanker/Number 8	1970
Matches: France 1970					
36=	1	Bucknall	Tony	Flanker	1971
Matches: Wales 1971					
36=	1	Harding	Richard	Scrum half	1988
Matches: Fiji 1988					
36=	1	Diprose	Tony	Number 8	1998
Matches: Australia (Brisbane) 1998					
41	0 (2)	*Tindall*	Mike	Centre	2004-2006
Matches: (Canada 2004), (Scotland 2006)					
42=	0 (1)	Davis (1)	Mike	Lock	1969
Matches: (South Africa 1969)					
42=	0 (1)	Colclough	Maurice	Lock	1986
Matches: (France 1986)					
42=	0 (1)	Clarke	Ben	Flanker/Number 8	1996
Matches: (Wales 1996)					
42=	0 (1)	Richards	Dean	Number 8	1996
Matches: (Ireland 1996)					
42=	0 (1)	Hill (2)	Richard	Flanker/Number 8	1999
Matches: (Tonga 1999)					
42=	0 (1)	Kay	Ben	Lock	2001
Matches: (Canada [Toronto] 2001)					
42=	0 (1)	Grayson	Paul	Fly half	2003
Matches: (France [Marseille] 2003)					
42=	0 (1)	*Easter*	Nick	Flanker/Number 8	2010
Matches: (Australia [Perth] 2010)					

2) ENGLAND NON-CAP MATCHES 1969-2010:

[In numerical order; current players in italics; Acting captains shown in brackets; data up to and including an England XV v Barbarians 30th May 2010]

Rank	Matches	Surname	Forename	Position	Captaincy
1	9 (1)	Beaumont	Bill	**Lock**	1977-1981

Matches: USA 1977, The Rest 1978, Argentina 1978, (The Rest 1979), Japan (Osaka) 1979, Japan (Tokyo) 1979, Fiji 1979, The Rest 1980, The Rest (Twickenham I) 1981, The Rest (Twickenham II) 1981

Rank	Matches	Surname	Forename	Position	Captaincy
2=	5	Rogers	Budge	**Flanker**	1971-1971

Matches: Japan (Tokyo) 1971, Hong Kong 1971, Singapore 1971, Ceylon (Colombo I) 1971, Ceylon (Colombo II) 1971

Rank	Matches	Surname	Forename	Position	Captaincy
2=	5	Carling	Will	**Centre**	1990-1992

Matches: Italy XV 1990, Barbarians 1990, USSR 1991, Gloucester 1991, Leicester 1992

Rank	Matches	Surname	Forename	Position	Captaincy
4=	4	Pullin	John	**Hooker**	1972-1974

Matches: The Rest (Twickenham II) 1972, Fiji 1973, The Rest (Burton-on-Trent) 1974, France XV 1974

Rank	Matches	Surname	Forename	Position	Captaincy
4=	4	Smith (1)	Steve	**Scrum half**	1982-1982

Matches: Canada 1982, USA 1982, Fiji 1982, The Rest 1982

Rank	Matches	Surname	Forename	Position	Captaincy
6=	2	Hiller	Bob	**Full back**	1970-1972

Matches: The Rest 1970, The Rest (Twickenham I) 1972

Rank	Matches	Surname	Forename	Position	Captaincy
6=	2	Uttley	Roger	Lock/Flanker/**Number 8**	1977-1979

Matches: The Rest 1977, The Rest 1979

Rank	Matches	Surname	Forename	Position	Captaincy
6=	2	Wheeler	Peter	Hooker	1979-1983

Matches: Tonga 1979, Canada 1983

Rank	Matches	Surname	Forename	Position	Captaincy
6=	2	Hill (1)	Richard	Scrum half	1986-1987

Matches: Japan 1986, The Rest 1987

Rank	Matches	Surname	Forename	Position	Captaincy
6=	2	de Glanville	Phil	Centre	1996-1999

Matches: New Zealand Barbarians 1996, Premiership All Stars (Anfield) 1999

Rank	Matches	Surname	Forename	Position	Captaincy
6=	2	Vickery	Phil	**Prop**	2002-2003

Matches: Barbarians 2002, Barbarians 2003

Rank	Matches	Surname	Forename	Position	Captaincy
6=	2	Sanderson	Pat	Flanker	2005-2006

Matches: Barbarians 2005, Barbarians 2006

Rank	Matches	Surname	Forename	Position	Captaincy
6=	2	*Easter*	Nick	Flanker/Number 8	2008-2010

Matches: Barbarians 2008, Barbarians 2010

Rank	Matches	Surname	Forename	Position	Captaincy
14	1 (1)	Andrew	Rob	**Fly half**	1990-1991

Matches: (Italy XV 1990), England Students 1991

Rank	Matches	Surname	Forename	Position	Captaincy
15=	1	Greenwood	Dick	Flanker	1969

Matches: The Rest 1969

Rank	Matches	Surname	Forename	Position	Captaincy
15=	1	Bucknall	Tony	Flanker	1971

Matches: The Rest 1971

Rank	Matches	Surname	Forename	Position	Captaincy
15=	1	Lloyd	Bob	Centre	1971

Matches: Japan (Osaka) 1971

Rank	Matches	Surname	Forename	Position	Captaincy
15=	1	Cotton	Fran	Prop	1974

Matches: The Rest (Twickenham) 1974

Rank	Matches	Surname	Forename	Position	Captaincy
15=	1	Neary	Tony	Flanker	1975

Matches: The Rest 1975

Rank	Matches	Surname	Forename	Position	Captaincy
15=	1	Colclough	Maurice	Lock	1984
Matches: The Rest 1984					
15=	1	Scott	John	Lock/Number 8	1984
Matches: President's XV 1984					
15=	1	Simpson	Paul	Flanker	1986
Matches: Portugal XV 1986					
15=	1	Bailey	Mark	**Wing**	1987
Matches: Portugal XV 1987					
15=	1	Harrison	Mike	**Wing**	1988
Matches: England B XV 1988					
15=	1	Johnson	Martin	Lock	1999
Matches: Premiership All Stars (Twickenham) 1999					
15=	1	Bracken	Kyran	Scrum half	2001
Matches: Barbarians 2001					
15=	1	Hill (2)	Richard	Flanker/Number 8	2003
Matches: New Zealand Barbarians 2003					
15=	1	*Vyvyan*	Hugh	Lock/Number 8	2004
Matches: Barbarians 2004					
15=	1	*Borthwick*	Steve	Lock	2009
Matches: Barbarians 2009					
30=	0 (1)	Redman	Nigel	Lock	1986
Matches: (Portugal XV 1986)					
30=	0 (1)	Lewsey	Josh	Fly half/Centre/Wing/Full back	2001
Matches: (Barbarians 2001)					
30=	0 (1)	*Gomarsall*	Andy	Scrum half	2003
Matches: (New Zealand Barbarians 2003)					

3) ENGLAND TOUR MATCHES 1969-2010:

[In numerical order; current players in italics; Acting captains shown in brackets; data up to and including an England XV v New Zealand Maori 23rd June 2010]

Rank Matches Surname Forename Position Captaincy

1= 7 Beaumont Bill **Lock** 1979-1981
Matches: Japan Select 1979, Kyushu 1979, Fiji Juniors 1979, San Isidro Club 1981, Northern Region XV 1981, Buenos Aires Selection 1981, Littoral Region XV 1981

1= 7 Scott John Lock/Number 8 1982-1984
Matches: US Cougars 1982, Western Rugby Football Union 1982, Currie Cup 'B' Section 1984, Proteas 1984, Western Province 1984, South African Rugby Association 1984, South African Country Districts 1984

1= 7 Carling Will **Centre** 1990-1994
Matches: Banco Nación 1990, Buenos Aires Selection 1990, New South Wales 1991, Queensland 1991, Natal 1994, Western Transvaal 1994, Transvaal 1994

4 6 Pullin John **Hooker** 1972-1975
Matches: Natal 1972, Western Province 1972, Northern Transvaal 1972, Taranaki 1973, Canterbury 1973, Queensland 1975

5 5 Orwin John Lock 1988-1988
Matches: Queensland Country Invitation XV 1988, Queensland 1988, Queensland B 1988, New South Wales 1988, New South Wales B 1988

6= 4 Neary Tony **Flanker** 1975-1975
Matches: Western Australia 1975, Sydney 1975, New South Wales 1975, New South Wales Country 1975

6= 4 Olver John Hooker 1990-1991
Matches: Córdoba 1990, Victorian President's XV 1991, Fiji B 1991, Emerging Wallabies 1991

8= 3 Smith (1) Steve **Scrum half** 1982-1982
Matches: Eastern Canada 1982, Pacific Coast Grizzlies 1982, Mid-Western Rugby Football Union 1982

8= 3 Dodge Paul Centre 1985-1985
Matches: North Auckland 1985, Poverty Bay 1985, Auckland 1985

8= 3 Ryan Dean **Number 8** 1994-1994
Matches: Orange Free State 1994, South Africa A 1994, Eastern Province 1994

8= 3 Diprose Tony **Number 8** 1997-1998
Matches: Argentina A 1997, New Zealand Academy 1998, New Zealand Maori 1998

12= 2 Cotton Fran **Prop** 1972-1973
Matches: Bantu XV 1972, Wellington 1973

12= 2 de Glanville Phil Centre 1997-1997
Matches: Córdoba 1997, Buenos Aires 1997

12= 2 Clarke Ben Flanker/Number 8 2000-2000
Matches: North West Leopards 2000, Griqualand West 2000

12= 2 Sanderson Alex Flanker/Number 8 2001-2001
Matches: British Columbia 2001, USA A 2001

12= 2 *Robshaw* Chris Flanker/Number 8 2010-2010
Matches: Australian Barbarians (Perth) 2010, New Zealand Maori 2010

17 1 (1) Corry Martin Lock/Flanker/Number 8 2000-2000
Matches: (Griqualand West 2000), Gauteng Falcons 2000

Rank	Matches	Surname	Forename	Position	Captaincy
18=	1	Rogers	Budge	Flanker	1971
Matches: Waseda University Past and Present 1971					
18=	1	Spencer	John	Centre	1972
Matches: Proteas 1972					
18=	1	Stevens	Stack	Prop	1972
Matches: Griqualand West 1972					
18=	1	Old	Alan	**Fly half**/Centre	1975
Matches: Queensland Country 1975					
18=	1	Rafter	Mike	Flanker	1981
Matches: Southern Region XV 1981					
18=	1	Colclough	Maurice	Lock	1982
Matches: Eastern Rugby Union 1982					
18=	1	Hesford	Bob	Number 8	1985
Matches: Otago 1985					
18=	1	Cooke (2)	David	Flanker	1985
Matches: Southland 1985					
18=	1	Andrew	Rob	**Fly half**	1988
Matches: South Australia Invitation XV 1988					
18=	1	Winterbottom	Peter	Flanker	1990
Matches: Tucumán Selection 1990					
18=	1	Moore	Brian	Hooker	1990
Matches: Cuyo Selection 1990					
18=	1	Sheasby	Chris	Flanker/Number 8	1997
Matches: Cuyo 1997					
18=	1	Dawson	Matt	Scrum half	1998
Matches: New Zealand A 1998					
18=	1	Johnson	Martin	Lock	1999
Matches: Queensland Reds 1999					
18=	1	*Vyvyan*	Hugh	Lock/Number 8	2002
Matches: Argentina A 2002					
18=	1	Vickery	Phil	Prop	2003
Matches: New Zealand Maori 2003					
18=	1	Worsley	Joe	Flanker/Number 8	2010
Matches: Australian Barbarians (Gosford) 2010					
35=	0 (1)	Rodber	Tim	Lock/Flanker/Number 8	1994
Matches: (Eastern Province 1994)					
35=	0 (1)	Bates	Steve	Scrum half	1994
Matches: (Eastern Province 1994)					

4) ENGLAND SEVENS COMPETITION* 1973-2009:

[In numerical order; current players in italics; uncapped players in bold or bold italics; Acting captains shown in brackets; data up to and including Rugby World Cup Sevens 5th-7th March 2009]

[*excludes IRB World Sevens competition]

Rank	Comps	Surname	Forename	Position	Period
1	2 (2)	Sheasby	Chris	Forward	1992-1998

Competitions: (Harlequin 1992), Dubai 1992, (Rugby World Cup 1993), Commonwealth 1998

2	2	***Amor***	Simon	Scrum half/Fly half	2005-2006

Competitions: Rugby World Cup 2005, Commonwealth 2006

3	1 (1)	**Friday**	Mike	Scrum half	1998-2001

Competitions: (Commonwealth 1998), Rugby World Cup 2001

4= 1 Cotton Fran Prop 1973
Competitions: International 1973

4= 1 Ripley Andy Prop 1986
Competitions: International 1986

4= 1 Morris Dewi Scrum half 1992
Competitions: Harlequin 1992

4= 1 Harriman Andy Wing 1993
Competitions: Rugby World Cup 1993

4= 1 **Eves** Derek Hooker 1995
Competitions: Hong Kong 1995

4= 1 **Kitchin** Rob Scrum half 1995
Competitions: Melun 1995

4= 1 Hopley Damian Hooker/Centre 1996
Competitions: Hong Kong 1996

4= 1 Rodber Tim Forward 1997
Competitions: Rugby World Cup 1997

4= 1 ***Chesney*** Kris Forward 1999
Competitions: Air France 1999

4= 1 Greening Phil Hooker 2002
Competitions: Commonwealth 2002

4= 1 ***Phillips*** Ollie Centre/Wing 2009
Competitions: Rugby World Cup 2009

15 0 (2) ***Gollings*** Ben Fly half/Centre 2005-2006
Competitions: (Rugby World Cup 2005), (Commonwealth 2006)

16= 0 (1) **Thompson** Adrian Fly half/Centre 1992
Competitions: (Dubai 1992)

16= 0 (1) **Scully** Dave Scrum half 1996
Competitions: (Hong Kong 1996)

16= 0 (1) Back Neil Hooker 1997
Competitions: (Rugby World Cup 1997)

16= 0 (1) Worsley Joe Forward 2001
Competitions: (Rugby World Cup 2001)

5) ENGLAND IRB WORLD SEVENS COMPETITION 2000-2010:

[In numerical order; current players in italics; uncapped players in bold or bold italics; Acting captains shown in brackets; data up to and including Edinburgh Sevens 29th-30th May 2010]

Rank Comps Surname Forename Position Period

1 32 (2) ***Amor*** Simon Scrum half/Fly half 2002-2007

Competitions: (Hong Kong 2002), Dubai 2002, South Africa 2002, Brisbane 2003, New Zealand 2003, Hong Kong 2003, Cardiff 2003, (London 2003), Dubai 2003, New Zealand 2004, USA 2004, Hong Kong 2004, Singapore 2004, Bordeaux 2004, London 2004, Dubai 2004, New Zealand 2005, Singapore 2005, London 2005, Paris 2005, Dubai 2005, South Africa 2005, New Zealand 2006, Hong Kong 2006, Singapore 2006, Paris 2006, London 2006, Dubai 2006, South Africa 2006, New Zealand 2007, USA 2007, Hong Kong 2007, Adelaide 2007, London 2007

2 8 ***Vilk*** Andy Back/Forward 2007-2008

Competitions: Dubai 2007, South Africa 2007, New Zealand 2008, USA 2008, Hong Kong 2008, Adelaide 2008, London 2008, Edinburgh 2008

3 7 ***Phillips*** Ollie Centre/Wing 2008-2009

Competitions: Dubai 2008, New Zealand 2009, USA 2009, Hong Kong 2009, Adelaide 2009, London 2009, Edinburgh 2009

4 6 (19) ***Gollings*** Ben Fly half/Centre 2003-2010

Competitions: (Dubai 2003), (Bordeaux 2004), (South Africa 2004), (New Zealand 2005), (USA 2005), (Singapore 2005), (Paris 2005), (Dubai 2005), (South Africa 2005), (New Zealand 2006), (Hong Kong 2006), (Singapore 2006), (London 2006), (London 2008), South Africa 2008, (Hong Kong 2009), (London 2009), (Edinburgh 2009), (South Africa 2009), (New Zealand 2010), USA 2010, Adelaide 2010, Hong Kong 2010, London 2010, Edinburgh 2010

5 5 **Friday** Mike Scrum half 2000-2002

Competitions: Air France 2000, Santiago 2002, Mar del Plata 2002, New Zealand 2002, Beijing 2002

6 4 (1) Greening Phil Hooker 2002-2003

Competitions: Hong Kong 2002, London 2002, Cardiff 2002, (Hong Kong 2003), London 2003

7 3 (2) ***Roques*** Tony Forward 2003-2007

Competitions: (New Zealand 2003), South Africa 2003, South Africa 2004, (Adelaide 2007), Edinburgh 2007

8 3 (1) ***Barrett*** Kevin Scrum half 2009-2010

Competitions: Dubai 2009, South Africa 2009, New Zealand 2010, (London 2010)

9 3 **Sowerby** Mark Forward 2000-2001

Competitions: South Africa 2000, Dubai 2000, New Zealand 2001

10= 2 *Gomarsall* Andy Scrum half/Fly half 2000-2001

Competitions: Hong Kong 2000, Shanghai 2001

10= 2 **Davis** Chris Forward 2001-2001

Competitions: Malaysia 2001, Japan 2001

10= 2 **Simpson** Nigel Back/Forward 2001-2001

Competitions: London 2001, Wales 2001

13 1 (2) Sanderson Pat Forward 2001-2003

Competitions: South Africa 2001, (Cardiff 2003), (London 2003)

Rank	**Comps**	**Surname**	**Forename**	**Position**	**Period**
14=	1	Sleightholme	Jon	Wing	2001
Competitions: Hong Kong 2001					
14=	1	***Thirlby***	Rob	Back/Forward	2002
Competitions: Brisbane 2002					
14=	1	*Noon*	Jamie	Back/Forward	2002
Competitions: Singapore 2002					
14=	1	***Graham***	Howard	Back/Forward	2002
Competitions: Malaysia 2002					
14=	1	Richards	Peter	Scrum half/Hooker	2005
Competitions: USA 2005					
14=	1	*Paul*	Henry	Back/Forward	2006
Competitions: USA 2006					
20=	0 (1)	Appleford	Geoff	Back/Forward	2003
Competitions: (South Africa 2003)					
20=	0 (1)	***Turner***	Mat	Centre/Wing	2010
Competitions: (Hong Kong 2010)					

BIBLIOGRAPHY

Back, Neil. 2002. *Size Doesn't Matter – My Rugby Life.* Ramsbottom: Milo Books Ltd.
Catt, Mike. 2007. *Landing on my Feet – My Story.* London: Hodder & Stoughton.
Cleary, Mick & Griffiths, John. 2001. Eds., *IRB International Rugby Yearbook 2001-02.* London: CollinsWillow.
Cleary, Mick & Griffiths, John. 2002. Eds., *IRB International Rugby Yearbook 2002-03.* London: CollinsWillow.
Dallaglio, Lawrence & Walsh, David. 2007. *It's In The Blood: My Life.* London: Headline Publishing Group.
Dawson, Matt & Spink, Alex. 2004. *Nine lives – The Autobiography.* London: CollinsWillow.
Deltéral, Francis & Navarro, Gilles. 2010. *La Légende Continue…* Champagne: Castor & Pollux.
Evans, Alan. 2005. *The Barbarians – the united nations of rugby.* Edinburgh: Mainstream Publishing Company.
Greenwood, Will. 2005. *Will: The Autobiography of Will Greenwood.* London: Arrow Books.
Healey, Austin & Spink, Alex. 2001. *The Austin Healey Story: Lions, Tigers & Roses.* Exeter: Greenwater Publishing.
Johnson, Martin. 2003. *Martin Johnson – The Autobiography.* London: Headline Book Publishing.
Leonard, Jason & Kervin, Alison. 2001. *The Autobiography.* London: CollinsWillow.
Malin, Ian & Griffiths, John. 2003. *The Essential History of Rugby Union – England.* London: Headline Book Publishing.
Robertson, Ian. 2000. Ed., *Wooden Spoon Society Rugby World '01.* Harpenden: Queen Anne Press.
Robinson, Jason & Folley, Malcolm. 2003. *Finding my Feet – My Autobiography.* London: Hodder and Stoughton.
Various. 1969-2001. Assorted articles IN the *Argus*. Cape Town.
Various. 1969-2001. Assorted articles IN the *Cape Times*. Cape Town.
Various. 1969-2009. Assorted articles IN the *Daily Nation*. Nairobi.
Various. 1969-2011. Assorted articles IN the *Daily Telegraph*. London.
Various. 1969-2002. Assorted articles IN the *Oxford Times*. Oxford.
Various. 1969-2011. Assorted Rugby Union programmes. Various.
Various. 1969-2011. Assorted articles IN the *Scotsman*. Edinburgh.
Various. 1969-2011. Assorted articles IN the *Sunday Telegraph*. London.
Various. 1969-2011. Assorted articles IN the *Sunday Times*. London.
Various. 1969-2011. Assorted articles IN the *Times*. London.
Various. 1969-2003. Assorted articles IN the *West Briton*. Truro.
Various. 1969-2005. Assorted articles IN the *Western Mail*. Cardiff.
Various. 1970-2004. Assorted articles IN the *Los Angeles Times*. Los Angeles.
Various. 1971-2002. Assorted articles IN the *Buenos Aires Herald*. Buenos Aires.
Various. 1971-2001. Assorted articles IN the *Courier Mail*. Brisbane.
Various. 1971-2001. Assorted articles IN the *Japan Times*. Tokyo.
Various. 1971-2004. Assorted articles IN the *New Zealand Herald*. Auckland.
Various. 1971-2001. Assorted articles IN the *Press*. Christchurch.
Various. 1971-2004. Assorted articles IN the *South China Morning Post*. Hong Kong.
Various. 1971-2004. Assorted articles IN the *Straits Times*. Singapore.
Various. 1971-2003. Assorted articles IN the *Sydney Morning Herald*. Sydney.
Various. 1972-2001. Assorted articles IN the *Cambridge Evening News*. Cambridge.

Various. 1973-2004. Assorted articles IN *L'Équipe*. Paris.
Various. 1984-2009. Assorted articles IN the *South Wales Evening Post*. Swansea.
Various. 1986-2011. Assorted articles IN the *Independent*. London.
Various. 1988-2001. Assorted articles IN *Rugby Magazine*. Paris: Fédération Française de Rugby.
Various. 1989-2003. Assorted articles IN the *Canberra Times*. Canberra.
Various. 1990-2011. Assorted articles IN the *Independent on Sunday*. London.
Various. 1993-2002. Assorted articles IN the *New Straits Times*. Kuala Lumpur.
Various. 1997-2001. Assorted articles IN the *Pontypridd & Llantrisant Observer*. Pontypridd.
Various. 1997-2003. Assorted articles IN the *Star*. Johannesburg.
Various. 1999-2004. Assorted articles IN the *Richmond & Twickenham Times*. London.
Various. 2000-2002. Assorted articles IN the *Gulf News*. Dubai.
Various. 2000. *Cornwall R.F.U. Official Handbook - Season 2000-2001*. Camborne: Cornwall Rugby Football Union.
Various. 2001. *Cornwall R.F.U. Official Handbook - Season 2001-2002*. Camborne: Cornwall Rugby Football Union.
Various. 2002-2004. Assorted articles IN the *Rugby Times*. Brighouse.
Various. 2002. *Cornwall R.F.U. Official Handbook - Season 2002-2003*. Camborne: Cornwall Rugby Football Union.
Various. 2002. *Great Rugby Headlines.* London: Michael O'Mara Books Limited.
Various. 2003. *Cornwall R.F.U. Official Handbook - 2003-2004*. Camborne: Cornwall Rugby Football Union.
Various. 2004. *Cornwall R.F.U. Official Handbook - 2004-2005*. Camborne: Cornwall Rugby Football Union.
Various. 2005. Assorted articles IN the *Daily Mirror*. Colombo.
Various. 2005. Assorted articles IN the *Daily News*. Colombo.
Various. 2005. Assorted articles IN the *Sunday Observer*. Colombo.
Various. 2005. Assorted articles IN *The Island*. Colombo.
Various. 2005. *Cornwall R.F.U. Official Handbook - 2005-2006*. Camborne: Cornwall Rugby Football Union.
Various. 2006. *Cornwall R.F.U. Official Handbook - 2006-2007*. Camborne: Cornwall Rugby Football Union.
Wilkinson, Jonny. 2006. *My World.* London: Headline Book Publishing.
Woodward, Clive. 2004. *Winning!* London: Hodder & Stoughton.

Printed in Great Britain
by Amazon.co.uk, Ltd.,
Marston Gate.